kimmel
weygandt
kieso
team for success

**FOURTH EDITION**

# ACCOUNTING

## TOOLS FOR BUSINESS DECISION MAKING

## CUSTOM VOLUME 1

WILEY *Custom*
LEARNING SOLUTIONS

To order books or for customer service, please call 1(800)-CALL-WILEY (225-5945).

Printed in the United States of America.

ISBN 978-1-118-10635-8
Printed and bound by Dunn & Company.

10 9 8 7 6 5 4

# Custom
# Brief Contents

## APPENDICES

*Available at the book's companion website, *www.wiley.com/college/kimmel.*

## ACCOUNT CLASSIFICATION AND PRESENTATION

| Account Title | Classification | Financial Statement | Normal Balance |
|---|---|---|---|
| **A** | | | |
| Accounts Payable | Current Liability | Balance Sheet | Credit |
| Accounts Receivable | Current Asset | Balance Sheet | Debit |
| Accumulated Depreciation—Buildings | Plant Asset—Contra | Balance Sheet | Credit |
| Accumulated Depreciation—Equipment | Plant Asset—Contra | Balance Sheet | Credit |
| Administrative Expenses | Operating Expense | Income Statement | Debit |
| Allowance for Doubtful Accounts | Current Asset—Contra | Balance Sheet | Credit |
| Amortization Expense | Operating Expense | Income Statement | Debit |
| **B** | | | |
| Bad Debts Expense | Operating Expense | Income Statement | Debit |
| Bonds Payable | Long-Term Liability | Balance Sheet | Credit |
| Buildings | Plant Assets | Balance Sheet | Debit |
| **C** | | | |
| Cash | Current Asset | Balance Sheet | Debit |
| Common Stock | Stockholder's Equity | Balance Sheet | Credit |
| Copyright | Intangible Asset | Balance Sheet | Debit |
| Cost of Goods Sold | Cost of Goods Sold | Income Statement | Debit |
| **D** | | | |
| Depreciation Expense | Operating Expense | Income Statement | Debit |
| Discount on Bonds Payable | Long-Term Liability—Contra | Balance Sheet | Debit |
| Dividends | Temporary account closed to Retained Earnings | Retained Earnings Statement | Debit |
| Dividends Payable | Current Liability | Balance Sheet | Credit |
| **E** | | | |
| Equipment | Plant Asset | Balance Sheet | Debit |
| **F** | | | |
| Freight-out | Operating Expense | Income Statement | Debit |
| **G** | | | |
| Gain on Disposal of Plant Assets | Other Income | Income Statement | Credit |
| Goodwill | Intangible Asset | Balance Sheet | Debit |
| **I** | | | |
| Income Summary | Temporary account closed to Retained Earnings | Not Applicable | (1) |
| Income Tax Expense | Income Tax Expense | Income Statement | Debit |
| Income Taxes Payable | Current Liability | Balance Sheet | Credit |
| Insurance Expense | Operating Expense | Income Statement | Debit |
| Interest Expense | Other Expense | Income Statement | Debit |
| Interest Payable | Current Liability | Balance Sheet | Credit |
| Interest Receivable | Current Asset | Balance Sheet | Debit |
| Interest Revenue | Other Income | Income Statement | Credit |
| Inventory | Current Asset | Balance Sheet (2) | Debit |

| Account Title | Classification | Financial Statement | Normal Balance |
|---|---|---|---|
| **L** | | | |
| Land | Plant Asset | Balance Sheet | Debit |
| Loss on Disposal of Plant Assets | Other Expense | Income Statement | Debit |
| **M** | | | |
| Maintenance and Repairs Expense | Operating Expense | Income Statement | Debit |
| Mortgage Payable | Long-Term Liability | Balance Sheet | Credit |
| **N** | | | |
| Notes Payable | Current Liability/ Long-Term Liability | Balance Sheet | Credit |
| **P** | | | |
| Patent | Intangible Asset | Balance Sheet | Debit |
| Paid-in Capital in Excess of Par Value—Common Stock | Stockholders' Equity | Balance Sheet | Credit |
| Paid-in Capital in Excess of Par Value—Preferred Stock | Stockholders' Equity | Balance Sheet | Credit |
| Preferred Stock | Stockholders' Equity | Balance Sheet | Credit |
| Premium on Bonds Payable | Long-Term Liability—Contra | Balance Sheet | Credit |
| Prepaid Insurance | Current Asset | Balance Sheet | Debit |
| Prepaid Rent | Current Asset | Balance Sheet | Debit |
| **R** | | | |
| Rent Expense | Operating Expense | Income Statement | Debit |
| Retained Earnings | Stockholders' Equity | Balance Sheet and Retained Earnings Statement | Credit |
| **S** | | | |
| Salaries and Wages Expense | Operating Expense | Income Statement | Debit |
| Salaries and Wages Payable | Current Liability | Balance Sheet | Credit |
| Sales Discounts | Revenue—Contra | Income Statement | Debit |
| Sales Returns and Allowances | Revenue—Contra | Income Statement | Debit |
| Sales Revenue | Revenue | Income Statement | Credit |
| Selling Expenses | Operating Expense | Income Statement | Debit |
| Service Revenue | Revenue | Income Statement | Credit |
| Short-Term Investments | Current Asset | Balance Sheet | Debit |
| Supplies | Current Asset | Balance Sheet | Debit |
| Supplies Expense | Operating Expense | Income Statement | Debit |
| **T** | | | |
| Treasury Stock—Common | Stockholders' Equity | Balance Sheet | Debit |
| **U** | | | |
| Unearned Service Revenue | Current Liability | Balance Sheet | Credit |
| Utilities Expense | Operating Expense | Income Statement | Debit |

(1) The normal balance for Income Summary will be credit when there is a net income, debit when there is a net loss. The Income Summary account does not appear on any financial statement.

(2) If a periodic system is used, Inventory also appears on the income statement in the calculation of cost of goods sold.

The following is a sample chart of accounts. It does not represent a comprehensive chart of all the accounts used in this textbook but rather those accounts that are commonly used. This sample chart of accounts is for a company that generates both service revenue as well as sales revenue. It uses the perpetual approach to inventory. If a periodic system was used, the following temporary accounts would be needed to record inventory purchases: Purchases; Freight-in; Purchase Returns and Allowances; and Purchase Discounts.

## CHART OF ACCOUNTS

| Assets | Liabilities | Stockholders' Equity | Revenues | Expenses |
|---|---|---|---|---|
| Cash | Notes Payable | Common Stock | Service Revenue | Administrative Expenses |
| Accounts Receivable | Accounts Payable | Paid-in Capital in Excess of Par Value—Common Stock | Sales Revenue | Amortization Expense |
| Allowance for Doubtful Accounts | Unearned Service Revenue | | Sales Discounts | |
| | Salaries and Wages Payable | Preferred Stock | Sales Returns and Allowances | Bad Debts Expense |
| Interest Receivable | Interest Payable | Paid-in Capital in Excess of Par Value—Preferred Stock | Interest Revenue | Cost of Goods Sold |
| Inventory | Dividends Payable | Stock | Gain on Disposal of Plant Assets | Depreciation Expense |
| Supplies | Income Taxes Payable | Treasury Stock—Common | | Freight-out |
| Prepaid Insurance | Bonds Payable | Retained Earnings | | Income Tax Expense |
| Prepaid Rent | Discount on Bonds Payable | Dividends | | Insurance Expense |
| Land | | Income Summary | | Interest Expense |
| Equipment | Premium on Bonds Payable | | | Loss on Disposal of Plant Assets |
| Accumulated Depreciation—Equipment | Mortgage Payable | | | Maintenance and Repairs Expense |
| Buildings | | | | Rent Expense |
| Accumulated Depreciation—Buildings | | | | Salaries and Wages Expense |
| Copyright | | | | Selling Expenses |
| Goodwill | | | | Supplies Expense |
| Patent | | | | Utilities Expense |

www.wileyplus.com

# ALL THE HELP, **RESOURCES**, AND PERSONAL **SUPPORT** YOU AND YOUR STUDENTS NEED!

## www.wileyplus.com/resources

2-Minute Tutorials and all of the resources you & your students need to get started.

Student support from an experienced student user.

Collaborate with your colleagues, find a mentor, attend virtual and live events, and view resources.
www.WhereFacultyConnect.com

Pre-loaded, ready-to-use assignments and presentations. Created by subject matter experts.

Technical Support 24/7 FAQs, online chat, and phone support.
www.wileyplus.com/support

Your *WileyPLUS* Account Manager. Personal training and implementation support.

kimmel
weygandt
kieso
team for success

# ACCOUNTING
## TOOLS FOR BUSINESS DECISION MAKING

4E

**Paul D. Kimmel PhD, CPA**
University of Wisconsin—Milwaukee
Milwaukee, Wisconsin

**Jerry J. Weygandt PhD, CPA**
University of Wisconsin—Madison
Madison, Wisconsin

**Donald E. Kieso PhD, CPA**
Northern Illinois University
DeKalb, Illinois

WILEY

# John Wiley & Sons, Inc.

| | |
|---|---|
| Vice President & Publisher | George Hoffman |
| Associate Publisher | Christopher DeJohn |
| Project Editor | Ed Brislin |
| Development Editor | Terry Ann Tatro |
| Project Manager | Paul Lopez |
| Production Manager | Dorothy Sinclair |
| Project Editor | Yana Mermel |
| Production Editor | Erin Bascom |
| Senior Production Editor | Trisha McFadden |
| Associate Director of Marketing | Amy Scholz |
| Senior Marketing Manager | Ramona Sherman |
| Executive Media Editor | Allison Morris |
| Media Editor | Greg Chaput |
| Creative Director | Harry Nolan |
| Senior Designer | Madelyn Lesure |
| Production Management Services | Ingrao Associates |
| Senior Illustration Editor | Sandra Rigby |
| Senior Photo Editor | Mary Ann Price |
| Editorial Assistant | Jacqueline Kepping |
| Senior Marketing Assistant | Laura Finley |
| Assistant Marketing Manager | Diane Mars |
| Cover Design | Maureen Eide |
| Cover Photo | ©Peter McBride/Getty Image, Inc. |

This book was set in New Aster by Aptara®, Inc. and printed and bound by RR Donnelley. The cover was printed by RR Donnelley.

To order books or for customer service please, call 1-800-CALL WILEY (225-5945).

Paul D. Kimmel, PhD, CPA; Jerry J. Weygandt, PhD, CPA;
and Donald E. Kieso, PhD, CPA
Accounting, Fourth Edition

ISBN-13 978-0-470-53478-6

Printed in the United States of America

10 9 8 7 6 5

# From the Authors

Dear Student,

**Why This Course?** *Remember your biology course in high school? Did you have one of those "invisible man" models (or maybe something more high-tech than that) that gave you the opportunity to look "inside" the human body? This accounting course offers something similar: To understand a business, you have to understand the financial insides of a business organization. An accounting course will help you understand the essential financial components of businesses. Whether you are looking at a large multinational company like Microsoft or Starbucks or a single-owner software consulting business or coffee shop, knowing the fundamentals of accounting will help you understand what is happening. As an employee, a manager, an investor, a business owner, or a director of your own personal finances—any of which roles you will have at some point in your life—you will be much the wiser for having taken this course.*

**Why This Book?** *Hundreds of thousands of students have used this textbook. Your instructor has chosen it for you because of its trusted reputation. The authors have worked hard to keep the book fresh, timely, and accurate.*

*This textbook contains features to help you learn best, whatever your learning style. To understand what your learning style is, spend about ten minutes to take the learning style quiz at the textbook companion website. Then, look at page xxv for how you can apply an understanding of your learning style to this course. When you know more about your own learning style, browse through the Student Owner's Manual on pages xxxi–xxxv. It shows you the main features you will find in this textbook and explains their purpose.*

**How To Succeed?** *We've asked many students and many instructors whether there is a secret for success in this course. The nearly unanimous answer turns out to be not much of a secret: "Do the homework." This is one course where doing is learning, and the more time you spend on the homework assignments—using the various tools that this textbook provides—the more likely you are to learn the essential concepts, techniques, and methods of accounting. Besides the textbook itself, the textbook companion website offers various support resources.*

*Good luck in this course. We hope you enjoy the experience and that you put to good use throughout a lifetime of success the knowledge you obtain in this course. We are sure you will not be disappointed.*

*Paul D. Kimmel*
*Jerry J. Weygandt*
*Donald E. Kieso*

# Your Team for Success in Accounting

Wiley Accounting is your partner in accounting education. We want to be the first publisher you think of when it comes to quality content, reliable technology, innovative resources, professional training, and unparalleled support for your accounting classroom.

Your Wiley Accounting Team for Success is comprised of three distinctive advantages that you won't find with any other publisher:

- Author Commitment
- Wiley Faculty Network
- WileyPLUS

kieso
weygandt
kimmel
warfield
team for success

## Author Commitment:

*A Proven Author Team of Inspired Teachers*

The Team for Success authors bring years of industry and academic experience to the development of each textbook that relates accounting concepts to real-world experiences. This cohesive team brings continuity of writing style, pedagogy, and problem material to each course from Principles to Intermediate so you and your students can seamlessly progress from introductory through advanced courses in accounting.

The authors understand the mindset and time limitations of today's students. They demonstrate an intangible ability to effectively deliver complex information so it is clear and understandable while staying one step ahead of emerging global trends in business.

## Wiley Faculty Network:
*A Team of Educators Dedicated to Your Professional Development*

The Wiley Faculty Network (WFN) is a global group of seasoned accounting professionals who share best practices in teaching with their peers. Our Virtual Guest Lecture Series provides the opportunity you need for professional development in an online environment that is relevant, convenient, and collaborative. The quality of these seminars and workshops meet the strictest standards, so we are proud to be able to offer valuable CPE credits to attendees.

With 24 faculty mentors in accounting, it's easy to find help with your most challenging curriculum questions—just ask our experts!

www.wileyplus.com

## WileyPLUS:
*An Experienced Team of Support Professionals*

The *WileyPLUS* Account Managers understand the time constraints of busy instructors who want to provide the best resources available to their students with minimal headaches and planning time. They know how intimidating new software can be, so they are sure to make the transition easy and painless.

Account Managers act as your personal contact and expert resource for training, course set-up, and shortcuts throughout the *WileyPLUS* experience.

Your success as an educator directly correlates to student success, and that's our goal. The Wiley Accounting Team for Success truly strives for YOUR success! Partner with us today!

www.wileyteamforsuccess.com

# Author Commitment.
## Collaboration. Innovation. Experience.

After decades of success as authors of textbooks like this one, Paul Kimmel, Jerry Weygandt, and Don Kieso understand that teaching accounting goes beyond simply presenting data. The authors are truly effective because they know that teaching is about telling compelling stories in ways that make each concept come-to-life.

## Teacher / Author / Professional

Through their textbooks, supplements, online learning tools, and classrooms, these authors have developed a comprehensive pedagogy that engages students in learning and faculty with teaching.

These authors collaborate throughout the entire process. The end result is a true collaboration where each author brings his individual experience and talent to the development of every paragraph, page, and chapter, thus creating a truly well-rounded, thorough view on any given accounting topic.

## Many Ways in One Direction

Our **Team for Success** has developed a learning system that addresses every learning style. Each year brings new insights, feedback, ideas, and improvements on how to deliver the material to every student with a passion for the subject in a format that gives them the best chance to succeed.

The key to the team's approach is in understanding that, just as there are many different ways to learn, there are also many different ways to teach.

## In Their Own Words

Visit the Wiley **Team for Success** website to hear from the authors first-hand as they discuss their teaching styles, collaboration, and the future of accounting.

www.wileyteamforsuccess.com

# Author Commitment

## Jerry Weygandt

Jerry J. Weygandt, PhD, CPA, is Arthur Andersen Alumni Emeritus Professor of Accounting at the University of Wisconsin—Madison. He holds a Ph.D. in accounting from the University of Illinois. Articles by Professor Weygandt have appeared in the Accounting Review, Journal of Accounting Research, Accounting Horizons, Journal of Accountancy, and other academic and professional journals. These articles have examined such financial reporting issues as accounting for price-level adjustments, pensions, convertible securities, stock option contracts, and interim reports. Professor Weygandt is author of other accounting and financial reporting books and is a member of the American Accounting Association, the American Institute of Certified Public Accountants, and the Wisconsin Society of Certified Public Accountants. He has served on numerous committees of the American Accounting Association and as a member of the editorial board of the Accounting Review; he also has served as President and Secretary-Treasurer of the American Accounting Association. In addition, he has been actively involved with the American Institute of Certified Public Accountants and has been a member of the Accounting Standards Executive Committee (AcSEC) of that organization. He has served on the FASB task force that examined the reporting issues related to accounting for income taxes and served as a trustee of the Financial Accounting Foundation. Professor Weygandt has received the Chancellor's Award for Excellence in Teaching and the Beta Gamma Sigma Dean's Teaching Award. He is on the board of directors of M & I Bank of Southern Wisconsin. He is the recipient of the Wisconsin Institute of CPA's Outstanding Educator's Award and the Lifetime Achievement Award. In 2001 he received the American Accounting Association's Outstanding Educator Award.

## Paul Kimmel

Paul D. Kimmel, PhD, CPA, received his bachelor's degree from the University of Minnesota and his doctorate in accounting from the University of Wisconsin. He is an Associate Professor at the University of Wisconsin—Milwaukee, and has public accounting experience with Deloitte & Touche (Minneapolis). He was the recipient of the UWM School of Business Advisory Council Teaching Award, the Reggie Taite Excellence in Teaching Award and a three-time winner of the Outstanding Teaching Assistant Award at the University of Wisconsin. He is also a recipient of the Elijah Watts Sells Award for Honorary Distinction for his results on the CPA exam. He is a member of the American Accounting Association and the Institute of Management Accountants and has published articles in Accounting Review, Accounting Horizons, Advances in Management Accounting, Managerial Finance, Issues in Accounting Education, Journal of Accounting Education, as well as other journals. His research interests include accounting for financial instruments and innovation in accounting education. He has published papers and given numerous talks on incorporating critical thinking into accounting education, and helped prepare a catalog of critical thinking resources for the Federated Schools of Accountancy.

## Don Kieso

Donald E. Kieso, PhD, CPA, received his bachelor's degree from Aurora University and his doctorate in accounting from the University of Illinois. He has served as chairman of the Department of Accountancy and is currently the KPMG Emeritus Professor of Accountancy at Northern Illinois University. He has public accounting experience with Price Waterhouse & Co. (San Francisco and Chicago) and Arthur Andersen & Co. (Chicago) and research experience with the Research Division of the American Institute of Certified Public Accountants (New York). He has done post doctorate work as a Visiting Scholar at the University of California at Berkeley and is a recipient of NIU's Teaching Excellence Award and four Golden Apple Teaching Awards. Professor Kieso is the author of other accounting and business books and is a member of the American Accounting Association, the American Institute of Certified Public Accountants, and the Illinois CPA Society. He has served as a member of the Board of Directors of the Illinois CPA Society, then AACSB's Accounting Accreditation Committees, the State of Illinois Comptroller's Commission, as Secretary-Treasurer of the Federation of Schools of Accountancy, and as Secretary-Treasurer of the American Accounting Association. Professor Kieso is currently serving on the Board of Trustees and Executive Committee of Aurora University, as a member of the Board of Directors of Kishwaukee Community Hospital, and as Treasurer and Director of Valley West Community Hospital. From 1989 to 1993 he served as a charter member of the national Accounting Education Change Commission. He is the recipient of the Outstanding Accounting Educator Award from the Illinois CPA Society, the FSA's Joseph A. Silvoso Award of Merit, the NIU Foundation's Humanitarian Award for Service to Higher Education, a Distinguished Service Award from the Illinois CPA Society, and in 2003 an honorary doctorate from Aurora University.

# for Students

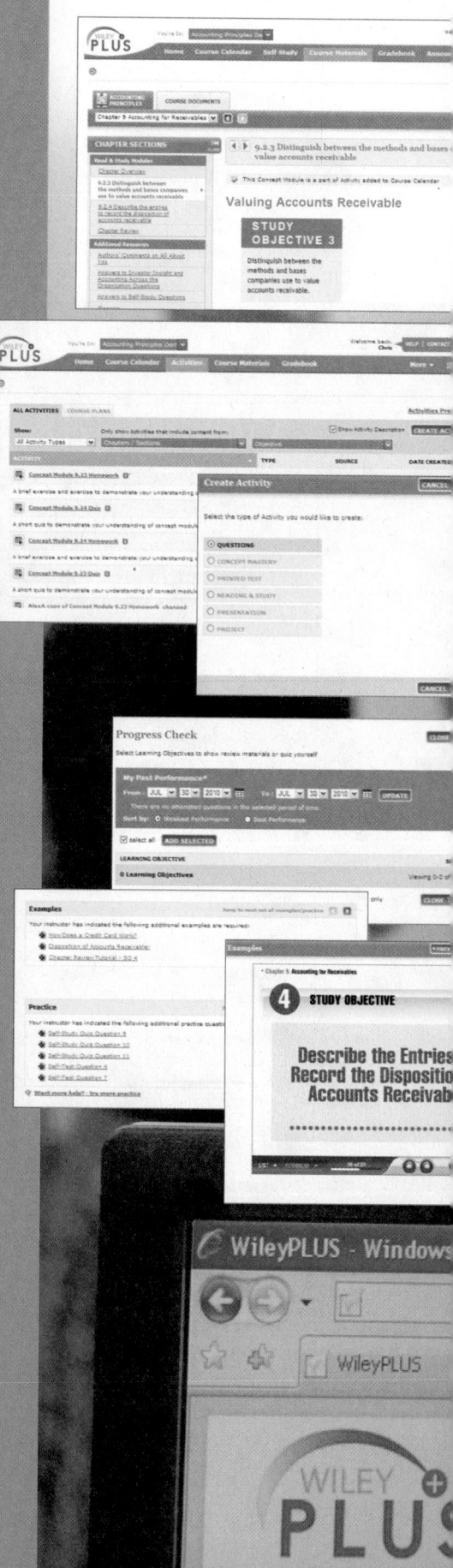

# WileyPLUS

*WileyPLUS* is an innovative, research-based, online environment for effective teaching and learning.

## What do STUDENTS receive with *WileyPLUS*?

*WileyPLUS* increases confidence through an innovative **design** that allows greater **engagement**, which leads to improved learning **outcomes**.

## Design

The *WileyPLUS* design integrates relevant resources, including the entire digital textbook, in an easy-to-navigate framework that helps students study more effectively and ensures student engagement. Innovative features, such as calendars and visual progress tracking, as well as a variety of self-evaluation tools, are all designed to improve time-management and increase student confidence.

## Engagement

*WileyPLUS* organizes the textbook content into smaller, more manageable learning units with demonstrable study objectives and outcomes. Related media, examples, and sample practice items are integrated within each section to reinforce the study objectives. Throughout each study session, students can assess progress and gain immediate feedback on strengths and weaknesses in order to ensure they are spending their time most effectively.

## Outcomes

Throughout each study session, students can assess their progress and gain immediate feedback. *WileyPLUS* provides precise reporting of strengths and weaknesses, as well as individualized quizzes, so that students are confident they are spending their time on the right things. With *WileyPLUS*, students always know the exact outcome of their efforts.

With increased confidence, motivation is sustained so students stay on task longer, leading to success.

## for Instructors

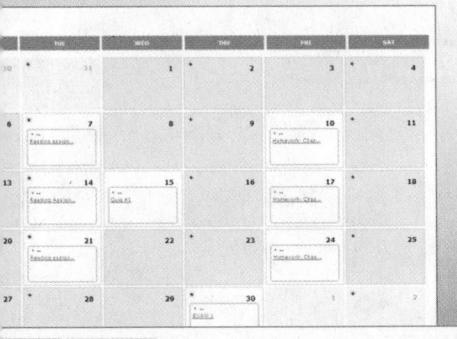

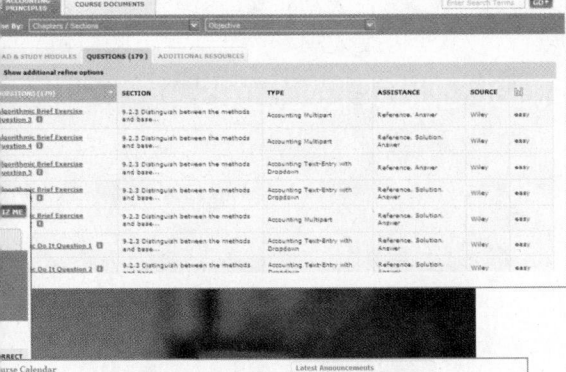

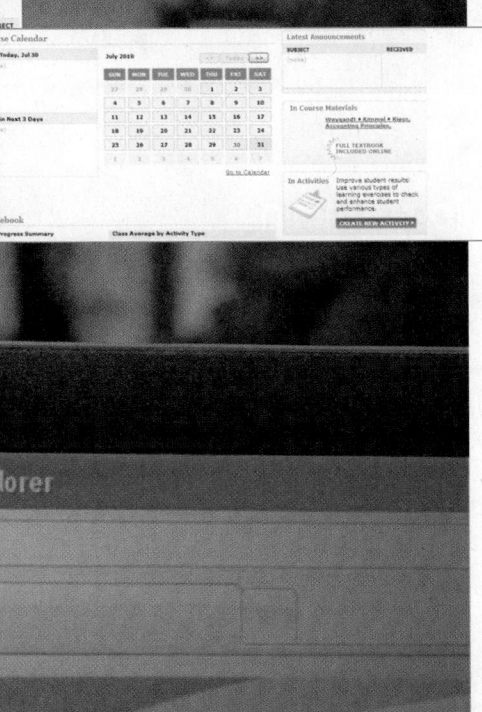

**What do INSTRUCTORS receive with *WileyPLUS*?
Support and Insight into Student Progress**

*WileyPLUS* provides reliable, customizable resources that reinforce course goals inside and outside of the classroom, as well as visibility into individual student progress. Pre-created materials and activities help instructors optimize their time.

**For class preparation and classroom use:**
- Lecture Notes, PowerPoint Slides, and Tutorials
- Classroom Response System (Clicker) Questions
- Image Gallery

**For assignments and testing:**
- Gradable Reading Assignment Questions (embedded with online text)
- Question Assignments: all end-of-chapter problems coded algorithmically with hints, links to text

**For course planning:** *WileyPLUS* comes with a pre-created **Course Plan** designed by a subject matter expert uniquely for this course. Simple drag-and-drop tools make it easy to assign the course plan as-is or modify it to reflect your course syllabus.

**For progress monitoring:** *WileyPLUS* provides instant access to reports on trends in class performance, student use of course materials, and progress toward learning objectives, helping inform decisions and drive classroom discussions.

Experience *WileyPLUS* for effective teaching and learning at **www.wileyplus.com**.

Powered by proven technology and built on a foundation of cognitive research, *WileyPLUS* has enriched the education of millions of students, in over 20 countries around the world.

# The Wiley Faculty Network

## The Place Where Faculty Connect ...

The Wiley Faculty Network is a global community of faculty connected by a passion for teaching and a drive to learn and share. Connect with the Wiley Faculty Network to collaborate with your colleagues, find a mentor, attend virtual and live events, and view a wealth of resources all designed to help you grow as an educator. Embrace the art of teaching—great things happen where faculty connect!

**Attend**

Discover innovative ideas and gain knowledge you can use.

- Training
- Virtual Guest Lectures
- Live Events

**View**

Explore your resources and development opportunities.

- Teaching Resources
- Archived Guest Lectures
- Recorded Presentations
- Professional Development Modules

**Collaborate**

Connect with colleagues— your greatest resource.

- Find a Mentor
- Interest Groups
- Blog

Find out more at
www.WHEREFACULTYCONNECT.com

## Virtual Guest Lectures

Connect with recognized leaders across disciplines and collaborate with your peers on timely topics and discipline specific issues, many of which offer CPE credit.

## Live and Virtual Events

These invitation-only, discipline-specific events are organized through a close partnership between the WFN, Wiley, and the academic community near the event location.

## Technology Training

Discover a wealth of topic- and technology-specific training presented by subject matter experts, authors, and faculty where and when you need it.

## Teaching Resources

Propel your teaching and student learning to the next level with quality peer-reviewed case studies, testimonials, classroom tools, and checklists.

## Connect with Colleagues

Achieve goals and tackle challenges more easily by enlisting the help of your peers. Connecting with colleagues through the WFN can help you improve your teaching experience.

**IFRS**

*Ready When You Are*

TOKYO BEIJING PARIS LONDON NEW YORK

*The emerging importance of* International Financial Reporting Standards presents challenges in how you teach and how your students learn Accounting.

The **Wiley Accounting Team for Success** is ready when you are to help prepare you and your students for the integration of IFRS into your courses.

No matter where you are in this transition, Wiley Accounting is here to provide the tools you need to fully incorporate IFRS into your accounting courses. We offer the most extensive **Products**, **Content**, **Services**, **Support**, and **Training** available today—leading the way to prepare you and your students for success!

*Innovative Products:* New IFRS Editions of **Kieso, Intermediate Accounting** and **Weygandt, Financial Accounting** are the most current and only textbooks available based fully on International Financial Reporting Standards. Wiley Accounting also offers numerous IFRS resources that can serve to supplement your course.

*Exclusive Content:* Our accounting publications feature more quality and current coverage of IFRS topics than any other textbook available today! The Wiley Accounting Team for Success authors integrate IFRS content within each chapter through features like **A Look at IFRS**, which demonstrates how international standards apply to each U.S. GAAP topic, as well as provides an opportunity for practical application. **International Insights** also provide an international perspective of the accounting topic discussed in the text.

*Support & Services:* Wiley Accounting features a dedicated **IFRS website** (at *www.wileyifrs.com*) and an **Accounting Weekly Updates website** (at *www. wileyaccountingupdates.com*) to make sure you have the most current resources available.

*Timely Training:* Wiley Accounting and the **Wiley Faculty Network** provides free IFRS virtual training workshops, IFRS Guest Lectures, and IFRS "Boot Camps" featuring authors Paul Kimmel and Terry Warfield. You can also earn **CPE credit** for attending these sessions.

To learn more about how the Wiley Accounting Team for Success can help your students succeed, visit **www.wileyteamforsuccess.com** or contact your Wiley sales representative today.

# What's new?

The Fourth Edition expands our emphasis on student learning and improves upon a teaching and learning package that instructors and students have rated the highest in customer satisfaction in the following ways:

## The Accounting Cycle

For many students, success in an introductory accounting course hinges on developing a sound conceptual understanding of the accounting cycle. In the past, we have received positive feedback regarding the framework that we have employed to introduce the recording process in Chapter 3. In this edition, we have expanded our use of this framework to cover the entire accounting cycle in Chapters 3 and 4.

## Anatomy of a Fraud

In the Third Edition, we added a new feature, called *Anatomy of a Fraud*, to Chapter 7 to illustrate how the lack of specific internal controls resulted in real-world frauds. Many users responded favorably to this new feature and requested that we expand it throughout the textbook to demonstrate the importance of internal controls to all assets and liabilities. Accordingly, in this edition, we have expanded the *Anatomy of a Fraud* feature to Chapters 5–13.

## Chart of Accounts

It is important to always try to eliminate unnecessary barriers to student understanding. Sometimes, the accounting course can seem unnecessarily complicated to students because so many account titles are used. In order to reduce possible confusion, and to keep students focused on those concepts that really matter, in this edition of the textbook we undertook to reduce the number of account titles used. In some chapters, we were able to cut the number of accounts used by more than half. See inside the front cover of the textbook for a sample chart of accounts, which represents the majority of account titles used in the text.

## Service Company Coverage

Because the U.S. economy is increasingly comprised of service companies, we have expanded our emphasis on service companies in this edition. We have added sections that specifically address the similarities and differences of applying managerial accounting techniques in a service company environment rather than a manufacturing environment, and expanded our use of service company examples.

## Enhanced Homework Material

In each chapter, we have revised all Self-Test Questions, Questions, Brief Exercises, Do it! Review, Exercises, Problems, and Research Cases. Financial analysis and reporting problems have been updated in accordance with the new Tootsie Roll and Hershey financial statements. Finally, new *FASB Codification Activities* now appear at the end of every chapter and offer students experience in using this system.

## Updated International Financial Reporting Standards (IFRS) Content

As we continue to strive to reflect the constant changes in the accounting environment, we have added new material on International Financial Reporting Standards (IFRS). A new end-of-chapter section, *A Look at IFRS*, includes an overview section, differences between GAAP and IFRS, IFRS/GAAP convergence efforts, and IFRS Self-Test Questions and IFRS Concepts and Applications. An international financial reporting problem is also included, based on Zetar plc (a U.K. candy company) financial statements, provided in a new Appendix C of the textbook. This will allow students to compare Zetar with U.S. companies Tootsie Roll and Hershey.

This edition was also subject to an overall, comprehensive revision to ensure that it is technically accurate, relevant, and up-to-date. A chapter-by-chapter summary of content changes is provided in the chart on the next page.

## Chapter 1 Introduction to Financial Statements
- More background information/student involvement with hypothetical company Sierra Corporation.
- Interrelationships of Statements illustration rewritten, using Tootsie Roll instead of Sierra Corporation as example.

## Chapter 2 A Further Look at Financial Statements
- Use of hhgregg instead of Circuit City, as comparison to Best Buy performance.
- Using the Statement of Cash Flows section deleted, as material covered in following *Keeping an Eye on Cash* section.
- Financial Reporting Concepts section heavily rewritten. The Standard-Setting Environment now includes IASB/IFRS discussion, as well as most recent conceptual framework material (e.g., fundamental and enhancing qualities of useful accounting information). Measurement principles now include cost and fair value; constraints are now materiality and cost (instead of conservatism).

## Chapter 3 The Accounting Information System
- For all transaction events, have reformatted to be consistent, that is, have added Basic Analysis and Equation Analysis sections.

## Chapter 4 Accrual Accounting Concepts
- Terminology changes: Matching principle to expense recognition principle; time period assumption to periodicity assumption.
- 2 new *Insight boxes*: one *Business Insight* on iPhone/Apple, other *Int'l Insight* on China's inconsistent use of accrual/cash basis of accounting.
- Consistent use of transaction analysis format (e.g., Basic Analysis, Equation Analysis, Debit-Credit Analysis, Journal Entry, and Posting) for Adjusting Entries examples, carried over from Chapter 3.

## Chapter 5 Merchandising Operations and the Multiple-Step Income Statement
- Addition of *Anatomy of a Fraud* box (previously only included in Chapter 7).

## Chapter 6 Reporting and Analyzing Inventory
- Addition of *Anatomy of a Fraud* box.

## Chapter 7 Fraud, Internal Control, and Cash
- Replaced Investor Insight box with new one on Madoff's Ponzi scheme.

## Chapter 8 Reporting and Analyzing Receivables
- More journal entry detail in the Recognizing Accounts Receivable section.
- Additional explanation about percentage of receivables basis.
- New *Anatomy of a Fraud* box.
- Explanation of maturity date of promissory note, in *Determining the Maturity Date* section.
- New *Int'l Insight* box on fair value, and new *AATO* box on eBay for receivables (Receivables Exchange).

## Chapter 9 Reporting and Analyzing Long-Lived Assets
- Expanded explanation for how to determine revised depreciation, including new *Do it!* box.
- New *Anatomy of a Fraud* box about WorldCom.

## Chapter 10 Reporting and Analyzing Liabilities
- Heavy edit of Feature Story, about U.S. auto industry.
- New *Anatomy of a Fraud* box about school district substitute-teacher fraud scheme.
- New *Investor Insight* box on debt masking.

## Chapter 11 Reporting and Analyzing Stockholders' Equity
- New *AATO* box on Facebook maintaining its private-company status.
- New *Anatomy of a Fraud* box on SafeNet's stock options being misused by top officers.
- New *Investor Insight* box on Warren Buffet's philosophy of keeping Berkshire Hathaway's stock prices high as well as avoiding stock splits.

## Chapter 12 Statement of Cash Flows
- New *Anatomy of a Fraud* box, about Parmalat's multiple frauds.
- **New Appendix 12B**, on preparing statement of cash flows using T accounts.

## Chapter 13 Financial Analysis: The Big Picture
- New Feature Story with profile of Warren Buffett.
- Replaced financial data with hypothetical company, as better basis for later comparison with General Mills.
- New *Anatomy of a Fraud* box, about how relationships between numbers can be used to detect fraud.
- New *Investor Insight* box, about credit rating agencies.

## Chapter 14 Managerial Accounting
- Rewritten Feature Story on Dell and Hewlett-Packard.
- Completely revised Cost Concepts section, featuring different company.
- New section, "Product Costing for Service Industries."
- New Service Company Insight box on Allegiant Airlines.

## Chapter 15 Job Order Costing
- New sections, "Job Order Costing for Service Companies" and "Advantages and Disadvantages of Job Order Costing."
- New Service Company Insight box, about General Electric's use of job order costing for its sales and service on jet engines.

## Chapter 16 Process Costing
- New section, "Process Costing for Service Companies."
- New Ethics Note on equivalent units.

## Chapter 17 Activity-Based Costing
- International Insight box, "The Origins of ABC," now incorporated as text discussion.
- New Service Company Insight boxes on baggage fees imposed by the airlines and the use of ABC as an employee evaluation tool in a small service company.

## Chapter 18 Cost-Volume-Profit
- New Feature Story on accounting for health-care costs.
- New Management Insight box on how skilled labor is essential to manufacturers.

## Chapter 20 Budgetary Planning
- New Service Company Insight box about budgetary concerns at museums and universities.

## Chapter 21 Budgetary Control and Responsibility Accounting
- New Feature Story, "Turning Trash into Treasure."
- New Management Insight box, about Honda's flexible manufacturing facilities.

## End-of-Textbook
**New Appendix C**, financial statements of Zetar plc (U.K. candy company).

# Acknowledgments

*Accounting* has benefited greatly from the input of focus group participants, manuscript reviewers, those who have sent comments by letter or e-mail, ancillary authors, and proofers. We greatly appreciate the constructive suggestions and innovative ideas of reviewers and the creativity and accuracy of the ancillary authors and checkers.

## Prior Editions

*Thanks to the following reviewers and focus group participants of prior editions of Accounting:*

Dawn Addington, *Central New Mexico Community College*; Gilda Agacer, *Monmouth University*; Solochidi Ahiarah, *Buffalo State College*; C. Richard Aldridge, *Western Kentucky University*; Sheila Ammons, *Austin Community College*; Thomas G. Amyot, *College of Santa Rose*; Brian Baick, *Montgomery College*; Cheryl Bartlett, *Central New Mexico Community College*; Timothy Baker, *California State University—Fresno*; Benjamin Bean, *Utah Valley State College.*

Victoria Beard, *University of North Dakota*; Angela H. Bell, *Jacksonville State University*; Charles Bokemeier, *Michigan State University*; John A. Booker, *Tennessee Technological University*; Robert L. Braun, *Southeastern Louisiana University*; Daniel Brickner, *Eastern Michigan University*; Sarah Ruth Brown, *University of North Alabama*; Charles Bunn, *Wake Technical Community College*; Thane Butt, *Champlain College*; James Byrne, *Oregon State University*; and Sandra Byrd, *Missouri State University.*

Judy Cadle, *Tarleton State University*; Julia Camp, *University of Massachusetts—Boston*; David Carr, *Austin Community College*; Jack Cathey, *University of North Carolina—Charlotte*; Andy Chen, *Northeast Illinois University*; Jim Christianson, *Austin Community College*; Laura Claus, *Louisiana State University*; Leslie A. Cohen, *University of Arizona*; Teresa L. Conover, *University of North Texas*; Samantha Cox, *Wake Technical Community College*; Janet Courts, *San Bernadino Valley College*; Dori Danko, *Grand Valley State University*; Helen Davis, *Johnson and Wales University*; Cheryl Dickerson, *Western Washington University*; George M. Dow, *Valencia Community College—West*; Kathy J. Dow, *Salem State College*; and Lola Dudley, *Eastern Illinois University.*

Mary Emery, *St. Olaf College*; Martin L. Epstein, *Central New Mexico Community College*; Larry R. Falcetto, *Emporia State University*; Scott Fargason, *Louisiana State University*; Janet Farler, *Pima Community College*; Sheila D. Foster, *The Citadel*; Jessica J. Frazier, *Eastern Kentucky University*; Lisa Gillespie, *Loyola University—Chicago*; Norman H. Godwin, *Auburn University*; David Gotlob, *Indiana University—Purdue University—Fort Wayne*; Emmett Griner, *Georgia State University*; Leon J. Hanouille, *Syracuse University*; Kenneth M. Hiltebeitel, *Villanova University*; Harry Hooper, *Santa Fe Community College*; Judith A. Hora, *University of San Diego*; and Carol Olson Houston, *San Diego State University*; and Sam Isley, *Wake Technical Community College.*

Norma Jacobs, *Austin Community College*; Marianne L. James, *California State University—Los Angeles*; Stanley Jenne, *University of Montana*; Christopher Jones, *George Washington University*; Jane Kaplan, *Drexel University*; John E. Karayan, *California State University—Pomona*; Susan Kattelus, *Eastern Michigan University*; Dawn Kelly, *Texas Tech University*; Cindi Khanlarian, *University of North Carolina—Greensboro*; Robert Kiddoo, *California State University—Northridge*; Robert J. Kirsch, *Southern Connecticut State University*; Frank Korman, *Mountain View College*; and Jerry G. Kreuze, *Western Michigan University.*

John Lacey, *California State University—Long Beach*; Doug Laufer, *Metropolitan State College of Denver*; Doulas Larson, *Salem State College*; Keith Leeseberg, *Manatee Community College*; Glenda Levendowski, *Arizona State University*; Seth Levine, *DeVry University*; James Lukawitz, *University of Memphis*; Noel McKeon, *Florida Community College*; P. Merle Maddocks, *University of Alabama—Huntsville*; Janice Mardon, *Green River Community College*; John Marts, *University of North Carolina—Wilmington*; Alan Mayer-Sommer, *Georgetown University*; Sara Melendy, *Gonzaga University*; Barbara Merino, *University of North Texas*; Jeanne Miller, *Cypress College*; Robert Miller, *California State University—Fullerton*; Elizabeth Minbiole, *Northwood University*; Sherry Mirbod, *Montgomery College*; Andrew Morgret, *University of Memphis*; Michelle Moshier, *SUNY Albany*; Marguerite Muise, *Santa Ana College*; James Neurath, *Central Michigan University*; and Gale E. Newell, *Western Michigan University*; Jim Neurath, *Central Michigan University*; and Garth Novack, *Utah State University.*

Suzanne Ogilby, *Sacramento State University*; Sarah N. Palmer, *University of North Carolina—Charlotte*; Patricia Parker, *Columbus State Community College*; Charles Pier, *Appalachian State University*; Meg Pollard, *American River College*; Franklin J. Plewa, *Idaho State University*; John Purisky, *Salem State College*; Donald J. Raux, *Siena College*; Judith Resnick, *Borough of Manhattan Community College*; Mary Ann Reynolds, *Western Washington University*; Carla Rich, *Pensacola Junior College*; Ray Rigoli, *Ramapo College of New Jersey*; Jeff Ritter, *St. Norbert College*; Brandi Roberts, *Southeastern Louisiana University*; Patricia A. Robinson, *Johnson and Wales University*; Nancy Rochman, *University of Arizona*; Marc A. Rubin, *Miami University*; and John A. Rude, *Bloomsburg University.*

Alfredo Salas, *El Paso Community College*; Christine Schalow, *California State University—San Bernardino*; Michael Schoderbek, *Rutgers University*; Richard Schroeder, *University of North Carolina—Charlotte*; Bill N. Schwartz, *Stevens Institute of Technology*; Jerry Searfoss, *University of Utah*; Cindy Seipel, *New Mexico State University*; Anne E. Selk, *University of Wisconsin—Green Bay*; William Seltz, *University of Massachusetts*; Suzanne Sevalstad, *University of Nevada*; Mary Alice Seville, *Oregon State University*; Donald Smillie, *Southwest Missouri State University*; Aileen Smith, *Stephen F. Austin State University*; Talitha Smith, *Auburn University*; Pam Smith, *Northern Illinois University*; William E. Smith, *Xavier University*; Will Snyder, *San Diego State University*; Chris Solomon, *Trident Technical College*; Teresa A. Speck, *St. Mary's University of Minnesota*; Charles Stanley, *Baylor University*; Ron Stone, *California State University—Northridge*; Gary Stout, *California State University—Northridge*; Gracelyn Stuart, *Palm Beach Community College*; and Ellen L. Sweatt, *Georgia Perimeter College.*

William Talbot, *Montgomery College*; Diane Tanner, *University of North Florida*; Pamadda Tantral, *Fairleigh Dickinson University*; Steve Teeter, *Utah Valley State College*; Andrea B. Weickgenannt, *Northern Kentucky University*; David P. Weiner, *University of San Francisco*; Frederick Weis, *Claremont McKenna College*; T. Sterling Wetzel, *Oklahoma State University*; Allan Young, *DeVry University*; Michael F. van Breda, *Texas Christian University*; Linda G. Wade, *Tarleton State University*; Stuart K. Webster, *University of Wyoming*; V. Joyce Yearley, *New Mexico State University*; and Joan Van Hise, *Fairfield University.*

# Fourth Edition

*Thanks to the following reviewers, focus group participants,
and others who provided suggestions for the Fourth Edition:*

| | |
|---|---|
| Sylvia Allen | *Los Angeles Valley College* |
| Juanita Ardavany | *Los Angeles Valley College* |
| Eric Blazer | *Millersville University* |
| Evangelie Brodie | *North Carolina State University* |
| Thane Butt | *Champlain College* |
| Sandra Byrd | *Missouri State University* |
| Lisa Capozzoli | *College of DuPage* |
| Siu Chung | *Los Angeles Valley College* |
| Leslie Cohen | *University of Arizona* |
| Rita Kingery Cook | *University of Delaware* |
| Cheryl Copeland | *California State University—Fresno* |
| Cheryl Crespi | *Central Connecticut State University* |
| Sue Counte | *St. Louis Community College—Meramec* |
| Robin D'Agati | *Palm Beach Community College* |
| Brent W. Darwin | *Allan Hancock College* |
| Michael Deschamps | *Mira Costa College* |
| Gadis Dillon | *Oakland University* |
| Rafik Elias | *University of California, Los Angeles* |
| Alan Falcon | *Loyola Marymount University* |
| Annette Fisher | *Glendale Community College* |
| Lance Fisher | *Oklahoma State University* |
| Roger Gee | *San Diego Mesa College* |
| Lisa Gray | *Seminole State College and Valencia Community College* |
| Michael Haselkorn | *Bentley University* |
| Hassan Hefzi | *California State PolyTech University—Pomona* |
| M.A. "Maggie" Houston | *Wright State University* |
| Ryan Huldah | *Iona College* |
| Ann Kelly | *Providence College* |
| Mehmet Kocakulah | *University of Southern Indiana* |
| Wikil Kwak | *University of Nebraska—Omaha* |
| Barbara Lamberton | *University of Hartford* |
| Lihon Liang | *Syracuse University* |
| D. Jordan Lowe | *Arizona State University* |
| James Lukawitz | *University of Memphis* |
| Sue Marcum | *American University* |
| Sal Marino | *Westchester Community College* |
| Florence McGovern | *Bergen Community College* |
| Noel McKeon | *Florida Community College at Jacksonville* |
| Paul Mihalek | *Central Connecticut State University* |
| Jeanne Miller | *Cypress College* |
| William J. Nealon | *Schenectady County Community College* |
| Joseph M. Nicassio | *Westmoreland County Community College* |
| Garth Novack | *University of Washington* |
| Rosemary Nurre | *San Mateo Community College* |
| Marge O'Reilly-Allen | *Rider University* |
| Terry Patton | *Midwestern State University* |
| Sandra Pelfrey | *Oakland University* |
| Ronald Pierno | *Florida State University* |
| John Purisky | *Salem State University* |
| Karl Putnam | *University of Texas—El Paso* |
| Ray Reisig | *Pace University, Pleasantville* |
| Rod Ridenour | *Montana State University—Bozeman* |
| Larry Rittenberg | *University of Wisconsin* |
| Cecile M. Roberti | *Community College of Rhode Island* |
| Lawrence Roman | *Cuyahoga Community College* |
| Luther L. Ross | *Central Piedmont Community College* |
| Robert Russ | *Northern Kentucky University* |
| Nancy Sill | *Modesto Junior College* |
| Gerald Smith | *University of Northern Iowa* |
| Vic Stanton | *University of California, Berkley* |
| Howard Switkay | *Community College of Philadelphia* |
| Diane Tanner | *University of North Florida* |
| Michael Tydlaska | *Mountain View College* |
| Joan Van Hise | *Fairfield University* |
| Richard Van Ness | *Schenectady County Community College* |
| Ron Vogel | *College of Eastern Utah* |
| Barbara Warschawski | *Schenectady County Community College* |
| Wendy Wilson | *Southern Methodist University* |

# Ancillary Authors, Contributors, and Proofers

*We sincerely thank the following individuals for their hard work
in preparing the content that accompanies this textbook:*

| | |
|---|---|
| LuAnn Bean | *Florida Institute of Technology* |
| Jack Borke | *University of Wisconsin—Platteville* |
| Richard Campbell | *University of Rio Grande* |
| Sandra Cohen | *Columbia College—Chicago* |
| Nancy Everett | *Pima Community College* |
| Larry R. Falcetto | *Emporia State University* |
| Cecelia M. Fewox | *College of Charleston* |
| Coby Harmon | *University of California, Santa Barbara* |
| Harry Howe | *State University of New York—Geneseo* |
| Laura McNally | *Black Hills State College* |
| Kevin McNelis | *New Mexico State University* |
| Barb Muller | *Arizona State University* |
| Rex Schildhouse | *San Diego Community College* |
| Eileen M. Shifflett | *James Madison University* |
| Diane Tanner | *University of North Florida* |
| Sheila Viel | *University of Wisconsin—Milwaukee* |
| Dick D. Wasson | *Southwestern College* |
| Bernie Weinrich | *Lindenwood University* |
| Melanie Yon | |

*We also greatly appreciate the expert assistance provided
by the following individuals in checking the accuracy
of the content that accompanies this textbook:*

| | |
|---|---|
| LuAnn Bean | *Florida Institute of Technology* |
| Terry Elliott | *Morehead State University* |
| James M. Emig | *Villanova University* |
| Larry R. Falcetto | *Emporia State University* |
| Lance Fisher | *Oklahoma State University* |
| Kirk Lynch | *Sandhills Community College* |
| Jill Misuraca | *Central Connecticut State University* |
| Patricia Mounce | *University of Central Arkansas* |
| Barb Muller | *Arizona State University* |
| Yvonne Phang | *Borough of Manhattan Community College* |
| John Plouffe | *California State University—Los Angeles* |
| Rex Schildhouse | *San Diego Community College* |
| Alice Sineath | *Forsyth Technical Community College* |
| Teresa Speck | *Saint Mary's University of Minnesota* |
| Lynn Stallworth | *Appalachian State University* |
| Sheila Viel | *University of Wisconsin* |
| Dick D. Wasson | *Southwestern College* |
| Bernie Weinrich | *Lindenwood University* |

We appreciate the exemplary support and commitment given to us by associate publisher Chris DeJohn, senior marketing manager Ramona Sherman, project editor Ed Brislin, project editor Yana Mermel, development editor Terry Ann Tatro, senior media editor Allie Morris, media editor Greg Chaput, vice president of higher education production and manufacturing Ann Berlin, designer Maddy Lesure, illustration editor Anna Melhorn, photo editor Mary Ann Price, permissions editor Joan Naples, project editor Suzanne Ingrao of Ingrao Associates, indexer Steve Ingle, Denise Showers at Aptara, Cyndy Taylor, and project manager Danielle Urban at Elm Street Publishing Services. All of these professionals provided innumerable services that helped the textbook take shape.

Finally, our thanks to Amy Scholz, Susan Elbe, George Hoffman, Tim Stookesberry, Joe Heider, Bonnie Lieberman, and Will Pesce, for their support and leadership in Wiley's College Division. We will appreciate suggestions and comments from users—instructors and students alike. You can send your thoughts and ideas about the textbook to us via email at: *AccountingAuthors@yahoo.com.*

| | | |
|---|---|---|
| Paul D. Kimmel | Jerry J. Weygandt | Donald E. Kieso |
| *Milwaukee, Wisconsin* | *Madison, Wisconsin* | *DeKalb, Illinois* |

# Brief Contents

\*Available at the book's companion website, *www.wiley.com/college/kimmel*.

# Contents

# What TYPE of learner are you?

By understanding each of these basic learning styles it enables the authors to engage students minds and motivate them to do their best work, ultimately improving the experience for both students and faculty.

| | Intake: To take in the information | To make a study package | Text features that may help you the most | Output: To do well on exams |
|---|---|---|---|---|
| **VISUAL** | • Pay close attention to charts, drawings, and handouts your instructors use.<br>• Underline.<br>• Use different colors.<br>• Use symbols, flow charts, graphs, different arrangements on the page, white spaces. | Convert your lecture notes into "page pictures."<br><br>To do this:<br>• Use the "Intake" strategies.<br>• Reconstruct images in different ways.<br>• Redraw pages from memory.<br>• Replace words with symbols and initials.<br>• Look at your pages. | The Navigator/Feature Story/Preview<br>Infographics/Illustrations<br>Accounting Equation Analyses<br>Highlighted words<br>Demonstration Problem/ Action Plan<br>Questions/Exercises/Problems<br>Financial Reporting Problem<br>Comparative Analysis Problem<br>Exploring the Web | • Recall your "page pictures."<br>• Draw diagrams where appropriate.<br>• Practice turning your visuals back into words. |
| **AURAL** | • Attend lectures and tutorials.<br>• Discuss topics with students and instructors.<br>• Explain new ideas to other people.<br>• Use a tape recorder.<br>• Leave spaces in your lecture notes for later recall.<br>• Describe overheads, pictures, and visuals to somebody who was not in class. | You may take poor notes because you prefer to listen. Therefore:<br>• Expand your notes by talking with others and with information from your textbook.<br>• Tape-record summarized notes and listen.<br>• Read summarized notes out loud.<br>• Explain your notes to another "aural" person. | Preview<br>Insight Boxes<br>Review It/Do it!/Action Plan<br>Summary of Study Objectives<br>Glossary<br>Demonstration Problem/Action Plan<br>Self-Study Questions<br>Questions/Exercises/Problems<br>Financial Reporting Problem<br>Comparative Analysis Problem<br>Exploring the Web<br>Decision Making Across the Organization | Communication Activity<br>Ethics Case<br>• Talk with the instructor.<br>• Spend time in quiet places recalling the ideas.<br>• Practice writing answers to old exam questions.<br>• Say your answers out loud. |
| **READING/ WRITING** | • Use lists and headings.<br>• Use dictionaries, glossaries, and definitions.<br>• Read handouts, textbooks, and supplementary library readings.<br>• Use lecture notes. | • Write out words again and again.<br>• Reread notes silently.<br>• Rewrite ideas and principles into other words.<br>• Turn charts, diagrams, and other illustrations into statements. | The Navigator/Feature Story/Study Objectives/Preview<br>Review It/Do it!/Action Plan<br>Summary of Study Objectives<br>Glossary/Self-Study Questions<br>Questions/Exercises/Problems<br>Writing Problems<br>Financial Reporting Problem<br>Comparative Analysis Problem<br>"All About You" Activity<br>Exploring the Web<br>Decision Making Across the Organization<br>Communication Activity | • Write exam answers.<br>• Practice with multiple-choice questions.<br>• Write paragraphs, beginning and endings.<br>• Write your lists in outline form.<br>• Arrange your words into hierarchies and points. |
| **KINESTHETIC** | • Use all your senses.<br>• Go to labs, take field trips.<br>• Listen to real-life examples.<br>• Pay attention to applications.<br>• Use hands-on approaches.<br>• Use trial-and-error methods. | You may take poor notes because topics do not seem concrete or relevant. Therefore:<br>• Put examples in your summaries.<br>• Use case studies and applications to help with principles and abstract concepts.<br>• Talk about your notes with another "kinesthetic" person.<br>• Use pictures and photographs that illustrate an idea. | The Navigator/Feature Story/Preview<br>Infographics/Illustrations<br>Review It/Do it!/Action Plan<br>Summary of Study Objectives<br>Demonstration Problem/ Action Plan<br>Self-Study Questions<br>Questions/Exercises/Problems<br>Financial Reporting Problem<br>Comparative Analysis Problem<br>Exploring the Web<br>Decision Making Across the Organization<br>Communication Activity<br>"All About You" Activity | • Write practice answers.<br>• Role-play the exam situation |

# Active Teaching and Learning Supplementary Material

*Accounting*, Fourth Edition, features a full line of teaching and learning resources. Driven by the same basic beliefs as the textbook, these supplements provide a consistent and well-integrated learning system. This hands-on, real-world package guides instructors through the process of active learning and gives them the tools to create an interactive learning environment. With its emphasis on activities, exercises, and the Internet, the package encourages students to take an active role in the course and prepares them for decision making in a real-world context.

## KIMMEL'S INTEGRATED TECHNOLOGY SOLUTIONS HELPING TEACHERS TEACH AND STUDENT LEARN—
www.wiley.com/college/kimmel

# For Instructors

## Textbook Companion Website

On this website, instructors will find electronic versions of the Solutions Manual, Test Bank, Instructor's Manual, Computerized Test Bank, and other resources.

## Wiley Faculty Network

When it comes to improving the classroom experience, there is no better source of ideas and inspiration than your fellow colleagues. The Wiley Faculty Network connects teachers with technologies, facilitates the exchange of best practices, and helps to enhance instructional efficiency and effectiveness. For details, visit *www.wherefacultyconnect.com*.

## Active-Teaching Aids

An extensive support package, including print and technology tools, helps you maximize your teaching effectiveness. We offer useful supplements for instructors with varying levels of experience and different instructional circumstances.

### Instructor's Resource CD.
The Instructor's Resource CD (IRCD) contains an electronic version of all instructor supplements. The IRCD gives you the flexibility to access and prepare instructional materials based on your individual needs.

## Solutions Manual.
The Solutions Manual contains detailed solutions to all questions, brief exercises, exercises, and problems in the textbook as well as suggested answers to the questions and cases.

## Solution Transparencies.
The solution transparencies feature detailed solutions to brief exercises, exercises, problems, and "Broadening Your Perspectives" activities. Transparencies can be easily ordered from the Instructor's textbook companion website.

## Instructor's Manual.
Included in each chapter are lecture outlines with teaching tips, chapter reviews, illustrations, and review quizzes.

## Teaching Transparencies.
The teaching transparencies are 4-color acetate images of the illustrations found in the Instructor's Manual. Transparencies can be easily ordered from the Instructor's textbook companion website.

## Test Bank and Computerized Test Bank.
The test bank and computerized test bank allow instructors to tailor examinations according to study objectives and Bloom's taxonomy. Achievement tests, comprehensive examinations, and a final exam are included.

## PowerPoint™.
The new PowerPoint™ presentations contain a combination of key concepts, images and problems from the textbook. Review exercises and "All About You" summaries are included in each chapter to encourage classroom participation.

## WebCT and Desire2Learn.
WebCT or Desire2Learn offer an integrated set of course management tools that enable instructors to easily design, develop, and manage Web-based and Web-enhanced courses.

# For Students

## Active-Learning Aids

### Textbook Companion Website.
The Financial Accounting student website provides a wealth of support materials that will help students develop their conceptual understanding of class material and increase their ability to solve problems. On this website, students will find Excel templates, PowerPoint presentations, web quizzing, and other resources. In addition, students can access the new B Exercises and C Problems at this site. Finally, full versions of the Continuing Cookie Chronicle and Waterways problems are included at the student website.

### Excel Working Papers.
Excel working papers are partially completed accounting forms (templates) for all end-of-chapter brief exercises, exercises, problems, and cases. They are a convenient resource for organizing and completing homework assignments, and they demonstrate how to correctly set up solution formats. Also available on CD-ROM and within *WileyPLUS* is an electronic version of the print working papers, which are Excel-formatted templates that will help you learn to properly format and present end-of-chapter textbook solutions.

### Study Guide.
The Study Guide is a comprehensive review of accounting. It guides you through chapter content, tied to study objectives. Each chapter of the Study Guide includes a chapter review and for extra practice, true/false, multiple-choice, matching questions, and problems, with solutions. The Study Guide is an excellent tool for use on a regular basis during the course and also when preparing for exams.

### Primer on Using Excel in Accounting.
This online manual and collection of Excel templates allow students to complete select end-of-chapter exercises and problems identified by a spreadsheet icon in the textbook.

### Mobile Applications.
Quizzing and reviewing content is available for download to an iPod.

# Student Owner's Manual

## *Using Your Textbook Effectively*

**Helpful Hints** in the margins further clarify concepts being discussed. They are like having an instructor with you as you read.

> **Helpful Hint** Stock is sometimes issued in exchange for services (payment to attorneys or consultants, for example) or for noncash assets (land or buildings). The value recorded for the shares issued is determined by either the market value of the shares or the value of the good or service received, depending upon which value the company can more readily determine.

we discuss the accounting for paid-in capital. In a later section, we discuss retained earnings.

Let's now look at how to account for new issues of common stock. The primary objectives in accounting for the issuance of common stock are (1) to identify the specific sources of paid-in capital and (2) to maintain the distinction between paid-in capital and retained earnings. As shown below, **the issuance of common stock affects only paid-in capital accounts**.

As discussed earlier, par value does not indicate a stock's market value. The cash proceeds from issuing par value stock may be equal to, greater than, or less than par value. When a company records the issuance of common stock for cash, it credits the par value of the shares to Common Stock, and records in a separate paid-in capital account the portion of the proceeds that is above or below par value.

> **Ethics Note** Managers who are not owners are often compensated based on the performance of the company. They thus may be tempted to exaggerate company performance by inflating income figures.

The chief executive officer (CEO) has overall responsibility [for managing the] business. As the organization chart shows, the CEO delegates [responsibilities to] other officers. The chief accounting officer is the **controller**. [The controller's re]sponsibilities are to (1) maintain the accounting records, (2) [maintain an ade]quate system of internal control, and (3) prepare financial statements, tax returns, and internal reports. The **treasurer** has custody of the corporation's funds and is responsible for maintaining the company's cash position.

The organizational structure of a corporation enables a company to hire professional managers to run the business. On the other hand, the separation of ownership and management often reduces an owner's ability to actively manage the company.

**Ethics Notes and International Notes** point out ethical and international points related to the nearby text discussion.

**Insight examples** give you more glimpses into how actual companies make decisions using accounting information. These high-interest boxes focus on various themes—ethics, international, and investor concerns.

A **critical thinking question** asks you to apply your accounting learning to the story in the example. *Guideline Answers* appear at the end of the chapter.

### Investor Insight
#### How to Read Stock Quotes

Organized exchanges trade the stock of publicly held companies at dollar prices per share established by the interaction between buyers and sellers. For each listed security, the financial press reports the high and low prices of the stock during the year, the total volume of stock traded on a given day, the high and low prices for the day, and the closing market price, with the net change for the day. Nike is listed on the New York Stock Exchange. Here is a recent listing for Nike:

| Stock | 52 Weeks High | 52 Weeks Low | Volume | High | Low | Close | Net Change |
|-------|------|-----|--------|------|-----|-------|------------|
| Nike | 78.55 | 48.76 | 5,375,651 | 72.44 | 69.78 | 70.61 | −1.69 |

These numbers indicate the following: The high and low market prices for the last 52 weeks have been $78.55 and $48.76. The trading volume for the day was 5,375,651 shares. The high, low, and closing prices for that date were $72.44, $69.78, and $70.61, respectively. The net change for the day was a decrease of $1.69 per share.

For stocks traded on organized exchanges, how are the dollar prices per share established? What factors might influence the price of shares in the marketplace? (See page 619.)

**Accounting Across the Organization** examples show the use of accounting by people in non-accounting functions—such as finance, marketing, or management.

*Guideline Answers* to the critical thinking questions appear at the end of the chapter.

### Accounting Across the Organization
#### Wall Street No Friend of Facebook

In the 1990s, it was the dream of every young technology entrepreneur to start a company and do an initial public offering (IPO), that is, list company shares on a stock exchange. It seemed like there was a never-ending supply of 20-something year-old technology entrepreneurs that made millions doing IPOs of companies that never made a profit and eventually failed. In sharp contrast to this is Mark Zuckerberg, the 25-year-old founder and CEO of Facebook. If Facebook did an IPO, he would make billions of dollars. But, he is in no hurry to go public. Because his company doesn't need to invest in factories, distribution systems, or even marketing, it doesn't need to raise a lot of cash. Also, by not going public, Zuckerberg has more control over the direction of the company. Right now, he and the other founders don't have to answer to outside shareholders, who might be more concerned about short-term investment horizons rather than long-term goals. In addition, publicly traded companies face many more financial reporting disclosure requirements.

*Source:* Jessica E. Vascellaro, "Facebook CEO in No Rush to 'Friend' Wall Street," *Wall Street Journal Online* (March 4, 2010).

Why has Mark Zuckerberg, the CEO and founder of Facebook, delayed taking his company's shares public through an initial public offering (IPO)? (See page 618.)

**Anatomy of a Fraud** boxes illustrate how the lack of specific internal controls resulted in real-world frauds.

### ANATOMY OF A FRAUD

The president, chief operating officer, and chief financial officer of SafeNet, a software encryption company, were each awarded employee stock options by the company's board of directors as part of their compensation package. Stock options enable an employee to buy a company's stock sometime in the future at the price that existed when the stock option was awarded. For example, suppose that you received stock options today, when the stock price of your company was $30. Three years later, if the stock price rose to $100, you could "exercise" your options and buy the stock for $30 per share, thereby making $70 per share. After being awarded their stock options, the three employees changed the award dates in the company's records to dates in the past, when the company's stock was trading at historical lows. For example, using the previous example, they would choose a past date when the stock was selling for $10 per share, rather than the $30 price on the actual

Brief **Do it!** exercises ask you to put to work your newly acquired knowledge. They outline an **Action Plan** necessary to complete the exercise, and they show a **Solution**.

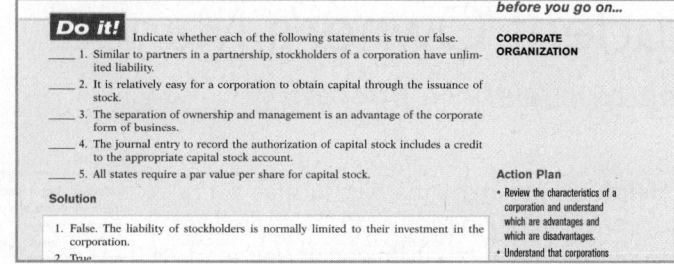

**Do it!**   Indicate whether each of the following statements is true or false.

_____ 1. Similar to partners in a partnership, stockholders of a corporation have unlimited liability.
_____ 2. It is relatively easy for a corporation to obtain capital through the issuance of stock.
_____ 3. The separation of ownership and management is an advantage of the corporate form of business.
_____ 4. The journal entry to record the authorization of capital stock includes a credit to the appropriate capital stock account.
_____ 5. All states require a par value per share for capital stock.

**Solution**

1. False. The liability of stockholders is normally limited to their investment in the corporation.
2. True

before you go on...

**CORPORATE ORGANIZATION**

**Action Plan**
• Review the characteristics of a corporation and understand which are advantages and which are disadvantages.
• Understand that corporations

---

**Comprehensive Do it!**

Rolman Corporation is authorized to issue 1,000,000 shares of $5 par value common stock. In its first year, the company has the following stock transactions.

Jan. 10   Issued 400,000 shares of stock at $8 per share.
Sept. 1   Purchased 10,000 shares of common stock for the treasury at $9 per share.
Dec. 24   Declared a cash dividend of 10 cents per share on common stock outstanding.

**Instructions**

(a) Journalize the transactions.
(b) Prepare the stockholders' equity section of the balance sheet, assuming the company had retained earnings of $150,600 at December 31.

**Comprehensive Do it!** problem with **Action Plan** gives students an opportunity to see a detailed solution to a representative problem before they do their homework. Coincides with the Do it! problems within the chapter.

**Do it! Review** problems appear in the homework material and provide another way for students to determine whether they have mastered the content in the chapters.

---

**Accounting equation analyses** appear next to key journal entries. They will help students understand the impact of an accounting transaction on the components of the accounting equation, on the stockholders' equity accounts, and on the company's cash flows.

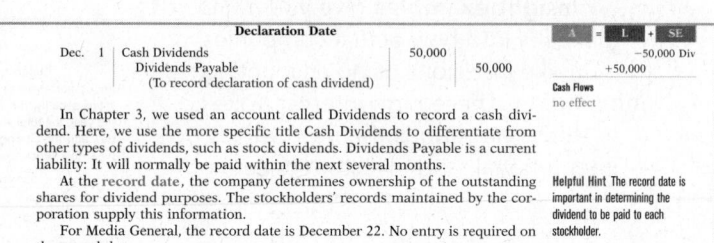

**Declaration Date**

| Dec. 1 | Cash Dividends | 50,000 | |
| | Dividends Payable | | 50,000 |
| | (To record declaration of cash dividend) | | |

A = L + SE
−50,000 Div
+50,000

Cash Flows
no effect

In Chapter 3, we used an account called Dividends to record a cash dividend. Here, we use the more specific title Cash Dividends to differentiate from other types of dividends, such as stock dividends. Dividends Payable is a current liability: It will normally be paid within the next several months.

At the record date, the company determines ownership of the outstanding shares for dividend purposes. The stockholders' records maintained by the corporation supply this information.

For Media General, the record date is December 22. No entry is required on the record date.

Helpful Hint The record date is important in determining the dividend to be paid to each stockholder.

---

**Financial Statements** appear regularly. Those from actual companies are identified by a company logo or a photo.

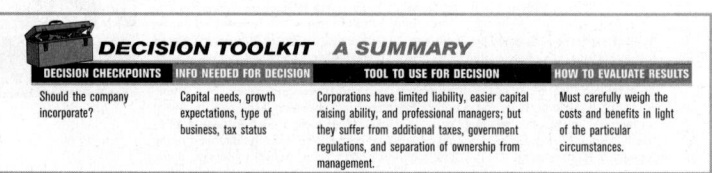

**Illustration 11-15**
Disclosure of unrestricted retained earnings

**TEKTRONIX INC.**
Notes to the Financial Statements

Certain of the Company's debt agreements require compliance with debt covenants. The Company had unrestricted retained earnings of $223.8 million after meeting those requirements.

---

**Decision Toolkits** highlight the important analytical tools integrated throughout the textbook, designed to assist students in evaluating and using the information at hand.

**DECISION TOOLKIT   A SUMMARY**

| DECISION CHECKPOINTS | INFO NEEDED FOR DECISION | TOOL TO USE FOR DECISION | HOW TO EVALUATE RESULTS |
|---|---|---|---|
| Should the company incorporate? | Capital needs, growth expectations, type of business, tax status | Corporations have limited liability, easier capital raising ability, and professional managers; but they suffer from additional taxes, government regulations, and separation of ownership from management. | Must carefully weigh the costs and benefits in light of the particular circumstances. |

---

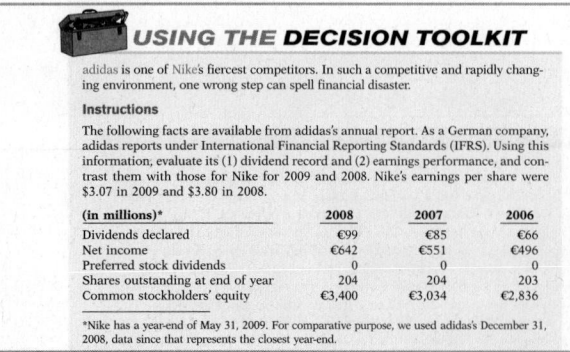

**USING THE DECISION TOOLKIT**

adidas is one of Nike's fiercest competitors. In such a competitive and rapidly changing environment, one wrong step can spell financial disaster.

**Instructions**

The following facts are available from adidas's annual report. As a German company, adidas reports under International Financial Reporting Standards (IFRS). Using this information, evaluate its (1) dividend record and (2) earnings performance, and contrast them with those for Nike for 2009 and 2008. Nike's earnings per share were $3.07 in 2009 and $3.80 in 2008.

| (in millions)* | 2008 | 2007 | 2006 |
|---|---|---|---|
| Dividends declared | €99 | €85 | €66 |
| Net income | €642 | €551 | €496 |
| Preferred stock dividends | 0 | 0 | 0 |
| Shares outstanding at end of year | 204 | 204 | 203 |
| Common stockholders' equity | €3,400 | €3,034 | €2,836 |

*Nike has a year-end of May 31, 2009. For comparative purpose, we used adidas's December 31, 2008, data since that represents the closest year-end.

A **Using the Decision Toolkit** exercise, just before the chapter summary, asks students to use the decision tools presented in the chapter and takes them through the problem-solving steps.

**KEEPING AN EYE ON CASH**

The balance sheet presents the balances of a company's stockholders' equity accounts at a point in time. Companies report in the "Financing Activities" section of the statement of cash flows information regarding cash inflows and outflows during the year that resulted from equity transactions. The excerpt below presents the cash flows from financing activities from the statement of cash flows of Sara Lee Corporation in a recent year. From this information, we learn that the company's purchases of

**Keeping an Eye on Cash** sections highlight differences between accrual accounting and cash accounting while increasing students' understanding of the statement of cash flows.

**Exercises: Set B and Challenge Exercises** are available online at *www.wiley.com/college/kimmel.*

In the textbook, two similar sets of **Problems**—**A** and **B**—are keyed to the same study objectives.

Selected problems, identified by this icon, can be solved using the **General Ledger Software (GLS)** package.

An icon identifies **Exercises** and **Problems** that can be solved using Excel templates at the student website.

### Exercises: Set B and Challenge Exercises

Visit the book's companion website, at **www.wiley.com/college/kimmel,** and choose the Student Companion site to access Exercise Set B and Challenge Exercises.

### Problems: Set A

*Journalize stock transactions, post, and prepare paid-in capital section.*

*(SO 2, 4, 7), AN*

**GLS**

**P11-1A** Whitten Corporation was organized on January 1, 2012. It is authorized to issue 20,000 shares of 6%, $50 par value preferred stock and 500,000 shares of no-par common stock with a stated value of $1 per share. The following stock transactions were completed during the first year.

| | | |
|---|---|---|
| Jan. | 10 | Issued 70,000 shares of common stock for cash at $4 per share. |
| Mar. | 1 | Issued 12,000 shares of preferred stock for cash at $53 per share. |
| May | 1 | Issued 120,000 shares of common stock for cash at $6 per share. |
| Sept. | 1 | Issued 5,000 shares of common stock for cash at $5 per share. |

*Prepare a stockholders' equity section.*

*(SO 7), AP*

**P11-6A** On January 1, 2012, Neville Inc. had these stockholders' equity balances.

| | |
|---|---|
| Common Stock, $1 par (2,000,000 shares authorized, 600,000 shares issued and outstanding) | $ 600,000 |
| Paid-in Capital in Excess of Par Value | 1,500,000 |
| Retained Earnings | 700,000 |

### Service Company Insight

**Sales Are Nice, but Service Revenue Pays the Bills**

Jet engines are one of the many products made by the industrial operations division of General Electric (GE). At prices as high as $30 million per engine, you can bet that GE does its best to keep track of costs. It might surprise you that GE doesn't make much profit on the sale of each engine. So why does it bother making them? Service revenue—during one recent year, about 75% of the division's revenues came from servicing its own products. One estimate is that the $13 billion in aircraft engines sold during a recent three-year period will generate about $90 billion in service revenue over the 30-year life of the engines. Because of the high product costs, both the engines themselves and the subsequent service are most likely accounted for using job order costing. Accurate service cost records are important because GE needs to generate high profit margins on its service jobs to make up for the low margins on the original sale. It also needs good cost records for its service jobs in order to control its costs. Otherwise, a competitor, such as Pratt and Whitney, might submit lower bids for service contracts and take lucrative service jobs away from GE.

Those exercises and problems that focus on accounting situations faced by **service companies** are identified by the icon shown here.

An additional parallel set of **C Problems** appears at the textbook companion website.

### Problems: Set C

Visit the book's companion website, at **www.wiley.com/college/kimmel**, and choose the Student Companion site to access Problem Set C.

### Comprehensive Problem: Chapters 14 to 23

**CP23** You would like to start a business manufacturing a unique model of bicycle helmet. In preparation for an interview with the bank to discuss your financing needs, you develop answers to the following questions. A number of assumptions are required; clearly note all assumptions that you make.

**Comprehensive Problems** combine material from the current chapter with previous chapters so that students understand how "it all fits together."

The **Continuing Cookie Chronicle** exercise follows the continuing saga of accounting for a small business begun by an entrepreneurial student.

### Continuing Cookie Chronicle

(*Note:* This is a continuation of the Cookie Chronicle from Chapters 1 through 10.)

**CCC11**

**Part 1** Because Natalie has been so successful with Cookie Creations and her friend Curtis Lesperance has been just as successful with his coffee shop, they conclude that they could benefit from each other's business expertise. Curtis and Natalie next evaluate the different types of business organization. Because of the advantage of limited personal liability, they decide to form a corporation.

Natalie and Curtis are very excited about this new business venture. They come to you

### Waterways Continuing Problem

(This is a continuation of the Waterways Problem from Chapters 14 through 22.)

**WCP23** Waterways Corporation puts much emphasis on cash flow when it plans for capital investments. The company chose its discount rate of 8% based on the rate of return it must pay its owners and creditors. Using that rate, Waterways then uses different methods to determine the best decisions for making capital outlays. Waterways is considering buying five new backhoes to replace the backhoes it now has. This problem asks you to evaluate that decision, using various capital budgeting techniques.

The **Waterways Continuing Problem** uses the business activities of a fictional company, to help students apply managerial accounting topics to a realistic entrepreneurial situation.

The **Broadening Your Perspective** section helps to pull together concepts from the chapter and apply them to real-world business situations.

The **Financial Reporting Problem** focuses on reading and understanding the financial statements of Tootsie Roll, which are printed in Appendix A.

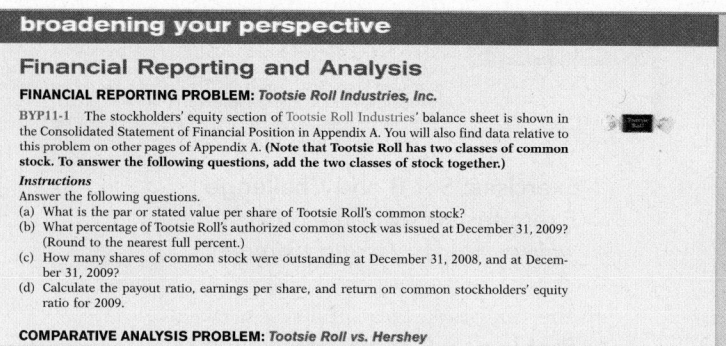

## broadening your perspective

### Financial Reporting and Analysis

**FINANCIAL REPORTING PROBLEM: *Tootsie Roll Industries, Inc.***

**BYP11-1** The stockholders' equity section of Tootsie Roll Industries' balance sheet is shown in the Consolidated Statement of Financial Position in Appendix A. You will also find data relative to this problem on other pages of Appendix A. **(Note that Tootsie Roll has two classes of common stock. To answer the following questions, add the two classes of stock together.)**

*Instructions*
Answer the following questions.
(a) What is the par or stated value per share of Tootsie Roll's common stock?
(b) What percentage of Tootsie Roll's authorized common stock was issued at December 31, 2009? (Round to the nearest full percent.)
(c) How many shares of common stock were outstanding at December 31, 2008, and at December 31, 2009?
(d) Calculate the payout ratio, earnings per share, and return on common stockholders' equity ratio for 2009.

**COMPARATIVE ANALYSIS PROBLEM: *Tootsie Roll vs. Hershey***

---

**COMPARATIVE ANALYSIS PROBLEM: *Tootsie Roll vs. Hershey***

**BYP11-2** The financial statements of The Hershey Company are presented in Appendix B, following the financial statements for Tootsie Roll in Appendix A.

A **Comparative Analysis Problem** compares and contrasts the financial reporting of Tootsie Roll and Hershey.

---

**FINANCIAL ANALYSIS ON THE WEB**

**BYP11-5** *Purpose:* Use the stockholders' equity section of an annual report and identify the major components.

*Address:* **www.annualreports.com**, or go to **www.wiley.com/college/kimmel**

*Steps*
1. Select a particular company.
2. Search by company name.
3. Follow instructions below.

**Exploring the Web** exercises guide students to websites where they can find and analyze information related to the chapter topic.

---

**Decision Making Across the Organization** cases help students build decision-making skills by analyzing accounting information in a less structured situation. These cases require teams of students to evaluate a manager's decision or lead to a decision among alternative courses of action.

## Critical Thinking

**DECISION MAKING ACROSS THE ORGANIZATION**

**BYP11-6** During a recent period, the fast-food chain Wendy's International purchased many treasury shares. This caused the number of shares outstanding to fall from 124 million to 105 million. The following information was drawn from the company's financial statements (in millions).

| | Information for the Year after Purchase of Treasury Stock | Information for the Year before Purchase of Treasury Stock |
|---|---|---|
| Net income | $ 193.6 | $ 123.4 |
| Total assets | 2,076.0 | 1,837.9 |
| Average total assets | 2,016.9 | 1,889.8 |
| Total common stockholders' equity | 1,029.8 | 1,068.1 |
| Average common stockholders' equity | 1,078.0 | 1,126.2 |
| Total liabilities | 1,046.3 | 769.9 |
| Average total liabilities | 939.0 | 763.7 |
| Interest expense | 30.2 | 19.8 |
| Income taxes | 113.7 | 84.3 |
| Cash provided by operations | 305.2 | 233.8 |
| Cash dividends paid on common stock | 26.8 | 31.0 |
| Preferred stock dividends | 0 | 0 |
| Average number of common shares outstanding | 109.7 | 119.9 |

---

**ETHICS CASES**

**BYP11-8** The R&D division of Mozy Corp. has just developed a chemical for sterilizing the vicious Brazilian "killer bees" which are invading Mexico and the southern United States. The president of Mozy is anxious to get the chemical on the market because Mozy profits need a boost—and his job is in jeopardy because of decreasing sales and profits. Mozy has an opportunity to sell this chemical in Central American countries, where the laws are much more relaxed than in the United States.

The director of Mozy's R&D division strongly recommends further research in the laboratory to test the side effects of this chemical on other insects, birds, animals, plants, and even humans. He cautions the president, "We could be sued from all sides if the chemical has tragic side effects that we didn't even test for in the lab." The president answers, "We can't wait an additional year for your lab tests. We can avoid losses from such lawsuits by establishing a separate wholly owned

**Ethics Cases** ask students to reflect on typical ethical dilemmas, analyze the stakeholders and the issues involved, and decide on an appropriate course of action.

---

**Managerial Analysis** assignments build analytical and decision-making skills in situations created by managers. They also require students to apply and practice business communication skills.

**MANAGERIAL ANALYSIS**

*BYP22-2** Al Finney and Associates is a medium-sized company located near a large metropolitan area in the Midwest. The company manufactures cabinets of mahogany, oak, and other fine woods for use in expensive homes, restaurants, and hotels. Although some of the work is custom, many of the cabinets are a standard size.

One such non-custom model is called Luxury Base Frame. Normal production is 1,000 units. Each unit has a direct labor hour standard of 5 hours. Overhead is applied to production based on standard direct labor hours. During the most recent month, only 900 units were produced; 4,500 direct labor hours were allowed for standard production, but only 4,000 hours were used. Standard and actual overhead costs were as follows.

| | Standard (1,000 units) | Actual (900 units) |
|---|---|---|
| Indirect materials | $ 12,000 | $ 12,300 |
| Indirect labor | 43,000 | 51,000 |
| (Fixed) Manufacturing supervisors salaries | 22,000 | 22,000 |
| (Fixed) Manufacturing office employees salaries | 13,000 | 11,500 |
| (Fixed) Engineering costs | 27,000 | 25,000 |
| Computer costs | 10,000 | 10,000 |

For **Real-World Focus** problems, students apply techniques and concepts presented in the chapter to specific situations faced by actual companies. These problems often have a global focus.

**A Look at IFRS** provides an overview of the International Financial Reporting Standards (IFRS) that relate to the chapter topics, highlights the differences between GAAP and IFRS, discusses IFRS/GAAP convergence efforts, and tests students' understanding through *IFRS Self-Test Questions* and *IFRS Concepts and Application.*

**IFRS** A Look at IFRS

It is often difficult for companies to determine in what time period they should report particular revenues and expenses. Both the IASB and FASB are working on a joint project to develop a common conceptual framework, as well as a revenue recognition project, that will enable companies to better use the same principles to record transactions consistently over time.

**KEY POINTS**

- In this chapter, you learned accrual-basis accounting applied under GAAP. Companies applying IFRS also use accrual-basis accounting to ensure that they record transactions that change a company's financial statements in the period in which events occur.
- Similar to GAAP, cash-basis accounting is not in accordance with IFRS.
- IFRS also divides the economic life of companies into artificial time periods. Under both GAAP and IFRS, this is referred to as the *periodicity assumption.*
- IFRS requires that companies present a complete set of financial statements, including comparative information annually.
- GAAP has more than 100 rules dealing with revenue recognition. Many of these rules are industry-specific. In contrast, revenue recognition under IFRS is determined primarily by a single standard. Despite this large disparity in the amount of detailed guidance devoted to revenue recognition, the **general** revenue recognition principles required by GAAP that are used in this textbook are similar to those under IFRS.
- As the Feature Story illustrates, revenue recognition fraud is a major issue in U.S. financial reporting. The same situation occurs in other countries, as evidenced by revenue recognition breakdowns at Dutch software company Baan NV, Japanese electronics giant NEC, and Dutch

# chapter 1

# INTRODUCTION TO FINANCIAL STATEMENTS

## ✔ the navigator

- Scan **Study Objectives** ○
- Read **Feature Story** ○
- Scan **Preview** ○
- Read **Text and Answer** **Do it!**
  p. 5 ○   p. 11 ○   p. 18 ○   p. 20 ○
- Work **Using the Decision Toolkit** ○
- Review **Summary of Study Objectives** ○
- Work **Comprehensive** **Do it!** p. 23 ○
- Answer **Self-Test Questions** ○
- Complete **Assignments** ○
- Go to **WileyPLUS** for practice and tutorials ○
- 🌐 Read **A Look at IFRS** p. 42 ○

## study objectives

**After studying this chapter, you should be able to:**

1 Describe the primary forms of business organization.

2 Identify the users and uses of accounting information.

3 Explain the three principal types of business activity.

4 Describe the content and purpose of each of the financial statements.

5 Explain the meaning of assets, liabilities, and stockholders' equity, and state the basic accounting equation.

6 Describe the components that supplement the financial statements in an annual report.

✔ the navigator

**The Navigator** is a learning system designed to prompt you to use the learning aids in the chapter and to set priorities as you study.

## KNOWING THE NUMBERS

Many students who take this course do not plan to be accountants. If you are in that group, you might be thinking, "If I'm not going to be an accountant, why do I need to know accounting?" In response, consider this quote from Harold Geneen, the former chairman of IT&T: "To be good at your business, you have to know the numbers—cold." Success in any business comes back to the numbers. You will rely on them to make decisions, and managers will use them to evaluate your performance. That is true whether your job involves marketing, production, management, or information systems.

In business, accounting and financial statements are the means for communicating the numbers. If you don't know how to read financial statements, you can't really know your business.

Many companies spend significant resources teaching their employees basic accounting so that they can read financial statements and understand how their actions affect the company's financial results. One such company is Springfield ReManufacturing Corporation (SRC). When Jack Stack and 11 other managers purchased SRC for 10 cents a share, it was a failing division of International Harvester. Jack's 119 employees were counting on him for their livelihood. He decided that for the company to survive, every employee needed to think like a businessperson and to act like an owner. To accomplish this, all employees at SRC took basic accounting courses and participated in weekly reviews of the company's financial statements. SRC survived, and eventually thrived. To this day, every employee (now numbering more than 1,000) undergoes this same training.

Many other companies have adopted this approach, which is called "open-book management." Even in companies that do not practice open-book management, employers generally assume that managers in all areas of the company are "financially literate."

Taking this course will go a long way to making you financially literate. In this book you will learn how to read and prepare financial statements, and how to use basic tools to evaluate financial results. In this first chapter we will introduce you to the financial statements of a real company whose products you are probably familiar with—Tootsie Roll. Tootsie Roll's presentation of its financial results is complete, yet also relatively easy to understand.

Tootsie Roll started off humbly in 1896 in a small New York City candy shop owned by an Austrian immigrant, Leo Hirshfield. The candy's name came from his five-year-old daughter's nickname—"Tootsie." Today the Chicago-based company produces more than 49 million Tootsie Rolls and 16 million Tootsie Pops *each day*. In fact, Tootsie Pops are at the center of one of science's most challenging questions: How many licks does it take to get to the Tootsie Roll center of a Tootsie Pop? The answer varies: Licking machines created at Purdue University and the University of Michigan report an average of 364 and 411 licks, respectively. In studies using human lickers, the answer ranges from 144 to 252. We recommend that you take a few minutes today away from your studies to determine your own results.

*Source:* Tootsie Roll information adapted from *www.tootsie.com.*

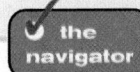

INSIDE CHAPTER 1 . . .

How do you start a business? How do you determine whether your business is making or losing money? How should you finance expansion—should you borrow, should you issue stock, should you use your own funds? How do you convince lenders to lend you money or investors to buy your stock? Success in business requires making countless decisions, and decisions require financial information.

The purpose of this chapter is to show you what role accounting plays in providing financial information. The content and organization of the chapter are as follows.

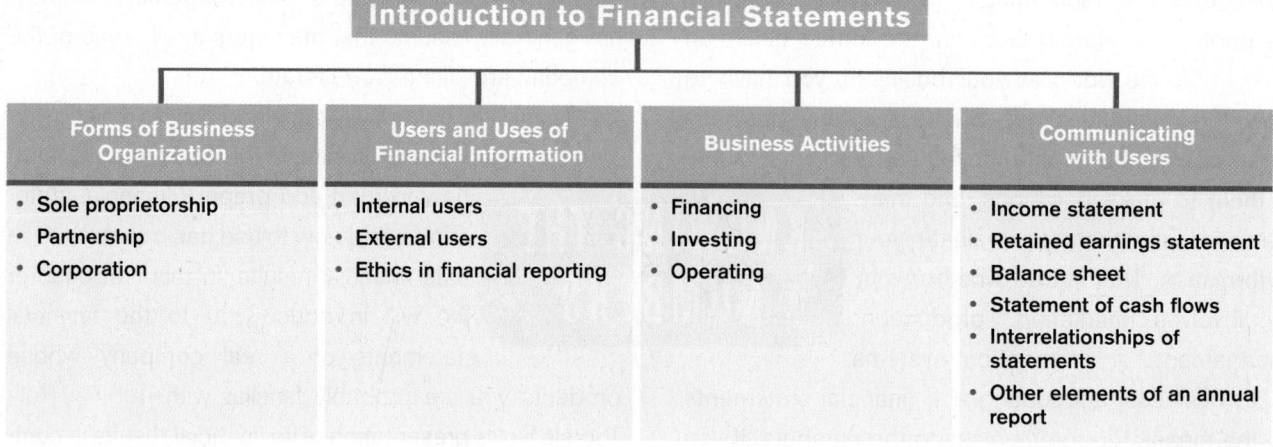

# Forms of Business Organization

**study objective** **1**

Describe the primary forms of business organization.

### Sole Proprietorship

-Simple to establish
-Owner controlled
-Tax advantages

### Partnership

-Simple to establish
-Shared control
-Broader skills and resources
-Tax advantages

### Corporation

-Easier to transfer ownership
-Easier to raise funds
-No personal liability

Suppose you graduate with a business degree and decide you want to start your own business. But what kind of business? You know that you enjoy working with people, especially teaching them new skills. And, ever since you were young, you have spent most of your free time outdoors, kayaking, backpacking, skiing, rock climbing, and mountain biking. You therefore realize that you might be most successful in opening an outdoor guide service where you grew up, in the Sierra Nevada mountains.

Your next decision is to determine what organizational form your business will have. You have three choices—sole proprietorship, partnership, or corporation.

You might choose the sole proprietorship form for your outdoor guide service. A business owned by one person is a sole proprietorship. It is **simple to set up** and **gives you control** over the business. Small owner-operated businesses such as barber shops, law offices, and auto repair shops are often sole proprietorships, as are farms and small retail stores.

Another possibility is for you to join forces with other individuals to form a partnership. A business owned by two or more persons associated as partners is a partnership. Partnerships often are formed because one individual does not have **enough economic resources** to initiate or expand the business. Sometimes, **partners bring unique skills or resources** to the partnership. You and your partners should formalize your duties and contributions in a written partnership agreement. Retail and service-type businesses, including professional practices (lawyers, doctors, architects, and certified public accountants), often organize as partnerships.

As a third alternative, you might organize as a corporation. A business organized as a separate legal entity owned by stockholders is a corporation. Investors in a corporation receive shares of stock to indicate their ownership claim. Buying stock in a corporation is often more attractive than investing in a partnership because shares of stock are **easy to sell** (transfer ownership). Selling a proprietorship or partnership interest is much more involved. Also, individuals can become **stockholders** by investing relatively small amounts of money. There-fore, it is **easier for corporations to raise funds**. Successful corporations of-ten have thousands of stockholders, and their stock is traded on organized stock exchanges like the New York Stock Exchange. Many businesses start as sole pro-prietorships or partnerships and eventually incorporate. For example, in 1896 Leo Hirshfield started Tootsie Roll as a sole proprietorship, and by 1919 the com-pany had incorporated.

Other factors to consider in deciding which organizational form to choose are **taxes and legal liability**. If you choose a sole proprietorship or partnership, you generally receive more favorable tax treatment than a corporation. However, proprietors and partners are personally liable for all debts of the business; cor-porate stockholders are not. In other words, corporate stockholders generally pay higher taxes but have no personal liability. We will discuss these issues in more depth in a later chapter.

The combined number of proprietorships and partnerships in the United States is more than five times the number of corporations. However, the revenue produced by corporations is eight times greater. Most of the largest enterprises in the United States—for example, Coca-Cola, ExxonMobil, General Motors, Citigroup, and Microsoft—are corporations. Because the majority of U.S. busi-ness is transacted by corporations, the emphasis in this book is on the corpo-rate form of organization.

**Alternative Terminology**
Stockholders are sometimes called *shareholders*.

**Alternative Terminology** notes present synonymous terms that you may come across in practice.

*before you go on...*

# Do it!

In choosing the organizational form for your outdoor guide service, you should consider the pros and cons of each. Identify each of the following organizational characteristics with the organizational form or forms with which it is associated.

1. Easier to raise funds
2. Simple to establish
3. No personal legal liability
4. Tax advantages
5. Easier to transfer ownership

**Solution**

1. Easier to raise funds: Corporation.
2. Simple to establish: Sole proprietorship and partnership.
3. No personal legal liability: Corporation.
4. Tax advantages: Sole proprietorship and partnership.
5. Easier to transfer ownership: Corporation.

Related exercise material: **BE1-1** and *Do it!* **1-1**.

**BUSINESS ORGANIZATION FORMS**

**Do it!** exercises prompt you to stop and review the key points you have just studied.

**Action Plan**
• Know which organizational form best matches the business type, size, and preferences of the owner(s).

**Action Plans** give you tips about how to approach the problem.

the navigator

# Users and Uses of Financial Information

The purpose of financial information is to provide inputs for decision making. Accounting is the information system that identifies, records, and communicates the economic events of an organization to interested users. **Users** of accounting in-formation can be divided broadly into two groups: internal users and external users.

**study objective 2**
Identify the users and uses of accounting information.

## INTERNAL USERS

**Internal users** of accounting information are managers who plan, organize, and run a business. These include **marketing managers**, **production supervisors**, **finance directors**, **and company officers**. In running a business, managers must answer many important questions, as shown in Illustration 1-1 (page 6).

## Questions Asked by Internal Users

**Finance**
Is cash sufficient to pay dividends to Microsoft stockholders?

**Marketing**
What price for an Apple iPod will maximize the company's net income?

**Human Resources**
Can we afford to give General Motors employees pay raises this year?

**Management**
Which PepsiCo product line is the most profitable? Should any product lines be eliminated?

**Illustration 1-1**
Questions that internal users ask

**Illustrations** like this one convey information in pictorial form to help you visualize and apply the ideas as you study.

To answer these and other questions, you need detailed information on a timely basis. For internal users, accounting provides internal reports, such as financial comparisons of operating alternatives, projections of income from new sales campaigns, and forecasts of cash needs for the next year. In addition, companies present summarized financial information in the form of financial statements.

## Accounting Across the Organization

### The Scoop on Accounting

Accounting can serve as a useful recruiting tool even for the human resources department. Rhino Foods, located in Burlington, Vermont, is a manufacturer of specialty ice cream. Its corporate website includes the following:

"Wouldn't it be great to work where you were part of a team? Where your input and hard work made a difference? Where you weren't kept in the dark about what management was thinking? . . . Well–it's not a dream! It's the way we do business . . . Rhino Foods believes in family, honesty and open communication–we really care about and appreciate our employees–and it shows. Operating results are posted and monthly group meetings inform all employees about what's happening in the Company. Employees also share in the Company's profits, in addition to having an excellent comprehensive *benefits* package."

Source: www.rhinofoods.com/workforus/workforus.html.

**Accounting Across the Organization** stories show applications of accounting information in various business functions.

**?** What are the benefits to the company and to the employees of making the financial statements available to all employees? (See page 41.)

### EXTERNAL USERS

There are several types of **external users** of accounting information. **Investors** (owners) use accounting information to make decisions to buy, hold, or sell stock. **Creditors** such as suppliers and bankers use accounting information to evaluate the risks of selling on credit or lending money. Some questions that investors and creditors may ask about a company are shown in Illustration 1-2.

**Illustration 1-2**
Questions that external users ask

## Questions Asked by External Users

**Investors**
Is General Electric earning satisfactory income?

**Investors**
How does Disney compare in size and profitability with Time Warner?

**Creditors**
Will United Airlines be able to pay its debts as they come due?

The information needs and questions of other external users vary considerably. **Taxing authorities**, such as the Internal Revenue Service, want to know whether the company complies with the tax laws. **Customers** are interested in whether a company like General Motors will continue to honor product warranties and otherwise support its product lines. **Labor unions**, such as the Major League Baseball Players Association, want to know whether the owners have the ability to pay increased wages and benefits. **Regulatory agencies**, such as the Securities and Exchange Commission or the Federal Trade Commission, want to know whether the company is operating within prescribed rules. For example, Enron, Dynegy, Duke Energy, and other big energy-trading companies reported record profits at the same time as California was paying extremely high prices for energy and suffering from blackouts. This disparity caused regulators to investigate the energy traders to make sure that the profits were earned by legitimate and fair practices.

## Accounting Across the Organization

### Spinning the Career Wheel

One question that business students frequently ask is, "How will the study of accounting help me?" It should help you a great deal, because a working knowledge of accounting is desirable for virtually every field of business. Some examples of how accounting is used in business careers include:

**General management:** Imagine running Ford Motors, Massachusetts General Hospital, California State University–Fullerton, a McDonald's franchise, a Trek bike shop. All general managers need to understand accounting data in order to make wise business decisions.

**Marketing:** A marketing specialist at a company like Procter & Gamble develops strategies to help the sales force be successful. But making a sale is meaningless unless it is a profitable sale. Marketing people must be sensitive to costs and benefits, which accounting helps them quantify and understand.

**Finance:** Do you want to be a banker for Citicorp, an investment analyst for Goldman Sachs, a stock broker for Merrill Lynch? These fields rely heavily on accounting. In all of them you will regularly examine and analyze financial statements. In fact, it is difficult to get a good job in a finance function without two or three courses in accounting.

**Real estate:** Are you interested in being a real estate broker for Prudential Real Estate? Because a third party—the bank—is almost always involved in financing a real estate transaction, brokers must understand the numbers involved: Can the buyer afford to make the payments to the bank? Does the cash flow from an industrial property justify the purchase price? What are the tax benefits of the purchase?

? How might accounting help you? (See page 41.)

## ETHICS IN FINANCIAL REPORTING

People won't gamble in a casino if they think it is "rigged." Similarly, people won't "play" the stock market if they think stock prices are rigged. In recent years the financial press has been full of articles about financial scandals at Enron, WorldCom, HealthSouth, and AIG. As more scandals came to light, a mistrust of financial reporting in general seemed to be developing. One article in the *Wall Street Journal* noted that "repeated disclosures about questionable accounting practices have bruised investors' faith in the reliability of earnings reports, which in turn has sent stock prices tumbling."[1] Imagine trying to carry on a business or invest money if you could not depend on the financial statements to be honestly prepared.

---

[1]"U.S. Share Prices Slump," *Wall Street Journal* (February 21, 2002).

Information would have no credibility. There is no doubt that a sound, well-functioning economy depends on accurate and dependable financial reporting.

United States regulators and lawmakers were very concerned that the economy would suffer if investors lost confidence in corporate accounting because of unethical financial reporting. In 2002, Congress passed the **Sarbanes-Oxley Act (SOX)** to reduce unethical corporate behavior and decrease the likelihood of future corporate scandals. As a result of SOX, top management must now certify the accuracy of financial information. In addition, penalties for fraudulent financial activity are much more severe. Also, SOX increased the independence of the outside auditors who review the accuracy of corporate financial statements, and increased the oversight role of boards of directors.

Effective financial reporting depends on sound ethical behavior. To sensitize you to ethical situations and to give you practice at solving ethical dilemmas, we address ethics in a number of ways in this book: (1) A number of the *Feature Stories* and other parts of the text discuss the central importance of ethical behavior to financial reporting. (2) *Insight boxes* with an ethics perspective highlight ethics situations and issues in actual business settings. (3) At the end of the chapter, an *Ethics Case* simulates a business situation and asks you to put yourself in the position of a decision maker in that case.

When analyzing these various ethics cases and your own ethical experiences, you should apply the three steps outlined in Illustration 1-3.

**Ethics Note** Circus-founder P.T. Barnum is alleged to have said, "Trust everyone, but cut the deck." What Sarbanes-Oxley does is to provide measures that (like cutting the deck of playing cards) help ensure that fraud will not occur.

**Illustration 1-3** Steps in analyzing ethics cases

### Solving an Ethical Dilemma

| **1. Recognize an ethical situation and the ethical issues involved.** | **2. Identify and analyze the principal elements in the situation.** | **3. Identify the alternatives, and weigh the impact of each alternative on various stakeholders.** |
|---|---|---|
| Use your personal ethics to identify ethical situations and issues. Some businesses and professional organizations provide written codes of ethics for guidance in some business situations. | Identify the *stakeholders*—persons or groups who may be harmed or benefited. Ask the question: What are the responsibilities and obligations of the parties involved? | Select the most ethical alternative, considering all the consequences. Sometimes there will be one right answer. Other situations involve more than one right solution; these situations require you to evaluate each alternative and select the best one. |

### Ethics Insight

#### The Numbers Behind Not-for-Profit Organizations

Accounting plays an important role for a wide range of business organizations worldwide. Just as the integrity of the numbers matters for business, it matters at least as much for not-for-profit organizations. Proper control and reporting help ensure that money is used the way donors intended. Donors are less inclined to give to an organization if they think the organization is subject to waste or theft. The accounting challenges of some large international not-for-profits rival those of the world's largest businesses. For example, after the Haitian earthquake, the Haitian-born musician Wyclef Jean was criticized for the poor accounting controls in a relief fund that he founded. Since then, he has hired a new accountant and improved the transparency regarding funds raised and spent.

**Insights** provide examples of business situations from various perspectives—ethics, investor, and international.

**?** What benefits does a sound accounting system provide to a not-for-profit organization? (See page 41.)

# Business Activities

All businesses are involved in three types of activity—financing, investing, and operating. For example, Leo Hirshfield, the founder of Tootsie Roll, obtained cash through financing to start and grow his business. Some of this **financing** came from personal savings, and some likely came from outside sources like banks. Hirshfield then **invested** the cash in equipment to run the business, such as mixing equipment and delivery vehicles. Once this equipment was in place, he could begin the **operating** activities of making and selling candy.

The **accounting information system** keeps track of the results of each of the various business activities—financing, investing, and operating. Let's look in more detail at each type of business activity.

**study objective** **3**

Explain the three principal types of business activity.

## FINANCING ACTIVITIES

It takes money to make money. The two primary sources of outside funds for corporations are borrowing money and issuing (selling) shares of stock in exchange for cash.

Tootsie Roll Industries may borrow money in a variety of ways. For example, it can take out a loan at a bank or borrow directly from investors by issuing debt securities called bonds. Persons or entities to whom Tootsie Roll owes money are its **creditors**. Amounts owed to creditors—in the form of debt and other obligations—are called liabilities. Specific names are given to different types of liabilities, depending on their source. Tootsie Roll may have a **note payable** to a bank for the money borrowed to purchase delivery trucks. Debt securities sold to investors that must be repaid at a particular date some years in the future are **bonds payable**.

A corporation may also obtain funds by selling shares of stock to investors. Common stock is the term used to describe the total amount paid in by stockholders for the shares they purchase.

The claims of creditors differ from those of stockholders. If you loan money to a company, you are one of its creditors. In lending money, you specify a payment schedule (e.g., payment at the end of three months). As a creditor, you have a legal right to be paid at the agreed time. In the event of nonpayment, you may legally force the company to sell property to pay its debts. In the case of financial difficulty, creditor claims must be paid before stockholders' claims.

Stockholders, on the other hand, have no claim to corporate cash until the claims of creditors are satisfied. If you buy a company's stock instead of loaning it money, you have no legal right to expect any payments until all of its creditors are paid. However, many corporations make payments to stockholders on a regular basis as long as there is sufficient cash to cover required payments to creditors. These payments to stockholders are called dividends.

**Financing**

Essential terms are printed in blue. They are defined again in the **glossary** at the end of the chapter.

## INVESTING ACTIVITIES

Once the company has raised cash through financing activities, it will then use that cash in investing activities. Investing activities involve the purchase of the resources a company needs in order to operate. A growing company purchases many resources, such as computers, delivery trucks, furniture, and buildings. Resources owned by a business are called assets. Different types of assets are given different names. Tootsie Roll's mixing equipment is a type of asset referred to as **property**, **plant**, **and equipment**.

**Cash** is one of the more important assets owned by Tootsie Roll or any other business. If a company has excess cash that it does not need for a while, it might

**Investing**

**Alternative Terminology**
Property, plant, and equipment is sometimes called *fixed assets*.

choose to invest in securities (stocks or bonds) of other corporations. **Investments** are another example of an investing activity.

### OPERATING ACTIVITIES

**Operating**

Once a business has the assets it needs to get started, it can begin its operations. Tootsie Roll is in the business of selling all things that taste, look, or smell like candy. It sells Tootsie Rolls, Tootsie Pops, Blow Pops, Caramel Apple Pops, Mason Dots, Mason Crows, Sugar Daddy, and Sugar Babies. We call amounts earned on the sale of these products *revenues*. Revenue is the increase in assets resulting from the sale of a product or service in the normal course of business. For example, Tootsie Roll records revenue when it sells a candy product.

Revenues arise from different sources and are identified by various names depending on the nature of the business. For instance, Tootsie Roll's primary source of revenue is the sale of candy products. However, it also generates interest revenue on debt securities held as investments. Sources of revenue common to many businesses are **sales revenue**, **service revenue**, and **interest revenue**.

The company purchases its longer-lived assets through investing activities as described earlier. Other assets with shorter lives, however, result from operating activities. For example, supplies are assets used in day-to-day operations. Goods available for future sales to customers are assets called **inventory**. Also, if Tootsie Roll sells goods to a customer and does not receive cash immediately, then the company has a right to expect payment from that customer in the near future. This right to receive money in the future is called an **account receivable**.

Before Tootsie Roll can sell a single Tootsie Roll, Tootsie Pop, or Blow Pop, it must purchase sugar, corn syrup, and other ingredients, mix these ingredients, process the mix, and wrap and ship the finished product. It also incurs costs like salaries, rents, and utilities. All of these costs, referred to as *expenses*, are necessary to produce and sell the product. In accounting language, expenses are the cost of assets consumed or services used in the process of generating revenues.

Expenses take many forms and are identified by various names depending on the type of asset consumed or service used. For example, Tootsie Roll keeps track of these types of expenses: **cost of goods sold** (such as the cost of ingredients); **selling expenses** (such as the cost of salespersons' salaries); **marketing expenses** (such as the cost of advertising); **administrative expenses** (such as the salaries of administrative staff, and telephone and heat costs incurred at the corporate office); **interest expense** (amounts of interest paid on various debts); and **income taxes** (corporate taxes paid to government).

Tootsie Roll may also have liabilities arising from these expenses. For example, it may purchase goods on credit from suppliers; the obligations to pay for these goods are called **accounts payable**. Additionally, Tootsie Roll may have **interest payable** on the outstanding amounts owed to the bank. It may also have **wages payable** to its employees and **sales taxes payable**, **property taxes payable**, and **income taxes payable** to the government.

Tootsie Roll compares the revenues of a period with the expenses of that period to determine whether it earned a profit. When revenues exceed expenses, net income results. When expenses exceed revenues, a net loss results.

*before you go on...*

 Classify each item as an asset, liability, common stock, revenue, or expense.

**BUSINESS ACTIVITIES**

1. Cost of renting property
2. Truck purchased
3. Notes payable
4. Issuance of ownership shares
5. Amount earned from providing service
6. Amounts owed to suppliers

**Action Plan**

- Classify each item based on its economic characteristics. Proper classification of items is critical if accounting is to provide useful information.

### Solution

1. Cost of renting property: Expense.
2. Truck purchased: Asset.
3. Notes payable: Liabilities.
4. Issuance of ownership shares: Common stock.
5. Amount earned from providing service: Revenue.
6. Amounts owed to suppliers: Liabilities.

 the navigator

Related exercise material: **BE1-3,** Do it! **1-2,** and **E1-3.**

## Communicating with Users

Assets, liabilities, expenses, and revenues are of interest to users of accounting information. This information is arranged in the format of four different **financial statements**, which form the backbone of financial accounting:

**study objective 4**

Describe the content and purpose of each of the financial statements.

- To present a picture at a point in time of what your business owns (its assets) and what it owes (its liabilities), you prepare a **balance sheet**.
- To show how successfully your business performed during a period of time, you report its revenues and expenses in an **income statement**.
- To indicate how much of previous income was distributed to you and the other owners of your business in the form of dividends, and how much was retained in the business to allow for future growth, you present a **retained earnings statement**.
- To show where your business obtained cash during a period of time and how that cash was used, you present a **statement of cash flows**.

**International Note** The primary types of financial statements required by International Financial Reporting Standards (IFRS) and U.S. generally accepted accounting principles (GAAP) are the same. Neither IFRS nor GAAP is very specific regarding format requirements for the primary financial statements. However, in practice, some format differences do exist in presentations commonly employed by IFRS companies compared to GAAP companies.

To introduce you to these statements, we have prepared the financial statements for your outdoor guide service, Sierra Corporation, after your first month of operations. To summarize, you officially started your business in Truckee, California, on October 1, 2012. Sierra provides guide services in the Lake Tahoe area of the Sierra Nevada mountains. Its promotional materials describe outdoor day trips, such as rafting, snowshoeing, and hiking, as well as multi-day backcountry experiences. To minimize your initial investment, at this point the company has limited outdoor equipment for customer use. Instead, your customers either bring their own equipment or you arrange for them to rent equipment through local outfitters. The financial statements for Sierra's first month of business are provided in the following pages.

### INCOME STATEMENT

The **income statement** reports the success or failure of the company's operations for a period of time. To indicate that its income statement reports the results of operations for a **period of time**, Sierra dates the income statement "For the Month Ended October 31, 2012." The income statement lists the company's revenues followed by its expenses. Finally, Sierra determines the net income (or net loss) by deducting expenses from revenues. Sierra Corporation's income statement is shown in Illustration 1-4. Congratulations, you are already showing a profit!

**Illustration 1-4** Sierra Corporation's income statement

**SIERRA CORPORATION**
Income Statement
For the Month Ended October 31, 2012

| Revenues | | |
|---|---|---|
| Service revenue | | $10,600 |
| Expenses | | |
| Salaries expense | $5,200 | |
| Supplies expense | 1,500 | |
| Rent expense | 900 | |
| Insurance expense | 50 | |
| Interest expense | 50 | |
| Depreciation expense | 40 | |
| Total expenses | | 7,740 |
| Net income | | $ 2,860 |

**Helpful Hint** The heading identifies the company, the type of statement, and the time period covered. Sometimes, another line indicates the unit of measure, e.g., "in thousands" or "in millions."

**Ethics Note** When companies find errors in previously released income statements, they restate those numbers. Perhaps because of the increased scrutiny shortly after Sarbanes-Oxley was implemented, companies filed a record 1,195 restatements.

Why are financial statement users interested in net income? **Investors are interested in a company's past net income because it provides useful information for predicting future net income**. Investors buy and sell stock based on their beliefs about a company's future performance. If investors believe that Sierra will be successful in the future and that this will result in a higher stock price, they will buy its stock. Creditors also use the income statement to predict future earnings. When a bank loans money to a company, it believes that it will be repaid in the future. If it didn't think it would be repaid, it wouldn't loan the money. Therefore, prior to making the loan the bank loan officer uses the income statement as a source of information to predict whether the company will be profitable enough to repay its loan. Thus, reporting a strong profit will make it easier for Sierra to raise additional cash either by issuing shares of stock or borrowing.

**Amounts received from issuing stock are not revenues, and amounts paid out as dividends are not expenses.** As a result, they are not reported on the income statement. For example, Sierra Corporation does not treat as revenue the $10,000 of cash received from issuing new stock, nor does it regard as a business expense the $500 of dividends paid.

**Decision Toolkits** summarize the financial decision-making process.

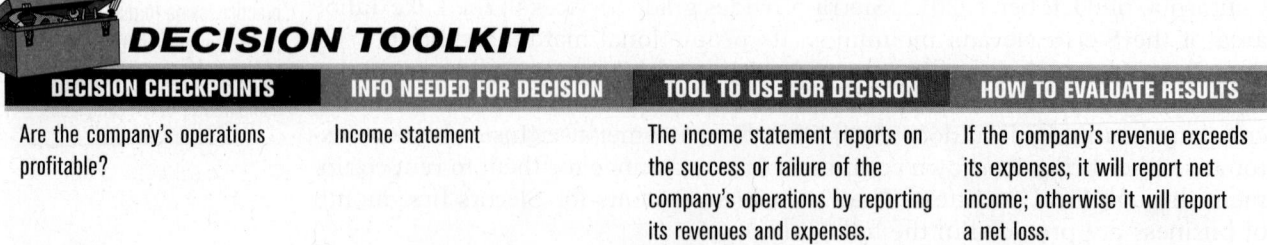

## DECISION TOOLKIT

| DECISION CHECKPOINTS | INFO NEEDED FOR DECISION | TOOL TO USE FOR DECISION | HOW TO EVALUATE RESULTS |
|---|---|---|---|
| Are the company's operations profitable? | Income statement | The income statement reports on the success or failure of the company's operations by reporting its revenues and expenses. | If the company's revenue exceeds its expenses, it will report net income; otherwise it will report a net loss. |

### RETAINED EARNINGS STATEMENT

If Sierra is profitable, at the end of each period it must decide what portion of profits to pay to shareholders in dividends. In theory, it could pay all of its current-period profits, but few companies do this. Why? Because they want to retain part of the profits to allow for further expansion. High-growth companies, such as Google and Cisco Systems, often pay no dividends. **Retained earnings** is the net income retained in the corporation.

The **retained earnings statement** shows the amounts and causes of changes in retained earnings during the period. The time period is the same as that covered by the income statement. The beginning retained earnings amount appears on the first line of the statement. Then the company adds net income and deducts dividends to determine the retained earnings at the end of the period. If a company has a net loss, it deducts (rather than adds) that amount in the retained earnings statement. Illustration 1-5 presents Sierra Corporation's retained earnings statement.

| SIERRA CORPORATION | | |
|---|---|---|
| Retained Earnings Statement | | |
| For the Month Ended October 31, 2012 | | |
| Retained earnings, October 1 | $ | 0 |
| Add: Net income | | 2,860 |
| | | 2,860 |
| Less: Dividends | | 500 |
| Retained earnings, October 31 | | $2,360 |

**Illustration 1-5**  Sierra Corporation's retained earnings statement

**Helpful Hint** The heading of this statement identifies the company, the type of statement, and the time period covered by the statement.

By monitoring the retained earnings statement, financial statement users can evaluate dividend payment practices. Some investors seek companies, such as Dow Chemical, that have a history of paying high dividends. Other investors seek companies, such as Amazon.com, that reinvest earnings to increase the company's growth instead of paying dividends. Lenders monitor their corporate customers' dividend payments because any money paid in dividends reduces a company's ability to repay its debts.

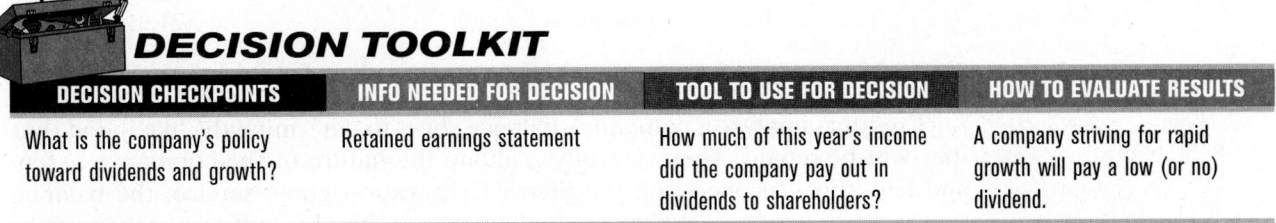

## DECISION TOOLKIT

| DECISION CHECKPOINTS | INFO NEEDED FOR DECISION | TOOL TO USE FOR DECISION | HOW TO EVALUATE RESULTS |
|---|---|---|---|
| What is the company's policy toward dividends and growth? | Retained earnings statement | How much of this year's income did the company pay out in dividends to shareholders? | A company striving for rapid growth will pay a low (or no) dividend. |

## BALANCE SHEET

The **balance sheet** reports assets and claims to assets at a specific **point** in time. Claims to assets are subdivided into two categories: claims of creditors and claims of owners. As noted earlier, claims of creditors are called **liabilities**. Claims of owners are called **stockholders' equity**.

Illustration 1-6 shows the relationship among the categories on the balance sheet in equation form. This equation is referred to as the **basic accounting equation**.

**study objective 5**

Explain the meaning of assets, liabilities, and stockholders' equity, and state the basic accounting equation.

**Assets = Liabilities + Stockholders' Equity**

**Illustration 1-6**  Basic accounting equation

This relationship is where the name "balance sheet" comes from. Assets must balance with the claims to assets.

As you can see from looking at Sierra's balance sheet in Illustration 1-7, the balance sheet presents the company's financial position as of a specific date—in this case, October 31, 2012. It lists assets first, followed by liabilities and stockholders' equity. Stockholders' equity is comprised of two parts: (1) common stock and (2) retained earnings. As noted earlier, common stock results when the company sells new shares of stock; retained earnings is the net income retained in the corporation. Sierra has common stock of $10,000 and retained earnings of $2,360, for total stockholders' equity of $12,360.

**Alternative Terminology**
Liabilities are also referred to as *debt*.

**Illustration 1-7** Sierra Corporation's balance sheet

**SIERRA CORPORATION**
Balance Sheet
October 31, 2012

### Assets

| | |
|---|---:|
| Cash | $15,200 |
| Accounts receivable | 200 |
| Supplies | 1,000 |
| Prepaid insurance | 550 |
| Equipment, net | 4,960 |
| Total assets | $21,910 |

### Liabilities and Stockholders' Equity

| | | |
|---|---:|---:|
| Liabilities | | |
|   Notes payable | $ 5,000 | |
|   Accounts payable | 2,500 | |
|   Salaries payable | 1,200 | |
|   Unearned service revenue | 800 | |
|   Interest payable | 50 | |
|     Total liabilities | | $ 9,550 |
| Stockholders' equity | | |
|   Common stock | 10,000 | |
|   Retained earnings | 2,360 | |
|     Total stockholders' equity | | 12,360 |
| Total liabilities and stockholders' equity | | $21,910 |

**Helpful Hint** The heading of a balance sheet must identify the company, the statement, and the date.

Creditors analyze a company's balance sheet to determine the likelihood that they will be repaid. They carefully evaluate the nature of the company's assets and liabilities. In operating the Sierra Corporation guide service, the balance sheet will be used to determine whether cash on hand is sufficient for immediate cash needs. The balance sheet will also be used to evaluate the relationship between debt and stockholders' equity to determine whether the company has a satisfactory proportion of debt and common stock financing.

## DECISION TOOLKIT

| DECISION CHECKPOINTS | INFO NEEDED FOR DECISION | TOOL TO USE FOR DECISION | HOW TO EVALUATE RESULTS |
|---|---|---|---|
| Does the company rely primarily on debt or stockholders' equity to finance its assets? | Balance sheet | The balance sheet reports the company's resources and claims to those resources. There are two types of claims: liabilities and stockholders' equity. | Compare the amount of debt versus the amount of stockholders' equity to determine whether the company relies more on creditors or owners for its financing. |

## Ethics Insight

### Rocking the Bottom Line

What topic has performers such as Tom Waits, Clint Black, Sheryl Crow, and Madonna so concerned that they are pushing for new laws regarding its use? Accounting. Recording-company accounting to be more precise. Musicians receive royalty payments based on the accounting done by their recording companies. Many performers say that the recording companies—either intentionally or unintentionally—have very poor accounting systems, which, the performers say, has resulted in many inaccurate royalty payments. They would like to see laws created that would hit the recording companies with stiff fines for accounting errors.

**?** What is one way that some of these disputes might be resolved? (See page 41.)

## STATEMENT OF CASH FLOWS

The primary purpose of a **statement of cash flows** is to provide financial information about the cash receipts and cash payments of a business for a specific period of time. To help investors, creditors, and others in their analysis of a company's cash position, the statement of cash flows reports the cash effects of a company's **operating**, **investing**, and **financing** activities. In addition, the statement shows the net increase or decrease in cash during the period, and the amount of cash at the end of the period.

Users are interested in the statement of cash flows because they want to know what is happening to a company's most important resource. In operating Sierra, the statement of cash flows will provide answers to these simple but important questions:

• Where did cash come from during the period?
• How was cash used during the period?
• What was the change in the cash balance during the period?

The statement of cash flows for Sierra, in Illustration 1-8, shows that cash increased $15,200 during the month. This increase resulted because operating

**SIERRA CORPORATION**
Statement of Cash Flows
For the Month Ended October 31, 2012

| | | |
|---|---:|---:|
| Cash flows from operating activities | | |
| Cash receipts from operating activities | $11,200 | |
| Cash payments for operating activities | (5,500) | |
| Net cash provided by operating activities | | $ 5,700 |
| Cash flows from investing activities | | |
| Purchased office equipment | (5,000) | |
| Net cash used by investing activities | | (5,000) |
| Cash flows from financing activities | | |
| Issuance of common stock | 10,000 | |
| Issued note payable | 5,000 | |
| Payment of dividend | (500) | |
| Net cash provided by financing activities | | 14,500 |
| Net increase in cash | | 15,200 |
| Cash at beginning of period | | 0 |
| Cash at end of period | | $15,200 |

**Illustration 1-8** Sierra Corporation's statement of cash flows

**Helpful Hint** The heading of this statement identifies the company, the type of statement, and the time period covered by the statement. Negative numbers are shown in parentheses.

activities (services to clients) increased cash $5,700, and financing activities increased cash $14,500. Investing activities used $5,000 of cash for the purchase of equipment.

## DECISION TOOLKIT

| DECISION CHECKPOINTS | INFO NEEDED FOR DECISION | TOOL TO USE FOR DECISION | HOW TO EVALUATE RESULTS |
|---|---|---|---|
| Does the company generate sufficient cash from operations to fund its investing activities? | Statement of cash flows | The statement of cash flows shows the amount of cash provided or used by operating activities, investing activities, and financing activities. | Compare the amount of cash provided by operating activities with the amount of cash used by investing activities. Any deficiency in cash from operating activities must be made up with cash from financing activities. |

**PLUS**

Tootsie Roll Annual
Report Walkthrough

### INTERRELATIONSHIPS OF STATEMENTS

Illustration 1-9 shows simplified financial statements of Tootsie Roll Industries, Inc. (We have simplified the financial statements to assist your learning.) Tootsie Roll's **actual financial statements** are presented in **Appendix A**, at the end of the textbook. Note that the numbers in Tootsie Roll's statements are presented in thousands—that is, the last three 000s are omitted. Thus, Tootsie Roll's net income in 2009 is $53,475,000, not $53,475. Because the results on some financial statements become inputs to other statements, the statements are interrelated. These interrelationships can be seen in Tootsie Roll's financial statements, as follows.

1. The retained earnings statement depends on the results of the income statement. Tootsie Roll reported net income of $53,475,000 for the period. It adds the net income amount to the beginning amount of retained earnings in order to determine ending retained earnings.

2. The balance sheet and retained earnings statement are also interrelated. Tootsie Roll reports the ending amount of $145,928,000 on the retained earnings statement as the retained earnings amount on the balance sheet.

3. Finally, the statement of cash flows relates to information on the balance sheet. The statement of cash flows shows how the Cash account changed during the period. It shows the amount of cash at the beginning of the period, the sources and uses of cash during the period, and the $90,990,000 of cash at the end of the period. The ending amount of cash shown on the statement of cash flows must agree with the amount of cash on the balance sheet.

Study these interrelationships carefully. To prepare financial statements, you must understand the sequence in which these amounts are determined and how each statement impacts the next.

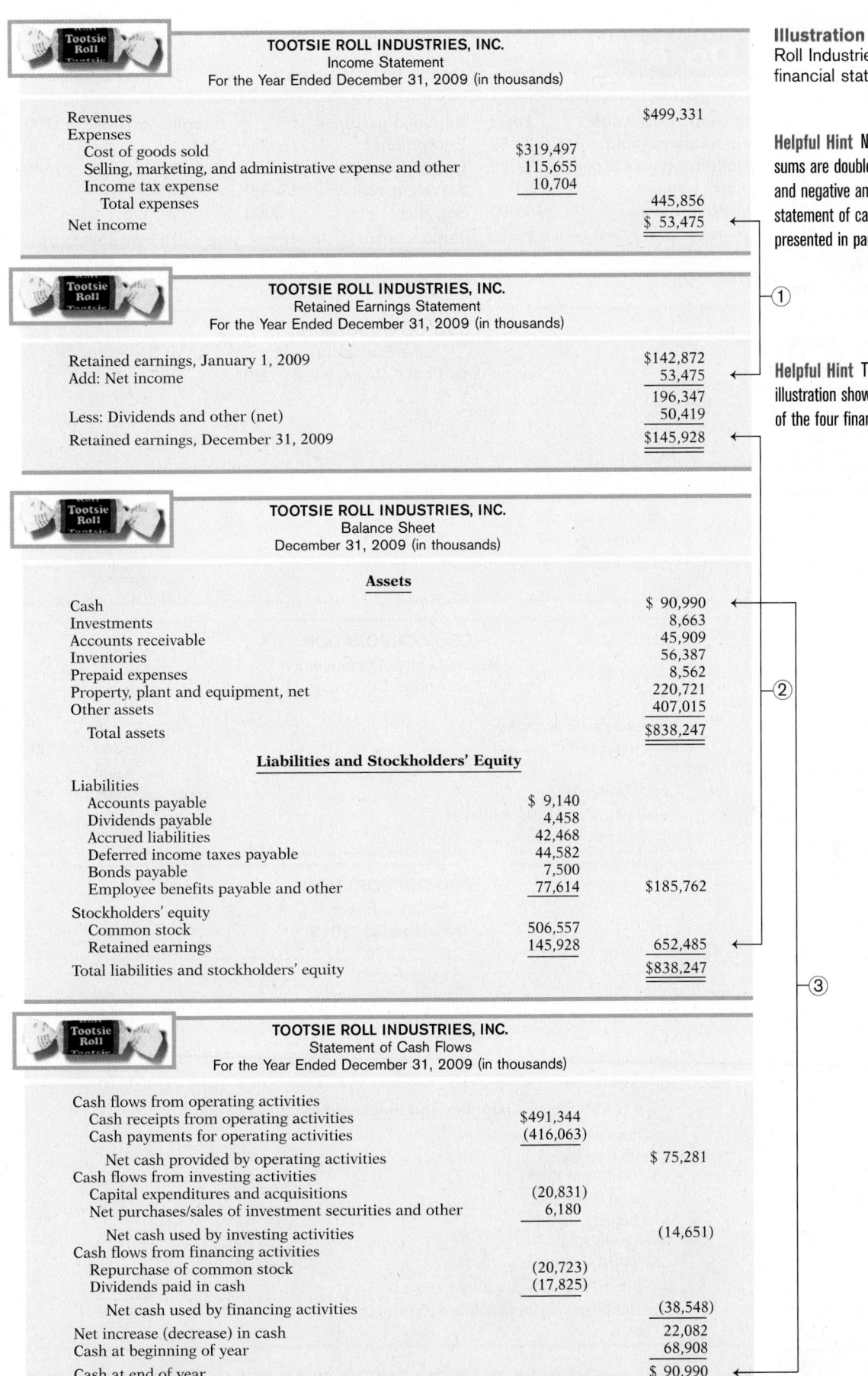

**Illustration 1-9**  Tootsie Roll Industries, Inc.'s financial statements

**Helpful Hint** Note that final sums are double-underlined, and negative amounts (in the statement of cash flows) are presented in parentheses.

**Helpful Hint** The arrows in this illustration show interrelationships of the four financial statements.

**TOOTSIE ROLL INDUSTRIES, INC.**
Income Statement
For the Year Ended December 31, 2009 (in thousands)

| | | |
|---|---:|---:|
| Revenues | | $499,331 |
| Expenses | | |
| Cost of goods sold | $319,497 | |
| Selling, marketing, and administrative expense and other | 115,655 | |
| Income tax expense | 10,704 | |
| Total expenses | | 445,856 |
| Net income | | $ 53,475 |

**TOOTSIE ROLL INDUSTRIES, INC.**
Retained Earnings Statement
For the Year Ended December 31, 2009 (in thousands)

| | |
|---|---:|
| Retained earnings, January 1, 2009 | $142,872 |
| Add: Net income | 53,475 |
| | 196,347 |
| Less: Dividends and other (net) | 50,419 |
| Retained earnings, December 31, 2009 | $145,928 |

**TOOTSIE ROLL INDUSTRIES, INC.**
Balance Sheet
December 31, 2009 (in thousands)

**Assets**

| | | |
|---|---:|---:|
| Cash | | $ 90,990 |
| Investments | | 8,663 |
| Accounts receivable | | 45,909 |
| Inventories | | 56,387 |
| Prepaid expenses | | 8,562 |
| Property, plant and equipment, net | | 220,721 |
| Other assets | | 407,015 |
| Total assets | | $838,247 |

**Liabilities and Stockholders' Equity**

| | | |
|---|---:|---:|
| Liabilities | | |
| Accounts payable | $ 9,140 | |
| Dividends payable | 4,458 | |
| Accrued liabilities | 42,468 | |
| Deferred income taxes payable | 44,582 | |
| Bonds payable | 7,500 | |
| Employee benefits payable and other | 77,614 | $185,762 |
| Stockholders' equity | | |
| Common stock | 506,557 | |
| Retained earnings | 145,928 | 652,485 |
| Total liabilities and stockholders' equity | | $838,247 |

**TOOTSIE ROLL INDUSTRIES, INC.**
Statement of Cash Flows
For the Year Ended December 31, 2009 (in thousands)

| | | |
|---|---:|---:|
| Cash flows from operating activities | | |
| Cash receipts from operating activities | $491,344 | |
| Cash payments for operating activities | (416,063) | |
| Net cash provided by operating activities | | $ 75,281 |
| Cash flows from investing activities | | |
| Capital expenditures and acquisitions | (20,831) | |
| Net purchases/sales of investment securities and other | 6,180 | |
| Net cash used by investing activities | | (14,651) |
| Cash flows from financing activities | | |
| Repurchase of common stock | (20,723) | |
| Dividends paid in cash | (17,825) | |
| Net cash used by financing activities | | (38,548) |
| Net increase (decrease) in cash | | 22,082 |
| Cash at beginning of year | | 68,908 |
| Cash at end of year | | $ 90,990 |

## before you go on...

**Do it!** CSU Corporation began operations on January 1, 2012. The following information is available for CSU Corporation on December 31, 2012:

| | | | | | |
|---|---|---|---|---|---|
| Accounts receivable | 1,800 | Retained earnings | ? | Supplies expense | 200 |
| Accounts payable | 2,000 | Equipment | 16,000 | Cash | 1,400 |
| Building rental expense | 9,000 | Insurance expense | 1,000 | Dividends | 600 |
| Notes payable | 5,000 | Service revenue | 17,000 | | |
| Common stock | 10,000 | Supplies | 4,000 | | |

Prepare an income statement, a retained earnings statement, and a balance sheet.

**Action Plan**

- Report the revenues and expenses for a period of time in an income statement.
- Show the amounts and causes (net income and dividends) of changes in retained earnings during the period in the retained earnings statement.
- Present the assets and claims to those assets at a specific point in time in the balance sheet.

**Solution**

**CSU CORPORATION**
Income Statement
For the Year Ended December 31, 2012

| | | |
|---|---|---|
| Revenues | | |
| Service revenue | | $17,000 |
| Expenses | | |
| Rent expense | $9,000 | |
| Insurance expense | 1,000 | |
| Supplies expense | 200 | |
| Total expenses | | 10,200 |
| Net income | | $ 6,800 |

**CSU CORPORATION**
Retained Earnings Statement
For the Year Ended December 31, 2012

| | |
|---|---|
| Retained earnings, January 1 | $ 0 |
| Add: Net income | 6,800 |
| | 6,800 |
| Less: Dividends | 600 |
| Retained earnings, December 31 | $6,200 |

**CSU CORPORATION**
Balance Sheet
December 31, 2012

| Assets | |
|---|---|
| Cash | $ 1,400 |
| Accounts receivable | 1,800 |
| Supplies | 4,000 |
| Equipment | 16,000 |
| Total assets | $23,200 |

| Liabilities and Stockholders' Equity | | |
|---|---|---|
| Liabilities | | |
| Notes payable | $ 5,000 | |
| Accounts payable | 2,000 | |
| Total liabilities | | $ 7,000 |
| Stockholders' equity | | |
| Common stock | 10,000 | |
| Retained earnings | 6,200 | |
| Total stockholders' equity | | 16,200 |
| Total liabilities and stockholders' equity | | $23,200 |

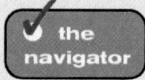

Related exercise material: **BE1-5, BE1-6, BE1-7, BE1-8, BE1-9, BE1-10, Do it! 1-3, E1-4, E1-5, E1-6, E1-7, E1-8, E1-9, E1-10, E1-11,** and **E1-14.**

## OTHER ELEMENTS OF AN ANNUAL REPORT

U.S. companies that are publicly traded must provide shareholders with an **annual report**. The annual report always includes the financial statements introduced in this chapter. The annual report also includes other important information such as a management discussion and analysis section, notes to the financial statements, and an independent auditor's report. No analysis of a company's financial situation and prospects is complete without a review of these items.

**study objective 6**

Describe the components that supplement the financial statements in an annual report.

### Management Discussion and Analysis

The **management discussion and analysis (MD&A)** section covers various financial aspects of a company, including **its ability to pay near-term obligations, its ability to fund operations and expansion, and its results of operations**. Management must highlight favorable or unfavorable trends and identify significant events and uncertainties that affect these three factors. This discussion obviously involves a number of subjective estimates and opinions. A brief excerpt from the MD&A section of Tootsie Roll's annual report is presented in Illustration 1-10.

**TOOTSIE ROLL INDUSTRIES, INC.**
Management's Discussion and Analysis of
Financial Condition and Results of Operations

The Company has a relatively straightforward financial structure and has historically maintained a conservative financial position. Except for an immaterial amount of operating leases, the Company has no special financing arrangements or "off-balance sheet" special purpose entities. Cash flows from operations plus maturities of short-term investments are expected to be adequate to meet the Company's overall financing needs, including capital expenditures, in 2010.

**Illustration 1-10** Tootsie Roll's management discussion and analysis

### Notes to the Financial Statements

Explanatory notes and supporting schedules accompany every set of financial statements and are an integral part of the statements. The **notes to the financial statements** clarify the financial statements, and provide additional detail. Information in the notes does not have to be quantifiable (numeric). Examples of notes are descriptions of the significant accounting policies and methods used in preparing the statements, explanations of uncertainties and contingencies, and various statistics and details too voluminous to be included in the statements. The notes are essential to understanding a company's operating performance and financial position.

Illustration 1-11 is an excerpt from the notes to Tootsie Roll's financial statements. It describes the methods that Tootsie Roll uses to account for revenues.

**TOOTSIE ROLL INDUSTRIES, INC.**
Notes to Financial Statements

**Revenue recognition**
Revenue, net of applicable provisions for discounts, returns, allowances, and certain advertising and promotional costs, is recognized when products are delivered to customers based on a customer purchase order, and collectibility is reasonably assured.

**Illustration 1-11** Notes to Tootsie Roll's financial statements

### Auditor's Report

An **auditor's report** is prepared by an independent outside auditor. It states the auditor's opinion as to the fairness of the presentation of the financial position and results of operations and their conformance with generally accepted accounting standards.

An **auditor** is an accounting professional who conducts an independent examination of a company's financial statements. Only accountants who meet certain criteria and thereby attain the designation Certified Public Accountant (CPA) may perform audits. If the auditor is satisfied that the financial statements provide a fair representation of the company's financial position and results of operations in accordance with generally accepted accounting principles, then the auditor expresses an **unqualified opinion**. If the auditor expresses anything other than an unqualified opinion, then readers should only use the financial statements with caution. That is, without an unqualified opinion, we cannot have complete confidence that the financial statements give an accurate picture of the company's financial health. For example, in April 2009 Blockbuster, Inc.'s auditor stated that its financial situation raised "substantial doubt about the Company's ability to continue as a going concern."

Illustration 1-12 is an excerpt from the auditor's report from Tootsie Roll's 2009 annual report. Tootsie Roll received an unqualified opinion from its auditor, PricewaterhouseCoopers.

**Illustration 1-12** Excerpt from auditor's report on Tootsie Roll's financial statements

### TOOTSIE ROLL INDUSTRIES, INC.
Excerpt from Auditor's Report

To the Board of Directors and Shareholders of Tootsie Roll Industries, Inc.

In our opinion, the accompanying consolidated statements of financial position and the related consolidated statements of earnings, comprehensive earnings and retained earnings, and of cash flows present fairly, in all material respects, the financial position of Tootsie Roll Industries, Inc. and its subsidiaries at December 31, 2009 and December 31, 2008, and the results of their operations and their cash flows for each of the three years in the period ended December 31, 2009 in conformity with accounting principles generally accepted in the United States of America. Also in our opinion, the Company maintained, in all material respects, effective internal control over financial reporting as of December 31, 2009, based on criteria established in Internal Control—Integrated Framework issued by the Committee of Sponsoring Organizations of the Treadway Commission (COSO).

## before you go on...

**COMPONENTS OF ANNUAL REPORTS**

**Do it!** State whether each of the following items is most closely associated with the management discussion and analysis (MD&A), the notes to the financial statements, or the auditor's report.

1. Descriptions of significant accounting policies
2. Unqualified opinion
3. Explanations of uncertainties and contingencies
4. Description of ability to fund operations and expansion
5. Description of results of operations
6. Certified Public Accountant (CPA)

**Action Plan**
- Realize that financial statements provide information about a company's performance and financial position.
- Be familiar with the other elements of the annual report in order to gain a fuller understanding of a company.

### Solution

1. Descriptions of significant accounting policies: Notes.
2. Unqualified opinion: Auditor's report.
3. Explanations of uncertainties and contingencies: Notes.
4. Description of ability to fund operations and expansion: MD&A.
5. Description of results of operations: MD&A.
6. Certified Public Accountant (CPA): Auditor's report.

Related exercise material: **BE1-11**, *Do it!* **1-4**, and **E1-17**.

# USING THE *DECISION TOOLKIT*

The Hershey Company, located in Hershey, Pennsylvania, is the leading North American manufacturer of chocolate—for example, Hershey's Kisses, Reese's Peanut Butter Cups, Kit Kat, and Take 5 bars. Imagine that you are considering the purchase of shares of Hershey's common stock.

**Using the Decision Toolkit** exercises ask you to use information from financial statements to make financial decisions.

### Instructions

Answer these questions related to your decision whether to invest.
(a) What financial statements should you request from the company?
(b) What should these financial statements tell you?
(c) Should you request audited financial statements? Explain.
(d) Appendix B at the end of this book contains financial statements for Hershey. What comparisons can you make between Tootsie Roll and Hershey in terms of their respective results from operations and financial position?

### Solution

(a) Before you invest, you should investigate the income statement, retained earnings statement, statement of cash flows, and balance sheet.
(b) You would probably be most interested in the income statement because it tells about past performance and thus gives an indication of future performance. The retained earnings statement provides a record of the company's dividend history. The statement of cash flows reveals where the company is getting and spending its cash. This is especially important for a company that wants to grow. Finally, the balance sheet reveals the relationship between assets and liabilities.
(c) You would want audited financial statements. These statements indicate that a CPA (certified public accountant) has examined and expressed an opinion that the statements present fairly the financial position and results of operations of the company. Investors and creditors should not make decisions without studying audited financial statements.
(d) Many interesting comparisons can be made between the two companies. Tootsie Roll is smaller, with total assets of $838,247,000 versus $3,675,031,000 for Hershey, and it has lower revenue—$499,331,000 versus $5,298,660,000 for Hershey. In addition, Tootsie Roll's cash provided by operating activities of $75,281,000 is less than Hershey's $1,065,749,000.

While useful, these basic measures are not enough to determine whether one company is a better investment than the other. In later chapters, you will learn of tools that will allow you to compare the relative profitability and financial health of these and other companies.

✔ the navigator

# Summary of Study Objectives

**1 Describe the primary forms of business organization.** A sole proprietorship is a business owned by one person. A partnership is a business owned by two or more people associated as partners. A corporation is a separate legal entity for which evidence of ownership is provided by shares of stock.

**2 Identify the users and uses of accounting information.** Internal users are managers who need accounting information to plan, organize, and run business operations. The primary external users are investors and creditors. Investors (stockholders) use accounting information to help them decide whether to buy, hold, or sell shares of a company's stock. Creditors (suppliers and bankers) use accounting information to assess the risk of granting credit or loaning money to a business. Other groups who have an indirect interest in a business are taxing authorities, customers, labor unions, and regulatory agencies.

**3 Explain the three principal types of business activity.** Financing activities involve collecting the necessary funds to support the business. Investing activities involve acquiring the resources necessary to run the business. Operating activities involve putting the resources of the business into action to generate a profit.

**4 Describe the content and purpose of each of the financial statements.** An income statement presents the revenues and expenses of a company for a specific period of time. A retained earnings statement summarizes the changes in retained earnings that have occurred for a specific period of time. A balance sheet reports the assets, liabilities, and stockholders' equity of a business at a specific date. A statement of cash flows summarizes information concerning the cash inflows (receipts) and outflows (payments) for a specific period of time.

**5 Explain the meaning of assets, liabilities, and stockholders' equity, and state the basic accounting equation.** Assets are resources owned by a business. Liabilities are the debts and obligations of the business. Liabilities represent claims of creditors on the assets of the business. Stockholders' equity represents the claims of

owners on the assets of the business. Stockholders' equity is subdivided into two parts: common stock and retained earnings. The basic accounting equation is: Assets = Liabilities + Stockholders' Equity.

**6 Describe the components that supplement the financial statements in an annual report.** The management discussion and analysis provides management's interpretation of the company's results and financial position as well as a discussion of plans for the future. Notes to the financial statements provide additional explanation or detail to make the financial statements more informative. The auditor's report expresses an opinion as to whether the financial statements present fairly the company's results of operations and financial position.

the navigator

## *DECISION TOOLKIT* A SUMMARY

| DECISION CHECKPOINTS | INFO NEEDED FOR DECISION | TOOL TO USE FOR DECISION | HOW TO EVALUATE RESULTS |
|---|---|---|---|
| Are the company's operations profitable? | Income statement | The income statement reports on the success or failure of the company's operations by reporting its revenues and expenses. | If the company's revenue exceeds its expenses, it will report net income; otherwise it will report a net loss. |
| What is the company's policy toward dividends and growth? | Retained earnings statement | How much of this year's income did the company pay out in dividends to shareholders? | A company striving for rapid growth will pay a low (or no) dividend. |
| Does the company rely primarily on debt or stockholders' equity to finance its assets? | Balance sheet | The balance sheet reports the company's resources and claims to those resources. There are two types of claims: liabilities and stockholders' equity. | Compare the amount of debt versus the amount of stockholders' equity to determine whether the company relies more on creditors or owners for its financing. |
| Does the company generate sufficient cash from operations to fund its investing activities? | Statement of cash flows | The statement of cash flows shows the amount of cash provided or used by operating activities, investing activities, and financing activities. | Compare the amount of cash provided by operating activities with the amount of cash used by investing activities. Any deficiency in cash from operating activities must be made up with cash from financing activities. |

# Glossary

**Accounting** *(p. 5)* The information system that identifies, records, and communicates the economic events of an organization to interested users.

**Annual report** *(p. 19)* A report prepared by corporate management that presents financial information including financial statements, notes, a management discus-

sion and analysis section, and an independent auditor's report.

**Assets** *(p. 9)* Resources owned by a business.

**Auditor's report** *(p. 19)* A report prepared by an independent outside auditor stating the auditor's opinion as to the fairness of the presentation of the financial position and results of operations and their conformance with generally accepted accounting standards.

**Balance sheet** *(p. 13)* A financial statement that reports the assets and claims to those assets at a specific point in time.

**Basic accounting equation** *(p. 13)* Assets = Liabilities + Stockholders' Equity.

**Certified Public Accountant (CPA)** *(p. 20)* An individual who has met certain criteria and is thus allowed to perform audits of corporations.

**Common stock** *(p. 9)* Term used to describe the total amount paid in by stockholders for the shares they purchase.

**Corporation** *(p. 4)* A business organized as a separate legal entity having ownership divided into transferable shares of stock.

**Dividends** *(p. 9)* Payments of cash from a corporation to its stockholders.

**Expenses** *(p. 10)* The cost of assets consumed or services used in the process of generating revenues.

**Income statement** *(p. 11)* A financial statement that presents the revenues and expenses and resulting net income or net loss of a company for a specific period of time.

**Liabilities** *(p. 9)* The debts and obligations of a business. Liabilities represent the amounts owed to creditors.

**Management discussion and analysis (MD&A)** *(p. 19)* A section of the annual report that presents management's views on the company's ability to pay near-term obligations, its ability to fund operations and expansion, and its results of operations.

**Net income** *(p. 10)* The amount by which revenues exceed expenses.

**Net loss** *(p. 10)* The amount by which expenses exceed revenues.

**Notes to the financial statements** *(p. 19)* Notes that clarify information presented in the financial statements, as well as expand upon it where additional detail is needed.

**Partnership** *(p. 4)* A business owned by two or more persons associated as partners.

**Retained earnings** *(p. 13)* The amount of net income retained in the corporation.

**Retained earnings statement** *(p. 13)* A financial statement that summarizes the amounts and causes of changes in retained earnings for a specific period of time.

**Revenue** *(p. 10)* The increase in assets that result from the sale of a product or service in the normal course of business.

**Sarbanes-Oxley Act** *(p. 8)* Regulations passed by Congress in 2002 to try to reduce unethical corporate behavior.

**Sole proprietorship** *(p. 4)* A business owned by one person.

**Statement of cash flows** *(p. 15)* A financial statement that provides financial information about the cash receipts and cash payments of a business for a specific period of time.

**Stockholders' equity** *(p. 13)* The owners' claim to assets.

# Comprehensive Do it!

Jeff Andringa, a former college hockey player, quit his job and started Ice Camp, a hockey camp for kids ages 8 to 18. Eventually, he would like to open hockey camps nationwide. Jeff has asked you to help him prepare financial statements at the end of his first year of operations. He relates the following facts about his business activities.

In order to get the business off the ground, he decided to incorporate. He sold shares of common stock to a few close friends, as well as buying some of the shares himself. He initially raised $25,000 through the sale of these shares. In addition, the company took out a $10,000 loan at a local bank.

Ice Camp purchased, for $12,000 cash, a bus for transporting kids. The company also bought hockey goals and other miscellaneous equipment with $1,500 cash. The company earned camp tuition during the year of $100,000 but had collected only $80,000 of this amount. Thus, at the end of the year its customers still owed $20,000. The company rents time at a local rink for $50 per hour. Total rink rental costs during the year were $8,000, insurance was $10,000, salary expense was $20,000, and supplies used totaled $9,000, all of which were paid in cash. The company incurred $800 in interest expense on the bank loan, which it still owed at the end of the year.

The company paid dividends during the year of $5,000 cash. The balance in the corporate bank account at December 31, 2012, was $49,500.

*The Comprehensive Do it! is a final review before you begin homework.*

## Action Plan

- On the income statement: Show revenues and expenses for a period of time.
- On the retained earnings statement: Show the changes in retained earnings for a period of time.
- On the balance sheet: Report assets, liabilities, and stockholders' equity at a specific date.
- On the statement of cash flows: Report sources and uses of cash from operating, investing, and financing activities for a period of time.

## Instructions

Using the format of the Sierra Corporation statements in this chapter, prepare an income statement, retained earnings statement, balance sheet, and statement of cash flows. (*Hint:* Prepare the statements in the order stated to take advantage of the flow of information from one statement to the next, as shown in Illustration 1-9 on page 17.)

### Solution to Comprehensive Do it!

#### ICE CAMP
#### Income Statement
#### For the Year Ended December 31, 2012

| | | |
|---|---:|---:|
| Revenues | | |
| Service revenue | | $100,000 |
| Expenses | | |
| Salaries and wages expense | $20,000 | |
| Insurance expense | 10,000 | |
| Supplies expense | 9,000 | |
| Rent expense | 8,000 | |
| Interest expense | 800 | |
| Total expenses | | 47,800 |
| Net income | | $ 52,200 |

#### ICE CAMP
#### Retained Earnings Statement
#### For the Year Ended December 31, 2012

| | |
|---|---:|
| Retained earnings, January 1, 2012 | $ 0 |
| Add: Net income | 52,200 |
| | 52,200 |
| Less: Dividends | 5,000 |
| Retained earnings, December 31, 2012 | $47,200 |

#### ICE CAMP
#### Balance Sheet
#### December 31, 2012

##### Assets

| | | |
|---|---:|---:|
| Cash | | $49,500 |
| Accounts receivable | | 20,000 |
| Equipment | | 13,500 |
| Total assets | | $83,000 |

##### Liabilities and Stockholders' Equity

| | | |
|---|---:|---:|
| Liabilities | | |
| Notes payable | $10,000 | |
| Interest payable | 800 | |
| Total liabilities | | $10,800 |
| Stockholders' equity | | |
| Common stock | 25,000 | |
| Retained earnings | 47,200 | |
| Total stockholders' equity | | 72,200 |
| Total liabilities and stockholders' equity | | $83,000 |

**ICE CAMP**

**Statement of Cash Flows**

**For the Year Ended December 31, 2012**

| | | |
|---|---|---|
| Cash flows from operating activities | | |
| Cash receipts from operating activities | $80,000 | |
| Cash payments for operating activities | (47,000) | |
| Net cash provided by operating activities | | $33,000 |
| Cash flows from investing activities | | |
| Purchase of equipment | (13,500) | |
| Net cash used by investing activities | | (13,500) |
| Cash flows from financing activities | | |
| Issuance of common stock | 25,000 | |
| Issuance of notes payable | 10,000 | |
| Dividends paid | (5,000) | |
| Net cash provided by financing activities | | 30,000 |
| Net increase in cash | | 49,500 |
| Cash at beginning of period | | 0 |
| Cash at end of period | | $49,500 |

This would be a good time to look at the **Student Owner's Manual** in the Preface to the book. Knowing the purpose of the different types of homework will help you understand what each contributes to your accounting skills and competencies.

The tool icon ⚬━━━⚬ indicates that an activity employs one of the decision tools presented in the chapter. The ◀━━ indicates that an activity relates to a business function beyond accounting. The pencil icon ▭▭▭▷ indicates that an activity requires written communication.

**Self-Test, Brief Exercises, Exercises, Problem Set A, and many more resources are available for practice in WileyPLUS**

# Self-Test Questions

Answers are on page 42.

(SO 1)  **1.** Which is *not* one of the three forms of business organization?
 (a) Sole proprietorship.    (c) Partnership.
 (b) Creditorship.           (d) Corporation.

(SO 1)  **2.** Which is an advantage of corporations relative to partnerships and sole proprietorships?
 (a) Lower taxes.
 (b) Harder to transfer ownership.
 (c) Reduced legal liability for investors.
 (d) Most common form of organization.

(SO 2)  **3.** Which statement about users of accounting information is *incorrect*?
 (a) Management is considered an internal user.
 (b) Taxing authorities are considered external users.
 (c) Present creditors are considered external users.
 (d) Regulatory authorities are considered internal users.

(SO 2)  **4.** Which of the following did *not* result from the Sarbanes-Oxley Act?

 (a) Top management must now certify the accuracy of financial information.
 (b) Penalties for fraudulent activity increased.
 (c) Independence of auditors increased.
 (d) Tax rates on corporations increased.

**5.** Which is *not* one of the three primary business (SO 3) activities?
 (a) Financing.       (c) Advertising.
 (b) Operating.       (d) Investing.

**6.** Which of the following is an example of a financing (SO 3) activity?
 (a) Issuing shares of common stock.
 (b) Selling goods on account.
 (c) Buying delivery equipment.
 (d) Buying inventory.

**7.** Net income will result during a time period when: (SO 4)
 (a) assets exceed liabilities.
 (b) assets exceed revenues.
 (c) expenses exceed revenues.
 (d) revenues exceed expenses.

(SO 4) **8.** The financial statements for Joseph Corporation contained the following information.

| | |
|---|---|
| Accounts receivable | $ 5,000 |
| Sales revenue | 75,000 |
| Cash | 15,000 |
| Salaries and wages expense | 20,000 |
| Rent expense | 10,000 |

What was Joseph Corporation's net income?
(a) $60,000.    (c) $65,000.
(b) $15,000.    (d) $45,000.

(SO 4, 5) **9.** What section of a statement of cash flows indicates the cash spent on new equipment during the past accounting period?
(a) The investing section.
(b) The operating section.
(c) The financing section.
(d) The cash flow statement does not give this information.

(SO 4, 5) **10.** Which statement presents information as of a specific point in time?
(a) Income statement.
(b) Balance sheet.
(c) Statement of cash flows.
(d) Retained earnings statement.

(SO 5) **11.** Which financial statement reports assets, liabilities, and stockholders' equity?
(a) Income statement.
(b) Retained earnings statement.
(c) Balance sheet.
(d) Statement of cash flows.

(SO 5) **12.** Stockholders' equity represents:
(a) claims of creditors.
(b) claims of employees.
(c) the difference between revenues and expenses.
(d) claims of owners.

(SO 5) **13.** As of December 31, 2012, Stoneland Corporation has assets of $3,500 and stockholders' equity of $1,500. What are the liabilities for Stoneland Corporation as of December 31, 2012?
(a) $1,500.    (c) $2,500.
(b) $1,000.    (d) $2,000.

(SO 6) **14.** The element of a corporation's annual report that describes the corporation's accounting methods is the:
(a) notes to the financial statements.
(b) management discussion and analysis.
(c) auditor's report.
(d) income statement.

(SO 6) **15.** The element of the annual report that presents an opinion regarding the fairness of the presentation of the financial position and results of operations is/are the:
(a) income statement.
(b) auditor's opinion.
(c) balance sheet.
(d) comparative statements.

Go to the book's companion website, **www.wiley.com/college/kimmel**, to access additional Self-Test Questions.

## Questions

1. What are the three basic forms of business organizations?

2. What are the advantages to a business of being formed as a corporation? What are the disadvantages?

3. What are the advantages to a business of being formed as a partnership or sole proprietorship? What are the disadvantages?

4. "Accounting is ingrained in our society and is vital to our economic system." Do you agree? Explain.

5. Who are the internal users of accounting data? How does accounting provide relevant data to the internal users?

6. Who are the external users of accounting data? Give examples.

7. What are the three main types of business activity? Give examples of each activity.

8. Listed here are some items found in the financial statements of Ellyn Toth, Inc. Indicate in which financial statement(s) each item would appear.
(a) Service revenue.    (d) Accounts receivable.
(b) Equipment.    (e) Common stock.
(c) Advertising expense.    (f) Interest payable.

9. Why would a bank want to monitor the dividend payment practices of the corporations it lends money to?

10. "A company's net income appears directly on the income statement and the retained earnings statement, and it is included indirectly in the company's balance sheet." Do you agree? Explain.

11. What is the primary purpose of the statement of cash flows?

12. What are the three main categories of the statement of cash flows? Why do you think these categories were chosen?

13. What is retained earnings? What items increase the balance in retained earnings? What items decrease the balance in retained earnings?

14. What is the basic accounting equation?

15. (a) Define the terms *assets*, *liabilities*, and *stockholders'* equity.
(b) What items affect stockholders' equity?

16. Which of these items are liabilities of White Glove Cleaning Service?
(a) Cash.    (c) Dividends.
(b) Accounts payable.    (d) Accounts receivable.

(e) Supplies.       (h) Service revenue.
(f) Equipment.       (i) Rent expense.
(g) Salaries and wages payable.

17. How are each of the following financial statements interrelated? (a) Retained earnings statement and income statement. (b) Retained earnings statement and balance sheet. (c) Balance sheet and statement of cash flows.

18. ⟢═══⟜ What is the purpose of the management discussion and analysis section (MD&A)?

19. ⟢═══⟜ Why is it important for financial statements to receive an unqualified auditor's opinion?

20. ⟢═══⟜ What types of information are presented in the notes to the financial statements?

21. 🍬 The accounting equation is: Assets = Liabilities + Stockholders' Equity. Appendix A, at the end of this book, reproduces Tootsie Roll's financial statements. Replacing words in the equation with dollar amounts, what is Tootsie Roll's accounting equation at December 31, 2009?

# Brief Exercises

**BE1-1** Match each of the following forms of business organization with a set of characteristics: sole proprietorship (SP), partnership (P), corporation (C).
(a) _____ Shared control, tax advantages, increased skills and resources.
(b) _____ Simple to set up and maintains control with founder.
(c) _____ Easier to transfer ownership and raise funds, no personal liability.

*Describe forms of business organization.*
*(SO 1),* **K**

**BE1-2** Match each of the following types of evaluation with one of the listed users of accounting information.
1. Trying to determine whether the company complied with tax laws.
2. Trying to determine whether the company can pay its obligations.
3. Trying to determine whether a marketing proposal will be cost effective.
4. Trying to determine whether the company's net income will result in a stock price increase.
5. Trying to determine whether the company should employ debt or equity financing.
(a) _____ Investors in common stock.       (d) _____ Chief Financial Officer.
(b) _____ Marketing managers.       (e) _____ Internal Revenue Service.
(c) _____ Creditors.

*Identify users of accounting information.*
*(SO 2),* **K**

**BE1-3** Indicate in which part of the statement of cash flows each item would appear: operating activities (O), investing activities (I), or financing activities (F).
(a) _____ Cash received from customers.
(b) _____ Cash paid to stockholders (dividends).
(c) _____ Cash received from issuing new common stock.
(d) _____ Cash paid to suppliers.
(e) _____ Cash paid to purchase a new office building.

*Classify items by activity.*
*(SO 3, 4),* **K**

**BE1-4** Presented below are a number of transactions. Determine whether each transaction affects common stock (C), dividends (D), revenue (R), expense (E), or does not affect stockholders' equity (NSE). Provide titles for the revenues and expenses.
(a) Costs incurred for advertising.
(b) Assets received for services performed.
(c) Costs incurred for insurance.
(d) Amounts paid to employees.
(e) Cash distributed to stockholders.
(f) Assets received in exchange for allowing the use of the company's building.
(g) Costs incurred for utilities used.
(h) Cash purchase of equipment.
(i) Issued common stock for cash.

*Determine effect of transactions on stockholders' equity.*
*(SO 4),* **C**

**BE1-5** In alphabetical order below are balance sheet items for Wyoming Company at December 31, 2012. Prepare a balance sheet following the format of Illustration 1-7.

*Prepare a balance sheet.*
*(SO 4, 5),* **AP**

| | |
|---|---|
| Accounts payable | $65,000 |
| Accounts receivable | 71,000 |
| Cash | 22,000 |
| Common stock | 28,000 |

*Determine where items appear on financial statements.*
(SO 4, 5), **K**

**BE1-6** Eskimo Pie Corporation markets a broad range of frozen treats, including its famous Eskimo Pie ice cream bars. The following items were taken from a recent income statement and balance sheet. In each case, identify whether the item would appear on the balance sheet (BS) or income statement (IS).

(a) _____ Income tax expense.      (f) _____ Net sales.
(b) _____ Inventories.             (g) _____ Cost of goods sold.
(c) _____ Accounts payable.        (h) _____ Common stock.
(d) _____ Retained earnings.       (i) _____ Receivables.
(e) _____ Property, plant, and equipment.   (j) _____ Interest expense.

*Determine proper financial statement.*
(SO 4), **K**

**BE1-7** Indicate which statement you would examine to find each of the following items: income statement (I), balance sheet (B), retained earnings statement (R), or statement of cash flows (C).
(a) Revenue during the period.
(b) Supplies on hand at the end of the year.
(c) Cash received from issuing new bonds during the period.
(d) Total debts outstanding at the end of the period.

*Use basic accounting equation.*
(SO 5), **AP**

**BE1-8** Use the basic accounting equation to answer these questions.
(a) The liabilities of Daley Company are $90,000 and the stockholders' equity is $230,000. What is the amount of Daley Company's total assets?
(b) The total assets of Laven Company are $170,000 and its stockholders' equity is $80,000. What is the amount of its total liabilities?
(c) The total assets of Peterman Co. are $800,000 and its liabilities are equal to one-fourth of its total assets. What is the amount of Peterman Co.'s stockholders' equity?

*Use basic accounting equation.*
(SO 5), **AP**

**BE1-9** At the beginning of the year, Peale Company had total assets of $800,000 and total liabilities of $500,000.
(a) If total assets increased $150,000 during the year and total liabilities decreased $80,000, what is the amount of stockholders' equity at the end of the year?
(b) During the year, total liabilities increased $100,000 and stockholders' equity decreased $70,000. What is the amount of total assets at the end of the year?
(c) If total assets decreased $80,000 and stockholders' equity increased $110,000 during the year, what is the amount of total liabilities at the end of the year?

*Identify assets, liabilities, and stockholders' equity.*
(SO 5), **K**

**BE1-10** Indicate whether each of these items is an asset (A), a liability (L), or part of stockholders' equity (SE).
(a) Accounts receivable.          (d) Supplies.
(b) Salaries and wages payable.   (e) Common stock.
(c) Equipment.                    (f) Notes payable.

*Determine required parts of annual report.*
(SO 6), **K**

**BE1-11** Which is *not* a required part of an annual report of a publicly traded company?
(a) Statement of cash flows.
(b) Notes to the financial statements.
(c) Management discussion and analysis.
(d) All of these are required.

# Do it! Review

*Identify benefits of business organization forms.*
(SO 1), **C**

**Do it! 1-1** Identify each of the following organizational characteristics with the organizational form or forms with which it is associated.
(a) Easier to transfer ownership     (d) Tax advantages
(b) Easier to raise funds            (e) No personal legal liability
(c) More owner control

*Classify business activities.*
(SO 3), **K**

**Do it! 1-2** Classify each item as an asset, liability, common stock, revenue, or expense.
(a) Issuance of ownership shares
(b) Land purchased
(c) Amounts owed to suppliers
(d) Bonds payable
(e) Amount earned from selling a product
(f) Cost of advertising

**Do it!** 1-3    Gould Corporation began operations on January 1, 2012. The following information is available for Gould Corporation on December 31, 2012.

| | | | |
|---|---|---|---|
| Accounts payable | $ 5,000 | Notes payable | $ 7,000 |
| Accounts receivable | 2,000 | Rent expense | 10,000 |
| Advertising expense | 4,000 | Retained earnings | ? |
| Cash | 3,100 | Service revenue | 25,000 |
| Common stock | 15,000 | Supplies | 1,900 |
| Dividends | 2,500 | Supplies expense | 1,700 |
| Equipment | 26,800 | | |

Prepare an income statement, a retained earnings statement, and a balance sheet for Gould Corporation.

**Do it!** 1-4    Indicate whether each of the following items is most closely associated with the management discussion and analysis (MD&A), the notes to the financial statements, or the auditor's report.

(a)  Description of ability to pay near-term obligations
(b)  Unqualified opinion
(c)  Details concerning liabilities, too voluminous to be included in the statements
(d)  Description of favorable and unfavorable trends
(e)  Certified Public Accountant (CPA)
(f)  Descriptions of significant accounting policies

# Exercises

**E1-1**    Here is a list of words or phrases discussed in this chapter:

1.  Corporation
2.  Creditor
3.  Accounts receivable
4.  Partnership
5.  Stockholder
6.  Common stock
7.  Accounts payable
8.  Auditor's opinion

**Instructions**
Match each word or phrase with the best description of it.

_____ (a) An expression about whether financial statements conform with generally accepted accounting principles.
_____ (b) A business enterprise that raises money by issuing shares of stock.
_____ (c) The portion of stockholders' equity that results from receiving cash from investors.
_____ (d) Obligations to suppliers of goods.
_____ (e) Amounts due from customers.
_____ (f) A party to whom a business owes money.
_____ (g) A party that invests in common stock.
_____ (h) A business that is owned jointly by two or more individuals but does not issue stock.

**E1-2**    All businesses are involved in three types of activities—financing, investing, and operating. Listed below are the names and descriptions of companies in several different industries.

Abitibi Consolidated Inc.—manufacturer and marketer of newsprint
Cal State–Northridge Stdt Union—university student union
Oracle Corporation—computer software developer and retailer
Sportsco Investments—owner of the Vancouver Canucks hockey club
Grant Thornton LLP—professional accounting and business advisory firm
Southwest Airlines—discount airline

**Instructions**
(a)  For each of the above companies, provide examples of (1) a financing activity, (2) an investing activity, and (3) an operating activity that the company likely engages in.
(b)  Which of the activities that you identified in (a) are common to most businesses? Which activities are not?

*Classify accounts.*
(SO 3, 4), **C**

**E1-3** The Fair View Golf & Country Club details the following accounts in its financial statements.

|  | (a) | (b) |
|---|---|---|
| Accounts payable | ____ | ____ |
| Accounts receivable | ____ | ____ |
| Equipment | ____ | ____ |
| Sales revenue | ____ | ____ |
| Service revenue | ____ | ____ |
| Inventory | ____ | ____ |
| Mortgage payable | ____ | ____ |
| Supplies expense | ____ | ____ |
| Rent expense | ____ | ____ |
| Salaries and wages expense | ____ | ____ |

*Instructions*
(a) Classify each of the above accounts as an asset (A), liability (L), stockholders' equity (SE), revenue (R), or expense (E) item.
(b) Classify each of the above accounts as a financing activity (F), investing activity (I), or operating activity (O). If you believe a particular account doesn't fit in any of these activities, explain why.

*Prepare income statement and retained earnings statement.*
(SO 4), **AP**

**E1-4** This information relates to Alexis Co. for the year 2012.

| | |
|---|---|
| Retained earnings, January 1, 2012 | $67,000 |
| Advertising expense | 1,800 |
| Dividends paid during 2012 | 6,000 |
| Rent expense | 10,400 |
| Service revenue | 58,000 |
| Utilities expense | 2,400 |
| Salaries and wages expense | 30,000 |

*Instructions*
After analyzing the data, prepare an income statement and a retained earnings statement for the year ending December 31, 2012.

*Prepare income statement and retained earnings statement.*
(SO 4), **AP**

**E1-5** The following information was taken from the 2009 financial statements of pharmaceutical giant Merck and Co. All dollar amounts are in millions.

| | |
|---|---|
| Retained earnings, January 1, 2009 | $43,698.8 |
| Materials and production expense | 9,018.9 |
| Marketing and administrative expense | 8,543.2 |
| Dividends | 3,597.7 |
| Sales revenue | 27,428.3 |
| Research and development expense | 5,845.0 |
| Tax expense | 2,267.6 |
| Other revenue | 11,147.7 |

*Instructions*
(a) After analyzing the data, prepare an income statement and a retained earnings statement for the year ending December 31, 2009.
(b) Suppose that Merck decided to reduce its research and development expense by 50%. What would be the short-term implications? What would be the long-term implications? How do you think the stock market would react?

*Prepare a retained earnings statement.*
(SO 4), **AP**

**E1-6** Presented here is information for Packee Inc. for 2012.

| | |
|---|---|
| Retained earnings, January 1 | $130,000 |
| Revenue from legal services | 400,000 |
| Total expenses | 175,000 |
| Dividends | 65,000 |

*Instructions*
Prepare the 2012 retained earnings statement for Packee Inc.

*Interpret financial facts.*
(SO 4), **AP**

**E1-7** Consider each of the following independent situations.
(a) The retained earnings statement of Scott Corporation shows dividends of $68,000, while net income for the year was $75,000.

(b) The statement of cash flows for Silberman Corporation shows that cash provided by operating activities was $10,000, cash used in investing activities was $110,000, and cash provided by financing activities was $130,000.

**Instructions**

For each company provide a brief discussion interpreting these financial facts. For example, you might discuss the company's financial health or its apparent growth philosophy.

**E1-8** The following items and amounts were taken from Linus Inc.'s 2012 income statement and balance sheet.

*Identify financial statement components and prepare income statement.*
*(SO 4), C*

| | | | | |
|---|---|---|---|---|
| _____ Cash | $ 84,700 | | _____ Accounts receivable | 88,419 |
| _____ Retained earnings | 123,192 | | _____ Sales revenue | 584,951 |
| _____ Cost of goods sold | 438,458 | | _____ Income taxes payable | 6,499 |
| _____ Salaries and wages expense | 115,131 | | _____ Accounts payable | 49,384 |
| _____ Prepaid insurance | 7,818 | | _____ Service revenue | 4,806 |
| _____ Inventory | $ 64,618 | | _____ Interest expense | 1,882 |

**Instructions**
(a) In each, case, identify on the blank line whether the item is an asset (A), liability (L), stockholder's equity (SE), revenue (R), or expense (E) item.
(b) Prepare an income statement for Linus Inc. for the year ended December 31, 2012.

**E1-9** Here are incomplete financial statements for Liam, Inc.

*Calculate missing amounts.*
*(SO 4, 5), AP*

**LIAM, INC.**
**Balance Sheet**

| Assets | | Liabilities and Stockholders' Equity | |
|---|---|---|---|
| Cash | $ 7,000 | Liabilities | |
| Inventory | 10,000 |   Accounts payable | $ 5,000 |
| Buildings | 45,000 | Stockholders' equity | |
| | |   Common stock | (a) |
| Total assets | $62,000 |   Retained earnings | (b) |
| | | Total liabilities and | |
| | |   stockholders' equity | $62,000 |

**Income Statement**

| | |
|---|---|
| Revenues | $85,000 |
| Cost of goods sold | (c) |
| Salaries and wages expense | 10,000 |
| Net income | $ (d) |

**Retained Earnings Statement**

| | |
|---|---|
| Beginning retained earnings | $12,000 |
| Add: Net income | (e) |
| Less: Dividends | 5,000 |
| Ending retained earnings | $27,000 |

**Instructions**
Calculate the missing amounts.

**E1-10** Deer Track Park is a private camping ground near the Lathom Peak Recreation Area. It has compiled the following financial information as of December 31, 2012.

*Compute net income and prepare a balance sheet.*
*(SO 4, 5), AP*

| | | | |
|---|---|---|---|
| Revenues during 2012: camping fees | $132,000 | Dividends | $ 9,000 |
| Revenues during 2012: general store | 25,000 | Notes payable | 50,000 |
| Accounts payable | 11,000 | Expenses during 2012 | 126,000 |
| Cash | 8,500 | Supplies | 5,500 |
| Equipment | 114,000 | Common stock | 40,000 |
| | | Retained earnings (1/1/2012) | 5,000 |

**Instructions**
(a) Determine Deer Track Park's net income for 2012.
(b) Prepare a retained earnings statement and a balance sheet for Deer Track Park as of December 31, 2012.
(c) Upon seeing this income statement, Ken Zilber, the campground manager, immediately concluded, "The general store is more trouble than it is worth—let's get rid of it." The marketing director isn't so sure this is a good idea. What do you think?

*Identify financial statement components and prepare an income statement.*
*(SO 4, 5),* **AP**

**E1-11**  Kellogg Company is the world's leading producer of ready-to-eat cereal and a leading producer of grain-based convenience foods such as frozen waffles and cereal bars. The following items were taken from its 2009 income statement and balance sheet. All dollars are in millions.

| | | | | | |
|---|---|---|---|---|---|
| ____ | Retained earnings | $5,481 | ____ | Long-term debt | $ 4,835 |
| ____ | Cost of goods sold | 7,184 | ____ | Inventories | 910 |
| ____ | Selling and | | ____ | Net sales | 12,575 |
| | administrative expenses | 3,390 | ____ | Accounts payable | 1,077 |
| ____ | Cash | 334 | ____ | Common stock | 105 |
| ____ | Notes payable | 44 | ____ | Income tax expense | 476 |
| ____ | Interest expense | 295 | ____ | Other expense | 22 |

**Instructions**
Perform each of the following.
(a) In each case identify whether the item is an asset (A), liability (L), stockholders' equity (SE), revenue (R), or expense (E).
(b) Prepare an income statement for Kellogg Company for the year ended December 31, 2009.

*Prepare a statement of cash flows.*
*(SO 5),* **AP**

**E1-12**  This information is for O'Brien Corporation for the year ended December 31, 2012.

| | |
|---|---|
| Cash received from lenders | $20,000 |
| Cash received from customers | 50,000 |
| Cash paid for new equipment | 28,000 |
| Cash dividends paid | 8,000 |
| Cash paid to suppliers | 16,000 |
| Cash balance 1/1/12 | 12,000 |

**Instructions**
(a) Prepare the 2012 statement of cash flows for O'Brien Corporation.
(b) Suppose you are one of O'Brien's creditors. Referring to the statement of cash flows, evaluate O'Brien's ability to repay its creditors.

*Prepare a statement of cash flows.*
*(SO 5),* **AP**

**E1-13**  The following data are derived from the 2009 financial statements of Southwest Airlines. All dollars are in millions. Southwest has a December 31 year-end.

| | |
|---|---|
| Cash balance, January 1, 2009 | $1,390 |
| Cash paid for repayment of debt | 122 |
| Cash received from issuance of common stock | 144 |
| Cash received from issuance of long-term debt | 500 |
| Cash received from customers | 9,823 |
| Cash paid for property and equipment | 1,529 |
| Cash paid for dividends | 14 |
| Cash paid for repurchase of common stock | 1,001 |
| Cash paid for goods and services | 6,978 |

**Instructions**
(a) After analyzing the data, prepare a statement of cash flows for Southwest Airlines for the year ended December 31, 2009.
(b) Discuss whether the company's cash from operations was sufficient to finance its investing activities. If it was not, how did the company finance its investing activities?

*Correct an incorrectly prepared balance sheet.*
*(SO 5),* **AP**

**E1-14**  Andrew Davis is the bookkeeper for Cheyenne Company. Andrew has been trying to get the balance sheet of Cheyenne Company to balance. It finally balanced, but now he's not sure it is correct.

## CHEYENNE COMPANY
### Balance Sheet
### December 31, 2012

| Assets | | Liabilities and Stockholders' Equity | |
|---|---|---|---|
| Cash | $18,000 | Accounts payable | $16,000 |
| Supplies | 9,500 | Accounts receivable | (12,000) |
| Equipment | 40,000 | Common stock | 40,000 |
| Dividends | 8,000 | Retained earnings | 31,500 |
| Total assets | $75,500 | Total liabilities and stockholders' equity | $75,500 |

**Instructions**
Prepare a correct balance sheet.

**E1-15** The following items were taken from the balance sheet of Nike, Inc.

*Classify items as assets, liabilities, and stockholders' equity and prepare accounting equation.*
*(SO 5),* **AP**

| | | | |
|---|---|---|---|
| 1. Cash | $2,291.1 | 7. Inventories | $2,357.0 |
| 2. Accounts receivable | 2,883.9 | 8. Income taxes payable | 86.3 |
| 3. Common stock | 2,874.2 | 9. Property, plant, and equipment | 1,957.7 |
| 4. Notes payable | 342.9 | 10. Retained earnings | 5,818.9 |
| 5. Other assets | 3,759.9 | 11. Accounts payable | 2,815.8 |
| 6. Other liabilities | 1,311.5 | | |

**Instructions**
Perform each of the following.
(a) Classify each of these items as an asset, liability, or stockholders' equity and determine the total dollar amount for each classification. (All dollars are in millions.)
(b) Determine Nike's accounting equation by calculating the value of total assets, total liabilities, and total stockholders' equity.
(c) To what extent does Nike rely on debt versus equity financing?

**E1-16** The summaries of data from the balance sheet, income statement, and retained earnings statement for two corporations, Bates Corporation and Wilson Enterprises, are presented below for 2012.

*Use financial statement relationships to determine missing amounts.*
*(SO 5),* **AP**

| | Bates Corporation | Wilson Enterprises |
|---|---|---|
| **Beginning of year** | | |
| Total assets | $110,000 | $150,000 |
| Total liabilities | 70,000 | (d) |
| Total stockholders' equity | (a) | 70,000 |
| **End of year** | | |
| Total assets | (b) | 180,000 |
| Total liabilities | 120,000 | 55,000 |
| Total stockholders' equity | 60,000 | (e) |
| **Changes during year in retained earnings** | | |
| Dividends | (c) | 5,000 |
| Total revenues | 215,000 | (f) |
| Total expenses | 165,000 | 80,000 |

**Instructions**
Determine the missing amounts. Assume all changes in stockholders' equity are due to changes in retained earnings.

**E1-17** The annual report provides financial information in a variety of formats, including the following.

*Classify various items in an annual report.*
*(SO 6),* **K**

> Management discussion and analysis (MD&A)
> Financial statements
> Notes to the financial statements
> Auditor's opinion

**Instructions**
For each of the following, state in what area of the annual report the item would be presented. If the item would probably not be found in an annual report, state "Not disclosed."

(a) The total cumulative amount received from stockholders in exchange for common stock.

(b) An independent assessment concerning whether the financial statements present a fair depiction of the company's results and financial position.

(c) The interest rate that the company is being charged on all outstanding debts.

(d) Total revenue from operating activities.

(e) Management's assessment of the company's results.

(f) The names and positions of all employees hired in the last year.

# Exercises: Set B and Challenge Exercises

Visit the book's companion website, at **www.wiley.com/college/kimmel**, and choose the Student Companion site to access Exercise Set B and Challenge Exercises.

# Problems: Set A

*Determine forms of business organization.*

*(SO 1),* C

**P1-1A** Presented below are five independent situations.

(a) Three physics professors at MIT have formed a business to improve the speed of information transfer over the Internet for stock exchange transactions. Each has contributed an equal amount of cash and knowledge to the venture. Although their approach looks promising, they are concerned about the legal liabilities that their business might confront.

(b) Ed Toth, a college student looking for summer employment, opened a bait shop in a small shed at a local marina.

(c) Joan Stuebben and Ron Klinke each owned separate shoe manufacturing businesses. They have decided to combine their businesses. They expect that within the coming year they will need significant funds to expand their operations.

(d) Crystal, Allie, and Harry recently graduated with marketing degrees. They have been friends since childhood. They have decided to start a consulting business focused on marketing sporting goods over the Internet.

(e) Mark Willis wants to rent CD players and CDs in airports across the country. His idea is that customers will be able to rent equipment and CDs at one airport, listen to the CDs on their flights, and return the equipment and CDs at their destination airport. Of course, this will require a substantial investment in equipment and CDs, as well as employees and locations in each airport. Mark has no savings or personal assets. He wants to maintain control over the business.

*Instructions*

In each case, explain what form of organization the business is likely to take—sole proprietorship, partnership, or corporation. Give reasons for your choice.

*Identify users and uses of financial statements.*

*(SO 2, 4, 5),* K

**P1-2A** Financial decisions often place heavier emphasis on one type of financial statement over the others. Consider each of the following hypothetical situations independently.

(a) The North Face, Inc. is considering extending credit to a new customer. The terms of the credit would require the customer to pay within 30 days of receipt of goods.

(b) An investor is considering purchasing common stock of Amazon.com. The investor plans to hold the investment for at least 5 years.

(c) Chase Manhattan is considering extending a loan to a small company. The company would be required to make interest payments at the end of each year for 5 years, and to repay the loan at the end of the fifth year.

(d) The president of Campbell Soup is trying to determine whether the company is generating enough cash to increase the amount of dividends paid to investors in this and future years, and still have enough cash to buy equipment as it is needed.

*Instructions*

In each situation, state whether the decision maker would be most likely to place primary emphasis on information provided by the income statement, balance sheet, or statement of cash flows. In each case provide a brief justification for your choice. Choose only one financial statement in each case.

**P1-3A** On June 1, Beardsley Service Co. was started with an initial investment in the company of $22,100 cash. Here are the assets and liabilities of the company at June 30, and the revenues and expenses for the month of June, its first month of operations:

| | | | |
|---|---|---|---|
| Cash | $ 4,600 | Notes payable | $12,000 |
| Accounts receivable | 4,000 | Accounts payable | 500 |
| Service revenue | 7,500 | Supplies expense | 1,000 |
| Supplies | 2,400 | Maintenance and repairs expense | 600 |
| Advertising expense | 400 | Utilities expense | 300 |
| Equipment | 26,000 | Salaries and wages expense | 1,400 |

In June, the company issued no additional stock, but paid dividends of $1,400.

**Instructions**
(a) Prepare an income statement and a retained earnings statement for the month of June and a balance sheet at June 30, 2012.
(b) Briefly discuss whether the company's first month of operations was a success.
(c) Discuss the company's decision to distribute a dividend.

**P1-4A** Presented below is selected financial information for Yvonne Corporation for December 31, 2012.

| | | | |
|---|---|---|---|
| Inventory | $ 25,000 | Cash paid to purchase equipment | $ 12,000 |
| Cash paid to suppliers | 104,000 | Equipment | 40,000 |
| Building | 200,000 | Revenues | 100,000 |
| Common stock | 50,000 | Cash received from customers | 132,000 |
| Cash dividends paid | 7,000 | Cash received from issuing common stock | 22,000 |

**Instructions**
(a) Determine which items should be included in a statement of cash flows and then prepare the statement for Yvonne Corporation.
(b) Comment on the adequacy of net cash provided by operating activities to fund the company's investing activities and dividend payments.

**P1-5A** Gabelli Corporation was formed on January 1, 2012. At December 31, 2012, John Paulus, the president and sole stockholder, decided to prepare a balance sheet, which appeared as follows.

**GABELLI CORPORATION**
**Balance Sheet**
**December 31, 2012**

| Assets | | Liabilities and Stockholders' Equity | |
|---|---|---|---|
| Cash | $20,000 | Accounts payable | $30,000 |
| Accounts receivable | 50,000 | Notes payable | 15,000 |
| Inventory | 36,000 | Boat loan | 22,000 |
| Boat | 24,000 | Stockholders' equity | 64,000 |

John willingly admits that he is not an accountant by training. He is concerned that his balance sheet might not be correct. He has provided you with the following additional information.

1. The boat actually belongs to Paulus, not to Gabelli Corporation. However, because he thinks he might take customers out on the boat occasionally, he decided to list it as an asset of the company. To be consistent, he also listed as a liability of the corporation his personal loan that he took out at the bank to buy the boat.
2. The inventory was originally purchased for $25,000, but due to a surge in demand John now thinks he could sell it for $36,000. He thought it would be best to record it at $36,000.
3. Included in the accounts receivable balance is $10,000 that John loaned to his brother 5 years ago. John included this in the receivables of Gabelli Corporation so he wouldn't forget that his brother owes him money.

**Instructions**
(a) Comment on the proper accounting treatment of the three items above.
(b) Provide a corrected balance sheet for Gabelli Corporation. (*Hint:* To get the balance sheet to balance, adjust stockholders' equity.)

*Prepare an income statement, retained earnings statement, and balance sheet; discuss results.*
(SO 4, 5), **AP**

**Marginal check figures** (in blue) provide a key number to let you know you are on the right track.
(a) Net income    $3,800
    Ret. earnings    $2,400
    Tot. assets    $37,000

*Determine items included in a statement of cash flows, prepare the statement, and comment.*
(SO 4, 5), **AP**

(a) Net increase $31,000

*Comment on proper accounting treatment and prepare a corrected balance sheet.*
(SO 4, 5), **AP**

Tot. assets $85,000

# Problems: Set B

*Determine forms of business organization.*

(SO 1), **C**

**P1-1B**   Presented below are five independent situations.

(a)  Rachel Jackson, a college student looking for summer employment, opened a vegetable stand along a busy local highway. Each morning she buys produce from local farmers, then sells it in the afternoon as people return home from work.

(b)  Colin Doyle and Jason Elliot each owned separate swing-set manufacturing businesses. They have decided to combine their businesses and try to expand their reach beyond their local market. They expect that within the coming year they will need significant funds to expand their operations.

(c)  Three chemistry professors at FIU have formed a business to employ bacteria to clean up toxic waste sites. Each has contributed an equal amount of cash and knowledge to the venture. The use of bacteria in this situation is experimental, and legal obligations could result.

(d)  Brittany Medler has run a successful, but small cooperative health food store for over 20 years. The increased sales of her store have made her believe that the time is right to open a national chain of health food stores across the country. Of course, this will require a substantial investment in stores, inventory, and employees in each store. Brittany has no savings or personal assets. She wants to maintain control over the business.

(e)  Cheryl Lamb and Tom Majors recently graduated with masters degrees in economics. They have decided to start a consulting business focused on teaching the basics of international economics to small business owners interested in international trade.

### Instructions

In each case, explain what form of organization the business is likely to take—sole proprietorship, partnership, or corporation. Give reasons for your choice.

*Identify users and uses of financial statements.*

(SO 2, 4, 5), **K**

**P1-2B**   Financial decisions often place heavier emphasis on one type of financial statement over the others. Consider each of the following hypothetical situations independently.

(a)  An investor is considering purchasing common stock of the Bally Total Fitness company. The investor plans to hold the investment for at least 3 years.

(b)  Boeing is considering extending credit to a new customer. The terms of the credit would require the customer to pay within 60 days of receipt of goods.

(c)  The president of Northwest Airlines is trying to determine whether the company is generating enough cash to increase the amount of dividends paid to investors in this and future years, and still have enough cash to buy new flight equipment as it is needed.

(d)  Bank of America is considering extending a loan to a small company. The company would be required to make interest payments at the end of each year for 5 years, and to repay the loan at the end of the fifth year.

### Instructions

In each of the situations above, state whether the decision maker would be most likely to place primary emphasis on information provided by the income statement, balance sheet, or statement of cash flows. In each case, provide a brief justification for your choice. Choose only one financial statement in each case.

*Prepare an income statement, retained earnings statement, and balance sheet; discuss results.*

(SO 4, 5), **AP**

(a)  Net income    $4,300
     Ret. earnings  $2,600
     Tot. assets    $78,000

**P1-3B**   Special Delivery was started on May 1 with an investment of $45,000 cash. Following are the assets and liabilities of the company on May 31, 2012, and the revenues and expenses for the month of May, its first month of operations.

| | | | |
|---|---|---|---|
| Accounts receivable | $ 6,200 | Notes payable | $28,000 |
| Service revenue | 10,400 | Salaries and wages expense | 2,000 |
| Advertising expense | 800 | Equipment | 56,000 |
| Accounts payable | 2,400 | Maintenance and repairs expense | 2,900 |
| Cash | 15,800 | Insurance expense | 400 |

No additional common stock was issued in May, but a dividend of $1,700 in cash was paid.

### Instructions

(a)  Prepare an income statement and a retained earnings statement for the month of May and a balance sheet at May 31, 2012.

(b) Briefly discuss whether the company's first month of operations was a success.

(c) Discuss the company's decision to distribute a dividend.

**P1-4B** Presented below are selected financial statement items for Rowe Corporation for December 31, 2012.

*Determine items included in a statement of cash flows, prepare the statement, and comment.*

*(SO 4, 5),* **AP**

| | | | |
|---|---|---|---|
| Inventory | $ 55,000 | Cash paid to purchase equipment | $ 30,000 |
| Cash paid to suppliers | 154,000 | Equipment | 40,000 |
| Buildings | 400,000 | Revenues | 200,000 |
| Common stock | 20,000 | Cash received from customers | 172,000 |
| Cash dividends paid | 6,000 | Cash received from issuing bonds payable | 40,000 |

**Instructions**

(a) Determine which items should be included in a statement of cash flows, and then prepare the statement for Rowe Corporation.

(b) Comment on the adequacy of net cash provided by operating activities to fund the company's investing activities and dividend payments.

*(a) Net increase $22,000*

**P1-5B** Austin Corporation was formed during 2011 by Joanna Kay. Joanna is the president and sole stockholder. At December 31, 2012, Joanna prepared an income statement for Austin Corporation. Joanna is not an accountant, but she thinks she did a reasonable job preparing the income statement by looking at the financial statements of other companies. She has asked you for advice. Joanna's income statement appears as follows.

*Comment on proper accounting treatment and prepare a corrected income statement.*

*(SO 4, 5),* **AP**

**AUSTIN CORPORATION**
**Income Statement**
**For the Year Ended December 31, 2012**

| | |
|---|---|
| Accounts receivable | $17,000 |
| Service revenue | 47,000 |
| Rent expense | 10,000 |
| Insurance expense | 7,000 |
| Vacation expense | 4,000 |
| Net income | $43,000 |

Joanna has also provided you with these facts.

1. Included in the service revenue account is $3,000 of revenue that the company earned and received payment for in 2011. She forgot to include it in the 2011 income statement, so she put it in this year's statement.

2. Joanna operates her business out of the basement of her parents' home. They do not charge her anything, but she thinks that if she paid rent it would cost her about $10,000 per year. Therefore, she included $10,000 of rent expense in the income statement.

3. To reward herself for a year of hard work, Joanna went to Greece. She did not use company funds to pay for the trip, but she reported it as an expense on the income statement since it was her job that made her need the vacation.

**Instructions**

(a) Comment on the proper accounting treatment of the three items above.

(b) Prepare a corrected income statement for Austin Corporation.

*(a) Net income $37,000*

# Problems: Set C

Visit the book's companion website, at **www.wiley.com/college/kimmel**, and choose the Student Companion site to access Problem Set C.

# Continuing Cookie Chronicle

**CCC1** Natalie Koebel spent much of her childhood learning the art of cookie-making from her grandmother. They spent many happy hours mastering every type of cookie imaginable and later devised new recipes that were both healthy and delicious. Now at

This serial problem starts in Chapter 1 and continues in every chapter. You can also find this problem at the book's companion website, **www.wiley.com/ college/kimmel**.

the start of her second year in college, Natalie is investigating possibilities for starting her own business as part of the entrepreneurship program in which she is enrolled.

A long-time friend insists that Natalie has to include cookies in her business plan. After a series of brainstorming sessions, Natalie settles on the idea of operating a cookie-making school. She will start on a part-time basis and offer her services in people's homes. Now that she has started thinking about it, the possibilities seem endless. During the fall, she will concentrate on holiday cookies. She will offer group sessions (which will probably be more entertainment than education) and individual lessons. Natalie also decides to include children in her target market. The first difficult decision is coming up with the perfect name for her business. She settles on "Cookie Creations," and then moves on to more important issues.

*Instructions*
(a) What form of business organization—proprietorship, partnership, or corporation—do you recommend that Natalie use for her business? Discuss the benefits and weaknesses of each form that Natalie might consider.
(b) Will Natalie need accounting information? If yes, what information will she need and why? How often will she need this information?
(c) Identify specific asset, liability, revenue, and expense accounts that Cookie Creations will likely use to record its business transactions.
(d) Should Natalie open a separate bank account for the business? Why or why not?
(e) Natalie expects she will have to use her car to drive to people's homes and to pick up supplies, but she also needs to use her car for personal reasons. She recalls from her first-year accounting course something about keeping business and personal assets separate. She wonders what she should do for accounting purposes. What do you recommend?

# broadening your perspective

# Financial Reporting and Analysis

**FINANCIAL REPORTING PROBLEM:** *Tootsie Roll Industries Inc.*

**BYP1-1** The 2009 financial statements of Tootsie Roll Industries, Inc. are provided in Appendix A.

*Instructions*
Refer to Tootsie Roll's financial statements to answer the following questions.
(a) What were Tootsie Roll's total assets at December 31, 2009? At December 31, 2008?
(b) How much cash did Tootsie Roll have on December 31, 2009?
(c) What amount of accounts payable did Tootsie Roll report on December 31, 2009? On December 31, 2008?
(d) What were Tootsie Roll's total revenues in 2009? In 2008?
(e) What is the amount of the change in Tootsie Roll's net income from 2008 to 2009?

**COMPARATIVE ANALYSIS PROBLEM:** *Tootsie Roll vs. Hershey*

**BYP1-2** Tootsie Roll's financial statements are presented in Appendix A, and the financial statements of The Hershey Company are presented in Appendix B.

*Instructions*
(a) Based on the information in these financial statements, determine the following for each company.
    (1) Total assets at December 31, 2009.
    (2) Net property, plant, and equipment at December 31, 2009.
    (3) Total revenue for 2009.
    (4) Net income for 2009.
(b) What conclusions concerning the two companies can you draw from these data?

## RESEARCH CASE

**BYP1-3** The September 3, 2009, issue of *BusinessWeek* includes an article by Lindsey Gerdes entitled "The Best Places to Launch a Career." It provides interesting information regarding the job opportunities for accounting students.

*Instructions*
Read the article and answer the following questions. (The article can be found at *www.businessweek.com/magazine/content/09_37/b4146032027785.htm.*)
(a) What position did each of the "Big Four" (the four largest international accounting firms) receive in the survey?
(b) To what did the article attribute the accounting firms' success?
(c) What was the starting salary for a new employee at Deloitte and Touche?
(d) The accounting firms' hiring was affected by the recession although not as much as many of the other employers in the survey. Which one of the Big Four firms had the smallest decline in hiring, and which had the largest?

## INTERPRETING FINANCIAL STATEMENTS

**BYP1-4** Xerox was not having a particularly pleasant year. The company's stock price had already fallen in the previous year from $60 per share to $30. Just when it seemed things couldn't get worse, Xerox's stock fell to $4 per share. The data below were taken from the statement of cash flows of Xerox. All dollars are in millions.

| | | |
|---|---|---|
| Cash used in operating activities | | $ (663) |
| Cash used in investing activities | | (644) |
| Financing activities | | |
| Dividends paid | $ (587) | |
| Net cash received from issuing debt | 3,498 | |
| Cash provided by financing activities | | 2,911 |

*Instructions*
Analyze the information above, and then answer the following questions.
(a) If you were a creditor of Xerox, what reaction might you have to the above information?
(b) If you were an investor in Xerox, what reaction might you have to the above information?
(c) If you were evaluating the company as either a creditor or a stockholder, what other information would you be interested in seeing?
(d) Xerox decided to pay a cash dividend. This dividend was approximately equal to the amount paid in the previous year. Discuss the issues that were probably considered in making this decision.

## FINANCIAL ANALYSIS ON THE WEB

**BYP1-5** *Purpose:* Identify summary information about companies. This information includes basic descriptions of the company's location, activities, industry, financial health, and financial performance.

*Address:* **http://biz.yahoo.com/i**, or go to **www.wiley.com/college/kimmel**

*Steps*
1. Type in a company name, or use the index to find company name.
2. Choose **Quote**, then choose **Profile**, then choose **Income Statement**. Perform instructions (a) and (b) below.
3. Choose **Industry** to identify others in this industry. Perform instructions (c)–(e) below.

*Instructions*
Answer the following questions.
(a) What was the company's net income? Over what period was this measured?
(b) What was the company's total sales? Over what period was this measured?
(c) What is the company's industry?
(d) What are the names of four companies in this industry?
(e) Choose one of the competitors. What is this competitor's name? What were its sales? What was its net income?

# Critical Thinking

## DECISION MAKING ACROSS THE ORGANIZATION

**BYP1-6**  Kim Walters recently accepted a job in the production department at Tootsie Roll. Before she starts work, she decides to review the company's annual report to better understand its operations.

*Instructions*
Use the annual report provided in Appendix A to answer the following questions.
(a) What CPA firm performed the audit of Tootsie Roll's financial statements?
(b) What was the amount of Tootsie Roll's earnings per share in 2009?
(c) What are the company's net sales in foreign countries in 2009?
(d) What did management suggest as the cause of the decrease in the earnings from operations in 2009?
(e) What were net sales in 2005?
(f) How many shares of Class B common stock have been authorized?
(g) How much cash was spent on capital expenditures in 2009?
(h) Over what life does the company depreciate its buildings?
(i) What was the value of raw material and supplies inventory in 2008?

## COMMUNICATION ACTIVITY

**BYP1-7**  Jane Noonan is the bookkeeper for Wilson Company, Inc. Jane has been trying to get the company's balance sheet to balance. She finally got it to balance, but she still isn't sure that it is correct.

### WILSON COMPANY, INC.
### Balance Sheet
### For the Month Ended December 31, 2012

| Assets | | Liabilities and Stockholders' Equity | |
|---|---|---|---|
| Equipment | $18,000 | Common stock | $12,000 |
| Cash | 9,000 | Accounts receivable | (6,000) |
| Supplies | 1,000 | Dividends | (2,000) |
| Accounts payable | (4,000) | Notes payable | 10,000 |
| Total assets | $24,000 | Retained earnings | 10,000 |
| | | Total liabilities and stockholders' equity | $24,000 |

*Instructions*
Explain to Jane Noonan in a memo (a) the purpose of a balance sheet, and (b) why this balance sheet is incorrect and what she should do to correct it.

## ETHICS CASE

**BYP1-8**  Rules governing the investment practices of individual certified public accountants prohibit them from investing in the stock of a company that their firm audits. The Securities and Exchange Commission (SEC) became concerned that some accountants were violating this rule. In response to an SEC investigation, PricewaterhouseCoopers fired 10 people and spent $25 million educating employees about the investment rules and installing an investment tracking system.

*Instructions*
Answer the following questions.
(a) Why do you think rules exist that restrict auditors from investing in companies that are audited by their firms?
(b) Some accountants argue that they should be allowed to invest in a company's stock as long as they themselves aren't involved in working on the company's audit or consulting. What do you think of this idea?
(c) Today a very high percentage of publicly traded companies are audited by only four very large public accounting firms. These firms also do a high percentage of the consulting work that

is done for publicly traded companies. How does this fact complicate the decision regarding whether CPAs should be allowed to invest in companies audited by their firm?

(d) Suppose you were a CPA and you had invested in IBM when IBM was not one of your firm's clients. Two years later, after IBM's stock price had fallen considerably, your firm won the IBM audit contract. You will be involved in working with the IBM audit. You know that your firm's rules require that you sell your shares immediately. If you do sell immediately, you will sustain a large loss. Do you think this is fair? What would you do?

(e) Why do you think PricewaterhouseCoopers took such extreme steps in response to the SEC investigation?

## "ALL ABOUT YOU" ACTIVITY

**BYP1-9**  Some people are tempted to make their finances look worse to get financial aid. Companies sometimes also manage their financial numbers in order to accomplish certain goals. Earnings management is the planned timing of revenues, expenses, gains, and losses to smooth out bumps in net income. In managing earnings, companies' actions vary from being within the range of ethical activity, to being both unethical and illegal attempts to mislead investors and creditors.

### Instructions
Provide responses for each of the following questions.
(a) Discuss whether you think each of the following actions (adapted from *www.finaid. org/fafsa/maximize.phtml*) to increase the chances of receiving financial aid is ethical.
  (i) Spend down the student's assets and income first, before spending parents' assets and income.
  (ii) Accelerate necessary expenses to reduce available cash. For example, if you need a new car, buy it before applying for financial aid.
  (iii) State that a truly financially dependent child is independent.
  (iv) Have a parent take an unpaid leave of absence for long enough to get below the "threshold" level of income.
(b) What are some reasons why a *company* might want to overstate its earnings?
(c) What are some reasons why a *company* might want to understate its earnings?
(d) Under what circumstances might an otherwise ethical person decide to illegally overstate or understate earnings?

## FASB CODIFICATION ACTIVITY

**BYP1-10**  The FASB has developed the Financial Accounting Standards Board Accounting Standards Codification (or more simply "the Codification"). The FASB's primary goal in developing the Codification is to provide in one place all the authoritative literature related to a particular topic. To provide easy access to the Codification, the FASB also developed the Financial Accounting Standards Board Codification Research System (CRS). CRS is an online, real-time database that provides easy access to the Codification. The Codification and the related CRS provide a topically organized structure, subdivided into topic, subtopics, sections, and paragraphs, using a numerical index system.

 You may find this system useful in your present and future studies, and so we have provided an opportunity to use this online system as part of the *Broadening Your Perspective* section.

### Instructions
Academic access to the FASB Codification is available through university subscriptions, obtained from the American Accounting Association (at **http://aaahq.org/FASB/Access.cfm**), for an annual fee of $150. This subscription covers an unlimited number of students within a single institution. Once this access has been obtained by your school, you should login (at **http://aaahq.org/ascLogin.cfm**) and familiarize yourself with the resources that are accessible at the FASB Codification site.

### Answers to Insight and Accounting Across the Organization Questions

**p. 6 The Scoop on Accounting  Q:** What are the benefits to the company and to the employees of making the financial statements available to all employees?  **A:** If employees can read and use financial reports, a company will benefit in the following ways. The *marketing department* will make better decisions about products to offer and prices to charge. The *finance department* will make better decisions about debt and equity financing and how much to distribute in dividends. The *production department* will make better decisions about when to buy new equipment and how much inventory to produce. The *human resources department* will be better able to determine whether employees can be given raises. Finally, *all employees* will be better informed about the basis on which they are evaluated, which will increase employee morale.

**p. 7 Spinning the Career Wheel  Q:** How might accounting help you? **A:** You will need to understand financial reports in any enterprise with which you are associated. Whether you become a manager, a doctor, a lawyer, a social worker, a teacher, an engineer, an architect, or an entrepreneur, a working knowledge of accounting is relevant.

**p. 8 The Numbers Behind Not-for-Profit Organizations  Q:** What benefits does a sound accounting system provide to a not-for-profit organization? **A:** Accounting provides at least two benefits to not-for-profit organizations. First, it helps to ensure that money is used in the way that donors intended. Second, it assures donors that their money is not going to waste and thus increases the likelihood of future donations.

**p. 15 Rocking the Bottom Line  Q:** What is one way that some of these disputes might be resolved? **A:** Frequently, when contractual payments depend on accounting-based financial results, interested parties employ outside auditors to evaluate whether the financial information has been prepared fairly and accurately. The musicians would like auditors to have easy access to inventory and manufacturing information of the recording companies.

### Answers to Self-Test Questions

**1.** b  **2.** c  **3.** d  **4.** d  **5.** c  **6.** a  **7.** d  **8.** d  **9.** a  **10.** b  **11.** c  **12.** d  **13.** d  **14.** a  **15.** b

# IFRS  A Look at IFRS

Most agree that there is a need for one set of international accounting standards. Here is why:

**Multinational corporations.** Today's companies view the entire world as their market. For example, Coca-Cola, Intel, and McDonald's generate more than 50% of their sales outside the United States, and many foreign companies, such as Toyota, Nestlé, and Sony, find their largest market to be the United States.

**Mergers and acquisitions.** The mergers between Fiat/Chrysler and Vodafone/Mannesmann suggest that we will see even more such business combinations in the future.

**Information technology.** As communication barriers continue to topple through advances in technology, companies and individuals in different countries and markets are becoming more comfortable buying and selling goods and services from one another.

**Financial markets.** Financial markets are of international significance today. Whether it is currency, equity securities (stocks), bonds, or derivatives, there are active markets throughout the world trading these types of instruments.

## KEY POINTS

- International standards are referred to as *International Financial Reporting Standards (IFRS)*, developed by the International Accounting Standards Board (IASB).
- Recent events in the global capital markets have underscored the importance of financial disclosure and transparency not only in the United States but in markets around the world. As a result, many are examining which accounting and financial disclosure rules should be followed. As indicated in the graphic on the next page, much of the world has voted for the standards issued by the IASB. Over 115 countries require or permit use of IFRS.

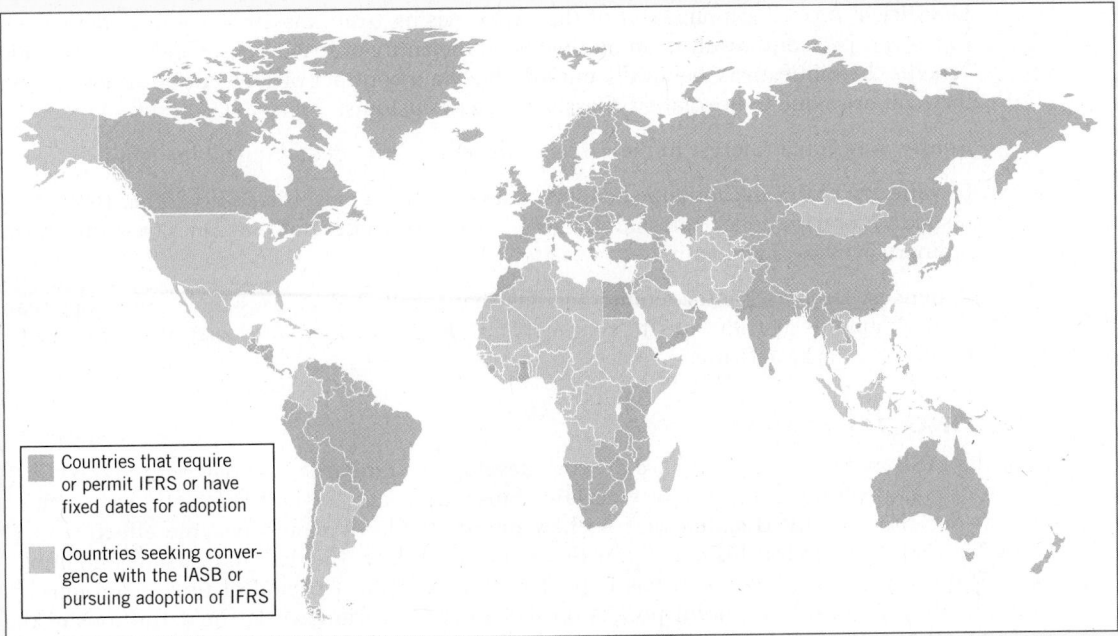

Countries that require or permit IFRS or have fixed dates for adoption

Countries seeking convergence with the IASB or pursuing adoption of IFRS

*Source: http://www.pwc.com/us/en/issues/ifrs-reporting/country-adoption/index.jhtml.*

- U.S standards, referred to as generally accepted accounting principles (GAAP), are developed by the Financial Accounting Standards Board (FASB). The fact that there are differences between what is in this textbook (which is based on U.S. standards) and IFRS should not be surprising because the FASB and IASB have responded to different user needs. In some countries, the primary users of financial statements are private investors; in others, the primary users are tax authorities or central government planners. It appears that the United States and the international standard-setting environment are primarily driven by meeting the needs of investors and creditors.

- The internal control standards applicable to Sarbanes-Oxley (SOX) apply only to large public companies listed on U.S. exchanges. There is a continuing debate as to whether non-U.S. companies should have to comply with this extra layer of regulation. Debate about international companies (non-U.S.) adopting SOX-type standards centers on whether the benefits exceed the costs. The concern is that the higher costs of SOX compliance are making the U.S. securities markets less competitive.

- The textbook mentions a number of ethics violations, such as Enron, WorldCom, and AIG. These problems have also occurred internationally, for example, at Satyam Computer Services (India), Parmalat (Italy), and Royal Ahold (the Netherlands).

- IFRS tends to be simpler in its accounting and disclosure requirements; some people say it is more "principles-based." GAAP is more detailed; some people say it is more "rules-based." This difference in approach has resulted in a debate about the merits of "principles-based" versus "rules-based" standards.

- U.S. regulators have recently eliminated the need for foreign companies that trade shares in U.S. markets to reconcile their accounting with GAAP.

- The three most common forms of business organization, proprietorships, partnerships, and corporations, are also found in countries that use IFRS. Because the choice of business organization is influenced by factors such as legal environment, tax rates and regulations, and degree of entrepreneurism, the relative use of each form will vary across countries.

- The conceptual framework that underlies IFRS is very similar to that used to develop GAAP. The basic definitions provided in this textbook for the key elements of financial statements, that is, assets, liabilities, equity, revenues, and expenses, are simplified versions of the official definitions provided by the FASB. The more substantive definitions, using the IASB definitional structure, are as follows.

  **Assets.** A resource controlled by the entity as a result of past events and from which future economic benefits are expected to flow to the entity.

**Liabilities.** A present obligation of the entity arising from past events, the settlement of which is expected to result in an outflow from the entity of resources embodying economic benefits. Liabilities may be legally enforceable via a contract or law, but need not be, i.e., they can arise due to normal business practice or customs.

**Equity.** A residual interest in the assets of the entity after deducting all its liabilities.

**Income.** Increases in economic benefits that result in increases in equity (other than those related to contributions from shareholders). Income includes both revenues (resulting from ordinary activities) and gains.

**Expenses.** Decreases in economic benefits that result in decreases in equity (other than those related to distributions to shareholders). Expenses includes losses that are not the result of ordinary activities.

## LOOKING TO THE FUTURE

Both the IASB and the FASB are hard at work developing standards that will lead to the elimination of major differences in the way certain transactions are accounted for and reported. In fact, at one time the IASB stated that no new major standards would become effective until 2009. The major reason for this policy was to provide companies the time to translate and implement IFRS into practice, as much has happened in a very short period of time. Consider, for example, that as a result of a joint project on the conceptual framework, the definitions of the most fundamental elements (assets, liabilities, equity, revenues, and expenses) may actually change. However, whether the IASB adopts internal control provisions similar to those in SOX remains to be seen.

## IFRS Self-Test Questions

1. Which of the following is *not* a reason why a single set of high-quality international accounting standards would be beneficial?
   (a) Mergers and acquisition activity.
   (b) Financial markets.
   (c) Multinational corporations.
   (d) GAAP is widely considered to be a superior reporting system.
2. The Sarbanes-Oxley Act determines:
   (a) international tax regulations.
   (b) internal control standards as enforced by the IASB.
   (c) internal control standards of U.S. publicly traded companies.
   (d) U.S. tax regulations.
3. IFRS is considered to be more:
   (a) principles-based and less rules-based than GAAP.
   (b) rules-based and less principles-based than GAAP.
   (c) detailed than GAAP.
   (d) None of the above.
4. Which of the following statements is *false*?
   (a) IFRS is based on a conceptual framework that is similar to that used to develop GAAP.
   (b) Assets are defined by the IASB as resources controlled by the entity as a result of past events and from which future economic benefits are expected to flow to the entity.
   (c) Non-U.S. companies that trade shares in U.S. markets must reconcile their accounting with GAAP.
   (d) Proprietorships, partnerships, and corporations are also found in countries that use IFRS.
5. Which of the following statements is *true*?
   (a) Under IFRS, the term income refers to what would be called revenues and gains under GAAP.
   (b) The term income is not used under IFRS.
   (c) The term income refers only to gains on investments.
   (d) Under IFRS, expenses include distributions to owners.

## IFRS Concepts and Application

IFRS1–1   Who are the two key international players in the development of international accounting standards? Explain their role.

**IFRS1-2**  What might explain the fact that different accounting standard-setters have developed accounting standards that are sometimes quite different in nature?

**IFRS1-3**  What is the benefit of a single set of high-quality accounting standards?

**IFRS1-4**  Discuss the potential advantages and disadvantages that countries outside the United States should consider before adopting regulations, such as those in the Sarbanes-Oxley Act, that increase corporate internal control requirements.

## INTERNATIONAL FINANCIAL REPORTING PROBLEM: *Zetar plc*

**IFRS1-5**  The financial statements of Zetar plc are presented in Appendix C. The company's complete annual report, including the notes to its financial statements, is available at **www.zetarplc.com**.

*Instructions*
Visit Zetar's corporate website and answer the following questions from Zetar's 2009 annual report.
  (a) What accounting firm performed the audit of Zetar's financial statements?
  (b) Over what life does the company depreciate its buildings?
  (c) What is the address of the company's corporate headquarters?
  (d) What is the company's reporting currency?
  (e) What two segments does the company operate in, and what were the sales for each segment in the year ended April 30, 2009?

### Answers to IFRS Self-Test Questions

**1.** d  **2.** c  **3.** a  **4.** c  **5.** a

 **Remember to go back to the navigator box on the chapter opening page and check off your completed work.**

# chapter 2

# A FURTHER LOOK AT FINANCIAL STATEMENTS

## ✓ the navigator

- Scan **Study Objectives** ○
- Read **Feature Story** ○
- Scan **Preview** ○
- Read **Text and Answer** **Do it!**
  p. 52 ○   p. 53 ○   p. 62 ○   p. 68 ○
- Work **Using the Decision Toolkit** ○
- Review **Summary of Study Objectives** ○
- Work **Comprehensive** **Do it!** p. 72 ○
- Answer **Self-Test Questions** ○
- Complete **Assignments** ○
- Go to **WileyPLUS** for practice and tutorials ○
- 🌐 Read **A Look at IFRS** p. 96 ○

## study objectives

**After studying this chapter, you should be able to:**

1 Identify the sections of a classified balance sheet.

2 Identify and compute ratios for analyzing a company's profitability.

3 Explain the relationship between a retained earnings statement and a statement of stockholders' equity.

4 Identify and compute ratios for analyzing a company's liquidity and solvency using a balance sheet.

5 Use the statement of cash flows to evaluate solvency.

6 Explain the meaning of generally accepted accounting principles.

7 Discuss financial reporting concepts.

✓ the navigator

Few people could have predicted how dramatically the Internet would change the investment world. One of the most interesting results is how it has changed the way ordinary people invest their savings. More and more people are striking out on their own, making their own investment decisions.

Two early pioneers in providing investment information to the masses were Tom and David Gardner, brothers who created an online investor bulletin board called The Motley Fool. The name comes from Shakespeare's *As You Like It*. The fool in Shakespeare's plays was the only one who could speak unpleasant truths to kings and queens without being killed. Tom and David view themselves as 21st-century "fools," revealing the "truths" of Wall Street to the small investor, who they feel has been taken advantage of by Wall Street insiders. Their online bulletin board enables investors to exchange information and insights about companies.

Critics of these bulletin boards contend that they are high-tech rumor mills. They suggest that the fervor created by bulletin board chatter causes investors to bid up stock prices to unreasonable levels. Because bulletin board participants typically use aliases, there is little to stop people from putting misinformation on the board to influence a stock's price. For example, the stock of PairGain Technologies jumped 32 percent in a single day as a result of a bogus takeover rumor on an investment bulletin board. Some observers are concerned that small investors—ironically, the very people the Gardner brothers are trying to help—will be hurt the most by misinformation and intentional scams.

## JUST FOOLING AROUND?

To show how these bulletin boards work, suppose that in a recent year you had $10,000 to invest. You were considering Best Buy Company, the largest seller of electronics equipment in the United States. You scanned the Internet investment bulletin boards and found messages posted by two different investors. Here are excerpts from actual postings during the same year:

*TMPVenus:* "Where are the prospects for positive movement for this company? Poor margins, poor management, astronomical P/E!"

*broachman:* "I believe that this is a LONG TERM winner, and presently at a good price."

One says sell, and one says buy. Whom should you believe? If you had taken "broachman's" advice and purchased the stock, the $10,000 you invested would have been worth over $300,000 five years later. Best Buy was one of America's best-performing stocks during that period of time.

Deciding what information to rely on is becoming increasingly complex. For example, shortly before its share price completely collapsed, nearly every professional analyst who followed Enron was recommending its stock as a "buy."

Rather than getting swept away by rumors, investors must sort out the good information from the bad. One thing is certain—as information services such as The Motley Fool increase in number, gathering information will become even easier. Evaluating it will be the harder task.

the navigator

## INSIDE CHAPTER 2...

If you are thinking of purchasing Best Buy stock, or any stock, how can you decide what the stock is worth? If you manage J. Crew's credit department, how should you determine whether to extend credit to a new customer? If you are a financial executive of IBM, how do you decide whether your company is generating adequate cash to expand operations without borrowing? Your decision in each of these situations will be influenced by a variety of considerations. One of them should be your careful analysis of a company's financial statements. The reason: Financial statements offer relevant and reliable information, which will help you in your decision making.

In this chapter, we take a closer look at the balance sheet and introduce some useful ways for evaluating the information provided by the financial statements. We also examine the financial reporting concepts underlying the financial statements.

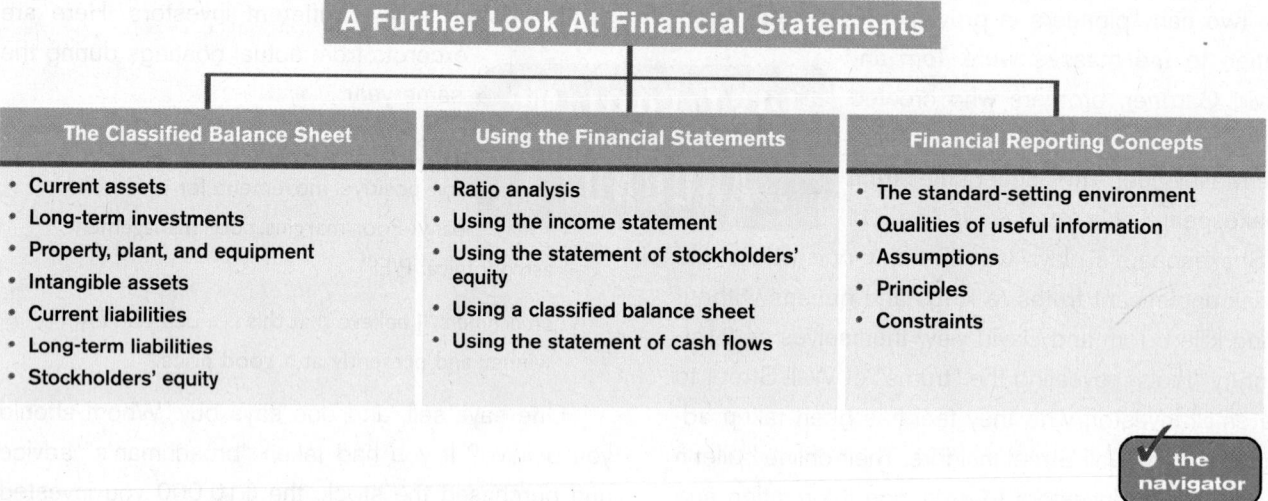

## A Further Look At Financial Statements

| The Classified Balance Sheet | Using the Financial Statements | Financial Reporting Concepts |
|---|---|---|
| • Current assets<br>• Long-term investments<br>• Property, plant, and equipment<br>• Intangible assets<br>• Current liabilities<br>• Long-term liabilities<br>• Stockholders' equity | • Ratio analysis<br>• Using the income statement<br>• Using the statement of stockholders' equity<br>• Using a classified balance sheet<br>• Using the statement of cash flows | • The standard-setting environment<br>• Qualities of useful information<br>• Assumptions<br>• Principles<br>• Constraints |

✔ the navigator

In Chapter 1, we introduced the four financial statements. In this section, we review the financial statements and present tools that are useful for evaluating them. We begin by introducing the classified balance sheet.

# The Classified Balance Sheet

In Chapter 1, you learned that a balance sheet presents a snapshot of a company's financial position at a point in time. The balance sheet in Chapter 1 listed individual asset, liability and stockholders' equity items in no particular order. To improve users' understanding of a company's financial position, companies often use a classified balance sheet. A **classified balance sheet** groups together similar assets and similar liabilities, using a number of standard classifications and sections. This is useful because items within a group have similar economic characteristics. A classified balance sheet generally contains the standard classifications listed in Illustration 2-1.

**Illustration 2-1** Standard balance sheet classifications

| Assets | Liabilities and Stockholders' Equity |
|---|---|
| Current assets<br>Long-term investments<br>Property, plant, and equipment<br>Intangible assets | Current liabilities<br>Long-term liabilities<br>Stockholders' equity |

These groupings help readers determine such things as (1) whether the company has enough assets to pay its debts as they come due, and (2) the claims of short- and long-term creditors on the company's total assets. Many of these groupings can be seen in the balance sheet of Franklin Corporation shown in Illustration 2-2. In the sections that follow, we explain each of these groupings.

## CURRENT ASSETS

Current assets are assets that a company expects to convert to cash or use up within one year or its operating cycle, whichever is longer. In Illustration 2-2, Franklin Corporation had current assets of $22,100. For most businesses, the cutoff for classification as current assets is one year from the balance sheet date. For example, accounts receivable are current assets because the company will

**Illustration 2-2** Classified balance sheet

**FRANKLIN CORPORATION**
Balance Sheet
October 31, 2012

### Assets

| Current assets | | |
|---|---:|---:|
| Cash | $ 6,600 | |
| Short-term investments | 2,000 | |
| Accounts receivable | 7,000 | |
| Notes receivable | 1,000 | |
| Inventory | 3,000 | |
| Supplies | 2,100 | |
| Prepaid insurance | 400 | |
| Total current assets | | $22,100 |
| **Long-term investments** | | |
| Investment in stock of Walters Corp. | 5,200 | |
| Investment in real estate | 2,000 | 7,200 |
| **Property, plant, and equipment** | | |
| Land | 10,000 | |
| Equipment $24,000 | | |
| Less: Accumulated | | |
| depreciation—equipment 5,000 | 19,000 | 29,000 |
| **Intangible assets** | | |
| Patents | | 3,100 |
| Total assets | | $61,400 |

### Liabilities and Stockholders' Equity

| Current liabilities | | |
|---|---:|---:|
| Notes payable | $11,000 | |
| Accounts payable | 2,100 | |
| Salaries and wages payable | 1,600 | |
| Unearned sales revenue | 900 | |
| Interest payable | 450 | |
| Total current liabilities | | $16,050 |
| **Long-term liabilities** | | |
| Mortgage payable | 10,000 | |
| Notes payable | 1,300 | |
| Total long-term liabilities | | 11,300 |
| Total liabilities | | 27,350 |
| **Stockholders' equity** | | |
| Common stock | 14,000 | |
| Retained earnings | 20,050 | |
| Total stockholders' equity | | 34,050 |
| Total liabilities and stockholders' equity | | $61,400 |

**Helpful Hint** Recall that the accounting equation is Assets = Liabilities + Stockholders' Equity.

collect them and convert them to cash within one year. Supplies is a current asset because the company expects to use them up in operations within one year.

Some companies use a period longer than one year to classify assets and liabilities as current because they have an operating cycle longer than one year. The **operating cycle** of a company is the average time that it takes to go from cash to cash in producing revenue—to purchase inventory, sell it on account, and then collect cash from customers. For most businesses, this cycle takes less than a year, so they use a one-year cutoff. But, for some businesses, such as vineyards or airplane manufacturers, this period may be longer than a year. **Except where noted, we will assume that companies use one year to determine whether an asset or liability is current or long-term.**

Common types of current assets are (1) cash, (2) short-term investments (such as short-term U.S. government securities), (3) receivables (notes receivable, accounts receivable, and interest receivable), (4) inventories, and (5) prepaid expenses (insurance and supplies). **Companies list current assets in the order in which they expect to convert them into cash**. *Follow this rule when doing your homework.*

Illustration 2-3 presents the current assets of Southwest Airlines Co. in a recent year.

**Illustration 2-3** Current assets section

**SOUTHWEST AIRLINES CO.**
Balance Sheet (partial)
(in millions)

| Current assets | |
|---|---|
| Cash and cash equivalents | $1,390 |
| Short-term investments | 369 |
| Accounts receivable | 241 |
| Inventories | 181 |
| Prepaid expenses and other current assets | 420 |
| Total current assets | $2,601 |

As explained later in the chapter, a company's current assets are important in assessing its short-term debt-paying ability.

### LONG-TERM INVESTMENTS

**Alternative Terminology** Long-term investments are often referred to simply as *investments.*

**Long-term investments** are generally: (1) investments in stocks and bonds of other corporations that are held for more than one year, and (2) long-term assets such as land or buildings that a company is not currently using in its operating activities. In Illustration 2-2, Franklin Corporation reported total long-term investments of $7,200 on its balance sheet.

Yahoo! Inc. reported long-term investments on its balance sheet in a recent year as shown in Illustration 2-4.

**Illustration 2-4** Long-term investments section

**YAHOO! INC.**
Balance Sheet (partial)
(in thousands)

| Long-term investments | |
|---|---|
| Long-term investments in marketable securities | $90,266 |

## PROPERTY, PLANT, AND EQUIPMENT

**Property, plant, and equipment** are assets with relatively long useful lives that are currently used in operating the business. This category includes land, buildings, equipment, delivery vehicles, and furniture. In Illustration 2-2, Franklin Corporation reported property, plant, and equipment of $29,000.

**Depreciation** is the practice of allocating the cost of assets to a number of years. Companies do this by systematically assigning a portion of an asset's cost as an expense each year (rather than expensing the full purchase price in the year of purchase). The assets that the company depreciates are reported on the balance sheet at cost less accumulated depreciation. The **accumulated depreciation** account shows the total amount of depreciation that the company has expensed thus far in the asset's life. In Illustration 2-2, Franklin Corporation reported accumulated depreciation of $5,000.

Illustration 2-5 presents the property, plant, and equipment of Cooper Tire & Rubber Company in a recent year.

**Alternative Terminology**
Property, plant, and equipment is sometimes called *fixed assets* or *plant assets.*

**International Note** In 2007, China adopted International Financial Reporting Standards (IFRS). This was done in an effort to reduce fraud and increase investor confidence in financial reports. Under these standards, many items, such as property, plant, and equipment, may be reported at current fair values, rather than historical cost.

**COOPER TIRE & RUBBER COMPANY**
Balance Sheet (partial)
(in thousands)

| Property, plant, and equipment | | |
|---|---:|---:|
| Land and land improvements | $ 41,553 | |
| Buildings | 298,706 | |
| Machinery and equipment | 1,636,091 | |
| Molds, cores, and rings | 268,158 | $2,244,508 |
| Less: Accumulated depreciation | | 1,252,692 |
| | | $ 991,816 |

**Illustration 2-5** Property, plant, and equipment section

## INTANGIBLE ASSETS

Many companies have assets that do not have physical substance yet often are very valuable. We call these assets intangible assets. One common intangible is goodwill. Others include patents, copyrights, and trademarks or trade names that give the company **exclusive right** of use for a specified period of time. Franklin Corporation reported intangible assets of $3,100.

Illustration 2-6 shows the intangible assets of media giant Time Warner, Inc. in a recent year.

**Helpful Hint** Sometimes intangible assets are reported under a broader heading called *"Other assets."*

**TIME WARNER, INC.**
Balance Sheet (partial)
(in millions)

| Intangible assets | |
|---|---:|
| Goodwill | $40,953 |
| Film library | 2,690 |
| Customer lists | 2,540 |
| Cable television franchises | 38,048 |
| Sports franchises | 262 |
| Brands, trademarks, and other intangible assets | 8,313 |
| | $92,806 |

**Illustration 2-6** Intangible assets section

*before you go on...*

## ASSETS SECTION OF BALANCE SHEET

**Do it!** Baxter Hoffman recently received the following information related to Hoffman Corporation's December 31, 2012, balance sheet.

| | | | |
|---|---|---|---|
| Prepaid insurance | $ 2,300 | Inventory | $3,400 |
| Cash | 800 | Accumulated depreciation— | |
| Equipment | 10,700 | equipment | 2,700 |
| | | Accounts receivable | 1,100 |

Prepare the assets section of Hoffman Corporation's balance sheet.

### Action Plan

- Present current assets first. Current assets are cash and other resources that the company expects to convert to cash or use up within one year.
- Present current assets in the order in which the company expects to convert them into cash.
- Subtract accumulated depreciation–equipment from equipment to determine net equipment.

### Solution

**HOFFMAN CORPORATION**
Balance Sheet (partial)
December 31, 2012

| Assets | | |
|---|---|---|
| Current assets | | |
| Cash | $  800 | |
| Accounts receivable | 1,100 | |
| Inventory | 3,400 | |
| Prepaid insurance | 2,300 | |
| Total current assets | | $ 7,600 |
| Equipment | 10,700 | |
| Less: Accumulated depreciation—equipment | 2,700 | 8,000 |
| Total assets | | $15,600 |

Related exercise material: **BE2-2**, **Do it!** **2-1**, and **E2-4**.

the navigator

## CURRENT LIABILITIES

In the liabilities and stockholders' equity section of the balance sheet, the first grouping is current liabilities. **Current liabilities** are obligations that the company is to pay within the coming year or operating cycle, whichever is longer. Common examples are accounts payable, wages payable, bank loans payable, interest payable, and taxes payable. Also included as current liabilities are current maturities of long-term obligations—payments to be made within the next year on long-term obligations. In Illustration 2-2, Franklin Corporation reported five different types of current liabilities, for a total of $16,050.

Within the current liabilities section, companies usually list notes payable first, followed by accounts payable. Other items then follow in the order of their magnitude. *In your homework, you should present notes payable first, followed by accounts payable.*

Illustration 2-7 shows the current liabilities section adapted from the balance sheet of Marcus Corporation in a recent year.

## LONG-TERM LIABILITIES

**Long-term liabilities** are obligations that a company expects to pay **after** one year. Liabilities in this category include bonds payable, mortgages payable, long-term notes payable, lease liabilities, and pension liabilities. Many companies report long-term debt maturing after one year as a single amount in the balance sheet and show the details of the debt in notes that accompany the financial

**Illustration 2-7**  Current liabilities section

**MARCUS CORPORATION**
Balance Sheet (partial)
(in thousands)

| Current liabilities | |
|---|---|
| Notes payable | $    239 |
| Accounts payable | 24,242 |
| Current maturities of long-term debt | 57,250 |
| Other current liabilities | 27,477 |
| Taxes payable | 11,215 |
| Accrued compensation payable | 6,720 |
| Total current liabilities | $127,143 |

statements. Others list the various types of long-term liabilities. In Illustration 2-2, Franklin Corporation reported long-term liabilities of $11,300.

Illustration 2-8 shows the long-term liabilities that The Procter & Gamble Company reported in its balance sheet in a recent year.

**Illustration 2-8**  Long-term liabilities section

**THE PROCTER & GAMBLE COMPANY**
Balance Sheet (partial)
(in millions)

| Long-term liabilities | |
|---|---|
| Long-term debt | $23,375 |
| Deferred income taxes | 12,015 |
| Other noncurrent liabilities | 5,147 |
| Total long-term liabilities | $40,537 |

## STOCKHOLDERS' EQUITY

Stockholders' equity consists of two parts: common stock and retained earnings. Companies record as **common stock** the investments of assets into the business by the stockholders. They record as **retained earnings** the income retained for use in the business. These two parts, combined, make up **stockholders' equity** on the balance sheet. In Illustration 2-2, Franklin reported common stock of $14,000 and retained earnings of $20,050.

**Alternative Terminology**
Common stock is sometimes called *capital stock.*

*before you go on...*

**Do it!**  The following financial statement items were taken from the financial statements of Callahan Corp.

**BALANCE SHEET CLASSIFICATIONS**

_____ Salaries and wages payable
_____ Service revenue
_____ Interest payable
_____ Goodwill
_____ Short-term investments
_____ Mortgage payable (due in 3 years)
_____ Investment in real estate

_____ Equipment
_____ Accumulated depreciation— equipment
_____ Depreciation expense
_____ Retained earnings
_____ Unearned service revenue

Match each of the items to its proper balance sheet classification, shown below. If the item would not appear on a balance sheet, use "NA."

Current assets (CA)                           Current liabilities (CL)
Long-term investments (LTI)                   Long-term liabilities (LTL)
Property, plant, and equipment (PPE)          Stockholders' equity (SE)
Intangible assets (IA)

**Action Plan**

• Analyze whether each financial statement item is an asset, liability, or stockholders' equity item.

• Determine if asset and liability items are current or long-term.

**Solution**

| | | | |
|---|---|---|---|
| CL | Salaries and wages payable | LTI | Investment in real estate |
| NA | Service revenue | PPE | Equipment |
| CL | Interest payable | PPE | Accumulated depreciation—equipment |
| IA | Goodwill | NA | Depreciation expense |
| CA | Short-term investments | SE | Retained earnings |
| LTL | Mortgage payable (due in 3 years) | CL | Unearned service revenue |

Related exercise material: **BE2-1, Do it! 2-2, E2-1, E2-2, E2-3, E2-5 and E2-6.**

# Using the Financial Statements

In Chapter 1, we introduced the four financial statements. We discussed how these statements provide information about a company's performance and financial position. In this chapter, we extend this discussion by showing you specific tools that you can use to analyze financial statements in order to make a more meaningful evaluation of a company.

### RATIO ANALYSIS

**Ratio analysis** expresses the relationship among selected items of financial statement data. A **ratio** expresses the mathematical relationship between one quantity and another. For analysis of the primary financial statements, we classify ratios as follows.

**Illustration 2-9** Financial ratio classifications

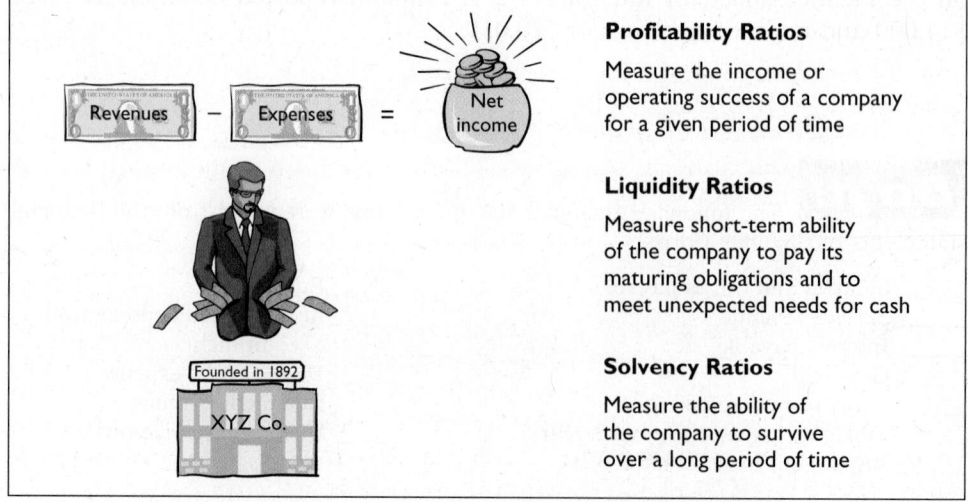

**Profitability Ratios**

Measure the income or operating success of a company for a given period of time

**Liquidity Ratios**

Measure short-term ability of the company to pay its maturing obligations and to meet unexpected needs for cash

**Solvency Ratios**

Measure the ability of the company to survive over a long period of time

A single ratio by itself is not very meaningful. Accordingly, in this and the following chapters, we will use various comparisons to shed light on company performance:

1. **Intracompany comparisons** covering two years for the same company.
2. **Industry-average comparisons** based on average ratios for particular industries.
3. **Intercompany comparisons** based on comparisons with a competitor in the same industry.

## USING THE INCOME STATEMENT

Best Buy Company generates profits for its stockholders by selling electronics. The income statement reports how successful it is at generating a profit from its sales. The income statement reports the amount earned during the period (revenues) and the costs incurred during the period (expenses). Illustration 2-10 shows a simplified income statement for Best Buy.

**study objective** **2**

Identify and compute ratios for analyzing a company's profitability.

**Illustration 2-10**  Best Buy's income statement

**BEST BUY CO., INC.**
Income Statements
For the Years Ended February 28, 2009,
and March 1, 2008 (in millions)

|  | 2009 | 2008 |
|---|---|---|
| **Revenues** | | |
| Net sales and other revenue | $45,015 | $40,023 |
| **Expenses** | | |
| Cost of goods sold | 34,017 | 30,477 |
| Selling, general, and administrative expenses and other | 9,321 | 7,324 |
| Income tax expense | 674 | 815 |
| Total expenses | 44,012 | 38,616 |
| **Net income** | $ 1,003 | $ 1,407 |

From this income statement, we can see that Best Buy's sales increased but net income decreased during the period. Net income decreased from $1,407 million to $1,003 million. A much smaller competitor of Best Buy is hhgregg. It operates 111 stores in 9 states and is headquartered in Indianapolis, Indiana. It reported net income of $36.5 million for the year ended March 31, 2009.

To evaluate the profitability of Best Buy, we will use ratio analysis. **Profitability ratios** measure the operating success of a company for a given period of time.

## Earnings per Share

**Earnings per share (EPS)** measures the net income earned on each share of common stock. We compute EPS by dividing **net income** by the **average number of common shares outstanding during the year**. Stockholders usually think in terms of the number of shares they own or plan to buy or sell, so stating net income earned as a per share amount provides a useful perspective for determining the investment return. Advanced accounting courses present more refined techniques for calculating earnings per share.

For now, a basic approach for calculating earnings per share is to divide earnings available to common stockholders by average common shares outstanding during the year. What is "earnings available to common stockholders"? It is an earnings amount calculated as net income less dividends paid on another type of stock, called preferred stock (Net income − Preferred stock dividends).

By comparing earnings per share of **a single company over time**, one can evaluate its relative earnings performance from the perspective of a stockholder—that is, on a per share basis. It is very important to note that comparisons of earnings per share across companies are **not meaningful** because of the wide variations in the numbers of shares of outstanding stock among companies.

Illustration 2-11 shows the earnings per share calculation for Best Buy in 2009 and 2008, based on the information presented below. (Note that to simplify our calculations, we assumed that any change in the number of shares for Best Buy occurred in the middle of the year.)

| (in millions) | 2009 | 2008 |
| --- | --- | --- |
| Net income | $1,003 | $1,407 |
| Preferred stock dividends | –0– | –0– |
| Shares outstanding at beginning of year | 411 | 481 |
| Shares outstanding at end of year | 414 | 411 |

**Illustration 2-11** Best Buy's earnings per share

| Earnings per Share | = | Net Income − Preferred Stock Dividends |
| --- | --- | --- |
| | | Average Common Shares Outstanding |

| ($ and shares in millions) | 2009 | 2008 |
| --- | --- | --- |
| Earnings per share | $\dfrac{\$1,003 - \$0}{(414 + 411)/2} = \$2.43$ | $\dfrac{\$1,407 - \$0}{(411 + 481)/2} = \$3.15$ |

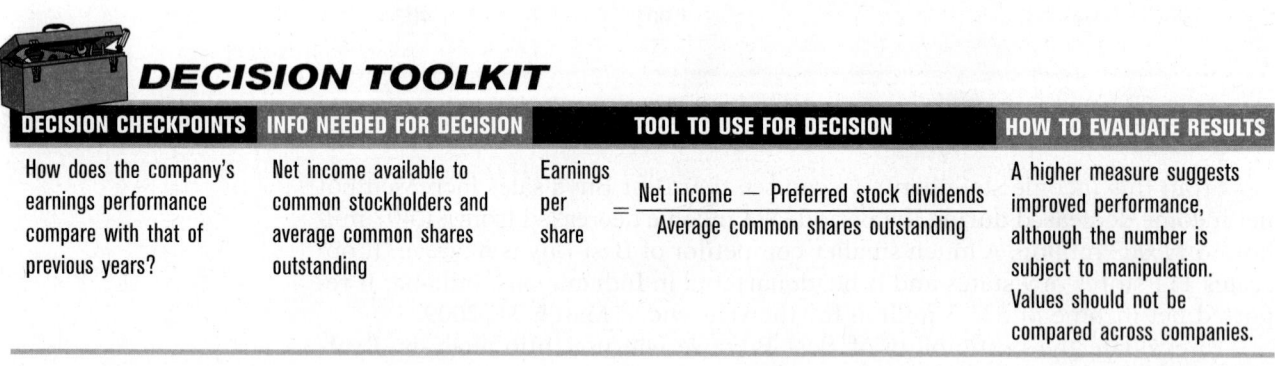

## DECISION TOOLKIT

| DECISION CHECKPOINTS | INFO NEEDED FOR DECISION | TOOL TO USE FOR DECISION | HOW TO EVALUATE RESULTS |
| --- | --- | --- | --- |
| How does the company's earnings performance compare with that of previous years? | Net income available to common stockholders and average common shares outstanding | Earnings per share $= \dfrac{\text{Net income} - \text{Preferred stock dividends}}{\text{Average common shares outstanding}}$ | A higher measure suggests improved performance, although the number is subject to manipulation. Values should not be compared across companies. |

## USING THE STATEMENT OF STOCKHOLDERS' EQUITY

**study objective 3**

Explain the relationship between a retained earnings statement and a statement of stockholders' equity.

As discussed in Chapter 1, the retained earnings statement describes the changes in retained earnings during the year. This statement adds net income and then subtracts dividends from the beginning retained earnings to arrive at ending retained earnings.

Stockholders' equity is comprised of two parts: retained earnings and common stock. Therefore, the stockholders' equity of most companies is affected by factors other than just changes in retained earnings. For example, the company may issue or retire shares of common stock. Most companies, therefore, use what is called a **statement of stockholders' equity,** rather than a retained earnings statement, so that they can report **all changes** in stockholders' equity accounts. Illustration 2-12 is a simplified statement of stockholders' equity for Best Buy.

**Illustration 2-12**  Best Buy's statement of stockholders' equity

**BEST BUY CO., INC.**
Statement of Stockholders' Equity
(in millions)

| | Common Stock | Retained Earnings |
|---|---|---|
| Balances at March 3, 2007 | $ 478 | $5,723 |
| Issuance of common stock | 268 | |
| Repurchase of common stock | (697) | |
| Net income | | 1,407 |
| Dividends | | (204) |
| Other adjustments | | (2,491) |
| Balances at March 1, 2008 | 49 | 4,435 |
| Issuance of common stock | 197 | |
| Net income | | 1,003 |
| Dividends | | (222) |
| Other adjustments | | (819) |
| Balances at February 28, 2009 | $ 246 | $4,397 |

We can observe from this financial statement that Best Buy's common stock decreased during the first year. Even though it had an issuance of common stock, that increase was much smaller than the decrease caused by a stock repurchase. It increased in the second year as the result of an issuance of shares. Another observation from this financial statement is that Best Buy paid dividends each year. This is a relatively recent practice for Best Buy. Prior to 2003, it did not pay dividends, even though it was profitable and could do so. You might wonder why Best Buy paid no dividends during prior years when it was profitable. In fact, in a prior year, two Best Buy stockholders discussed this question about the company's dividend policy on an investor bulletin board. Here are excerpts:

> *Katwoman:* "Best Buy has a nice price increase. Earnings are on the way up. But why no dividends?"

> *AngryCandy:* "I guess they feel they can make better use of the money by investing back in the business. They still view Best Buy as a rapidly growing company and would prefer to invest in expanding the infrastructure (building new stores, advertising, etc.) than in paying out dividends. . . . If Best Buy gets to the stage of 'stable, big company' with little room for expansion, then I'm sure you'll see them elect to pay out a dividend."

AngryCandy's response is an excellent explanation of the thought process that management goes through in deciding whether to pay a dividend. Management must evaluate what its cash needs are. If it has uses for cash that will increase the value of the company (for example, building a new, centralized warehouse), then it should retain cash in the company. However, if it has more cash than it has valuable opportunities, it should distribute its excess cash as a dividend.

study objective 4

Identify and compute ratios for analyzing a company's liquidity and solvency using a balance sheet.

## USING A CLASSIFIED BALANCE SHEET

You can learn a lot about a company's financial health by also evaluating the relationship between its various assets and liabilities. Illustration 2-13 provides a simplified balance sheet for Best Buy.

**Illustration 2-13** Best Buy's balance sheet

### BEST BUY CO., INC.
### Balance Sheets
### (in millions)

| Assets | February 28, 2009 | March 1, 2008 |
|---|---|---|
| Current assets | | |
| Cash and cash equivalents | $ 498 | $ 1,438 |
| Short-term investments | 11 | 64 |
| Receivables | 1,868 | 549 |
| Merchandise inventories | 4,753 | 4,708 |
| Other current assets | 1,062 | 583 |
| Total current assets | 8,192 | 7,342 |
| Property and equipment | 6,940 | 5,608 |
| Less: Accumulated depreciation | 2,766 | 2,302 |
| Net property and equipment | 4,174 | 3,306 |
| Other assets | 3,460 | 2,110 |
| Total assets | $15,826 | $12,758 |
| **Liabilities and Stockholders' Equity** | | |
| Current liabilities | | |
| Accounts payable | $ 4,997 | $ 4,297 |
| Accrued liabilities | 1,382 | 975 |
| Accrued income taxes | 281 | 404 |
| Accrued compensation payable | 459 | 373 |
| Other current liabilities | 1,316 | 720 |
| Total current liabilities | 8,435 | 6,769 |
| Long-term liabilities | | |
| Long-term debt | 1,126 | 627 |
| Other long-term liabilities | 1,622 | 878 |
| Total long-term liabilities | 2,748 | 1,505 |
| Total liabilities | 11,183 | 8,274 |
| Stockholders' equity | | |
| Common stock | 246 | 49 |
| Retained earnings | 4,397 | 4,435 |
| Total stockholders' equity | 4,643 | 4,484 |
| Total liabilities and stockholders' equity | $15,826 | $12,758 |

## Liquidity

Suppose you are a banker at CitiGroup considering lending money to Best Buy, or you are a sales manager at Hewlett-Packard interested in selling computers to Best Buy on credit. You would be concerned about Best Buy's liquidity—its ability to pay obligations expected to become due within the next year or operating cycle. You would look closely at the relationship of its current assets to current liabilities.

**WORKING CAPITAL.**   One measure of liquidity is working capital, which is the difference between the amounts of current assets and current liabilities:

**Illustration 2-14**   Working capital

> **Working Capital = Current Assets − Current Liabilities**

When current assets exceed current liabilities, working capital is positive. When this occurs, there is greater likelihood that the company will pay its liabilities. When working capital is negative, a company might not be able to pay short-term creditors, and the company might ultimately be forced into bankruptcy. Best Buy had working capital in 2009 of −$243 million ($8,192 million − $8,435 million). Best Buy's negative working capital does not necessarily mean the company has liquidity problems. It does warrant further investigation though.

**CURRENT RATIO.** Liquidity ratios measure the short-term ability of the company to pay its maturing obligations and to meet unexpected needs for cash. One liquidity ratio is the current ratio, computed as current assets divided by current liabilities.

The current ratio is a more dependable indicator of liquidity than working capital. Two companies with the same amount of working capital may have significantly different current ratios. Illustration 2-15 shows the 2009 and 2008 current ratios for Best Buy and for hhgregg, along with the 2009 industry average.

**Illustration 2-15**   Current ratio

$$\text{Current Ratio} = \frac{\text{Current Assets}}{\text{Current Liabilities}}$$

| Best Buy ($ in millions) | | hhgregg | Industry Average |
|---|---|---|---|
| 2009 | 2008 | 2009 | 2009 |
| $\dfrac{\$8,192}{\$8,435} = .97{:}1$ | 1.08:1 | 1.68:1 | 1.50:1 |

What does the ratio actually mean? Best Buy's 2009 current ratio of .97:1 means that for every dollar of current liabilities, Best Buy has 97¢ of current assets. Best Buy's current ratio decreased in 2009. When compared to the industry average of 1.5:1, Best Buy's liquidity seems low. It is also less than hhgregg's.

One potential weakness of the current ratio is that it does not take into account the **composition** of the current assets. For example, a satisfactory current ratio does not disclose whether a portion of the current assets is tied up in slow-moving inventory. The composition of the current assets matters because a dollar of cash is more readily available to pay the bills than is a dollar of inventory. For example, suppose a company's cash balance declined while its merchandise inventory increased substantially. If inventory increased because the company is having difficulty selling its products, then the current ratio might not fully reflect the reduction in the company's liquidity.

**Ethics Note** A company that has more current assets than current liabilities can increase the ratio of current assets to current liabilities by using cash to pay off some current liabilities. This gives the appearance of being more liquid. Do you think this move is ethical?

## Accounting Across the Organization

### Can a Company Be Too Liquid?

There actually is a point where a company can be too liquid—that is, it can have too much working capital. While it is important to be liquid enough to be able to pay short-term bills as they come due, a company does not want to tie up its cash in extra inventory or receivables that are not earning the company money.

By one estimate from the REL Consultancy Group, the thousand largest U.S. companies have on their books cumulative excess working capital of $764 billion. Based on this figure, companies could have reduced debt by 36% or increased net income by 9%. Given that managers throughout a company are interested in improving profitability, it is clear that they should have an eye toward managing working capital. They need to aim for a "Goldilocks solution"—not too much, not too little, but just right.

*Source:* K. Richardson, "Companies Fall Behind in Cash Management," *Wall Street Journal* (June 19, 2007).

**?** What can various company managers do to ensure that working capital is managed efficiently to maximize net income? (See page 96.)

## Solvency

Now suppose that instead of being a short-term creditor, you are interested in either buying Best Buy's stock or extending the company a long-term loan. Long-term creditors and stockholders are interested in a company's solvency—its ability to pay interest as it comes due and to repay the balance of a debt due at its maturity. Solvency ratios measure the ability of the company to survive over a long period of time.

**DEBT TO TOTAL ASSETS RATIO.** The debt to total assets ratio is one source of information about long-term debt-paying ability. It measures the percentage of total financing provided by creditors rather than stockholders. Debt financing is more risky than equity financing because debt must be repaid at specific points in time, whether the company is performing well or not. Thus, the higher the percentage of debt financing, the riskier the company.

**Helpful Hint** Some users evaluate solvency using a ratio of liabilities divided by stockholders' equity. The higher this "debt to equity" ratio, the lower is a company's solvency.

We compute the debt to total assets ratio as total debt (both current and long-term liabilities) divided by total assets. The higher the percentage of total liabilities (debt) to total assets, the greater the risk that the company may be unable to pay its debts as they come due. Illustration 2-16 shows the debt to total assets ratios for Best Buy and hhgregg, along with the 2009 industry average.

**Illustration 2-16** Debt to total assets ratio

| Debt to Total Assets Ratio = $\dfrac{\text{Total Liabilities}}{\text{Total Assets}}$ | | | |
|---|---|---|---|
| **Best Buy**<br>($ in millions) | | **hhgregg** | **Industry Average** |
| 2009 | 2008 | 2009 | 2009 |
| $\dfrac{\$11,183}{\$15,826} = 71\%$ | 65% | 64% | 57% |

The 2009 ratio of 71% means that every dollar of assets was financed by 71 cents of debt. Best Buy's ratio exceeds the industry average of 57% and is higher than hhgregg's ratio of 64%. The higher the ratio, the more reliant the company is on debt financing. This means the company has a lower equity "buffer" available to creditors if the company becomes insolvent. Thus, from the creditors' point of view, a high ratio of debt to total assets is undesirable. Best Buy's solvency appears lower than hhgregg's and lower than the average company in the industry.

The adequacy of this ratio is often judged in the light of the company's earnings. Generally, companies with relatively stable earnings, such as public utilities, can support higher debt to total assets ratios than can cyclical companies with widely fluctuating earnings, such as many high-tech companies. In later chapters, you will learn additional ways to evaluate solvency.

## Investor Insight

### When Debt Is Good

Debt financing differs greatly across industries and companies. Here are some debt to total assets ratios for selected companies in a recent year:

| | Debt to Total Assets Ratio |
|---|---|
| American Pharmaceutical Partners | 19% |
| Callaway Golf Company | 20% |
| Microsoft | 21% |
| Sears Holdings Corporation | 73% |
| Eastman Kodak Company | 78% |
| General Motors Corporation | 94% |

Discuss the difference in the debt to total assets ratio of Microsoft and General Motors. (See page 96.)

## DECISION TOOLKIT

| DECISION CHECKPOINTS | INFO NEEDED FOR DECISION | TOOL TO USE FOR DECISION | HOW TO EVALUATE RESULTS |
|---|---|---|---|
| Can the company meet its near-term obligations? | Current assets and current liabilities | $\text{Current ratio} = \dfrac{\text{Current assets}}{\text{Current liabilities}}$ | Higher ratio suggests favorable liquidity. |
| Can the company meet its long-term obligations? | Total debt and total assets | $\text{Debt to total assets ratio} = \dfrac{\text{Total liabilities}}{\text{Total assets}}$ | Lower value suggests favorable solvency. |

In the statement of cash flows, cash provided by operating activities is intended to indicate the cash-generating capability of the company. Analysts have noted, however, that **cash provided by operating activities fails to take into account that a company must invest in new property, plant, and equipment** (capital expenditures) just to maintain its current level of operations. Companies also must at least **maintain dividends at current levels** to satisfy investors. A measurement to provide additional insight regarding a company's cash-generating ability is free cash flow. **Free cash flow** describes the cash remaining from operating activities after adjusting for capital expenditures and dividends paid.

Consider the following example: Suppose that MPC produced and sold 10,000 personal computers this year. It reported $100,000 cash provided by operating

**KEEPING AN EYE ON CASH**

study objective **5**
Use the statement of cash flows to evaluate solvency.

activities. In order to maintain production at 10,000 computers, MPC invested $15,000 in equipment. It chose to pay $5,000 in dividends. Its free cash flow was $80,000 ($100,000 − $15,000 − $5,000). The company could use this $80,000 to purchase new assets to expand the business, to pay off debts, or to increase its dividend distribution. In practice, analysts often calculate free cash flow with the formula shown below. (Alternative definitions also exist.)

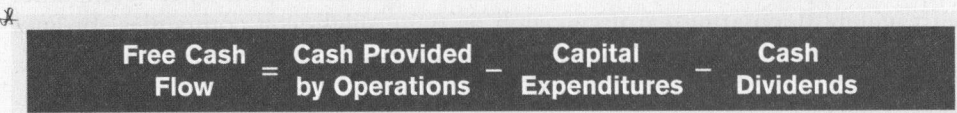

$$\text{Free Cash Flow} = \text{Cash Provided by Operations} - \text{Capital Expenditures} - \text{Cash Dividends}$$

We can calculate Best Buy's 2009 free cash flow as follows (dollars in millions).

| | |
|---|---:|
| Cash provided by operating activities | $1,877 |
| Less: Expenditures on property, plant, and equipment | 1,303 |
| Dividends paid | 222 |
| Free cash flow | $ 352 |

Best Buy generated free cash flow of $352 million which is available for the acquisition of new assets, the retirement of stock or debt, or the payment of additional dividends. Long-term creditors consider a high free cash flow amount an indication of solvency. hhgregg's free cash flow for 2009 is $7.7 million. Given that hhgregg is considerably smaller than Best Buy, we would expect its free cash flow to be much lower.

## DECISION TOOLKIT

| DECISION CHECKPOINTS | INFO NEEDED FOR DECISION | TOOL TO USE FOR DECISION | HOW TO EVALUATE RESULTS |
|---|---|---|---|
| How much cash did the company generate to expand operations, pay off debts, or distribute dividends? | Cash provided by operating activities, cash spent on fixed assets, and cash dividends | $$\text{Free cash flow} = \text{Cash provided by operations} - \text{Capital expenditures} - \text{Cash dividends}$$ | Significant free cash flow indicates greater potential to finance new investment and pay additional dividends. |

## before you go on...

**RATIO ANALYSIS**     **Do it!**     The following information is available for Ozone Inc.

| | 2012 | 2011 |
|---|---:|---:|
| Current assets | $ 88,000 | $ 60,800 |
| Total assets | 400,000 | 341,000 |
| Current liabilities | 40,000 | 38,000 |
| Total liabilities | 120,000 | 150,000 |
| Net income | 100,000 | 50,000 |
| Cash provided by operating activities | 110,000 | 70,000 |
| Preferred stock dividends | 10,000 | 10,000 |
| Common stock dividends | 5,000 | 2,500 |
| Expenditures on property, plant, and equipment | 45,000 | 20,000 |
| Shares outstanding at beginning of year | 60,000 | 40,000 |
| Shares outstanding at end of year | 120,000 | 60,000 |

(a) Compute earnings per share for 2012 and 2011 for Ozone, and comment on the change. Ozone's primary competitor, Frost Corporation, had earnings per share of $2 in 2012. Comment on the difference in the ratios of the two companies.

(b) Compute the current ratio and debt to total assets ratio for each year, and comment on the changes.

(c) Compute free cash flow for each year, and comment on the changes.

## Solution

(a) Earnings per share

| 2012 | 2011 |
|---|---|
| $\dfrac{(\$100{,}000 - \$10{,}000)}{(120{,}000 + 60{,}000)/2} = \$1.00$ | $\dfrac{(\$50{,}000 - \$10{,}000)}{(60{,}000 + 40{,}000)/2} = \$0.80$ |

Ozone's profitability, as measured by the amount of income available to each share of common stock, increased by 25% [($1.00 − $0.80) ÷ $0.80] during 2012. Earnings per share should not be compared across companies because the number of shares issued by companies varies widely. Thus, we cannot conclude that Frost Corporation is more profitable than Ozone based on its higher EPS.

(b)

| | 2012 | 2011 |
|---|---|---|
| Current ratio | $\dfrac{\$88{,}000}{\$40{,}000} = 2.20{:}1$ | $\dfrac{\$60{,}800}{\$38{,}000} = 1.60{:}1$ |
| Debt to total assets ratio | $\dfrac{\$120{,}000}{\$400{,}000} = 30\%$ | $\dfrac{\$150{,}000}{\$341{,}000} = 44\%$ |

The company's liquidity, as measured by the current ratio, improved from 1:60:1 to 2.20:1. Its solvency also improved, as measured by the debt to total assets ratio, which declined from 44% to 30%.

(c) Free cash flow

2012: $110,000 − $45,000 − ($10,000 + $5,000) = $50,000
2011: $70,000 − $20,000 − ($10,000 + $2,500) = $37,500

The amount of cash generated by the company above its needs for dividends and capital expenditures increased from $37,500 to $50,000.

Related exercise material: **BE2-3, BE2-5, BE2-6, Do it! 2-3, E2-7, E2-9, E2-10,** and **E2-11.**

**Action Plan**
- Use the formula for earnings per share (EPS): (Net income − Preferred stock dividends) ÷ (Average common shares outstanding).
- Use the formula for the current ratio: Current assets ÷ Current liabilities.
- Use the formula for the debt to total assets ratio: Total liabilities ÷ Total assets.
- Use the formula for free cash flow: Cash provided by operating activities − Capital expenditures − Cash dividends.

# Financial Reporting Concepts

In Chapter 1, you learned about the four financial statements, and in this chapter, we introduced you to some basic ways to interpret those statements. In this last section, we will discuss concepts that underly these financial statements. It would be unwise to make business decisions based on financial statements without understanding the implications of these concepts.

**study objective 6**

Explain the meaning of generally accepted accounting principles.

## THE STANDARD-SETTING ENVIRONMENT

How does Best Buy decide on the type of financial information to disclose? What format should it use? How should it measure assets, liabilities, revenues, and expenses? Best Buy and all other U.S. companies get guidance from a set of rules and practices that have authoritative support, referred to as **generally accepted accounting principles (GAAP).** Standard-setting bodies, in consultation with the accounting profession and the business community, determine these accounting standards.

**International Note** Over 100 countries use international standards (called IFRS). For example, all companies in the European Union follow international standards. The differences between U.S. and international standards are not generally significant. In this book, we highlight any major differences using International Notes like this one, as well as a more in-depth discussion in the *A Look at IFRS* section at the end of each chapter.

The **Securities and Exchange Commission (SEC)** is the agency of the U.S. government that oversees U.S. financial markets and accounting standard-setting bodies. The **Financial Accounting Standards Board (FASB)** is the primary accounting standard-setting body in the United States. The **International Accounting Standards Board (IASB)** issues standards called **International Financial Reporting Standards (IFRS)**, which have been adopted by many countries outside of the United States. Today, the FASB and IASB are working closely together to minimize the differences in their standards. Recently, the SEC announced that foreign companies that wish to have their shares traded on U.S stock exchanges no longer have to prepare reports that conform with GAAP, as long as their reports conform with IFRS. The SEC is currently evaluating whether the United States should eventually adopt IFRS as the required set of standards for U.S. publicly traded companies. Another relatively recent change to the financial reporting environment was that, as a result of the Sarbanes-Oxley Act, the **Public Company Accounting Oversight Board (PCAOB)** was created. Its job is to determine auditing standards and review the performance of auditing firms. If the United States adopts IFRS for its accounting standards, it will also have to coordinate its auditing regulations with those of other countries.

## International Insight

### The Korean Discount

If you think that accounting standards don't matter, consider recent events in South Korea. For many years, international investors complained that the financial reports of South Korean companies were inadequate and inaccurate. Accounting practices there often resulted in huge differences between stated revenues and actual revenues. Because investors did not have faith in the accuracy of the numbers, they were unwilling to pay as much for the shares of these companies relative to shares of comparable companies in different countries. This difference in share price was often referred to as the "Korean discount."

In response, Korean regulators decided that, beginning in 2011, companies will have to comply with international accounting standards. This change was motivated by a desire to "make the country's businesses more transparent" in order to build investor confidence and spur economic growth. Many other Asian countries, including China, India, Japan, and Hong Kong, have also decided either to adopt international standards or to create standards that are based on the international standards.

*Source:* Evan Ramstad, "End to 'Korea Discount'?" *Wall Street Journal* (March 16, 2007).

 What is meant by the phrase "make the country's businesses more transparent"? Why would increasing transparency spur economic growth? (See page 96.)

## QUALITIES OF USEFUL INFORMATION

**study objective 7**
Discuss financial reporting concepts.

Recently, the FASB and IASB completed the first phase of a joint project in which they developed a conceptual framework to serve as the basis for future accounting standards. The framework begins by stating that the primary objective of financial reporting is to provide financial information that is **useful** to investors and creditors for making decisions about providing capital. According to the FASB, useful information should possess two fundamental qualities, relevance and faithful representation, as shown in Illustration 2-17.

**Relevance** Accounting information is considered relevant if it would make a difference in a business decision. Information is considered relevant if it provides information that has **predictive value**, that is, helps provide accurate expectations about the future, and has **confirmatory value**, that is, confirms or corrects prior expectations.

**Faithful Representation** Faithful representation means that information accurately depicts what really happened. To provide a faithful representation, information must be **complete** (nothing important has been omitted) and **neutral** (is not biased toward one position or another).

**Illustration 2-17**
Fundamental qualities of useful information

## Enhancing Qualities

In addition to the two fundamental qualities, the FASB and IASB also describe a number of enhancing qualities of useful information. These include **comparability, consistency, verifiability, timeliness,** and **understandability**. In accounting, comparability results when different companies use the same accounting principles. Another characteristic that enhances comparability is consistency. Consistency means that a company uses the same accounting principles and methods from year to year. Information is verifiable if we are able to prove that it is free from error. As noted in Chapter 1, certified public accountants (CPAs) perform audits of financial statements to verify their accuracy. For accounting information to be relevant, it must be timely. That is, it must be available to decision makers before it loses its capacity to influence decisions. The SEC requires that public companies provide their annual reports to investors within 60 days of their year-end. Information has the quality of understandability if it is presented in a clear and concise fashion, so that reasonably informed users of that information can interpret it and comprehend its meaning.

 ## Accounting Across the Organization

### What Do These Companies Have in Common?

Another issue related to comparability is the accounting time period. An accounting period that is one-year long is called a **fiscal year**. But a fiscal year need not match the calendar year. For example, a company could end its fiscal year on April 30, rather than December 31.

Why do companies choose the particular year-ends that they do? For example, why doesn't every company use December 31 as the accounting year-end? Many companies choose to end their accounting year when inventory or operations are at a low point. This is advantageous because compiling accounting information requires much time and effort by managers, so they would rather do it when they aren't as busy operating the business. Also, inventory is easier and less costly to count when its volume is low.

Some companies whose year-ends differ from December 31 are Delta Air Lines, June 30; Walt Disney Productions, September 30; and Dunkin' Donuts, Inc., October 31. In the notes to its financial statements, Best Buy states that its accounting year-end is the Saturday nearest the end of February.

 What problems might Best Buy's year-end create for analysts? (See page 96.)

## ASSUMPTIONS IN FINANCIAL REPORTING

To develop accounting standards, the FASB relies on some key assumptions, as shown in Illustration 2-18. These include assumptions about the monetary unit, economic entity, periodicity, going concern, and accrual basis.

**Illustration 2-18** Key assumptions in financial reporting

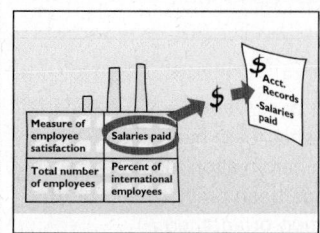

**Monetary Unit Assumption** The monetary unit assumption requires that only those things that can be expressed in money are included in the accounting records. This means that certain important information needed by investors, creditors, and managers, such as customer satisfaction, is not reported in the financial statements.

**Ethics Note** The importance of the economic entity assumption is illustrated by scandals involving Adelphia. In this case, senior company employees entered into transactions that blurred the line between the employees' financial interests and those of the company. For example, Adelphia guaranteed over $2 billion of loans to the founding family.

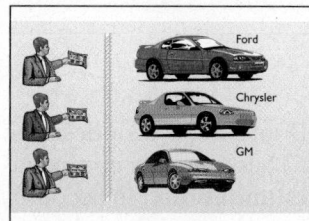

**Economic Entity Assumption** The economic entity assumption states that every economic entity can be separately identified and accounted for. In order to assess a company's performance and financial position accurately, it is important that we not blur company transactions with personal transactions (especially those of its managers) or transactions of other companies.

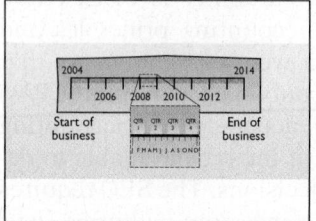

**Periodicity Assumption** Notice that the income statement, retained earnings statement, and statement of cash flows all cover periods of one year, and the balance sheet is prepared at the end of each year. The periodicity assumption states that the life of a business can be divided into artificial time periods and that useful reports covering those periods can be prepared for the business.

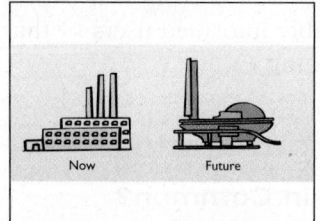

**Going Concern Assumption** The going concern assumption states that the business will remain in operation for the foreseeable future. Of course, many businesses do fail, but in general, it is reasonable to assume that the business will continue operating.

**Accrual Basis** Accrual-basis accounting means that transactions that change a company's financial statements are recorded in the periods in which the events occur. Accrual-basis accounting is addressed in more detail in Chapter 4.

## PRINCIPLES IN FINANCIAL REPORTING
### Measurement Principles

GAAP generally uses one of two measurement principles, the cost principle or the fair value principle. Selection of which principle to follow generally relates to trade-offs between relevance and faithful representation.

**COST PRINCIPLE.** The cost principle (or historical cost principle) dictates that companies record assets at their cost. This is true not only at the time the asset is purchased but also over the time the asset is held. For example, if land that was purchased for $30,000 increases in value to $40,000, it continues to be reported at $30,000.

**FAIR VALUE PRINCIPLE.** The fair value principle indicates that assets and liabilities should be reported at fair value (the price received to sell an asset or settle a liability). Fair value information may be more useful than historical cost for certain types of assets and liabilities. For example, certain investment securities are reported at fair value because market price information is often readily available for these types of assets. In choosing between cost and fair value, the FASB uses two qualities that make accounting information useful for decision making—relevance and faithful representation. In determining which measurement principle to use, the FASB weighs the factual nature of cost figures versus the relevance of fair value. In general, the FASB indicates that most assets must follow the cost principle because market values may not be representationally faithful. Only in situations where assets are actively traded, such as investment securities, is the fair value principle applied.

## Full Disclosure Principle

The full disclosure principle requires that companies disclose all circumstances and events that would make a difference to financial statement users. If an important item cannot reasonably be reported directly in one of the four types of financial statements, then it should be discussed in notes that accompany the statements.

### CONSTRAINTS IN FINANCIAL REPORTING

Efforts to provide useful financial information can be costly to a company. Therefore, the profession has agreed upon **constraints** to ensure that companies apply accounting rules in a reasonable fashion, from the perspectives of both the company and the user. The constraints are the materiality and cost constraints, as shown in Illustration 2-19.

**Materiality Constraint** The materiality constraint relates to a financial statement item's impact on a company's overall financial condition and operations. An item is **material** when its **size** makes it likely to influence the decision of an investor or creditor. It is **immaterial** if it is too small to impact a decision maker. If the item does not make a difference, the company does not have to follow GAAP in reporting it.

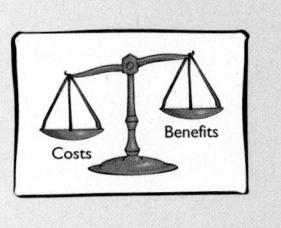

**Cost Constraint** The cost constraint relates to the fact that providing information is costly. In deciding whether companies should be required to provide a certain type of information, accounting standard-setters weigh the cost that companies will incur to provide the information against the benefit that financial statement users will gain from having the information available.

**Illustration 2-19**
Constraints in financial reporting

## before you go on...

**Do it!** The following are characteristics, assumptions, principles, or constraints that guide the FASB when it creates accounting standards.

| | |
|---|---|
| Relevance | Periodicity assumption |
| Faithful representation | Going concern assumption |
| Comparability | Cost principle |
| Consistency | Full disclosure principle |
| Monetary unit assumption | Materiality constraint |
| Economic entity assumption | |

Match each item above with a description below.

1. _____ Ability to easily evaluate one company's results relative to another's.

2. _____ Belief that a company will continue to operate for the foreseeable future.

3. _____ The judgment concerning whether an item is large enough to matter to decision makers.

4. _____ The reporting of all information that would make a difference to financial statement users.

5. _____ The practice of preparing financial statements at regular intervals.

6. _____ The quality of information that indicates the information makes a difference in a decision.

7. _____ A belief that items should be reported on the balance sheet at the price that was paid to acquire the item.

8. _____ A company's use of the same accounting principles and methods from year to year.

9. _____ Tracing accounting events to particular companies.

10. _____ The desire to minimize errors and bias in financial statements.

11. _____ Reporting only those things that can be measured in dollars.

### Action Plan

- Understand the need for conceptual guidelines in accounting.
- List the characteristics of useful financial information.
- Review the assumptions, principles, and constraints that comprise the guidelines in accounting.

### Solution

| | |
|---|---|
| 1. Comparability | 7. Cost principle |
| 2. Going concern assumption | 8. Consistency |
| 3. Materiality constraint | 9. Economic entity assumption |
| 4. Full disclosure principle | 10. Faithful representation |
| 5. Periodicity assumption | 11. Monetary unit assumption |
| 6. Relevance | |

Related exercise material: **BE2-8, BE2-9, BE2-10, BE2-11, Do it! 2-4, E2-12,** and **E2-13.**

the navigator

# USING THE *DECISION TOOLKIT*

In this chapter, we evaluated a home electronics giant, Best Buy. Tweeter Home Entertainment sold consumer electronics products from 154 stores on the East Coast under various names. It specialized in products with high-end features. Tweeter filed for bankruptcy in June 2007 and was acquired by another company in July 2007. Financial data for Tweeter, prior to its bankruptcy, are provided below.

| | September 30 | |
|---|---|---|
| (amounts in millions) | **2006** | **2005** |
| Current assets | $146.4 | $158.2 |
| Total assets | 258.6 | 284.0 |
| Current liabilities | 107.1 | 119.0 |
| Total liabilities | 190.4 | 201.1 |
| Total common stockholders' equity | 68.2 | 82.9 |
| Net income (loss) | (16.5) | (74.4) |
| Cash provided (used) by operating activities | 15.6 | (26.7) |
| Capital expenditures (net) | 17.4 | 22.2 |
| Dividends paid | 0 | 0 |
| Average shares of common stock (millions) | 25.2 | 24.6 |

## Instructions

Using the data provided, answer the following questions and discuss how these results might have provided an indication of Tweeter's financial troubles.

1. Calculate the current ratio for Tweeter for 2006 and 2005 and discuss its liquidity position.

2. Calculate the debt to total assets ratio and free cash flow for Tweeter for 2006 and 2005 and discuss its solvency.

3. Calculate the earnings per share for Tweeter for 2006 and 2005, and discuss its change in profitability.

4. Best Buy's accounting year-end was February 28, 2007; Tweeter's was September 30, 2006. How does this difference affect your ability to compare their profitability?

## Solution

1. Current ratio:

   *2006:*   $146.4 ÷ $107.1 = 1.37:1      *2005:*   $158.2 ÷ $119.0 = 1.33:1

   Tweeter's liquidity improved slightly from 2005 to 2006, but in both years it would most likely have been considered inadequate. In 2006 Tweeter had only $1.37 in current assets for every dollar of current liabilities. Sometimes larger companies, such as Best Buy, can function with lower current ratios because they have alternative sources of working capital. But a company of Tweeter's size would normally want a higher ratio.

2. Debt to total assets:

   *2006:*   $190.4 ÷ $258.6 = 73.6%      *2005:*   $201.1 ÷ $284.0 = 70.8%

   Tweeter's solvency, as measured by its debt to total assets ratio, declined from 2005 to 2006. Its ratio of 73.6% meant that every dollar of assets was financed by 73.6 cents of debt. For a retailer, this is extremely high reliance on debt. This low solvency suggests Tweeter's ability to meet its debt payments was questionable.

   Free cash flow:

   *2006:*   $15.6 − $17.4 − $0 = −$1.8 million
   *2005:*   −$26.7 − $22.2 − $0 = −$48.9 million

   Tweeter's free cash flow was negative in both years. The company did not generate enough cash from operations even to cover its capital expenditures, and it was not paying a dividend. While this is not unusual for new companies in their early years, it is also not sustainable for very long. Part of the reason that its debt to assets ratio, discussed above, was so high was that it had to borrow money to make up for its deficient free cash flow.

3. Loss per share:
   *2006:*  $-\$16.5 \div 25.2 = -\$0.65$ per share
   *2005:*  $-\$74.4 \div 24.6 = -\$3.02$ per share

   Tweeter's loss per share declined substantially. However, this was little consolation for its shareholders, who experienced losses in previous years as well. The company's lack of profitability, combined with its poor liquidity and solvency, increased the likelihood that it would eventually file for bankruptcy.

4. Tweeter's income statement covers 7 months not covered by Best Buy's. Suppose that the economy changed dramatically during this 7-month period, either improving or declining. This change in the economy would be reflected in Tweeter's income statement but would not be reflected in Best Buy's income statement until the following March, thus reducing the usefulness of a comparison of the income statements of the two companies.

# Summary of Study Objectives

**1** **Identify the sections of a classified balance sheet.** In a classified balance sheet, companies classify assets as current assets; long-term investments; property, plant, and equipment; and intangibles. They classify liabilities as either current or long-term. A stockholders' equity section shows common stock and retained earnings.

**2** **Identify and compute ratios for analyzing a company's profitability.** Profitability ratios, such as earnings per share (EPS), measure aspects of the operating success of a company for a given period of time.

**3** **Explain the relationship between a retained earnings statement and a statement of stockholders' equity.** The retained earnings statement presents the factors that changed the retained earnings balance during the period. A statement of stockholders' equity presents the factors that changed stockholders' equity during the period, including those that changed retained earnings. Thus, a statement of stockholders' equity is more inclusive.

**4** **Identify and compute ratios for analyzing a company's liquidity and solvency using a balance sheet.** Liquidity ratios, such as the current ratio, measure the short-term ability of a company to pay its maturing obligations and to meet unexpected needs for cash. Solvency ratios, such as the debt to total assets ratio, measure the ability of a company to survive over a long period.

**5** **Use the statement of cash flows to evaluate solvency.** Free cash flow indicates a company's ability to generate cash from operations that is sufficient to pay debts, acquire assets, and distribute dividends.

**6** **Explain the meaning of generally accepted accounting principles.** Generally accepted accounting principles

are a set of rules and practices recognized as a general guide for financial reporting purposes. The basic objective of financial reporting is to provide information that is useful for decision making.

**7** **Discuss financial reporting concepts.** To be judged useful, information should have the primary characteristics of relevance and faithful representation. In addition, it should be comparable, consistent, verifiable, timely, and understandable.

The *monetary unit assumption* requires that companies include in the accounting records only transaction data that can be expressed in terms of money. The *economic entity assumption* states that economic events can be identified with a particular unit of accountability. The *periodicity assumption* states that the economic life of a business can be divided into artificial time periods and that meaningful accounting reports can be prepared for each period. The *going concern assumption* states that the company will continue in operation long enough to carry out its existing objectives and commitments. *Accrual-basis accounting* means that transactions are recorded in the periods in which the events occur.

The *cost principle* states that companies should record assets at their cost. The *fair value principle* indicates that assets and liabilities should be reported at fair value. The *full disclosure principle* requires that companies disclose circumstances and events that matter to financial statement users.

The major constraints are materiality and cost.

## DECISION TOOLKIT  A SUMMARY

| DECISION CHECKPOINTS | INFO NEEDED FOR DECISION | TOOL TO USE FOR DECISION | HOW TO EVALUATE RESULTS |
|---|---|---|---|
| How does the company's earnings performance compare with that of previous years? | Net income available to common stockholders and average common shares outstanding | $$\text{Earnings per share} = \frac{\text{Net income} - \text{Preferred stock dividends}}{\text{Average common shares outstanding}}$$ | A higher measure suggests improved performance, although the number is subject to manipulation. Values should not be compared across companies. |
| Can the company meet its near-term obligations? | Current assets and current liabilities | $$\text{Current ratio} = \frac{\text{Current assets}}{\text{Current liabilities}}$$ | Higher ratio suggests favorable liquidity. |
| Can the company meet its long-term obligations? | Total debt and total assets | $$\text{Debt to total assets ratio} = \frac{\text{Total liabilities}}{\text{Total assets}}$$ | Lower value suggests favorable solvency. |
| How much cash did the company generate to expand operations, pay off debts, or distribute dividends? | Cash provided by operating activities, cash spent on fixed assets, and cash dividends | $$\text{Free cash flow} = \frac{\text{Cash provided by operations}}{} - \frac{\text{Capital expenditures}}{} - \frac{\text{Cash dividends}}{}$$ | Significant free cash flow indicates greater potential to finance new investment and pay additional dividends. |

## Glossary

**Accrual-basis accounting** (p. 66) Transactions that change a company's financial statements are recorded in the periods in which the events occur.

**Classified balance sheet** (p. 48) A balance sheet that contains a number of standard classifications and sections.

**Comparability** (p. 65) Ability to compare the accounting information of different companies because they use the same accounting principles.

**Consistency** (p. 65) Use of the same accounting principles and methods from year to year within a company.

**Cost constraint** (p. 67) Constraint of determining whether the cost that companies will incur to provide the information will outweigh the benefit that financial statement users will gain from having the information available.

**Cost principle** (p. 67) An accounting principle that states that companies should record assets at their cost.

**Current assets** (p. 49) Cash and other resources that companies reasonably expect to convert to cash or use up within one year or the operating cycle, whichever is longer.

**Current liabilities** (p. 52) Obligations that a company reasonably expects to pay within the next year or operating cycle, whichever is longer.

**Current ratio** (p. 59) A measure used to evaluate a company's liquidity and short-term debt-paying ability; computed as current assets divided by current liabilities.

**Debt to total assets ratio** (p. 60) Measures the percentage of total financing provided by creditors; computed as total debt divided by total assets.

**Earnings per share (EPS)** (p. 55) A measure of the net income earned on each share of common stock; computed as net income minus preferred stock dividends divided by the average number of common shares outstanding during the year.

**Economic entity assumption** (p. 66) An assumption that every economic entity can be separately identified and accounted for.

**Fair value principle** (p. 67) Assets and liabilities should be reported at fair value (the price received to sell an asset or settle a liability).

**Faithful representation** (p. 65) Information that is complete, neutral, and free from error.

**Financial Accounting Standards Board (FASB)** (p. 64) The primary accounting standard-setting body in the United States.

**Free cash flow** (p. 61) Cash remaining from operating activities after adjusting for capital expenditures and dividends paid.

**Full disclosure principle** (p. 67) Accounting principle that dictates that companies disclose circumstances and events that make a difference to financial statement users.

**Generally accepted accounting principles (GAAP)** (p. 63) A set of rules and practices, having substantial authoritative support, that the accounting profession recognizes as a general guide for financial reporting purposes.

**Going concern assumption** (p. 66) The assumption that the company will continue in operation for the foreseeable future.

**Intangible assets** (p. 51) Assets that do not have physical substance.

**International Accounting Standards Board (IASB)** (p. 64) An accounting standard-setting body that issues standards adopted by many countries outside of the United States.

**International Financial Reporting Standards (IFRS)** (p. 64) Accounting standards, issued by the IASB, that have been adopted by many countries outside of the United States.

**Liquidity** *(p. 58)*   The ability of a company to pay obligations that are expected to become due within the next year or operating cycle.

**Liquidity ratios** *(p. 59)*   Measures of the short-term ability of the company to pay its maturing obligations and to meet unexpected needs for cash.

**Long-term investments** *(p. 50)*   Generally, (1) investments in stocks and bonds of other corporations that companies hold for more than one year, and (2) long-term assets, such as land and buildings, not currently being used in the company's operations.

**Long-term liabilities (Long-term debt)** *(p. 52)*   Obligations that a company expects to pay after one year.

**Materiality constraint** *(p. 67)*   The constraint of determining whether an item is large enough to likely influence the decision of an investor or creditor.

**Monetary unit assumption** *(p. 66)*   An assumption that requires that only those things that can be expressed in money are included in the accounting records.

**Operating cycle** *(p. 50)*   The average time required to go from cash to cash in producing revenue.

**Periodicity assumption** *(p. 66)*   An assumption that the life of a business can be divided into artificial time periods and that useful reports covering those periods can be prepared for the business.

**Profitability ratios** *(p. 55)*   Measures of the operating success of a company for a given period of time.

**Property, plant, and equipment** *(p. 51)*   Assets with relatively long useful lives that companies use in operating the business.

**Public Company Accounting Oversight Board (PCAOB)** *(p. 64)*   The group charged with determining auditing standards and reviewing the performance of auditing firms.

**Ratio** *(p. 54)*   An expression of the mathematical relationship between one quantity and another.

**Ratio analysis** *(p. 54)*   A technique for evaluating financial statements that expresses the relationship among selected items of financial statement data.

**Relevance** *(p. 65)*   The quality of information that indicates the information makes a difference in a decision.

**Securities and Exchange Commission (SEC)** *(p. 64)*   The agency of the U.S. government that oversees U.S. financial markets and accounting standard-setting bodies.

**Solvency** *(p. 60)*   The ability of a company to pay interest as it comes due and to repay the balance of debt at its maturity.

**Solvency ratios** *(p. 60)*   Measures of the ability of the company to survive over a long period of time.

**Statement of stockholders' equity** *(p. 57)*   A financial statement that presents the factors that caused stockholders' equity to change during the period, including those that caused retained earnings to change.

**Timely** *(p. 65)*   Information that is available to decision makers before it loses its capacity to influence decisions.

**Understandability** *(p. 65)*   Information presented in a clear and concise fashion so that users can interpret it and comprehend its meaning.

**Verifiable** *(p. 65)*   Information that is proven to be free from error.

**Working capital** *(p. 59)*   The difference between the amounts of current assets and current liabilities.

# Comprehensive  Do it!

Listed here are items taken from the income statement and balance sheet of Bargain Electronics, Inc. for the year ended December 31, 2012. Certain items have been combined for simplification. Amounts are given in thousands.

| | |
|---|---|
| Notes payable (due in 3 years) | $    50.5 |
| Cash | 141.1 |
| Salaries and wages expense | 2,933.6 |
| Common stock | 454.9 |
| Accounts payable | 922.2 |
| Accounts receivable | 723.3 |
| Equipment, net | 921.0 |
| Cost of goods sold | 9,501.4 |
| Income taxes payable | 7.2 |
| Interest expense | 1.5 |
| Mortgage payable | 451.5 |
| Retained earnings | 1,336.3 |
| Inventory | 1,636.5 |
| Sales revenue | 12,456.9 |
| Short-term investments | 382.6 |
| Income tax expense | 30.5 |
| Goodwill | 202.7 |
| Notes payable (due in 6 months) | 784.6 |

## Instructions

Prepare an income statement and a classified balance sheet using the items listed. Do not use any item more than once.

## Solution to Comprehensive Do it!

**Action Plan**

• In preparing the income statement, list revenues, then expenses.

• In preparing a classified balance sheet, list current assets in order of liquidity.

**BARGAIN ELECTRONICS, INC.**
Income Statement
For the Year Ended December 31, 2012
(in thousands)

| | | |
|---|---:|---:|
| Sales revenue | | $12,456.9 |
| Cost of goods sold | $9,501.4 | |
| Salaries and wages expense | 2,933.6 | |
| Interest expense | 1.5 | |
| Income tax expense | 30.5 | |
| Total expenses | | 12,467.0 |
| Net loss | | $(10.1) |

**BARGAIN ELECTRONICS, INC.**
Balance Sheet
December 31, 2012
(in thousands)

### Assets

| | | |
|---|---:|---:|
| Current assets | | |
| Cash | $ 141.1 | |
| Short-term investments | 382.6 | |
| Accounts receivable | 723.3 | |
| Inventory | 1,636.5 | |
| Total current assets | | $2,883.5 |
| Equipment, net | | 921.0 |
| Goodwill | | 202.7 |
| Total assets | | $4,007.2 |

### Liabilities and Stockholders' Equity

| | | |
|---|---:|---:|
| Current liabilities | | |
| Notes payable | $ 784.6 | |
| Accounts payable | 922.2 | |
| Income taxes payable | 7.2 | |
| Total current liabilities | | $1,714.0 |
| Long-term liabilities | | |
| Mortgage payable | 451.5 | |
| Notes payable | 50.5 | 502.0 |
| Total liabilities | | 2,216.0 |
| Stockholders' equity | | |
| Common stock | 454.9 | |
| Retained earnings | 1,336.3 | |
| Total stockholders' equity | | 1,791.2 |
| Total liabilities and stockholders' equity | | $4,007.2 |

 Self-Test, Brief Exercises, Exercises, Problem Set A, and many more resources are available for practice in WileyPLUS

# Self-Test Questions

Answers are on page 96.

(SO 1) **1.** In a classified balance sheet, assets are usually classified as:
   (a) current assets; long-term assets; property, plant, and equipment; and intangible assets.
   (b) current assets; long-term investments; property, plant, and equipment; and common stock.
   (c) current assets; long-term investments; tangible assets; and intangible assets.
   (d) current assets; long-term investments; property, plant, and equipment; and intangible assets.

(SO 1) **2.** Current assets are listed:
   (a) by order of expected conversion to cash.
   (b) by importance.
   (c) by longevity.
   (d) alphabetically.

(SO 1) **3.** The correct order of presentation in a classified balance sheet for the following current assets is:
   (a) accounts receivable, cash, prepaid insurance, inventory.
   (b) cash, inventory, accounts receivable, prepaid insurance.
   (c) cash, accounts receivable, inventory, prepaid insurance.
   (d) inventory, cash, accounts receivable, prepaid insurance.

(SO 1) **4.** A company has purchased a tract of land. It expects to build a production plant on the land in approximately 5 years. During the 5 years before construction, the land will be idle. The land should be reported as:
   (a) property, plant, and equipment.
   (b) land expense.
   (c) a long-term investment.
   (d) an intangible asset.

(SO 2) **5.** Which is an indicator of profitability?
   (a) Current ratio.
   (b) Earnings per share.
   (c) Debt to total assets ratio.
   (d) Free cash flow.

(SO 2) **6.** For 2012, Ganos Corporation reported net income $26,000; net sales $400,000; and average shares outstanding 4,000. There were preferred stock dividends of $2,000. What was the 2012 earnings per share?
   (a) $6.00         (c) $99.50
   (b) $6.50         (d) $100.00

(SO 3) **7.** The balance in retained earnings is *not* affected by:
   (a) net income.
   (b) net loss.
   (c) issuance of common stock.
   (d) dividends.

(SO 4) **8.** Which of these measures is an evaluation of a company's ability to pay current liabilities?
   (a) Earnings per share.
   (b) Current ratio.
   (c) Both (a) and (b).
   (d) None of the above.

(SO 2, 4) **9.** The following ratios are available for Bachus Inc. and Newton Inc.

| | Current Ratio | Debt to Assets Ratio | Earnings per Share |
|---|---|---|---|
| Bachus Inc. | 2:1 | 75% | $3.50 |
| Newton Inc. | 1.5:1 | 40% | $2.75 |

Compared to Newton Inc., Bachus Inc. has:
   (a) higher liquidity, higher solvency, and higher profitability.
   (b) lower liquidity, higher solvency, and higher profitability.
   (c) higher liquidity, lower solvency, and higher profitability.
   (d) higher liquidity and lower solvency, but profitability cannot be compared based on information provided.

(SO 5) **10.** Companies can use free cash flow to:
   (a) pay additional dividends.
   (b) acquire property, plant, and equipment.
   (c) pay off debts.
   (d) All of the above.

(SO 6) **11.** Generally accepted accounting principles are:
   (a) a set of standards and rules that are recognized as a general guide for financial reporting.
   (b) usually established by the Internal Revenue Service.
   (c) the guidelines used to resolve ethical dilemmas.
   (d) fundamental truths that can be derived from the laws of nature.

(SO 6) **12.** What organization issues U.S. accounting standards?
   (a) Financial Accounting Standards Board.
   (b) International Accounting Standards Committee.
   (c) International Auditing Standards Committee.
   (d) None of the above.

(SO 7) **13.** What is the primary criterion by which accounting information can be judged?
   (a) Consistency.
   (b) Predictive value.
   (c) Usefulness for decision making.
   (d) Comparability.

(SO 7)  **14.** Neutrality is an ingredient of:

|  | Faithful representation | Relevance |
|---|---|---|
| (a) | Yes | Yes |
| (b) | No | No |
| (c) | Yes | No |
| (d) | No | Yes |

**15.** What accounting constraint allows a company to ignore (SO 7) GAAP if an item is too small to impact a decision?
(a) Comparability.    (c) Cost.
(b) Materiality.      (d) Consistency.

Go to the book's companion website, **www. wiley.com/college/kimmel**, to access additional Self-Test Questions.

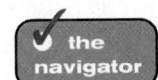

# Questions

**1.** What is meant by the term *operating cycle?*

**2.** Define current assets. What basis is used for ordering individual items within the current assets section?

**3.** Distinguish between long-term investments and property, plant, and equipment.

**4.** How do current liabilities differ from long-term liabilities?

**5.** Identify the two parts of stockholders' equity in a corporation and indicate the purpose of each.

**6.**
(a) Julia Alter believes that the analysis of financial statements is directed at two characteristics of a company: liquidity and profitability. Is Julia correct? Explain.
(b) Are short-term creditors, long-term creditors, and stockholders primarily interested in the same characteristics of a company? Explain.

**7.** Name ratios useful in assessing (a) liquidity, (b) solvency, and (c) profitability.

**8.** Jon Baird, the founder of Water-boots Inc., needs to raise $500,000 to expand his company's operations. He has been told that raising the money through debt will increase the riskiness of his company much more than issuing stock. He doesn't understand why this is true. Explain it to him.

**9.** What do these classes of ratios measure?
(a) Liquidity ratios.
(b) Profitability ratios.
(c) Solvency ratios.

**10.** Holding all other factors constant, indicate whether each of the following signals generally good or bad news about a company.

(a) Increase in earnings per share.
(b) Increase in the current ratio.
(c) Increase in the debt to total assets ratio.
(d) Decrease in free cash flow.

**11.** Which ratio or ratios from this chapter do you think should be of greatest interest to:
(a) a pension fund considering investing in a corporation's 20-year bonds?
(b) a bank contemplating a short-term loan?
(c) an investor in common stock?

**12.** (a) What are generally accepted accounting principles (GAAP)?
(b) What body provides authoritative support for GAAP?

**13.** (a) What is the primary objective of financial reporting?
(b) Identify the characteristics of useful accounting information.

**14.** Dan Fineman, the president of King Company, is pleased. King substantially increased its net income in 2012 while keeping its unit inventory relatively the same. Howard Gross, chief accountant, cautions Dan, however. Gross says that since King changed its method of inventory valuation, there is a consistency problem and it is difficult to determine whether King is better off. Is Gross correct? Why or why not?

**15.** What is the distinction between comparability and consistency?

**16.** Describe the two constraints inherent in the presentation of accounting information.

**17.** Your roommate believes that international accounting standards are uniform throughout the world. Is your roommate correct? Explain.

**18.** Laurie Belk is president of Better Books. She has no accounting background. Belk cannot understand why fair value is not used as the basis for all accounting measurement and reporting. Discuss.

**19.** What is the economic entity assumption? Give an example of its violation.

**20.** What was Tootsie Roll's largest current asset, largest current liability, and largest item under "Other assets" at December 31, 2009?

# Brief Exercises

*Classify accounts on balance sheet.*

(SO 1), **K**

**BE2-1**   The following are the major balance sheet classifications:

Current assets (CA)                         Current liabilities (CL)
Long-term investments (LTI)                 Long-term liabilities (LTL)
Property, plant, and equipment (PPE)        Common stock (CS)
Intangible assets (IA)                      Retained earnings (RE)

Match each of the following accounts to its proper balance sheet classification.

_____ Accounts payable                 _____ Income taxes payable
_____ Accounts receivable              _____ Investment in long-term bonds
_____ Accumulated depreciation         _____ Land
_____ Buildings                        _____ Inventory
_____ Cash                             _____ Patent
_____ Goodwill                         _____ Supplies

*Prepare the current assets section of a balance sheet.*

(SO 1), **AP**

**BE2-2**   A list of financial statement items for Georges Company includes the following: accounts receivable $14,000; prepaid insurance $2,600; cash $10,400; supplies $3,800, and short-term investments $8,200. Prepare the current assets section of the balance sheet listing the items in the proper sequence.

*Compute earnings per share.*

(SO 2), **AP**

**BE2-3**   The following information (in millions of dollars) is available for Limited Brands for 2008: Sales revenue $9,043; net income $220; preferred stock dividend $0; average shares outstanding 333 million. Compute the earnings per share for Limited Brands for 2008.

*Identify items affecting stockholders' equity.*

(SO 3), **K**

**BE2-4**   For each of the following events affecting the stockholders' equity of Willis, indicate whether the event would: increase retained earnings (IRE), decrease retained earnings (DRE), increase common stock (ICS), or decrease common stock (DCS).

_____ (a) Issued new shares of common stock.
_____ (b) Paid a cash dividend.
_____ (c) Reported net income of $75,000.
_____ (d) Reported a net loss of $20,000.

*Calculate liquidity ratios.*

(SO 4), **AP**

**BE2-5**   These selected condensed data are taken from a recent balance sheet of Bob Evans Farms (in millions of dollars).

| | |
|---|---|
| Cash | $ 29.3 |
| Accounts receivable | 20.5 |
| Inventory | 28.7 |
| Other current assets | 24.0 |
| Total current assets | $102.5 |
| Total current liabilities | $201.2 |

Compute working capital and the current ratio.

*Calculate liquidity and solvency ratios.*

(SO 4, 5), **AP**

**BE2-6**   Kalb's Books & Music Inc. reported the following selected information at March 31.

| | 2012 |
|---|---|
| Total current assets | $262,787 |
| Total assets | 439,832 |
| Total current liabilities | 293,625 |
| Total liabilities | 376,002 |
| Cash provided by operating activities | 62,300 |

Calculate (a) the current ratio, (b) the debt to total assets ratio, and (c) free cash flow for March 31, 2012. The company paid dividends of $12,000 and spent $24,787 on capital expenditures.

*Recognize generally accepted accounting principles.*

(SO 6), **K**

**BE2-7**   Indicate whether each statement is *true* or *false*.
(a) GAAP is a set of rules and practices established by accounting standard-setting bodies to serve as a general guide for financial reporting purposes.
(b) Substantial authoritative support for GAAP usually comes from two standards-setting bodies: the FASB and the IRS.

**BE2-8** The accompanying chart shows the qualitative characteristics of useful accounting information. Fill in the blanks.

*Identify characteristics of useful information.*
(SO 7), **K**

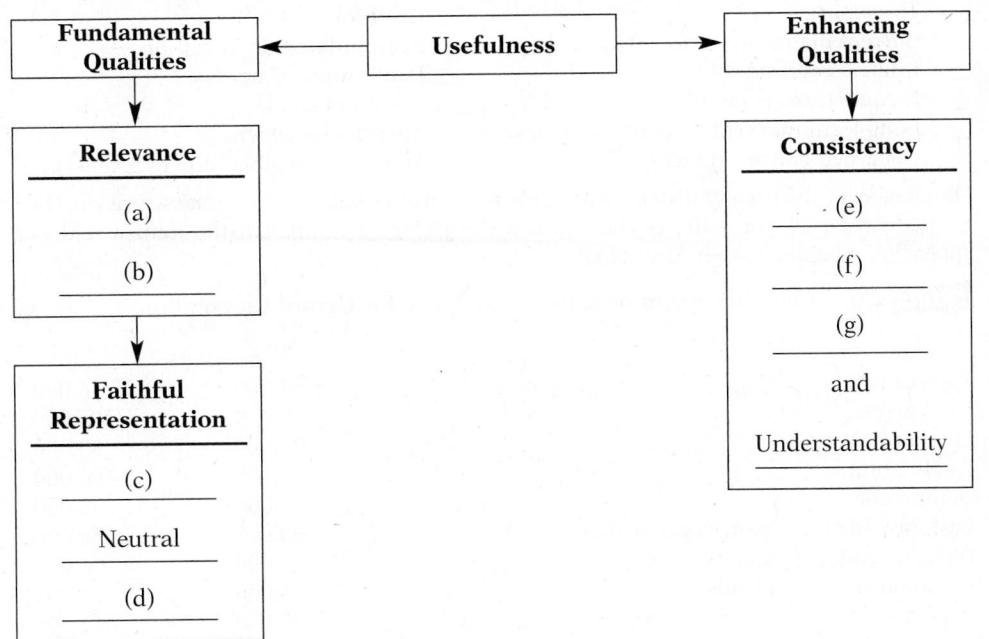

**BE2-9** Given the *characteristics* of useful accounting information, complete each of the following statements.

(a) For information to be _____, it should have predictive and confirmatory value.

(b) _____ is the quality of information that gives assurance that it is free from error and bias.

(c) _____ means using the same accounting principles and methods from year to year within a company.

*Identify characteristics of useful information.*
(SO 7), **K**

**BE2-10** Here are some qualitative characteristics of useful accounting information:

1. Predictive value        3. Verifiable
2. Neutral                 4. Timely

*Identify characteristics of useful information.*
(SO 7), **K**

Match each qualitative characteristic to one of the following statements.

_____ (a) Accounting information should help provide accurate expectations about future events.

_____ (b) Accounting information cannot be selected, prepared, or presented to favor one set of interested users over another.

_____ (c) Accounting information must be proved to be free of error.

_____ (d) Accounting information must be available to decision makers before it loses its capacity to influence their decisions.

**BE2-11** The full disclosure principle dictates that:

(a) financial statements should disclose all assets at their cost.

(b) financial statements should disclose only those events that can be measured in dollars.

(c) financial statements should disclose all events and circumstances that would matter to users of financial statements.

(d) financial statements should not be relied on unless an auditor has expressed an unqualified opinion on them.

*Define full disclosure principle.*
(SO 7), **K**

# Do it! Review

*Prepare assets section of balance sheet.*
(SO 1), **AP**

**Do it! 2-1** Heather Corporation has collected the following information related to its December 31, 2012, balance sheet.

| | | | |
|---|---|---|---|
| Accounts receivable | $22,000 | Equipment | $180,000 |
| Accumulated depreciation—equipment | 50,000 | Inventory | 58,000 |
| Cash | 13,000 | Supplies | 7,000 |

Prepare the assets section of Heather Corporation's balance sheet.

*Classify financial statement items by balance sheet classification.*
(SO 1), **AP**

**Do it!** 2-2 The following financial statement items were taken from the financial statements of Jing Corp.

____ Trademarks      ____ Inventory
____ Current maturities of long-term debt      ____ Accumulated depreciation
____ Interest revenue      ____ Land improvements
____ Income taxes payable      ____ Common stock
____ Long-term marketable debt securities      ____ Advertising expense
____ Unearned consulting fees      ____ Mortgage payable (due in 3 years)

Match each of the financial statement items to its proper balance sheet classification. (See E2-1, on page 79, for a list of the balance sheet classifications.) If the item would not appear on a balance sheet, use "NA."

*Compute ratios and analyze.*
(SO 4, 5), **K**

**Do it!** 2-3 The following information is available for Gerard Corporation.

|  | 2012 | 2011 |
|---|---|---|
| Current assets | $ 54,000 | $ 36,000 |
| Total assets | 240,000 | 205,000 |
| Current liabilities | 22,000 | 30,000 |
| Total liabilities | 72,000 | 100,000 |
| Net income | 80,000 | 40,000 |
| Cash provided by operating activities | 90,000 | 56,000 |
| Preferred stock dividends | 6,000 | 6,000 |
| Common stock dividends | 3,000 | 1,500 |
| Expenditures on property, plant, and equipment | 27,000 | 12,000 |
| Shares outstanding at beginning of year | 40,000 | 30,000 |
| Shares outstanding at end of year | 75,000 | 40,000 |

(a) Compute earnings per share for 2012 and 2011 for Gerard, and comment on the change. Gerard's primary competitor, Thorpe Corporation, had earnings per share of $1 per share in 2012. Comment on the difference in the ratios of the two companies.
(b) Compute the current ratio and debt to total assets ratio for each year, and comment on the changes.
(c) Compute free cash flow for each year, and comment on the changes.

*Identify financial accounting concepts and principles.*
(SO 7), **K**

**Do it!** 2-4 The following are characteristics, assumptions, principles, or constraints that guide the FASB when it creates accounting standards.

Relevance      Periodicity assumption
Faithful representation      Going concern assumption
Comparability      Cost principle
Consistency      Full disclosure principle
Monetary unit assumption      Materiality constraint
Economic entity assumption      Cost constraint

Match each item above with a description below.

1. _____ Items not easily quantified in dollar terms are not reported in the financial statements.
2. _____ Accounting information must be complete, neutral, and free from error.
3. _____ Personal transactions are not mixed with the company's transactions.
4. _____ The cost to provide information should be weighed against the benefit that users will gain from having the information available.
5. _____ A company's use of the same accounting principles from year to year.
6. _____ Assets are recorded and reported at original purchase price.
7. _____ Accounting information should help users predict future events, and should confirm or correct prior expectations.
8. _____ The life of a business can be divided into artificial segments of time.
9. _____ The reporting of all information that would make a difference to financial statement users.
10. _____ The judgment concerning whether an item's size makes it likely to influence a decision maker.
11. _____ Assumes a business will remain in operation for the foreseeable future.
12. _____ Different companies use the same accounting principles.

# Exercises

**E2-1**  The following are the major balance sheet classifications.

Current assets (CA)
Long-term investments (LTI)
Property, plant, and equipment (PPE)
Intangible assets (IA)

Current liabilities (CL)
Long-term liabilities (LTL)
Stockholders' equity (SE)

**Instructions**
Classify each of the following financial statement items taken from Inshore Corporation's balance sheet.

____ Accounts payable
____ Accounts receivable
____ Accumulated depreciation—
     equipment
____ Buildings
____ Cash
____ Interest payable
____ Goodwill

____ Income taxes payable
____ Inventory
____ Investments
____ Land
____ Mortgage payable
____ Supplies
____ Equipment
____ Prepaid rent

**E2-2**  The major balance sheet classifications are listed in E2-1 above.

**Instructions**
Classify each of the following financial statement items based upon the major balance sheet classifications listed in E2-1.

____ Prepaid advertising
____ Equipment
____ Trademarks
____ Salaries and wages payable
____ Income taxes payable
____ Retained earnings
____ Accounts receivable
____ Land held for future use

____ Patents
____ Bonds payable
____ Common stock
____ Accumulated depreciation—
     equipment
____ Unearned sales revenue
____ Inventory

**E2-3**  The following items were taken from the December 31, 2009, assets section of the Boeing Company balance sheet. (All dollars are in millions.)

| | | | |
|---|---|---|---|
| Inventories | $16,933 | Other current assets | $ 966 |
| Notes receivable—due after | | Property, plant, and | |
|   December 31, 2010 | 5,466 |   equipment | 21,579 |
| Notes receivable—due before | | Cash and cash equivalents | 9,215 |
|   December 31, 2010 | 368 | Accounts receivable | 5,785 |
| Accumulated depreciation | 12,795 | Short-term investments | 2,008 |
| Intangible and other assets | 12,528 | | |

**Instructions**
Prepare the assets section of a classified balance sheet, listing the current assets in order of their liquidity.

**E2-4**  The following information (in thousands of dollars) is available for H.J. Heinz Company—famous for ketchup and other fine food products—for the year ended April 29, 2009.

| | | | |
|---|---|---|---|
| Prepaid expenses | $ 125,765 | Inventories | $1,237,613 |
| Land | 76,193 | Buildings and equipment | 4,033,369 |
| Other current assets | 36,701 | Cash and cash equivalents | 373,145 |
| Intangible assets | 3,982,954 | Accounts receivable | 1,171,797 |
| Other noncurrent assets | 757,907 | Accumulated depreciation | 2,131,260 |

**Instructions**
Prepare the assets section of a classified balance sheet, listing the items in proper sequence and including a statement heading.

*Prepare a classified balance sheet.*
*(SO 1), AP*

**E2-5** These items are taken from the financial statements of Victory Co. at December 31, 2012.

| | |
|---|---:|
| Buildings | $105,800 |
| Accounts receivable | 12,600 |
| Prepaid insurance | 3,200 |
| Cash | 11,840 |
| Equipment | 82,400 |
| Land | 61,200 |
| Insurance expense | 780 |
| Depreciation expense | 5,300 |
| Interest expense | 2,600 |
| Common stock | 60,000 |
| Retained earnings (January 1, 2012) | 40,000 |
| Accumulated depreciation—buildings | 45,600 |
| Accounts payable | 9,500 |
| Notes payable | 93,600 |
| Accumulated depreciation—equipment | 18,720 |
| Interest payable | 3,600 |
| Service revenue | 14,700 |

**Instructions**
Prepare a classified balance sheet. Assume that $13,600 of the note payable will be paid in 2013.

*Prepare a classified balance sheet.*
*(SO 1), AP*

**E2-6** The following items were taken from the 2009 financial statements of Texas Instruments, Inc. (All dollars are in millions.)

| | | | |
|---|---:|---|---:|
| Common stock | $2,826 | Cash and cash equivalents | $1,182 |
| Prepaid expenses | 164 | Accumulated depreciation | 3,547 |
| Property, plant, and equipment | 6,705 | Accounts payable | 1,344 |
| Other current assets | 546 | Other noncurrent assets | 2,210 |
| Other current liabilities | 115 | Noncurrent liabilities | 810 |
| Long-term investments | 637 | Retained earnings | 6,896 |
| Short-term investments | 1,743 | Accounts receivable | 1,277 |
| Income taxes payable | 128 | Inventories | 1,202 |

**Instructions**
Prepare a classified balance sheet in good form as of December 31, 2009.

*Compute and interpret profitability ratio.*
*(SO 2), AP*

**E2-7** The following information is available for Callaway Golf Company for the years 2008 and 2007. (Dollars are in thousands, except share information.)

| | 2008 | 2007 |
|---|---:|---:|
| Net sales | $ 1,117,204 | $ 1,124,591 |
| Net income (loss) | 66,176 | 54,587 |
| Total assets | 855,338 | 838,078 |
| **Share information** | | |
| Shares outstanding at year-end | 64,507,000 | 66,282,000 |
| Preferred dividends | –0– | –0– |

There were 73,139,000 shares outstanding at the end of 2006.

**Instructions**
(a)  What was the company's earnings per share for each year?
(b)  Based on your findings above, how did the company's profitability change from 2007 to 2008?
(c)  Suppose the company had paid dividends on preferred stock and on common stock during the year. How would this affect your calculation in part (a)?

*Prepare financial statements.*
*(SO 1, 3, 4), AP*

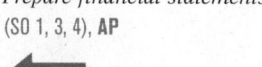

**E2-8** These financial statement items are for Whitnall Corporation at year-end, July 31, 2012.

| | |
|---|---:|
| Salaries and wages payable | $ 2,080 |
| Salaries and wages expense | 57,500 |
| Supplies expense | 15,600 |

| | |
|---|---|
| Equipment | $18,500 |
| Accounts payable | 4,100 |
| Service revenue | 66,100 |
| Rent revenue | 8,500 |
| Notes payable (due in 2015) | 1,800 |
| Common stock | 16,000 |
| Cash | 29,200 |
| Accounts receivable | 9,780 |
| Accumulated depreciation—equipment | 6,000 |
| Dividends | 4,000 |
| Depreciation expense | 4,000 |
| Retained earnings (beginning of the year) | 34,000 |

*Instructions*

(a) Prepare an income statement and a retained earnings statement for the year. Whitnall Corporation did not issue any new stock during the year.

(b) Prepare a classified balance sheet at July 31.

(c) Compute the current ratio and debt to total assets ratio.

(d) Suppose that you are the president of Crescent Equipment. Your sales manager has approached you with a proposal to sell $20,000 of equipment to Whitnall. He would like to provide a loan to Whitnall in the form of a 10%, 5-year note payable. Evaluate how this loan would change Whitnall's current ratio and debt to total assets ratio, and discuss whether you would make the sale.

**E2-9** Nordstrom, Inc. operates department stores in numerous states. Selected financial statement data (in millions of dollars) for the year ended January 31, 2009, follow.

*Compute liquidity ratios and compare results.*

(SO 4), **AP**

| | End of Year | Beginning of Year |
|---|---|---|
| Cash and cash equivalents | $ 72 | $ 358 |
| Receivables (net) | 1,942 | 1,788 |
| Merchandise inventory | 900 | 956 |
| Other current assets | 303 | 259 |
| Total current assets | $3,217 | $3,361 |
| Total current liabilities | $1,601 | $1,635 |

*Instructions*

(a) Compute working capital and the current ratio at the beginning of the year and at the end of the current year.

(b) Did Nordstrom's liquidity improve or worsen during the year?

(c) Using the data in the chapter, compare Nordstrom's liquidity with Best Buy's.

**E2-10** The chief financial officer (CFO) of Padilla Corporation requested that the accounting department prepare a preliminary balance sheet on December 30, 2012, so that the CFO could get an idea of how the company stood. He knows that certain debt agreements with its creditors require the company to maintain a current ratio of at least 2:1. The preliminary balance sheet is as follows.

*Compute liquidity measures and discuss findings.*

(SO 4), **AP**

**PADILLA CORP.**
**Balance Sheet**
**December 30, 2012**

| Current assets | | | Current liabilities | | |
|---|---|---|---|---|---|
| Cash | $25,000 | | Accounts payable | $ 20,000 | |
| Accounts receivable | 30,000 | | Salaries and wages payable | 10,000 | $ 30,000 |
| Prepaid insurance | 5,000 | $ 60,000 | Long-term liabilities | | |
| Equipment (net) | | 200,000 | Notes payable | | 80,000 |
| Total assets | | $260,000 | Total liabilities | | 110,000 |
| | | | Stockholders' equity | | |
| | | | Common stock | 100,000 | |
| | | | Retained earnings | 50,000 | 150,000 |
| | | | Total liabilities and stockholders' equity | | $260,000 |

*Instructions*

(a) Calculate the current ratio and working capital based on the preliminary balance sheet.

(b) Based on the results in (a), the CFO requested that $20,000 of cash be used to pay off the balance of the accounts payable account on December 31, 2012. Calculate the new current ratio and working capital after the company takes these actions.

(c) Discuss the pros and cons of the current ratio and working capital as measures of liquidity.

(d) Was it unethical for the CFO to take these steps?

*Compute and interpret solvency ratios.*
(SO 4, 5), **AP**

**E2-11**   The following data were taken from the 2009 and 2008 financial statements of American Eagle Outfitters. (All dollars are in thousands.)

|  | 2009 | 2008 |
|---|---|---|
| Current assets | $ 925,359 | $1,020,834 |
| Total assets | 1,963,676 | 1,867,680 |
| Current liabilities | 401,763 | 376,178 |
| Total liabilities | 554,645 | 527,216 |
| Total stockholders' equity | 1,409,031 | 1,340,464 |
| Cash provided by operating activities | 302,193 | 464,270 |
| Capital expenditures | 265,335 | 250,407 |
| Dividends paid | 82,394 | 80,796 |

*Instructions*

Perform each of the following.

(a) Calculate the debt to total assets ratio for each year.

(b) Calculate the free cash flow for each year.

(c) Discuss American Eagle's solvency in 2009 versus 2008.

(d) Discuss American Eagle's ability to finance its investment activities with cash provided by operating activities, and how any deficiency would be met.

*Identify accounting assumptions and principles.*
(SO 7), **K**

**E2-12**   Presented below are the assumptions and principles discussed in this chapter.

1. Full disclosure principle.
2. Going concern assumption.
3. Monetary unit assumption.
4. Periodicity assumption.
5. Cost principle.
6. Economic entity assumption.

*Instructions*

Identify by number the accounting assumption or principle that is described below. Do not use a number more than once.

——— (a)  Is the rationale for why plant assets are not reported at liquidation value. (*Note:* Do not use the cost principle.)

——— (b)  Indicates that personal and business record-keeping should be separately maintained.

——— (c)  Assumes that the dollar is the "measuring stick" used to report on financial performance.

——— (d)  Separates financial information into time periods for reporting purposes.

——— (e)  Measurement basis used when a reliable estimate of fair value is not available.

——— (f)  Dictates that companies should disclose all circumstances and events that make a difference to financial statement users.

*Identify the assumption or principle that has been violated.*
(SO 7), **C**

**E2-13**   Rosman Co. had three major business transactions during 2012.

(a) Reported at its fair value of $260,000 merchandise inventory with a cost of $208,000.

(b) The president of Rosman Co., Jay Rosman, purchased a truck for personal use and charged it to his expense account.

(c) Rosman Co. wanted to make its 2012 income look better, so it added 2 more weeks to the year (a 54-week year). Previous years were 52 weeks.

*Instructions*

In each situation, identify the assumption or principle that has been violated, if any, and discuss what the company should have done.

# Exercises: Set B and Challenge Exercises

Visit the book's companion website, at **www.wiley.com/college/kimmel**, and choose the Student Companion site to access Exercise Set B and Challenge Exercises.

# Problems: Set A

**P2-1A**  The following items are taken from the 2008 balance sheet of Yahoo! Inc. (All dollars are in thousands.)

*Prepare a classified balance sheet.*
(SO 1), **AP**

| | |
|---|---|
| Intangible assets | $3,926,749 |
| Common stock | 6,282,504 |
| Property and equipment, net | 1,536,181 |
| Accounts payable | 151,897 |
| Other assets | 233,989 |
| Long-term investments | 3,247,431 |
| Accounts receivable | 1,060,450 |
| Prepaid expenses and other current assets | 233,061 |
| Short-term investments | 1,159,691 |
| Retained earnings | 4,968,438 |
| Cash and cash equivalents | 2,292,296 |
| Long-term debt | 733,891 |
| Accrued expenses and other current liabilities | 1,139,894 |
| Unearned revenue—current | 413,224 |

**Instructions**

Prepare a classified balance sheet for Yahoo! Inc. as of December 31, 2008.

Tot. current assets    $4,745,498
Tot. assets    $13,689,848

**P2-2A**  These items are taken from the financial statements of Xenox Corporation for 2012.

*Prepare financial statements.*
(SO 1, 3), **AP**

| | |
|---|---|
| Retained earnings (beginning of year) | $31,000 |
| Utilities expense | 2,000 |
| Equipment | 66,000 |
| Accounts payable | 18,300 |
| Cash | 10,100 |
| Salaries and wages payable | 3,000 |
| Common stock | 12,000 |
| Dividends | 12,000 |
| Service revenue | 68,000 |
| Prepaid insurance | 3,500 |
| Maintenance and repairs expense | 1,800 |
| Depreciation expense | 3,600 |
| Accounts receivable | 11,700 |
| Insurance expense | 2,200 |
| Salaries and wages expense | 37,000 |
| Accumulated depreciation—equipment | 17,600 |

**Instructions**

Prepare an income statement, a retained earnings statement, and a classified balance sheet as of December 31, 2012.

Net income    $21,400
Tot. assets    $73,700

**P2-3A**  You are provided with the following information for Merrell Enterprises, effective as of its April 30, 2012, year-end.

*Prepare financial statements.*
(SO 1, 3), **AP**

| | |
|---|---|
| Accounts payable | $ 834 |
| Accounts receivable | 810 |
| Accumulated depreciation—equipment | 670 |
| Cash | 1,270 |
| Common stock | 900 |
| Cost of goods sold | 1,060 |

| | |
|---|---:|
| Depreciation expense | $ 335 |
| Dividends | 325 |
| Equipment | 2,420 |
| Income tax expense | 165 |
| Income taxes payable | 135 |
| Insurance expense | 210 |
| Interest expense | 400 |
| Inventory | 967 |
| Land | 3,100 |
| Mortgage payable | 3,500 |
| Notes payable | 61 |
| Prepaid insurance | 60 |
| Retained earnings (beginning) | 1,600 |
| Sales revenue | 5,100 |
| Short-term investments | 1,200 |
| Salaries and wages expense | 700 |
| Salaries and wages payable | 222 |

*Net income* $2,230
*Tot. current assets* $4,307
*Tot. assets* $9,157

*Compute ratios; comment on relative profitability, liquidity, and solvency.*

(SO 2, 4, 5), **AN**

**Instructions**

(a) Prepare an income statement and a retained earnings statement for Merrell Enterprises for the year ended April 30, 2012.

(b) Prepare a classified balance sheet for Merrell Enterprises as of April 30, 2012.

**P2-4A** Comparative financial statement data for Duran Corporation and Kiepert Corporation, two competitors, appear below. All balance sheet data are as of December 31, 2012.

| | Duran Corporation 2012 | Kiepert Corporation 2012 |
|---|---:|---:|
| Net sales | $1,800,000 | $620,000 |
| Cost of goods sold | 1,175,000 | 340,000 |
| Operating expenses | 283,000 | 98,000 |
| Interest expense | 9,000 | 3,800 |
| Income tax expense | 85,000 | 36,000 |
| Current assets | 407,200 | 190,336 |
| Plant assets (net) | 532,000 | 139,728 |
| Current liabilities | 66,325 | 33,716 |
| Long-term liabilities | 108,500 | 40,684 |
| Cash from operating activities | 138,000 | 36,000 |
| Capital expenditures | 90,000 | 20,000 |
| Dividends paid on common stock | 36,000 | 15,000 |
| Average number of shares outstanding | 80,000 | 50,000 |

**Instructions**

(a) Comment on the relative profitability of the companies by computing the net income and earnings per share for each company for 2012.

(b) Comment on the relative liquidity of the companies by computing working capital and the current ratios for each company for 2012.

(c) Comment on the relative solvency of the companies by computing the debt to total assets ratio and the free cash flow for each company for 2012.

*Compute and interpret liquidity, solvency, and profitability ratios.*

(SO 2, 4, 5), **AP**

**P2-5A** Here and on page 85 are financial statements of Batcha Company.

**BATCHA COMPANY**
**Income Statement**
**For the Year Ended December 31, 2012**

| | |
|---|---:|
| Net sales | $2,218,500 |
| Cost of goods sold | 1,012,400 |
| Selling and administrative expenses | 906,000 |
| Interest expense | 78,000 |
| Income tax expense | 69,000 |
| Net income | $ 153,100 |

**BATCHA COMPANY**
**Balance Sheet**
**December 31, 2012**

**Assets**

| | |
|---|---:|
| Current assets | |
| Cash | $    60,100 |
| Short-term investments | 84,000 |
| Accounts receivable (net) | 169,800 |
| Inventory | 145,000 |
| Total current assets | 458,900 |
| Plant assets (net) | 575,300 |
| Total assets | $1,034,200 |

**Liabilities and Stockholders' Equity**

| | |
|---|---:|
| Current liabilities | |
| Accounts payable | $  160,000 |
| Income taxes payable | 35,500 |
| Total current liabilities | 195,500 |
| Bonds payable | 200,000 |
| Total liabilities | 395,500 |
| Stockholders' equity | |
| Common stock | 350,000 |
| Retained earnings | 288,700 |
| Total stockholders' equity | 638,700 |
| Total liabilities and stockholders' equity | $1,034,200 |

Additional information: The cash provided by operating activities for 2012 was $190,800. The cash used for capital expenditures was $92,000. The cash used for dividends was $31,000. The average number of shares outstanding during the year was 50,000.

**Instructions**

(a) Compute the following values and ratios for 2012. (We provide the results from 2011 for comparative purposes.)
  (i) Working capital. (2011:    $160,500)
 (ii) Current ratio. (2011:    1.65:1)
(iii) Free cash flow. (2011:    $48,700)
(iv) Debt to total assets ratio. (2011:    31%)
 (v) Earnings per share. (2011:    $3.15)

(b) Using your calculations from part (a), discuss changes from 2011 in liquidity, solvency, and profitability.

**P2-6A** Condensed balance sheet and income statement data for Sievert Corporation are presented here and on the next page.

*Compute and interpret liquidity, solvency, and profitability ratios.*
(SO 2, 4, 5), **AP**

**SIEVERT CORPORATION**
**Balance Sheets**
**December 31**

| Assets | 2012 | 2011 |
|---|---:|---:|
| Cash | $  28,000 | $  20,000 |
| Receivables (net) | 70,000 | 62,000 |
| Other current assets | 90,000 | 73,000 |
| Long-term investments | 62,000 | 60,000 |
| Plant and equipment (net) | 510,000 | 470,000 |
| Total assets | $760,000 | $685,000 |

| Liabilities and Stockholders' Equity | | |
|---|---:|---:|
| Current liabilities | $  75,000 | $  70,000 |
| Long-term debt | 80,000 | 90,000 |
| Common stock | 330,000 | 300,000 |
| Retained earnings | 275,000 | 225,000 |
| Total liabilities and stockholders' equity | $760,000 | $685,000 |

**SIEVERT CORPORATION**
**Income Statements**
**For the Years Ended December 31**

|  | 2012 | 2011 |
|---|---|---|
| Sales | $750,000 | $680,000 |
| Cost of goods sold | 440,000 | 400,000 |
| Operating expenses (including income taxes) | 240,000 | 220,000 |
| Net income | $ 70,000 | $ 60,000 |

Additional information:

|  | | |
|---|---|---|
| Cash from operating activities | $82,000 | $56,000 |
| Cash used for capital expenditures | $45,000 | $38,000 |
| Dividends paid | $20,000 | $15,000 |
| Average number of shares outstanding | 33,000 | 30,000 |

**Instructions**

Compute these values and ratios for 2011 and 2012.

(a) Earnings per share.

(b) Working capital.

(c) Current ratio.

(d) Debt to total assets ratio.

(e) Free cash flow.

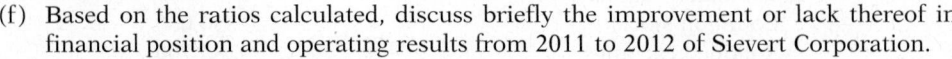 (f) Based on the ratios calculated, discuss briefly the improvement or lack thereof in financial position and operating results from 2011 to 2012 of Sievert Corporation.

*Compute ratios and compare liquidity, solvency, and profitability for two companies.*

(SO 2, 4, 5), **AP**

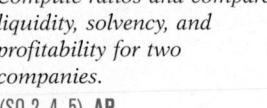

**P2-7A** Selected financial data of two competitors, Target and Wal-Mart, are presented here. (All dollars are in millions.)

|  | Target (1/31/09) | Wal-Mart (1/31/09) |
|---|---|---|
| **Income Statement Data for Year** | | |
| Net sales | $64,948 | $401,244 |
| Cost of goods sold | 44,157 | 306,158 |
| Selling and administrative expenses | 16,389 | 76,651 |
| Interest expense | 894 | 2,103 |
| Other income | 28 | 4,213 |
| Income taxes | 1,322 | 7,145 |
| Net income | $ 2,214 | $ 13,400 |

|  | Target | Wal-Mart |
|---|---|---|
| **Balance Sheet Data (End of Year)** | | |
| Current assets | $17,488 | $ 48,949 |
| Noncurrent assets | 26,618 | 114,480 |
| Total assets | $44,106 | $163,429 |
| Current liabilities | $10,512 | $ 55,390 |
| Long-term debt | 19,882 | 42,754 |
| Total stockholders' equity | 13,712 | 65,285 |
| Total liabilities and stockholders' equity | $44,106 | $163,429 |
| Cash from operating activities | $4,430 | $23,147 |
| Cash paid for capital expenditures | 3,547 | 11,499 |
| Dividends declared and paid on common stock | 465 | 3,746 |
| Average shares outstanding (millions) | 774 | 3,951 |

**Instructions**

For each company, compute these values and ratios.

(a) Working capital.

(b) Current ratio.

(c) Debt to total assets ratio.
(d) Free cash flow.
(e) Earnings per share.
(f) Compare the liquidity and solvency of the two companies.

**P2-8A** A friend of yours, Ana Gehrig, recently completed an undergraduate degree in science and has just started working with a biotechnology company. Ana tells you that the owners of the business are trying to secure new sources of financing which are needed in order for the company to proceed with development of a new health care product. Ana said that her boss told her that the company must put together a report to present to potential investors.

*Comment on the objectives and qualitative characteristics of financial reporting.*
*(SO 6, 7),* **E**
◀▬▬▭▯

Ana thought that the company should include in this package the detailed scientific findings related to the Phase I clinical trials for this product. She said, "I know that the biotech industry sometimes has only a 10% success rate with new products, but if we report all the scientific findings, everyone will see what a sure success this is going to be! The president was talking about the importance of following some set of accounting principles. Why do we need to look at some accounting rules? What they need to realize is that we have scientific results that are quite encouraging, some of the most talented employees around, and the start of some really great customer relationships. We haven't made any sales yet, but we will. We just need the funds to get through all the clinical testing and get government approval for our product. Then these investors will be quite happy that they bought in to our company early!"

*Instructions*
(a) What is accounting information? Explain to Ana what is meant by generally accepted accounting principles.
(b) Comment on how Ana's suggestions for what should be reported to prospective investors conforms to the qualitative characteristics of accounting information. Do you think that the things that Ana wants to include in the information for investors will conform to financial reporting guidelines?

# Problems: Set B

**P2-1B** The following items are from the 2009 balance sheet of Kellogg Company. (All dollars are in millions.)

*Prepare a classified balance sheet.*
*(SO 1),* **AP**

| | |
|---|---:|
| Common stock | $ 577 |
| Other assets | 5,632 |
| Notes payable—current | 44 |
| Other current assets | 221 |
| Cash and cash equivalents | 334 |
| Other long-term liabilities | 1,802 |
| Retained earnings | 1,698 |
| Accounts payable | 1,077 |
| Other current liabilities | 1,167 |
| Accounts receivable, net | 1,093 |
| Property, net | 3,010 |
| Inventories | 910 |
| Long-term debt | 4,835 |

*Instructions*
Prepare a classified balance sheet for Kellogg Company as of December 31, 2009.

Tot. current assets $2,558
Tot. assets $11,200

**P2-2B** These items are taken from the financial statements of Tilley, Inc.

*Prepare financial statements.*
*(SO 1, 3),* **AP**

| | |
|---|---:|
| Prepaid insurance | $ 1,400 |
| Equipment | 31,000 |
| Salaries and wages expense | 36,000 |
| Utilities expense | 2,100 |
| Accumulated depreciation—equipment | 8,600 |
| Accounts payable | 8,200 |
| Cash | 5,100 |

| | |
|---|---:|
| Accounts receivable | $ 4,900 |
| Salaries and wages payable | 2,000 |
| Common stock | 6,000 |
| Depreciation expense | 4,300 |
| Retained earnings (beginning) | 14,000 |
| Dividends | 2,600 |
| Service revenue | 53,000 |
| Maintenance and repairs expense | 2,600 |
| Insurance expense | 1,800 |

**Instructions**

Net income $6,200
Tot. assets $33,800

Prepare an income statement, a retained earnings statement, and a classified balance sheet as of December 31, 2012.

*Prepare financial statements.*
(SO 1, 3), **AP**

**P2-3B** You are provided with the following information for Rapp Corporation, effective as of its April 30, 2012, year-end.

| | |
|---|---:|
| Accounts payable | $ 2,100 |
| Accounts receivable | 9,150 |
| Accumulated depreciation—equipment | 6,600 |
| Depreciation expense | 2,200 |
| Cash | 21,955 |
| Common stock | 20,000 |
| Dividends | 2,800 |
| Equipment | 24,250 |
| Sales revenue | 21,450 |
| Income tax expense | 1,600 |
| Income taxes payable | 300 |
| Interest expense | 350 |
| Interest payable | 175 |
| Notes payable (due in 2016) | 5,700 |
| Prepaid rent | 380 |
| Rent expense | 760 |
| Retained earnings, beginning | 13,960 |
| Salaries and wages expense | 6,840 |

**Instructions**

Net income $9,700
Tot. current assets $31,485
Tot. assets $49,135

(a) Prepare an income statement and a retained earnings statement for Rapp Corporation for the year ended April 30, 2012.

(b) Prepare a classified balance sheet for Rapp as of April 30, 2012.

(c) Explain how each financial statement interrelates with the others.

*Compute ratios; comment on relative profitability, liquidity, and solvency.*
(SO 2, 4, 5), **AN**

**P2-4B** Comparative statement data for Al Sharif Company and Weber Company, two competitors, are presented below. All balance sheet data are as of December 31, 2012.

| | Al Sharif Company 2012 | Weber Company 2012 |
|---|---:|---:|
| Net sales | $450,000 | $890,000 |
| Cost of goods sold | 260,000 | 620,000 |
| Operating expenses | 130,000 | 59,000 |
| Interest expense | 6,000 | 10,000 |
| Income tax expense | 10,000 | 65,000 |
| Current assets | 180,000 | 700,000 |
| Plant assets (net) | 600,000 | 800,000 |
| Current liabilities | 75,000 | 300,000 |
| Long-term liabilities | 190,000 | 200,000 |
| Cash from operating activities | 46,000 | 180,000 |
| Capital expenditures | 20,000 | 50,000 |
| Dividends paid | 4,000 | 15,000 |
| Average number of shares outstanding | 200,000 | 400,000 |

**Instructions**

(a) Compute the net income and earnings per share for each company for 2012.

(b) Comment on the relative liquidity of the companies by computing working capital and the current ratio for each company for 2012.

(c) Comment on the relative solvency of the companies by computing the debt to total assets ratio and the free cash flow for each company for 2012.

**P2-5B**    The financial statements of DeVoe Company are presented here.

*Compute and interpret liquidity, solvency, and profitability ratios.*

(SO 2, 4, 5), **AP**

### DEVOE COMPANY
### Income Statement
### For the Year Ended December 31, 2012

| | |
|---|---:|
| Net sales | $700,000 |
| Cost of goods sold | 400,000 |
| Selling and administrative expenses | 150,000 |
| Interest expense | 7,800 |
| Income tax expense | 43,000 |
| Net income | $ 99,200 |

### DEVOE COMPANY
### Balance Sheet
### December 31, 2012

**Assets**

Current assets

| | |
|---|---:|
| Cash | $ 18,100 |
| Short-term investments | 34,800 |
| Accounts receivable (net) | 90,700 |
| Inventory | 155,000 |
| Total current assets | 298,600 |
| Plant assets (net) | 465,300 |
| Total assets | $763,900 |

**Liabilities and Stockholders' Equity**

Current liabilities

| | |
|---|---:|
| Accounts payable | $119,700 |
| Income taxes payable | 29,000 |
| Total current liabilities | 148,700 |
| Bonds payable | 110,000 |
| Total liabilities | 258,700 |

Stockholders' equity

| | |
|---|---:|
| Common stock | 170,000 |
| Retained earnings | 335,200 |
| Total stockholders' equity | 505,200 |
| Total liabilities and stockholders' equity | $763,900 |

| | |
|---|---:|
| Cash from operating activities | $ 71,300 |
| Capital expenditures | $ 42,000 |
| Dividends paid | $ 10,000 |
| Average number of shares outstanding | 65,000 |

*Instructions*

(a) Compute the following values and ratios for 2012. (We provide the results from 2011 for comparative purposes.)
  (i)  Current ratio. (2011:   2.4:1)
  (ii)  Working capital. (2011:   $178,000)
  (iii)  Debt to total assets ratio. (2011:   31%)
  (iv)  Free cash flow. (2011:   $13,000)
  (v)  Earnings per share. (2011:   $1.35)

(b) Using your calculations from part (a), discuss changes from 2011 in liquidity, solvency, and profitability.

*Compute and interpret liquidity, solvency, and profitability ratios.*
(SO 2, 4, 5), **AP**

**P2-6B** Condensed balance sheet and income statement data for Fellenz Corporation are presented below.

### FELLENZ CORPORATION
### Balance Sheets
### December 31

| Assets | 2012 | 2011 |
|---|---|---|
| Cash | $ 40,000 | $ 24,000 |
| Receivables (net) | 90,000 | 55,000 |
| Other current assets | 74,000 | 73,000 |
| Long-term investments | 78,000 | 60,000 |
| Plant and equipment (net) | 520,000 | 407,000 |
| Total assets | $802,000 | $619,000 |

| Liabilities and Stockholders' Equity | 2012 | 2011 |
|---|---|---|
| Current liabilities | $ 88,000 | $ 65,000 |
| Long-term debt | 90,000 | 70,000 |
| Common stock | 370,000 | 320,000 |
| Retained earnings | 254,000 | 164,000 |
| Total liabilities and stockholders' equity | $802,000 | $619,000 |

### FELLENZ CORPORATION
### Income Statements
### For the Years Ended December 31

| | 2012 | 2011 |
|---|---|---|
| Sales | $770,000 | $800,000 |
| Cost of goods sold | 420,000 | 400,000 |
| Operating expenses (including income taxes) | 200,000 | 237,000 |
| Net income | $150,000 | $163,000 |
| | | |
| Cash from operating activities | $165,000 | $178,000 |
| Cash used for capital expenditures | 85,000 | 45,000 |
| Dividends paid | 50,000 | 43,000 |
| | | |
| Average number of shares outstanding | 370,000 | 320,000 |

**Instructions**
Compute the following values and ratios for 2011 and 2012.
(a) Earnings per share.
(b) Working capital.
(c) Current ratio.
(d) Debt to total assets ratio.
(e) Free cash flow.
(f) Based on the ratios calculated, discuss briefly the improvement or lack thereof in the financial position and operating results of Fellenz from 2011 to 2012.

*Compute ratios and compare liquidity, solvency, and profitability for two companies.*
(SO 2, 4, 5), **AP**

**P2-7B** Selected financial data of two competitors, Blockbuster Inc. and Movie Gallery, Inc., in a recent year are presented below and on page 91. (All dollars are in millions.)

| | Blockbuster Inc. | Movie Gallery, Inc. |
|---|---|---|
| | Income Statement Data for Year | |
| Net sales | $ 5,524 | $2,542 |
| Cost of goods sold | 2,476 | 1,012 |
| Selling and administrative expenses | 2,755 | 1,431 |
| Interest expense | 102 | 120 |
| Other expense | 212 | 3 |
| Income tax expense (refund) | (76) | 2 |
| Net income (loss) | $    55 | $ (26) |

| | Blockbuster Inc. | Movie Gallery, Inc. |
|---|---|---|
| | Balance Sheet Data (End of Year) | |
| Current assets | $ 1,566 | $ 239 |
| Property, plant, and equipment (net) | 580 | 243 |
| Intangible assets | 835 | 297 |
| Other assets | 156 | 374 |
| Total assets | $ 3,137 | $1,153 |
| | | |
| Current liabilities | $ 1,395 | $ 268 |
| Long-term debt | 851 | 1,122 |
| Total stockholders' equity | 891 | (237) |
| Total liabilities and stockholders' equity | $ 3,137 | $1,153 |
| | | |
| Cash from operating activities | $329 | $(10) |
| Cash used for capital expenditures | 79 | 20 |
| Dividends paid | 11 | –0– |
| | | |
| Average shares outstanding | 189.0 | 31.8 |

### Instructions

For each company, compute these values and ratios.
(a) Working capital.
(b) Current ratio. (Round to two decimal places.)
(c) Debt to total assets ratio.
(d) Free cash flow.
(e) Earnings per share.
(f) Compare the liquidity, profitability, and solvency of the two companies.

**P2-8B**   Net Nanny Software International Inc., headquartered in Vancouver, specializes in Internet safety and computer security products for both the home and commercial markets. In a recent balance sheet, it reported a deficit (negative retained earnings) of US $5,678,288. It has reported only net losses since its inception. In spite of these losses, Net Nanny's common shares have traded anywhere from a high of $3.70 to a low of $0.32 on the Canadian Venture Exchange.

*Comment on the objectives and qualitative characteristics of accounting information.* (SO 6, 7), **E**

   Net Nanny's financial statements have historically been prepared in Canadian dollars. Recently, the company adopted the U.S. dollar as its reporting currency.

### Instructions

(a) What is the objective of financial reporting? How does this objective meet or not meet Net Nanny's investors' needs?
(b) Why would investors want to buy Net Nanny's shares if the company has consistently reported losses over the last few years? Include in your answer an assessment of the relevance of the information reported on Net Nanny's financial statements.
(c) Comment on how the change in reporting information from Canadian dollars to U.S. dollars likely affected the readers of Net Nanny's financial statements. Include in your answer an assessment of the comparability of the information.

# Problems: Set C

Visit the book's companion website, at **www.wiley.com/college/kimmel**, and choose the Student Companion site to access Problem Set C.

# Continuing Cookie Chronicle

(*Note:* This is a continuation of the Cookie Chronicle from Chapter 1.)

**CCC2**   After investigating the different forms of business organization, Natalie Koebel decides to operate her business as a corporation, Cookie Creations Inc., and she begins the process of getting her business running.

While at a trade show, Natalie is introduced to Gerry Richards, operations manager of "Biscuits," a national food retailer. After much discussion, Gerry asks Natalie to consider being Biscuits' major supplier of oatmeal chocolate chip cookies. He provides Natalie with the most recent copy of the financial statements of Biscuits. He expects that Natalie will need to supply Biscuits' Watertown warehouse with approximately 1,500 dozen cookies a week. Natalie is to send Biscuits a monthly invoice, and she will be paid approximately 30 days from the date the invoice is received in Biscuits' Chicago office.

Natalie is thrilled with the offer. However, she has recently read in the newspaper that Biscuits has a reputation for selling cookies and donuts with high amounts of sugar and fat, and as a result, consumer demand for the company's products has decreased.

### Instructions
Natalie has several questions. Answer the following questions for Natalie.
(a) What type of information does each financial statement provide?
(b) What financial statements would Natalie need in order to evaluate whether Biscuits will have enough cash to meet its current liabilities? Explain what to look for.
(c) What financial statements would Natalie need in order to evaluate whether Biscuits will be able to survive over a long period of time? Explain what to look for.
(d) What financial statement would Natalie need in order to evaluate Biscuits' profitability? Explain what to look for.
(e) Where can Natalie find out whether Biscuits has outstanding debt? How can Natalie determine whether Biscuits would be able to meet its interest and debt payments on any debts it has?
(f) How could Natalie determine whether Biscuits pays a dividend?
(g) In deciding whether to go ahead with this opportunity, are there other areas of concern that Natalie should be aware of?

# broadening your perspective

## Financial Reporting and Analysis

### FINANCIAL REPORTING PROBLEM: *Tootsie Roll Industries Inc.*

**BYP2-1** The financial statements of Tootsie Roll Industries, Inc., appear in Appendix A at the end of this book.

### Instructions
Answer the following questions using the financial statements and the notes to the financial statements.
(a) What were Tootsie Roll's total current assets at December 31, 2009, and December 31, 2008?
(b) Are the assets included in current assets listed in the proper order? Explain.
(c) How are Tootsie Roll's assets classified?
(d) What were Tootsie Roll's current liabilities at December 31, 2009, and December 31, 2008?

### COMPARATIVE ANALYSIS PROBLEM: *Tootsie Roll vs. Hershey*

**BYP2-2** The financial statements of The Hershey Company appear in Appendix B, following the financial statements for Tootsie Roll in Appendix A. Assume Hershey's average number of shares outstanding was 227,517,000, and Tootsie Roll's was 56,072,000.

### Instructions
(a) For each company calculate the following values for 2009.
    (1) Working capital.               (4) Free cash flow.
    (2) Current ratio.                 (5) Earnings per share.
    (3) Debt to total assets ratio
    (*Hint:* When calculating free cash flow, **do not** consider business acquisitions to be part of capital expenditures.)
(b) Based on your findings above, discuss the relative liquidity and solvency of the two companies.

## RESEARCH CASE

**BYP2-3**   The April 27, 2009, edition of the *Wall Street Journal Online* includes an article by Cari Tuna entitled "Corporate Blogs and 'Tweets' Must Keep SEC in Mind."

*Instructions*
Read the article and answer the following questions.
(a) At the time of the article, how many of the Fortune 500 companies sponsored public blogs? Of these blogs, how many had links to corporate Twitter accounts?
(b) What potential advantages might Twitter provide to companies in their efforts to communicate with investors?
(c) Why are some companies, such as Intel, wary of using Twitter and blogs to communicate to investors?
(d) What recommendations does Lisa Wood, of Foley Hoag LLP, make to companies if they use blogs or Twitter to communicate to investors?

## INTERPRETING FINANCIAL STATEMENTS

**BYP2-4**   The following information was reported by Gap, Inc. in its 2009 annual report.

|  | 2009 | 2008 | 2007 | 2006 | 2005 |
|---|---|---|---|---|---|
| Total assets (millions) | $7,985 | $7,564 | $7,838 | $ 8,544 | $ 8,821 |
| Working capital | 2,533 | 1,847 | 1,653 | $ 2,757 | $ 3,297 |
| Current ratio | 2.19:1 | 1.86:1 | 1.68:1 | 2.21:1 | 2.70:1 |
| Debt to total assets ratio | .39:1 | .42:1 | .45:1 | .39:1 | .38:1 |
| Earnings per share | $1.59 | $1.35 | $1.05 | $0.94 | $1.26 |

(a) Determine the overall percentage decrease in Gap's total assets from 2005 to 2009. What was the average decrease per year?
(b) Comment on the change in Gap's liquidity. Does working capital or the current ratio appear to provide a better indication of Gap's liquidity? What might explain the change in Gap's liquidity during this period?
(c) Comment on the change in Gap's solvency during this period.
(d) Comment on the change in Gap's profitability during this period. How might this affect your prediction about Gap's future profitability?

## FINANCIAL ANALYSIS ON THE WEB

**BYP2-5**   *Purpose:* Identify summary liquidity, solvency, and profitability information about companies, and compare this information across companies in the same industry.

*Address:*  **http://biz.yahoo.com/i**, or go to **www.wiley.com/college/kimmel**

*Steps*
1. Type in a company name, or use the index to find a company name. Choose **Profile**. Choose **Key Statistics**. Perform instruction (a) below.
2. Go back to **Profile**. Click on the company's particular industry behind the heading "Industry." Perform instructions (b), (c), and (d).

*Instructions*
Answer the following questions.
(a) What is the company's name? What was the company's current ratio and debt to equity ratio (a variation of the debt to total assets ratio)?
(b) What is the company's industry?
(c) What is the name of a competitor? What is the competitor's current ratio and its debt to equity ratio?
(d) Based on these measures: Which company is more liquid? Which company is more solvent?

**BYP2-6**   The opening story described the dramatic effect that investment bulletin boards are having on the investment world. This exercise will allow you to evaluate a bulletin board discussing a company of your choice.

*Address:*  **http://biz.yahoo.com/i**, or go to **www.wiley.com/college/kimmel**

*Steps*
1. Type in a company name, or use the index to find a company name.
2. Choose **Msgs** or **Message Board**. (for messages).
3. Read the ten most recent messages.

*Instructions*
Answer the following questions.
(a) State the nature of each of these messages (e.g., offering advice, criticizing company, predicting future results, ridiculing other people who have posted messages).
(b) For those messages that expressed an opinion about the company, was evidence provided to support the opinion?
(c) What effect do you think it would have on bulletin board discussions if the participants provided their actual names? Do you think this would be a good policy?

# Critical Thinking

## DECISION MAKING ACROSS THE ORGANIZATION

**BYP2-7**   As a financial analyst in the planning department for Lindemann Industries, Inc., you have been requested to develop some key ratios from the comparative financial statements. This information is to be used to convince creditors that Lindemann Industries, Inc. is liquid, solvent, and profitable, and that it deserves their continued support. Lenders are particularly concerned about the company's ability to continue as a going concern.
   Here are the data requested and the computations developed from the financial statements:

|                          | 2012    | 2011     |
|--------------------------|---------|----------|
| Current ratio            | 3.1     | 2.1      |
| Working capital          | Up 22%  | Down 7%  |
| Free cash flow           | Up 25%  | Up 18%   |
| Debt to total assets ratio | 0.60  | 0.70     |
| Net income               | Up 32%  | Down 8%  |
| Earnings per share       | $2.40   | $1.15    |

*Instructions*
Lindemann Industries, Inc. asks you to prepare brief comments stating how each of these items supports the argument that its financial health is improving. The company wishes to use these comments to support presentation of data to its creditors. With the class divided into groups, prepare the comments as requested, giving the implications and the limitations of each item regarding Lindemann's financial well-being.

## COMMUNICATION ACTIVITY

**BYP2-8**   T. J. Cerrillo is the chief executive officer of Tomorrow's Products. T. J. is an expert engineer but a novice in accounting.

*Instructions*
Write a letter to T. J. Cerrillo that explains (a) the three main types of ratios; (b) examples of each, how they are calculated, and what they measure; and (c) the bases for comparison in analyzing Tomorrow's Products' financial statements.

## ETHICS CASE

**BYP2-9**   At one time, Boeing closed a giant deal to acquire another manufacturer, McDonnell Douglas. Boeing paid for the acquisition by issuing shares of its own stock to the stockholders of McDonnell Douglas. In order for the deal not to be revoked, the value of Boeing's stock could not decline below a certain level for a number of months after the deal.

During the first half of the year, Boeing suffered significant cost overruns because of inefficiencies in its production methods. Had these problems been disclosed in the quarterly financial statements during the first and second quarter of the year, the company's stock most likely would have plummeted, and the deal would have been revoked. Company managers spent considerable time debating when the bad news should be disclosed. One public relations manager suggested that the company's problems be revealed on the date of either Princess Diana's or Mother Teresa's funeral, in the hope that it would be lost among those big stories that day. Instead, the company waited until October 22 of that year to announce a $2.6 billion write-off due to cost overruns. Within one week, the company's stock price had fallen 20%, but by this time the McDonnell Douglas deal could not be reversed.

*Instructions*
Answer the following questions.
(a) Who are the stakeholders in this situation?
(b) What are the ethical issues?
(c) What assumptions or principles of accounting are relevant to this case?
(d) Do you think it is ethical to try to "time" the release of a story so as to diminish its effect?
(e) What would you have done if you were the chief executive officer of Boeing?
(f) Boeing's top management maintains that it did not have an obligation to reveal its problems during the first half of the year. What implications does this have for investors and analysts who follow Boeing's stock?

## "ALL ABOUT YOU" ACTIVITY

**BYP2-10** Every company needs to plan in order to move forward. Its top management must consider where it wants the company to be in three to five years. Like a company, you need to think about where you want to be three to five years from now, and you need to start taking steps now in order to get there.

*Instructions*
Provide responses to each of the following items.
(a) Where would you like to be working in three to five years? Describe your plan for getting there by identifying between five and 10 specific steps that you need to take in order to get there.
(b) In order to get the job you want, you will need a résumé. Your résumé is the equivalent of a company's annual report. It needs to provide relevant and reliable information about your past accomplishments so that employers can decide whether to "invest" in you. Do a search on the Internet to find a good résumé format. What are the basic elements of a résumé?
(c) A company's annual report provides information about a company's accomplishments. In order for investors to use the annual report, the information must be reliable; that is, users must have faith that the information is accurate and believable. How can you provide assurance that the information on your résumé is reliable?
(d) Prepare a résumé assuming that you have accomplished the five to 10 specific steps you identified in part (a). Also, provide evidence that would give assurance that the information is reliable.

## FASB CODIFICATION ACTIVITY

**BYP2-11** If your school has a subscription to the FASB Codification, go to **http://aaahq.org/ ascLogin.cfm** to log in and prepare responses to the following.

*Instructions*
(a) Access the glossary ("Master Glossary") at the FASB Codification website to answer the following.
(1) What is the definition of current assets?
(2) What is the definition of current liabilities?
(b) A company wants to offset its accounts payable against its cash account and show a cash amount net of accounts payable on its balance sheet. Identify the criteria (found in the FASB Codification) under which a company has the right of set off. Does the company have the right to offset accounts payable against the cash account?

## Answers to Insight and Accounting Across the Organization Questions

**p. 60 Can a Company Be Too Liquid?  Q:** What can various company managers do to ensure that working capital is managed efficiently to maximize net income?  **A:** Marketing and sales managers must understand that by extending generous repayment terms, they are expanding the company's receivables balance and slowing the company's cash flow. Production managers must strive to minimize the amount of excess inventory on hand. Managers must coordinate efforts to speed up the collection of receivables, while also ensuring that the company pays its payables on time but never too early.

**p. 61 When Debt Is Good  Q:** Discuss the difference in the debt to total assets ratio of Microsoft and General Motors.  **A:** Microsoft has a very low debt to total assets ratio. The company is in a rapidly changing industry and thus should try to minimize the risk associated with increased debt. Also, because Microsoft generates significant amounts of cash and has minimal needs for large investments in plant assets, it does not need to borrow a lot of cash. General Motors needs to make huge investments in plant assets, and it has a very large credit operation. Thus, it has large borrowing needs.

**p. 64 The Korean Discount  Q:** What is meant by the phrase "make the country's businesses more transparent"? Why would increasing transparency spur economic growth?  **A:** Transparency refers to the extent to which outsiders have knowledge regarding a company's financial performance and financial position. If a company lacks transparency, its financial reports do not adequately inform investors of critical information that is needed to make investment decisions. If corporate transparency is increased, investors will be more willing to supply the financial capital that businesses need in order to grow, which would spur the country's economic growth.

**p. 65 What Do These Companies Have in Common?  Q:** What problems might Best Buy's year-end create for analysts?  **A:** First, if Best Buy's competitors use a different year-end, then when you compare their financial results, you are not comparing performance over the same period of time or financial position at the same point in time. Also, by not picking a particular date, the number of weeks in Best Buy's fiscal year will change. For example, fiscal years 2008 and 2009 had 52 weeks, but fiscal year 2007 had 53 weeks.

## Answers to Self-Test Questions

**1.** d  **2.** a  **3.** c  **4.** c  **5.** b  **6.** a  **7.** c  **8.** b  **9.** d  **10.** d  **11.** a  **12.** a  **13.** c  **14.** c  **15.** b

# IFRS   A Look at IFRS

The classified balance sheet, although generally required internationally, contains certain variations in format when reporting under IFRS.

## KEY POINTS

- IFRS recommends but does not require the use of the title "statement of financial position" rather than balance sheet.
- The format of statement of financial position information is often presented differently under IFRS. Although no specific format is required, most companies that follow IFRS present statement of financial position information in this order:
  - Noncurrent assets
  - Current assets
  - Equity
  - Noncurrent liabilities
  - Current liabilities
- IFRS requires a classified statement of financial position except in very limited situations. IFRS follows the same guidelines as this textbook for distinguishing between current and noncurrent assets and liabilities.
- Under IFRS, current assets are usually listed in the reverse order of liquidity. For example, under GAAP cash is listed first, but under IFRS it is listed last.
- Some companies report the subtotal *net assets*, which equals total assets minus total liabilities. See, for example, the statement of financial position of Zetar plc in Appendix C.

- IFRS has many differences in terminology that you will notice in this textbook. For example, in the sample statement of financial position illustrated below, notice in the investment category that stock is called shares, and in the equity section common stock is called share capital–ordinary.

---

**FRANKLIN CORPORATION**
Statement of Financial Position
October 31, 2012

**Assets**

| | | | |
|---|--:|--:|--:|
| **Intangible assets** | | | |
| Patents | | | $ 3,100 |
| **Property, plant, and equipment** | | | |
| Land | | $10,000 | |
| Office equipment | $24,000 | | |
| Less: Accumulated depreciation | 5,000 | 19,000 | 29,000 |
| **Long-term investments** | | | |
| Investment in shares of Walters Corp. | | 5,200 | |
| Investment in real estate | | 2,000 | 7,200 |
| **Current assets** | | | |
| Prepaid insurance | | 400 | |
| Supplies | | 2,100 | |
| Inventories | | 3,000 | |
| Notes receivable | | 1,000 | |
| Accounts receivable | | 7,000 | |
| Short-term investments | | 2,000 | |
| Cash | | 6,600 | 22,100 |
| Total assets | | | $61,400 |

**Equity and Liabilities**

| | | | |
|---|--:|--:|--:|
| **Equity** | | | |
| Share capital—ordinary | | $20,000 | |
| Retained earnings | | 14,050 | $34,050 |
| **Non-current liabilities** | | | |
| Mortgage note payable | | 10,000 | |
| Notes payable | | 1,300 | 11,300 |
| **Current liabilities** | | | |
| Notes payable | | 11,000 | |
| Accounts payable | | 2,100 | |
| Salaries payable | | 1,600 | |
| Unearned revenue | | 900 | |
| Interest payable | | 450 | 16,050 |
| Total equity and liabilities | | | $61,400 |

---

- Both IFRS and GAAP require disclosures about (1) accounting policies followed, (2) judgments that management has made in the process of applying the entity's accounting policies, and (3) the key assumptions and estimation uncertainty that could result in a material adjustment to the carrying amounts of assets and liabilities within the next financial year.
- Comparative prior-period information must be presented and financial statements must be prepared annually.
- Both GAAP and IFRS are increasing the use of fair value to report assets. However, at this point IFRS has adopted it more broadly. As examples, under IFRS companies can apply fair value to property, plant, and equipment; natural resources; and in some cases intangible assets.
- Recently, the IASB and FASB completed the first phase of a jointly created conceptual framework. In this first phase, they agreed on the objective of financial reporting and a common set of desired qualitative characteristics. These were presented in the Chapter 2 discussion.

- The monetary unit assumption is part of each framework. However, the unit of measure will vary depending on the currency used in the country in which the company is incorporated (e.g., Chinese yuan, Japanese yen, and British pound).
- The economic entity assumption is also part of each framework although some cultural differences result in differences in its application. For example, in Japan many companies have formed alliances that are so strong that they act similar to related corporate divisions although they are not actually part of the same company.

## LOOKING TO THE FUTURE

The IASB and the FASB are working on a project to converge their standards related to financial statement presentation. A key feature of the proposed framework is that each of the statements will be organized in the same format, to separate an entity's financing activities from its operating and investing activities and, further, to separate financing activities into transactions with owners and creditors. Thus, the same classifications used in the statement of financial position would also be used in the income statement and the statement of cash flows. The project has three phases. You can follow the joint financial presentation project at the following link: *http://www.fasb.org/project/financial_statement_presentation.shtml.*

The IASB and the FASB face a difficult task in attempting to update, modify, and complete a converged conceptual framework. For example, how do companies choose between information that is highly relevant but difficult to verify versus information that is less relevant but easy to verify? How do companies define control when developing a definition of an asset? Is a liability the future sacrifice itself or the obligation to make the sacrifice? Should a single measurement method, such as historical cost or fair value, be used, or does it depend on whether it is an asset or liability that is being measured? It appears that the new document will be a significant improvement over its predecessors and will lead to principle-based standards, which will help financial statement users make better decisions.

## IFRS Self-Test Questions

1. Which of the following statements is *false*?
   (a) The monetary unit assumption is used under IFRS.
   (b) Under IFRS, companies sometimes net liabilities against assets to report "net assets."
   (c) The FASB and IASB are working on a joint conceptual framework project.
   (d) Under IFRS, the statement of financial position is usually referred to as the statement of assets and equity.
2. A company has purchased a tract of land and expects to build a production plant on the land in approximately 5 years. During the 5 years before construction, the land will be idle. Under IFRS, the land should be reported as:
   (a) land expense.
   (b) property, plant, and equipment.
   (c) an intangible asset.
   (d) a long-term investment.
3. Current assets under IFRS are listed generally:
   (a) by importance.
   (b) in the reverse order of their expected conversion to cash.
   (c) by longevity.
   (d) alphabetically.
4. Companies that use IFRS:
   (a) may report all their assets on the statement of financial position at fair value.
   (b) may offset assets against liabilities and show net assets and net liabilities on their statement of financial positions, rather than the underlying detailed line items.
   (c) may report noncurrent assets before current assets on the statement of financial position.
   (d) do not have any guidelines as to what should be reported on the statement of financial position.
5. Companies that follow IFRS to prepare a statement of financial position generally use the following order of classification:
   (a) current assets, current liabilities, noncurrent assets, noncurrent liabilities, equity.
   (b) noncurrent assets, noncurrent liabilities, current assets, current liabilities, equity.
   (c) noncurrent assets, current assets, equity, noncurrent liabilities, current liabilities.
   (d) equity, noncurrent assets, current assets, noncurrent liabilities, current liabilities.

## IFRS Concepts and Application

**IFRS2–1**   In what ways does the format of a statement of financial of position under IFRS often differ from a balance sheet presented under GAAP?

**IFRS2–2**   Do the IFRS and GAAP conceptual frameworks differ in terms of the objective of financial reporting? Explain.

**IFRS2–3**   What terms commonly used under IFRS are synonymous with common stock and balance sheet?

**IFRS2–4**   The statement of financial position for Diaz Company includes the following accounts: Accounts Receivable £12,500; Prepaid Insurance £3,600; Cash £15,400; Supplies £5,200; and Short-Term Investments £6,700. Prepare the current assets section of the statement of financial position, listing the accounts in proper sequence.

**IFRS2–5**   Zurich Company recently received the following information related to the company's December 31, 2012, statement of financial position.

| | | | |
|---|---|---|---|
| Inventories | CHF 2,900 | Short-term investments | CHF 120 |
| Cash | 13,400 | Accumulated depreciation | 5,700 |
| Equipment | 21,700 | Accounts receivable | 4,300 |
| Investments in ordinary shares (long-term) | 6,500 | | |

Prepare the assets section of the company's classified statement of financial position.

**IFRS2–6**   The following information is available for Karr Bowling Alley at December 31, 2012.

| | | | |
|---|---|---|---|
| Buildings | $128,800 | Share Capital—Ordinary | $100,000 |
| Accounts Receivable | 14,520 | Retained Earnings | 15,000 |
| Prepaid Insurance | 4,680 | Accumulated Depreciation—Buildings | 42,600 |
| Cash | 18,040 | Accounts Payable | 12,300 |
| Equipment | 62,400 | Notes Payable | 97,780 |
| Land | 64,000 | Accumulated Depreciation—Equipment | 18,720 |
| Insurance Expense | 780 | Interest Payable | 2,600 |
| Depreciation Expense | 7,360 | Bowling Revenues | 14,180 |
| Interest Expense | 2,600 | | |

Prepare a classified statement of financial position; assume that $13,900 of the notes payable will be paid in 2013.

**IFRS2–7**   Brian Hopkins is interested in comparing the liquidity and solvency of a U.S. software company with a Chinese competitor. Is this possible if the two companies report using different currencies?

## INTERNATIONAL COMPARATIVE ANALYSIS PROBLEM: *Tootsie Roll vs. Zetar plc*

**IFRS2–8**   The financial statements of Zetar plc are presented in Appendix C. The company's complete annual report, including the notes to its financial statements, is available at **www.zetarplc.com**.

*Instructions*
Identify five differences in the format of the statement of financial position used by Zetar plc compared to a company, such as Tootsie Roll, that follows GAAP. (Tootsie Roll's financial statements are available in Appendix A.)

### Answers to IFRS Self-Test Questions

**1.** d   **2.** d   **3.** b   **4.** c   **5.** c

✔ Remember to go back to the navigator box on the chapter opening page and check off your completed work.

# chapter 3

# THE ACCOUNTING INFORMATION SYSTEM

## ✔ the navigator

- Scan **Study Objectives** ◯
- Read **Feature Story** ◯
- Scan **Preview** ◯
- Read **Text and Answer** **Do it!**
  p. 110 ◯  p. 116 ◯  p. 119 ◯  p. 128 ◯
- Work **Using the Decision Toolkit** ◯
- Review **Summary of Study Objectives** ◯
- Work **Comprehensive** **Do it!** p. 133 ◯
- Answer **Self-Test Questions** ◯
- Complete **Assignments** ◯
- Go to **WileyPLUS** for practice and tutorials ◯
- 🌐 Read **A Look at IFRS** p. 159 ◯

## study objectives

**After studying this chapter, you should be able to:**

1 Analyze the effect of business transactions on the basic accounting equation.
2 Explain what an account is and how it helps in the recording process.
3 Define debits and credits and explain how they are used to record business transactions.
4 Identify the basic steps in the recording process.
5 Explain what a journal is and how it helps in the recording process.
6 Explain what a ledger is and how it helps in the recording process.
7 Explain what posting is and how it helps in the recording process.
8 Explain the purposes of a trial balance.
9 Classify cash activities as operating, investing, or financing.

✔ the navigator

How organized are you financially? Take a short quiz. Answer *yes* or *no* to each question:

- Does your wallet contain so many cash machine receipts that you've been declared a walking fire hazard?

- Is your wallet such a mess that it is often faster to fish for money in the crack of your car seat than to dig around in your wallet?

- Was Steve Nash playing high school basketball the last time you balanced your bank account?

- Have you ever been tempted to burn down your house so you don't have to try to find all of the receipts and records that you need to fill out your tax returns?

**ACCIDENTS HAPPEN**

If you think it is hard to keep track of the many transactions that make up *your* life, imagine what it is like for a major corporation like Fidelity Investments. Fidelity is one of the largest mutual fund management firms in the world. If you had your life savings invested at Fidelity Investments, you might be just slightly displeased if, when you called to find out your balance, the representative said, "You know, I kind of remember someone with a name like yours sending us some money—now what did we do with that?"

To ensure the accuracy of your balance and the security of your funds, Fidelity Investments, like all other companies large and small, relies on a sophisticated accounting information system. That's not to say that Fidelity or any other company is error-free. In fact, if you've ever really messed up your checkbook register, you may take some comfort from one accountant's mistake at Fidelity Investments. The accountant failed to include a minus sign while doing a calculation, making what was actually a $1.3 billion loss look like a $1.3 billion gain—yes, *billion!* Fortunately, like most accounting errors, it was detected before any real harm was done.

No one expects that kind of mistake at a company like Fidelity, which has sophisticated computer systems and top investment managers. In explaining the mistake to shareholders, a spokesperson wrote, "Some people have asked how, in this age of technology, such a mistake could be made. While many of our processes are computerized, accounting systems are complex and dictate that some steps must be handled manually by our managers and accountants, and people can make mistakes."

✓ the navigator

---

**INSIDE CHAPTER 3 . . .**

As indicated in the Feature Story, a reliable information system is a necessity for any company. The purpose of this chapter is to explain and illustrate the features of an accounting information system. The organization and content of the chapter are as follows.

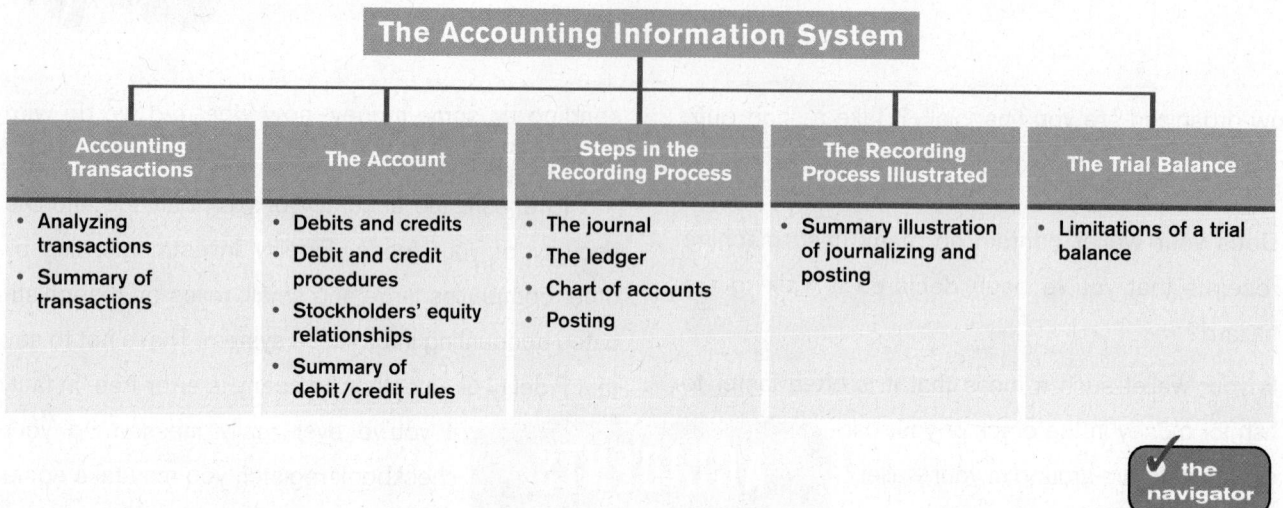

## The Accounting Information System

The system of collecting and processing transaction data and communicating financial information to decision makers is known as the **accounting information system**. Factors that shape these systems include: the nature of the company's business, the types of transactions, the size of the company, the volume of data, and the information demands of management and others.

Most businesses use computerized accounting systems—sometimes referred to as electronic data processing (EDP) systems. These systems handle all the steps involved in the recording process, from initial data entry to preparation of the financial statements. In order to remain competitive, companies continually improve their accounting systems to provide accurate and timely data for decision making. For example, in a recent annual report, Tootsie Roll states, "We also invested in additional processing and data storage hardware during the year. We view information technology as a key strategic tool, and are committed to deploying leading edge technology in this area." In addition, many companies have upgraded their accounting information systems in response to the requirements of Sarbanes-Oxley.

In this chapter, we focus on a manual accounting system because the accounting concepts and principles do not change whether a system is computerized or manual, and manual systems are easier to illustrate.

## Accounting Transactions

To use an accounting information system, you need to know which economic events to recognize (record). Not all events are recorded and reported in the financial statements. For example, suppose General Motors hired a new employee or purchased a new computer. Are these events entered in its accounting records? The first event would not be recorded, but the second event would. We call economic events that require recording in the financial statements **accounting transactions**.

An accounting transaction occurs when assets, liabilities, or stockholders' equity items change as a result of some economic event. The purchase of a computer by General Motors, the payment of rent by Microsoft, and the sale of a multi-day guided trip by Sierra Corporation are examples of events that change a company's assets, liabilities, or stockholders' equity. Illustration 3-1 summarizes the decision process companies use to decide whether or not to record economic events.

**Illustration 3-1**
Transaction identification
process

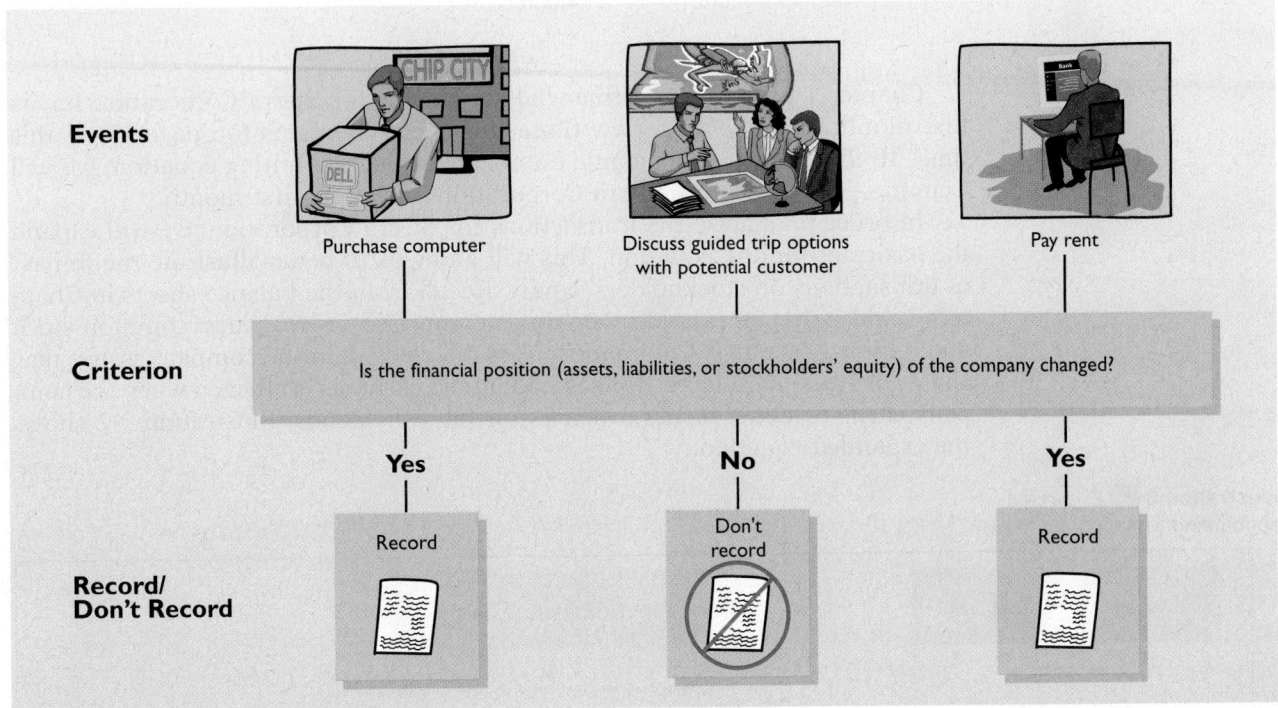

## ANALYZING TRANSACTIONS

In Chapter 1, you learned the basic accounting equation:

**study objective** **1**

Analyze the effect of
business transactions
on the basic accounting
equation.

$$\textbf{Assets = Liabilities + Stockholders' Equity}$$

In this chapter, you will learn how to analyze transactions in terms of their effect on assets, liabilities, and stockholders' equity. **Transaction analysis** is the process of identifying the specific effects of economic events on the accounting equation.

The accounting equation must always balance. Each transaction has a dual (double-sided) effect on the equation. For example, if an individual asset is increased, there must be a corresponding:

Decrease in another asset, *or*

Increase in a specific liability, *or*

Increase in stockholders' equity.

Two or more items could be affected when an asset is increased. For example, if a company purchases a computer for $10,000 by paying $6,000 in cash and signing a note for $4,000, one asset (equipment) increases $10,000, another asset (cash) decreases $6,000, and a liability (notes payable) increases $4,000.

The result is that the accounting equation remains in balance—assets increased by a net $4,000 and liabilities increased by $4,000, as shown below.

| Assets | = | Liabilities | + | Stockholders' Equity |
|---|---|---|---|---|
| +$10,000 | | +$4,000 | | |
| − 6,000 | | | | |
| $ 4,000 | = | $4,000 | | |

Chapter 1 presented the financial statements for Sierra Corporation for its first month. You should review those financial statements (on page 17) at this time. To illustrate how economic events affect the accounting equation, we will examine events affecting Sierra Corporation during its first month.

In order to analyze the transactions for Sierra Corporation, we will expand the basic accounting equation. This will allow us to better illustrate the impact of transactions on stockholders' equity. Recall from the balance sheets in Chapters 1 and 2 that stockholders' equity is comprised of two parts: common stock and retained earnings. Common stock is affected when the company issues new shares of stock in exchange for cash. Retained earnings is affected when the company earns revenue, incurs expenses, or pays dividends. Illustration 3-2 shows the expanded equation.

**Illustration 3-2** Expanded accounting equation

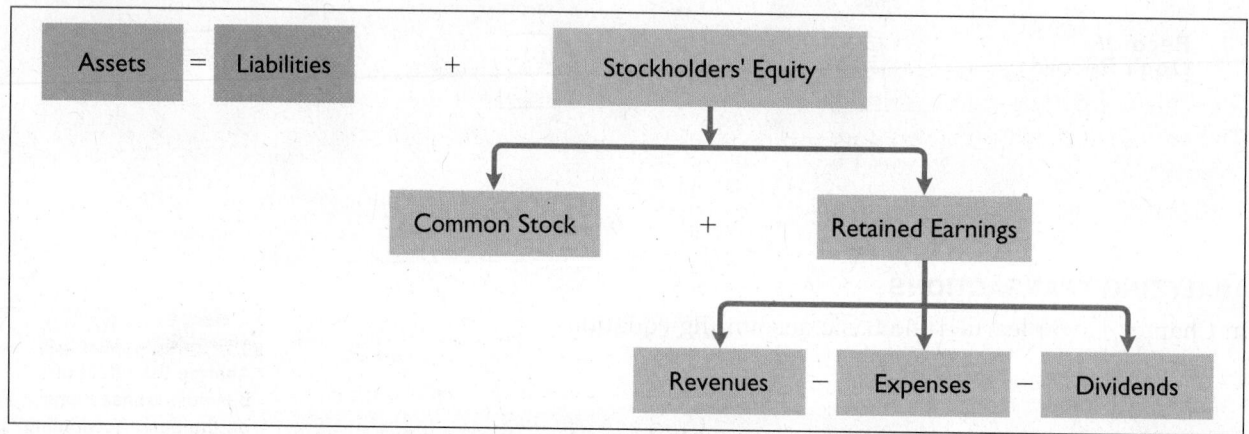

If you are tempted to skip ahead after you've read a few of the following transaction analyses, don't do it. Each has something unique to teach, something you'll need later. (We assure you that we've kept them to the minimum needed!)

**EVENT (1). INVESTMENT OF CASH BY STOCKHOLDERS.** On October 1, cash of $10,000 is invested in the business by investors (primarily your friends and family) in exchange for $10,000 of common stock. This event is an accounting transaction because it results in an increase in both assets and stockholders' equity.

| Basic Analysis | The asset Cash is increased $10,000, and stockholders' equity (specifically Common Stock) is increased $10,000. |
|---|---|

| Equation Analysis | | Assets | = | Liabilities | + | Stockholders' Equity | |
|---|---|---|---|---|---|---|---|
| | | Cash | = | | | Common Stock | |
| | (1) | +$10,000 | = | | | +$10,000 | Issued stock |

The equation is in balance after the issuance of common stock. Keeping track of the source of each change in stockholders' equity is essential for later accounting activities. In particular, items recorded in the revenue and expense columns are used for the calculation of net income.

**EVENT (2). NOTE ISSUED IN EXCHANGE FOR CASH.** On October 1, Sierra borrowed $5,000 from Castle Bank by signing a 3-month, 12%, $5,000 note payable. This transaction results in an equal increase in assets and liabilities. The specific effect of this transaction and the cumulative effect of the first two transactions are:

| Basic Analysis | The asset Cash is increased $5,000, and the liability Notes Payable is increased $5,000. | | | |
|---|---|---|---|---|
| | **Assets** = | **Liabilities** + | **Stockholders' Equity** | |
| | Cash = | Notes Payable + | Common Stock | |
| Equation Analysis | $10,000 | | $10,000 | |
| (2) | +5,000 | +$5,000 | | |
| | $15,000 = | $5,000 + | $10,000 | |
| | | $15,000 | | |

Total assets are now $15,000, and liabilities plus stockholders' equity also total $15,000.

**EVENT (3). PURCHASE OF OFFICE EQUIPMENT FOR CASH.** On October 2, Sierra purchased equipment by paying $5,000 cash to Superior Equipment Sales Co. This event is a transaction because an equal increase and decrease in Sierra's assets occur.

| Basic Analysis | The asset Equipment is increased $5,000; the asset Cash is decreased $5,000. | | | | | |
|---|---|---|---|---|---|---|
| | **Assets** | | = | **Liabilities** + | **Stockholders' Equity** | |
| | Cash + | Equipment | = | Notes Payable + | Common Stock | |
| Equation Analysis | $15,000 | | | $5,000 | $10,000 | |
| (3) | −5,000 | +$5,000 | | | | |
| | $10,000 + | $5,000 | = | $5,000 + | $10,000 | |
| | $15,000 | | | $15,000 | | |

The total assets are now $15,000, and liabilities plus stockholders' equity also total $15,000.

**EVENT (4). RECEIPT OF CASH IN ADVANCE FROM CUSTOMER.** On October 2, Sierra received a $1,200 cash advance from R. Knox, a client. This event is a transaction because Sierra received cash (an asset) for guide services for multi-day trips that are expected to be completed by Sierra in the future. Although Sierra received cash, **it does not record revenue until it has performed the work**. In some industries, such as the magazine and airline industries, customers are expected to prepay. These companies have a liability to the customer until they deliver the magazines or provide the flight. When the company eventually provides the product or service, it records the revenue.

Since Sierra received cash prior to performance of the service, Sierra has a liability for the work due.

| Basic Analysis | The asset Cash is increased $1,200; the liability Unearned Service Revenue is increased $1,200 because the service has not been provided yet. That is, when an advance payment is received, an unearned revenue (a liability) should be recorded in order to recognize the obligation that exists. |
|---|---|

**Equation Analysis**

| | Assets | | | = | Liabilities | | | + | Stockholders' Equity |
|---|---|---|---|---|---|---|---|---|---|
| | Cash | + | Equipment | = | Notes Payable | + | Unearned Service Revenue | + | Common Stock |
| | $10,000 | | $5,000 | | $5,000 | | | | $10,000 |
| (4) | +1,200 | | | | | | +$1,200 | | |
| | $11,200 | + | $5,000 | = | $5,000 | + | $1,200 | + | $10,000 |

$16,200     $16,200

**EVENT (5). SERVICES PROVIDED FOR CASH.** On October 3, Sierra received $10,000 in cash from Copa Company for guide services performed for a corporate event. This event is a transaction because Sierra received an asset (cash) in exchange for services.

Guide service is the principal revenue-producing activity of Sierra. **Revenue increases stockholders' equity.** This transaction, then, increases both assets and stockholders' equity.

| Basic Analysis | The asset Cash is increased $10,000; the revenue Service Revenue is increased $10,000. |
|---|---|

**Equation Analysis**

| | Assets | | | = | Liabilities | | | + | Stockholders' Equity | | | | | |
|---|---|---|---|---|---|---|---|---|---|---|---|---|---|---|
| | Cash | + | Equipment | = | Notes Pay. | + | Unearned Serv. Rev. | + | Common Stock | + | Rev. | − | Exp. | − Div. |
| | $11,200 | | $5,000 | | $5,000 | | $1,200 | | $10,000 | | | | | |
| (5) | +10,000 | | | | | | | | | | +$10,000 | | | Service Revenue |
| | $21,200 | + | $5,000 | = | $5,000 | + | $1,200 | + | $10,000 | + | $10,000 | | | |

$26,200     $26,200

Often companies provide services "on account." That is, they provide service for which they are paid at a later date. Revenue, however, is earned when services are performed. Therefore, revenues would increase when services are performed, even though cash has not been received. Instead of receiving cash, the company receives a different type of asset, an **account receivable**. Accounts receivable represent the right to receive payment at a later date. Suppose that Sierra had provided these services on account rather than for cash. This event would be reported using the accounting equation as:

| Assets | = | Liabilities | + | Stockholders' Equity |
|---|---|---|---|---|
| Accounts Receivable | = | | | Revenues |
| +$10,000 | | | | +$10,000 Service Revenue |

Later, when Sierra collects the $10,000 from the customer, Accounts Receivable declines by $10,000, and Cash increases by $10,000.

| Assets | | = | Liabilities | + | Stockholders' Equity |
|---|---|---|---|---|---|
| Cash | Accounts Receivable | | | | |
| +$10,000 | −$10,000 | | | | |

Note that in this case, revenues are not affected by the collection of cash. Instead we record an exchange of one asset (Accounts Receivable) for a different asset (Cash).

**EVENT (6). PAYMENT OF RENT.** On October 3, Sierra Corporation paid its office rent for the month of October in cash, $900. This rent payment is a transaction because it results in a decrease in an asset, cash.

Rent is an expense incurred by Sierra Corporation in its effort to generate revenues. **Expenses decrease stockholders' equity.** Sierra records the rent payment by decreasing cash and increasing expenses to maintain the balance of the accounting equation.

| Basic Analysis | The expense account Rent Expense is increased $900 because the payment pertains only to the current month; the asset Cash is decreased $900. |
|---|---|

**Equation Analysis**

| | Assets | | | = | Liabilities | | | + | Stockholders' Equity | | | | |
|---|---|---|---|---|---|---|---|---|---|---|---|---|---|
| | Cash | + | Equipment | = | Notes Pay. | + | Unearned Serv. Rev. | + | Common Stock | + | Retained Earnings Rev. | − Exp. | − Div. |
| | $21,200 | | $5,000 | | $5,000 | | $1,200 | | $10,000 | | $10,000 | | |
| (6) | −900 | | | | | | | | | | | −$900 | Rent Expense |
| | $20,300 | + | $5,000 | = | $5,000 | + | $1,200 | + | $10,000 | + | $10,000 | − $900 | |
| | | $25,300 | | | | | | | | $25,300 | | | |

**EVENT (7). PURCHASE OF INSURANCE POLICY FOR CASH.** On October 4, Sierra paid $600 for a one-year insurance policy that will expire next year on September 30. Payments of expenses that will benefit more than one accounting period are identified as assets called prepaid expenses or prepayments.

| Basic Analysis | The asset Cash is decreased $600. The asset Prepaid Insurance is increased $600. |
|---|---|

**Equation Analysis**

| | Assets | | | | | = | Liabilities | | | + | Stockholders' Equity | | | |
|---|---|---|---|---|---|---|---|---|---|---|---|---|---|---|
| | Cash | + | Prepaid Insurance | + | Equipment | = | Notes Pay. | + | Unearned Serv. Rev. | + | Common Stock | + | Retained Earnings Rev. − Exp. − Div. | |
| | $20,300 | | | | $5,000 | | $5,000 | | $1,200 | | $10,000 | | $10,000 $900 | |
| (7) | −600 | | +$600 | | | | | | | | | | | |
| | $19,700 | + | $600 | + | $5,000 | = | $5,000 | + | $1,200 | + | $10,000 | + | $10,000 − $900 | |
| | | | $25,300 | | | | | | | | $25,300 | | | |

The balance in total assets did not change; one asset account decreased by the same amount that another increased.

**EVENT (8). PURCHASE OF SUPPLIES ON ACCOUNT.** On October 5, Sierra purchased supplies on account from Aero Supply for $2,500. In this case, "on account" means that the company receives goods or services that it will pay for at a later date.

| Basic Analysis | The asset Supplies is increased $2,500; the liability Accounts Payable is increased $2,500. |
| --- | --- |

**Equation Analysis**

| | | Assets | | | = | Liabilities | | | + | Stockholders' Equity | | | |
| --- | --- | --- | --- | --- | --- | --- | --- | --- | --- | --- | --- | --- | --- |
| | | | Prepd. | Equip- | | Notes | Accounts | Unearned | | Common | | Retained Earnings | |
| | Cash + | Supplies + | Insur. + | ment = | | Pay. + | Payable + | Serv. Rev. + | | Stock + | Rev. − | Exp. − | Div. |
| | $19,700 | | $600 | $5,000 | | $5,000 | | $1,200 | | $10,000 | $10,000 | $900 | |
| (8) | | +$2,500 | | | | | +$2,500 | | | | | | |
| | $19,700 + | $2,500 + | $600 + | $5,000 = | | $5,000 + | $2,500 + | $1,200 + | | $10,000 + | $10,000 − | $900 | |
| | | $27,800 | | | | | | $27,800 | | | | | |

**EVENT (9). HIRING OF NEW EMPLOYEES.** On October 9, Sierra hired four new employees to begin work on October 15. Each employee will receive a weekly salary of $500 for a five-day work week, payable every two weeks. Employees will receive their first paychecks on October 26. On the date Sierra hires the employees, there is no effect on the accounting equation because the assets, liabilities, and stockholders' equity of the company have not changed.

| Basic Analysis | An accounting transaction has not occurred. There is only an agreement that the employees will begin work on October 15. (See Event (11) for the first payment.) |
| --- | --- |

**EVENT (10). PAYMENT OF DIVIDEND.** On October 20, Sierra paid a $500 dividend. **Dividends** are a reduction of stockholders' equity but not an expense. Dividends are not included in the calculation of net income. Instead, a dividend is a distribution of the company's assets to its stockholders.

| Basic Analysis | The dividends account is increased $500; the asset Cash is decreased $500. |
| --- | --- |

**Equation Analysis**

| | | Assets | | | = | Liabilities | | | + | Stockholders' Equity | | | |
| --- | --- | --- | --- | --- | --- | --- | --- | --- | --- | --- | --- | --- | --- |
| | | Sup- | Prepd. | Equip- | | Notes | Accts. | Unearned | | Common | | Retained Earnings | |
| | Cash + | plies + | Insur. + | ment = | | Pay. + | Pay. + | Serv. Rev. + | | Stock + | Rev. − | Exp. − | Div. |
| | $19,700 | $2,500 | $600 | $5,000 | | $5,000 | $2,500 | $1,200 | | $10,000 | $10,000 | $900 | |
| (10) | −500 | | | | | | | | | | | | − $500 |
| | $19,200 + | $2,500 + | $600 + | $5,000 = | | $5,000 + | $2,500 + | $1,200 + | | $10,000 + | $10,000 − | $900 − | $500 |
| | | $27,300 | | | | | | $27,300 | | | | | |

**EVENT (11). PAYMENT OF CASH FOR EMPLOYEE SALARIES.** Employees have worked two weeks, earning $4,000 in salaries, which were paid on October 26.

Salaries Expense is an expense that reduces stockholders' equity. This event is a transaction because assets and stockholders' equity are affected.

| Basic Analysis | The asset Cash is decreased $4,000; the expense account Salaries Expense is increased $4,000. |
|---|---|

**Equation Analysis**

| | Assets | | | | = | Liabilities | | | + | Stockholders' Equity | | | | |
|---|---|---|---|---|---|---|---|---|---|---|---|---|---|---|
| | | Sup- | Prepd. | Equip- | | Notes | Accts. | Unearned | | Common | | Retained Earnings | | |
| | Cash + | plies + | Insur. + | ment = | | Pay. + | Pay. + | Serv. Rev. + | | Stock + | Rev. − | Exp. − | Div. | |
| | $19,200 | $2,500 | $600 | $5,000 | | $5,000 | $2,500 | $1,200 | | $10,000 | $10,000 | $ 900 | $500 | |
| (11) | −4,000 | | | | | | | | | | | − 4,000 | | Salaries |
| | $15,200 + | $2,500 + | $600 + | $5,000 = | | $5,000 + | $2,500 + | $1,200 + | | $10,000 + | $10,000 − | $4,900 − | $500 | Expense |

$23,300            $23,300

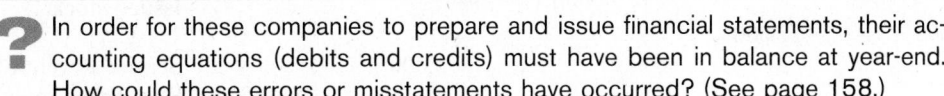

## Investor Insight
### Why Accuracy Matters

While most companies record transactions very carefully, the reality is that mistakes still happen. For example, bank regulators fined Bank One Corporation (now Chase) $1.8 million because they felt that the unreliability of the bank's accounting system caused it to violate regulatory requirements.

Also, in recent years Fannie Mae, the government-chartered mortgage association, announced a series of large accounting errors. These announcements caused alarm among investors, regulators, and politicians because they fear that the errors may suggest larger, undetected problems. This is important because the home-mortgage market depends on Fannie Mae to buy hundreds of billions of dollars of mortgages each year from banks, thus enabling the banks to issue new mortgages.

Finally, before a major overhaul of its accounting system, the financial records of Waste Management Company were in such disarray that of the company's 57,000 employees, 10,000 were receiving pay slips that were in error.

The Sarbanes-Oxley Act of 2002 was created to minimize the occurrence of errors like these by increasing every employee's responsibility for accurate financial reporting.

In order for these companies to prepare and issue financial statements, their accounting equations (debits and credits) must have been in balance at year-end. How could these errors or misstatements have occurred? (See page 158.)

## SUMMARY OF TRANSACTIONS

Illustration 3-3 (page 110) summarizes the transactions of Sierra Corporation to show their cumulative effect on the basic accounting equation. It includes the transaction number in the first column on the left. The right-most column shows the specific effect of any transaction that affects stockholders' equity. Remember that Event (9) did not result in a transaction, so no entry is included for that event. The illustration demonstrates three important points:

1. Each transaction is analyzed in terms of its effect on assets, liabilities, and stockholders' equity.
2. The two sides of the equation must always be equal.
3. The cause of each change in stockholders' equity must be indicated.

**Illustration 3-3** Summary of transactions

| | Assets | | | | = | Liabilities | | | + | Stockholders' Equity | | | | |
|---|---|---|---|---|---|---|---|---|---|---|---|---|---|---|
| | | Sup- | Prepd. | Equip- | | Notes | Accts. | Unearned | | Common | | Retained Earnings | | |
| | Cash + | plies | + Insur. + | ment | = Pay. | + | Pay. | + Serv. Rev. | + | Stock | + Rev. | − Exp. | − Div. | |
| (1) | +$10,000 | | | | = | | | | | +$10,000 | | | | Issued stock |
| (2) | +5,000 | | | | +$5,000 | | | | | | | | | |
| (3) | −5,000 | | | +$5,000 | | | | | | | | | | |
| (4) | +1,200 | | | | | | | +$1,200 | | | | | | |
| (5) | +10,000 | | | | | | | | | | +$10,000 | | | Service Revenue |
| (6) | −900 | | | | | | | | | | | −$ 900 | | Rent Expense |
| (7) | −600 | | +$600 | | | | | | | | | | | |
| (8) | +$2,500 | | | | | + | $2,500 | | | | | | | |
| (10) | −500 | | | | | | | | | | | | −$500 | Dividends |
| (11) | −4,000 | | | | | | | | | | | −4,000 | | Salaries Expense |
| | $15,200 + | $2,500 + | $600 + | $5,000 = | $5,000 + | $2,500 + | | $1,200 | + | $10,000 + | $10,000 | − $4,900 | − $500 | |

$23,300 = $23,300

## DECISION TOOLKIT

| DECISION CHECKPOINTS | INFO NEEDED FOR DECISION | TOOL TO USE FOR DECISION | HOW TO EVALUATE RESULTS |
|---|---|---|---|
| Has an accounting transaction occurred? | Details of the event | Accounting equation | If the event affected assets, liabilities, or stockholders' equity, then record as a transaction. |

## before you go on...

**TRANSACTION ANALYSIS**

**Do it!** A tabular analysis of the transactions made by Roberta Mendez & Co., a certified public accounting firm, for the month of August is shown below. Each increase and decrease in stockholders' equity is explained.

| | Assets | | | = | Liabilities | + | | Stockholders' Equity | | | |
|---|---|---|---|---|---|---|---|---|---|---|---|
| | | | | | Accounts | | Common | | Retained Earnings | | |
| | Cash | + | Equipment | = | Payable | + | Stock | + | Revenue | − Expenses | |
| 1. | +$25,000 | | | | | | +$25,000 | | | | Issued stock |
| 2. | | | +$7,000 | = | +$7,000 | | | | | | |
| 3. | +8,000 | | | | | | | | +$8,000 | | Service Revenue |
| 4. | −850 | | | | | | | | | −$850 | Rent Expense |
| | $32,150 | + | $7,000 | = | $7,000 | + | $25,000 | + | $8,000 | − $850 | |

$39,150 = $39,150

**Action Plan**

- Analyze the tabular analysis to determine the nature and effect of each transaction.
- Keep the accounting equation in balance.
- Remember that a change in an asset will require a change in another asset, a liability, or in stockholders' equity.

Describe each transaction that occurred for the month.

**Solution**

1. The company issued shares of stock to stockholders for $25,000 cash.
2. The company purchased $7,000 of equipment on account.
3. The company received $8,000 of cash in exchange for services performed.
4. The company paid $850 for this month's rent.

Related exercise material: **BE3-1, BE3-2, BE3-3,** **Do it!** **3-1, E3-1, E3-2, E3-3,** and **E3-4.**

the navigator

# The Account

Rather than using a tabular summary like the one in Illustration 3-3 for Sierra Corporation, an accounting information system uses accounts. An **account** is an individual accounting record of increases and decreases in a specific asset, liability, stockholders' equity, revenue, or expense item. For example, Sierra Corporation has separate accounts for Cash, Accounts Receivable, Accounts Payable, Service Revenue, Salaries Expense, and so on. (Note that whenever we are referring to a specific account, we capitalize the name.)

In its simplest form, an account consists of three parts: (1) the title of the account, (2) a left or debit side, and (3) a right or credit side. Because the alignment of these parts of an account resembles the letter T, it is referred to as a **T account**. The basic form of an account is shown in Illustration 3-4.

**study objective 2**

Explain what an account is and how it helps in the recording process.

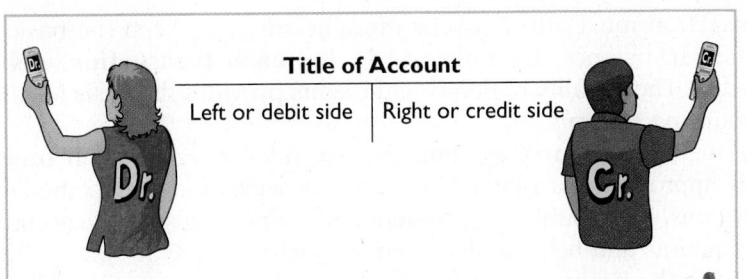

**Title of Account**

| Left or debit side | Right or credit side |

**Illustration 3-4** Basic form of account

We use this form of account often throughout this book to explain basic accounting relationships.

## DEBITS AND CREDITS

The term **debit** indicates the left side of an account, and **credit** indicates the right side. They are commonly abbreviated as **Dr.** for debit and **Cr.** for credit. They **do not** mean increase or decrease, as is commonly thought. We use the terms *debit* and *credit* repeatedly in the recording process to describe **where** entries are made in accounts. For example, the act of entering an amount on the left side of an account is called **debiting** the account. Making an entry on the right side is **crediting** the account.

When comparing the totals of the two sides, an account shows a **debit balance** if the total of the debit amounts exceeds the credits. An account shows a **credit balance** if the credit amounts exceed the debits. Note the position of the debit side and credit side in Illustration 3-4.

The procedure of recording debits and credits in an account is shown in Illustration 3-5 for the transactions affecting the Cash account of Sierra Corporation. The data are taken from the Cash column of the tabular summary in Illustration 3-3.

**study objective 3**

Define debits and credits and explain how they are used to record business transactions.

**Illustration 3-5** Tabular summary and account form for Sierra Corporation's Cash account

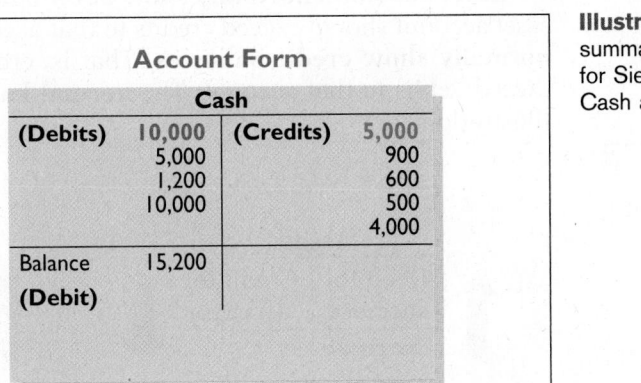

| Tabular Summary | Account Form |
|---|---|
| **Cash** | **Cash** |
| $10,000 | (Debits) 10,000 (Credits) 5,000 |
| 5,000 | 5,000 900 |
| −5,000 | 1,200 600 |
| 1,200 | 10,000 500 |
| 10,000 | 4,000 |
| −900 | |
| −600 | Balance 15,200 |
| −500 | (Debit) |
| −4,000 | |
| $15,200 | |

Every positive item in the tabular summary represents a receipt of cash; every negative amount represents a payment of cash. **Notice that in the account form we record the increases in cash as debits, and the decreases in cash as credits.** For example, the $10,000 receipt of cash (in red) is debited to Cash, and the −$5,000 payment of cash (in blue) is credited to Cash.

Having increases on one side and decreases on the other reduces recording errors and helps in determining the totals of each side of the account as well as the account balance. The balance is determined by netting the two sides (subtracting one amount from the other). The account balance, a debit of $15,200, indicates that Sierra had $15,200 more increases than decreases in cash. That is, since it started with a balance of zero, it has $15,200 in its Cash account.

## DEBIT AND CREDIT PROCEDURES

**International Note** Rules for accounting for specific events sometimes differ across countries. For example, European companies rely less on historical cost and more on fair value than U.S. companies. Despite the differences, the double-entry accounting system is the basis of accounting systems worldwide.

Each transaction must affect two or more accounts to keep the basic accounting equation in balance. In other words, **for each transaction, debits must equal credits**. The equality of debits and credits provides the basis for the double-entry accounting system.

Under the double-entry system, the two-sided effect of each transaction is recorded in appropriate accounts. This system provides a logical method for recording transactions. The double-entry system also helps to ensure the accuracy of the recorded amounts and helps to detect errors such as those at Fidelity Investments as discussed in the Feature Story. If every transaction is recorded with equal debits and credits, then the sum of all the debits to the accounts must equal the sum of all the credits. The double-entry system for determining the equality of the accounting equation is much more efficient than the plus/minus procedure used earlier.

### Dr./Cr. Procedures for Assets and Liabilities

In Illustration 3-5 for Sierra Corporation, increases in Cash—an asset—were entered on the left side, and decreases in Cash were entered on the right side. We know that both sides of the basic equation (Assets = Liabilities + Stockholders' Equity) must be equal. It therefore follows that increases and decreases in liabilities will have to be recorded *opposite from* increases and decreases in assets. Thus, increases in liabilities must be entered on the right or credit side, and decreases in liabilities must be entered on the left or debit side. The effects that debits and credits have on assets and liabilities are summarized in Illustration 3-6.

**Illustration 3-6** Debit and credit effects–assets and liabilities

| Debits | Credits |
|---|---|
| Increase assets | Decrease assets |
| Decrease liabilities | Increase liabilities |

**Asset accounts normally show debit balances**. That is, debits to a specific asset account should exceed credits to that account. Likewise, **liability accounts normally show credit balances**. That is, credits to a liability account should exceed debits to that account. The **normal balances** may be diagrammed as in Illustration 3-7.

**Illustration 3-7** Normal balances–assets and liabilities

| Assets | | Liabilities | |
|---|---|---|---|
| Debit for increase | Credit for decrease | Debit for decrease | Credit for increase |
| Normal balance | | | Normal balance |

Knowing which is the normal balance in an account may help when you are trying to identify errors. For example, a credit balance in an asset account, such as Land, or a debit balance in a liability account, such as Salaries Payable, usually indicates errors in recording. Occasionally, however, an abnormal balance may be correct. The Cash account, for example, will have a credit balance when a company has overdrawn its bank balance (written a check that "bounced"). In automated accounting systems, the computer is programmed to flag violations of the normal balance and to print out error or exception reports. In manual systems, careful visual inspection of the accounts is required to detect normal balance problems.

**Helpful Hint** The normal balance is the side where increases in the account are recorded.

### Dr./Cr. Procedures for Stockholders' Equity

In Chapter 1, we indicated that stockholders' equity is comprised of two parts: common stock and retained earnings. In the transaction events earlier in this chapter, you saw that revenues, expenses, and the payment of dividends affect retained earnings. Therefore, the subdivisions of stockholders' equity are: common stock, retained earnings, dividends, revenues, and expenses.

**COMMON STOCK.** Common stock is issued to investors in exchange for the stockholders' investment. The common stock account is increased by credits and decreased by debits. For example, when cash is invested in the business, cash is debited and common stock is credited. The effects of debits and credits on the common stock account are shown in Illustration 3-8.

| **Debits** | **Credits** |
|---|---|
| Decrease Common Stock | Increase Common Stock |

**Illustration 3-8** Debit and credit effects—Common Stock

The normal balance in the Common Stock account may be diagrammed as in Illustration 3-9.

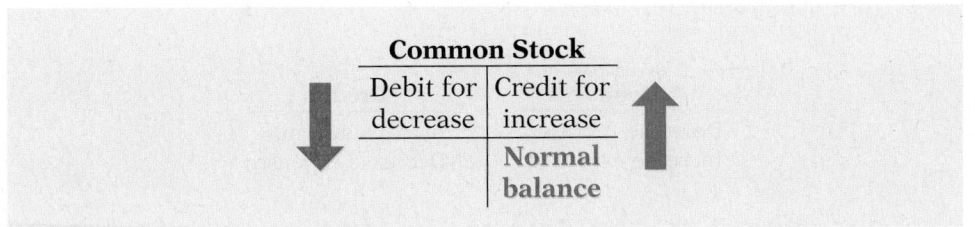

**Illustration 3-9** Normal balance—Common Stock

**RETAINED EARNINGS.** Retained earnings is net income that is retained in the business. It represents the portion of stockholders' equity that has been accumulated through the profitable operation of the company. Retained earnings is increased by credits (for example, by net income) and decreased by debits (for example, by a net loss), as shown in Illustration 3-10.

| **Debits** | **Credits** |
|---|---|
| Decrease Retained Earnings | Increase Retained Earnings |

**Illustration 3-10** Debit and credit effects—Retained Earnings

The normal balance for Retained Earnings may be diagrammed as in Illustration 3-11.

**Illustration 3-11** Normal balance–Retained Earnings

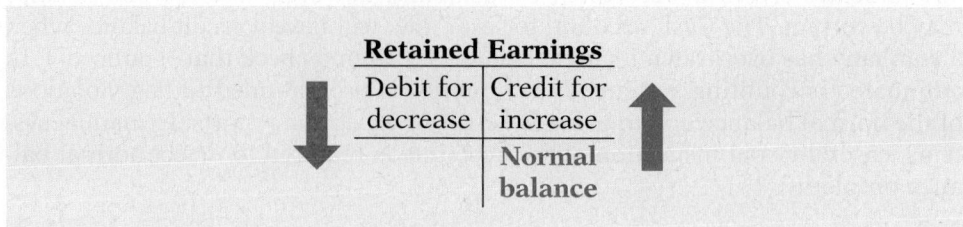

**DIVIDENDS.** A dividend is a distribution by a corporation to its stockholders. The most common form of distribution is a cash dividend. Dividends result in a reduction of the stockholders' claims on retained earnings. Because dividends reduce stockholders' equity, increases in the Dividends account are recorded with debits. As shown in Illustration 3-12, the Dividends account normally has a debit balance.

**Illustration 3-12** Normal balance–Dividends

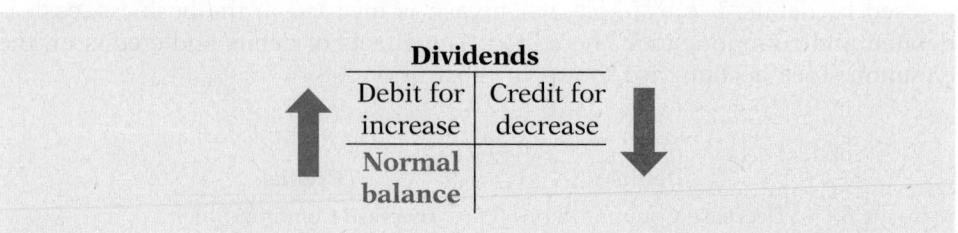

**REVENUES AND EXPENSES.** When a company earns revenues, stockholders' equity is increased. Revenue accounts are increased by credits and decreased by debits.

**Expenses decrease stockholders' equity.** Thus, expense accounts are increased by debits and decreased by credits. The effects of debits and credits on revenues and expenses are shown in Illustration 3-13.

**Illustration 3-13** Debit and credit effects–revenues and expenses

| Debits | Credits |
| --- | --- |
| Decrease revenue | Increase revenue |
| Increase expenses | Decrease expenses |

Credits to revenue accounts should exceed debits; debits to expense accounts should exceed credits. Thus, **revenue accounts normally show credit balances, and expense accounts normally show debit balances.** The normal balances may be diagrammed as in Illustration 3-14.

**Illustration 3-14** Normal balances–revenues and expenses

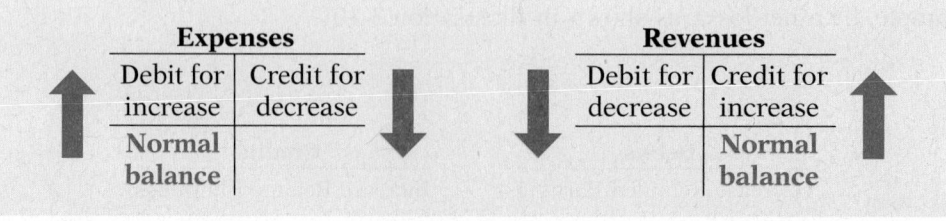

## Investor Insight

### Keeping Score

The Chicago Cubs baseball team has these major revenue and expense accounts:

| Revenues | Expenses |
|---|---|
| Admissions (ticket sales) | Players' salaries |
| Concessions | Administrative salaries |
| Television and radio | Travel |
| Advertising | Ballpark maintenance |

**?** Do you think that the Chicago Bears football team would be likely to have the same major revenue and expense accounts as the Cubs? (See page 158.)

## STOCKHOLDERS' EQUITY RELATIONSHIPS

Companies report the subdivisions of stockholders' equity in various places in the financial statements:

- Common stock and retained earnings: in the stockholders' equity section of the balance sheet.
- Dividends: on the retained earnings statement.
- Revenues and expenses: on the income statement.

Dividends, revenues, and expenses are eventually transferred to retained earnings at the end of the period. As a result, a change in any one of these three items affects stockholders' equity. Illustration 3-15 shows the relationships of the accounts affecting stockholders' equity.

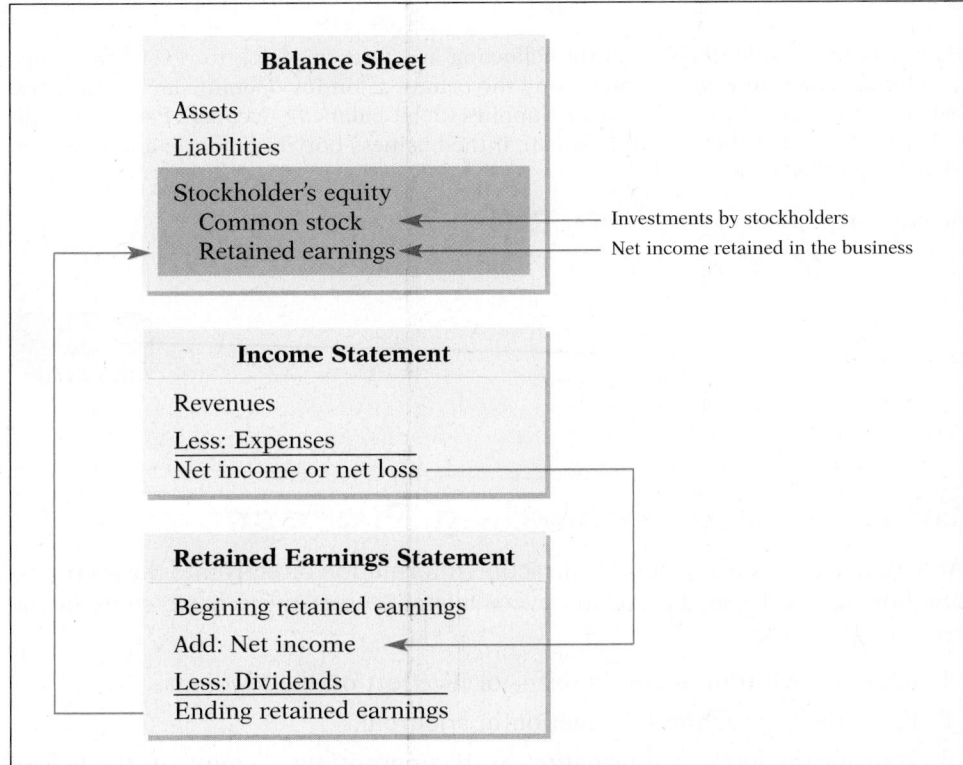

**Illustration 3-15**
Stockholders' equity relationships

## SUMMARY OF DEBIT/CREDIT RULES

Illustration 3-16 summarizes the debit/credit rules and effects on each type of account. **Study this diagram carefully.** It will help you understand the fundamentals of the double-entry system. No matter what the transaction, total debits must equal total credits in order to keep the accounting equation in balance.

**Illustration 3-16** Summary of debit/credit rules

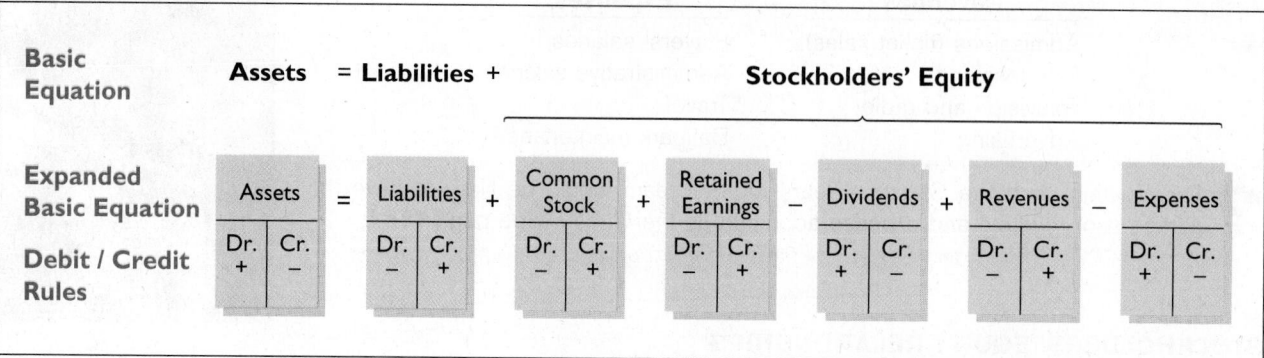

**Basic Equation**   Assets   = Liabilities +                Stockholders' Equity

| | Assets | Liabilities | Common Stock | Retained Earnings | Dividends | Revenues | Expenses |
|---|---|---|---|---|---|---|---|
| Expanded Basic Equation | = | + | + | − | + | − | |
| Debit / Credit Rules | Dr. + / Cr. − | Dr. − / Cr. + | Dr. − / Cr. + | Dr. − / Cr. + | Dr. + / Cr. − | Dr. − / Cr. + | Dr. + / Cr. − |

## before you go on...

### DEBITS AND CREDITS FOR BALANCE SHEET ACCOUNTS

### Action Plan

- First identify asset accounts for each different type of asset invested in the business.
- Then identify liability accounts for debts incurred by the business.
- Remember that Hair It Is Inc. will need only one stockholders' equity account for common stock when it begins the business. The other stockholders' equity accounts will be needed only after the business is operating.

## Do it!

Kate Browne, president of Hair It Is Inc., has just rented space in a shopping mall for the purpose of opening and operating a beauty salon. Long before opening day and before purchasing equipment, hiring assistants, and remodeling the space, Kate was strongly advised to set up a double-entry set of accounting records in which to record all of her business transactions.

Identify the balance sheet accounts that Hair It Is Inc. will likely need to record the transactions necessary to establish and open for business. Also, indicate whether the normal balance of each account is a debit or a credit.

### Solution

Hair It Is Inc. would likely need the following accounts in which to record the transactions necessary to establish and ready the beauty salon for opening day: Cash (debit balance); Equipment (debit balance); Supplies (debit balance); Accounts Payable (credit balance); Notes Payable (credit balance), if the business borrows money; and Common Stock (credit balance).

Related exercise material: **BE3-4, BE3-5, Do it! 3-2,** and **E3-7.**

# Steps in the Recording Process

**study objective 4**

Identify the basic steps in the recording process.

Although it is possible to enter transaction information directly into the accounts, few businesses do so. Practically every business uses these basic steps in the recording process:

1. Analyze each transaction in terms of its effect on the accounts.
2. Enter the transaction information in a journal.
3. Transfer the journal information to the appropriate accounts in the ledger.

The actual sequence of events begins with the transaction. Evidence of the transaction comes in the form of a **source document**, such as a sales slip, a check, a bill, or a cash register tape. This evidence is analyzed to determine the effect of the transaction on specific accounts. The transaction is then entered in the **journal**. Finally, the journal entry is transferred to the designated accounts in the **ledger**. The sequence of events in the recording process is shown in Illustration 3-17.

**Illustration 3-17**  The recording process

The Recording Process

Analyze each transaction     Enter transaction in a journal     Transfer journal information to ledger accounts

## THE JOURNAL

Transactions are initially recorded in chronological order in journals before they are transferred to the accounts. For each transaction the journal shows the debit and credit effects on specific accounts. (In a computerized system, journals are kept as files, and accounts are recorded in computer databases.)

Companies may use various kinds of journals, but every company has at least the most basic form of journal, a general journal. **The journal makes three significant contributions to the recording process:**

1. It discloses in one place the **complete effect of a transaction**.
2. It provides a **chronological record** of transactions.
3. It **helps to prevent or locate errors** because the debit and credit amounts for each entry can be readily compared.

Entering transaction data in the journal is known as journalizing. To illustrate the technique of journalizing, let's look at the first three transactions of Sierra Corporation in equation form.

On October 1, Sierra issued common stock in exchange for $10,000 cash:

study objective **5**

Explain what a journal is and how it helps in the recording process.

**Ethics Note** Business documents provide evidence that transactions actually occurred. International Outsourcing Services, LLC, was accused of submitting fraudulent documents (store coupons) to companies such as Kraft Foods and PepsiCo for reimbursement of as much as $250 million. Ensuring that all recorded transactions are backed up by proper business documents reduces the likelihood of fraudulent activity.

| **Assets** | **=** | **Liabilities** | **+** | **Stockholders' Equity** | |
|---|---|---|---|---|---|
| Cash | = | | | Common Stock | |
| +$10,000 | | | | +$10,000 | Issued stock |

On October 1, Sierra borrowed $5,000 by signing a note:

| Assets | = | Liabilities | + | Stockholders' Equity |
|---|---|---|---|---|
| | | Notes | | |
| Cash | = | Payable | | |
| +$5,000 | | +$5,000 | | |

On October 2, Sierra purchased equipment for $5,000:

| Assets | | = | Liabilities | + | Stockholders' Equity |
|---|---|---|---|---|---|
| Cash | Equipment | | | | |
| −$5,000 | +$5,000 | | | | |

Sierra makes separate journal entries for each transaction. A complete entry consists of: (1) the date of the transaction, (2) the accounts and amounts to be debited and credited, and (3) a brief explanation of the transaction. These transactions are journalized in Illustration 3-18.

**Illustration 3-18**
Recording transactions in journal form

**GENERAL JOURNAL**

| Date | | Account Titles and Explanation | Debit | Credit |
|---|---|---|---|---|
| 2012 | | | | |
| Oct. | 1 | Cash | 10,000 | |
| | | Common Stock | | 10,000 |
| | | (Issued stock for cash) | | |
| | 1 | Cash | 5,000 | |
| | | Notes Payable | | 5,000 |
| | | (Issued 3-month, 12% note payable for cash) | | |
| | 2 | Equipment | 5,000 | |
| | | Cash | | 5,000 |
| | | (Purchased equipment for cash) | | |

Note the following features of the journal entries.

1. The date of the transaction is entered in the Date column.
2. The account to be debited is entered first at the left. The account to be credited is then entered on the next line, indented under the line above. The indentation differentiates debits from credits and decreases the possibility of switching the debit and credit amounts.
3. The amounts for the debits are recorded in the Debit (left) column, and the amounts for the credits are recorded in the Credit (right) column.
4. A brief explanation of the transaction is given.

**It is important to use correct and specific account titles in journalizing.** Erroneous account titles lead to incorrect financial statements. Some flexibility exists initially in selecting account titles. The main criterion is that each title must appropriately describe the content of the account. For example, a company could use any of these account titles for recording the cost of delivery trucks: Equipment, Delivery Equipment, Delivery Trucks, or Trucks. Once the company chooses the specific title to use, however, it should record under that account title all subsequent transactions involving the account.

## Accounting Across the Organization
### Boosting Microsoft's Profits

Bryan Lee is head of finance at Microsoft's Home and Entertainment Division. In recent years the division lost over $4 billion, mostly due to losses on the original Xbox videogame player. With the Xbox 360 videogame player, Mr. Lee hoped the division would become profitable. He set strict goals for sales, revenue, and profit. "A manager seeking to spend more on a feature such as a disk drive has to find allies in the group to cut spending elsewhere, or identify new revenue to offset the increase," he explains.

For example, Microsoft originally designed the new Xbox to have 256 megabytes of memory. But the design department said that amount of memory wouldn't support the best special effects. The purchasing department said that adding more memory would cost $30—which was 10% of the estimated selling price of $300. But the marketing department "determined that adding the memory would let Microsoft reduce marketing costs and attract more game developers, boosting royalty revenue. It would also extend the life of the console, generating more sales." Microsoft doubled the memory to 512 megabytes.

*Source:* Robert A. Guth, "New Xbox Aim for Microsoft: Profitability," *Wall Street Journal* (May 24, 2005), p. C1.

**?** In what ways is this Microsoft division using accounting to assist in its effort to become more profitable? (See page 158.)

*before you go on...*

**Do it!** The following events occurred during the first month of business of Hair It Is Inc., Kate Browne's beauty salon:

**JOURNAL ENTRIES**

1. Issued common stock to shareholders in exchange for $20,000 cash.
2. Purchased $4,800 of equipment on account (to be paid in 30 days).
3. Interviewed three people for the position of beautician.

In what form (type of record) should the company record these three activities? Prepare the entries to record the transactions.

**Action Plan**

- Record the transactions in a journal, which is a chronological record of the transactions.
- Make sure to provide a complete and accurate representation of the transactions' effects on the assets, liabilities, and stockholders' equity of the business.

### Solution

Each transaction that is recorded is entered in the general journal. The three activities are recorded as follows.

| | | | |
|---|---|---|---|
| 1. | Cash | 20,000 | |
| | Common Stock | | 20,000 |
| | (Issued stock for cash) | | |
| 2. | Equipment | 4,800 | |
| | Accounts Payable | | 4,800 |
| | (Purchased equipment on account) | | |
| 3. | No entry because no transaction occurred. | | |

Related exercise material: **BE3-6, BE3-9, Do it! 3-3, E3-6, E3-8,** and **E3-9.**

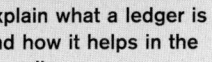

### THE LEDGER

The entire group of accounts maintained by a company is referred to collectively as the **ledger**. The ledger keeps in one place all the information about changes in specific account balances.

Companies may use various kinds of ledgers, but every company has a general ledger. A **general ledger** contains all the assets, liabilities, stockholders' equity, revenue, and expense accounts, as shown in Illustration 3-19 (page 120). Whenever we use the term *ledger* in this textbook without additional specification, it will mean the general ledger.

**study objective 6**

Explain what a ledger is and how it helps in the recording process.

**Illustration 3-19** The general ledger

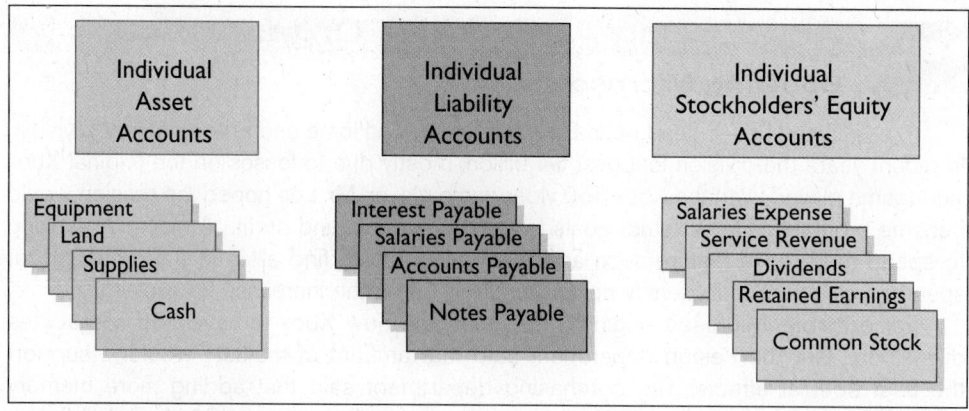

## CHART OF ACCOUNTS

The number and type of accounts used differ for each company, depending on the size, complexity, and type of business. For example, the number of accounts depends on the amount of detail desired by management. The management of one company may want one single account for all types of utility expense. Another may keep separate expense accounts for each type of utility expenditure, such as gas, electricity, and water. A small corporation like Sierra Corporation will not have many accounts compared with a corporate giant like Ford Motor Company. Sierra may be able to manage and report its activities in 20 to 30 accounts, whereas Ford requires thousands of accounts to keep track of its worldwide activities.

Most companies list the accounts in a **chart of accounts**. They may create new accounts as needed during the life of the business. Illustration 3-20 shows the chart of accounts for Sierra Corporation in the order that they are typically listed (assets, liabilities, stockholders' equity, revenues, and expenses). **Accounts shown in red are used in this chapter**; accounts shown in black are explained in later chapters.

**Illustration 3-20** Chart of accounts for Sierra Corporation

### SIERRA CORPORATION—CHART OF ACCOUNTS

| Assets | Liabilities | Stockholders' Equity | Revenues | Expenses |
|---|---|---|---|---|
| Cash | Notes Payable | Common Stock | Service Revenue | Salaries Expense |
| Accounts Receivable | Accounts Payable | Retained Earnings | | Supplies Expense |
| Supplies | Interest Payable | Dividends | | Rent Expense |
| Prepaid Insurance | Unearned | Income Summary | | Insurance Expense |
| Equipment | Service Revenue | | | Interest Expense |
| Accumulated Depreciation— | Salaries Payable | | | Depreciation Expense |
| Equipment | | | | |

## POSTING

The procedure of transferring journal entry amounts to ledger accounts is called posting. **This phase of the recording process accumulates the effects of journalized transactions in the individual accounts.** Posting involves these steps:

1. In the ledger, enter in the appropriate columns of the debited account(s) the date and debit amount shown in the journal.

2. In the ledger, enter in the appropriate columns of the credited account(s) the date and credit amount shown in the journal.

# The Recording Process Illustrated

Illustrations 3-21 through 3-31 on the following pages show the basic steps in the recording process using the October transactions of Sierra Corporation. Sierra's accounting period is a month. A basic analysis and a debit–credit analysis precede the journalizing and posting of each transaction. Study these transaction analyses carefully. **The purpose of transaction analysis is first to identify the type of account involved and then to determine whether a debit or a credit to the account is required.** You should always perform this type of analysis before preparing a journal entry. Doing so will help you understand the journal entries discussed in this chapter as well as more complex journal entries to be described in later chapters.

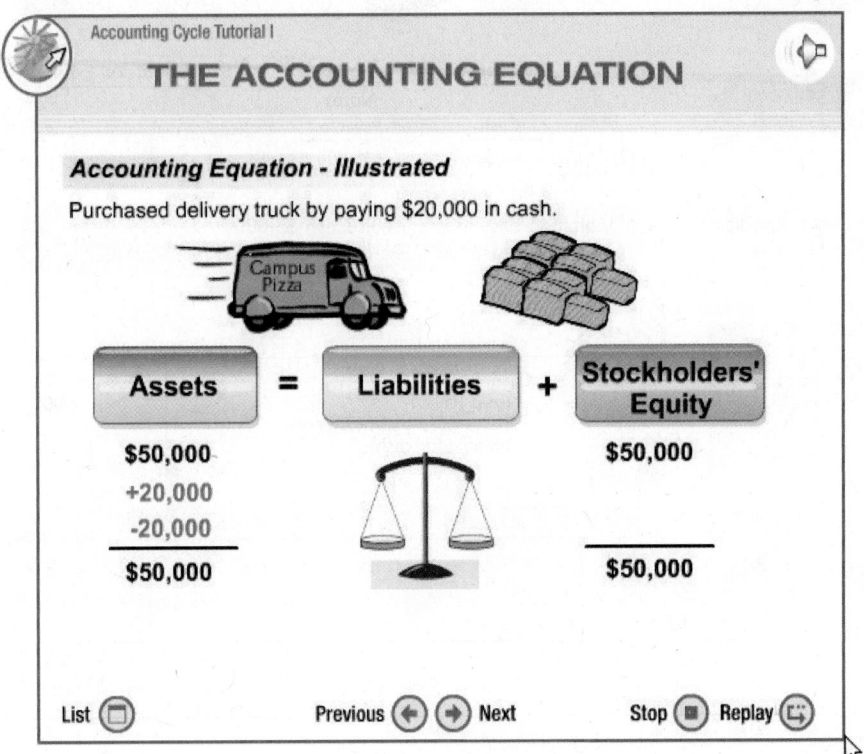

Accounting Cycle Tutorial

The diagrams in Illustrations 3-21 to 3-31 review the accounting cycle. If you would like additional practice, an Accounting Cycle Tutorial is available on WileyPLUS. The illustration to the left is an example of a screen from the tutorial.

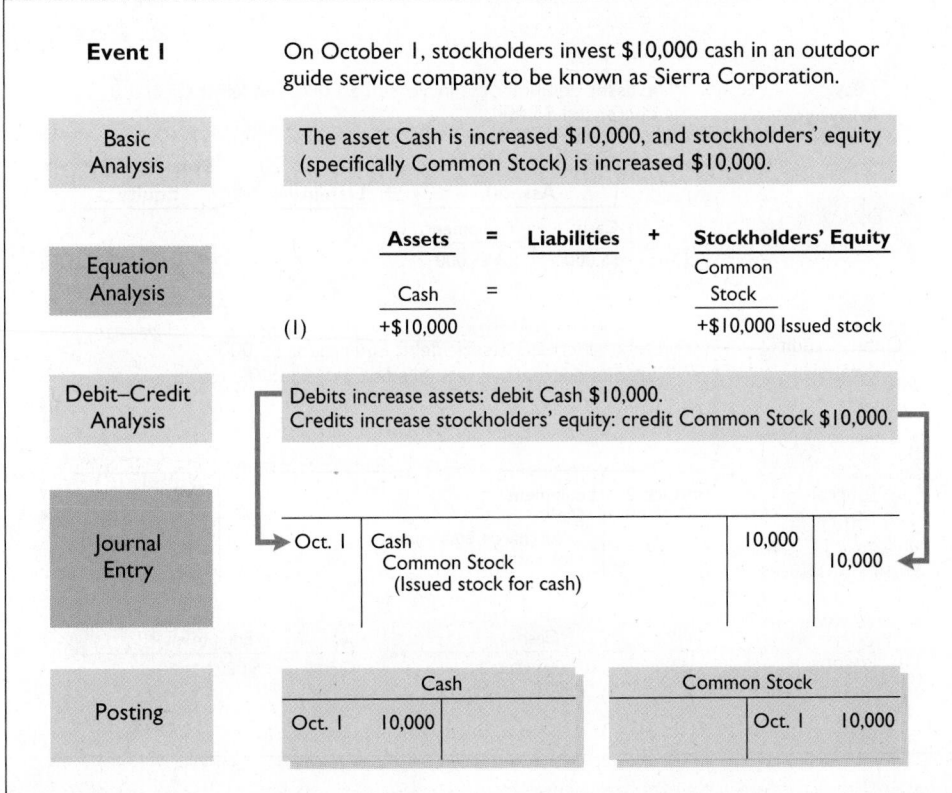

**Illustration 3-21**
Investment of cash by stockholders

**Illustration 3-22**   Issue
of note payable

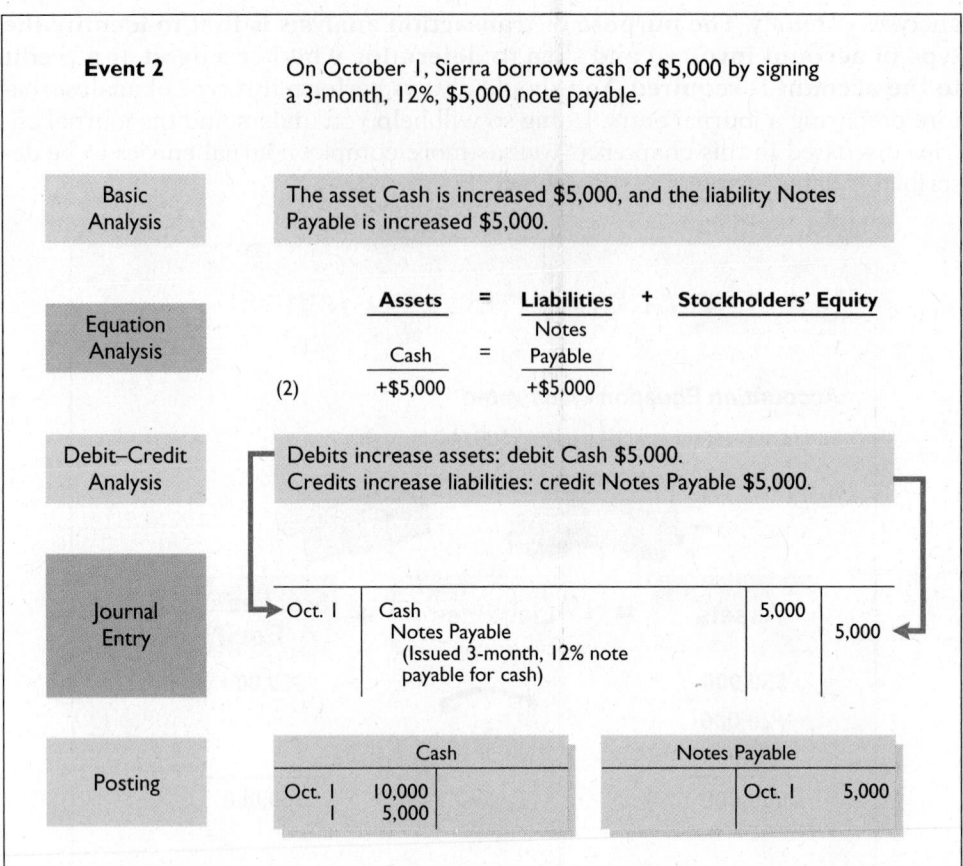

**Illustration 3-23**
Purchase of equipment

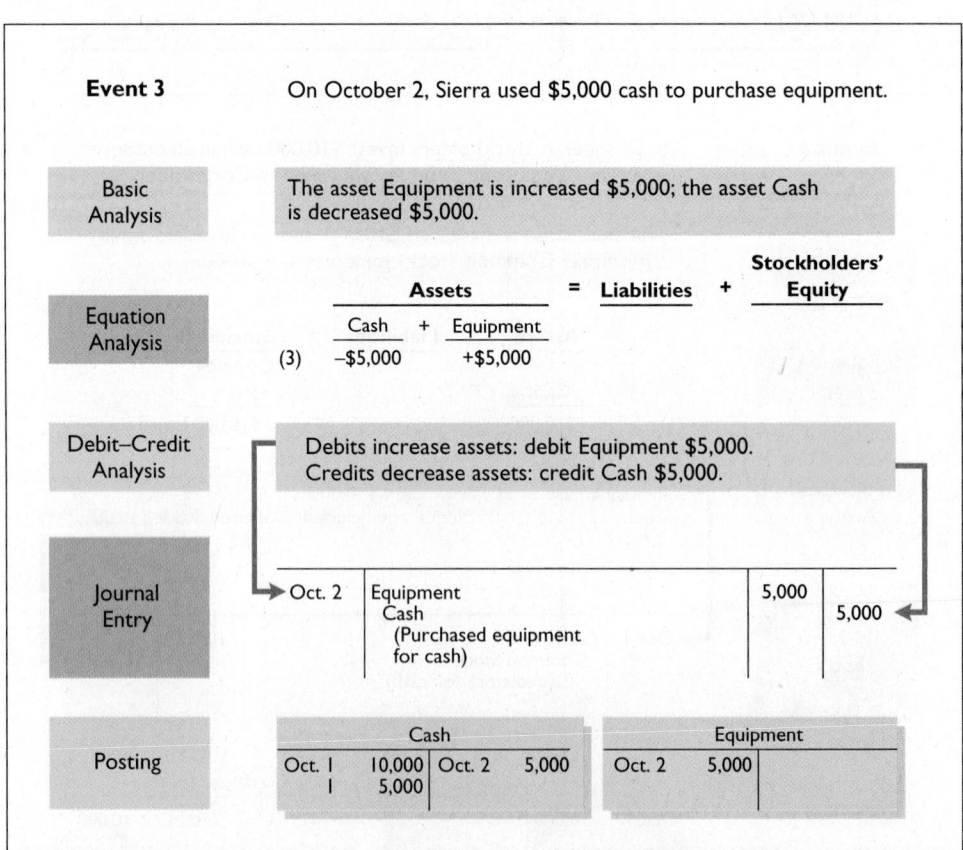

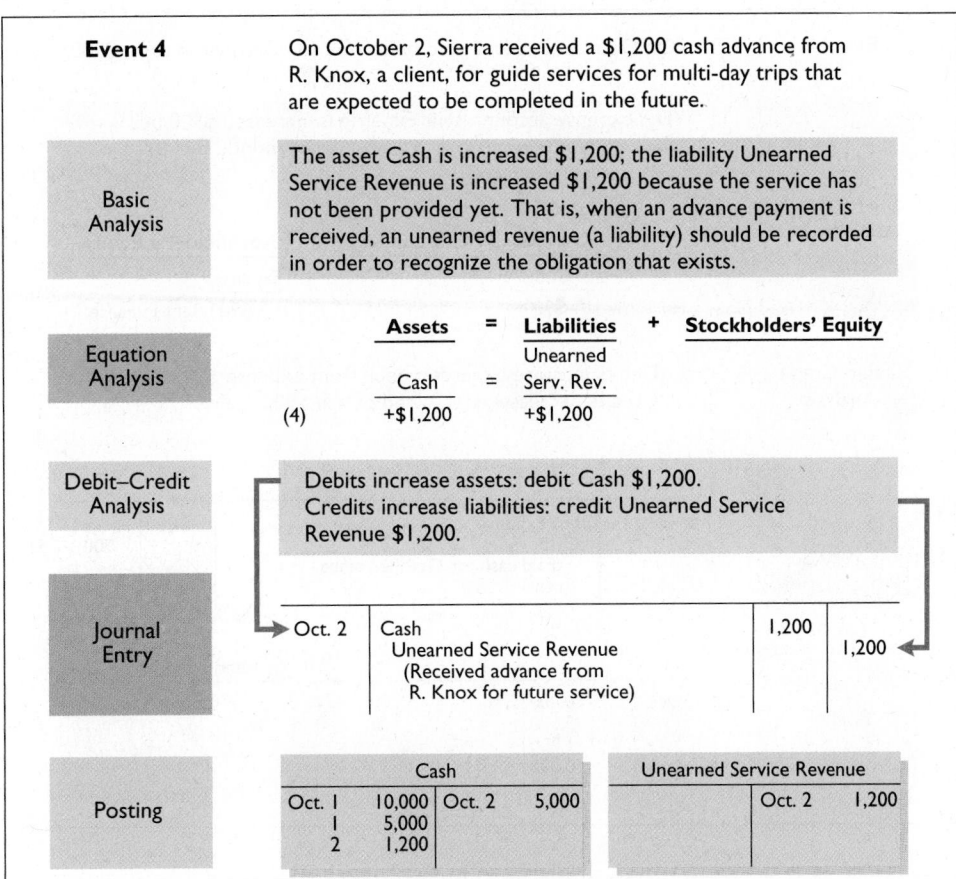

**Illustration 3-24**
Receipt of cash in advance
from customer

**Event 4** — On October 2, Sierra received a $1,200 cash advance from R. Knox, a client, for guide services for multi-day trips that are expected to be completed in the future.

**Basic Analysis** — The asset Cash is increased $1,200; the liability Unearned Service Revenue is increased $1,200 because the service has not been provided yet. That is, when an advance payment is received, an unearned revenue (a liability) should be recorded in order to recognize the obligation that exists.

**Equation Analysis**

| | Assets | = | Liabilities | + | Stockholders' Equity |
|---|---|---|---|---|---|
| | Cash | = | Unearned Serv. Rev. | | |
| (4) | +$1,200 | | +$1,200 | | |

**Debit–Credit Analysis** — Debits increase assets: debit Cash $1,200. Credits increase liabilities: credit Unearned Service Revenue $1,200.

**Journal Entry**

| Oct. 2 | Cash | 1,200 | |
|---|---|---|---|
| | Unearned Service Revenue | | 1,200 |
| | (Received advance from R. Knox for future service) | | |

**Posting**

| Cash | | | | Unearned Service Revenue | |
|---|---|---|---|---|---|
| Oct. 1 | 10,000 | Oct. 2 | 5,000 | Oct. 2 | 1,200 |
| 1 | 5,000 | | | | |
| 2 | 1,200 | | | | |

**Helpful Hint** Many liabilities have the word "payable" in their title. But, note that Unearned Service Revenue is considered a liability even though the word *payable* is not used.

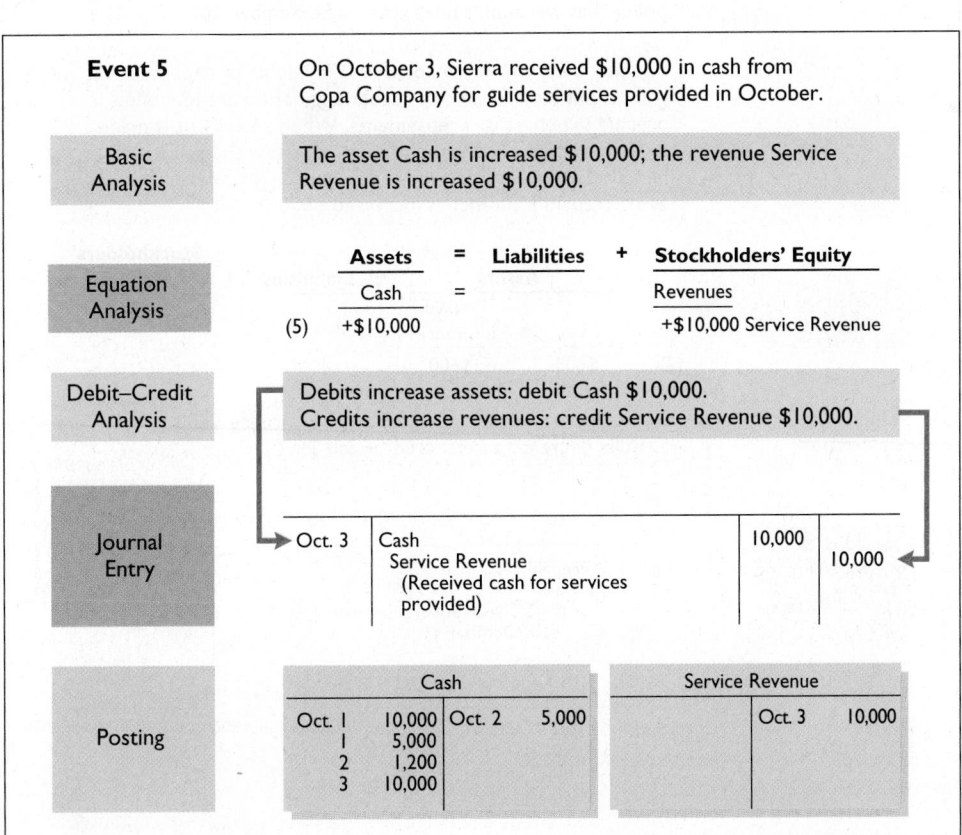

**Illustration 3-25**
Services provided for cash

**Event 5** — On October 3, Sierra received $10,000 in cash from Copa Company for guide services provided in October.

**Basic Analysis** — The asset Cash is increased $10,000; the revenue Service Revenue is increased $10,000.

**Equation Analysis**

| | Assets | = | Liabilities | + | Stockholders' Equity |
|---|---|---|---|---|---|
| | Cash | = | | | Revenues |
| (5) | +$10,000 | | | | +$10,000 Service Revenue |

**Debit–Credit Analysis** — Debits increase assets: debit Cash $10,000. Credits increase revenues: credit Service Revenue $10,000.

**Journal Entry**

| Oct. 3 | Cash | 10,000 | |
|---|---|---|---|
| | Service Revenue | | 10,000 |
| | (Received cash for services provided) | | |

**Posting**

| Cash | | | | Service Revenue | |
|---|---|---|---|---|---|
| Oct. 1 | 10,000 | Oct. 2 | 5,000 | Oct. 3 | 10,000 |
| 1 | 5,000 | | | | |
| 2 | 1,200 | | | | |
| 3 | 10,000 | | | | |

**Illustration 3-26**
Payment of rent with cash

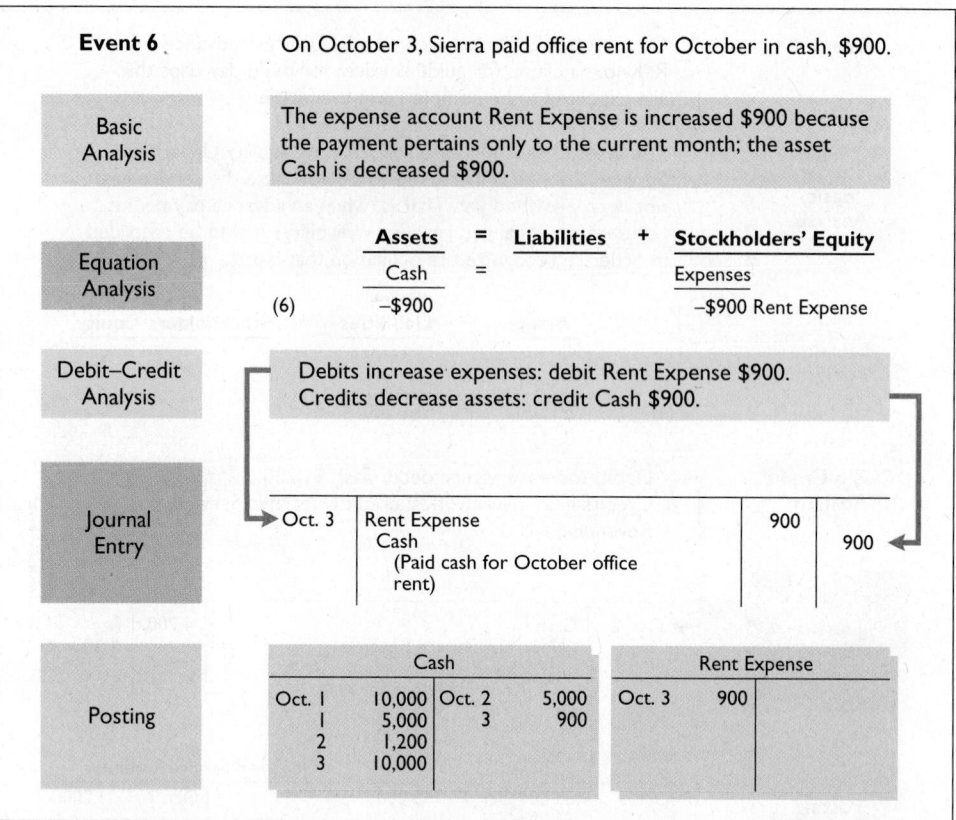

**Event 6** — On October 3, Sierra paid office rent for October in cash, $900.

**Basic Analysis** — The expense account Rent Expense is increased $900 because the payment pertains only to the current month; the asset Cash is decreased $900.

**Equation Analysis**

| Assets | = | Liabilities | + | Stockholders' Equity |
|---|---|---|---|---|
| Cash | = | | | Expenses |
| (6) −$900 | | | | −$900 Rent Expense |

**Debit–Credit Analysis** — Debits increase expenses: debit Rent Expense $900. Credits decrease assets: credit Cash $900.

**Journal Entry**

Oct. 3 | Rent Expense | 900 |
| Cash | | 900 |
| (Paid cash for October office rent) | | |

**Posting**

| Cash | | | | Rent Expense | |
|---|---|---|---|---|---|
| Oct. 1 | 10,000 | Oct. 2 | 5,000 | Oct. 3 | 900 |
| 1 | 5,000 | 3 | 900 | | |
| 2 | 1,200 | | | | |
| 3 | 10,000 | | | | |

**Illustration 3-27**
Purchase of insurance policy with cash

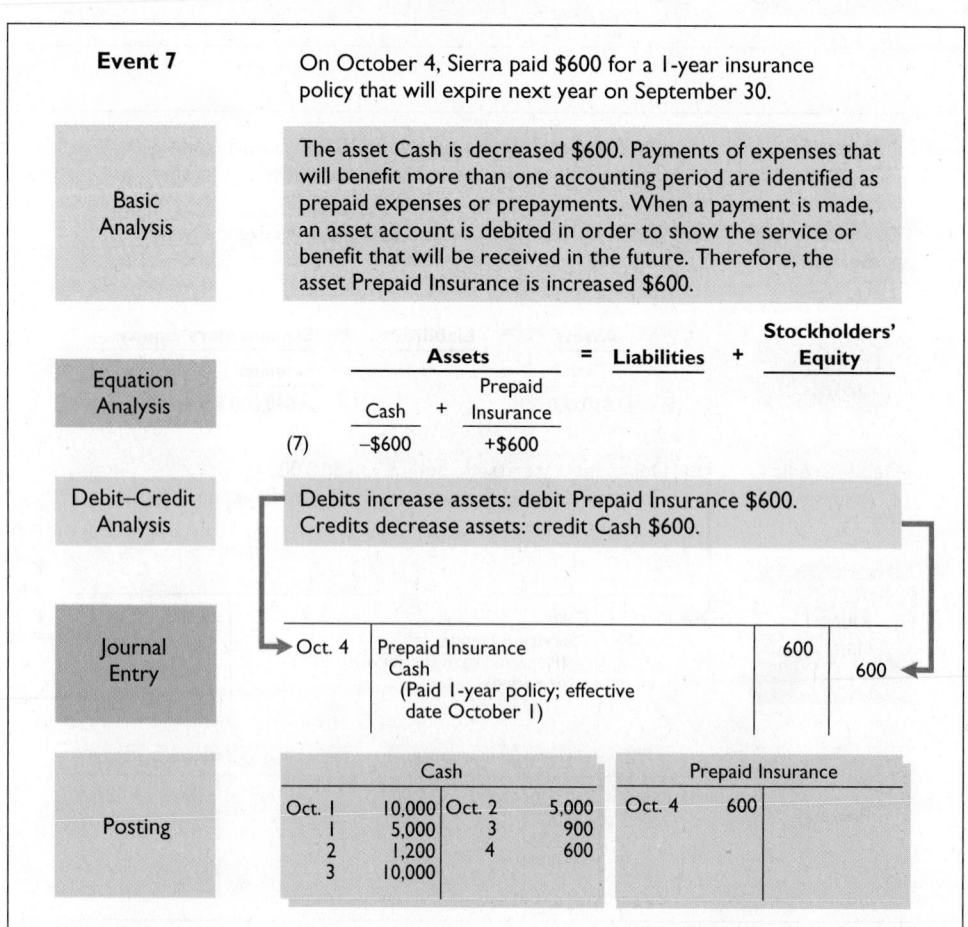

**Event 7** — On October 4, Sierra paid $600 for a 1-year insurance policy that will expire next year on September 30.

**Basic Analysis** — The asset Cash is decreased $600. Payments of expenses that will benefit more than one accounting period are identified as prepaid expenses or prepayments. When a payment is made, an asset account is debited in order to show the service or benefit that will be received in the future. Therefore, the asset Prepaid Insurance is increased $600.

**Equation Analysis**

| Assets | | | = | Liabilities | + | Stockholders' Equity |
|---|---|---|---|---|---|---|
| Cash | + | Prepaid Insurance | = | | | |
| (7) −$600 | | +$600 | | | | |

**Debit–Credit Analysis** — Debits increase assets: debit Prepaid Insurance $600. Credits decrease assets: credit Cash $600.

**Journal Entry**

Oct. 4 | Prepaid Insurance | 600 |
| Cash | | 600 |
| (Paid 1-year policy; effective date October 1) | | |

**Posting**

| Cash | | | | Prepaid Insurance | |
|---|---|---|---|---|---|
| Oct. 1 | 10,000 | Oct. 2 | 5,000 | Oct. 4 | 600 |
| 1 | 5,000 | 3 | 900 | | |
| 2 | 1,200 | 4 | 600 | | |
| 3 | 10,000 | | | | |

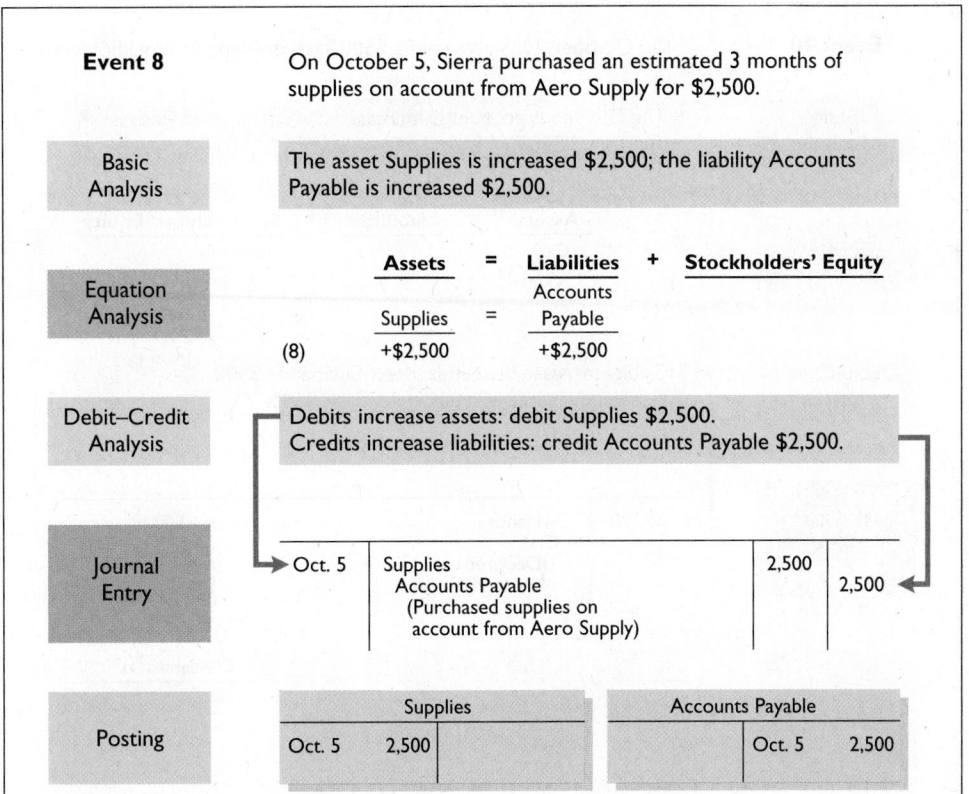

**Illustration 3-28**
Purchase of supplies on
account

**Event 8**    On October 5, Sierra purchased an estimated 3 months of
supplies on account from Aero Supply for $2,500.

**Basic Analysis**    The asset Supplies is increased $2,500; the liability Accounts Payable is increased $2,500.

**Equation Analysis**

|   | **Assets** | **=** | **Liabilities** | **+** | **Stockholders' Equity** |
|---|---|---|---|---|---|
|   |  |  | Accounts |  |  |
|   | Supplies | = | Payable |  |  |
| (8) | +$2,500 |  | +$2,500 |  |  |

**Debit–Credit Analysis**    Debits increase assets: debit Supplies $2,500.
Credits increase liabilities: credit Accounts Payable $2,500.

**Journal Entry**

| Oct. 5 | Supplies | 2,500 |  |
|---|---|---|---|
|  | Accounts Payable |  | 2,500 |
|  | (Purchased supplies on account from Aero Supply) |  |  |

**Posting**

| Supplies | | Accounts Payable | |
|---|---|---|---|
| Oct. 5    2,500 | | | Oct. 5    2,500 |

**Illustration 3-29**    Hiring
of new employees

**Event 9**    On October 9, Sierra hired four employees to begin work on
October 15. Each employee will receive a weekly salary
of $500 for a 5-day work week, payable every 2 weeks—first
payment made on October 26.

**Basic Analysis**    An accounting transaction has not occurred. There is only an
agreement that the employees will begin work on October 15.
Thus, a debit–credit analysis is not needed because there is no
accounting entry. (See transaction of October 26 (Event II) for
first payment.)

**Illustration 3-30**
Payment of dividend

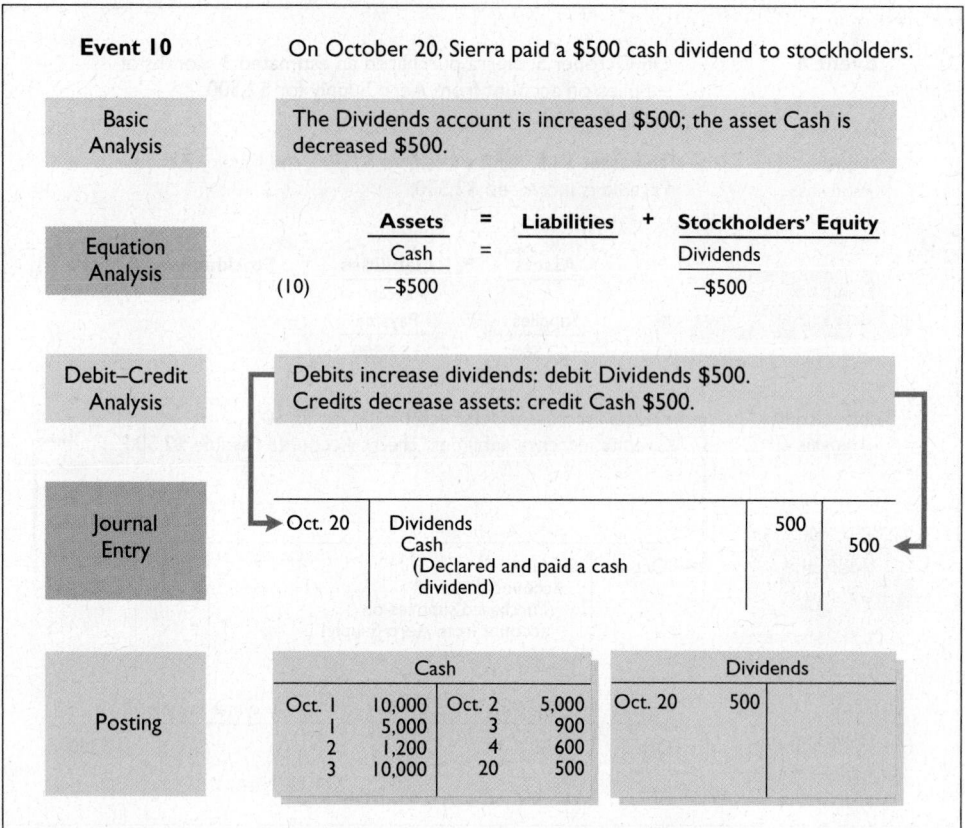

**Illustration 3-31** Payment of cash for employee salaries

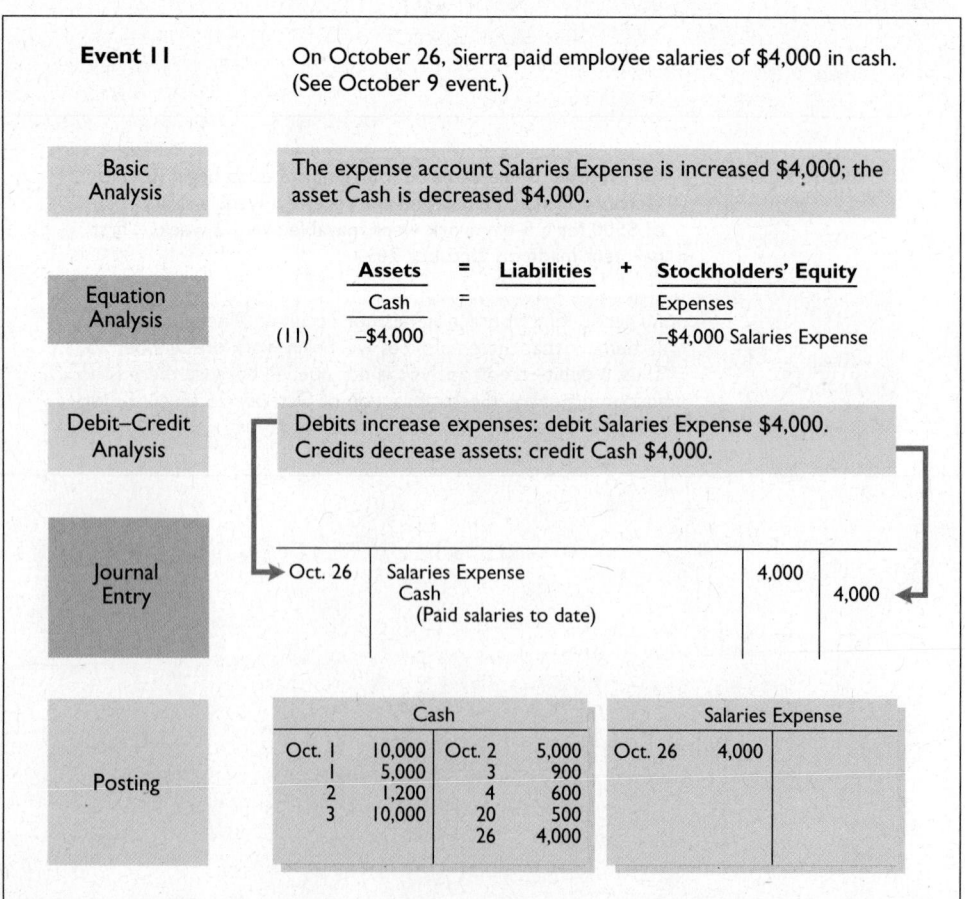

## SUMMARY ILLUSTRATION OF JOURNALIZING AND POSTING

The journal for Sierra Corporation for the month of October is summarized in Illustration 3-32. The ledger is shown in Illustration 3-33 (on page 128) with all balances highlighted in red.

Illustration 3-33 (on page 128)

**Illustration 3-32** General journal for Sierra Corporation

### GENERAL JOURNAL

| Date | | Account Titles and Explanation | Debit | Credit |
|---|---|---|---|---|
| 2012 | | | | |
| Oct. | 1 | Cash | 10,000 | |
| | | Common Stock | | 10,000 |
| | | (Issued stock for cash) | | |
| | 1 | Cash | 5,000 | |
| | | Notes Payable | | 5,000 |
| | | (Issued 3-month, 12% note payable for cash) | | |
| | 2 | Equipment | 5,000 | |
| | | Cash | | 5,000 |
| | | (Purchased equipment for cash) | | |
| | 2 | Cash | 1,200 | |
| | | Unearned Service Revenue | | 1,200 |
| | | (Received advance from R. Knox for future service) | | |
| | 3 | Cash | 10,000 | |
| | | Service Revenue | | 10,000 |
| | | (Received cash for services provided) | | |
| | 3 | Rent Expense | 900 | |
| | | Cash | | 900 |
| | | (Paid cash for October office rent) | | |
| | 4 | Prepaid Insurance | 600 | |
| | | Cash | | 600 |
| | | (Paid 1-year policy; effective date October 1) | | |
| | 5 | Supplies | 2,500 | |
| | | Accounts Payable | | 2,500 |
| | | (Purchased supplies on account from Aero Supply) | | |
| | 20 | Dividends | 500 | |
| | | Cash | | 500 |
| | | (Paid a cash dividend) | | |
| | 26 | Salaries Expense | 4,000 | |
| | | Cash | | 4,000 |
| | | (Paid salaries to date) | | |

**Illustration 3-33** General ledger for Sierra Corporation

## GENERAL LEDGER

| Cash | | | | | |
|------|------|------|------|------|------|
| Oct. 1 | 10,000 | Oct. 2 | 5,000 | | |
| 1 | 5,000 | 3 | 900 | | |
| 2 | 1,200 | 4 | 600 | | |
| 3 | 10,000 | 20 | 500 | | |
| | | 26 | 4,000 | | |
| Bal. | 15,200 | | | | |

| Unearned Service Revenue | | | |
|------|------|------|------|
| | | Oct. 2 | 1,200 |
| | | Bal. | 1,200 |

| Supplies | | |
|------|------|------|
| Oct. 5 | 2,500 | |
| Bal. | 2,500 | |

| Common Stock | | |
|------|------|------|
| | Oct. 1 | 10,000 |
| | Bal. | 10,000 |

| Prepaid Insurance | | |
|------|------|------|
| Oct. 4 | 600 | |
| Bal. | 600 | |

| Dividends | | |
|------|------|------|
| Oct. 20 | 500 | |
| Bal. | 500 | |

| Equipment | | |
|------|------|------|
| Oct. 2 | 5,000 | |
| Bal. | 5,000 | |

| Service Revenue | | |
|------|------|------|
| | Oct. 3 | 10,000 |
| | Bal. | 10,000 |

| Notes Payable | | |
|------|------|------|
| | Oct. 1 | 5,000 |
| | Bal. | 5,000 |

| Salaries Expense | | |
|------|------|------|
| Oct. 26 | 4,000 | |
| Bal. | 4,000 | |

| Accounts Payable | | |
|------|------|------|
| | Oct. 5 | 2,500 |
| | Bal. | 2,500 |

| Rent Expense | | |
|------|------|------|
| Oct. 3 | 900 | |
| Bal. | 900 | |

## before you go on...

**POSTING**

# Do it!

Selected transactions from the journal of Faital Inc. during its first month of operations are presented below. Post these transactions to T accounts.

| Date | | Account Titles | Debit | Credit |
|------|------|------|------|------|
| July | 1 | Cash | 30,000 | |
| | | Common Stock | | 30,000 |
| | 9 | Accounts Receivable | 6,000 | |
| | | Service Revenue | | 6,000 |
| | 24 | Cash | 4,000 | |
| | | Accounts Receivable | | 4,000 |

### Action Plan

- Journalize transactions to keep track of financial activities (receipts, payments, receivables, payables, etc.).
- To make entries useful, classify and summarize them by posting the entries to specific ledger accounts.

### Solution

| Cash | | |
|------|------|------|
| July 1 | 30,000 | |
| 24 | 4,000 | |

| Accounts Receivable | | | |
|------|------|------|------|
| July 9 | 6,000 | July 24 | 4,000 |

| Common Stock | | |
|------|------|------|
| | July 1 | 30,000 |

| Service Revenue | | |
|------|------|------|
| | July 9 | 6,000 |

the navigator

Related exercise material: **BE3-10**, *Do it!* **3-4**, and **E3-11**.

# The Trial Balance

A **trial balance** lists accounts and their balances at a given time. A company usually prepares a trial balance at the end of an accounting period. The accounts are listed in the order in which they appear in the ledger. Debit balances are listed in the left column and credit balances in the right column. The totals of the two columns must be equal.

**study objective 8**

Explain the purposes of a trial balance.

**The trial balance proves the mathematical equality of debits and credits after posting.** Under the double-entry system this equality occurs when the sum of the debit account balances equals the sum of the credit account balances. **A trial balance may also uncover errors in journalizing and posting.** For example, a trial balance may well have detected the error at Fidelity Investments discussed in the Feature Story. **In addition, a trial balance is useful in the preparation of financial statements.**

These are the procedures for preparing a trial balance:

1. List the account titles and their balances.
2. Total the debit column and total the credit column.
3. Verify the equality of the two columns.

Illustration 3-34 presents the trial balance prepared from the ledger of Sierra Corporation. Note that the total debits, $28,700, equal the total credits, $28,700.

**Illustration 3-34** Sierra Corporation trial balance

| SIERRA CORPORATION Trial Balance October 31, 2012 | | |
|---|---|---|
| | **Debit** | **Credit** |
| Cash | $15,200 | |
| Supplies | 2,500 | |
| Prepaid Insurance | 600 | |
| Equipment | 5,000 | |
| Notes Payable | | $ 5,000 |
| Accounts Payable | | 2,500 |
| Unearned Service Revenue | | 1,200 |
| Common Stock | | 10,000 |
| Dividends | 500 | |
| Service Revenue | | 10,000 |
| Salaries Expense | 4,000 | |
| Rent Expense | 900 | |
| | $28,700 | $28,700 |

**Helpful Hint** Note that the order of presentation in the trial balance is:
  Assets
  Liabilities
  Stockholders' equity
  Revenues
  Expenses

## LIMITATIONS OF A TRIAL BALANCE

A trial balance does not prove that all transactions have been recorded or that the ledger is correct. Numerous errors may exist even though the trial balance column totals agree. For example, the trial balance may balance even when any of the following occurs: (1) a transaction is not journalized, (2) a correct journal entry is not posted, (3) a journal entry is posted twice, (4) incorrect accounts are used in journalizing or posting, or (5) offsetting errors are made in recording the amount of a transaction. In other words, as long as equal debits and credits are posted, even to the wrong account or in the wrong amount, the total debits will equal the total credits. Nevertheless, despite these limitations, the trial balance is a useful screen for finding errors and is frequently used in practice.

**Ethics Note** An *error* is the result of an unintentional mistake; it is neither ethical nor unethical. An *irregularity* is an intentional misstatement, which *is* viewed as unethical.

# DECISION TOOLKIT

| DECISION CHECKPOINTS | INFO NEEDED FOR DECISION | TOOL TO USE FOR DECISION | HOW TO EVALUATE RESULTS |
|---|---|---|---|
| How do you determine that debits equal credits? | All account balances | Trial balance | List the account titles and their balances; total the debit and credit columns; verify equality. |

## KEEPING AN EYE ON CASH

The Cash account shown below reflects all of the inflows and outflows of cash that occurred during October. We have also provided a description of each transaction that affected the Cash account.

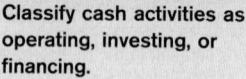

|        | Cash |        |         |   |       |
|--------|------|--------|---------|---|-------|
| Oct. 1 | 10,000 | Oct. | 2 |   | 5,000 |
|      1 | 5,000  |      | 3 |   | 900   |
|      2 | 1,200  |      | 4 |   | 600   |
|      3 | 10,000 |      | 20 |  | 500   |
|        |        |      | 26 |  | 4,000 |
| Bal.   | **15,200** |  |   |   |       |

1. Oct. 1 Issued stock for $10,000 cash.
2. Oct. 1 Issued note payable for $5,000 cash.
3. Oct. 2 Purchased equipment for $5,000 cash.
4. Oct. 2 Received $1,200 cash in advance from customer.
5. Oct. 3 Received $10,000 cash for services provided.
6. Oct. 3 Paid $900 cash for October rent.
7. Oct. 4 Paid $600 cash for one-year insurance policy.
8. Oct. 20 Paid $500 cash dividend to stockholders.
9. Oct. 26 Paid $4,000 cash salaries.

The Cash account and the related cash transactions indicate why cash changed during October. However, to make this information useful for analysis, it is summarized in a statement of cash flows. The statement of cash flows classifies each transaction as an operating activity, an investing activity, or a financing activity. A user of this statement can then determine the amount of cash provided by operations, the amount of cash used for investing purposes, and the amount of cash provided by financing activities.

*Operating activities* are the types of activities the company performs to generate profits. Sierra Corporation is an outdoor guide business, so its operating activities involve providing guide services. Activities 4, 5, 6, 7, and 9 relate to cash received or spent to directly support its guide services.

**study objective** 9

Classify cash activities as operating, investing, or financing.

*Investing activities* include the purchase or sale of long-lived assets used in operating the business, or the purchase or sale of investment securities (stocks and bonds of companies other than Sierra). Activity 3, the purchase of equipment, is an investment activity.

The primary types of *financing activities* are borrowing money, issuing shares of stock, and paying dividends. The financing activities of Sierra Corporation are activities 1, 2, and 8.

# USING THE DECISION TOOLKIT

The Kansas Farmers' Vertically Integrated Cooperative, Inc. (K-VIC) was formed by over 200 northeast Kansas farmers in the late 1980s. Its purpose is to use raw materials, primarily grain and meat products grown by K-VIC's members, to process this material into end-user food products, and to distribute the products nationally. Profits not needed for expansion or investment are returned to the members annually, on a pro-rata basis, according to the fair value of the grain and meat products received from each farmer.

Assume that the following trial balance was prepared for K-VIC.

## KANSAS FARMERS' VERTICALLY INTEGRATED COOPERATIVE, INC.
### Trial Balance
### December 31, 2012
### (in thousands)

|  | Debit | Credit |
|---|---|---|
| Accounts Receivable | $ 712,000 | |
| Accounts Payable | | $ 673,000 |
| Buildings | 365,000 | |
| Cash | 32,000 | |
| Cost of Goods Sold | 2,384,000 | |
| Notes Payable (due in 2013) | | 12,000 |
| Inventory | 1,291,000 | |
| Land | 110,000 | |
| Mortgage Payable | | 873,000 |
| Equipment | 63,000 | |
| Retained Earnings | | 822,000 |
| Sales Revenue | | 3,741,000 |
| Salaries and Wages Payable | | 62,000 |
| Salaries and Wages Expense | 651,000 | |
| Maintenance and Repairs Expense | 500,000 | |
| | $6,108,000 | $6,183,000 |

Because the trial balance is not in balance, you have checked with various people responsible for entering accounting data and have discovered the following.

1. The purchase of 35 new trucks, costing $7 million and paid for with cash, was not recorded.

2. A data entry clerk accidentally deleted the account name for an account with a credit balance of $472 million, so the amount was added to the Mortgage Payable account in the trial balance.

3. December cash sales revenue of $75 million was credited to the Sales Revenue account, but the other half of the entry was not made.

4. $50 million of salaries expenses were mistakenly charged to Maintenance and Repairs Expense.

### Instructions

Answer these questions.

(a) Which mistake(s) have caused the trial balance to be out of balance?

(b) Should all of the items be corrected? Explain.

(c) What is the name of the account the data entry clerk deleted?

(d) Make the necessary corrections and prepare a correct trial balance with accounts listed in proper order.

(e) On your trial balance, write BAL beside the accounts that go on the balance sheet and INC beside those that go on the income statement.

### Solution

(a) Only mistake #3 has caused the trial balance to be out of balance.

(b) All of the items should be corrected. The misclassification error (mistake #4) on the salaries expense would not affect bottom-line net income, but it does affect the amounts reported in the two expense accounts.

(c) There is no Common Stock account, so that must be the account that was deleted by the data entry clerk.

(d) and (e):

### KANSAS FARMERS' VERTICALLY INTEGRATED COOPERATIVE, INC.
### Trial Balance
### December 31, 2012
### (in thousands)

|  | Debit | Credit |  |
|---|---|---|---|
| Cash ($32,000 − $7,000 + $75,000) | $ 100,000 |  | BAL |
| Accounts Receivable | 712,000 |  | BAL |
| Inventory | 1,291,000 |  | BAL |
| Land | 110,000 |  | BAL |
| Equipment ($63,000 + $7,000) | 70,000 |  | BAL |
| Buildings | 365,000 |  | BAL |
| Accounts Payable |  | $ 673,000 | BAL |
| Salaries and Wages Payable |  | 62,000 | BAL |
| Notes Payable (due in 2013) |  | 12,000 | BAL |
| Mortgage Payable ($873,000 − $472,000) |  | 401,000 | BAL |
| Common Stock |  | 472,000 | BAL |
| Retained Earnings |  | 822,000 | BAL |
| Sales Revenue |  | 3,741,000 | INC |
| Cost of Goods Sold | 2,384,000 |  | INC |
| Salaries and Wages Expense | 701,000 |  | INC |
| Maintenance and Repairs Expense | 450,000 |  | INC |
|  | $6,183,000 | $6,183,000 |  |

# Summary of Study Objectives

**1** **Analyze the effect of business transactions on the basic accounting equation.** Each business transaction must have a dual effect on the accounting equation. For example, if an individual asset is increased, there must be a corresponding (a) decrease in another asset, or (b) increase in a specific liability, or (c) increase in stockholders' equity.

**2** **Explain what an account is and how it helps in the recording process.** An account is an individual accounting record of increases and decreases in specific asset, liability, and stockholders' equity items.

**3** **Define debits and credits and explain how they are used to record business transactions.** The terms *debit* and *credit* are synonymous with *left* and *right*. Assets, dividends, and expenses are increased by debits and decreased by credits. Liabilities, common stock, retained earnings, and revenues are increased by credits and decreased by debits.

**4** **Identify the basic steps in the recording process.** The basic steps in the recording process are: (a) analyze each transaction in terms of its effect on the accounts, (b) enter the transaction information in a journal, and (c) transfer the journal information to the appropriate accounts in the ledger.

**5** **Explain what a journal is and how it helps in the recording process.** The initial accounting record of a transaction is entered in a journal before the data are entered in the accounts. A journal (a) discloses in one place the complete effect of a transaction, (b) provides a chronological record of transactions, and (c) prevents or locates errors because the debit and credit amounts for each entry can be readily compared.

**6** **Explain what a ledger is and how it helps in the recording process.** The entire group of accounts maintained by a company is referred to collectively as a ledger. The ledger keeps in one place all the information about changes in specific account balances.

**7** **Explain what posting is and how it helps in the recording process.** Posting is the procedure of transferring journal entries to the ledger accounts. This phase of the recording process accumulates the effects of journalized transactions in the individual accounts.

**8** **Explain the purposes of a trial balance.** A trial balance is a list of accounts and their balances at a given time. The primary purpose of the trial balance is to prove the mathematical equality of debits and credits after posting. A trial balance also uncovers errors in journalizing and posting and is useful in preparing financial statements.

**9 Classify cash activities as operating, investing, or financing.** Operating activities are the types of activities the company uses to generate profits. Investing activities relate to the purchase or sale of long-lived assets used in operating the business, or to the purchase or sale of investment securities (stock and bonds of other companies). Financing activities are borrowing money, issuing shares of stock, and paying dividends.

## DECISION TOOLKIT   A SUMMARY

| DECISION CHECKPOINTS | INFO NEEDED FOR DECISION | TOOL TO USE FOR DECISION | HOW TO EVALUATE RESULTS |
|---|---|---|---|
| Has an accounting transaction occurred? | Details of the event | Accounting equation | If the event affected assets, liabilities, or stockholders' equity, then record as a transaction. |
| How do you determine that debits equal credits? | All account balances | Trial balance | List the account titles and their balances; total the debit and credit colums; verify equality. |

## Glossary

**Account** *(p. 111)* An individual accounting record of increases and decreases in specific asset, liability, stockholders' equity, revenue or expense items.

**Accounting information system** *(p. 102)* The system of collecting and processing transaction data and communicating financial information to decision makers.

**Accounting transactions** *(p. 102)* Events that require recording in the financial statements because they affect assets, liabilities, or stockholders' equity.

**Chart of accounts** *(p. 120)* A list of a company's accounts.

**Credit** *(p. 111)* The right side of an account.

**Debit** *(p. 111)* The left side of an account.

**Double-entry system** *(p. 112)* A system that records the two-sided effect of each transaction in appropriate accounts.

**General journal** *(p. 117)* The most basic form of journal.

**General ledger** *(p. 119)* A ledger that contains all asset, liability, stockholders' equity, revenue, and expense accounts.

**Journal** *(p. 117)* An accounting record in which transactions are initially recorded in chronological order.

**Journalizing** *(p. 117)* The procedure of entering transaction data in the journal.

**Ledger** *(p. 119)* The group of accounts maintained by a company.

**Posting** *(p. 120)* The procedure of transferring journal entry amounts to the ledger accounts.

**T account** *(p. 111)* The basic form of an account.

**Trial balance** *(p. 129)* A list of accounts and their balances at a given time.

## Comprehensive Do it!

Bob Sample and other student investors opened Campus Carpet Cleaning, Inc. on September 1, 2012. During the first month of operations, the following transactions occurred.

Sept. 1 Stockholders invested $20,000 cash in the business.
2 Paid $1,000 cash for store rent for the month of September.
3 Purchased industrial carpet-cleaning equipment for $25,000, paying $10,000 in cash and signing a $15,000 6-month, 12% note payable.
4 Paid $1,200 for 1-year accident insurance policy.
10 Received bill from the *Daily News* for advertising the opening of the cleaning service, $200.
15 Performed services on account for $6,200.
20 Paid a $700 cash dividend to stockholders.
30 Received $5,000 from customers billed on September 15.

The chart of accounts for the company is the same as for Sierra Corporation except for the following additional account: Advertising Expense.

### Instructions

(a) Journalize the September transactions.
(b) Open ledger accounts and post the September transactions.
(c) Prepare a trial balance at September 30, 2012.

## Action Plan

• Proceed through the accounting cycle in the following sequence:

1. Make separate journal entries for each transaction.

2. Note that all debits precede all credit entries.

3. In journalizing, make sure debits equal credits.

4. In journalizing, use specific account titles taken from the chart of accounts.

5. Provide an appropriate explanation of each journal entry.

6. Arrange ledger in statement order, beginning with the balance sheet accounts.

7. Post in chronological order.

8. Prepare a trial balance, which lists accounts in the order in which they appear in the ledger.

9. List debit balances in the left column and credit balances in the right column.

## Solution to Comprehensive Do it!

(a)

### GENERAL JOURNAL

| Date | | Account Titles and Explanation | Debit | Credit |
|---|---|---|---|---|
| 2012 Sept. | 1 | Cash | 20,000 | |
| | | Common Stock | | 20,000 |
| | | (Issued stock for cash) | | |
| | 2 | Rent Expense | 1,000 | |
| | | Cash | | 1,000 |
| | | (Paid September rent) | | |
| | 3 | Equipment | 25,000 | |
| | | Cash | | 10,000 |
| | | Notes Payable | | 15,000 |
| | | (Purchased cleaning equipment for cash and 6-month, 12% note payable) | | |
| | 4 | Prepaid Insurance | 1,200 | |
| | | Cash | | 1,200 |
| | | (Paid 1-year insurance policy) | | |
| | 10 | Advertising Expense | 200 | |
| | | Accounts Payable · | | 200 |
| | | (Received bill from *Daily News* for advertising) | | |
| | 15 | Accounts Receivable | 6,200 | |
| | | Service Revenue | | 6,200 |
| | | (Services performed on account) | | |
| | 20 | Dividends | 700 | |
| | | Cash | | 700 |
| | | (Declared and paid a cash dividend) | | |
| | 30 | Cash | 5,000 | |
| | | Accounts Receivable | | 5,000 |
| | | (Collection of accounts receivable) | | |

(b)

### GENERAL LEDGER

**Cash**

| Sept. | 1 | 20,000 | Sept. | 2 | 1,000 |
|---|---|---|---|---|---|
| | 30 | 5,000 | | 3 | 10,000 |
| | | | | 4 | 1,200 |
| | | | | 20 | 700 |
| Bal. | | 12,100 | | | |

**Common Stock**

| | | | Sept. | 1 | 20,000 |
|---|---|---|---|---|---|
| | | | Bal. | | 20,000 |

**Accounts Receivable**

| Sept. | 15 | 6,200 | Sept. | 30 | 5,000 |
|---|---|---|---|---|---|
| Bal. | | 1,200 | | | |

**Dividends**

| Sept. | 20 | 700 | | | |
|---|---|---|---|---|---|
| Bal. | | 700 | | | |

| Prepaid Insurance | | | |
|---|---|---|---|
| Sept. 4 | 1,200 | | |
| Bal. | 1,200 | | |

| Service Revenue | | | |
|---|---|---|---|
| | | Sept. 15 | 6,200 |
| | | Bal. | 6,200 |

| Equipment | | | |
|---|---|---|---|
| Sept. 3 | 25,000 | | |
| Bal. | 25,000 | | |

| Advertising Expense | | | |
|---|---|---|---|
| Sept. 10 | 200 | | |
| Bal. | 200 | | |

| Notes Payable | | | |
|---|---|---|---|
| | | Sept. 3 | 15,000 |
| | | Bal. | 15,000 |

| Rent Expense | | | |
|---|---|---|---|
| Sept. 2 | 1,000 | | |
| Bal. | 1,000 | | |

| Accounts Payable | | | |
|---|---|---|---|
| | | Sept. 10 | 200 |
| | | Bal. | 200 |

(c)

**CAMPUS CARPET CLEANING, INC.**
**Trial Balance**
**September 30, 2012**

| | Debit | Credit |
|---|---|---|
| Cash | $12,100 | |
| Accounts Receivable | 1,200 | |
| Prepaid Insurance | 1,200 | |
| Equipment | 25,000 | |
| Notes Payable | | $15,000 |
| Accounts Payable | | 200 |
| Common Stock | | 20,000 |
| Dividends | 700 | |
| Service Revenue | | 6,200 |
| Advertising Expense | 200 | |
| Rent Expense | 1,000 | |
| | $41,400 | $41,400 |

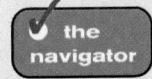

 Self-Test, Brief Exercises, Exercises, Problem Set A, and many more resources are available for practice in WileyPLUS

# Self-Test Questions

Answers are on page 159.

(SO 1)  **1.** The effects on the basic accounting equation of performing services for cash are to:
(a) increase assets and decrease stockholders' equity.
(b) increase assets and increase stockholders' equity.
(c) increase assets and increase liabilities.
(d) increase liabilities and increase stockholders' equity.

**2.** Genesis Company buys a $900 machine on credit. (SO 1) This transaction will affect the:
(a) income statement only.
(b) balance sheet only.
(c) income statement and retained earnings statement only.
(d) income statement, retained earnings statement, and balance sheet.

(SO 1) 3. Which of the following events is *not* recorded in the accounting records?
(a) Equipment is purchased on account.
(b) An employee is terminated.
(c) A cash investment is made into the business.
(d) Company pays dividend to stockholders.

(SO 1) 4. During 2012, Gibson Company assets decreased $50,000 and its liabilities decreased $90,000. Its stockholders' equity therefore:
(a) increased $40,000.
(b) decreased $140,000.
(c) decreased $40,000.
(d) increased $140,000.

(SO 2) 5. Which statement about an account is *true*?
(a) In its simplest form, an account consists of two parts.
(b) An account is an individual accounting record of increases and decreases in specific asset, liability, and stockholders' equity items.
(c) There are separate accounts for specific assets and liabilities but only one account for stockholders' equity items.
(d) The left side of an account is the credit or decrease side.

(SO 3) 6. Debits:
(a) increase both assets and liabilities.
(b) decrease both assets and liabilities.
(c) increase assets and decrease liabilities.
(d) decrease assets and increase liabilities.

(SO 3) 7. A revenue account:
(a) is increased by debits.
(b) is decreased by credits.
(c) has a normal balance of a debit.
(d) is increased by credits.

(SO 3) 8. Which accounts normally have debit balances?
(a) Assets, expenses, and revenues.
(b) Assets, expenses, and retained earnings.
(c) Assets, liabilities, and dividends.
(d) Assets, dividends, and expenses.

(SO 3) 9. Paying an account payable with cash affects the components of the accounting equation in the following way:
(a) Decreases stockholders' equity and decreases liabilities.
(b) Increases assets and decreases liabilities.
(c) Decreases assets and increases stockholders' equity.
(d) Decreases assets and decreases liabilities.

10. Which is *not* part of the recording process? (SO 4)
(a) Analyzing transactions.
(b) Preparing a trial balance.
(c) Entering transactions in a journal.
(d) Posting transactions.

11. Which of these statements about a journal is *false*? (SO 5)
(a) It contains only revenue and expense accounts.
(b) It provides a chronological record of transactions.
(c) It helps to locate errors because the debit and credit amounts for each entry can be readily compared.
(d) It discloses in one place the complete effect of a transaction.

12. A ledger: (SO 6)
(a) contains only asset and liability accounts.
(b) should show accounts in alphabetical order.
(c) is a collection of the entire group of accounts maintained by a company.
(d) provides a chronological record of transactions.

13. Posting: (SO 7)
(a) normally occurs before journalizing.
(b) transfers ledger transaction data to the journal.
(c) is an optional step in the recording process.
(d) transfers journal entries to ledger accounts.

14. A trial balance: (SO 8)
(a) is a list of accounts with their balances at a given time.
(b) proves that proper account titles were used.
(c) will not balance if a correct journal entry is posted twice.
(d) proves that all transactions have been recorded.

15. A trial balance will *not* balance if: (SO 8)
(a) a correct journal entry is posted twice.
(b) the purchase of supplies on account is debited to Supplies and credited to Cash.
(c) a $100 cash dividend is debited to Dividends for $1,000 and credited to Cash for $100.
(d) a $450 payment on account is debited to Accounts Payable for $45 and credited to Cash for $45.

Go to the book's companion website, **www.wiley.com/college/kimmel**, to access additional Self-Test Questions.

## Questions

1. Describe the accounting information system.

2. Can a business enter into a transaction that affects only the left side of the basic accounting equation? If so, give an example.

3. Are the following events recorded in the accounting records? Explain your answer in each case.

(a) A major stockholder of the company dies.
(b) Supplies are purchased on account.
(c) An employee is fired.
(d) The company pays a cash dividend to its stockholders.

4. Indicate how each business transaction affects the basic accounting equation.
(a) Paid cash for janitorial services.
(b) Purchased equipment for cash.

(c) Issued common stock to investors in exchange for cash.

(d) Paid an account payable in full.

5. Why is an account referred to as a T account?

6. The terms *debit* and *credit* mean "increase" and "decrease," respectively. Do you agree? Explain.

7. James Quest, a fellow student, contends that the double-entry system means each transaction must be recorded twice. Is James correct? Explain.

8. Gayle Weir, a beginning accounting student, believes debit balances are favorable and credit balances are unfavorable. Is Gayle correct? Discuss.

9. State the rules of debit and credit as applied to (a) asset accounts, (b) liability accounts, and (c) the common stock account.

10. What is the normal balance for each of these accounts?
(a) Accounts Receivable.
(b) Cash.
(c) Dividends.
(d) Accounts Payable.
(e) Service Revenue.
(f) Salaries and Wages Expense.
(g) Common Stock.

11. Indicate whether each account is an asset, a liability, or a stockholders' equity account, and whether it would have a normal debit or credit balance.
(a) Accounts Receivable.    (d) Dividends.
(b) Accounts Payable.    (e) Supplies.
(c) Equipment.

12. For the following transactions, indicate the account debited and the account credited.
(a) Supplies are purchased on account.
(b) Cash is received on signing a note payable.
(c) Employees are paid salaries in cash.

13. For each account listed here, indicate whether it generally will have debit entries only, credit entries only, or both debit and credit entries.
(a) Cash.
(b) Accounts Receivable.
(c) Dividends.
(d) Accounts Payable.

(e) Salaries and Wages Expense.
(f) Service Revenue.

14. [Tootsie Roll]    What are the normal balances for the following accounts of Tootsie Roll Industries? (a) Accounts Receivable, (b) Income Taxes Payable, (c) Sales, and (d) Selling, Marketing, and Administrative Expenses.

15. What are the basic steps in the recording process?

16. (a) When entering a transaction in the journal, should the debit or credit be written first?
(b) Which should be indented, the debit or the credit?

17. (a) Should accounting transaction debits and credits be recorded directly in the ledger accounts?
(b) What are the advantages of first recording transactions in the journal and then posting to the ledger?

18. Journalize these accounting transactions.
(a) Stockholders invested $12,000 in the business in exchange for common stock.
(b) Insurance of $800 is paid for the year.
(c) Supplies of $1,800 are purchased on account.
(d) Cash of $7,500 is received for services rendered.

19. (a) What is a ledger?
(b) Why is a chart of accounts important?

20. What is a trial balance and what are its purposes?

21. Kevin Haden is confused about how accounting information flows through the accounting system. He believes information flows in this order:
(a) Debits and credits are posted to the ledger.
(b) Accounting transaction occurs.
(c) Information is entered in the journal.
(d) Financial statements are prepared.
(e) Trial balance is prepared.
Indicate to Kevin the proper flow of the information.

22. Two students are discussing the use of a trial balance. They wonder whether the following errors, each considered separately, would prevent the trial balance from balancing. What would you tell them?
(a) The bookkeeper debited Cash for $600 and credited Wages Expense for $600 for payment of wages.
(b) Cash collected on account was debited to Cash for $800, and Service Revenue was credited for $80.

# Brief Exercises

**BE3-1**    Presented below are three economic events. On a sheet of paper, list the letters (a), (b), and (c) with columns for assets, liabilities, and stockholders' equity. In each column, indicate whether the event increased (+), decreased (−), or had no effect (NE) on assets, liabilities, and stockholders' equity.
(a) Purchased supplies on account.
(b) Received cash for providing a service.
(c) Expenses paid in cash.

*Determine effect of transactions on basic accounting equation.*
(SO 1), **C**

**BE3-2**    During 2012, Gavin Corp. entered into the following transactions.
1. Borrowed $60,000 by issuing bonds.
2. Paid $9,000 cash dividend to stockholders.
3. Received $13,000 cash from a previously billed customer for services provided.
4. Purchased supplies on account for $3,100.

*Determine effect of transactions on basic accounting equation.*
(SO 1), **AP**

Using the following tabular analysis, show the effect of each transaction on the accounting equation. Put explanations for changes to Stockholders' Equity in the right-hand margin. For Retained Earnings, use separate columns for Revenues, Expenses, and Dividends if necessary. Use Illustration 3-3 (page 110) as a model.

| Assets | | | = | Liabilities | | + | Stockholders' Equity | |
|---|---|---|---|---|---|---|---|---|
| | Accounts | | | Accounts | Bonds | | Common | Retained |
| Cash + | Receivable + | Supplies = | | Payable + | Payable + | | Stock + | Earnings |

*Determine effect of transactions on basic accounting equation.*
(SO 1), **AP**

**BE3-3**  During 2012, Newberry Company entered into the following transactions.
1. Purchased equipment for $286,176 cash.
2. Issued common stock to investors for $137,590 cash.
3. Purchased inventory of $68,480 on account.

Using the following tabular analysis, show the effect of each transaction on the accounting equation. Put explanations for changes to Stockholders' Equity in the right-hand margin. For Retained Earnings, use separate columns for Revenues, Expenses, and Dividends if necessary. Use Illustration 3-3 (page 110) as a model.

| Assets | | | = | Liabilities | + | Stockholders' Equity | |
|---|---|---|---|---|---|---|---|
| | | | | Accounts | | Common | Retained |
| Cash + | Inventory + | Equipment = | | Payable | + | Stock + | Earnings |

*Indicate debit and credit effects.*
(SO 3), **K**

**BE3-4**  For each of the following accounts, indicate the effect of a debit or a credit on the account and the normal balance.
(a) Accounts Payable.        (d) Accounts Receivable.
(b) Advertising Expense.     (e) Retained Earnings.
(c) Service Revenue.         (f) Dividends.

*Identify accounts to be debited and credited.*
(SO 3), **C**

**BE3-5**  Transactions for Marlin Company for the month of June are presented below. Identify the accounts to be debited and credited for each transaction.

June 1  Issues common stock to investors in exchange for $5,000 cash.
     2  Buys equipment on account for $1,100.
     3  Pays $740 to landlord for June rent.
    12  Bills Matt Wilfer $700 for welding work done.

*Journalize transactions.*
(SO 5), **AP**

**BE3-6**  Use the data in BE3-5 and journalize the transactions. (You may omit explanations.)

*Identify steps in the recording process.*
(SO 4), **C**

**BE3-7**  Eugenie Steckler, a fellow student, is unclear about the basic steps in the recording process. Identify and briefly explain the steps in the order in which they occur.

*Indicate basic debit–credit analysis.*
(SO 4), **C**

**BE3-8**  Acker Corporation has the following transactions during August of the current year. Indicate (a) the basic analysis and (b) the debit–credit analysis illustrated on pages 121–126.
Aug. 1  Issues shares of common stock to investors in exchange for $10,000.
     4  Pays insurance in advance for 3 months, $1,500.
    16  Receives $900 from clients for services rendered.
    27  Pays the secretary $620 salary.

*Journalize transactions.*
(SO 5), **AP**

**BE3-9**  Use the data in BE3-8 and journalize the transactions. (You may omit explanations.)

*Post journal entries to T accounts.*
(SO 7), **AP**

**BE3-10**  Selected transactions for Rojas Company are presented below in journal form (without explanations). Post the transactions to T accounts.

| Date | Account Title | Debit | Credit |
|---|---|---|---|
| May  5 | Accounts Receivable | 3,800 | |
| | Service Revenue | | 3,800 |
| 12 | Cash | 1,600 | |
| | Accounts Receivable | | 1,600 |
| 15 | Cash | 2,000 | |
| | Service Revenue | | 2,000 |

**BE3-11** From the ledger balances below, prepare a trial balance for Lyndon Company at June 30, 2012. All account balances are normal.

*Prepare a trial balance.*
(SO 8), **AP**

| Accounts Payable | $ 1,000 | Service Revenue | $8,600 |
| Cash | 5,400 | Accounts Receivable | 3,000 |
| Common Stock | 18,000 | Salaries and Wages Expense | 4,000 |
| Dividends | 1,200 | Rent Expense | 1,000 |
| Equipment | 13,000 | | |

**BE3-12** An inexperienced bookkeeper prepared the following trial balance that does not balance. Prepare a correct trial balance, assuming all account balances are normal.

*Prepare a corrected trial balance.*
(SO 8), **AP**

**PELICAN COMPANY**
**Trial Balance**
**December 31, 2012**

| | Debit | Credit |
| --- | --- | --- |
| Cash | $20,800 | |
| Prepaid Insurance | | $ 3,500 |
| Accounts Payable | | 2,500 |
| Unearned Service Revenue | 1,800 | |
| Common Stock | | 10,000 |
| Retained Earnings | | 6,600 |
| Dividends | | 5,000 |
| Service Revenue | | 25,600 |
| Salaries and Wages Expense | 14,600 | |
| Rent Expense | | 2,600 |
| | $37,200 | $55,800 |

# Do it! Review

**Do it! 3-1** Transactions made by Leonardo Bloom Co. for the month of March are shown below. Prepare a tabular analysis that shows the effects of these transactions on the expanded accounting equation, similar to that shown in Illustration 3-3 (page 110).

*Prepare tabular analysis.*
(SO 1), **C**

1. The company provided $20,000 of services for customers on account.
2. The company received $20,000 in cash from customers who had been billed for services [in transaction (1)].
3. The company received a bill for $1,800 of advertising but will not pay it until a later date.
4. Leonardo Bloom Co. paid a cash dividend of $3,000.

**Do it! 3-2** Phil Eubanks has just rented space in a strip mall. In this space, he will open a photography studio, to be called Picture This! A friend has advised Phil to set up a double-entry set of accounting records in which to record all of his business transactions.

*Identify normal balances.*
(SO 2, 3), **C**

Identify the balance sheet accounts that Phil will likely need to record the transactions needed to open his business (a corporation). Indicate whether the normal balance of each account is a debit or credit.

**Do it! 3-3** Phil Eubanks engaged in the following activities in establishing his photography studio, Picture This!:

*Record business activities.*
(SO 4, 5), **AP**

1. Opened a bank account in the name of Picture This! and deposited $8,000 of his own money into this account in exchange for common stock.
2. Purchased photography supplies at a total cost of $950. The business paid $400 in cash, and the balance is on account.
3. Obtained estimates on the cost of photography equipment from three different manufacturers.

In what form (type of record) should Phil record these three activities? Prepare the entries to record the transactions.

*Post transactions.*
*(SO 6, 7),* **AP**

**Do it!** 3-4 Phil Eubanks recorded the following transactions during the month of April.

| Apr. 3 | Cash | 3,400 | |
|---|---|---|---|
| | Service Revenue | | 3,400 |
| 16 | Rent Expense | 500 | |
| | Cash | | 500 |
| 20 | Salaries and Wages Expense | 300 | |
| | Cash | | 300 |

Post these entries to the Cash account of the general ledger to determine the ending balance in cash. The beginning balance in cash on April 1 was $1,900.

# Exercises

*Analyze the effect of transactions.*
*(SO 1),* **C**

**E3-1** Selected transactions for Arnett Advertising Company, Inc., are listed here.

1. Issued common stock to investors in exchange for cash received from investors.
2. Paid monthly rent.
3. Received cash from customers when service was provided.
4. Billed customers for services performed.
5. Paid dividend to stockholders.
6. Incurred advertising expense on account.
7. Received cash from customers billed in (4).
8. Purchased additional equipment for cash.
9. Purchased equipment on account.

*Instructions*
Describe the effect of each transaction on assets, liabilities, and stockholders' equity. For example, the first answer is: (1) Increase in assets and increase in stockholders' equity.

*Analyze the effect of transactions on assets, liabilities, and stockholders' equity.*
*(SO 1),* **AP**

**E3-2** Delmont Company entered into these transactions during May 2012.

1. Purchased computers for office use for $30,000 from Dell on account.
2. Paid $4,000 cash for May rent on storage space.
3. Received $12,000 cash from customers for contracts billed in April.
4. Provided computer services to Lawton Construction Company for $5,000 cash.
5. Paid Southern States Power Co. $8,000 cash for energy usage in May.
6. Stockholders invested an additional $40,000 in the business in exchange for common stock of the company.
7. Paid Dell for the computers purchased in (1).
8. Incurred advertising expense for May of $1,300 on account.

*Instructions*
Using the following tabular analysis, show the effect of each transaction on the accounting equation. Put explanations for changes to Stockholders' Equity in the right-hand margin. Use Illustration 3-3 (page 110) as a model.

| Assets | | | = | Liabilities | + | | | Stockholders' Equity | | | |
|---|---|---|---|---|---|---|---|---|---|---|---|
| | Accounts | | | Accounts | | Common | | | Retained Earnings | | |
| Cash | + Receivable | + Equipment | = | Payable | + | Stock | + | Revenues | − Expenses | − | Dividends |

*Determine effect of transactions on basic accounting equation.*
*(SO 1),* **AP**

**E3-3** During 2012, its first year of operations as a delivery service, Underwood Corp. entered into the following transactions.

1. Issued shares of common stock to investors in exchange for $100,000 in cash.
2. Borrowed $45,000 by issuing bonds.
3. Purchased delivery trucks for $60,000 cash.
4. Received $16,000 from customers for services provided.
5. Purchased supplies for $4,700 on account.
6. Paid rent of $5,200.
7. Performed services on account for $10,000.

8. Paid salaries of $28,000.
9. Paid a dividend of $11,000 to shareholders.

**Instructions**

Using the following tabular analysis, show the effect of each transaction on the accounting equation. Put explanations for changes to Stockholders' Equity in the right-hand margin. Use Illustration 3-3 (page 110) as a model.

| Assets | | | | | = | Liabilities | | + | Stockholders' Equity | | | | |
|---|---|---|---|---|---|---|---|---|---|---|---|---|---|
| | | Accounts | | Equip- | | Accounts | Bonds | | Common | | Retained Earnings | | |
| Cash | + | Receivable | + Supplies | + ment | = | Payable | + Payable | + | Stock | + | Revenues − | Expenses − | Dividends |

**E3-4** A tabular analysis of the transactions made during August 2012 by Nigel Company during its first month of operations is shown below. Each increase and decrease in stockholders' equity is explained.

*Analyze transactions and compute net income.*
*(SO 1),* **AP**

| | Assets | | | | | = Liabilities | + | Stockholders' Equity | | | | | |
|---|---|---|---|---|---|---|---|---|---|---|---|---|---|
| | | | | | | Accounts | | Common | | Retained Earnings | | | |
| | Cash | + A/R | + Supp. | + Equip. | = | Payable | + | Stock | + | Rev. − | Exp. − | Div. | |
| 1. | +$20,000 | | | | | | | +$20,000 | | | | | Com. Stock |
| 2. | −1,000 | | | +$5,000 | | +$4,000 | | | | | | | |
| 3. | −750 | | +$750 | | | | | | | | | | |
| 4. | +4,100 | +$5,400 | | | | | | | | +$9,500 | | | Serv. Rev. |
| 5. | −1,500 | | | | | −1,500 | | | | | | | |
| 6. | −2,000 | | | | | | | | | | | −$2,000 | Div. |
| 7. | −800 | | | | | | | | | | −$ 800 | | Rent Exp. |
| 8. | +450 | −450 | | | | | | | | | | | |
| 9. | −3,000 | | | | | | | | | | −3,000 | | Sal. Exp. |
| 10. | | | | | | +300 | | | | | −300 | | Util. Exp. |

**Instructions**
(a) Describe each transaction.
(b) Determine how much stockholders' equity increased for the month.
(c) Compute the net income for the month.

**E3-5** The tabular analysis of transactions for Nigel Company is presented in E3-4.

*Prepare an income statement, retained earnings statement, and balance sheet.*
*(SO 1),* **AP**

**Instructions**
Prepare an income statement and a retained earnings statement for August and a classified balance sheet at August 31, 2012.

**E3-6** Selected transactions for Home Place, an interior decorator corporation, in its first month of business, are as follows.

*Identify debits, credits, and normal balances and journalize transactions.*
*(SO 3, 5),* **AP**

1. Issued stock to investors for $15,000 in cash.
2. Purchased used car for $10,000 cash for use in business.
3. Purchased supplies on account for $300.
4. Billed customers $3,700 for services performed.
5. Paid $200 cash for advertising start of the business.
6. Received $1,100 cash from customers billed in transaction (4).
7. Paid creditor $300 cash on account.
8. Paid dividends of $400 cash to stockholders.

**Instructions**
(a) For each transaction indicate (a) the basic type of account debited and credited (asset, liability, stockholders' equity); (b) the specific account debited and credited (Cash, Rent Expense, Service Revenue, etc.); (c) whether the specific account is increased or decreased; and (d) the normal balance of the specific account. Use the format shown on page 142, in which transaction 1 is given as an example.

| | | Account Debited | | | | Account Credited | | |
|---|---|---|---|---|---|---|---|---|
| | (a) | (b) | (c) | (d) | (a) | (b) | (c) | (d) |
| Trans-action | Basic Type | Specific Account | Effect | Normal Balance | Basic Type | Specific Account | Effect | Normal Balance |
| 1 | Asset | Cash | Increase | Debit | Stock-holders' equity | Common Stock | Increase | Credit |

(b) Journalize the transactions. Do not provide explanations.

*Analyze transactions and determine their effect on accounts.*

*(SO 3),* **C**

**E3-7** This information relates to Plunkett Real Estate Agency.

Oct. 1 Stockholders invest $30,000 in exchange for common stock of the corporation.
   2 Hires an administrative assistant at an annual salary of $36,000.
   3 Buys office furniture for $3,800, on account.
   6 Sells a house and lot for M.E. Petty; commissions due from Petty, $10,800 (not paid by Petty at this time).
   10 Receives cash of $140 as commission for acting as rental agent renting an apartment.
   27 Pays $700 on account for the office furniture purchased on October 3.
   30 Pays the administrative assistant $3,000 in salary for October.

**Instructions**
Prepare the debit–credit analysis for each transaction, as illustrated on pages 121–126.

*Journalize transactions.*

*(SO 5),* **AP**

**E3-8** Transaction data for Plunkett Real Estate Agency are presented in E3-7.

**Instructions**
Journalize the transactions. Do not provide explanations.

*Journalize a series of transactions.*

*(SO 3, 4, 5),* **AP**

**E3-9** The May transactions of StepAside Corporation were as follows.

May 4 Paid $700 due for supplies previously purchased on account.
   7 Performed advisory services on account for $6,800.
   8 Purchased supplies for $850 on account.
   9 Purchased equipment for $1,000 in cash.
   17 Paid employees $530 in cash.
   22 Received bill for equipment repairs of $900.
   29 Paid $1,200 for 12 months of insurance policy. Coverage begins June 1.

**Instructions**
Journalize the transactions. Do not provide explanations.

*Post journal entries and prepare a trial balance.*

*(SO 7, 8),* **AP**

**E3-10** Transaction data and journal entries for Plunkett Real Estate Agency are presented in E3-7 and E3-8.

**Instructions**
(a) Post the transactions to T accounts.
(b) Prepare a trial balance at October 31, 2012.

*Analyze transactions, prepare journal entries, and post transactions to T accounts.*

*(SO 1, 5, 7),* **AP**

**E3-11** Selected transactions for Charlotte Corporation during its first month in business are presented below.

Sept. 1 Issued common stock in exchange for $20,000 cash received from investors.
   5 Purchased equipment for $9,000, paying $3,000 in cash and the balance on account.
   25 Paid $4,000 cash on balance owed for equipment.
   30 Paid $500 cash dividend.

Charlotte's chart of accounts shows: Cash, Equipment, Accounts Payable, Common Stock, and Dividends.

**Instructions**
(a) Prepare a tabular analysis of the September transactions. The column headings should be: Cash + Equipment = Accounts Payable + Stockholders' Equity. For transactions affecting stockholders' equity, provide explanations in the right margin, as shown on page 110.
(b) Journalize the transactions. Do not provide explanations.
(c) Post the transactions to T accounts.

*Journalize transactions from T accounts and prepare a trial balance.*

*(SO 5, 8),* **AP**

**E3-12** The T accounts on the next page summarize the ledger of McGregor Gardening Company, Inc. at the end of the first month of operations.

| Cash | | | | | |
|---|---|---|---|---|---|
| Apr. | 1 | 15,000 | Apr. | 15 | 800 |
| | 12 | 700 | | 25 | 3,500 |
| | 29 | 800 | | | |
| | 30 | 900 | | | |

| Unearned Service Revenue | | |
|---|---|---|
| | Apr. 30 | 900 |

| Accounts Receivable | | | | | |
|---|---|---|---|---|---|
| Apr. | 7 | 3,400 | Apr. | 29 | 800 |

| Common Stock | | |
|---|---|---|
| | Apr. 1 | 15,000 |

| Supplies | | |
|---|---|---|
| Apr. | 4 | 5,200 |

| Service Revenue | | |
|---|---|---|
| | Apr. 7 | 3,400 |
| | 12 | 700 |

| Accounts Payable | | | | | |
|---|---|---|---|---|---|
| Apr. | 25 | 3,500 | Apr. | 4 | 5,200 |

| Salaries and Wages Expense | | |
|---|---|---|
| Apr. | 15 | 800 |

**Instructions**

(a) Prepare in the order they occurred the journal entries (including explanations) that resulted in the amounts posted to the accounts.

(b) Prepare a trial balance at April 30, 2012. (*Hint:* Compute ending balances of T accounts first.)

**E3-13** Selected transactions from the journal of Galaxy Inc. during its first month of operations are presented here.

*Post journal entries and prepare a trial balance.*
(SO 7, 8), **AP**

| Date | | Account Titles | Debit | Credit |
|---|---|---|---|---|
| Aug. | 1 | Cash | 8,000 | |
| | | Common Stock | | 8,000 |
| | 10 | Cash | 1,700 | |
| | | Service Revenue | | 1,700 |
| | 12 | Equipment | 6,200 | |
| | | Cash | | 1,200 |
| | | Notes Payable | | 5,000 |
| | 25 | Accounts Receivable | 3,400 | |
| | | Service Revenue | | 3,400 |
| | 31 | Cash | 600 | |
| | | Accounts Receivable | | 600 |

**Instructions**

(a) Post the transactions to T accounts.

(b) Prepare a trial balance at August 31, 2012.

**E3-14** Here is the ledger for Stampfer Co.

*Journalize transactions from T accounts and prepare a trial balance.*
(SO 5, 8), **AP**

| Cash | | | | | |
|---|---|---|---|---|---|
| Oct. | 1 | 7,000 | Oct. | 4 | 400 |
| | 10 | 980 | | 12 | 1,500 |
| | 10 | 8,000 | | 15 | 250 |
| | 20 | 700 | | 30 | 300 |
| | 25 | 2,000 | | 31 | 500 |

| Common Stock | | |
|---|---|---|
| | Oct. 1 | 7,000 |
| | 25 | 2,000 |

| Accounts Receivable | | | | | |
|---|---|---|---|---|---|
| Oct. | 6 | 800 | Oct. | 20 | 700 |
| | 20 | 920 | | | |

| Dividends | | |
|---|---|---|
| Oct. | 30 | 300 |

| Supplies | | | | | |
|---|---|---|---|---|---|
| Oct. | 4 | 400 | Oct. | 31 | 180 |

| Service Revenue | | |
|---|---|---|
| | Oct. 6 | 800 |
| | 10 | 980 |
| | 20 | 920 |

| Equipment | | |
|---|---|---|
| Oct. | 3 | 3,000 |

| Salaries and Wages Expense | | |
|---|---|---|
| Oct. | 31 | 500 |

| Notes Payable | | |
|---|---|---|
| | Oct. 10 | 8,000 |

| Supplies Expense | | |
|---|---|---|
| Oct. | 31 | 180 |

| Accounts Payable | | | | | |
|---|---|---|---|---|---|
| Oct. | 12 | 1,500 | Oct. | 3 | 3,000 |

| Rent Expense | | |
|---|---|---|
| Oct. | 15 | 250 |

**Instructions**

(a) Reproduce the journal entries for only the transactions that **occurred on October 1, 10, and 20,** and provide explanations for each.

(b) Prepare a trial balance at October 31, 2012. (*Hint:* Compute ending balances of T accounts first.)

*Analyze errors and their effects on trial balance.*

(SO 8), **AN**

**E3-15** The bookkeeper for Bullwinkle Corporation made these errors in journalizing and posting.

1. A credit posting of $400 to Accounts Receivable was omitted.
2. A debit posting of $750 for Prepaid Insurance was debited to Insurance Expense.
3. A collection on account of $100 was journalized and posted as a debit to Cash $100 and a credit to Accounts Payable $100.
4. A credit posting of $300 to Property Taxes Payable was made twice.
5. A cash purchase of supplies for $250 was journalized and posted as a debit to Supplies $25 and a credit to Cash $25.
6. A debit of $395 to Advertising Expense was posted as $359.

**Instructions**

For each error, indicate (a) whether the trial balance will balance; if the trial balance will not balance, indicate (b) the amount of the difference, and (c) the trial balance column that will have the larger total. Consider each error separately. Use the following form, in which error 1 is given as an example.

| | **(a)** | **(b)** | **(c)** |
|---|---|---|---|
| **Error** | **In Balance** | **Difference** | **Larger Column** |
| 1 | No | $400 | Debit |

*Prepare a trial balance and financial statements.*

(SO 8), **AP**

**E3-16** The accounts in the ledger of Roshek Delivery Service contain the following balances on July 31, 2012.

| | | | |
|---|---|---|---|
| Accounts Receivable | $13,400 | Prepaid Insurance | $ 2,200 |
| Accounts Payable | 8,400 | Service Revenue | 15,500 |
| Cash | ? | Dividends | 700 |
| Equipment | 59,360 | Common Stock | 40,000 |
| Maintenance and | | Salaries and Wages Expense | 7,428 |
| Repairs Expense | 1,958 | Salaries and Wages Payable | 820 |
| Insurance Expense | 900 | Retained Earnings | 5,200 |
| Notes Payable (due 2015) | 28,450 | (July 1, 2012) | |

**Instructions**

(a) Prepare a trial balance with the accounts arranged as illustrated in the chapter, and fill in the missing amount for Cash.

(b) Prepare an income statement, a retained earnings statement, and a classified balance sheet for the month of July 2012.

*Identify normal account balance and corresponding financial statement.*

(SO 3), **K**

**E3-17** The following accounts, in alphabetical order, were selected from recent financial statements of Krispy Kreme Doughnuts, Inc.

| | |
|---|---|
| Accounts payable | Interest income |
| Accounts receivable | Inventories |
| Common stock | Prepaid expenses |
| Depreciation expense | Property and equipment |
| Interest expense | Revenues |

**Instructions**

For each account, indicate (a) whether the normal balance is a debit or a credit, and (b) the financial statement—balance sheet or income statement—where the account should be presented.

*Classify transactions as cash-flow activities.*

(SO 9), **AP**

**E3-18** Review the transactions listed in E3-1 for Arnett Advertising Company, and classify each transaction as either an operating activity, investing activity, or financing activity, or if no cash is exchanged, as a noncash event.

*Classify transactions as cash-flow activities.*

(SO 9), **AP**

**E3-19** Review the transactions listed in E3-3 for Underwood Corp. and classify each transaction as either an operating activity, investing activity, or financing activity, or if no cash is exchanged, as a noncash event.

# Exercises: Set B and Challenge Exercises

Visit the book's companion website, at **www.wiley.com/college/kimmel**, and choose the Student Companion site to access Exercise Set B and Challenge Exercises.

# Problems: Set A

**P3-1A**  On April 1, Vagabond Travel Agency Inc. was established. These transactions were completed during the month.

1. Stockholders invested $30,000 cash in the company in exchange for common stock.
2. Paid $900 cash for April office rent.
3. Purchased office equipment for $3,400 cash.
4. Purchased $200 of advertising in the *Chicago Tribune*, on account.
5. Paid $500 cash for office supplies.
6. Earned $12,000 for services provided: Cash of $3,000 is received from customers, and the balance of $9,000 is billed to customers on account.
7. Paid $400 cash dividends.
8. Paid *Chicago Tribune* amount due in transaction (4).
9. Paid employees' salaries $1,800.
10. Received $9,000 in cash from customers billed previously in transaction (6).

*Analyze transactions and compute net income.*
(SO 1), **AP**

**Instructions**
(a) Prepare a tabular analysis of the transactions using these column headings: Cash, Accounts Receivable, Supplies, Equipment, Accounts Payable, Common Stock, and Retained Earnings (with separate columns for Revenues, Expenses, and Dividends). Include margin explanations for any changes in Retained Earnings.
(b) From an analysis of the Retained Earnings columns, compute the net income or net loss for April.

(a) Cash          $34,800
   Total assets   $38,700

**P3-2A**  Susan Taylor started her own consulting firm, Taylor Made Consulting Inc., on May 1, 2012. The following transactions occurred during the month of May.

*Analyze transactions and prepare financial statements.*
(SO 1), **AP**

GLS

| May | 1 | Stockholders invested $15,000 cash in the business in exchange for common stock. |
| | 2 | Paid $600 for office rent for the month. |
| | 3 | Purchased $500 of supplies on account. |
| | 5 | Paid $150 to advertise in the *County News*. |
| | 9 | Received $1,400 cash for services provided. |
| | 12 | Paid $200 cash dividend. |
| | 15 | Performed $4,200 of services on account. |
| | 17 | Paid $2,500 for employee salaries. |
| | 20 | Paid for the supplies purchased on account on May 3. |
| | 23 | Received a cash payment of $1,200 for services provided on account on May 15. |
| | 26 | Borrowed $5,000 from the bank on a note payable. |
| | 29 | Purchased office equipment for $2,000 paying $200 in cash and the balance on account. |
| | 30 | Paid $180 for utilities. |

**Instructions**
(a) Show the effects of the previous transactions on the accounting equation using the following format. Assume the note payable is to be repaid within the year.

(a) Cash          $18,270
   Total assets   $23,770

| | Assets | | | = | Liabilities | | + | Stockholders' Equity | | | |
|---|---|---|---|---|---|---|---|---|---|---|---|
| Date | Cash + | Accounts Receivable + | Supplies + Equipment | = | Notes Payable + | Accounts Payable | + | Common Stock | + Revenues | Retained Earnings − Expenses | − Dividends |

(b) Net income  $2,170

Include margin explanations for any changes in Retained Earnings.
(b) Prepare an income statement for the month of May 2012.
(c) Prepare a classified balance sheet at May 31, 2012.

*Analyze transactions and prepare an income statement, retained earnings statement, and balance sheet.*

(SO 1), **AP**

**P3-3A**  Robin Klann created a corporation providing legal services, Robin Klann Inc., on July 1, 2012. On July 31 the balance sheet showed: Cash $4,000; Accounts Receivable $2,500; Supplies $500; Equipment $5,000; Accounts Payable $4,200; Common Stock $6,200; and Retained Earnings $1,600. During August the following transactions occurred.

| Aug. | | |
|---|---|---|
| | 1 | Collected $1,100 of accounts receivable due from customers. |
| | 4 | Paid $2,700 cash for accounts payable due. |
| | 9 | Earned revenue of $5,400, of which $3,600 is collected in cash and the balance is due in September. |
| | 15 | Purchased additional office equipment for $4,000, paying $700 in cash and the balance on account. |
| | 19 | Paid salaries $1,400, rent for August $700, and advertising expenses $350. |
| | 23 | Paid a cash dividend of $700. |
| | 26 | Received $5,000 from Standard Federal Bank; the money was borrowed on a 4-month note payable. |
| | 31 | Incurred utility expenses for the month on account $380. |

**Instructions**

(a) Cash  $7,150

(a) Prepare a tabular analysis of the August transactions beginning with July 31 balances. The column heading should be: Cash + Accounts Receivable + Supplies + Equipment = Notes Payable + Accounts Payable + Common Stock + Retained Earnings + Revenues − Expenses − Dividends. Include margin explanations for any changes in Retained Earnings.

(b) Ret. earnings  $3,470
Net income  $2,570

(b) Prepare an income statement for August, a retained earnings statement for August, and a classified balance sheet at August 31.

*Journalize a series of transactions.*

(SO 3, 5), **AP**

**P3-4A**  Clear View Miniature Golf and Driving Range Inc. was opened on March 1 by Roger Prince. These selected events and transactions occurred during March.

| Mar. | | |
|---|---|---|
| | 1 | Stockholders invested $50,000 cash in the business in exchange for common stock of the corporation. |
| | 3 | Purchased Arnie's Golf Land for $38,000 cash. The price consists of land $23,000, building $9,000, and equipment $6,000. (Record this in a single entry.) |
| | 5 | Advertised the opening of the driving range and miniature golf course, paying advertising expenses of $1,200 cash. |
| | 6 | Paid cash $2,400 for a 1-year insurance policy. |
| | 10 | Purchased golf clubs and other equipment for $5,500 from Golden Bear Company, payable in 30 days. |
| | 18 | Received golf fees of $1,600 in cash from customers for golf fees earned. |
| | 19 | Sold 100 coupon books for $25 each in cash. Each book contains ten coupons that enable the holder to play one round of miniature golf or to hit one bucket of golf balls. (*Hint:* The revenue is not earned until the customers use the coupons.) |
| | 25 | Paid a $500 cash dividend. |
| | 30 | Paid salaries of $800. |
| | 30 | Paid Golden Bear Company in full for equipment purchased on March 10. |
| | 31 | Received $900 in cash from customers for golf fees earned. |

The company uses these accounts: Cash, Prepaid Insurance, Land, Buildings, Equipment, Accounts Payable, Unearned Service Revenue, Common Stock, Retained Earnings, Dividends, Service Revenue, Advertising Expense, and Salaries and Wages Expense.

**Instructions**

Journalize the March transactions, including explanations. Clear View records golf fees as service revenue.

**P3-5A** Towne Architects incorporated as licensed architects on April 1, 2012. During the first month of the operation of the business, these events and transactions occurred:

*Journalize transactions, post, and prepare a trial balance.*
(SO 3, 5, 6, 7, 8), **AP**

| Apr. | 1 | Stockholders invested $18,000 cash in exchange for common stock of the corporation. |
|---|---|---|
| | 1 | Hired a secretary-receptionist at a salary of $375 per week, payable monthly. |
| | 2 | Paid office rent for the month $900. |
| | 3 | Purchased architectural supplies on account from Spring Green Company $1,300. |
| | 10 | Completed blueprints on a carport and billed client $1,900 for services. |
| | 11 | Received $700 cash advance from J. Madison to design a new home. |
| | 20 | Received $2,800 cash for services completed and delivered to M. Svetlana. |
| | 30 | Paid secretary-receptionist for the month $1,500. |
| | 30 | Paid $300 to Spring Green Company for accounts payable due. |

The company uses these accounts: Cash, Accounts Receivable, Supplies, Accounts Payable, Unearned Service Revenue, Common Stock, Service Revenue, Salaries and Wages Expense, and Rent Expense.

**Instructions**
(a) Journalize the transactions, including explanations.
(b) Post to the ledger T accounts.
(c) Prepare a trial balance on April 30, 2012.

(c) Cash $18,800
Tot. trial
balance $24,400

**P3-6A** This is the trial balance of Mimosa Company on September 30.

*Journalize transactions, post, and prepare a trial balance.*
(SO 3, 5, 6, 7, 8), **AP**

**MIMOSA COMPANY**
**Trial Balance**
**September 30, 2012**

| | Debit | Credit |
|---|---|---|
| Cash | $ 8,200 | |
| Accounts Receivable | 2,600 | |
| Supplies | 2,100 | |
| Equipment | 8,000 | |
| Accounts Payable | | $ 4,800 |
| Unearned Service Revenue | | 1,100 |
| Common Stock | | 15,000 |
| | $20,900 | $20,900 |

The October transactions were as follows.

| Oct. | 5 | Received $1,300 in cash from customers for accounts receivable due. |
|---|---|---|
| | 10 | Billed customers for services performed $5,100. |
| | 15 | Paid employee salaries $1,200. |
| | 17 | Performed $600 of services for customers who paid in advance in August. |
| | 20 | Paid $1,900 to creditors for accounts payable due. |
| | 29 | Paid a $300 cash dividend. |
| | 31 | Paid utilities $400. |

**Instructions**
(a) Prepare a general ledger using T accounts. Enter the opening balances in the ledger accounts as of October 1. Provision should be made for these additional accounts: Dividends, Service Revenue, Salaries and Wages Expense, and Utilities Expense.
(b) Journalize the transactions, including explanations.
(c) Post to the ledger accounts.
(d) Prepare a trial balance on October 31, 2012.

(d) Cash $ 5,700
Tot. trial
balance $24,100

*Prepare a correct trial balance.*

(SO 8), **AN**

**P3-7A** This trial balance of Michels Co. does not balance.

**MICHELS CO.**
**Trial Balance**
**June 30, 2012**

|  | Debit | Credit |
|---|---|---|
| Cash |  | $ 3,090 |
| Accounts Receivable | $ 3,190 |  |
| Supplies | 800 |  |
| Equipment | 3,000 |  |
| Accounts Payable |  | 3,686 |
| Unearned Service Revenue | 1,200 |  |
| Common Stock |  | 9,000 |
| Dividends | 800 |  |
| Service Revenue |  | 3,480 |
| Salaries and Wages Expense | 3,600 |  |
| Utilities Expense | 910 |  |
|  | $13,500 | $19,256 |

Each of the listed accounts has a normal balance per the general ledger. An examination of the ledger and journal reveals the following errors:

1. Cash received from a customer on account was debited for $780, and Accounts Receivable was credited for the same amount. The actual collection was for $870.
2. The purchase of a printer on account for $340 was recorded as a debit to Supplies for $340 and a credit to Accounts Payable for $340.
3. Services were performed on account for a client for $900. Accounts Receivable was debited for $90 and Service Revenue was credited for $900.
4. A debit posting to Salaries and Wages Expense of $700 was omitted.
5. A payment on account for $206 was credited to Cash for $206 and credited to Accounts Payable for $260.
6. Payment of a $600 cash dividend to Michels' stockholders was debited to Salaries and Wages Expense for $600 and credited to Cash for $600.

*Instructions*

Tot. trial balance $16,900

Prepare the correct trial balance. (*Hint:* All accounts have normal balances.)

*Journalize transactions, post, and prepare a trial balance.*

(SO 3, 5, 6, 7, 8), **AP**

**GLS**

**P3-8A** The SciFi Theater Inc. was recently formed. It began operations in March 2012. The SciFi is unique in that it will show only triple features of sequential theme movies. On March 1, the ledger of The SciFi showed: Cash $16,000; Land $38,000; Buildings (concession stand, projection room, ticket booth, and screen) $22,000; Equipment $16,000; Accounts Payable $12,000; and Common Stock $80,000. During the month of March the following events and transactions occurred.

| Mar. | 2 | Rented the three Star Wars movies (*Star Wars®*, *The Empire Strikes Back*, and *The Return of the Jedi*) to be shown for the first three weeks of March. The film rental was $10,000; $2,000 was paid in cash and $8,000 will be paid on March 10. |
|---|---|---|
|  | 3 | Ordered the first three *Star Trek* movies to be shown the last 10 days of March. It will cost $500 per night. |
|  | 9 | Received $9,900 cash from admissions. |
|  | 10 | Paid balance due on *Star Wars* movies rental and $2,900 on March 1 accounts payable. |
|  | 11 | Hired J. Carne to operate the concession stand. Carne agrees to pay The SciFi Theater 15% of gross receipts, payable monthly. |
|  | 12 | Paid advertising expenses $500. |
|  | 20 | Received $8,300 cash from customers for admissions. |
|  | 20 | Received the *Star Trek* movies and paid rental fee of $5,000. |
|  | 31 | Paid salaries of $3,800. |

31    Received statement from J. Carne showing gross receipts from concessions of $10,000 and the balance due to The SciFi of $1,500 for March. Carne paid half the balance due and will remit the remainder on April 5.

31    Received $20,000 cash from customers for admissions.

In addition to the accounts identified above, the chart of accounts includes: Accounts Receivable, Service Revenue, Sales Revenue, Advertising Expense, Rent Expense, and Salaries and Wages Expense.

### Instructions

(a)  Using T accounts, enter the beginning balances to the ledger.

(b)  Journalize the March transactions, including explanations. SciFi records admission revenue as service revenue, concession revenue as sales revenue, and film rental expense as rent expense.

(c)  Post the March journal entries to the ledger.

(d)  Prepare a trial balance on March 31, 2012.

(d) Cash          $ 32,750

Tot. trial

balance        $128,800

---

**P3-9A**   The bookkeeper for Fred Kelley's dance studio made the following errors in journalizing and posting.

*Analyze errors and their effects on the trial balance.*

(SO 8), **AN**

1.  A credit to Supplies of $600 was omitted.
2.  A debit posting of $300 to Accounts Payable was inadvertently debited to Accounts Receivable.
3.  A purchase of supplies on account of $450 was debited to Supplies for $540 and credited to Accounts Payable for $540.
4.  A credit posting of $680 to Interest Payable was posted twice.
5.  A debit posting to Income Taxes Payable for $250 and a credit posting to Cash for $250 were made twice.
6.  A debit posting for $1,200 of Dividends was inadvertently posted to Salaries and Wages Expense instead.
7.  A credit to Service Revenue for $450 was inadvertently posted as a debit to Service Revenue.
8.  A credit to Accounts Receivable of $250 was credited to Accounts Payable.

### Instructions

For each error, indicate (a) whether the trial balance will balance; (b) the amount of the difference if the trial balance will not balance; and (c) the trial balance column that will have the larger total. Consider each error separately. Use the following form, in which error 1 is given as an example.

| Error | (a) In Balance | (b) Difference | (c) Larger Column |
|-------|------------|------------|---------------|
| 1. | No | $600 | Debit |

# Problems: Set B

**P3-1B**   New Dawn Window Washing Inc. was started on May 1. Here is a summary of the May transactions.

*Analyze transactions and compute net income.*

(SO 1), **AP**

1.  Stockholders invested $20,000 cash in the company in exchange for common stock.
2.  Purchased equipment for $9,000 cash.
3.  Paid $700 cash for May office rent.
4.  Paid $300 cash for supplies.
5.  Purchased $750 of advertising in the *Beacon News* on account.
6.  Received $7,200 in cash from customers for service.
7.  Paid a $500 cash dividend.
8.  Paid part-time employee salaries $1,700.
9.  Paid utility bills $140.
10.  Provided service on account to customers $1,000.
11.  Collected cash of $650 for services billed in transaction (10).

**Instructions**

(a) Prepare a tabular analysis of the transactions using these column headings: Cash, Accounts Receivable, Supplies, Equipment, Accounts Payable, Common Stock, and Retained Earnings (with separate columns for Revenues, Expenses, and Dividends). Revenue is called Service Revenue. Include margin explanations for any changes in Retained Earnings.

(b) Net income $4,910

(b) From an analysis of the Retained Earnings columns, compute the net income or net loss for May.

*Analyze transactions and prepare financial statements.*
(SO 1), **AP**

GLS

**P3-2B** Samuel Aldrich started his own delivery service, Aldrich Service Inc., on June 1, 2012. The following transactions occurred during the month of June.

June   1   Stockholders invested $15,000 cash in the business in exchange for common stock.
      2   Purchased a used van for deliveries for $15,000. Samuel paid $2,000 cash and signed a note payable for the remaining balance.
      3   Paid $600 for office rent for the month.
      5   Performed $2,400 of services on account.
      9   Paid $300 in cash dividends.
     12   Purchased supplies for $240 on account.
     15   Received a cash payment of $750 for services provided on June 5.
     17   Received a bill for $200 to cover advertisements in *Tri-State News*.
     20   Received a cash payment of $1,500 for services provided.
     23   Made a cash payment of $500 on the note payable.
     26   Paid $180 for utilities.
     29   Paid for the supplies purchased on account on June 12.
     30   Paid $750 for employee salaries.

**Instructions**

(a) Cash $12,680

(a) Show the effects of the previous transactions on the accounting equation using the following format. Assume the note payable is to be repaid within the year.

| | | Assets | | | = | Liabilities | + | | Stockholders' Equity | | | |
|---|---|---|---|---|---|---|---|---|---|---|---|---|
| | | Accounts | | | | Notes | Accounts | Common | | Retained Earnings | | |
| Date | Cash + | Receivable + | Supplies + | Equipment = | | Payable + | Payable + | Stock + | Revenues − | Expenses − | Dividends | |

(b) Net income $2,170

Include margin explanations for any changes in Retained Earnings.
(b) Prepare an income statement for the month of June.
(c) Prepare a classified balance sheet at June 30, 2012.

*Analyze transactions and prepare an income statement, retained earnings statement, and balance sheet.*
(SO 1), **AP**

GLS

**P3-3B** Joy Tiede opened Tiede Company, a veterinary business in Neosho, Wisconsin, on August 1, 2012. On August 31, the balance sheet showed: Cash $9,000; Accounts Receivable $1,700; Supplies $600; Equipment $5,000; Accounts Payable $3,600; Common Stock $12,000; and Retained Earnings $700. During September, the following transactions occurred.

Sept.   2   Paid $3,400 cash for accounts payable due.
      5   Received $1,200 from customers in payment of accounts receivable.
      8   Purchased additional office equipment for $5,100, paying $1,000 in cash and the balance on account.
     13   Earned revenue of $10,600, of which $2,300 is paid in cash and the balance is due in October.
     17   Paid a $600 cash dividend.
     22   Paid salaries $900, rent for September $1,100, and advertising expense $250.
     26   Incurred utility expenses for the month on account $220.
     30   Received $5,000 from Hilldale Bank on a 6-month note payable.

**Instructions**

(a) Cash          $10,250

(a) Prepare a tabular analysis of the September transactions beginning with August 31 balances. The column headings should be: Cash + Accounts Receivable + Supplies + Equipment = Notes Payable + Accounts Payable + Common Stock + Retained Earnings + Revenues − Expenses − Dividends. Include margin explanations for any changes in Retained Earnings.

(b) Ret. earnings     $ 8,230

(b) Prepare an income statement for September, a retained earnings statement for September, and a classified balance sheet at September 30, 2012.

**P3-4B**   RV Oasis was started on April 1 by Taras Dankert. These selected events and transactions occurred during April.

*Journalize a series of transactions.*
*(SO 3, 5),* **AP**

GLS

Apr.  1    Stockholders invested $70,000 cash in the business in exchange for common stock.
4    Purchased land costing $50,000 for cash.
8    Purchased advertising in local newspaper for $1,200 on account.
11   Paid salaries to employees $2,700.
12   Hired park manager at a salary of $3,600 per month, effective May 1.
13   Paid $7,200 for a 1-year insurance policy.
17   Paid $600 cash dividends.
20   Received $6,000 in cash from customers for admission fees.
25   Sold 100 coupon books for $90 each. Each book contains ten coupons that entitle the holder to one admission to the park. (*Hint*: The revenue is not earned until the coupons are used.)
30   Received $7,900 in cash from customers for admission fees.
30   Paid $400 of the balance owed for the advertising purchased on account on April 8.

The company uses the following accounts: Cash, Prepaid Insurance, Land, Accounts Payable, Unearned Service Revenue, Common Stock, Dividends, Service Revenue, Advertising Expense, and Salaries and Wages Expense.

*Instructions*

Journalize the April transactions, including explanations. (*Note*: RV Oasis records admission revenue as service revenue.)

**P3-5B**   Troy Ridgell incorporated Ridgell Consulting, an accounting practice, on May 1, 2012. During the first month of operations, these events and transactions occurred.

*Journalize transactions, post, and prepare a trial balance.*
*(SO 3, 5, 6, 7, 8),* **AP**

GLS

May   1    Stockholders invested $40,000 cash in exchange for common stock of the corporation.
2    Hired a secretary-receptionist at a salary of $2,000 per month.
3    Purchased $800 of supplies on account from Fleming Supply Company.
7    Paid office rent of $1,400 for the month.
11   Completed a tax assignment and billed client $1,500 for services provided.
12   Received $4,200 advance on a management consulting engagement.
17   Received cash of $3,300 for services completed for Goodman Co.
31   Paid secretary-receptionist $2,000 salary for the month.
31   Paid 50% of balance due Fleming Supply Company.

The company uses the following chart of accounts: Cash, Accounts Receivable, Supplies, Accounts Payable, Unearned Service Revenue, Common Stock, Service Revenue, Salaries and Wages Expense, and Rent Expense.

*Instructions*
(a) Journalize the transactions, including explanations.
(b) Post to the ledger T accounts.
(c) Prepare a trial balance on May 31, 2012.

(c) Cash                    $43,700
    Tot. trial
    balance              $49,400

**P3-6B**   The trial balance of Kinnear Dry Cleaners on June 30 is given here.

*Journalize transactions, post, and prepare a trial balance.*
*(SO 3, 5, 6, 7, 8),* **AP**

GLS

**KINNEAR DRY CLEANERS**
**Trial Balance**
**June 30, 2012**

|                           | Debit    | Credit   |
|---------------------------|----------|----------|
| Cash                      | $12,532  |          |
| Accounts Receivable       | 10,536   |          |
| Supplies                  | 3,592    |          |
| Equipment                 | 25,950   |          |
| Accounts Payable          |          | $15,800  |
| Unearned Service Revenue  |          | 1,810    |
| Common Stock              |          | 35,000   |
|                           | $52,610  | $52,610  |

The July transactions were as follows.

July 8 Received $5,189 in cash on June 30 accounts receivable.
9 Paid employee salaries $2,100.
11 Received $7,320 in cash for services provided.
14 Paid creditors $9,810 of accounts payable.
17 Purchased supplies on account $720.
22 Billed customers for services provided $4,700.
30 Paid employee salaries $3,114, utilities $1,767, and repairs $386.
31 Paid $400 cash dividend.

**Instructions**
(a) Prepare a general ledger using T accounts. Enter the opening balances in the ledger accounts as of July 1. Provision should be made for the following additional accounts: Dividends, Service Revenue, Maintenance and Repairs Expense, Salaries and Wages Expense, and Utilities Expense.

(d) Cash $ 7,464
Tot. trial
balance $55,540

(b) Journalize the transactions, including explanations.
(c) Post to the ledger accounts.
(d) Prepare a trial balance on July 31, 2012.

*Prepare a correct trial balance.*
(SO 8), **AN**

**P3-7B** This trial balance of Lagerstrom Company does not balance.

**LAGERSTROM COMPANY**
**Trial Balance**
**May 31, 2012**

| | Debit | Credit |
|---|---|---|
| Cash | $ 6,340 | |
| Accounts Receivable | | $ 2,750 |
| Prepaid Insurance | 700 | |
| Equipment | 8,000 | |
| Accounts Payable | | 4,100 |
| Income Taxes Payable | 850 | |
| Common Stock | | 5,700 |
| Retained Earnings | | 6,000 |
| Service Revenue | 7,690 | |
| Salaries and Wages Expense | 4,200 | |
| Advertising Expense | | 1,100 |
| Income Tax Expense | 900 | |
| | $28,680 | $19,650 |

Your review of the ledger reveals that each account has a normal balance. You also discover the following errors.

1. The totals of the debit sides of Prepaid Insurance, Accounts Payable, and Income Tax Expense were each understated $100.
2. Transposition errors were made in Accounts Receivable and Service Revenue. Based on postings made, the correct balances were $2,570 and $7,960, respectively.
3. A debit posting to Salaries and Wages Expense of $500 was omitted.
4. A $600 cash dividend was debited to Common Stock for $600 and credited to Cash for $600.
5. A $350 purchase of supplies on account was debited to Equipment for $350 and credited to Cash for $350.
6. A cash payment of $490 for advertising was debited to Advertising Expense for $49 and credited to Cash for $49.
7. A collection from a customer for $240 was debited to Cash for $240 and credited to Accounts Payable for $240.

**Instructions**

Cash $ 6,249
Tot. trial balance $25,220

Prepare the correct trial balance, assuming all accounts have normal balances. (*Note:* The chart of accounts also includes the following: Dividends and Supplies.)

**P3-8B** Riviera Theater Inc. was recently formed. All facilities were completed on March 31. On April 1, the ledger showed: Cash $6,300; Land $10,000; Buildings (concession stand, projection room, ticket booth, and screen) $8,000; Equipment $6,000; Accounts Payable $2,300; Mortgage Payable $8,000; and Common Stock $20,000. During April, the following events and transactions occurred.

*Journalize transactions, post, and prepare a trial balance.*
*(SO 3, 5, 6, 7, 8),* **AP**

| Apr. | 2 | Paid film rental fee of $800 on first movie. |
|---|---|---|
| | 3 | Ordered two additional films at $750 each. |
| | 9 | Received $4,700 cash from admissions. |
| | 10 | Paid $2,000 of mortgage payable and $1,200 of accounts payable. |
| | 11 | Hired M. Gavin to operate the concession stand. Gavin agrees to pay Riviera Theater 17% of gross receipts, payable monthly. |
| | 12 | Paid advertising expenses $410. |
| | 20 | Received one of the films ordered on April 3 and was billed $750. The film will be shown in April. |
| | 25 | Received $3,000 cash from customers for admissions. |
| | 29 | Paid salaries $1,900. |
| | 30 | Received statement from M. Gavin showing gross receipts of $2,000 and the balance due to Riviera Theater of $340 for April. Gavin paid half of the balance due and will remit the remainder on May 5. |
| | 30 | Prepaid $1,200 rental fee on special film to be run in May. |

In addition to the accounts identified above, the chart of accounts shows: Accounts Receivable, Prepaid Rent, Service Revenue, Sales Revenue, Advertising Expense, Rent Expense, Salaries and Wages Expense.

**Instructions**
(a) Enter the beginning balances in the ledger T accounts as of April 1.
(b) Journalize the April transactions, including explanations. (*Note:* Riviera records admission revenue as service revenue, concession revenue as sales revenue, and film rental expense as rent expense.)
(c) Post the April journal entries to the ledger T accounts.
(d) Prepare a trial balance on April 30, 2012.

| (d) Cash | $ 6,660 |
|---|---|
| Tot. trial | |
| balance | $35,890 |

**P3-9B** A first year co-op student working for Solutions.com recorded the transactions for the month. He wasn't exactly sure how to journalize and post, but he did the best he could. He had a few questions, however, about the following transactions.

*Analyze errors and their effects on the trial balance.*
*(SO 8),* **AN**

1. Cash received from a customer on account was recorded as a debit to Cash of $360 and a credit to Accounts Receivable of $630, instead of $360.
2. A service provided for cash was posted as a debit to Cash of $2,000 and a credit to Service Revenue of $2,000.
3. A debit of $880 for services provided on account was neither recorded nor posted. The credit was recorded correctly.
4. The debit to record $1,000 of cash dividends was posted to the Salaries and Wages Expense account.
5. The purchase, on account, of a computer that cost $2,500 was recorded as a debit to Supplies and a credit to Accounts Payable.
6. A cash payment of $495 for salaries was recorded as a debit to Dividends and a credit to Cash.
7. Payment of month's rent was debited to Rent Expense and credited to Cash, $850.
8. Issue of $5,000 of common shares was credited to the Common Stock account, but no debit was recorded.

**Instructions**
(a) Indicate which of the above transactions are correct, and which are incorrect.
(b) For each error identified in (a), indicate (1) whether the trial balance will balance; (2) the amount of the difference if the trial balance will not balance; and (3) the trial balance column that will have the larger total. Consider each error separately. Use the following form, in which transaction 1 is given as an example.

| | (1) | (2) | (3) |
|---|---|---|---|
| Error | In Balance | Difference | Larger Column |
| 1. | No | $270 | Credit |

# Problems: Set C

Visit the book's companion website, at **www.wiley.com/college/kimmel**, and choose the Student Companion site to access Problem Set C.

# Continuing Cookie Chronicle

(*Note*: This is a continuation of the Cookie Chronicle from Chapters 1 and 2.)

**CCC3** In November 2011, after having incorporated Cookie Creations Inc., Natalie begins operations. She has decided not to pursue the offer to supply cookies to Biscuits. Instead, she will focus on offering cooking classes. The following events occur.

Nov. 8    Natalie cashes in her U.S. Savings Bonds and receives $520, which she deposits in her personal bank account.

8    Natalie opens a bank account for Cookie Creations Inc.

8    Natalie purchases $500 of Cookie Creations' common stock.

11    Cookie Creations purchases paper and other office supplies for $95. (Use Supplies.)

14    Cookie Creations pays $125 to purchase baking supplies, such as flour, sugar, butter, and chocolate chips. (Use Supplies.)

15    Natalie starts to gather some baking equipment to take with her when teaching the cookie classes. She has an excellent top-of-the-line food processor and mixer that originally cost her $550. Natalie decides to start using it only in her new business. She estimates that the equipment is currently worth $300, and she transfers the equipment into the business in exchange for additional common stock.

16    The company needs more cash to sustain its operations. Natalie's grandmother lends the company $2,000 cash, in exchange for a two-year, 9% note payable. Interest and the principal are repayable at maturity.

17    Cookie Creations pays $900 for additional baking equipment.

18    Natalie schedules her first class for November 29. She will receive $100 on the date of the class.

25    Natalie books a second class for December 5 for $150. She receives a $60 cash down payment, in advance.

29    Natalie teaches her first class, booked on November 18, and collects the $100 cash.

30    Natalie's brother develops a website for Cookie Creations Inc. that the company will use for advertising. He charges the company $600 for his work, payable at the end of December. (Because the website is expected to have a useful life of two years before upgrades are needed, it should be treated as an asset called Website.)

30    Cookie Creations pays $1,200 for a one-year insurance policy.

30    Natalie teaches a group of elementary school students how to make Santa Claus cookies. At the end of the class, Natalie leaves an invoice for $300 with the school principal. The principal says that he will pass it along to the business office and it will be paid some time in December.

30    Natalie receives a $50 invoice for use of her cell phone. She uses the cell phone exclusively for Cookie Creations Inc. business. The invoice is for services provided in November, and payment is due on December 15.

*Instructions*

(a) Prepare journal entries to record the November transactions.

(b) Post the journal entries to the general ledger accounts.

(c) Prepare a trial balance at November 30, 2011.

(c) Trial balance total    3,910

# broadening your perspective

# Financial Reporting and Analysis

**FINANCIAL REPORTING PROBLEM:** *Tootsie Roll Industries Inc.*

**BYP3-1** The financial statements of Tootsie Roll in Appendix A at the back of this book contain the following selected accounts, all in thousands of dollars.

| | |
|---|---|
| Common Stock | $ 24,862 |
| Accounts Payable | 9,140 |
| Accounts Receivable | 37,512 |
| Selling, Marketing, and Administrative Expenses | 103,755 |
| Prepaid Expenses | 8,562 |
| Net Property, Plant, and Equipment | 220,721 |
| Net Product Sales | 495,592 |

*Instructions*
(a) What is the increase and decrease side for each account? What is the normal balance for each account?
(b) Identify the probable other account in the transaction and the effect on that account when:
   (1) Accounts Receivable is decreased.
   (2) Accounts Payable is decreased.
   (3) Prepaid Expenses is increased.
(c) Identify the other account(s) that ordinarily would be involved when:
   (1) Interest Expense is increased.
   (2) Property, Plant, and Equipment is increased.

**COMPARATIVE ANALYSIS PROBLEM:** *Tootsie Roll vs. Hershey*

**BYP3-2** The financial statements of The Hershey Company appear in Appendix B, following the financial statements for Tootsie Roll in Appendix A.

*Instructions*
(a) Based on the information contained in these financial statements, determine the normal balance for:

| **Tootsie Roll Industries** | **The Hershey Company** |
|---|---|
| (1) Accounts Receivable | (1) Inventories |
| (2) Net Property, Plant, and Equipment | (2) Provision for Income Taxes |
| (3) Accounts Payable | (3) Accrued Liabilities |
| (4) Retained Earnings | (4) Common Stock |
| (5) Net Product Sales | (5) Interest Expense |

(b) Identify the other account ordinarily involved when:
   (1) Accounts Receivable is increased.
   (2) Notes Payable is decreased.
   (3) Machinery is increased.
   (4) Interest Revenue is increased.

**RESEARCH CASE**

**BYP3-3** Sid Cato provides critiques of corporate annual reports. He maintains a website at **www.sidcato.com** that provides many useful resources for those who are interested in preparing or using annual reports.

*Instructions*
Go to the website and answer the following questions.
(a) Read the section, "What makes a good annual report?" and choose which three factors you think are most important. Explain why you think each item is important.
(b) For the most recent year presented, which companies were listed in the section "Producers of the best annuals for (*most recent year*)"?
(c) What potential benefits might a company gain by receiving a high rating from Sid Cato's organization?

## INTERPRETING FINANCIAL STATEMENTS

**BYP3-4**  Chieftain International, Inc., is an oil and natural gas exploration and production company. A recent balance sheet reported $208 million in assets with only $4.6 million in liabilities, all of which were short-term accounts payable.

During the year, Chieftain expanded its holdings of oil and gas rights, drilled 37 new wells, and invested in expensive 3-D seismic technology. The company generated $19 million cash from operating activities and paid no dividends. It had a cash balance of $102 million at the end of the year.

### Instructions
(a)  Name at least two advantages to Chieftain from having no long-term debt. Can you think of disadvantages?
(b)  What are some of the advantages to Chieftain from having this large a cash balance? What is a disadvantage?
(c)  Why do you suppose Chieftain has the $4.6 million balance in accounts payable, since it appears that it could have made all its purchases for cash?

## FINANCIAL ANALYSIS ON THE WEB

**BYP3-5**  *Purpose:* This activity provides information about career opportunities for CPAs.

*Address:* **www.icpas.org**, or go to **www.wiley.com/college/kimmel**

### Steps
1.  Go to the address shown above and click on **Students/Educators**.
2.  Click on **High School**, then **CPA101** for parts a, b, and c.
3.  Click **College** to answer part d.

### Instructions
Answer the following questions.
(a)  What does CPA stand for? Where do CPAs work?
(b)  What is meant by "public accounting"?
(c)  What skills does a CPA need?
(d)  What is the salary range for a CPA at a large firm during the first three years? What is the salary range for chief financial officers and treasurers at large corporations?

# Critical Thinking

## DECISION MAKING ACROSS THE ORGANIZATION

**BYP3-6**  Donna Dye operates Double D Riding Academy, Inc. The academy's primary sources of revenue are riding fees and lesson fees, which are provided on a cash basis. Donna also boards horses for owners, who are billed monthly for boarding fees. In a few cases, boarders pay in advance of expected use. For its revenue transactions, the academy maintains these accounts: Cash, Accounts Receivable, Unearned Revenue, Riding Revenue, Lesson Revenue, and Boarding Revenue.

The academy owns 10 horses, a stable, a riding corral, riding equipment, and office equipment. These assets are accounted for in the following accounts: Horses, Building, Riding Corral, Riding Equipment, and Office Equipment.

The academy employs stable helpers and an office employee, who receive weekly salaries. At the end of each month, the mail usually brings bills for advertising, utilities, and veterinary service. Other expenses include feed for the horses and insurance. For its expenses, the academy maintains the following accounts: Hay and Feed Supplies, Prepaid Insurance, Accounts Payable, Salaries Expense, Advertising Expense, Utilities Expense, Veterinary Expense, Hay and Feed Expense, and Insurance Expense.

Donna Dye's sole source of personal income is dividends from the academy. Thus, the corporation declares and pays periodic dividends. To account for  stockholders' equity in the business and dividends, two accounts are maintained: Common Stock and Dividends.

During the first month of operations an inexperienced bookkeeper was employed. Donna Dye asks you to review the following eight entries of the 50 entries made during the month. In each case, the explanation for the entry is correct.

| May | 1 | Cash | 15,000 | |
|---|---|---|---|---|
| | | Unearned Revenue | | 15,000 |
| | | (Issued common stock in exchange for $15,000 cash) | | |
| | 5 | Cash | 250 | |
| | | Lesson Revenue | | 250 |
| | | (Received $250 cash for lesson fees) | | |
| | 7 | Cash | 500 | |
| | | Boarding Revenue | | 500 |
| | | (Received $500 for boarding of horses beginning June 1) | | |
| | 9 | Hay and Feed Expense | 1,500 | |
| | | Cash | | 1,500 |
| | | (Purchased estimated 5 months' supply of feed and hay for $1,500 on account) | | |
| | 14 | Riding Equipment | 80 | |
| | | Cash | | 800 |
| | | (Purchased desk and other office equipment for $800 cash) | | |
| | 15 | Salaries Expense | 400 | |
| | | Cash | | 400 |
| | | (Issued check to Donna Dye for personal use) | | |
| | 20 | Cash | 145 | |
| | | Riding Revenue | | 154 |
| | | (Received $154 cash for riding fees) | | |
| | 31 | Veterinary Expense | 75 | |
| | | Accounts Receivable | | 75 |
| | | (Received bill of $75 from veterinarian for services provided) | | |

**Instructions**

With the class divided into groups, answer the following.

(a) For each journal entry that is correct, so state. For each journal entry that is incorrect, prepare the entry that should have been made by the bookkeeper.

(b) Which of the incorrect entries would prevent the trial balance from balancing?

(c) What was the correct net income for May, assuming the bookkeeper originally reported net income of $4,500 after posting all 50 entries?

(d) What was the correct cash balance at May 31, assuming the bookkeeper reported a balance of $12,475 after posting all 50 entries?

## COMMUNICATION ACTIVITY

**BYP3-7**    Clean Sweep Company offers home cleaning service. Two recurring transactions for the company are billing customers for services provided and paying employee salaries. For example, on March 15 bills totaling $6,000 were sent to customers, and $2,000 was paid in salaries to employees.

**Instructions**

Write a memorandum to your instructor that explains and illustrates the steps in the recording process for each of the March 15 transactions. Use the format illustrated in the text under the heading "The Recording Process Illustrated" (pp. 121–126).

## ETHICS CASES

**BYP3-8**    Courtney Delacey is the assistant chief accountant at BIT Company, a manufacturer of computer chips and cellular phones. The company presently has total sales of $20 million. It is the end of the first quarter and Courtney is hurriedly trying to prepare a general ledger trial balance so that quarterly financial statements can be prepared and released to management and the regulatory agencies. The total credits on the trial balance exceed the debits by $1,000.

In order to meet the 4 P.M. deadline, Courtney decides to force the debits and credits into balance by adding the amount of the difference to the Equipment account. She chose Equipment because it is one of the larger account balances; percentage-wise it will be the least misstated. Courtney plugs the difference! She believes that the difference is quite small and will not affect anyone's decisions. She wishes that she had another few days to find the error but realizes that the financial statements are already late.

*Instructions*
(a) Who are the stakeholders in this situation?
(b) What ethical issues are involved?
(c) What are Courtney's alternatives?

**BYP3-9** The July 28, 2007, issue of the *Wall Street Journal* includes an article by Kathryn Kranhold entitled "GE's Accounting Draws Fresh Focus on News of Improper Sales Bookings."

*Instructions*
Read the article and answer the following questions.
(a) What improper activity did the employees at GE engage in?
(b) Why might the employees have engaged in this activity?
(c) What were the implications for the employees who engaged in this activity?
(d) What does it mean to "restate" financial results? Why didn't GE restate its results to correct for the improperly reported locomotive sales?

## "ALL ABOUT YOU" ACTIVITY

**BYP3-10** In their annual reports to stockholders, companies must report or disclose information about all liabilities, including potential liabilities related to environmental clean-up. There are many situations in which you will be asked to provide personal financial information about your assets, liabilities, revenue, and expenses. Sometimes you will face difficult decisions regarding what to disclose and how to disclose it.

*Instructions*
Suppose that you are putting together a loan application to purchase a home. Based on your income and assets, you qualify for the mortgage loan, but just barely. How would you address each of the following situations in reporting your financial position for the loan application? Provide responses for each of the following questions.

(a) You signed a guarantee for a bank loan that a friend took out for $20,000. If your friend doesn't pay, you will have to pay. Your friend has made all of the payments so far, and it appears he will be able to pay in the future.
(b) You were involved in an auto accident in which you were at fault. There is the possibility that you may have to pay as much as $50,000 as part of a settlement. The issue will not be resolved before the bank processes your mortgage request.
(c) The company at which you work isn't doing very well, and it has recently laid off employees. You are still employed, but it is quite possible that you will lose your job in the next few months.

### Answers to Insight and Accounting Across the Organization Questions

**p. 109 Why Accuracy Matters Q:** In order for these companies to prepare and issue financial statements, their accounting equations (debit and credits) must have been in balance at year-end. How could these errors or misstatements have occurred? **A:** A company's accounting equation (its books) can be in balance yet its financial statements have errors or misstatements because of the following: entire transactions were not recorded; transactions were recorded at wrong amounts; transactions were recorded in the wrong accounts; transactions were recorded in the wrong accounting period. Audits of financial statements uncover some, but obviously not all, errors or misstatements.

**p. 115 Keeping Score Q:** Do you think that the Chicago Bears football team would be likely to have the same major revenue and expense accounts as the Cubs? **A:** Because their businesses are similar—professional sports—many of the revenue and expense accounts for the baseball and football teams might be similar.

**p. 119 Boosting Microsoft's Profits Q:** In what ways is this Microsoft division using accounting to assist in its effort to become more profitable? **A:** The division has used accounting to set very strict sales, revenue, and profit goals. In addition, the managers in this division use accounting to keep a tight reign on product costs. Also, accounting serves as the basis of communication so that the marketing managers and product designers can work with production managers, engineers, and accountants to create an exciting product within specified cost constraints.

### Answers to Self-Test Questions

**1.** b   **2.** b   **3.** b   **4.** a (−$50,000 = −$90,000 + $40,000)   **5.** b   **6.** c   **7.** d   **8.** d   **9.** d   **10.** b   **11.** a   **12.** c   **13.** d   **14.** a   **15.** c

## IFRS A Look at IFRS

International companies use the same set of procedures and records to keep track of transaction data. Thus, the material in Chapter 3 dealing with the account, general rules of debit and credit, and steps in the recording process—the journal, ledger, and chart of accounts—is the same under both GAAP and IFRS.

### KEY POINTS

- Transaction analysis is the same under IFRS and GAAP but, as you will see in later chapters, different standards sometimes impact how transactions are recorded.
- Rules for accounting for specific events sometimes differ across countries. For example, European companies rely less on historical cost and more on fair value than U.S. companies. Despite the differences, the double-entry accounting system is the basis of accounting systems worldwide.
- Both the IASB and FASB go beyond the basic definitions provided in this textbook for the key elements of financial statements, that is, assets, liabilities, equity, revenues, and expenses. The more substantive definitions, using the IASB definitional structure, are provided in the Chapter 1 *A Look at IFRS* discussion.
- A trial balance under IFRS follows the same format as shown in the textbook.
- As shown in the textbook, dollars signs are typically used only in the trial balance and the financial statements. The same practice is followed under IFRS, using the currency of the country that the reporting company is headquartered.
- In February 2010, the SEC expressed a desire to continue working toward a single set of high-quality standards. In deciding whether the United States should adopt IFRS, some of the issues the SEC said should be considered are:
  - ◆ Whether IFRS is sufficiently developed and consistent in application.
  - ◆ Whether the IASB is sufficiently independent.
  - ◆ Whether IFRS is established for the benefit of investors.
  - ◆ The issues involved in educating investors about IFRS.
  - ◆ The impact of a switch to IFRS on U.S. laws and regulations.
  - ◆ The impact on companies including changes to their accounting systems, contractual arrangements, corporate governance, and litigation.
  - ◆ The issues involved in educating accountants, so they can prepare statements under IFRS.

### LOOKING TO THE FUTURE

The basic recording process shown in this textbook is followed by companies across the globe. It is unlikely to change in the future. The definitional structure of assets, liabilities, equity, revenues, and expenses may change over time as the IASB and FASB evaluate their overall conceptual framework for establishing accounting standards.

## IFRS Self-Test Questions

1. Which statement is *correct* regarding IFRS?
   (a) IFRS reverses the rules of debits and credits, that is, debits are on the right and credits are on the left.
   (b) IFRS uses the same process for recording transactions as GAAP.
   (c) The chart of accounts under IFRS is different because revenues follow assets.
   (d) None of the above statements are correct.

2. The expanded accounting equation under IFRS is as follows:
   (a) Assets = Liabilities + Share Capital + Dividends + Revenues − Expenses.
   (b) Assets + Liabilities = Share Capital + Dividends + Revenues − Expenses.
   (c) Assets = Liabilities + Share Capital − Dividends + Revenues − Expenses.
   (d) Assets = Liabilities + Share Capital + Dividends − Revenues − Expenses.

3. A trial balance:
   (a) is the same under IFRS and GAAP.
   (b) proves that transactions are recorded correctly.
   (c) proves that all transactions have been recorded.
   (d) will not balance if a correct journal entry is posted twice.

4. One difference between IFRS and GAAP is that:
   (a) GAAP uses accrual-accounting concepts and IFRS uses primarily the cash basis of accounting.
   (b) IFRS uses a different posting process than GAAP.
   (c) IFRS uses more fair value measurements than GAAP.
   (d) the limitations of a trial balance are different between IFRS and GAAP.

5. The general policy for using proper currency signs (dollar, yen, pound, etc.) is the same for both IFRS and this textbook. This policy is as follows:
   (a) Currency signs only appear in ledgers and journal entries.
   (b) Currency signs are only shown in the trial balance.
   (c) Currency signs are shown for all compound journal entries.
   (d) Currency signs are shown in trial balances and financial statements.

## IFRS Concepts and Application

**IFRS3–1**   Describe some of the issues the SEC must consider in deciding whether the United States should adopt IFRS.

## INTERNATIONAL FINANCIAL REPORTING PROBLEM: *Zetar plc*

**IFRS3–2**   The financial statements of Zetar plc are presented in Appendix C. The company's complete annual report, including the notes to its financial statements, is available at **www.zetarplc.com.**

*Instructions*
Describe in which statement each of the following items is reported, and the position in the statement (e.g., current asset).
   (a) Share capital.
   (b) Goodwill.
   (c) Borrowings and overdrafts.
   (d) Amortisation of intangible assets.
   (e) Derivative financial asset.

## Answers to IFRS Self-Test Questions

1. b   2. c   3. a   4. c   5. d

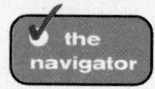

 **Remember to go back to the navigator box on the chapter opening page and check off your completed work.**

# chapter 4

# ACCRUAL ACCOUNTING CONCEPTS

## ✓ the navigator

- Scan **Study Objectives** ○
- Read **Feature Story** ○
- Scan **Preview** ○
- Read **Text and Answer** **Do it!** 
  p. 175 ○  p. 180 ○  p. 185 ○  p. 189 ○
- Work **Using the Decision Toolkit** ○
- Review **Summary of Study Objectives** ○
- Work **Comprehensive** **Do it!** p. 197 ○
- Answer **Self-Test Questions** ○
- Complete **Assignments** ○
- Go to **WileyPLUS** for practice and tutorials ○
- 🌐 Read **A Look at IFRS** p. 224 ○

## study objectives

**After studying this chapter, you should be able to:**

1 Explain the revenue recognition principle and the expense recognition principle.

2 Differentiate between the cash basis and the accrual basis of accounting.

3 Explain why adjusting entries are needed, and identify the major types of adjusting entries.

4 Prepare adjusting entries for deferrals.

5 Prepare adjusting entries for accruals.

6 Describe the nature and purpose of the adjusted trial balance.

7 Explain the purpose of closing entries.

8 Describe the required steps in the accounting cycle.

9 Understand the causes of differences between net income and cash provided by operating activities.

✓ the navigator

The accuracy of the financial reporting system depends on answers to a few fundamental questions. At what point has revenue been earned? At what point is the earnings process complete? When have expenses really been incurred?

During the 1990s, the stock prices of dot-com companies boomed. Many dot-com companies earned most of their revenue from selling advertising space on their websites. To boost reported revenue, some dot-coms began swapping website ad space. Company A would put an ad for its website on company B's website, and company B would put an ad for its website on company A's website. No money ever changed hands, but each company recorded revenue (for the value of the space that it gave up on its site). This practice did little to boost net income and resulted in no additional cash flow—but it did boost *reported revenue*. Regulators eventually put an end to the practice.

Another type of transgression results from companies recording revenue or expenses in the wrong year. In fact, shifting revenues and expenses is one of the

## WHAT WAS YOUR PROFIT?

most common abuses of financial accounting. Xerox admitted reporting billions of dollars of lease revenue in periods earlier than it should have been reported. And WorldCom stunned the financial markets with its admission that it had boosted net income by billions of dollars by delaying the recognition of expenses until later years.

Unfortunately, revelations such as these have become all too common in the corporate world. It is no wonder that the U.S. Trust Survey of affluent Americans reported that 85 percent of its respondents believed that there should be tighter regulation of financial disclosures, and 66 percent said they did not trust the management of publicly traded companies.

Why did so many companies violate basic financial reporting rules and sound ethics? Many speculate that as stock prices climbed, executives were under increasing pressure to meet higher and higher earnings expectations. If actual results weren't as good as hoped for, some gave in to temptation and "adjusted" their numbers to meet market expectations.

*the navigator*

**INSIDE CHAPTER 4 . . .**

As indicated in the Feature Story, making adjustments is necessary to avoid misstatement of revenues and expenses such as those at Xerox and WorldCom. In this chapter, we introduce you to the accrual accounting concepts that make such adjustments possible.

The organization and content of the chapter are as follows.

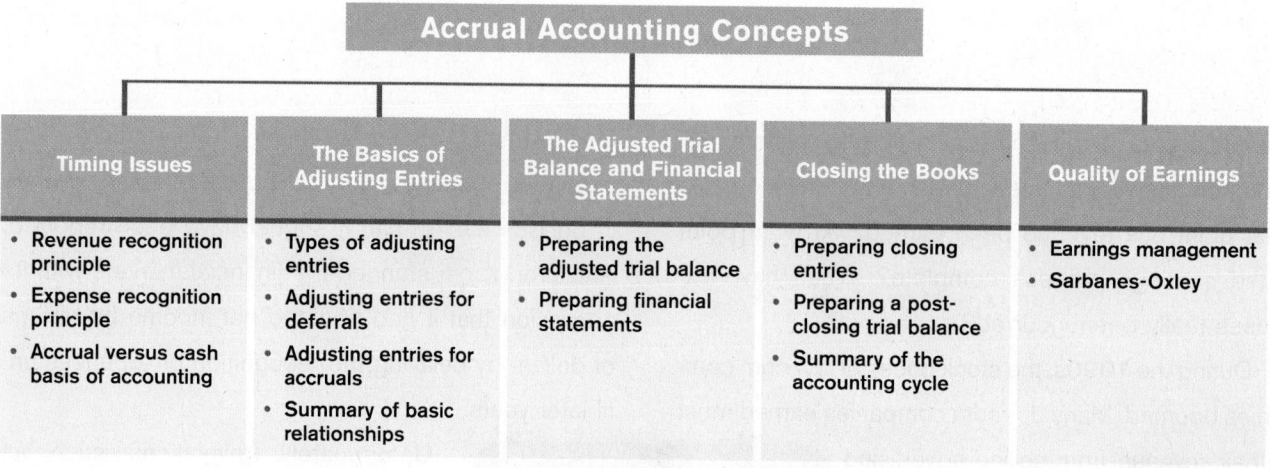

# Timing Issues

**Helpful Hint** An accounting time period that is one year long is called a fiscal year.

Most businesses need immediate feedback about how well they are doing. For example, management usually wants monthly reports on financial results, most large corporations are required to present quarterly and annual financial statements to stockholders, and the Internal Revenue Service requires all businesses to file annual tax returns. **Accounting divides the economic life of a business into artificial time periods.** As indicated in Chapter 2, this is the periodicity assumption. **Accounting time periods are generally a month, a quarter, or a year.**

Many business transactions affect more than one of these arbitrary time periods. For example, a new building purchased by Citigroup or a new airplane purchased by Delta Air Lines will be used for many years. It doesn't make sense to expense the full cost of the building or the airplane at the time of purchase because each will be used for many subsequent periods. Instead, we determine the impact of each transaction on specific accounting periods.

Determining the amount of revenues and expenses to report in a given accounting period can be difficult. Proper reporting requires an understanding of the nature of the company's business. Two principles are used as guidelines: the revenue recognition principle and the expense recognition principle.

### THE REVENUE RECOGNITION PRINCIPLE

The revenue recognition principle requires that companies recognize revenue in the accounting period **in which it is earned**. In a service company, revenue is considered to be earned at the time the service is performed. To illustrate, assume Conrad Dry Cleaners cleans clothing on June 30, but customers do not claim and pay for their clothes until the first week of July. Under the revenue recognition principle, Conrad earns revenue in June when it performs the service, not in July when it receives the cash. At June 30, Conrad would report a receivable on its balance sheet and revenue in its income statement for the service performed. The journal entries for June and July would be as follows.

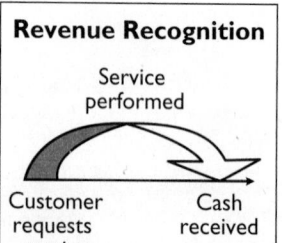

**Revenue Recognition**

Service performed

Customer requests service

Cash received

Revenue should be recognized in the accounting period in which it is earned (generally when service is performed).

| | | | |
|---|---|---|---|
| June | Accounts Receivable | xxx | |
| | Service Revenue | | xxx |
| July | Cash | xxx | |
| | Accounts Receivable | | xxx |

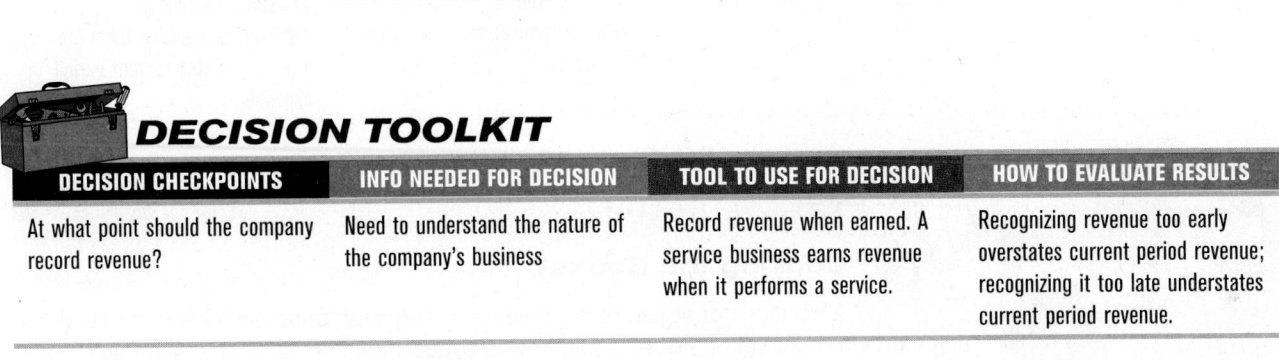

## DECISION TOOLKIT

| DECISION CHECKPOINTS | INFO NEEDED FOR DECISION | TOOL TO USE FOR DECISION | HOW TO EVALUATE RESULTS |
|---|---|---|---|
| At what point should the company record revenue? | Need to understand the nature of the company's business | Record revenue when earned. A service business earns revenue when it performs a service. | Recognizing revenue too early overstates current period revenue; recognizing it too late understates current period revenue. |

## THE EXPENSE RECOGNITION PRINCIPLE

In recognizing expenses, a simple rule is followed: "Let the expenses follow the revenues." Thus, expense recognition is tied to revenue recognition. Applied to the preceding example, this means that the salary expense Conrad incurred in performing the cleaning service on June 30 should be reported in the same period in which it recognizes the service revenue. The critical issue in expense recognition is determining when the expense makes its contribution to revenue. This may or may not be the same period in which the expense is paid. If Conrad does not pay the salary incurred on June 30 until July, it would report salaries payable on its June 30 balance sheet.

The practice of expense recognition is referred to as the **expense recognition principle** (often referred to as the **matching principle**). It dictates that efforts (expenses) be matched with results (revenues). Illustration 4-1 shows these relationships.

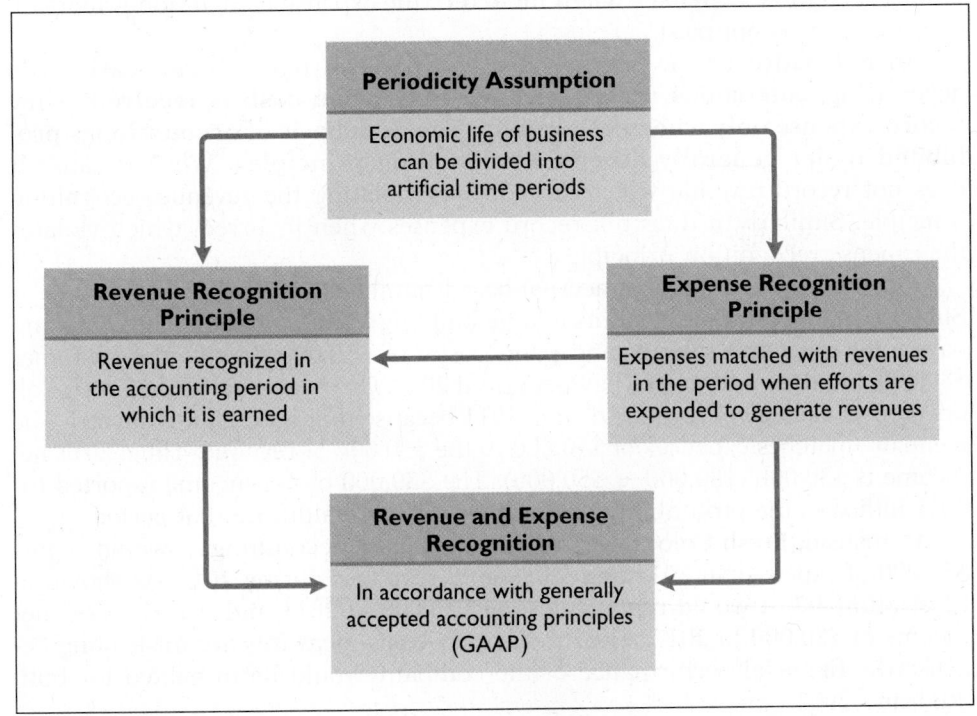

**Illustration 4-1** GAAP relationships in revenue and expense recognition

# DECISION TOOLKIT

| DECISION CHECKPOINTS | INFO NEEDED FOR DECISION | TOOL TO USE FOR DECISION | HOW TO EVALUATE RESULTS |
|---|---|---|---|
| At what point should the company record expenses? | Need to understand the nature of the company's business | Expenses should "follow" revenues—that is, match the effort (expense) with the result (revenue). | Recognizing expenses too early overstates current period expense; recognizing them too late understates current period expense. |

## Ethics Insight

### Cooking the Books?

Allegations of abuse of the revenue recognition principle have become all too common in recent years. For example, it was alleged that Krispy Kreme sometimes doubled the number of doughnuts shipped to wholesale customers at the end of a quarter to boost quarterly results. The customers shipped the unsold doughnuts back after the beginning of the next quarter for a refund. Conversely, Computer Associates International was accused of backdating sales—that is, saying that a sale that occurred at the beginning of one quarter occurred at the end of the previous quarter in order to achieve the previous quarter's sales targets.

 What motivates sales executives and finance and accounting executives to participate in activities that result in inaccurate reporting of revenues? (See page 223.)

## ACCRUAL VERSUS CASH BASIS OF ACCOUNTING

**study objective 2**

Differentiate between the cash basis and the accrual basis of accounting.

**International Note** Although different accounting standards are often used by companies in other countries, the accrual basis of accounting is central to all of these standards.

**Accrual-basis accounting** means that transactions that change a company's financial statements are recorded **in the periods in which the events occur**, even if cash was not exchanged. For example, using the accrual basis means that companies recognize revenues **when earned** (the revenue recognition principle), even if cash was not received. **Likewise, under the accrual basis, companies recognize expenses when incurred** (the expense recognition principle), even if cash was not paid.

An alternative to the accrual basis is the cash basis. Under **cash-basis accounting, companies record revenue only when cash is received. They record expense only when cash is paid. The cash basis of accounting is prohibited under generally accepted accounting principles.** Why? Because it does not record revenue when earned, thus violating the revenue recognition principle. Similarly, it does not record expenses when incurred, which violates the expense recognition principle.

Illustration 4-2 compares accrual-based numbers and cash-based numbers. Suppose that Fresh Colors paints a large building in 2011. In 2011, it incurs and pays total expenses (salaries and paint costs) of $50,000. It bills the customer $80,000, but does not receive payment until 2012. On an accrual basis, Fresh Colors reports $80,000 of revenue during 2011 because that is when it is earned. The company matches expenses of $50,000 to the $80,000 of revenue. Thus, 2011 net income is $30,000 ($80,000 − $50,000). The $30,000 of net income reported for 2011 indicates the profitability of Fresh Colors' efforts during that period.

If, instead, Fresh Colors were to use cash-basis accounting, it would report $50,000 of expenses in 2011 and $80,000 of revenues during 2012. As shown in Illustration 4-2, it would report a loss of $50,000 in 2011 and would report net income of $80,000 in 2012. Clearly, the cash-basis measures are misleading because the financial performance of the company would be misstated for both 2011 and 2012.

**Illustration 4-2** Accrual-versus cash-basis accounting

| | 2011 | 2012 |
|---|---|---|
| **Activity** | Purchased paint, painted building, paid employees | Received payment for work done in 2011 |
| **Accrual basis** | Revenue $80,000<br>Expense 50,000<br>Net income $30,000 | Revenue $    0<br>Expense 0<br>Net income $    0 |
| **Cash basis** | Revenue $    0<br>Expense 50,000<br>Net loss $(50,000) | Revenue $80,000<br>Expense 0<br>Net income $80,000 |

## Investor Insight

### Reporting Revenue Accurately

Until recently, electronics manufacturer Apple was required to spread the revenues earned from iPhone sales over the two-year period following the sale of the phone. Accounting standards required this because it was argued that Apple was obligated to provide software updates after the phone was sold. Therefore, since Apple had service obligations after the initial date of sale, it was forced to spread the revenue over a two-year period. However, since the company received full payment upfront, the cash flows from iPhones significantly exceeded the revenue reported from iPhone sales in each accounting period. It also meant that the rapid growth of iPhone sales was not fully reflected in the revenue amounts reported in Apple's income statement. A new accounting standard now enables Apple to report nearly all of its iPhone revenue at the point of sale. It was estimated that 2009 revenues would have been about 17% higher, and earnings per share would have been almost 50% higher, under the new rule.

**?** In the past, why was it argued that Apple should spread the recognition of iPhone revenue over a two-year period, rather than recording it upfront? (See page 223.)

# The Basics of Adjusting Entries

In order for revenues to be recorded in the period in which they are earned, and for expenses to be recognized in the period in which they are incurred, companies make adjusting entries. **Adjusting entries ensure that the revenue recognition and expense recognition principles are followed**.

Adjusting entries are necessary because the **trial balance**—the first pulling together of the transaction data—may not contain up-to-date and complete data. This is true for several reasons:

1. Some events are not recorded daily because it is not efficient to do so. Examples are the use of supplies and the earning of wages by employees.

**study objective** 3

Explain why adjusting entries are needed, and identify the major types of adjusting entries.

**International Note** Internal controls are a system of checks and balances designed to detect and prevent fraud and errors. The Sarbanes-Oxley Act requires U.S. companies to enhance their systems of internal control. However, many foreign companies do not have to meet strict internal control requirements. Some U.S. companies believe that this gives foreign firms an unfair advantage because developing and maintaining internal controls can be very expensive.

2. Some costs are not recorded during the accounting period because these costs expire with the passage of time rather than as a result of recurring daily transactions. Examples are charges related to the use of buildings and equipment, rent, and insurance.

3. Some items may be unrecorded. An example is a utility service bill that will not be received until the next accounting period.

**Adjusting entries are required every time a company prepares financial statements.** The company analyzes each account in the trial balance to determine whether it is complete and up to date for financial statement purposes. **Every adjusting entry will include one income statement account and one balance sheet account.**

## TYPES OF ADJUSTING ENTRIES

Adjusting entries are classified as either deferrals or accruals. As Illustration 4-3 shows, each of these classes has two subcategories.

**Illustration 4-3**
Categories of adjusting entries

**Deferrals:**

1. Prepaid expenses: Expenses paid in cash and recorded as assets before they are used or consumed.

2. Unearned revenues: Cash received and recorded as liabilities before revenue is earned.

**Accruals:**

1. Accrued revenues: Revenues earned but not yet received in cash or recorded.

2. Accrued expenses: Expenses incurred but not yet paid in cash or recorded.

Subsequent sections give examples of each type of adjustment. Each example is based on the October 31 trial balance of Sierra Corporation, from Chapter 3, reproduced in Illustration 4-4. Note that Retained Earnings, with a zero balance, has been added to this trial balance. We will explain its use later.

**Illustration 4-4** Trial balance

**SIERRA CORPORATION**
Trial Balance
October 31, 2012

|  | Debit | Credit |
| --- | --- | --- |
| Cash | $15,200 | |
| Supplies | 2,500 | |
| Prepaid Insurance | 600 | |
| Equipment | 5,000 | |
| Notes Payable | | $ 5,000 |
| Accounts Payable | | 2,500 |
| Unearned Service Revenue | | 1,200 |
| Common Stock | | 10,000 |
| Retained Earnings | | 0 |
| Dividends | 500 | |
| Service Revenue | | 10,000 |
| Salaries Expense | 4,000 | |
| Rent Expense | 900 | |
|  | $28,700 | $28,700 |

We assume that Sierra Corporation uses an accounting period of one month. Thus, monthly adjusting entries are made. The entries are dated October 31.

## ADJUSTING ENTRIES FOR DEFERRALS

**study objective** **4**

Prepare adjusting entries for deferrals.

To defer means to postpone or delay. Deferrals are costs or revenues that are recognized at a date later than the point when cash was originally exchanged. Companies make adjusting entries for deferrals to record the portion of the deferred item that was incurred as an expense or earned as revenue during the current accounting period. The two types of deferrals are prepaid expenses and unearned revenues.

### Prepaid Expenses

Companies record payments of expenses that will benefit more than one accounting period as assets called **prepaid expenses** or **prepayments**. When expenses are prepaid, an asset account is increased (debited) to show the service or benefit that the company will receive in the future. Examples of common prepayments are insurance, supplies, advertising, and rent. In addition, companies make prepayments when they purchase buildings and equipment.

**Prepaid expenses are costs that expire either with the passage of time** (e.g., rent and insurance) **or through use** (e.g., supplies). The expiration of these costs does not require daily entries, which would be impractical and unnecessary. Accordingly, companies postpone the recognition of such cost expirations until they prepare financial statements. At each statement date, they make adjusting entries to record the expenses applicable to the current accounting period and to show the remaining amounts in the asset accounts.

Prior to adjustment, assets are overstated and expenses are understated. Therefore, as shown in Illustration 4-5, **an adjusting entry for prepaid expenses results in an increase (a debit) to an expense account and a decrease (a credit) to an asset account**.

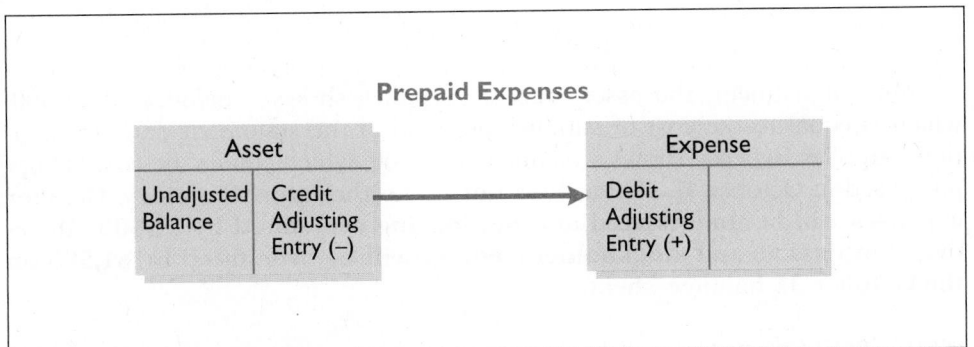

**Illustration 4-5**  Adjusting entries for prepaid expenses

Let's look in more detail at some specific types of prepaid expenses, beginning with supplies.

**SUPPLIES.** The purchase of supplies, such as paper and envelopes, results in an increase (a debit) to an asset account. During the accounting period, the company uses supplies. Rather than record supplies expense as the supplies are used, companies recognize supplies expense at the **end** of the accounting period. At the end of the accounting period, the company counts the remaining supplies. The difference between the unadjusted balance in the Supplies (asset) account and the actual cost of supplies on hand represents the supplies used (an expense) for that period.

Recall from Chapter 3 that Sierra Corporation purchased supplies costing $2,500 on October 5. Sierra recorded the purchase by increasing (debiting) the asset Supplies. This account shows a balance of $2,500 in the October 31 trial balance. An inventory count at the close of business on October 31 reveals that $1,000 of supplies are still on hand. Thus, the cost of supplies used is

**Supplies**

Oct. 5

Supplies purchased; record asset

Oct. 31
Supplies used; record supplies expense

$1,500 ($2,500 − $1,000). This use of supplies decreases an asset, Supplies. It also decreases stockholders' equity by increasing an expense account, Supplies Expense. This is shown in Illustration 4-6.

**Illustration 4-6**
Adjustment for supplies

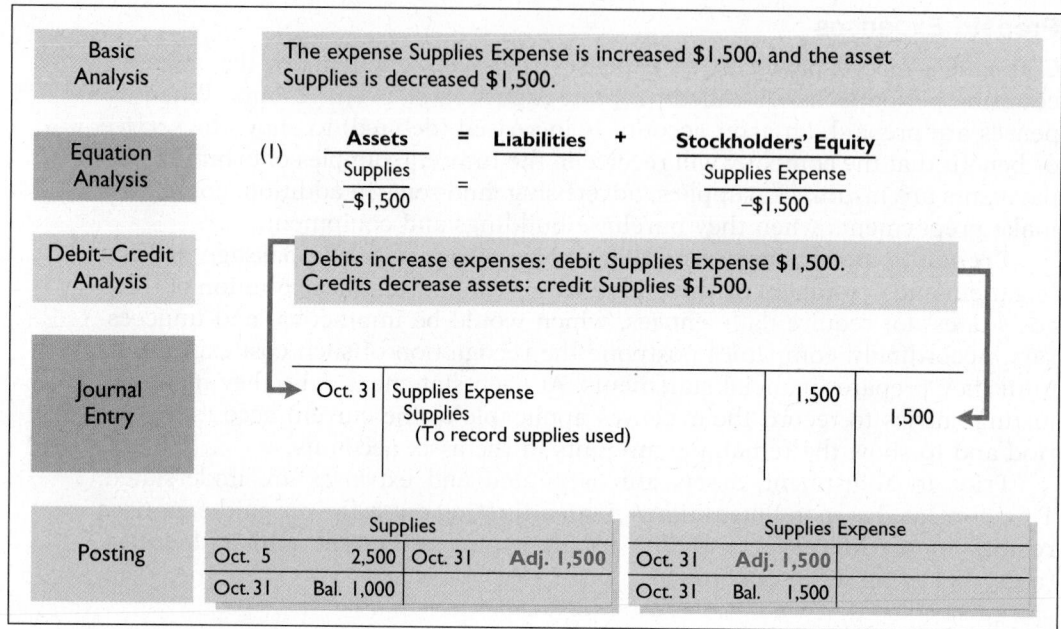

After adjustment, the asset account Supplies shows a balance of $1,000, which is equal to the cost of supplies on hand at the statement date. In addition, Supplies Expense shows a balance of $1,500, which equals the cost of supplies used in October. **If Sierra does not make the adjusting entry, October expenses will be understated and net income overstated by $1,500. Moreover, both assets and stockholders' equity will be overstated by $1,500 on the October 31 balance sheet.**

**Insurance**

Oct. 4

Insurance purchased; record asset

| Insurance Policy | | | |
|------|------|------|------|
| Oct | Nov | Dec | Jan |
| $50 | $50 | $50 | $50 |
| Feb | March | April | May |
| $50 | $50 | $50 | $50 |
| June | July | Aug | Sept |
| $50 | $50 | $50 | $50 |
| I YEAR $600 | | | |

Oct. 31
Insurance expired; record insurance expense

**INSURANCE.** Companies purchase insurance to protect themselves from losses due to fire, theft, and unforeseen events. Insurance must be paid in advance, often for more than one year. The cost of insurance (premiums) paid in advance is recorded as an increase (debit) in the asset account Prepaid Insurance. At the financial statement date, companies increase (debit) Insurance Expense and decrease (credit) Prepaid Insurance for the cost of insurance that has expired during the period.

On October 4, Sierra Corporation paid $600 for a one-year fire insurance policy. Coverage began on October 1. Sierra recorded the payment by increasing (debiting) Prepaid Insurance. This account shows a balance of $600 in the October 31 trial balance. Insurance of $50 ($600 ÷ 12) expires each month. The expiration of prepaid insurance decreases an asset, Prepaid Insurance. It also decreases stockholders' equity by increasing an expense account, Insurance Expense.

As shown in Illustration 4-7, the asset Prepaid Insurance shows a balance of $550, which represents the unexpired cost for the remaining 11 months of coverage. At the same time, the balance in Insurance Expense equals the insurance cost that expired in October. If Sierra does not make this adjustment, October expenses are understated by $50 and net income is overstated by $50. Moreover, as the accounting equation shows, both assets and stockholders' equity will be overstated by $50 on the October 31 balance sheet.

**Illustration 4-7**
Adjustment for insurance

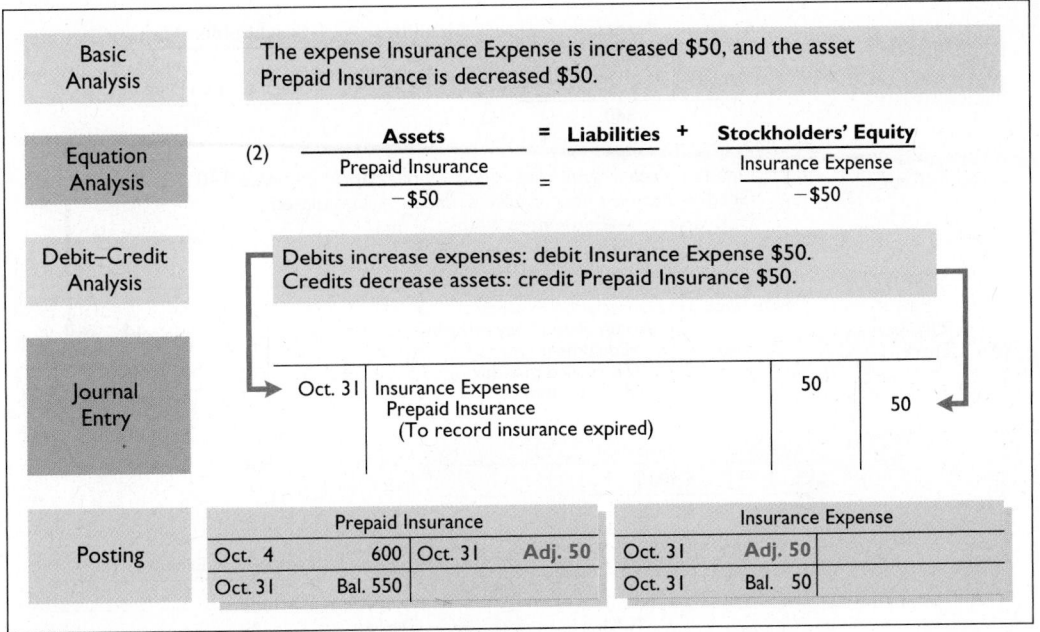

| | | | |
|---|---|---|---|
| **Basic Analysis** | The expense Insurance Expense is increased $50, and the asset Prepaid Insurance is decreased $50. | | |

| **Equation Analysis** | (2) | **Assets** = **Liabilities** + **Stockholders' Equity** |
|---|---|---|

Prepaid Insurance −$50 = Insurance Expense −$50

**Debit–Credit Analysis**
Debits increase expenses: debit Insurance Expense $50.
Credits decrease assets: credit Prepaid Insurance $50.

**Journal Entry**
Oct. 31 | Insurance Expense ... 50
Prepaid Insurance ... 50
(To record insurance expired)

**Posting**

| Prepaid Insurance | | Insurance Expense | |
|---|---|---|---|
| Oct. 4   600 | Oct. 31   Adj. 50 | Oct. 31   Adj. 50 | |
| Oct. 31   Bal. 550 | | Oct. 31   Bal. 50 | |

**DEPRECIATION.** A company typically owns a variety of assets that have long lives, such as buildings, equipment, and motor vehicles. The period of service is referred to as the **useful life** of the asset. Because a building is expected to provide service for many years, it is recorded as an asset, rather than an expense, on the date it is acquired. As explained in chapter 2, companies record such assets **at cost**, as required by the cost principle. To follow the expense recognition principle, companies allocate a portion of this cost as an expense during each period of the asset's useful life. **Depreciation** is the process of allocating the cost of an asset to expense over its useful life.

*Need for adjustment.* The acquisition of long-lived assets is essentially a long-term prepayment for the use of an asset. An adjusting entry for depreciation is needed to recognize the cost that has been used (an expense) during the period and to report the unused cost (an asset) at the end of the period. One very important point to understand: **Depreciation is an allocation concept, not a valuation concept.** That is, depreciation **allocates an asset's cost to the periods in which it is used. Depreciation does not attempt to report the actual change in the value of the asset.**

For Sierra Corporation, assume that depreciation on the equipment is $480 a year, or $40 per month. As shown in Illustration 4-8 (page 172), rather than decrease (credit) the asset account directly, Sierra instead credits Accumulated Depreciation—Equipment. Accumulated Depreciation is called a **contra asset account.** Such an account is offset against an asset account on the balance sheet. Thus, the Accumulated Depreciation—Equipment account offsets the asset Equipment. This account keeps track of the total amount of depreciation expense taken over the life of the asset. To keep the accounting equation in balance, Sierra decreases stockholders' equity by increasing an expense account, Depreciation Expense.

The balance in the Accumulated Depreciation—Equipment account will increase $40 each month, and the balance in Equipment remains $5,000.

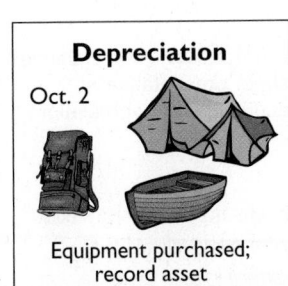

**Depreciation**

Oct. 2

Equipment purchased; record asset

| Equipment | | | |
|---|---|---|---|
| Oct | Nov | Dec | Jan |
| $40 | $40 | $40 | $40 |
| Feb | March | April | May |
| $40 | $40 | $40 | $40 |
| June | July | Aug | Sept |
| $40 | $40 | $40 | $40 |
| Depreciation = $480/year | | | |

Oct. 31
Depreciation recognized; record depreciation expense

**Illustration 4-8**
Adjustment for depreciation

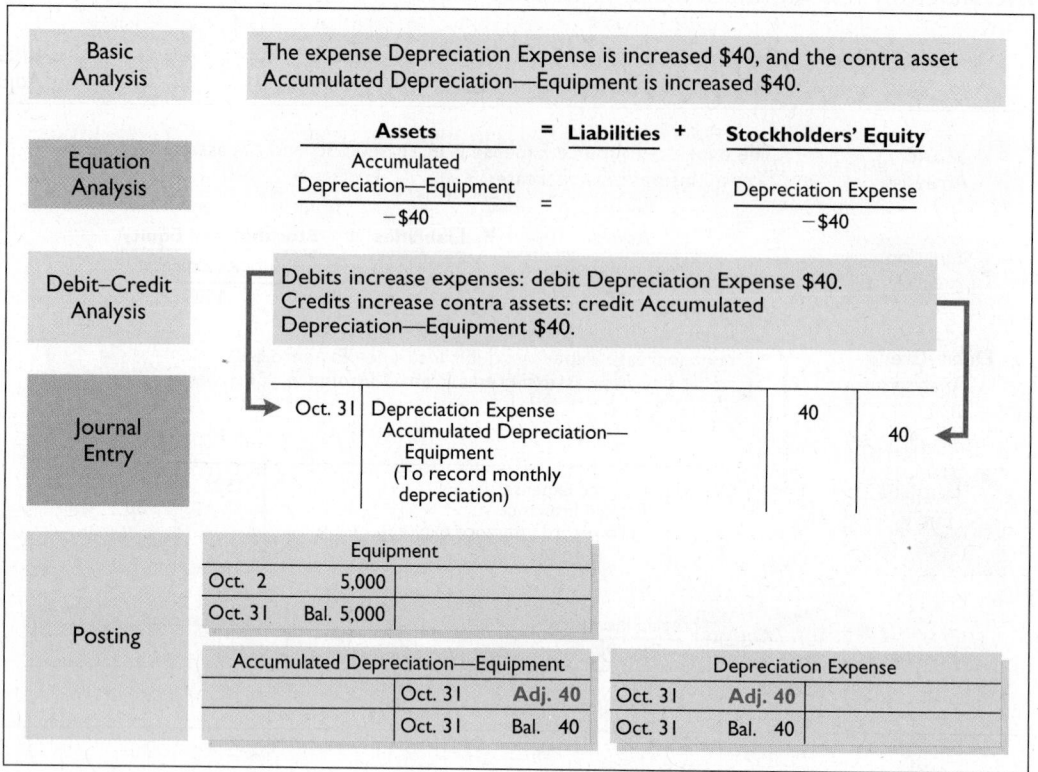

**Helpful Hint** All contra accounts have increases, decreases, and normal balances **opposite to** the account to which they relate.

***Statement presentation.*** As noted above, Accumulated Depreciation—Equipment is a contra asset account. It is offset against Equipment on the balance sheet. The normal balance of a contra asset account is a credit. A theoretical alternative to using a contra asset account would be to decrease (credit) the asset account by the amount of depreciation each period. But using the contra account is preferable for a simple reason: It discloses *both* the original cost of the equipment *and* the total cost that has expired to date. Thus, in the balance sheet, Sierra deducts Accumulated Depreciation—Equipment from the related asset account, as shown in Illustration 4-9.

**Illustration 4-9** Balance sheet presentation of accumulated depreciation

| Equipment | $ 5,000 |
|---|---|
| Less: Accumulated depreciation—equipment | 40 |
| | $4,960 |

**Alternative Terminology** Book value is also referred to as *carrying value.*

**Book value** is the difference between the cost of any depreciable asset and its related accumulated depreciation. In Illustration 4-9, the book value of the equipment at the balance sheet date is $4,960. The book value and the fair value of the asset are generally two different values. As noted earlier, **the purpose of depreciation is not valuation but a means of cost allocation.**

Depreciation expense identifies the portion of an asset's cost that expired during the period (in this case, in October). The accounting equation shows that without this adjusting entry, total assets, total stockholders' equity, and net income are overstated by $40 and depreciation expense is understated by $40.

Illustration 4-10 summarizes the accounting for prepaid expenses.

**Unearned Revenues**

Companies record cash received before revenue is earned by increasing (crediting) a liability account called **unearned revenues**. Items like rent, magazine subscriptions,

**Illustration 4-10**
Accounting for prepaid expenses

### ACCOUNTING FOR PREPAID EXPENSES

| Examples | Reason for Adjustment | Accounts Before Adjustment | Adjusting Entry |
|---|---|---|---|
| Insurance, supplies, advertising, rent, depreciation | Prepaid expenses recorded in asset accounts have been used. | Assets overstated. Expenses understated. | Dr. Expenses<br>　Cr. Assets |

**Unearned Revenues**

Cash is received in advance; liability is recorded

Oct. 31
Some service has been provided; some revenue is recorded

and customer deposits for future service may result in unearned revenues. Airlines such as United, American, and Delta, for instance, treat receipts from the sale of tickets as unearned revenue until the flight service is provided.

Unearned revenues are the opposite of prepaid expenses. Indeed, unearned revenue on the books of one company is likely to be a prepaid expense on the books of the company that has made the advance payment. For example, if identical accounting periods are assumed, a landlord will have unearned rent revenue when a tenant has prepaid rent.

When a company receives payment for services to be provided in a future accounting period, it increases (credits) an unearned revenue (a liability) account to recognize the liability that exists. The company subsequently earns revenues by providing service. During the accounting period it is not practical to make daily entries as the company earns the revenue. Instead, we delay recognition of earned revenue until the adjustment process. Then the company makes an adjusting entry to record the revenue earned during the period and to show the liability that remains at the end of the accounting period. Typically, prior to adjustment, liabilities are overstated and revenues are understated. Therefore, as shown in Illustration 4-11, **the adjusting entry for unearned revenues results in a decrease (a debit) to a liability account and an increase (a credit) to a revenue account**.

**Illustration 4-11**
Adjusting entries for unearned revenues

**Unearned Revenues**

| Liability | | Revenue | |
|---|---|---|---|
| Debit Adjusting Entry (–) | Unadjusted Balance | | Credit Adjusting Entry (+) |

Sierra Corporation received $1,200 on October 2 from R. Knox for guide services for multi-day trips expected to be completed by December 31. Sierra credited the payment to Unearned Service Revenue, and this liability account shows a balance of $1,200 in the October 31 trial balance. From an evaluation of the service Sierra performed for Knox during October, the company determines that it has earned $400 in October. The liability (Unearned Service Revenue) is therefore decreased, and stockholders' equity (Service Revenue) is increased.

As shown in Illustration 4-12 (page 174), the liability Unearned Service Revenue now shows a balance of $800. That amount represents the remaining guide services expected to be performed in the future. At the same time, Service Revenue shows total revenue earned in October of $10,400. **Without this adjustment, revenues and net income are understated by $400 in the income statement.**

**Illustration 4-12** Service revenue accounts after adjustment

Moreover, liabilities are overstated and stockholders' equity is understated by $400 on the October 31 balance sheet.

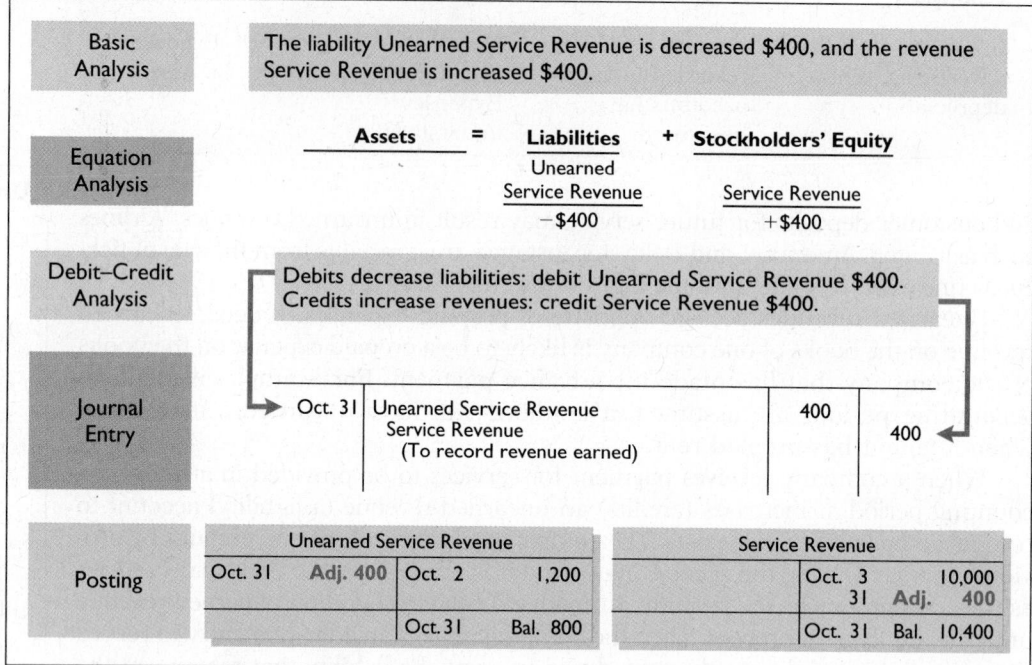

Illustration 4-13 summarizes the accounting for unearned revenues.

**Illustration 4-13**
Accounting for unearned revenues

### ACCOUNTING FOR UNEARNED REVENUES

| Examples | Reason for Adjustment | Accounts Before Adjustment | Adjusting Entry |
|---|---|---|---|
| Rent, magazine subscriptions, customer deposits for future service | Unearned revenues recorded in liability accounts have been earned. | Liabilities overstated. Revenues understated. | Dr. Liabilities  Cr. Revenues |

## Accounting Across the Organization

### Turning Gift Cards into Revenue

Those of you who are marketing majors (and even most of you who are not) know that gift cards are among the hottest marketing tools in merchandising today. Customers purchase gift cards and give them to someone for later use. In a recent year, gift-card sales topped $95 billion.

Although these programs are popular with marketing executives, they create accounting questions. Should revenue be recorded at the time the gift card is sold, or when it is exercised? How should expired gift cards be accounted for? In its 2009 balance sheet, Best Buy reported unearned revenue related to gift cards of $479 million.

*Source:* Robert Berner, "Gift Cards: No Gift to Investors," *Business Week* (March 14, 2005), p. 86.

**?** Suppose that Robert Jones purchases a $100 gift card at Best Buy on December 24, 2011, and gives it to his wife, Mary Jones, on December 25, 2011. On January 3, 2012, Mary uses the card to purchase $100 worth of CDs. When do you think Best Buy should recognize revenue and why? (See page 223.)

# Do it!

The ledger of Hammond, Inc., on March 31, 2012, includes these selected accounts before adjusting entries are prepared.

|  | Debit | Credit |
|---|---|---|
| Prepaid Insurance | $ 3,600 | |
| Supplies | 2,800 | |
| Equipment | 25,000 | |
| Accumulated Depreciation—Equipment | | $5,000 |
| Unearned Service Revenue | | 9,200 |

An analysis of the accounts shows the following.

1. Insurance expires at the rate of $100 per month.
2. Supplies on hand total $800.
3. The equipment depreciates $200 a month.
4. One-half of the unearned service revenue was earned in March.

Prepare the adjusting entries for the month of March.

### Solution

| | | |
|---|---|---|
| 1. Insurance Expense | 100 | |
|     Prepaid Insurance | | 100 |
|       (To record insurance expired) | | |
| 2. Supplies Expense | 2,000 | |
|     Supplies | | 2,000 |
|       (To record supplies used) | | |
| 3. Depreciation Expense | 200 | |
|     Accumulated Depreciation—Equipment | | 200 |
|       (To record monthly depreciation) | | |
| 4. Unearned Service Revenue | 4,600 | |
|     Service Revenue | | 4,600 |
|       (To record revenue earned) | | |

### Action Plan

- Make adjusting entries at the end of the period for revenues earned and expenses incurred in the period.
- Don't forget to make adjusting entries for deferrals. Failure to adjust for deferrals leads to overstatement of the asset or liability and understatement of the related expense or revenue.

Related exercise material: **BE4-4, BE4-5, BE4-6, BE4-7,** and **Do it!** **4-1.**

## ADJUSTING ENTRIES FOR ACCRUALS

The second category of adjusting entries is **accruals**. Prior to an accrual adjustment, the revenue account (and the related asset account) or the expense account (and the related liability account) are understated. Thus, the adjusting entry for accruals will **increase both a balance sheet and an income statement account**.

### Accrued Revenues

Revenues earned but not yet recorded at the statement date are accrued revenues. Accrued revenues may accumulate (accrue) with the passing of time, as in the case of interest revenue. These are unrecorded because the earning of interest does not involve daily transactions. Companies do not record interest revenue on a daily basis because it is often impractical to do so. Accrued revenues also may result from services that have been performed but not yet billed nor collected, as in the case of commissions and fees. These may be unrecorded because only a portion of the total service has been provided and the clients won't be billed until the service has been completed.

An adjusting entry records the receivable that exists at the balance sheet date and the revenue earned during the period. Prior to adjustment, both assets and revenues are understated. As shown in Illustration 4-14 (page 176), **an adjusting entry for accrued revenues results in an increase (a debit) to an asset account and an increase (a credit) to a revenue account**.

**Accrued Revenues**

Oct. 31

My fee is $200

Revenue and receivable are recorded for unbilled services

Nov. 10

Cash is received; receivable is reduced

**Illustration 4-14** Adjusting entries for accrued revenues

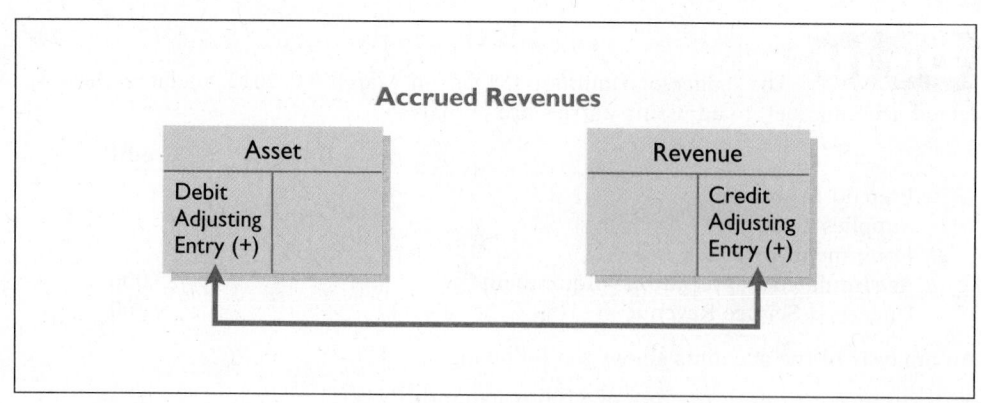

**Helpful Hint** For accruals, there may have been no prior entry, and the accounts requiring adjustment may both have zero balances prior to adjustment.

**Ethics Note** Computer Associates International was accused of backdating sales–that is, saying that a sale that occurred at the beginning of one quarter occurred at the end of the previous quarter, in order to achieve the previous quarter's sales targets.

In October, Sierra Corporation earned $200 for guide services that were not billed to clients on or before October 31. Because these services are not billed, they are not recorded. The accrual of unrecorded service revenue increases an asset account, Accounts Receivable. It also increases stockholders' equity by increasing a revenue account, Service Revenue, as shown in Illustration 4-15.

**Illustration 4-15** Adjustment for accrued revenue

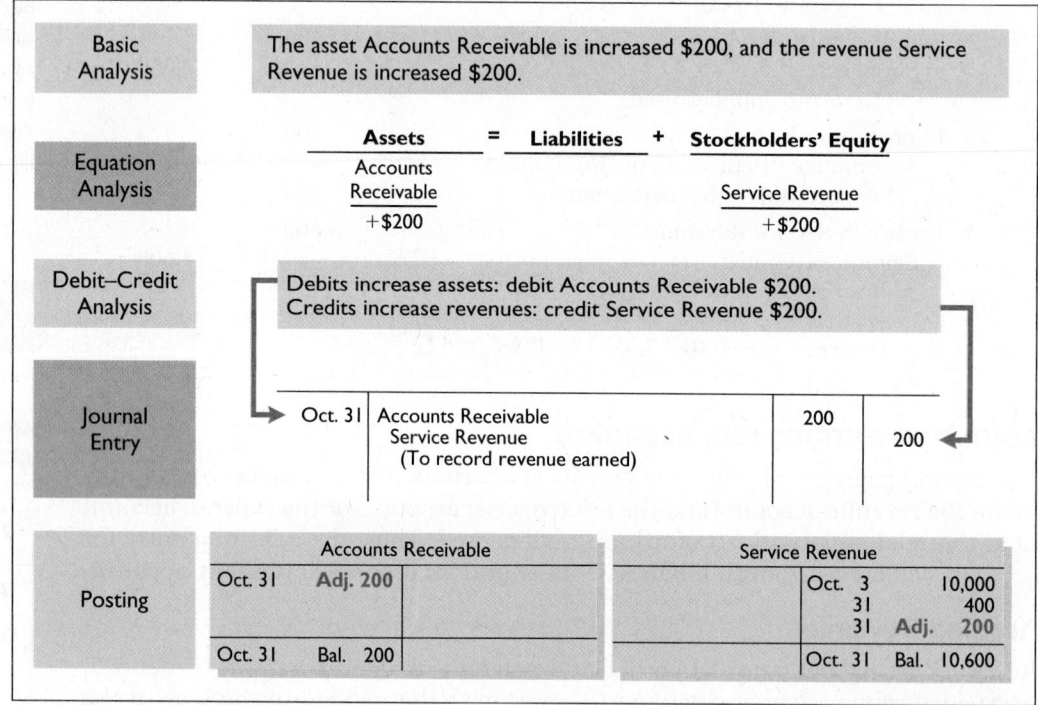

**Equation analyses** summarize the effects of transactions on the three elements of the accounting equation, as well as the effect on cash flows.

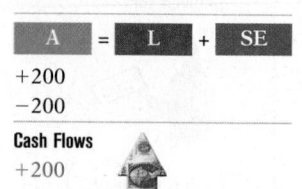

The asset Accounts Receivable shows that clients owe Sierra $200 at the balance sheet date. The balance of $10,600 in Service Revenue represents the total revenue Sierra earned during the month ($10,000 + $400 + $200). **Without the adjusting entry, assets and stockholders' equity on the balance sheet and revenues and net income on the income statement are understated.**

On November 10, Sierra receives cash of $200 for the services performed in October and makes the following entry.

| Nov. 10 | Cash | 200 | |
| | Accounts Receivable | | 200 |
| | (To record cash collected on account) | | |

The company records the collection of the receivables by a debit (increase) to Cash and a credit (decrease) to Accounts Receivable.

Illustration 4-16 summarizes the accounting for accrued revenues.

**Illustration 4-16**
Accounting for accrued revenues

| | | ACCOUNTING FOR ACCRUED REVENUES | |
|---|---|---|---|
| **Examples** | **Reason for Adjustment** | **Accounts Before Adjustment** | **Adjusting Entry** |
| Interest, rent, services performed but not collected | Revenues have been earned but not yet received in cash or recorded. | Assets understated. Revenues understated. | Dr. Assets <br> Cr. Revenues |

## Accrued Expenses

Expenses incurred but not yet paid or recorded at the statement date are called **accrued expenses**. Interest, taxes, and salaries are common examples of accrued expenses.

Companies make adjustments for accrued expenses to record the obligations that exist at the balance sheet date and to recognize the expenses that apply to the current accounting period. Prior to adjustment, both liabilities and expenses are understated. Therefore, **an adjusting entry for accrued expenses results in an increase (a debit) to an expense account and an increase (a credit) to a liability account.**

**Ethics Note** A report released by Fannie Mae's board of directors stated that improper adjusting entries at the mortgage-finance company resulted in delayed recognition of expenses caused by interest-rate changes. The motivation for such accounting apparently was the desire to hit earnings estimates.

**Illustration 4-17**
Adjusting entries for accrued expenses

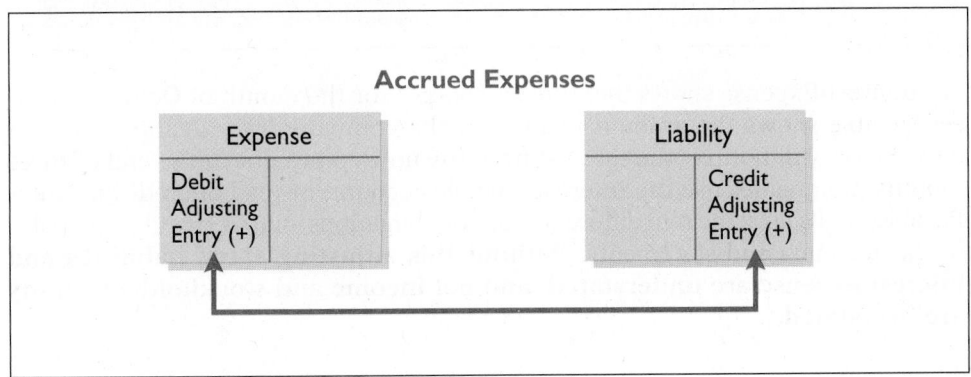

Let's look in more detail at some specific types of accrued expenses, beginning with accrued interest.

**ACCRUED INTEREST.** Sierra Corporation signed a three-month note payable in the amount of $5,000 on October 1. The note requires Sierra to pay interest at an annual rate of 12%.

The amount of the interest recorded is determined by three factors: (1) the face value of the note; (2) the interest rate, which is always expressed as an annual rate; and (3) the length of time the note is outstanding. For Sierra, the total interest due on the $5,000 note at its maturity date three months in the future is $150 ($5,000 $\times$ 12% $\times \frac{3}{12}$), or $50 for one month. Illustration 4-18 shows the formula for computing interest and its application to Sierra Corporation for the month of October.

**Illustration 4-18** Formula for computing interest

| Face Value of Note | $\times$ | Annual Interest Rate | $\times$ | Time in Terms of One Year | = | Interest |
|---|---|---|---|---|---|---|
| $5,000 | $\times$ | 12% | $\times$ | $\frac{1}{12}$ | = | $50 |

**Helpful Hint** In computing interest, we express the time period as a fraction of a year.

As Illustration 4-19 shows, the accrual of interest at October 31 increases a liability account, Interest Payable. It also decreases stockholders' equity by increasing an expense account, Interest Expense.

**Illustration 4-19**
Adjustment for accrued interest

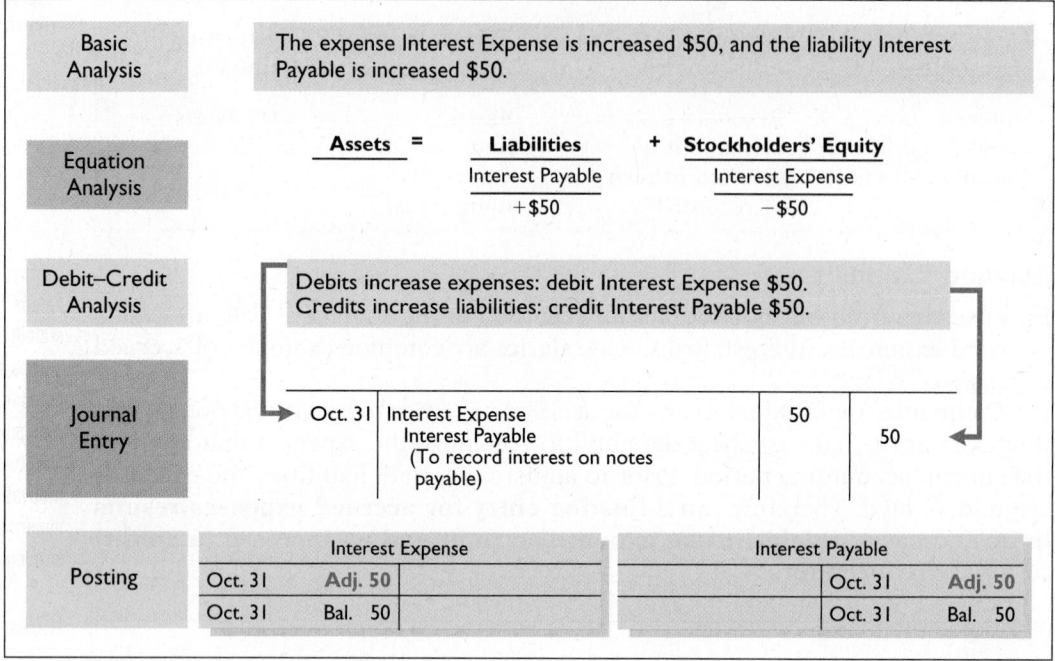

| Basic Analysis | The expense Interest Expense is increased $50, and the liability Interest Payable is increased $50. |

Equation Analysis

| Assets | = | Liabilities | + | Stockholders' Equity |
|---|---|---|---|---|
| | | Interest Payable | | Interest Expense |
| | | +$50 | | −$50 |

Debit–Credit Analysis

Debits increase expenses: debit Interest Expense $50.
Credits increase liabilities: credit Interest Payable $50.

Journal Entry

| Oct. 31 | Interest Expense | 50 | |
| | Interest Payable | | 50 |
| | (To record interest on notes payable) | | |

Posting

| Interest Expense | | | | Interest Payable | | |
|---|---|---|---|---|---|---|
| Oct. 31 | Adj. 50 | | | | Oct. 31 | Adj. 50 |
| Oct. 31 | Bal. 50 | | | | Oct. 31 | Bal. 50 |

Interest Expense shows the interest charges for the month of October. Interest Payable shows the amount of interest the company owes at the statement date. Sierra will not pay the interest until the note comes due at the end of three months. Companies use the Interest Payable account, instead of crediting Notes Payable, to disclose the two different types of obligations—interest and principal—in the accounts and statements. **Without this adjusting entry, liabilities and interest expense are understated, and net income and stockholders' equity are overstated.**

## International Insight

### Cashing In on Accrual Accounting

The Chinese government, like most governments, uses cash accounting. It was therefore interesting when it was recently reported that for about $38 billion of expenditures in a recent budget projection, the Chinese government decided to use accrual accounting versus cash accounting. It decided to expense the amount in the year in which it was originally allocated rather than when the payments would be made. Why did it do this? It enabled the government to keep its projected budget deficit below a 3% threshold. While it was able to keep its projected shortfall below 3%, China did suffer some criticism for its inconsistent accounting. Critics charge that this inconsistent treatment reduces the transparency of China's accounting information. That is, it is not easy for outsiders to accurately evaluate what is really going on.

*Source:* Andrew Batson, "China Altered Budget Accounting to Reduce Deficit Figure," *Wall Street Journal Online* (March 15, 2010).

 Accrual accounting is often considered superior to cash accounting. Why, then, were some people critical of China's use of accrual accounting in this instance? (See page 223.)

**ACCRUED SALARIES.** Companies pay for some types of expenses, such as employee salaries and commissions, after the services have been performed. Sierra paid salaries on October 26 for its employees' first two weeks of work; the next payment of salaries will not occur until November 9. As Illustration 4-20 shows, three working days remain in October (October 29–31).

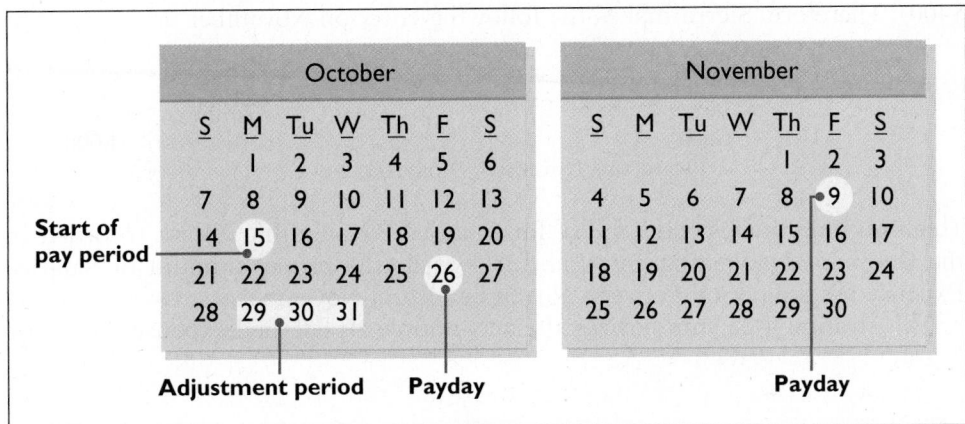

**Illustration 4-20** Calendar showing Sierra Corporation's pay periods

At October 31, the salaries for these three days represent an accrued expense and a related liability to Sierra. The employees receive total salaries of $2,000 for a five-day work week, or $400 per day. Thus, accrued salaries at October 31 are $1,200 ($400 × 3). This accrual increases a liability, Salaries Payable. It also decreases stockholders' equity by increasing an expense account, Salaries Expense, as shown in Illustration 4-21.

**Illustration 4-21** Adjustment for accrued salaries

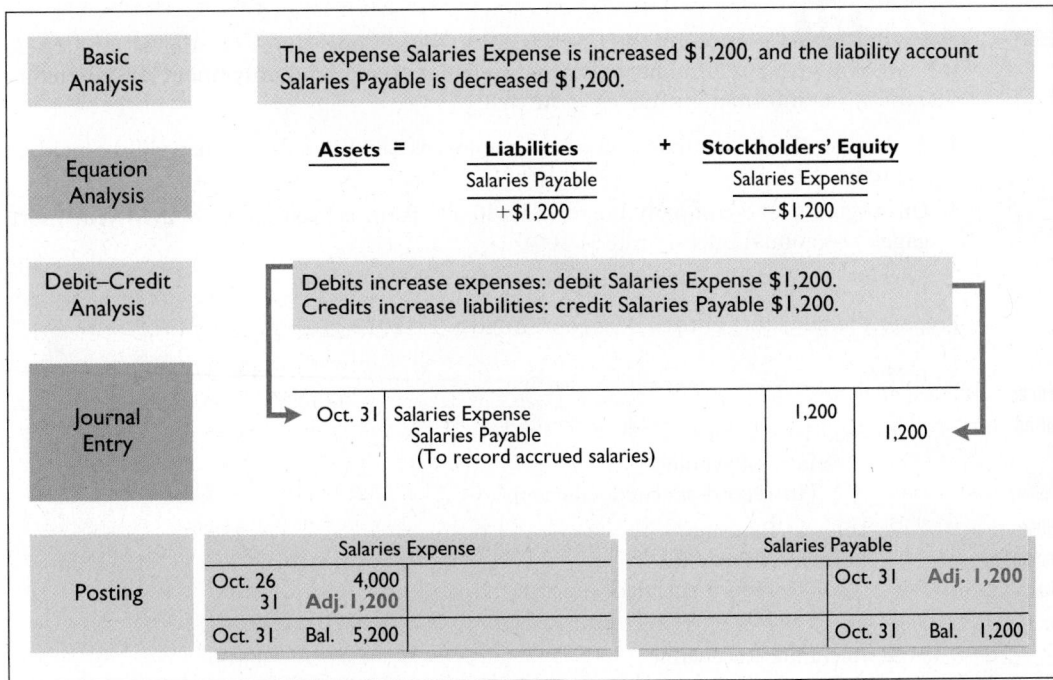

After this adjustment, the balance in Salaries Expense of $5,200 (13 days × $400) is the actual salary expense for October. The balance in Salaries Payable

of $1,200 is the amount of the liability for salaries Sierra owes as of October 31. **Without the $1,200 adjustment for salaries, Sierra's expenses are understated $1,200 and its liabilities are understated $1,200.**

Sierra Corporation pays salaries every two weeks. Consequently, the next payday is November 9, when the company will again pay total salaries of $4,000. The payment consists of $1,200 of salaries payable at October 31 plus $2,800 of salaries expense for November (7 working days, as shown in the November calendar × $400). Therefore, Sierra makes the following entry on November 9.

| Nov. 9 | Salaries Payable | 1,200 | |
| | Salaries Expense | 2,800 | |
| | Cash | | 4,000 |
| | (To record November 9 payroll) | | |

This entry eliminates the liability for Salaries Payable that Sierra recorded in the October 31 adjusting entry, and it records the proper amount of Salaries Expense for the period between November 1 and November 9.

Illustration 4-22 summarizes the accounting for accrued expenses.

**Illustration 4-22**
Accounting for accrued expenses

| | ACCOUNTING FOR ACCRUED EXPENSES | | |
|---|---|---|---|
| **Examples** | **Reason for Adjustment** | **Accounts Before Adjustment** | **Adjusting Entry** |
| Interest, rent, salaries | Expenses have been incurred but not yet paid in cash or recorded. | Expenses understated. Liabilities understated. | Dr. Expenses Cr. Liabilities |

## before you go on...

**ADJUSTING ENTRIES FOR ACCRUALS**

**Do it!** Micro Computer Services Inc. began operations on August 1, 2012. At the end of August 2012, management attempted to prepare monthly financial statements. The following information relates to August.

1. At August 31, the company owed its employees $800 in salaries that will be paid on September 1.
2. On August 1, the company borrowed $30,000 from a local bank on a 15-year mortgage. The annual interest rate is 10%.
3. Revenue earned but unrecorded for August totaled $1,100.

Prepare the adjusting entries needed at August 31, 2012.

**Action Plan**

• Make adjusting entries at the end of the period for revenues earned and expenses incurred in the period.

• Don't forget to make adjusting entries for accruals. Adjusting entries for accruals will increase both a balance sheet and an income statement account.

**Solution**

| 1. Salaries Expense | 800 | |
| Salaries Payable | | 800 |
| (To record accrued salaries) | | |
| 2. Interest Expense | 250 | |
| Interest Payable | | 250 |
| (To record accrued interest: $30,000 \times 10\% \times \frac{1}{12} = \$250$) | | |
| 3. Accounts Receivable | 1,100 | |
| Service Revenue | | 1,100 |
| (To record revenue earned) | | |

✓ the navigator

Related exercise material: **BE4-8, Do it! 4-2, E4-8, E4-9, E4-10, and E4-11.**

## SUMMARY OF BASIC RELATIONSHIPS

Illustration 4-23 summarizes the four basic types of adjusting entries. Take some time to study and analyze the adjusting entries. Be sure to note that **each adjusting entry affects one balance sheet account and one income statement account**.

| Type of Adjustment | Accounts Before Adjustment | Adjusting Entry |
|---|---|---|
| Prepaid expenses | Assets overstated<br>Expenses understated | Dr. Expenses<br>Cr. Assets |
| Unearned revenues | Liabilities overstated<br>Revenues understated | Dr. Liabilities<br>Cr. Revenues |
| Accrued revenues | Assets understated<br>Revenues understated | Dr. Assets<br>Cr. Revenues |
| Accrued expenses | Expenses understated<br>Liabilities understated | Dr. Expenses<br>Cr. Liabilities |

**Illustration 4-23**
Summary of adjusting entries

Illustrations 4-24 and 4-25 (page 182) show the journalizing and posting of adjusting entries for Sierra Corporation on October 31. When reviewing the general ledger in Illustration 4-25, note that for learning purposes, we have highlighted the adjustments in color.

**GENERAL JOURNAL**

| Date | Account Titles and Explanation | Debit | Credit |
|---|---|---|---|
| 2010 | Adjusting Entries | | |
| Oct. 31 | Supplies Expense | 1,500 | |
| | Supplies | | 1,500 |
| | (To record supplies used) | | |
| 31 | Insurance Expense | 50 | |
| | Prepaid Insurance | | 50 |
| | (To record insurance expired) | | |
| 31 | Depreciation Expense | 40 | |
| | Accumulated Depreciation—Equipment | | 40 |
| | (To record monthly depreciation) | | |
| 31 | Unearned Service Revenue | 400 | |
| | Service Revenue | | 400 |
| | (To record revenue earned) | | |
| 31 | Accounts Receivable | 200 | |
| | Service Revenue | | 200 |
| | (To record revenue earned) | | |
| 31 | Interest Expense | 50 | |
| | Interest Payable | | 50 |
| | (To record interest on notes payable) | | |
| 31 | Salaries Expense | 1,200 | |
| | Salaries Payable | | 1,200 |
| | (To record accrued salaries) | | |

**Illustration 4-24** General journal showing adjusting entries

**Illustration 4-25** General ledger after adjustments

## GENERAL LEDGER

### Cash

| | | | | | |
|---|---|---|---|---|---|
| Oct. | 1 | 10,000 | Oct. | 2 | 5,000 |
| | 1 | 5,000 | | 3 | 900 |
| | 2 | 1,200 | | 4 | 600 |
| | 3 | 10,000 | | 20 | 500 |
| | | | | 26 | 4,000 |
| Oct. 31 | Bal. 15,200 | | | | |

### Accounts Receivable

| | | |
|---|---|---|
| Oct. 31 | 200 | |
| Oct. 31 | Bal. 200 | |

### Supplies

| | | | | |
|---|---|---|---|---|
| Oct. | 5 | 2,500 | Oct. 31 | 1,500 |
| Oct. 31 | Bal. 1,000 | | | |

### Prepaid Insurance

| | | | | |
|---|---|---|---|---|
| Oct. | 4 | 600 | Oct. 31 | 50 |
| Oct. 31 | Bal. 550 | | | |

### Equipment

| | | |
|---|---|---|
| Oct. | 2 | 5,000 |
| Oct. 31 | Bal. 5,000 | |

### Accumulated Depreciation—Equipment

| | | |
|---|---|---|
| | Oct. 31 | 40 |
| | Oct. 31 | Bal. 40 |

### Notes Payable

| | | |
|---|---|---|
| | Oct. 1 | 5,000 |
| | Oct. 31 | Bal. 5,000 |

### Accounts Payable

| | | |
|---|---|---|
| | Oct. 5 | 2,500 |
| | Oct. 31 | Bal. 2,500 |

### Interest Payable

| | | |
|---|---|---|
| | Oct. 31 | 50 |
| | Oct. 31 | Bal. 50 |

### Unearned Service Revenue

| | | | | |
|---|---|---|---|---|
| Oct. 31 | 400 | Oct. | 2 | 1,200 |
| | | Oct. 31 | Bal. 800 | |

### Salaries Payable

| | | |
|---|---|---|
| | Oct. 31 | 1,200 |
| | Oct. 31 | Bal. 1,200 |

### Common Stock

| | | |
|---|---|---|
| | Oct. 1 | 10,000 |
| | Oct. 31 | Bal. 10,000 |

### Retained Earnings

| | | |
|---|---|---|
| | Oct. 31 | Bal. 0 |

### Dividends

| | | |
|---|---|---|
| Oct. 20 | 500 | |
| Oct. 31 | Bal. 500 | |

### Service Revenue

| | | | |
|---|---|---|---|
| | Oct. | 3 | 10,000 |
| | | 31 | 400 |
| | | 31 | 200 |
| | Oct. 31 | Bal. 10,600 | |

### Salaries Expense

| | | |
|---|---|---|
| Oct. 26 | 4,000 | |
| 31 | 1,200 | |
| Oct. 31 | Bal. 5,200 | |

### Supplies Expense

| | | |
|---|---|---|
| Oct. 31 | 1,500 | |
| Oct. 31 | Bal. 1,500 | |

### Rent Expense

| | | |
|---|---|---|
| Oct. 3 | 900 | |
| Oct. 31 | Bal. 900 | |

### Insurance Expense

| | | |
|---|---|---|
| Oct. 31 | 50 | |
| Oct. 31 | Bal. 50 | |

### Interest Expense

| | | |
|---|---|---|
| Oct. 31 | 50 | |
| Oct. 31 | Bal. 50 | |

### Depreciation Expense

| | | |
|---|---|---|
| Oct. 31 | 40 | |
| Oct. 31 | Bal. 40 | |

# The Adjusted Trial Balance and Financial Statements

After a company has journalized and posted all adjusting entries, it prepares another trial balance from the ledger accounts. This trial balance is called an **adjusted trial balance**. It shows the balances of all accounts, including those adjusted, at the end of the accounting period. The purpose of an adjusted trial balance is to **prove the equality** of the total debit balances and the total credit balances in the ledger after all adjustments. Because the accounts contain all data needed for financial statements, the adjusted trial balance is the **primary basis for the preparation of financial statements**.

**study objective 6**

Describe the nature and purpose of the adjusted trial balance.

### PREPARING THE ADJUSTED TRIAL BALANCE

Illustration 4-26 presents the adjusted trial balance for Sierra Corporation prepared from the ledger accounts in Illustration 4-25. The amounts affected by the adjusting entries are highlighted in color.

**Illustration 4-26**
Adjusted trial balance

### SIERRA CORPORATION
Adjusted Trial Balance
October 31, 2012

|  | Dr. | Cr. |
|---|---|---|
| Cash | $ 15,200 | |
| Accounts Receivable | 200 | |
| Supplies | 1,000 | |
| Prepaid Insurance | 550 | |
| Equipment | 5,000 | |
| Accumulated Depreciation—Equipment | | $ 40 |
| Notes Payable | | 5,000 |
| Accounts Payable | | 2,500 |
| Interest Payable | | 50 |
| Unearned Service Revenue | | 800 |
| Salaries Payable | | 1,200 |
| Common Stock | | 10,000 |
| Retained Earnings | | 0 |
| Dividends | 500 | |
| Service Revenue | | 10,600 |
| Salaries Expense | 5,200 | |
| Supplies Expense | 1,500 | |
| Rent Expense | 900 | |
| Insurance Expense | 50 | |
| Interest Expense | 50 | |
| Depreciation Expense | 40 | |
| | $30,190 | $30,190 |

## PREPARING FINANCIAL STATEMENTS

**Companies can prepare financial statements directly from an adjusted trial balance.** Illustrations 4-27 and 4-28 present the interrelationships of data in the adjusted trial balance of Sierra Corporation. As Illustration 4-27 shows, companies prepare the income statement from the revenue and expense accounts. Similarly, they derive the retained earnings statement from the retained earnings account, dividends account, and the net income (or net loss) shown in the income statement. As Illustration 4-28 shows, companies then prepare the balance sheet from the asset, liability, and stockholders' equity accounts. They obtain the amount reported for retained earnings on the balance sheet from the ending balance in the retained earnings statement.

**Illustration 4-27**
Preparation of the income statement and retained earnings statement from the adjusted trial balance

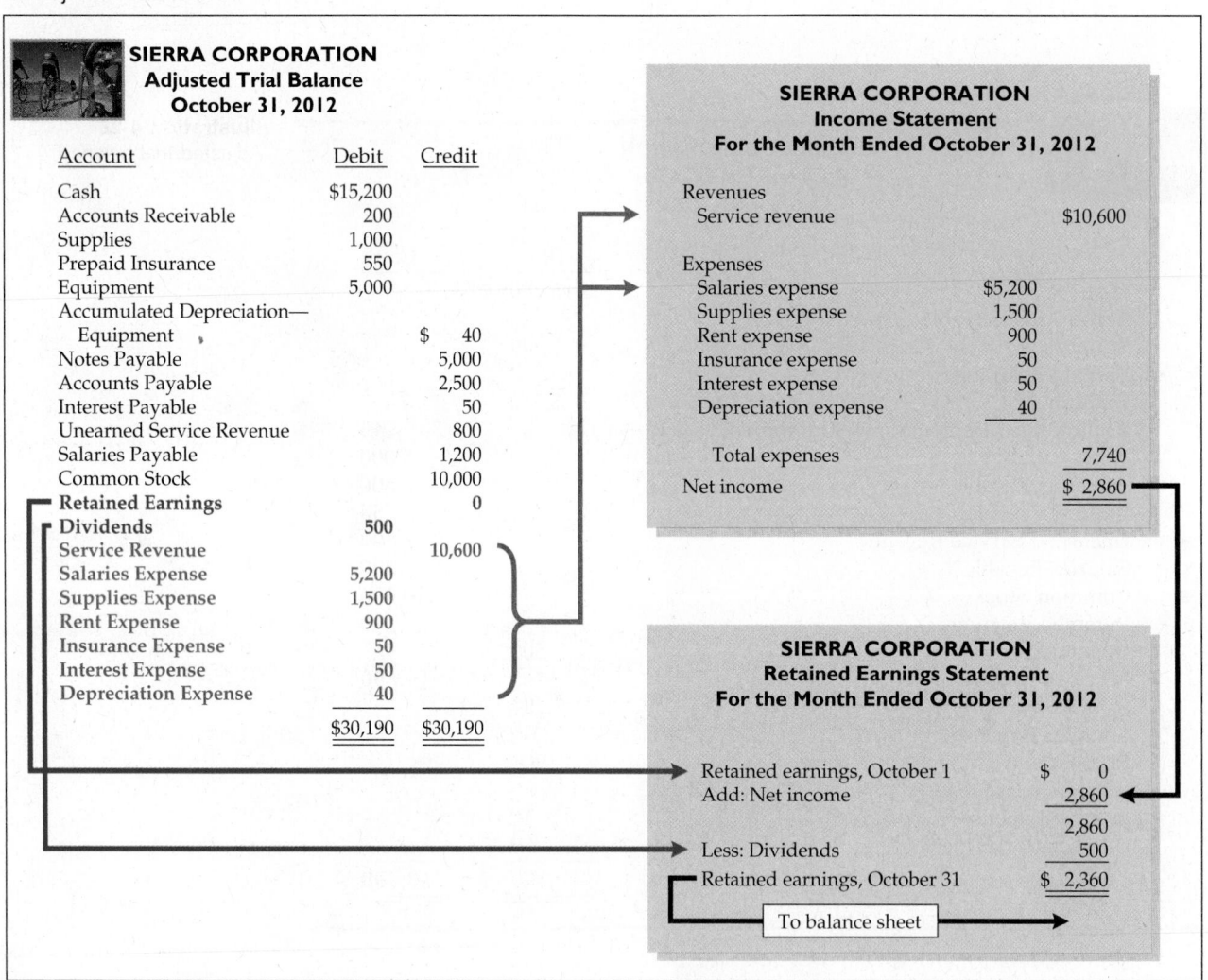

**Illustration 4-28**
Preparation of the balance
sheet from the adjusted
trial balance

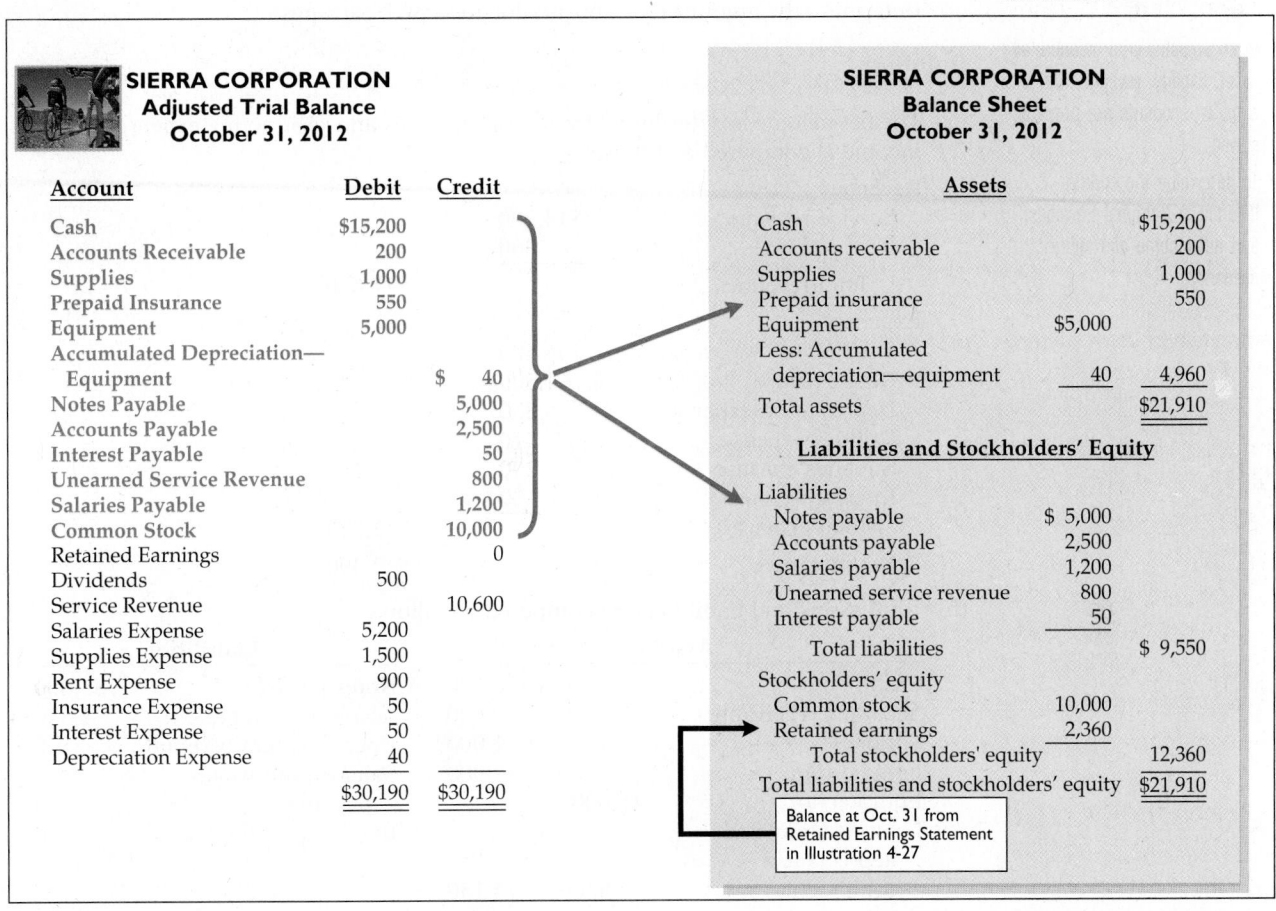

**before you go on...**

| **Do it!** | | |
|---|---|---|

Skolnick Co. was organized on April 1, 2012. The company prepares **TRIAL BALANCE**
quarterly financial statements. The adjusted trial balance amounts at June 30 are shown
below:

| | **Debits** | | **Credits** |
|---|---|---|---|
| Cash | $ 6,700 | Accumulated Depreciation—Equipment | $    850 |
| Accounts Receivable | 600 | Notes Payable | 5,000 |
| Prepaid Rent | 900 | Accounts Payable | 1,510 |
| Supplies | 1,000 | Salaries and Wages Payable | 400 |
| Equipment | 15,000 | Interest Payable | 50 |
| Dividends | 600 | Unearned Rent Revenue | 500 |
| Salaries and Wages Expense | 9,400 | Common Stock | 14,000 |
| Rent Expense | 1,500 | Service Revenue | 14,200 |
| Depreciation Expense | 850 | Rent Revenue | 800 |
| Supplies Expense | 200 | | |
| Utilities Expense | 510 | | |
| Interest Expense | 50 | | |
| Total debits | $37,310 | Total credits | $37,310 |

(a) Determine the net income for the quarter April 1 to June 30.

(b) Determine the total assets and total liabilities at June 30, 2012 for Skolnick Co.

(c) Determine the amount that appears for Retained Earnings.

**Action Plan**

• In an adjusted trial balance, all asset, liability, revenue, and expense accounts are properly stated.

• To determine the ending balance in Retained Earnings, add net income and subtract dividends.

## Solution

(a) The net income is determined by adding revenues and subtracting expenses. The net income is computed as follows.

Revenues

| Service revenue | $14,200 | |
| Rent revenue | 800 | |
| Total revenues | | $15,000 |

Expenses

| Salaries and wages expense | $ 9,400 | |
| Rent expense | 1,500 | |
| Depreciation expense | 850 | |
| Utilities expense | 510 | |
| Supplies expense | 200 | |
| Interest expense | 50 | |
| Total expenses | | 12,510 |
| Net income | | $ 2,490 |

(b) Total assets and liabilities are computed as follows.

| **Assets** | | | **Liabilities** | |
|---|---|---|---|---|
| Cash | | $ 6,700 | Notes payable | $5,000 |
| Accounts receivable | | 600 | Accounts payable | 1,510 |
| Supplies | | 1,000 | Unearned rent revenue | 500 |
| Prepaid rent | | 900 | Salaries and wages | |
| Equipment | 15,000 | | payable | 400 |
| Less: Accumulated | | | Interest payable | 50 |
| depreciation— | | | | |
| equipment | 850 | 14,150 | | |
| Total assets | | $23,350 | Total liabilities | $7,460 |

(c)

| Retained earnings, April 1 | $    0 |
|---|---|
| Add: Net income | 2,490 |
| Less: Dividends | 600 |
| Retained earnings, June 30 | $1,890 |

Related exercise material: **BE4-9, BE4-10, BE4-11, BE4-12,** **Do it!** **4-3, E4-12, E4-13, E4-15, and E4-16.**

# Closing the Books

**Alternative Terminology**
Temporary accounts are sometimes called *nominal accounts*, and permanent accounts are sometimes called *real accounts*.

In previous chapters, you learned that revenue and expense accounts and the dividends account are subdivisions of retained earnings, which is reported in the stockholders' equity section of the balance sheet. Because revenues, expenses, and dividends relate to only a given accounting period, they are considered **temporary accounts**. In contrast, all balance sheet accounts are considered **permanent accounts** because their balances are carried forward into future accounting periods. Illustration 4-29 identifies the accounts in each category.

### PREPARING CLOSING ENTRIES

**study objective 7**
Explain the purpose of closing entries.

At the end of the accounting period, companies transfer the temporary account balances to the permanent stockholders' equity account—Retained Earnings—through the preparation of closing entries. **Closing entries** transfer net income

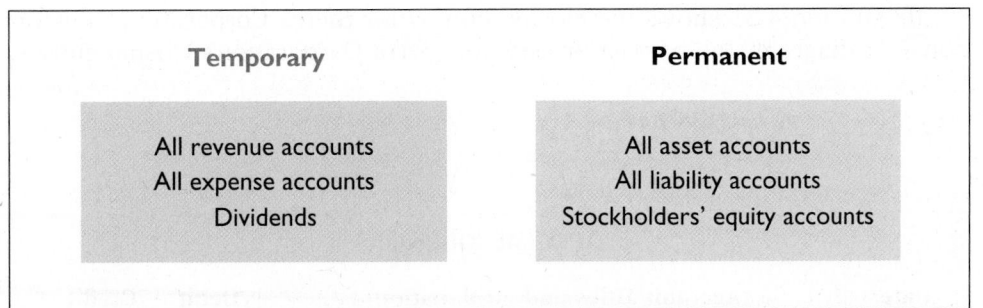

**Illustration 4-29**
Temporary versus
permanent accounts

(or net loss) and dividends to Retained Earnings, so the balance in Retained Earnings agrees with the retained earnings statement. For example, notice that in the adjusted trial balance in Illustration 4-24 (page 183). Retained Earnings has a balance of zero. Prior to the closing entries, the balance in Retained Earnings will be its beginning-of-the-period balance. (For Sierra, this is zero because it is Sierra's first month of operations.)

In addition to updating Retained Earnings to its correct ending balance, closing entries produce a **zero balance in each temporary account**. As a result, these accounts are ready to accumulate data about revenues, expenses, and dividends that occur in the next accounting period. **Permanent accounts are not closed.**

When companies prepare closing entries, they could close each income statement account directly to Retained Earnings. However, to do so would result in excessive detail in the retained earnings account. Accordingly, companies close the revenue and expense accounts to another temporary account, **Income Summary**, and they transfer only the resulting net income or net loss from this account to Retained Earnings. Illustration 4-30 depicts the closing process. While it still takes the average large company seven days to close, some companies such as Cisco employ technology that allows them to do a so-called "virtual close" almost instantaneously any time during the year. Besides dramatically reducing the cost of closing, the virtual close provides companies with accurate data for decision making whenever they desire it.

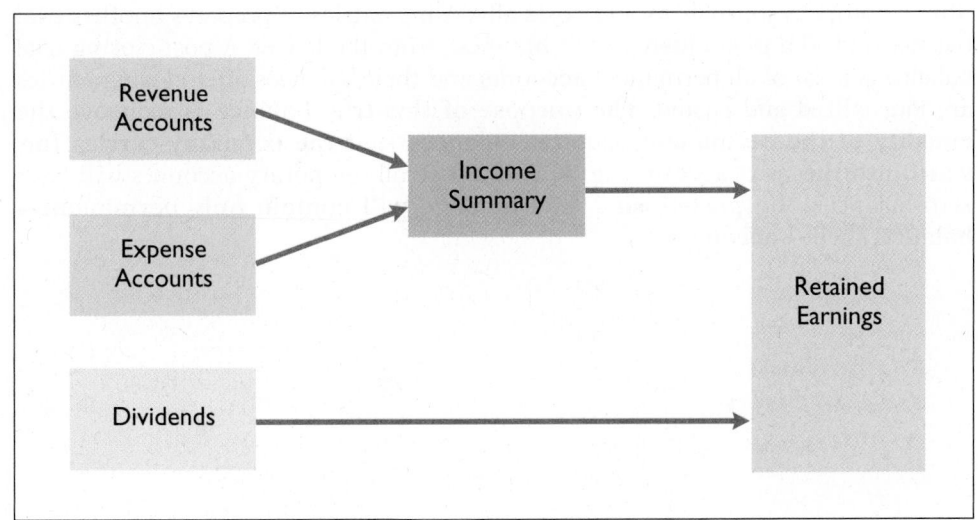

**Illustration 4-30** The closing process

Illustration 4-31 shows the closing entries for Sierra Corporation. Illustration 4-32 diagrams the posting process for Sierra Corporation's closing entries.

**Illustration 4-31** Closing entries journalized

**Helpful Hint** Income Summary is a very descriptive title: Companies close total revenues to Income Summary and total expenses to Income Summary. The balance in the Income Summary is a net income or net loss.

| GENERAL JOURNAL | | | |
|---|---|---|---|
| **Date** | **Account Titles and Explanation** | **Debit** | **Credit** |
| | <u>Closing Entries</u> | | |
| 2012 | (1) | | |
| Oct. 31 | Service Revenue | 10,600 | |
| |    Income Summary | | 10,600 |
| |    (To close revenue account) | | |
| | (2) | | |
| 31 | Income Summary | 7,740 | |
| |    Salaries Expense | | 5,200 |
| |    Supplies Expense | | 1,500 |
| |    Rent Expense | | 900 |
| |    Insurance Expense | | 50 |
| |    Interest Expense | | 50 |
| |    Depreciation Expense | | 40 |
| |    (To close expense accounts) | | |
| | (3) | | |
| 31 | Income Summary | 2,860 | |
| |    Retained Earnings | | 2,860 |
| |    (To close net income to retained earnings) | | |
| | (4) | | |
| 31 | Retained Earnings | 500 | |
| |    Dividends | | 500 |
| |    (To close dividends to retained earnings) | | |

## PREPARING A POST-CLOSING TRIAL BALANCE

After a company journalizes and posts all closing entries, it prepares another trial balance, called a post-closing trial balance, from the ledger. A post-closing trial balance is a list of all permanent accounts and their balances after closing entries are journalized and posted. **The purpose of this trial balance is to prove the equality of the permanent account balances that the company carries forward into the next accounting period.** Since all temporary accounts will have zero balances, **the post-closing trial balance will contain only permanent— balance sheet—accounts**.

**Illustration 4-32**  Posting of closing entries

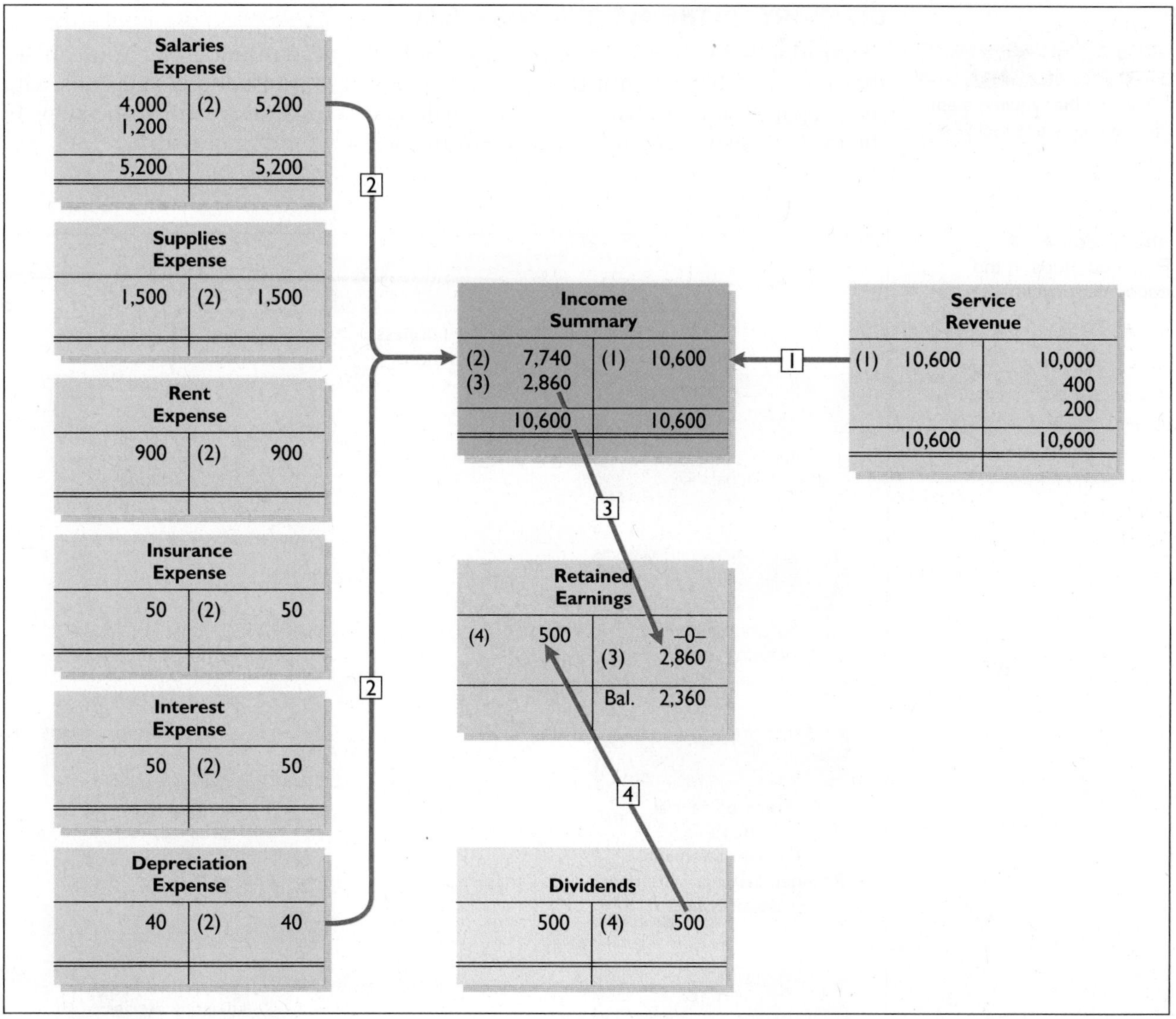

## Salaries Expense

| | | | |
|---|---|---|---|
| 4,000 | (2) | 5,200 |
| 1,200 | | |
| 5,200 | | 5,200 |

## Supplies Expense

| | | | |
|---|---|---|---|
| 1,500 | (2) | 1,500 |

## Rent Expense

| | | | |
|---|---|---|---|
| 900 | (2) | 900 |

## Insurance Expense

| | | | |
|---|---|---|---|
| 50 | (2) | 50 |

## Interest Expense

| | | | |
|---|---|---|---|
| 50 | (2) | 50 |

## Depreciation Expense

| | | | |
|---|---|---|---|
| 40 | (2) | 40 |

2

2

## Income Summary

| | | | | |
|---|---|---|---|---|
| (2) | 7,740 | (1) | 10,600 |
| (3) | 2,860 | | |
| | 10,600 | | 10,600 |

1

## Service Revenue

| | | | | |
|---|---|---|---|---|
| (1) | 10,600 | | 10,000 |
| | | | 400 |
| | | | 200 |
| | 10,600 | | 10,600 |

3

## Retained Earnings

| | | | | |
|---|---|---|---|---|
| (4) | 500 | | –0– |
| | | (3) | 2,860 |
| | | Bal. | 2,360 |

4

## Dividends

| | | | |
|---|---|---|---|
| 500 | (4) | 500 |

---

*before you go on...*

# Do it!

After making entries to close its revenue and expense accounts to Income Summary, Hancock Company has the following balances.

| | |
|---|---|
| Dividends | $15,000 |
| Retained Earnings | 42,000 |
| Income Summary | 18,000  (credit balance) |

Prepare the closing entries at December 31 that affect the stockholders' equity accounts.

## Solution

| Dec. 31 | Income Summary | 18,000 | |
|---|---|---|---|
| |     Retained Earnings | | 18,000 |
| |       (To close net income to retained earnings) | | |
| 31 | Retained Earnings | 15,000 | |
| |     Dividends | | 15,000 |
| |       (To close dividends to retained earnings) | | |

**CLOSING ENTRIES**

**Action Plan**

- Close Income Summary to Retained Earnings.
- Close Dividends to Retained Earnings.

Related exercise material: **BE4-13, BE4-14,** **Do it!** **4-4, E4-14,** and **E4-18.**

**SUMMARY OF THE ACCOUNTING CYCLE**

**study objective 8**

Describe the required steps in the accounting cycle.

## SUMMARY OF THE ACCOUNTING CYCLE

Illustration 4-33 shows the required steps in the accounting cycle. You can see that the cycle begins with the analysis of business transactions and ends with the preparation of a post-closing trial balance. Companies perform the steps in the cycle in sequence and repeat them in each accounting period.

**Illustration 4-33**
Required steps in the accounting cycle

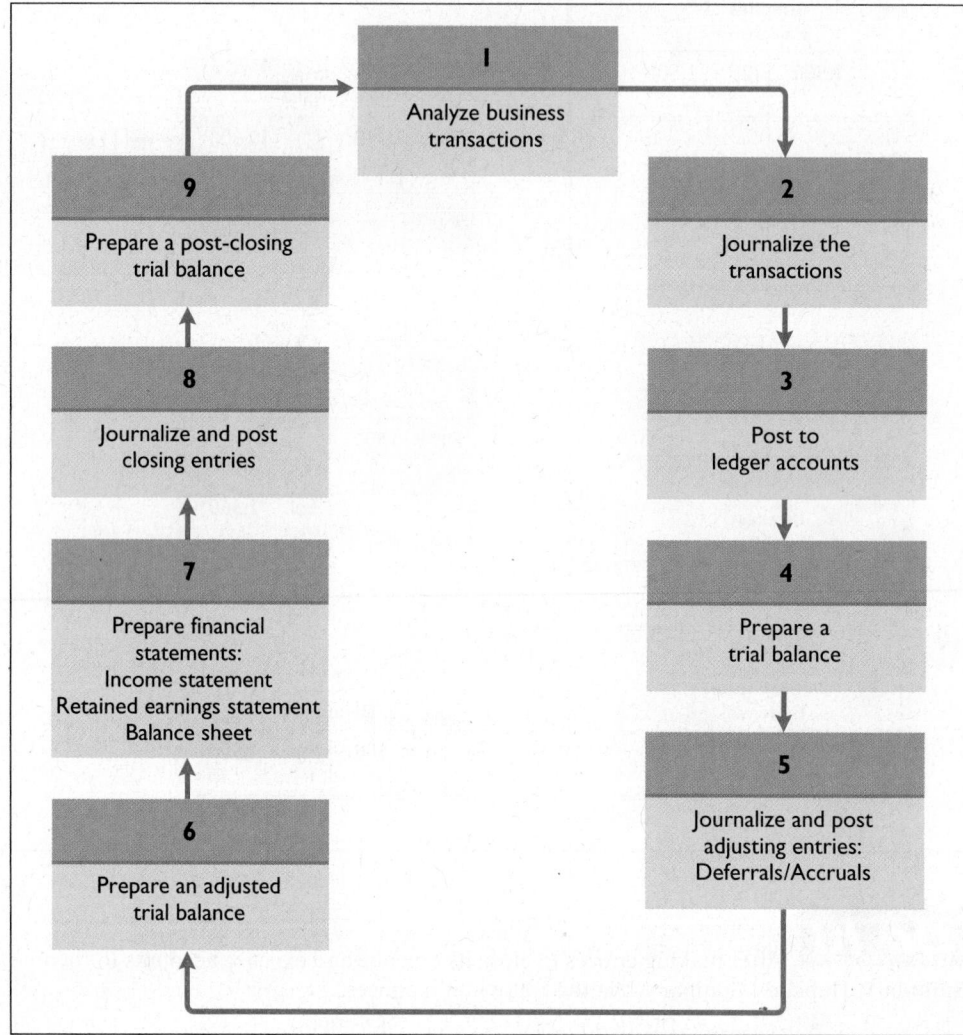

**Helpful Hint** Some companies prefer to reverse certain adjusting entries at the beginning of a new accounting period. The company makes a reversing entry at the beginning of the next accounting period; this entry is the exact opposite of the adjusting entry made in the previous period.

Steps 1–3 may occur daily during the accounting period, as explained in Chapter 3. Companies perform Steps 4–7 on a periodic basis, such as monthly, quarterly, or annually. Steps 8 and 9, closing entries and a post-closing trial balance, usually take place only at the end of a company's **annual** accounting period.

## Quality of Earnings

"Did you make your numbers today?" is a question asked often in both large and small businesses. Companies and employees are continually under pressure to "make the numbers"—that is, to have earnings that are in line with expectations. As a consequence it is not surprising that many companies practice earnings management. **Earnings management** is the planned timing of revenues, expenses, gains, and losses to smooth out bumps in net income. The quality of earnings is greatly affected when a company manages earnings up or down to meet some targeted earnings number. A company that has a high **quality of earnings** provides full and transparent information that will not confuse or mislead users of the financial statements. A company with questionable quality of earnings may mislead investors and creditors, who believe they are relying on relevant and reliable information. As a consequence, investors and creditors lose confidence in financial reporting, and it becomes difficult for our capital markets to work efficiently.

Companies manage earnings in a variety of ways. One way is through the use of **one-time items** to prop up earnings numbers. For example, ConAgra Foods recorded a nonrecurring gain from the sale of Pilgrim's Pride stock for $186 million to help meet an earnings projection for the quarter.

Another way is to **inflate revenue** numbers in the short-run to the detriment of the long-run. For example, Bristol-Myers Squibb provided sales incentives to its wholesalers to encourage them to buy products at the end of the quarter (often referred to as channel-stuffing). As a result Bristol-Myers was able to meet its sales projections. The problem was that the wholesalers could not sell that amount of merchandise and ended up returning it to Bristol-Myers. The result was that Bristol-Myers had to restate its income numbers.

Companies also manage earnings through **improper adjusting entries**. Regulators investigated Xerox for accusations that it was booking too much revenue up-front on multi-year contract sales. Financial executives at Office Max resigned amid accusations that the company was recognizing rebates from its vendors too early and therefore overstating revenue. Finally, WorldCom's abuse of adjusting entries to meet its net income targets is unsurpassed: It used adjusting entries to increase net income by reclassifying liabilities as revenue and reclassifying expenses as assets. Investigations of the company's books after it went bankrupt revealed adjusting entries of more than a billion dollars that had no supporting documentation.

The good news is that, as a result of investor pressure as well as the **Sarbanes-Oxley Act**, many companies are trying to improve the quality of their financial reporting. For example, hotel operator Marriott is now providing detailed information on the write-offs it has on loan guarantees it gives hotels. General Electric has decided to provide more detail on its revenues and operating profits for individual businesses it owns. IBM is attempting to provide a better breakdown of its earnings. At the same time, regulators are taking a tough stand on the issue of quality of earnings. For example, one regulator noted that companies may be required to restate their financials every single time that they account for any transaction that had no legitimate purpose but was done solely for an accounting purpose, such as to smooth net income.

---

**KEEPING AN EYE ON CASH**

In this chapter, you learned that adjusting entries are used to adjust numbers that would otherwise be stated on a cash basis. Sierra Corporation's income statement (Illustration 4-27, page 184) shows net income of $2,860. The statement of cash flows reports a form of cash basis income referred to as "Net cash provided by operating activities." For example, Illustration 1-8 (page 15), which shows a statement of cash flows, reports net cash provided by operating activities of $5,700 for Sierra. Net income and net cash provided by operating activities often differ. The difference for Sierra is $2,840 ($5,700 − $2,860). The following summary shows the causes of this difference of $2,840.

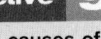 **study objective 9**

Understand the causes of differences between net income and cash provided by operating activities.

| | Computation of Net Cash Provided by Operating Activities | Computation of Net Income |
|---|---|---|
| (1) Cash received in advance from customer | $ 1,200 | $ 0 |
| (2) Cash received from customers for services provided | 10,000 | 10,000 |
| (3) Services provided for cash received previously in (1) | 0 | 400 |
| (4) Services provided on account | 0 | 200 |
| (5) Payment of rent | (900) | (900) |
| (6) Purchase of insurance | (600) | 0 |
| (7) Payment of employee salaries | (4,000) | (4,000) |
| (8) Use of supplies | 0 | (1,500) |
| (9) Use of insurance | 0 | (50) |
| (10) Depreciation | 0 | (40) |
| (11) Interest cost incurred, but not paid | 0 | (50) |
| (12) Salaries incurred, but not paid | 0 | (1,200) |
| | $ 5,700 | $ 2,860 |

For each item included in the computation of net cash provided by operating activities, you should confirm that cash was either received or paid. For each item in the income statement, the company should confirm that revenue was earned (even when cash was not received) or that an expense was incurred (even when cash was not paid).

# USING THE DECISION TOOLKIT

Humana Corporation provides managed health care services to approximately 7 million people. Headquartered in Louisville, Kentucky, it has over 13,700 employees in 15 states and Puerto Rico. A simplified version of Humana's December 31, 2009, adjusted trial balance is shown at the top of the next page.

## Instructions

From the trial balance, prepare an income statement, retained earnings statement, and classified balance sheet. **Be sure to prepare them in that order, since each statement depends on information determined in the preceding statement.**

**HUMANA CORPORATION**
Adjusted Trial Balance
December 31, 2009
(in millions)

| Account | Dr. | Cr. |
|---|---|---|
| Cash | $ 1,613 | |
| Short-Term Investments | 6,190 | |
| Receivables | 824 | |
| Other Current Assets | 626 | |
| Property and Equipment, Net | 679 | |
| Long-Term Investments | 1,307 | |
| Goodwill | 1,993 | |
| Other Long-Term Assets | 921 | |
| Benefits Payable | | $ 3,222 |
| Accounts Payable | | 1,308 |
| Other Current Liabilities | | 730 |
| Long-Term Debt | | 3,117 |
| Common Stock | | 1,690 |
| Dividends | 0 | |
| Retained Earnings | | 3,046 |
| Revenues | | 30,960 |
| Medical Cost Expense | 24,775 | |
| Selling, General, and Administrative Expense | 4,227 | |
| Depreciation Expense | 250 | |
| Interest Expense | 106 | |
| Income Tax Expense | 562 | |
| | $44,073 | $44,073 |

**Solution**

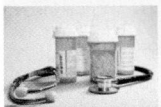

**HUMANA CORPORATION**
Income Statement
For the Year Ended December 31, 2009
(in millions)

| | | |
|---|---|---|
| Revenues | | $30,960 |
| Medical cost expense | $24,775 | |
| Selling, general, and administrative expense | 4,227 | |
| Depreciation expense | 250 | |
| Interest expense | 106 | |
| Income tax expense | 562 | 29,920 |
| Net income | | $ 1,040 |

**HUMANA CORPORATION**
Retained Earnings Statement
For the Year Ended December 31, 2009
(in millions)

| | |
|---|---|
| Beginning retained earnings | $3,046 |
| Add: Net income | 1,040 |
| Less: Dividends | 0 |
| Ending retained earnings | $4,086 |

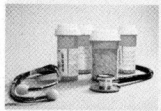

**HUMANA CORPORATION**
Balance Sheet
December 31, 2009
(in millions)

## Assets

| | | |
|---|---|---|
| Current assets | | |
| Cash | $ 1,613 | |
| Short-term investments | 6,190 | |
| Receivables | 824 | |
| Other current assets | 626 | |
| Total current assets | | $9,253 |
| Long-term investments | | 1,307 |
| Property and equipment, | | |
| net of accumulated depreciation | | 679 |
| Goodwill | | 1,993 |
| Other long-term assets | | 921 |
| Total assets | | $14,153 |

## Liabilities and Stockholders' Equity

| | | |
|---|---|---|
| Liabilities | | |
| Current liabilities | | |
| Accounts payable | $1,308 | |
| Benefits payable | 3,222 | |
| Other current liabilities | 730 | |
| Total current liabilities | | $5,260 |
| Long-term debt | | 3,117 |
| Total liabilities | | 8,377 |
| Stockholders' equity | | |
| Common stock | 1,690 | |
| Retained earnings | 4,086 | |
| Total stockholders' equity | | 5,776 |
| Total liabilities and stockholders' equity | | $14,153 |

# Summary of Study Objectives

**1 Explain the revenue recognition principle and the expense recognition principle.** The revenue recognition principle dictates that companies recognize revenue in the accounting period in which it is earned. The expense recognition principle dictates that companies recognize expenses when expenses make their contribution to revenues.

**2 Differentiate between the cash basis and the accrual basis of accounting.** Under the cash basis, companies record events only in the periods in which the company receives or pays cash. Accrual-based accounting means that companies record, in the periods in which the events occur, events that change a company's financial statements even if cash has not been exchanged.

**3 Explain why adjusting entries are needed, and identify the major types of adjusting entries.** Companies make adjusting entries at the end of an accounting period.

These entries ensure that companies record revenues in the period in which they are earned and that companies recognize expenses in the period in which they are incurred. The major types of adjusting entries are prepaid expenses, unearned revenues, accrued revenues, and accrued expenses.

**4 Prepare adjusting entries for deferrals.** Deferrals are either prepaid expenses or unearned revenues. Companies make adjusting entries for deferrals at the statement date to record the portion of the deferred item that represents the expense incurred or the revenue earned in the current accounting period.

**5 Prepare adjusting entries for accruals.** Accruals are either accrued revenues or accrued expenses. Adjusting entries for accruals record revenues earned and expenses incurred in the current accounting period that have not been recognized through daily entries.

**6** **Describe the nature and purpose of the adjusted trial balance.** An adjusted trial balance is a trial balance that shows the balances of all accounts, including those that have been adjusted, at the end of an accounting period. The purpose of an adjusted trial balance is to show the effects of all financial events that have occurred during the accounting period.

**7** **Explain the purpose of closing entries.** One purpose of closing entries is to transfer net income or net loss for the period to Retained Earnings. A second purpose is to "zero-out" all temporary accounts (revenue accounts, expense accounts, and dividends) so that they start each new period with a zero balance. To accomplish this, companies "close" all temporary accounts at the end of an accounting period. They make separate entries to close revenues and expenses to Income Summary; Income Summary to Retained Earnings; and Dividends to Retained Earnings. Only temporary accounts are closed.

**8** **Describe the required steps in the accounting cycle.** The required steps in the accounting cycle are: (a) analyze business transactions, (b) journalize the transactions, (c) post to ledger accounts, (d) prepare a trial balance, (e) journalize and post adjusting entries, (f) prepare an adjusted trial balance, (g) prepare financial statements, (h) journalize and post closing entries, and (i) prepare a post-closing trial balance.

**9** **Understand the causes of differences between net income and net cash provided by operating activities.** Net income is based on accrual accounting, which relies on the adjustment process. Net cash provided by operating activities is determined by adding cash received from operating the business and subtracting cash expended during operations.

*the navigator*

## DECISION TOOLKIT   A SUMMARY

| DECISION CHECKPOINTS | INFO NEEDED FOR DECISION | TOOL TO USE FOR DECISION | HOW TO EVALUATE RESULTS |
|---|---|---|---|
| At what point should the company record revenue? | Need to understand the nature of the company's business | Record revenue when earned. A service business earns revenue when it performs a service. | Recognizing revenue too early overstates current period revenue; recognizing it too late understates current period revenue. |
| At what point should the company record expenses? | Need to understand the nature of the company's business | Expenses should "follow" revenues—that is, match the effort (expense) with the result (revenue). | Recognizing expenses too early overstates current period expense; recognizing them too late understates current period expense. |

## appendix 4A

# Adjusting Entries in an Automated World—Using a Worksheet

**study objective 10**

Describe the purpose and the basic form of a worksheet.

In the previous discussion, we used T accounts and trial balances to arrive at the amounts used to prepare financial statements. Accountants frequently use a device known as a worksheet to determine these amounts. A **worksheet** is a multiple-column form that may be used in the adjustment process and in preparing financial statements. Accountants can prepare worksheets manually, but today most use computer spreadsheets.

As its name suggests, the worksheet is a working tool for the accountant. **A worksheet is not a permanent accounting record**; it is neither a journal nor a part of the general ledger. The worksheet is merely a supplemental device used to make it easier to prepare adjusting entries and the financial statements. Small companies with relatively few accounts and adjustments may not need a worksheet. In large companies with numerous accounts and many adjustments, a worksheet is almost indispensable.

**Illustration 4A-1** Form and procedure for a worksheet

**Sierra Corporation.xls**

File   Exit   View   Insert   Format   Tools   Data   Window   Help

### SIERRA CORPORATION
#### Worksheet
#### For the Month Ended October 31, 2012

| Account Titles | Trial Balance Dr. | Trial Balance Cr. | Adjustments Dr. | Adjustments Cr. | Adjusted Trial Balance Dr. | Adjusted Trial Balance Cr. | Income Statement Dr. | Income Statement Cr. | Balance Sheet Dr. | Balance Sheet Cr. |
|---|---|---|---|---|---|---|---|---|---|---|
| Cash | 15,200 | | | | 15,200 | | | | 15,200 | |
| Supplies | 2,500 | | | (a) 1,500 | 1,000 | | | | 1,000 | |
| Prepaid Insurance | 600 | | | (b) 50 | 550 | | | | 550 | |
| Equipment | 5,000 | | | | 5,000 | | | | 5,000 | |
| Notes Payable | | 5,000 | | | | 5,000 | | | | 5,000 |
| Accounts Payable | | 2,500 | | | | 2,500 | | | | 2,500 |
| Unearned Service Revenue | | 1,200 | (d) 400 | | | 800 | | | | 800 |
| Common Stock | | 10,000 | | | | 10,000 | | | | 10,000 |
| Retained Earnings | | –0– | | | | –0– | | | | –0– |
| Dividends | 500 | | | | 500 | | | | 500 | |
| Service Revenue | | 10,000 | | (d) 400 | | 10,600 | | 10,600 | | |
| | | | | (e) 200 | | | | | | |
| Salaries Expense | 4,000 | | (g) 1,200 | | 5,200 | | 5,200 | | | |
| Rent Expense | 900 | | | | 900 | | 900 | | | |
| Totals | 28,700 | 28,700 | | | | | | | | |
| | | | | | | | | | | |
| Supplies Expense | | | (a) 1,500 | | 1,500 | | 1,500 | | | |
| Insurance Expense | | | (b) 50 | | 50 | | 50 | | | |
| Accum. Depreciation— Equipment | | | | (c) 40 | | 40 | | | | 40 |
| Depreciation Expense | | | (c) 40 | | 40 | | 40 | | | |
| Interest Expense | | | (f) 50 | | 50 | | 50 | | | |
| Accounts Receivable | | | (e) 200 | | 200 | | | | 200 | |
| Interest Payable | | | | (f) 50 | | 50 | | | | 50 |
| Salaries Payable | | | | (g) 1,200 | | 1,200 | | | | 1,200 |
| Totals | | | 3,440 | 3,440 | 30,190 | 30,190 | 7,740 | 10,600 | 22,450 | 19,590 |
| | | | | | | | | | | |
| Net Income | | | | | | | 2,860 | | | 2,860 |
| Totals | | | | | | | 10,600 | 10,600 | 22,450 | 22,450 |

1.
Prepare a trial balance on the worksheet

2.
Enter adjustment data

3.
Enter adjusted balances

4.
Extend adjusted balances to appropriate statement columns

5.
Total the statement columns, compute net income (or net loss), and complete worksheet

Illustration 4A-1 shows the basic form of a worksheet. Note the headings: The worksheet starts with two columns for the Trial Balance. The next two columns record all Adjustments. Next is the Adjusted Trial Balance. The last two sets of columns correspond to the Income Statement and the Balance Sheet. All items listed in the Adjusted Trial Balance columns are included in either the Income Statement or the Balance Sheet columns.

# Summary of Study Objective for Appendix 4A

**10** **Describe the purpose and the basic form of a worksheet.** The worksheet is a device to make it easier to prepare adjusting entries and the financial statements. Companies often prepare a worksheet on a computer spreadsheet. The sets of columns of the worksheet are, from left to right, the unadjusted trial balance, adjustments, adjusted trial balance, income statement, and balance sheet.

# Glossary

**Accrual-basis accounting** (p. 166)   Accounting basis in which companies record, in the periods in which the events occur, transactions that change a company's financial statements, even if cash was not exchanged.

**Accrued expenses** (p. 177)   Expenses incurred but not yet paid in cash or recorded.

**Accrued revenues** (p. 175)   Revenues earned but not yet received in cash or recorded.

**Adjusted trial balance** (p. 183)   A list of accounts and their balances after all adjustments have been made.

**Adjusting entries** (p. 167)   Entries made at the end of an accounting period to ensure that the revenue recognition and expense recognition principles are followed.

**Book value** (p. 172)   The difference between the cost of a depreciable asset and its related accumulated depreciation.

**Cash-basis accounting** (p. 166)   Accounting basis in which a company records revenue only when it receives cash, and an expense only when it pays cash.

**Closing entries** (p. 186)   Entries at the end of an accounting period to transfer the balances of temporary accounts to a permanent stockholders' equity account, Retained Earnings.

**Contra asset account** (p. 171)   An account that is offset against an asset account on the balance sheet.

**Depreciation** (p. 171)   The process of allocating the cost of an asset to expense over its useful life.

**Earnings management** (p. 190)   The planned timing of revenues, expenses, gains, and losses to smooth out bumps in net income.

**Expense recognition principle (matching principle)** (p. 165)   The principle that dictates that companies match efforts (expenses) with results (revenues).

**Fiscal year** (p. 164, in margin)   An accounting period that is one year long.

**Income Summary** (p. 187)   A temporary account used in closing revenue and expense accounts.

**Periodicity assumption** (p. 164)   An assumption that the economic life of a business can be divided into artificial time periods.

**Permanent accounts** (p. 186)   Balance sheet accounts whose balances are carried forward to the next accounting period.

**Post-closing trial balance** (p. 188)   A list of permanent accounts and their balances after a company has journalized and posted closing entries.

**Prepaid expenses (prepayments)** (p. 169)   Assets that result from the payment of expenses that benefit more than one accounting period.

**Quality of earnings** (p. 191)   Indicates the level of full and transparent information that a company provides to users of its financial statements.

**Revenue recognition principle** (p. 164)   The principle that companies recognize revenue in the accounting period in which it is earned.

**Reversing entry** (p. 190, in margin)   An entry made at the beginning of the next accounting period; the exact opposite of the adjusting entry made in the previous period.

**Temporary accounts** (p. 186)   Revenue, expense, and dividend accounts whose balances a company transfers to Retained Earnings at the end of an accounting period.

**Unearned revenues** (p. 172)   Cash received before a company earns revenues and recorded as a liability until earned.

**Useful life** (p. 171)   The length of service of a productive asset.

**Worksheet** (p. 195)   A multiple-column form that companies may use in the adjustment process and in preparing financial statements.

# Comprehensive Do it!

Terry Thomas and a group of investors incorporate the Green Thumb Lawn Care Corporation on April 1. At April 30, the trial balance shows the following balances for selected accounts.

| | |
|---|---|
| Prepaid Insurance | $ 3,600 |
| Equipment | 28,000 |
| Notes Payable | 20,000 |
| Unearned Service Revenue | 4,200 |
| Service Revenue | 1,800 |

Analysis reveals the following additional data pertaining to these accounts.

1. Prepaid insurance is the cost of a 2-year insurance policy, effective April 1.
2. Depreciation on the equipment is $500 per month.
3. The note payable is dated April 1. It is a 6-month, 12% note.

4. Seven customers paid for the company's 6-month lawn service package of $600 beginning in April. These customers received the first month of services in April.

5. Lawn services performed for other customers but not billed at April 30 totaled $1,500.

### Instructions

Prepare the adjusting entries for the month of April. Show computations.

**Action Plan**

- Note that adjustments are being made for one month.
- Make computations carefully.
- Select account titles carefully.
- Make sure debits are made first and credits are indented.
- Check that debits equal credits for each entry.

### Solution to Comprehensive Do it!

**GENERAL JOURNAL**

| Date | Account Titles and Explanation | Debit | Credit |
|------|-------------------------------|-------|--------|
| | Adjusting Entries | | |
| Apr. 30 | Insurance Expense | 150 | |
| |     Prepaid Insurance | | 150 |
| |     (To record insurance expired: $3,600 \div 24 = \$150$ per month) | | |
| 30 | Depreciation Expense | 500 | |
| |     Accumulated Depreciation—Equipment | | 500 |
| |     (To record monthly depreciation) | | |
| 30 | Interest Expense | 200 | |
| |     Interest Payable | | 200 |
| |     (To accrue interest on notes payable: $\$20,000 \times 12\% \times \frac{1}{12} = \$200$) | | |
| 30 | Unearned Service Revenue | 700 | |
| |     Service Revenue | | 700 |
| |     (To record revenue earned: $\$600 \div 6 = \$100$; $\$100$ per month $\times 7 = \$700$) | | |
| 30 | Accounts Receivable | 1,500 | |
| |     Service Revenue | | 1,500 |
| |     (To accrue revenue earned but not billed or collected) | | |

**Self-Test, Brief Exercises, Exercises, Problem Set A, and many more resources are available for practice in WileyPLUS**

# Self-Test Questions

Answers are on page 223.

(SO 1) 1. What is the periodicity assumption?
    (a) Companies should recognize revenue in the accounting period in which it is earned.
    (b) Companies should match expenses with revenues.
    (c) The economic life of a business can be divided into artificial time periods.
    (d) The fiscal year should correspond with the calendar year.

(SO 1) 2. Which principle dictates that efforts (expenses) be recorded with accomplishments (revenues)?
    (a) Expense recognition principle.
    (b) Cost principle.
    (c) Periodicity principle.
    (d) Revenue recognition principle.

3. Which one of these statements about the (SO 2) accrual basis of accounting is *false*?
    (a) Companies record events that change their financial statements in the period in which events occur, even if cash was not exchanged.
    (b) Companies recognize revenue in the period in which it is earned.
    (c) This basis is in accord with generally accepted accounting principles.
    (d) Companies record revenue only when they receive cash, and record expense only when they pay out cash.

4. Adjusting entries are made to ensure that: (SO 3)
    (a) expenses are recognized in the period in which they are incurred.

(b) revenues are recorded in the period in which they are earned.

(c) balance sheet and income statement accounts have correct balances at the end of an accounting period.

(d) All of the above.

(SO 4, 5) **5.** Each of the following is a major type (or category) of adjusting entry *except:*

(a) prepaid expenses.  (c) accrued expenses.

(b) accrued revenues.  (d) earned expenses.

(SO 4) **6.** The trial balance shows Supplies $1,350 and Supplies Expense $0. If $600 of supplies are on hand at the end of the period, the adjusting entry is:

| (a) Supplies | 600 | |
| Supplies Expense | | 600 |
| (b) Supplies | 750 | |
| Supplies Expense | | 750 |
| (c) Supplies Expense | 750 | |
| Supplies | | 750 |
| (d) Supplies Expense | 600 | |
| Supplies | | 600 |

(SO 4) **7.** Adjustments for unearned revenues:

(a) decrease liabilities and increase revenues.

(b) increase liabilities and increase revenues.

(c) increase assets and increase revenues.

(d) decrease revenues and decrease assets.

(SO 4) **8.** Adjustments for prepaid expenses:

(a) decrease assets and increase revenues.

(b) decrease expenses and increase assets.

(c) decrease assets and increase expenses.

(d) decrease revenues and increase assets.

(SO 4) **9.** Queenan Company computes depreciation on delivery equipment at $1,000 for the month of June. The adjusting entry to record this depreciation is as follows:

| (a) Depreciation Expense | 1,000 | |
| Accumulated Depreciation— Queenan Company | | 1,000 |
| (b) Depreciation Expense | 1,000 | |
| Equipment | | 1,000 |
| (c) Depreciation Expense | 1,000 | |
| Accumulated Depreciation— Equipment | | 1,000 |
| (d) Equipment Expense | 1,000 | |
| Accumulated Depreciation— Equipment | | 1,000 |

(SO 5) **10.** Adjustments for accrued revenues:

(a) increase assets and increase liabilities.

(b) increase assets and increase revenues.

(c) decrease assets and decrease revenues.

(d) decrease liabilities and increase revenues.

(SO 5) **11.** Colleen Mooney earned a salary of $400 for the last week of September. She will be paid on October 1. The adjusting entry for Colleen's employer at September 30 is:

(a) No entry is required.

| (b) Salaries and Wages Expense | 400 | |
| Salaries and Wages Payable | | 400 |
| (c) Salaries and Wages Expense | 400 | |
| Cash | | 400 |
| (d) Salaries and Wages Payable | 400 | |
| Cash | | 400 |

(SO 6) **12.** Which statement is *incorrect* concerning the adjusted trial balance?

(a) An adjusted trial balance proves the equality of the total debit balances and the total credit balances in the ledger after all adjustments are made.

(b) The adjusted trial balance provides the primary basis for the preparation of financial statements.

(c) The adjusted trial balance does not list temporary accounts.

(d) The company prepares the adjusted trial balance after it has journalized and posted the adjusting entries.

(SO 7) **13.** Which account will have a zero balance after a company has journalized and posted closing entries?

(a) Service Revenue.

(b) Supplies.

(c) Prepaid Insurance.

(d) Accumulated Depreciation.

(SO 7) **14.** Which types of accounts will appear in the post-closing trial balance?

(a) Permanent accounts.

(b) Temporary accounts.

(c) Expense accounts.

(d) None of the above.

(SO 8) **15.** All of the following are required steps in the accounting cycle *except:*

(a) journalizing and posting closing entries.

(b) preparing an adjusted trial balance.

(c) preparing a post-closing trial balance.

(d) reversing entries.

Go to the book's companion website, **www.wiley.com/college/kimmel**, to access additional Self-Test Questions.

*Note:* All asterisked Questions relate to material in the appendix to the chapter.

# Questions

**1.** (a) How does the periodicity assumption affect an accountant's analysis of accounting transactions?

(b) Explain the term *fiscal year.*

**2.** Identify and state two generally accepted accounting principles that relate to adjusting the accounts.

3. Don Wishne, a lawyer, accepts a legal engagement in March, performs the work in April, and is paid in May. If Wishne's law firm prepares monthly financial statements, when should it recognize revenue from this engagement? Why?

4. In completing the engagement in question 3, Wishne pays no costs in March, $2,500 in April, and $2,200 in May (incurred in April). How much expense should the firm deduct from revenues in the month when it recognizes the revenue? Why?

5. "The cost principle of accounting requires adjusting entries." Do you agree? Explain.

6. Why may the financial information in an unadjusted trial balance not be up-to-date and complete?

7. Distinguish between the two categories of adjusting entries, and identify the types of adjustments applicable to each category.

8. What types of accounts does a company debit and credit in a prepaid expense adjusting entry?

9. "Depreciation is a process of valuation that results in the reporting of the fair value of the asset." Do you agree? Explain.

10. Explain the differences between depreciation expense and accumulated depreciation.

11. Greenstreet Company purchased equipment for $15,000. By the current balance sheet date, the company had depreciated $7,000. Indicate the balance sheet presentation of the data.

12. What types of accounts are debited and credited in an unearned revenue adjusting entry?

13. Data Technologies provides maintenance service for computers and office equipment for companies throughout the Northeast. The sales manager is elated because she closed a $300,000 three-year maintenance contract on December 29, 2011, two days before the company's year-end. "Now we will hit this year's net income target for sure," she crowed. The customer is required to pay $100,000 on December 29 (the day the deal was closed). Two more payments of $100,000 each are also required on December 29, 2012 and 2013. Discuss the effect that this event will have on the company's financial statements.

14. ValuMart, a large national retail chain, is nearing its fiscal year-end. It appears that the company is not going to hit its revenue and net income targets. The company's marketing manager, Chris Ahrentzen, suggests running a promotion selling $50 gift cards for $45. He believes that this would be very popular and would enable the company to meet its targets for revenue and net income. What do you think of this idea?

15. A company fails to recognize revenue earned but not yet received. Which of the following types of accounts are involved in the adjusting entry: (a) asset, (b) liability, (c) revenue, or (d) expense? For the accounts selected, indicate whether they would be debited or credited in the entry.

16. A company fails to recognize an expense incurred but not paid. Indicate which of the following types of accounts is debited and which is credited in the adjusting entry: (a) asset, (b) liability, (c) revenue, or (d) expense.

17. A company makes an accrued revenue adjusting entry for $780 and an accrued expense adjusting entry for $510. How much was net income understated prior to these entries? Explain.

18. On January 9 a company pays $6,200 for salaries, of which $1,100 was reported as Salaries and Wages Payable on December 31. Give the entry to record the payment.

19. For each of the following items before adjustment, indicate the type of adjusting entry—prepaid expense, unearned revenue, accrued revenue, and accrued expense—that is needed to correct the misstatement. If an item could result in more than one type of adjusting entry, indicate each of the types.
(a) Assets are understated.
(b) Liabilities are overstated.
(c) Liabilities are understated.
(d) Expenses are understated.
(e) Assets are overstated.
(f) Revenue is understated.

20. One-half of the adjusting entry is given below. Indicate the account title for the other half of the entry.
(a) Salaries and Wages Expense is debited.
(b) Depreciation Expense is debited.
(c) Interest Payable is credited.
(d) Supplies is credited.
(e) Accounts Receivable is debited.
(f) Unearned Service Revenue is debited.

21. "An adjusting entry may affect more than one balance sheet or income statement account." Do you agree? Why or why not?

22. Which balance sheet account provides evidence that Tootsie Roll records sales on an accrual basis rather than a cash basis? Explain.

23. Why is it possible to prepare financial statements directly from an adjusted trial balance?

24. 
(a) What information do accrual basis financial statements provide that cash basis statements do not?
(b) What information do cash basis financial statements provide that accrual basis statements do not?

25. What is the relationship, if any, between the amount shown in the adjusted trial balance column for an account and that account's ledger balance?

26. Identify the account(s) debited and credited in each of the four closing entries, assuming the company has net income for the year.

27. Some companies employ technologies that allow them to do a so-called "virtual close." This enables them to close their books nearly instantaneously any time during the year. What advantages does a "virtual close" provide?

28. Describe the nature of the Income Summary account, and identify the types of summary data that may be posted to this account.

29. What items are disclosed on a post-closing trial balance, and what is its purpose?

30. Which of these accounts would not appear in the post-closing trial balance? Interest Payable, Equipment, Depreciation Expense, Dividends, Unearned Service Revenue, Accumulated Depreciation—Equipment, and Service Revenue.

31. Indicate, in the sequence in which they are made, the three required steps in the accounting cycle that involve journalizing.

32. Identify, in the sequence in which they are prepared, the three trial balances that are required in the accounting cycle.

33. Explain the terms earnings management and quality of earnings.

34. Give examples of how companies manage earnings.

*35. What is the purpose of a worksheet?

*36. What is the basic form of a worksheet?

# Brief Exercises

**BE4-1** Transactions that affect earnings do not necessarily affect cash. Identify the effect, if any, that each of the following transactions would have upon cash and net income. The first transaction has been completed as an example.

*Identify impact of transactions on cash and net income.*
*(SO 2, 9), C*

|  | Cash | Net Income |
|---|---|---|
| (a) Purchased $100 of supplies for cash. | −$100 | $ 0 |

(b) Recorded an adjusting entry to record use of $20 of the above supplies.
(c) Made sales of $1,300, all on account.
(d) Received $800 from customers in payment of their accounts.
(e) Purchased equipment for cash, $2,500.
(f) Recorded depreciation of building for period used, $600.

**BE4-2** The ledger of Hubbard Company includes the following accounts. Explain why each account may require adjustment.

*Indicate why adjusting entries are needed.*
*(SO 3), C*

(a) Prepaid Insurance.
(b) Depreciation Expense.
(c) Unearned Service Revenue.
(d) Interest Payable.

**BE4-3** Dicker Company accumulates the following adjustment data at December 31. Indicate (1) the type of adjustment (prepaid expense, accrued revenue, and so on) and (2) the status of the accounts before adjustment (overstated or understated).

*Identify the major types of adjusting entries.*
*(SO 3), AN*

(a) Supplies of $400 are on hand. Supplies account shows $1,600 balance.
(b) Service Revenue earned but unbilled total $700.
(c) Interest of $300 has accumulated on a note payable.
(d) Rent collected in advance totaling $1,100 has been earned.

**BE4-4** Stagg Advertising Company's trial balance at December 31 shows Supplies $8,800 and Supplies Expense $0. On December 31 there are $1,100 of supplies on hand. Prepare the adjusting entry at December 31 and, using T accounts, enter the balances in the accounts, post the adjusting entry, and indicate the adjusted balance in each account.

*Prepare adjusting entry for supplies.*
*(SO 4), AP*

**BE4-5** At the end of its first year, the trial balance of Jules Company shows Equipment $22,000 and zero balances in Accumulated Depreciation—Equipment and Depreciation Expense. Depreciation for the year is estimated to be $2,750. Prepare the adjusting entry for depreciation at December 31, post the adjustments to T accounts, and indicate the balance sheet presentation of the equipment at December 31.

*Prepare adjusting entry for depreciation.*
*(SO 4), AP*

**BE4-6** On July 1, 2012, Ryhn Co. pays $12,400 to Craig Insurance Co. for a 2-year insurance contract. Both companies have fiscal years ending December 31. For Ryhn Co., journalize and post the entry on July 1 and the adjusting entry on December 31.

*Prepare adjusting entry for prepaid expense.*
*(SO 4), AP*

**BE4-7** Using the data in BE4-6, journalize and post the entry on July 1 and the adjusting entry on December 31 for Craig Insurance Co. Craig uses the accounts Unearned Service Revenue and Service Revenue.

*Prepare adjusting entry for unearned revenue.*
*(SO 4), AP*

**BE4-8** The bookkeeper for Forseth Company asks you to prepare the following accrual adjusting entries at December 31.

*Prepare adjusting entries for accruals.*
*(SO 5), AP*

(a) Interest on notes payable of $300 is accrued.
(b) Service revenue earned but unbilled totals $1,700.
(c) Salaries of $780 earned by employees have not been recorded.
Use these account titles: Service Revenue, Accounts Receivable, Interest Expense, Interest Payable, Salaries and Wages Expense, and Salaries and Wages Payable.

*Analyze accounts in an adjusted trial balance.*
(SO 6), **AN**

**BE4-9** The trial balance of LaGrace Company includes the following balance sheet accounts. Identify the accounts that might require adjustment. For each account that requires adjustment, indicate (1) the type of adjusting entry (prepaid expenses, unearned revenues, accrued revenues, and accrued expenses) and (2) the related account in the adjusting entry.
(a) Accounts Receivable.
(b) Prepaid Insurance.
(c) Equipment.
(d) Accumulated Depreciation—Equipment.
(e) Notes Payable.
(f) Interest Payable.
(g) Unearned Service Revenue.

*Prepare an income statement from an adjusted trial balance.*
(SO 6), **AP**

**BE4-10** The adjusted trial balance of Hanlon Corporation at December 31, 2012, includes the following accounts: Retained Earnings $17,200; Dividends $6,000; Service Revenue $32,000; Salaries and Wages Expense $14,000; Insurance Expense $1,800; Rent Expense $3,900; Supplies Expense $1,500; and Depreciation Expense $1,000. Prepare an income statement for the year.

*Prepare a retained earnings statement from an adjusted trial balance.*
(SO 6), **AP**

**BE4-11** Partial adjusted trial balance data for Hanlon Corporation are presented in BE4-10. The balance in Retained Earnings is the balance as of January 1. Prepare a retained earnings statement for the year assuming net income is $10,400.

*Identify financial statement for selected accounts.*
(SO 6), **K**

**BE4-12** The following selected accounts appear in the adjusted trial balance for Cohen Company. Indicate the financial statement on which each account would be reported.
(a) Accumulated Depreciation.
(b) Depreciation Expense.
(c) Retained Earnings (beginning).
(d) Dividends.
(e) Service Revenue.
(f) Supplies.
(g) Accounts Payable.

*Identify post-closing trial balance accounts.*
(SO 7), **K**

**BE4-13** Using the data in BE4-12, identify the accounts that would be included in a post-closing trial balance.

*Prepare and post closing entries.*
(SO 7), **AP**

**BE4-14** The income statement for the Timberline Golf Club Inc. for the month ended July 31 shows Service Revenue $16,000; Salaries and Wages Expense $8,400; Maintenance and Repairs Expense $2,500; and Income Tax Expense $1,000. The statement of retained earnings shows an opening balance for Retained Earnings of $20,000 and Dividends $1,300.
(a) Prepare closing journal entries.
(b) What is the ending balance in Retained Earnings?

*List required steps in the accounting cycle sequence.*
(SO 8), **K**

**BE4-15** The required steps in the accounting cycle are listed in random order below. List the steps in proper sequence.
(a) Prepare a post-closing trial balance.
(b) Prepare an adjusted trial balance.
(c) Analyze business transactions.
(d) Prepare a trial balance.
(e) Journalize the transactions.
(f) Journalize and post closing entries.
(g) Prepare financial statements.
(h) Journalize and post adjusting entries.
(i) Post to ledger accounts.

# Do it! Review

*Prepare adjusting entries for deferrals.*
(SO 4), **AP**

**Do it! 4-1** The ledger of Witzling, Inc. on March 31, 2012, includes the following selected accounts before adjusting entries.

|                          | Debit  | Credit |
| ------------------------ | ------ | ------ |
| Prepaid Insurance        | 2,400  |        |
| Supplies                 | 2,500  |        |
| Equipment                | 30,000 |        |
| Unearned Service Revenue |        | 10,000 |

An analysis of the accounts shows the following:

1. Insurance expires at the rate of $300 per month.
2. Supplies on hand total $900.
3. The office equipment depreciates $200 per month.
4. 2/5 of the unearned service revenue was earned in March.

Prepare the adjusting entries for the month of March.

**Do it!** 4-2   Tammy Krause is the new owner of Tammy's Computer Services. At the end of July 2012, her first month of ownership, Tammy is trying to prepare monthly financial statements. She has the following information for the month.

*Prepare adjusting entries for accruals.*
*(SO 5), AP*

1. At July 31, Krause owed employees $1,100 in salaries that the company will pay in August.
2. On July 1, Krause borrowed $20,000 from a local bank on a 10-year note. The annual interest rate is 9%.
3. Service revenue unrecorded in July totaled $1,600.

Prepare the adjusting entries needed at July 31, 2012.

**Do it!** 4-3   Indicate in which financial statement each of the following adjusted trial balance accounts would be presented.

*Prepare financial statements from adjusted trial balance.*
*(SO 6), C*

| | |
|---|---|
| Service Revenue | Accounts Receivable |
| Notes Payable | Accumulated Depreciation |
| Common Stock | Utilities Expense |

**Do it!** 4-4   After closing revenues and expense, Natraj Company shows the following account balances.

*Prepare closing entries.*
*(SO 7), AP*

| | |
|---|---|
| Dividends | $22,000 |
| Retained Earnings | 70,000 |
| Income Summary | 36,000  (credit balance) |

Prepare the remaining closing entries at December 31.

# Exercises

**E4-1**   The following independent situations require professional judgment for determining when to recognize revenue from the transactions.

*Identify point of revenue recognition.*
*(SO 1), C*

(a) Southwest Airlines sells you an advance-purchase airline ticket in September for your flight home at Christmas.
(b) Ultimate Electronics sells you a home theatre on a "no money down and full payment in three months" promotional deal.
(c) The Toronto Blue Jays sell season tickets online to games in the Skydome. Fans can purchase the tickets at any time, although the season doesn't officially begin until April. The major league baseball season runs from April through October.
(d) You borrow money in August from RBC Financial Group. The loan and the interest are repayable in full in November.
(e) In August, you order a sweater from Sears using its online catalog. The sweater arrives in September, and you charge it to your Sears credit card. You receive and pay the Sears bill in October.

*Instructions*
Identify when revenue should be recognized in each of the above situations.

**E4-2**   These are the assumptions, principles, and constraints discussed in this and previous chapters.

*Identify accounting assumptions, principles, and constraints.*
*(SO 1), K*

1. Economic entity assumption.
2. Expense recognition principle.
3. Monetary unit assumption.
4. Periodicity assumption.
5. Cost principle.

6. Materiality constraint.
7. Full disclosure principle.
8. Going concern assumption.
9. Revenue recognition principle.
10. Cost constraint.

*Instructions*

Identify by number the accounting assumption, principle, or constraint that describes each situation below. Do not use a number more than once.

_____ (a) Is the rationale for why plant assets are not reported at liquidation value. (Do not use the cost principle.)

_____ (b) Indicates that personal and business record-keeping should be separately maintained.

_____ (c) Ensures that all relevant financial information is reported.

_____ (d) Assumes that the dollar is the "measuring stick" used to report on financial performance.

_____ (e) Requires that accounting standards be followed for all *significant* items.

_____ (f) Separates financial information into time periods for reporting purposes.

_____ (g) Requires recognition of expenses in the same period as related revenues.

_____ (h) Indicates that fair value changes subsequent to purchase are not recorded in the accounts.

*Identify the violated assumption, principle, or constraint.*

(SO 1), **C**

**E4-3** Here are some accounting reporting situations.

(a) Dorfner Company recognizes revenue at the end of the production cycle but before sale. The price of the product, as well as the amount that can be sold, is not certain.

(b) Rayms Company is in its fifth year of operation and has yet to issue financial statements. (Do not use the full disclosure principle.)

(c) Tariq, Inc. is carrying inventory at its original cost of $100,000. Inventory has a fair value of $110,000.

(d) Leer Hospital Supply Corporation reports only current assets and current liabilities on its balance sheet. Property, plant, and equipment and bonds payable are reported as current assets and current liabilities, respectively. Liquidation of the company is unlikely.

(e) Kim Company has inventory on hand that cost $400,000. Kim reports inventory on its balance sheet at its current fair value of $425,000.

(f) Kris Piwek, president of Classic Music Company, bought a computer for her personal use. She paid for the computer by using company funds and debited the "Computers" account.

*Instructions*

For each situation, list the assumption, principle, or constraint that has been violated, if any. Some of these assumptions, principles, and constraints were presented in earlier chapters. List only one answer for each situation.

*Convert earnings from cash to accrual basis.*

(SO 2, 4, 5, 9), **AP**

**E4-4** Your examination of the records of a company that follows the cash basis of accounting tells you that the company's reported cash basis earnings in 2012 are $33,640. If this firm had followed accrual basis accounting practices, it would have reported the following year-end balances.

|  | 2012 | 2011 |
| --- | --- | --- |
| Accounts receivable | $3,400 | $2,800 |
| Supplies on hand | 1,300 | 1,460 |
| Unpaid wages owed | 2,000 | 2,400 |
| Other unpaid amounts | 1,400 | 1,100 |

*Instructions*

Determine the company's net earnings on an accrual basis for 2012. Show all your calculations in an orderly fashion.

*Determine cash-basis and accrual-basis earnings.*

(SO 2, 9), **AP**

**E4-5** In its first year of operations, Lazirko Company earned $28,000 in service revenue, $6,000 of which was on account and still outstanding at year-end. The remaining $22,000 was received in cash from customers.

The company incurred operating expenses of $15,800. Of these expenses, $12,000 were paid in cash; $3,800 was still owed on account at year-end. In addition, Lazirko prepaid $2,400 for insurance coverage that would not be used until the second year of operations.

*Instructions*

(a) Calculate the first year's net earnings under the cash basis of accounting, and calculate the first year's net earnings under the accrual basis of accounting.

(b) Which basis of accounting (cash or accrual) provides more useful information for decision makers?

**E4-6** Mt. Horeb Company, a ski tuning and repair shop, opened in November 2011. The company carefully kept track of all its cash receipts and cash payments. The following information is available at the end of the ski season, April 30, 2012.

*Convert earnings from cash to accrual basis; prepare accrual-based financial statements.*

*(SO 2, 4, 5, 9), AP*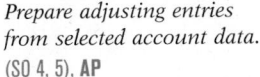

|  | Cash Receipts | Cash Payments |
|---|---|---|
| Issue of common shares | $20,000 | |
| Payment for repair equipment | | $ 9,200 |
| Rent payments | | 1,225 |
| Newspaper advertising payment | | 375 |
| Utility bills payments | | 970 |
| Part-time helper's wages payments | | 2,600 |
| Income tax payment | | 10,000 |
| Cash receipts from ski and snowboard repair services | 32,150 | |
| Subtotals | 52,150 | 24,370 |
| Cash balance | | 27,780 |
| Totals | $52,150 | $52,150 |

You learn that the repair equipment has an estimated useful life of 4 years. The company rents space at a cost of $175 per month on a one-year lease. The lease contract requires payment of the first and last months' rent in advance, which was done. The part-time helper is owed $420 at April 30, 2012, for unpaid wages. At April 30, 2012, customers owe Mt. Horeb Company $420 for services they have received but have not yet paid for.

**Instructions**
(a) Prepare an accrual-basis income statement for the 6 months ended April 30, 2012.
(b) Prepare the April 30, 2012, classified balance sheet.

**E4-7** KidVid, a maker of electronic games for kids, has just completed its first year of operations. The company's sales growth was explosive. To encourage large national stores to carry its products, KidVid offered 180-day financing—meaning its largest customers do not pay for nearly 6 months. Because KidVid is a new company, its components suppliers insist on being paid cash on delivery. Also, it had to pay up front for 2 years of insurance. At the end of the year, KidVid owed employees for one full month of salaries, but due to a cash shortfall, it promised to pay them the first week of next year.

*Identify differences between cash and accrual accounting.*

*(SO 2, 3, 9), C*

**Instructions**
(a) Explain how cash and accrual accounting would differ for each of the events listed above and describe the proper accrual accounting.
(b) Assume that at the end of the year KidVid reported a favorable net income, yet the company's management is concerned because the company is very short of cash. Explain how KidVid could have positive net income and yet run out of cash.

**E4-8** Peng Company accumulates the following adjustment data at December 31.
(a) Service Revenue earned but unbilled totals $600.
(b) Store supplies of $160 are on hand. Supplies account shows $1,900 balance.
(c) Utility expenses of $275 are unpaid.
(d) Service revenue of $490 collected in advance has been earned.
(e) Salaries of $620 are unpaid.
(f) Prepaid insurance totaling $400 has expired.

*Identify types of adjustments and accounts before adjustment.*

*(SO 3, 4, 5), AN*

**Instructions**
For each item, indicate (1) the type of adjustment (prepaid expense, unearned revenue, accrued revenue, or accrued expense) and (2) the status of the accounts before adjustment (overstated or understated).

**E4-9** The ledger of Sagovic Rental Agency on March 31 of the current year includes the selected accounts on page 206 before adjusting entries have been prepared.

*Prepare adjusting entries from selected account data.*

*(SO 4, 5), AP*

|  | Debits | Credits |
|---|---|---|
| Prepaid Insurance | $ 3,600 | |
| Supplies | 3,000 | |
| Equipment | 25,000 | |
| Accumulated Depreciation—Equipment | | $ 8,400 |
| Notes Payable | | 20,000 |
| Unearned Rent Revenue | | 12,400 |
| Rent Revenue | | 60,000 |
| Interest Expense | 0 | |
| Salaries and Wages Expense | 14,000 | |

An analysis of the accounts shows the following.

1. The equipment depreciates $280 per month.
2. Half of the unearned rent revenue was earned during the quarter.
3. Interest of $400 is accrued on the notes payable.
4. Supplies on hand total $850.
5. Insurance expires at the rate of $400 per month.

**Instructions**

Prepare the adjusting entries at March 31, assuming that adjusting entries are made quarterly. Additional accounts are: Depreciation Expense, Insurance Expense, Interest Payable, and Supplies Expense.

*Prepare adjusting entries.*
(SO 4, 5), **AP**

**E4-10** Adam Singh, D.D.S., opened an incorporated dental practice on January 1, 2012. During the first month of operations the following transactions occurred:

1. Performed services for patients who had dental plan insurance. At January 31, $760 of such services was earned but not yet billed to the insurance companies.
2. Utility expenses incurred but not paid prior to January 31 totaled $450.
3. Purchased dental equipment on January 1 for $80,000, paying $20,000 in cash and signing a $60,000, 3-year note payable (Interest is paid each December 31). The equipment depreciates $400 per month. Interest is $500 per month.
4. Purchased a 1-year malpractice insurance policy on January 1 for $24,000.
5. Purchased $1,750 of dental supplies (recorded as increase to Supplies). On January 31 determined that $550 of supplies were on hand.

**Instructions**

Prepare the adjusting entries on January 31. Account titles are: Accumulated Depreciation—Equipment, Depreciation Expense, Service Revenue, Accounts Receivable, Insurance Expense, Interest Expense, Interest Payable, Prepaid Insurance, Supplies, Supplies Expense, Utilities Expense, and Utilities Payable.

*Prepare adjusting entries.*
(SO 4, 5), **AP**

**E4-11** The unadjusted trial balance for Sierra Corp. is shown in Illustration 4-4 (page 168). In lieu of the adjusting entries shown in the text at October 31, assume the following adjustment data.

1. Supplies on hand at October 31 total $500.
2. Expired insurance for the month is $100.
3. Depreciation for the month is $75.
4. As of October 31, $800 of the previously recorded unearned revenue had been earned.
5. Services provided but unbilled (and no receivable has been recorded) at October 31 are $280.
6. Interest expense accrued at October 31 is $70.
7. Accrued salaries at October 31 are $1,400.

**Instructions**

Prepare the adjusting entries for the items above.

*Prepare a correct income statement.*
(SO 1, 4, 5, 6), **AP**

**E4-12** The income statement of Kaleta Co. for the month of July shows net income of $2,000 based on Service Revenue $5,500; Salaries and Wages Expense $2,100; Supplies Expense $900, and Utilities Expense $500. In reviewing the statement, you discover the following:

1. Insurance expired during July of $350 was omitted.
2. Supplies expense includes $200 of supplies that are still on hand at July 31.
3. Depreciation on equipment of $150 was omitted.
4. Accrued but unpaid wages at July 31 of $360 were not included.
5. Revenue earned but unrecorded totaled $700.

**Instructions**
Prepare a correct income statement for July 2012.

**E4-13** This is a partial adjusted trial balance of Fenske Company.

*Analyze adjusted data.*
(SO 1, 4, 5, 6), **AN**

### FENSKE COMPANY
### Adjusted Trial Balance
### January 31, 2012

|  | Debit | Credit |
|---|---|---|
| Supplies | $ 700 | |
| Prepaid Insurance | 1,560 | |
| Salaries and Wages Payable | | $1,060 |
| Unearned Service Revenue | | 750 |
| Supplies Expense | 950 | |
| Insurance Expense | 520 | |
| Salaries and Wages Expense | 1,800 | |
| Service Revenue | | 2,000 |

**Instructions**
Answer these questions, assuming the year begins January 1.
(a) If the amount in Supplies Expense is the January 31 adjusting entry, and $300 of supplies was purchased in January, what was the balance in Supplies on January 1?
(b) If the amount in Insurance Expense is the January 31 adjusting entry, and the original insurance premium was for 1 year, what was the total premium and when was the policy purchased?
(c) If $2,500 of salaries was paid in January, what was the balance in Salaries and Wages Payable at December 31, 2011?
(d) If $1,800 was received in January for services performed in January, what was the balance in Unearned Service Revenue at December 31, 2011?

**E4-14** A partial adjusted trial balance for Fenske Company is given in E4-13.

*Prepare closing entries.*
(SO 7), **AP**

**Instructions**
Prepare the closing entries at January 31, 2012.

**E4-15** Selected accounts of Sandin Company are shown here.

*Journalize basic transactions and adjusting entries.*
(SO 4, 5, 6), **AN**

| Supplies Expense | | | | Salaries and Wages Payable | |
|---|---|---|---|---|---|
| July 31 | 750 | | | July 31 | 1,000 |

| Salaries and Wages Expense | | | | Accounts Receivable | |
|---|---|---|---|---|---|
| July 15 | 1,000 | | | July 31 | 500 |
| 31 | 1,000 | | | | |

| Service Revenue | | | | Unearned Service Revenue | | | |
|---|---|---|---|---|---|---|---|
| | July 14 | 3,800 | July 31 | 900 | July 1 | Bal. 1,500 |
| | 31 | 900 | | | 20 | 600 |
| | 31 | 500 | | | | |

| Supplies | | | |
|---|---|---|---|
| July 1 | Bal. 1,100 | July 31 | 750 |
| 10 | 200 | | |

**Instructions**
After analyzing the accounts, journalize (a) the July transactions and (b) the adjusting entries that were made on July 31. (*Hint:* July transactions were for cash.)

**E4-16** The trial balances shown on page 208 are before and after adjustment for Amit Company at the end of its fiscal year.

*Prepare adjusting entries from analysis of trial balance.*
(SO 4, 5, 6), **AP**

**AMIT COMPANY**
**Trial Balance**
**August 31, 2012**

| | Before Adjustment Dr. | Before Adjustment Cr. | After Adjustment Dr. | After Adjustment Cr. |
|---|---|---|---|---|
| Cash | $10,900 | | $10,900 | |
| Accounts Receivable | 8,800 | | 9,400 | |
| Supplies | 2,500 | | 500 | |
| Prepaid Insurance | 4,000 | | 2,500 | |
| Equipment | 16,000 | | 16,000 | |
| Accumulated Depreciation—Equipment | | $ 3,600 | | $ 4,800 |
| Accounts Payable | | 5,800 | | 5,800 |
| Salaries and Wages Payable | | 0 | | 1,100 |
| Unearned Rent Revenue | | 1,800 | | 800 |
| Common Stock | | 10,000 | | 10,000 |
| Retained Earnings | | 5,500 | | 5,500 |
| Dividends | 2,800 | | 2,800 | |
| Service Revenue | | 34,000 | | 34,600 |
| Rent Revenue | | 12,100 | | 13,100 |
| Salaries and Wages Expense | 17,000 | | 18,100 | |
| Supplies Expense | 0 | | 2,000 | |
| Rent Expense | 10,800 | | 10,800 | |
| Insurance Expense | 0 | | 1,500 | |
| Depreciation Expense | 0 | | 1,200 | |
| | $72,800 | $72,800 | $75,700 | $75,700 |

**Instructions**
Prepare the adjusting entries that were made.

**E4-17** The adjusted trial balance for Amit Company is given in E4-16.

**Instructions**
Prepare the income and retained earnings statements for the year and the classified balance sheet at August 31.

**E4-18** The adjusted trial balance for Amit Company is given in E4-16.

**Instructions**
Prepare the closing entries for the temporary accounts at August 31.

# Exercises: Set B and Challenge Exercises

Visit the book's companion website, at **www.wiley.com/college/kimmel**, and choose the Student Companion site to access Exercise Set B and Challenge Exercises.

# Problems: Set A

**P4-1A** The following selected data are taken from the comparative financial statements of Superior Curling Club. The club prepares its financial statements using the accrual basis of accounting.

| September 30 | 2012 | 2011 |
|---|---|---|
| Accounts receivable for member dues | $ 15,000 | $ 19,000 |
| Unearned sales revenue | 20,000 | 23,000 |
| Service revenue (from member dues) | 151,000 | $135,000 |

Dues are billed to members based upon their use of the club's facilities. Unearned sales revenues arise from the sale of tickets to events, such as the Skins Game.

### Instructions

(*Hint:* You will find it helpful to use T accounts to analyze the following data. You must analyze these data sequentially, as missing information must first be deduced before moving on. Post your journal entries as you progress, rather than waiting until the end.)

(a) Prepare journal entries for each of the following events that took place during 2012.
1. Dues receivable from members from 2011 were all collected during 2012.
2. Unearned sales revenue at the end of 2011 was all earned during 2012.
3. Additional tickets were sold for $44,000 cash during 2012; a portion of these were used by the purchasers during the year. The entire balance remaining in Unearned Sales Revenue relates to the upcoming Skins Game in 2012.
4. Dues for the 2011–2012 fiscal year were billed to members.
5. Dues receivable for 2012 (i.e., those billed in item (4) above) were partially collected.

(b) Determine the amount of cash received by the Club from the above transactions during the year ended September 30, 2012.

(b) Cash received        $199,000

---

**P4-2A**  Gil Vogel started his own consulting firm, Vogel Consulting, on June 1, 2012. The trial balance at June 30 is as follows.

*Prepare adjusting entries, post to ledger accounts, and prepare adjusted trial balance.*

(SO 4, 5, 6), **AP**

### VOGEL CONSULTING
### Trial Balance
### June 30, 2012

|  | Debit | Credit |
|---|---|---|
| Cash | $ 6,850 | |
| Accounts Receivable | 7,000 | |
| Prepaid Insurance | 2,880 | |
| Supplies | 2,000 | |
| Equipment | 15,000 | |
| Accounts Payable | | $ 4,230 |
| Unearned Service Revenue | | 5,200 |
| Common Stock | | 22,000 |
| Service Revenue | | 8,300 |
| Salaries and Wages Expense | 4,000 | |
| Rent Expense | 2,000 | |
|  | $39,730 | $39,730 |

In addition to those accounts listed on the trial balance, the chart of accounts for Vogel also contains the following accounts: Accumulated Depreciation—Equipment, Utilities Payable, Salaries and Wages Payable, Depreciation Expense, Insurance Expense, Utilities Expense, and Supplies Expense.

Other data:

1. Supplies on hand at June 30 total $720.
2. A utility bill for $180 has not been recorded and will not be paid until next month.
3. The insurance policy is for a year.
4. $4,100 of unearned service revenue has been earned at the end of the month.
5. Salaries of $1,250 are accrued at June 30.
6. The equipment has a 5-year life with no salvage value and is being depreciated at $250 per month for 60 months.
7. Invoices representing $3,900 of services performed during the month have not been recorded as of June 30.

### Instructions

(a) Prepare the adjusting entries for the month of June.
(b) Post the adjusting entries to the ledger accounts. Enter the totals from the trial balance as beginning account balances. Use T accounts.
(c) Prepare an adjusted trial balance at June 30, 2012.

(b) Service rev.        $16,300
(c) Tot. trial
    balance             $45,310

*Prepare adjusting entries,
adjusted trial balance, and
financial statements.*
(SO 4, 5, 6, 7), **AP**

**P4-3A** The Vang Hotel opened for business on May 1, 2012. Here is its trial balance before adjustment on May 31.

**VANG HOTEL**
**Trial Balance**
**May 31, 2012**

|  | Debit | Credit |
|---|---|---|
| Cash | $ 2,500 | |
| Prepaid Insurance | 1,800 | |
| Supplies | 2,600 | |
| Land | 15,000 | |
| Buildings | 70,000 | |
| Equipment | 16,800 | |
| Accounts Payable | | $ 4,700 |
| Unearned Rent Revenue | | 3,300 |
| Mortgage Payable | | 36,000 |
| Common Stock | | 60,000 |
| Rent Revenue | | 9,000 |
| Salaries and Wages Expense | 3,000 | |
| Utilities Expense | 800 | |
| Advertising Expense | 500 | |
| | $113,000 | $113,000 |

Other data:

1. Insurance expires at the rate of $450 per month.
2. A count of supplies shows $1,050 of unused supplies on May 31.
3. Annual depreciation is $3,600 on the building and $3,000 on equipment.
4. The mortgage interest rate is 6%. (The mortgage was taken out on May 1.)
5. Unearned rent of $2,500 has been earned.
6. Salaries of $900 are accrued and unpaid at May 31.

*Instructions*
(a) Journalize the adjusting entries on May 31.
(b) Prepare a ledger using T accounts. Enter the trial balance amounts and post the adjusting entries.
(c) Prepare an adjusted trial balance on May 31.
(d) Prepare an income statement and a retained earnings statement for the month of May and a classified balance sheet at May 31.
(e) Identify which accounts should be closed on May 31.

(c) Rent revenue $11,500
Tot. adj. trial
balance $114,630
(d) Net income $3,570

*Prepare adjusting entries and
financial statements; identify
accounts to be closed.*
(SO 4, 5, 6, 7), **AP**

**P4-4A** Rolling Hills Golf Inc. was organized on July 1, 2012. Quarterly financial statements are prepared. The trial balance and adjusted trial balance on September 30 are shown here.

**ROLLING HILLS GOLF INC.**
**Trial Balance**
**September 30, 2012**

|  | Unadjusted | | Adjusted | |
|---|---|---|---|---|
|  | Dr. | Cr. | Dr. | Cr. |
| Cash | $ 6,700 | | $ 6,700 | |
| Accounts Receivable | 400 | | 1,000 | |
| Prepaid Rent | 1,800 | | 900 | |
| Supplies | 1,200 | | 180 | |
| Equipment | 15,000 | | 15,000 | |
| Accumulated Depreciation—Equipment | | | | $ 350 |
| Notes Payable | | $ 5,000 | | 5,000 |
| Accounts Payable | | 1,070 | | 1,070 |
| Salaries and Wages Payable | | | | 600 |
| Interest Payable | | | | 50 |
| Unearned Rent Revenue | | 1,000 | | 800 |
| Common Stock | | 14,000 | | 14,000 |
| Retained Earnings | | 0 | | 0 |
| Dividends | 600 | | 600 | |

|  | Unadjusted | | Adjusted | |
| --- | --- | --- | --- | --- |
|  | **Dr.** | **Cr.** | **Dr.** | **Cr.** |
| Service Revenue |  | 14,100 |  | 14,700 |
| Rent Revenue |  | 700 |  | 900 |
| Salaries and Wages Expense | 8,800 |  | 9,400 |  |
| Rent Expense | 900 |  | 1,800 |  |
| Depreciation Expense |  |  | 350 |  |
| Supplies Expense |  |  | 1,020 |  |
| Utilities Expense | 470 |  | 470 |  |
| Interest Expense |  |  | 50 |  |
|  | $35,870 | $35,870 | $37,470 | $37,470 |

## Instructions

(a) Journalize the adjusting entries that were made.

(b) Prepare an income statement and a retained earnings statement for the 3 months ending September 30 and a classified balance sheet at September 30.

(c) Identify which accounts should be closed on September 30.

(d) If the note bears interest at 12%, how many months has it been outstanding?

(b) Net income    $2,510
Tot. assets    $23,430

**P4-5A**   A review of the ledger of Terrell Company at December 31, 2012, produces these data pertaining to the preparation of annual adjusting entries.

*Prepare adjusting entries.*
(SO 4, 5), **AP**

1. Prepaid Insurance $15,200. The company has separate insurance policies on its buildings and its motor vehicles. Policy B4564 on the building was purchased on July 1, 2011, for $9,600. The policy has a term of 3 years. Policy A2958 on the vehicles was purchased on January 1, 2012, for $7,200. This policy has a term of 18 months.

2. Unearned Sales Revenue $22,800: The company began selling magazine subscriptions on October 1, 2012, on an annual basis. The selling price of a subscription is $24. A review of subscription contracts reveals the following.

| Subscription Start Date | Number of Subscriptions |
| --- | --- |
| October 1 | 250 |
| November 1 | 300 |
| December 1 | 400 |
|  | 950 |

3. Notes Payable, $40,000: This balance consists of a note for 6 months at an annual interest rate of 7%, dated October 1.

4. Salaries Payable $0: There are eight salaried employees. Salaries are paid every Friday for the current week. Five employees receive a salary of $600 each per week, and three employees earn $700 each per week. Assume December 31 is a Wednesday. Employees do not work weekends. All employees worked the last 3 days of December.

## Instructions

Prepare the adjusting entries at December 31, 2012.

**P4-6A**   Open Road Travel Court was organized on July 1, 2011, by Tiffany Lampkins. Tiffany is a good manager but a poor accountant. From the trial balance prepared by a part-time bookkeeper, Tiffany prepared the following income statement for her fourth quarter, which ended June 30, 2012.

*Prepare adjusting entries and a corrected income statement.*
(SO 4, 5), **AN**

### OPEN ROAD TRAVEL COURT
### Income Statement
### For the Quarter Ended June 30, 2012

| | | |
| --- | --- | --- |
| Revenues | | |
|   Rent revenues | | $212,000 |
| Operating expenses | | |
|   Advertising | $ 3,800 | |
|   Salaries and wages | 80,500 | |
|   Utilities | 900 | |
|   Depreciation | 2,700 | |
|   Maintenance and repairs | 4,300 | |
|   Total operating expenses | | 92,200 |
| Net income | | $119,800 |

Tiffany suspected that something was wrong with the statement because net income had never exceeded $30,000 in any one quarter. Knowing that you are an experienced accountant, she asks you to review the income statement and other data.

You first look at the trial balance. In addition to the account balances reported above in the income statement, the trial balance contains the following additional selected balances at June 30, 2012.

| | |
|---|---|
| Supplies | $ 8,200 |
| Prepaid Insurance | 14,400 |
| Note Payable | 14,000 |

You then make inquiries and discover the following.

1. Travel court rental revenues include advanced rental payments received for summer occupancy, in the amount of $57,000.

2. There were $1,800 of supplies on hand at June 30.

3. Prepaid insurance resulted from the payment of a one-year policy on April 1, 2012.

4. The mail in July 2012 brought the following bills: advertising for the week of June 24, $110; repairs made June 18, $4,450; and utilities for the month of June, $215.

5. There are three employees who receive wages that total $300 per day. At June 30, four days' wages have been incurred but not paid.

6. The note payable is a 6% note dated May 1, 2012, and due on July 31, 2012.

7. Income tax of $13,400 for the quarter is due in July but has not yet been recorded.

**Instructions**

(a) Prepare any adjusting journal entries required at June 30, 2012.

(b) Net income      $33,285     (b) Prepare a correct income statement for the quarter ended June 30, 2012.

(c) Explain to Tiffany the generally accepted accounting principles that she did not recognize in preparing her income statement and their effect on her results.

*Journalize transactions and follow through accounting cycle to preparation of financial statements.*

(SO 4, 5, 6), **AP**

GLS

**P4-7A** On November 1, 2012, the following were the account balances of Tate Equipment Repair.

| | **Debits** | | **Credits** |
|---|---|---|---|
| Cash | $ 2,790 | Accumulated Depreciation—Equipment | $ 500 |
| Accounts Receivable | 2,910 | Accounts Payable | 2,300 |
| Supplies | 1,120 | Unearned Service Revenue | 400 |
| Equipment | 10,000 | Salaries and Wages Payable | 620 |
| | | Common Stock | 10,000 |
| | | Retained Earnings | 3,000 |
| | $16,820 | | $16,820 |

During November, the following summary transactions were completed.

Nov. 8   Paid $1,220 for salaries due employees, of which $600 is for November and $620 is for October salaries payable.

     10   Received $1,800 cash from customers in payment of account.

     12   Received $1,700 cash for services performed in November.

     15   Purchased store equipment on account $3,600.

     17   Purchased supplies on account $1,300.

     20   Paid creditors $2,500 of accounts payable due.

     22   Paid November rent $480.

     25   Paid salaries $1,000.

     27   Performed services on account and billed customers for services provided $900.

     29   Received $750 from customers for services to be provided in the future.

Adjustment data:

1. Supplies on hand are valued at $1,100.

2. Accrued salaries payable are $480.

3. Depreciation for the month is $250.

4. Unearned service revenue of $500 is earned.

## Instructions

(a) Enter the November 1 balances in the ledger accounts. (Use T accounts.)
(b) Journalize the November transactions.
(c) Post to the ledger accounts. Use Service Revenue, Depreciation Expense, Supplies Expense, Salaries and Wages Expense, and Rent Expense.
(d) Prepare a trial balance at November 30.
(e) Journalize and post adjusting entries.
(f) Prepare an adjusted trial balance.
(g) Prepare an income statement and a retained earnings statement for November and a classified balance sheet at November 30.

| | |
|---|---|
| (f) Cash | $1,840 |
| Tot. adj. trial balance | $22,680 |
| (g) Net loss | $1,030 |

**P4-8A**    Dana La Fontsee opened Pro Window Washing Inc. on July 1, 2012. During July the following transactions were completed.

*Complete all steps in accounting cycle.*
(SO 4, 5, 6, 7, 8), **AP**

GLS

| July | 1 | Issued 12,000 shares of common stock for $12,000 cash. |
|---|---|---|
| | 1 | Purchased used truck for $8,000, paying $2,000 cash and the balance on account. |
| | 3 | Purchased cleaning supplies for $900 on account. |
| | 5 | Paid $1,800 cash on 1-year insurance policy effective July 1. |
| | 12 | Billed customers $3,700 for cleaning services. |
| | 18 | Paid $1,000 cash on amount owed on truck and $500 on amount owed on cleaning supplies. |
| | 20 | Paid $2,000 cash for employee salaries. |
| | 21 | Collected $1,600 cash from customers billed on July 12. |
| | 25 | Billed customers $2,500 for cleaning services. |
| | 31 | Paid $290 for maintenance of the truck during month. |
| | 31 | Declared and paid $600 cash dividend. |

The chart of accounts for Pro Window Washing contains the following accounts: Cash, Accounts Receivable, Supplies, Prepaid Insurance, Equipment, Accumulated Depreciation—Equipment, Accounts Payable, Salaries and Wages Payable, Common Stock, Retained Earnings, Dividends, Income Summary, Service Revenue, Maintenance and Repairs Expense, Supplies Expense, Depreciation Expense, Insurance Expense, Salaries and Wages Expense.

## Instructions

(a) Journalize the July transactions.
(b) Post to the ledger accounts. (Use T accounts.)
(c) Prepare a trial balance at July 31.
(d) Journalize the following adjustments.
   (1) Services provided but unbilled and uncollected at July 31 were $1,700.
   (2) Depreciation on equipment for the month was $180.
   (3) One-twelfth of the insurance expired.
   (4) An inventory count shows $320 of cleaning supplies on hand at July 31.
   (5) Accrued but unpaid employee salaries were $400.
(e) Post adjusting entries to the T accounts.
(f) Prepare an adjusted trial balance.
(g) Prepare the income statement and a retained earnings statement for July and a classified balance sheet at July 31.
(h) Journalize and post closing entries and complete the closing process.
(i) Prepare a post-closing trial balance at July 31.

| | |
|---|---|
| (f) Cash | $5,410 |
| (g) Tot. assets | $21,500 |

# Problems: Set B

**P4-1B**    The following data are taken from the comparative balance sheets of Glenview Club, which prepares its financial statements using the accrual basis of accounting.

*Record transactions on accrual basis; convert revenue to cash receipts.*
(SO 2, 4, 9), **AP**

| December 31 | 2012 | 2011 |
|---|---|---|
| Accounts receivable for member fees | $12,000 | $18,000 |
| Unearned service revenue | 17,000 | 11,000 |

Fees are billed to members based upon their use of the club's facilities. Unearned service revenues arise from the sale of gift certificates, which members can apply to their future use of club facilities. The 2012 income statement for the club showed that service revenue of $172,000 was earned during the year.

**Instructions**

(*Hint:* You will find it helpful to use T accounts to analyze these data.)

(a) Prepare journal entries for each of the following events that took place during 2012.

1. Fees receivable from 2011 were all collected during 2012.
2. Gift certificates outstanding at the end of 2011 were all redeemed during 2012.
3. An additional $40,000 worth of gift certificates were sold during 2012; a portion of these were used by the recipients during the year; the remainder were still outstanding at the end of 2012.
4. Fees for 2012 were billed to members.
5. Fees receivable for 2012 (i.e., those billed in item (4) above) were partially collected.

(b) Cash
received $184,000

(b) Determine the amount of cash received by the club with respect to fees during 2012.

*Prepare adjusting entries, post to ledger accounts, and prepare an adjusted trial balance.*
(SO 4, 5, 6), **AP**

**P4-2B** Pamela Quinn started her own consulting firm, Quinn Consulting, on May 1, 2012. The trial balance at May 31 is as shown below.

**QUINN CONSULTING**
**Trial Balance**
**May 31, 2012**

| | Debit | Credit |
|---|---|---|
| Cash | $ 7,500 | |
| Accounts Receivable | 3,000 | |
| Prepaid Insurance | 3,600 | |
| Supplies | 2,500 | |
| Equipment | 12,000 | |
| Accounts Payable | | $ 3,500 |
| Unearned Service Revenue | | 4,000 |
| Common Stock | | 19,100 |
| Service Revenue | | 7,500 |
| Salaries and Wages Expense | 4,000 | |
| Rent Expense | 1,500 | |
| | $34,100 | $34,100 |

In addition to those accounts listed on the trial balance, the chart of accounts for Quinn Consulting also contains the following accounts: Accumulated Depreciation—Equipment, Salaries and Wages Payable, Depreciation Expense, Insurance Expense, Utilities Expense, and Supplies Expense.

Other data:

1. $750 of supplies have been used during the month.
2. Utility costs incurred but not paid are $260.
3. The insurance policy is for 2 years.
4. $1,500 of the balance in the Unearned Service Revenue account remains unearned at the end of the month.
5. Assume May 31 is a Thursday and employees are paid on Fridays. Quinn Consulting has two employees that are paid $600 each for a 5-day work week.
6. The equipment has a 5-year life with no salvage value and is being depreciated at $200 per month for 60 months.
7. Invoices representing $1,980 of services performed during the month have not been recorded as of May 31.

**Instructions**

(a) Prepare the adjusting entries for the month of May.
(b) Post the adjusting entries to the ledger accounts. Enter the totals from the trial balance as beginning account balances. Use T accounts.

(c) Tot. trial
balance $37,500

(c) Prepare an adjusted trial balance at May 31, 2012.

**P4-3B**    Maquoketa Valley Resort opened for business on June 1 with eight air-conditioned units. Its trial balance before adjustment on August 31 is presented here.

*Prepare adjusting entries, adjusted trial balance, and financial statements.*

(SO 4, 5, 6, 7), **AP**

### MAQUOKETA VALLEY RESORT
### Trial Balance
### August 31, 2012

|  | Debit | Credit |
|---|---|---|
| Cash | $ 24,600 | |
| Prepaid Insurance | 5,400 | |
| Supplies | 4,300 | |
| Land | 40,000 | |
| Buildings | 132,000 | |
| Equipment | 36,000 | |
| Accounts Payable | | $  6,500 |
| Unearned Rent Revenue | | 6,800 |
| Mortgage Payable | | 120,000 |
| Common Stock | | 100,000 |
| Dividends | 5,000 | |
| Rent Revenue | | 80,000 |
| Salaries and Wages Expense | 53,000 | |
| Utilities Expense | 9,400 | |
| Maintenance and Repairs Expense | 3,600 | |
| | $313,300 | $313,300 |

Other data:

1. Insurance expires at the rate of $450 per month.
2. A count of supplies on August 31 shows $700 of supplies on hand.
3. Annual depreciation is $6,600 on buildings and $4,000 on equipment.
4. Unearned rent of $5,000 was earned prior to August 31.
5. Salaries of $600 were unpaid at August 31.
6. Rentals of $1,600 were due from tenants at August 31. (Use Accounts Receivable.)
7. The mortgage interest rate is 9% per year. (The mortgage was taken out August 1.)

**Instructions**
(a) Journalize the adjusting entries on August 31 for the 3-month period June 1–August 31.
(b) Prepare a ledger using T accounts. Enter the trial balance amounts and post the adjusting entries.
(c) Prepare an adjusted trial balance on August 31.
(d) Prepare an income statement and a retained earnings statement for the 3 months ended August 31 and a classified balance sheet as of August 31.
(e) Identify which accounts should be closed on August 31.

(c) Tot. adj. trial
    balance        $319,050
(d) Net income     $11,500

**P4-4B**    Vedula Advertising Agency was founded by Murali Vedula in January 2007. Presented here are both the adjusted and unadjusted trial balances as of December 31, 2012.

*Prepare adjusting entries and financial statements; identify accounts to be closed.*

(SO 4, 5, 6, 7), **AP**

### VEDULA ADVERTISING AGENCY
### Trial Balance
### December 31, 2012

|  | Unadjusted | | Adjusted | |
|---|---|---|---|---|
|  | Dr. | Cr. | Dr. | Cr. |
| Cash | $ 11,000 | | $ 11,000 | |
| Accounts Receivable | 16,000 | | 19,500 | |
| Supplies | 9,400 | | 6,500 | |
| Prepaid Insurance | 3,350 | | 1,790 | |
| Equipment | 60,000 | | 60,000 | |
| Accumulated Depreciation— | | | | |
| Equipment | | $ 25,000 | | $ 30,000 |
| Notes Payable | | 8,000 | | 8,000 |
| Accounts Payable | | 2,000 | | 2,000 |
| Interest Payable | | 0 | | 560 |

| | Unadjusted | | Adjusted | |
|---|---|---|---|---|
| | **Dr.** | **Cr.** | **Dr.** | **Cr.** |
| Unearned Service Revenue | | 5,000 | | 3,100 |
| Salaries and Wages Payable | | 0 | | 820 |
| Common Stock | | 20,000 | | 20,000 |
| Retained Earnings | | 5,500 | | 5,500 |
| Dividends | 10,000 | | 10,000 | |
| Service Revenue | | 57,600 | | 63,000 |
| Salaries and Wages Expense | 9,000 | | 9,820 | |
| Insurance Expense | | | 1,560 | |
| Interest Expense | | | 560 | |
| Depreciation Expense | | | 5,000 | |
| Supplies Expense | | | 2,900 | |
| Rent Expense | 4,350 | | 4,350 | |
| | $123,100 | $123,100 | $132,980 | $132,980 |

**Instructions**

(a) Journalize the annual adjusting entries that were made.

(b) Prepare an income statement and a retained earnings statement for the year ended December 31, and a classified balance sheet at December 31.

(c) Identify which accounts should be closed on December 31.

(d) If the note has been outstanding 10 months, what is the annual interest rate on that note?

(e) If the company paid $10,500 in salaries in 2012, what was the balance in Salaries and Wages Payable on December 31, 2011?

*(b) Net income $38,810*
*Tot. assets $68,790*

*Prepare adjusting entries.*
*(SO 4, 5), AP*

**P4-5B** A review of the ledger of Felipe Company at December 31, 2012, produces the following data pertaining to the preparation of annual adjusting entries.

1. Salaries and Wages Payable $0: There are eight salaried employees. Salaries are paid every Friday for the current week. Six employees receive a salary of $800 each per week, and two employees earn $600 each per week. Assume December 31 is a Tuesday. Employees do not work weekends. All employees worked the last 2 days of December.

2. Unearned Rent Revenue $300,000: The company began subleasing office space in its new building on November 1. Each tenant is required to make a $5,000 security deposit that is not refundable until occupancy is terminated. At December 31 the company had the following rental contracts that are paid in full for the entire term of the lease.

| Date | Term (in months) | Monthly Rent | Number of Leases |
|---|---|---|---|
| Nov. 1 | 6 | $4,000 | 5 |
| Dec. 1 | 6 | 7,500 | 4 |

3. Prepaid Advertising $13,200: This balance consists of payments on two advertising contracts. The contracts provide for monthly advertising in two trade magazines. The terms of the contracts are as follows.

| Contract | Date | Amount | Number of Magazine Issues |
|---|---|---|---|
| A650 | May 1 | $6,000 | 12 |
| B974 | Sept. 1 | 7,200 | 18 |

The first advertisement runs in the month in which the contract is signed.

4. Notes Payable $80,000: This balance consists of a note for 1 year at an annual interest rate of 8%, dated April 1, 2012.

**Instructions**

Prepare the adjusting entries at December 31, 2012. Show all computations.

**P4-6B**   The Fly Right Travel Agency was organized on January 1, 2010, by Joe Kirkpatrick. Joe is a good manager but a poor accountant. From the trial balance prepared by a part-time bookkeeper, Joe prepared the following income statement for the quarter that ended March 31, 2012.

*Prepare adjusting entries and a corrected income statement.*
*(SO 4, 5),* **AN**

### FLY RIGHT TRAVEL AGENCY
### Income Statement
### For the Quarter Ended March 31, 2012

| | | |
|---|---|---|
| Revenues | | |
| Service revenue | | $50,000 |
| Operating expenses | | |
| Advertising | $ 2,600 | |
| Depreciation | 400 | |
| Income tax | 1,500 | |
| Salaries and wages | 11,000 | |
| Utilities | 400 | 15,900 |
| Net income | | $34,100 |

Joe knew that something was wrong with the statement because net income had never exceeded $8,000 in any one quarter. Knowing that you are an experienced account-ant, he asks you to review the income statement and other data.

You first look at the trial balance. In addition to the account balances reported above in the income statement, the trial balance contains the following additional selected bal-ances at March 31, 2012.

| | |
|---|---|
| Supplies | $ 2,900 |
| Prepaid insurance | 3,360 |
| Notes payable | 12,000 |

You then make inquiries and discover the following:

1. Travel service revenue includes advance payments for cruises, $20,000.
2. There were $800 of supplies on hand at March 31.
3. Prepaid insurance resulted from the payment of a one-year policy on January 1, 2012.
4. The mail on April 1, 2012, brought the utility bill for the month of March's heat, light, and power, $210.
5. There are two employees who receive salaries of $80 each per day. At March 31, four days' salaries have been incurred but not paid.
6. The note payable is a 6-month, 7% note dated January 1, 2012.

**Instructions**
(a) Prepare any adjusting journal entries required at March 31, 2012.
(b) Prepare a correct income statement for the quarter ended March 31, 2012.
(c) Explain to Joe the generally accepted accounting principles that he did not recog-nize in preparing his income statement and their effect on his results.

*(b) Net income          $10,100*

**P4-7B**   On September 1, 2012, the following were the account balances of Worthington Equipment Repair.

*Journalize transactions and follow through accounting cycle to preparation of financial statements.*
*(SO 4, 5, 6),* **AP**

| | **Debits** | | **Credits** |
|---|---|---|---|
| Cash | $ 4,880 | Accumulated Depreciation—Equipment | $ 1,600 |
| Accounts Receivable | 3,420 | Accounts Payable | 3,100 |
| Supplies | 800 | Unearned Service Revenue | 400 |
| Equipment | 15,000 | Salaries and Wages Payable | 700 |
| | | Common Stock | 10,000 |
| | | Retained Earnings | 8,300 |
| | $24,100 | | $24,100 |

During September, the following summary transactions were completed.

Sept.  8   Paid $1,100 for salaries due employees, of which $400 is for September and $700 is for August salaries payable.
     10   Received $1,500 cash from customers in payment of account.
     12   Received $3,400 cash for services performed in September.
     15   Purchased store equipment on account $3,000.

Sept. 17 Purchased supplies on account $2,000.
20 Paid creditors $4,500 of accounts payable due.
22 Paid September rent $520.
25 Paid salaries $1,200.
27 Performed services on account and billed customers for services provided $2,040.
29 Received $650 from customers for services to be provided in the future.

Adjustment data:

1. Supplies on hand $1,100.
2. Accrued salaries payable $400.
3. Depreciation $200 per month.
4. Unearned service revenue of $280 earned.

**Instructions**
(a) Enter the September 1 balances in the ledger T accounts.
(b) Journalize the September transactions.
(c) Post to the ledger T accounts. Use Service Revenue, Depreciation Expense, Supplies Expense, Salaries and Wages Expense, and Rent Expense.
(d) Prepare a trial balance at September 30.
(e) Journalize and post adjusting entries.
(f) Prepare an adjusted trial balance.
(g) Prepare an income statement and a retained earnings statement for September and a classified balance sheet at September 30.

(f) Tot. adj. trial
    balance     $30,590
(g) Tot. assets     $24,370

*Complete all steps in accounting cycle.*
(SO 4, 5, 6, 7, 8), **AP**

**P4-8B** Gina Balistrieri opened Genie Cleaners on March 1, 2012. During March, the following transactions were completed.

Mar. 1 Issued 10,000 shares of common stock for $15,000 cash.
1 Purchased used truck for $8,000, paying $3,000 cash and the balance on account.
3 Purchased cleaning supplies for $1,500 on account.
5 Paid $2,400 cash on a 6-month insurance policy effective March 1.
14 Billed customers $3,700 for cleaning services.
18 Paid $1,500 cash on amount owed on truck and $500 on amount owed on cleaning supplies.
20 Paid $1,750 cash for employee salaries.
21 Collected $1,600 cash from customers billed on March 14.
28 Billed customers $4,200 for cleaning services.
31 Paid $350 for gas and oil used in truck during month (use Maintenance and Repairs Expense).
31 Declared and paid a $900 cash dividend.

The chart of accounts for Genie Cleaners contains the following accounts: Cash, Accounts Receivable, Supplies, Prepaid Insurance, Equipment, Accumulated Depreciation—Equipment, Accounts Payable, Salaries and Wages Payable, Common Stock, Retained Earnings, Dividends, Income Summary, Service Revenue, Maintenance and Repairs Expense, Supplies Expense, Depreciation Expense, Insurance Expense, Salaries and Wages Expense.

**Instructions**
(a) Journalize the March transactions.
(b) Post to the ledger accounts. (Use T accounts.)
(c) Prepare a trial balance at March 31.
(d) Journalize the following adjustments.
    1. Earned but unbilled revenue at March 31 was $200.
    2. Depreciation on equipment for the month was $250.
    3. One-sixth of the insurance expired.
    4. An inventory count shows $280 of cleaning supplies on hand at March 31.
    5. Accrued but unpaid employee salaries were $1,080.
(e) Post adjusting entries to the T accounts.
(f) Prepare an adjusted trial balance.

(f) Tot. adj. trial
    balance     $28,930
(g) Tot. assets     $22,730

(g) Prepare the income statement and a retained earnings statement for March and a classified balance sheet at March 31.
(h) Journalize and post closing entries and complete the closing process.
(i) Prepare a post-closing trial balance at March 31.

# Problems: Set C

Visit the book's companion website, at **www.wiley.com/college/kimmel**, and choose the Student Companion site to access Problem Set C.

# Continuing Cookie Chronicle

(*Note:* This is a continuation of the Cookie Chronicle from Chapters 1 through 3.)

**CCC4**  Cookie Creations is gearing up for the winter holiday season. During the month of December 2011, the following transactions occur.

Dec. 1   Natalie hires an assistant at an hourly wage of $8 to help with cookie making and some administrative duties.

  5   Natalie teaches the class that was booked on November 25. The balance outstanding is received.

  8   Cookie Creations receives a check for the amount due from the neighborhood school for the class given on November 30.

  9   Cookie Creations receives $750 in advance from the local school board for five classes that the company will give during December and January.

 15   Pays the cell phone invoice outstanding at November 30.

 16   Issues a check to Natalie's brother for the amount owed for the design of the website.

 19   Receives a deposit of $60 on a cookie class scheduled for early January.

 23   Additional revenue earned during the month for cookie-making classes amounts to $4,000. (Natalie has not had time to account for each class individually.) $3,000 in cash has been collected and $1,000 is still outstanding. (This is in addition to the December 5 and December 9 transactions.)

 23   Additional baking supplies purchased during the month for sugar, flour, and chocolate chips amount to $1,250 cash.

 23   Issues a check to Natalie's assistant for $800. Her assistant worked approximately 100 hours from the time in which she was hired until December 23.

 28   Pays a dividend of $500 to the common shareholder (Natalie).

As of December 31, Cookie Creations' year-end, the following adjusting entry data are provided.

 1. A count reveals that $45 of brochures and posters were used.
 2. Depreciation is recorded on the baking equipment purchased in November. The baking equipment has a useful life of 5 years. Assume that 2 months' worth of depreciation is required.
 3. Amortization (which is similar to depreciation) is recorded on the website. (Credit the Website account directly for the amount of the amortization.) The website is amortized over a useful life of 2 years and was available for use on December 1.
 4. Interest on the note payable is accrued. (Assume that 1.5 months of interest accrued during November and December.) Round to nearest dollar.
 5. One month's worth of insurance has expired.
 6. Natalie is unexpectedly telephoned on December 28 to give a cookie class at the neighborhood community center on December 31. In early January Cookie Creations sends an invoice for $450 to the community center.
 7. A count reveals that $1,025 of baking supplies were used.
 8. A cell phone invoice is received for $75. The invoice is for services provided during the month of December and is due on January 15.
 9. Because the cookie-making class occurred unexpectedly on December 28 and is for such a large group of children, Natalie's assistant helps out. Her assistant worked 7 hours at a rate of $8 per hour.
10. An analysis of the unearned revenue account reveals that two of the five classes paid for by the local school board on December 9 still have not been taught by the end of December. The $60 deposit received on December 19 for another class also remains unearned.

## Instructions

Using the information that you have gathered and the general ledger accounts that you have prepared through Chapter 3, plus the new information above, do the following.
(a) Journalize the above transactions.
(b) Post the December transactions. (Use the general ledger accounts prepared in Chapter 3.)

(c) Totals      $8,160      (c) Prepare a trial balance at December 31, 2011.

                                    (d) Prepare and post adjusting journal entries for the month of December.

(e) Totals      $8,804      (e) Prepare an adjusted trial balance as of December 31, 2011.

(f) Net income      $3,211      (f) Prepare an income statement and a retained earnings statement for the 2-month period ending December 31, 2011, and a classified balance sheet as of December 31, 2011.

                                    (g) Prepare and post closing entries as of December 31, 2011.

(h) Totals      $6,065      (h) Prepare a post-closing trial balance.

# broadening your perspective

# Financial Reporting and Analysis

### FINANCIAL REPORTING PROBLEM: *Tootsie Roll Industries, Inc.*

**BYP4-1** The financial statements of Tootsie Roll are presented in Appendix A at the end of this book.

*Instructions*

(a) Using the consolidated income statement and balance sheet, identify items that may result in adjusting entries for deferrals.

(b) Using the consolidated income statement, identify two items that may result in adjusting entries for accruals.

(c) What was the amount of depreciation expense for 2009 and 2008? (You will need to examine the notes to the financial statements or the statement of cash flows.) Where was accumulated depreciation reported?

(d) What was the cash paid for income taxes during 2009, reported at the bottom of the consolidated statement of cash flows? What was income tax expense (provision for income taxes) for 2009?

### COMPARATIVE ANALYSIS PROBLEM: *Tootsie Roll vs. Hershey*

**BYP4-2** The financial statements of The Hershey Company are presented in Appendix B, following the financial statements for Tootsie Roll in Appendix A.

*Instructions*

(a) Identify two accounts on Hershey's balance sheet that provide evidence that Hershey uses accrual accounting. In each case, identify the income statement account that would be affected by the adjustment process.

(b) Identify two accounts on Tootsie Roll's balance sheet that provide evidence that Tootsie Roll uses accrual accounting (different from the two you listed for Hershey). In each case, identify the income statement account that would be affected by the adjustment process.

### RESEARCH CASE

**BYP4-3** The February 13, 2010, issue of the *Wall Street Journal* includes an article by Scott Thurm entitled "For Some Firms, a Case of 'Quadrophobia'."

*Instructions*

Read the article and answer the following.

(a) What method did the study's authors use to determine that companies were "managing" their earnings per share calculation?

(b) For the average company in the study, how much would the company have to boost earnings in order to increase earnings per share by 1/10 of a cent?

(c) What examples did the authors cite of accounting adjustments that companies can make to boost net income enough that they can round up to the next highest cent? Why aren't these methods of adjustment considered illegal?

(d) What is an earnings restatement? What relationship did the authors identify about companies that restate earnings?

(e) What incentive do companies have to round up their earnings per share to the next highest cent?

## INTERPRETING FINANCIAL STATEMENTS

**BYP4-4** Laser Recording Systems, founded in 1981, produces disks for use in the home market. The following is an excerpt from Laser Recording Systems' financial statements (all dollars in thousands).

---

### LASER RECORDING SYSTEMS
#### Management Discussion

Accrued liabilities increased to $1,642 at January 31, from $138 at the end of the previous fiscal year. Compensation and related accruals increased $195 due primarily to increases in accruals for severance, vacation, commissions, and relocation expenses. Accrued professional services increased by $137 primarily as a result of legal expenses related to several outstanding contractual disputes. Other expenses increased $35, of which $18 was for interest payable.

---

*Instructions*

(a) Can you tell from the discussion whether Laser Recording Systems has prepaid its legal expenses and is now making an adjustment to the asset account Prepaid Legal Expenses, or whether the company is handling the legal expense via an accrued expense adjustment?

(b) Identify each of the adjustments Laser Recording Systems is discussing as one of the four types of possible adjustments discussed in the chapter. How is net income ultimately affected by each of the adjustments?

(c) What journal entry did Laser Recording make to record the accrued interest?

## FINANCIAL ANALYSIS ON THE WEB

**BYP4-5** *Purpose:* To learn about the functions of the Securities and Exchange Commission (SEC).

*Address:* **www.sec.gov/about/whatwedo.shtml,** or go to **www.wiley.com/college/kimmel**

*Instructions*
Use the information in this site to answer the following questions.

(a) What event spurred the creation of the SEC? Why was the SEC created?

(b) What are the four divisions of the SEC? Briefly describe the purpose of each.

(c) What are the responsibilities of the chief accountant?

# Critical Thinking

## DECISION MAKING ACROSS THE ORGANIZATION

**BYP4-6** Council Bluff Park was organized on April 1, 2011, by Lori Delzer. Lori is a good manager but a poor accountant. From the trial balance prepared by a part-time bookkeeper, Lori prepared the following income statement for the quarter that ended March 31, 2012.

**COUNCIL BLUFF PARK**
**Income Statement**
**For the Quarter Ended March 31, 2012**

| | | |
|---|---:|---:|
| Revenues | | |
|    Rental revenues | | $83,000 |
| Operating expenses | | |
|    Advertising | $ 4,200 | |
|    Wages | 27,600 | |
|    Utilities | 1,500 | |
|    Depreciation | 800 | |
|    Repairs | 2,800 | |
|      Total operating expenses | | 36,900 |
| Net income | | $46,100 |

Lori knew that something was wrong with the statement because net income had never exceeded $20,000 in any one quarter. Knowing that you are an experienced accountant, she asks you to review the income statement and other data.

You first look at the trial balance. In addition to the account balances reported in the income statement, the ledger contains these selected balances at March 31, 2012.

| | |
|---|---|
| Supplies | $ 4,500 |
| Prepaid Insurance | 7,200 |
| Notes Payable | 20,000 |

You then make inquiries and discover the following.

1. Rental revenues include advanced rentals for summer-month occupancy, $21,000.
2. There were $600 of supplies on hand at March 31.
3. Prepaid insurance resulted from the payment of a 1-year policy on January 1, 2012.
4. The mail on April 1, 2012, brought the following bills: advertising for week of March 24, $110; repairs made March 10, $1,040; and utilities $240.
5. There are four employees who receive wages totaling $290 per day. At March 31, 3 days' wages have been incurred but not paid.
6. The note payable is a 3-month, 7% note dated January 1, 2012.

*Instructions*
With the class divided into groups, answer the following.
(a) Prepare a correct income statement for the quarter ended March 31, 2012.
(b) Explain to Lori the generally accepted accounting principles that she did not follow in preparing her income statement and their effect on her results.

## COMMUNICATION ACTIVITY

BYP4-7   On numerous occasions, proposals have surfaced to put the federal government on the accrual basis of accounting. This is no small issue because if this basis were used, it would mean that billions in unrecorded liabilities would have to be booked and the federal deficit would increase substantially.

*Instructions*
(a) What is the difference between accrual-basis accounting and cash-basis accounting?
(b) Comment on why politicians prefer a cash-basis accounting system over an accrual-basis system.
(c) Write a letter to your senators explaining why you think the federal government should adopt the accrual basis of accounting.

## ETHICS CASE

BYP4-8   Prism Company is a pesticide manufacturer. Its sales declined greatly this year due to the passage of legislation outlawing the sale of several of Prism's chemical pesticides. During the coming year, Prism will have environmentally safe and competitive replacement chemicals to replace these discontinued products. Sales in the next year are expected to greatly exceed those of any prior year. Therefore, the decline in this year's sales and profits appears to be a one-year aberration.

Even so, the company president believes that a large dip in the current year's profits could cause a significant drop in the market price of Prism's stock and make it a takeover target. To avoid this possibility, he urges Brad Ellis, controller, in making this period's year-end adjusting entries to accrue every possible revenue and to defer as many expenses as possible. The president says to Brad, "We need the revenues this year, and next year we can easily absorb expenses deferred from this year. We can't let our stock price be hammered down!" Brad didn't get around to recording the adjusting entries until January 17, but she dated the entries December 31 as if they were recorded then. Brad also made every effort to comply with the president's request.

*Instructions*
(a) Who are the stakeholders in this situation?
(b) What are the ethical considerations of the president's request and Brad's dating the adjusting entries December 31?
(c) Can Brad accrue revenues and defer expenses and still be ethical?

## "ALL ABOUT YOU" ACTIVITY

BYP4-9   Companies prepare balance sheets in order to know their financial position at a specific point in time. This enables them to make a comparison to their position at previous points in time and gives them a basis for planning for the future. In order to evaluate *your* financial position, you can prepare a personal balance sheet. Assume that you have compiled the following information regarding your finances. (*Hint:* Some of the items might not be used in your personal balance sheet.)

| | |
|---|---:|
| Amount owed on student loan balance (long-term) | $5,000 |
| Balance in checking account | 1,200 |
| Certificate of deposit (6-month) | 3,000 |
| Annual earnings from part-time job | 11,300 |
| Automobile | 7,000 |
| Balance on automobile loan (current portion) | 1,500 |
| Balance on automobile loan (long-term portion) | 4,000 |
| Home computer | 800 |
| Amount owed to you by younger brother | 300 |
| Balance in money market account | 1,800 |
| Annual tuition | 6,400 |
| Video and stereo equipment | 1,250 |
| Balance owed on credit card (current portion) | 150 |
| Balance owed on credit card (long-term portion) | 1,650 |

*Instructions*

Prepare a personal balance sheet using the format you have learned for a classified balance sheet for a company. For the equity account, use M. Y. Own, Capital.

## FASB CODIFICATION ACTIVITY

**BYP4-10** If your school has a subscription to the FASB Codification, go to **http://aaahq.org/ ascLogin.cfm** to log in and prepare responses to the following.

*Instructions*

Access the glossary ("Master Glossary") to answer the following.
(a) What is the definition of revenue?
(b) What is the definition of compensation?

## Answers to Insight and Accounting Across the Organization Questions

**p. 166 Cooking the Books? Q:** What motivates sales executives and finance and accounting executives to participate in activities that result in inaccurate reporting of revenues? **A:** Sales executives typically receive bonuses based on their ability to meet quarterly sales targets. In addition, they often face the possibility of losing their jobs if they miss those targets. Executives in accounting and finance are very aware of the earnings targets of Wall Street analysts and investors. If they fail to meet these targets, the company's stock price will fall. As a result of these pressures, executives sometimes knowingly engage in unethical efforts to misstate revenues. As a result of the Sarbanes-Oxley Act of 2002, the penalties for such behavior are now much more severe.

**p. 167 Reporting Revenue Accurately Q:** In the past, why was it argued that Apple should spread the recognition of iPhone revenue over a two-year period, rather than recording it upfront? **A:** Apple promises to provide software updates over the life of the phone's use. Because this represents an unfulfilled service obligation, it was argued that Apple should spread its revenue recognition over a two-year estimated life of the phone.

**p. 174 Turning Gift Cards into Revenue Q:** Suppose that Robert Jones purchases a $100 gift card at Best Buy on December 24, 2011, and gives it to his wife, Mary Jones, on December 25, 2011. On January 3, 2012, Mary uses the card to purchase $100 worth of CDs. When do you think Best Buy should recognize revenue and why? **A:** According to the revenue recognition principle, companies should recognize revenue when earned. In this case, revenue is not earned until Best Buy provides the goods. Thus, when Best Buy receives cash in exchange for the gift card on December 24, 2011, it should recognize a liability, Unearned Revenue, for $100. On January 3, 2012, when Mary Jones exchanges the card for merchandise, Best Buy should recognize revenue and eliminate $100 from the balance in the Unearned Revenue account.

**p. 178 Cashing In on Accrual Accounting Q:** Accrual accounting is often considered superior to cash accounting. Why, then, were some people critical of China's use of accrual accounting in this instance? **A:** In this case, some people were critical because, in general, China uses cash accounting. By switching to accrual accounting for this transaction, China was not being consistent in its accounting practices. Lack of consistency reduces the transparency and usefulness of accounting information.

## Answers to Self-Test Questions

**1.** c   **2.** a   **3.** d   **4.** d   **5.** d   **6.** c ($1,350 − $600 = $750)   **7.** a   **8.** c   **9.** c   **10.** b   **11.** b   **12.** c
**13.** a   **14.** a   **15.** d

 **A Look at IFRS**

It is often difficult for companies to determine in what time period they should report particular revenues and expenses. Both the IASB and FASB are working on a joint project to develop a common conceptual framework, as well as a revenue recognition project, that will enable companies to better use the same principles to record transactions consistently over time.

## KEY POINTS

- In this chapter, you learned accrual-basis accounting applied under GAAP. Companies applying IFRS also use accrual-basis accounting to ensure that they record transactions that change a company's financial statements in the period in which events occur.
- Similar to GAAP, cash-basis accounting is not in accordance with IFRS.
- IFRS also divides the economic life of companies into artificial time periods. Under both GAAP and IFRS, this is referred to as the *periodicity assumption*.
- IFRS requires that companies present a complete set of financial statements, including comparative information annually.
- GAAP has more than 100 rules dealing with revenue recognition. Many of these rules are industry-specific. In contrast, revenue recognition under IFRS is determined primarily by a single standard. Despite this large disparity in the amount of detailed guidance devoted to revenue recognition, the **general** revenue recognition principles required by GAAP that are used in this textbook are similar to those under IFRS.
- As the Feature Story illustrates, revenue recognition fraud is a major issue in U.S. financial reporting. The same situation occurs in other countries, as evidenced by revenue recognition breakdowns at Dutch software company Baan NV, Japanese electronics giant NEC, and Dutch grocer AHold NV.
- A specific standard exists for revenue recognition under IFRS *(IAS 18)*. In general, the standard is based on the **probability that the economic benefits associated with the transaction will flow to the company** selling the goods, providing the service, or receiving investment income. In addition, the revenues and costs **must be capable of being measured reliably**. GAAP uses concepts such as *realized*, *realizable* (that is, it is received, or expected to be received), and *earned* as a basis for revenue recognition.
- Under IFRS, revaluation of items such as land and buildings is permitted. IFRS allows depreciation based on revaluation of assets, which is not permitted under GAAP.
- The terminology used for revenues and gains, and expenses and losses, differs somewhat between IFRS and GAAP. For example, income is defined as:

    Increases in economic benefits during the accounting period in the form of inflows or enhancements of assets or decreases of liabilities that result in increases in equity, other than those relating to contributions from shareholders.

Income includes *both* revenues, which arise during the normal course of operating activities, and gains, which arise from activities outside of the normal sales of goods and services. The term income is not used this way under GAAP. Instead, under GAAP income refers to the net difference between revenues and expenses. Expenses are defined as:

    Decreases in economic benefits during the accounting period in the form of outflows or depletions of assets or incurrences of liabilities that result in decreases in equity other than those relating to distributions to shareholders.

Note that under IFRS, expenses include both those costs incurred in the normal course of operations, as well as losses that are not part of normal operations. This in contrast to GAAP, which defines each separately.

- The procedures of the closing process are applicable to all companies whether they are using IFRS or GAAP.

## LOOKING TO THE FUTURE

The IASB and FASB are now involved in a joint project on revenue recognition. The purpose of this project is to develop comprehensive guidance on when to recognize revenue. Presently, the Boards are considering an approach that focuses on changes in assets and liabilities (rather than on earned and realized) as the basis for revenue recognition. It is hoped that this approach will lead to more consistent accounting in this area. For more on this topic, see *www.fasb.org/project/revenue_recognition.shtml*.

## IFRS Self-Test Questions

1. GAAP:
   (a) provides very detailed, industry-specific guidance on revenue recognition, compared to the general guidance provided by IFRS.
   (b) provides only general guidance on revenue recognition, compared to the detailed guidance provided by IFRS.
   (c) allows revenue to be recognized when a customer makes an order.
   (d) requires that revenue not be recognized until cash is received.
2. Which of the following statements is *false*?
   (a) IFRS employs the periodicity assumption.
   (b) IFRS employs accrual accounting.
   (c) IFRS requires that revenues and costs must be capable of being measured reliably.
   (d) IFRS uses the cash basis of accounting.
3. As a result of the revenue recognition project being undertaken by the FASB and IASB:
   (a) revenue recognition will place more emphasis on when revenue is earned.
   (b) revenue recognition will place more emphasis on when revenue is realized.
   (c) revenue recognition will place more emphasis on when changes occur in assets and liabilities.
   (d) revenue will no longer be recorded unless cash has been received.
4. Which of the following is *false*?
   (a) Under IFRS, the term *income* describes both revenues and gains.
   (b) Under IFRS, the term *expenses* includes losses.
   (c) Under IFRS, firms do not engage in the closing process.
   (d) IFRS has fewer standards than GAAP that address revenue recognition.
5. Accrual-basis accounting:
   (a) is optional under IFRS.
   (b) results in companies recording transactions that change a company's financial statements in the period in which events occur.
   (c) will likely be eliminated as a result of the IASB/FASB joint project on revenue recognition.
   (d) is not consistent with the IASB conceptual framework.

## IFRS Concepts and Application

**IFRS4-1**  Compare and contrast the rules regarding revenue recognition under IFRS versus GAAP.

**IFRS4-2**  Under IFRS, do the definitions of revenues and expenses include gains and losses? Explain.

## INTERNATIONAL FINANCIAL REPORTING PROBLEM: *Zetar plc*

**IFRS4-3**  The financial statements of Zetar plc are presented in Appendix C. The company's complete annual report, including the notes to its financial statements, is available at **www.zetarplc.com**. Visit Zetar's corporate website and answer the following questions from Zetar's 2009 annual report.
   (a) From the notes to the financial statements, how does the company determine the amount of revenue to record at the time of a sale?
   (b) From the notes to the financial statements, how does the company determine whether a sale has occurred?
   (c) Using the consolidated income statement and consolidated statement of financial position, identify items that may result in adjusting entries for deferrals.
   (d) Using the consolidated income statement, identify two items that may result in adjusting entries for accruals.

## Answers to IFRS Self-Test Questions

1. a  2. d  3. c  4. c  5. b

**Remember to go back to the navigator box on the chapter opening page and check off your completed work.**

chapter 5

# MERCHANDISING OPERATIONS AND THE MULTIPLE-STEP INCOME STATEMENT

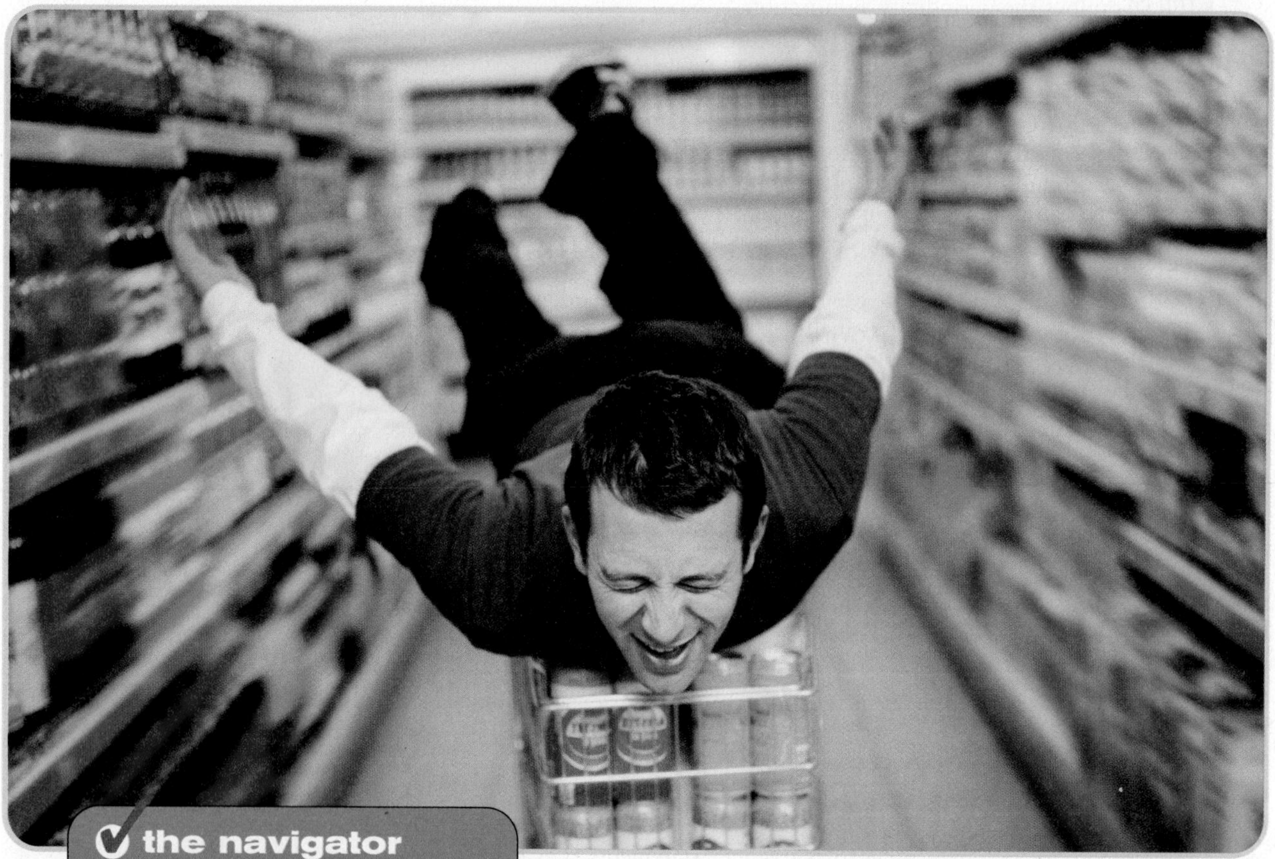

## the navigator

- Scan Study Objectives ○
- Read Feature Story ○
- Scan Preview ○
- Read Text and Answer **Do it!** p. 235 ○ p. 239 ○ p. 243 ○ p. 245 ○
- Work Using the Decision Toolkit ○
- Review Summary of Study Objectives ○
- Work Comprehensive **Do it!** p. 254 ○
- Answer Self-Test Questions ○
- Complete Assignments ○
- Go to WileyPLUS for practice and tutorials ○
- Read A Look at IFRS p. 276 ○

## study objectives

**After studying this chapter, you should be able to:**

1 Identify the differences between a service company and a merchandising company.

2 Explain the recording of purchases under a perpetual inventory system.

3 Explain the recording of sales revenues under a perpetual inventory system.

4 Distinguish between a single-step and a multiple-step income statement.

5 Determine cost of goods sold under a periodic system.

6 Explain the factors affecting profitability.

7 Identify a quality of earnings indicator.

the navigator

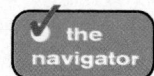

In his book *The End of Work,* Jeremy Rifkin notes that until the 20th century the word *consumption* evoked negative images; to be labeled a "consumer" was an insult. (In fact, one of the deadliest diseases in history, tuberculosis, was often referred to as "consumption.") Twentieth-century merchants realized, however, that in order to prosper, they had to convince people of the need for things not previously needed. For example, General Motors made annual changes in its cars so that people would be discontented with the cars they already owned. Thus began consumerism.

## WHO DOESN'T SHOP AT WAL-MART?

Today, consumption describes the U.S. lifestyle in a nutshell. We consume twice as much today per person as we did at the end of World War II. The amount of U.S. retail space per person is vastly greater than that of any other country. It appears that we live to shop.

The first great retail giant was Sears, Roebuck. It started as a catalog company enabling people in rural areas to buy things by mail. For decades it was the uncontested merchandising leader.

Today, Wal-Mart is the undisputed champion provider of basic (and perhaps not-so-basic) human needs. Wal-Mart opened its first store in 1962, and it now has almost 8,000 stores, serving more than 100 million customers every week. A key cause of Wal-Mart's incredible growth is its amazing system of inventory control and distribution. Wal-Mart has a management information system that employs six satellite channels, from which company computers receive 8.4 million updates every minute on what items customers buy and the relationship among items sold to each person.

Measured by sales revenues, Wal-Mart is the largest company in the world. In six years, it went from selling almost no groceries to being America's largest grocery retailer.

It would appear that things have never looked better at Wal-Mart. On the other hand, a *Wall Street Journal* article, entitled "How to Sell More to Those Who Think It's Cool to Be Frugal," suggests that consumerism as a way of life might be dying. Don't bet your high-definition 3D TV on it though.

✔ **the navigator**

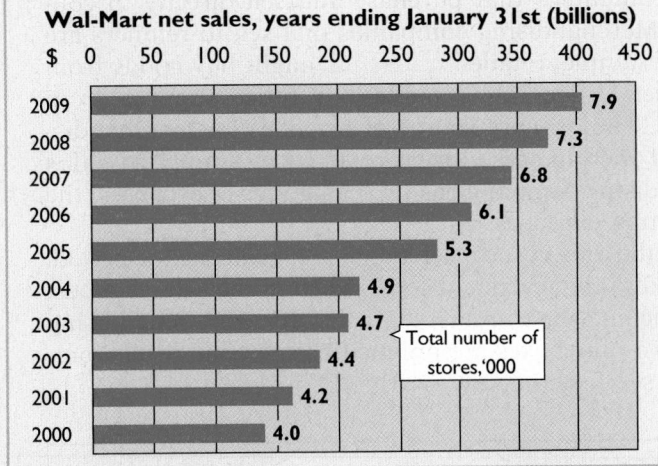

**Wal-Mart net sales, years ending January 31st (billions)**

| Year | Net sales | Total number of stores, '000 |
|------|-----------|------------------------------|
| 2009 | | 7.9 |
| 2008 | | 7.3 |
| 2007 | | 6.8 |
| 2006 | | 6.1 |
| 2005 | | 5.3 |
| 2004 | | 4.9 |
| 2003 | | 4.7 |
| 2002 | | 4.4 |
| 2001 | | 4.2 |
| 2000 | | 4.0 |

*Source:* "How Big Can It Grow?" *The Economist* (April 17, 2004), pp. 67–69, and *www.walmart.com* (accessed March 17, 2008).

## INSIDE CHAPTER 5 . . .

Merchandising is one of the largest and most influential industries in the United States. It is likely that a number of you will work for a merchandiser. Therefore, understanding the financial statements of merchandising companies is important. In this chapter, you will learn the basics about reporting merchandising transactions. In addition, you will learn how to prepare and analyze a commonly used form of the income statement—the multiple-step income statement. The content and organization of the chapter are as follows.

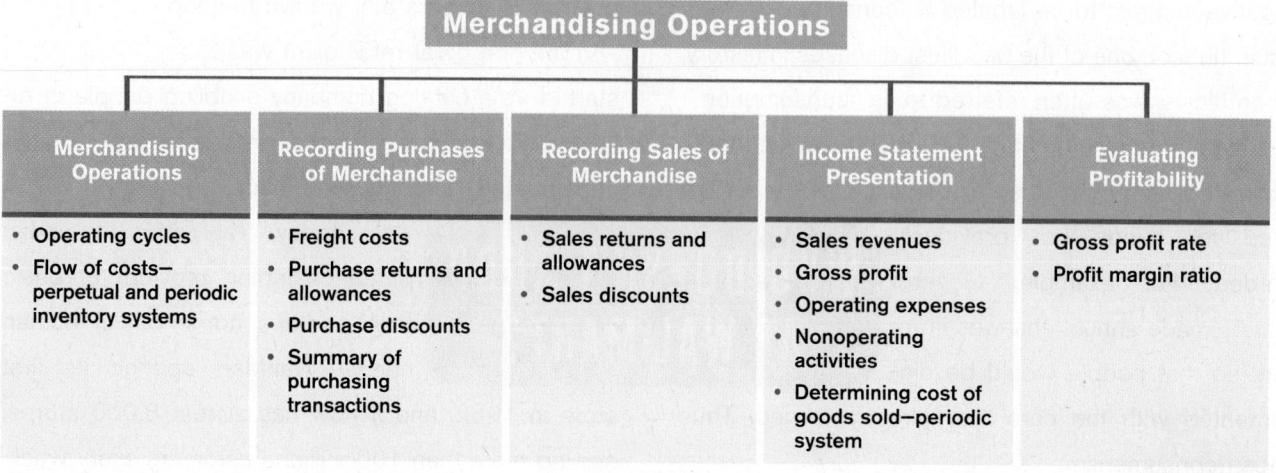

# Merchandising Operations

Wal-Mart, Kmart, and Target are called merchandising companies because they buy and sell merchandise rather than perform services as their primary source of revenue. Merchandising companies that purchase and sell directly to consumers are called **retailers**. Merchandising companies that sell to retailers are known as **wholesalers**. For example, retailer Walgreens might buy goods from wholesaler McKesson; retailer Office Depot might buy office supplies from wholesaler United Stationers. The primary source of revenues for merchandising companies is the sale of merchandise, often referred to simply as **sales revenue** or **sales**. A merchandising company has two categories of expenses: the cost of goods sold and operating expenses.

The **cost of goods sold** is the total cost of merchandise sold during the period. This expense is directly related to the revenue recognized from the sale of goods. Illustration 5-1 shows the income measurement process for a merchandising company. The items in the two blue boxes are unique to a merchandising company; they are not used by a service company.

**Illustration 5-1** Income measurement process for a merchandising company

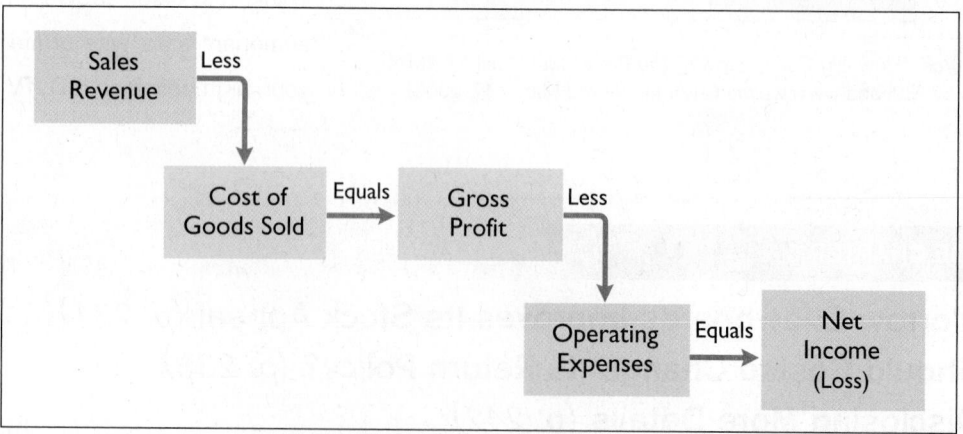

## OPERATING CYCLES

The operating cycle of a merchandising company ordinarily is longer than that of a service company. The purchase of merchandise inventory and its eventual sale lengthen the cycle. Illustration 5-2 contrasts the operating cycles of service and merchandising companies. Note that the added asset account for a merchandising company is the Inventory account.

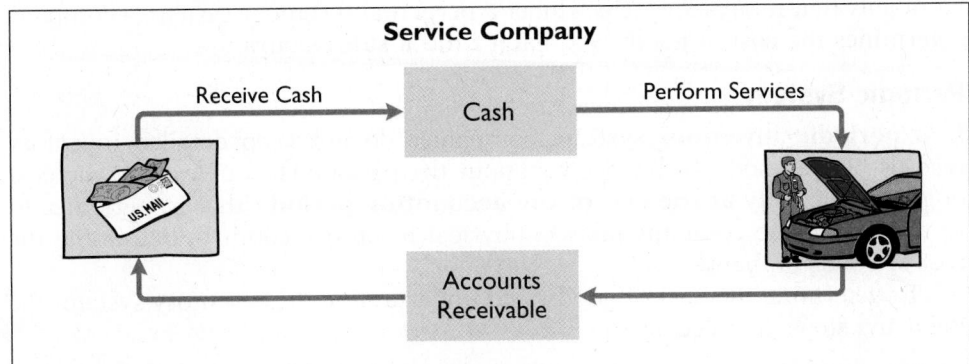

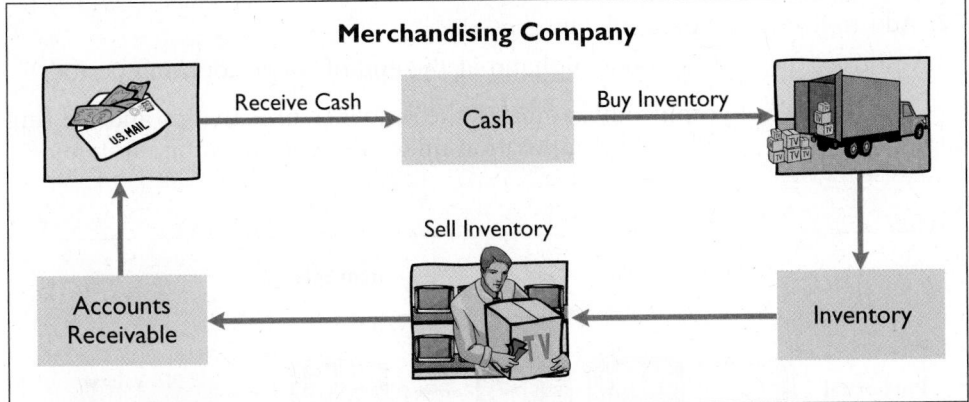

## FLOW OF COSTS

The flow of costs for a merchandising company is as follows: Beginning inventory plus the cost of goods purchased is the cost of goods available for sale. As goods are sold, they are assigned to cost of goods sold. Those goods that are not sold by the end of the accounting period represent ending inventory. Illustration 5-3 describes these relationships. Companies use one of two systems to account for inventory: a **perpetual inventory system** or a **periodic inventory system**.

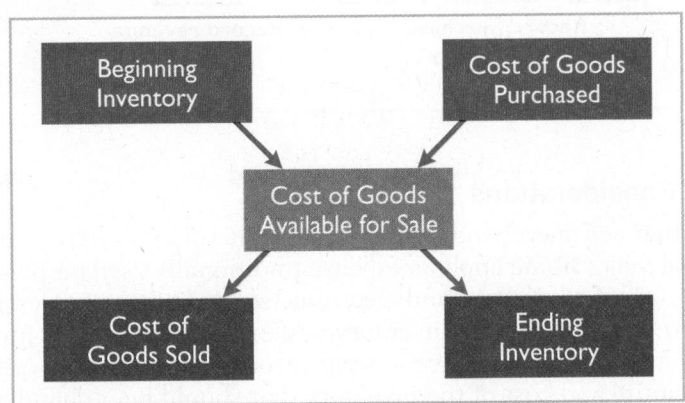

**Illustration 5-3**   Flow of costs

### Perpetual System

In a **perpetual inventory system**, companies maintain detailed records of the cost of each inventory purchase and sale. These records continuously—perpetually—show the inventory that should be on hand for every item. For example, a Ford dealership has separate inventory records for each automobile, truck, and van on its lot and showroom floor. Similarly, a grocery store uses bar codes and optical scanners to keep a daily running record of every box of cereal and every jar of jelly that it buys and sells. Under a perpetual inventory system, a company determines the cost of goods sold **each time a sale occurs**.

### Periodic System

In a **periodic inventory system**, companies do not keep detailed inventory records of the goods on hand throughout the period. They determine the cost of goods sold **only at the end of the accounting period**—that is, periodically. At that point, the company takes a physical inventory count to determine the cost of goods on hand.

To determine the cost of goods sold under a periodic inventory system, the following steps are necessary:

1. Determine the cost of goods on hand at the beginning of the accounting period.
2. Add to it the cost of goods purchased.
3. Subtract the cost of goods on hand at the end of the accounting period.

Illustration 5-4 graphically compares the sequence of activities and the timing of the cost of goods sold computation under the two inventory systems.

**Illustration 5-4**
Comparing perpetual and periodic inventory systems

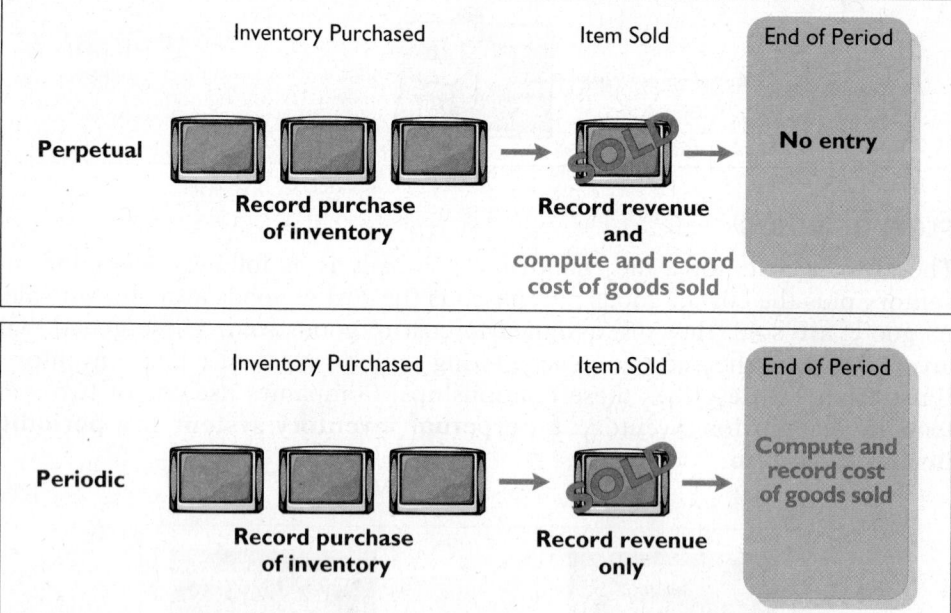

### Additional Considerations

Companies that sell merchandise with high unit values, such as automobiles, furniture, and major home appliances, have traditionally used perpetual systems. The growing use of computers and electronic scanners has enabled many more companies to install perpetual inventory systems. The perpetual inventory system is so named because the accounting records continuously—perpetually—show the quantity and cost of the inventory that should be on hand at any time.

A perpetual inventory system provides better control over inventories than a periodic system. Since the inventory records show the quantities that should be on hand, the company can count the goods at any time to see whether the amount of goods actually on hand agrees with the inventory records. If shortages are uncovered, the company can investigate immediately. Although a perpetual inventory system requires additional clerical work and additional cost to maintain inventory records, a computerized system can minimize this cost. As noted in the Feature Story, much of Wal-Mart's success is attributed to its sophisticated inventory system.

Some businesses find it either unnecessary or uneconomical to invest in a sophisticated, computerized perpetual inventory system such as Wal-Mart's. However, many small merchandising businesses, in particular, find that basic computerized accounting packages provide some of the essential benefits of a perpetual inventory system. Yet, managers of some small businesses still find that they can control their merchandise and manage day-to-day operations using a periodic inventory system.

Because the perpetual inventory system is growing in popularity and use, we illustrate it in this chapter. An appendix to this chapter describes the journal entries for the periodic system.

---

### Investor Insight

#### Morrow Snowboards Improves Its Stock Appeal

Investors are often eager to invest in a company that has a hot new product. However, when snowboard maker Morrow Snowboards, Inc., issued shares of stock to the public for the first time, some investors expressed reluctance to invest in Morrow because of a number of accounting control problems. To reduce investor concerns, Morrow implemented a perpetual inventory system to improve its control over inventory. In addition, it stated that it would perform a physical inventory count every quarter until it felt that the perpetual inventory system was reliable.

**?** If a perpetual system keeps track of inventory on a daily basis, why do companies ever need to do a physical count? (See page 276.)

---

## Recording Purchases of Merchandise

Companies may purchase inventory for cash or on account (credit). They normally record purchases when they receive the goods from the seller. Every purchase should be supported by business documents that provide written evidence of the transaction. Each cash purchase should be supported by a canceled check or a cash register receipt indicating the items purchased and amounts paid. Companies record cash purchases by an increase in Inventory and a decrease in Cash.

Each purchase should be supported by a **purchase invoice**, which indicates the total purchase price and other relevant information. However, the purchaser does not prepare a separate purchase invoice. Instead, the purchaser uses as a purchase invoice the copy of the sales invoice sent by the seller. In Illustration 5-5 (page 232), for example, Sauk Stereo (the buyer) uses as a purchase invoice the sales invoice prepared by PW Audio Supply, Inc. (the seller).

The associated entry for Sauk Stereo for the invoice from PW Audio Supply increases Inventory and increases Accounts Payable.

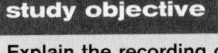

**study objective** 2

Explain the recording of purchases under a perpetual inventory system.

| | | | | |
|---|---|---|---|---|
| May 4 | Inventory | | 3,800 | |
| | Accounts Payable | | | 3,800 |
| | (To record goods purchased on account from PW Audio Supply) | | | |

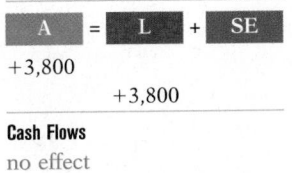

| A | = | L | + | SE |
|---|---|---|---|---|
| +3,800 | | | | |
| | | | | +3,800 |

**Cash Flows**
no effect

**Illustration 5-5** Sales invoice used as purchase invoice by Sauk Stereo

**Helpful Hint** To better understand the contents of this invoice, identify these items:
1. Seller
2. Invoice date
3. Purchaser
4. Salesperson
5. Credit terms
6. Freight terms
7. Goods sold: catalog number, description, quantity, price per unit
8. Total invoice amount

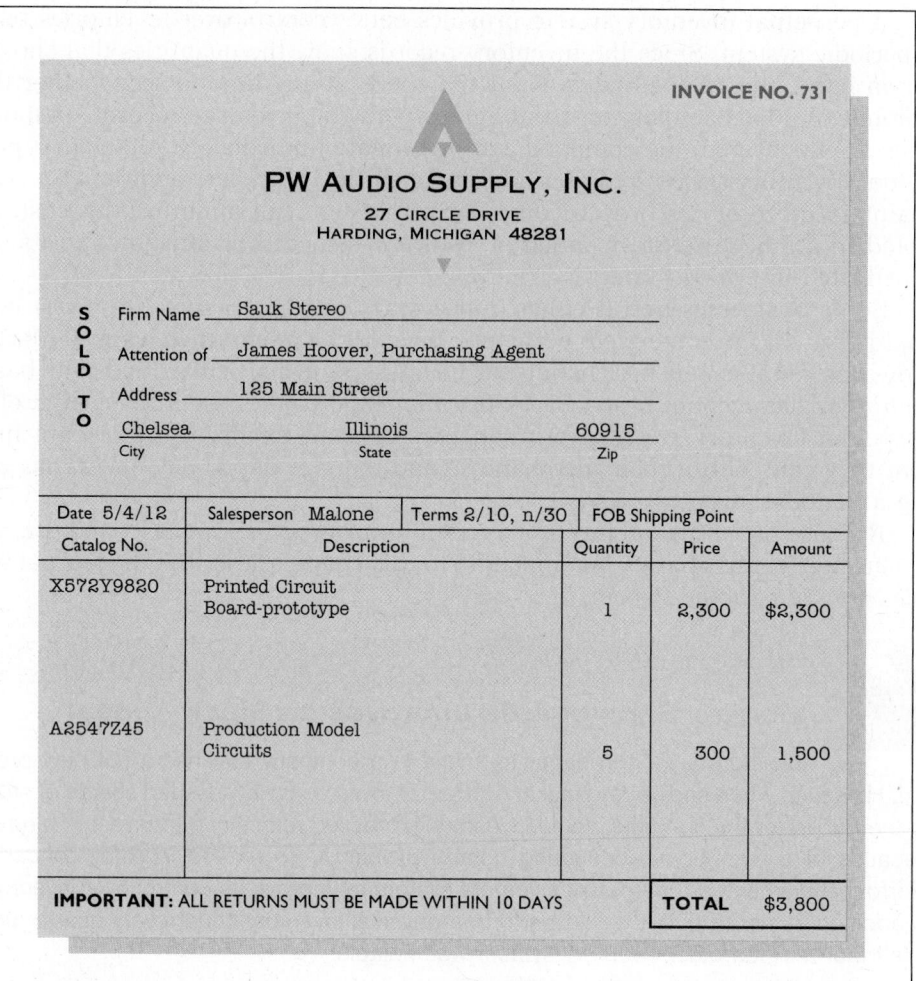

INVOICE NO. 731

# PW AUDIO SUPPLY, INC.
### 27 CIRCLE DRIVE
### HARDING, MICHIGAN 48281

**SOLD TO**

Firm Name ___Sauk Stereo___

Attention of ___James Hoover, Purchasing Agent___

Address ___125 Main Street___

Chelsea / Illinois / 60915
City / State / Zip

| Date 5/4/12 | Salesperson Malone | Terms 2/10, n/30 | FOB Shipping Point | | |
|---|---|---|---|---|---|
| Catalog No. | Description | | Quantity | Price | Amount |
| X572Y9820 | Printed Circuit Board-prototype | | 1 | 2,300 | $2,300 |
| A2547Z45 | Production Model Circuits | | 5 | 300 | 1,500 |

**IMPORTANT:** ALL RETURNS MUST BE MADE WITHIN 10 DAYS | **TOTAL** | $3,800

Under the perpetual inventory system, companies record purchases of merchandise for sale in the Inventory account. Thus, Wal-Mart would increase (debit) Inventory for clothing, sporting goods, and anything else purchased for resale to customers. Not all purchases are debited to Inventory, however. Companies record purchases of assets acquired for use and not for resale, such as supplies, equipment, and similar items, as increases to specific asset accounts rather than to Inventory. For example, to record the purchase of materials used to make shelf signs or for cash register receipt paper, Wal-Mart would increase (debit) Supplies.

## FREIGHT COSTS

The sales agreement should indicate who—the seller or the buyer—is to pay for transporting the goods to the buyer's place of business. When a common carrier such as a railroad, trucking company, or airline transports the goods, the carrier prepares a freight bill in accord with the sales agreement.

Freight terms are expressed as either FOB shipping point or FOB destination. The letters FOB mean **free on board**. Thus, **FOB shipping point** means that the seller places the goods free on board the carrier, and the buyer pays the freight costs. Conversely, **FOB destination** means that the seller places the goods free on board to the buyer's place of business, and the seller pays the freight. For example, the sales invoice in Illustration 5-5 indicates FOB shipping point.

Thus, the buyer (Sauk Stereo) pays the freight charges. Illustration 5-6 illustrates these shipping terms.

**Illustration 5-6** Shipping terms

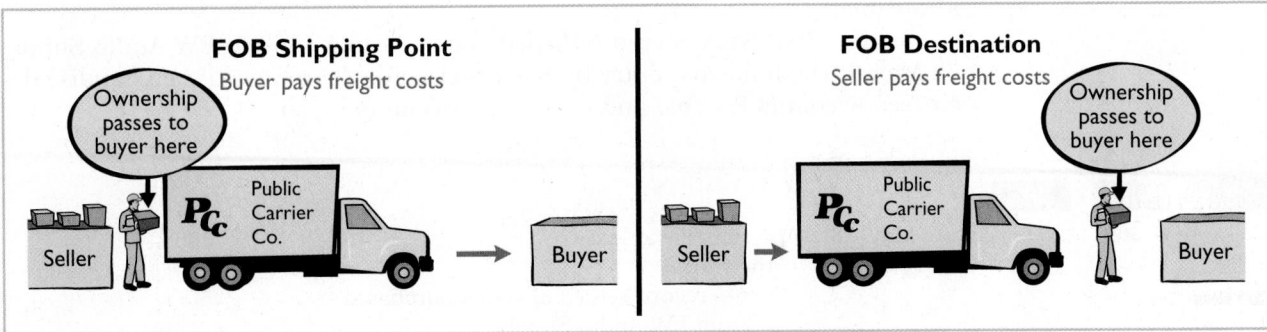

### Freight Costs Incurred by Buyer

When the buyer pays the transportation costs, these costs are considered part of the cost of purchasing inventory. As a result, the account **Inventory is increased**. For example, if Sauk Stereo (the buyer) pays Haul-It Freight Company $150 for freight charges on May 6, the entry on Sauk Stereo's books is:

| | | | | |
|---|---|---|---|---|
| May 6 | Inventory | | 150 | |
| | Cash | | | 150 |
| | (To record payment of freight on goods purchased) | | | |

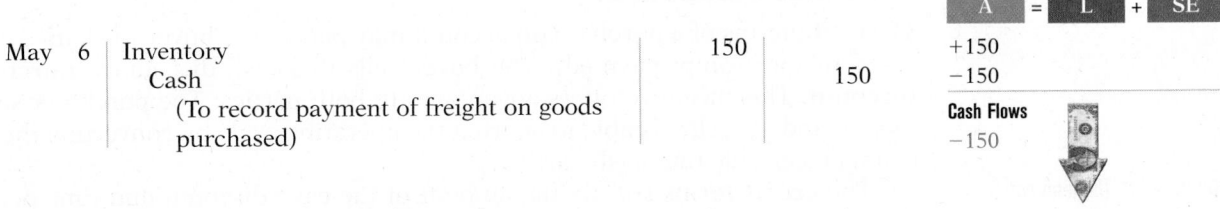

Thus, any freight costs incurred by the buyer are part of the cost of merchandise purchased. The reason: Inventory cost should include any freight charges necessary to deliver the goods to the buyer.

### Freight Costs Incurred by Seller

In contrast, **freight costs incurred by the seller on outgoing merchandise are an operating expense to the seller**. These costs increase an expense account titled Freight-out or Delivery Expense. For example, if the freight terms on the invoice in Illustration 5-5 had required that PW Audio Supply (the seller) pay the $150 freight charges, the entry by PW Audio Supply would be:

| | | | | |
|---|---|---|---|---|
| May 4 | Freight-out | | 150 | |
| | Cash | | | 150 |
| | (To record payment of freight on goods sold) | | | |

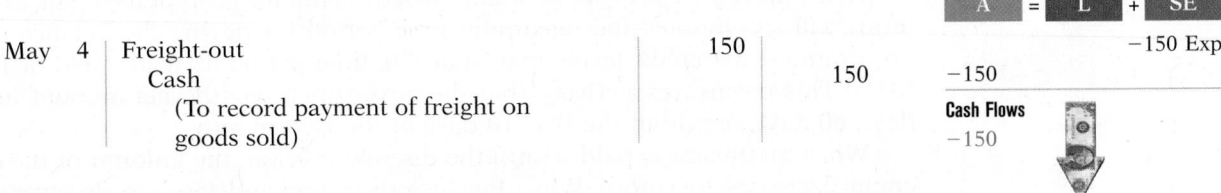

When the seller pays the freight charges, the seller will usually establish a higher invoice price for the goods, to cover the expense of shipping.

### PURCHASE RETURNS AND ALLOWANCES

A purchaser may be dissatisfied with the merchandise received because the goods are damaged or defective, of inferior quality, or do not meet the purchaser's specifications. In such cases, the purchaser may return the goods to the seller for credit if the sale was made on credit, or for a cash refund if the purchase was for cash. This transaction is known as a **purchase return**. Alternatively, the purchaser may choose to keep the merchandise if the seller is willing to grant a reduction of the purchase price. This transaction is known as a **purchase allowance**.

Assume that Sauk Stereo returned goods costing $300 to PW Audio Supply on May 8. The following entry by Sauk Stereo for the returned merchandise decreases Accounts Payable and decreases Inventory.

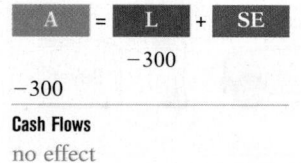

-300
-300
**Cash Flows**
no effect

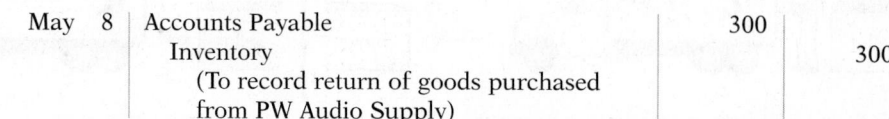

| May | 8 | Accounts Payable | 300 | |
| | | Inventory | | 300 |
| | | (To record return of goods purchased from PW Audio Supply) | | |

Because Sauk Stereo increased Inventory when the goods were received, Inventory is decreased (credited) when Sauk Stereo returns the goods.

Suppose instead that Sauk Stereo chose to keep the goods after being granted a $50 allowance (reduction in price). It would reduce (debit) Accounts Payable and reduce (credit) Inventory for $50.

### PURCHASE DISCOUNTS

The credit terms of a purchase on account may permit the buyer to claim a cash discount for prompt payment. The buyer calls this cash discount a **purchase discount**. This incentive offers advantages to both parties: The purchaser saves money, and the seller is able to shorten the operating cycle by converting the accounts receivable into cash earlier.

The **credit terms** specify the amount of the cash discount and time period during which it is offered. They also indicate the length of time in which the purchaser is expected to pay the full invoice price. In the sales invoice in Illustration 5-5 (page 232), credit terms are 2/10, n/30, which is read "two-ten, net thirty." This means that a 2% cash discount may be taken on the invoice price less ("net of") any returns or allowances, if payment is made within 10 days of the invoice date (the **discount period**). Otherwise, the invoice price, less any returns or allowances, is due 30 days from the invoice date. Alternatively, the discount period may extend to a specified number of days following the month in which the sale occurs. For example, 1/10 EOM (end of month) means that a 1% discount is available if the invoice is paid within the first 10 days of the next month.

When the seller elects not to offer a cash discount for prompt payment, credit terms will specify only the maximum time period for paying the balance due. For example, the credit terms may state the time period as n/30, n/60, or n/10 EOM. This means, respectively, that the buyer must pay the net amount in 30 days, 60 days, or within the first 10 days of the next month.

When an invoice is paid within the discount period, the amount of the discount decreases Inventory. Why? Because the merchandiser records inventory at its cost and, by paying within the discount period, it has reduced that cost. To illustrate, assume Sauk Stereo pays the balance due of $3,500 (gross invoice price of $3,800 less purchase returns and allowances of $300) on May 14, the last day of the discount period. The cash discount is $70 ($3,500 × 2%), and the amount of cash Sauk Stereo paid is $3,430 ($3,500 − $70). The entry Sauk Stereo makes to record its May 14 payment decreases (debits) Accounts Payable by the amount of the gross invoice price, reduces (credits) Inventory by the $70 discount, and reduces (credits) Cash by the net amount owed.

**Helpful Hint** The term *net* in "net 30" means the remaining amount due after subtracting any returns and allowances and partial payments.

| May 14 | Accounts Payable | 3,500 | |
| | Cash | | 3,430 |
| | Inventory | | 70 |
| | (To record payment within discount period) | | |

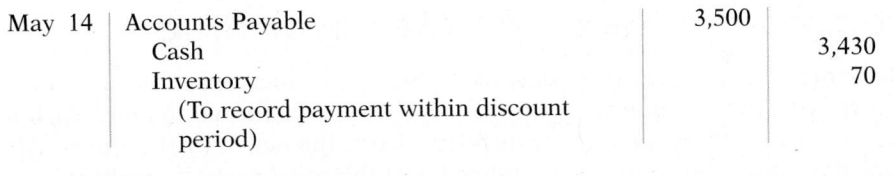

If Sauk Stereo failed to take the discount and instead made full payment of $3,500 on June 3, Sauk Stereo would reduce (debit) Accounts Payable and reduce (credit) Cash for $3,500 each.

| June 3 | Accounts Payable | 3,500 | |
| | Cash | | 3,500 |
| | (To record payment with no discount taken) | | |

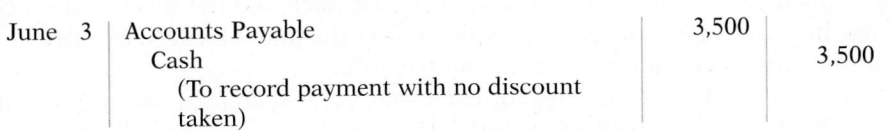

A merchandising company usually should take all available discounts. Passing up the discount may be viewed as **paying interest** for use of the money. For example, passing up the discount offered by PW Audio Supply would be like Sauk Stereo paying an interest rate of 2% for the use of $3,500 for 20 days. This is the equivalent of an annual interest rate of approximately 36.5% (2% × 365/20). Obviously, it would be better for Sauk Stereo to borrow at prevailing bank interest rates of 6% to 10% than to lose the discount.

### SUMMARY OF PURCHASING TRANSACTIONS

The following T account (with transaction descriptions in blue) provides a summary of the effect of the previous transactions on Inventory. Sauk Stereo originally purchased $3,800 worth of inventory for resale. It then returned $300 of goods. It paid $150 in freight charges, and finally, it received a $70 discount off the balance owed because it paid within the discount period. This results in a balance in Inventory of $3,580.

| | Inventory | | | |
|---|---|---|---|---|
| Purchase | May 4 | 3,800 | May 8    300 | Purchase return |
| Freight-in | 6 | 150 | 14    70 | Purchase discount |
| Balance | | 3,580 | | |

*before you go on...*

---

**Do it!**   On September 5, De La Hoya Company buys merchandise on account from Junot Diaz Company. The selling price of the goods is $1,500. On September 8, De La Hoya returns defective goods with a selling price of $200. Record the transactions on the books of De La Hoya Company.

**PURCHASE TRANSACTIONS**

**Action Plan**

- Purchaser records goods at cost.
- When goods are returned, purchaser reduces Inventory.

### Solution

| Sept. 5 | Inventory | 1,500 | |
| | Accounts Payable | | 1,500 |
| | (To record goods purchased on account) | | |
| 8 | Accounts Payable | 200 | |
| | Inventory | | 200 |
| | (To record return of defective goods) | | |

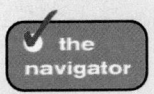
the navigator

Related exercise material: **BE5-4,** *Do it!* **5-1,** and **E5-1.**

# Recording Sales of Merchandise

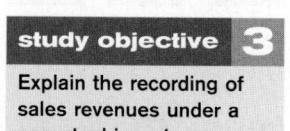

Companies record sales revenues, like service revenues, when earned, in compliance with the revenue recognition principle. Typically, companies earn sales revenues when the goods are transferred from the seller to the buyer. At this point the sales transaction is completed and the sales price is established.

Sales may be made on credit or for cash. Every sales transaction should be supported by a **business document** that provides written evidence of the sale. **Cash register tapes** provide evidence of cash sales. A sales invoice, like the one that was shown in Illustration 5-5 (page 232), provides support for each sale. The original copy of the invoice goes to the customer, and the seller keeps a copy for use in recording the sale. The invoice shows the date of sale, customer name, total sales price, and other relevant information.

The seller makes two entries for each sale: (1) It increases (debits) Accounts Receivable or Cash, as well as increases (credits) Sales Revenue. (2) It increases (debits) Cost of Goods Sold and decreases (credits) Inventory. As a result, the Inventory account will show at all times the amount of inventory that should be on hand.

To illustrate a credit sales transaction, PW Audio Supply records the sale of $3,800 on May 4 to Sauk Stereo (see Illustration 5-5) as follows (assume the merchandise cost PW Audio Supply $2,400).

| A | = | L | + | SE |
|---|---|---|---|---|
| +3,800 | | | | |
| | | | | +3,800 Rev |

**Cash Flows**
no effect

| May | 4 | Accounts Receivable | 3,800 | |
|---|---|---|---|---|
| | |    Sales Revenue | | 3,800 |
| | |    (To record credit sale to Sauk Stereo per invoice #731) | | |

| A | = | L | + | SE |
|---|---|---|---|---|
| | | | | −2,400 Exp |
| −2,400 | | | | |

**Cash Flows**
no effect

| | 4 | Cost of Goods Sold | 2,400 | |
|---|---|---|---|---|
| | |    Inventory | | 2,400 |
| | |    (To record cost of merchandise sold on invoice #731 to Sauk Stereo) | | |

**Helpful Hint** The merchandiser credits the Sales Revenue account only for sales of goods held for resale. Sales of assets not held for resale, such as equipment or land, are credited directly to the asset account.

For internal decision-making purposes, merchandising companies may use more than one sales account. For example, PW Audio Supply may decide to keep separate sales accounts for its sales of TV sets, DVD players, and microwave ovens. Wal-Mart might use separate accounts for sporting goods, children's clothing, and hardware—or it might have even more narrowly defined accounts. By using separate sales accounts for major product lines, rather than a single combined sales account, company management can monitor sales trends more closely and respond more strategically to changes in sales patterns. For example, if TV sales are increasing while microwave oven sales are decreasing, the company might reevaluate both its advertising and pricing policies on each of these items to ensure they are optimal.

**Ethics Note** Many companies are trying to improve the quality of their financial reporting. For example, General Electric now provides more detail on its revenues and operating profits.

On its income statement presented to outside investors a merchandising company would normally provide only a single sales figure—the sum of all of its individual sales accounts. This is done for two reasons. First, providing detail on all of its individual sales accounts would add considerable length to its income statement. Second, companies do not want their competitors to know the details of their operating results. However, at one time Microsoft expanded its disclosure of revenue from three to five types. The reason: The additional categories will better enable financial statement users to evaluate the growth of the company's consumer and Internet businesses.

## ANATOMY OF A FRAUD[1]

Holly Harmon was a cashier at a national superstore for only a short while when she began stealing merchandise using three methods. First, her husband or friends took UPC labels from cheaper items and put them on more expensive items. Holly then scanned the goods at the register. Second, Holly rang an item up but then voided the sale and left the merchandise in the shopping cart. A third approach was to put goods into large plastic containers. She rang up the plastic containers but not the goods within them. One day, Holly did not call in sick or show up for work. In such instances, the company reviews past surveillance tapes to look for suspicious activity by employees. This enabled the store to observe the thefts and to identify the participants.

**Total take: $12,000**

### THE MISSING CONTROLS

*Human resource controls.* A background check would have revealed Holly's previous criminal record. She would not have been hired as a cashier.

*Physical controls.* Software can flag high numbers of voided transactions or a high number of sales of low-priced goods. Random comparisons of video records with cash register records can ensure that the goods reported as sold on the register are the same goods that are shown being purchased on the video recording. Finally, employees should be aware that they are being monitored.

*Source:* Adapted from Wells, *Fraud Casebook* (2007), pp. 251–259.

## SALES RETURNS AND ALLOWANCES

We now look at the "flipside" of purchase returns and allowances, which the seller records as **sales returns and allowances**. These are transactions where the seller either accepts goods back from a purchaser (a return) or grants a reduction in the purchase price (an allowance) so that the buyer will keep the goods. PW Audio Supply's entries to record credit for returned goods involve (1) an increase (debit) in Sales Returns and Allowances (a contra account to Sales Revenue) and a decrease (credit) in Accounts Receivable at the $300 selling price, and (2) an increase (debit) in Inventory (assume a $140 cost) and a decrease (credit) in Cost of Goods Sold, as shown below. (We have assumed that the goods were not defective. If they were defective, PW Audio Supply would make an adjustment to the Inventory account to reflect their decline in value.)

| May 8 | Sales Returns and Allowances | 300 | |
| | Accounts Receivable | | 300 |
| | (To record credit granted to Sauk Stereo for returned goods) | | |
| 8 | Inventory | 140 | |
| | Cost of Goods Sold | | 140 |
| | (To record cost of goods returned) | | |

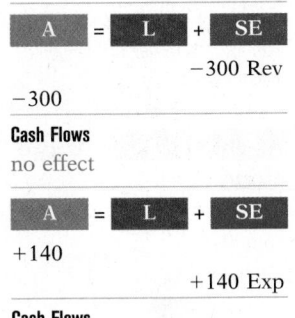

A = L + SE
−300        −300 Rev
**Cash Flows** no effect

A = L + SE
+140        +140 Exp
**Cash Flows** no effect

Suppose instead that the goods were not returned, but the seller granted the buyer an allowance by reducing the purchase price. In this case, the seller would debit Sales Returns and Allowances and credit Accounts Receivable for the amount of the allowance.

[1]The "Anatomy of a Fraud" stories in this textbook are adapted from *Fraud Casebook: Lessons from the Bad Side of Business,* edited by Joseph T. Wells (Hoboken, NJ: John Wiley & Sons, Inc., 2007). Used by permission. The names of some of the people and organizations in the stories are fictitious, but the facts in the stories are true.

As mentioned previously, Sales Returns and Allowances is a **contra revenue account** to Sales Revenue. The normal balance of Sales Returns and Allowances is a debit. Companies use a contra account, instead of debiting Sales Revenue, to disclose in the accounts and in the income statement the amount of sales returns and allowances. Disclosure of this information is important to management. Excessive returns and allowances suggest problems—inferior merchandise, inefficiencies in filling orders, errors in billing customers, or mistakes in delivery or shipment of goods. Moreover, a decrease (debit) recorded directly to Sales Revenue would obscure the relative importance of sales returns and allowances as a percentage of sales. It also could distort comparisons between total sales in different accounting periods.

## Accounting Across the Organization

### Should Costco Change Its Return Policy?

In most industries, sales returns are relatively minor. But returns of consumer electronics can really take a bite out of profits. Recently, the marketing executives at Costco Wholesale Corp. faced a difficult decision. Costco has always prided itself on its generous return policy. Most goods have had an unlimited grace period for returns. A new policy will require that certain electronics must be returned within 90 days of their purchase. The reason? The cost of returned products such as high-definition TVs, computers, and iPods cut an estimated 8¢ per share off Costco's earnings per share, which was $2.30.

*Source:* Kris Hudson, "Costco Tightens Policy on Returning Electronics," *Wall Street Journal* (February 27, 2007), p. B4.

 If a company expects significant returns, what are the implications for revenue recognition? (See page 276.)

## SALES DISCOUNTS

As mentioned in our discussion of purchase transactions, the seller may offer the customer a cash discount—called by the seller a **sales discount**—for the prompt payment of the balance due. Like a purchase discount, a sales discount is based on the invoice price less returns and allowances, if any. The seller increases (debits) the Sales Discounts account for discounts that are taken. The entry by PW Audio Supply to record the cash receipt on May 14 from Sauk Stereo within the discount period is:

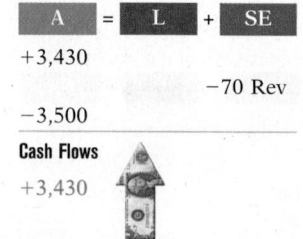

A = L + SE
+3,430
     −70 Rev
−3,500

**Cash Flows**
+3,430

| May 14 | Cash | 3,430 | |
| | Sales Discounts | 70 | |
| | Accounts Receivable | | 3,500 |
| | (To record collection within 2/10, n/30 | | |
| | discount period from Sauk Stereo) | | |

Like Sales Returns and Allowances, Sales Discounts is a **contra revenue account** to Sales Revenue. Its normal balance is a debit. Sellers use this account, instead of debiting sales, to disclose the amount of cash discounts taken by customers. If the customer does not take the discount, PW Audio Supply increases (debits) Cash for $3,500 and decreases (credits) Accounts Receivable for the same amount at the date of collection.

The following T accounts summarize the three sales-related transactions and show their combined effect on net sales.

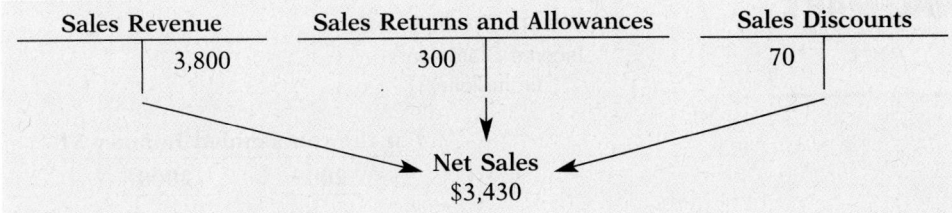

| Sales Revenue | Sales Returns and Allowances | Sales Discounts |
| --- | --- | --- |
| 3,800 | 300 | 70 |

Net Sales
$3,430

*before you go on...*

## Do it!

On September 5, De La Hoya Company buys merchandise on account from Junot Diaz Company. The selling price of the goods is $1,500, and the cost to Diaz Company was $800. On September 8, De La Hoya returns goods with a selling price of $200 and a cost of $105. Record the transactions on the books of Junot Diaz Company.

**SALES TRANSACTIONS**

### Solution

| | | | | |
| --- | --- | --- | --- | --- |
| Sept. | 5 | Accounts Receivable | 1,500 | |
| | |     Sales Revenue | | 1,500 |
| | |       (To record credit sale) | | |
| | 5 | Cost of Goods Sold | 800 | |
| | |     Inventory | | 800 |
| | |       (To record cost of goods sold on | | |
| | |       account) | | |
| Sept. | 8 | Sales Returns and Allowances | 200 | |
| | |     Accounts Receivable | | 200 |
| | |       (To record credit granted for receipt of | | |
| | |       returned goods) | | |
| | 8 | Inventory | 105 | |
| | |     Cost of Goods Sold | | 105 |
| | |       (To record cost of goods returned) | | |

### Action Plan

- Seller records both the sale and the cost of goods sold at the time of the sale.
- When goods are returned, the seller records the return in a contra account, Sales Returns and Allowances, and reduces Accounts Receivable.
- Any goods returned increase Inventory and reduce Cost of Goods Sold. The merchandise inventory should be recorded at its fair value (scrap value).

Related exercise material: **BE5-2, BE5-3, Do it! 5-2, E5-2, E5-3,** and **E5-4.**

# Income Statement Presentation

Companies widely use two forms of the income statement. One is the **single-step income statement**. The statement is so named because only one step, subtracting total expenses from total revenues, is required in determining net income (or net loss).

In a single-step statement, all data are classified into two categories: (1) **revenues**, which include both operating revenues and nonoperating revenues and gains (for example, interest revenue and gain on sale of equipment); and (2) **expenses**, which include cost of goods sold, operating expenses, and nonoperating expenses and losses (for example, interest expense, loss on sale of equipment, or income tax expense). The single-step income statement is the form we have used thus far in the text. Illustration 5-7 (page 240) shows a single-step statement for Wal-Mart.

There are two primary reasons for using the single-step form: (1) A company does not realize any type of profit or income until total revenues exceed total expenses, so it makes sense to divide the statement into these two categories. (2) The form is simple and easy to read.

**study objective 4**

Distinguish between a single-step and a multiple-step income statement.

**Illustration 5-7** Single-step income statements

**WAL-MART STORES, INC.**
Income Statements
(in millions)

| | 2009 | 2008 |
|---|---|---|
| **For the years ended January 31** | | |
| **Revenues** | | |
| Net sales | $401,244 | $374,307 |
| Other revenues | 4,363 | 4,169 |
| | 405,607 | 378,476 |
| **Expenses** | | |
| Cost of goods sold | 306,158 | 286,350 |
| Selling, general, and administrative expenses | 76,651 | 70,174 |
| Interest expense | 1,900 | 1,794 |
| Other expense | 353 | 538 |
| Income taxes | 7,145 | 6,889 |
| | 392,207 | 365,745 |
| **Net income** | $ 13,400 | $ 12,731 |

**International Note** The IASB and FASB are involved in a joint project to evaluate the format of financial statements. The first phase of that project involves a focus on how to best present revenues and expenses. One longer-term result of the project may well be an income statement format that better reflects how businesses are run.

A second form of the income statement is the **multiple-step income statement**. The multiple-step income statement is often considered more useful because it highlights the components of net income. The Wal-Mart income statement in Illustration 5-8 is an example.

The multiple-step income statement has three important line items: gross profit, income from operations, and net income. They are determined as follows.

1. Subtract cost of goods sold from net sales to determine **gross profit**.
2. Deduct operating expenses from gross profit to determine **income from operations**.
3. Add or subtract the results of activities not related to operations to determine **net income**.

**Illustration 5-8** Multiple-step income statements

**WAL-MART STORES, INC.**
Income Statements
(in millions)

| | 2009 | 2008 |
|---|---|---|
| **For the years ended January 31** | | |
| Net sales | $401,244 | $374,307 |
| Cost of goods sold | 306,158 | 286,350 |
| **Gross profit** | 95,086 | 87,957 |
| Operating expenses | | |
| Selling, general, and administrative expenses | 76,651 | 70,174 |
| **Income from operations** | 18,435 | 17,783 |
| Other revenues and gains | | |
| Other revenues | 4,363 | 4,169 |
| Other expenses and losses | | |
| Interest expense | 1,900 | 1,794 |
| Other expense | 353 | 538 |
| Income before income taxes | 20,545 | 19,620 |
| Income tax expense | 7,145 | 6,889 |
| **Net income** | $ 13,400 | $ 12,731 |

Note that companies report income tax expense in a separate section of the income statement before net income. The net incomes in Illustrations 5-7 and 5-8 are the same. The difference in the two income statements is the amount of detail displayed and the order presented. The following discussion provides additional information about the components of a multiple-step income statement.

## SALES REVENUES

The income statement for a merchandising company typically presents gross sales revenues for the period. The company deducts sales returns and allowances and sales discounts (both contra accounts) from sales revenue in the income statement to arrive at **net sales**. Illustration 5-9 shows the sales revenues section of the income statement for PW Audio Supply.

| PW AUDIO SUPPLY, INC.<br>Income Statement (partial) | | |
|---|---|---|
| Sales revenues | | |
| Sales revenue | | $ 480,000 |
| Less: Sales returns and allowances | $12,000 | |
| Sales discounts | 8,000 | 20,000 |
| Net sales | | $460,000 |

**Illustration 5-9**   Statement presentation of sales revenues section

## GROSS PROFIT

Companies deduct **cost of goods sold** from sales revenue to determine **gross profit**. As shown in Illustration 5-8, for example, Wal-Mart had a gross profit of $95.1 billion in fiscal year 2009. Sales revenue used for this computation is **net sales**, which takes into account sales returns and allowances and sales discounts.

**Alternative Terminology** Gross profit is sometimes referred to as *gross margin.*

On the basis of the PW Audio Supply sales data presented in Illustration 5-9 (net sales of $460,000) and the cost of goods sold (assume a balance of $316,000), PW Audio Supply's gross profit is $144,000, computed as follows.

| | |
|---|---|
| Net sales | $ 460,000 |
| Cost of goods sold | 316,000 |
| Gross profit | $144,000 |

It is important to understand what gross profit is—and what it is not. Gross profit represents the **merchandising profit** of a company. Because operating expenses have not been deducted, it is *not* a measure of the overall profit of a company. Nevertheless, management and other interested parties closely watch the amount and trend of gross profit. Comparisons of current gross profit with past amounts and rates and with those in the industry indicate the effectiveness of a company's purchasing and pricing policies.

## OPERATING EXPENSES

Operating expenses are the next component in measuring net income for a merchandising company. At Wal-Mart, for example, operating expenses were $76.7 billion in fiscal year 2009.

At PW Audio Supply, operating expenses were $114,000. The firm determines its income from operations by subtracting operating expenses from gross profit. Thus, income from operations is $30,000, as shown below.

| | |
|---|---|
| Gross profit | $144,000 |
| Operating expenses | 114,000 |
| Income from operations | $ 30,000 |

## NONOPERATING ACTIVITIES

**Nonoperating activities** consist of various revenues and expenses and gains and losses that are unrelated to the company's main line of operations. When nonoperating items are included, the label "**Income from operations**" (or "Operating income") precedes them. This label clearly identifies the results of the company's normal operations, an amount determined by subtracting cost of goods sold and operating expenses from net sales. The results of nonoperating activities are shown in the categories "**Other revenues and gains**" and "**Other expenses and losses.**" Illustration 5-10 lists examples of each.

Nonoperating income is sometimes very significant. For example, in a recent quarter Sears Holdings earned more than half of its net income from investments in derivative securities.

**Illustration 5-10**
Examples of nonoperating activities

| **Other Revenues and Gains** |
| --- |
| **Interest revenue** from notes receivable and marketable securities. |
| **Dividend revenue** from investments in capital stock. |
| **Rent revenue** from subleasing a portion of the store. |
| **Gain** from the sale of property, plant, and equipment. |

| **Other Expenses and Losses** |
| --- |
| **Interest expense** on notes and loans payable. |
| **Casualty losses** from recurring causes, such as vandalism and accidents. |
| **Loss** from the sale or abandonment of property, plant, and equipment. |
| **Loss** from strikes by employees and suppliers. |

**Ethics Note** Companies manage earnings in various ways. ConAgra Foods recorded a nonrecurring gain for $186 million from the sale of Pilgrim's Pride stock to help meet an earnings projection for the quarter.

The distinction between operating and nonoperating activities is crucial to external users of financial data. These users view operating income as sustainable and many nonoperating activities as nonrecurring. When forecasting next year's income, analysts put the most weight on this year's operating income, and less weight on this year's nonoperating activities.

## Ethics Insight

### Disclosing More Details

After Enron, increased investor criticism and regulator scrutiny forced many companies to improve the clarity of their financial disclosures. For example, IBM announced that it would begin providing more detail regarding its "Other gains and losses." It had previously included these items in its selling, general, and administrative expenses, with little disclosure.

Disclosing other gains and losses in a separate line item on the income statement will not have any effect on bottom-line income. However, analysts complained that burying these details in the selling, general, and administrative expense line reduced their ability to fully understand how well IBM was performing. For example, previously if IBM sold off one of its buildings at a gain, it would include this gain in the selling, general, and administrative expense line item, thus reducing that expense. This made it appear that the company had done a better job of controlling operating expenses than it actually had.

Other companies that also recently announced changes to increase the informativeness of their income statements included PepsiCo and General Electric.

**?** Why have investors and analysts demanded more accuracy in isolating "Other gains and losses" from operating items? (See page 276.)

The nonoperating activities are reported in the income statement immediately after the operating activities. Included among these activities in Illustration 5-8 (page 240) for Wal-Mart is interest expense of $1.9 billion for fiscal year 2009. The amount remaining, after adding the operating and nonoperating sections together, is Wal-Mart's net income of $13.4 billion.

In Illustration 5-11 we have provided the multiple-step income statement of a hypothetical company. This statement provides more detail than that of Wal-Mart and thus is useful as a guide for homework. **(For WileyPLUS homework, individual revenues and expenses are listed in order of magnitude.)** *For homework problems, use the multiple-step form of the income statement unless the requirements state otherwise.*

**Illustration 5-11** Multiple-step income statement

**PW AUDIO SUPPLY, INC.**
Income Statement
For the Year Ended December 31, 2012

| | | | |
|---|---:|---:|---|
| **Sales revenues** | | | ⎫ |
| Sales revenue | | $480,000 | |
| Less: Sales returns and allowances | $12,000 | | |
| Sales discounts | 8,000 | 20,000 | Calculation of |
| Net sales | | 460,000 | gross profit |
| **Cost of goods sold** | | 316,000 | |
| **Gross profit** | | 144,000 | ⎭ |
| **Operating expenses** | | | ⎫ |
| Salaries and wages expense | 64,000 | | |
| Utilities expense | 17,000 | | |
| Advertising expense | 16,000 | | Calculation of |
| Depreciation expense | 8,000 | | income from |
| Freight-out | 7,000 | | operations |
| Insurance expense | 2,000 | | |
| Total operating expenses | | 114,000 | |
| Income from operations | | 30,000 | ⎭ |
| **Other revenues and gains** | | | ⎫ |
| Interest revenue | 3,000 | | |
| Gain on disposal of | | | |
| plant assets | 600 | | |
| | 3,600 | | Results of |
| | | | activities not |
| **Other expenses and losses** | | | related to |
| Interest expense | 1,800 | | operations |
| Casualty loss from vandalism | 200 | | |
| | 2,000 | | |
| | | 1,600 | ⎭ |
| Income before income taxes | | 31,600 | |
| Income tax expense | | 10,100 | |
| **Net income** | | $ 21,500 | |

*before you go on...*

**Do it!** The following information is available for Art Center Corp. for the year ended December 31, 2012.

**MULTIPLE-STEP INCOME STATEMENT**

| | | | |
|---|---:|---|---:|
| Other revenues and gains | $ 8,000 | Net sales | $442,000 |
| Other expenses and losses | 3,000 | Operating expenses | 187,000 |
| Cost of goods sold | 147,000 | | |

Prepare a multiple-step income statement for Art Center Corp. The company has a tax rate of 25%.

## Action Plan

- Subtract cost of goods sold from net sales to determine gross profit.
- Subtract operating expenses from gross profit to determine income from operations.
- Multiply the tax rate by income before tax to determine tax expense.

## Solution

**ART CENTER CORP.**
Income Statement
For the Year Ended December 31, 2012

| | | |
|---|---:|---:|
| Net sales | | $442,000 |
| Cost of goods sold | | 147,000 |
| Gross profit | | 295,000 |
| Operating expenses | | 187,000 |
| Income from operations | | 108,000 |
| Other revenues and gains | 8,000 | |
| Other expenses and losses | 3,000 | 5,000 |
| Income before income taxes | | 113,000 |
| Income tax expense | | 28,250 |
| Net income | | $ 84,750 |

Related exercise material: **BE5-5, BE5-6, Do it! 5-3, and E5-5.**

## DETERMINING COST OF GOODS SOLD UNDER A PERIODIC SYSTEM

**study objective** **5**

Determine cost of goods sold under a periodic system.

Determining cost of goods sold is different when a periodic inventory system is used rather than a perpetual system. As you have seen, a company using a **perpetual system** makes an entry to record cost of goods sold and to reduce inventory *each time a sale is made*. A company using a **periodic system** does not determine cost of goods sold *until the end of the period*. At the end of the period the company performs a count to determine the ending balance of inventory. It then **calculates cost of goods sold by subtracting ending inventory from the goods available for sale.** Goods available for sale is the sum of beginning inventory plus purchases, as shown in Illustration 5-12.

**Illustration 5-12** Basic formula for cost of goods sold using the periodic system

| |
|---|
| Beginning Inventory |
| + Cost of Goods Purchased |
| Cost of Goods Available for Sale |
| − Ending Inventory |
| Cost of Goods Sold |

Another difference between the two approaches is that the perpetual system directly adjusts the Inventory account for any transaction that affects inventory (such as freight costs, returns, and discounts). The periodic system does not do this. Instead, it creates different accounts for purchases, freight costs, returns, and discounts. These various accounts are shown in Illustration 5-13 (page 245), which presents the calculation of cost of goods sold for PW Audio Supply using the periodic approach. Note that the basic elements from Illustration 5-12 are highlighted in Illustration 5-13. You will learn more in Chapter 6 about how to determine cost of goods sold using the periodic system.

The use of the periodic inventory system does not affect the form of presentation in the balance sheet. As under the perpetual system, a company reports inventory in the current assets section.

Appendix 5A provides further detail on the use of the periodic system.

**Illustration 5-13** Cost of goods sold for a merchandiser using a periodic inventory system

### PW AUDIO SUPPLY, INC.
Cost of Goods Sold
For the Year Ended December 31, 2012

| | | | |
|---|---:|---:|---:|
| Cost of goods sold | | | |
| Inventory, January 1 | | | $ 36,000 |
| Purchases | | $325,000 | |
| Less: Purchase returns and | | | |
| allowances | $10,400 | | |
| Purchase discounts | 6,800 | 17,200 | |
| Net purchases | | 307,800 | |
| Add: Freight-in | | 12,200 | |
| Cost of goods purchased | | | 320,000 |
| Cost of goods available for sale | | | 356,000 |
| Inventory, December 31 | | | 40,000 |
| Cost of goods sold | | | $316,000 |

**Helpful Hint** The far right column identifies the primary items that make up cost of goods sold of $316,000. The middle column explains cost of goods purchased of $320,000. The left column reports contra purchase items of $17,200.

*before you go on...*

## Do it!

Aerosmith Company's accounting records show the following at the year-end December 31, 2012.

| | |
|---|---:|
| Purchase Discounts | $ 3,400 |
| Freight-in | 6,100 |
| Purchases | 162,500 |
| Beginning Inventory | 18,000 |
| Ending Inventory | 20,000 |
| Purchase Returns | 5,200 |

Assuming that Aerosmith Company uses the periodic system, compute (a) cost of goods purchased and (b) cost of goods sold.

**COST OF GOODS SOLD–PERIODIC SYSTEM**

**Action Plan**

• To determine cost of goods purchased, adjust purchases for returns, discounts, and freight-in.

• To determine cost of goods sold, add cost of goods purchased to beginning inventory, and subtract ending inventory.

### Solution

(a) Cost of goods purchased = $160,000:

Purchases − Purchase returns − Purchase discounts + Freight-in
$162,500 −    $5,200    −    $3,400    +    $6,100    = $160,000

(b) Cost of goods sold = $158,000:

Beginning inventory + Cost of goods purchased − Ending inventory
$18,000    +    $160,000    −    $20,000    = $158,000

Related exercise material: **BE5-7, BE5-8, BE5-9, Do it! 5-4, E5-10,** and **E5-11.**

# Evaluating Profitability

## GROSS PROFIT RATE

A company's gross profit may be expressed as a **percentage** by dividing the amount of gross profit by net sales. This is referred to as the **gross profit rate**. For PW Audio Supply, the gross profit rate is 31.3% ($144,000 ÷ $460,000).

Analysts generally consider the gross profit *rate* to be more informative than the gross profit *amount* because it expresses a more meaningful (qualitative) relationship between gross profit and net sales. For example, a gross profit amount of $1,000,000 may sound impressive. But if it was the result of sales of $100,000,000, the company's gross profit rate was only 1%. A 1% gross profit rate is acceptable in very few industries. Illustration 5-14 (page 246) demonstrates that gross profit rates differ greatly across industries.

**study objective 6**

Explain the factors affecting profitability.

**Illustration 5-14** Gross profit rate by industry

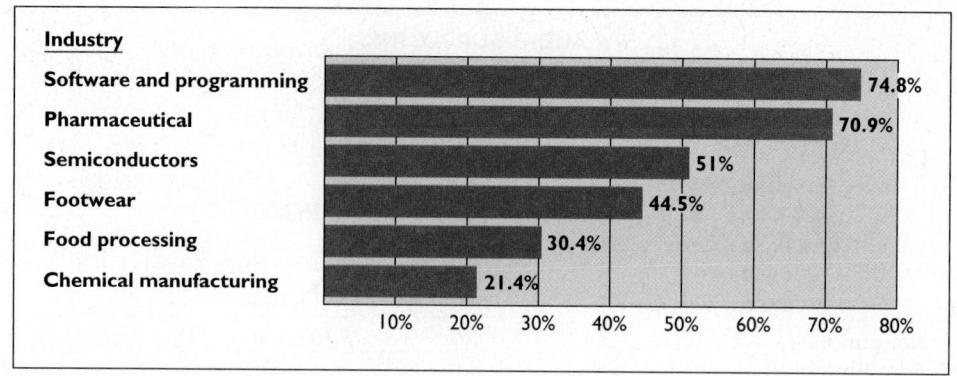

| Industry | |
|---|---|
| Software and programming | 74.8% |
| Pharmaceutical | 70.9% |
| Semiconductors | 51% |
| Footwear | 44.5% |
| Food processing | 30.4% |
| Chemical manufacturing | 21.4% |

A decline in a company's gross profit rate might have several causes. The company may have begun to sell products with a lower "markup"—for example, budget blue jeans versus designer blue jeans. Increased competition may have resulted in a lower selling price. Or, the company may be forced to pay higher prices to its suppliers without being able to pass these costs on to its customers. The gross profit rates for Wal-Mart and Target, and the industry average, are presented in Illustration 5-15.

**Illustration 5-15** Gross profit rate

$$\text{Gross Profit Rate} = \frac{\text{Gross Profit}}{\text{Net Sales}}$$

| Wal-Mart ($ in millions) | | Target | Industry Average |
|---|---|---|---|
| 2009 | 2008 | 2009 | 2009 |
| $\dfrac{\$95{,}086}{\$401{,}244} = 23.7\%$ | 23.5% | 30.0% | 25.1% |

Wal-Mart's gross profit rate increased from 23.5% in 2008 to 23.7% in 2009. In its Management Discussion and Analysis (MD&A), Wal-Mart explained, "The gross profit margin increase in fiscal 2009 compared to fiscal 2008 was primarily due to lower inventory shrinkage and less markdown activity as a result of more effective merchandising in the Wal-Mart U.S. segment. Additionally, the increase in gross profit margin in fiscal 2008 included a $97 million refund of excise taxes previously paid on past merchandise sales of prepaid phone cards."

At first glance, it might be surprising that Wal-Mart has a lower gross profit rate than Target and the industry average. It is likely, however, that this can be explained by the fact that grocery products are becoming an increasingly large component of Wal-Mart's sales. (In 2010, Wal-Mart announced that groceries now represent more than 50% of its sales.) In fact, in its MD&A, Wal-Mart once stated, "Because food items carry a lower gross margin than our other merchandise, increasing food sales tends to have an unfavorable impact on our total gross margin." Also, Wal-Mart has substantial warehouse-style sales in its Sam's Club stores, which are a low-margin, high-volume operation. In later chapters, we will provide further discussion of the trade-off between sales volume and gross profit.

## DECISION TOOLKIT

| DECISION CHECKPOINTS | INFO NEEDED FOR DECISION | TOOL TO USE FOR DECISION | HOW TO EVALUATE RESULTS |
|---|---|---|---|
| Is the price of goods keeping pace with changes in the cost of inventory? | Gross profit and net sales | $\text{Gross profit rate} = \dfrac{\text{Gross profit}}{\text{Net sales}}$ | Higher ratio suggests the average margin between selling price and inventory cost is increasing. Too high a margin may result in lost sales. |

## PROFIT MARGIN RATIO

The **profit margin ratio** measures the percentage of each dollar of sales that results in net income. We compute this ratio by dividing net income by net sales (revenue) for the period.

How do the gross profit rate and profit margin ratio differ? The gross profit rate measures the margin by which selling price exceeds cost of goods sold. **The profit margin ratio measures the extent by which selling price covers all expenses** (including cost of goods sold). A company can improve its profit margin ratio by either increasing its gross profit rate and/or by controlling its operating expenses and other costs. For example, at one time Radio Shack reported increased profit margins which it accomplished by closing stores and slashing costs. While its total sales have been declining, its profitability as measured by its profit margin has increased.

Profit margins vary across industries. Businesses with high turnover, such as grocery stores (Safeway and Kroger) and discount stores (Target and Wal-Mart), generally experience low profit margins. Low-turnover businesses, such as high-end jewelry stores (Tiffany and Co.) or major drug manufacturers (Merck), have high profit margins. Illustration 5-16 shows profit margin ratios from a variety of industries.

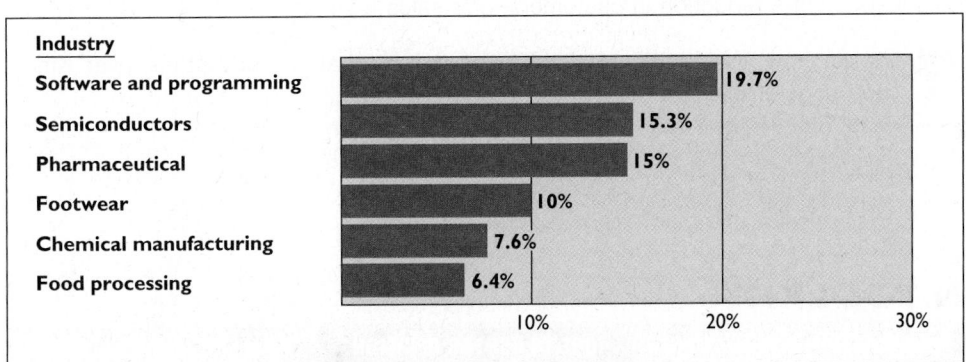

**Illustration 5-16**  Profit margin ratio by industry

Profit margins for Wal-Mart and Target and the industry average are presented in Illustration 5-17.

**Illustration 5-17**  Profit margin ratio

| Profit Margin Ratio = $\dfrac{\text{Net Income}}{\text{Net Sales}}$ | | | |
|---|---|---|---|
| **Wal-Mart** ($ in millions) | | **Target** | **Industry Average** |
| 2009 | 2008 | 2009 | 2009 |
| $\dfrac{\$13,400}{\$401,244} = 3.3\%$ | 3.4% | 3.4% | 3.5% |

Wal-Mart's profit margin declined from 3.4% to 3.3% between 2008 and 2009. This means that the company generated 3.3¢ of profit on each dollar of sales. This occurred even though the gross profit rate increased. The cause of the decline in the profit margin ratio was increased operating expenses. Wal-Mart's MD&A discussion states: "In fiscal 2009, operating expenses increased primarily due to higher utility costs, a pre-tax charge of approximately $352 million resulting from the settlement of 63 wage and hour class action lawsuits, higher health benefit costs and increased corporate expenses compared to fiscal 2008. Corporate expenses have increased primarily due to our long-term transformation projects to enhance our information systems for merchandising, finance and human resources."

How does Wal-Mart compare to its competitors? Its profit margin ratio was lower than Target's in 2009 and was less than the industry average. Thus, its profit margin ratio does not suggest exceptional profitability. However, we must again keep in mind that an increasing percentage of Wal-Mart's sales is from low-margin groceries.

## Accounting Across the Organization

### Strategic Errors Can Be Costly

In its death spiral toward bankruptcy, Kmart appeared to make two very costly strategic errors. First, in an effort to attract customers, it decided to reduce selling prices on over 30,000 items. The problem was that this reduced its gross profit rate–and didn't even have the intended effect of increasing sales because Wal-Mart quickly matched these price cuts. Because Wal-Mart operated much more efficiently than Kmart, Wal-Mart could afford to absorb these price cuts and still operate at a profit. Kmart could not. Its second error was to try to reduce operating costs by cutting its advertising expenditures. This resulted in a reduction in customers–and sales revenue.

**?** Explain how Wal-Mart's profitability gave it a strategic advantage over Kmart.
(See page 276.)

## DECISION TOOLKIT

| DECISION CHECKPOINTS | INFO NEEDED FOR DECISION | TOOL TO USE FOR DECISION | HOW TO EVALUATE RESULTS |
|---|---|---|---|
| Is the company maintaining an adequate margin between sales and expenses? | Net income and net sales | $\text{Profit margin ratio} = \dfrac{\text{Net income}}{\text{Net sales}}$ | Higher value suggests favorable return on each dollar of sales. |

## KEEPING AN EYE ON CASH

In Chapter 4, you learned that **earnings have high quality if they provide a full and transparent depiction of how a company performed**. In order to quickly assess earnings quality, analysts sometimes employ the **quality of earnings ratio**. It is calculated as net cash provided by operating activities divided by net income.

**study objective 7**

Identify a quality of earnings indicator.

$$\text{Quality of Earnings Ratio} = \frac{\text{Net Cash Provided by Operating Activities}}{\text{Net Income}}$$

In general, a measure significantly less than 1 suggests that a company may be using more aggressive accounting techniques in order to accelerate income recognition (record income in earlier periods). A measure significantly greater than 1 suggests that a company is using conservative accounting techniques, which cause it to delay the recognition of income.

Measures that are significantly less than 1 do not provide definitive evidence of low-quality earnings. Low measures do, however, indicate that analysts should investigate the company's earnings quality by evaluating the causes of the difference between net income and net cash provided by operating activities. Examples of factors that would cause differences are presented in Chapter 4 (pp. 191–192).

Here are recent quality of earnings ratios for a number of well-known companies, all of which have measures in excess of 1.

| Company Name ($ in millions) | Net Cash Provided by Operating Activities | ÷ | Net Income | = | Quality of Earnings Ratio |
|---|---|---|---|---|---|
| DuPont | $4,741 | | $1,769 | | 2.7 |
| Intel | $11,170 | | $4,369 | | 2.6 |
| Nike | $1,736 | | $1,487 | | 1.2 |
| Microsoft | $19,037 | | $14,569 | | 1.3 |
| Wal-Mart | $26,249 | | $14,335 | | 1.8 |

# USING THE *DECISION TOOLKIT*

After having once been as dominant as Wal-Mart, in recent years Sears has struggled to survive. It has enacted many changes trying to turn itself around. In the 1990s, it shocked and disappointed many loyal customers by closing its catalog business. It also closed 113 stores and eliminated 50,000 jobs. None of these changes was enough to make Sears truly competitive, so in March 2005 Sears merged with Kmart to form the third largest U.S. retailer. Here is recent data for Sears Holdings, Inc.

| | Year ended | |
|---|---|---|
| ($ in millions) | 01/30/10 | 01/31/09 |
| Net income | $ 235 | $ 53 |
| Sales revenue | 44,043 | 46,770 |
| Cost of goods sold | 31,824 | 34,118 |

## Instructions

Using the basic facts in the table, evaluate the following components of Sears's profitability for the years ended January 30, 2010, and January 31, 2009.

    Profit margin ratio
    Gross profit rate

How do Sears's profit margin ratio and gross profit rate compare to those of Wal-Mart and Target for 2009?

## Solution

| | Year ended | |
|---|---|---|
| ($ in millions) | 01/30/10 | 01/31/09 |
| Profit margin ratio | $\frac{\$235}{\$44,043} = 0.5\%$ | $\frac{\$53}{\$46,770} = 0.1\%$ |
| Gross profit rate | $\frac{\$12,219^*}{\$44,043} = 27.7\%$ | $\frac{\$12,652^{**}}{\$46,770} = 27.1\%$ |

*$44,043 − $31,824    **$46,770 − $34,118

Sears's profit margin ratio (income per dollar of sales) increased from 0.1% to 0.5%. This is well below both Wal-Mart's (3.3%) and Target's (3.4%). Thus, Sears is not as effective at turning its sales into net income as these two competitors.

Sears's gross profit rate improved from 27.1% to 27.7%. This suggests that its ability to maintain its mark-up above its cost of goods sold improved during this period. Sears's gross profit rate of 27.7% is lower than Target's (30.0%) but higher than Wal-Mart's (23.7%). As discussed in the chapter, Wal-Mart's gross profit is depressed by the fact that it sells many grocery products, which are very low-margin. Target is superior to Sears both in its ability to maintain its mark-up above its costs of goods sold (its gross profit rate) and in its ability to control operating costs (its profit margin ratio).

# Summary of Study Objectives

**1 Identify the differences between a service company and a merchandising company.** Because of the presence of inventory, a merchandising company has sales revenue, cost of goods sold, and gross profit. To account for inventory, a merchandising company must choose between a perpetual inventory system and a periodic inventory system.

**2 Explain the recording of purchases under a perpetual inventory system.** The Inventory account is debited for all purchases of merchandise and for freight costs, and it is credited for purchase discounts and purchase returns and allowances.

**3 Explain the recording of sales revenues under a perpetual inventory system.** When inventory is sold, Accounts Receivable (or Cash) is debited and Sales Revenue is credited for the selling price of the merchandise. At the same time, Cost of Goods Sold is debited and Inventory is credited for the cost of inventory items sold. Subsequent entries are required for (a) sales returns and allowances and (b) sales discounts.

**4 Distinguish between a single-step and a multiple-step income statement.** In a single-step income statement, companies classify all data under two categories, revenues or expenses, and net income is determined in one step. A multiple-step income statement shows numerous steps in determining net income, including results of nonoperating activities.

**5 Determine cost of goods sold under a periodic system.** The periodic system uses multiple accounts to keep track of transactions that affect inventory. To determine cost of goods sold, first calculate cost of goods purchased by adjusting purchases for returns, allowances, discounts, and freight-in. Then calculate cost of goods sold by adding cost of goods purchased to beginning inventory and subtracting ending inventory.

**6 Explain the factors affecting profitability.** Profitability is affected by gross profit, as measured by the gross profit rate, and by management's ability to control costs, as measured by the profit margin ratio.

**7 Identify a quality of earnings indicator.** Earnings have high quality if they provide a full and transparent depiction of how a company performed. An indicator of the quality of earnings is the quality of earnings ratio, which is net cash provided by operating activities divided by net income. Measures above 1 suggest the company is employing conservative accounting practices. Measures significantly below 1 might suggest the company is using aggressive accounting to accelerate the recognition of income.

# DECISION TOOLKIT  A SUMMARY

| DECISION CHECKPOINTS | INFO NEEDED FOR DECISION | TOOL TO USE FOR DECISION | HOW TO EVALUATE RESULTS |
|---|---|---|---|
| Is the price of goods keeping pace with changes in the cost of inventory? | Gross profit and net sales | Gross profit rate $=\dfrac{\text{Gross profit}}{\text{Net sales}}$ | Higher ratio suggests the average margin between selling price and inventory cost is increasing. Too high a margin may result in lost sales. |
| Is the company maintaining an adequate margin between sales and expenses? | Net income and net sales | Profit margin ratio $=\dfrac{\text{Net income}}{\text{Net sales}}$ | Higher value suggests favorable return on each dollar of sales. |

**appendix 5A**

# Periodic Inventory System

As described in this chapter, companies may use one of two basic systems of accounting for inventories: (1) the perpetual inventory system or (2) the periodic inventory system. In the chapter, we focused on the characteristics of the perpetual inventory system. In this appendix, we discuss and illustrate the **periodic inventory system**. One key difference between the two systems is the point at which the company computes cost of goods sold. For a visual reminder of this difference, you may want to refer back to Illustration 5-4 on page 230.

**study objective   8**

Explain the recording of purchases and sales of inventory under a periodic inventory system.

## RECORDING MERCHANDISE TRANSACTIONS

In a **periodic inventory system**, companies record revenues from the sale of merchandise when sales are made, just as in a perpetual system. Unlike the perpetual system, however, companies **do not attempt on the date of sale to record the cost of the merchandise sold**. Instead, they take a physical inventory count at the **end of the period** to determine (1) the cost of the merchandise then on hand and (2) the cost of the goods sold during the period. And, **under a periodic system, companies record purchases of merchandise in the Purchases account rather than the Inventory account**. Also, in a periodic system, purchase returns and allowances, purchase discounts, and freight costs on purchases are recorded in separate accounts.

To illustrate the recording of merchandise transactions under a periodic inventory system, we will use purchase/sale transactions between PW Audio Supply, Inc. and Sauk Stereo, as illustrated for the perpetual inventory system in this chapter.

## RECORDING PURCHASES OF MERCHANDISE

On the basis of the sales invoice (Illustration 5-5, shown on page 232) and receipt of the merchandise ordered from PW Audio Supply, Sauk Stereo records the $3,800 purchase as follows.

| | | | | |
|---|---|---|---|---|
| May 4 | Purchases | | 3,800 | |
| |     Accounts Payable | | | 3,800 |
| |       (To record goods purchased on account | | | |
| |       from PW Audio Supply) | | | |

Purchases is a temporary account whose normal balance is a debit.

## FREIGHT COSTS

When the purchaser directly incurs the freight costs, it debits the account Freight-in (or Transportation-in). For example, if Sauk Stereo pays Haul-It Freight Company $150 for freight charges on its purchase from PW Audio Supply on May 6, the entry on Sauk Stereo's books is:

| | | | | |
|---|---|---|---|---|
| May 6 | Freight-in (Transportation-in) | | 150 | |
| |     Cash | | | 150 |
| |       (To record payment of freight on goods | | | |
| |       purchased) | | | |

Like Purchases, Freight-in is a temporary account whose normal balance is a debit. **Freight-in is part of cost of goods purchased**. The reason is that cost of goods purchased should include any freight charges necessary to bring the goods to the purchaser. Freight costs are not subject to a purchase discount. Purchase discounts apply on the invoice cost of the merchandise.

### Purchase Returns and Allowances

Because $300 of merchandise received from PW Audio Supply is inoperable, Sauk Stereo returns the goods and prepares the following entry to recognize the return.

| | | | | |
|---|---|---|---|---|
| May | 8 | Accounts Payable | 300 | |
| | | Purchase Returns and Allowances | | 300 |
| | | (To record return of goods | | |
| | | purchased from PW Audio Supply) | | |

Purchase Returns and Allowances is a temporary account whose normal balance is a credit.

### Purchase Discounts

On May 14, Sauk Stereo pays the balance due on account to PW Audio Supply, taking the 2% cash discount allowed by PW Audio Supply for payment within 10 days. Sauk Stereo records the payment and discount as follows.

| | | | | |
|---|---|---|---|---|
| May | 14 | Accounts Payable ($3,800 − $300) | 3,500 | |
| | | Purchase Discounts ($3,500 × .02) | | 70 |
| | | Cash | | 3,430 |
| | | (To record payment within the | | |
| | | discount period) | | |

Purchase Discounts is a temporary account whose normal balance is a credit.

### RECORDING SALES OF MERCHANDISE

The seller, PW Audio Supply, records the sale of $3,800 of merchandise to Sauk Stereo on May 4 (sales invoice No. 731, Illustration 5-5, page 232) as follows.

| | | | | |
|---|---|---|---|---|
| May | 4 | Accounts Receivable | 3,800 | |
| | | Sales Revenue | | 3,800 |
| | | (To record credit sales to Sauk Stereo | | |
| | | per invoice #731) | | |

### Sales Returns and Allowances

To record the returned goods received from Sauk Stereo on May 8, PW Audio Supply records the $300 sales return as follows.

| | | | | |
|---|---|---|---|---|
| May | 8 | Sales Returns and Allowances | 300 | |
| | | Accounts Receivable | | 300 |
| | | (To record credit granted to Sauk | | |
| | | Stereo for returned goods) | | |

### Sales Discounts

On May 14, PW Audio Supply receives payment of $3,430 on account from Sauk Stereo. PW Audio Supply honors the 2% cash discount and records the payment of Sauk Stereo's account receivable in full as follows.

| May 14 | Cash | 3,430 | |
| | Sales Discounts ($3,500 ×.02) | 70 | |
| | Accounts Receivable ($3,800 − $300) | | 3,500 |
| | (To record collection within 2/10, n/30 discount period from Sauk Stereo) | | |

## COMPARISON OF ENTRIES– PERPETUAL vs. PERIODIC

### ENTRIES ON SAUK STEREO'S BOOKS *Buyer*

| | Transaction | Perpetual Inventory System | | Periodic Inventory System | |
|---|---|---|---|---|---|
| May 4 | Purchase of merchandise on credit. | Inventory<br>  Accounts Payable | 3,800<br>3,800 | Purchases<br>  Accounts Payable | 3,800<br>3,800 |
| May 6 | Freight costs on purchases. | Inventory<br>  Cash | 150<br>150 | Freight-in<br>  Cash | 150<br>150 |
| May 8 | Purchase returns and allowances. | Accounts Payable<br>  Inventory | 300<br>300 | Accounts Payable<br>  Purchase Returns and Allowances | 300<br>300 |
| May 14 | Payment on account with a discount. | Accounts Payable<br>  Cash<br>  Inventory | 3,500<br>3,430<br>70 | Accounts Payable<br>  Cash<br>  Purchase Discounts | 3,500<br>3,430<br>70 |

### ENTRIES ON PW AUDIO SUPPLY'S BOOKS *Seller*

| | Transaction | Perpetual Inventory System | | Periodic Inventory System | |
|---|---|---|---|---|---|
| May 4 | Sale of merchandise on credit. | Accounts Receivable<br>  Sales Revenue | 3,800<br>3,800 | Accounts Receivable<br>  Sales Revenue | 3,800<br>3,800 |
| | | Cost of Goods Sold<br>  Inventory | 2,400<br>2,400 | No entry for cost of goods sold | |
| May 8 | Return of merchandise sold. | Sales Returns and Allowances<br>  Accounts Receivable | 300<br>300 | Sales Returns and Allowances<br>  Accounts Receivable | 300<br>300 |
| | | Inventory<br>  Cost of Goods Sold | 140<br>140 | No entry | |
| May 14 | Cash received on account with a discount. | Cash<br>Sales Discounts<br>  Accounts Receivable | 3,430<br>70<br>3,500 | Cash<br>Sales Discounts<br>  Accounts Receivable | 3,430<br>70<br>3,500 |

# Summary of Study Objective for Appendix 5A

**8** **Explain the recording of purchases and sales of inventory under a periodic inventory system.** To record purchases, entries are required for (a) cash and credit purchases, (b) purchase returns and allowances, (c) purchase discounts, and (d) freight costs. To record sales, entries are required for (a) cash and credit sales, (b) sales returns and allowances, and (c) sales discounts.

# Glossary

**Contra revenue account** *(p. 238)* An account that is offset against a revenue account on the income statement.

**Cost of goods sold** *(p. 228)* The total cost of merchandise sold during the period.

**Gross profit** *(p. 241)* The excess of net sales over the cost of goods sold.

**Gross profit rate** *(p. 245)* Gross profit expressed as a percentage by dividing the amount of gross profit by net sales.

**Net sales** (p. 241) Sales less sales returns and allowances and sales discounts.

**Periodic inventory system** (p. 230) An inventory system in which a company does not maintain detailed records of goods on hand and determines the cost of goods sold only at the end of an accounting period.

**Perpetual inventory system** (p. 230) A detailed inventory system in which a company maintains the cost of each inventory item and the records continuously show the inventory that should be on hand.

**Profit margin ratio** (p. 247) Measures the percentage of each dollar of sales that results in net income, computed by dividing net income by net sales.

**Purchase allowance** (p. 234) A deduction made to the selling price of merchandise, granted by the seller so that the buyer will keep the merchandise.

**Purchase discount** (p. 234) A cash discount claimed by a buyer for prompt payment of a balance due.

**Purchase invoice** (p. 231) A document that supports each purchase.

**Purchase return** (p. 234) A return of goods from the buyer to the seller for cash or credit.

**Quality of earnings ratio** (p. 248) A measure used to indicate the extent to which a company's earnings provide a full and transparent depiction of its performance; computed as net cash provided by operating activities divided by net income.

**Sales discount** (p. 238) A reduction given by a seller for prompt payment of a credit sale.

**Sales invoice** (p. 236) A document that provides support for each sale.

**Sales returns and allowances** (p. 237) Transactions in which the seller either accepts goods back from the purchaser (a return) or grants a reduction in the purchase price (an allowance) so that the buyer will keep the goods.

**Sales revenue** (p. 228) Primary source of revenue in a merchandising company.

## Comprehensive Do it!

The adjusted trial balance for the year ended December 31, 2012, for Dykstra Company is shown below.

**DYKSTRA COMPANY**
**Adjusted Trial Balance**
**For the Year Ended December 31, 2012**

|  | Dr. | Cr. |
| --- | --- | --- |
| Cash | $ 14,500 | |
| Accounts Receivable | 11,100 | |
| Inventory | 29,000 | |
| Prepaid Insurance | 2,500 | |
| Equipment | 95,000 | |
| Accumulated Depreciation—Equipment | | $ 18,000 |
| Notes Payable | | 25,000 |
| Accounts Payable | | 10,600 |
| Common Stock | | 70,000 |
| Retained Earnings | | 11,000 |
| Dividends | 12,000 | |
| Sales Revenue | | 536,800 |
| Sales Returns and Allowances | 6,700 | |
| Sales Discounts | 5,000 | |
| Cost of Goods Sold | 363,400 | |
| Freight-out | 7,600 | |
| Advertising Expense | 12,000 | |
| Salaries and Wages Expense | 56,000 | |
| Utilities Expense | 18,000 | |
| Rent Expense | 24,000 | |
| Depreciation Expense | 9,000 | |
| Insurance Expense | 4,500 | |
| Interest Expense | 3,600 | |
| Interest Revenue | | 2,500 |
| | $673,900 | $673,900 |

## Instructions

Prepare a multiple-step income statement for Dykstra Company. Assume a tax rate of 30 percent.

## Solution to Comprehensive **Do it!**

**DYKSTRA COMPANY**
**Income Statement**
**For the Year Ended December 31, 2012**

| | | |
|---|---:|---:|
| Sales revenues | | |
| Sales revenue | | $536,800 |
| Less: Sales returns and allowances | $ 6,700 | |
| Sales discounts | 5,000 | 11,700 |
| Net sales | | 525,100 |
| Cost of goods sold | | 363,400 |
| Gross profit | | 161,700 |
| Operating expenses | | |
| Salaries and wages expense | 56,000 | |
| Rent expense | 24,000 | |
| Utilities expense | 18,000 | |
| Advertising expense | 12,000 | |
| Depreciation expense | 9,000 | |
| Freight-out | 7,600 | |
| Insurance expense | 4,500 | |
| Total operating expenses | | 131,100 |
| Income from operations | | 30,600 |
| Other revenues and gains | | |
| Interest revenue | 2,500 | |
| Other expenses and losses | | |
| Interest expense | 3,600 | 1,100 |
| Income before income taxes | | 29,500 |
| Income tax expense | | 8,850 |
| Net income | | $ 20,650 |

### Action Plan

- In preparing the income statement, remember that the key components are net sales, cost of goods sold, gross profit, total operating expenses, and net income (loss). These components are reported in the right-hand column of the income statement.
- Present nonoperating items after income from operations.

**Self-Test, Brief Exercises, Exercises, Problem Set A, and many more resources are available for practice in WileyPLUS**

*Note:* All Questions, Exercises, and Problems marked with an asterisk relate to material in the appendix to the chapter.

# Self-Test Questions

Answers are on page 276.

(SO 1)
1. Which of the following statements about a periodic inventory system is true?
   (a) Companies determine cost of goods sold only at the end of the accounting period.
   (b) Companies continuously maintain detailed records of the cost of each inventory purchase and sale.
   (c) The periodic system provides better control over inventories than a perpetual system.
   (d) The increased use of computerized systems has increased the use of the periodic system.

(SO 2)
2. Which of the following items does *not* result in an adjustment in the Inventory account under a perpetual system?
   (a) A purchase of merchandise.
   (b) A return of merchandise inventory to the supplier.
   (c) Payment of freight costs for goods shipped to a customer.
   (d) Payment of freight costs for goods received from a supplier.

(SO 3)
3. Which sales accounts normally have a debit balance?
   (a) Sales discounts.
   (b) Sales returns and allowances.

(c) Both (a) and (b).

(d) Neither (a) nor (b).

(SO 3) **4.** A company makes a credit sale of $750 on June 13, terms 2/10, n/30, on which it grants a return of $50 on June 16. What amount is received as payment in full on June 23?

(a) $700.       (c) $685.

(b) $686.       (d) $650.

(SO 3) **5.** To record the sale of goods for cash in a perpetual inventory system:

(a) only one journal entry is necessary to record cost of goods sold and reduction of inventory.

(b) only one journal entry is necessary to record the receipt of cash and the sales revenue.

(c) two journal entries are necessary: one to record the receipt of cash and sales revenue, and one to record the cost of goods sold and reduction of inventory.

(d) two journal entries are necessary: one to record the receipt of cash and reduction of inventory, and one to record the cost of goods sold and sales revenue.

(SO 4) **6.** Gross profit will result if:

(a) operating expenses are less than net income.

(b) sales revenues are greater than operating expenses.

(c) sales revenues are greater than cost of goods sold.

(d) operating expenses are greater than cost of goods sold.

(SO 4) **7.** If sales revenues are $400,000, cost of goods sold is $310,000, and operating expenses are $60,000, what is the gross profit?

(a) $30,000.       (c) $340,000.

(b) $90,000.       (d) $400,000.

(SO 4) **8.** The multiple-step income statement for a merchandising company shows each of these features *except*:

(a) gross profit.

(b) cost of goods sold.

(c) a sales revenue section.

(d) All of these are present.

(SO 5) **9.** If beginning inventory is $60,000, cost of goods purchased is $380,000, and ending inventory is $50,000, what is cost of goods sold under a periodic system?

(a) $390,000.       (c) $330,000.

(b) $370,000.       (d) $420,000.

(SO 5) **10.** Bufford Corporation had reported the following amounts at December 31, 2012: Sales revenue $184,000;

ending inventory $11,600; beginning inventory $17,200; purchases $60,400; purchase discounts $3,000; purchase returns and allowances $1,100; freight-in $600; freight-out $900. Calculate the cost of goods available for sale.

(a) $69,400.       (c) $56,900.

(b) $74,100.       (d) $197,700.

**11.** Which of the following would affect the (SO 6) gross profit rate? (Assume sales remains constant.)

(a) An increase in advertising expense.

(b) A decrease in depreciation expense.

(c) An increase in cost of goods sold.

(d) A decrease in insurance expense.

**12.** The gross profit *rate* is equal to:       (SO 6)

(a) net income divided by sales.

(b) cost of goods sold divided by sales.

(c) net sales minus cost of goods sold, divided by net sales.

(d) sales minus cost of goods sold, divided by cost of goods sold.

**13.** During the year ended December 31, 2012, Bjornstad (SO 6) Corporation had the following results: Sales revenue $267,000; cost of good sold $107,000; net income $92,400; operating expenses $55,400; net cash provided by operating activities $108,950. What was the company's profit margin ratio?

(a) 40%.       (c) 20.5%.

(b) 60%.       (d) 34.6%.

**14.** A quality of earnings ratio:       (SO 7)

(a) is computed as net income divided by net cash provided by operating activities.

(b) that is less than 1 indicates that a company might be using aggressive accounting tactics.

(c) that is greater than 1 indicates that a company might be using aggressive accounting tactics.

(d) is computed as net cash provided by operating activities divided by total assets.

*15. When goods are purchased for resale by a company (SO 8) using a periodic inventory system:

(a) purchases on account are debited to Inventory.

(b) purchases on account are debited to Purchases.

(c) purchase returns are debited to Purchase Returns and Allowances.

(d) freight costs are debited to Purchases.

Go to the book's companion website, **www.wiley.com/college/kimmel**, to access additional Self-Test Questions.

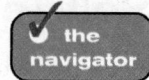

# Questions

**1.** (a) "The steps in the accounting cycle for a merchandising company differ from the steps in the accounting cycle for a service company." Do you agree or disagree?

(b) Is the measurement of net income in a merchandising company conceptually the same as in a service company? Explain.

**2.** How do the components of revenues and expenses differ between a merchandising company and a service company?

**3.** Rachel Harpole, CEO of Bargain Den Stores, is considering a recommendation made by both the company's purchasing manager and director of finance that the company should invest in a sophisticated new perpetual inventory system to replace its periodic system. Explain the primary difference between the two systems, and discuss the potential benefits of a perpetual inventory system.

4. (a) Explain the income measurement process in a merchandising company.
   (b) How does income measurement differ between a merchandising company and a service company?

5. Markoff Co. has sales revenue of $100,000, cost of goods sold of $70,000, and operating expenses of $18,000. What is its gross profit?

6. Peggy Wilder believes revenues from credit sales may be earned before they are collected in cash. Do you agree? Explain.

7. (a) What is the primary source document for recording (1) cash sales and (2) credit sales?
   (b) Using XXs for amounts, give the journal entry for each of the transactions in part (a), assuming perpetual inventory.

8. A credit sale is made on July 10 for $900, terms 1/15, n/30. On July 12, the purchaser returns $100 of goods for credit. Give the journal entry on July 19 to record the receipt of the balance due within the discount period.

9. As the end of Agnew Company's fiscal year-end approached, it became clear that the company had considerable excess inventory. Belden Glass, the head of marketing and sales, ordered salespeople to "add 20% more units to each order that you ship. The customers can always ship the extra back next period if they decide they don't want it. We've got to do it to meet this year's sales goal." Discuss the accounting implications of Belden's action.

10. To encourage bookstores to buy a broader range of book titles, and to discourage price discounting, the publishing industry allows bookstores to return unsold books to the publisher. This results in very significant returns each year. To ensure proper recognition of revenues, how should publishing companies account for these returns?

11. Goods costing $1,900 are purchased on account on July 15 with credit terms of 2/10, n/30. On July 18, the purchaser receives a $300 credit from the supplier for damaged goods. Give the journal entry on July 24 to record payment of the balance due within the discount period.

12. Frattura Company reports net sales of $800,000, gross profit of $560,000, and net income of $230,000. What are its operating expenses?

13. Rai Company has always provided its customers with payment terms of 1/10, n/30. Members of its sale force have commented that competitors are offering customers 2/10, n/45. Explain what these terms mean, and discuss the implications to Rai of switching its payment terms to those of its competitors.

14. In its year-end earnings announcement press release, Longwell Corp. announced that its earnings increased by $15 million relative to the previous year. This

represented a 20% increase. Inspection of its income statement reveals that the company reported a $20 million gain under "Other revenues and gains" from the sale of one of its factories. Discuss the implications of this gain from the perspective of a potential investor.

15. Identify the distinguishing features of an income statement for a merchandising company.

16. Why is the normal operating cycle for a merchandising company likely to be longer than for a service company?

17. What title does Tootsie Roll use for gross profit? How did it present gross profit? By how much did its total gross profit change, and in what direction, in 2009?

18. What merchandising account(s) will appear in the post-closing trial balance?

19. What types of businesses are most likely to use a perpetual inventory system?

20. Identify the accounts that are added to or deducted from purchases to determine the cost of goods purchased under a periodic system. For each account, indicate (a) whether it is added or deducted, and (b) its normal balance.

21. In the following cases, use a periodic inventory system to identify the item(s) designated by the letters $X$ and $Y$.
   (a) Purchases $-X-Y=$ Net purchases.
   (b) Cost of goods purchased $-$ Net purchases $=X$.
   (c) Beginning inventory $+X=$ Cost of goods available for sale.
   (d) Cost of goods available for sale $-$ Cost of goods sold $=X$.

22. What two ratios measure factors that affect profitability?

23. What factors affect a company's gross profit rate—that is, what can cause the gross profit rate to increase and what can cause it to decrease?

24. Corliss Ford, director of marketing, wants to reduce the selling price of his company's products by 15% to increase market share. He says, "I know this will reduce our gross profit rate, but the increased number of units sold will make up for the lost margin." Before this action is taken, what other factors does the company need to consider?

25. Howard Paulson is considering investing in Stevenson Pet Food Company. Stevenson's net income increased considerably during the most recent year, even though many other companies in the same industry reported disappointing earnings. Howard wants to know whether the company's earnings provide a reasonable depiction of its results. What initial step can Howard take to help determine whether he needs to investigate further?

*26. On July 15, a company purchases on account goods costing $1,900, with credit terms of 2/10, n/30. On July 18, the company receives a $400 credit memo from the supplier for damaged goods. Give the journal entry on July 24 to record payment of the balance due within the discount period assuming a periodic inventory system.

# Brief Exercises

*Compute missing amounts in determining net income.*
*(SO 1, 4),* **AP**

**BE5-1** Presented here are the components in Korinek Company's income statement. Determine the missing amounts.

| Sales Revenue | Cost of Goods Sold | Gross Profit | Operating Expenses | Net Income |
|---|---|---|---|---|
| $ 71,200 | (b) | $ 30,000 | (d) | $12,100 |
| $108,000 | $70,000 | (c) | (e) | $29,500 |
| (a) | $71,900 | $109,600 | $46,200 | (f) |

*Journalize perpetual inventory entries.*
*(SO 2, 3),* **AP**

**BE5-2** Pocras Company buys merchandise on account from Wedell Company. The selling price of the goods is $900 and the cost of the goods sold is $590. Both companies use perpetual inventory systems. Journalize the transactions on the books of both companies.

*Journalize sales transactions.*
*(SO 3),* **AP**

**BE5-3** Prepare the journal entries to record the following transactions on Graff Company's books using a perpetual inventory system.
(a) On March 2, Graff Company sold $800,000 of merchandise to Rodriguez Company, terms 2/10, n/30. The cost of the merchandise sold was $540,000.
(b) On March 6, Rodriguez Company returned $140,000 of the merchandise purchased on March 2. The cost of the merchandise returned was $94,000.
(c) On March 12, Graff Company received the balance due from Rodriguez Company.

*Journalize purchase transactions.*
*(SO 2),* **AP**

**BE5-4** From the information in BE5-3, prepare the journal entries to record these transactions on Rodriguez Company's books under a perpetual inventory system.

*Prepare sales revenue section of income statement.*
*(SO 4),* **AP**

**BE5-5** Bangura Company provides this information for the month ended October 31, 2012: sales on credit $300,000; cash sales $150,000; sales discounts $5,000; and sales returns and allowances $19,000. Prepare the sales revenues section of the income statement based on this information.

*Identify placement of items on a multiple-step income statement.*
*(SO 4),* **AP**

**BE5-6** Explain where each of these items would appear on a multiple-step income statement: gain on disposal of plant assets; cost of goods sold; depreciation expense; and sales returns and allowances.

*Determine cost of goods sold using basic periodic formula.*
*(SO 5),* **AP**

**BE5-7** Berry Company sold goods with a total selling price of $800,000 during the year. It purchased goods for $380,000 and had beginning inventory of $67,000. A count of its ending inventory determined that goods on hand was $50,000. What was its cost of goods sold?

*Compute net purchases and cost of goods purchased.*
*(SO 5),* **AP**

**BE5-8** Assume that Logan Company uses a periodic inventory system and has these account balances: Purchases $404,000; Purchase Returns and Allowances $13,000; Purchase Discounts $9,000; and Freight-in $16,000. Determine net purchases and cost of goods purchased.

*Compute cost of goods sold and gross profit.*
*(SO 5),* **C**

**BE5-9** Assume the same information as in BE5-8 and also that Logan Company has beginning inventory of $60,000, ending inventory of $90,000, and net sales of $612,000. Determine the amounts to be reported for cost of goods sold and gross profit.

*Calculate profitability ratios.*
*(SO 6),* **AP**

**BE5-10** Modder Corporation reported net sales of $250,000, cost of goods sold of $150,000, operating expenses of $50,000, net income of $32,500, beginning total assets of $520,000, and ending total assets of $600,000. Calculate each of the following values and explain what they mean: (a) profit margin ratio and (b) gross profit rate.

*Calculate profitability ratios.*
*(SO 6),* **AP**

**BE5-11** Delzer Corporation reported net sales $800,000; cost of goods sold $520,000; operating expenses $210,000; and net income $68,000. Calculate the following values and explain what they mean: (a) profit margin ratio and (b) gross profit rate.

*Evaluate quality of earnings.*
*(SO 7),* **C**

**BE5-12** Wasley Corporation reported net income of $346,000, cash of $67,800, and net cash provided by operating activities of $221,200. What does this suggest about the quality of the company's earnings? What further steps should be taken?

*Journalize purchase transactions.*
*(SO 8),* **AP**

**\*BE5-13** Prepare the journal entries to record these transactions on Koeller Company's books using a periodic inventory system.
(a) On March 2, Koeller Company purchased $800,000 of merchandise from Reeves Company, terms 2/10, n/30.
(b) On March 6, Koeller Company returned $95,000 of the merchandise purchased on March 2.
(c) On March 12, Koeller Company paid the balance due to Reeves Company.

# Do it! Review

**Do it! 5-1**   On October 5, Longhini Company buys merchandise on account from Okern Company. The selling price of the goods is $5,000, and the cost to Okern Company is $3,000. On October 8, Longhini returns defective goods with a selling price of $640 and a scrap value of $240. Record the transactions of Longhini Company, assuming a perpetual approach.

*Record transactions of purchasing company.*
*(SO 2), AP*

**Do it! 5-2**   Assume information similar to that in **Do it!** 5-1. That is: On October 5, Longhini Company buys merchandise on account from Okern Company. The selling price of the goods is $5,000, and the cost to Okern Company is $3,000. On October 8, Longhini returns defective goods with a selling price of $640 and a scrap value of $240. Record the transactions on the books of Okern Company, assuming a perpetual approach.

*Record transactions of selling company.*
*(SO 3), AP*

**Do it! 5-3**   The following information is available for Jain Corp. for the year ended December 31, 2012:

*Prepare multiple-step income statement.*
*(SO 4 ), AP*

| | | | |
|---|---|---|---|
| Other revenues and gains | $ 12,700 | Net sales | $552,000 |
| Other expenses and losses | 13,300 | Operating expenses | 186,000 |
| Cost of goods sold | 156,000 | | |

Prepare a multiple-step income statement for Jain Corp. The company has a tax rate of 30%.

**Do it! 5-4**   Crystal Lake Corporation's accounting records show the following at year-end December 31, 2012:

*Determine cost of goods sold using periodic system.*
*(SO 5), AP*

| | | | |
|---|---|---|---|
| Purchase Discounts | $ 5,900 | Beginning Inventory | $31,720 |
| Freight-in | 8,400 | Ending Inventory | 27,950 |
| Freight-out | 11,100 | Purchase Returns | 3,600 |
| Purchases | 162,500 | | |

Assuming that Crystal Lake Corporation uses the periodic system, compute (a) cost of goods purchased and (b) cost of goods sold.

# Exercises

**E5-1**   This information relates to Percy Co.
1. On April 5, purchased merchandise from Lyman Company for $28,000, terms 2/10, n/30.
2. On April 6, paid freight costs of $700 on merchandise purchased from Lyman.
3. On April 7, purchased equipment on account for $30,000.
4. On April 8, returned some of April 5 merchandise to Lyman Company, which cost $3,600.
5. On April 15, paid the amount due to Lyman Company in full.

*Journalize purchase transactions.*
*(SO 2), AP*

*Instructions*
(a) Prepare the journal entries to record the transactions listed above on the books of Percy Co. Percy Co. uses a perpetual inventory system.
(b) Assume that Percy Co. paid the balance due to Lyman Company on May 4 instead of April 15. Prepare the journal entry to record this payment.

**E5-2**   Assume that on September 1, Office Depot had an inventory that included a variety of calculators. The company uses a perpetual inventory system. During September, these transactions occurred.

*Journalize perpetual inventory entries.*
*(SO 2, 3), AP*

| | | |
|---|---|---|
| Sept. | 6 | Purchased calculators from Abacus Co. at a total cost of $1,650, terms n/30. |
| | 9 | Paid freight of $50 on calculators purchased from Abacus Co. |
| | 10 | Returned calculators to Abacus Co. for $66 credit because they did not meet specifications. |
| | 12 | Sold calculators costing $520 for $690 to Union Book Store, terms n/30. |
| | 14 | Granted credit of $45 to Union Book Store for the return of one calculator that was not ordered. The calculator cost $34. |
| | 20 | Sold calculators costing $570 for $760 to Commons Card Shop, terms n/30. |

*Instructions*

Journalize the September transactions.

*Journalize sales transactions.*
*(SO 3), **AP***

**E5-3**   The following transactions are for Masland Company.

1. On December 3, Masland Company sold $500,000 of merchandise to Parker Co., terms 1/10, n/30. The cost of the merchandise sold was $330,000.
2. On December 8, Parker Co. was granted an allowance of $25,000 for merchandise purchased on December 3.
3. On December 13, Masland Company received the balance due from Parker Co.

*Instructions*

(a) Prepare the journal entries to record these transactions on the books of Masland Company. Masland uses a perpetual inventory system.

(b) Assume that Masland Company received the balance due from Parker Co. on January 2 of the following year instead of December 13. Prepare the journal entry to record the receipt of payment on January 2.

*Journalize perpetual inventory entries.*
*(SO 2, 3), **AP***

**E5-4**   On June 10, Harris Company purchased $9,000 of merchandise from Goetz Company, terms 3/10, n/30. Harris pays the freight costs of $400 on June 11. Goods totaling $600 are returned to Goetz for credit on June 12. On June 19, Harris Company pays Goetz Company in full, less the purchase discount. Both companies use a perpetual inventory system.

*Instructions*

(a) Prepare separate entries for each transaction on the books of Harris Company.

(b) Prepare separate entries for each transaction for Goetz Company. The merchandise purchased by Harris on June 10 cost Goetz $5,000, and the goods returned cost Goetz $310.

*Prepare sales revenues section of income statement.*
*(SO 4), **AP***

**E5-5**   The adjusted trial balance of Dredge Company shows these data pertaining to sales at the end of its fiscal year, October 31, 2012: Sales Revenue $900,000; Freight-out $14,000; Sales Returns and Allowances $22,000; and Sales Discounts $13,500.

*Instructions*

Prepare the sales revenues section of the income statement.

*Prepare an income statement and calculate profitability ratios.*
*(SO 4, 6), **AP***

**E5-6**   Presented below is information for Yu Co. for the month of January 2012.

| | | | |
|---|---|---|---|
| Cost of goods sold | $212,000 | Rent expense | $32,000 |
| Freight-out | 7,000 | Sales discounts | 8,000 |
| Insurance expense | 12,000 | Sales returns and allowances | 20,000 |
| Salaries and wages expense | 60,000 | Sales revenue | 370,000 |

*Instructions*

(a) Prepare an income statement using the format presented on page 243. Assume a 25% tax rate.

(b) Calculate the profit margin ratio and the gross profit rate.

*Compute missing amounts and calculate profitability ratios.*
*(SO 4, 6), **AP***

**E5-7**   Financial information is presented here for two companies.

| | Indig Company | Perez Company |
|---|---|---|
| Sales revenue | $90,000 | ? |
| Sales returns | ? | $ 5,000 |
| Net sales | 84,000 | 100,000 |
| Cost of goods sold | 58,000 | ? |
| Gross profit | ? | 40,000 |
| Operating expenses | 14,380 | ? |
| Net income | ? | 17,000 |

*Prepare multiple-step income statement and calculate profitability ratios.*
*(SO 4, 6), **AP***

*Instructions*

(a) Fill in the missing amounts. Show all computations.

(b) Calculate the profit margin ratio and the gross profit rate for each company.

(c) Discuss your findings in part (b).

**E5-8**   In its income statement for the year ended December 31, 2012, Misra Company reported the following condensed data.

| | | | |
|---|---|---|---|
| Administrative expenses | $465,000 | Loss on disposal of | |
| Cost of goods sold | 987,000 | plant assets | $ 83,500 |
| Interest expense | 71,000 | Net sales | 2,050,000 |
| Interest revenue | 65,000 | Income tax expense | 25,000 |
| Selling expenses | 420,000 | | |

**Instructions**
(a) Prepare a multiple-step income statement.
(b) Calculate the profit margin ratio and gross profit rate.
(c) In 2011, Misra had a profit margin ratio of 5%. Is the decline in 2012 a cause for concern? (Ignore income tax effects.)

**E5-9** In its income statement for the year ended June 30, 2009, The Clorox Company reported the following condensed data (dollars in millions).

*Prepare multiple-step income statement and calculate profitability ratios.*
*(SO 4, 6), C .*

| | | | |
|---|---|---|---|
| Selling and | | Research and | |
| administrative expenses | $ 715 | development expense | $ 114 |
| Net sales | 5,450 | Income tax expense | 274 |
| Interest expense | 161 | Other expense | 46 |
| Advertising expense | 499 | Cost of goods sold | 3,104 |

**Instructions**
(a) Prepare a multiple-step income statement.
(b) Calculate the gross profit rate and the profit margin ratio and explain what each means.
(c) Assume the marketing department has presented a plan to increase advertising expenses by $340 million. It expects this plan to result in an increase in both net sales and cost of goods sold of 25%. Redo parts (a) and (b) and discuss whether this plan has merit. (Assume a tax rate of 34%, and round all amounts to whole dollars.)

**E5-10** The trial balance of Pollard Company at the end of its fiscal year, August 31, 2012, includes these accounts: Beginning Inventory $18,700; Purchases $154,000; Sales Revenue $190,000; Freight-in $8,000; Sales Returns and Allowances $3,000; Freight-out $1,000; and Purchase Returns and Allowances $5,000. The ending merchandise inventory is $21,000.

*Prepare cost of goods sold section using periodic system.*
*(SO 5), AP*

**Instructions**
Prepare a cost of goods sold section (periodic system) for the year ending August 31.

**E5-11** Below is a series of cost of goods sold sections for companies A, F, L, and V.

*Prepare cost of goods sold section using periodic system.*
*(SO 5), AP*

| | A | F | L | V |
|---|---|---|---|---|
| Beginning inventory | $ 250 | $ 120 | $ 700 | $ (j) |
| Purchases | 1,500 | 1,080 | (g) | 43,590 |
| Purchase returns and allowances | 80 | (d) | 290 | (k) |
| Net purchases | (a) | 1,040 | 7,410 | 42,290 |
| Freight-in | 130 | (e) | (h) | 2,240 |
| Cost of goods purchased | (b) | 1,230 | 8,050 | (l) |
| Cost of goods available for sale | 1,800 | 1,350 | (i) | 49,530 |
| Ending inventory | 310 | (f) | 1,150 | 6,230 |
| Cost of goods sold | (c) | 1,230 | 7,600 | 43,300 |

**Instructions**
Fill in the lettered blanks to complete the cost of goods sold sections.

**E5-12** Pardow Corporation reported sales revenue of $257,000, net income of $45,300, cash of $9,300, and net cash provided by operating activities of $23,200. Accounts receivable have increased at three times the rate of sales during the last 3 years.

*Evaluate quality of earnings.*
*(SO 7), C*

**Instructions**
(a) Explain what is meant by high quality of earnings.
(b) Evaluate the quality of the company's earnings. Discuss your findings.
(c) What factors might have contributed to the company's quality of earnings?

**\*E5-13** This information relates to Edyburn Co.

*Journalize purchase transactions.*
*(SO 8), AP*

1. On April 5, purchased merchandise from Hansen Company for $27,000, terms 2/10, n/30.
2. On April 6, paid freight costs of $1,200 on merchandise purchased from Hansen Company.

3. On April 7, purchased equipment on account for $30,000.
4. On April 8, returned some of the April 5 merchandise to Hansen Company, which cost $3,600.
5. On April 15, paid the amount due to Hansen Company in full.

**Instructions**

(a) Prepare the journal entries to record these transactions on the books of Edyburn Co. using a periodic inventory system.
(b) Assume that Edyburn Co. paid the balance due to Hansen Company on May 4 instead of April 15. Prepare the journal entry to record this payment.

# Exercises: Set B and Challenge Exercises

Visit the book's companion website, at **www.wiley.com/college/kimmel**, and choose the Student Companion site to access Exercise Set B and Challenge Exercises.

# Problems: Set A

*Journalize, post, prepare partial income statement, and calculate ratios.*

(SO 2, 3, 4, 6), **AP**

GLS

**P5-1A** Janssen Hardware Store completed the following merchandising transactions in the month of May. At the beginning of May, Janssen's ledger showed Cash of $8,000 and Common Stock of $8,000.

| May | 1 | Purchased merchandise on account from Vanco Wholesale Supply for $8,000, terms 1/10, n/30. |
| | 2 | Sold merchandise on account for $4,400, terms 2/10, n/30. The cost of the merchandise sold was $3,300. |
| | 5 | Received credit from Vanco Wholesale Supply for merchandise returned $200. |
| | 9 | Received collections in full, less discounts, from customers billed on May 2. |
| | 10 | Paid Vanco Wholesale Supply in full, less discount. |
| | 11 | Purchased supplies for cash $900. |
| | 12 | Purchased merchandise for cash $3,100. |
| | 15 | Received $230 refund for return of poor-quality merchandise from supplier on cash purchase. |
| | 17 | Purchased merchandise from Strickler Distributors for $2,500, terms 2/10, n/30. |
| | 19 | Paid freight on May 17 purchase $250. |
| | 24 | Sold merchandise for cash $5,500. The cost of the merchandise sold was $4,100. |
| | 25 | Purchased merchandise from Fasteners Inc. for $800, terms 3/10, n/30. |
| | 27 | Paid Strickler Distributors in full, less discount. |
| | 29 | Made refunds to cash customers for returned merchandise $124. The returned merchandise had cost $90. |
| | 31 | Sold merchandise on account for $1,280, terms n/30. The cost of the merchandise sold was $830. |

Janssen Hardware's chart of accounts includes Cash, Accounts Receivable, Inventory, Supplies, Accounts Payable, Common Stock, Sales Revenue, Sales Returns and Allowances, Sales Discounts, and Cost of Goods Sold.

**Instructions**

(a) Journalize the transactions using a perpetual inventory system.
(b) Post the transactions to T accounts. Be sure to enter the beginning cash and common stock balances.

(c) Gross profit $2,828

(c) Prepare an income statement through gross profit for the month of May 2012.
(d) Calculate the profit margin ratio and the gross profit rate. (Assume operating expenses were $1,400.)

*Journalize purchase and sale transactions under a perpetual system.*

(SO 2, 3), **AP**

**P5-2A** Hayes Warehouse distributes hardback books to retail stores and extends credit terms of 2/10, n/30 to all of its customers. During the month of June, the following merchandising transactions occurred.

June    1    Purchased books on account for $1,040 (including freight) from Brooks Publishers, terms 2/10, n/30.

3    Sold books on account to the Mission Viejo bookstore for $1,200. The cost of the merchandise sold was $720.

6    Received $40 credit for books returned to Brooks Publishers.

9    Paid Brooks Publishers in full.

15    Received payment in full from the Mission Viejo bookstore.

17    Sold books on account to Book Nook for $1,200. The cost of the merchandise sold was $730.

20    Purchased books on account for $720 from Cook Book Publishers, terms 1/15, n/30.

24    Received payment in full from Book Nook.

26    Paid Cook Book Publishers in full.

28    Sold books on account to NewTown Bookstore for $1,300. The cost of the merchandise sold was $780.

30    Granted NewTown Bookstore $130 credit for books returned costing $80.

### Instructions

Journalize the transactions for the month of June for Hayes Warehouse, using a perpetual inventory system.

**P5-3A**    At the beginning of the current season on April 1, the ledger of Thousand Oaks Pro Shop showed Cash $2,500; Inventory $3,500; and Common Stock $6,000. The following transactions were completed during April 2012.

*Journalize, post, and prepare trial balance and partial income statement.*

(SO 2, 3, 4), **AP**

Apr.    5    Purchased golf bags, clubs, and balls on account from Ryder Co. $1,500, terms 3/10, n/60.

7    Paid freight on Ryder purchase $80.

9    Received credit from Ryder Co. for merchandise returned $200.

10    Sold merchandise on account to members $1,340, terms n/30. The merchandise sold had a cost of $820.

12    Purchased golf shoes, sweaters, and other accessories on account from Birdie Sportswear $830, terms 1/10, n/30.

14    Paid Ryder Co. in full.

17    Received credit from Birdie Sportswear for merchandise returned $30.

20    Made sales on account to members $810, terms n/30. The cost of the merchandise sold was $550.

21    Paid Birdie Sportswear in full.

27    Granted an allowance to members for clothing that did not fit properly $80.

30    Received payments on account from members $1,220.

The chart of accounts for the pro shop includes Cash, Accounts Receivable, Inventory, Accounts Payable, Common Stock, Sales Revenue, Sales Returns and Allowances, and Cost of Goods Sold.

### Instructions

(a) Journalize the April transactions using a perpetual inventory system.

(b) Using T accounts, enter the beginning balances in the ledger accounts and post the April transactions.

(c) Prepare a trial balance on April 30, 2012.

(d) Prepare an income statement through gross profit.

(c) Tot. trial balance    $8,150
(d) Gross profit    $ 700

**P5-4A**    Chapman Department Store is located in midtown Metropolis. During the past several years, net income has been declining because suburban shopping centers have been attracting business away from city areas. At the end of the company's fiscal year on November 30, 2012, these accounts appeared in its adjusted trial balance.

*Prepare financial statements and calculate profitability ratios.*

(SO 4, 6), **AP**

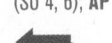

| | |
|---|---|
| Accounts Payable | $ 26,800 |
| Accounts Receivable | 17,200 |
| Accumulated Depreciation—Equipment | 68,000 |
| Cash | 8,000 |
| Common Stock | 35,000 |
| Cost of Goods Sold | 614,300 |
| Freight-out | 6,200 |

| | |
|---|---|
| Equipment | $157,000 |
| Depreciation Expense | 13,500 |
| Dividends | 12,000 |
| Gain on Disposal of Plant Assets | 2,000 |
| Income Tax Expense | 10,000 |
| Insurance Expense | 9,000 |
| Interest Expense | 5,000 |
| Inventory | 26,200 |
| Notes Payable | 43,500 |
| Prepaid Insurance | 6,000 |
| Advertising Expense | 33,500 |
| Rent Expense | 34,000 |
| Retained Earnings | 14,200 |
| Salaries and Wages Expense | 117,000 |
| Sales Revenue | 904,000 |
| Salaries and Wages Payable | 6,000 |
| Sales Returns and Allowances | 20,000 |
| Utilities Expense | 10,600 |

Additional data: Notes payable are due in 2016.

**Instructions**

(a) Net income    $ 32,900
Tot. assets    $146,400

(a) Prepare a multiple-step income statement, a retained earnings statement, and a classified balance sheet.

(b) Calculate the profit margin ratio and the gross profit rate.

(c) The vice president of marketing and the director of human resources have developed a proposal whereby the company would compensate the sales force on a strictly commission basis. Given the increased incentive, they expect net sales to increase by 15%. As a result, they estimate that gross profit will increase by $40,443 and expenses by $58,600. Compute the expected new net income. (*Hint*: You do not need to prepare an income statement.) Then, compute the revised profit margin ratio and gross profit rate. Comment on the effect that this plan would have on net income and on the ratios, and evaluate the merit of this proposal. (Ignore income tax effects.)

*Prepare a correct multiple-step income statement.*

*(SO 4),* **AP**

**P5-5A** An inexperienced accountant prepared this condensed income statement for McDowell Company, a retail firm that has been in business for a number of years.

### MCDOWELL COMPANY
### Income Statement
### For the Year Ended December 31, 2012

| | | |
|---|---|---|
| Revenues | | |
| Net sales | $850,000 | |
| Other revenues | 22,000 | |
| | | 872,000 |
| Cost of goods sold | | 555,000 |
| Gross profit | | 317,000 |
| Operating expenses | | |
| Selling expenses | 109,000 | |
| Administrative expenses | 103,000 | |
| | | 212,000 |
| Net earnings | | $105,000 |

As an experienced, knowledgeable accountant, you review the statement and determine the following facts.

1. Net sales consist of sales $911,000, less freight-out expense on merchandise sold $33,000, and sales returns and allowances $28,000.

2. Other revenues consist of sales discounts $18,000 and rent revenue $8,000.

3. Selling expenses consist of salespersons' salaries $80,000; depreciation on equipment $10,000; advertising $15,000; and sales commissions $6,000. The commissions represent commissions paid. At December 31, $3,000 of commissions have been earned by salespersons but have not been paid. All compensation should be recorded as Salaries and Wages Expense.

4. Administrative expenses consist of office salaries $47,000; dividends $18,000; utilities $12,000; interest expense $2,000; and rent expense $24,000, which includes prepayments totaling $6,000 for the first quarter of 2013.

**Instructions**
Prepare a correct detailed multiple-step income statement. Assume a 25% tax rate.

*Net income $69,500*

**P5-6A** The trial balance of Dealer's Choice Wholesale Company contained the accounts shown at December 31, the end of the company's fiscal year.

*Journalize, post, and prepare adjusted trial balance and financial statements.*
(SO 4), **AP**

### DEALER'S CHOICE WHOLESALE COMPANY
### Trial Balance
### December 31, 2012

|  | Debit | Credit |
|---|---|---|
| Cash | $ 31,400 | |
| Accounts Receivable | 37,600 | |
| Inventory | 70,000 | |
| Land | 92,000 | |
| Buildings | 200,000 | |
| Accumulated Depreciation—Buildings | | $ 60,000 |
| Equipment | 83,500 | |
| Accumulated Depreciation—Equipment | | 40,500 |
| Notes Payable | | 54,700 |
| Accounts Payable | | 17,500 |
| Common Stock | | 160,000 |
| Retained Earnings | | 67,200 |
| Dividends | 10,000 | |
| Sales Revenue | | 922,100 |
| Sales Discounts | 6,000 | |
| Cost of Goods Sold | 709,900 | |
| Salaries and Wages Expense | 51,300 | |
| Utilities Expense | 11,400 | |
| Maintenance and Repairs Expense | 8,900 | |
| Advertising Expense | 5,200 | |
| Insurance Expense | 4,800 | |
|  | $1,322,000 | $1,322,000 |

Adjustment data:
1. Depreciation is $8,000 on buildings and $7,000 on equipment. (Both are operating expenses.)
2. Interest of $4,500 is due and unpaid on notes payable at December 31.
3. Income tax due and unpaid at December 31 is $24,000.
Other data: $15,000 of the notes payable are payable next year.

**Instructions**
(a) Journalize the adjusting entries.
(b) Create T accounts for all accounts used in part (a). Enter the trial balance amounts into the T accounts and post the adjusting entries.
(c) Prepare an adjusted trial balance.
(d) Prepare a multiple-step income statement and a retained earnings statement for the year, and a classified balance sheet at December 31, 2012.

(c) Tot. trial balance    $1,365,500
(d) Net income    $81,100
     Tot. assets    $399,000

**P5-7A** At the end of Snyder Department Store's fiscal year on November 30, 2012, these accounts appeared in its adjusted trial balance.

*Determine cost of goods sold and gross profit under a periodic system.*
(SO 4, 5), **AP**

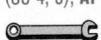

| | |
|---|---|
| Freight-in | $ 5,060 |
| Inventory (beginning) | 41,300 |
| Purchases | 613,000 |
| Purchase Discounts | 7,000 |
| Purchase Returns and Allowances | 6,760 |
| Sales Revenue | 902,000 |
| Sales Returns and Allowances | 20,000 |

Additional facts:
1. Merchandise inventory on November 30, 2012, is $36,200.
2. Note that Snyder Department Store uses a periodic system.

**Instructions**

Prepare an income statement through gross profit for the year ended November 30, 2012.

Gross profit $272,600

**P5-8A**  Reza Inc. operates a retail operation that purchases and sells snowmobiles, amongst other outdoor products. The company purchases all merchandise inventory on credit and uses a periodic inventory system. The Accounts Payable account is used for recording inventory purchases only; all other current liabilities are accrued in separate accounts. You are provided with the following selected information for the fiscal years 2010 through 2013, inclusive.

*Calculate missing amounts and assess profitability.*
(SO 4, 5, 6), **AN**

|  | 2010 | 2011 | 2012 | 2013 |
|---|---|---|---|---|
| **Income Statement Data** | | | | |
| Sales revenue | | $96,890 | $ (e) | $82,220 |
| Cost of goods sold | | (a) | 28,060 | 26,490 |
| Gross profit | | 67,800 | 59,620 | (i) |
| Operating expenses | | 63,640 | (f) | 52,870 |
| Net income | | $ (b) | $ 3,510 | $ (j) |
| **Balance Sheet Data** | | | | |
| Inventory | $13,000 | $ (c) | $14,700 | $ (k) |
| Accounts payable | 5,800 | 6,500 | 4,600 | (l) |
| **Additional Information** | | | | |
| Purchases of merchandise inventory on account | | $25,890 | $ (g) | $24,050 |
| Cash payments to suppliers | | (d) | (h) | 24,650 |

**Instructions**

(a) Calculate the missing amounts.

(b) The vice presidents of sales, marketing, production, and finance are discussing the company's results with the CEO. They note that sales declined over the 3-year fiscal period, 2011–2013. Does that mean that profitability necessarily also declined? Explain, computing the gross profit rate and the profit margin ratio for each fiscal year to help support your answer.

*Journalize, post, and prepare trial balance and partial income statement under a periodic system.*
(SO 5, 8), **AP**

**GLS**

***P5-9A**  At the beginning of the current season on April 1, the ledger of Thousand Oaks Pro Shop showed Cash $2,500; Inventory $3,500; and Common Stock $6,000. These transactions occurred during April 2012.

| Apr. | 5 | Purchased golf bags, clubs, and balls on account from Ryder Co. $1,500, terms 3/10, n/60. |
|---|---|---|
| | 7 | Paid freight on Ryder Co. purchases $80. |
| | 9 | Received credit from Ryder Co. for merchandise returned $200. |
| | 10 | Sold merchandise on account to members $1,340, terms n/30. |
| | 12 | Purchased golf shoes, sweaters, and other accessories on account from Birdie Sportswear $830, terms 1/10, n/30. |
| | 14 | Paid Ryder Co. in full. |
| | 17 | Received credit from Birdie Sportswear for merchandise returned $30. |
| | 20 | Made sales on account to members $810, terms n/30. |
| | 21 | Paid Birdie Sportswear in full. |
| | 27 | Granted credit to members for clothing that did not fit properly $80. |
| | 30 | Received payments on account from members $1,220. |

The chart of accounts for the pro shop includes Cash, Accounts Receivable, Inventory, Accounts Payable, Common Stock, Sales Revenue, Sales Returns and Allowances, Purchases, Purchase Returns and Allowances, Purchase Discounts, and Freight-in.

**Instructions**

(a) Journalize the April transactions using a periodic inventory system.
(b) Using T accounts, enter the beginning balances in the ledger accounts and post the April transactions.
(c) Prepare a trial balance on April 30, 2012.

(c) Tot. trial balance  $8,427
Gross profit  $700

(d) Prepare an income statement through gross profit, assuming merchandise inventory on hand at April 30 is $4,263.

# Problems: Set B

**P5-1B**  Curtain Distributing Company completed these merchandising transactions in the month of April. At the beginning of April, the ledger of Curtain showed Cash of $9,000 and Common Stock of $9,000.

*Journalize, post, prepare partial income statement, and calculate ratios.*

*(SO 2, 3, 4, 6),* **AP**

**GLS**

| | | |
|---|---|---|
| Apr. | 2 | Purchased merchandise on account from Luebke Supply Co. $8,700, terms 2/10, n/30. |
| | 4 | Sold merchandise on account $6,000, terms 2/10, n/30. The cost of the merchandise sold was $3,700. |
| | 5 | Paid $200 freight on April 4 sale. |
| | 6 | Received credit from Luebke Supply Co. for merchandise returned $400. |
| | 11 | Paid Luebke Supply Co. in full, less discount. |
| | 13 | Received collections in full, less discounts, from customers billed on April 4. |
| | 14 | Purchased merchandise for cash $4,700. |
| | 16 | Received refund from supplier for returned merchandise on cash purchase of April 14, $500. |
| | 18 | Purchased merchandise from Cascade Distributors $5,500, terms 2/10, n/30. |
| | 20 | Paid freight on April 18 purchase $180. |
| | 23 | Sold merchandise for cash $8,300. The cost of the merchandise sold was $5,580. |
| | 26 | Purchased merchandise for cash $2,300. |
| | 27 | Paid Cascade Distributors in full, less discount. |
| | 29 | Made refunds to cash customers for returned merchandise $180. The returned merchandise had a cost of $120. |
| | 30 | Sold merchandise on account $3,980, terms n/30. The cost of the merchandise sold was $2,500. |

Curtain Distributing Company's chart of accounts includes Cash, Accounts Receivable, Inventory, Accounts Payable, Common Stock, Sales Revenue, Sales Returns and Allowances, Sales Discounts, Cost of Goods Sold, and Freight-out.

## Instructions
(a) Journalize the transactions.
(b) Post the transactions to T accounts. Be sure to enter the beginning cash and common stock balances.
(c) Prepare the income statement through gross profit for the month of April 2012.
(d) Calculate the profit margin ratio and the gross profit rate. (Assume operating expenses were $2,050.)

*(c) Gross profit $6,320*

**P5-2B**  Holiday Warehouse distributes suitcases to retail stores and extends credit terms of 1/10, n/30 to all of its customers. During the month of July, the following merchandising transactions occurred.

*Journalize purchase and sale transactions under a perpetual system.*

*(SO 2, 3),* **AP**

| | | |
|---|---|---|
| July | 1 | Purchased suitcases on account for $2,700 from Satchel Manufacturers, terms 2/15, n/30. |
| | 3 | Sold suitcases on account to Triptik for $2,900. The cost of the merchandise sold was $1,800. |
| | 9 | Paid Satchel Manufacturers in full. |
| | 12 | Received payment in full from Triptik. |
| | 17 | Sold suitcases on account to PassPort for $2,000. The cost of the merchandise sold was $1,200. |
| | 18 | Purchased suitcases on account for $2,200 (including freight) from Steamer Manufacturers, terms 1/10, n/30. |
| | 20 | Received $300 credit for suitcases returned to Steamer Manufacturers. |
| | 21 | Received payment in full from PassPort. |
| | 22 | Sold suitcases on account to Carry On for $3,120. The cost of the merchandise sold was $1,800. |
| | 30 | Paid Steamer Manufacturers in full. |
| | 31 | Granted Carry On $310 credit for suitcases returned costing $170. |

### Instructions

Journalize the transactions for the month of July for Holiday Warehouse, using a perpetual inventory system.

*Journalize, post, and prepare trial balance and partial income statement.*

(SO 2, 3, 4), **AP**

**P5-3B** At the beginning of the current season, the ledger of Highland Tennis Shop showed Cash $2,500; Inventory $1,700; and Common Stock $4,200. The following transactions were completed during April.

| Apr. | 4 | Purchased racquets and balls from Harris Co. $980, terms 2/10, n/30. |
|---|---|---|
| | 6 | Paid freight on Harris Co. purchase $60. |
| | 8 | Sold merchandise to members $750, terms n/30. The merchandise sold cost $480. |
| | 10 | Received credit of $130 from Harris Co. for damaged racquets that were returned. |
| | 11 | Purchased tennis shoes from Happy Feet for cash $300. |
| | 13 | Paid Harris Co. in full. |
| | 14 | Purchased tennis shirts and shorts from Rivera Sportswear $1,300, terms 3/10, n/60. |
| | 15 | Received cash refund of $50 from Happy Feet for damaged merchandise that was returned. |
| | 17 | Paid freight on Rivera Sportswear purchase $60. |
| | 18 | Sold merchandise to members $660, terms n/30. The cost of the merchandise sold was $440. |
| | 20 | Received $500 in cash from members in settlement of their accounts. |
| | 21 | Paid Rivera Sportswear in full. |
| | 27 | Granted an allowance of $30 to members for tennis clothing that did not fit properly. |
| | 30 | Received cash payments on account from members $550. |

The chart of accounts for the tennis shop includes Cash, Accounts Receivable, Inventory, Accounts Payable, Common Stock, Sales Revenue, Sales Returns and Allowances, and Cost of Goods Sold.

### Instructions

(a) Journalize the April transactions using a perpetual inventory system.
(b) Using T accounts, enter the beginning balances in the ledger accounts and post the April transactions.

(c) Tot. trial balance     $5,610     (c) Prepare a trial balance on April 30, 2012.
(d) Gross profit          $460     (d) Prepare an income statement through gross profit.

*Prepare financial statements and calculate profitability ratios.*

(SO 4, 6), **AP**

**P5-4B** Parkland Department Store is located near the Lyndale Shopping Mall. At the end of the company's fiscal year on December 31, 2012, the following accounts appeared in its adjusted trial balance.

| | |
|---|---|
| Accounts Payable | $ 73,300 |
| Accounts Receivable | 45,500 |
| Accumulated Depreciation—Buildings | 52,500 |
| Accumulated Depreciation—Equipment | 42,600 |
| Buildings | 190,000 |
| Cash | 28,000 |
| Common Stock | 140,000 |
| Cost of Goods Sold | 412,000 |
| Depreciation Expense | 23,400 |
| Dividends | 15,000 |
| Equipment | 100,000 |
| Gain on Disposal of Plant Assets | 4,300 |
| Income Tax Expense | 15,000 |
| Insurance Expense | 8,400 |
| Interest Expense | 7,000 |
| Interest Payable | 2,000 |
| Inventory | 43,000 |
| Mortgage Payable | 62,500 |
| Prepaid Insurance | 2,400 |

| | |
|---|---:|
| Maintenance and Repairs Expense | $ 6,200 |
| Retained Earnings | 19,200 |
| Salaries and Wages Expense | 111,000 |
| Sales Revenue | 626,000 |
| Salaries and Wages Payable | 3,500 |
| Sales Returns and Allowances | 8,000 |
| Utilities Expense | 11,000 |

Additional data: $20,000 of the mortgage payable is due for payment next year.

**Instructions**
(a) Prepare a multiple-step income statement, a retained earnings statement, and a classified balance sheet.
(b) Calculate the profit margin ratio and the gross profit rate.
(c) The vice president of marketing and the director of human resources have developed a proposal whereby the company would compensate the sales force on a strictly commission basis. Given the increased incentive, they expect net sales to increase by 25%. As a result, they estimate that gross profit will increase by $50,500 and expenses by $27,800. Compute the expected new net income. (*Hint:* You do not need to prepare an income statement.) Then, compute the revised profit margin ratio and gross profit rate. Comment on the effect that this plan would have on net income and the ratios, and evaluate the merit of this proposal.

(a) Net income     $28,300
Tot. assets     $313,800

**P5-5B**  A part-time bookkeeper prepared this income statement for Kritek Company for the year ending December 31, 2012.

*Prepare a correct multiple-step income statement.*
*(SO 4),* **AP**

**KRITEK COMPANY**
**Income Statement**
**December 31, 2012**

| | | |
|---|---:|---:|
| Revenues | | |
| Sales revenue | | $720,000 |
| Less: Freight-out | $14,000 | |
| Sales discounts | 11,300 | 25,300 |
| Net sales | | 694,700 |
| Other revenues (net) | | 1,300 |
| Total revenues | | 696,000 |
| Expenses | | |
| Cost of goods sold | | 460,000 |
| Selling expenses | | 103,000 |
| Administrative expenses | | 54,000 |
| Dividends | | 12,000 |
| Total expenses | | 629,000 |
| Net income | | $ 67,000 |

As an experienced, knowledgeable accountant, you review the statement and determine the following facts.

1. Sales include $12,000 of deposits from customers for future sales orders.
2. Other revenues contain two items: interest expense $4,000 and interest revenue $5,300.
3. Selling expenses consist of sales salaries and wages $82,500, advertising $13,000, and depreciation on store equipment $7,500.
4. Administrative expenses consist of office salaries $23,000; utilities expense $9,500; rent expense $14,500; and insurance expense $7,000. Insurance expense includes $1,200 of insurance applicable to 2013.

Operating expenses     $169,800
Net income     $51,150

**Instructions**
Prepare a correct detailed multiple-step income statement. Assume a tax rate of 25%.

*Journalize, post, and prepare adjusted trial balance and financial statements.*
*(SO 4),* **AP**

**P5-6B**  The trial balance of Runway Fashion Center contained the accounts on the next page at November 30, the end of the company's fiscal year.

**RUNWAY FASHION CENTER**
**Trial Balance**
**November 30, 2012**

| | Debit | Credit |
|---|---|---|
| Cash | $ 37,700 | |
| Accounts Receivable | 33,700 | |
| Inventory | 43,000 | |
| Supplies | 8,800 | |
| Equipment | 143,000 | |
| Accumulated Depreciation—Equipment | | $ 41,000 |
| Notes Payable | | 62,000 |
| Accounts Payable | | 17,800 |
| Common Stock | | 80,000 |
| Retained Earnings | | 30,000 |
| Dividends | 12,000 | |
| Sales Revenue | | 757,200 |
| Sales Returns and Allowances | 6,200 | |
| Cost of Goods Sold | 505,400 | |
| Salaries and Wages Expense | 110,000 | |
| Advertising Expense | 26,400 | |
| Utilities Expense | 14,000 | |
| Maintenance and Repairs Expense | 12,100 | |
| Freight-out | 11,700 | |
| Rent Expense | 24,000 | |
| | $988,000 | $988,000 |

Adjustment data:

1. Store supplies on hand total $3,100.
2. Depreciation is $14,000 on the store equipment and $6,000 on the delivery equipment.
3. Interest of $4,400 is accrued on notes payable at November 30.
4. Income tax due and unpaid at November 30 is $3,000.

Other data: $24,000 of notes payable are due for payment next year.

***Instructions***
(a) Journalize the adjusting entries.
(b) Prepare T accounts for all accounts used in part (a). Enter the trial balance amounts into the T accounts and post the adjusting entries.

(c) Tot. trial balance $1,015,400

(c) Prepare an adjusted trial balance.

(d) Net income $14,300
Tot. assets $199,500

(d) Prepare a multiple-step income statement and a retained earnings statement for the year, and a classified balance sheet at November 30, 2012.

*Determine cost of goods sold and gross profit under a periodic system.*

(SO 4, 5), **AP**

**P5-7B** At the end of Ehlinger Department Store's fiscal year on December 31, 2012, these accounts appeared in its adjusted trial balance.

| | |
|---|---|
| Freight-in | $ 7,200 |
| Inventory (beginning) | 40,500 |
| Purchases | 456,000 |
| Purchase Discounts | 12,000 |
| Purchase Returns and Allowances | 6,400 |
| Sales Revenue | 702,000 |
| Sales Returns and Allowances | 8,000 |

Additional facts:

1. Merchandise inventory on December 31, 2012, is $58,300.
2. Note that Ehlinger Department Store uses a periodic system.

***Instructions***
Prepare an income statement through gross profit for the year ended December 31, 2012.

Gross profit $267,000

*Calculate missing amounts and assess profitability.*

(SO 4, 5, 6), **AN**

**P5-8B** Sandra McLellan operates a clothing retail operation. She purchases all merchandise inventory on credit and uses a periodic inventory system. The Accounts Payable account is used for recording inventory purchases only; all other current liabilities are accrued in separate accounts. You are provided with the following selected information for the fiscal years 2010, 2011, 2012, and 2013.

|  | 2010 | 2011 | 2012 | 2013 |
|---|---|---|---|---|
| Inventory (ending) | $16,000 | $ 11,300 | $ 16,400 | $ 12,200 |
| Accounts payable (ending) | 17,000 | | | |
| Sales revenue | | 229,700 | 227,600 | 222,000 |
| Purchases of merchandise inventory on account | | 146,900 | 155,700 | 139,200 |
| Cash payments to suppliers | | 135,900 | 159,000 | 127,000 |

**Instructions**
(a) Calculate cost of goods sold for each of the 2011, 2012, and 2013 fiscal years.
(b) Calculate the gross profit for each of the 2011, 2012, and 2013 fiscal years.
(c) Calculate the ending balance of accounts payable for each of the 2011, 2012, and 2013 fiscal years.
(d) The vice presidents of sales, marketing, production, and finance are discussing the company's results with the CEO. They note that sales declined in fiscal 2013. They wonder whether that means that profitability, as measured by the gross profit rate, necessarily also declined. Explain, calculating the gross profit rate for each fiscal year to help support your answer.

(a) 2012 $150,600

(c) 2012 $24,700

*P5-9B At the beginning of the current season, the ledger of Highland Tennis Shop showed Cash $2,500; Inventory $1,700; and Common Stock $4,200. The following transactions were completed during April.

*Journalize, post, and prepare trial balance and partial income statement under a periodic system.*
(SO 5, 8), **AP**

| Apr. | 4 | Purchased racquets and balls from Harris Co. $980, terms 2/10, n/30. |
|---|---|---|
| | 6 | Paid freight on Harris Co. purchase $60. |
| | 8 | Sold merchandise to members $750, terms n/30. |
| | 10 | Received credit of $130 from Harris Co. for damaged racquets that were returned. |
| | 11 | Purchased tennis shoes from Happy Feet for cash $300. |
| | 13 | Paid Harris Co. in full. |
| | 14 | Purchased tennis shirts and shorts from Rivera Sportswear $1,300, terms 3/10, n/60. |
| | 15 | Received cash refund of $50 from Happy Feet for damaged merchandise that was returned. |
| | 17 | Paid freight on Rivera Sportswear purchase $60. |
| | 18 | Sold merchandise to members $660, terms n/30. |
| | 20 | Received $500 in cash from members in settlement of their accounts. |
| | 21 | Paid Rivera Sportswear in full. |
| | 27 | Granted an allowance of $30 to members for tennis clothing that did not fit properly. |
| | 30 | Received cash payments on account from members $550. |

The chart of accounts for the tennis shop includes Cash, Accounts Receivable, Inventory, Accounts Payable, Common Stock, Sales Revenue, Sales Returns and Allowances, Purchases, Purchase Returns and Allowances, Purchase Discounts, and Freight-in.

**Instructions**
(a) Journalize the April transactions using a periodic inventory system.
(b) Using T accounts, enter the beginning balances in the ledger accounts and post the April transactions.
(c) Prepare a trial balance on April 30, 2012.
(d) Prepare an income statement through Gross Profit, assuming merchandise inventory on hand at April 30 is $3,244.

(c) Tot. trial balance      $5,846
(d) Gross profit                 $460

# Problems: Set C

Visit the book's companion website, at **www.wiley.com/college/kimmel**, and choose the Student Companion site to access Problem Set C.

# Comprehensive Problem

**CP5** On December 1, 2012, Shiras Distributing Company had the following account balances.

| | Debits | | Credits |
|---|---|---|---|
| Cash | $ 7,200 | Accumulated Depreciation— | |
| Accounts Receivable | 4,600 | Equipment | $ 2,200 |
| Inventory | 12,000 | Accounts Payable | 4,500 |
| Supplies | 1,200 | Salaries and Wages Payable | 1,000 |
| Equipment | 22,000 | Common Stock | 15,000 |
| | $47,000 | Retained Earnings | 24,300 |
| | | | $47,000 |

During December, the company completed the following summary transactions.

Dec. 6 Paid $1,600 for salaries due employees, of which $600 is for December and $1,000 is for November salaries payable.

8 Received $1,900 cash from customers in payment of account (no discount allowed).

10 Sold merchandise for cash $6,300. The cost of the merchandise sold was $4,100.

13 Purchased merchandise on account from Gong Co. $9,000, terms 2/10, n/30.

15 Purchased supplies for cash $2,000.

18 Sold merchandise on account $12,000, terms 3/10, n/30. The cost of the merchandise sold was $8,000.

20 Paid salaries $1,800.

23 Paid Gong Co. in full, less discount.

27 Received collections in full, less discounts, from customers billed on December 18.

Adjustment data:

1. Accrued salaries payable $800.
2. Depreciation $200 per month.
3. Supplies on hand $1,500.
4. Income tax due and unpaid at December 31 is $200.

## Instructions

(a) Journalize the December transactions using a perpetual inventory system.

(b) Enter the December 1 balances in the ledger T accounts and post the December transactions. Use Cost of Goods Sold, Depreciation Expense, Salaries and Wages Expense, Sales Revenue, Sales Discounts, Supplies Expense, Income Tax Expense, and Income Taxes Payable.

(c) Journalize and post adjusting entries.

(d) Totals $65,500    (d) Prepare an adjusted trial balance.

(e) Net income $540    (e) Prepare an income statement and a retained earnings statement for December and a classified balance sheet at December 31.

# Continuing Cookie Chronicle

(*Note:* This is a continuation of the Cookie Chronicle from Chapters 1 through 4.)

**CCC5** Because Natalie has had such a successful first few months, she is considering other opportunities to develop her business. One opportunity is to become the exclusive distributor of a line of fine European mixers. Natalie comes to you for advice on how to account for these mixers.

Go to the book's companion website, at **www.wiley.com/college/kimmel**, to see the completion of this problem.

# broadening your perspective

## Financial Reporting and Analysis

### FINANCIAL REPORTING PROBLEM: *Tootsie Roll Industries Inc.*

**BYP5-1**   The financial statements for Tootsie Roll Industries appear in Appendix A at the end of this book.

*Instructions*
Answer these questions using the Consolidated Income Statement.
(a)  What was the percentage change in total revenue and in net income from 2008 to 2009?
(b)  What was the profit margin ratio in each of the 3 years? (Use "Total Revenue.") Comment on the trend.
(c)  What was Tootsie Roll's gross profit rate in each of the 3 years? (Use "Product" amounts.) Comment on the trend.

### COMPARATIVE ANALYSIS PROBLEM: *Tootsie Roll vs. Hershey*

**BYP5-2**   The financial statements of The Hershey Company appear in Appendix B, following the financial statements for Tootsie Roll in Appendix A.

*Instructions*
(a)  Based on the information contained in these financial statements, determine the following values for each company.
   (1)  Profit margin ratio for 2009. (For Tootsie Roll, use "Total Revenue.")
   (2)  Gross profit for 2009. (For Tootsie Roll, use "Product" amounts.)
   (3)  Gross profit rate for 2009. (For Tootsie Roll, use "Product" amounts.)
   (4)  Operating income for 2009.
   (5)  Percentage change in operating income from 2009 to 2008.
(b)  What conclusions concerning the relative profitability of the two companies can be drawn from these data?

### RESEARCH CASE

**BYP5-3**   The April 23, 2008, issue of the *Wall Street Journal* includes an article by Vanessa O'Connell entitled "Coach Profit Is Up but Margins Are Tightening."

*Instructions*
Read the article and answer the following questions.
(a)  Referring to the ratios that were presented in this chapter, interpret the first paragraph of the article.
(b)  Explain why investors would be angry that the company has stopped reporting the amount of its sales from outlet malls separately from its sales at full-priced stores.
(c)  The article says that the gross margin (gross profit rate) fell from 77.8% to 75%. According to the article, what were the two causes of this decline?

### INTERPRETING FINANCIAL STATEMENTS

**BYP5-4**   Recently, it was announced that two giant French retailers, Carrefour SA and Promodes SA, would merge. A headline in the *Wall Street Journal* blared, "French Retailers Create New Wal-Mart Rival." While Wal-Mart's total sales would still exceed those of the combined company, Wal-Mart's international sales are far less than those of the combined company. This is a serious concern for Wal-Mart, since its primary opportunity for future growth lies outside of the United States.

Below are basic financial data for the combined corporation (in euros) and Wal-Mart (in U.S. dollars). Even though their results are presented in different currencies, by employing ratios we can make some basic comparisons.

|  | Carrefour (in millions) | Wal-Mart (in millions) |
|---|---|---|
| Sales | €70,486 | $256,329 |
| Cost of goods sold | 54,630 | 198,747 |
| Net income | 1,738 | 9,054 |
| Total assets | 39,063 | 104,912 |
| Current assets | 14,521 | 34,421 |
| Current liabilities | 13,660 | 37,418 |
| Total liabilities | 29,434 | 61,289 |

*Instructions*

Compare the two companies by answering the following.

(a) Calculate the gross profit rate for each of the companies, and discuss their relative abilities to control cost of goods sold.

(b) Calculate the profit margin ratio, and discuss the companies' relative profitability.

(c) Calculate the current ratio and debt to total assets ratios for the two companies, and discuss their relative liquidity and solvency.

(d) What concerns might you have in relying on this comparison?

## FINANCIAL ANALYSIS ON THE WEB

**BYP5-5** *Purpose*: No financial decision maker should ever rely solely on the financial information reported in the annual report to make decisions. It is important to keep abreast of financial news. This activity demonstrates how to search for financial news on the Web.

*Address:* **http://biz.yahoo.com/i**, or go to **www.wiley.com/college/kimmel**

*Steps*

1. Type in either Wal-Mart, Target Corp., or Kmart.
2. Choose **News**.
3. Select an article that sounds interesting to you and that would be relevant to an investor in these companies.

*Instructions*

(a) What was the source of the article (e.g., Reuters, Businesswire, Prnewswire)?

(b) Assume that you are a personal financial planner and that one of your clients owns stock in the company. Write a brief memo to your client summarizing the article and explaining the implications of the article for their investment.

# Critical Thinking

## DECISION MAKING ACROSS THE ORGANIZATION

**BYP5-6** Three years ago, Amy Blodgett and her brother-in-law Dennis Torres opened Megamart Department Store. For the first 2 years, business was good, but the following condensed income statement results for 2012 were disappointing.

**MEGAMART DEPARTMENT STORE**
**Income Statement**
**For the Year Ended December 31, 2012**

| | | |
|---|---:|---:|
| Net sales | | $700,000 |
| Cost of goods sold | | 560,000 |
| Gross profit | | 140,000 |
| Operating expenses | | |
| Selling expenses | $100,000 | |
| Administrative expenses | 20,000 | |
| | | 120,000 |
| Net income | | $ 20,000 |

Amy believes the problem lies in the relatively low gross profit rate of 20%. Dennis believes the problem is that operating expenses are too high. Amy thinks the gross profit rate can be improved by making two changes: (1) Increase average selling prices by 15%; this increase is expected to lower sales volume so that total sales dollars will increase only 4%. (2) Buy merchandise in larger quantities and take all purchase discounts; these changes are expected to increase the gross profit rate from 20% to 25%. Amy does not anticipate that these changes will have any effect on operating expenses.

Dennis thinks expenses can be cut by making these two changes: (1) Cut 2012 sales salaries of $60,000 in half and give sales personnel a commission of 2% of net sales. (2) Reduce store deliveries to one day per week rather than twice a week; this change will reduce 2012 delivery expenses of $40,000 by 40%. Dennis feels that these changes will not have any effect on net sales.

Amy and Dennis come to you for help in deciding the best way to improve net income.

*Instructions*

With the class divided into groups, answer the following.

(a) Prepare a condensed income statement for 2013 assuming (1) Amy's changes are implemented and (2) Dennis's ideas are adopted.

(b) What is your recommendation to Amy and Dennis?

(c) Prepare a condensed income statement for 2013 assuming both sets of proposed changes are made.

(d) Discuss the impact that other factors might have. For example, would increasing the quantity of inventory increase costs? Would a salary cut affect employee morale? Would decreased morale affect sales? Would decreased store deliveries decrease customer satisfaction? What other suggestions might be considered?

## COMMUNICATION ACTIVITY

**BYP5-7**   The following situation is presented in chronological order.

1. Finley decides to buy a surfboard.
2. He calls Surfing USA Co. to inquire about their surfboards.
3. Two days later he requests Surfing USA Co. to make him a surfboard.
4. Three days later Surfing USA Co. sends him a purchase order to fill out.
5. He sends back the purchase order.
6. Surfing USA Co. receives the completed purchase order.
7. Surfing USA Co. completes the surfboard.
8. Finley picks up the surfboard.
9. Surfing USA Co. bills Finley.
10. Surfing USA Co. receives payment from Finley.

*Instructions*

In a memo to the president of Surfing USA Co., answer the following questions.

(a) When should Surfing USA Co. record the sale?

(b) Suppose that with his purchase order, Finley is required to make a down payment. Would that change your answer to part (a)?

## ETHICS CASE

**BYP5-8**   Margie Anunson was just hired as the assistant treasurer of Northshore Stores, a specialty chain store company that has nine retail stores concentrated in one metropolitan area. Among other things, the payment of all invoices is centralized in one of the departments Margie will manage. Her primary responsibility is to maintain the company's high credit rating by paying all bills when due and to take advantage of all cash discounts.

Michael Hauer, the former assistant treasurer, who has been promoted to treasurer, is training Margie in her new duties. He instructs Margie that she is to continue the practice of preparing all checks "net of discount" and dating the checks the last day of the discount period. "But," Michael continues, "we always hold the checks at least 4 days beyond the discount period before mailing them. That way we get another 4 days of interest on our money. Most of our creditors need our business and don't complain. And, if they scream about our missing the discount period, we blame it on the mail room or the post office. We've only lost one discount out of every hundred we take that way. I think everybody does it. By the way, welcome to our team!"

*Instructions*

(a) What are the ethical considerations in this case?

(b) What stakeholders are harmed or benefited?

(c) Should Margie continue the practice started by Michael? Does she have any choice?

## "ALL ABOUT YOU" ACTIVITY

**BYP5-9**   There are many situations in business where it is difficult to determine the proper period in which to record revenue. Suppose that after graduation with a degree in finance, you take a job as a manager at a consumer electronics store called Pacifica Electronics. The company has expanded rapidly in order to compete with Best Buy.

Pacifica has also begun selling gift cards. The cards are available in any dollar amount and allow the holder of the card to purchase an item for up to 2 years from the time the card is purchased. If the card is not used during that 2 years, it expires.

*Instructions*

Answer the following questions.

At what point should the revenue from the gift cards be recognized? Should the revenue be recognized at the time the card is sold, or should it be recorded when the card is redeemed? Explain the reasoning to support your answers.

## FASB CODIFICATION ACTIVITY

**BYP5-10** Access the FASB Codification at *http://asc.fasb.org* to prepare responses to the following.
(a) Access the glossary ("Master Glossary") to answer the following.
   (1) What is the definition provided for inventory?
   (2) What is a customer?
(b) What guidance does the Codification provide concerning reporting inventories above cost?

## Answers to Insight and Accounting Across the Organization Questions

**p. 231 Morrow Snowboards Improves Its Stock Appeal Q:** If a perpetual system keeps track of inventory on a daily basis, why do companies ever need to do a physical count? **A:** A perpetual system keeps track of all sales and purchases on a continuous basis. This provides a constant record of the number of units in the inventory. However, if employees make errors in recording sales or purchases, or if there is theft, the inventory value will not be correct. As a consequence, all companies do a physical count of inventory at least once a year.

**p. 238 Should Costco Change Its Return Policy? Q:** If a company expects significant returns, what are the implications for revenue recognition? **A:** If a company expects significant returns, it should make an adjusting entry at the end of the year reducing sales by the estimated amount of sales returns. This is necessary so as not to overstate the amount of revenue recognized in the period.

**p. 242 Disclosing More Details Q:** Why have investors and analysts demanded more accuracy in isolating "Other gains and losses" from operating items? **A:** Greater accuracy in the classification of operating versus nonoperating ("Other gains and losses") items permits investors and analysts to judge the real operating margin, the results of continuing operations, and management's ability to control operating expenses.

**p. 248 Strategic Errors Can Be Costly Q:** Explain how Wal-Mart's profitability gave it a strategic advantage over Kmart. **A:** If two competitors get into a "price war," the company with the lower costs can reduce prices further (thus eroding its gross profit rate), but still operate at a profit. Thus, Wal-Mart's success at minimizing its operating costs has enabled it to drive many competitors out of business.

## Answers to Self-Test Questions

**1.** a   **2.** c   **3.** c   **4.** b (($750 − $50) × .98)   **5.** c   **6.** c   **7.** b ($400,000 − $310,000)   **8.** d   **9.** a ($60,000 + $380,000 − $50,000)   **10.** b ($17,200 + ($60,400 − $3,000 − $1,100 + $600))   **11.** c **12.** c   **13.** d ($92,400 ÷ $267,000)   **14.** b   *15.** b

## IFRS A Look at IFRS

The basic accounting entries for merchandising are the same under both GAAP and IFRS. The income statement is a required statement under both sets of standards. The basic format is similar although some differences do exist.

### KEY POINTS

- Under both GAAP and IFRS, a company can choose to use either a perpetual or a periodic system.
- Inventories are defined by IFRS as held-for-sale in the ordinary course of business, in the process of production for such sale, or in the form of materials or supplies to be consumed in the production process or in the providing of services.

- Under GAAP, companies generally classify income statement items by function. Classification by function leads to descriptions like administration, distribution, and manufacturing. Under IFRS, companies must classify expenses by either nature or function. Classification by nature leads to descriptions such as the following: salaries, depreciation expense, and utilities expense. If a company uses the functional-expense method on the income statement, disclosure by nature is required in the notes to the financial statements.

- Presentation of the income statement under GAAP follows either a single-step or multiple-step format. IFRS does not mention a single-step or multiple-step approach.

- Under IFRS, revaluation of land, buildings, and intangible assets is permitted. The initial gains and losses resulting from this revaluation are reported as adjustments to equity, often referred to as *other comprehensive income*. The effect of this difference is that the use of IFRS results in more transactions affecting equity (other comprehensive income) but not net income.

- *IAS 1*, "Presentation of Financial Statements," provides general guidelines for the reporting of income statement information. Subsequently, a number of international standards have been issued that provide additional guidance to issues related to income statement presentation.

- Similar to GAAP, comprehensive income under IFRS includes unrealized gains and losses (such as those on so-called "available-for-sale securities") that are not included in the calculation of net income.

- IFRS requires that two years of income statement information be presented, whereas GAAP requires three years.

## LOOKING TO THE FUTURE

The IASB and FASB are working on a project that would rework the structure of financial statements. Specifically, this project will address the issue of how to classify various items in the income statement. A main goal of this new approach is to provide information that better represents how businesses are run. In addition, this approach draws attention away from just one number—net income. It will adopt major groupings similar to those currently used by the statement of cash flows (operating, investing, and financing), so that numbers can be more readily traced across statements. For example, the amount of income that is generated by operations would be traceable to the assets and liabilities used to generate the income. Finally, this approach would also provide detail, beyond that currently seen in most statements (either GAAP or IFRS), by requiring that line items be presented both by function and by nature. The new financial statement format was heavily influenced by suggestions from financial statement analysts.

### IFRS Self-Test Questions

**1.** Which of the following would *not* be included in the definition of inventory under IFRS?
  (a) Photocopy paper held for sale by an office-supply store.
  (b) Stereo equipment held for sale by an electronics store.
  (c) Used office equipment held for sale by the human relations department of a plastics company.
  (d) All of the above would meet the definition.

**2.** Which of the following would *not* be a line item of a company reporting costs by nature?
  (a) Depreciation expense.
  (b) Salaries expense.
  (c) Interest expense.
  (d) Manufacturing expense.

**3.** Which of the following would *not* be a line item of a company reporting costs by function?
  (a) Administration.
  (b) Manufacturing.
  (c) Utilities expense.
  (d) Distribution.

**4.** Which of the following statements is *false*?
  (a) IFRS specifically requires use of a multiple-step income statement.
  (b) Under IFRS, companies can use either a perpetual or periodic system.
  (c) The proposed new format for financial statements was heavily influenced by the suggestions of financial statement analysts.
  (d) The new income statement format will try to de-emphasize the focus on the "net income" line item.

**5.** Under the new format for financial statements being proposed under a joint IASB/FASB project:

(a) all financial statements would adopt headings similar to the current format of the balance sheet.

(b) financial statements would be presented consistent with the way management usually run companies.

(c) companies would be required to report income statement line items by function only.

(d) the amount of detail shown in the income statement would decrease compared to current presentations.

## IFRS Concepts and Application

**IFRS5–1** Explain the difference between the "nature-of-expense" and "function-of-expense" classifications.

**IFRS5–2** For each of the following income statement line items, state whether the item is a "by nature" expense item or a "by function" expense item.

_____ Cost of goods sold
_____ Depreciation expense
_____ Wages and salaries expense
_____ Selling expenses
_____ Utilities expense
_____ Delivery expense
_____ General and administrative expenses

**IFRS5–3** Gribble Company reported the following amounts in 2012: Net income, €150,000; Unrealized gain related to revaluation of buildings, €10,000; and Unrealized loss on available-for-sale securities, €(35,000). Determine Gribble's total comprehensive income for 2012.

## INTERNATIONAL FINANCIAL REPORTING PROBLEM: *Zetar plc*

**IFRS5–4** The financial statements of Zetar plc are presented in Appendix C. The company's complete annual report, including the notes to its financial statements, is available at **www.zetarplc.com.**

*Instructions*

(a) Is Zetar using a multiple-step or a single-step income statement format? Explain how you made your determination.

(b) Instead of "interest expense," what label does Zetar use for interest costs that it incurs?

(c) What is the approximate tax rate of Zetar's "Tax on profit from continuing activities"?

(d) Using the notes to the company's financial statements, explain what each of the following are:

(1) Adjusted results.

(2) One-off items.

## Answers to IFRS Self-Test Questions

**1.** c  **2.** d  **3.** c  **4.** a  **5.** b

# REPORTING AND ANALYZING INVENTORY

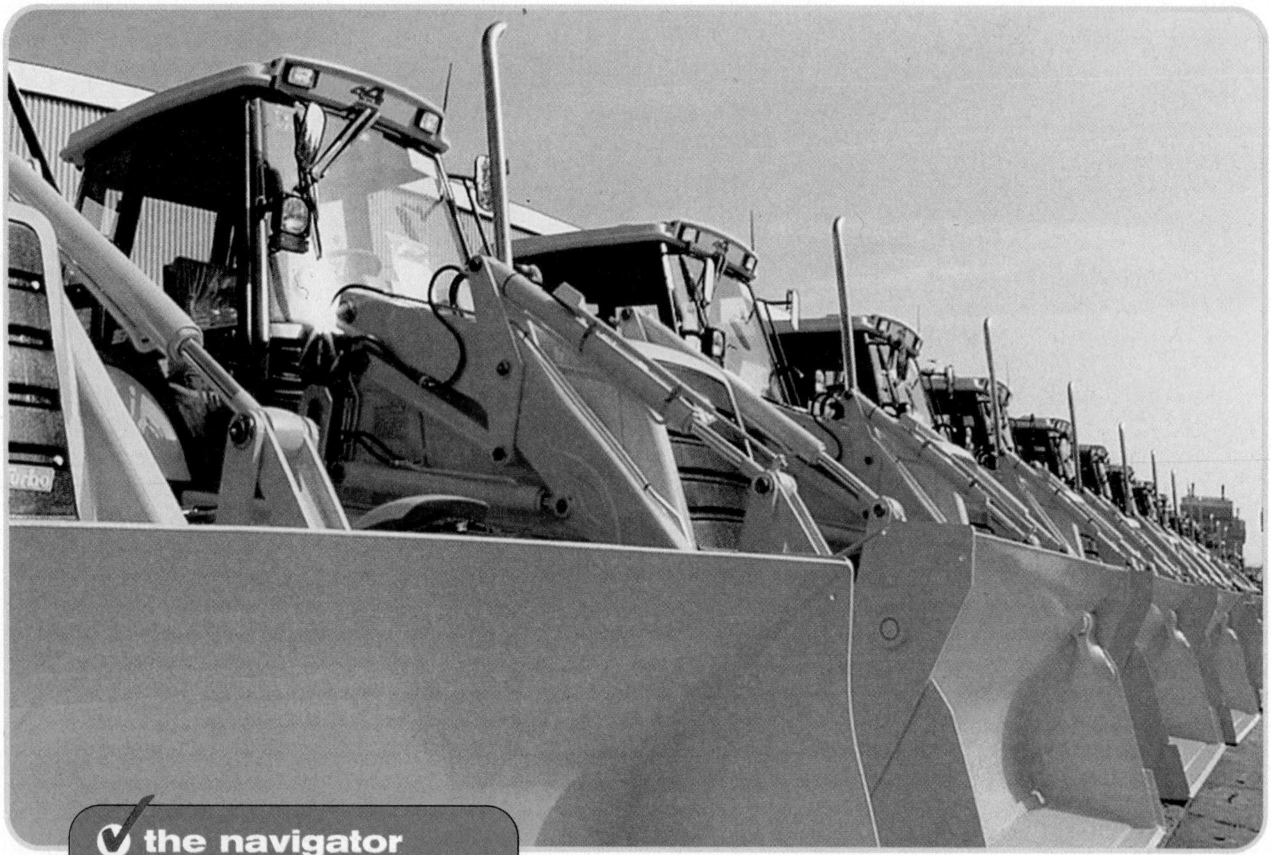

## study objectives

**After studying this chapter, you should be able to:**

1 Describe the steps in determining inventory quantities.

2 Explain the basis of accounting for inventories and apply the inventory cost flow methods under a periodic inventory system.

3 Explain the financial statement and tax effects of each of the inventory cost flow assumptions.

4 Explain the lower-of-cost-or-market basis of accounting for inventories.

5 Compute and interpret the inventory turnover ratio.

6 Describe the LIFO reserve and explain its importance for comparing results of different companies.

✔ the navigator

Let's talk inventory—big, bulldozer-size inventory. Caterpillar Inc. is the world's largest manufacturer of construction and mining equipment, diesel and natural gas engines, and industrial gas turbines. It sells its products in over 200 countries, making it one of the most successful U.S. exporters. More than 70% of its productive assets are located domestically, and nearly 50% of its sales are foreign.

During the 1980s, Caterpillar's profitability suffered, but today it is very successful. A big part of this turnaround can be attributed to effective management of its inventory. Imagine what a bulldozer costs. Now imagine what it costs Caterpillar to have too many bulldozers sitting around in inventory—a situation the company definitely wants to avoid. Conversely, Caterpillar must make sure it has enough inventory to meet demand.

At one time during a 7-year period, Caterpillar's sales increased by 100%, while its inventory increased by only 50%. To achieve this dramatic reduction in the amount of resources tied up in inventory, while continuing to meet customers' needs, Caterpillar used a two-pronged approach. First, it completed a factory modernization program, which dramatically increased its production efficiency. The program reduced by 60% the amount of inventory the company processed

## "WHERE IS THAT SPARE BULLDOZER BLADE?"

at any one time. It also reduced by an incredible 75% the time it takes to manufacture a part.

Second, Caterpillar dramatically improved its parts distribution system. It ships more than 100,000 items daily from its 23 distribution centers strategically located around the world (10 *million* square feet of warehouse space—remember, we're talking bulldozers). The company can virtually guarantee that it can get any part to anywhere in the world within 24 hours.

After these changes, Caterpillar had record exports, profits, and revenues. It would have seemed that things couldn't have been better. But industry analysts, as well as the company's managers, thought otherwise. In order to maintain Caterpillar's position as the industry leader, management began another major overhaul of inventory production and inventory management processes. The goal: to cut the number of repairs in half, increase productivity by 20%, and increase inventory turnover by 40%. In short, Caterpillar's ability to manage its inventory has been a key reason for its past success, and inventory management will very likely play a huge part in its ability to succeed in the future.

*the navigator*

## INSIDE CHAPTER 6 . . .

In the previous chapter, we discussed the accounting for merchandise inventory using a perpetual inventory system. In this chapter, we explain the methods used to calculate the cost of inventory on hand at the balance sheet date and the cost of goods sold. We conclude by illustrating methods for analyzing inventory.

The content and organization of this chapter are as follows.

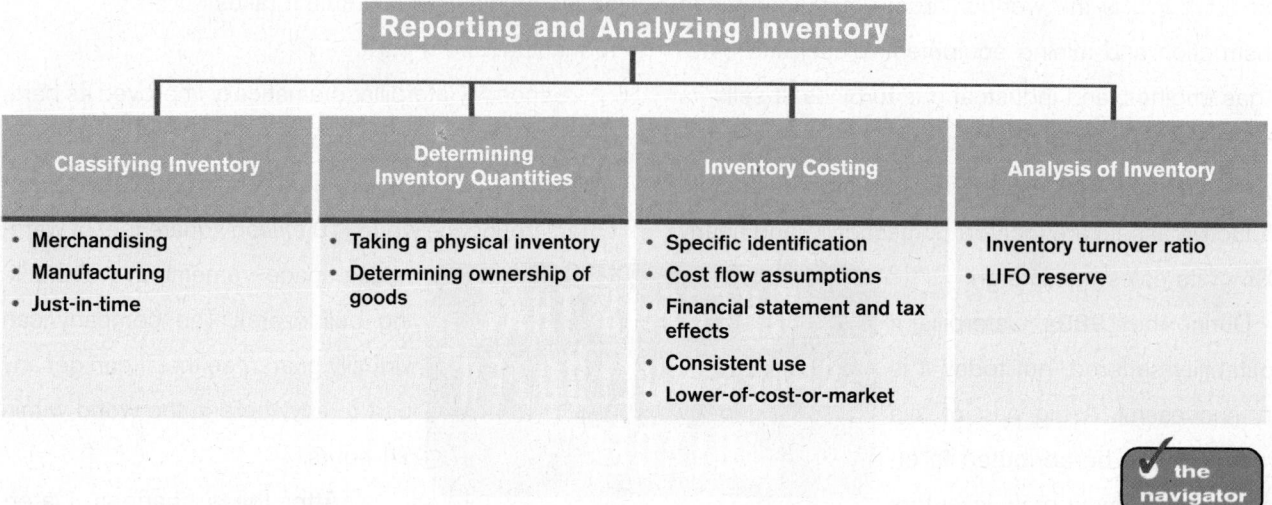

## Classifying Inventory

How a company classifies its inventory depends on whether the firm is a merchandiser or a manufacturer. In a **merchandising** company, such as those described in Chapter 5, inventory consists of many different items. For example, in a grocery store, canned goods, dairy products, meats, and produce are just a few of the inventory items on hand. These items have two common characteristics: (1) They are owned by the company, and (2) they are in a form ready for sale to customers in the ordinary course of business. Thus, merchandisers need only one inventory classification, **merchandise inventory**, to describe the many different items that make up the total inventory.

In a **manufacturing** company, some inventory may not yet be ready for sale. As a result, manufacturers usually classify inventory into three categories: finished goods, work in process, and raw materials. **Finished goods inventory** is manufactured items that are completed and ready for sale. **Work in process** is that portion of manufactured inventory that has begun the production process but is not yet complete. **Raw materials** are the basic goods that will be used in production but have not yet been placed into production.

*Helpful Hint* Regardless of the classification, companies report all inventories under Current Assets on the balance sheet.

For example, Caterpillar classifies earth-moving tractors completed and ready for sale as **finished goods**. It classifies the tractors on the assembly line in various stages of production as **work in process**. The steel, glass, tires, and other components that are on hand waiting to be used in the production of tractors are identified as **raw materials**.

The accounting concepts discussed in this chapter apply to the inventory classifications of both merchandising and manufacturing companies. Our focus throughout most of this chapter is on merchandise inventory.

**By observing the levels and changes in the levels of these three inventory types, financial statement users can gain insight into management's production plans.** For example, low levels of raw materials and high levels of finished goods suggest that management believes it has enough inventory on hand, and production will be slowing down—perhaps in anticipation of a recession. On the other hand, high levels of raw materials and low levels of finished goods probably indicate that management is planning to step up production.

Many companies have significantly lowered inventory levels and costs using **just-in-time (JIT) inventory** methods. Under a just-in-time method, companies manufacture or purchase goods just in time for use. Dell is famous for having developed a system for making computers in response to individual customer requests. Even though it makes computers to meet a customer's particular specifications, Dell is able to assemble the computer and put it on a truck in less than 48 hours. The success of a JIT system depends on reliable suppliers. By integrating its information systems with those of its suppliers, Dell reduced its inventories to nearly zero. This is a huge advantage in an industry where products become obsolete nearly overnight.

## Accounting Across the Organization

### A Big Hiccup

JIT can save a company a lot of money, but it isn't without risk. An unexpected disruption in the supply chain can cost a company a lot of money. Japanese automakers experienced just such a disruption when a 6.8-magnitude earthquake caused major damage to the company that produces 50% of their piston rings. The rings themselves cost only $1.50, but without them you cannot make a car. No other supplier could quickly begin producing sufficient quantities of the rings to match the desired specifications. As a result, the automakers were forced to shut down production for a few days—a loss of tens of thousands of cars.

*Source:* Amy Chozick, "A Key Strategy of Japan's Car Makers Backfires," *Wall Street Journal* (July 20, 2007).

**?** What steps might the companies take to avoid such a serious disruption in the future? (See page 330.)

# Determining Inventory Quantities

No matter whether they are using a periodic or perpetual inventory system, all companies need to determine inventory quantities at the end of the accounting period. If using a perpetual system, companies take a physical inventory for two purposes: The first purpose is to check the accuracy of their perpetual inventory records. The second is to determine the amount of inventory lost due to wasted raw materials, shoplifting, or employee theft.

Companies using a periodic inventory system must take a physical inventory for two *different* purposes: to determine the inventory on hand at the balance sheet date, and to determine the cost of goods sold for the period.

Determining inventory quantities involves two steps: (1) taking a physical inventory of goods on hand and (2) determining the ownership of goods.

### TAKING A PHYSICAL INVENTORY

Companies take the physical inventory at the end of the accounting period. Taking a physical inventory involves actually counting, weighing, or measuring each kind of inventory on hand. In many companies, taking an inventory is a formidable task. Retailers such as Target, True Value Hardware, or Home Depot have thousands of different inventory items. An inventory count is generally more accurate when a limited number of goods are being sold or received during the counting. Consequently, companies often "take inventory" when the business is closed or when business is slow. Many retailers close early on a chosen day in January—after the holiday sales and returns, when inventories are at their lowest level—to count inventory. Recall from Chapter 5 that Wal-Mart had a year-end of January 31.

**study objective** **1**

Describe the steps in determining inventory quantities.

**Ethics Note** In a famous fraud, a salad oil company filled its storage tanks mostly with water. The oil rose to the top, so auditors thought the tanks were full of oil. The company also said it had more tanks than it really did: it repainted numbers on the tanks to confuse auditors.

## Ethics Insight

### Falsifying Inventory to Boost Income

Managers at women's apparel maker Leslie Fay were convicted of falsifying inventory records to boost net income—and consequently to boost management bonuses. In another case, executives at Craig Consumer Electronics were accused of defrauding lenders by manipulating inventory records. The indictment said the company classified "defective goods as new or refurbished" and claimed that it owned certain shipments "from overseas suppliers" when, in fact, Craig either did not own the shipments or the shipments did not exist.

**?** What effect does an overstatement of inventory have on a company's financial statements? (See page 330.)

## DETERMINING OWNERSHIP OF GOODS

One challenge in determining inventory quantities is making sure a company owns the inventory. To determine ownership of goods, two questions must be answered: Do all of the goods included in the count belong to the company? Does the company own any goods that were not included in the count?

### Goods in Transit

A complication in determining ownership is **goods in transit** (on board a truck, train, ship, or plane) at the end of the period. The company may have purchased goods that have not yet been received, or it may have sold goods that have not yet been delivered. To arrive at an accurate count, the company must determine ownership of these goods.

Goods in transit should be included in the inventory of the company that has legal title to the goods. Legal title is determined by the terms of the sale, as shown in Illustration 6-1 and described below.

**Illustration 6-1** Terms of sale

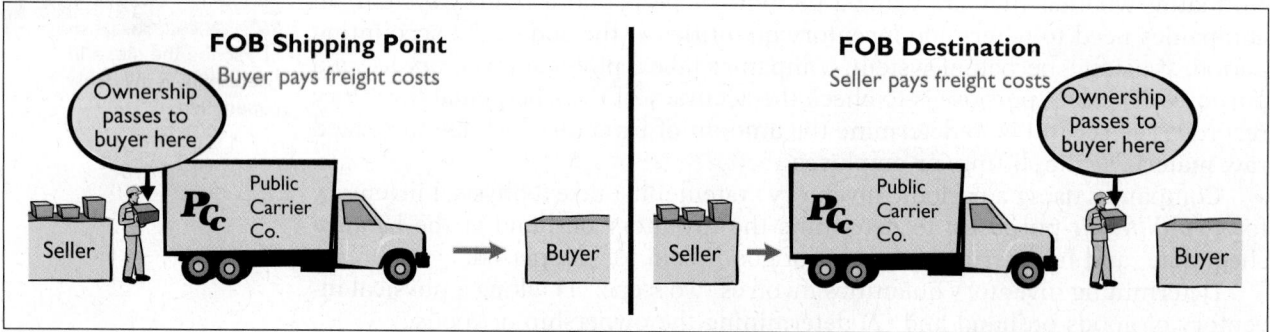

1. When the terms are FOB (free on board) shipping point, ownership of the goods passes to the buyer when the public carrier accepts the goods from the seller.
2. When the terms are FOB destination, ownership of the goods remains with the seller until the goods reach the buyer.

### Consigned Goods

In some lines of business, it is common to hold the goods of other parties and try to sell the goods for them for a fee, but without taking ownership of the goods. These are called consigned goods.

For example, you might have a used car that you would like to sell. If you take the item to a dealer, the dealer might be willing to put the car on its lot and charge you a commission if it is sold. Under this agreement, the dealer **would not take ownership** of the car, which would still belong to you. If an inventory count were taken, the car would not be included in the dealer's inventory because the dealer does not own it.

Many car, boat, and antique dealers sell goods on consignment to keep their inventory costs down and to avoid the risk of purchasing an item that they won't be able to sell. Today, even some manufacturers are making consignment agreements with their suppliers in order to keep their inventory levels low.

*before you go on...*

## Do it!

Hasbeen Company completed its inventory count. It arrived at a total inventory value of $200,000. You have been given the information listed below. Discuss how this information affects the reported cost of inventory.

1. Hasbeen included in the inventory goods held on consignment for Falls Co., costing $15,000.
2. The company did not include in the count purchased goods of $10,000, which were in transit (terms: FOB shipping point).
3. The company did not include in the count inventory that had been sold with a cost of $12,000, which was in transit (terms: FOB shipping point).

### Solution

The goods of $15,000 held on consignment should be deducted from the inventory count. The goods of $10,000 purchased FOB shipping point should be added to the inventory count. Sold goods of $12,000 which were in transit FOB shipping point should not be included in the ending inventory. Inventory should be $195,000 ($200,000 − $15,000 + $10,000).

Related exercise material: **BE6-1,** Do it! **6-1, E6-1, E6-2,** and **E6-3.**

**RULES OF OWNERSHIP**

### Action Plan
- Apply the rules of ownership to goods held on consignment.
- Apply the rules of ownership to goods in transit.

---

## ANATOMY OF A FRAUD

Ted Nickerson, CEO of clock manufacturer Dally Industries, was feared by all of his employees. Ted had expensive tastes. To support his expensive tastes, Ted took out large loans, which he collateralized with his shares of Dally Industries stock. If the price of Dally's stock fell, he was required to provide the bank with more shares of stock. To achieve target net income figures and thus maintain the stock price, Ted coerced employees in the company to alter inventory figures. Inventory quantities were manipulated by changing the amounts on inventory control tags after the year-end physical inventory count. For example, if a tag said there were 20 units of a particular item, the tag was changed to 220. Similarly, the unit costs that were used to determine the value of ending inventory were increased from, for example, $125 per unit to $1,250. Both of these fraudulent changes had the effect of increasing the amount of reported ending inventory. This reduced cost of goods sold and increased net income.

**Total take: $245,000**

### THE MISSING CONTROL

*Independent internal verification.* The company should have spot-checked its inventory records periodically, verifying that the number of units in the records agreed with the amount on hand and that the unit costs agreed with vendor price sheets.

*Source:* Adapted from Wells, *Fraud Casebook* (2007), pp. 502–509.

# Inventory Costing

**study objective** **2**

Explain the basis of accounting for inventories and apply the inventory cost flow methods under a periodic inventory system.

Inventory is accounted for at cost. Cost includes all expenditures necessary to acquire goods and place them in a condition ready for sale. For example, freight costs incurred to acquire inventory are added to the cost of inventory, but the cost of shipping goods to a customer are a selling expense. After a company has determined the quantity of units of inventory, it applies unit costs to the quantities to determine the total cost of the inventory and the cost of goods sold. This process can be complicated if a company has purchased inventory items at different times and at different prices.

For example, assume that Crivitz TV Company purchases three identical 50-inch TVs on different dates at costs of $700, $750, and $800. During the year, Crivitz sold two sets at $1,200 each. These facts are summarized in Illustration 6-2.

**Illustration 6-2** Data for inventory costing example

| Purchases | | | |
|---|---|---|---|
| Feb. 3 | 1 TV | at | $700 |
| March 5 | 1 TV | at | $750 |
| May 22 | 1 TV | at | $800 |
| **Sales** | | | |
| June 1 | 2 TVs | for | $2,400 ($1,200 × 2) |

Cost of goods sold will differ depending on which two TVs the company sold. For example, it might be $1,450 ($700 + $750), or $1,500 ($700 + $800), or $1,550 ($750 + $800). In this section, we discuss alternative costing methods available to Crivitz.

## SPECIFIC IDENTIFICATION

If Crivitz can positively identify which particular units it sold and which are still in ending inventory, it can use the **specific identification method** of inventory costing. For example, if Crivitz sold the TVs it purchased on February 3 and May 22, then its cost of goods sold is $1,500 ($700 + $800), and its ending inventory is $750 (see Illustration 6-3). Using this method, companies can accurately determine ending inventory and cost of goods sold.

**Illustration 6-3** Specific identification method

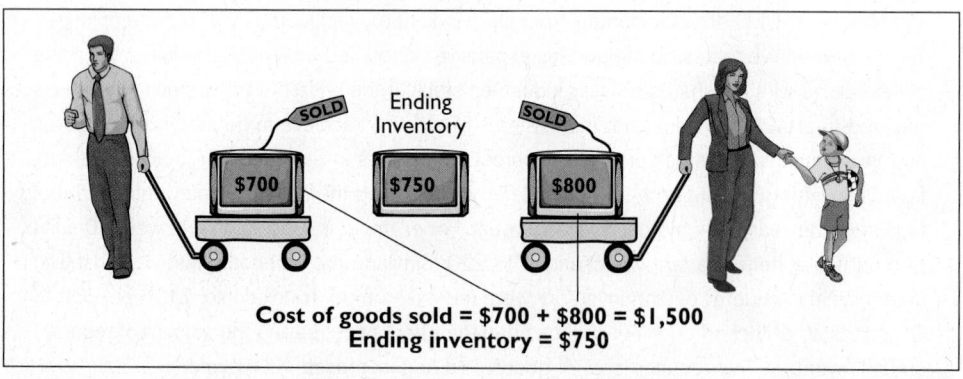

Cost of goods sold = $700 + $800 = $1,500
Ending inventory = $750

**Ethics Note** A major disadvantage of the specific identification method is that management may be able to manipulate net income. For example, it can boost net income by selling units purchased at a low cost, or reduce net income by selling units purchased at a high cost.

Specific identification requires that companies keep records of the original cost of each individual inventory item. Historically, specific identification was possible only when a company sold a limited variety of high-unit-cost items that could be identified clearly from the time of purchase through the time of sale. Examples of such products are cars, pianos, or expensive antiques.

Today, with bar coding, electronic product codes, and radio frequency identification, it is theoretically possible to do specific identification with nearly any type of product. The reality is, however, that this practice is still relatively rare. Instead, rather than keep track of the cost of each particular item sold, most companies make assumptions, called **cost flow assumptions**, about which units were sold.

## COST FLOW ASSUMPTIONS

Because specific identification is often impractical, other cost flow methods are permitted. These differ from specific identification in that they **assume** flows of costs that may be unrelated to the actual physical flow of goods. There are three assumed cost flow methods:

1. First-in, first-out (FIFO)
2. Last-in, first-out (LIFO)
3. Average-cost

**There is no accounting requirement that the cost flow assumption be consistent with the physical movement of the goods.** Company management selects the appropriate cost flow method.

To demonstrate the three cost flow methods, we will use a *periodic* inventory system. We assume a periodic system for two main reasons. First, many small companies use periodic rather than perpetual systems. Second, **very few companies use *perpetual* LIFO, FIFO, or average-cost** to cost their inventory and related cost of goods sold. Instead, companies that use perpetual systems often use an assumed cost (called a standard cost) to record cost of goods sold at the time of sale. Then, at the end of the period when they count their inventory, they **recalculate cost of goods sold using *periodic* FIFO, LIFO, or average-cost** and adjust cost of goods sold to this recalculated number.[1]

To illustrate the three inventory cost flow methods, we will use the data for Houston Electronics' Astro condensers, shown in Illustration 6-4.

**Illustration 6-4** Data for Houston Electronics

**HOUSTON ELECTRONICS**
Astro Condensers

| Date | Explanation | Units | Unit Cost | Total Cost |
|---|---|---|---|---|
| Jan. 1 | Beginning inventory | 100 | $10 | $ 1,000 |
| Apr. 15 | Purchase | 200 | 11 | 2,200 |
| Aug. 24 | Purchase | 300 | 12 | 3,600 |
| Nov. 27 | Purchase | 400 | 13 | 5,200 |
| | Total units available for sale | 1,000 | | $12,000 |
| | Units in ending inventory | 450 | | |
| | Units sold | 550 | | |

From Chapter 5, the cost of goods sold formula in a periodic system is:

**(Beginning Inventory + Purchases) − Ending Inventory = Cost of Goods Sold**

Houston Electronics had a total of 1,000 units available to sell during the period (beginning inventory plus purchases). The total cost of these 1,000 units is $12,000, referred to as *cost of goods available for sale*. A physical inventory taken at December 31 determined that there were 450 units in ending inventory. Therefore, Houston sold 550 units (1,000 − 450) during the period. To determine the cost of the 550 units that were sold (the cost of goods sold), we assign a cost to the ending inventory and subtract that value from the cost of goods available for sale. The

[1]Also, some companies use a perpetual system to keep track of units, but they do not make an entry for perpetual cost of goods sold. In addition, firms that employ LIFO tend to use *dollar-value LIFO*, a method discussed in upper-level courses. FIFO periodic and FIFO perpetual give the same result; therefore firms should not incur the additional cost to use FIFO perpetual. Few firms use perpetual average-cost because of the added cost of record-keeping. Finally, for instructional purposes, we believe it is easier to demonstrate the cost flow assumptions under the periodic system, which makes it more pedagogically appropriate.

value assigned to the ending inventory **will depend on which cost flow method we use**. No matter which cost flow assumption we use, though, the sum of cost of goods sold plus the cost of the ending inventory must equal the cost of goods available for sale—in this case, $12,000.

## First-In, First-Out (FIFO)

The **FIFO (first-in, first-out) method** assumes that the **earliest goods** purchased are the first to be sold. FIFO often parallels the actual physical flow of merchandise because it generally is good business practice to sell the oldest units first. Under the FIFO method, therefore, the **costs** of the earliest goods purchased are the first to be recognized in determining cost of goods sold, regardless which units were actually sold. (Note that this does not mean that the oldest units *are* sold first, but that the costs of the oldest units are *recognized* first. In a bin of picture hangers at the hardware store, for example, no one really knows, nor would it matter, which hangers are sold first.) Illustration 6-5 shows the allocation of the cost of goods available for sale at Houston Electronics under FIFO.

**Illustration 6-5** Allocation of costs—FIFO method

**Helpful Hint** Note the sequencing of the allocation: (1) Compute ending inventory, and (2) determine cost of goods sold.

**Helpful Hint** Another way of thinking about the calculation of FIFO **ending inventory** is the *LISH assumption*—last in still here.

### COST OF GOODS AVAILABLE FOR SALE

| Date | Explanation | Units | Unit Cost | Total Cost |
|---|---|---|---|---|
| Jan. 1 | Beginning inventory | 100 | $10 | $ 1,000 |
| Apr. 15 | Purchase | 200 | 11 | 2,200 |
| Aug. 24 | Purchase | 300 | 12 | 3,600 |
| Nov. 27 | Purchase | 400 | 13 | 5,200 |
| | Total | 1,000 | | $12,000 |

### STEP 1: ENDING INVENTORY

| Date | Units | Unit Cost | Total Cost |
|---|---|---|---|
| Nov. 27 | 400 | $13 | $ 5,200 |
| Aug. 24 | 50 | 12 | 600 |
| Total | 450 | | $5,800 |

### STEP 2: COST OF GOODS SOLD

| | |
|---|---|
| Cost of goods available for sale | $12,000 |
| Less: Ending inventory | 5,800 |
| Cost of goods sold | $ 6,200 |

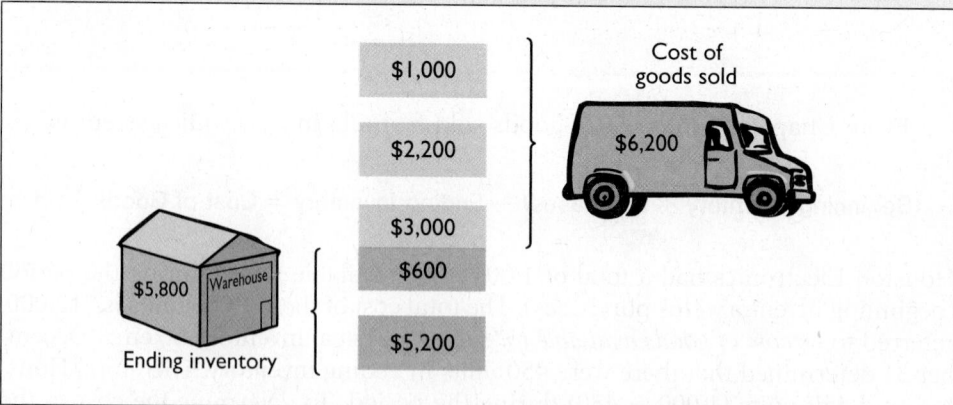

Under FIFO, since it is assumed that the first goods purchased were the first goods sold, ending inventory is based on the prices of the most recent units purchased. That is, **under FIFO, companies determine the cost of the ending inventory by taking the unit cost of the most recent purchase and working backward until all units of inventory have been costed.** In this example, Houston Electronics prices the 450 units of ending inventory using the *most recent* prices. The last purchase was 400 units at $13 on November 27. The remaining 50 units are priced using the unit cost of the second most recent purchase, $12, on August 24. Next, Houston Electronics calculates cost of goods sold by subtracting the cost of the units **not sold** (ending inventory) from the cost of all goods available for sale.

Illustration 6-6 demonstrates that companies also can calculate cost of goods sold by pricing the 550 units sold using the prices of the first 550 units acquired. Note that of the 300 units purchased on August 24, only 250 units are assumed sold. This agrees with our calculation of the cost of ending inventory, where 50 of these units were assumed unsold and thus included in ending inventory.

**Illustration 6-6**  Proof of cost of goods sold

| Date | Units | Unit Cost | Total Cost |
|---|---|---|---|
| Jan.  1 | 100 | $10 | $ 1,000 |
| Apr. 15 | 200 | 11 | 2,200 |
| Aug. 24 | 250 | 12 | 3,000 |
| Total | 550 | | $6,200 |

## Last-In, First-Out (LIFO)

The **LIFO (last-in, first-out) method** assumes that the **latest goods** purchased are the first to be sold. LIFO seldom coincides with the actual physical flow of inventory. (Exceptions include goods stored in piles, such as coal or hay, where goods are removed from the top of the pile as they are sold.) Under the LIFO method, the **costs** of the latest goods purchased are the first to be recognized in determining cost of goods sold. Illustration 6-7 shows the allocation of the cost of goods available for sale at Houston Electronics under LIFO.

**Illustration 6-7**  Allocation of costs–LIFO method

### COST OF GOODS AVAILABLE FOR SALE

| Date | Explanation | Units | Unit Cost | Total Cost |
|---|---|---|---|---|
| Jan.  1 | Beginning inventory | 100 | $10 | $ 1,000 |
| Apr. 15 | Purchase | 200 | 11 | 2,200 |
| Aug. 24 | Purchase | 300 | 12 | 3,600 |
| Nov. 27 | Purchase | 400 | 13 | 5,200 |
| | Total | 1,000 | | $12,000 |

### STEP 1: ENDING INVENTORY

| Date | Units | Unit Cost | Total Cost |
|---|---|---|---|
| Jan.  1 | 100 | $10 | $ 1,000 |
| Apr. 15 | 200 | 11 | 2,200 |
| Aug. 24 | 150 | 12 | 1,800 |
| Total | 450 | | $5,000 |

### STEP 2: COST OF GOODS SOLD

| | |
|---|---|
| Cost of goods available for sale | $12,000 |
| Less: Ending inventory | 5,000 |
| Cost of goods sold | $ 7,000 |

**Helpful Hint** Another way of thinking about the calculation of LIFO **ending inventory** is the *FISH assumption*–first in still here.

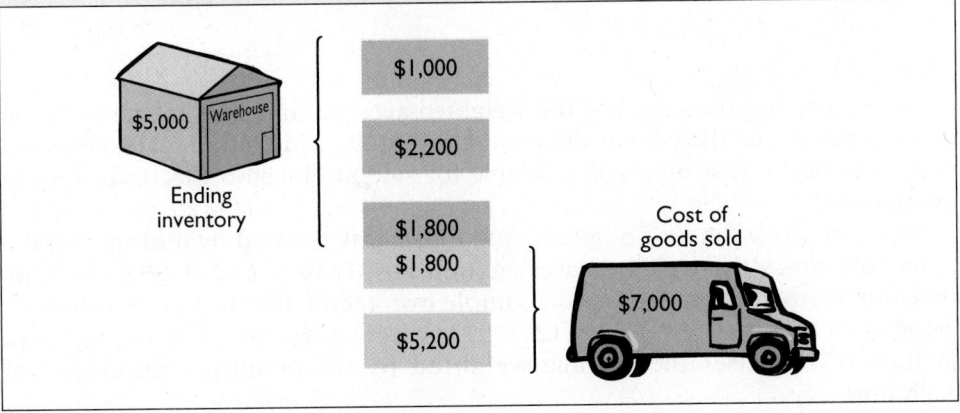

Under LIFO, since it is assumed that the first goods sold were those that were most recently purchased, ending inventory is based on the prices of the oldest units purchased. That is, **under LIFO, companies obtain the cost of the ending inventory by taking the unit cost of the earliest goods available for sale and working forward until all units of inventory have been costed.** In this example, Houston Electronics prices the 450 units of ending inventory using the *earliest* prices. The first purchase was 100 units at $10 in the January 1 beginning inventory. Then 200 units were purchased at $11. The remaining 150 units needed are priced at $12 per unit (August 24 purchase). Next, Houston Electronics calculates cost of goods sold by subtracting the cost of the units **not sold** (ending inventory) from the cost of all goods available for sale.

Illustration 6-8 demonstrates that we can also calculate cost of goods sold by pricing the 550 units sold using the prices of the last 550 units acquired. Note that of the 300 units purchased on August 24, only 150 units are assumed sold. This agrees with our calculation of the cost of ending inventory, where 150 of these units were assumed unsold and thus included in ending inventory.

**Illustration 6-8** Proof of cost of goods sold

| Date | Units | Unit Cost | Total Cost |
|---|---|---|---|
| Nov. 27 | 400 | $13 | $ 5,200 |
| Aug. 24 | 150 | 12 | 1,800 |
| Total | 550 | | $7,000 |

Under a periodic inventory system, which we are using here, **all goods purchased during the period are assumed to be available for the first sale**, regardless of the date of purchase.

### Average-Cost

The **average-cost method** allocates the cost of goods available for sale on the basis of the **weighted-average unit cost** incurred. Illustration 6-9 presents the formula and a sample computation of the weighted-average unit cost.

**Illustration 6-9** Formula for weighted-average unit cost

| Cost of Goods Available for Sale | ÷ | Total Units Available for Sale | = | Weighted- Average Unit Cost |
|---|---|---|---|---|
| $12,000 | ÷ | 1,000 | = | $12.00 |

The company then applies the weighted-average unit cost to the units on hand to determine the cost of the ending inventory. Illustration 6-10 shows the allocation of the cost of goods available for sale at Houston Electronics using average-cost.

We can verify the cost of goods sold under this method by multiplying the units sold times the weighted-average unit cost (550 × $12 = $6,600). Note that this method does not use the simple average of the unit costs. That average is $11.50 ($10 + $11 + $12 + $13 = $46; $46 ÷ 4). The average-cost method instead uses the average **weighted by** the quantities purchased at each unit cost.

**Illustration 6-10**
Allocation of costs—
average-cost method

### COST OF GOODS AVAILABLE FOR SALE

| Date | Explanation | Units | Unit Cost | Total Cost |
|------|-------------|-------|-----------|-----------|
| Jan. 1 | Beginning inventory | 100 | $10 | $ 1,000 |
| Apr. 15 | Purchase | 200 | 11 | 2,200 |
| Aug. 24 | Purchase | 300 | 12 | 3,600 |
| Nov. 27 | Purchase | 400 | 13 | 5,200 |
| | Total | 1,000 | | $12,000 |

### STEP 1: ENDING INVENTORY  STEP 2: COST OF GOODS SOLD

$12,000 ÷ 1,000 = $12.00

| Units | Unit Cost | Total Cost |
|-------|-----------|-----------|
| | Unit Cost | Total Cost |
| 450 | $12.00 | $5,400 |

Cost of goods available for sale $12,000
Less: Ending inventory 5,400
Cost of goods sold $ 6,600

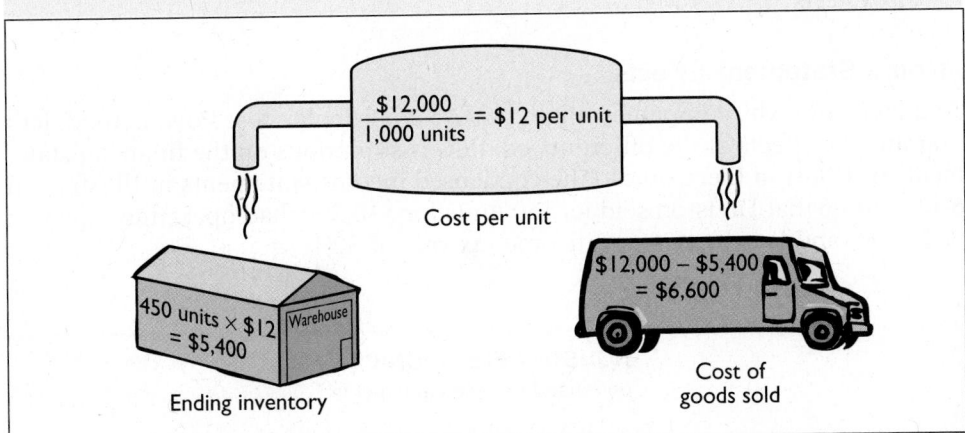

$\frac{\$12,000}{1,000 \text{ units}} = \$12 \text{ per unit}$

Cost per unit

450 units × $12 = $5,400  Warehouse

Ending inventory

$12,000 − $5,400 = $6,600

Cost of
goods sold

---

*before you go on...*

## Do it!

The accounting records of Shumway Ag Implement show the following data.

| | |
|---|---|
| Beginning inventory | 4,000 units at $3 |
| Purchases | 6,000 units at $4 |
| Sales | 7,000 units at $12 |

Determine (a) the cost of goods available for sale and (b) the cost of goods sold during the period under a periodic system using (i) FIFO, (ii) LIFO, and (iii) average-cost.

### Solution

(a) Cost of goods available for sale: (4,000 × $3) + (6,000 × $4) = $36,000
(b) Cost of goods sold using:
    (i) FIFO: $36,000 − (3,000* × $4) = $24,000
    (ii) LIFO: $36,000 − (3,000 × $3) = $27,000
    (iii) Average-cost: Weighted-average price = ($36,000 ÷ 10,000) = $3.60
        $36,000 − (3,000 × $3.60) = $25,200

*(4,000 + 6,000 − 7,000)

Related exercise material: **BE6-2, BE6-3, Do it! 6-2, E6-4,** and **E6-5.**

**COST FLOW METHODS**

**Action Plan**
- Understand the periodic inventory system.
- Allocate costs between goods sold and goods on hand (ending inventory) for each cost flow method.
- Compute cost of goods sold for each cost flow method.

the navigator

## FINANCIAL STATEMENT AND TAX EFFECTS OF COST FLOW METHODS

Each of the three assumed cost flow methods is acceptable for use under GAAP. For example, Reebok International Ltd. and Wendy's International currently use the FIFO method of inventory costing. Campbell Soup Company, Krogers, and Walgreens use LIFO for part or all of their inventory. Bristol-Myers Squibb, Starbucks, and Motorola use the average-cost method. In fact, a company may also use more than one cost flow method at the same time. Stanley Black & Decker Manufacturing Company, for example, uses LIFO for domestic inventories and FIFO for foreign inventories. Illustration 6-11 shows the use of the three cost flow methods in the 600 largest U.S. companies.

The reasons companies adopt different inventory cost flow methods are varied, but they usually involve at least one of the following three factors:

1. Income statement effects
2. Balance sheet effects
3. Tax effects

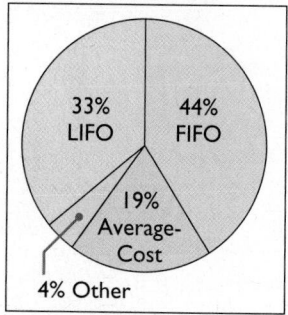

**Illustration 6-11** Use of cost flow methods in major U.S. companies

### Income Statement Effects

To understand why companies might choose a particular cost flow method, let's examine the effects of the different cost flow assumptions on the financial statements of Houston Electronics. The condensed income statements in Illustration 6-12 assume that Houston sold its 550 units for $18,500, had operating expenses of $9,000, and is subject to an income tax rate of 30%.

**Illustration 6-12**
Comparative effects of cost flow methods

| HOUSTON ELECTRONICS | | | |
|---|---|---|---|
| Condensed Income Statements | | | |
| | **FIFO** | **LIFO** | **Average-Cost** |
| Sales revenue | $18,500 | $18,500 | $18,500 |
| Beginning inventory | 1,000 | 1,000 | 1,000 |
| Purchases | 11,000 | 11,000 | 11,000 |
| Cost of goods available for sale | 12,000 | 12,000 | 12,000 |
| Less: Ending inventory | 5,800 | 5,000 | 5,400 |
| Cost of goods sold | 6,200 | 7,000 | 6,600 |
| Gross profit | 12,300 | 11,500 | 11,900 |
| Operating expenses | 9,000 | 9,000 | 9,000 |
| Income before income taxes | 3,300 | 2,500 | 2,900 |
| Income tax expense (30%) | 990 | 750 | 870 |
| Net income | $ 2,310 | $ 1,750 | $ 2,030 |

Note the cost of goods available for sale ($12,000) is the same under each of the three inventory cost flow methods. However, the ending inventories and the costs of goods sold are different. This difference is due to the unit costs that the company allocated to cost of goods sold and to ending inventory. Each dollar of difference in ending inventory results in a corresponding dollar difference in income before income taxes. For Houston, an $800 difference exists between FIFO and LIFO cost of goods sold.

In periods of changing prices, the cost flow assumption can have a significant impact on income and on evaluations based on income. In most instances, prices are rising (inflation). In a period of inflation, FIFO produces a higher net income because the lower unit costs of the first units purchased are matched against revenues. In a period of rising prices (as is the case in the Houston example), FIFO reports the highest net income ($2,310) and LIFO the lowest ($1,750); average-cost falls in the middle ($2,030). If prices are falling, the results from the use of FIFO and LIFO are reversed: FIFO will report the lowest net income and LIFO the highest.

To management, higher net income is an advantage: It causes external users to view the company more favorably. In addition, management bonuses, if based on net income, will be higher. Therefore, when prices are rising (which is usually the case), companies tend to prefer FIFO because it results in higher net income.

Some argue that the use of LIFO in a period of inflation reduces the likelihood that the company will report **paper** (or **phantom**) **profit** as economic gain. To illustrate, assume that Kralik Company buys 200 units of a product at $20 per unit on January 10 and 200 more on December 31 at $24 each. During the year, Kralik sells 200 units at $30 each. Illustration 6-13 shows the results under FIFO and LIFO.

**Illustration 6-13** Income statement effects compared

|  | FIFO | LIFO |
|---|---|---|
| Sales revenue (200 × $30) | $6,000 | $6,000 |
| Cost of goods sold | 4,000 (200 × $20) | 4,800 (200 × $24) |
| Gross profit | $2,000 | $1,200 |

Under LIFO, Kralik Company has recovered the current replacement cost ($4,800) of the units sold. Thus, the gross profit in economic terms is real. However, under FIFO, the company has recovered only the January 10 cost ($4,000). To replace the units sold, it must reinvest $800 (200 × $4) of the gross profit. Thus, $800 of the gross profit is said to be phantom or illusory. As a result, reported net income is also overstated in real terms.

## Balance Sheet Effects

A major advantage of the FIFO method is that in a period of inflation, the costs allocated to ending inventory will approximate their current cost. For example, for Houston Electronics, 400 of the 450 units in the ending inventory are costed under FIFO at the higher November 27 unit cost of $13.

Conversely, a major shortcoming of the LIFO method is that in a period of inflation, the costs allocated to ending inventory may be significantly understated in terms of current cost. The understatement becomes greater over prolonged periods of inflation if the inventory includes goods purchased in one or more prior accounting periods. For example, Caterpillar has used LIFO for 50 years. Its balance sheet shows ending inventory of $4,675 million. But, the inventory's actual current cost if FIFO had been used is $6,799 million.

## Tax Effects

We have seen that both inventory on the balance sheet and net income on the income statement are higher when companies use FIFO in a period of inflation. Yet, many companies use LIFO. Why? The reason is that LIFO results in the lowest income taxes (because of lower net income) during times of rising prices. For example, in Illustration 6-12, income taxes are $750 under LIFO, compared to $990 under FIFO. The tax savings of $240 makes more cash available for use in the business.

**Helpful Hint** A tax rule, often referred to as the *LIFO conformity rule*, requires that if companies use LIFO for tax purposes, they must also use it for financial reporting purposes. This means that if a company chooses the LIFO method to reduce its tax bills, it will also have to report lower net income in its financial statements.

## International Insight

### Is LIFO Fair?

 ExxonMobil Corporation, like many U.S. companies, uses LIFO to value its inventory for financial reporting and tax purposes. In one recent year, this resulted in a cost of goods sold figure that was $5.6 billion higher than under FIFO. By increasing cost of goods sold, ExxonMobil reduces net income, which reduces taxes. Critics say that LIFO provides an unfair "tax dodge." As Congress looks for more sources of tax revenue, some lawmakers favor the elimination of LIFO. Supporters of LIFO argue that the method is conceptually sound because it matches current costs with current revenues. In addition, they point out that this matching provides protection against inflation.

International accounting standards do not allow the use of LIFO. Because of this, the net income of foreign oil companies, such as BP and Royal Dutch Shell, are not directly comparable to U.S. companies, which makes analysis difficult.

*Source:* David Reilly, "Big Oil's Accounting Methods Fuel Criticism," *Wall Street Journal* (August 8, 2006), p. C1.

**?** What are the arguments for and against the use of LIFO? (See page 330.)

## KEEPING AN EYE ON CASH

You have just seen that when prices are rising the use of LIFO can have a big effect on taxes. The lower taxes paid using LIFO can significantly increase cash flows. To demonstrate the effect of the cost flow assumptions on cash flow, we will calculate net cash provided by operating activities, using the data for Houston Electronics from Illustration 6-12. To simplify our example, we assume that Houston's sales and purchases are all cash transactions. We also assume that operating expenses, other than $4,600 of depreciation, are cash transactions.

|  | FIFO | LIFO | Average-Cost |
|---|---|---|---|
| Cash received from customers | $18,500 | $18,500 | $18,500 |
| Cash purchases of goods | 11,000 | 11,000 | 11,000 |
| Cash paid for operating expenses ($9,000 − $4,600) | 4,400 | 4,400 | 4,400 |
| Cash paid for taxes | 990 | 750 | 870 |
| Net cash provided by operating activities | $ 2,110 | $ 2,350 | $ 2,230 |

LIFO has the highest net cash provided by operating activities because it results in the lowest tax payments. Since cash flow is the lifeblood of any organization, the choice of inventory method is very important.

LIFO also impacts the quality of earnings ratio. Recall that the quality of earnings ratio is net cash provided by operating activities divided by net income. Here, we calculate the quality earnings ratio under each cost flow assumption.

|  | FIFO | LIFO | Average-Cost |
|---|---|---|---|
| Net income (from Illustration 6-12) | $2,310 | $1,750 | $2,030 |
| Quality of earnings ratio | 0.91 | 1.34 | 1.1 |

LIFO has the highest quality of earnings ratio for two reasons: (1) It has the highest net cash provided by operating activities, which increases the ratio's numerator. (2) It reports a conservative measure of net income, which decreases the ratio's denominator. As discussed earlier, LIFO provides a conservative measure of net income because it does not include the phantom profits reported under FIFO.

## DECISION TOOLKIT

| DECISION CHECKPOINTS | INFO NEEDED FOR DECISION | TOOL TO USE FOR DECISION | HOW TO EVALUATE RESULTS |
|---|---|---|---|
| Which inventory costing method should be used? | Are prices increasing, or are they decreasing? | Income statement, balance sheet, and tax effects | Depends on objective. In a period of rising prices, income and inventory are higher and cash flow is lower under FIFO. LIFO provides opposite results. Average-cost can moderate the impact of changing prices. |

## USING INVENTORY COST FLOW METHODS CONSISTENTLY

Whatever cost flow method a company chooses, it should use that method consistently from one accounting period to another. Consistent application enhances the ability to analyze a company's financial statements over successive time periods. In contrast, using the FIFO method one year and the LIFO method the next year would make it difficult to compare the net incomes of the two years.

Although consistent application is preferred, it does not mean that a company may *never* change its method of inventory costing. When a company adopts a different method, it should disclose in the financial statements the change and its effects on net income. A typical disclosure is shown in Illustration 6-14, using information from recent financial statements of the Quaker Oats Company.

**Helpful Hint** As you learned in Chapter 2, consistency and comparability are important characteristics of accounting information.

**QUAKER OATS COMPANY**
Notes to the Financial Statements

**Illustration 6-14**
Disclosure of change in cost flow method

**Note 1:** Effective July 1, the Company adopted the LIFO cost flow assumption for valuing the majority of U.S. Grocery Products inventories. The Company believes that the use of the LIFO method better matches current costs with current revenues. The effect of this change on the current year was to decrease net income by $16.0 million.

## LOWER-OF-COST-OR-MARKET

The value of inventory for companies selling high-technology or fashion goods can drop very quickly due to changes in technology or changes in fashions. These circumstances sometimes call for inventory valuation methods other than those presented so far. For example, in a recent year, purchasing managers at Ford decided to make a large purchase of palladium, a precious metal used in vehicle emission devices. They made this large purchase because they feared a future shortage. The shortage did not materialize, and by the end of the year the price of palladium had plummeted. Ford's inventory was then worth $1 billion less than its original cost. Do you think Ford's inventory should have been stated at cost, in accordance with the cost principle, or at its lower replacement cost?

As you probably reasoned, this situation requires a departure from the cost basis of accounting. When the value of inventory is lower than its cost, companies write down the inventory to its market value. This is done by valuing the inventory at the **lower-of-cost-or-market (LCM)** in the period in which the price decline occurs. LCM is an example of the accounting **concept of conservatism**, which means that the best choice among accounting alternatives is the method that is least likely to overstate assets and net income.

Companies apply LCM to the items in inventory after they have used one of the cost flow methods (specific identification, FIFO, LIFO, or average-cost) to determine cost. Under the LCM basis, market is defined as **current replacement cost**, not selling price. For a merchandising company, market is the cost of

**study objective** **4**

Explain the lower-of-cost-or-market basis of accounting for inventories.

**International Note** Under U.S. GAAP, companies cannot reverse inventory write-downs if inventory increases in value in subsequent periods. IFRS permits companies to reverse write-downs in some circumstances.

purchasing the same goods at the present time from the usual suppliers in the usual quantities. Current replacement cost is used because a decline in the replacement cost of an item usually leads to a decline in the selling price of the item.

To illustrate the application of LCM, assume that Ken Tuckie TV has the following lines of merchandise with costs and market values as indicated. LCM produces the results shown in Illustration 6-15. Note that the amounts shown in the final column are the lower-of-cost-or-market amounts for each item.

**Illustration 6-15**
Computation of inventory at lower-of-cost-or-market

|  | Cost | Market | Lower-of-Cost-or-Market |
|---|---|---|---|
| Flat-panel TVs | $60,000 | $55,000 | $ 55,000 |
| Satellite radios | 45,000 | 52,000 | 45,000 |
| DVD recorders | 48,000 | 45,000 | 45,000 |
| DVDs | 15,000 | 14,000 | 14,000 |
| Total inventory |  |  | $159,000 |

Adherence to LCM is important. A Chinese manufacturer of silicon wafers for solar energy panels, LDK Solar Co., was accused of violating LCM. When the financial press reported accusations that two-thirds of its inventory of silicon was unsuitable for processing, the company's stock price fell by 40%.

**before you go on...**

**LCM BASIS**

**Do it!** Tracy Company sells three different types of home heating stoves (wood, gas, and pellet). The cost and market value of its inventory of stoves are as follows.

|  | Cost | Market |
|---|---|---|
| Gas | $ 84,000 | $ 79,000 |
| Wood | 250,000 | 280,000 |
| Pellet | 112,000 | 101,000 |

Determine the value of the company's inventory under the lower-of-cost-or-market approach.

**Action Plan**

• Determine whether cost or market value is lower for each inventory type.

• Sum the lower value of each inventory type to determine the total value of inventory.

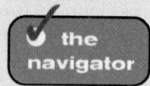
the navigator

**Solution**

The lower value for each inventory type is: gas $79,000, wood $250,000, and pellet $101,000. The total inventory value is the sum of these figures, $430,000.

Related exercise material: **BE6-7**, **Do it!** **6-3**, and **E6-9**.

# Analysis of Inventory

For companies that sell goods, managing inventory levels can be one of the most critical tasks. Having too much inventory on hand costs the company money in storage costs, interest cost (on funds tied up in inventory), and costs associated with the obsolescence of technical goods (e.g., computer chips) or shifts in fashion (e.g., clothes). But having too little inventory on hand results in lost sales. In this section, we discuss some issues related to evaluating inventory levels.

**study objective 5**
Compute and interpret the inventory turnover ratio.

## INVENTORY TURNOVER RATIO

The **inventory turnover ratio** is calculated as cost of goods sold divided by average inventory. It indicates how quickly a company sells its goods—the number of times the average inventory "turns over" (is sold) during the year.

Inventory turnover can be divided into 365 days to compute **days in inventory**, which indicates the average number of days inventory is held.

High inventory turnover (low days in inventory) indicates the company has minimal funds tied up in inventory—that it has a minimal amount of inventory on hand at any one time. Although minimizing the funds tied up in inventory is efficient, too high an inventory turnover ratio may indicate that the company is losing sales opportunities because of inventory shortages. For example, investment analysts at one time suggested that Office Depot had gone too far in reducing its inventory—they said they were seeing too many empty shelves. Thus, management should closely monitor this ratio to achieve the best balance between too much and too little inventory.

In Chapter 5, we discussed the increasingly competitive environment of retailers like Wal-Mart and Target. Wal-Mart has implemented **just-in-time inventory procedures** as well as many technological innovations to improve the efficiency of its inventory management. The following data are available for Wal-Mart.

| (in millions) | **2009** | **2008** |
|---|---|---|
| Ending inventory | $ 34,511 | $35,159 |
| Cost of goods sold | 306,158 | |

Illustration 6-16 presents the inventory turnover ratios and days in inventory for Wal-Mart and Target, using data from the financial statements of those corporations for 2009 and 2008.

**Illustration 6-16** Inventory turnover ratio and days in inventory

$$\text{Inventory Turnover Ratio} = \frac{\text{Cost of Goods Sold}}{\text{Average Inventory}}$$

$$\text{Days in Inventory} = \frac{365}{\text{Inventory Turnover Ratio}}$$

| Ratio | Wal-Mart ($ in millions) | | | Target | Industry Average |
|---|---|---|---|---|---|
| | 2009 | | 2008 | 2009 | 2009 |
| Inventory turnover ratio | $\dfrac{\$306,158}{(\$34,511 + \$35,159)/2}$ | = 8.8 times | 7.8 times | 6.5 times | 8.6 times |
| Days in inventory | $\dfrac{365 \text{ days}}{8.8}$ | = 41.5 days | 46.8 days | 56.2 days | 42.4 days |

The calculations in Illustration 6-16 show that Wal-Mart turns its inventory more frequently than Target and the industry average (8.8 times for Wal-Mart versus 6.5 times for Target and 8.6 for the industry). Consequently, the average time an item spends on a Wal-Mart shelf is shorter (41.5 days for Wal-Mart versus 56.2 days for Target and 42.4 days for the industry). This suggests that Wal-Mart is more efficient than Target in its inventory management.

Note also that Wal-Mart's inventory turnover, which was already very good in 2008, improved significantly in 2009. Wal-Mart's sophisticated inventory tracking and distribution system allows it to keep minimum amounts of inventory on hand, while still keeping the shelves full of what customers are looking for.

## Accounting Across the Organization
### Improving Inventory Control with RFID

Wal-Mart improved its inventory control with the introduction of radio frequency identification (RFID). Much like bar codes, which tell a retailer the number of boxes of a specific product it has, RFID goes a step farther, helping to distinguish one box of a specific product from another. RFID uses technology similar to that used by keyless remotes that unlock car doors.

Companies currently use RFID to track shipments from supplier to distribution center to store. Other potential uses include monitoring product expiration dates and acting quickly on product recalls. Wal-Mart also anticipates faster returns and warranty processing using RFID. This technology will further assist Wal-Mart managers in their efforts to ensure that their store has just the right type of inventory, in just the right amount, in just the right place. Other companies are also interested in RFID. Best Buy has spent millions researching possible applications in its stores.

 Why is inventory control important to managers such as those at Wal-Mart and Best Buy? (See page 330.)

## DECISION TOOLKIT

| DECISION CHECKPOINTS | INFO NEEDED FOR DECISION | TOOL TO USE FOR DECISION | HOW TO EVALUATE RESULTS |
|---|---|---|---|
| How long is an item in inventory? | Cost of goods sold; beginning and ending inventory | $\text{Inventory turnover ratio} = \dfrac{\text{Cost of goods sold}}{\text{Average inventory}}$ $\text{Days in inventory} = \dfrac{365 \text{ days}}{\text{Inventory turnover ratio}}$ | A higher inventory turnover ratio or lower average days in inventory suggests that management is reducing the amount of inventory on hand, relative to cost of goods sold. |

*before you go on...*

**INVENTORY TURNOVER** **Do it!** Early in 2012, Westmoreland Company switched to a just-in-time inventory system. Its sales, cost of goods sold, and inventory amounts for 2011 and 2012 are shown below.

| | 2011 | 2012 |
|---|---|---|
| Sales revenue | $2,000,000 | $1,800,000 |
| Cost of goods sold | 1,000,000 | 910,000 |
| Beginning inventory | 290,000 | 210,000 |
| Ending inventory | 210,000 | 50,000 |

Determine the inventory turnover and days in inventory for 2011 and 2012. Discuss the changes in the amount of inventory, the inventory turnover and days in inventory, and the amount of sales across the two years.

## Solution

| | 2011 | | 2012 | |
|---|---|---|---|---|
| Inventory turnover ratio | $\dfrac{\$1,000,000}{(\$290,000 + \$210,000)/2}$ | $= 4$ | $\dfrac{\$910,000}{(\$210,000 + \$50,000)/2}$ | $= 7$ |
| Days in inventory | $365 \div 4 = 91.3$ days | | $365 \div 7 = 52.1$ days | |

The company experienced a very significant decline in its ending inventory as a result of the just-in-time inventory. This decline improved its inventory turnover ratio and its days in inventory. However, its sales declined by 10%. It is possible that this decline was caused by the dramatic reduction in the amount of inventory that was on hand, which increased the likelihood of "stock-outs." To determine the optimal inventory level, management must weigh the benefits of reduced inventory against the potential lost sales caused by stock-outs.

**Action Plan**

- To find the inventory turnover ratio, divide cost of goods sold by average inventory.
- To determine days in inventory, divide 365 days by the inventory turnover ratio.
- Just-in-time inventory reduces the amount of inventory on hand, which reduces carrying costs. Reducing inventory levels by too much has potential negative implications for sales.

the navigator

Related exercise material: **BE6-8,** Do it! **6-4,** and **E6-10.**

## ANALYSTS' ADJUSTMENTS FOR LIFO RESERVE

Earlier we noted that using LIFO rather than FIFO can result in significant differences in the results reported in the balance sheet and the income statement. With increasing prices, FIFO will result in higher income than LIFO. On the balance sheet, FIFO will result in higher reported inventory. The financial statement differences from using LIFO normally increase the longer a company uses LIFO.

Use of different inventory cost flow assumptions complicates analysts' attempts to compare companies' results. Fortunately, companies using LIFO are required to report the difference between inventory reported using LIFO and inventory using FIFO. This amount is referred to as the **LIFO reserve**. Reporting the LIFO reserve enables analysts to make adjustments to compare companies that use different cost flow methods.

Illustration 6-17 presents an excerpt from the notes to Caterpillar's 2009 financial statements that discloses and discusses Caterpillar's LIFO reserve.

**study objective 6**

Describe the LIFO reserve and explain its importance for comparing results of different companies.

**CATERPILLAR INC.**
Notes to the Financial Statements

**Inventories:** Inventories are stated at the lower of cost or market. Cost is principally determined using the last-in, first-out (LIFO) method . . . . If the FIFO (first-in, first-out) method had been in use, inventories would have been $3,003, $3,183, and $2,617 million higher than reported at December 31, 2009, 2008, and 2007, respectively.

**Illustration 6-17**
Caterpillar LIFO reserve

Caterpillar has used LIFO for over 50 years. Thus, the cumulative difference between LIFO and FIFO reflected in the Inventory account is very large. In fact, the 2009 LIFO reserve of $3,003 million is 47% of the 2009 LIFO inventory of $6,360 million. Such a huge difference would clearly distort any comparisons you might try to make with one of Caterpillar's competitors that used FIFO.

To adjust Caterpillar's inventory balance, we add the LIFO reserve to reported inventory, as shown in Illustration 6-18. That is, if Caterpillar had used FIFO all along, its inventory would be $9,363 million, rather than $6,360 million.

**Illustration 6-18**
Conversion of inventory from LIFO to FIFO

|  | (in millions) |
|---|---|
| 2009 inventory using LIFO | $ 6,360 |
| 2009 LIFO reserve | 3,003 |
| **2009 inventory assuming FIFO** | **$9,363** |

The LIFO reserve can have a significant effect on ratios that analysts commonly use. Using the LIFO reserve adjustment, Illustration 6-19 calculates the value of the current ratio (current assets ÷ current liabilities) for Caterpillar under both the LIFO and FIFO cost flow assumptions.

**Illustration 6-19**   Impact of LIFO reserve on ratios

| ($ in millions) | LIFO | FIFO |
|---|---|---|
| **Current ratio** | $\dfrac{\$26,789}{\$19,292} = 1.39{:}1$ | $\dfrac{\$26,789 + \$3,003}{\$19,292} = 1.54{:}1$ |

As Illustration 6-19 shows, if Caterpillar used FIFO, its current ratio would be 1.54:1 rather than 1.39:1 under LIFO. Thus, Caterpillar's liquidity appears stronger if a FIFO assumption were used in valuing inventories. If a similar adjustment is made for the inventory turnover ratio, Caterpillar's inventory turnover actually would look worse under FIFO than under LIFO, dropping from 3.2 times for LIFO to 2.3 times for FIFO.[2] The reason: LIFO reports low inventory amounts, which cause inventory turnover to be higher.

CNH Global, a competitor of Caterpillar, uses FIFO to account for its inventory. Comparing Caterpillar to CNH without converting Caterpillar's inventory to FIFO would lead to distortions and potentially erroneous decisions.

# DECISION TOOLKIT

| DECISION CHECKPOINTS | INFO NEEDED FOR DECISION | TOOL TO USE FOR DECISION | HOW TO EVALUATE RESULTS |
|---|---|---|---|
| What is the impact of LIFO on the company's reported inventory? | LIFO reserve, cost of goods sold, ending inventory, current assets, current liabilities | $\dfrac{\text{LIFO}}{\text{inventory}} + \dfrac{\text{LIFO}}{\text{reserve}} = \dfrac{\text{FIFO}}{\text{inventory}}$ | If these adjustments are material, they can significantly affect such measures as the current ratio and the inventory turnover ratio. |

---

[2]The LIFO reserve also affects cost of goods sold although typically by a much less material amount. The cost of goods sold adjustment is discussed in more advanced financial statement analysis texts.

# USING THE DECISION TOOLKIT

The Manitowoc Company is located in Manitowoc, Wisconsin. In recent years, it has made a series of strategic acquisitions to grow and enhance its market-leading positions in each of its three business segments. These include: cranes and related products (crawler cranes, tower cranes, and boom trucks); food service equipment (commercial ice-cube machines, ice-beverage dispensers, and commercial refrigeration equipment); and marine operations (shipbuilding and ship-repair services). The company reported inventory of $595.5 million for 2009 and of $925.3 million for 2008. Here is the inventory note taken from the 2009 financial statements.

**THE MANITOWOC COMPANY**
Notes to the Financial Statements

**Inventories:** The components of inventories at December 31 are summarized as follows (in millions).

|  | 2009 | 2008 |
|---|---|---|
| Inventories—gross |  |  |
| Raw materials | $244.5 | $ 416.0 |
| Work-in-process | 163.5 | 262.9 |
| Finished goods | 310.8 | 352.3 |
| Total | 718.8 | 1,031.2 |
| Less: Excess and obsolete inventory reserve | (90.9) | (70.1) |
| Net inventories at FIFO cost | 627.9 | 961.1 |
| Less: Excess of FIFO costs over LIFO value | (32.4) | (35.8) |
| Inventories—net (as reported on balance sheet) | $595.5 | $ 925.3 |

Manitowoc carries inventory at the lower-of-cost-or-market using the first-in, first-out (FIFO) method for approximately 90% of total inventory for 2009 and 2008. The remainder of the inventory is costed using the last-in, first-out (LIFO) method.

Additional facts:

| | |
|---|---|
| 2009 Current liabilities | $1,142.2 |
| 2009 Current assets (as reported) | 1,259.9 |
| 2009 Cost of goods sold | 2,958.0 |

### Instructions

Answer the following questions.
1. Why does the company report its inventory in three components?
2. Why might the company use two methods (LIFO and FIFO) to account for its inventory?
3. Perform each of the following.
   (a) Calculate the inventory turnover ratio and days in inventory using the LIFO inventory.
   (b) Calculate the 2009 current ratio using LIFO and the current ratio using FIFO. Discuss the difference.

### Solution

1. The Manitowoc Company is a manufacturer, so it purchases raw materials and makes them into finished products. At the end of each period, it has some goods that have been started but are not yet complete (work in process).

By reporting all three components of inventory, a company reveals important information about its inventory position. For example, if amounts of raw materials have increased significantly compared to the previous year, we might assume the company is planning to step up production. On the other hand, if levels of finished goods have increased relative to last year and raw materials have declined, we might conclude that sales are slowing down—that the company has too much inventory on hand and is cutting back production.

2. Companies are free to choose different cost flow assumptions for different types of inventory. A company might choose to use FIFO for a product that is expected to decrease in price over time. One common reason for choosing a method other than LIFO is that many foreign countries do not allow LIFO; thus, the company cannot use LIFO for its foreign operations.

3. (a) $\dfrac{\text{Inventory turnover}}{\text{ratio}} = \dfrac{\text{Cost of goods sold}}{\text{Average inventory}} = \dfrac{\$2,958.0}{(\$595.5 + \$925.3)/2} = 3.9$

$\dfrac{\text{Days in}}{\text{inventory}} = \dfrac{365}{\text{Inventory turnover ratio}} = \dfrac{365}{3.9} = 93.6 \text{ days}$

(b) Current ratio

| | **LIFO** | **FIFO** |
|---|---|---|
| $\dfrac{\text{Current assets}}{\text{Current liabilities}}$ | $\dfrac{\$1,259.9}{\$1,142.2} = 1.10{:}1$ | $\dfrac{\$1,259.9 + \$32.4}{\$1,142.2} = 1.13{:}1$ |

This represents a 2.7% increase in the current ratio $(1.13 - 1.10)/1.10$.

# Summary of Study Objectives

**1** **Describe the steps in determining inventory quantities.** The steps are (1) take a physical inventory of goods on hand and (2) determine the ownership of goods in transit or on consignment.

**2** **Explain the basis of accounting for inventories and apply the inventory cost flow methods under a periodic inventory system.** The primary basis of accounting for inventories is cost. Cost includes all expenditures necessary to acquire goods and place them in a condition ready for sale. Cost of goods available for sale includes (a) cost of beginning inventory and (b) cost of goods purchased. The inventory cost flow methods are: specific identification and three assumed cost flow methods—FIFO, LIFO, and average-cost.

**3** **Explain the financial statement and tax effects of each of the inventory cost flow assumptions.** The cost of goods available for sale may be allocated to cost of goods sold and ending inventory by specific identification or by a method based on an assumed cost flow. When prices are rising, the first-in, first-out (FIFO) method results in lower cost of goods sold and higher net income than the average-cost and the last-in, first-out (LIFO) methods. The reverse is true when prices are falling. In the balance sheet, FIFO results in an ending inventory that is closest to current value, whereas the inventory under LIFO is the farthest from current value. LIFO

results in the lowest income taxes (because of lower taxable income).

**4** **Explain the lower-of-cost-or-market basis of accounting for inventories.** Companies use the lower-of-cost-or-market (LCM) basis when the current replacement cost (market) is less than cost. Under LCM, companies recognize the loss in the period in which the price decline occurs.

**5** **Compute and interpret the inventory turnover ratio.** The inventory turnover ratio is calculated as cost of goods sold divided by average inventory. It can be converted to average days in inventory by dividing 365 days by the inventory turnover ratio. A higher turnover ratio or lower average days in inventory suggests that management is trying to keep inventory levels low relative to its sales level.

**6** **Describe the LIFO reserve and explain its importance for comparing results of different companies.** The LIFO reserve represents the difference between ending inventory using LIFO and ending inventory if FIFO were employed instead. For some companies this difference can be significant, and ignoring it can lead to inappropriate conclusions when using the current ratio or inventory turnover ratio.

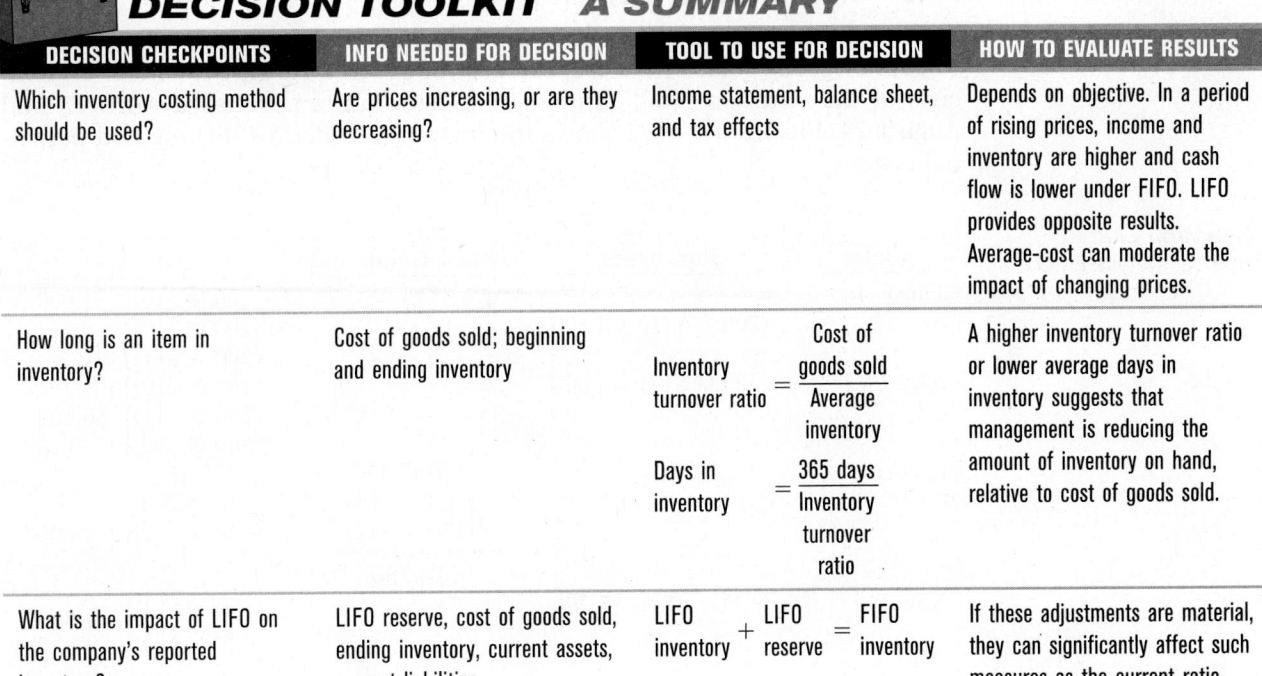

## DECISION TOOLKIT   A SUMMARY

| DECISION CHECKPOINTS | INFO NEEDED FOR DECISION | TOOL TO USE FOR DECISION | HOW TO EVALUATE RESULTS |
|---|---|---|---|
| Which inventory costing method should be used? | Are prices increasing, or are they decreasing? | Income statement, balance sheet, and tax effects | Depends on objective. In a period of rising prices, income and inventory are higher and cash flow is lower under FIFO. LIFO provides opposite results. Average-cost can moderate the impact of changing prices. |
| How long is an item in inventory? | Cost of goods sold; beginning and ending inventory | $$\text{Inventory turnover ratio} = \frac{\text{Cost of goods sold}}{\text{Average inventory}}$$ $$\text{Days in inventory} = \frac{365 \text{ days}}{\text{Inventory turnover ratio}}$$ | A higher inventory turnover ratio or lower average days in inventory suggests that management is reducing the amount of inventory on hand, relative to cost of goods sold. |
| What is the impact of LIFO on the company's reported inventory? | LIFO reserve, cost of goods sold, ending inventory, current assets, current liabilities | $$\text{LIFO inventory} + \text{LIFO reserve} = \text{FIFO inventory}$$ | If these adjustments are material, they can significantly affect such measures as the current ratio and the inventory turnover ratio. |

## appendix 6A

# Inventory Cost Flow Methods in Perpetual Inventory Systems

Each of the inventory cost flow methods described in the chapter for a periodic inventory system may be used in a perpetual inventory system. To illustrate the application of the three assumed cost flow methods (FIFO, LIFO, and average-cost), we will use the data shown in Illustration 6A-1 and in this chapter for Houston Electronics' Astro condensers.

**study objective 7**

Apply the inventory cost flow methods to perpetual inventory records.

**Illustration 6A-1**
Inventoriable units and costs

### HOUSTON ELECTRONICS
Astro Condensers

| Date | Explanation | Units | Unit Cost | Total Cost | Balance in Units |
|---|---|---|---|---|---|
| 1/1 | Beginning inventory | 100 | $10 | $ 1,000 | 100 |
| 4/15 | Purchase | 200 | 11 | 2,200 | 300 |
| 8/24 | Purchase | 300 | 12 | 3,600 | 600 |
| 9/10 | Sale | 550 | | | 50 |
| 11/27 | Purchase | 400 | 13 | 5,200 | 450 |
| | | | | $12,000 | |

### FIRST-IN, FIRST-OUT (FIFO)

Under FIFO, the cost of the earliest goods on hand **prior to each sale** is charged to cost of goods sold. Therefore, the cost of goods sold on September 10 consists of the units on hand January 1 and the units purchased April 15 and August 24. Illustration 6A-2 shows the inventory under a FIFO method perpetual system.

**Illustration 6A-2**
Perpetual system–FIFO

| Date | Purchases | Cost of Goods Sold | Balance | |
|------|-----------|--------------------|---------|---|
| Jan. 1 | | | (100 @ $10) | $1,000 |
| Apr. 15 | (200 @ $11)  $2,200 | | (100 @ $10)<br>(200 @ $11) | $3,200 |
| Aug. 24 | (300 @ $12)  $3,600 | | (100 @ $10)<br>(200 @ $11)<br>(300 @ $12) | $6,800 |
| Sept. 10 | | (100 @ $10)<br>(200 @ $11)<br>(250 @ $12)<br>———————<br>$6,200 | ( 50 @ $12) | $ 600 |
| Nov. 27 | (400 @ $13)  $5,200 | | ( 50 @ $12)<br>(400 @ $13) | $5,800 |

The ending inventory in this situation is $5,800, and the cost of goods sold is $6,200 [(100 @ $10) + (200 @ $11) + (250 @ $12)].

The results under FIFO in a perpetual system are the **same as in a periodic system**. (See Illustration 6-5 on page 288 where, similarly, the ending inventory is $5,800 and cost of goods sold is $6,200.) Regardless of the system, the first costs in are the costs assigned to cost of goods sold.

### LAST-IN, FIRST-OUT (LIFO)

Under the LIFO method using a perpetual system, the cost of the most recent purchase prior to sale is allocated to the units sold. Therefore, the cost of the goods sold on September 10 consists of all the units from the August 24 and April 15 purchases plus 50 of the units in beginning inventory. The ending inventory under the LIFO method is computed in Illustration 6A-3.

**Illustration 6A-3**
Perpetual system–LIFO

| Date | Purchases | Cost of Goods Sold | Balance | |
|------|-----------|--------------------|---------|---|
| Jan. 1 | | | (100 @ $10) | $1,000 |
| Apr. 15 | (200 @ $11) $2,200 | | (100 @ $10)<br>(200 @ $11) | $3,200 |
| Aug. 24 | (300 @ $12) $3,600 | | (100 @ $10)<br>(200 @ $11)<br>(300 @ $12) | $6,800 |
| Sept. 10 | | (300 @ $12)<br>(200 @ $11)<br>(50 @ $10)<br>———————<br>$6,300 | (50 @ $10) | $ 500 |
| Nov. 27 | (400 @ $13) $5,200 | | (50 @ $10)<br>(400 @ $13) | $5,700 |

The use of LIFO in a perpetual system will usually produce cost allocations that differ from use of LIFO in a periodic system. In a perpetual system, the latest units purchased *prior to each sale* are allocated to cost of goods sold. In contrast, in a periodic system, the latest units purchased *during the period* are allocated to cost of goods sold. Thus, when a purchase is made after the last sale, the LIFO periodic system will apply this purchase to the previous sale. See Illustration 6-8 (on page 290) where the proof shows the 400 units at $13 purchased on November 27 applied to the sale of 550 units on September 10.

As shown above, under the LIFO perpetual system the 400 units at $13 purchased on November 27 are all applied to the ending inventory.

The ending inventory in this LIFO perpetual illustration is $5,700 and cost of goods sold is $6,300. Compare this to the LIFO periodic illustration (Illustration 6-7 on page 289) where the ending inventory is $5,000 and cost of goods sold is $7,000.

## AVERAGE-COST

The average-cost method in a perpetual inventory system is called the **moving-average method**. Under this method, the company computes a new average **after each purchase**. The average cost is computed by dividing the cost of goods available for sale by the units on hand. The average cost is then applied to: (1) the units sold, to determine the cost of goods sold, and (2) the remaining units on hand, to determine the ending inventory amount. Illustration 6A-4 shows the application of the average-cost method by Houston Electronics.

| Date | Purchases | Cost of Goods Sold | Balance |
|---|---|---|---|
| Jan. 1 | | | (100 @ $10) $ 1,000 |
| Apr. 15 | (200 @ $11) $2,200 | | (300 @ $10.667) $ 3,200 |
| Aug. 24 | (300 @ $12) $3,600 | | (600 @ $11.333) $ 6,800 |
| Sept. 10 | | (550 @ $11.333) $6,233 | (50 @ $11.333) $ 567 |
| Nov. 27 | (400 @ $13) $5,200 | | (450 @ $12.816) $5,767 |

**Illustration 6A-4**
Perpetual system–average-cost method

As indicated above, the company computes **a new average each time it makes a purchase**. On April 15, after 200 units are purchased for $2,200, a total of 300 units costing $3,200 ($1,000 + $2,200) are on hand. The average unit cost is $10.667 ($3,200 ÷ 300). On August 24, after 300 units are purchased for $3,600, a total of 600 units costing $6,800 ($1,000 + $2,200 + $3,600) are on hand at an average cost per unit of $11.333 ($6,800 ÷ 600). Houston Electronics uses this unit cost of $11.333 in costing sales until another purchase is made, when the company computes a new unit cost. Accordingly, the unit cost of the 550 units sold on September 10 is $11.333, and the total cost of goods sold is $6,233. On November 27, following the purchase of 400 units for $5,200, there are 450 units on hand costing $5,767 ($567 + $5,200) with a new average cost of $12.816 ($5,767 ÷ 450).

Compare this moving-average cost under the perpetual inventory system to Illustration 6-10 (on page 291) showing the weighted-average method under a periodic inventory system.

# Summary of Study Objective for Appendix 6A

**7 Apply the inventory cost flow methods to perpetual inventory records.** Under FIFO, the cost of the earliest goods on hand prior to each sale is charged to cost of goods sold. Under LIFO, the cost of the most recent purchase prior to sale is charged to cost of goods sold. Under the average-cost method, a new average cost is computed after each purchase.

## appendix 6B

# Inventory Errors

Unfortunately, errors occasionally occur in accounting for inventory. In some cases, errors are caused by failure to count or price the inventory correctly. In other cases, errors occur because companies do not properly recognize the transfer of legal title to goods that are in transit. When inventory errors occur, they affect both the income statement and the balance sheet.

### INCOME STATEMENT EFFECTS

Under a periodic inventory system, both the beginning and ending inventories appear in the income statement. The ending inventory of one period automatically becomes the beginning inventory of the next period. Thus, inventory errors affect the computation of cost of goods sold and net income in two periods.

The effects on cost of goods sold can be computed by entering incorrect data in the formula in Illustration 6B-1 and then substituting the correct data.

**Illustration 6B-1**
Formula for cost of goods sold

| Beginning Inventory | + | Cost of Goods Purchased | − | Ending Inventory | = | Cost of Goods Sold |
|---|---|---|---|---|---|---|

If *beginning* inventory is understated, cost of goods sold will be understated. If *ending* inventory is understated, cost of goods sold will be overstated. Illustration 6B-2 shows the effects of inventory errors on the current year's income statement.

**Illustration 6B-2** Effects of inventory errors on current year's income statement

| Inventory Error | Cost of Goods Sold | Net Income |
|---|---|---|
| Beginning inventory understated | Understated | Overstated |
| Beginning inventory overstated | Overstated | Understated |
| Ending inventory understated | Overstated | Understated |
| Ending inventory overstated | Understated | Overstated |

An error in the ending inventory of the current period will have a **reverse effect on net income of the next accounting period**. This is shown in Illustration 6B-3. Note that the understatement of ending inventory in 2011 results in an understatement of beginning inventory in 2012 and an overstatement of net income in 2012.

Over the two years, total net income is correct because the errors offset each other. Notice that total income using incorrect data is $35,000 ($22,000 + $13,000), which is the same as the total income of $35,000 ($25,000 + $10,000) using correct data. Also note in this example that an error in the beginning inventory does not result in a corresponding error in the ending inventory for that period. The correctness of the ending inventory depends entirely on the accuracy of taking and costing the inventory at the balance sheet date under the periodic inventory system.

**SAMPLE COMPANY**
Condensed Income Statements

| | 2011 | | | | 2012 | | | |
| --- | --- | --- | --- | --- | --- | --- | --- | --- |
| | **Incorrect** | | **Correct** | | **Incorrect** | | **Correct** | |
| Sales revenue | | $80,000 | | $80,000 | | $90,000 | | $90,000 |
| Beginning inventory | $20,000 | | $20,000 | | **$12,000** | | **$15,000** | |
| Cost of goods purchased | 40,000 | | 40,000 | | 68,000 | | 68,000 | |
| Cost of goods available for sale | 60,000 | | 60,000 | | 80,000 | | 83,000 | |
| Ending inventory | **12,000** | | **15,000** | | 23,000 | | 23,000 | |
| Cost of goods sold | | 48,000 | | 45,000 | | 57,000 | | 60,000 |
| Gross profit | | 32,000 | | 35,000 | | 33,000 | | 30,000 |
| Operating expenses | | 10,000 | | 10,000 | | 20,000 | | 20,000 |
| Net income | | $22,000 | | $25,000 | | $13,000 | | $10,000 |

$(3,000)
Net income
understated

$3,000
Net income
overstated

**The errors cancel. Thus, the combined total
income for the 2-year period is correct.**

**Illustration 6B-3**  Effects of inventory errors on two years' income statements

## BALANCE SHEET EFFECTS

The effect of ending inventory errors on the balance sheet can be determined by using the basic accounting equation: Assets = Liabilities + Stockholders' equity. Errors in the ending inventory have the effects shown in Illustration 6B-4.

**Illustration 6B-4**  Effects of ending inventory errors on balance sheet

| Ending Inventory Error | Assets | Liabilities | Stockholders' Equity |
| --- | --- | --- | --- |
| Overstated | Overstated | No effect | Overstated |
| Understated | Understated | No effect | Understated |

The effect of an error in ending inventory on the subsequent period was shown in Illustration 6B-3. Recall that if the error is not corrected, the combined total net income for the two periods would be correct. Thus, total stockholders' equity reported on the balance sheet at the end of 2012 will also be correct.

# Summary of Study Objective for Appendix 6B

**8** **Indicate the effects of inventory errors on the financial statements.** In the income statement of the current year: (1) An error in beginning inventory will have a reverse effect on net income (e.g., overstatement of inventory results in understatement of net income, and vice versa). (2) An error in ending inventory will have a similar effect on net income (e.g., overstatement of inventory results in overstatement of net income). If ending inventory errors are not corrected in the following period, their effect on net income for that period is reversed, and total net income for the two years will be correct.

*In the balance sheet:* Ending inventory errors will have the same effect on total assets and total stockholders' equity and no effect on liabilities.

# Glossary

**Average-cost method** (p. 290) An inventory costing method that uses the weighted-average unit cost to allocate the cost of goods available for sale to ending inventory and cost of goods sold.

**Consigned goods** (p. 284) Goods held for sale by one party although ownership of the goods is retained by another party.

**Current replacement cost** (p. 295) The cost of purchasing the same goods at the present time from the usual suppliers in the usual quantities.

**Days in inventory** (p. 297) Measure of the average number of days inventory is held; calculated as 365 divided by inventory turnover ratio.

**Finished goods inventory** (p. 282) Manufactured items that are completed and ready for sale.

**First-in, first-out (FIFO) method** (p. 288) An inventory costing method that assumes that the earliest goods purchased are the first to be sold.

**FOB destination** (p. 284) Freight terms indicating that ownership of goods remains with the seller until the goods reach the buyer.

**FOB shipping point** (p. 284) Freight terms indicating that ownership of goods passes to the buyer when the public carrier accepts the goods from the seller.

**Inventory turnover ratio** (p. 296) A ratio that measures the liquidity of inventory by measuring the number of times average inventory sold during the period; computed by dividing cost of goods sold by the average inventory during the period.

**Just-in-time (JIT) inventory** (p. 283) Inventory system in which companies manufacture or purchase goods just in time for use.

**Last-in, first-out (LIFO) method** (p. 289) An inventory costing method that assumes that the latest units purchased are the first to be sold.

**LIFO reserve** (p. 299) For a company using LIFO, the difference between inventory reported using LIFO and inventory using FIFO.

**Lower-of-cost-or-market (LCM)** (p. 295) A basis whereby inventory is stated at the lower of either its cost or its market value as determined by current replacement cost.

**Raw materials** (p. 282) Basic goods that will be used in production but have not yet been placed in production.

**Specific identification method** (p. 286) An actual physical flow costing method in which items sold and items still in inventory are specifically costed to arrive at cost of goods sold and ending inventory.

**Weighted-average unit cost** (p. 290) Average cost that is weighted by the number of units purchased at each unit cost.

**Work in process** (p. 282) That portion of manufactured inventory that has begun the production process but is not yet complete.

# Comprehensive Do it!

Englehart Company has the following inventory, purchases, and sales data for the month of March.

| Inventory, March 1 | 200 units @ $4.00 | $ 800 |
| --- | --- | --- |
| Purchases | | |
| March 10 | 500 units @ $4.50 | 2,250 |
| March 20 | 400 units @ $4.75 | 1,900 |
| March 30 | 300 units @ $5.00 | 1,500 |
| Sales | | |
| March 15 | 500 units | |
| March 25 | 400 units | |

The physical inventory count on March 31 shows 500 units on hand.

## Instructions

Under a **periodic inventory system**, determine the cost of inventory on hand at March 31 and the cost of goods sold for March under (a) the first-in, first-out (FIFO) method; (b) the last-in, first-out (LIFO) method; and (c) the average-cost method. (For average-cost, carry cost per unit to three decimal places.)

## Solution to Comprehensive *Do it!*

The cost of goods available for sale is $6,450:

|  | Inventory Purchases | 200 units @ $4.00 | $  800 |
|--|--|--|--|
|  | March 10 | 500 units @ $4.50 | 2,250 |
|  | March 20 | 400 units @ $4.75 | 1,900 |
|  | March 30 | 300 units @ $5.00 | 1,500 |
|  | Total cost of goods available for sale |  | $6,450 |

**(a)**                 **FIFO Method**

Ending inventory:

| Date | Units | Unit Cost | Total Cost |  |
|--|--|--|--|--|
| Mar. 30 | 300 | $5.00 | $1,500 |  |
| Mar. 20 | 200 | 4.75 | 950 | $2,450 |

Cost of goods sold: $6,450 − $2,450 =      $4,000

**(b)**                 **LIFO Method**

Ending inventory:

| Date | Units | Unit Cost | Total Cost |  |
|--|--|--|--|--|
| Mar. 1 | 200 | $4.00 | $  800 |  |
| Mar. 10 | 300 | 4.50 | 1,350 | $2,150 |

Cost of goods sold: $6,450 − $2,150 =      $4,300

**(c)**              **Average-Cost Method**

Weighted-average unit cost: $6,450 ÷ 1,400 = $4.607
Ending inventory: 500 × $4.607 =      $2,303.50
Cost of goods sold: $6,450 − $2,303.50 =      $4,146.50

### Action Plan

- For FIFO, allocate the latest costs to inventory.
- For LIFO, allocate the earliest costs to inventory.
- For average-cost, use a weighted average.
- Remember, the costs allocated to cost of goods sold can be proved.
- Total purchases are the same under all three cost flow assumptions.

---

 **Self-Test, Brief Exercises, Exercises, Problem Set A, and many more resources are available for practice in WileyPLUS**

---

*Note:* All Questions, Exercises, and Problems marked with an asterisk relate to material in the appendices to the chapter.

# Self-Test Questions

Answers are on page 330.

(SO 1)   **1.** When is a physical inventory usually taken?
     (a) When the company has its greatest amount of inventory.
     (b) When a limited number of goods are being sold or received.
     (c) At the end of the company's fiscal year.
     (d) Both (b) and (c).

(SO 1)   **2.** Which of the following should *not* be included in the physical inventory of a company?
     (a) Goods held on consignment from another company.

     (b) Goods shipped on consignment to another company.
     (c) Goods in transit from another company shipped FOB shipping point.
     (d) All of the above should be included.

**3.** As a result of a thorough physical inventory, Railway (SO 1) Company determined that it had inventory worth $180,000 at December 31, 2012. This count did not take into consideration the following facts: Rogers Consignment store currently has goods worth $35,000 on its sales floor that belong to Railway but

are being sold on consignment by Rogers. The selling price of these goods is $50,000. Railway purchased $13,000 of goods that were shipped on December 27, FOB destination, that will be received by Railway on January 3. Determine the correct amount of inventory that Railway should report.
(a) $230,000.
(b) $215,000.
(c) $228,000.
(d) $193,000.

(SO 2) **4.** Kam Company has the following units and costs.

| | Units | Unit Cost |
|---|---|---|
| Inventory, Jan. 1 | 8,000 | $11 |
| Purchase, June 19 | 13,000 | 12 |
| Purchase, Nov. 8 | 5,000 | 13 |

If 9,000 units are on hand at December 31, what is the cost of the ending inventory under FIFO?
(a) $99,000.      (c) $113,000.
(b) $108,000.     (d) $117,000.

(SO 2) **5.** From the data in question 4, what is the cost of the ending inventory under LIFO?
(a) $113,000.     (c) $99,000.
(b) $108,000.     (d) $100,000.

(SO 2) **6.** Davidson Electronics has the following:

| | Units | Unit Cost |
|---|---|---|
| Inventory, Jan. 1 | 5,000 | $ 8 |
| Purchase, April 2 | 15,000 | 10 |
| Purchase, Aug. 28 | 20,000 | 12 |

If Davidson has 7,000 units on hand at December 31, the cost of ending inventory under the average-cost method is:
(a) $84,000.      (c) $56,000.
(b) $70,000.      (d) $75,250.

(SO 3) **7.** In periods of rising prices, LIFO will produce:
(a) higher net income than FIFO.
(b) the same net income as FIFO.
(c) lower net income than FIFO.
(d) higher net income than average-cost.

(SO 3) **8.** Considerations that affect the selection of an inventory costing method do *not* include:
(a) tax effects.
(b) balance sheet effects.
(c) income statement effects.
(d) perpetual versus periodic inventory system.

(SO 4) **9.** The lower-of-cost-or-market rule for inventory is an example of the application of:
(a) the conservatism constraint.
(b) the historical cost principle.
(c) the materiality constraint.
(d) the economic entity assumption.

(SO 5) **10.** Which of these would cause the inventory turnover ratio to increase the most?

(a) Increasing the amount of inventory on hand.
(b) Keeping the amount of inventory on hand constant but increasing sales.
(c) Keeping the amount of inventory on hand constant but decreasing sales.
(d) Decreasing the amount of inventory on hand and increasing sales.

(SO 5) **11.** Carlos Company had beginning inventory of $80,000, ending inventory of $110,000, cost of goods sold of $285,000, and sales of $475,000. Carlos's days in inventory is:
(a) 73 days.
(b) 121.7 days.
(c) 102.5 days.
(d) 84.5 days.

(SO 6) **12.** The LIFO reserve is:
(a) the difference between the value of the inventory under LIFO and the value under FIFO.
(b) an amount used to adjust inventory to the lower-of-cost-or-market.
(c) the difference between the value of the inventory under LIFO and the value under average-cost.
(d) an amount used to adjust inventory to historical cost.

(SO 7) *****13.** In a perpetual inventory system,
(a) LIFO cost of goods sold will be the same as in a periodic inventory system.
(b) average costs are based entirely on unit-cost simple averages.
(c) a new average is computed under the average-cost method after each sale.
(d) FIFO cost of goods sold will be the same as in a periodic inventory system.

(SO 8) *****14.** Fran Company's ending inventory is understated by $4,000. The effects of this error on the current year's cost of goods sold and net income, respectively, are:
(a) understated and overstated.
(b) overstated and understated.
(c) overstated and overstated.
(d) understated and understated.

(SO 4) *****15.** Harold Company overstated its inventory by $15,000 at December 31, 2012. It did not correct the error in 2012 or 2013. As a result, Harold's stockholders' equity was:
(a) overstated at December 31, 2012, and understated at December 31, 2013.
(b) overstated at December 31, 2012, and properly stated at December 31, 2013.
(c) understated at December 31, 2012, and understated at December 31, 2013.
(d) overstated at December 31, 2012, and overstated at December 31, 2013.

Go to the book's companion website, **www.wiley.com/college/kimmel**, to access additional Self-Test Questions.

# Questions

1. "The key to successful business operations is effective inventory management." Do you agree? Explain.

2. An item must possess two characteristics to be classified as inventory. What are these two characteristics?

3. ➡ What is just-in-time inventory management? What are its potential advantages?

4. Your friend Sara Hovey has been hired to help take the physical inventory in Malaby's Hardware Store. Explain to Sara what this job will entail.

5. (a) Brandt Company ships merchandise to England Corporation on December 30. The merchandise reaches the buyer on January 5. Indicate the terms of sale that will result in the goods being included in (1) Brandt's December 31 inventory and (2) England's December 31 inventory.
   (b) Under what circumstances should Brandt Company include consigned goods in its inventory?

6. Katz Hat Shop received a shipment of hats for which it paid the wholesaler $2,940. The price of the hats was $3,000, but Katz was given a $60 cash discount and required to pay freight charges of $75. What amount should Katz include in inventory? Why?

7. What is the primary basis of accounting for inventories? What is the major objective in accounting for inventories?

8. Brad Watters believes that the allocation of cost of goods available for sale should be based on the actual physical flow of the goods. Explain to Brad why this may be both impractical and inappropriate.

9. What is the major advantage and major disadvantage of the specific identification method of inventory costing?

10. ➡ "The selection of an inventory cost flow method is a decision made by accountants." Do you agree? Explain. Once a method has been selected, what accounting requirement applies?

11. Which assumed inventory cost flow method:
    (a) usually parallels the actual physical flow of merchandise?
    (b) divides cost of goods available for sale by total units available for sale to determine a unit cost?
    (c) assumes that the latest units purchased are the first to be sold?

12. In a period of rising prices, the inventory reported in King Company's balance sheet is close to the current cost of the inventory, whereas Ritchie Company's inventory is considerably below its current cost. Identify the inventory cost flow method used by each company. Which company probably has been reporting the higher gross profit?

13. Azenabor Corporation has been using the FIFO cost flow method during a prolonged period of inflation. During the same time period, Azenabor has been paying out all of its net income as dividends. What adverse effects may result from this policy?

14. Thomas Holme, a mid-level product manager for Dorothy's Shoes, thinks his company should switch from LIFO to FIFO. He says, "My bonus is based on net income. If we switch it will increase net income and increase my bonus. The company would be better off and so would I." Is he correct? Explain.

15. Discuss the impact the use of LIFO has on taxes paid, cash flows, and the quality of earnings ratio relative to the impact of FIFO when prices are increasing.

16. 🔲 What inventory cost flow method does Tootsie Roll Industries use for U.S. inventories? What method does it use for foreign inventories? (*Hint:* You will need to examine the notes for Tootsie Roll's financial statements.) Why does it use a different method for foreign inventories?

17. Olivia Dietz is studying for the next accounting midterm examination. What should Olivia know about (a) departing from the cost basis of accounting for inventories and (b) the meaning of "market" in the lower-of-cost-or-market method?

18. Cataldi Music Center has five TVs on hand at the balance sheet date that cost $400 each. The current replacement cost is $350 per unit. Under the lower-of-cost-or-market basis of accounting for inventories, what value should Cataldi report for the TVs on the balance sheet? Why?

19. 🔧 What cost flow assumption may be used under the lower-of-cost-or-market basis of accounting for inventories?

20. Why is it inappropriate for a company to include freight-out expense in the Cost of Goods Sold account?

21. Berges Company's balance sheet shows Inventory $162,800. What additional disclosures should be made?

22. ➡ 🔧 Under what circumstances might the inventory turnover ratio be too high—that is, what possible negative consequences might occur?

23. 🔧 What is the LIFO reserve? What are the consequences of ignoring a large LIFO reserve when analyzing a company?

*24. "When perpetual inventory records are kept, the results under the FIFO and LIFO methods are the same as they would be in a periodic inventory system." Do you agree? Explain.

*25. How does the average-cost method of inventory costing differ between a perpetual inventory system and a periodic inventory system?

*26. Nicholas Company discovers in 2012 that its ending inventory at December 31, 2011, was $5,000 understated. What effect will this error have on (a) 2011 net income, (b) 2012 net income, and (c) the combined net income for the 2 years?

# Brief Exercises

*Identify items to be included in taking a physical inventory.*
(SO 1), **C**

**BE6-1** Susan Cashin Company identifies the following items for possible inclusion in the physical inventory. Indicate whether each item should be included or excluded from the inventory taking.
(a) 900 units of inventory shipped on consignment by Cashin to another company.
(b) 3,000 units of inventory in transit from a supplier shipped FOB destination.
(c) 1,200 units of inventory sold but being held for customer pickup.
(d) 500 units of inventory held on consignment from another company.

*Compute ending inventory using FIFO and LIFO.*
(SO 2), **AP**

**BE6-2** In its first month of operations, Cisler Company made three purchases of merchandise in the following sequence: (1) 300 units at $6, (2) 400 units at $8, and (3) 500 units at $9. Assuming there are 200 units on hand at the end of the period, compute the cost of the ending inventory under (a) the FIFO method and (b) the LIFO method. Cisler uses a periodic inventory system.

*Compute the ending inventory using average-cost.*
(SO 2), **AP**

**BE6-3** Data for Cisler Company are presented in BE6-2. Compute the cost of the ending inventory under the average-cost method. (Round the cost per unit to three decimal places.)

*Explain the financial statement effect of inventory cost flow assumptions.*
(SO 3), **C**

**BE6-4** The management of Easterling Corp. is considering the effects of various inventory-costing methods on its financial statements and its income tax expense. Assuming that the price the company pays for inventory is increasing, which method will:
(a) provide the highest net income?
(b) provide the highest ending inventory?
(c) result in the lowest income tax expense?
(d) result in the most stable earnings over a number of years?

*Explain the financial statement effect of inventory cost flow assumptions.*
(SO 3), **AP**

**BE6-5** In its first month of operation, Moraine Company purchased 100 units of inventory for $6, then 200 units for $7, and finally 140 units for $8. At the end of the month, 180 units remained. Compute the amount of phantom profit that would result if the company used FIFO rather than LIFO. Explain why this amount is referred to as phantom profit. The company uses the periodic method.

*Identify the impact of LIFO versus FIFO.*
(SO 3), **C**

**BE6-6** For each of the following cases, state whether the statement is true for LIFO or for FIFO. Assume that prices are rising.
(a) Results in a higher quality of earnings ratio.
(b) Results in higher phantom profits.
(c) Results in higher net income.
(d) Results in lower taxes.
(e) Results in lower net cash provided by operating activities.

*Determine the LCM valuation.*
(SO 4), **AP**

**BE6-7** Olsson Video Center accumulates the following cost and market data at December 31.

| Inventory Categories | Cost Data | Market Data |
|---|---|---|
| Cameras | $12,500 | $13,400 |
| Camcorders | 9,000 | 9,500 |
| DVDs | 13,000 | 12,200 |

Compute the lower-of-cost-or-market valuation for Olsson inventory.

*Compute inventory turnover ratio and days in inventory.*
(SO 5), **AP**

**BE6-8** At December 31 of a recent year, the following information (in thousands) was available for sunglasses manufacturer Oakley, Inc.: ending inventory $155,377; beginning inventory $119,035; cost of goods sold $349,114; and sales revenue $761,865. Calculate the inventory turnover ratio and days in inventory for Oakley, Inc.

*Determine ending inventory and cost of goods sold using LIFO reserve.*
(SO 6), **C**

**BE6-9** Winnebago Industries, Inc. is a leading manufacturer of motor homes. Winnebago reported ending inventory at August 29, 2009, of $46,850,000 under the LIFO inventory method. In the notes to its financial statements, Winnebago reported a LIFO reserve of $30,346,000 at August 29, 2009. What would Winnebago Industries' ending inventory have been if it had used FIFO?

*Apply cost flow methods to perpetual inventory records.*
(SO 7), **AP**

*BE6-10** Dewey's Department Store uses a perpetual inventory system. Data for product E2-D2 include the purchases shown on page 313.

| Date | Number of Units | Unit Price |
|---|---|---|
| May 7 | 50 | $10 |
| July 28 | 30 | 15 |

On June 1, Dewey sold 25 units, and on August 27, 30 more units. Compute the cost of goods sold using (1) FIFO, (2) LIFO, and (3) average-cost. (Round the cost per unit to three decimal places.)

*BE6-11  Roskopf Company reports net income of $92,000 in 2012. However, ending inventory was understated by $7,000. What is the correct net income for 2012? What effect, if any, will this error have on total assets as reported in the balance sheet at December 31, 2012?

*Determine correct financial statement amount.*
*(SO 8),* **AN**

# Do it! Review

**Do it! 6-1**  Newell Company just took its physical inventory. The count of inventory items on hand at the company's business locations resulted in a total inventory cost of $300,000. In reviewing the details of the count and related inventory transactions, you have discovered the following items that had not been considered.

*Apply rules of ownership to determine inventory cost.*
*(SO 1),* **AN**

1. Newell has sent inventory costing $28,000 on consignment to Victoria Company. All of this inventory was at Victoria's showrooms on December 31.
2. The company did not include in the count inventory (cost, $20,000) that was sold on December 28, terms FOB shipping point. The goods were in transit on December 31.
3. The company did not include in the count inventory (cost, $13,000) that was purchased with terms of FOB shipping point. The goods were in transit on December 31.

Compute the correct December 31 inventory.

**Do it! 6-2**  The accounting records of Orth Electronics show the following data.

*Compute cost of goods sold under different cost flow methods.*
*(SO 2),* **AP**

| Beginning inventory | 3,000 units at $5 |
| Purchases | 8,000 units at $7 |
| Sales | 9,400 units at $10 |

Determine cost of goods sold during the period under a periodic inventory system using (a) the FIFO method, (b) the LIFO method, and (c) the average-cost method. (Round unit cost to three decimal places.)

**Do it! 6-3**  Bardell Company sells three different categories of tools (small, medium and large). The cost and market value of its inventory of tools are as follows.

*Compute inventory value under LCM.*
*(SO 4),* **AP**

| | Cost | Market |
|---|---|---|
| Small | $ 64,000 | $ 61,000 |
| Medium | 290,000 | 260,000 |
| Large | 152,000 | 167,000 |

Determine the value of the company's inventory under the lower-of-cost-or-market approach.

**Do it! 6-4**  Early in 2012, Aragon Company switched to a just-in-time inventory system. Its sales and inventory amounts for 2011 and 2012 are shown below.

*Compute inventory turnover ratio and assess inventory level.*
*(SO 5),* **AN**

| | 2011 | 2012 |
|---|---|---|
| Sales revenue | $3,120,000 | $3,713,000 |
| Cost of goods sold | 1,200,000 | 1,425,000 |
| Beginning inventory | 170,000 | 210,000 |
| Ending inventory | 210,000 | 90,000 |

Determine the inventory turnover and days in inventory for 2011 and 2012. Discuss the changes in the amount of inventory, the inventory turnover and days in inventory, and the amount of sales across the two years.

# Exercises

*Determine the correct inventory amount.*
(SO 1), **AN**

**E6-1** Worthmore Bank and Trust is considering giving Madsen Company a loan. Before doing so, it decides that further discussions with Madsen's accountant may be desirable. One area of particular concern is the Inventory account, which has a year-end balance of $275,000. Discussions with the accountant reveal the following.

1. Madsen sold goods costing $55,000 to Allen Company FOB shipping point on December 28. The goods are not expected to reach Allen until January 12. The goods were not included in the physical inventory because they were not in the warehouse.
2. The physical count of the inventory did not include goods costing $95,000 that were shipped to Madsen FOB destination on December 27 and were still in transit at year-end.
3. Madsen received goods costing $25,000 on January 2. The goods were shipped FOB shipping point on December 26 by Lynch Co. The goods were not included in the physical count.
4. Madsen sold goods costing $51,000 to Finet of Canada FOB destination on December 30. The goods were received in Canada on January 8. They were not included in Madsen's physical inventory.
5. Madsen received goods costing $42,000 on January 2 that were shipped FOB destination on December 29. The shipment was a rush order that was supposed to arrive December 31. This purchase was included in the ending inventory of $275,000.

*Instructions*
Determine the correct inventory amount on December 31.

*Determine the correct inventory amount.*
(SO 1), **AN**

**E6-2** Jerry Karron, an auditor with Joshi CPAs, is performing a review of Duncan Company's Inventory account. Duncan did not have a good year, and top management is under pressure to boost reported income. According to its records, the inventory balance at year-end was $740,000. However, the following information was not considered when determining that amount.

1. Included in the company's count were goods with a cost of $228,000 that the company is holding on consignment. The goods belong to Arnold Corporation.
2. The physical count did not include goods purchased by Duncan with a cost of $40,000 that were shipped FOB shipping point on December 28 and did not arrive at Duncan's warehouse until January 3.
3. Included in the Inventory account was $17,000 of office supplies that were stored in the warehouse and were to be used by the company's supervisors and managers during the coming year.
4. The company received an order on December 29 that was boxed and was sitting on the loading dock awaiting pick-up on December 31. The shipper picked up the goods on January 1 and delivered them on January 6. The shipping terms were FOB shipping point. The goods had a selling price of $40,000 and a cost of $29,000. The goods were not included in the count because they were sitting on the dock.
5. On December 29, Duncan shipped goods with a selling price of $80,000 and a cost of $50,000 to Siebring Sales Corporation FOB shipping point. The goods arrived on January 3. Siebring Sales had only ordered goods with a selling price of $10,000 and a cost of $6,000. However, a sales manager at Duncan had authorized the shipment and said that if Siebring wanted to ship the goods back next week, it could.
6. Included in the count was $50,000 of goods that were parts for a machine that the company no longer made. Given the high-tech nature of Duncan's products, it was unlikely that these obsolete parts had any other use. However, management would prefer to keep them on the books at cost, "since that is what we paid for them, after all."

*Instructions*
Prepare a schedule to determine the correct inventory amount. Provide explanations for each item above, stating why you did or did not make an adjustment for each item.

*Identify items in inventory.*
(SO 1), **K**

**E6-3** Trinh Inc. had the following inventory situations to consider at January 31, its year-end.
(a) Goods held on consignment for MailBoxes Corp. since December 12.
(b) Goods shipped on consignment to Reddy Holdings Inc. on January 5.
(c) Goods shipped to a customer, FOB destination, on January 29 that are still in transit.

(d) Goods shipped to a customer, FOB shipping point, on January 29 that are still in transit.

(e) Goods purchased FOB destination from a supplier on January 25, that are still in transit.

(f) Goods purchased FOB shipping point from a supplier on January 25, that are still in transit.

(g) Office supplies on hand at January 31.

**Instructions**

Identify which of the preceding items should be included in inventory. If the item should not be included in inventory, state in what account, if any, it should have been recorded.

**E6-4** Sunburst sells a snowboard, Xpert, that is popular with snowboard enthusiasts. Below is information relating to Sunburst's purchases of Xpert snowboards during September. During the same month, 116 Xpert snowboards were sold. Sunburst uses a periodic inventory system.

*Compute inventory and cost of goods sold using periodic FIFO and LIFO.*
*(SO 2), AN*

| Date | Explanation | Units | Unit Cost | Total Cost |
|---|---|---|---|---|
| Sept. 1 | Inventory | 12 | $100 | $ 1,200 |
| Sept. 12 | Purchases | 45 | 103 | 4,635 |
| Sept. 19 | Purchases | 20 | 104 | 2,080 |
| Sept. 26 | Purchases | 50 | 105 | 5,250 |
| | Totals | 127 | | $13,165 |

**Instructions**

(a) Compute the ending inventory at September 30 using the FIFO and LIFO methods. Prove the amount allocated to cost of goods sold under each method.

(b) For both FIFO and LIFO, calculate the sum of ending inventory and cost of goods sold. What do you notice about the answers you found for each method?

**E6-5** Klumb Inc. uses a periodic inventory system. Its records show the following for the month of May, in which 74 units were sold.

*Calculate inventory and cost of goods sold using FIFO, average-cost, and LIFO in a periodic inventory system.*
*(SO 2), AP*

| Date | Explanation | Units | Unit Cost | Total Cost |
|---|---|---|---|---|
| May 1 | Inventory | 30 | $ 9 | $270 |
| 15 | Purchase | 25 | 10 | 250 |
| 24 | Purchase | 38 | 11 | 418 |
| | Total | 93 | | $938 |

**Instructions**

Calculate the ending inventory at May 31 using the (a) FIFO, (b) average-cost, and (c) LIFO methods. (For average-cost, round the average unit cost to three decimal places.) Prove the amount allocated to cost of goods sold under each method.

**E6-6** On December 1, LoPrice Electronics has three DVD players left in stock. All are identical, all are priced to sell at $85. One of the three DVD players left in stock, with serial #1012, was purchased on June 1 at a cost of $52. Another, with serial #1045, was purchased on November 1 for $48. The last player, serial #1056, was purchased on November 30 for $40.

*Calculate cost of goods sold using specific identification and FIFO periodic.*
*(SO 2, 3), AN*

**Instructions**

(a) Calculate the cost of goods sold using the FIFO periodic inventory method, assuming that two of the three players were sold by the end of December, LoPrice Electronics' year-end.

(b) If LoPrice Electronics used the specific identification method instead of the FIFO method, how might it alter its earnings by "selectively choosing" which particular players to sell to the two customers? What would LoPrice's cost of goods sold be if the company wished to minimize earnings? Maximize earnings?

(c) Which inventory method, FIFO or specific identification, do you recommend that LoPrice use? Explain why.

*Compute inventory and cost of goods sold using periodic FIFO, LIFO, and average-cost.*

(SO 2, 3), **AP**

**E6-7** Kuchin Company reports the following for the month of June.

| Date | Explanation | Units | Unit Cost | Total Cost |
|---|---|---|---|---|
| June 1 | Inventory | 120 | $5 | $ 600 |
| 12 | Purchase | 370 | 6 | 2,220 |
| 23 | Purchase | 500 | 7 | 3,500 |
| 30 | Inventory | 240 | | |

**Instructions**
(a) Compute the cost of the ending inventory and the cost of goods sold under (1) FIFO, (2) LIFO, and (3) average-cost.
(b) Which costing method gives the highest ending inventory? The highest cost of goods sold? Why?
(c) How do the average-cost values for ending inventory and cost of goods sold relate to ending inventory and cost of goods sold for FIFO and LIFO?
(d) Explain why the average cost is not $6.

*Evaluate impact of LIFO and FIFO on cash flows and earnings quality.*

(SO 3), **AP**

**E6-8** The following comparative information is available for Prasad Company for 2012.

| | LIFO | FIFO |
|---|---|---|
| Sales revenue | $86,000 | $86,000 |
| Cost of goods sold | 38,000 | 29,000 |
| Operating expenses (including depreciation) | 27,000 | 27,000 |
| Depreciation | 10,000 | 10,000 |
| Cash paid for inventory purchases | 32,000 | 32,000 |

**Instructions**
(a) Determine net income under each approach. Assume a 30% tax rate.
(b) Determine net cash provided by operating activities under each approach. Assume that all sales were on a cash basis and that income taxes and operating expenses, other than depreciation, were on a cash basis.
(c) Calculate the quality of earnings ratio under each approach and explain your findings.

*Determine LCM valuation.*

(SO 4), **AP**

**E6-9** Laib Camera Shop Inc. uses the lower-of-cost-or-market basis for its inventory. The following data are available at December 31.

| | Units | Cost/Unit | Market Value/Unit |
|---|---|---|---|
| Cameras | | | |
| Minolta | 5 | $170 | $158 |
| Canon | 7 | 145 | 152 |
| Light Meters | | | |
| Vivitar | 12 | 125 | 114 |
| Kodak | 10 | 120 | 135 |

**Instructions**
What amount should be reported on Laib Camera Shop's financial statements, assuming the lower-of-cost-or-market rule is applied?

*Compute inventory turnover ratio, days in inventory, and gross profit rate.*

(SO 5), **AP**

**E6-10** This information is available for PepsiCo, Inc. for 2007, 2008, and 2009.

| (in millions) | 2007 | 2008 | 2009 |
|---|---|---|---|
| Beginning inventory | $ 1,926 | $ 2,290 | $ 2,522 |
| Ending inventory | 2,290 | 2,522 | 2,618 |
| Cost of goods sold | 18,038 | 20,351 | 20,099 |
| Sales revenue | 39,474 | 43,251 | 43,232 |

*Instructions*

Calculate the inventory turnover ratio, days in inventory, and gross profit rate for PepsiCo., Inc. for 2007, 2008, and 2009. Comment on any trends.

**E6-11** Deere & Company is a global manufacturer and distributor of agricultural, construction, and forestry equipment. It reported the following information in its 2009 annual report.

*Determine the effect of the LIFO reserve on current ratio.*
*(SO 5, 6), AP*

| (in millions) | **2009** | **2008** |
|---|---|---|
| Inventories (LIFO) | $ 2,397 | 3,042 |
| Current assets | 30,857 | |
| Current liabilities | 12,753 | |
| LIFO reserve | 1,367 | |
| Cost of goods sold | 16,255 | |

*Instructions*

(a) Compute Deere's inventory turnover ratio and days in inventory for 2009.
(b) Compute Deere's current ratio using the 2009 data as presented, and then again after adjusting for the LIFO reserve.
(c) Comment on how ignoring the LIFO reserve might affect your evaluation of Deere's liquidity.

*\*E6-12* Inventory data for Kuchin Company are presented in E6-7.

*Calculate inventory and cost of goods sold using three cost flow methods in a perpetual inventory system.*
*(SO 7), AP*

*Instructions*

(a) Calculate the cost of the ending inventory and the cost of goods sold for each cost flow assumption, using a perpetual inventory system. Assume a sale of 410 units occurred on June 15 for a selling price of $8 and a sale of 340 units on June 27 for $9. (*Note:* For the moving-average method, round unit cost to three decimal places.)
(b) How do the results differ from E6-7?
(c) Why is the average unit cost not $6 [($5 + $6 + $7) ÷ 3 = $6]?

*\*E6-13* Information about Sunburst is presented in E6-4. Additional data regarding the company's sales of Xpert snowboards are provided below. Assume that Sunburst uses a perpetual inventory system.

*Apply cost flow methods to perpetual records.*
*(SO 7), AP*

| **Date** | | **Units** |
|---|---|---|
| Sept.  5 | Sale | 8 |
| Sept. 16 | Sale | 48 |
| Sept. 29 | Sale | 60 |
| | Totals | 116 |

*Instructions*

Compute ending inventory at September 30 using FIFO, LIFO, and moving-average. (*Note:* For moving-average, round unit cost to three decimal places.)

*\*E6-14* Brooks Hardware reported cost of goods sold as follows.

*Determine effects of inventory errors.*
*(SO 8), AN*

| | **2012** | **2011** |
|---|---|---|
| Beginning inventory | $ 30,000 | $ 20,000 |
| Cost of goods purchased | 175,000 | 164,000 |
| Cost of goods available for sale | 205,000 | 184,000 |
| Less: Ending inventory | 37,000 | 30,000 |
| Cost of goods sold | $168,000 | $154,000 |

Brooks made two errors:
1. 2011 ending inventory was overstated by $2,000.
2. 2012 ending inventory was understated by $5,000.

*Instructions*

Compute the correct cost of goods sold for each year.

*Prepare correct income statements.*
(SO 8), **AN**

**\*E6-15** Sprague Company reported these income statement data for a 2-year period.

| | 2012 | 2011 |
|---|---|---|
| Sales revenue | $250,000 | $210,000 |
| Beginning inventory | 40,000 | 32,000 |
| Cost of goods purchased | 202,000 | 173,000 |
| Cost of goods available for sale | 242,000 | 205,000 |
| Less: Ending inventory | 55,000 | 40,000 |
| Cost of goods sold | 187,000 | 165,000 |
| Gross profit | $ 63,000 | $ 45,000 |

Sprague Company uses a periodic inventory system. The inventories at January 1, 2011, and December 31, 2012, are correct. However, the ending inventory at December 31, 2011, is overstated by $8,000.

**Instructions**
(a) Prepare correct income statement data for the 2 years.
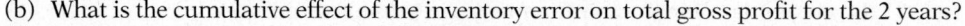
(b) What is the cumulative effect of the inventory error on total gross profit for the 2 years?
(c) Explain in a letter to the president of Sprague Company what has happened—that is, the nature of the error and its effect on the financial statements.

# Exercises: Set B and Challenge Exercises

Visit the book's companion website, at **www.wiley.com/college/kimmel**, and choose the Student Companion site to access Exercise Set B and Challenge Exercises.

# Problems: Set A

*Determine items and amounts to be recorded in inventory.*
(SO 1), **AN**

**P6-1A** Kirk Limited is trying to determine the value of its ending inventory as of February 28, 2012, the company's year-end. The accountant counted everything that was in the warehouse, as of February 28, which resulted in an ending inventory valuation of $48,000. However, she didn't know how to treat the following transactions so she didn't record them.
(a) On February 26, Kirk shipped to a customer goods costing $800. The goods were shipped FOB shipping point, and the receiving report indicates that the customer received the goods on March 2.
(b) On February 26, Seller Inc. shipped goods to Kirk FOB destination. The invoice price was $350 plus $25 for freight. The receiving report indicates that the goods were received by Kirk on March 2.
(c) Kirk had $500 of inventory at a customer's warehouse "on approval." The customer was going to let Kirk know whether it wanted the merchandise by the end of the week, March 4.
(d) Kirk also had $400 of inventory at a Balena craft shop, on consignment from Kirk.
(e) On February 26, Kirk ordered goods costing $750. The goods were shipped FOB shipping point on February 27. Kirk received the goods on March 1.
(f) On February 28, Kirk packaged goods and had them ready for shipping to a customer FOB destination. The invoice price was $350 plus $25 for freight; the cost of the items was $280. The receiving report indicates that the goods were received by the customer on March 2.
(g) Kirk had damaged goods set aside in the warehouse because they are no longer saleable. These goods originally cost $400 and, originally, Kirk expected to sell these items for $600.

## Instructions

For each of the above transactions, specify whether the item in question should be included in ending inventory, and if so, at what amount. For each item that is not included in ending inventory, indicate who owns it and what account, if any, it should have been recorded in.

**P6-2A**   Turner Distribution markets CDs of numerous performing artists. At the beginning of March, Turner had in beginning inventory 2,500 CDs with a unit cost of $7. During March, Turner made the following purchases of CDs.

| March 5 | 2,000 @ $8 | March 21 | 5,000 @ $10 |
|---------|------------|----------|-------------|
| March 13 | 3,500 @ $9 | March 26 | 2,000 @ $11 |

During March 12,000 units were sold. Turner uses a periodic inventory system.

*Determine cost of goods sold and ending inventory using FIFO, LIFO, and average-cost with analysis.*
(SO 2, 3), **AP**

## Instructions
(a) Determine the cost of goods available for sale.
(b) Determine (1) the ending inventory and (2) the cost of goods sold under each of the assumed cost flow methods (FIFO, LIFO, and average-cost). Prove the accuracy of the cost of goods sold under the FIFO and LIFO methods. (*Note:* For average-cost, round cost per unit to three decimal places.)
(c) Which cost flow method results in (1) the highest inventory amount for the balance sheet and (2) the highest cost of goods sold for the income statement?

Cost of goods sold:
| FIFO | $105,000 |
|------|----------|
| LIFO | $115,500 |
| Average | $109,601 |

**P6-3A**   Remsen Company Inc. had a beginning inventory of 100 units of Product MLN at a cost of $8 per unit. During the year, purchases were:

| Feb. 20 | 600 units at $ 9 | Aug. 12 | 400 units at $11 |
|---------|------------------|---------|------------------|
| May  5 | 500 units at $10 | Dec.  8 | 100 units at $12 |

Remsen Company uses a periodic inventory system. Sales totalled 1,500 units.

*Determine cost of goods sold and ending inventory using FIFO, LIFO, and average-cost in a periodic inventory system and assess financial statement effects.*
(SO 2, 3), **AP**

## Instructions
(a) Determine the cost of goods available for sale.
(b) Determine the ending inventory and the cost of goods sold under each of the assumed cost flow methods (FIFO, LIFO, and average-cost). Prove the accuracy of the cost of goods sold under the FIFO and LIFO methods. (Round average unit cost to three decimal places.)
(c) Which cost flow method results in the lowest inventory amount for the balance sheet? The lowest cost of goods sold for the income statement?

Cost of goods sold:
| FIFO | $14,500 |
|------|---------|
| LIFO | $15,100 |
| Average | $14,824 |

**P6-4A**   The management of Kuiper Inc. asks your help in determining the comparative effects of the FIFO and LIFO inventory cost flow methods. For 2012, the accounting records show these data.

*Compute ending inventory, prepare income statements, and answer questions using FIFO and LIFO.*
(SO 2, 3), **AN**

| Inventory, January 1 (10,000 units) | $ 35,000 |
|--------------------------------------|----------|
| Cost of 120,000 units purchased | 468,500 |
| Selling price of 98,000 units sold | 750,000 |
| Operating expenses | 124,000 |

Units purchased consisted of 35,000 units at $3.70 on May 10; 60,000 units at $3.90 on August 15; and 25,000 units at $4.20 on November 20. Income taxes are 28%.

## Instructions
(a) Prepare comparative condensed income statements for 2012 under FIFO and LIFO. (Show computations of ending inventory.)
(b) Answer the following questions for management in the form of a business letter.
   (1) Which inventory cost flow method produces the inventory amount that most closely approximates the amount that would have to be paid to replace the inventory? Why?
   (2) Which inventory cost flow method produces the net income amount that is a more likely indicator of next period's net income? Why?
   (3) Which inventory cost flow method is most likely to approximate the actual physical flow of the goods? Why?
   (4) How much more cash will be available under LIFO than under FIFO? Why?
   (5) How much of the gross profit under FIFO is illusionary in comparison with the gross profit under LIFO?

Gross profit:
| FIFO | $378,800 |
|------|----------|
| LIFO | $362,900 |

*Calculate ending inventory, cost of goods sold, gross profit, and gross profit rate under periodic method; compare results.*

*(SO 2, 3),* **AP**

**P6-5A** You have the following information for McBride Inc. for the month ended October 31, 2012. McBride uses a periodic method for inventory.

| Date | Description | Units | Unit Cost or Selling Price |
|------|-------------|-------|----------------------------|
| Oct. 1 | Beginning inventory | 60 | $24 |
| Oct. 9 | Purchase | 120 | 26 |
| Oct. 11 | Sale | 100 | 35 |
| Oct. 17 | Purchase | 100 | 27 |
| Oct. 22 | Sale | 60 | 40 |
| Oct. 25 | Purchase | 70 | 29 |
| Oct. 29 | Sale | 110 | 40 |

Gross profit:
| | |
|---|---|
| LIFO | $2,970 |
| FIFO | $3,310 |
| Average | $3,133 |

**Instructions**
(a) Calculate (i) ending inventory, (ii) cost of goods sold, (iii) gross profit, and (iv) gross profit rate under each of the following methods.
   (1) LIFO.
   (2) FIFO.
   (3) Average-cost. (Round cost per unit to three decimal places.)
(b) Compare results for the three cost flow assumptions.

*Compare specific identification, FIFO, and LIFO under periodic method; use cost flow assumption to influence earnings.*

*(SO 2, 3),* **AP**

**P6-6A** You have the following information for Prospector Gems. Prospector uses the periodic method of accounting for its inventory transactions. Prospector only carries one brand and size of diamonds—all are identical. Each batch of diamonds purchased is carefully coded and marked with its purchase cost.

March 1   Beginning inventory 150 diamonds at a cost of $310 per diamond.
March 3   Purchased 200 diamonds at a cost of $350 each.
March 5   Sold 180 diamonds for $600 each.
March 10  Purchased 330 diamonds at a cost of $375 each.
March 25  Sold 390 diamonds for $650 each.

Gross profit:
| | |
|---|---|
| Maximum | $162,500 |
| Minimum | $155,350 |

**Instructions**
(a) Assume that Prospector Gems uses the specific identification cost flow method.
   (1) Demonstrate how Prospector could maximize its gross profit for the month by specifically selecting which diamonds to sell on March 5 and March 25.
   (2) Demonstrate how Prospector could minimize its gross profit for the month by selecting which diamonds to sell on March 5 and March 25.
(b) Assume that Prospector uses the FIFO cost flow assumption. Calculate cost of goods sold. How much gross profit would Prospector report under this cost flow assumption?
(c) Assume that Prospector uses the LIFO cost flow assumption. Calculate cost of goods sold. How much gross profit would the company report under this cost flow assumption?
(d) Which cost flow method should Prospector Gems select? Explain.

*Compute inventory turnover ratio and days in inventory; compute current ratio based on LIFO and after adjusting for LIFO reserve.*

*(SO 5, 6),* **AP**

**P6-7A** This information (in millions) is available for the Automotive and Other Operations Divisions of General Motors Corporation for a recent year. General Motors uses the LIFO inventory method.

| | |
|---|---|
| Beginning inventory | $ 13,921 |
| Ending inventory | 14,939 |
| LIFO reserve | 1,423 |
| Current assets | 60,135 |
| Current liabilities | 70,308 |
| Cost of goods sold | 166,259 |
| Sales revenue | 178,199 |

**Instructions**
(a) Calculate the inventory turnover ratio and days in inventory.
(b) Calculate the current ratio based on inventory as reported using LIFO.
(c) Calculate the current ratio after adjusting for the LIFO reserve.
(d) Comment on any difference between parts (b) and (c).

\*P6-8A   Singer Inc. is a retailer operating in Edmonton, Alberta. Singer uses the perpetual inventory method. All sales returns from customers result in the goods being returned to inventory. (Assume that the inventory is not damaged.) Assume that there are no credit transactions; all amounts are settled in cash. You are provided with the following information for Singer Inc. for the month of January 2012.

*Calculate cost of goods sold, ending inventory, and gross profit for LIFO, FIFO, and moving-average under the perpetual system; compare results.*

(SO 3, 7), **AP**

| Date | Description | Quantity | Unit Cost or Selling Price |
|---|---|---|---|
| Dec. 31 | Ending inventory | 160 | $20 |
| Jan. 2 | Purchase | 100 | 22 |
| Jan. 6 | Sale | 180 | 40 |
| Jan. 9 | Sale return | 10 | 40 |
| Jan. 9 | Purchase | 75 | 24 |
| Jan. 10 | Purchase return | 15 | 24 |
| Jan. 10 | Sale | 50 | 45 |
| Jan. 23 | Purchase | 100 | 25 |
| Jan. 30 | Sale | 130 | 48 |

### Instructions

(a) For each of the following cost flow assumptions, calculate (i) cost of goods sold, (ii) ending inventory, and (iii) gross profit.
   (1) LIFO. (Assume sales returns had a cost of $20 and purchase returns had a cost of $24.)
   (2) FIFO. (Assume sales returns had a cost of $20 and purchase returns had a cost of $24.)
   (3) Moving-average. (Round cost per unit to three decimal places.)
(b) Compare results for the three cost flow assumptions.

Gross profit:

| | |
|---|---|
| LIFO | $7,350 |
| FIFO | $7,700 |
| Average | $7,597 |

\*P6-9A   Premier Center began operations on July 1. It uses a perpetual inventory system. During July, the company had the following purchases and sales.

*Determine ending inventory under a perpetual inventory system.*

(SO 3, 7), **AP**

| Date | Purchases Units | Unit Cost | Sales Units |
|---|---|---|---|
| July 1 | 7 | $62 | |
| July 6 | | | 5 |
| July 11 | 3 | $66 | |
| July 14 | | | 3 |
| July 21 | 4 | $71 | |
| July 27 | | | 3 |

### Instructions

(a) Determine the ending inventory under a perpetual inventory system using (1) FIFO, (2) moving-average (round unit cost to three decimal places), and (3) LIFO.
(b) Which costing method produces the highest ending inventory valuation?

| | |
|---|---|
| FIFO | $213 |
| Average | $207 |
| LIFO | $195 |

# Problems: Set B

**P6-1B**   Equitz Limited is trying to determine the value of its ending inventory as of February 28, 2012, the company's year-end. The following transactions occurred, and the accountant asked your help in determining whether they should be recorded or not.

(a) On February 26, Equitz shipped goods costing $800 to a customer and charged the customer $1,000. The goods were shipped with terms FOB destination and the receiving report indicates that the customer received the goods on March 2.

*Determine items and amounts to be recorded in inventory.*

(SO 1), **AN**

(b) On February 26, Seller Inc. shipped goods to Equitz under terms FOB shipping point. The invoice price was $300 plus $25 for freight. The receiving report indicates that the goods were received by Equitz on March 2.

(c) Equitz had $500 of inventory isolated in the warehouse. The inventory is designated for a customer who has requested that the goods be shipped on March 10.

(d) Also included in Equitz's warehouse is $400 of inventory that Meredith Producers shipped to Equitz on consignment.

(e) On February 26, Equitz issued a purchase order to acquire goods costing $750. The goods were shipped with terms FOB destination on February 27. Equitz received the goods on March 2.

(f) On February 26, Equitz shipped goods to a customer under terms FOB shipping point. The invoice price was $350 plus $25 for freight; the cost of the items was $260. The receiving report indicates that the goods were received by the customer on March 2.

### Instructions
For each of the above transactions, specify whether the item in question should be included in ending inventory, and if so, at what amount.

*Determine cost of goods sold and ending inventory using FIFO, LIFO, and average-cost with analysis.*
(SO 2, 3), **AP**

Cost of goods sold:
FIFO      $60,600
LIFO      $70,400
Average   $65,867

**P6-2B** Savage Distribution markets CDs of the performing artist Little Sister. At the beginning of October, Savage had in beginning inventory 1,200 Sister's CDs with a unit cost of $5. During October, Savage made the following purchases of Sister's CDs.

| Oct. 3 | 4,000 @ $6 | Oct. 19 | 2,500 @ $8 |
| Oct. 9 | 3,000 @ $7 | Oct. 25 | 2,000 @ $9 |

During October 9,400 units were sold. Savage uses a periodic inventory system.

### Instructions
(a) Determine the cost of goods available for sale.
(b) Determine (1) the ending inventory and (2) the cost of goods sold under each of the assumed cost flow methods (FIFO, LIFO, and average-cost). Prove the accuracy of the cost of goods sold under the FIFO and LIFO methods. (Round cost per unit to three decimal places.)
(c) Which cost flow method results in (1) the highest inventory amount for the balance sheet and (2) the highest cost of goods sold for the income statement?

*Determine cost of goods sold and ending inventory using FIFO, LIFO, and average-cost in a periodic inventory system and assess financial statement effects.*
(SO 2, 3), **AP**

Cost of goods sold:
FIFO      $19,350
LIFO      $21,260
Average   $20,314

**P6-3B** Trattner Company had a beginning inventory on January 1 of 100 units of Product SXL at a cost of $20 per unit. During the year, purchases were:

| Mar. 15 | 300 units at $23 | Sept. 4 | 290 units at $28 |
| July 20 | 250 units at $25 | Dec. 2 | 130 units at $30 |

Trattner Company sold 800 units, and it uses a periodic inventory system.

### Instructions
(a) Determine the cost of goods available for sale.
(b) Determine the ending inventory and the cost of goods sold under each of the assumed cost flow methods (FIFO, LIFO, and average-cost). Prove the accuracy of the cost of goods sold under each method. (Round cost per unit to three decimal places.)
(c) Which cost flow method results in the highest inventory amount for the balance sheet? The highest cost of goods sold for the income statement?

*Compute ending inventory, prepare income statements, and answer questions using FIFO and LIFO.*
(SO 2, 3), **AN**

**P6-4B** The management of Howland is reevaluating the appropriateness of using its present inventory cost flow method, which is average-cost. The company requests your help in determining the results of operations for 2012 if either the FIFO or the LIFO method had been used. For 2012, the accounting records show these data:

| Inventories | | Purchases and Sales | |
|---|---|---|---|
| Beginning (10,000 units) | $22,500 | Total net sales (220,000 units) | $862,000 |
| Ending (20,000 units) | | Total cost of goods purchased (230,000 units) | 567,500 |

Purchases were made quarterly as follows.

| Quarter | Units | Unit Cost | Total Cost |
|---|---|---|---|
| 1 | 60,000 | $2.30 | $138,000 |
| 2 | 50,000 | 2.40 | 120,000 |
| 3 | 50,000 | 2.55 | 127,500 |
| 4 | 70,000 | 2.60 | 182,000 |
| | 230,000 | | $567,500 |

Operating expenses were $147,000, and the company's income tax rate is 32%.

**Instructions**
(a) Prepare comparative condensed income statements for 2012 under FIFO and LIFO. (Show computations of ending inventory.)
(b) Answer the following questions for management in business-letter form.
   (1) Which cost flow method (FIFO or LIFO) produces the inventory amount that most closely approximates the amount that would have to be paid to replace the inventory? Why?
   (2) Which cost flow method (FIFO or LIFO) produces the net income amount that is a more likely indicator of next period's net income? Why?
   (3) Which cost flow method (FIFO or LIFO) is more likely to approximate the actual physical flow of goods? Why?
   (4) How much more cash will be available for management under LIFO than under FIFO? Why?
   (5) Will gross profit under the average-cost method be higher or lower than FIFO? Than LIFO? (*Note:* It is not necessary to quantify your answer.)

*Gross profit:*
FIFO    $324,000
LIFO    $317,500

**P6-5B** You have the following information for Wirth Inc. for the month ended June 30, 2012. Wirth uses the periodic method for inventory.

| Date | Description | Quantity | Unit Cost or Selling Price |
|---|---|---|---|
| June 1 | Beginning inventory | 25 | $60 |
| June 4 | Purchase | 85 | 63 |
| June 10 | Sale | 60 | 90 |
| June 11 | Sale return | 5 | 90 |
| June 18 | Purchase | 35 | 66 |
| June 18 | Purchase return | 15 | 66 |
| June 25 | Sale | 55 | 95 |
| June 28 | Purchase | 20 | 70 |

*Calculate ending inventory, cost of goods sold, gross profit, and gross profit rate under periodic method; compare results.*
(SO 2, 3), **AP**

**Instructions**
(a) Calculate (i) ending inventory, (ii) cost of goods sold, (iii) gross profit, and (iv) gross profit rate under each of the following methods.
   (1) LIFO.
   (2) FIFO.
   (3) Average-cost. (Round cost per unit to three decimal places.)
(b) Compare results for the three cost flow assumptions.

*Gross profit:*
LIFO    $3,045
FIFO    $3,320
Average    $3,153

**P6-6B** You have the following information for Gas Saver Plus. Gas Saver Plus uses the periodic method of accounting for its inventory transactions.

March 1   Beginning inventory 1,500 litres at a cost of 40¢ per litre.
March 3   Purchased 2,200 litres at a cost of 45¢ per litre.
March 5   Sold 1,800 litres for 60¢ per litre.
March 10   Purchased 3,500 litres at a cost of 49¢ per litre.
March 20   Purchased 2,000 litres at a cost of 52¢ per litre.
March 30   Sold 5,000 litres for 70¢ per litre.

*Compare specific identification, FIFO, and LIFO under periodic method; use cost flow assumption to justify price increase.*
(SO 2, 3), **AP**

**Instructions**
(a) Prepare partial income statements through gross profit, and calculate the value of ending inventory that would be reported on the balance sheet, under each of the cost flow assumptions on the next page.

*Gross profit:*
Specific identification    $1,371
FIFO    $1,471
LIFO    $1,240

(1) Specific identification method assuming:
    (i) the March 5 sale consisted of 800 litres from the March 1 beginning inventory and 1,000 litres from the March 3 purchase; and
    (ii) the March 30 sale consisted of the following number of units sold from each purchase: 400 litres from March 1; 500 litres from March 3; 2,600 litres from March 10; 1,500 litres from March 20.
(2) FIFO.
(3) LIFO.
(b) How can companies use a cost flow method to justify price increases? Which cost flow method would best support an argument to increase prices?

*Compute inventory turnover ratio and days in inventory; compute current ratio based on LIFO and after adjusting for LIFO reserve.*
(SO 5, 6), **AP**

**P6-7B** The following information is available for the automotive division of Ford Motor Company for 2009. The company uses the LIFO inventory method.

| (in millions) | **2009** |
| --- | --- |
| Beginning inventory | $ 6,988 |
| Ending inventory | 5,450 |
| LIFO reserve | 798 |
| Current assets | 40,560 |
| Current liabilities | 37,037 |
| Cost of goods sold | 100,016 |
| Sales revenue | 105,893 |

*Instructions*
(a) Calculate the inventory turnover ratio and days in inventory.
(b) Calculate the current ratio based on LIFO inventory.
(c) After adjusting for the LIFO reserve, calculate the current ratio.
(d) Comment on any difference between parts (b) and (c).

*Calculate cost of goods sold, ending inventory, and gross profit under LIFO, FIFO, and moving-average under the perpetual system; compare results.*
(SO 3, 7), **AP**

Gross profit:
| LIFO | $1,345 |
| FIFO | $1,395 |
| Average | $1,374 |

*P6-8B** Morse Inc. is a retail company that uses the perpetual inventory method. All sales returns from customers result in the goods being returned to inventory. (Assume that the inventory is not damaged.) Assume that there are no credit transactions; all amounts are settled in cash. You have the following information for Morse Inc. for the month of January 2012.

| Date | Description | Quantity | Unit Cost or Selling Price |
| --- | --- | --- | --- |
| January 1 | Beginning inventory | 40 | $13 |
| January 5 | Purchase | 90 | 16 |
| January 8 | Sale | 75 | 25 |
| January 10 | Sale return | 10 | 25 |
| January 15 | Purchase | 30 | 18 |
| January 16 | Purchase return | 5 | 18 |
| January 20 | Sale | 80 | 25 |
| January 25 | Purchase | 20 | 21 |

*Instructions*
(a) For each of the following cost flow assumptions, calculate (i) cost of goods sold, (ii) ending inventory, and (iii) gross profit.
    (1) LIFO. (Assume sales returns had a cost of $16 and purchase returns had a cost of $18.)
    (2) FIFO. (Assume sales returns had a cost of $16 and purchase returns had a cost of $18.)
    (3) Moving-average. (Round cost per unit to three decimal places.)
(b) Compare results for the three cost flow assumptions.

**\*P6-9B**  Dollar Saver Center began operations on July 1. It uses a perpetual inventory system. During July, the company had the following purchases and sales.

*Determine ending inventory under a perpetual inventory system.*
(SO 3, 7), **AP**

|  | Purchases | | |
|---|---|---|---|
| **Date** | **Units** | **Unit Cost** | **Sales Units** |
| July  1 | 7 | $47 | |
| July  6 | | | 3 |
| July 11 | 5 | $50 | |
| July 14 | | | 4 |
| July 21 | 3 | $54 | |
| July 27 | | | 2 |

**Instructions**
(a) Determine the ending inventory under a perpetual inventory system using (1) FIFO, (2) moving-average, and (3) LIFO. (*Note:* For moving-average, round cost per unit to three decimal places.)
(b) Which costing method produces the highest ending inventory valuation?

| FIFO | $312 |
|---|---|
| Average | $304 |
| LIFO | $292 |

# Problems: Set C

Visit the book's companion website, at **www.wiley.com/college/kimmel**, and choose the Student Companion site to access Problem Set C.

# Comprehensive Problem

**CP6**  On December 1, 2012, Ruggiero Company had the account balances shown below.

| | **Debits** | | **Credits** |
|---|---|---|---|
| Cash | $ 4,800 | Accumulated Depreciation—Equipment | $ 1,500 |
| Accounts Receivable | 3,900 | Accounts Payable | 3,000 |
| Inventory | 1,800* | Common Stock | 10,000 |
| Equipment | 21,000 | Retained Earnings | 17,000 |
| | $31,500 | | $31,500 |

*(3,000 × $0.60)

The following transactions occurred during December.

Dec.  3  Purchased 4,000 units of inventory on account at a cost of $0.72 per unit.
  5  Sold 4,400 units of inventory on account for $0.90 per unit. (It sold 3,000 of the $0.60 units and 1,400 of the $0.72.)
  7  Granted the December 5 customer $180 credit for 200 units of inventory returned costing $150. These units were returned to inventory.
  17  Purchased 2,200 units of inventory for cash at $0.80 each.
  22  Sold 2,000 units of inventory on account for $0.95 per unit. (It sold 2,000 of the $0.72 units.)

**Adjustment data:**
1. Accrued salaries payable $400.
2. Depreciation $200 per month.
3. Income tax expense was $215, to be paid next year.

**Instructions**
(a) Journalize the December transactions and adjusting entries, assuming Ruggiero uses the perpetual inventory method.

(b) Enter the December 1 balances in the ledger T accounts and post the December transactions. In addition to the accounts mentioned above, use the following additional accounts: Cost of Goods Sold, Depreciation Expense, Salaries and Wages Expense, Salaries and Wages Payable, Sales Revenue, Sales Returns and Allowances, Income Tax Expense, and Income Taxes Payable.

(c) Prepare an adjusted trial balance as of December 31, 2012.

(d) Prepare an income statement for December 2012 and a classified balance sheet at December 31, 2012.

(e) Compute ending inventory and cost of goods sold under FIFO, assuming Ruggiero Company uses the periodic inventory system.

(f) Compute ending inventory and cost of goods sold under LIFO, assuming Ruggiero Company uses the periodic inventory system.

# Continuing Cookie Chronicle

(*Note:* This is a continuation of the Cookie Chronicle from Chapters 1 through 5.)

**CCC6** Natalie is busy establishing both divisions of her business (cookie classes and mixer sales) and completing her business degree. Her goals for the next 11 months are to sell one mixer per month and to give two to three classes per week. Natalie has decided to use a periodic inventory system and now must choose a cost flow assumption for her mixer inventory.

---

Go to the book's companion website, at **www.wiley.com/college/kimmel**, to see the completion of this problem.

---

# broadening your perspective

## Financial Reporting and Analysis

### FINANCIAL REPORTING PROBLEM: *Tootsie Roll, Industries Inc.*

**BYP6-1**   The notes that accompany a company's financial statements provide informative details that would clutter the amounts and descriptions presented in the statements. Refer to the financial statements of Tootsie Roll and the accompanying Notes to Consolidated Financial Statements in Appendix A.

*Instructions*

Answer the following questions. (Give the amounts in thousands of dollars, as shown in Tootsie Roll's annual report.)

(a) What did Tootsie Roll report for the amount of inventories in its Consolidated Balance Sheet at December 31, 2009? At December 31, 2008?

(b) Compute the dollar amount of change and the percentage change in inventories between 2008 and 2009. Compute inventory as a percentage of current assets for 2009.

(c) What are the (product) cost of goods sold reported by Tootsie Roll for 2009, 2008, and 2007? Compute the ratio of (product) cost of goods sold to net (product) sales in 2009.

### COMPARATIVE ANALYSIS PROBLEM: *Tootsie Roll vs. Hershey*

**BYP6-2**   The financial statements of The Hershey Company appear in Appendix B, following the financial statements for Tootsie Roll in Appendix A.

*Instructions*

(a) Based on the information in the financial statements, compute these 2009 values for each company. (Do not adjust for the LIFO reserve.)
   (1) Inventory turnover ratio. (Use product cost of goods sold and total inventory.)
   (2) Days in inventory.

(b) What conclusions concerning the management of the inventory can you draw from these data?

## RESEARCH CASE

**BYP6-3** The January 27, 2010, issue of the *Wall Street Journal* contains an article by Timothy Aeppel entitled "'Bullwhip' Hits Firms as Growth Snaps Back."

*Instructions*
Read the article and answer the following questions.
(a) Explain why Caterpillar would more than double its purchases of steel this year even if its own sales don't rise relative to the previous year.
(b) Why did Caterpillar meet with its key suppliers during the previous year?
(c) What are some of the barriers and concerns that suppliers faced at the time of the article?
(d) How rapidly did Caterpillar grow in recent years and what did it learn from that experience, that is, what changes did it implement with regard to suppliers?

## INTERPRETING FINANCIAL STATEMENTS

**BYP6-4** The following information is from the 2009 annual report of American Greetings Corporation (all dollars in thousands).

|  | Feb. 28, 2009 | Feb. 29, 2008 |
|---|---|---|
| Inventories |  |  |
| Finished goods | $232,893 | $244,379 |
| Work in process | 7,068 | 10,516 |
| Raw materials and supplies | 49,937 | 43,861 |
|  | 289,898 | 298,756 |
| Less: LIFO reserve | 86,025 | 82,085 |
| Total (as reported) | $203,873 | $216,671 |
|  |  |  |
| Cost of goods sold | $809,956 | $780,771 |
| Current assets (as reported) | $561,395 | $669,340 |
| Current liabilities | $343,405 | $432,321 |

The following information comes from the notes to the company's financial statements.

Finished products, work in process, and raw material inventories are carried at the lower-of-cost-or-market. The last-in, first-out (LIFO) cost method is used for approximately 75% of the domestic inventories in 2009 and approximately 70% in 2008. The foreign subsidiaries principally use the first-in, first-out method. Display material and factory supplies are carried at average-cost.

*Instructions*
(a) Define each of the following: finished goods, work in process, and raw materials.
(b) What might be a possible explanation for why the company uses FIFO for its nondomestic inventories?
(c) Calculate the company's inventory turnover ratio and days in inventory for 2008 and 2009. (2007 inventory was $182,618.) Discuss the implications of any change in the ratios.
(d) What percentage of total inventory does the 2009 LIFO reserve represent? If the company used FIFO in 2009, what would be the value of its inventory? Do you consider this difference a "material" amount from the perspective of an analyst? Which value accurately represents the value of the company's inventory?
(e) Calculate the company's 2009 current ratio with the numbers as reported, then recalculate after adjusting for the LIFO reserve.

## FINANCIAL ANALYSIS ON THE WEB

**BYP6-5** *Purpose:* Use SEC filings to learn about a company's inventory accounting practices.

*Address:* **http://biz.yahoo.com/p/_capgds-bldmch.html**,
or go to **www.wiley.com/college/kimmel**

*Steps*

1. Go to this site and click on the name of an equipment manufacturer other than those discussed in the chapter.
2. Click on **SEC filings**.
3. Under "Recent filings" choose **Form 10K** (annual report) and click on **Full Filing at Edgar Online**.
4. Choose option "3," **Online HTML Version**.

If the 10K is not listed among the recent filings then click on **View All Filings on EDGAR Online**.

*Instructions*

Review the 10K to answer the following questions.

(a) What is the name of the company?
(b) How has its inventory changed from the previous year?
(c) What is the amount of raw materials, work in process, and finished goods inventory?
(d) What inventory method does the company use?
(e) Calculate the inventory turnover ratio and days in inventory for the current year.
(f) If the company uses LIFO, what was the amount of its LIFO reserve?

# Critical Thinking

## DECISION MAKING ACROSS THE ORGANIZATION

**BYP6-6** Crescent Electronics has enjoyed tremendous sales growth during the last 10 years. However, even though sales have steadily increased, the company's CEO, Anne Healy, is concerned about certain aspects of its performance. She has called a meeting with the corporate controller and the vice presidents of finance, operations, sales, and marketing to discuss the company's performance. Anne begins the meeting by making the following observations:

> We have been forced to take significant write-downs on inventory during each of the last three years because of obsolescence. In addition, inventory storage costs have soared. We rent four additional warehouses to store our increasingly diverse inventory. Five years ago inventory represented only 20% of the value of our total assets. It now exceeds 35%. Yet, even with all of this inventory, "stockouts" (measured by complaints by customers that the desired product is not available) have increased by 40% during the last three years. And worse yet, it seems that we constantly must discount merchandise that we have too much of.

Anne asks the group to review the following data and make suggestions as to how the company's performance might be improved.

| (in millions) | 2012 | 2011 | 2010 | 2009 |
|---|---|---|---|---|
| Inventory | | | | |
| Raw materials | $242 | $198 | $155 | $128 |
| Work in process | 116 | 77 | 49 | 33 |
| Finished goods | 567 | 482 | 398 | 257 |
| Total inventory | $925 | $757 | $602 | $418 |
| | | | | |
| Current assets | $1,800 | $1,423 | $1,183 | $841 |
| Total assets | $2,643 | $2,523 | $2,408 | $2,090 |
| Current liabilities | $600 | $590 | $525 | $420 |
| Sales revenue | $9,428 | $8,674 | $7,536 | $6,840 |
| Cost of goods sold | $6,328 | $5,474 | $4,445 | $3,557 |
| Net income | $754 | $987 | $979 | $958 |

*Instructions*

Using the information provided, answer the following questions.

(a) Compute the current ratio, gross profit rate, profit margin ratio, inventory turnover ratio, and days in inventory for 2010, 2011, and 2012.
(b) Discuss the trends and potential causes of the changes in the ratios in part (a).
(c) Discuss potential remedies to any problems discussed in part (b).
(d) What concerns might be raised by some members of management with regard to your suggestions in part (c)?

## COMMUNICATION ACTIVITIES

**BYP6-7** In a discussion of dramatic increases in coffee bean prices, a *Wall Street Journal* article noted the following fact about Starbucks.

> Before this year's bean-price hike, Starbucks added several defenses that analysts say could help it maintain earnings and revenue. The company last year began accounting for its coffee-bean purchases by taking the average price of all beans in inventory.
>
> *Source:* Aaron Lucchetti, "Crowded Coffee Market May Keep a Lid on Starbucks After Price Rise Hurt Stock," *Wall Street Journal* (June 4, 1997), p. C1.

Prior to this change the company was using FIFO.

***Instructions***

Your client, the CEO of Supreme Coffee, Inc., read this article and sent you an e-mail message requesting that you explain why Starbucks might have taken this action. Your response should explain what impact this change in accounting method has on earnings, why the company might want to do this, and any possible disadvantages of such a change.

***BYP6-8** You are the controller of Emjay Inc. M. J. Danner, the president, recently mentioned to you that she found an error in the 2011 financial statements which she believes has corrected itself. She determined, in discussions with the purchasing department, that 2011 ending inventory was overstated by $1 million. M. J. says that the 2012 ending inventory is correct, and she assumes that 2012 income is correct. M. J. says to you, "What happened has happened—there's no point in worrying about it anymore."

***Instructions***

You conclude that M. J. is incorrect. Write a brief, tactful memo to her, clarifying the situation.

## ETHICS CASE

**BYP6-9** Yelich Wholesale Corp. uses the LIFO cost flow method. In the current year, profit at Yelich is running unusually high. The corporate tax rate is also high this year, but it is scheduled to decline significantly next year. In an effort to lower the current year's net income and to take advantage of the changing income tax rate, the president of Yelich Wholesale instructs the plant accountant to recommend to the purchasing department a large purchase of inventory for delivery 3 days before the end of the year. The price of the inventory to be purchased has doubled during the year, and the purchase will represent a major portion of the ending inventory value.

***Instructions***

(a) What is the effect of this transaction on this year's and next year's income statement and income tax expense? Why?

(b) If Yelich Wholesale had been using the FIFO method of inventory costing, would the president give the same directive?

(c) Should the plant accountant order the inventory purchase to lower income? What are the ethical implications of this order?

## "ALL ABOUT YOU" ACTIVITY

**BYP6-10** Some of the largest business frauds ever perpetrated have involved the misstatement of inventory. Two classics were at Leslie Fay Cos, and McKesson Corporation.

***Instructions***

There is considerable information regarding inventory frauds available on the Internet. Search for information about one of the two cases mentioned above, or inventory fraud at any other company, and prepare a short explanation of the nature of the inventory fraud.

## FASB CODIFICATION ACTIVITY

**BYP6-11** If your school has a subscription to the FASB Codification, go to **http://aaahq.org/ ascLogin.cfm** to log in and prepare responses to the following.

(a) The primary basis for accounting for inventories is cost. How is cost defined in the Codification?

(b) What does the Codification state regarding the use of consistency in the selection or employment of a basis for inventory?

(c) What does the Codification indicate is a justification for the use of the lower-of-cost-or-market for inventory valuation?

## Answers to Insight and Accounting Across the Organization Questions

**p. 283 A Big Hiccup Q:** What steps might the companies take to avoid such a serious disruption in the future? **A:** The manufacturer of the piston rings should spread its manufacturing facilities across a few locations that are far enough apart that they would not all be at risk at once. In addition, the automakers might consider becoming less dependent on a single supplier.

**p. 284 Falsifying Inventory to Boost Income Q:** What effect does an overstatement of inventory have on a company's financial statements? **A:** The balance sheet looks stronger because inventory and retained earnings are overstated. The income statement looks better because cost of goods sold is understated and income is overstated.

**p. 294 Is LIFO Fair? Q:** What are the arguments for and against the use of LIFO? **A:** Proponents of LIFO argue that it is conceptually superior because it matches the most recent cost with the most recent selling price. Critics contend that it artificially understates the company's net income and consequently reduces tax payments. Also, because most foreign companies are not allowed to use LIFO, its use by U.S. companies reduces the ability of investors to compare U.S. companies with foreign companies.

**p. 298 Improving Inventory Control with RFID Q:** Why is inventory control important to managers such as those at Wal-Mart and Best Buy? **A:** In the very competitive environment of discount retailing, where Wal-Mart and Best Buy are the major players, small differences in price matter to the customer. Wal-Mart sells a high volume of inventory at a low gross profit rate. When operating in a high-volume, low-margin environment, small cost savings can mean the difference between being profitable or going out of business.

## Answers to Self-Test Questions

**1.** d  **2.** a  **3.** b ($180,000 + $35,000)  **4.** c ((5,000 × $13) + (4,000 × $12))  **5.** d ((8,000 × $11) + (1,000 × $12))  **6.** d ((5,000 × $8) + (15,000 × $10) + (20,000 × $12)) ÷ 40,000 = $10.75; $10.75 × 7,000  **7.** c  **8.** d  **9.** a  **10.** d  **11.** b ($285,000 ÷ (($80,000 + $110,000) ÷ 2) = 3; 365 ÷ 3)  **12.** a  *13.** d  *14.** b  *15.** b

# IFRS A Look at IFRS

The major IFRS requirements related to accounting and reporting for inventories are the same as GAAP. The major differences are that IFRS prohibits the use of the LIFO cost flow assumption and determines market in the lower-of-cost-or-market inventory valuation differently.

## KEY POINTS

- The requirements for accounting for and reporting inventories are more principles-based under IFRS. That is, GAAP provides more detailed guidelines in inventory accounting.

- The definitions for inventory are essentially similar under IFRS and GAAP. Both define inventory as assets held-for-sale in the ordinary course of business, in the process of production for sale (work in process), or to be consumed in the production of goods or services (e.g., raw materials).

- Who owns the goods—goods in transit or consigned goods—as well as the costs to include in inventory, are accounted for the same under IFRS and GAAP.

- Both GAAP and IFRS permit specific identification where appropriate. IFRS actually requires that the specific identification method be used where the inventory items are not interchangeable (i.e., can be specifically identified). If the inventory items are not specifically identifiable, a cost flow assumption is used. GAAP does not specify situations in which specific identification must be used.

- A major difference between IFRS and GAAP relates to the LIFO cost flow assumption. GAAP permits the use of LIFO for inventory valuation. IFRS prohibits its use. FIFO and average-cost are the only two acceptable cost flow assumptions permitted under IFRS.

- IFRS requires companies to use the same cost flow assumption for all goods of a similar nature. GAAP has no specific requirement in this area.

- In the lower-of-cost-or-market test for inventory valuation, IFRS defines market as net realizable value. Net realizable value is the estimated selling price in the ordinary course of business, less the estimated costs of completion and estimated selling expenses. In other words, net realizable value is the best estimate of the net amounts that inventories are expected to realize. GAAP, on the other hand, defines market as essentially replacement cost.

- Under GAAP, if inventory is written down under the lower-of-cost-or-market valuation, the new value becomes its cost basis. As a result, the inventory may not be written back up to its original cost in a subsequent period. Under IFRS, the write-down may be reversed in a subsequent period up to the amount of the previous write-down. Both the write-down and any subsequent reversal should be reported on the income statement as an expense. An item-by-item approach is generally followed under IFRS.

- An example of the use of lower-of-cost-or-net realizable value under IFRS follows.

---

Mendel Company has the following four items in its ending inventory as of December 31, 2012. The company uses the lower-of-cost-or-net realizable value approach for inventory valuation following IFRS.

| Item No. | Cost | Net Realizable Value |
|---|---|---|
| 1320 | $3,600 | $3,400 |
| 1333 | 4,000 | 4,100 |
| 1428 | 2,800 | 2,100 |
| 1510 | 5,000 | 4,700 |

The computation of the ending inventory value to be reported in the financial statements at December 31, 2012, is as follows.

| Item No. | Cost | Net Realizable Value | Lower-of-Cost-or-NRV |
|---|---|---|---|
| 1320 | $ 3,600 | $ 3,400 | $ 3,400 |
| 1333 | 4,000 | 4,100 | 4,000 |
| 1428 | 2,800 | 2,100 | 2,100 |
| 1510 | 5,000 | 4,700 | 4,700 |
| Total | $15,400 | $14,300 | $14,200 |

---

- Unlike property, plant, and equipment, IFRS does not permit the option of valuing inventories at fair value. As indicated above, IFRS requires inventory to be written down, but inventory cannot be written up above its original cost.

- Similar to GAAP, certain agricultural products and mineral products can be reported at net realizable value using IFRS.

## LOOKING TO THE FUTURE

One convergence issue that will be difficult to resolve relates to the use of the LIFO cost flow assumption. As indicated, IFRS specifically prohibits its use. Conversely, the LIFO cost flow assumption is widely used in the United States because of its favorable tax advantages. In addition, many argue that LIFO from a financial reporting point of view provides a better matching of current costs against revenue and, therefore, enables companies to compute a more realistic income.

With a new conceptual framework being developed, it is highly probable that the use of the concept of conservatism will be eliminated. Similarly, the concept of "prudence" in the IASB literature will also be eliminated. This may ultimately have implications for the application of the lower-of-cost-or-net realizable value.

## IFRS Self-Test Questions

1. Which of the following should *not* be included in the inventory of a company using IFRS?
   (a) Goods held on consignment from another company.
   (b) Goods shipped on consignment to another company.
   (c) Goods in transit from another company shipped FOB shipping point.
   (d) None of the above.

2. Which method of inventory costing is prohibited under IFRS?
   (a) Specific identification.
   (c) FIFO.
   (b) LIFO.
   (d) Average-cost.

3. Yang Company purchased 2,000 phones and has 400 phones in its ending inventory at a cost of $90 each and a current replacement cost of $80 each. The net realizable value of each phone in the ending inventory is $70. The ending inventory under lower-of-cost-or-net realizable value is:
   (a) $36,000.
   (c) $28,000.
   (b) $32,000.
   (d) None of the above.

4. Specific identification:
   (a) must be used under IFRS if the inventory items are not interchangeable.
   (b) cannot be used under IFRS.
   (c) cannot be used under GAAP.
   (d) must be used under IFRS if it would result in the most conservative net income.

5. IFRS requires the following:
   (a) Ending inventory is written up and down to net realizable value each reporting period.
   (b) Ending inventory is written down to net realizable value but cannot be written up.
   (c) Ending inventory is written down to net realizable value and may be written up in future periods to its net realizable value but not above its original cost.
   (d) Ending inventory is written down to net realizable value and may be written up in future periods to its net realizable value.

## IFRS Concepts and Application

**IFRS6–1** Briefly describe some of the similarities and differences between GAAP and IFRS with respect to the accounting for inventories.

**IFRS6–2** LaTour Inc. is based in France and prepares its financial statements in accordance with IFRS. In 2012, it reported cost of goods sold of €578 million and average inventory of €154 million. Briefly discuss how analysis of LaTour's inventory turnover ratio (and comparisons to a company using GAAP) might be affected by differences in inventory accounting between IFRS and GAAP.

**IFRS6–3** Franklin Company has the following four items in its ending inventory as of December 31, 2012. The company uses the lower-of-cost-or-net realizable value approach for inventory valuation following IFRS.

| Item No. | Cost | Net Realizable Value |
|---|---|---|
| AB | $1,700 | $1,400 |
| TRX | 2,200 | 2,300 |
| NWA | 7,800 | 7,100 |
| SGH | 3,000 | 3,700 |

Compute the lower-of-cost-or-net realizable value.

## INTERNATIONAL FINANCIAL REPORTING PROBLEM: *Zetar plc*

**IFRS6–4** The financial statements of Zetar plc are presented in Appendix C. The company's complete annual report, including the notes to its financial statements, is available at **www.zetarplc.com**. Using the notes to the company's financial statements, answer the following questions.

*Instructions*
   (a) What cost flow assumption does the company use to value inventory?
   (b) What was the amount of expense that the company reported for inventory write-downs during 2009?
   (c) What amount of raw materials, work in process, and finished goods inventory did the company report at April 30, 2009?

## Answers to IFRS Self-Test Questions

**1.** a  **2.** b  **3.** c  **4.** a  **5.** c

Remember to go back to the navigator box on the chapter opening page and check off your completed work.

# chapter 7

# FRAUD, INTERNAL CONTROL, AND CASH

## the navigator

## study objectives

**After studying this chapter, you should be able to:**

1 Define fraud and internal control.

2 Identify the principles of internal control activities.

3 Explain the applications of internal control principles to cash receipts.

4 Explain the applications of internal control principles to cash disbursements.

5 Prepare a bank reconciliation.

6 Explain the reporting of cash.

7 Discuss the basic principles of cash management.

8 Identify the primary elements of a cash budget.

the navigator

If you're ever looking for a cappuccino in Moose Jaw, Saskatchewan, stop by Stephanie's Gourmet Coffee and More, located on Main Street. Staff there serve, on average, 650 cups of coffee a day, including both regular and specialty coffees, not to mention soups, Italian sandwiches, and a wide assortment of gourmet cheesecakes.

"We've got high school students who come here, and students from the community college," says owner/manager Stephanie Mintenko, who has run the place since opening it in 1995. "We have customers who are retired, and others who are working people and have only 30 minutes for lunch. We have to be pretty quick."

That means that the cashiers have to be efficient. Like most businesses where purchases are low-cost and high-volume, cash control has to be simple.

"We have an electronic cash register, but it's not the fancy new kind where you just punch in the item," explains Ms. Mintenko. "You have to punch in the prices." The machine does keep track of sales in several categories, however. Cashiers punch a button to indicate whether each item is a beverage, a meal, or

# MINDING THE MONEY IN MOOSE JAW

a charge for the cafe's Internet connections. An internal tape in the machine keeps a record of all transactions; the customer receives a receipt only upon request.

There is only one cash register. "Up to three of us might operate it on any given shift, including myself," says Ms. Mintenko.

She and her staff do two "cashouts" each day—one with the shift change at 5:00 p.m. and one when the shop closes at 10:00 p.m. At each cashout, they count the cash in the register drawer. That amount, minus the cash change carried forward (the float), should match the shift total on the register tape. If there's a discrepancy, they do another count. Then, if necessary, "we go through the whole tape to find the mistake," she explains. "It usually turns out to be someone who punched in $18 instead of $1.80, or something like that."

Ms. Mintenko sends all the cash tapes and float totals to a bookkeeper, who double-checks everything and provides regular reports. "We try to keep the accounting simple, so we can concentrate on making great coffee and food."

the navigator

**INSIDE CHAPTER 7 . . .**

As the story about recording cash sales at Stephanie's Gourmet Coffee and More indicates, control of cash is important to ensure that fraud does not occur. Companies also need controls to safeguard other types of assets. For example, Stephanie's undoubtedly has controls to prevent the theft of food and supplies, and controls to prevent the theft of tableware and dishes from its kitchen.

In this chapter, we explain the essential features of an internal control system and how it prevents fraud. We also describe how those controls apply to a specific asset–cash. The applications include some controls with which you may be already familiar, such as the use of a bank.

The content and organization of Chapter 7 are as follows.

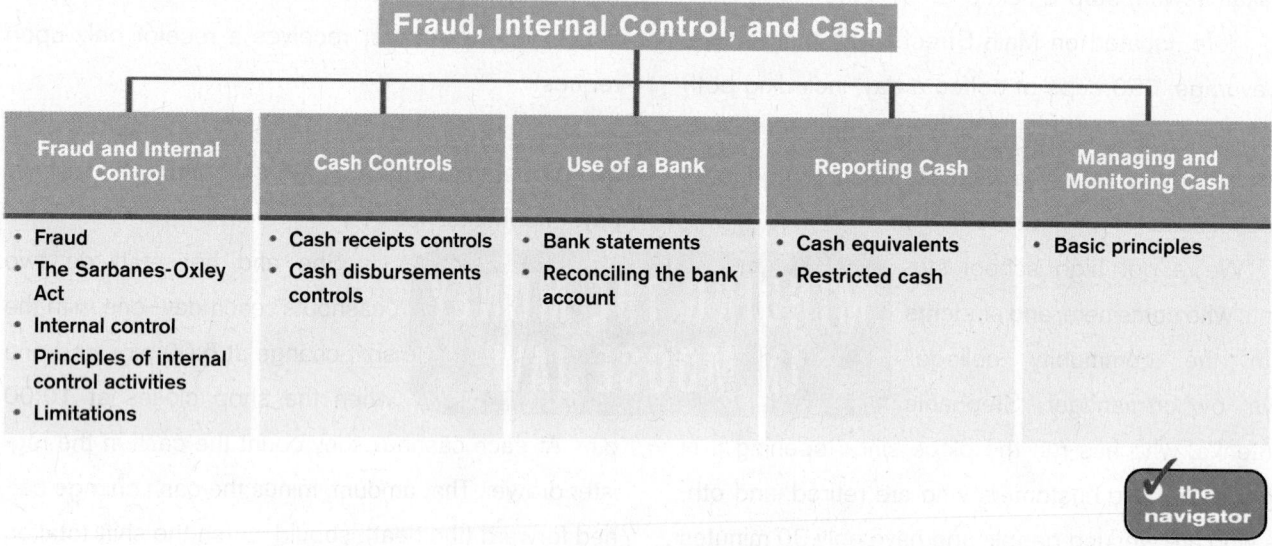

the navigator

# Fraud and Internal Control

The Feature Story describes many of the internal control procedures used by Stephanie's Gourmet Coffee and More. These procedures are necessary to discourage employees from fraudulent activities.

### FRAUD

A **fraud** is a dishonest act by an employee that results in personal benefit to the employee at a cost to the employer. Examples of fraud reported in the financial press include:

- A bookkeeper in a small company diverted $750,000 of bill payments to a personal bank account over a three-year period.
- A shipping clerk with 28 years of service shipped $125,000 of merchandise to himself.
- A computer operator embezzled $21 million from Wells Fargo Bank over a two-year period.
- A church treasurer "borrowed" $150,000 of church funds to finance a friend's business dealings.

Why does fraud occur? The three main factors that contribute to fraudulent activity are depicted by the **fraud triangle** in Illustration 7-1.

The most important element of the fraud triangle is **opportunity**. For an employee to commit fraud, the workplace environment must provide opportunities that an employee can exploit. Opportunities occur when the workplace lacks sufficient controls to deter and detect fraud. For example, inadequate monitoring of employee actions can create opportunities for theft and can embolden employees because they believe they will not be caught.

A second factor that contributes to fraud is **financial pressure**. Employees sometimes commit fraud because of personal financial problems caused by too much debt. Or they might commit fraud because they want to lead a lifestyle that they cannot afford on their current salary.

The third factor that contributes to fraud is **rationalization**. In order to justify their fraud, employees rationalize their dishonest actions. For example, employees sometimes justify fraud because they believe they are underpaid while the employer is making lots of money. These employees feel justified in stealing because they believe they deserve to be paid more.

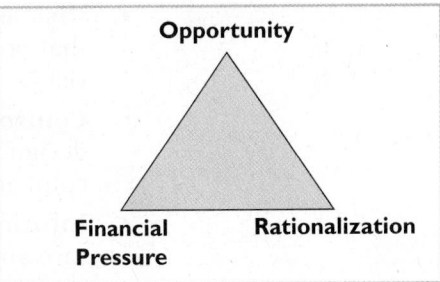

**Illustration 7-1**   Fraud triangle

## THE SARBANES-OXLEY ACT

What can be done to prevent or to detect fraud? After numerous corporate scandals came to light in the early 2000s, Congress addressed this issue by passing the **Sarbanes-Oxley Act of 2002 (SOX)**. Under SOX, all publicly traded U.S. corporations are required to maintain an adequate system of internal control. Corporate executives and boards of directors must ensure that these controls are reliable and effective. In addition, independent outside auditors must attest to the adequacy of the internal control system. Companies that fail to comply are subject to fines, and company officers can be imprisoned. SOX also created the Public Company Accounting Oversight Board (PCAOB) to establish auditing standards and regulate auditor activity.

One poll found that 60% of investors believe that SOX helps safeguard their stock investments. Many say they would be unlikely to invest in a company that fails to follow SOX requirements. Although some corporate executives have criticized the time and expense involved in following the SOX requirements, SOX appears to be working well. For example, the chief accounting officer of Eli Lily noted that SOX triggered a comprehensive review of how the company documents controls. This review uncovered redundancies and pointed out controls that needed to be added. In short, it added up to time and money well spent. And the finance chief at General Electric noted, "We have seen value in SOX. It helps build investors' trust and gives them more confidence."[1]

## INTERNAL CONTROL

**Internal control** consists of all the related methods and measures adopted within an organization to safeguard its assets, enhance the reliability of its accounting records, increase efficiency of operations, and ensure compliance with laws and regulations. Internal control systems have five primary components as listed below.[2]

- **A control environment.** It is the responsibility of top management to make it clear that the organization values integrity and that unethical activity will not be tolerated. This component is often referred to as the "tone at the top."

---

[1]"Corporate Regulation Must Be Working—There's a Backlash," *Wall Street Journal* (June 16, 2004), p. C1; and Judith Burns, "Is Sarbanes-Oxley Working?" *Wall Street Journal* (June 21, 2004), pp. R8–R9.
[2]The Committee of Sponsoring Organizations of the Treadway Commission, "Internal Control—Integrated Framework," *www.coso.org/publications/executive_summary_integrated_framework.htm* (accessed March 2008).

- **Risk assessment.** Companies must identify and analyze the various factors that create risk for the business and must determine how to manage these risks.

- **Control activities.** To reduce the occurrence of fraud, management must design policies and procedures to address the specific risks faced by the company.

- **Information and communication.** The internal control system must capture and communicate all pertinent information both down and up the organization, as well as communicate information to appropriate external parties.

- **Monitoring.** Internal control systems must be monitored periodically for their adequacy. Significant deficiencies need to be reported to top management and/or the board of directors.

## PRINCIPLES OF INTERNAL CONTROL ACTIVITIES

**study objective 2**

Identify the principles of internal control activities.

Each of the five components of an internal control system is important. Here, we will focus on one component, the control activities. The reason? These activities are the backbone of the company's efforts to address the risks it faces, such as fraud. The specific control activities used by a company will vary, depending on management's assessment of the risks faced. This assessment is heavily influenced by the size and nature of the company.

The six principles of control activities are as follows.

- Establishment of responsibility
- Segregation of duties
- Documentation procedures
- Physical controls
- Independent internal verification
- Human resource controls

We explain these principles in the following sections. You should recognize that they apply to most companies and are relevant to both manual and computerized accounting systems.

### Establishment of Responsibility

An essential principle of internal control is to assign responsibility to specific employees. **Control is most effective when only one person is responsible for a given task.**

To illustrate, assume that the cash on hand at the end of the day in a Safeway supermarket is $10 short of the cash rung up on the cash register. If only one person has operated the register, the shift manager can quickly determine responsibility for the shortage. If two or more individuals have worked the register, it may be impossible to determine who is responsible for the error. In the Feature Story, the principle of establishing responsibility does not appear to be strictly applied by Stephanie's, since three people operate the cash register on any given shift.

Establishing responsibility often requires limiting access only to authorized personnel, and then identifying those personnel. For example, the automated systems used by many companies have mechanisms such as identifying passcodes that keep track of who made a journal entry, who rang up a sale, or who entered an inventory storeroom at a particular time. Use of identifying passcodes enables the company to establish responsibility by identifying the particular employee who carried out the activity.

It's your shift now. I'm turning in my cash drawer and heading home.

**Transfer of cash drawers**

## ANATOMY OF A FRAUD

Maureen Frugali was a training supervisor for claims processing at Colossal Healthcare. As a standard part of the claims processing training program, Maureen created fictitious claims for use by trainees. These fictitious claims were then sent to the accounts payable department. After the training claims had been processed, she was to notify Accounts Payable of all fictitious claims, so that they would not be paid. However, she did not inform Accounts Payable about every fictitious claim. She created some fictitious claims for entities that she controlled (that is, she would receive the payment), and she let Accounts Payable pay her.

**Total take: $11 million**

### THE MISSING CONTROL

*Establishment of responsibility.* The healthcare company did not adequately restrict the responsibility for authoring and approving claims transactions. The training supervisor should not have been authorized to create claims in the company's "live" system.

*Source:* Adapted from Wells, *Fraud Casebook* (2007), pp. 61–70.

### Segregation of Duties

Segregation of duties is indispensable in an internal control system. There are two common applications of this principle:

1. Different individuals should be responsible for related activities.
2. The responsibility for record-keeping for an asset should be separate from the physical custody of that asset.

The rationale for segregation of duties is this: **The work of one employee should, without a duplication of effort, provide a reliable basis for evaluating the work of another employee.** For example, the personnel that design and program computerized systems should not be assigned duties related to day-to-day use of the system. Otherwise, they could design the system to benefit them personally and conceal the fraud through day-to-day use.

**SEGREGATION OF RELATED ACTIVITIES.  Making one individual responsible for related activities increases the potential for errors and irregularities.**

For example, companies should assign related *purchasing activities* to different individuals. Related purchasing activities include ordering merchandise, order approval, receiving goods, authorizing payment, and paying for goods or services. Various frauds are possible when one person handles related purchasing activities. For example:

- If a purchasing agent is allowed to order goods without supervisory approval, the likelihood of the agent receiving kickbacks from suppliers increases.
- If an employee who orders goods also handles receipt of the goods and invoice, as well as payment authorization, he or she might authorize payment for a fictitious invoice.

These abuses are less likely to occur when companies divide the purchasing tasks.

Similarly, companies should assign related *sales activities* to different individuals. Related selling activities include making a sale, shipping (or delivering) the goods to the customer, billing the customer, and receiving payment. Various frauds are possible when one person handles related sales transactions. For example:

- If a salesperson can make a sale without obtaining supervisory approval, he or she might make sales at unauthorized prices to increase sales commissions.

- A shipping clerk who also has access to accounting records could ship goods to himself.
- A billing clerk who handles billing and cash receipts could understate the amount billed for sales made to friends and relatives.

These abuses are less likely to occur when companies divide the sales tasks: the salespeople make the sale; the shipping department ships the goods on the basis of the sales order; and the billing department prepares the sales invoice after comparing the sales order with the report of goods shipped.

## ANATOMY OF A FRAUD

Lawrence Fairbanks, the assistant vice-chancellor of communications at Aesop University, was allowed to make purchases of under $2,500 for his department without external approval. Unfortunately, he also sometimes bought items for himself, such as expensive antiques and other collectibles. How did he do it? He replaced the vendor invoices he received with fake vendor invoices that he created. The fake invoices had descriptions that were more consistent with communications department purchases. He submitted these fake invoices to the accounting department as the basis for their journal entries and to the accounts payable department as the basis for payment.

Total take: $475,000

### THE MISSING CONTROL

*Segregation of duties.* The university had not properly segregated related purchasing activities. Lawrence was ordering items, receiving the items, and receiving the invoice. By receiving the invoice, he had control over the documents that were used to account for the purchase and thus was able to substitute a fake invoice.

*Source:* Adapted from Wells, *Fraud Casebook* (2007), pp. 3–15.

**SEGREGATION OF RECORD-KEEPING FROM PHYSICAL CUSTODY.** The accountant should have neither physical custody of the asset nor access to it. Likewise, the custodian of the asset should not maintain or have access to the accounting records. **The custodian of the asset is not likely to convert the asset to personal use when one employee maintains the record of the asset, and a different employee has physical custody of the asset.** The separation of accounting responsibility from the custody of assets is especially important for cash and inventories because these assets are very vulnerable to fraud.

**Accounting employee A**
Maintains cash balances per books

**Segregation of duties**
(Accountability for assets)

**Assistant cashier B**
Maintains custody of cash on hand

## ANATOMY OF A FRAUD

Angela Bauer was an accounts payable clerk for Aggasiz Construction Company. She prepared and issued checks to vendors and reconciled bank statements. She perpetrated a fraud in this way: She wrote checks for costs that the company had not actually incurred (e.g., fake taxes). A supervisor then approved and signed the checks. Before issuing the check, though, Angela would "white-out" the payee line on the check and change it to personal accounts that she controlled. She was able to conceal the theft because she also reconciled the bank account. That is, nobody else ever saw that the checks had been altered.

Total take: $570,000

**THE MISSING CONTROL**

*Segregation of duties.* Aggasiz Construction Company did not properly segregate record-keeping from physical custody. Angela had physical custody of the blank checks, which essentially was control of the cash. She also had record-keeping responsibility because she prepared the bank reconciliation.

*Source:* Adapted from Wells, *Fraud Casebook* (2007), pp. 100–107.

## Documentation Procedures

Documents provide evidence that transactions and events have occurred. At Stephanie's Gourmet Coffee and More, the cash register tape is the restaurant's documentation for the sale and the amount of cash received. Similarly, a shipping document indicates that the goods have been shipped, and a sales invoice indicates that the company has billed the customer for the goods. By requiring signatures (or initials) on the documents, the company can identify the individual(s) responsible for the transaction or event. Companies should document transactions when the transaction occurs.

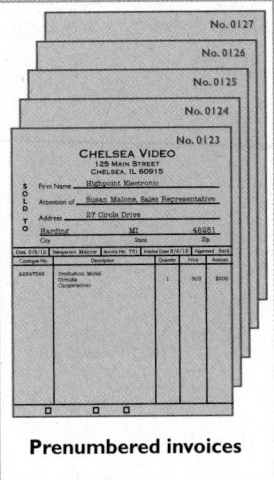

**Prenumbered invoices**

Companies should establish procedures for documents. First, whenever possible, companies should use **prenumbered documents, and all documents should be accounted for**. Prenumbering helps to prevent a transaction from being recorded more than once, or conversely, from not being recorded at all. Second, the control system should require that employees **promptly forward source documents for accounting entries to the accounting department. This control measure helps to ensure timely recording of the transaction** and contributes directly to the accuracy and reliability of the accounting records.

## ANATOMY OF A FRAUD

To support their reimbursement requests for travel costs incurred, employees at Mod Fashions Corporation's design center were required to submit receipts. The receipts could include the detailed bill provided for a meal, or the credit card receipt provided when the credit card payment is made, or a copy of the employee's monthly credit card bill that listed the item. A number of the designers who frequently traveled together came up with a fraud scheme: They submitted claims for the same expenses. For example, if they had a meal together that cost $200, one person submitted the detailed meal bill, another submitted the credit card receipt, and a third submitted a monthly credit card bill showing the meal as a line item. Thus, all three received a $200 reimbursement.

**Total take: $75,000**

**THE MISSING CONTROL**

*Documentation procedures.* Mod Fashions should require the original, detailed receipt. It should not accept photocopies, and it should not accept credit card statements. In addition, documentation procedures could be further improved by requiring the use of a corporate credit card (rather than personal credit card) for all business expenses.

*Source:* Adapted from Wells, *Fraud Casebook* (2007), pp. 79–90.

## Physical Controls

Use of physical controls is essential. *Physical controls* relate to the safeguarding of assets and enhance the accuracy and reliability of the accounting records. Illustration 7-2 (page 342) shows examples of these controls.

**Physical Controls**

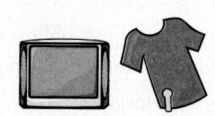

Safes, vaults, and safety deposit boxes for cash and business papers

Locked warehouses and storage cabinets for inventories and records

Computer facilities with pass key access or fingerprint or eyeball scans

Alarms to prevent break-ins

Television monitors and garment sensors to deter theft

Time clocks for recording time worked

**Illustration 7-2** Physical controls

---

## ANATOMY OF A FRAUD

At Centerstone Health, a large insurance company, the mailroom each day received insurance applications from prospective customers. Mailroom employees scanned the applications into electronic documents before the applications were processed. Once the applications are scanned they can be accessed online by authorized employees.

Insurance agents at Centerstone Health earn commissions based upon successful applications. The sales agent's name is listed on the application. However, roughly 15% of the applications are from customers who did not work with a sales agent. Two friends—Alex, an employee in record keeping, and Parviz, a sales agent—thought up a way to perpetrate a fraud. Alex identified scanned applications that did not list a sales agent. After business hours, he entered the mailroom and found the hardcopy applications that did not show a sales agent. He wrote in Parviz's name as the sales agent and then rescanned the application for processing. Parviz received the commission, which the friends then split.

**Total take: $240,000**

### THE MISSING CONTROL

*Physical controls.* Centerstone Health lacked two basic physical controls that could have prevented this fraud. First, the mailroom should have been locked during nonbusiness hours, and access during business hours should have been tightly controlled. Second, the scanned applications supposedly could be accessed only by authorized employees using their password. However, the password for each employee was the same as the employee's user ID. Since employee user ID numbers were available to all other employees, all employees knew all other employees' passwords. Thus, Alex could enter the system using another employee's password and access the scanned applications.

*Source:* Adapted from Wells, *Fraud Casebook* (2007), pp. 316–326.

---

### Independent Internal Verification

Most internal control systems provide for **independent internal verification**. This principle involves the review of data prepared by employees. To obtain maximum benefit from independent internal verification:

1. Companies should verify records periodically or on a surprise basis.

2. An employee who is independent of the personnel responsible for the information should make the verification.

3. Discrepancies and exceptions should be reported to a management level that can take appropriate corrective action.

Independent internal verification is especially useful in comparing recorded transactions with existing assets. The reconciliation of the cash register tape with the cash in the register at Stephanie's Gourmet Coffee and More is an example of this internal control principle. Another common example is the reconciliation of a company's cash balance per books with the cash balance per bank and the verification of the perpetual inventory records through a count of physical inventory. Illustration 7-3 shows the relationship between this principle and the segregation of duties principle.

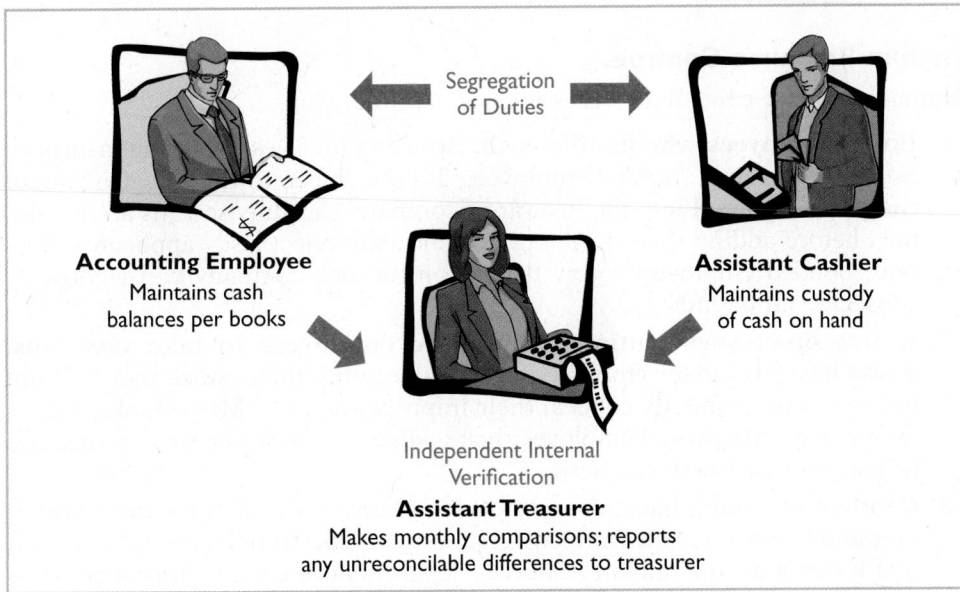

**Illustration 7-3**
Comparison of segregation of duties principle with independent internal verification principle

Large companies often assign independent internal verification to internal auditors. **Internal auditors** are company employees who continuously evaluate the effectiveness of the company's internal control systems. They review the activities of departments and individuals to determine whether prescribed internal controls are being followed. They also recommend improvements when needed. In fact, most fraud is discovered by the company through internal mechanisms such as existing internal controls and internal audits. For example, the fraud at World-Com, involving billions of dollars, was uncovered by an internal auditor.

## ANATOMY OF A FRAUD

Bobbi Jean Donnelly, the office manager for Mod Fashions Corporation's design center, was responsible for preparing the design center budget and reviewing expense reports submitted by design center employees. Her desire to upgrade her wardrobe got the better of her, and she enacted a fraud that involved filing expense-reimbursement requests for her own personal clothing purchases. She was able to conceal the fraud because she was responsible for reviewing all expense reports, including her own. In addition, she sometimes was given ultimate responsibility for signing off on the expense reports when her boss was "too busy." Also, because she controlled the budget, when she submitted her expenses, she coded them to budget items that she knew were running under budget, so that they would not catch anyone's attention.

Total take: $275,000

---

**THE MISSING CONTROL**

*Independent internal verification.* Bobbi Jean's boss should have verified her expense reports. When asked what he thought her expenses for a year were, the boss said about $10,000. At $115,000 per year, her actual expenses were more than ten times what would have been expected. However, because he was "too busy" to verify her expense reports or to review the budget, he never noticed.

*Source:* Adapted from Wells, *Fraud Casebook* (2007), pp. 79–90.

## Human Resource Controls

Human resource control activities include the following.

1. **Bond employees who handle cash. Bonding** involves obtaining insurance protection against theft by employees. It contributes to the safeguarding of cash in two ways: First, the insurance company carefully screens all individuals before adding them to the policy and may reject risky applicants. Second, bonded employees know that the insurance company will vigorously prosecute all offenders.

2. **Rotate employees' duties and require employees to take vacations.** These measures deter employees from attempting thefts since they will not be able to permanently conceal their improper actions. Many banks, for example, have discovered employee thefts when the employee was on vacation or assigned to a new position.

3. **Conduct thorough background checks.** Many believe that the most important and inexpensive measure any business can take to reduce employee theft and fraud is for the human resources department to conduct thorough background checks. Two tips: (1) Check to see whether job applicants actually graduated from the schools they list. (2) Never use the telephone numbers for previous employers given on the reference sheet; always look them up yourself.

### ANATOMY OF A FRAUD

Ellen Lowry was the desk manager and Josephine Rodriquez was the head of housekeeping at the Excelsior Inn, a luxury hotel. The two best friends were so dedicated to their jobs that they never took vacations, and they frequently filled in for other employees. In fact, Ms. Rodriquez, whose job as head of housekeeping did not include cleaning rooms, often cleaned rooms herself, "just to help the staff keep up." These two "dedicated" employees, working as a team, found a way to earn a little more cash. Ellen, the desk manager, provided significant discounts to guests who paid with cash. She kept the cash and did not register the guest in the hotel's computerized system. Instead, she took the room out of circulation "due to routine maintenance." Because the room did not show up as being used, it did not receive a normal housekeeping assignment. Instead, Josephine, the head of housekeeping, cleaned the rooms during the guests' stay.

Total take: $95,000

**THE MISSING CONTROL**

*Human resource controls.* Ellen, the desk manager, had been fired by a previous employer after being accused of fraud. If the Excelsior Inn had conducted a thorough background check, it would not have hired her. The hotel fraud was detected when Ellen missed work for a few days due to illness. A system of mandatory vacations and rotating days off would have increased the chances of detecting the fraud before it became so large.

*Source:* Adapted from Wells, *Fraud Casebook* (2007), pp. 145–155.

## Accounting Across the Organization
### SOX Boosts the Role of Human Resources

Under SOX, a company needs to keep track of employees' degrees and certifications to ensure that employees continue to meet the specified requirements of a job. Also, to ensure proper employee supervision and proper separation of duties, companies must develop and monitor an organizational chart. When one corporation went through this exercise it found that out of 17,000 employees, there were 400 people who did not report to anyone, and they had 35 people who reported to each other. In addition, SOX also mandates that, if an employee complains of an unfair firing and mentions financial issues at the company, HR must refer the case to the company audit committee and possibly to its legal counsel.

 Why would unsupervised employees or employees who report to each other represent potential internal control threats? (See page 392.)

## LIMITATIONS OF INTERNAL CONTROL

Companies generally design their systems of internal control to provide **reasonable assurance** of proper safeguarding of assets and reliability of the accounting records. The concept of reasonable assurance rests on the premise that the costs of establishing control procedures should not exceed their expected benefit.

To illustrate, consider shoplifting losses in retail stores. Stores could eliminate such losses by having a security guard stop and search customers as they leave the store. But store managers have concluded that the negative effects of such a procedure cannot be justified. Instead, stores have attempted to control shoplifting losses by less costly procedures: They post signs saying, "We reserve the right to inspect all packages" and "All shoplifters will be prosecuted." They use hidden TV cameras and store detectives to monitor customer activity, and they install sensor equipment at exits.

The **human element** is an important factor in every system of internal control. A good system can become ineffective as a result of employee fatigue, carelessness, or indifference. For example, a receiving clerk may not bother to count goods received and may just "fudge" the counts. Occasionally, two or more individuals may work together to get around prescribed controls. Such **collusion** can significantly reduce the effectiveness of a system, eliminating the protection offered by segregation of duties. No system of internal control is perfect.

The size of the business also may impose limitations on internal control. A small company, for example, may find it difficult to segregate duties or to provide for independent internal verification.

**Helpful Hint** Controls may vary with the risk level of the activity. For example, management may consider cash to be high risk and maintaining inventories in the stockroom as lower risk. Thus, management would have stricter controls for cash.

## Ethics Insight
### Big Theft at Small Companies

A study by the Association of Certified Fraud Examiners indicates that businesses with fewer than 100 employees are most at risk for employee theft. In fact, 38% of frauds occurred at companies with fewer than 100 employees. The median loss at small companies was $200,000, which was higher than the median fraud at companies with more than 10,000 employees ($147,000). A $200,000 loss can threaten the very existence of a small company.

*Source: 2008 Report to the Nation on Occupational Fraud and Abuse,* Association of Certified Fraud Examiners, *www.acfe.com/documents/2008-rttn.pdf,* p. 26.

 Why are small companies more susceptible to employee theft? (See page 392.)

# DECISION TOOLKIT

| DECISION CHECKPOINTS | INFO NEEDED FOR DECISION | TOOL TO USE FOR DECISION | HOW TO EVALUATE RESULTS |
|---|---|---|---|
| Are the company's financial statements supported by adequate internal controls? | Auditor's report, management discussion and analysis, articles in financial press | The principles of internal control activities are (1) establishment of responsibility, (2) segregation of duties, (3) documentation procedures, (4) physical controls, (5) independent internal verification, and (6) human resource controls. | If any indication is given that these or other controls are lacking, use the financial statements with caution. |

## before you go on...

**CONTROL ACTIVITIES**

### Action Plan

- Familiarize yourself with each of the control activities listed on page 338.
- Understand the nature of the frauds that each control activity is intended to address.

✔ the navigator

**Do it!** Identify which control activity is violated in each of the following situations, and explain how the situation creates an opportunity for a fraud.

1. The person with primary responsibility for reconciling the bank account is also the company's accountant and makes all bank deposits.
2. Wellstone Company's treasurer received an award for distinguished service because he had not taken a vacation in 30 years.
3. In order to save money on order slips, and to reduce time spent keeping track of order slips, a local bar/restaurant does not buy prenumbered order slips.

### Solution

1. Violates the control activity of segregation of duties. Record-keeping should be separate from physical custody. As a consequence, the employee could embezzle cash and make journal entries to hide the theft.
2. Violates the control activity of human resource controls. Key employees, such as a treasurer, should be required to take vacations. The treasurer, who manages the company's cash, might embezzle cash and use his position to conceal the theft.
3. Violates the control activity of documentation procedures. If pre-numbered documents are not used, then it is virtually impossible to account for the documents. As a consequence, an employee could write up a dinner sale, receive the cash from the customer, and then throw away the order slip and keep the cash.

Related exercise material: **BE7-1, BE7-2, BE7-3, Do it! 7-1, E7-1,** and **E7-2.**

## Cash Controls

Cash is the one asset that is readily convertible into any other type of asset. It also is easily concealed and transported, and is highly desired. Because of these characteristics, **cash is the asset most susceptible to fraudulent activities**. In addition, because of the large volume of cash transactions, numerous errors may occur in executing and recording them. To safeguard cash and to ensure the accuracy of the accounting records for cash, effective internal control over cash is critical.

**study objective 3**

Explain the applications of internal control principles to cash receipts.

### CASH RECEIPTS CONTROLS

Illustration 7-4 shows how the internal control principles explained earlier apply to cash receipts transactions. As you might expect, companies vary considerably in how they apply these principles. To illustrate internal control over

**Cash Receipts Controls**

**Establishment of Responsibility**

Only designated personnel are authorized to handle cash receipts (cashiers)

**Segregation of Duties**

Different individuals receive cash, record cash receipts, and hold the cash

**Documentation Procedures**

Use remittance advice (mail receipts), cash register tapes, and deposit slips

**Physical Controls**

Store cash in safes and bank vaults; limit access to storage areas; use cash registers

**Independent Internal Verification**

Supervisors count cash receipts daily; treasurer compares total receipts to bank deposits daily

**Human Resource Controls**

Bond personnel who handle cash; require employees to take vacations; conduct background checks

**Illustration 7-4**
Application of internal control principles to cash receipts

cash receipts, we will examine control activities for a retail store with both over-the-counter and mail receipts.

### Over-the-Counter Receipts

In retail businesses, control of over-the-counter receipts centers on cash registers that are visible to customers. A cash sale is rung-up on a cash register with the amount clearly visible to the customer. This activity prevents the cashier from ringing up a lower amount and pocketing the difference. The customer receives an itemized cash register receipt slip and is expected to count the change received. The cash register's tape is locked in the register until a supervisor removes it. This tape accumulates the daily transactions and totals.

At the end of the clerk's shift, the clerk counts the cash and sends the cash and the count to the cashier. The cashier counts the cash, prepares a deposit slip, and deposits the cash at the bank. The cashier also sends a duplicate of the deposit slip to the accounting department to indicate cash received. The supervisor removes the cash register tape and sends it to the accounting department as the basis for a journal entry to record the cash received. The tape is compared to the deposit slip for any discrepancies. Illustration 7-5 (page 348) summarizes this process.

This system for handling cash receipts uses an important internal control principle—segregation of record-keeping from physical custody. The supervisor has access to the cash register tape, but **not** to the cash. The clerk and the cashier have access to the cash, but **not** to the register tape. In addition, the cash register tape provides documentation and enables independent internal verification with the deposit slip. Use of these three principles of internal control (segregation of record-keeping from physical custody, documentation, and independent internal verification) provides an effective system of internal control. Any attempt at fraudulent activity should be detected unless there is collusion among the employees.

**Illustration 7-5**   Control of over-the-counter receipts

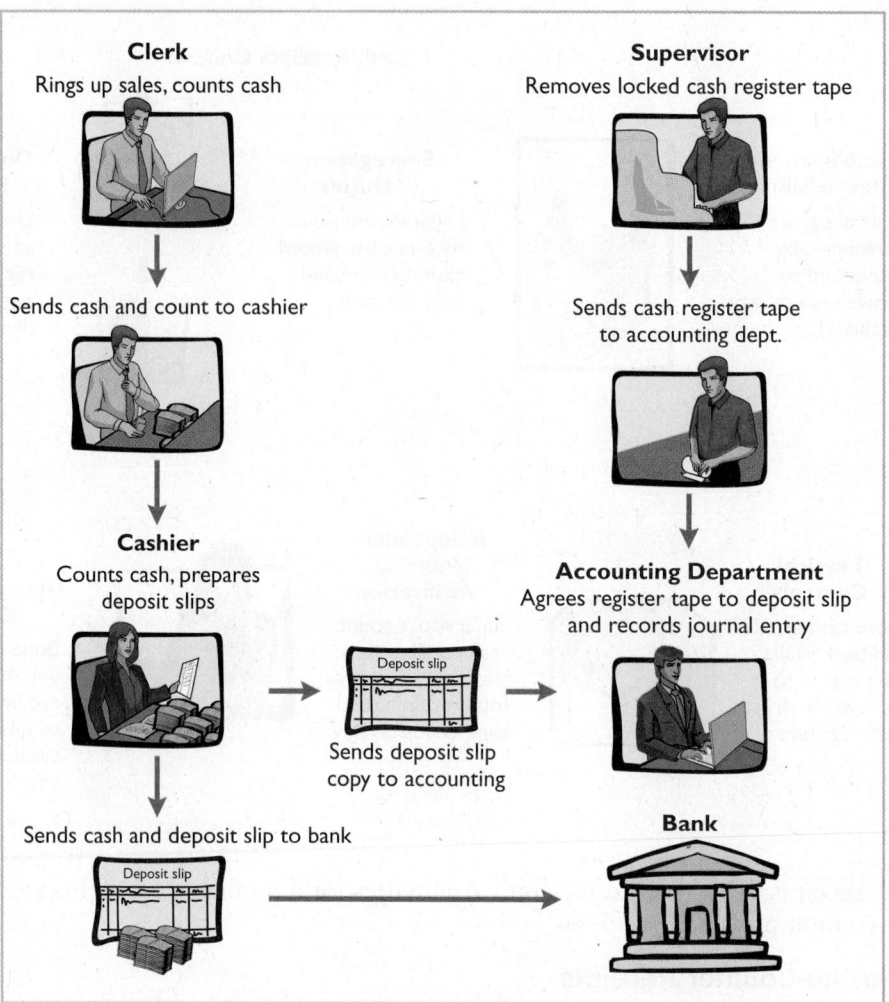

**Clerk**
Rings up sales, counts cash

Sends cash and count to cashier

**Cashier**
Counts cash, prepares deposit slips

Sends deposit slip copy to accounting

Sends cash and deposit slip to bank

Deposit slip

**Supervisor**
Removes locked cash register tape

Sends cash register tape to accounting dept.

**Accounting Department**
Agrees register tape to deposit slip and records journal entry

**Bank**

**Helpful Hint** Flowcharts such as this one enhance the understanding of the flow of documents, the processing steps, and the internal control procedures.

In some instances, the amount deposited at the bank will not agree with the cash recorded in the accounting records based on the cash register tape. These differences often result because the clerk hands incorrect change back to the retail customer. In this case, the difference between the actual cash and the amount reported on the cash register tape is reported in a Cash Over and Short account. For example, suppose that the cash register tape indicated sales of $6,956.20 but the amount of cash was only $6,946.10. A cash shortfall of $10.10 exists. To account for this cash shortfall and related cash, the company makes the following entry.

| A | = | L | + | SE |
|---|---|---|---|---|
| +6,946.10 | | | | |
| | | | | −10.10 |
| | | | | +6,956.20 |

**Cash Flows**
+6,946.10

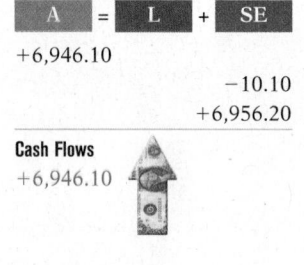

| | | |
|---|---|---|
| Cash | 6,946.10 | |
| Cash Over and Short | 10.10 | |
|     Sales Revenue | | 6,956.20 |
|       (To record cash shortfall) | | |

Cash Over and Short is an income statement item. It is reported as miscellaneous expense when there is a cash shortfall, and as miscellaneous revenue when there is an overage. Clearly, the amount should be small. Any material amounts in this account should be investigated.

### Mail Receipts

All mail receipts should be opened in the presence of at least two mail clerks. These receipts are generally in the form of checks. A mail clerk should endorse each check "For Deposit Only." This restrictive endorsement reduces the likelihood that someone could divert the check to personal use. Banks will not give an individual cash when presented with a check that has this type of endorsement.

The mail-receipt clerks prepare, in triplicate, a list of the checks received each day. This list shows the name of the check issuer, the purpose of the payment, and the amount of the check. Each mail clerk signs the list to establish responsibility for the data. The original copy of the list, along with the checks, is then sent to the cashier's department. A copy of the list is sent to the accounting department for recording in the accounting records. The clerks also keep a copy.

This process provides excellent internal control for the company. By employing two clerks, the chance of fraud is reduced; each clerk knows he or she is being observed by the other clerk(s). To engage in fraud, they would have to collude. The customers who submit payments also provide control, because they will contact the company with a complaint if they are not properly credited for payment. Because the cashier has access to cash but not the records, and the accounting department has access to records but not cash, neither can engage in undetected fraud.

*before you go on...*

## **Do it!**

L. R. Cortez is concerned about the control over cash receipts in his fast-food restaurant, Big Cheese. The restaurant has two cash registers. At no time do more than two employees take customer orders and ring up sales. Work shifts for employees range from 4 to 8 hours. Cortez asks your help in installing a good system of internal control over cash receipts.

### Solution

Cortez should assign a cash register to each employee at the start of each work shift, with register totals set at zero. Each employee should be instructed to use only the assigned register and to ring up all sales. Each customer should be given a receipt. At the end of the shift, the employee should do a cash count. A separate employee should compare the cash count with the register tape, to be sure they agree. In addition, Cortez should install an automated system that would enable the company to compare orders rung up on the register to orders processed by the kitchen.

Related exercise material: **BE7-4, BE7-5, Do it! 7-2,** and **E7-3.**

**CONTROL OVER CASH RECEIPTS**

**Action Plan**

- Differentiate among the internal control principles of (1) establishment of responsibility, (2) physical controls, and (3) independent internal verification.

- Design an effective system of internal control over cash receipts.

## CASH DISBURSEMENTS CONTROLS

Companies disburse cash for a variety of reasons, such as to pay expenses and liabilities or to purchase assets. **Generally, internal control over cash disbursements is more effective when companies pay by check, rather than by cash.** One exception is **for incidental amounts that are paid out of petty cash.**[3]

Companies generally issue checks only after following specified control procedures. Illustration 7-6 (page 350) shows how principles of internal control apply to cash disbursements.

## Voucher System Controls

Most medium and large companies use vouchers as part of their internal control over cash disbursements. A **voucher system** is a network of approvals by authorized individuals, acting independently, to ensure that all disbursements by check are proper.

Explain the applications of internal control principles to cash disbursements.

---

[3]We explain the operation of a petty cash fund in the appendix to this chapter on pages 366–368.

## Cash Disbursements Controls

**Establishment of Responsibility**

Only designated personnel are authorized to sign checks (treasurer) and approve vendors

**Physical Controls**

Store blank checks in safes, with limited access; print check amounts by machine in indelible ink

**Segregation of Duties**

Different individuals approve and make payments; check signers do not record disbursements

**Independent Internal Verification**

Compare checks to invoices; reconcile bank statement monthly

**Documentation Procedures**

Use prenumbered checks and account for them in sequence; each check must have an approved invoice; require employees to use corporate credit cards for reimbursable expenses; stamp invoices "paid."

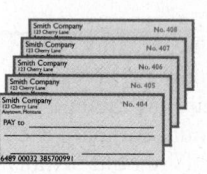

**Human Resource Controls**

Bond personnel who handle cash; require employees to take vacations; conduct background checks

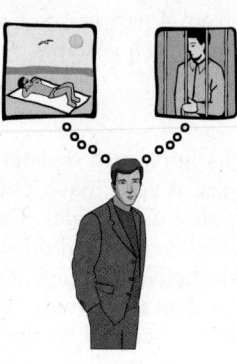

**Illustration 7-6**
Application of internal control principles to cash disbursements

The system begins with the authorization to incur a cost or expense. It ends with the issuance of a check for the liability incurred. A **voucher** is an authorization form prepared for each expenditure in a voucher system. Companies require vouchers for all types of cash disbursements except those from petty cash.

The starting point in preparing a voucher is to fill in the appropriate information about the liability on the face of the voucher. The vendor's invoice provides most of the needed information. Then, an employee in accounts payable records the voucher (in a journal called a **voucher register**) and files it according to the date on which it is to be paid. The company issues and sends a check on that date, and stamps the voucher "paid." The paid voucher is sent to the accounting department for recording (in a journal called the **check register**). A voucher system involves two journal entries, one to record the liability when the voucher is issued and a second to pay the liability that relates to the voucher.

The use of a voucher system improves internal control over cash disbursements. First, the authorization process inherent in a voucher system establishes responsibility. Each individual has responsibility to review the underlying documentation to ensure that it is correct. In addition, the voucher system keeps track of the documents that back up each transaction. By keeping these documents in one place, a supervisor can independently verify the authenticity of each transaction. Consider, for example, the case of Aesop University presented on page 340. Aesop did not use a voucher system for transactions under $2,500. As a consequence, there was no independent verification of the documents, which enabled the employee to submit fake invoices to hide his unauthorized purchases.

### Petty Cash Fund

As you learned earlier in the chapter, better internal control over cash disbursements is possible when companies make payments by check. However, using checks to pay such small amounts as those for postage due, employee working lunches, and taxi fares is both impractical and a nuisance. A common way of handling such payments, while maintaining satisfactory control, is to use a petty cash fund. A **petty cash fund** is a cash fund used to pay relatively small amounts. We explain the operation of a petty cash fund in the appendix at the end of this chapter.

**Ethics Note** Internal control over a petty cash fund is strengthened by: (1) having a supervisor make surprise counts of the fund to confirm whether the paid petty cash receipts and fund cash equal the fund amount, and (2) canceling or mutilating the paid petty cash receipts so they cannot be resubmitted for reimbursement.

## Ethics Insight

### How Employees Steal

A recent study by the Association of Certified Fraud Examiners found that two-thirds of all employee thefts involved a fraudulent disbursement by an employee. The most common form (28.3% of cases) was fraudulent billing schemes. In these, the employee causes the company to issue a payment to the employee by submitting a bill for nonexistent goods or services, purchases of personal goods by the employee, or inflated invoices. The following graph shows various types of fraudulent disbursements and the median loss from each.

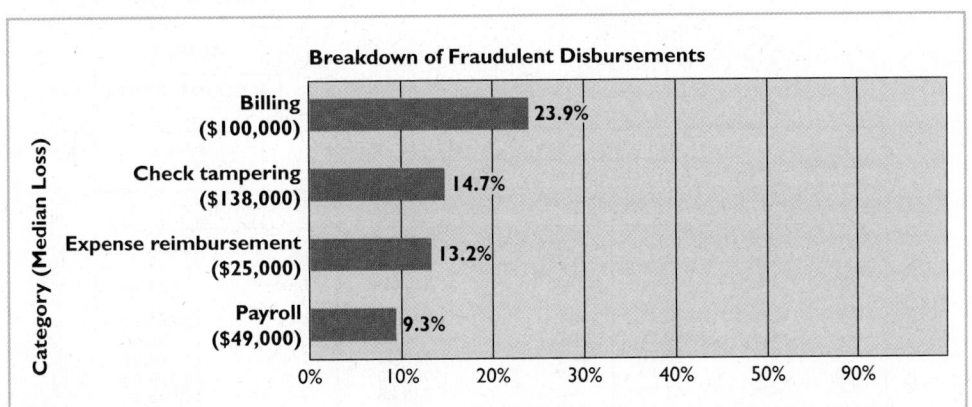

**Breakdown of Fraudulent Disbursements**

Category (Median Loss):
- Billing ($100,000): 23.9%
- Check tampering ($138,000): 14.7%
- Expense reimbursement ($25,000): 13.2%
- Payroll ($49,000): 9.3%

*Source: 2008 Report to the Nation on Occupational Fraud and Abuse,* Association of Certified Fraud Examiners, *www.acfe.com/documents/2008_rttn.pdf,* p. 13.

**?** How can companies reduce the likelihood of fraudulent disbursements? (See page 392.)

## Control Features: Use of a Bank

**The use of a bank contributes significantly to good internal control over cash.** A company can safeguard its cash by using a bank as a depository and clearinghouse for checks received and checks written. The use of a bank checking account minimizes the amount of currency that must be kept on hand. It also facilitates control of cash because a double record is maintained of all bank transactions—one by the business and the other by the bank. The asset account

Cash maintained by the company is the "flip-side" of the bank's liability account for that company. A **bank reconciliation** is the process of comparing the bank's balance with the company's balance, and explaining the differences to make them agree.

Many companies have more than one bank account. For efficiency of operations and better control, national retailers like Wal-Mart and Target often have regional bank accounts. Similarly, a company such as ExxonMobil with more than 100,000 employees may have a payroll bank account as well as one or more general bank accounts. In addition, a company may maintain several bank accounts in order to have more than one source for short-term loans.

## BANK STATEMENTS

Each month, the company receives from the bank a **bank statement** showing its bank transactions and balances.[4] For example, the statement for Laird Company in Illustration 7-7 shows the following: (1) checks paid and other debits that reduce the balance in the depositor's account, (2) deposits and other credits that increase the balance in the depositor's account, and (3) the account balance after each day's transactions.

**Illustration 7-7** Bank statement

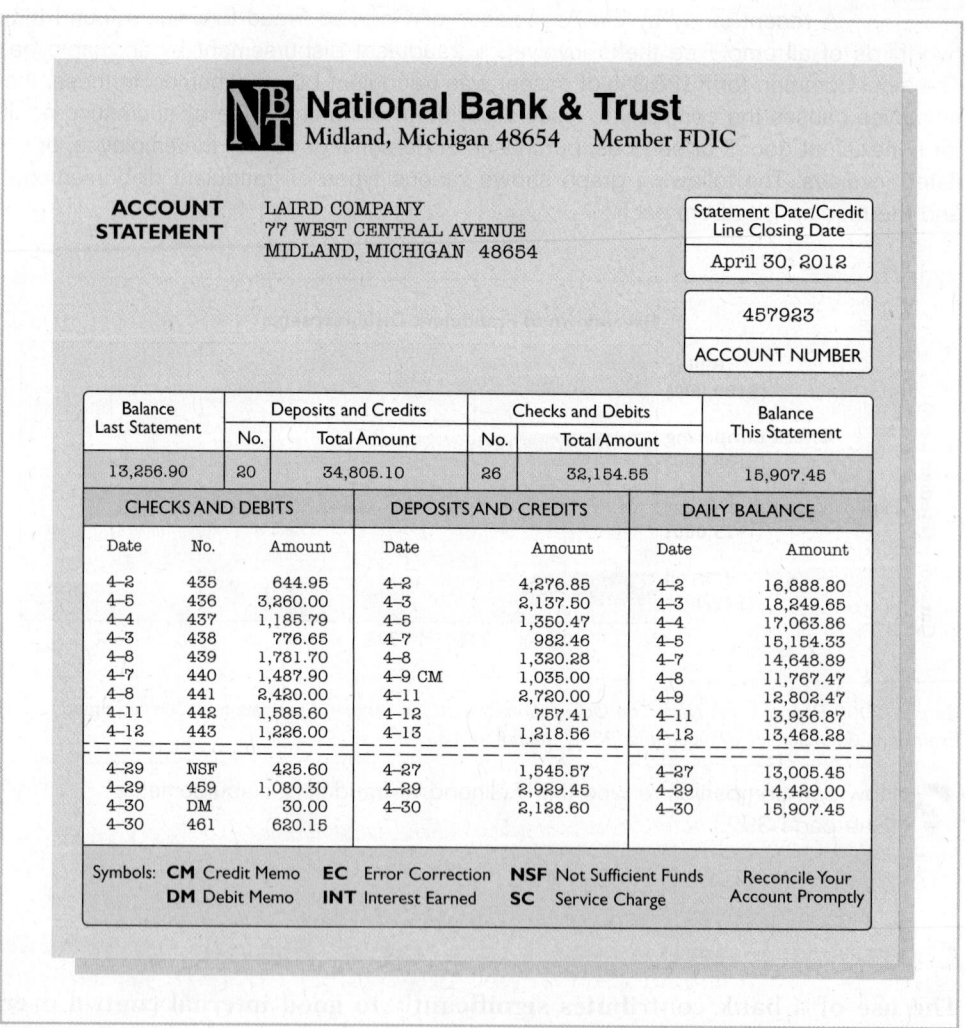

---

[4]Our presentation assumes that a company makes all adjustments at the end of the month. In practice, a company may also make journal entries during the month as it receives information from the bank regarding its account.

Remember that bank statements are prepared from the *bank's* perspective. For example, every deposit the bank receives is an increase in the bank's liabilities (an account payable to the depositor). Therefore, in Illustration 7-7, National Bank and Trust *credits* to Laird Company every deposit it received from Laird. The reverse occurs when the bank "pays" a check issued by Laird Company on its checking account balance: Payment reduces the bank's liability and is therefore *debited* to Laird's account with the bank.

The bank statement lists in numerical sequence all paid checks along with the date the check was paid and its amount. Upon paying a check, the bank stamps the check "paid"; a paid check is sometimes referred to as a **canceled** check. In addition, the bank includes with the bank statement memoranda explaining other debits and credits it made to the depositor's account.

A check that is not paid by a bank because of insufficient funds in a bank account is called an **NSF check** (not sufficient funds). The bank uses a debit memorandum when a previously deposited customer's check "bounces" because of insufficient funds. In such a case, the customer's bank marks the check NSF (not sufficient funds) and returns it to the depositor's bank. The bank then debits (decreases) the depositor's account, as shown by the symbol NSF in Illustration 7-7, and sends the NSF check and debit memorandum to the depositor as notification of the charge. The NSF check creates an account receivable for the depositor and reduces cash in the bank account.

> **Helpful Hint** Essentially, the bank statement is a copy of the bank's records sent to the customer for periodic review.

## RECONCILING THE BANK ACCOUNT

Because the bank and the company maintain independent records of the company's checking account, you might assume that the respective balances will always agree. In fact, the two balances are seldom the same at any given time, and both balances differ from the "correct or true" balance. Therefore, it is necessary to make the balance per books and the balance per bank agree with the correct or true amount—a process called **reconciling the bank account**. The need for reconciliation has two causes:

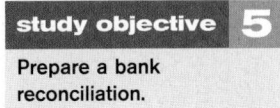

**study objective 5**

Prepare a bank reconciliation.

1. **Time lags** that prevent one of the parties from recording the transaction in the same period.

2. **Errors** by either party in recording transactions.

Time lags occur frequently. For example, several days may elapse between the time a company pays by check and the date the bank pays the check. Similarly, when a company uses the bank's night depository to make its deposits, there will be a difference of one day between the time the company records the receipts and the time the bank does so. A time lag also occurs whenever the bank mails a debit or credit memorandum to the company.

The incidence of errors depends on the effectiveness of the internal controls maintained by the company and the bank. Bank errors are infrequent. However, either party could accidentally record a $450 check as $45 or $540. In addition, the bank might mistakenly charge a check drawn by C. D. Berg to the account of C. D. Burg.

## Reconciliation Procedure

In reconciling the bank account, it is customary to reconcile the balance per books and balance per bank to their adjusted (correct or true) cash balances. **To obtain maximum benefit from a bank reconciliation, an employee who has no other responsibilities related to cash should prepare the reconciliation.** When companies do not follow the internal control principle of independent internal verification in preparing the reconciliation, cash embezzlements may escape unnoticed. For example, in the Anatomy of a Fraud box at the bottom of page 340, a bank reconciliation by someone other than Angela Bauer might have exposed her embezzlement.

Illustration 7-8 shows the reconciliation process. The starting point in preparing the reconciliation is to enter the balance per bank statement and balance per books on a schedule. The following steps should reveal all the reconciling items that cause the difference between the two balances.

**Illustration 7-8** Bank reconciliation adjustments

**Helpful Hint** Deposits in transit and outstanding checks are reconciling items because of time lags.

Cash Balances

**Per Bank Statement**

Adjustments to the bank balance

Deposits in transit

Outstanding checks

Bank errors "Oops"

**Per Books**

Adjustments to the book balance

Notes collected by banks

NSF (bounced) checks

Check printing or other service charges

Company errors "Oops"

**Correct Cash Amount**

**Step 1. Deposits in transit.** Compare the individual deposits on the bank statement with the deposits in transit from the preceding bank reconciliation and with the deposits per company records or copies of duplicate deposit slips. Deposits recorded by the depositor that have not been recorded by the bank represent **deposits in transit**. Add these deposits to the balance per bank.

**Step 2. Outstanding checks.** Compare the paid checks shown on the bank statement or the paid checks returned with the bank statement with (a) checks outstanding from the preceding bank reconciliation, and (b) checks issued by the company as recorded in the cash payments journal. Issued checks recorded by the company that have not been paid by the bank represent **outstanding checks**. Deduct outstanding checks from the balance per the bank.

**Step 3. Errors.** Note any errors discovered in the previous steps and list them in the appropriate section of the reconciliation schedule. For example, if the company mistakenly recorded as $159 a paid check correctly written for $195, the company would deduct the error of $36 from the balance per books. All errors made by the depositor are reconciling items in determining the adjusted cash balance per books. In contrast, all errors made by the bank are reconciling items in determining the adjusted cash balance per the bank.

**Step 4. Bank memoranda.** Trace bank memoranda to the depositor's records. The company lists in the appropriate section of the reconciliation schedule any unrecorded memoranda. For example, the company would deduct from the balance per books a $5 debit memorandum for bank service charges. Similarly, it would add to the balance per books a $32 credit memorandum for interest earned.

## Bank Reconciliation Illustrated

Illustration 7-7 presented the bank statement for Laird Company. It shows a balance per bank of $15,907.45 on April 30, 2012. On this date the balance of cash per books is $11,589.45. From the foregoing steps, Laird determines the following reconciling items.

**Helpful Hint** Note in the bank statement that the bank has paid checks No. 459 and 461, but check No. 460 is not listed. Thus, this check is outstanding. If a complete bank statement were provided, checks No. 453 and 457 also would not be listed. Laird obtains the amounts for these three checks from its cash payments records.

| | |
|---|---:|
| **Step 1. Deposits in transit:** April 30 deposit (received by bank on May 1). | $2,201.40 |
| **Step 2. Outstanding checks:** No. 453, $3,000.00; No. 457, $1,401.30; No. 460, $1,502.70. | 5,904.00 |
| **Step 3. Errors:** Check No. 443 was correctly written by Laird for $1,226.00 and was correctly paid by the bank. However, Laird recorded the check as $1,262.00. | 36.00 |
| **Step 4. Bank memoranda:** | |
| (a) Debit—NSF check from J. R. Baron for $425.60 | 425.60 |
| (b) Debit—Printing company checks charge, $30 | 30.00 |
| (c) Credit—Collection of note receivable for $1,000 plus interest earned $50, less bank collection fee $15 | 1,035.00 |

Illustration 7-9 shows Laird's bank reconciliation.

**Illustration 7-9** Bank reconciliation

### LAIRD COMPANY
### Bank Reconciliation
### April 30, 2012

| | | |
|---|---:|---:|
| Cash balance per bank statement | | $ 15,907.45 |
| Add: Deposits in transit | | 2,201.40 |
| | | 18,108.85 |
| | | |
| Less: Outstanding checks | | |
| No. 453 | $3,000.00 | |
| No. 457 | 1,401.30 | |
| No. 460 | 1,502.70 | 5,904.00 |
| **Adjusted cash balance per bank** | | **$12,204.85** ◄ |
| | | |
| Cash balance per books | | $ 11,589.45 |
| Add: Collection of note receivable for $1,000 plus interest earned $50, less collection fee $15 | $1,035.00 | |
| Error in recording check No. 443 | 36.00 | 1,071.00 |
| | | 12,660.45 |
| | | |
| Less: NSF check | 425.60 | |
| Bank service charge | 30.00 | 455.60 |
| **Adjusted cash balance per books** | | **$12,204.85** ◄ |

**Alternative Terminology** The terms *adjusted cash balance*, *true cash balance*, and *correct cash balance* are used interchangeably.

## Entries from Bank Reconciliation

The depositor (that is, the company) next must record each reconciling item used to determine the **adjusted cash balance per books**. If the company does not journalize and post these items, the Cash account will not show the correct balance. The adjusting entries for the Laird Company bank reconciliation on April 30 are as follows.

**COLLECTION OF NOTE RECEIVABLE.** This entry involves four accounts. Assuming that the interest of $50 has not been recorded and the collection fee is charged to Miscellaneous Expense, the entry is:

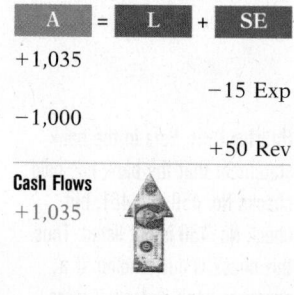

| Apr. 30 | Cash | 1,035 | |
| | Miscellaneous Expense | 15 | |
| | Notes Receivable | | 1,000 |
| | Interest Revenue | | 50 |
| | (To record collection of note receivable by bank) | | |

**BOOK ERROR.** An examination of the cash disbursements journal shows that check No. 443 was a payment on account to Andrea Company, a supplier. The correcting entry is:

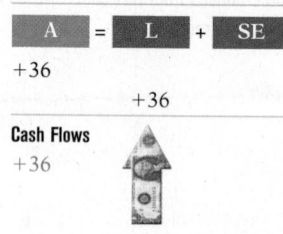

| Apr. 30 | Cash | 36 | |
| | Accounts Payable—Andrea Company | | 36 |
| | (To correct error in recording check No. 443) | | |

**NSF CHECK.** As indicated earlier, an NSF check becomes an accounts receivable to the depositor. The entry is:

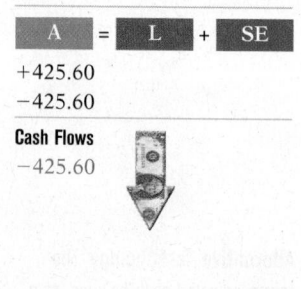

| Apr. 30 | Accounts Receivable—J. R. Baron | 425.60 | |
| | Cash | | 425.60 |
| | (To record NSF check) | | |

**BANK SERVICE CHARGES.** Companies typically debit to Miscellaneous Expense the check printing charges (DM) and other bank service charges (SC) because they are usually small in amount. Laird's entry is:

| Apr. 30 | Miscellaneous Expense | 30 | |
| | Cash | | 30 |
| | (To record charge for printing company checks) | | |

The foregoing entries could also be combined into one compound entry.

After Laird posts the entries, the Cash account will appear as in Illustration 7-10. The adjusted cash balance in the ledger should agree with the adjusted cash balance per books in the bank reconciliation in Illustration 7-9 (page 355).

Illustration 7-10
Adjusted balance in Cash
account

| | | Cash | | | |
|---|---|---|---|---|---|
| Apr. 30 | Bal. | 11,589.45 | Apr. 30 | 425.60 | |
| 30 | | 1,035.00 | 30 | 30.00 | |
| 30 | | 36.00 | | | |
| Apr. 30 | Bal. | 12,204.85 | | | |

What entries does the bank make? If the company discovers any bank errors in preparing the reconciliation, it should notify the bank so the bank can make the necessary corrections on its records. The bank does not make any entries for deposits in transit or outstanding checks. Only when these items reach the bank will the bank record these items.

## Electronic Funds Transfer (EFT) System

It is not surprising that companies and banks have developed approaches to transfer funds among parties without the use of paper (deposit tickets, checks, etc.). Such procedures, called **electronic funds transfers (EFTs)**, are disbursement systems that use wire, telephone, or computers to transfer cash from one location to another. Use of EFT is quite common. For example, many employees receive no formal payroll checks from their employers. Instead, employers send electronic payroll data to the appropriate banks. Also, individuals now frequently make regular payments such as those for house, car, and utilities by EFT.

EFT transactions normally result in better internal control since no cash or checks are handled by company employees. This does not mean that opportunities for fraud are eliminated. In fact, the same basic principles related to internal control apply to EFT transactions. For example, without proper segregation of duties and authorizations, an employee might be able to redirect electronic payments into a personal bank account and conceal the theft with fraudulent accounting entries.

## Investor Insight

### Madoff's Ponzi Scheme

No recent fraud has generated more interest and rage than the one perpetrated by Bernard Madoff. Madoff was an elite New York investment fund manager who was highly regarded by securities regulators. Investors flocked to him because he delivered very steady returns of between 10% and 15%, no matter whether the market was going up or going down. However, for many years, Madoff did not actually invest the cash that people gave to him. Instead, he was running a Ponzi scheme: He paid returns to existing investors using cash received from new investors. As long as the size of his investment fund continued to grow from new investments at a rate that exceeded the amounts that he needed to pay out in returns, Madoff was able to operate his fraud smoothly. To conceal his misdeeds, he fabricated false investment statements that were provided to investors. In addition, Madoff hired an auditor that never verified the accuracy of the investment records but automatically issued unqualified opinions each year. Although a competing fund manager warned the SEC a number of times over a nearly 10-year period that he thought Madoff was engaged in fraud, the SEC never aggressively investigated the allegations. Investors, many of which were charitable organizations, lost more than $18 billion. Madoff was sentenced to a jail term of 150 years.

How was Madoff able to conceal such a giant fraud? (See page 392.)

## before you go on...

### BANK RECONCILIATION

#### Action Plan

- Understand the purpose of a bank reconciliation.
- Identify time lags and explain how they cause reconciling items.

 Sally Kist owns Linen Kist Fabrics. Sally asks you to explain how she should treat the following reconciling items when reconciling the company's bank account: (1) a debit memorandum for an NSF check, (2) a credit memorandum for a note collected by the bank, (3) outstanding checks, and (4) a deposit in transit.

#### Solution

Sally should treat the reconciling items as follows.

(1) NSF check: Deduct from balance per books.
(2) Collection of note: Add to balance per books.
(3) Outstanding checks: Deduct from balance per bank.
(4) Deposit in transit: Add to balance per bank.

Related exercise material: **BE7-8, BE7-9, BE7-10, BE7-11, Do it! 7-3, E7-6, E7-7, E7-8, E7-9, E7-10, and E7-11.**

# Reporting Cash

**study objective 6**

Explain the reporting of cash.

**Cash** consists of coins, currency (paper money), checks, money orders, and money on hand or on deposit in a bank or similar depository. Checks that are dated later than the current date (post-dated checks) are not included in cash. Companies report cash in two different statements: the balance sheet and the statement of cash flows. The balance sheet reports the amount of cash available at a given point in time. The statement of cash flows shows the sources and uses of cash during a period of time. The cash flow statement was introduced in Chapters 1 and 2 and will be discussed in much detail in Chapter 12. In this section, we discuss some important points regarding the presentation of cash in the balance sheet.

When presented in a balance sheet, cash on hand, cash in banks, and petty cash are often combined and reported simply as **Cash**. Because it is the most liquid asset owned by the company, cash is listed first in the current assets section of the balance sheet.

### CASH EQUIVALENTS

Many companies use the designation "Cash and cash equivalents" in reporting cash. (See Illustration 7-11 for an example.) **Cash equivalents** are short-term, highly liquid investments that are both:

1. Readily convertible to known amounts of cash, and
2. So near their maturity that their market value is relatively insensitive to changes in interest rates.

**Illustration 7-11** Balance sheet presentation of cash

| DELTA AIR LINES, INC. Balance Sheet (partial) December 31, 2009 (in millions) | |
|---|---|
| **Assets** | |
| Current assets | |
| Cash and cash equivalents | $4,607 |
| Short-term investments | 71 |
| Restricted cash | 423 |
| Accounts receivable and other, net | 1,360 |
| Parts inventories | 327 |
| Prepaid expenses and other | 953 |
| Total current assets | $7,741 |

Examples of cash equivalents are Treasury bills, commercial paper (short-term corporate notes), and money market funds. All typically are purchased with cash that is in excess of immediate needs.

Occasionally a company will have a net negative balance in its bank account. In this case, the company should report the negative balance among current liabilities. For example, farm equipment manufacturer Ag-Chem recently reported "Checks outstanding in excess of cash balances" of $2,145,000 among its current liabilities.

### RESTRICTED CASH

A company may have **restricted cash**, cash that is not available for general use but rather is restricted for a special purpose. For example, landfill companies are often required to maintain a fund of restricted cash to ensure they will have adequate resources to cover closing and clean-up costs at the end of a landfill site's useful life. McKesson Corp. recently reported restricted cash of $962 million to be paid out as the result of investor lawsuits.

Cash restricted in use should be reported separately on the balance sheet as restricted cash. If the company expects to use the restricted cash within the next year, it reports the amount as a current asset. When this is not the case, it reports the restricted funds as a noncurrent asset.

Illustration 7-11 shows restricted cash reported in the financial statements of Delta Air Lines. The company is required to maintain restricted cash as collateral to support insurance obligations related to workers' compensation claims. Delta does not have access to these funds for general use, and so it must report them separately, rather than as part of cash and cash equivalents.

**Ethics Note** Recently, some companies were forced to restate their financial statements because they had too broadly interpreted which types of investments could be treated as cash equivalents. By reporting these items as cash equivalents, the companies made themselves look more liquid.

## DECISION TOOLKIT

| DECISION CHECKPOINTS | INFO NEEDED FOR DECISION | TOOL TO USE FOR DECISION | HOW TO EVALUATE RESULTS |
|---|---|---|---|
| Is all of the company's cash available for general use? | Balance sheet and notes to financial statements | Does the company report any cash as being restricted? | A restriction on the use of cash limits management's ability to use those resources for general obligations. This might be considered when assessing liquidity. |

# Managing and Monitoring Cash

Many companies struggle, not because they fail to generate sales, but because they can't manage their cash. A real-life example of this is a clothing manufacturing company owned by Sharon McCollick. McCollick gave up a stable, high-paying marketing job with Intel Corporation to start her own company. Soon she had more orders from stores such as JC Penney and Dayton Hudson (now Target) than she could fill. Yet she found herself on the brink of financial disaster, owing three mortgage payments on her house and $2,000 to the IRS. Her company could generate sales, but it was not collecting cash fast enough to support its operations. The bottom line is that a business must have cash.[5]

A merchandising company's operating cycle is generally shorter than that of a manufacturing company. Illustration 7-12 (page 360) shows the cash to cash operating cycle of a merchandising operation.

---

[5]Adapted from T. Petzinger, Jr., "The Front Lines—Sharon McCollick Got Mad and Tore Down a Bank's Barriers," *Wall Street Journal* (May 19, 1995), p. B1.

**Illustration 7-12**
Operating cycle of a
merchandising company

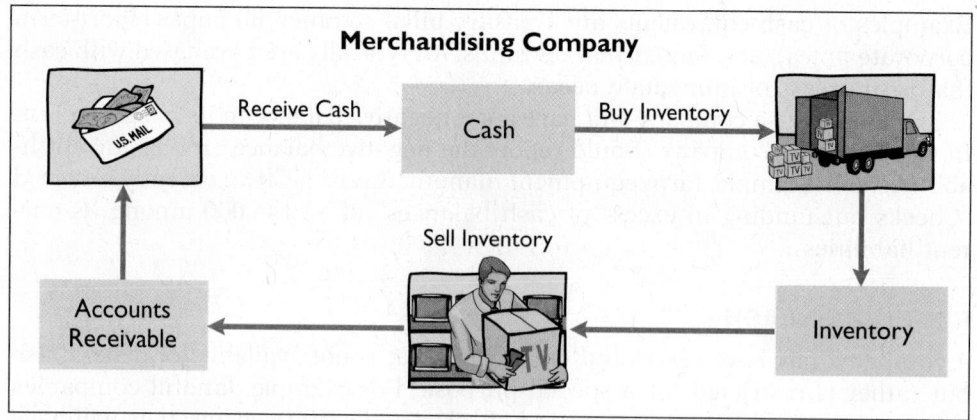

To understand cash management, consider the operating cycle of Sharon McCollick's clothing manufacturing company. First, it purchases cloth. Let's assume that it purchases the cloth on credit provided by the supplier, so the company owes its supplier money. Next, employees convert the cloth to clothing. Now the company also owes its employees money. Next, it sells the clothing to retailers, on credit. McCollick's company will have no money to repay suppliers or employees until it receives payments from customers. In a manufacturing operation there may be a significant lag between the original purchase of raw materials and the ultimate receipt of cash from customers.

Managing the often-precarious balance created by the ebb and flow of cash during the operating cycle is one of a company's greatest challenges. The objective is to ensure that a company has sufficient cash to meet payments as they come due, yet minimize the amount of non-revenue-generating cash on hand.

## BASIC PRINCIPLES OF CASH MANAGEMENT

**study objective  7**

Discuss the basic principles
of cash management.

Management of cash is the responsibility of the company **treasurer**. Any company can improve its chances of having adequate cash by following five basic principles of cash management.

1. **Increase the speed of receivables collection.** Money owed Sharon McCollick by her customers is money that she can't use. The more quickly customers pay her, the more quickly she can use those funds. Thus, rather than have an average collection period of 30 days, she may want an average collection period of 15 days. However, she must carefully weigh any attempt to force her customers to pay earlier against the possibility that she may anger or alienate customers. Perhaps her competitors are willing to provide a 30-day grace period. As noted in Chapter 5, one common way to encourage customers to pay more quickly is to offer cash discounts for early payment under such terms as 2/10, n/30.

2. **Keep inventory levels low.** Maintaining a large inventory of cloth and finished clothing is costly. It ties up large amounts of cash, as well as warehouse space. Increasingly, companies are using techniques to reduce the inventory on hand, thus conserving their cash. Of course, if Sharon McCollick has inadequate inventory, she will lose sales. The proper level of inventory is an important decision.

3. **Monitor payment of liabilities.** Sharon McCollick should monitor when her bills are due, so she avoids paying bills too early. Let's say her supplier

allows 30 days for payment. If she pays in 10 days, she has lost the use of that cash for 20 days. Therefore, she should use the full payment period. But, she should not pay late. This could damage her credit rating (and future borrowing ability). Also, late payments to suppliers can damage important supplier relationships and may even threaten a supplier's viability. Sharon McCollick's company also should conserve cash by taking cash discounts offered by suppliers, when possible.

4. **Plan the timing of major expenditures.** To maintain operations or to grow, all companies must make major expenditures. These often require some form of outside financing. In order to increase the likelihood of obtaining outside financing, McCollick should carefully consider the timing of major expenditures in light of her company's operating cycle. If at all possible, she should make any major expenditure when the company normally has excess cash—usually during the off-season.

5. **Invest idle cash.** Cash on hand earns nothing. An important part of the treasurer's job is to ensure that the company invests any excess cash, even if it is only overnight. Many businesses, such as Sharon McCollick's clothing company, are seasonal. During her slow season, when she has excess cash, she should invest it.

   To avoid a cash crisis, however, it is very important that investments of idle cash be highly liquid and risk-free. A *liquid investment* is one with a market in which someone is always willing to buy or sell the investment. A *risk-free investment* means there is no concern that the party will default on its promise to pay its principal and interest. For example, using excess cash to purchase stock in a small company because you heard that it was probably going to increase in value in the near term is totally inappropriate. First, the stock of small companies is often illiquid. Second, if the stock suddenly decreases in value, you might be forced to sell the stock at a loss in order to pay your bills as they come due. The most common form of liquid investments is interest-paying U.S. government securities.

Illustration 7-13 summarizes these five principles of cash management.

**International Note** International sales complicate cash management. For example, if Nike must repay a Japanese supplier 30 days from today in Japanese yen, Nike will be concerned about how the exchange rate of U.S. dollars for yen might change during those 30 days. Often, corporate treasurers make investments known as *hedges* to lock in an exchange rate to reduce the company's exposure to exchange-rate fluctuation.

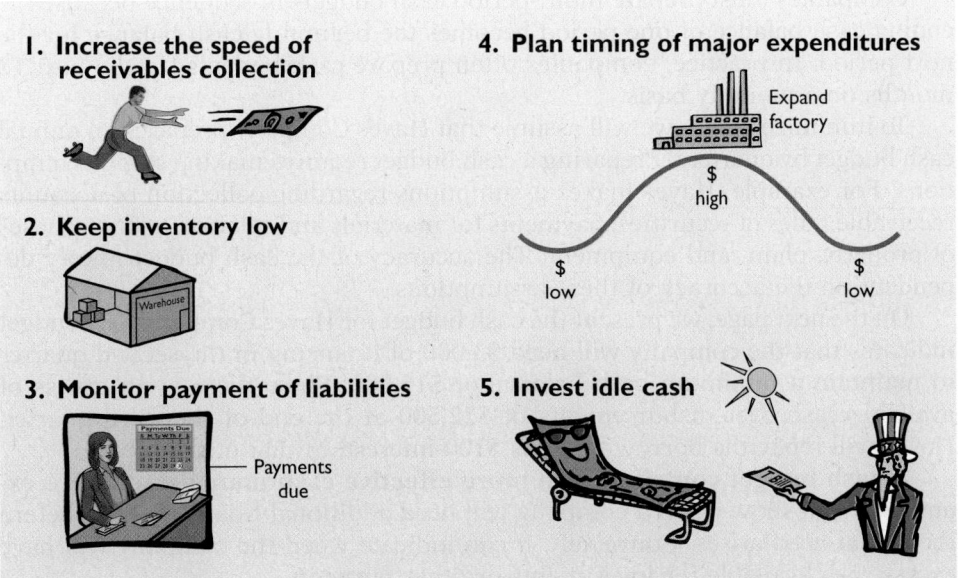

**Illustration 7-13** Five principles of sound cash management

1. **Increase the speed of receivables collection**

2. **Keep inventory low**

3. **Monitor payment of liabilities**

4. **Plan timing of major expenditures**

5. **Invest idle cash**

## KEEPING AN EYE ON CASH

study objective **8**

Identify the primary elements of a cash budget.

Because cash is so vital to a company, **planning the company's cash needs** is a key business activity. It enables the company to plan ahead to cover possible cash shortfalls and to make investments of idle funds. The cash budget shows anticipated cash flows, usually over a one- to two-year period. In this section, we introduce the basics of cash budgeting. More advanced discussion of cash budgets and budgets in general is provided in managerial accounting texts.

As shown below, the cash budget contains three sections—cash receipts, cash disbursements, and financing—and the beginning and ending cash balances.

**ANY COMPANY**
Cash Budget

| | |
|---|---|
| Beginning cash balance | $X,XXX |
| Add: **Cash receipts** (itemized) | X,XXX |
| Total available cash | X,XXX |
| Less: **Cash disbursements** (itemized) | X,XXX |
| Excess (deficiency) of available cash over cash disbursements | X,XXX |
| **Financing** | |
| Add: Borrowings | X,XXX |
| Less: Repayments | X,XXX |
| Ending cash balance | $X,XXX |

The **Cash receipts** section includes expected receipts from the company's principal source(s) of cash, such as cash sales and collections from customers on credit sales. This section also shows anticipated receipts of interest and dividends, and proceeds from planned sales of investments, plant assets, and the company's capital stock.

The **Cash disbursements** section shows expected payments for inventory, labor, overhead, and selling and administrative expenses. It also includes projected payments for income taxes, dividends, investments, and plant assets. Note that it does not include depreciation since depreciation expense does not use cash.

The **Financing** section shows expected borrowings and repayments of borrowed funds plus interest. Financing is needed when there is a cash deficiency or when the cash balance is less than management's minimum required balance.

Companies must prepare multi-period cash budgets in sequence because the ending cash balance of one period becomes the beginning cash balance for the next period. In practice, companies often prepare cash budgets for the next 12 months on a monthly basis.

To minimize detail, we will assume that Hayes Company prepares an annual cash budget by quarters. Preparing a cash budget requires making some assumptions. For example, Hayes makes assumptions regarding collection of accounts receivable, sales of securities, payments for materials and salaries, and purchases of property, plant, and equipment. The accuracy of the cash budget is very dependent on the accuracy of these assumptions.

On the next page, we present the cash budget for Hayes Company. The budget indicates that the company will need $3,000 of financing in the second quarter to maintain a minimum cash balance of $15,000. Since there is an excess of available cash over disbursements of $22,500 at the end of the third quarter, Hayes will repay the borrowing, plus $100 interest, in that quarter.

**A cash budget contributes to more effective cash management.** For example, it can show when a company will need additional financing, well before the actual need arises. Conversely, it can indicate when the company will have excess cash available for investments or other purposes.

**HAYES COMPANY**
Cash Budget
For the Year Ending December 31, 2012

| | Quarter | | | |
|---|---|---|---|---|
| | **1** | **2** | **3** | **4** |
| Beginning cash balance | $ 38,000 | $ 25,500 | $ 15,000 | $ 19,400 |
| Add: **Cash receipts** | | | | |
|   Collections from customers | 168,000 | 198,000 | 228,000 | 258,000 |
|   Sale of securities | 2,000 | 0 | 0 | 0 |
|     Total receipts | 170,000 | 198,000 | 228,000 | 258,000 |
| Total available cash | 208,000 | 223,500 | 243,000 | 277,400 |
| Less: **Cash disbursements** | | | | |
|   Inventory | 23,200 | 27,200 | 31,200 | 35,200 |
|   Salaries | 62,000 | 72,000 | 82,000 | 92,000 |
|   Selling and administrative expenses (excluding depreciation) | 94,300 | 99,300 | 104,300 | 109,300 |
|   Purchase of truck | 0 | 10,000 | 0 | 0 |
|   Income tax expense | 3,000 | 3,000 | 3,000 | 3,000 |
|     Total disbursements | 182,500 | 211,500 | 220,500 | 239,500 |
| Excess (deficiency) of available cash over disbursements | 25,500 | 12,000 | 22,500 | 37,900 |
| **Financing** | | | | |
|   Add: Borrowings | 0 | 3,000 | 0 | 0 |
|   Less: Repayments—plus $100 interest | 0 | 0 | 3,100 | 0 |
| Ending cash balance | $ 25,500 | $ 15,000 | $ 19,400 | $ 37,900 |

## DECISION TOOLKIT

| DECISION CHECKPOINTS | INFO NEEDED FOR DECISION | TOOL TO USE FOR DECISION | HOW TO EVALUATE RESULTS |
|---|---|---|---|
| Will the company be able to meet its projected cash needs? | Cash budget (typically available only to management) | The cash budget shows projected sources and uses of cash. If cash uses exceed internal cash sources, then the company must look for outside sources. | Two issues: (1) Are management's projections reasonable? (2) If outside sources are needed, are they available? |

*before you go on...*

**Do it!** Martian Company's management wants to maintain a minimum monthly cash balance of $15,000. At the beginning of March, the cash balance is $16,500; expected cash receipts for March are $210,000; and cash disbursements are expected to be $220,000. How much cash, if any, must Martian borrow to maintain the desired minimum monthly balance?

**CASH BUDGET**

## Action Plan

- Add the beginning cash balance to receipts to determine total available cash.
- Subtract disbursements to determine excess or deficiency.
- Compare excess or deficiency with desired minimum cash to determine borrowing needs.

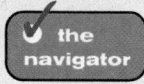

## Solution

| | |
|---|---:|
| Beginning cash balance | $ 16,500 |
| Add: Cash receipts for March | 210,000 |
| Total available cash | 226,500 |
| Less: Cash disbursements for March | 220,000 |
| Excess of available cash over cash disbursements | 6,500 |
| Financing | |
| Add: **Borrowings** | 8,500 |
| Ending cash balance | $ 15,000 |

To maintain the desired minimum cash balance of $15,000, Martian Company must borrow $8,500 of cash.

Related exercise material: **BE7-13, Do it! 7-4,** and **E7-14.**

## USING THE DECISION TOOLKIT

Presented below is hypothetical financial information for Mattel Corporation. Included in this information is financial statement data from the year ended December 31, 2011, which should be used to evaluate Mattel's cash position.

**Selected Financial Information**
**Year Ended December 31, 2011**
**(in millions)**

| | |
|---|---:|
| Net cash provided by operations | $325 |
| Capital expenditures | 162 |
| Dividends paid | 80 |
| Total expenses | 680 |
| Depreciation expense | 40 |
| Cash balance | 206 |

Also provided are projected data which are management's best estimate of its sources and uses of cash during 2012. This information should be used to prepare a cash budget for 2012.

**Projected Sources and Uses of Cash**
**(in millions)**

| | |
|---|---:|
| Beginning cash balance | $206 |
| Cash receipts from sales of product | 355 |
| Cash receipts from sale of short-term investments | 20 |
| Cash payments for inventory | 357 |
| Cash payments for selling and administrative costs | 201 |
| Cash payments for property, plant, and equipment | 45 |
| Cash payments for taxes | 17 |

Mattel Corporation's management believes it should maintain a balance of $200 million cash.

### Instructions

(a) Using the hypothetical projected sources and uses of cash information presented above, prepare a cash budget for 2012 for Mattel Corporation.
(b) Comment on the company's cash adequacy, and discuss steps that might be taken to improve its cash position.

**Solution**

(a)

**MATTEL CORPORATION**
**Cash Budget**
**For the Year 2012**
**(in millions)**

| | | |
|---|---:|---:|
| Beginning cash balance | | $206 |
| Add: Cash receipts | | |
| From sales of product | $355 | |
| From sale of short-term investments | 20 | 375 |
| Total available cash | | 581 |
| Less: Cash disbursements | | |
| Payments for inventory | 357 | |
| Payments for selling and administrative costs | 201 | |
| Payments for property, plant, and equipment | 45 | |
| Payments for taxes | 17 | |
| Total disbursements | | 620 |
| Excess (deficiency) of available cash over disbursements | | (39) |
| Financing | | |
| Add: **Borrowings** | | 239 |
| Ending cash balance | | $200 |

(b) Using these hypothetical data, Mattel's cash position appears adequate. For 2012, Mattel is projecting a cash shortfall. This is not necessarily of concern, but it should be investigated. Given that its primary line of business is toys, and that most toys are sold during December, we would expect Mattel's cash position to vary significantly during the course of the year. After the holiday season, it probably has a lot of excess cash. Earlier in the year, when it is making and selling its product but has not yet been paid, it may need to borrow to meet any temporary cash shortfalls.

    If Mattel's management is concerned with its cash position, it could take the following steps: (1) Offer its customers cash discounts for early payment, such as 2/10, n/30. (2) Implement inventory management techniques to reduce the need for large inventories of such things as the plastics used to make its toys. (3) Carefully time payments to suppliers by keeping track of when payments are due, so as not to pay too early. (4) If it has plans for major expenditures, time those expenditures to coincide with its seasonal period of excess cash.

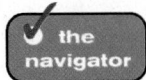

# Summary of Study Objectives

**1** **Define fraud and internal control.** A fraud is a dishonest act by an employee that results in personal benefit to the employee at a cost to the employer. The fraud triangle refers to the three factors that contribute to fraudulent activity by employees: opportunity, financial pressure, and rationalization. Internal control consists of all the related methods and measures adopted within an organization to safeguard its assets, enhance the reliability of its accounting records, increase efficiency of operations, and ensure compliance with laws and regulations.

**2** **Identify the principles of internal control activities.** The principles of internal control are: establishment of responsibility; segregation of duties; documentation procedures; physical controls; independent internal verification; and human resource controls.

**3** **Explain the applications of internal control principles to cash receipts.** Internal controls over cash receipts include: (a) designating only personnel such as cashiers to handle cash; (b) assigning the duties of receiving cash, recording cash, and having custody of cash to different individuals; (c) obtaining remittance advices for mail receipts, cash register tapes for over-the-counter receipts, and deposit slips for bank deposits; (d) using company safes and bank vaults to store cash with access limited to authorized personnel, and using cash registers in executing over-the-counter receipts; (e) making independent daily counts of register receipts and daily comparisons of total receipts with total deposits; and (f) conducting background checks and bonding personnel who handle cash, as well as requiring them to take vacations.

**4** **Explain the applications of internal control principles to cash disbursements.** Internal controls over cash disbursements include: (a) having only specified individuals such as the treasurer authorized to sign checks; (b) assigning the duties of approving items for payment, paying the items, and recording the payment to different individuals; (c) using prenumbered checks and accounting for all checks, with each check supported by an approved invoice; after payment, stamping each approved invoice "paid"; (d) storing blank checks in a safe or vault with access restricted to authorized personnel, and using a machine with indelible ink to imprint amounts on checks; (e) comparing each check with the approved invoice before issuing the check, and making monthly reconciliations of bank and book balances; and (f) bonding personnel who handle cash, requiring employees to take vacations, and conducting background checks.

**5** **Prepare a bank reconciliation.** In reconciling the bank account, it is customary to reconcile the balance per books and the balance per bank to their adjusted balance. The steps reconciling the Cash account are to determine deposits in transit, outstanding checks, errors by the depositor or the bank, and unrecorded bank memoranda.

**6** **Explain the reporting of cash.** Cash is listed first in the current assets section of the balance sheet. Companies often report cash together with cash equivalents. Cash restricted for a special purpose is reported separately as a current asset or as a noncurrent asset, depending on when the company expects to use the cash.

**7** **Discuss the basic principles of cash management.** The basic principles of cash management include: (a) increase the speed of receivables collection, (b) keep inventory levels low, (c) monitor the timing of payment of liabilities, (d) plan timing of major expenditures, and (e) invest idle cash.

**8** **Identify the primary elements of a cash budget.** The three main elements of a cash budget are the cash receipts section, cash disbursements section, and financing section.

✓ the navigator

## DECISION TOOLKIT A SUMMARY

| DECISION CHECKPOINTS | INFO NEEDED FOR DECISION | TOOL TO USE FOR DECISION | HOW TO EVALUATE RESULTS |
|---|---|---|---|
| Are the company's financial statements supported by adequate internal controls? | Auditor's report, management discussion and analysis, articles in financial press | The principles of internal control activities are (1) establishment of responsibility, (2) segregation of duties, (3) documentation procedures, (4) physical controls, (5) independent internal verification, and (6) human resource controls. | If any indication is given that these or other controls are lacking, use the financial statements with caution. |
| Is all of the company's cash available for general use? | Balance sheet and notes to financial statements | Does the company report any cash as being restricted? | A restriction on the use of cash limits management's ability to use those resources for general obligations. This might be considered when assessing liquidity. |
| Will the company be able to meet its projected cash needs? | Cash budget (typically available only to management) | The cash budget shows projected sources and uses of cash. If cash uses exceed internal cash sources, then the company must look for outside sources. | Two issues: (1) Are management's projections reasonable? (2) If outside sources are needed, are they available? |

## appendix 7A

# Operation of the Petty Cash Fund

**study objective 9**

Explain the operation of a petty cash fund.

The operation of a petty cash fund involves (1) establishing the fund, (2) making payments from the fund, and (3) replenishing the fund.

## ESTABLISHING THE PETTY CASH FUND

Two essential steps in establishing a petty cash fund are: (1) appointing a petty cash custodian who will be responsible for the fund, and (2) determining the size of the fund. Ordinarily, a company expects the amount in the fund to cover anticipated disbursements for a three- to four-week period.

When the company establishes the petty cash fund, it issues a check payable to the petty cash custodian for the stipulated amount. If Laird Company decides to establish a $100 fund on March 1, the entry in general journal form is:

| Mar. 1 | Petty Cash | 100 | |
| | Cash | | 100 |
| | (To establish a petty cash fund) | | |

A = L + SE

+100
−100

**Cash Flows**
no effect

The fund custodian cashes the check and places the proceeds in a locked petty cash box or drawer. Most petty cash funds are established on a fixed-amount basis. Moreover, the company will make no additional entries to the Petty Cash account unless the stipulated amount of the fund is changed. For example, if Laird Company decides on July 1 to increase the size of the fund to $250, it would debit Petty Cash $150 and credit Cash $150.

**Ethics Note** Petty cash funds are authorized and legitimate. In contrast, "slush" funds are unauthorized and hidden (under the table).

## MAKING PAYMENTS FROM PETTY CASH

The custodian of the petty cash fund has the authority to make payments from the fund that conform to prescribed management policies. Usually, management limits the size of expenditures that come from petty cash and does not permit use of the fund for certain types of transactions (such as making short-term loans to employees).

Each payment from the fund must be documented on a prenumbered petty cash receipt (or petty cash voucher). The signatures of both the custodian and the individual receiving payment are required on the receipt. If other supporting documents such as a freight bill or invoice are available, they should be attached to the petty cash receipt.

The custodian keeps the receipts in the petty cash box until the fund is replenished. As a result, the sum of the petty cash receipts and money in the fund should equal the established total at all times. This means that management can make surprise counts at any time by an independent person, such as an internal auditor, to determine the correctness of the fund.

The company does not make an accounting entry to record a payment at the time it is taken from petty cash. It is considered both inexpedient and unnecessary to do so. Instead, the company recognizes the accounting effects of each payment when the fund is replenished.

**Helpful Hint** From the standpoint of internal control, the receipt satisfies two principles: (1) establishing responsibility (signature of custodian), and (2) documentation procedures.

## REPLENISHING THE PETTY CASH FUND

When the money in the petty cash fund reaches a minimum level, the company replenishes the fund. The petty cash custodian initiates a request for reimbursement. This individual prepares a schedule (or summary) of the payments that have been made and sends the schedule, supported by petty cash receipts and other documentation, to the treasurer's office. The receipts and supporting documents are examined in the treasurer's office to verify that they were proper payments from the fund. The treasurer then approves the request, and a check is prepared to restore the fund to its established amount. At the same time, all supporting documentation is stamped "paid" so that it cannot be submitted again for payment.

To illustrate, assume that on March 15 the petty cash custodian requests a check for $87. The fund contains $13 cash and petty cash receipts for postage

**Helpful Hint** Replenishing involves three internal control procedures: segregation of duties, documentation procedures, and independent internal verification.

$44, supplies $38, and miscellaneous expenses $5. The entry, in general journal form, to record the check is:

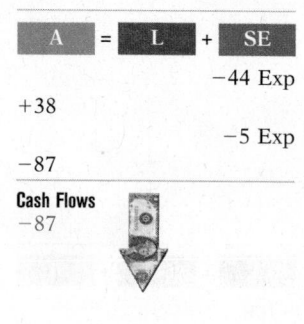

A = L + SE

−44 Exp
+38
−5 Exp
−87

**Cash Flows**
−87

| Mar. 15 | Postage Expense | 44 | |
| | Supplies | 38 | |
| | Miscellaneous Expense | 5 | |
| |     Cash | | 87 |
| |     (To replenish petty cash fund) | | |

Note that the reimbursement entry does not affect the Petty Cash account. Replenishment changes the composition of the fund by replacing the petty cash receipts with cash, but it does not change the balance in the fund.

Occasionally, in replenishing a petty cash fund the company may need to recognize a cash shortage or overage. To illustrate, assume in the preceding example that the custodian had only $12 in cash in the fund plus the receipts as listed. The request for reimbursement would therefore be for $88, and the following entry would be made.

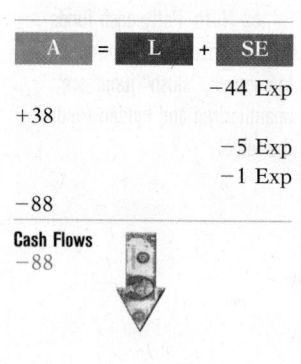

A = L + SE

−44 Exp
+38
−5 Exp
−1 Exp
−88

**Cash Flows**
−88

| Mar. 15 | Postage Expense | 44 | |
| | Supplies | 38 | |
| | Miscellaneous Expense | 5 | |
| | **Cash Over and Short** | 1 | |
| |     Cash | | 88 |
| |     (To replenish petty cash fund) | | |

Conversely, if the custodian had $14 in cash, the reimbursement request would be for $86, and Cash Over and Short would be credited for $1. A debit balance in Cash Over and Short is reported in the income statement as miscellaneous expense; a credit balance is reported as miscellaneous revenue. The company closes Cash Over and Short to Income Summary at the end of the year.

Companies should replenish a petty cash fund **at the end of the accounting period**, **regardless of the cash in the fund**. Replenishment at this time is necessary in order to recognize the effects of the petty cash payments on the financial statements.

Internal control over a petty cash fund is strengthened by (1) having a supervisor make surprise counts of the fund to ascertain whether the paid petty cash receipts and fund cash equal the designated amount, and (2) canceling or mutilating the paid petty cash receipts so they cannot be resubmitted for reimbursement.

# Summary of Study Objective for Appendix 7A

**9** **Explain the operation of a petty cash fund.** In operating a petty cash fund, a company establishes the fund by appointing a custodian and determining the size of the fund. The custodian makes payments from the fund for documented expenditures. The company replenishes the fund as needed, and at the end of each accounting period. Accounting entries to record payments are made each time the fund is replenished.

# Glossary

**Bank reconciliation** (p. 352) The process of comparing the bank's account balance with the company's balance, and explaining the differences to make them agree.

**Bank statement** (p. 352) A statement received monthly from the bank that shows the depositor's bank transactions and balances.

**Bonding** (p. 344) Obtaining insurance protection against theft by employees.

**Cash** (p. 358) Resources that consist of coins, currency, checks, money orders, and money on hand or on deposit in a bank or similar depository.

**Cash budget** (p. 362) A projection of anticipated cash flows, usually over a one- to two-year period.

**Cash equivalents** (p. 358) Short-term, highly liquid investments that can be readily converted to a specific amount of cash.

**Deposits in transit** (p. 354) Deposits recorded by the depositor that have not been recorded by the bank.

**Electronic funds transfer (EFT)** (p. 357) A disbursement system that uses wire, telephone, or computer to transfer cash from one location to another.

**Fraud** *(p. 336)* A dishonest act by an employee that results in personal benefit to the employee at a cost to the employer.

**Fraud triangle** *(p. 336)* The three factors that contribute to fraudulent activity by employees: opportunity, financial pressure, and rationalization.

**Internal auditors** *(p. 343)* Company employees who continuously evaluate the effectiveness of the company's internal control systems.

**Internal control** *(p. 337)* All the related methods and measures adopted within an organization to safeguard its assets and enhance the reliability of its accounting records, increase efficiency of operations, and ensure compliance with laws and regulations.

**NSF check** *(p. 353)* A check that is not paid by a bank because of insufficient funds in a bank account.

**Outstanding checks** *(p. 354)* Checks issued and recorded by a company that have not been paid by the bank.

**Petty cash fund** *(p. 351)* A cash fund used to pay relatively small amounts.

**Restricted cash** *(p. 359)* Cash that is not available for general use but instead is restricted for a particular purpose.

**Sarbanes-Oxley Act of 2002 (SOX)** *(p. 337)* Law that requires companies to maintain adequate systems of internal control.

**Treasurer** *(p. 360)* Employee responsible for the management of a company's cash.

**Voucher** *(p. 350)* An authorization form prepared for each expenditure in a voucher system.

**Voucher system** *(p. 349)* A network of approvals by authorized individuals, acting independently, to ensure that all disbursements by check are proper.

# Comprehensive Do it!

Trillo Company's bank statement for May 2012 shows these data.

| | | | |
|---|---|---|---|
| Balance May 1 | $12,650 | Balance May 31 | $14,280 |
| Debit memorandum: | | Credit memorandum: | |
| NSF check | 175 | Collection of note receivable | 505 |

The cash balance per books at May 31 is $13,319. Your review of the data reveals the following.

1. The NSF check was from Hup Co., a customer.
2. The note collected by the bank was a $500, 3-month, 12% note. The bank charged a $10 collection fee. No interest has been previously accrued.
3. Outstanding checks at May 31 total $2,410.
4. Deposits in transit at May 31 total $1,752.
5. A Trillo Company check for $352 dated May 10 cleared the bank on May 25. This check, which was a payment on account, was journalized for $325.

### Instructions

(a) Prepare a bank reconciliation at May 31.
(b) Journalize the entries required by the reconciliation.

### Solution to Comprehensive Do it!

(a)

| | | |
|---|---|---|
| Cash balance per bank statement | | $14,280 |
| Add: Deposits in transit | | 1,752 |
| | | 16,032 |
| Less: Outstanding checks | | 2,410 |
| Adjusted cash balance per bank | | $13,622 |
| Cash balance per books | | $13,319 |
| Add: Collection of note receivable $500, plus $15 interest less collection fee $10 | | 505 |
| | | 13,824 |
| Less: NSF check | $175 | |
| Error in recording check | 27 | 202 |
| Adjusted cash balance per books | | $13,622 |

### Action Plan

- Follow the four steps used in reconciling items (pp. 354–355).
- Work carefully to minimize mathematical errors in the reconciliation.
- Prepare entries based on reconciling items per books.
- Make sure the cash ledger balance after posting the reconciling entries agrees with the adjusted cash balance per books.

(b)

| | | | |
|---|---|---|---|
| May 31 | Cash | 505 | |
| | Miscellaneous Expense | 10 | |
| | Notes Receivable | | 500 |
| | Interest Revenue | | 15 |
| | (To record collection of note by bank) | | |
| 31 | Accounts Receivable—Hup Co. | 175 | |
| | Cash | | 175 |
| | (To record NSF check from Hup Co.) | | |
| 31 | Accounts Payable | 27 | |
| | Cash | | 27 |
| | (To correct error in recording check) | | |

the navigator

Self-Test, Brief Exercises, Exercises, Problem Set A, and many more resources are available for practice in WileyPLUS

*Note:* All Questions, Exercises, and Problems marked with an asterisk relate to material in the appendix to the chapter.

# Self-Test Questions

Answers are on page 392.

(SO 1) **1.** Which of the following is *not* an element of the fraud triangle?
  (a) Rationalization.
  (b) Financial pressure.
  (c) Segregation of duties.
  (d) Opportunity.

(SO 1) **2.** Internal control is used in a business to enhance the accuracy and reliability of its accounting records and to:
  (a) safeguard its assets.
  (b) create fraud.
  (c) analyze financial statements.
  (d) determine employee bonuses.

(SO 2) **3.** ◎━━━◎ The principles of internal control do *not* include:
  (a) establishment of responsibility.
  (b) documentation procedures.
  (c) financial performance measures.
  (d) independent internal verification.

(SO 2) **4.** Physical controls do *not* include:
  (a) safes and vaults to store cash.
  (b) independent bank reconciliations.
  (c) locked warehouses for inventories.
  (d) bank safety deposit boxes for important papers.

(SO 1) **5.** Which of the following was *not* a result of the Sarbanes-Oxley Act?
  (a) Companies must file financial statements with the Internal Revenue Service.
  (b) All publicly traded companies must maintain adequate internal controls.
  (c) The Public Company Accounting Oversight Board was created to establish auditing standards and regulate auditor activity.
  (d) Corporate executives and boards of directors must ensure that controls are reliable and effective, and they can be fined or imprisoned for failure to do so.

**6.** Permitting only designated personnel such as cashiers (SO 3) to handle cash receipts is an application of the principle of:
  (a) documentation procedures.
  (b) establishment of responsibility.
  (c) independent internal verification.
  (d) other controls.

**7.** The use of prenumbered checks in disbursing cash is (SO 4) an application of the principle of:
  (a) establishment of responsibility.
  (b) segregation of duties.
  (c) physical controls.
  (d) documentation procedures.

**8.** The control features of a bank account do *not* (SO 4) include:
  (a) having bank auditors verify the correctness of the bank balance per books.
  (b) minimizing the amount of cash that must be kept on hand.
  (c) providing a double record of all bank transactions.
  (d) safeguarding cash by using a bank as a depository.

**9.** Which of the following control activities is *not* rele- (SO 2) vant when a company uses a computerized (rather than manual) accounting system?
  (a) Establishment of responsibility.
  (b) Segregation of duties.
  (c) Independent internal verification.
  (d) All of these control activities are relevant to a computerized system.

**10.** In a bank reconciliation, deposits in transit are: (SO 5)
  (a) deducted from the book balance.
  (b) added to the book balance.
  (c) added to the bank balance.
  (d) deducted from the bank balance.

(SO 6)  11. Which of the following items in a cash drawer at November 30 is *not* cash?
  (a) Money orders.
  (b) Coins and currency.
  (c) A customer check dated December 1.
  (d) A customer check dated November 28.

(SO 6)  12.  Which statement correctly describes the reporting of cash?
  (a) Cash cannot be combined with cash equivalents.
  (b) Restricted cash funds may be combined with Cash.
  (c) Cash is listed first in the current assets section.
  (d) Restricted cash funds cannot be reported as a current asset.

(SO 7)  13. Which of the following would *not* be an example of good cash management?
  (a) Provide discounts to customers to encourage early payment.
  (b) Invest temporary excess cash in stock of a small company.
  (c) Carefully monitor payments so that payments are not made early.

  (d) Employ just-in-time inventory methods to keep inventory low.

14. Which of the following is *not* one of the sec-  (SO 8) tions of a cash budget?
  (a) Cash receipts section.
  (b) Cash disbursements section.
  (c) Financing section.
  (d) Cash from operations section.

*15. A check is written to replenish a $100 petty cash fund  (SO 9) when the fund contains receipts of $94 and $2 in cash. In recording the check:
  (a) Cash Over and Short should be debited for $4.
  (b) Petty Cash should be debited for $94.
  (c) Cash should be credited for $94.
  (d) Petty Cash should be credited for $4.

Go to the book's companion website, **www.wiley.com/college/kimmel**, to access additional Self-Test Questions.

# Questions

1. A local bank reported that it lost $150,000 as the result of employee fraud. Doug Steeber is not clear on what is meant by "employee fraud." Explain the meaning of fraud to Doug and give an example of fraud that might occur at a bank.

2. Fraud experts often say that there are three primary factors that contribute to employee fraud. Identify the three factors and explain what is meant by each.

3. Identify the five components of a good internal control system.

4. "Internal control is concerned only with enhancing the accuracy of the accounting records." Do you agree? Explain.

5. Discuss how the Sarbanes-Oxley Act has increased the importance of internal control to top managers of a company.

6. What principles of internal control apply to most businesses?

7. In the corner grocery store, all sales clerks make change out of one cash register drawer. Is this a violation of internal control? Why?

8. Graham Moran is reviewing the principle of segregation of duties. What are the two common applications of this principle?

9. How do documentation procedures contribute to good internal control?

10. What internal control objectives are met by physical controls?

11. (a) Explain the control principle of independent internal verification.
  (b) What practices are important in applying this principle?

12. As the company accountant, explain the following ideas to the management of Kovacic Company.
  (a) The concept of reasonable assurance in internal control.
  (b) The importance of the human factor in internal control.

13. Discuss the human resources department's involvement in internal controls.

14. Coggins Inc. owns the following assets at the balance sheet date.

| | |
|---|---|
| Cash in bank—savings account | $ 8,000 |
| Cash on hand | 1,100 |
| Cash refund due from the IRS | 1,000 |
| Checking account balance | 12,000 |
| Postdated checks | 500 |

What amount should be reported as Cash in the balance sheet?

15. What principle(s) of internal control is (are) involved in making daily cash counts of over-the-counter receipts?

16. Assume that Kohl's Department Stores installed new cash registers in its stores. How do cash registers improve internal control over cash receipts?

17. At Yorio Wholesale Company, two mail clerks open all mail receipts. How does this strengthen internal control?

18. "To have maximum effective internal control over cash disbursements, all payments should be made by check." Is this true? Explain.

19. Remsen Company's internal controls over cash disbursements provide for the treasurer to sign checks imprinted by a checkwriter after comparing the check

with the approved invoice. Identify the internal control principles that are present in these controls.

20. How do these principles apply to cash disbursements?
    (a) Physical controls.
    (b) Human resource controls.

21. What is the essential feature of an electronic funds transfer (EFT) procedure?

22. "The use of a bank contributes significantly to good internal control over cash." Is this true? Why?

23. Peter Dunn is confused about the lack of agreement between the cash balance per books and the balance per bank. Explain the causes for the lack of agreement to Peter and give an example of each cause.

24. ⚙━━⚙ Identify the basic principles of cash management.

25. Jennifer Earl asks your help concerning an NSF check. Explain to Jennifer (a) what an NSF check is, (b) how

it is treated in a bank reconciliation, and (c) whether it will require an adjusting entry on the company's books.

26. ⚙━━⚙
    (a) Describe cash equivalents and explain how they are reported.
    (b) How should restricted cash funds be reported on the balance sheet?

27. [Tootsie Roll] What was Tootsie Roll's balance in cash and cash equivalents at December 31, 2009? Did it report any restricted cash? How did Tootsie Roll define cash equivalents?

*28. (a) Identify the three activities that pertain to a petty cash fund, and indicate an internal control principle that is applicable to each activity.
    (b) When are journal entries required in the operation of a petty cash fund?

## Brief Exercises

*Identify fraud-triangle concepts.*
(SO 1), **C**

**BE7-1** Match each situation with the fraud triangle factor (opportunity, financial pressure, or rationalization) that best describes it.
(a) An employee's monthly credit card payments are nearly 75% of their monthly earnings.
(b) An employee earns minimum wage at a firm that has reported record earnings for each of the last five years.
(c) An employee has an expensive gambling habit.
(d) An employee has check writing and signing responsibilities for a small company, and is also responsible for reconciling the bank account.

*Explain the importance of internal control.*
(SO 2), **C** ⚙━━⚙

**BE7-2** Gwyn Wallander is the new owner of Bennett Co. She has heard about internal control but is not clear about its importance for her business. Explain to Gwyn the four purposes of internal control, and give her one application of each purpose for Bennett Co.

*Identify internal control principles.*
(SO 2), **C**

**BE7-3** The internal control procedures in Phillips Company make the following provisions. Identify the principles of internal control that are being followed in each case.
(a) Employees who have physical custody of assets do not have access to the accounting records.
(b) Each month the assets on hand are compared to the accounting records by an internal auditor.
(c) A prenumbered shipping document is prepared for each shipment of goods to customers.

*Identify the internal control principles applicable to cash receipts.*
(SO 3), **C**

**BE7-4** Aldstadt Company has the following internal control procedures over cash receipts. Identify the internal control principle that is applicable to each procedure.
(a) All over-the-counter receipts are registered on cash registers.
(b) All cashiers are bonded.
(c) Daily cash counts are made by cashier department supervisors.
(d) The duties of receiving cash, recording cash, and having custody of cash are assigned to different individuals.
(e) Only cashiers may operate cash registers.

*Make journal entry using cash count sheet.*
(SO 3), **AP**

**BE7-5** While examining cash receipts information, the accounting department determined the following information: opening cash balance $150, cash on hand $1,125.74, and cash sales per register tape $988.62. Prepare the required journal entry based upon the cash count sheet.

*Identify the internal control principles applicable to cash disbursements.*
(SO 4), **C**

**BE7-6** Ndon Company has the following internal control procedures over cash disbursements. Identify the internal control principle that is applicable to each procedure.
(a) Company checks are prenumbered.
(b) The bank statement is reconciled monthly by an internal auditor.

(c) Blank checks are stored in a safe in the treasurer's office.
(d) Only the treasurer or assistant treasurer may sign checks.
(e) Check signers are not allowed to record cash disbursement transactions.

**BE7-7** Jay Bauer is uncertain about the control features of a bank account. Explain the control benefits of (a) a checking account and (b) a bank statement.

*Identify the control features of a bank account.*
(SO 4), C

**BE7-8** The following reconciling items are applicable to the bank reconciliation for Gratz Co. Indicate how each item should be shown on a bank reconciliation.
(a) Outstanding checks.
(b) Bank debit memorandum for service charge.
(c) Bank credit memorandum for collecting a note for the depositor.
(d) Deposit in transit.

*Indicate location of reconciling items in a bank reconciliation.*
(SO 5), C

**BE7-9** Using the data in BE7-8, indicate (a) the items that will result in an adjustment to the depositor's records and (b) why the other items do not require adjustment.

*Identify reconciling items that require adjusting entries.*
(SO 5), C

**BE7-10** At July 31, Cisler Company has this bank information: cash balance per bank $7,291; outstanding checks $762; deposits in transit $1,350; and a bank service charge $40. Determine the adjusted cash balance per bank at July 31.

*Prepare partial bank reconciliation.*
(SO 5), AP

**BE7-11** In the month of November, Hasbrook Company Inc. wrote checks in the amount of $9,750. In December, checks in the amount of $11,762 were written. In November, $8,800 of these checks were presented to the bank for payment, and $10,889 in December. What is the amount of outstanding checks at the end of November? At the end of December?

*Analyze outstanding checks.*
(SO 5), AP

**BE7-12** Laib Company has these cash balances: cash in bank $12,742; payroll bank account $6,000; and plant expansion fund cash $25,000. Explain how each balance should be reported on the balance sheet.

*Explain the statement presentation of cash balances.*
(SO 6), C

**BE7-13** The following information is available for Eckman Company for the month of January: expected cash receipts $59,000; expected cash disbursements $67,000; and cash balance on January 1, $12,000. Management wishes to maintain a minimum cash balance of $9,000. Prepare a basic cash budget for the month of January.

*Prepare a cash budget.*
(SO 8), AP

*BE7-14** On March 20, Palasz's petty cash fund of $100 is replenished when the fund contains $19 in cash and receipts for postage $40, supplies $26, and travel expense $15. Prepare the journal entry to record the replenishment of the petty cash fund.

*Prepare entry to replenish a petty cash fund.*
(SO 9), AP

# Do it! Review

**Do it! 7-1** Identify which control activity is violated in each of the following situations, and explain how the situation creates an opportunity for fraud or inappropriate accounting practices.
1. Once a month, the sales department sends sales invoices to the accounting department to be recorded.
2. Greg Mursky orders merchandise for Ross Company; he also receives merchandise and authorizes payment for merchandise.
3. Several clerks at Terando's Groceries use the same cash register drawer.

*Identify violations of control activities.*
(SO 2), C

**Do it! 7-2** Mark Graziano is concerned with control over mail receipts at Grazi's Sporting Goods. All mail receipts are opened by Glen Schrag. Glen sends the checks to the accounting department, where they are stamped "For Deposit Only." The accounting department records and deposits the mail receipts weekly. Mark asks your help in installing a good system of internal control over mail receipts.

*Design system of internal control over cash receipts.*
(SO 3), C

**Do it! 7-3** Leon Holzner owns Leon Blankets. Leon asks you to explain how he should treat the following reconciling items when reconciling the company's bank account.
1. Outstanding checks
2. A deposit in transit
3. The bank charged to our account a check written by another company
4. A debit memorandum for a bank service charge

*Explain treatment of items in bank reconciliation.*
(SO 5), K

*Prepare a cash budget.*
*(SO 8),* **AP**

**Do it!** 7-4 Ross Corporation's management wants to maintain a minimum monthly cash balance of $8,000. At the beginning of September, the cash balance is $12,270; expected cash receipts for September are $97,200; cash disbursements are expected to be $115,000. How much cash, if any, must Ross borrow to maintain the desired minimum monthly balance? Determine your answer by using the basic form of the cash budget.

# Exercises

*Identify the principles of internal control.*
*(SO 2),* **C**

**E7-1** Bank employees use a system known as the "maker-checker" system. An employee will record an entry in the appropriate journal, and then a supervisor will verify and approve the entry. These days, as all of a bank's accounts are computerized, the employee first enters a batch of entries into the computer, and then the entries are posted automatically to the general ledger account after the supervisor approves them on the system.

Access to the computer system is password-protected and task-specific, which means that the computer system will not allow the employee to approve a transaction or the supervisor to record a transaction.

**Instructions**
Identify the principles of internal control inherent in the "maker-checker" procedure used by banks.

*Identify the principles of internal control.*
*(SO 2),* **C**

**E7-2** Lisa's Pizza operates strictly on a carryout basis. Customers pick up their orders at a counter where a clerk exchanges the pizza for cash. While at the counter, the customer can see other employees making the pizzas and the large ovens in which the pizzas are baked.

**Instructions**
Identify the six principles of internal control and give an example of each principle that you might observe when picking up your pizza. (*Note:* It may not be possible to observe all the principles.)

*List internal control weaknesses over cash receipts and suggest improvements.*
*(SO 2, 3),* **E**

**E7-3** The following control procedures are used in Danner Company for over-the-counter cash receipts.
1. Cashiers are experienced; thus, they are not bonded.
2. All over-the-counter receipts are registered by three clerks who share a cash register with a single cash drawer.
3. To minimize the risk of robbery, cash in excess of $100 is stored in an unlocked attaché case in the stock room until it is deposited in the bank.
4. At the end of each day the total receipts are counted by the cashier on duty and reconciled to the cash register total.
5. The company accountant makes the bank deposit and then records the day's receipts.

**Instructions**
(a) For each procedure, explain the weakness in internal control and identify the control principle that is violated.
(b) For each weakness, suggest a change in the procedure that will result in good internal control.

*List internal control weaknesses for cash disbursements and suggest improvements.*
*(SO 2, 4),* **E**

**E7-4** The following control procedures are used in Katja's Boutique Shoppe for cash disbursements.
1. Each week, Katja leaves 100 company checks in an unmarked envelope on a shelf behind the cash register.
2. The store manager personally approves all payments before signing and issuing checks.
3. The company checks are unnumbered.
4. After payment, bills are "filed" in a paid invoice folder.
5. The company accountant prepares the bank reconciliation and reports any discrepancies to the owner.

**Instructions**
(a) For each procedure, explain the weakness in internal control and identify the internal control principle that is violated.
(b) For each weakness, suggest a change in the procedure that will result in good internal control.

**E7-5**   At Reyes Company, checks are not prenumbered because both the purchasing agent and the treasurer are authorized to issue checks. Each signer has access to unissued checks kept in an unlocked file cabinet. The purchasing agent pays all bills pertaining to goods purchased for resale. Prior to payment, the purchasing agent determines that the goods have been received and verifies the mathematical accuracy of the vendor's invoice. After payment, the invoice is filed by vendor and the purchasing agent records the payment in the cash disbursements journal. The treasurer pays all other bills following approval by authorized employees. After payment, the treasurer stamps all bills "paid," files them by payment date, and records the checks in the cash disbursements journal. Reyes Company maintains one checking account that is reconciled by the treasurer.

*Identify internal control weaknesses for cash disbursements and suggest improvements.*

*(SO 2, 4),* **E**

**Instructions**
(a) List the weaknesses in internal control over cash disbursements.
(b) Identify improvements for correcting these weaknesses.

**E7-6**   Tasha Orin is unable to reconcile the bank balance at January 31. Tasha's reconciliation is shown here.

*Prepare bank reconciliation and adjusting entries.*

*(SO 5),* **AP**

| | |
|---|---:|
| Cash balance per bank | $3,677.20 |
| Add: NSF check | 450.00 |
| Less: Bank service charge | 28.00 |
| Adjusted balance per bank | $4,099.20 |
| Cash balance per books | $3,975.20 |
| Less: Deposits in transit | 590.00 |
| Add: Outstanding checks | 770.00 |
| Adjusted balance per books | $4,155.20 |

**Instructions**
(a) What is the proper adjusted cash balance per bank?
(b) What is the proper adjusted cash balance per books?
(c) Prepare the adjusting journal entries necessary to determine the adjusted cash balance per books.

**E7-7**   At April 30, the bank reconciliation of Silvestre Company shows three outstanding checks: No. 254 $650, No. 255 $700, and No. 257 $410. The May bank statement and the May cash payments journal are given here.

*Determine outstanding checks.*

*(SO 5),* **AP**

| Bank Statement Checks Paid | | | | Cash Payments Journal Checks Issued | | |
|---|---|---|---|---|---|---|
| **Date** | **Check No.** | **Amount** | | **Date** | **Check No.** | **Amount** |
| 5-4 | 254 | $650 | | 5-2 | 258 | $159 |
| 5-2 | 257 | 410 | | 5-5 | 259 | 275 |
| 5-17 | 258 | 159 | | 5-10 | 260 | 925 |
| 5-12 | 259 | 275 | | 5-15 | 261 | 500 |
| 5-20 | 260 | 925 | | 5-22 | 262 | 750 |
| 5-29 | 263 | 480 | | 5-24 | 263 | 480 |
| 5-30 | 262 | 750 | | 5-29 | 264 | 360 |

**Instructions**
Using step 2 in the reconciliation procedure (see page 354), list the outstanding checks at May 31.

**E7-8**   The following information pertains to Ghose Company.
1. Cash balance per bank, July 31, $7,328.
2. July bank service charge not recorded by the depositor $38.
3. Cash balance per books, July 31, $7,364.
4. Deposits in transit, July 31, $2,700.
5. Note for $2,000 collected for Ghose in July by the bank, plus interest $36 less fee $20. The collection has not been recorded by Ghose, and no interest has been accrued.
6. Outstanding checks, July 31, $686.

*Prepare bank reconciliation and adjusting entries.*

*(SO 5),* **AP**

**Instructions**
(a) Prepare a bank reconciliation at July 31, 2012.
(b) Journalize the adjusting entries at July 31 on the books of Ghose Company.

*Prepare bank reconciliation and adjusting entries.*
(SO 5), **AP**

**E7-9** This information relates to the Cash account in the ledger of Hawkins Company.

Balance September 1—$16,400; Cash deposited—$64,000
Balance September 30—$17,600; Checks written—$62,800

The September bank statement shows a balance of $16,500 at September 30 and the following memoranda.

| Credits | | Debits | |
|---|---|---|---|
| Collection of $1,800 note plus interest $30 | $1,830 | NSF check: H. Juno | $560 |
| Interest earned on checking account | 45 | Safety deposit box rent | 60 |

At September 30, deposits in transit were $4,738 and outstanding checks totaled $2,383.

**Instructions**
(a) Prepare the bank reconciliation at September 30, 2012.
(b) Prepare the adjusting entries at September 30, assuming (1) the NSF check was from a customer on account, and (2) no interest had been accrued on the note.

*Compute deposits in transit and outstanding checks for two bank reconciliations.*
(SO 5), **AP**

**E7-10** The cash records of Arora Company show the following.

For July:

1. The June 30 bank reconciliation indicated that deposits in transit total $580. During July, the general ledger account Cash shows deposits of $16,900, but the bank statement indicates that only $15,600 in deposits were received during the month.
2. The June 30 bank reconciliation also reported outstanding checks of $940. During the month of July, Arora Company books show that $17,500 of checks were issued, yet the bank statement showed that $16,400 of checks cleared the bank in July.

For September:

3. In September, deposits per bank statement totaled $25,900, deposits per books were $26,400, and deposits in transit at September 30 were $2,200.
4. In September, cash disbursements per books were $23,500, checks clearing the bank were $24,000, and outstanding checks at September 30 were $2,100.

There were no bank debit or credit memoranda, and no errors were made by either the bank or Arora Company.

**Instructions**
Answer the following questions.
(a) In situation 1, what were the deposits in transit at July 31?
(b) In situation 2, what were the outstanding checks at July 31?
(c) In situation 3, what were the deposits in transit at August 31?
(d) In situation 4, what were the outstanding checks at August 31?

*Prepare bank reconciliation and adjusting entries.*
(SO 5), **AP**

**E7-11** Mazor Inc.'s bank statement from Hometown Bank at August 31, 2012, gives the following information.

| | | | | |
|---|---|---|---|---|
| Balance, August 1 | $18,400 | Bank debit memorandum: | | |
| August deposits | 71,000 | Safety deposit box fee | $ | 25 |
| Checks cleared in August | 68,678 | Service charge | | 50 |
| Bank credit memorandum: | | Balance, August 31 | | 20,692 |
| Interest earned | 45 | | | |

A summary of the Cash account in the ledger for August shows the following: balance, August 1, $18,700; receipts $74,000; disbursements $73,570; and balance, August 31, $19,130. Analysis reveals that the only reconciling items on the July 31 bank reconciliation were a deposit in transit for $4,800 and outstanding checks of $4,500. In addition, you determine that there was an error involving a company check drawn in August: A check for $400 to a creditor on account that cleared the bank in August was journalized and posted for $40.

**Instructions**
(a) Determine deposits in transit.
(b) Determine outstanding checks. (*Hint:* You need to correct disbursements for the check error.)
(c) Prepare a bank reconciliation at August 31.
(d) Journalize the adjusting entry(ies) to be made by Mazor Inc. at August 31.

*Identify reporting of cash.*
(SO 6), **AP**

**E7-12** A new accountant at Netzloff Inc. is trying to identify which of the amounts shown on page 377 should be reported as the current asset "Cash and cash equivalents" in the year-end balance sheet, as of April 30, 2012.

1. $60 of currency and coin in a locked box used for incidental cash transactions.
2. A $10,000 U.S. Treasury bill, due May 31, 2012.
3. $260 of April-dated checks that Netzloff has received from customers but not yet deposited.
4. An $85 check received from a customer in payment of its April account, but post-dated to May 1.
5. $2,500 in the company's checking account.
6. $4,800 in its savings account.
7. $75 of prepaid postage in its postage meter.
8. A $25 IOU from the company receptionist.

### Instructions
(a) What balance should Netzloff report as its "Cash and cash equivalents" balance at April 30, 2012?
(b) In what account(s) and in what financial statement(s) should the items not included in "Cash and cash equivalents" be reported?

**E7-13** Amster, Lasca, and Vang, three law students who have joined together to open a law practice, are struggling to manage their cash flow. They haven't yet built up sufficient clientele and revenues to support their legal practice's ongoing costs. Initial costs, such as advertising, renovations to their premises, and the like, all result in outgoing cash flow at a time when little is coming in. Amster, Lasca, and Vang haven't had time to establish a billing system since most of their clients' cases haven't yet reached the courts, and the lawyers didn't think it would be right to bill them until "results were achieved."

*Review cash management practices.*

(SO 7), **C**

Unfortunately, Amster, Lasca, and Vang's suppliers don't feel the same way. Their suppliers expect them to pay their accounts payable within a few days of receiving their bills. So far, there hasn't even been enough money to pay the three lawyers, and they are not sure how long they can keep practicing law without getting some money into their pockets.

### Instructions
Can you provide any suggestions for Amster, Lasca, and Vang to improve their cash management practices?

**E7-14** Merrick Company expects to have a cash balance of $46,000 on January 1, 2012. These are the relevant monthly budget data for the first two months of 2012.
1. Collections from customers: January $71,000, February $146,000
2. Payments to suppliers: January $40,000, February $75,000
3. Wages: January $30,000, February $40,000. Wages are paid in the month they are incurred.
4. Administrative expenses: January $21,000, February $24,000. These costs include depreciation of $1,000 per month. All other costs are paid as incurred.
5. Selling expenses: January $15,000, February $20,000. These costs are exclusive of depreciation. They are paid as incurred.
6. Sales of short-term investments in January are expected to realize $12,000 in cash. Merrick has a line of credit at a local bank that enables it to borrow up to $25,000. The company wants to maintain a minimum monthly cash balance of $20,000.

*Prepare a cash budget for two months.*

(SO 8), **AP**

### Instructions
Prepare a cash budget for January and February.

**\*E7-15** During October, Central Light Company experiences the following transactions in establishing a petty cash fund.

*Prepare journal entries for a petty cash fund.*

(SO 9), **AP**

| | | |
|---|---|---|
| Oct. | 1 | A petty cash fund is established with a check for $150 issued to the petty cash custodian. |
| | 31 | A check was written to reimburse the fund and increase the fund to $200. A count of the petty cash fund disclosed the following items: |

|  |  |
|---|---|
| Currency | $59.00 |
| Coins | 0.70 |
| Expenditure receipts (vouchers): | |
|     Supplies | $26.10 |
|     Telephone, Internet, and fax | 16.40 |
|     Postage | 39.70 |
|     Freight-out | 6.80 |

*Journalize and post petty cash fund transactions.*
(SO 9), **AP**

**Instructions**
Journalize the entries in October that pertain to the petty cash fund.

*\*E7-16* Paik Company maintains a petty cash fund for small expenditures. These transactions occurred during the month of August.

Aug.   1   Established the petty cash fund by writing a check on Westown Bank for $200.

15   Replenished the petty cash fund by writing a check for $175. On this date, the fund consisted of $25 in cash and these petty cash receipts: freight-out $74.40, entertainment expense $36, postage expense $33.70 and miscellaneous expense $27.50.

16   Increased the amount of the petty cash fund to $400 by writing a check for $200.

31   Replenished the petty cash fund by writing a check for $283. On this date, the fund consisted of $117 in cash and these petty cash receipts: postage expense $145, entertainment expense $90.60, and freight-out $46.40.

**Instructions**
(a)  Journalize the petty cash transactions.
(b)  Post to the Petty Cash account.
(c)  What internal control features exist in a petty cash fund?

# Exercises: Set B and Challenge Exercises

Visit the book's companion website, at **www.wiley.com/college/kimmel**, and choose the Student Companion site to access Exercise Set B and Challenge Exercises.

# Problems: Set A

*Identify internal control weaknesses for cash receipts.*
(SO 2, 3), **C**

**P7-1A**   Classic Theater is in the Greenbelt Mall. A cashier's booth is located near the entrance to the theater. Two cashiers are employed. One works from 1:00 to 5:00 P.M., the other from 5:00 to 9:00 P.M. Each cashier is bonded. The cashiers receive cash from customers and operate a machine that ejects serially numbered tickets. The rolls of tickets are inserted and locked into the machine by the theater manager at the beginning of each cashier's shift.

After purchasing a ticket, the customer takes the ticket to a doorperson stationed at the entrance of the theater lobby some 60 feet from the cashier's booth. The doorperson tears the ticket in half, admits the customer, and returns the ticket stub to the customer. The other half of the ticket is dropped into a locked box by the doorperson.

At the end of each cashier's shift, the theater manager removes the ticket rolls from the machine and makes a cash count. The cash count sheet is initialed by the cashier. At the end of the day, the manager deposits the receipts in total in a bank night deposit vault located in the mall. In addition, the manager sends copies of the deposit slip and the initialed cash count sheets to the theater company treasurer for verification and to the company's accounting department. Receipts from the first shift are stored in a safe located in the manager's office.

**Instructions**
(a)  Identify the internal control principles and their application to the cash receipts transactions of Classic Theater.
(b)  If the doorperson and cashier decided to collaborate to misappropriate cash, what actions might they take?

*Identify internal control weaknesses in cash receipts and cash disbursements.*
(SO 2, 3, 4), **C**

**P7-2A**   Nature Hill Middle School wants to raise money for a new sound system for its auditorium. The primary fund-raising event is a dance at which the famous disc jockey Jay Dee will play classic and not-so-classic dance tunes. Barry Cameron, the music and theater instructor, has been given the responsibility for coordinating the fund-raising efforts. This is Barry's first experience with fund-raising. He decides to put the eighth-grade choir in charge of the event; he will be a relatively passive observer.

Barry had 500 unnumbered tickets printed for the dance. He left the tickets in a box on his desk and told the choir students to take as many tickets as they thought they could sell for $5 each. In order to ensure that no extra tickets would be floating around, he told them to dispose of any unsold tickets. When the students received payment for the tickets, they were to bring the cash back to Barry, and he would put it in a locked box in his desk drawer.

Some of the students were responsible for decorating the gymnasium for the dance. Barry gave each of them a key to the money box and told them that if they took money out to purchase materials, they should put a note in the box saying how much they took and what it was used for. After two weeks, the money box appeared to be getting full, so Barry asked Robin Herbert to count the money, prepare a deposit slip, and deposit the money in a bank account Barry had opened.

The day of the dance, Barry wrote a check from the account to pay Jay Dee. The DJ said, however, that he accepted only cash and did not give receipts. So Barry took $200 out of the cash box and gave it to Jay. At the dance, Barry had Amy Kuether working at the entrance to the gymnasium, collecting tickets from students and selling tickets to those who had not pre-purchased them. Barry estimated that 400 students attended the dance.

The following day, Barry closed out the bank account, which had $250 in it, and gave that amount plus the $180 in the cash box to Principal Skinner. Principal Skinner seemed surprised that, after generating roughly $2,000 in sales, the dance netted only $430 in cash. Barry did not know how to respond.

### Instructions
Identify as many internal control weaknesses as you can in this scenario, and suggest how each could be addressed.

**P7-3A** On July 31, 2012, Fraiser Company had a cash balance per books of $6,140. The statement from Nashota State Bank on that date showed a balance of $7,690.80. A comparison of the bank statement with the Cash account revealed the following facts.

*Prepare a bank reconciliation and adjusting entries.*
*(SO 5),* **AP**

1. The bank service charge for July was $25.

2. The bank collected a note receivable of $1,500 for Fraiser Company on July 15, plus $30 of interest. The bank made a $10 charge for the collection. Fraiser has not accrued any interest on the note.

3. The July 31 receipts of $1,193.30 were not included in the bank deposits for July. These receipts were deposited by the company in a night deposit vault on July 31.

4. Company check No. 2480 issued to T. Crain, a creditor, for $384 that cleared the bank in July was incorrectly entered in the cash payments journal on July 10 for $348.

5. Checks outstanding on July 31 totaled $1,860.10.

6. On July 31, the bank statement showed an NSF charge of $575 for a check received by the company from K. Fonner, a customer, on account.

### Instructions
(a) Prepare the bank reconciliation as of July 31.
(b) Prepare the necessary adjusting entries at July 31.

*(a) Cash bal.  $7,024.00*

**P7-4A** The bank portion of the bank reconciliation for Horsman Company at October 31, 2012, is shown here and on the next page.

*Prepare a bank reconciliation and adjusting entries from detailed data.*
*(SO 5),* **AP**

**HORSMAN COMPANY**
**Bank Reconciliation**
**October 31, 2012**

| | |
|---|---:|
| Cash balance per bank | $12,367.90 |
| Add: Deposits in transit | 1,530.20 |
| | 13,898.10 |

Less: Outstanding checks

| Check Number | Check Amount | |
|---|---|---|
| 2451 | $ 1,260.40 | |
| 2470 | 684.20 | |
| 2471 | 844.50 | |
| 2472 | 426.80 | |
| 2474 | 1,050.00 | 4,265.90 |
| Adjusted cash balance per bank | | $ 9,632.20 |

The adjusted cash balance per bank agreed with the cash balance per books at October 31. The November bank statement showed the following checks and deposits.

**Bank Statement**

| | Checks | | | Deposits | |
|---|---|---|---|---|---|
| **Date** | **Number** | **Amount** | **Date** | **Amount** | |
| 11-1 | 2470 | $ 684.20 | 11-1 | $ 1,530.20 | |
| 11-2 | 2471 | 844.50 | 11-4 | 1,211.60 | |
| 11-5 | 2474 | 1,050.00 | 11-8 | 990.10 | |
| 11-4 | 2475 | 1,640.70 | 11-13 | 2,575.00 | |
| 11-8 | 2476 | 2,830.00 | 11-18 | 1,472.70 | |
| 11-10 | 2477 | 600.00 | 11-21 | 2,945.00 | |
| 11-15 | 2479 | 1,750.00 | 11-25 | 2,567.30 | |
| 11-18 | 2480 | 1,330.00 | 11-28 | 1,650.00 | |
| 11-27 | 2481 | 695.40 | 11-30 | 1,186.00 | |
| 11-30 | 2483 | 575.50 | Total | $16,127.90 | |
| 11-29 | 2486 | 940.00 | | | |
| | Total | $12,940.30 | | | |

The cash records per books for November showed the following.

**Cash Payments Journal**

| Date | Number | Amount | Date | Number | Amount |
|---|---|---|---|---|---|
| 11-1 | 2475 | $1,640.70 | 11-20 | 2483 | $ 575.50 |
| 11-2 | 2476 | 2,830.00 | 11-22 | 2484 | 829.50 |
| 11-2 | 2477 | 600.00 | 11-23 | 2485 | 974.80 |
| 11-4 | 2478 | 538.20 | 11-24 | 2486 | 940.00 |
| 11-8 | 2479 | 1,705.00 | 11-29 | 2487 | 398.00 |
| 11-10 | 2480 | 1,330.00 | 11-30 | 2488 | 800.00 |
| 11-15 | 2481 | 695.40 | Total | | $14,469.10 |
| 11-18 | 2482 | 612.00 | | | |

**Cash Receipts Journal**

| Date | Amount |
|---|---|
| 11-3 | $ 1,211.60 |
| 11-7 | 990.10 |
| 11-12 | 2,575.00 |
| 11-17 | 1,472.70 |
| 11-20 | 2,954.00 |
| 11-24 | 2,567.30 |
| 11-27 | 1,650.00 |
| 11-29 | 1,186.00 |
| 11-30 | 1,304.00 |
| Total | $15,910.70 |

The bank statement contained two bank memoranda:

1. A credit of $2,242 for the collection of a $2,100 note for Horsman Company plus interest of $157 and less a collection fee of $15. Horsman Company has not accrued any interest on the note.

2. A debit for the printing of additional company checks $85.

At November 30, the cash balance per books was $11,073.80 and the cash balance per bank statement was $17,712.50. The bank did not make any errors, but **Horsman Company made two errors.**

*Instructions*
(a) Using the four steps in the reconciliation procedure described on pages 354–355, prepare a bank reconciliation at November 30, 2012.
(b) Prepare the adjusting entries based on the reconciliation. (*Note:* The correction of any errors pertaining to recording checks should be made to Accounts Payable. The correction of any errors relating to recording cash receipts should be made to Accounts Receivable.)

(a) Cash bal.  $13,176.80

**P7-5A**   Stromberg Company of Zwingle, Kansas, spreads herbicides and applies liquid fertilizer for local farmers. On May 31, 2012, the company's Cash account per its general ledger showed a balance of $6,738.90.

*Prepare a bank reconciliation and adjusting entries.*
(SO 5), **AP**

The bank statement from Zwingle State Bank on that date showed the following balance.

**ZWINGLE STATE BANK**

| Checks and Debits | Deposits and Credits | Daily Balance |
|---|---|---|
| XXX | XXX | 5-31  6,968.00 |

A comparison of the details on the bank statement with the details in the Cash account revealed the following facts.

1. The statement included a debit memo of $40 for the printing of additional company checks.
2. Cash sales of $883.15 on May 12 were deposited in the bank. The cash receipts journal entry and the deposit slip were incorrectly made for $933.15. The bank credited Stromberg Company for the correct amount.
3. Outstanding checks at May 31 totaled $276.25, and deposits in transit were $1,880.15.
4. On May 18, the company issued check No. 1181 for $685 to M. Dornbos, on account. The check, which cleared the bank in May, was incorrectly journalized and posted by Stromberg Company for $658.
5. A $2,600 note receivable was collected by the bank for Stromberg Company on May 31 plus $110 interest. The bank charged a collection fee of $20. No interest has been accrued on the note.
6. Included with the cancelled checks was a check issued by Strongberg Company to P. Jordan for $360 that was incorrectly charged to Stromberg Company by the bank.
7. On May 31, the bank statement showed an NSF charge of $380 for a check issued by Bev Fountain, a customer, to Stromberg Company on account.

*Instructions*
(a) Prepare the bank reconciliation at May 31, 2012.
(b) Prepare the necessary adjusting entries for Stromberg Company at May 31, 2012.

(a) Cash bal.  $8,931.90

**P7-6A**   You are provided with the following information taken from Washburne Inc.'s March 31, 2012, balance sheet.

*Prepare a cash budget.*
(SO 8), **AP**

| | |
|---|---|
| Cash | $ 11,000 |
| Accounts receivable | 20,000 |
| Inventory | 36,000 |
| Property, plant, and equipment, net of depreciation | 120,000 |
| Accounts payable | 22,400 |
| Common stock | 150,000 |
| Retained earnings | 11,600 |

Additional information concerning Washburne Inc. is as follows.

1. Gross profit is 25% of sales.
2. Actual and budgeted sales data:

| March (actual) | $46,000 |
|---|---|
| April (budgeted) | 70,000 |

3. Sales are both cash and credit. Cash collections expected in April are:

| | | |
|---|---|---|
| March | $18,400 | (40% of $46,000) |
| April | 42,000 | (60% of $70,000) |
| | $60,400 | |

4. Half of a month's purchases are paid for in the month of purchase and half in the following month. Cash disbursements expected in April are:

| | | |
|---|---|---|
| Purchases March | $22,400 | |
| Purchases April | 28,100 | |
| | $50,500 | |

5. Cash operating costs are anticipated to be $11,200 for the month of April.

6. Equipment costing $2,500 will be purchased for cash in April.

7. The company wishes to maintain a minimum cash balance of $9,000. An open line of credit is available at the bank. All borrowing is done at the beginning of the month, and all repayments are made at the end of the month. The interest rate is 12% per year, and interest expense is accrued at the end of the month and paid in the following month.

**Instructions**

*Apr. borrowings $1,800*

Prepare a cash budget for the month of April. Determine how much cash Washburne Inc. must borrow, or can repay, in April.

*Prepare a cash budget.*
*(SO 8),* **AP**

**P7-7A** Austin Corporation prepares monthly cash budgets. Here are relevant data from operating budgets for 2012.

| | January | February |
|---|---|---|
| Sales | $360,000 | $400,000 |
| Purchases | 120,000 | 130,000 |
| Salaries | 84,000 | 81,000 |
| Administrative expenses | 72,000 | 75,000 |
| Selling expenses | 79,000 | 88,000 |

All sales and purchases are on account. Budgeted collections and disbursement data are given below. All other expenses are paid in the month incurred except for administrative expenses, which include $1,000 of depreciation per month.

Other data.

1. Collections from customers: January $326,000; February $378,000.

2. Payments for purchases: January $110,000; February $135,000.

3. Other receipts: January: collection of December 31, 2011, notes receivable $15,000; February: proceeds from sale of securities $4,000.

4. Other disbursements: February $10,000 cash dividend.

The company's cash balance on January 1, 2012, is expected to be $46,000. The company wants to maintain a minimum cash balance of $40,000.

**Instructions**

*Jan. 31 cash bal.    $ 43,000*

Prepare a cash budget for January and February.

*Prepare a comprehensive*
*bank reconciliation with*
*theft and internal control*
*deficiencies.*
*(SO 2, 3, 4, 5),* **E**

**P7-8A** Fetter Company is a very profitable small business. It has not, however, given much consideration to internal control. For example, in an attempt to keep clerical and office expenses to a minimum, the company has combined the jobs of cashier and book-keeper. As a result, Allan Donay handles all cash receipts, keeps the accounting records, and prepares the monthly bank reconciliations.

The balance per the bank statement on October 31, 2012, was $18,380. Outstanding checks were: No. 62 for $140.75, No. 183 for $180, No. 284 for $253.25, No. 862 for $190.71, No. 863 for $226.80, and No. 864 for $165.28. Included with the statement was a credit memorandum of $185 indicating the collection of a note receivable for Fetter Company by the bank on October 25. This memorandum has not been recorded by Fetter.

The company's ledger showed one Cash account with a balance of $21,877.72. The balance included undeposited cash on hand. Because of the lack of internal controls, Allan took for personal use all of the undeposited receipts in excess of $3,795.51. He then prepared the following bank reconciliation in an effort to conceal his theft of cash.

| | | |
|---|---:|---:|
| Cash balance per books, October 31 | | $21,877.72 |
| Add: Outstanding checks | | |
| No. 862 | $190.71 | |
| No. 863 | 226.80 | |
| No. 864 | 165.28 | 482.79 |
| | | 22,360.51 |
| Less: Undeposited receipts | | 3,795.51 |
| Unadjusted balance per bank, October 31 | | 18,565.00 |
| Less: Bank credit memorandum | | 185.00 |
| Cash balance per bank statement, October 31 | | $18,380.00 |

**Instructions**

(a) Prepare a correct bank reconciliation. (*Hint:* Deduct the amount of the theft from the adjusted balance per books.)

(a) Cash bal. $21,018.72

(b) Indicate the three ways that Allan attempted to conceal the theft and the dollar amount involved in each method.

(c) What principles of internal control were violated in this case?

# Problems: Set B

**P7-1B**   Erin Company recently changed its system of internal control over cash disbursements. The system includes the following features.

*Identify internal control principles for cash disbursements.*

(SO 2, 4), **C**

1. Instead of being unnumbered and manually prepared, all checks must now be prenumbered and written by using the new checkwriter purchased by the company.

2. Before a check can be issued, each invoice must have the approval of Karen Noonan, the purchasing agent, and Tom Fah, the receiving department supervisor.

3. Checks must be signed by either Carl Merfeld, the treasurer, or Bonnie Kurt, the assistant treasurer. Before signing a check, the signer is expected to compare the amounts of the check with the amounts on the invoice.

4. After signing a check, the signer stamps the invoice "paid" and inserts within the stamp, the date, check number, and amount of the check. The "paid" invoice is then sent to the accounting department for recording.

5. Blank checks are stored in a safe in the treasurer's office. The combination to the safe is known by only the treasurer and assistant treasurer.

6. Each month the bank statement is reconciled with the bank balance per books by the assistant chief accountant.

7. All employees who handle or account for cash are bonded.

**Instructions**

Identify the internal control principles and their application to cash disbursements of Erin Company.

**P7-2B**   The board of trustees of a local church is concerned about the internal accounting controls pertaining to the offering collections made at weekly services. They ask you to serve on a three-person audit team with the internal auditor of a local university and a CPA who has just joined the church. At a meeting of the audit team and the board of trustees, you learn the following.

*Identify internal control weaknesses in cash receipts.*

(SO 2, 3), **C**

1. The church's board of trustees has delegated responsibility for the financial management and audit of the financial records to the finance committee. This group prepares

the annual budget and approves major disbursements but is not involved in collections or recordkeeping. No audit has been made in recent years because the same trusted employee has kept church records and served as financial secretary for 15 years. The church does not carry any fidelity insurance.

2. The collection at the weekly service is taken by a team of ushers who volunteer to serve for 1 month. The ushers take the collection plates to a basement office at the rear of the church. They hand their plates to the head usher and return to the church service. After all plates have been turned in, the head usher counts the cash received. The head usher then places the cash in the church safe along with a notation of the amount counted. The head usher volunteers to serve for 3 months.

3. The next morning, the financial secretary opens the safe and recounts the collection. The secretary withholds $150–$200 in cash, depending on the cash expenditures expected for the week, and deposits the remainder of the collections in the bank. To facilitate the deposit, church members who contribute by check are asked to make their checks payable to "Cash."

4. Each month, the financial secretary reconciles the bank statement and submits a copy of the reconciliation to the board of trustees. The reconciliations have rarely contained any bank errors and have never shown any errors per books.

**Instructions**
(a) Indicate the weaknesses in internal accounting control in the handling of collections.
(b) List the improvements in internal control procedures that you plan to make at the next meeting of the audit team for (1) the ushers, (2) the head usher, (3) the financial secretary, and (4) the finance committee.
(c) What church policies should be changed to improve internal control?

*Prepare a bank reconciliation and adjusting entries.*
(SO 5), **AP**

**P7-3B**  On May 31, 2012, Laban Company had a cash balance per books of $5,681.50. The bank statement from Citizens Bank on that date showed a balance of $7,964.60. A comparison of the statement with the Cash account revealed the following facts.

1. The statement included a debit memo of $70 for the printing of additional company checks.

2. Cash sales of $786.15 on May 12 were deposited in the bank. The cash receipts journal entry and the deposit slip were incorrectly made for $796.15. The bank credited Laban Company for the correct amount.

3. Outstanding checks at May 31 totaled $1,106.25, and deposits in transit were $799.15.

4. On May 18, the company issued check No. 1181 for $685 to A. Hawkins, on account. The check, which cleared the bank in May, was incorrectly journalized and posted by Laban Company for $658.

5. A $2,500 note receivable was collected by the bank for Laban Company on May 31 plus $80 interest. The bank charged a collection fee of $42. No interest has been accrued on the note.

6. Included with the cancelled checks was a check issued by Logan Company to D. Reyes for $290 that was incorrectly charged to Laban Company by the bank.

7. On May 31, the bank statement showed an NSF charge of $165 for a check issued by G. Verdier, a customer, to Laban Company on account.

**Instructions**
(a) Cash bal. $7,947.50
(a) Prepare the bank reconciliation as of May 31, 2012.
(b) Prepare the necessary adjusting entries at May 31, 2012.

*Prepare a bank reconciliation and adjusting entries from detailed data.*
(SO 5), **AP**

**P7-4B**  The bank portion of the bank reconciliation for Carlin Company at November 30, 2012, is shown here and on the next page.

**CARLIN COMPANY**
**Bank Reconciliation**
**November 30, 2012**

| | |
|---|---:|
| Cash balance per bank | $14,367.90 |
| Add: Deposits in transit | 2,530.20 |
| | 16,898.10 |

Less: Outstanding checks

| Check Number | Check Amount | |
|---|---|---|
| 3451 | $ 2,260.40 | |
| 3470 | 1,100.10 | |
| 3471 | 844.50 | |
| 3472 | 1,426.80 | |
| 3474 | 1,050.00 | 6,681.80 |
| Adjusted cash balance per bank | | $10,216.30 |

The adjusted cash balance per bank agreed with the cash balance per books at November 30. The December bank statement showed the following checks and deposits.

**Bank Statement**

| | Checks | | | Deposits | |
|---|---|---|---|---|---|
| Date | Number | Amount | Date | Amount | |
| 12-1 | 3451 | $ 2,260.40 | 12-1 | $ 2,530.20 | |
| 12-2 | 3470 | 1,100.10 | 12-4 | 1,211.60 | |
| 12-7 | 3472 | 1,426.80 | 12-8 | 2,365.10 | |
| 12-4 | 3475 | 1,640.70 | 12-16 | 2,632.70 | |
| 12-8 | 3476 | 1,300.00 | 12-21 | 2,945.00 | |
| 12-10 | 3477 | 2,130.00 | 12-26 | 2,567.30 | |
| 12-15 | 3479 | 3,080.00 | 12-29 | 2,836.00 | |
| 12-27 | 3480 | 600.00 | 12-30 | 1,025.00 | |
| 12-30 | 3482 | 475.50 | Total | $18,112.90 | |
| 12-29 | 3484 | 764.00 | | | |
| 12-31 | 3485 | 540.80 | | | |
| | Total | $15,318.30 | | | |

The cash records per books for December showed the following.

**Cash Payments Journal**

| Date | Number | Amount | Date | Number | Amount |
|---|---|---|---|---|---|
| 12-1 | 3475 | $1,640.70 | 12-20 | 3482 | $ 475.50 |
| 12-2 | 3476 | 1,300.00 | 12-22 | 3483 | 1,340.00 |
| 12-2 | 3477 | 2,130.00 | 12-23 | 3484 | 764.00 |
| 12-4 | 3478 | 538.20 | 12-24 | 3485 | 450.80 |
| 12-8 | 3479 | 3,080.00 | 12-30 | 3486 | 1,389.50 |
| 12-10 | 3480 | 600.00 | Total | | $14,516.10 |
| 12-17 | 3481 | 807.40 | | | |

**Cash Receipts Journal**

| Date | Amount |
|---|---|
| 12-3 | $ 1,211.60 |
| 12-7 | 2,365.10 |
| 12-15 | 2,672.70 |
| 12-20 | 2,945.00 |
| 12-25 | 2,567.30 |
| 12-28 | 2,836.00 |
| 12-30 | 1,025.00 |
| 12-31 | 1,190.40 |
| Total | $16,813.10 |

The bank statement contained two memoranda.

1. A credit of $2,645 for the collection of a $2,500 note for Carlin Company plus interest of $160 and less a collection fee of $15. Carlin Company has not accrued any interest on the note.

2. A debit of $819.10 for an NSF check written by K. Webster, a customer. At December 31, the check had not been redeposited in the bank.

At December 31, the cash balance per books was $12,513.30, and the cash balance per bank statement was $18,988.40. The bank did not make any errors, **but Carlin Company made two errors.**

*Instructions*

(a) Using the four steps in the reconciliation procedure described on pages 354–355, prepare a bank reconciliation at December 31, 2012.

(b) Prepare the adjusting entries based on the reconciliation. (*Note:* The correction of any errors pertaining to recording checks should be made to Accounts Payable. The correction of any errors relating to recording cash receipts should be made to Accounts Receivable.)

*(a) Cash bal. $14,209.20*

*Prepare a bank reconciliation and adjusting entries.*
*(SO 5),* **AP**

**P7-5B** Grossfeld Company of Omaha, Nebraska, provides liquid fertilizer and herbicides to regional farmers. On July 31, 2012, the company's Cash account per its general ledger showed a balance of $5,876.70.

The bank statement from Tri-State Bank on that date showed the following balance.

### TRI-STATE BANK

| Checks and Debits | Deposits and Credits | Daily Balance |
|---|---|---|
| XXX | XXX | 7-31  7,043.80 |

A comparison of the details on the bank statement with the details in the Cash account revealed the following facts.

1. The bank service charge for July was $32.

2. The bank collected a note receivable of $900 for Grossfeld Company on July 15, plus $48 of interest. The bank made an $18 charge for the collection. Grossfeld has not accrued any interest on the note.

3. The July 31 receipts of $1,339 were not included in the bank deposits for July. These receipts were deposited by the company in a night deposit vault on July 31.

4. Company check No. 2480 issued to S. Tully, a creditor, for $471 that cleared the bank in July was incorrectly entered in the cash payments journal on July 10 for $417.

5. Checks outstanding on July 31 totaled $2,480.10.

6. On July 31, the bank statement showed an NSF charge of $818 for a check received by the company from L. Weare, a customer, on account.

*Instructions*

(a) Prepare the bank reconciliation as of July 31, 2012.

(b) Prepare the necessary adjusting entries at July 31, 2012.

*(a) Cash bal. $5,902.70*

*Prepare a cash budget.*
*(SO 8),* **AP**

**P7-6B** Pincus Co. expects to have a cash balance of $26,000 on January 1, 2012. Relevant monthly budget data for the first two months of 2012 are as follows.

Collections from customers: January $70,000; February $147,000
Payments to suppliers: January $45,000; February $69,000
Salaries: January $38,000; February $40,000. Salaries are paid in the month they are incurred.
Selling and administrative expenses: January $27,000; February $32,000. These costs are exclusive of depreciation and are paid as incurred.
Sales of short-term investments in January are expected to realize $7,000 in cash.

Pincus has a line of credit at a local bank that enables it to borrow up to $45,000. The company wants to maintain a minimum monthly cash balance of $25,000. Any excess cash above the $25,000 minimum is used to pay off the line of credit.

*Instructions*

(a) Prepare a cash budget for January and February.

(b) Explain how a cash budget contributes to effective management.

*(a) Jan. cash bal. $25,000*

*Prepare a cash budget.*
*(SO 8),* **AP**

**P7-7B** Vaux Inc. prepares monthly cash budgets. Shown on page 387 are relevant data from operating budgets for 2012.

|  | January | February |
|---|---|---|
| Sales | $330,000 | $400,000 |
| Purchases | 110,000 | 130,000 |
| Salaries | 80,000 | 95,000 |
| Selling and administrative expenses | 132,000 | 150,000 |

All sales and purchases are on account. Collections and disbursement data are given below. All other items above are paid in the month incurred. Depreciation has been excluded from selling and administrative expenses.

Other data.

1. Collections from customers: January $293,000; February $358,000.

2. Payments for purchases: January $98,000; February $118,000.

3. Other receipts: January: collection of December 31, 2011, interest receivable $2,000; February: proceeds from sale of short-term investments $5,000

4. Other disbursements: February payment of $20,000 for land

The company's cash balance on January 1, 2012, is expected to be $58,000. The company wants to maintain a minimum cash balance of $40,000.

**Instructions**
Prepare a cash budget for January and February.

*Jan. 31 cash bal. $43,000*

**P7-8B** Monti Company is a very profitable small business. It has not, however, given much consideration to internal control. For example, in an attempt to keep clerical and office expenses to a minimum, the company has combined the jobs of cashier and book-keeper. As a result, L. Stark handles all cash receipts, keeps the accounting records, and prepares the monthly bank reconciliations.

*Prepare a comprehensive bank reconciliation with theft and internal control deficiencies.*
*(SO 2, 3, 4, 5), E*

The balance per the bank statement on October 31, 2012, was $13,600. Outstanding checks were: No. 62 for $126.75, No. 183 for $190, No. 284 for $253.25, No. 862 for $190.71, No. 863 for $226.80, and No. 864 for $165.28. Included with the statement was a credit memorandum of $440 indicating the collection of a note receivable for Monti Company by the bank on October 25. This memorandum has not been recorded by Monti Company.

The company's ledger showed one Cash account with a balance of $15,797.21. The balance included undeposited cash on hand. Because of the lack of internal controls, Stark took for personal use all of the undeposited receipts in excess of $2,240. He then prepared the following bank reconciliation in an effort to conceal his theft of cash.

| | | |
|---|---|---|
| Cash balance per books, October 31 | | $15,797.21 |
| Add: Outstanding checks | | |
| No. 862 | $190.71 | |
| No. 863 | 226.80 | |
| No. 864 | 165.28 | 482.79 |
| | | 16,280.00 |
| Less: Undeposited receipts | | 2,240.00 |
| Unadjusted balance per bank, October 31 | | 14,040.00 |
| Less: Bank credit memorandum | | 440.00 |
| Cash balance per bank statement, October 31 | | $13,600.00 |

**Instructions**
(a) Prepare a correct bank reconciliation. (*Hint:* Deduct the amount of the theft from the adjusted balance per books.)

(b) Indicate the three ways that Stark attempted to conceal the theft and the dollar amount pertaining to each method.

(c) What principles of internal control were violated in this case?

*(a) Cash bal. $14,687.21*

# Problems: Set C

Visit the book's companion website, at **www.wiley.com/college/kimmel**, and choose the Student Companion site to access Problem Set C.

# Comprehensive Problem

**CP7** On December 1, 2012, Bluemound Company had the following account balances.

|  | **Debits** |  | **Credits** |
|---|---|---|---|
| Cash | $18,200 | Accumulated Depreciation— | |
| Notes Receivable | 2,200 | Equipment | $ 3,000 |
| Accounts Receivable | 7,500 | Accounts Payable | 6,100 |
| Inventory | 16,000 | Common Stock | 20,000 |
| Prepaid Insurance | 1,600 | Retained Earnings | 44,400 |
| Equipment | 28,000 | | |
| | $73,500 | | $73,500 |

During December, the company completed the following transactions.

Dec. 7 Received $3,600 cash from customers in payment of account (no discount allowed).
  12 Purchased merchandise on account from Klump Co. $12,000, terms 1/10, n/30.
  17 Sold merchandise on account $15,000, terms 2/10, n/30. The cost of the merchandise sold was $10,000.
  19 Paid salaries $2,500.
  22 Paid Klump Co. in full, less discount.
  26 Received collections in full, less discounts, from customers billed on December 17.

Adjustment data:

1. Depreciation $200 per month.
2. Insurance expired $400.
3. Income tax expense was $425. It was unpaid at December 31.

*Instructions*
(a) Journalize the December transactions. (Assume a perpetual inventory system.)
(b) Enter the December 1 balances in the ledger T accounts and post the December transactions. Use Cost of Goods Sold, Depreciation Expense, Insurance Expense, Salaries and Wages Expense, Sales Revenue, Sales Discounts, Income Taxes Payable, and Income Tax Expense.
(c) The statement from Jackson County Bank on December 31 showed a balance of $21,994. A comparison of the bank statement with the Cash account revealed the following facts.
  1. The bank collected a note receivable of $2,200 for Bluemound Company on December 15.
  2. The December 31 receipts of $2,736 were not included in the bank deposits for December. The company deposited these receipts in a night deposit vault on December 31.
  3. Checks outstanding on December 31 totaled $1,210.
  4. On December 31, the bank statement showed a NSF charge of $800 for a check received by the company from L. Shur, a customer, on account.

Prepare a bank reconciliation as of December 31 based on the available information. (*Hint:* The cash balance per books is $22,120. This can be proven by finding the balance in the Cash account from parts (a) and (b).)
(d) Journalize the adjusting entries resulting from the bank reconciliation and adjustment data.
(e) Post the adjusting entries to the ledger T accounts.
(f) Prepare an adjusted trial balance.
(g) Prepare an income statement for December and a classified balance sheet at December 31.

(f) Totals $89,125
(g) Net income $ 1,175
  Total assets $72,100

# Continuing Cookie Chronicle

(*Note:* This is a continuation of the Cookie Chronicle from Chapters 1 through 6.)

**CCC7   Part 1**   Natalie is struggling to keep up with the recording of her accounting transactions. She is spending a lot of time marketing and selling mixers and giving her cookie classes. Her friend John is an accounting student who runs his own accounting service. He has asked Natalie if she would like to have him do her accounting. John and Natalie meet and discuss her business.

**Part 2**   Natalie decides that she cannot afford to hire John to do her accounting. One way that she can ensure that her Cash account does not have any errors and is accurate and up-to-date is to prepare a bank reconciliation at the end of each month. Natalie would like you to help her.

> Go to the book's companion website, at **www.wiley.com/college/kimmel**, to see the completion of this problem.

# broadening your perspective

# Financial Reporting and Analysis

## FINANCIAL REPORTING PROBLEM: *Tootsie Roll Industries Inc.*

**BYP7-1**   The financial statements of Tootsie Roll are presented in Appendix A of this book, together with an auditor's report—Report of Independent Auditors.

### Instructions
Using the financial statements and reports, answer these questions about Tootsie Roll's internal controls and cash.
(a)  What comments, if any, are made about cash in the "Report of Independent Registered Public Accounting Firm"?
(b)  What data about cash and cash equivalents are shown in the consolidated balance sheet (statement of financial position)?
(c)  What activities are identified in the consolidated statement of cash flows as being responsible for the changes in cash during 2009?
(d)  How are cash equivalents defined in the Notes to Consolidated Financial Statements?
(e)  Read the section of the report titled "Management's Report on Internal Control Over Financial Reporting." Summarize the statements made in that section of the report. ·

## COMPARATIVE ANALYSIS PROBLEM: *Tootsie Roll vs. Hershey*

**BYP7-2**   The financial statements of The Hershey Company are presented in Appendix B, following the financial statements for Tootsie Roll in Appendix A.

### Instructions
Answer the following questions for each company.
(a)  What is the balance in cash and cash equivalents at December 31, 2009?
(b)  What percentage of total assets does cash represent for each company over the last two years? Has it changed significantly for either company?
(c)  How much cash was provided by operating activities during 2009?
(d)  Comment on your findings in parts (a) through (c).

## RESEARCH CASE

**BYP7-3**   The website **www.cpa2biz.com** has an article dated February 4, 2010, by Mary Schaeffer entitled "Emerging Issues: Demise of Paper Checks."

*Instructions*

Go to the website and do a search on the article title. Read the article and answer the following questions.

(a) How many different forms of payment types does the article list? What are the payment types?

(b) What problems does the shift away from paper checks to alternative payment options present for companies?

(c) What five controls does the article suggest incorporating, to decrease problems associated with multiple payment options?

## INTERPRETING FINANCIAL STATEMENTS

**BYP7-4** The international accounting firm Ernst and Young performed a global survey. The results of that survey are summarized in a report titled "Fraud Risk in Emerging Markets." You can find this report at:

**http://www.ey.com/Global/assets.nsf/International/FIDS_-_9th_Global_Fraud_Survey_2006/ $file/EY_Fraud_Survey_June2006.pdf,** or do an Internet search for "9th Global Fraud Survey— Fraud Risk in Emerging Markets."

*Instructions*

Read the Executive Summary section, and then skim the remainder of the report to answer the following questions.

(a) What did survey respondents consider to be the top three factors to prevent fraud?

(b) What type of fraud poses the greatest threat in developed markets? What type of fraud poses the greatest threat in emerging markets?

(c) In what three regions are anti-fraud measures most likely to be considered when deciding whether to begin doing business in that region?

## FINANCIAL ANALYSIS ON THE WEB

**BYP7-5** The Financial Accounting Standards Board (FASB) is a private organization established to improve accounting standards and financial reporting. The FASB conducts extensive research before issuing a "Statement of Financial Accounting Standards," which represents an authoritative expression of generally accepted accounting principles.

*Address:* **www.fasb.org,** or go to **www.wiley.com/college/kimmel**

*Steps*

Choose **About FASB.**

*Instructions*

Answer the following questions.

(a) What is the mission of the FASB?

(b) How are topics added to the FASB technical agenda? (*Hint:* See Project Plans in Our Rules of Procedure.)

(c) What characteristics make the FASB's procedures an "open" decision-making process? (*Hint:* See Due Process in Our Rules of Procedure.)

**BYP7-6** The Public Company Accounting Oversight Board (PCAOB) was created as a result of the Sarbanes-Oxley Act. It has oversight and enforcement responsibilities over accounting firms in the U.S.

*Address:* **http://www.pcaobus.org/,** or go to **www.wiley.com/college/kimmel**

*Instructions*

Answer the following questions.

(a) What is the mission of the PCAOB?

(b) Briefly summarize its responsibilities related to inspections.

(c) Briefly summarize its responsibilities related to enforcement.

# Critical Thinking

## DECISION MAKING ACROSS THE ORGANIZATION

**BYP7-7** Alternative Distributor Corp., a distributor of groceries and related products, is headquartered in Medford, Massachusetts.

During a recent audit, Alternative Distributor Corp. was advised that existing internal controls necessary for the company to develop reliable financial statements were inadequate. The audit report stated that the current system of accounting for sales, receivables, and cash receipts constituted a material weakness. Among other items, the report focused on nontimely deposit of cash receipts, exposing Alternative Distributor to potential loss or misappropriation, excessive past due accounts receivable due to lack of collection efforts, disregard of advantages offered by vendors for prompt payment of invoices, absence of appropriate segregation of duties by personnel consistent with appropriate control objectives, inadequate procedures for applying accounting principles, lack of qualified management personnel, lack of supervision by an outside board of directors, and overall poor recordkeeping.

*Instructions*
(a) Identify the principles of internal control violated by Alternative Distributor Corporation.
(b) Explain why managers of various functional areas in the company should be concerned about internal controls.

## COMMUNICATION ACTIVITY

**BYP7-8**   As a new auditor for the CPA firm of Ticke and Tie, you have been assigned to review the internal controls over mail cash receipts of Perso Company. Your review reveals that checks are promptly endorsed "For Deposit Only," but no list of the checks is prepared by the person opening the mail. The mail is opened either by the cashier or by the employee who maintains the accounts receivable records. Mail receipts are deposited in the bank weekly by the cashier.

*Instructions*
Write a letter to S. A. Davis, owner of the Perso Company, explaining the weaknesses in internal control and your recommendations for improving the system.

## ETHICS CASES

**BYP7-9**   Banks charge fees for "bounced" checks—that is, checks that exceed the balance in the account. It has been estimated that processing bounced checks costs a bank roughly $1.50 per check. Thus, the profit margin on bounced checks is very high. Recognizing this, some banks have started to process checks from largest to smallest. By doing this, they maximize the number of checks that bounce if a customer overdraws an account. For example, NationsBank (now Bank of America) projected a $14 million increase in fee revenue as a result of processing largest checks first. In response to criticism, banks have responded that their customers prefer to have large checks processed first, because those tend to be the most important. At the other extreme, some banks will cover their customers' bounced checks, effectively extending them an interest-free loan while their account is overdrawn.

*Instructions*
Answer each of the following questions.
(a) William Preston had a balance of $1,500 in his checking account at First National Bank on a day when the bank received the following five checks for processing against his account.

| Check Number | Amount | Check Number | Amount |
|---|---|---|---|
| 3150 | $ 35 | 3165 | $ 550 |
| 3162 | 400 | 3166 | 1,510 |
| | | 3169 | 180 |

Assuming a $30 fee assessed by the bank for each bounced check, how much fee revenue would the bank generate if it processed checks (1) from largest to smallest, (2) from smallest to largest, and (3) in order of check number?
(b) Do you think that processing checks from largest to smallest is an ethical business practice?
(c) In addition to ethical issues, what other issues must a bank consider in deciding whether to process checks from largest to smallest?
(d) If you were managing a bank, what policy would you adopt on bounced checks?

**BYP7-10**   The NFIC was originally established in 1992 by the National Consumers League, the oldest nonprofit consumer organization in the United States, to fight the growing menace of telemarketing fraud by improving prevention and enforcement. It maintains a website that provides many useful fraud related resources.

*Address:* **www.fraud.org/scamsagainstbusinesses/bizscams.htm** or go to **www.wiley.com/college/ kimmel**

*Instructions*
Go to the site and find an item of interest to you. Write a short summary of your findings.

## "ALL ABOUT YOU" ACTIVITY

**BYP7-11** The print and electronic media are full of stories about potential security risks that can arise from your personal computer. It is important to keep in mind, however, that there are also many ways that your identity can be stolen other than from your computer. The federal government provides many resources to help protect you from identity thieves.

*Instructions*
Go to **http://onguardonline.gov/idtheft.html**, and click Games, then click ID Theft Faceoff. Complete the quiz provided there.

## FASB CODIFICATION ACTIVITY

**BYP7-12** If your school has a subscription to the FASB Codification, go to **http://aaahq.org/ ascLogin.cfm** to log in and prepare responses to the following.
(a) How is cash defined in the Codification?
(b) How are cash equivalents defined in the Codification?
(c) What are the disclosure requirements related to cash and cash equivalents?

### Answers to Insight and Accounting Across the Organization Questions

**p. 345 SOX Boosts the Role of Human Resources Q:** Why would unsupervised employees or employees who report to each other represent potential internal control threats? **A:** An unsupervised employee may have a fraudulent job (or may even be a fictitious person)—e.g., a person drawing a paycheck without working. Or, if two employees supervise each other, there is no real separation of duties, and they can conspire to defraud the company.

**p. 345 Big Theft at Small Companies Q:** Why are small companies more susceptible to employee theft? **A:** The high degree of trust often found in small companies makes them more vulnerable. Also, small companies tend to have less sophisticated systems of internal control, and they usually lack internal auditors. In addition, it is very hard to achieve some internal control features, such as segregation of duties, when you have very few employees.

**p. 351 How Employees Steal Q:** How can companies reduce the likelihood of fraudulent disbursements? **A:** To reduce the occurrence of fraudulent disbursements, a company should follow the procedures discussed in this chapter. These include having only designated personnel sign checks; having different personnel approve payments and make payments; ensuring that check signers do not record disbursements; using prenumbered checks and matching each check to an approved invoice; storing blank checks securely; reconciling the bank statement; and stamping invoices PAID.

**p. 357 Madoff's Ponzi Scheme Q:** How was Madoff able to conceal such a giant fraud? **A:** Madoff fabricated false investment statements that were provided to investors. In addition, his auditor never verified these investment statements even though the auditor gave him an unqualified opinion each year.

### Answers to Self-Test Questions

**1.** c **2.** a **3.** c **4.** b **5.** a **6.** b **7.** d **8.** a **9.** d **10.** c **11.** c **12.** c **13.** b **14.** d
***15.** a ($100 − ($94 + $2))

# IFRS A Look at IFRS

Fraud can occur anywhere. And because the three main factors that contribute to fraud are universal in nature, the principles of internal control activities are used globally by companies. While Sarbanes-Oxley (SOX) does not apply to international companies, most large international companies have internal controls similar to those indicated in the chapter. IFRS and GAAP are very similar in accounting for cash. *IAS No. 1 (revised)*, "Presentation of Financial Statements," is the only standard that discusses issues specifically related to cash.

## KEY POINTS

- The fraud triangle discussed in this chapter is applicable to all international companies. Some of the major frauds on an international basis are Parmalat (Italy), Royal Ahold (the Netherlands), and Satyam Computer Services (India).

- Rising economic crime poses a growing threat to companies, with nearly half of all organizations worldwide being victims of fraud in a recent two-year period (*PricewaterhouseCoopers' Global Economic Crime Survey*, 2005). Specifically, 44% of Romanian companies surveyed experienced fraud in the past two years.

- Globally, the number of companies reporting fraud increased from 37% to 45% since 2003, a 22% increase. The cost to companies was an average $1.7 million in losses from "tangible frauds," that is, those that result in an immediate and direct financial loss. These include asset misappropriation, false pretenses, and counterfeiting (*PricewaterhouseCoopers' Global Economic Crime Survey*, 2005).

- Accounting scandals both in the United States and internationally have re-ignited the debate over the relative merits of GAAP, which takes a "rules-based" approach to accounting, versus IFRS, which takes a "principles-based" approach. The FASB announced that it intends to introduce more principles-based standards.

- On a lighter note, at one time the Ig Nobel Prize in Economics went to the CEOs of those companies involved in the corporate accounting scandals of that year for "adapting the mathematical concept of imaginary numbers for use in the business world." The Ig Nobel Prizes (read Ignoble, as not noble) are a parody of the Nobel Prizes and are given each year in early October for 10 achievements that "first make people laugh, and then make them think." Organized by the scientific humor magazine *Annals of Improbable Research* (*AIR*), they are presented by a group that includes genuine Nobel laureates at a ceremony at Harvard University's Sanders Theater. (See *en.wikipedia.org/wiki/Ig_Nobel_Prize*.)

- Internal controls are a system of checks and balances designed to prevent and detect fraud and errors. While most companies have these systems in place, many have never completely documented them, nor had an independent auditor attest to their effectiveness. Both of these actions are required under SOX.

- Companies find that internal control review is a costly process but badly needed. One study estimates the cost of SOX compliance for U.S. companies at over $35 billion, with audit fees doubling in the first year of compliance. At the same time, examination of internal controls indicates lingering problems in the way companies operate. One study of first compliance with the internal-control testing provisions documented material weaknesses for about 13% of companies reporting in a two-year period (*PricewaterhouseCoopers' Global Economic Crime Survey*, 2005).

- The SOX internal control standards apply only to companies listed on U.S. exchanges. There is continuing debate over whether foreign issuers should have to comply with this extra layer of regulation.

- The accounting and internal control procedures related to cash are essentially the same under both IFRS and this textbook. In addition, the definition used for cash equivalents is the same.

- Most companies report cash and cash equivalents together under IFRS, as shown in this textbook. In addition, IFRS follows the same accounting policies related to the reporting of restricted cash.

- IFRS defines cash and cash equivalents as follows.
  - **Cash** is comprised of cash on hand and demand deposits.
  - **Cash equivalents** are short-term, highly liquid investments that are readily convertible to known amounts of cash and which are subject to an insignificant risk of changes in value.

## LOOKING TO THE FUTURE

Ethics has become a very important aspect of reporting. Different cultures have different perspectives on bribery and other questionable activities, and consequently penalties for engaging in such activities vary considerably across countries.

High-quality international accounting requires both high-quality accounting standards and high-quality auditing. Similar to the convergence of GAAP and IFRS, there is movement to improve international auditing standards. The International Auditing and Assurance Standards Board (IAASB) functions as an independent standard-setting body. It works to establish high-quality auditing and assurance and quality-control standards throughout the world. Whether the IAASB adopts internal control provisions similar to those in SOX remains to be seen. You can follow developments in the international audit arena at *http://www.ifac.org/iaasb/*.

Under proposed new standards for financial statements, companies would not be allowed to combine cash equivalents with cash.

## IFRS Self-Test Questions

1. Non-U.S companies that follow IFRS:
   (a) do not normally use the principles of internal control activities used in this textbook.
   (b) often offset cash with accounts payable on the balance sheet.
   (c) are not required to follow SOX.
   (d) None of the above.
2. Which of the following is the correct accounting under IFRS for cash?
   (a) Cash cannot be combined with cash equivalents.
   (b) Restricted cash funds may be reported as a current or non-current asset depending on the circumstances.
   (c) Restricted cash funds cannot be reported as a current asset.
   (d) Cash on hand is not reported on the balance sheet as Cash.
3. The Sarbanes-Oxley Act of 2002 applies to:
   (a) all U.S. companies listed on U.S. exchanges.
   (b) all companies that list stock on any stock exchange in any country.
   (c) all European companies listed on European exchanges.
   (d) Both (a) and (c).
4. High-quality international accounting requires both high-quality accounting standards and:
   (a) a reconsideration of SOX to make it less onerous.
   (b) high-quality auditing standards.
   (c) government intervention to ensure that the public interest is protected.
   (d) the development of new principles of internal control activities.
5. Cash equivalents under IFRS:
   (a) are significantly different than the cash equivalents discussed in the textbook.
   (b) are generally disclosed separately from cash.
   (c) may be required to be reported separately from cash in the future.
   (d) None of the above.

## IFRS Concepts and Application

**IFRS7–1** Some people argue that the internal control requirements of the Sarbanes-Oxley Act (SOX) put U.S. companies at a competitive disadvantage to companies outside the United States. Discuss the competitive implications (both pros and cons) of SOX.

**IFRS7–2** State whether each of the following is true or false. For those that are false, explain why.
   (a) A proposed new financial accounting standard would not allow cash equivalents to be reported in combination with cash.
   (b) Perspectives on bribery and penalties for engaging in bribery are the same across all countries.
   (c) Cash equivalents are comprised of cash on hand and demand deposits.
   (d) SOX was created by the International Accounting Standards Board.

## INTERNATIONAL FINANCIAL REPORTING PROBLEM: *Zetar plc*

**IFRS7–3** The financial statements of Zetar plc are presented in Appendix C. The company's complete annual report, including the notes to its financial statements, is available at **www.zetarplc.com.**

### Instructions

(a) Which committee of the board of directors is responsible for considering management's reports on internal control?

(b) What are the company's key control procedures?

(c) Does the company have an internal audit department?

(d) In what section or sections does Zetar report its bank overdrafts?

### Answers to IFRS Self-Test Questions

**1.** c  **2.** b  **3.** a  **4.** b  **5.** c

# REPORTING AND ANALYZING RECEIVABLES

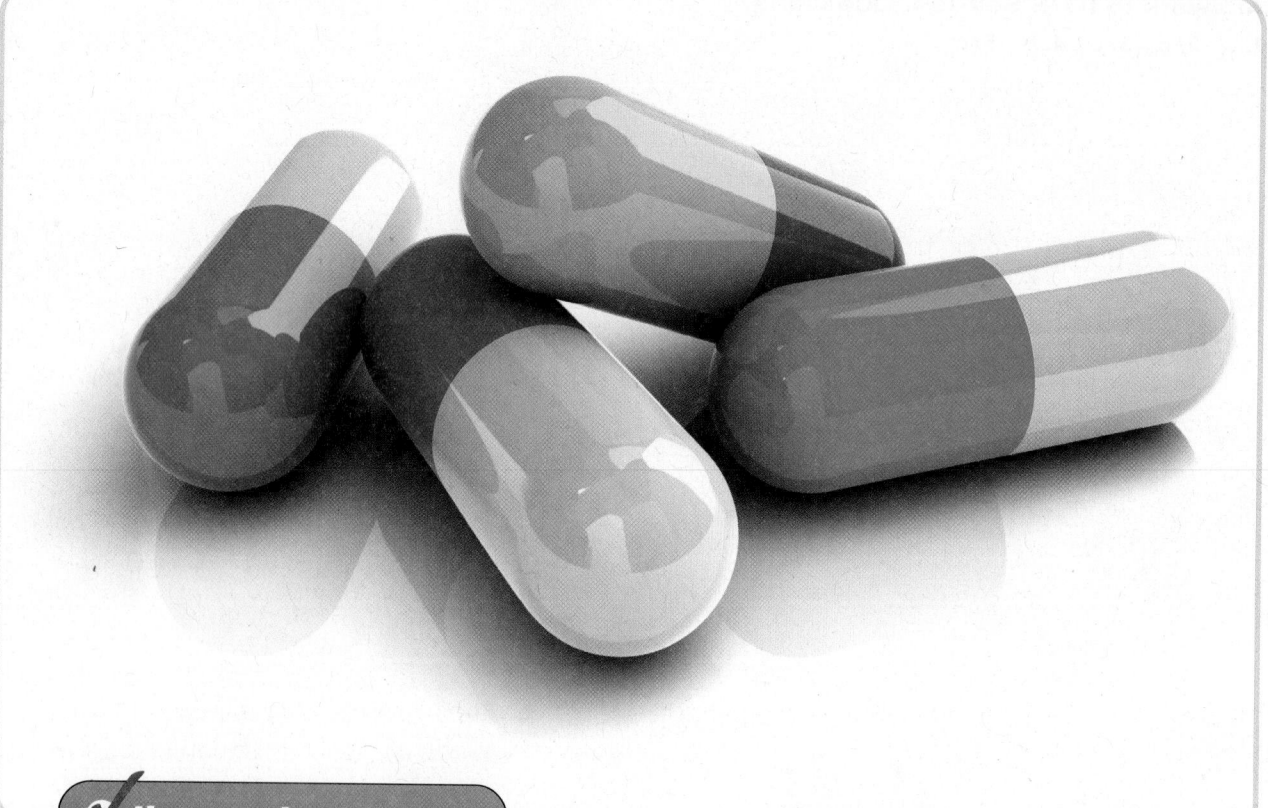

## study objectives

**After studying this chapter, you should be able to:**

1 Identify the different types of receivables.

2 Explain how accounts receivable are recognized in the accounts.

3 Describe the methods used to account for bad debts.

4 Compute the interest on notes receivable.

5 Describe the entries to record the disposition of notes receivable.

6 Explain the statement presentation of receivables.

7 Describe the principles of sound accounts receivable management.

8 Identify ratios to analyze a company's receivables.

9 Describe methods to accelerate the receipt of cash from receivables.

"Sometimes you have to know when to be very tough, and sometimes you can give them a bit of a break," says Vivi Su. She's not talking about her children, but about the customers of a subsidiary of pharmaceutical company Whitehall-Robins, where she works as supervisor of credit and collections.

For example, while the company's regular terms are 1/15, n/30 (1% discount if paid within 15 days), a customer might ask for and receive a few days of grace and still get the discount. Or a customer might place orders above its credit limit, in which case, depending on its payment history and the circumstances, Ms. Su might authorize shipment of the goods anyway.

"It's not about drawing a line in the sand, and that's all," she explains. "You want a good relationship with your customers—but you also need to bring in the money."

"The money," in Whitehall-Robins's case amounts to some $170 million in sales a year. Nearly all of it comes in through the credit accounts Ms. Su manages. The process starts with the decision to grant a customer an account in the first place, Ms. Su explains. The sales rep gives the customer a credit application. "My department reviews this application very carefully; a customer needs to supply three good references, and we also run a check with a credit firm like Equifax. If we accept them, then based on their size and history, we assign a credit limit."

Once accounts are established, the company supervises them very carefully. "I get an aging report every single day," says Ms. Su.

## DOSE OF CAREFUL MANAGEMENT KEEPS RECEIVABLES HEALTHY

"The rule of thumb is that we should always have at least 85% of receivables current—meaning they were billed less than 30 days ago," she continues. "But we try to do even better than that—I like to see 90%." Similarly, her guideline is never to have more than 5% of receivables at over 90 days. But long before that figure is reached, "we jump on it," she says firmly.

At 15 days overdue, Whitehall-Robins phones the client. Often there's a reasonable explanation for the delay—an invoice may have gone astray, or the payables clerk is away. "But if a customer keeps on delaying, and tells us several times that it'll only be a few more days, we know there's a problem," says Ms. Su. After 45 days, "I send a letter. Then a second notice is sent in writing. After the third and final notice, the client has 10 days to pay, and then I hand it over to a collection agency, and it's out of my hands."

Ms. Su's boss, Terry Norton, records an estimate for bad debts every year, based on a percentage of receivables. The percentage depends on the current aging history. He also calculates and monitors the company's receivables turnover ratio, which the company reports in its financial statements. "I think of it in terms of collection period of DSO—days of sales outstanding," he explains.

Ms. Su knows that she and Mr. Norton are crucial to the profitability of Whitehall-Robins. "Receivables are generally the second-largest asset of any company (after its capital assets)," she points out. "So it's no wonder we keep a very close eye on them."

✔ the navigator

## INSIDE CHAPTER 8 . . .

In this chapter, we discuss some of the decisions related to reporting and analyzing receivables. As indicated in the Feature Story, receivables are a significant asset on the books of pharmaceutical company Whitehall-Robins. Receivables are significant to companies in other industries as well, because a significant portion of sales are made on credit in the United States. As a consequence, companies must pay close attention to their receivables balances and manage them carefully.

The organization and content of the chapter are as follows.

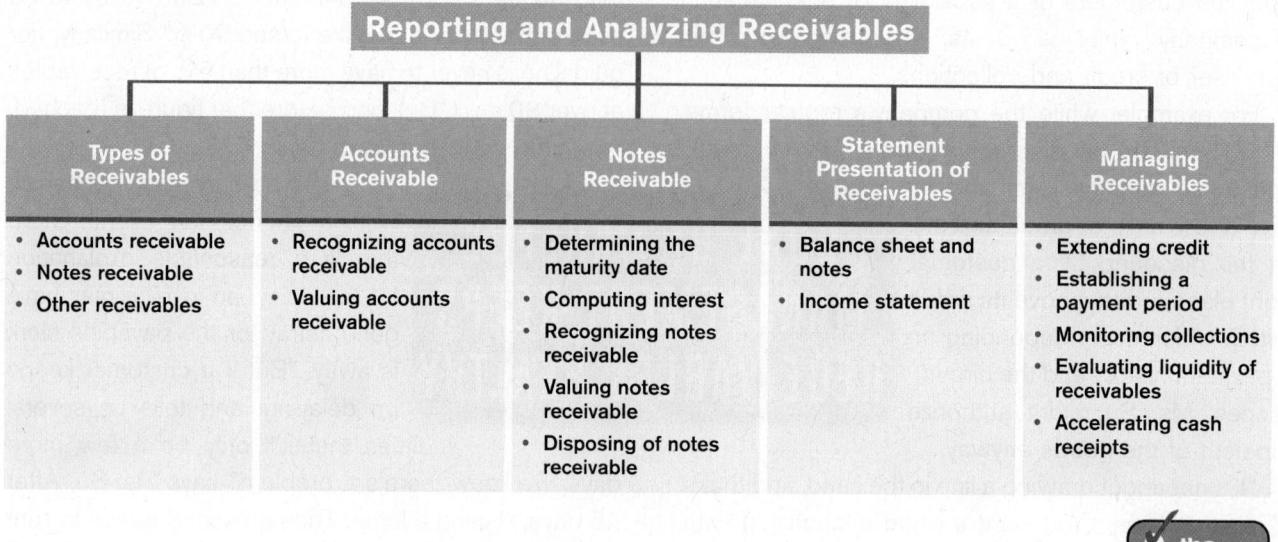

| Reporting and Analyzing Receivables | | | | |
|---|---|---|---|---|
| **Types of Receivables** | **Accounts Receivable** | **Notes Receivable** | **Statement Presentation of Receivables** | **Managing Receivables** |
| • Accounts receivable<br>• Notes receivable<br>• Other receivables | • Recognizing accounts receivable<br>• Valuing accounts receivable | • Determining the maturity date<br>• Computing interest<br>• Recognizing notes receivable<br>• Valuing notes receivable<br>• Disposing of notes receivable | • Balance sheet and notes<br>• Income statement | • Extending credit<br>• Establishing a payment period<br>• Monitoring collections<br>• Evaluating liquidity of receivables<br>• Accelerating cash receipts |

the navigator

# Types of Receivables

**study objective 1**

Identify the different types of receivables.

The term **receivables** refers to amounts due from individuals and companies. Receivables are claims that are expected to be collected in cash. The management of receivables is a very important activity for any company that sells goods or services on credit.

Receivables are important because they represent one of a company's most liquid assets. For many companies, receivables are also one of the largest assets. For example, receivables represented 30.8% of the current assets of pharmaceutical giant Rite Aid in 2009. Illustration 8-1 lists receivables as a percentage of total assets for five other well-known companies in a recent year.

**Illustration 8-1**
Receivables as a percentage of assets

| Company | Receivables as a Percentage of Total Assets |
|---|---|
| General Electric | 52% |
| Ford Motor Company | 42% |
| Minnesota Mining and Manufacturing Company (3M) | 14% |
| DuPont Co. | 17% |
| Intel Corporation | 5% |

The relative significance of a company's receivables as a percentage of its assets depends on various factors: its industry, the time of year, whether it extends long-term financing, and its credit policies. To reflect important differences among receivables, they are frequently classified as (1) accounts receivable, (2) notes receivable, and (3) other receivables.

**Accounts receivable** are amounts customers owe on account. They result from the sale of goods and services. Companies generally expect to collect accounts receivable within 30 to 60 days. They are usually the most significant type of claim held by a company.

**Notes receivable** represent claims for which formal instruments of credit are issued as evidence of the debt. The credit instrument normally requires the debtor to pay interest and extends for time periods of 60–90 days or longer. Notes and accounts receivable that result from sales transactions are often called **trade receivables**.

**Other receivables** include nontrade receivables such as interest receivable, loans to company officers, advances to employees, and income taxes refundable. These do not generally result from the operations of the business. Therefore, they are generally classified and reported as separate items in the balance sheet.

**Ethics Note** Companies report receivables from employees separately in the financial statements. The reason: Sometimes those assets are not the result of an "arm's-length" transaction.

## Accounts Receivable

Two accounting issues associated with accounts receivable are:

1. Recognizing accounts receivable.
2. Valuing accounts receivable.

A third issue, accelerating cash receipts from receivables, is discussed later in the chapter.

### RECOGNIZING ACCOUNTS RECEIVABLE

Recognizing accounts receivable is relatively straightforward. A service organization records a receivable when it provides service on account. A merchandiser records accounts receivable at the point of sale of merchandise on account. When a merchandiser sells goods, it increases (debits) Accounts Receivable and increases (credits) Sales Revenue.

**study objective 2**
Explain how accounts receivable are recognized in the accounts.

The seller may offer terms that encourage early payment by providing a discount. Sales returns also reduce receivables. The buyer might find some of the goods unacceptable and choose to return the unwanted goods.

To review, assume that Jordache Co. on July 1, 2012, sells merchandise on account to Polo Company for $1,000, terms 2/10, n/30. On July 5, Polo returns merchandise worth $100 to Jordache Co. On July 11, Jordache receives payment from Polo Company for the balance due. The journal entries to record these transactions on the books of Jordache Co. are as follows. **(Cost of goods sold entries are omitted.)**

| | | | |
|---|---|---|---|
| July 1 | Accounts Receivable—Polo Company | 1,000 | |
| | Sales Revenue | | 1,000 |
| | (To record sales on account) | | |
| July 5 | Sales Returns and Allowances | 100 | |
| | Accounts Receivable—Polo Company | | 100 |
| | (To record merchandise returned) | | |
| July 11 | Cash ($900 − $18) | 882 | |
| | Sales Discounts ($900 × .02) | 18 | |
| | Accounts Receivable—Polo Company | | 900 |
| | (To record collection of accounts receivable) | | |

**Helpful Hint** These entries are the same as those described in Chapter 5. For simplicity, we have omitted inventory and cost of goods sold from this set of journal entries and from end-of-chapter material.

Some retailers issue their own credit cards. When you use a retailer's credit card (JCPenney, for example), the retailer charges interest on the balance due if not paid within a specified period (usually 25–30 days).

To illustrate, assume that you use your JCPenney Company credit card to purchase clothing with a sales price of $300. JCPenney will increase (debit)

Accounts Receivable for $300 and increase (credit) Sales Revenue for $300 (cost of goods sold entry omitted) as follows.

| | | |
|---|---|---|
| Accounts Receivable | 300 | |
|    Sales Revenue | | 300 |
|     (To record sale of merchandise) | | |

Assuming that you owe $300 at the end of the month, and JCPenney charges 1.5% per month on the balance due, the adjusting entry that JCPenney makes to record interest revenue of $4.50 ($300 × 1.5%) is as follows.

| | | |
|---|---|---|
| Accounts Receivable | 4.50 | |
|    Interest Revenue | | 4.50 |
|     (To record interest on amount due) | | |

Interest revenue is often substantial for many retailers.

## ANATOMY OF A FRAUD

Tasanee was the accounts receivable clerk for a large non-profit foundation that provided performance and exhibition space for the performing and visual arts. Her responsibilities included activities normally assigned to an accounts receivable clerk, such as recording revenues from various sources that included donations, facility rental fees, ticket revenue, and bar receipts. However, she was also responsible for handling all cash and checks from the time they were received until the time she deposited them, as well as preparing the bank reconciliation. Tasanee took advantage of her situation by falsifying bank deposits and bank reconciliations so that she could steal cash from the bar receipts. Since nobody else logged the donations or matched the donation receipts to pledges prior to Tasanee receiving them, she was able to offset the cash that was stolen against donations that she received but didn't record. Her crime was made easier by the fact that her boss, the company's controller, only did a very superficial review of the bank reconciliation and thus didn't notice that some numbers had been cut out from other documents and taped onto the bank reconciliation.

**Total take: $1.5 million**

### THE MISSING CONTROLS

*Segregation of duties.* The foundation should not have allowed an accounts receivable clerk, whose job was to record receivables, to also handle cash, record cash, and make deposits, and especially prepare the bank reconciliation.

*Independent internal verification.* The controller was supposed to perform a thorough review of the bank reconciliation. Because he did not, he was terminated from his position.

*Source:* Adapted from Wells, *Fraud Casebook* (2007), pp. 183–194.

### VALUING ACCOUNTS RECEIVABLE

study objective **3**

Describe the methods used to account for bad debts.

Once companies record receivables in the accounts, the next question is: How should they report receivables in the financial statements? Companies report accounts receivable on the balance sheet as an asset. Determining the **amount** to report is sometimes difficult because some receivables will become uncollectible.

Although each customer must satisfy the credit requirements of the seller before the credit sale is approved, inevitably some accounts receivable become uncollectible. For example, a corporate customer may not be able to pay because it experienced a sales decline due to an economic downturn. Similarly, individuals may be laid off from their jobs or be faced with unexpected hospital bills. The seller records these losses that result from extending credit as **Bad Debts Expense**. Such losses are a normal and necessary risk of doing business on a credit basis.

**Alternative Terminology** You will sometimes see *Bad Debts Expense* called *Uncollectible Accounts Expense.*

Recently, when U.S. home prices fell, home foreclosures rose, and the economy in general slowed, lenders experienced huge increases in their bad debts expense. For example, during a recent quarter Wachovia, the fourth largest U.S. bank, increased bad debts expense from $108 million to $408 million. Similarly, American Express increased its bad debts expense by 70%.

The accounting profession uses two methods for uncollectible accounts: (1) the direct write-off method, and (2) the allowance method. We explain each of these methods in the following sections.

### Direct Write-Off Method for Uncollectible Accounts

Under the **direct write-off method**, when a company determines receivables from a particular company to be uncollectible, it charges the loss to Bad Debts Expense. Assume, for example, that Warden Co. writes off M. E. Doran's $200 balance as uncollectible on December 12. Warden's entry is:

| Dec. 12 | Bad Debts Expense | 200 | |
| | Accounts Receivable—M. E. Doran | | 200 |
| | (To record write-off of M. E. Doran account) | | |

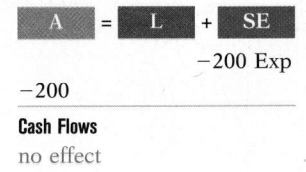

−200       −200 Exp

**Cash Flows**
no effect

Under this method, bad debts expense will show only **actual losses** from uncollectibles. The company reports accounts receivable at its gross amount without any adjustment for estimated losses for bad debts.

Use of the direct write-off method can reduce the usefulness of both the income statement and balance sheet. Consider the following example. In 2012, Quick Buck Computer Company decided it could increase its revenues by offering computers to college students without requiring any money down, and with no credit-approval process. It went on campuses across the country and sold one million computers at a selling price of $800 each. This promotion increased Quick Buck's revenues and receivables by $800,000,000. It was a huge success: The 2012 balance sheet and income statement looked wonderful. Unfortunately, during 2013, nearly 40% of the college student customers defaulted on their loans. The 2013 income statement and balance sheet looked terrible. Illustration 8-2 shows the effect of these events on the financial statements using the direct write-off method.

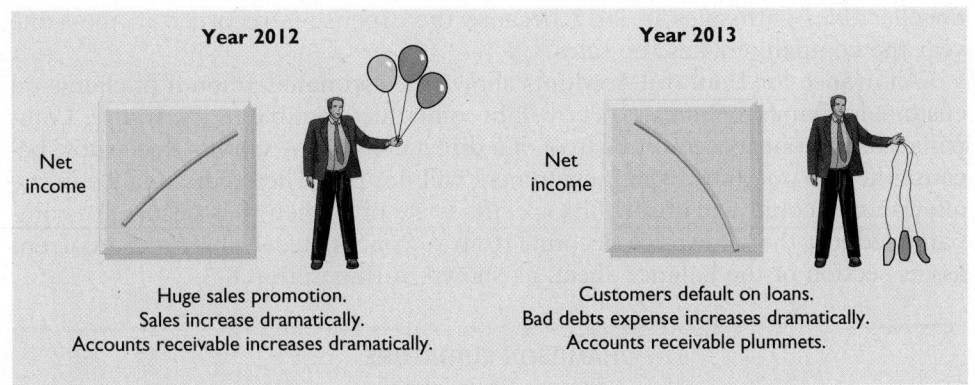

**Illustration 8-2** Effects of direct write-off method

Under the direct write-off method, companies often record bad debts expense in a period different from the period in which they recorded the revenue. Thus, no attempt is made to match bad debts expense to sales revenues in the income statement. Nor does the company try to show accounts receivable in the balance sheet at the amount actually expected to be received. **Consequently, unless a company expects bad debts losses to be insignificant, the direct write-off method is not acceptable for financial reporting purposes.**

## Allowance Method for Uncollectible Accounts

The **allowance method** of accounting for bad debts involves estimating uncollectible accounts at the end of each period. This provides better matching of expenses with revenues on the income statement. It also ensures that receivables are stated at their cash (net) realizable value on the balance sheet. **Cash (net) realizable value** is the net amount a company expects to receive in cash from receivables. It excludes amounts that the company estimates it will not collect. Estimated uncollectible receivables therefore reduce receivables on the balance sheet through use of the allowance method.

Companies must use the allowance method for financial reporting purposes when bad debts are material in amount. It has three essential features:

1. Companies **estimate** uncollectible accounts receivable and **match them against revenues** in the same accounting period in which the revenues are recorded.

2. Companies record estimated uncollectibles as an increase (a debit) to Bad Debts Expense and an increase (a credit) to Allowance for Doubtful Accounts through an adjusting entry at the end of each period. Allowance for Doubtful Accounts is a contra account to Accounts Receivable.

3. Companies debit actual uncollectibles to Allowance for Doubtful Accounts and credit them to Accounts Receivable at the time the specific account is written off as uncollectible.

**RECORDING ESTIMATED UNCOLLECTIBLES.** To illustrate the allowance method, assume that Hampson Furniture has credit sales of $1,200,000 in 2012, of which $200,000 remains uncollected at December 31. The credit manager estimates that $12,000 of these sales will prove uncollectible. The adjusting entry to record the estimated uncollectibles increases (debits) Bad Debts Expense and increases (credits) Allowance for Doubtful Accounts, as follows.

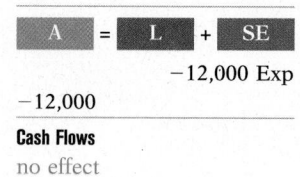

A = L + SE
−12,000 Exp
−12,000

**Cash Flows**
no effect

| Dec. 31 | Bad Debts Expense | 12,000 | |
| | Allowance for Doubtful Accounts | | 12,000 |
| | (To record estimate of uncollectible accounts) | | |

Companies report Bad Debts Expense in the income statement as an operating expense (usually as a selling expense). Thus, Hampson matches the estimated uncollectibles with sales in 2012 because the expense is recorded in the same year the company makes the sales.

Allowance for Doubtful Accounts shows the estimated amount of claims on customers that companies expect will become uncollectible in the future. Companies use a contra account instead of a direct credit to Accounts Receivable because they do not know *which* customers will not pay. The credit balance in the allowance account will absorb the specific write-offs when they occur. The company deducts the allowance account from Accounts Receivable in the current assets section of the balance sheet, as shown in Illustration 8-3.

**Illustration 8-3**
Presentation of allowance for doubtful accounts

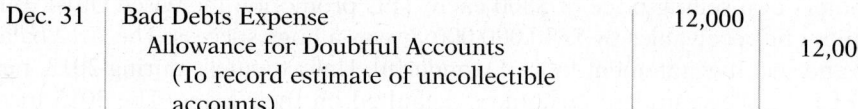

| HAMPSON FURNITURE | | |
|---|---|---|
| Balance Sheet (partial) | | |
| Current assets | | |
| Cash | | $ 14,800 |
| Accounts receivable | $200,000 | |
| Less: Allowance for doubtful accounts | 12,000 | 188,000 |
| Inventory | | 310,000 |
| Supplies | | 25,000 |
| Total current assets | | $537,800 |

The amount of $188,000 in Illustration 8-3 represents the expected **cash realizable value** of the accounts receivable at the statement date. **Companies do not close Allowance for Doubtful Accounts at the end of the fiscal year.**

**RECORDING THE WRITE-OFF OF AN UNCOLLECTIBLE ACCOUNT.** Various methods are used to collect past-due accounts, as discussed in the Feature Story. When a company exhausts all means of collecting a past-due account and collection appears unlikely, the company writes off the account. In the credit card industry, it is standard practice to write off accounts that are 210 days past due. To prevent premature or unauthorized write-offs, authorized management personnel should formally approve each write-off. **To maintain good internal control, companies should not authorize someone to write off accounts who also has daily responsibilities related to cash or receivables.**

To illustrate a receivables write-off, assume that the vice president of finance of Hampson Furniture on March 1, 2013, authorizes a write-off of the $500 balance owed by R. A. Ware. The entry to record the write-off is:

| | | | |
|---|---|---|---|
| Mar. 1 | Allowance for Doubtful Accounts | 500 | |
| | Accounts Receivable—R. A. Ware | | 500 |
| | (Write-off of R. A. Ware account) | | |

| A | = | L | + | SE |
|---|---|---|---|---|

+500
−500

**Cash Flows**
no effect

The company does not increase Bad Debts Expense when the write-off occurs. **Under the allowance method, a company debits every bad debt write-off to the allowance account and not to Bad Debts Expense.** A debit to Bad Debts Expense would be incorrect because the company has already recognized the expense when it made the adjusting entry for estimated bad debts. Instead, the entry to record the write-off of an uncollectible account reduces both Accounts Receivable and the Allowance for Doubtful Accounts. After posting, the general ledger accounts will appear as in Illustration 8-4.

| Accounts Receivable | | Allowance for Doubtful Accounts | |
|---|---|---|---|
| Jan. 1 Bal. 200,000 | Mar. 1    **500** | Mar. 1    **500** | Jan. 1    Bal. 12,000 |
| Mar. 1 Bal. 199,500 | | | Mar. 1    Bal. 11,500 |

**Illustration 8-4** General ledger balances after write-off

A write-off affects only balance sheet accounts. Cash realizable value in the balance sheet, therefore, remains the same before and after the write-off, as shown in Illustration 8-5.

| | Before Write-Off | After Write-Off |
|---|---|---|
| Accounts receivable | $ 200,000 | $ 199,500 |
| Allowance for doubtful accounts | 12,000 | 11,500 |
| **Cash realizable value** | **$188,000** | **$188,000** |

**Illustration 8-5** Cash realizable value comparison

**RECOVERY OF AN UNCOLLECTIBLE ACCOUNT.** Occasionally, a company collects from a customer after the account has been written off as uncollectible. The company must make two entries to record the recovery of a bad debt: (1) It reverses the entry made in writing off the account. This reinstates the customer's account. (2) It journalizes the collection in the usual manner.

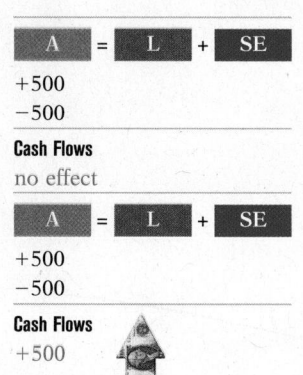

To illustrate, assume that on July 1, R. A. Ware pays the $500 amount that Hampson Furniture had written off on March 1. Hampson makes these entries:

(1)

| July | 1 | Accounts Receivable—R. A. Ware | 500 | |
|------|---|--------------------------------|-----|-----|
| | |     Allowance for Doubtful Accounts | | 500 |
| | |     (To reverse write-off of R. A. Ware | | |
| | |     account) | | |

(2)

| | 1 | Cash | 500 | |
|---|---|------|-----|-----|
| | |     Accounts Receivable—R. A. Ware | | 500 |
| | |     (To record collection from R. A. Ware) | | |

Note that the recovery of a bad debt, like the write-off of a bad debt, affects only balance sheet accounts. The net effect of the two entries is an increase in Cash and an increase in Allowance for Doubtful Accounts for $500. Accounts Receivable and the Allowance for Doubtful Accounts both increase in entry (1) for two reasons: First, the company made an error in judgment when it wrote off the account receivable. Second, R. A. Ware did pay, and therefore the Accounts Receivable account should show this reinstatement and collection for possible future credit purposes.

**ESTIMATING THE ALLOWANCE.** For Hampson Furniture in Illustration 8-3, the amount of the expected uncollectibles was given. However, in "real life," companies must estimate the amount of expected uncollectible accounts if they use the allowance method. Frequently they estimate the allowance as a percentage of the outstanding receivables.

Under the **percentage of receivables basis**, management establishes a percentage relationship between the amount of receivables and expected losses from uncollectible accounts. For example, suppose Steffen Company has an ending balance in Accounts Receivable of $200,000, and an unadjusted credit balance in the Allowance for Doubtful Accounts of $1,500. If it estimates that 5% of its accounts receivable will eventually be uncollectible, then it should report a balance in the Allowance for Doubtful Accounts of $10,000 (.05 × $200,000). This would require a debit to Bad Debts Expense and a credit to Allowance for Doubtful Accounts of $8,500.

To more accurately estimate the ending balance in the allowance account, a company often prepares a schedule, called **aging the accounts receivable**, in which customer balances are classified by the length of time they have been unpaid.

After the company arranges the accounts by age, it determines the expected bad debts losses by applying percentages, based on past experience, to the totals of each category. The longer a receivable is past due, the less likely it is to be collected. As a result, the estimated percentage of uncollectible debts increases as the number of days past due increases. Illustration 8-6 shows an aging schedule for Dart Company. Note the increasing uncollectible percentages from 2% to 40%.

Total estimated uncollectible accounts for Dart Company ($2,228) represent the existing customer claims expected to become uncollectible in the future. Thus, this amount represents the **required balance** in Allowance for Doubtful Accounts at the balance sheet date. Accordingly, **the amount of the bad debts expense adjusting entry is the difference between the required balance and the existing balance in the allowance account**. The existing, unadjusted balance in the Allowance for Doubtful Accounts is the net result of the beginning balance (a normal credit balance) less the write-offs of specific accounts during the year (debits to the allowance account).

| Customer | Total | Not Yet Due | Number of Days Past Due | | | |
|---|---|---|---|---|---|---|
| | | | 1–30 | 31–60 | 61–90 | Over 90 |
| T. E. Adert | $ 600 | | $ 300 | | $ 200 | $ 100 |
| R. C. Bortz | 300 | $ 300 | | | | |
| B. A. Carl | 450 | | 200 | $ 250 | | |
| O. L. Diker | 700 | 500 | | | 200 | |
| T. O. Ebbet | 600 | | | 300 | | 300 |
| Others | 36,950 | 26,200 | 5,200 | 2,450 | 1,600 | 1,500 |
| | $39,600 | $27,000 | $5,700 | $3,000 | $2,000 | $1,900 |
| Estimated percentage uncollectible | | 2% | 4% | 10% | 20% | 40% |
| Total estimated uncollectible accounts | **$ 2,228** | $ 540 | $ 228 | $ 300 | $ 400 | $ 760 |

**Illustration 8-6** Aging schedule

For example, if the unadjusted trial balance shows Allowance for Doubtful Accounts with a credit balance of $528, then an adjusting entry for $1,700 ($2,228 − $528) is necessary:

| | | | |
|---|---|---|---|
| Dec. 31 | Bad Debts Expense | 1,700 | |
| | Allowance for Doubtful Accounts | | 1,700 |
| | (To adjust allowance account to total estimated uncollectibles) | | |

| A | = | L | + | SE |
|---|---|---|---|---|
| | | | | −1,700 Exp |
| −1,700 | | | | |

**Cash Flows**
no effect

After Dart posts the adjusting entry, its accounts will appear as in Illustration 8-7.

| Bad Debts Expense | Allowance for Doubtful Accounts |
|---|---|
| Dec. 31 Adj. **1,700** | Dec. 31 Unadj. Bal. 528 |
| | Dec. 31 Adj. **1,700** |
| | Dec. 31 Bal. 2,228 |

**Illustration 8-7** Bad debts accounts after posting

An important aspect of accounts receivable management is simply maintaining a close watch on the accounts. Studies have shown that accounts more than 60 days past due lose approximately 50% of their value if no payment activity occurs within the next 30 days. For each additional 30 days that pass, the collectible value halves once again. As noted in our Feature Story, Vivi Su of Whitehall-Robins monitors accounts receivable closely, using an aging schedule to set the percentage of bad debts and computing the company's receivables turnover.

Occasionally, the allowance account will have a **debit balance** prior to adjustment. This occurs because the debits to the allowance account from write-offs during the year **exceeded** the beginning balance in the account which was based on previous estimates for bad debts. In such a case, the company **adds the debit balance to the required balance** when it makes the adjusting entry. Thus, if there had been a $500 debit balance in the allowance account before adjustment, the adjusting entry would have been for $2,728 ($2,228 + $500) in order to arrive at a credit balance of $2,228.

The percentage of receivables basis provides an estimate of the cash realizable value of the receivables. It also provides a reasonable matching of expense to revenue.

## DECISION TOOLKIT

| DECISION CHECKPOINTS | INFO NEEDED FOR DECISION | TOOL TO USE FOR DECISION | HOW TO EVALUATE RESULTS |
|---|---|---|---|
| Is the amount of past due accounts increasing? Which accounts require management's attention? | List of outstanding receivables and their due dates | Prepare an aging schedule showing the receivables in various stages: outstanding 0–30 days, 31–60 days, 61–90 days, and over 90 days. | Accounts in the older categories require follow-up: letters, phone calls, and possible renegotiation of terms. |

The following note regarding accounts receivable comes from the annual report of healthcare company McKesson Corp.

**Illustration 8-8** Note disclosure of accounts receivable

**McKESSON CORP.**
Notes to the Financial Statements

**Receivables, net**

| (In millions) | March 31, 2009 | 2008 |
|---|---|---|
| Customer accounts | $6,902 | $6,390 |
| Other | 1,033 | 984 |
| Total | 7,935 | 7,374 |
| Allowances | (161) | (161) |
| Net | $7,774 | $7,213 |

The allowances are primarily for uncollectible accounts and sales returns.

## Ethics Insight

### When Investors Ignore Warning Signs

At one time, Nortel Networks announced that half of its previous year's earnings were "fake." Should investors have seen this coming? Well, there were issues in its annual report that should have caused investors to ask questions. The company had cut its allowance for doubtful accounts on all receivables from $1,253 million to $544 million, even though its total balance of receivables remained relatively unchanged.

This reduction in bad debts expense was responsible for a very large part of the company's earnings that year. At the time, it was unclear whether Nortel might have set the reserves too high originally and needed to reduce them, or whether it slashed the allowance to artificially boost earnings. But one thing is certain—when a company makes an accounting change of this magnitude, investors need to ask questions.

*Source:* Jonathan Weil, "Outside Audit: At Nortel, Warning Signs Existed Months Ago," *Wall Street Journal* (May 18, 2004), p. C3.

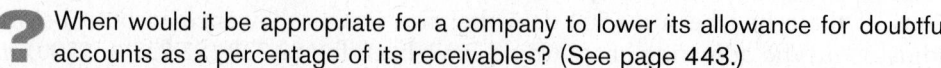

When would it be appropriate for a company to lower its allowance for doubtful accounts as a percentage of its receivables? (See page 443.)

**Do it!**  Brule Corporation has been in business for 5 years. The ledger at the end of the current year shows: Accounts Receivable $30,000; Sales Revenue $180,000; and Allowance for Doubtful Accounts with a debit balance of $2,000. Brule estimates bad debts to be 10% of accounts receivable. Prepare the entry necessary to adjust the Allowance for Doubtful Accounts.

### Solution

Brule should make the following entry to bring the debit balance in the Allowance for Doubtful Accounts up to a normal, credit balance of $3,000 (.1 × $30,000):

| | | |
|---|---|---|
| Bad Debts Expense | 5,000 | |
|     Allowance for Doubtful Accounts | | 5,000 |
|       (To record estimate of uncollectible accounts) | | |

Related exercise material: **BE8-3, BE8-4, BE8-5, Do it! 8-1, E8-3, E8-4, E8-5,** and **E8-6.**

**BAD DEBTS EXPENSE**

**Action Plan**

- Report receivables at their cash (net) realizable value–that is, the amount the company expects to collect in cash.
- Estimate the amount the company does not expect to collect.
- Consider the existing balance in the allowance account when using the percentage of receivables basis.

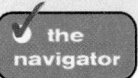
✓ the navigator

## Notes Receivable

Companies also may grant credit in exchange for a formal credit instrument known as a promissory note. A **promissory note** is a written promise to pay a specified amount of money on demand or at a definite time. Promissory notes may be used (1) when individuals and companies lend or borrow money, (2) when the amount of the transaction and the credit period exceed normal limits, and (3) in settlement of accounts receivable.

In a promissory note, the party making the promise to pay is called the **maker**. The party to whom payment is to be made is called the **payee**. The promissory note may specifically identify the payee by name or may designate the payee simply as the bearer of the note.

In the note shown in Illustration 8-9, Brent Company is the maker, and Wilma Company is the payee. To Wilma Company, the promissory note is a note receivable; to Brent Company, the note is a note payable.

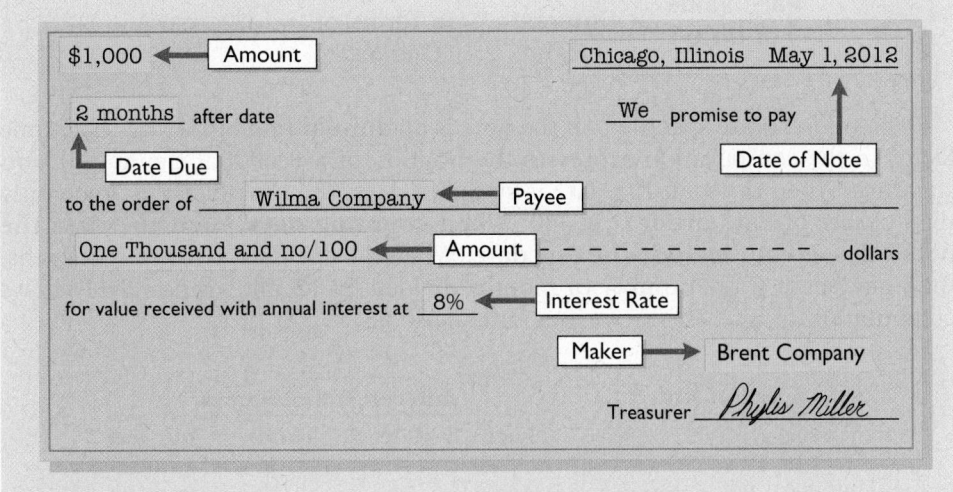

**Illustration 8-9**
Promissory note

**Helpful Hint** Who are the two key parties to a note? What entry does each party make when the note is issued?
Answer:
1. The maker, Brent Company, credits Notes Payable.
2. The payee, Wilma Company, debits Notes Receivable.

Notes receivable give the holder a stronger legal claim to assets than do accounts receivable. Like accounts receivable, notes receivable can be readily sold to another party. Promissory notes are negotiable instruments (as are checks), which means that, when sold, the seller can transfer them to another party by endorsement.

Companies frequently accept notes receivable from customers who need to extend the payment of an outstanding account receivable, and they often require them from high-risk customers. In some industries (e.g., the pleasure and sport boat industry), all credit sales are supported by notes. The majority of notes, however, originate from lending transactions.

There are three basic issues in accounting for notes receivable:

1. **Recognizing** notes receivable.
2. **Valuing** notes receivable.
3. **Disposing** of notes receivable.

We will look at each of these issues, but first we need to consider an issue that did not apply to accounts receivable: computing interest.

### DETERMINING THE MATURITY DATE

**Helpful Hint** The maturity date of a 60-day note dated July 17 is determined as follows:

| Term of note | | 60 days |
|---|---|---|
| July (31 − 17) | 14 | |
| August | 31 | 45 |
| September | | 15 |
| (Maturity date) | | |

The maturity date of a promissory note may be stated in one of three ways: (1) on demand, (2) on a stated date, and (3) at the end of a stated period of time. When it is stated to be at the end of a period of time, the parties to the note will need to determine the maturity date.

When the life of a note is expressed in terms of months, you find the date when it matures by counting the months from the date of issue. For example, the maturity date of a three-month note dated May 1 is August 1. A note drawn on the last day of a month matures on the last day of a subsequent month. That is, a July 31 note due in two months matures on September 30.

When the due date is stated in terms of days, you need to count the exact number of days to determine the maturity date. In counting, **omit the date the note is issued but include the due date**.

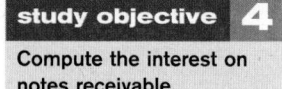

**study objective 4**

Compute the interest on notes receivable.

### COMPUTING INTEREST

Illustration 8-10 gives the basic formula for computing interest on an interest-bearing note.

**Illustration 8-10** Formula for computing interest

$$\text{Face Value of Note} \times \frac{\text{Annual Interest Rate}}{} \times \frac{\text{Time in Terms of One Year}}{} = \text{Interest}$$

The interest rate specified on the note is an **annual** rate of interest. The time factor in the computation expresses the fraction of a year that the note is outstanding. When the maturity date is stated in days, the time factor is frequently the number of days divided by 360. **When counting days, omit the date the note is issued but include the due date.** When the due date is stated in months, the time factor is the number of months divided by 12. Illustration 8-11 shows computation of interest for various time periods.

**Illustration 8-11** Computation of interest

| Terms of Note | Interest Computation | | | |
|---|---|---|---|---|
| | Face × | Rate × | Time | = Interest |
| $ 730, 12%, 120 days | $ 730 × | 12% × | 120/360 | = $ 29.20 |
| $1,000, 9%, 6 months | $1,000 × | 9% × | 6/12 | = $ 45.00 |
| $2,000, 6%, 1 year | $2,000 × | 6% × | 1/1 | = $120.00 |

There are different ways to calculate interest. For example, the computation in Illustration 8-11 assumed 360 days for the year. Most financial institutions use 365 days to compute interest. *For homework problems, assume 360 days to simplify computations*.

## RECOGNIZING NOTES RECEIVABLE

To illustrate the basic entry for notes receivable, we will use Brent Company's $1,000, two-month, 8% promissory note dated May 1. Assuming that Brent Company wrote the note to settle an open account, Wilma Company makes the following entry for the receipt of the note.

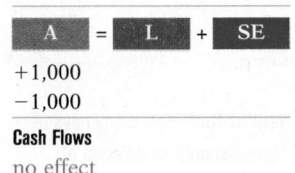

| | | | | |
|---|---|---|---|---|
| May | 1 | Notes Receivable | 1,000 | |
| | | Accounts Receivable—Brent Company | | 1,000 |
| | | (To record acceptance of Brent Company note) | | |

**A = L + SE**
+1,000
−1,000

**Cash Flows**
no effect

The company records the note receivable at its **face value**, the value shown on the face of the note. No interest revenue is reported when the company accepts the note because the revenue recognition principle does not recognize revenue until earned. Interest is earned (accrued) as time passes.

If a company issues cash in exchange for a note, the entry is a debit to Notes Receivable and a credit to Cash in the amount of the loan.

## VALUING NOTES RECEIVABLE

Like accounts receivable, companies report short-term notes receivable at their **cash (net) realizable value**. The notes receivable allowance account is Allowance for Doubtful Accounts. Valuing short-term notes receivable is the same as valuing accounts receivable. The computations and estimations involved in determining cash realizable value and in recording the proper amount of bad debts expense and related allowance are similar.

Long-term notes receivable, however, pose additional estimation problems. As an example, we need only look at the problems large U.S. banks sometimes have in collecting their receivables. Loans to less-developed countries are particularly worrisome. Developing countries need loans for development but often find repayment difficult. U.S. loans (notes) to less-developed countries at one time totaled approximately $135 billion. In Brazil alone, **Citigroup** at one time had loans equivalent to 80% of its stockholders' equity. In some cases, developed nations have intervened to provide financial assistance to the financially troubled borrowers so as to minimize the political and economic turmoil to the borrower and to ensure the survival of the lender.

### International Insight

#### Can Fair Value Be Unfair?

The FASB and the International Accounting Standards Board (IASB) are considering proposals for how to account for financial instruments. The FASB has proposed that loans and receivables be accounted for at their fair value (the amount they could currently be sold for), as are most investments. The FASB believes that this would provide a more accurate view of a company's financial position. It might be especially useful as an early warning when a bank is in trouble because of poor-quality loans. But, banks argue that fair values are difficult to estimate accurately. They are also concerned that volatile fair values could cause large swings in a bank's reported net income.

*Source:* David Reilly, "Banks Face a Mark-to-Market Challenge," *Wall Street Journal Online* (March 15, 2010).

**?** What are the arguments in favor of and against fair value accounting for loans and receivables? (See page 443.)

## DISPOSING OF NOTES RECEIVABLE

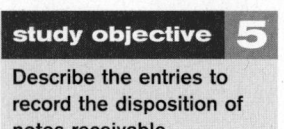

Notes may be held to their maturity date, at which time the face value plus accrued interest is due. In some situations, the maker of the note defaults, and the payee must make an appropriate adjustment. In other situations, similar to accounts receivable, the holder of the note speeds up the conversion to cash by selling the receivables as described later in this chapter.

### Honor of Notes Receivable

A note is **honored** when its maker pays in full at its maturity date. For each interest-bearing note, the **amount due at maturity** is the face value of the note plus interest for the length of time specified on the note.

To illustrate, assume that Wolder Co. lends Higley Inc. $10,000 on June 1, accepting a five-month, 9% interest note. In this situation, interest is $375 ($10,000 × 9% × $\frac{5}{12}$). The amount due, the maturity value, is $10,375 ($10,000 + $375). To obtain payment, Wolder (the payee) must present the note either to Higley Inc. (the maker) or to the maker's agent, such as a bank. If Wolder presents the note to Higley Inc. on November 1, the maturity date, Wolder's entry to record the collection is:

**Helpful Hint** How many days of interest should be accrued at September 30 for a 90-day note issued on August 16? *Answer:* 45 days (15 days in August plus 30 days in September).

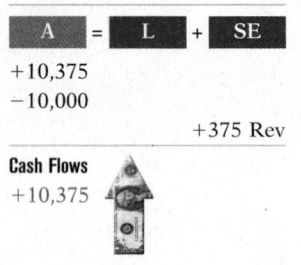

A = L + SE

+10,375
−10,000
            +375 Rev

**Cash Flows**
+10,375

| Nov. 1 | Cash | 10,375 | |
|---|---|---|---|
| | Notes Receivable | | 10,000 |
| | Interest Revenue ($10,000 × 9% × $\frac{5}{12}$) | | 375 |
| | (To record collection of Higley Inc. note and interest) | | |

### Accrual of Interest Receivable

Suppose instead that Wolder Co. prepares financial statements as of September 30. The timeline in Illustration 8-12 presents this situation.

**Illustration 8-12** Timeline of interest earned

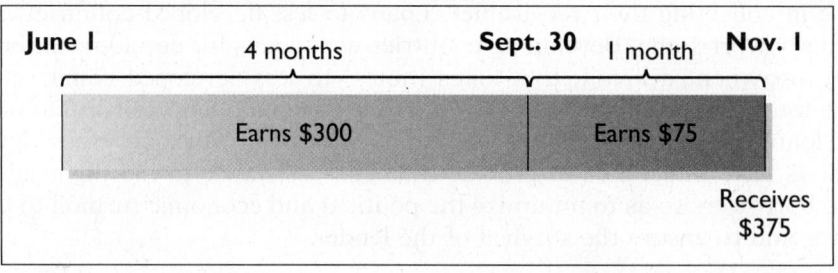

To reflect interest earned but not yet received, Wolder must accrue interest on September 30. In this case, the adjusting entry by Wolder is for four months of interest, or $300, as shown below.

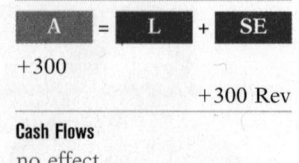

A = L + SE

+300
            +300 Rev

**Cash Flows**
no effect

| Sept. 30 | Interest Receivable ($10,000 × 9% × $\frac{4}{12}$) | 300 | |
|---|---|---|---|
| | Interest Revenue | | 300 |
| | (To accrue 4 months' interest on Higley note) | | |

At the note's maturity on November 1, Wolder receives $10,375. This amount represents repayment of the $10,000 note as well as five months of interest, or $375, as shown on the next page. The $375 is comprised of the $300 Interest

Receivable accrued on September 30 plus $75 earned during October. Wolder's entry to record the honoring of the Higley note on November 1 is:

| | | | | |
|---|---|---|---|---|
| Nov. 1 | Cash [$10,000 + ($10,000 × 9% × $\frac{5}{12}$)] | 10,375 | |
| |     Notes Receivable | | 10,000 |
| |     Interest Receivable | | 300 |
| |     Interest Revenue ($10,000 × 9% × $\frac{1}{12}$) | | 75 |
| |       (To record collection of Higley Inc. note | | |
| |       and interest) | | |

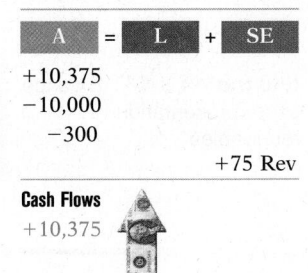

A = L + SE
+10,375
−10,000
−300
          +75 Rev

**Cash Flows**
+10,375

In this case, Wolder credits Interest Receivable because the receivable was established in the adjusting entry on September 30.

### Dishonor of Notes Receivable

A **dishonored note** is a note that is not paid in full at maturity. A dishonored note receivable is no longer negotiable; however, the payee still has a claim against the maker of the note for both the note and the interest. If the lender expects that it eventually will be able to collect, the two parties negotiate new terms to make it easier for the borrower to repay the debt. If there is no hope of collection, the payee should write off the face value of the note.

*before you go on...*

**Do it!** Gambit Stores accepts from Leonard Co. a $3,400, 90-day, 6% note dated May 10 in settlement of Leonard's overdue open account. The note matures on August 8. What entry does Gambit make at the maturity date, assuming Leonard pays the note and interest in full at that time?

**NOTES RECEIVABLE**

**Action Plan**

- Determine whether interest was accrued.
- Compute the accrued interest.
- Prepare the entry for payment of the note and the interest. The entry to record interest at maturity in this solution assumes that no interest has been previously accrued on this note.

#### Solution

The interest payable at maturity date is $51, computed as follows.

$$\text{Face} \times \text{Rate} \times \text{Time} = \text{Interest}$$
$$\$3,400 \times 6\% \times \frac{90}{360} = \$51$$

Gambit Stores records this entry at the maturity date:

| | | |
|---|---|---|
| Cash | 3,451 | |
|     Notes Receivable | | 3,400 |
|     Interest Revenue | | 51 |
|       (To record collection of Leonard note and interest) | | |

the navigator

Related exercise material: **BE8-6, BE8-7, Do it! 8-2, E8-7,** and **E8-8**.

# Financial Statement Presentation of Receivables

Companies should identify in the balance sheet or in the notes to the financial statements each of the major types of receivables. Short-term receivables are reported in the current assets section of the balance sheet, below short-term investments. Short-term investments appear before short-term receivables because these investments are nearer to cash. Companies report both the gross amount of receivables and the allowance for doubtful accounts.

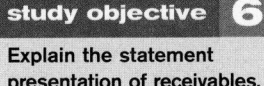
**study objective 6**
Explain the statement presentation of receivables.

Receivables represent 53% of the total assets of heavy equipment manufacturer Deere & Company. Illustration 8-13 shows a presentation of receivables for Deere & Company from its 2009 balance sheet and notes.

**Illustration 8-13** Balance sheet presentation of receivables

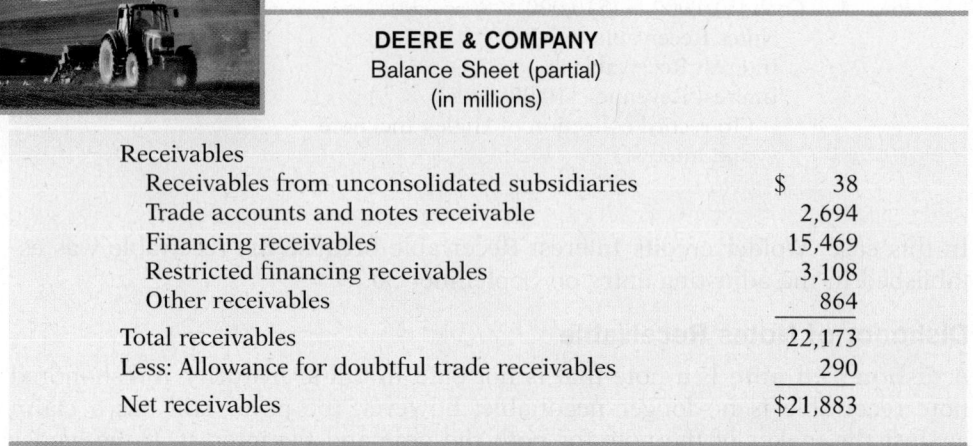

| DEERE & COMPANY Balance Sheet (partial) (in millions) | | |
| --- | --- | --- |
| Receivables | | |
| Receivables from unconsolidated subsidiaries | $ | 38 |
| Trade accounts and notes receivable | | 2,694 |
| Financing receivables | | 15,469 |
| Restricted financing receivables | | 3,108 |
| Other receivables | | 864 |
| Total receivables | | 22,173 |
| Less: Allowance for doubtful trade receivables | | 290 |
| Net receivables | | $21,883 |

In the income statement, companies report bad debts expense under "Selling expenses" in the operating expenses section. They show interest revenue under "Other revenues and gains" in the nonoperating section of the income statement.

If a company has significant risk of uncollectible accounts or other problems with its receivables, it is required to discuss this possibility in the notes to the financial statements.

# Managing Receivables

**study objective 7**

Describe the principles of sound accounts receivable management.

Managing accounts receivable involves five steps:

1. Determine to whom to extend credit.
2. Establish a payment period.
3. Monitor collections.
4. Evaluate the liquidity of receivables.
5. Accelerate cash receipts from receivables when necessary.

### EXTENDING CREDIT

A critical part of managing receivables is determining who should be extended credit and who should not. Many companies increase sales by being generous with their credit policy, but they may end up extending credit to risky customers who do not pay. If the credit policy is too tight, you will lose sales. If it is too loose, you may sell to "deadbeats" who will pay either very late or not at all. One CEO noted that prior to getting his credit and collection department in order, his salespeople had 300 square feet of office space **per person**, while the people in credit and collections had six people crammed into a single 300-square-foot space. Although this focus on sales boosted sales revenue, it had very expensive consequences in bad debts expense.

Companies can take certain steps to help minimize losses due to bad debts when they decide to relax credit standards for new customers. They might require risky customers to provide letters of credit or bank guarantees. Then, if the customer does not pay, the bank that provided the guarantee will do so. Particularly risky customers might be required to pay cash on delivery. For example, retailer Linens 'n Things, Inc. recently reported that it was paying its largest vendors cash before it had even received the goods. The vendors had cut off shipments because the company had been slow in paying. Kmart's suppliers also required it to pay cash in advance when it was financially troubled.

In addition, companies should ask potential customers for references from banks and suppliers, to determine their payment history. It is important to check these references on potential new customers as well as periodically to check the financial health of continuing customers. Many resources are available for investigating customers. For example, *The Dun & Bradstreet Reference Book of American Business* (*www.dnb.com*) lists millions of companies and provides credit ratings for many of them.

## Accounting Across the Organization

### Bad Information Can Lead to Bad Loans

Many factors have contributed to the recent credit crisis. One significant factor that resulted in many bad loans was a failure by lenders to investigate loan customers sufficiently. For example, Countrywide Financial Corporation wrote many loans under its "Fast and Easy" loan program. That program allowed borrowers to provide little or no documentation for their income or their assets. Other lenders had similar programs, which earned the nickname "liars' loans." One study found that in these situations 60% of applicants overstated their incomes by more than 50% in order to qualify for a loan. Critics of the banking industry say that because loan officers were compensated for loan volume, and because banks were selling the loans to investors rather than holding them, the lenders had little incentive to investigate the borrowers' creditworthiness.

*Source:* Glenn R. Simpson and James R. Hagerty, "Countrywide Loss Focuses Attention on Underwriting," *Wall Street Journal* (April 30, 2008), p. B1; and Michael Corkery, "Fraud Seen as Driver in Wave of Foreclosures," *Wall Street Journal* (December 21, 2007), p. A1.

**?** What steps should the banks have taken to ensure the accuracy of financial information provided on loan applications? (See page 443.)

### ESTABLISHING A PAYMENT PERIOD

Companies that extend credit should determine a required payment period and communicate that policy to their customers. It is important that the payment period is consistent with that of competitors. For example, if you decide to require payment within 15 days, but your competitors require payment within 45 days, you may lose sales to your competitors. However, to match competitors' terms yet still encourage prompt payment of accounts, you might allow up to 45 days to pay but offer a sales discount for people paying within 15 days.

### MONITORING COLLECTIONS

We discussed preparation of the accounts receivable aging schedule earlier in the chapter (pages 404–405). Companies should prepare an accounts receivable aging schedule at least monthly. In addition to estimating the allowance for doubtful accounts, the aging schedule has other uses: It helps managers estimate the timing of future cash inflows, which is very important to the treasurer's efforts to prepare a cash budget. It provides information about the overall collection experience of the company and identifies problem accounts. For example, as discussed in the Feature Story about Whitehall-Robins, management would compute and compare the percentage of receivables that are over 90 days past due.

The aging schedule identifies problem accounts that the company needs to pursue with phone calls, letters, and occasionally legal action. Sometimes, special arrangements must be made with problem accounts. For example, it was reported that Intel Corporation (a major manufacturer of computer chips) required that Packard Bell (at one time one of the largest U.S. sellers of personal computers) exchange its past-due account receivable for an interest-bearing note receivable. This caused concern within the investment community. The move suggested that Packard Bell was in trouble, which worried Intel investors concerned about Intel's accounts receivable.

## DECISION TOOLKIT

| DECISION CHECKPOINTS | INFO NEEDED FOR DECISION | TOOL TO USE FOR DECISION | HOW TO EVALUATE RESULTS |
|---|---|---|---|
| Is the company's credit risk increasing? | Customer account balances and due dates | Accounts receivable aging schedule | Compute and compare the percentage of receivables over 90 days old. |

If a company has significant concentrations of credit risk, it must discuss this risk in the notes to its financial statements. A **concentration of credit risk** is a threat of nonpayment from a single large customer or class of customers that could adversely affect the financial health of the company. Illustration 8-14 shows an excerpt from the credit risk note from the 2009 annual report of McKesson Corp. McKesson reports that its ten largest customers account for 52% of its total revenues and 49% of its receivables.

**Illustration 8-14** Excerpt from note on concentration of credit risk

**McKESSON CORP.**
Notes to the Financial Statements

*Concentrations of Credit Risk and Receivables:* Our trade receivables subject us to a concentration of credit risk with customers primarily in our Distribution Solutions segment. At March 31, 2009, revenues and accounts receivable from our ten largest customers accounted for approximately 52% of consolidated revenues and approximately 49% of accounts receivable. At March 31, 2009, revenues and accounts receivable from our two largest customers, CVS Caremark Corporation and Rite Aid Corporation, represented approximately 14% and 12% of total consolidated revenues and 14% and 10% of accounts receivable.

This note to McKesson Corp.'s financial statements indicates it has a high level of credit concentration. A default by any of these large customers could have a significant negative impact on its financial performance.

## DECISION TOOLKIT

| DECISION CHECKPOINTS | INFO NEEDED FOR DECISION | TOOL TO USE FOR DECISION | HOW TO EVALUATE RESULTS |
|---|---|---|---|
| Does the company have significant concentrations of credit risk? | Note to the financial statements on concentrations of credit risk | If risky credit customers are identified, the financial health of those customers should be evaluated to gain an independent assessment of the potential for a material credit loss. | If a material loss appears likely, the potential negative impact of that loss on the company should be carefully evaluated, along with the adequacy of the allowance for doubtful accounts. |

## EVALUATING LIQUIDITY OF RECEIVABLES

Investors and managers keep a watchful eye on the relationship among sales, accounts receivable, and cash collections. If sales increase, then accounts receivable are also expected to increase. But a disproportionate increase in accounts receivable might signal trouble. Perhaps the company increased its sales by loosening its credit policy, and these receivables may be difficult or impossible to collect. Such receivables are considered less liquid. Recall that liquidity is measured by how quickly certain assets can be converted to cash.

The ratio that analysts use to assess the liquidity of receivables is the **receivables turnover ratio**, computed by dividing net credit sales (net sales less cash sales) by the average net accounts receivables during the year. This ratio measures the number of times, on average, a company collects receivables during the period. Unless seasonal factors are significant, **average** accounts receivable outstanding can be computed from the beginning and ending balances of the net receivables.[1]

A popular variant of the receivables turnover ratio is the **average collection period**, which measures the average amount of time that a receivable is outstanding. This is done by dividing the receivables turnover ratio into 365 days. Companies use the average collection period to assess the effectiveness of a company's credit and collection policies. The average collection period should not greatly exceed the credit term period (i.e., the time allowed for payment).

The following data (in millions) are available for McKesson Corp.

|  | For the year ended March 31, | |
|---|---|---|
|  | **2009** | **2008** |
| Sales | $106,632 | $101,703 |
| Accounts receivable (net) | 7,774 | 7,213 |

Illustration 8-15 shows the receivables turnover ratio and average collection period for McKesson Corp., along with comparative industry data. These calculations assume that all sales were credit sales.

**Illustration 8-15**
Receivables turnover and average collection period

$$\text{Receivables Turnover Ratio} = \frac{\text{Net Credit Sales}}{\text{Average Net Receivables}}$$

$$\text{Average Collection Period} = \frac{365}{\text{Receivables Turnover Ratio}}$$

| Ratio | McKesson ($ in millions) | | Cardinal Health | Industry Average |
|---|---|---|---|---|
|  | 2009 | 2008 | 2009 | 2009 |
| Receivables turnover | $\dfrac{\$106,632}{(\$7,774 + \$7,213)/2}$ = 14.2 times | 14.8 times | 18.7 times | 16.2 times |
| Average collection period | $\dfrac{365 \text{ days}}{14.2}$ = 25.7 days | 24.7 days | 19.5 days | 22.5 days |

---

[1]If seasonal factors are significant, the company might determine the average accounts receivable balance by using monthly or quarterly amounts.

study objective 8

Identify ratios to analyze a company's receivables.

McKesson's receivables turnover was 14.2 times in 2009, with a corresponding average collection period of 25.7 days. This was slightly slower than its 2008 collection period. It was also slower than the industry average collection period of 22.5 days and considerably slower than Cardinal Health, which was 19.5 days. What this means is that McKesson turned its receivables into cash more slowly than most of its competitors. Therefore, it was less likely to pay its current obligations than a company with a quicker receivables turnover and is more likely to need outside financing to meet cash shortfalls.

## DECISION TOOLKIT

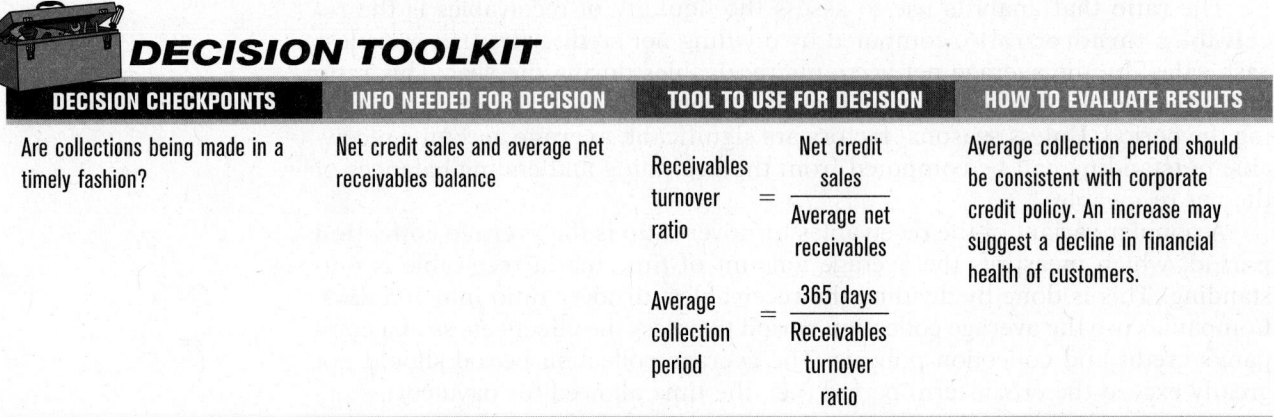

| DECISION CHECKPOINTS | INFO NEEDED FOR DECISION | TOOL TO USE FOR DECISION | HOW TO EVALUATE RESULTS |
|---|---|---|---|
| Are collections being made in a timely fashion? | Net credit sales and average net receivables balance | Receivables turnover ratio = $\dfrac{\text{Net credit sales}}{\text{Average net receivables}}$  Average collection period = $\dfrac{365 \text{ days}}{\text{Receivables turnover ratio}}$ | Average collection period should be consistent with corporate credit policy. An increase may suggest a decline in financial health of customers. |

In some cases, receivables turnover may be misleading. Some large retail chains that issue their own credit cards encourage customers to use these cards for purchases. If customers pay slowly, the stores earn a healthy return on the outstanding receivables in the form of interest at rates of 18% to 22%. On the other hand, companies that sell (factor) their receivables on a consistent basis will have a faster turnover than those that do not. Thus, to interpret receivables turnover, you must know how a company manages its receivables. In general, the faster the turnover, the greater the reliability of the current ratio for assessing liquidity.

## before you go on...

### ANALYSIS OF RECEIVABLES

#### Action Plan

- Review the formula to compute the receivables turnover.
- Make sure that both the beginning and ending accounts receivable are considered in the computation.
- Review the formula to compute the average collection period in days.

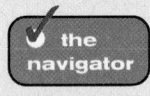

**Do it!**  In 2012, Lebron James Company had net credit sales of $923,795 for the year. It had a beginning accounts receivable (net) balance of $38,275 and an ending accounts receivable (net) balance of $35,988. Compute Lebron James Company's (a) receivables turnover and (b) average collection period in days.

**Solution**

**(a)**

| Net credit sales | ÷ | Average net receivables | = | Receivables turnover |
|---|---|---|---|---|
| $923,795 | ÷ | $\dfrac{\$38,275 + \$35,988}{2}$ | = | 24.9 times |

**(b)**

| Days in year | ÷ | Receivables turnover | = | Average collection period in days |
|---|---|---|---|---|
| 365 | ÷ | 24.9 times | = | 14.7 days |

Related exercise material: **BE8-10**, **Do it!** **8-3**, **E8-11**, and **E8-12**.

## ACCELERATING CASH RECEIPTS

In the normal course of events, companies collect accounts receivable in cash and remove them from the books. However, as credit sales and receivables have grown in size and significance, the "normal course of events" has changed. Two common expressions apply to the collection of receivables: (1) "Time is money"—that is, waiting for the normal collection process costs money. (2) "A bird in the hand is worth two in the bush"—that is, getting the cash now is better than getting it later or not at all. Therefore, in order to accelerate the receipt of cash from receivables, companies frequently sell their receivables to another company for cash, thereby shortening the cash-to-cash operating cycle.

There are three reasons for the sale of receivables. The first is their **size**. In recent years, for competitive reasons, sellers (retailers, wholesalers, and manufacturers) often have provided financing to purchasers of their goods. For example, many major companies in the automobile, truck, industrial and farm equipment, computer, and appliance industries have created companies that accept responsibility for accounts receivable financing. Caterpillar has Caterpillar Financial Services, General Electric has GE Capital, and Ford has Ford Motor Credit Corp. (FMCC). These companies are referred to as **captive finance companies** because they are owned by the company selling the product. The purpose of captive finance companies is to encourage the sale of the company's products by assuring financing to buyers. However, the parent companies involved do not necessarily want to hold large amounts of receivables, so they may sell them.

Second, **companies may sell receivables because they may be the only reasonable source of cash**. When credit is tight, companies may not be able to borrow money in the usual credit markets. Even if credit is available, the cost of borrowing may be prohibitive.

A final reason for selling receivables is that **billing and collection are often time-consuming and costly**. As a result, it is often easier for a retailer to sell the receivables to another party that has expertise in billing and collection matters. Credit card companies such as MasterCard, Visa, American Express, and Discover specialize in billing and collecting accounts receivable.

### National Credit Card Sales

Approximately one billion credit cards were in use recently—more than three credit cards for every man, woman, and child in this country. A common type of credit card is a national credit card such as Visa and MasterCard. Three parties are involved when national credit cards are used in making retail sales: (1) the credit card issuer, who is independent of the retailer, (2) the retailer, and (3) the customer. **A retailer's acceptance of a national credit card is another form of selling—factoring—the receivable by the retailer.**

The use of national credit cards translates to more sales and zero bad debts for the retailer. Both are powerful reasons for a retailer to accept such cards. Illustration 8-16 (page 418) shows the major advantages of national credit cards to the retailer. In exchange for these advantages, the retailer pays the credit card issuer a fee of 2% to 4% of the invoice price for its services.

The retailer considers sales resulting from the use of Visa and MasterCard as **cash sales**. Upon notification of a credit card charge from a retailer, the bank that issued the card immediately adds the amount to the seller's bank balance. Companies therefore record these credit card charges in the same manner as checks deposited from a cash sale.

To illustrate, Morgan Marie purchases $1,000 of compact discs for her restaurant from Sondgeroth Music Co., and she charges this amount on her Visa First

**Illustration 8-16**
Advantages of credit cards
to the retailer

Bank Card. The service fee that First Bank charges Sondgeroth Music is 3%. Sondgeroth Music's entry to record this transaction is:

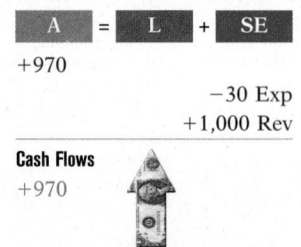

A = L + SE
+970

−30 Exp
+1,000 Rev

**Cash Flows**
+970

| | | |
|---|---|---|
| Cash | 970 | |
| Service Charge Expense | 30 | |
| Sales Revenue | | 1,000 |
| (To record Visa credit card sales) | | |

### Sale of Receivables to a Factor

A common way to accelerate receivables collection is a sale to a factor. A **factor** is a finance company or bank that buys receivables from businesses for a fee and then collects the payments directly from the customers.

Factoring was traditionally associated with the textiles, apparel, footwear, furniture, and home furnishing industries. It has now spread to other types of businesses and is a multibillion dollar industry. For example, Sears, Roebuck & Co. (now Sears Holdings) once sold $14.8 billion of customer accounts receivable. McKesson has a pre-arranged agreement allowing it to sell up to $700 million of its receivables.

Factoring arrangements vary widely, but typically the factor charges a commission. It ranges from 1% to 3% of the amount of receivables purchased. To illustrate, assume that Hendredon Furniture factors $600,000 of receivables to Federal Factors, Inc. Federal Factors assesses a service charge of 2% of the amount of receivables sold. The following journal entry records Hendredon's sale of receivables.

**International Note** GAAP has less stringent requirements regarding the sale of receivables. Thus, GAAP companies can more easily use factoring transactions as a form of financing without showing a related liability on their books. Some argue that this type of so-called "off-balance-sheet" financing would be more difficult to achieve under IFRS.

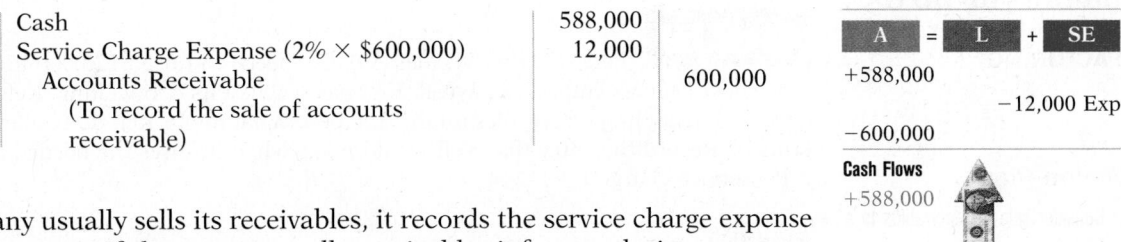

| | | | |
|---|---|---|---|
| Cash | 588,000 | | |
| Service Charge Expense (2% × $600,000) | 12,000 | | |
|    Accounts Receivable | | 600,000 | |
|      (To record the sale of accounts | | | |
|      receivable) | | | |

| A | = | L | + | SE |
|---|---|---|---|---|
| +588,000 | | | | |
| | | | | −12,000 Exp |
| −600,000 | | | | |

**Cash Flows**
+588,000

If the company usually sells its receivables, it records the service charge expense as a selling expense. If the company sells receivables infrequently, it may report this amount under "Other expenses and losses" in the income statement.

## Accounting Across the Organization

### eBay for Receivables

The credit crunch has hit small businesses especially hard. Because banks have been very reluctant to loan, entrepreneurs have had to look more frequently to factoring as a source of cash. This created an opportunity for a new business called The Receivables Exchange. It offers a website where small companies can anonymously display a list of their receivables that they would like to factor in exchange for cash. Parties that are interested in providing cash in exchange for the receivables can also view the receivables and bid on those they like without revealing their identity. It has been described as "eBay for receivables." Because of his continued use of the service, one experienced participant has reduced the monthly rate that he pays to The Receivables Exchange from 4% to below 3%.

*Source*: Simona Covel, "Getting Your Due," *Wall Street Journal Online* (May 11, 2009).

 What issues should management consider in deciding whether to factor its receivables? (See page 444.)

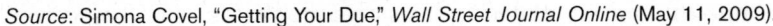

Illustration 8-17 summarizes the basic principles of managing accounts receivable.

**Illustration 8-17**
Managing receivables

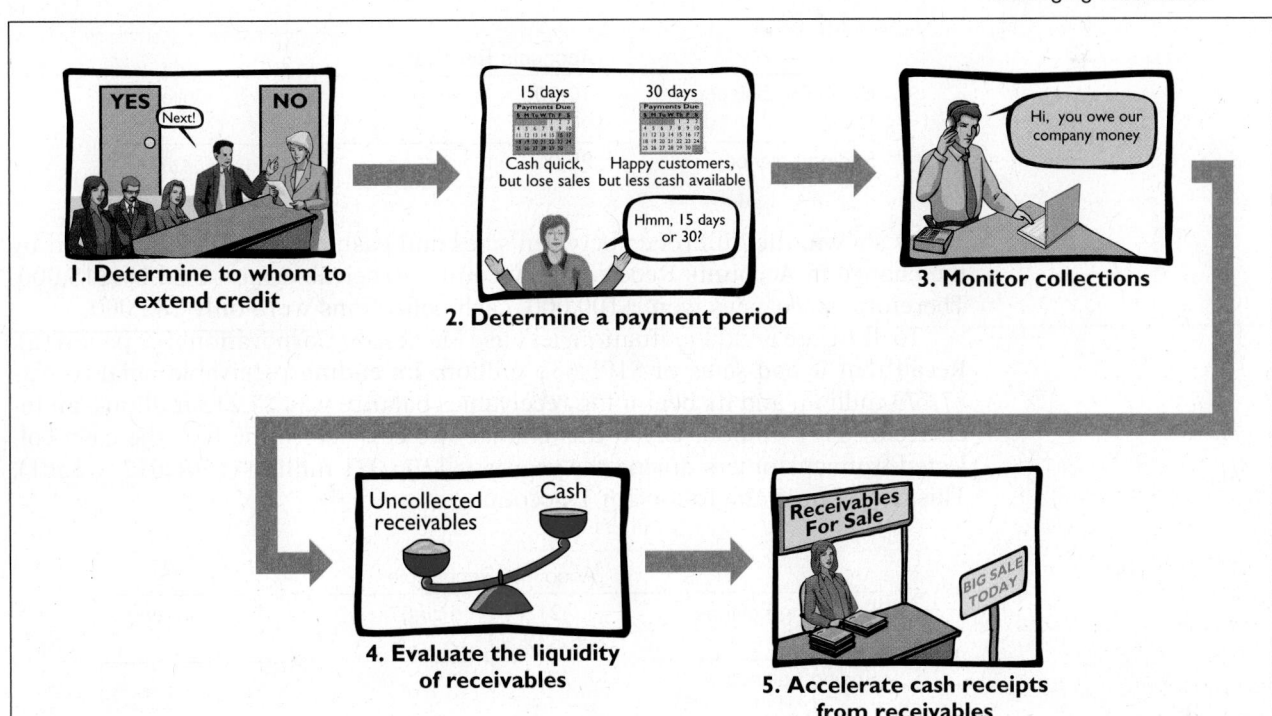

## before you go on...

**FACTORING**

**Action Plan**

- Consider sale of receivables to a factor.
- Weigh cost of factoring against benefit of having cash in hand.

the navigator

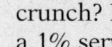 Peter M. Kell Wholesalers Co. needs to raise $120,000 in cash to safely cover next Friday's employee payroll. Kell has reached its debt ceiling. Kell's present balance of outstanding receivables totals $750,000. What might Kell do to alleviate this cash crunch? Record the entry that Kell would make when it raises the needed cash. (Assume a 1% service charge.)

**Solution**

If Kell Co. factors $125,000 of its accounts receivable at a 1% service charge, it would make this entry:

| | | |
|---|---|---|
| Cash | 123,750 | |
| Service Charge Expense | 1,250 | |
| Accounts Receivable | | 125,000 |
| (To record sale of receivables to factor) | | |

Related exercise material: **BE8-11**, **Do it! 8-4**, **E8-13**, and **E8-14**.

## KEEPING AN EYE ON CASH

A lot of companies report strong sales growth but have cash flow problems. How can this be? The reason for the difference is timing: Sales revenue is recorded when goods are delivered, even if cash is not received until later. For example, McKesson Corp. had sales of $106,632 million during 2009. Does that mean it received cash of $106,632 million from its customers? Most likely not. So how do we determine the amount of cash related to sales revenue that is actually received from customers? We analyze the changes that take place in Accounts Receivable.

To illustrate, suppose Bestor Corporation started the year with $10,000 in accounts receivable. During the year, it had sales of $100,000. At the end of the year, the balance in accounts receivable was $25,000. As a result, accounts receivable increased $15,000 during the year. How much cash did Bestor collect from customers during the year? Using the following T account, we can determine that collections were $85,000.

| Accounts Receivable | | | |
|---|---|---|---|
| Beginning balance | 10,000 | 85,000 | Collections |
| Sales | 100,000 | | |
| Ending balance | 25,000 | | |

As shown, the difference between sales and cash collections is explained by the change in Accounts Receivable. Accounts Receivable increased by $15,000. Therefore, since sales were $100,000, cash collections were only $85,000.

To illustrate another situation, let's use McKesson Corporation (see page 415). Recall that it had sales of $106,632 million. Its ending receivable balance was $7,774 million, and its beginning receivables balance was $7,213 million—an increase of $561 million. Given this change, we can determine that the cash collected from customers during the year was $106,071 million ($106,632 − $561). This is shown in the following T account.

| Accounts Receivable | | | |
|---|---|---|---|
| Beginning balance | 7,213 | 106,071 | Collections |
| Sales | 106,632 | | |
| Ending balance | 7,774 | | |

# USING THE DECISION TOOLKIT

The information below was taken from the September 30, 2009, financial statements of AmerisourceBergen Corp., Inc. Similar to McKesson Corp., AmerisourceBergen distributes drugs and related services to pharmaceutical manufacturers and health-care providers in the United States and Puerto Rico.

### Instructions

Comment on AmerisourceBergen's accounts receivable management and liquidity relative to that of McKesson, using (1) the current ratio and (2) the receivables turnover ratio and average collection period. McKesson's current ratio was 1.16:1. The other ratio values for McKesson were calculated earlier in the chapter.

**AMERISOURCEBERGEN CORP., INC.**
Selected Financial Information
(in millions)

|  | 2009 | 2008 |
|---|---|---|
| Sales | $71,760 | $70,190 |
| Current assets |  |  |
| Cash and cash equivalents | $ 1,009 | $ 878 |
| Short-term investment securities | — | — |
| Accounts receivable (net) | 3,917 | 3,480 |
| Merchandise inventories | 4,973 | 4,212 |
| Other | — | 44 |
| Total current assets | $ 9,899 | $ 8,614 |
| Total current liabilities | $ 9,480 | $ 8,168 |

### Solution

1. Here is the current ratio (Current assets ÷ Current liabilities) for each company.

**McKesson**

1.16:1

**AmerisourceBergen**

$$\frac{\$9,899}{\$9,480} = 1.04:1$$

This suggests that McKesson and AmerisourceBergen have similar liquidity, with McKesson slightly more liquid. Both have relatively low current ratios.

2. The receivables turnover ratio and average collection period for each company are:

|  | McKesson | AmerisourceBergen |
|---|---|---|
| Receivables turnover ratio | 14.2 times | $\frac{\$71,760}{(\$3,917 + \$3,480)/2} = 19.4$ times |
| Average collection period | 25.7 days | $\frac{365}{19.4} = 18.8$ days |

AmerisourceBergen's receivables turnover ratio of 19.4 compared to McKesson's 14.2, and its average collection period of 18.8 days versus McKesson's 25.7 days, suggest that AmerisourceBergen is able to collect from its customers much more rapidly. The high receivables turnover ratios of both companies help to compensate for their relatively low current ratios when evaluating their liquidity.

# Summary of Study Objectives

**1 Identify the different types of receivables.** Receivables are frequently classified as accounts, notes, and other. Accounts receivable are amounts customers owe on account. Notes receivable represent claims that are evidenced by formal instruments of credit. Other receivables include nontrade receivables such as interest receivable, loans to company officers, advances to employees, and income taxes refundable.

**2 Explain how accounts receivable are recognized in the accounts.** Accounts receivable are recorded at invoice price. They are reduced by sales returns and allowances. Cash discounts reduce the amount received on accounts receivable.

**3 Describe the methods used to account for bad debts.** The two methods of accounting for uncollectible accounts are the allowance method and the direct write-off method. Under the allowance method, companies estimate uncollectible accounts as a percentage of receivables. It emphasizes the cash realizable value of the accounts receivable. An aging schedule is frequently used with this approach.

**4 Compute the interest on notes receivable.** The formula for computing interest is: Face value × Interest rate × Time.

**5 Describe the entries to record the disposition of notes receivable.** Notes can be held to maturity, at which time the borrower (maker) pays the face value plus accrued interest and the payee removes the note from the accounts. In many cases, however, similar to accounts receivable, the holder of the note speeds up the conversion by selling the receivable to another party. In some situations, the maker of the note dishonors the note (defaults), and the note is written off.

**6 Explain the statement presentation of receivables.** Companies should identify each major type of receivable in the balance sheet or in the notes to the financial statements. Short-term receivables are considered current assets. Companies report the gross amount of receivables and allowance for doubtful accounts. They report bad debts and service charge expenses in the income statement as operating (selling) expenses, and interest revenue as other revenues and gains in the nonoperating section of the statement.

**7 Describe the principles of sound accounts receivable management.** To properly manage receivables, management must (a) determine to whom to extend credit, (b) establish a payment period, (c) monitor

(Summary continues on next page)

## DECISION TOOLKIT   A SUMMARY

| DECISION CHECKPOINTS | INFO NEEDED FOR DECISION | TOOL TO USE FOR DECISION | HOW TO EVALUATE RESULTS |
|---|---|---|---|
| Is the amount of past due accounts increasing? Which accounts require management's attention? | List of outstanding receivables and their due dates | Prepare an aging schedule showing the receivables in various stages: outstanding 0–30 days, 31–60 days, 61–90 days, and over 90 days. | Accounts in the older categories require follow-up: letters, phone calls, and possible renegotiation of terms. |
| Is the company's credit risk increasing? | Customer account balances and due dates | Accounts receivable aging schedule | Compute and compare the percentage of receivables over 90 days old. |
| Does the company have significant concentrations of credit risk? | Note to the financial statements on concentrations of credit risk | If risky credit customers are identified, the financial health of those customers should be evaluated to gain an independent assessment of the potential for a material credit loss. | If a material loss appears likely, the potential negative impact of that loss on the company should be carefully evaluated, along with the adequacy of the allowance for doubtful accounts. |
| Are collections being made in a timely fashion? | Net credit sales and average net receivables balance | $$\text{Receivables turnover ratio} = \frac{\text{Net credit sales}}{\text{Average net receivables}}$$ $$\text{Average collection period} = \frac{365 \text{ days}}{\text{Receivables turnover ratio}}$$ | Average collection period should be consistent with corporate credit policy. An increase may suggest a decline in financial health of customers. |

collections, (d) evaluate the liquidity of receivables, and (e) accelerate cash receipts from receivables when necessary.

**8** **Identify ratios to analyze a company's receivables.** The receivables turnover ratio and the average collection period both are useful in analyzing management's effectiveness in managing receivables. The accounts receivable aging schedule also provides useful information.

**9** **Describe methods to accelerate the receipt of cash from receivables.** If the company needs additional cash, management can accelerate the collection of cash from receivables by selling (factoring) its receivables or by allowing customers to pay with bank credit cards.

# Glossary

**Accounts receivable** *(p. 398)* Amounts customers owe on account.

**Aging the accounts receivable** *(p. 404)* A schedule of customer balances classified by the length of time they have been unpaid.

**Allowance method** *(p. 402)* A method of accounting for bad debts that involves estimating uncollectible accounts at the end of each period.

**Average collection period** *(p. 415)* The average amount of time that a receivable is outstanding, calculated by dividing 365 days by the receivables turnover ratio.

**Bad Debts Expense** *(p. 401)* An expense account to record losses from extending credit.

**Cash (net) realizable value** *(p. 402)* The net amount a company expects to receive in cash from receivables.

**Concentration of credit risk** *(p. 414)* The threat of nonpayment from a single large customer or class of customers that could adversely affect the financial health of the company.

**Direct write-off method** *(p. 401)* A method of accounting for bad debts that involves charging receivable balances to Bed Debts Expense at the time receivables from a particular company are determined to be uncollectible.

**Dishonored note** *(p. 411)* A note that is not paid in full at maturity.

**Factor** *(p. 418)* A finance company or bank that buys receivables from businesses for a fee and then collects the payments directly from the customers.

**Maker** *(p. 407)* The party in a promissory note who is making the promise to pay.

**Notes receivable** *(p. 399)* Claims for which formal instruments of credit are issued as evidence of the debt.

**Payee** *(p. 407)* The party to whom payment of a promissory note is to be made.

**Percentage of receivables basis** *(p. 404)* A method of estimating the amount of bad debts expense whereby management establishes a percentage relationship between the amount of receivables and the expected losses from uncollectible accounts.

**Promissory note** *(p. 407)* A written promise to pay a specified amount of money on demand or at a definite time.

**Receivables** *(p. 398)* Amounts due from individuals and companies that are expected to be collected in cash.

**Receivables turnover ratio** *(p. 415)* A measure of the liquidity of receivables, computed by dividing net credit sales by average net accounts receivable.

**Trade receivables** *(p. 399)* Notes and accounts receivable that result from sales transactions.

# Comprehensive Do it!

Presented here are selected transactions related to B. Dylan Corp.

| | | |
|---|---|---|
| Mar. | 1 | Sold $20,000 of merchandise to Potter Company, terms 2/10, n/30. |
| | 11 | Received payment in full from Potter Company for balance due. |
| | 12 | Accepted Juno Company's $20,000, 6-month, 12% note for balance due on outstanding account receivable. |
| | 13 | Made B. Dylan Corp. credit card sales for $13,200. |
| | 15 | Made Visa credit sales totaling $6,700. A 5% service fee is charged by Visa. |
| Apr. | 11 | Sold accounts receivable of $8,000 to Harcot Factor. Harcot Factor assesses a service charge of 2% of the amount of receivables sold. |
| | 13 | Received collections of $8,200 on B. Dylan Corp. credit card sales. |
| May | 10 | Wrote off as uncollectible $16,000 of accounts receivable. (B. Dylan Corp. uses the percentage of receivables basis to estimate bad debts.) |
| June | 30 | The balance in accounts receivable at the end of the first 6 months is $200,000 and the bad debts percentage is 10%. At June 30 the credit balance in the allowance account prior to adjustment is $3,500. Recorded bad debt expense. |
| July | 16 | One of the accounts receivable written off in May pays the amount due, $4,000, in full. |

## Action Plan

- Generally, record accounts receivable at invoice price.
- Recognize that sales returns and allowances and cash discounts reduce the amount received on accounts receivable.
- Record a service charge expense on the seller's books when accounts receivable are sold.
- Prepare an adjusting entry for bad debts expense.
- Recognize the balance in the allowance account under the percentage of receivables basis.
- Record write-offs of accounts receivable only in balance sheet accounts.

## Instructions

Prepare the journal entries for the transactions. (Omit cost of goods sold entries.)

### Solution to Comprehensive Do it!

| Date | Account | Debit | Credit |
|---|---|---|---|
| Mar. 1 | Accounts Receivable—Potter Company | 20,000 | |
| | Sales Revenue | | 20,000 |
| | (To record sales on account) | | |
| | * | | |
| 11 | Cash | 19,600 | |
| | Sales Discounts (2% × $20,000) | 400 | |
| | Accounts Receivable—Potter Company | | 20,000 |
| | (To record collection of accounts receivable) | | |
| 12 | Notes Receivable | 20,000 | |
| | Accounts Receivable—Juno Company | | 20,000 |
| | (To record acceptance of Juno Company note) | | |
| 13 | Accounts Receivable | 13,200 | |
| | Sales Revenue | | 13,200 |
| | (To record company credit card sales) | | |
| 15 | Cash | 6,365 | |
| | Service Charge Expense (5% × $6,700) | 335 | |
| | Sales Revenue | | 6,700 |
| | (To record credit card sales) | | |
| Apr. 11 | Cash | 7,840 | |
| | Service Charge Expense (2% × $8,000) | 160 | |
| | Accounts Receivable | | 8,000 |
| | (To record sale of receivables to factor) | | |
| 13 | Cash | 8,200 | |
| | Accounts Receivable | | 8,200 |
| | (To record collection of accounts receivable) | | |
| May 10 | Allowance for Doubtful Accounts | 16,000 | |
| | Accounts Receivable | | 16,000 |
| | (To record write-off of accounts receivable) | | |
| June 30 | Bad Debts Expense | 16,500 | |
| | Allowance for Doubtful Accounts | | 16,500 |
| | [($200,000 × 10%) − $3,500] | | |
| | (To record estimate of uncollectible accounts) | | |
| July 16 | Accounts Receivable | 4,000 | |
| | Allowance for Doubtful Accounts | | 4,000 |
| | (To reverse write-off of accounts receivable) | | |
| | Cash | 4,000 | |
| | Accounts Receivable | | 4,000 |
| | (To record collection of accounts receivable) | | |

*Cost of goods sold entries are omitted here as well as in homework material.

**Self-Test, Brief Exercises, Exercises, Problem Set A, and many more resources are available for practice in WileyPLUS**

# Self-Test Questions

Answers are on page 444.

(SO 1)   **1.** A receivable that is evidenced by a formal instrument and that normally requires the payment of interest is:
(a) an account receivable.
(b) a trade receivable.
(c) a note receivable.
(d) a classified receivable.

(SO 2)   **2.** Kersee Company on June 15 sells merchandise on account to Soo Eng Co. for $1,000, terms 2/10, n/30. On June 20, Eng Co. returns merchandise worth $300 to Kersee Company. On June 24, payment is received from Eng Co. for the balance due. What is the amount of cash received?
(a) $700.        (c) $686.
(b) $680.        (d) None of the above.

(SO 3, 6)   **3.** Accounts and notes receivable are reported in the current assets section of the balance sheet at:
(a) cash (net) realizable value
(b) net book value.
(c) lower-of-cost-or-market value.
(d) invoice cost.

(SO 3)   **4.** Net credit sales for the month are $800,000. The accounts receivable balance is $160,000. The allowance is calculated as 7.5% of the receivables balance using the percentage of receivables basis. If the Allowance for Doubtful Accounts has a credit balance of $5,000 before adjustment, what is the balance after adjustment?
(a) $12,000.        (c) $17,000.
(b) $7,000.        (d) $31,000.

(SO 3)   **5.** In 2012, Patterson Wholesale Company had net credit sales of $750,000. On January 1, 2012, Allowance for Doubtful Accounts had a credit balance of $18,000. During 2012, $30,000 of uncollectible accounts receivable were written off. Past experience indicates that the allowance should be 10% of the balance in receivables (percentage of receivables basis). If the accounts receivable balance at December 31 was $200,000, what is the required adjustment to the Allowance for Doubtful Accounts at December 31, 2012?
(a) $20,000.        (c) $32,000.
(b) $75,000.        (d) $30,000.

(SO 3)   **6.** An analysis and aging of the accounts receivable of Raja Company at December 31 reveal these data:

| | |
|---|---|
| Accounts receivable | $800,000 |
| Allowance for doubtful accounts per books before adjustment (credit) | 50,000 |
| Amounts expected to become uncollectible | 65,000 |

What is the cash realizable value of the accounts receivable at December 31, after adjustment?
(a) $685,000.        (c) $800,000.
(b) $750,000.        (d) $735,000.

(SO 4)   **7.** Which of these statements about promissory notes is *incorrect*?
(a) The party making the promise to pay is called the maker.
(b) The party to whom payment is to be made is called the payee.
(c) A promissory note is not a negotiable instrument.
(d) A promissory note is more liquid than an account receivable.

(SO 4)   **8.** Michael Co. accepts a $1,000, 3-month, 12% promissory note in settlement of an account with Tani Co. The entry to record this transaction is:

| | | |
|---|---|---|
| (a) Notes Receivable | 1,030 | |
|    Accounts Receivable | | 1,030 |
| (b) Notes Receivable | 1,000 | |
|    Accounts Receivable | | 1,000 |
| (c) Notes Receivable | 1,000 | |
|    Sales Revenue | | 1,000 |
| (d) Notes Receivable | 1,020 | |
|    Accounts Receivable | | 1,020 |

(SO 5)   **9.** Schleis Co. holds Murphy Inc.'s $10,000, 120-day, 9% note. The entry made by Schleis Co. when the note is collected, assuming no interest has previously been accrued, is:

| | | |
|---|---|---|
| (a) Cash | 10,300 | |
|    Notes Receivable | | 10,300 |
| (b) Cash | 10,000 | |
|    Notes Receivable | | 10,000 |
| (c) Accounts Receivable | 10,300 | |
|    Notes Receivable | | 10,000 |
|    Interest Revenue | | 300 |
| (d) Cash | 10,300 | |
|    Notes Receivable | | 10,000 |
|    Interest Revenue | | 300 |

(SO 7)   **10.** If a company is concerned about extending credit to a risky customer, it could do any of the following *except*:
(a) require the customer to pay cash in advance.
(b) require the customer to provide a letter of credit or a bank guarantee.
(c) contact references provided by the customer, such as banks and other suppliers.
(d) provide the customer a lengthy payment period to increase the chance of paying.

(SO 8) **11.** ◐━━━☉ Eddy Corporation had net credit sales during the year of $800,000 and cost of goods sold of $500,000. The balance in receivables at the beginning of the year was $100,000 and at the end of the year was $150,000. What was the receivables turnover ratio?
(a) 6.4       (c) 5.3
(b) 8.0       (d) 4.0

(SO 8) **12.** ◐━━━☉ Prall Corporation sells its goods on terms of 2/10, n/30. It has a receivables turnover ratio of 7. What is its average collection period (days)?
(a) 2,555    (b) 30    (c) 52    (d) 210

(SO 9) **13.** Which of these statements about Visa credit card sales is *incorrect*?
(a) The credit card issuer conducts the credit investigation of the customer.
(b) The retailer is not involved in the collection process.
(c) The retailer must wait to receive payment from the issuer.
(d) The retailer receives cash more quickly than it would from individual customers.

**14.** Good Stuff Retailers accepted $50,000 of Citibank Visa (SO 9) credit card charges for merchandise sold on July 1. Citibank charges 4% for its credit card use. The entry to record this transaction by Good Stuff Retailers will include a credit to Sales Revenue of $50,000 and a debit(s) to:
(a) Cash $48,000 and Service Charge Expense $2,000.
(b) Accounts Receivable $48,000 and Service Charge Expense $2,000.
(c) Cash $50,000.
(d) Accounts Receivable $50,000.

**15.** A company can accelerate its cash receipts by all of (SO 9) the following *except*:
(a) offering discounts for early payment.
(b) accepting national credit cards for customer purchases.
(c) selling receivables to a factor.
(d) writing off receivables.

Go to the book's companion website, **www.wiley.com/college/kimmel**, to access additional Self-Test Questions.

## Questions

1. What is the difference between an account receivable and a note receivable?

2. What are some common types of receivables other than accounts receivable or notes receivable?

3. What are the essential features of the allowance method of accounting for bad debts?

4. Tracy Buss cannot understand why the cash realizable value does not decrease when an uncollectible account is written off under the allowance method. Clarify this point for Tracy.

5. Coffaro Company has a credit balance of $2,200 in Allowance for Doubtful Accounts before adjustment. The estimated uncollectibles under the percentage of receivables basis is $5,100. Prepare the adjusting entry.

6. What types of receivables does Tootsie Roll report on its balance sheet? Does it use the allowance method or the direct write-off method to account for uncollectibles?

7. How are bad debts accounted for under the direct write-off method? What are the disadvantages of this method?

8. Andrea Herbert, the vice president of sales for Tropical Pools and Spas, wants the company's credit department to be less restrictive in granting credit. "How can we sell anything when you guys won't approve anybody?" she asks. Discuss the pros and cons of "easy credit." What are the accounting implications?

9. Your roommate is uncertain about the advantages of a promissory note. Compare the advantages of a note receivable with those of an account receivable.

10. How may the maturity date of a promissory note be stated?

11. Compute the missing amounts for each of the following notes.

| Principal | Annual Interest Rate | Time | Total Interest |
|---|---|---|---|
| (a) | 6% | 60 days | $ 270 |
| $30,000 | 8% | 3 years | (d) |
| $60,000 | (b) | 5 months | $2,500 |
| $50,000 | 11% | (c) | $2,750 |

12. DeSousa Company dishonors a note at maturity. What are the options available to the lender?

13. General Motors Company has accounts receivable and notes receivable. How should the receivables be reported on the balance sheet?

14. ⬅ ◐━━━☉ What are the steps to good receivables management?

15. ◐━━━☉ How might a company monitor the risk related to its accounts receivable?

16. ◐━━━☉ What is meant by a concentration of credit risk?

17. ◐━━━☉ The president of Gruenwald Inc. proudly announces her company's improved liquidity since its current ratio has increased substantially from one year to the next. Does an increase in the current ratio always indicate improved liquidity? What other ratio or ratios might you review to determine whether or not the increase in the current ratio is an improvement in financial health?

18. ⬅ Since hiring a new sales director, Palasz Inc. has enjoyed a 50% increase in sales. The CEO has also noticed, however, that the company's average collection period has increased from 17 days to 38 days. What might be the cause of this increase? What are the implications to management of this increase?

19. ◐━━━☉ The Coca-Cola Company's receivables turnover ratio was 9.05 in 2009, and its average amount of net receivables during the period was

$3,424 million. What is the amount of its net credit sales for the period? What is the average collection period in days?

20. JCPenney Company accepts both its own credit cards and national credit cards. What are the advantages of accepting both types of cards?

21. An article in the *Wall Street Journal* indicated that companies are selling their receivables at a record rate. Why do companies sell their receivables?

22. Calico Corners decides to sell $400,000 of its accounts receivable to First Central Factors Inc. First Central Factors assesses a service charge of 3% of the amount of receivables sold. Prepare the journal entry that Calico Corners makes to record this sale.

23. Ross Corp. has experienced tremendous sales growth this year, but it is always short of cash. What is one explanation for this occurrence?

24. How can the amount of collections from customers be determined?

# Brief Exercises

**BE8-1** Presented below are three receivables transactions. Indicate whether these receivables are reported as accounts receivable, notes receivable, or other receivables on a balance sheet.

(a) Advanced $10,000 to an employee.
(b) Received a promissory note of $34,000 for services performed.
(c) Sold merchandise on account for $60,000 to a customer.

*Identify different types of receivables.*
*(SO 1), C*

**BE8-2** Record the following transactions on the books of Kuist Co. (Omit cost of goods sold entries.)

(a) On July 1, Kuist Co. sold merchandise on account to Firer Inc. for $23,000, terms 2/10, n/30.
(b) On July 8, Firer Inc. returned merchandise worth $2,400 to Kuist Co.
(c) On July 11, Firer Inc. paid for the merchandise.

*Record basic accounts receivable transactions.*
*(SO 2), AP*

**BE8-3** At the end of 2011, Tatham Co. has accounts receivable of $700,000 and an allowance for doubtful accounts of $25,000. On January 24, 2012, it is learned that the company's receivable from Nardin Inc. is not collectible and therefore management authorizes a write-off of $4,300.

(a) Prepare the journal entry to record the write-off.
(b) What is the cash realizable value of the accounts receivable (1) before the write-off and (2) after the write-off?

*Prepare entry for write-off, and determine cash realizable value.*
*(SO 3), AP*

**BE8-4** Assume the same information as BE8-3 and that on March 4, 2012, Tatham Co. receives payment of $4,300 in full from Nardin Inc. Prepare the journal entries to record this transaction.

*Prepare entries for collection of bad debt write-off.*
*(SO 3), AP*

**BE8-5** Lynch Co. uses the percentage of receivables basis to record bad debts expense and concludes that 2% of accounts receivable will become uncollectible. Accounts receivable are $400,000 at the end of the year, and the allowance for doubtful accounts has a credit balance of $2,800.

(a) Prepare the adjusting journal entry to record bad debts expense for the year.
(b) If the allowance for doubtful accounts had a debit balance of $900 instead of a credit balance of $2,800, prepare the adjusting journal entry for bad debts expense.

*Prepare entry using percentage of receivables method.*
*(SO 3), AP*

**BE8-6** Compute interest and find the maturity date for the following notes.

*Compute interest and determine maturity dates on notes.*
*(SO 4), AP*

| | Date of Note | Principal | Interest Rate (%) | Terms |
|---|---|---|---|---|
| (a) | June 10 | $80,000 | 6% | 60 days |
| (b) | July 14 | $50,000 | 7% | 90 days |
| (c) | April 27 | $12,000 | 8% | 75 days |

**BE8-7** Presented below are data on three promissory notes. Determine the missing amounts.

*Determine maturity dates and compute interest and rates on notes.*
*(SO 4), AP*

| | Date of Note | Terms | Maturity Date | Principal | Annual Interest Rate | Total Interest |
|---|---|---|---|---|---|---|
| (a) | April 1 | 60 days | ? | $600,000 | 9% | ? |
| (b) | July 2 | 30 days | ? | 90,000 | ? | $600 |
| (c) | March 7 | 6 months | ? | 120,000 | 10% | ? |

**BE8-8** On January 10, 2012, Ruggiero Co. sold merchandise on account to Edwards for $8,000, terms n/30. On February 9, Edwards gave Ruggiero Co. a 7% promissory note in settlement of this account. Prepare the journal entry to record the sale and the settlement of the accounts receivable. (Omit cost of goods sold entries.)

*Prepare entry for note receivable exchanged for accounts receivable.*
*(SO 4), AP*

*Prepare entry for estimated uncollectibles and classifications, and compute ratios.*

*(SO 3, 6, 7, 8),* **AP**

**BE8-9** During its first year of operations, Ketter Company had credit sales of $3,000,000, of which $400,000 remained uncollected at year-end. The credit manager estimates that $18,000 of these receivables will become uncollectible.

(a) Prepare the journal entry to record the estimated uncollectibles. (Assume an unadjusted balance of zero in Allowance for Doubtful Accounts.)

(b) Prepare the current assets section of the balance sheet for Ketter Company, assuming that in addition to the receivables it has cash of $90,000, merchandise inventory of $180,000, and supplies of $13,000.

(c) Calculate the receivables turnover ratio and average collection period. Assume that average net receivables were $300,000. Explain what these measures tell us.

*Analyze accounts receivable.*

*(SO 8),* **AP**

**BE8-10** The 2009 financial statements of 3M Company report net sales of $23.1 billion. Accounts receivable (net) are $3.2 billion at the beginning of the year and $3.25 billion at the end of the year. Compute 3M's receivables turnover ratio. Compute 3M's average collection period for accounts receivable in days.

*Prepare entries for credit card sale and sale of accounts receivable.*

*(SO 9),* **AP**

**BE8-11** Consider these transactions:

(a) Galvao Restaurant accepted a Visa card in payment of a $200 lunch bill. The bank charges a 3% fee. What entry should Galvao make?

(b) Stone Company sold its accounts receivable of $65,000. What entry should Stone make, given a service charge of 3% on the amount of receivables sold?

*Determine cash collections.*

*(SO 9),* **AP**

**BE8-12** Roberts Corp. had a beginning balance in accounts receivable of $70,000 and an ending balance of $91,000. Sales during the period were $598,000. Determine cash collections.

## Do it! Review

*Prepare entry for uncollectible accounts.*

*(SO 3),* **AP**

**Do it! 8-1** Else Company has been in business several years. At the end of the current year, the ledger shows:

| | |
|---|---|
| Accounts Receivable | $ 310,000 Dr. |
| Sales Revenue | 2,200,000 Cr. |
| Allowance for Doubtful Accounts | 5,700 Cr. |

Bad debts are estimated to be 7% of receivables. Prepare the entry to adjust the Allowance for Doubtful Accounts.

*Prepare entries for notes receivable.*

*(SO 4, 5),* **AP**

**Do it! 8-2** Gilliam Wholesalers accepts from Perlman Stores a $6,200, 4-month, 9% note dated May 31 in settlement of Perlman's overdue account. The maturity date of the note is September 30. What entry does Gilliam make at the maturity date, assuming Perlman pays the note and interest in full at that time?

*Compute ratios for receivables.*

*(SO 8),* **AP**

**Do it! 8-3** In 2012, Grossfeld Company has net credit sales of $1,600,000 for the year. It had a beginning accounts receivable (net) balance of $108,000 and an ending accounts receivable (net) balance of $120,000. Compute Grossfeld Company's (a) receivables turnover and (b) average collection period in days.

*Prepare entry for factored accounts.*

*(SO 9),* **AP**

**Do it! 8-4** Vesely Distributors is a growing company whose ability to raise capital has not been growing as quickly as its expanding assets and sales. Vesely's local banker has indicated that the company cannot increase its borrowing for the foreseeable future. Vesely's suppliers are demanding payment for goods acquired within 30 days of the invoice date, but Vesely's customers are slow in paying for their purchases (60–90 days). As a result, Vesely has a cash flow problem.

Vesely needs $160,000 to cover next Friday's payroll. Its balance of outstanding accounts receivable totals $800,000. To alleviate this cash crunch, the company sells $170,000 of its receivables. Record the entry that Vesely would make. (Assume a 2% service charge.)

## Exercises

*Prepare entries for recognizing accounts receivable.*

*(SO 2),* **AP**

**E8-1** On January 6, Petro Co. sells merchandise on account to Chose Inc. for $9,200, terms 1/10, n/30. On January 16, Chose pays the amount due.

*Instructions*

Prepare the entries on Petro Co.'s books to record the sale and related collection. (Omit cost of goods sold entries.)

**E8-2** On January 10, Kristin Pitt uses her Stampfer Co. credit card to purchase merchandise from Stampfer Co. for $1,700. On February 10, Pitt is billed for the amount due of $1,700. On February 12, Pitt pays $1,100 on the balance due. On March 10, Pitt is billed for the amount due, including interest at 1% per month on the unpaid balance as of February 12.

*Prepare entries for recognizing accounts receivable.*
*(SO 2),* **AP**

**Instructions**
Prepare the entries on Stampfer Co.'s books related to the transactions that occurred on January 10, February 12, and March 10. (Omit cost of goods sold entries.)

**E8-3** At the beginning of the current period, Engseth Corp. had balances in Accounts Receivable of $200,000 and in Allowance for Doubtful Accounts of $9,000 (credit). During the period, it had net credit sales of $800,000 and collections of $763,000. It wrote off as uncollectible accounts receivable of $7,300. However, a $3,100 account previously written off as uncollectible was recovered before the end of the current period. Uncollectible accounts are estimated to total $25,000 at the end of the period. (Omit cost of goods sold entries.)

*Journalize receivables transactions.*
*(SO 2, 3),* **AP**

**Instructions**
(a) Prepare the entries to record sales and collections during the period.
(b) Prepare the entry to record the write-off of uncollectible accounts during the period.
(c) Prepare the entries to record the recovery of the uncollectible account during the period.
(d) Prepare the entry to record bad debts expense for the period.
(e) Determine the ending balances in Accounts Receivable and Allowance for Doubtful Accounts.
(f) What is the net realizable value of the receivables at the end of the period?

**E8-4** The ledger of Montgomery Company at the end of the current year shows Accounts Receivable $78,000; Credit Sales $810,000; and Sales Returns and Allowances $40,000.

*Prepare entries to record allowance for doubtful accounts.*
*(SO 3),* **AP**

**Instructions**
(a) If Montgomery uses the direct write-off method to account for uncollectible accounts, journalize the adjusting entry at December 31, assuming Montgomery determines that Baruth's $900 balance is uncollectible.
(b) If Allowance for Doubtful Accounts has a credit balance of $1,100 in the trial balance, journalize the adjusting entry at December 31, assuming bad debts are expected to be 10% of accounts receivable.
(c) If Allowance for Doubtful Accounts has a debit balance of $500 in the trial balance, journalize the adjusting entry at December 31, assuming bad debts are expected to be 8% of accounts receivable.

**E8-5** Parry Company has accounts receivable of $95,400 at March 31, 2012. An analysis of the accounts shows these amounts.

*Determine bad debts expense, and prepare the adjusting entry.*
*(SO 3),* **AP**

| | Balance, March 31 | |
| Month of Sale | 2012 | 2011 |
| --- | --- | --- |
| March | $65,000 | $75,000 |
| February | 12,900 | 8,000 |
| December and January | 10,100 | 2,400 |
| November and October | 7,400 | 1,100 |
| | $95,400 | $86,500 |

Credit terms are 2/10, n/30. At March 31, 2012, there is a $2,100 credit balance in Allowance for Doubtful Accounts prior to adjustment. The company uses the percentage of receivables basis for estimating uncollectible accounts. The company's estimates of bad debts are as shown below.

| Age of Accounts | Estimated Percentage Uncollectible |
| --- | --- |
| Current | 2% |
| 1–30 days past due | 5 |
| 31–90 days past due | 30 |
| Over 90 days past due | 50 |

**Instructions**
(a) Determine the total estimated uncollectibles.
(b) Prepare the adjusting entry at March 31, 2012, to record bad debts expense.
(c) Discuss the implications of the changes in the aging schedule from 2011 to 2012.

*Prepare entry for estimated uncollectibles, write-off, and recovery.*
(SO 3), **AP**

**E8-6** On December 31, 2011, when its Allowance for Doubtful Accounts had a debit balance of $1,400, Nova Co. estimates that 9% of its accounts receivable balance of $90,000 will become uncollectible and records the necessary adjustment to the Allowance for Doubtful Accounts. On May 11, 2012, Nova Co. determined that J. Rast's account was uncollectible and wrote off $1,200. On June 12, 2012, Rast paid the amount previously written off.

**Instructions**
Prepare the journal entries on December 31, 2011, May 11, 2012, and June 12, 2012.

*Prepare entries for notes receivable transactions.*
(SO 4, 5), **AP**

**E8-7** Gwynne Supply Co. has the following transactions related to notes receivable during the last 2 months of the year.

Nov.  1  Loaned $60,000 cash to B. Akey on a 1-year, 7% note.
Dec.  11  Sold goods to R. P. Mayrl, Inc., receiving a $3,600, 90-day, 8% note.
      16  Received a $12,000, 6-month, 9% note to settle an open account from M. Colvin.
      31  Accrued interest revenue on all notes receivable.

**Instructions**
Journalize the transactions for Gwynne Supply Co. (Omit cost of goods sold entries.)

*Journalize notes receivable transactions.*
(SO 4, 5), **AP**

**E8-8** These transactions took place for Renda Co.

**2011**

May  1  Received a $5,000, 1-year, 6% note in exchange for an outstanding account receivable from S. Dorsey.
Dec.  31  Accrued interest revenue on the S. Dorsey note.

**2012**

May  1  Received principal plus interest on the S. Dorsey note. (No interest has been accrued since December 31, 2011.)

**Instructions**
Record the transactions in the general journal.

*Prepare a balance sheet presentation of receivables.*
(SO 6), **AP**

**E8-9** Kopecky Corp. had the following balances in receivable accounts at October 31, 2012 (in thousands): Allowance for Doubtful Accounts $52; Accounts Receivable $2,910; Other Receivables $189; Notes Receivable $1,353.

**Instructions**
Prepare the balance sheet presentation of Kopecky Corp.'s receivables in good form.

*Identify the principles of receivables management.*
(SO 7), **K**

**E8-10** The following is a list of activities that companies perform in relation to their receivables.
1. Selling receivables to a factor.
2. Reviewing company ratings in *The Dun and Bradstreet Reference Book of American Business*.
3. Collecting information on competitors' payment period policies.
4. Preparing monthly accounts receivable aging schedule and investigating problem accounts.
5. Calculating the receivables turnover ratio and average collection period.

**Instructions**
Match each of the activities listed above with a purpose of the activity listed below.
(a) Determine to whom to extend credit.
(b) Establish a payment period.
(c) Monitor collections.
(d) Evaluate the liquidity of receivables.
(e) Accelerate cash receipts from receivables when necessary.

*Compute ratios to evaluate a company's receivables balance.*
(SO 7, 8), **AN**

**E8-11** The following information was taken from the 2009 financial statements of FedEx Corporation, a major global transportation/delivery company.

| (in millions) | 2009 | 2008 |
|---|---|---|
| Accounts receivable (gross) | $ 3,587 | $ 4,517 |
| Accounts receivable (net) | 3,391 | 4,359 |
| Allowance for doubtful accounts | 196 | 158 |
| Sales | 35,497 | 37,953 |
| Total current assets | 7,116 | 7,244 |

**Instructions**

Answer each of the following questions.

(a) Calculate the receivables turnover ratio and the average collection period for 2009 for FedEx.

(b) Is accounts receivable a material component of the company's total current assets?

(c) Evaluate the balance in FedEx's allowance for doubtful accounts.

**E8-12** The following ratios are available for Tym Inc.

*Evaluate liquidity.*
(SO 7, 8, 9), **AN**

|  | **2012** | **2011** |
|---|---|---|
| Current ratio | 1.3:1 | 1.5:1 |
| Receivables turnover | 12 times | 10 times |
| Inventory turnover | 11 times | 9 times |

**Instructions**

(a) Is Tym's short-term liquidity improving or deteriorating in 2012? Be specific in your answer, referring to relevant ratios.

(b) Do changes in turnover ratios affect profitability? Explain.

(c) Identify any steps Tym might have taken, or might wish to take, to improve its management of its receivables and inventory turnover.

**E8-13** On March 3, Pitrof Appliances sells $710,000 of its receivables to American Factors Inc. American Factors Inc. assesses a service charge of 4% of the amount of receivables sold.

*Prepare entry for sale of accounts receivable.*
(SO 9), **AN**

**Instructions**

Prepare the entry on Pitrof Appliances' books to record the sale of the receivables.

**E8-14** In a recent annual report, Office Depot, Inc. notes that the company entered into an agreement to sell all of its credit card program receivables to financial service companies.

*Identify reason for sale of receivables.*
(SO 9), **C**

**Instructions**

Explain why Office Depot, a financially stable company with positive cash flow, would choose to sell its receivables.

**E8-15** On May 10, Rose Company sold merchandise for $4,000 and accepted the customer's First Business Bank MasterCard. At the end of the day, the First Business Bank MasterCard receipts were deposited in the company's bank account. First Business Bank charges a 3.8% service charge for credit card sales.

*Prepare entry for credit card sale.*
(SO 9), **AP**

**Instructions**

Prepare the entry on Rose Company's books to record the sale of merchandise.

**E8-16** On July 4, Kathi's Restaurant accepts a Visa card for a $250 dinner bill. Visa charges a 4% service fee.

*Prepare entry for credit card sale.*
(SO 9), **AP**

**Instructions**

Prepare the entry on Kathi's books related to the transaction.

**E8-17** Redding Corp. significantly reduced its requirements for credit sales. As a result, sales during the current year increased dramatically. It had receivables at the beginning of the year of $38,000 and ending receivables of $191,000. Sales were $380,000.

*Determine cash flows and evaluate quality of earnings.*
(SO 9), **AN**

**Instructions**

(a) Determine cash collections during the period.

(b) Discuss how your findings in part (a) would affect Redding Corp.'s quality of earnings ratio. (Do not compute.)

(c) What concerns might you have regarding Redding's accounting?

# Exercises: Set B and Challenge Exercises

Visit the book's companion website, at **www.wiley.com/college/kimmel**, and choose the Student Companion site to access Exercise Set B and Challenge Exercises.

# Problems: Set A

*Journalize transactions related to bad debts.*
*(SO 2, 3),* **AP**

**P8-1A**   Sellmore.com uses the allowance method of accounting for bad debts. The company produced the following aging of the accounts receivable at year-end.

| | Total | Number of Days Outstanding | | | | |
| --- | --- | --- | --- | --- | --- | --- |
| | | 0–30 | 31–60 | 61–90 | 91–120 | Over 120 |
| Accounts receivable | $377,000 | $222,000 | $90,000 | $38,000 | $15,000 | $12,000 |
| % uncollectible | | 1% | 4% | 5% | 8% | 10% |
| Estimated bad debts | | | | | | |

**Instructions**

(a) Tot. est.
    bad debts $10,120

(a)  Calculate the total estimated bad debts based on the above information.
(b)  Prepare the year-end adjusting journal entry to record the bad debts using the aged uncollectible accounts receivable determined in (a). Assume the unadjusted balance in Allowance for Doubtful Accounts is a $4,000 debit.
(c)  Of the above accounts, $5,000 is determined to be specifically uncollectible. Prepare the journal entry to write off the uncollectible account.
(d)  The company collects $5,000 subsequently on a specific account that had previously been determined to be uncollectible in (c). Prepare the journal entry(ies) necessary to restore the account and record the cash collection.
(e)  Comment on how your answers to (a)–(d) would change if Sellmore.com used 3% of total accounts receivable, rather than aging the accounts receivable. What are the advantages to the company of aging the accounts receivable rather than applying a percentage to total accounts receivable?

*Prepare journal entries related to bad debts expense, and compute ratios.*
*(SO 2, 3, 8),* **AP**

**P8-2A**   At December 31, 2011, Ihrke Imports reported this information on its balance sheet.

| | |
| --- | --- |
| Accounts receivable | $600,000 |
| Less: Allowance for doubtful accounts | 37,000 |

During 2012, the company had the following transactions related to receivables.

| | |
| --- | --- |
| 1. Sales on account | $2,500,000 |
| 2. Sales returns and allowances | 50,000 |
| 3. Collections of accounts receivable | 2,200,000 |
| 4. Write-offs of accounts receivable deemed uncollectible | 41,000 |
| 5. Recovery of bad debts previously written off as uncollectible | 15,000 |

**Instructions**

(b) A/R bal.  $809,000

(a)  Prepare the journal entries to record each of these five transactions. Assume that no cash discounts were taken on the collections of accounts receivable. (Omit cost of goods sold entries.)
(b)  Enter the January 1, 2012, balances in Accounts Receivable and Allowance for Doubtful Accounts, post the entries to the two accounts (use T accounts), and determine the balances.
(c)  Prepare the journal entry to record bad debts expense for 2012, assuming that aging the accounts receivable indicates that estimated bad debts are $46,000.
(d)  Compute the receivables turnover ratio and average collection period.

**P8-3A**   Presented below is an aging schedule for Gille Company.

*Journalize transactions related to bad debts.*

(SO 2, 3), **AP**

| Customer | Total | Not Yet Due | Number of Days Past Due | | | |
| --- | --- | --- | --- | --- | --- | --- |
| | | | 1–30 | 31–60 | 61–90 | Over 90 |
| Aneesh | $ 24,000 | | $ 9,000 | $15,000 | | |
| Bird | 30,000 | $ 30,000 | | | | |
| Cope | 50,000 | 5,000 | 5,000 | | $40,000 | |
| DeSpears | 38,000 | | | | | $38,000 |
| Others | 120,000 | 72,000 | 35,000 | 13,000 | | |
| | $262,000 | $107,000 | $49,000 | $28,000 | $40,000 | $38,000 |
| Estimated percentage uncollectible | | 3% | 7% | 12% | 24% | 60% |
| Total estimated bad debts | $ 42,400 | $ 3,210 | $ 3,430 | $ 3,360 | $ 9,600 | $22,800 |

At December 31, 2011, the unadjusted balance in Allowance for Doubtful Accounts is a credit of $8,000.

**Instructions**
(a) Journalize and post the adjusting entry for bad debts at December 31, 2011. (Use T accounts.)
(b) Journalize and post to the allowance account these 2012 events and transactions:
   1. March 1, a $600 customer balance originating in 2011 is judged uncollectible.
   2. May 1, a check for $600 is received from the customer whose account was written off as uncollectible on March 1.
(c) Journalize the adjusting entry for bad debts at December 31, 2012, assuming that the unadjusted balance in Allowance for Doubtful Accounts is a debit of $1,400 and the aging schedule indicates that total estimated bad debts will be $36,700.

**P8-4A**   Here is information related to Shashko Company for 2012.

*Compute bad debts amounts.*

(SO 3), **AP**

| | |
| --- | --- |
| Total credit sales | $1,500,000 |
| Accounts receivable at December 31 | 840,000 |
| Bad debts written off | 37,000 |

**Instructions**
(a) What amount of bad debts expense will Shashko Company report if it uses the direct write-off method of accounting for bad debts?
(b) Assume that Shashko Company decides to estimate its bad debts expense based on 4% of accounts receivable. What amount of bad debts expense will the company record if Allowance for Doubtful Accounts has a credit balance of $3,000?
(c) Assume the same facts as in part (b), except that there is a $1,000 debit balance in Allowance for Doubtful Accounts. What amount of bad debts expense will Shashko record?
(d) ▭▭▭▶ What is a weakness of the direct write-off method of reporting bad debts expense?

**P8-5A**   At December 31, 2012, the trial balance of Oliker Company contained the following amounts before adjustment.

*Journalize entries to record transactions related to bad debts.*

(SO 2, 3), **AP**

| | Debits | Credits |
| --- | --- | --- |
| Accounts Receivable | $180,000 | |
| Allowance for Doubtful Accounts | | $  1,500 |
| Sales Revenue | | 875,000 |

**Instructions**
(a) Prepare the adjusting entry at December 31, 2012, to record bad debts expense, assuming that the aging schedule indicates that $10,200 of accounts receivable will be uncollectible.

(b) Repeat part (a), assuming that instead of a credit balance there is a $1,500 debit balance in the Allowance for Doubtful Accounts.

(c) During the next month, January 2013, a $2,100 account receivable is written off as uncollectible. Prepare the journal entry to record the write-off.

(d) Repeat part (c), assuming that Oliker Company uses the direct write-off method instead of the allowance method in accounting for uncollectible accounts receivable.

(e)  What are the advantages of using the allowance method in accounting for uncollectible accounts as compared to the direct write-off method?

*Journalize various receivables transactions.*
*(SO 1, 2, 4, 5),* **AP**

**P8-6A** On January 1, 2012, Sather Company had Accounts Receivable of $54,200 and Allowance for Doubtful Accounts of $3,700. Sather Company prepares financial statements annually. During the year, the following selected transactions occurred.

| | | |
|---|---|---|
| Jan. | 5 | Sold $4,000 of merchandise to Noel Company, terms n/30. |
| Feb. | 2 | Accepted a $4,000, 4-month, 9% promissory note from Noel Company for balance due. |
| | 12 | Sold $12,000 of merchandise to Lima Company and accepted Lima's $12,000, 2-month, 10% note for the balance due. |
| | 26 | Sold $5,200 of merchandise to Hubbard Co., terms n/10. |
| Apr. | 5 | Accepted a $5,200, 3-month, 8% note from Hubbard Co. for balance due. |
| | 12 | Collected Lima Company note in full. |
| June | 2 | Collected Noel Company note in full. |
| | 15 | Sold $2,000 of merchandise to Matthews Inc. and accepted a $2,000, 6-month, 12% note for the amount due. |

**Instructions**
Journalize the transactions. (Omit cost of goods sold entries.)

*Explain the impact of transactions on ratios.*
*(SO 8),* **C**

**P8-7A** The president of Screven Enterprises asks if you could indicate the impact certain transactions have on the following ratios.

| Transaction | Current Ratio (2:1) | Receivables Turnover (10×) | Average Collection Period (36.5 days) |
|---|---|---|---|
| 1. Received $5,000 on cash sale. The cost of the goods sold was $2,600. | | | |
| 2. Recorded bad debts expense of $500 using allowance method. | | | |
| 3. Wrote off a $100 account receivable as uncollectible (Uses allowance method.) | | | |
| 4. Recorded $2,500 sales on account. The cost of the goods sold was $1,500. | | | |

**Instructions**
Complete the table, indicating whether each transaction will increase (I), decrease (D), or have no effect (NE) on the specific ratios provided for Screven Enterprises.

*Prepare entries for various credit card and notes receivable transactions.*
*(SO 2, 4, 5, 6, 9),* **AP**

**P8-8A** Jander Company closes its books on July 31. On June 30, the Notes Receivable account balance is $23,800. Notes Receivable include the following.

| Date | Maker | Face Value | Term | Maturity Date | Interest Rate |
|---|---|---|---|---|---|
| April 21 | Allen Inc. | $ 6,000 | 90 days | July 20 | 8% |
| May 25 | Garnham Co. | 7,800 | 60 days | July 24 | 10% |
| June 30 | ERV Corp. | 10,000 | 6 months | December 31 | 6% |

During July, the following transactions were completed.

July 5    Made sales of $4,500 on Jander credit cards.
     14    Made sales of $600 on Visa credit cards. The credit card service charge
           is 3%.
     20    Received payment in full from Allen Inc. on the amount due.
     24    Received payment in full from Garnham Co. on the amount due.

**Instructions**
(a) Journalize the July transactions and the July 31 adjusting entry for accrued interest
    receivable. (Interest is computed using 360 days; omit cost of goods sold entries.)
(b) Enter the balances at July 1 in the receivable accounts and post the entries to all of
    the receivable accounts. (Use T accounts.)
(c) Show the balance sheet presentation of the receivable accounts at July 31.

(b) A/R bal.  $ 4,500

(c) Tot. receivables  $14,550

**P8-9A**  Presented here is basic financial information (in millions) from the 2009 annual
reports of Nike and Adidas.

*Calculate and interpret
various ratios.*
(SO 7, 8), **AN**

|  | Nike | Adidas |
|---|---|---|
| Sales | $19,176.1 | $10,381 |
| Allowance for doubtful accounts, beginning | 78.4 | 119 |
| Allowance for doubtful accounts, ending | 110.8 | 124 |
| Accounts receivable balance (gross), beginning | 2,873.7 | 1,743 |
| Accounts receivable balance (gross), ending | 2,994.7 | 1,553 |

**Instructions**
Calculate the receivables turnover ratio and average collection period for both companies. Comment on the difference in their collection experiences.

# Problems: Set B

**P8-1B**  The following represents selected information taken from a company's aging
schedule to estimate uncollectible accounts receivable at year-end.

*Journalize transactions
related to bad debts.*
(SO 2, 3), **AP**

|  | Total | Number of Days Outstanding | | | | |
|---|---|---|---|---|---|---|
|  |  | 0–30 | 31–60 | 61–90 | 91–120 | Over 120 |
| Accounts receivable | $285,000 | $107,000 | $60,000 | $50,000 | $38,000 | $30,000 |
| % uncollectible |  | 2% | 5% | 7.5% | 10% | 14% |
| Estimated bad debts |  |  |  |  |  |  |

**Instructions**
(a) Calculate the total estimated bad debts based on the above information.
(b) Prepare the year-end adjusting journal entry to record the bad debts using the al-
    lowance method and the aged uncollectible accounts receivable determined in (a).
    Assume the unadjusted balance in the Allowance for Doubtful Accounts account is
    a $7,000 credit.
(c) Of the above accounts, $2,600 is determined to be specifically uncollectible. Prepare
    the journal entry to write off the uncollectible accounts.
(d) The company subsequently collects $1,200 on a specific account that had previously
    been determined to be uncollectible in (c). Prepare the journal entry(ies) necessary
    to restore the account and record the cash collection.
(e) Explain how establishing an allowance account satisfies the expense recognition
    principle.

(a) Tot. est.
    bad debts  $16,890

*Prepare journal entries related to bad debts expense, and compute ratios.*
(SO 2, 3, 8), **AP**

**P8-2B** At December 31, 2011, Littman Company reported this information on its balance sheet.

| | |
|---|---|
| Accounts receivable | $960,000 |
| Less: Allowance for doubtful accounts | 78,000 |

During 2012, the company had the following transactions related to receivables.

1. Sales on account — $3,600,000
2. Sales returns and allowances — 50,000
3. Collections of accounts receivable — 3,100,000
4. Write-offs of accounts receivable deemed uncollectible — 92,000
5. Recovery of bad debts previously written off as uncollectible — 28,000

**Instructions**
(a) Prepare the journal entries to record each of these five transactions. Assume that no cash discounts were taken on the collections of accounts receivable. (Omit cost of goods sold entries.)

(b) A/R bal. $1,318,000

(b) Enter the January 1, 2012, balances in Accounts Receivable and Allowance for Doubtful Accounts, post the entries to the two accounts (use T accounts), and determine the balances.
(c) Prepare the journal entry to record bad debts expense for 2012, assuming that aging the accounts receivable indicates that expected bad debts are $109,000.
(d) Compute the receivables turnover ratio and average collection period.

*Journalize transactions related to bad debts.*
(SO 2, 3), **AP**

**P8-3B** Presented here is an aging schedule for Zander Company.

| Customer | Total | Not Yet Due | Number of Days Past Due | | | |
|---|---|---|---|---|---|---|
| | | | 1–30 | 31–60 | 61–90 | Over 90 |
| Amy | $ 22,000 | | $12,000 | $10,000 | | |
| Bergin | 40,000 | $ 40,000 | | | | |
| Curt | 65,000 | 14,000 | 6,000 | | $45,000 | |
| David | 28,000 | | | | | $28,000 |
| Others | 126,000 | 96,000 | 16,000 | 14,000 | | |
| | $281,000 | $150,000 | $34,000 | $24,000 | $45,000 | $28,000 |
| Estimated percentage uncollectible | | 4% | 9% | 15% | 25% | 50% |
| Total estimated bad debts | $ 37,910 | $ 6,000 | $ 3,060 | $ 3,600 | $11,250 | $14,000 |

At December 31, 2011, the unadjusted balance in Allowance for Doubtful Accounts is a credit of $11,700.

**Instructions**
(a) Journalize and post the adjusting entry for bad debts at December 31, 2011. (Use T accounts.)
(b) Journalize and post to the allowance account these 2012 events and transactions:
   1. March 31, a $500 customer balance originating in 2011 is judged uncollectible.
   2. May 31, a check for $500 is received from the customer whose account was written off as uncollectible on March 31.
(c) Journalize the adjusting entry for bad debts on December 31, 2012, assuming that the unadjusted balance in Allowance for Doubtful Accounts is a debit of $800 and the aging schedule indicates that total estimated bad debts will be $35,300.

*Compute bad debts amounts.*
(SO 3), **AP**

**P8-4B** Here is information related to Vansen Company for 2012.

| | |
|---|---|
| Total credit sales | $2,000,000 |
| Accounts receivable at December 31 | 400,000 |
| Bad debts written off | 15,000 |

*Instructions*

(a) What amount of bad debts expense will Vansen Company report if it uses the direct write-off method of accounting for bad debts?

(b) Assume that Vansen Company decides to estimate its bad debts expense based on 4% of accounts receivable. What amount of bad debts expense will the company record if it has an Allowance for Doubtful Accounts credit balance of $3,700?

(c) Assume the same facts as in part (b), except that there is a $2,000 debit balance in Allowance for Doubtful Accounts. What amount of bad debts expense will Vansen record?

(d) What is the weakness of the direct write-off method of reporting bad debts expense?

**P8-5B** At December 31, 2012, the trial balance of Seidl Company contained the following amounts before adjustment.

*Journalize entries to record transactions related to bad debts.*
(SO 2, 3), **AP**

| | Debits | Credits |
|---|---|---|
| Accounts Receivable | $500,000 | |
| Allowance for Doubtful Accounts | | $    4,800 |
| Sales Revenue | | 2,400,000 |

*Instructions*

(a) Based on the information given, which method of accounting for bad debts is Seidl Company using—the direct write-off method or the allowance method? How can you tell?

(b) Prepare the adjusting entry at December 31, 2012, for bad debts expense assuming that the aging schedule indicates that $26,000 of accounts receivable will be uncollectible.

(c) Repeat part (b), assuming that instead of a credit balance there is a $4,800 debit balance in the Allowance for Doubtful Accounts.

(d) During the next month, January 2013, a $5,000 account receivable is written off as uncollectible. Prepare the journal entry to record the write-off.

(e) Repeat part (d), assuming that Seidl uses the direct write-off method instead of the allowance method in accounting for uncollectible accounts receivable.

(f)  ▭▭▭▭▷ What type of account is the allowance for doubtful accounts? How does it affect how accounts receivable is reported on the balance sheet at the end of the accounting period?

**P8-6B** On January 1, 2012, Moline Company had Accounts Receivable $154,000; Notes Receivable of $12,000; and Allowance for Doubtful Accounts of $13,200. The note receivable is from Hartwig Company. It is a 4-month, 9% note dated December 31, 2011. Moline Company prepares financial statements annually. During the year, the following selected transactions occurred.

*Journalize various receivables transactions.*
(SO 1, 2, 4, 5), **AP**

| | | |
|---|---|---|
| Jan. | 5 | Sold $10,000 of merchandise to Flint Company, terms n/15. |
| | 20 | Accepted Flint Company's $10,000, 3-month, 9% note for balance due. |
| Feb. | 18 | Sold $4,000 of merchandise to Zinck Company and accepted Zinck's $4,000, 6-month, 8% note for the amount due. |
| Apr. | 20 | Collected Flint Company note in full. |
| | 30 | Received payment in full from Hartwig Company on the amount due. |
| May | 25 | Accepted Aberd Inc.'s $9,000, 6-month, 8% note in settlement of a past-due balance on account. |
| Aug. | 18 | Received payment in full from Zinck Company on note due. |
| Sept. | 1 | Sold $5,000 of merchandise to Cosier Company and accepted a $5,000, 6-month, 9% note for the amount due. |

*Instructions*

Journalize the transactions. (Omit cost of goods sold entries.)

**P8-7B** The president of Felder Enterprises Ltd., Emma Felder, is considering the impact that certain transactions have on the company's receivables turnover and average collection period ratios. Prior to the transactions on the next page, Felder's receivables turnover was 6 times, and its average collection period was 61 days.

*Explain the impact of transactions on ratios: discuss acceleration of receipt of cash from receivables.*
(SO 8, 9), **C**

| Transaction | Receivables Turnover (6×) | Average Collection Period (61 days) |
|---|---|---|
| 1. Recorded sales on account $100,000. | | |
| 2. Collected $25,000 owed by customers. | | |
| 3. Wrote off a $2,500 account from a customer as uncollectible. (Uses allowance method.) | | |
| 4. Recorded sales returns of $1,800 and credited the customers' accounts. | | |
| 5. Recorded bad debts expense for the year $7,900, using the allowance method. | | |

### Instructions

(a) Complete the table, indicating whether each transaction will increase (I), decrease (D), or have no effect (NE) on the ratios.

(b) Emma was reading through the financial statements for some publicly traded companies and noticed that they had recorded an expense related to the sale of receivables. She would like you to explain why companies sell their receivables.

*Prepare entries for various credit card and notes receivable transactions.*

*(SO 2, 4, 5, 6, 9),* **AP**

**P8-8B** Brockman Company closes its books on October 31. On September 30, the Notes Receivable account balance is $18,800. Notes Receivable include the following.

| Date | Maker | Face Value | Term | Maturity Date | Interest Rate |
|---|---|---|---|---|---|
| Aug. 16 | Stuhmer Inc. | $6,000 | 60 days | Oct. 15 | 9% |
| Aug. 25 | Moberg Co. | 3,000 | 2 months | Oct. 25 | 7% |
| Sept. 30 | Earnest Corp. | 9,800 | 6 months | Mar. 30 | 6% |

Interest is computed using a 360-day year. During October, the following transactions were completed.

Oct.  7 Made sales of $4,600 on Brockman credit cards.
  12 Made sales of $600 on Visa credit cards. The credit card service charge is 3%.
  15 Received payment in full from Stuhmer Inc. on the amount due.
  25 Received payment in full from Moberg Co. on amount due.

### Instructions

(a) Journalize the October transactions and the October 31 adjusting entry for accrued interest receivable. (Interest is computed using 360 days; omit cost of goods sold entries.)

(b) A/R bal.  $ 4,600

(b) Enter the balances at October 1 in the receivable accounts and post the entries to all of the receivable accounts. (Use T accounts.)

(c) Tot. receivables  $14,449

(c) Show the balance sheet presentation of the receivable accounts at October 31.

*Calculate and interpret various ratios.*

*(SO 7, 8),* **AN**

**P8-9B** Presented here is basic financial information from the 2009 annual reports of Intel and Advanced Micro Devices (AMD), the two primary manufacturers of silicon chips for personal computers.

| (in millions) | Intel | AMD |
|---|---|---|
| Sales | $35,127 | $5,403 |
| Allowance for doubtful accounts, Jan. 1 | 17 | 8 |
| Allowance for doubtful accounts, Dec. 31 | 19 | 7 |
| Accounts receivable balance (gross), Jan. 1 | 1,729 | 328 |
| Accounts receivable balance (gross), Dec. 31 | 2,292 | 752 |

### Instructions

Calculate the receivables turnover ratio and average collection period for both companies. Comment on the difference in their collection experiences.

# Problems: Set C

Visit the book's companion website, at **www.wiley.com/college/kimmel**, and choose the Student Companion site to access Problem Set C.

# Comprehensive Problem

**CP8**  Porter Corporation's balance sheet at December 31, 2011, is presented below.

**PORTER CORPORATION**
**Balance Sheet**
**December 31, 2011**

| | | | |
|---|---|---|---|
| Cash | $13,100 | Accounts payable | $ 8,750 |
| Accounts receivable | 19,780 | Common stock | 20,000 |
| Allowance for doubtful accounts | (800) | Retained earnings | 12,730 |
| Inventory | 9,400 | | $41,480 |
| | $41,480 | | |

During January 2012, the following transactions occurred. Porter uses the perpetual inventory method.

Jan.  1   Porter accepted a 4-month, 8% note from Anderko Company in payment of Anderko's $1,200 account.
  3   Porter wrote off as uncollectible the accounts of Elrich Corporation ($450) and Rios Company ($280).
  8   Porter purchased $17,200 of inventory on account.
  11   Porter sold for $25,000 on account inventory that cost $17,500.
  15   Porter sold inventory that cost $700 to Fred Berman for $1,000. Berman charged this amount on his Visa First Bank card. The service fee charged Porter by First Bank is 3%.
  17   Porter collected $22,900 from customers on account.
  21   Porter paid $16,300 on accounts payable.
  24   Porter received payment in full ($280) from Rios Company on the account written off on January 3.
  27   Porter purchased advertising supplies for $1,400 cash.
  31   Porter paid other operating expenses, $3,218.

**Adjustment data:**

1. Interest is recorded for the month on the note from January 1.
2. Bad debts are expected to be 6% of the January 31, 2012, accounts receivable.
3. A count of advertising supplies on January 31, 2012, reveals that $560 remains unused.
4. The income tax rate is 30%. (*Hint:* Prepare the income statement up to "Income before taxes" and multiply by 30% to compute the amount; round to whole dollars.)

*Instructions*
(You may want to set up T accounts to determine ending balances.)
(a) Prepare journal entries for the transactions listed above and adjusting entries. (Include entries for cost of goods sold using the perpetual system.)
(b) Prepare an adjusted trial balance at January 31, 2012.
(c) Prepare an income statement and a retained earnings statement for the month ending January 31, 2012, and a classified balance sheet as of January 31, 2012.

## Continuing Cookie Chronicle

(*Note:* This is a continuation of the Cookie Chronicle from Chapters 1 through 7.)

**CCC8** One of Natalie's friends, Curtis Lesperance, runs a coffee shop where he sells specialty coffees and prepares and sells muffins and cookies. He is eager to buy one of Natalie's fine European mixers, which would enable him to make larger batches of muffins and cookies. However, Curtis cannot afford to pay for the mixer for at least 30 days. He asks Natalie if she would be willing to sell him the mixer on credit. Natalie comes to you for advice.

> Go to the book's companion website, at **www.wiley.com/college/kimmel**, to see the completion of this problem.

# broadening your perspective

# Financial Reporting and Analysis

## FINANCIAL REPORTING PROBLEM: *Tootsie Roll Industries Inc.*

**BYP8-1** Refer to the financial statements of Tootsie Roll Industries and the accompanying notes to its financial statements in Appendix A.

### Instructions
(a) Calculate the receivables turnover ratio and average collection period for 2009. (Use "Net Product Sales." Assume all sales were credit sales.)
(b) Did Tootsie Roll have any potentially significant credit risks in 2009? (*Hint:* Review Note 1 under Revenue recognition and Note 9 to the financial statements.)
(c) What conclusions can you draw from the information in parts (a) and (b)?

## COMPARATIVE ANALYSIS PROBLEM: *Tootsie Roll vs. Hershey*

**BYP8-2** The financial statements of The Hershey Company are presented in Appendix B, following the financial statements for Tootsie Roll in Appendix A.

### Instructions
(a) Based on the information contained in these financial statements, compute the following 2009 values for each company.
   (1) Receivables turnover ratio. (For Tootsie Roll use "Net product sales." Assume all sales were credit sales.)
   (2) Average collection period for receivables.
(b) What conclusions concerning the management of accounts receivable can be drawn from these data?

## RESEARCH CASE

**BYP8-3** The August 31, 2009, issue of the *Wall Street Journal* includes an article by Serena Ng and Cari Tuna entitled "Big Firms Are Quick to Collect, Slow to Pay."

### Instructions
Read the article and answer the following questions.
(a) How many days did InBev tell its suppliers that it was going to take to pay? How many days did it take previously?
(b) What steps did General Electric take to free up cash? How much cash did it free up?
(c) On average, how many days did companies with more than $5 billion take to pay suppliers, and how many days did they take to collect from their customers? How did this compare to companies with less than $500 million in sales?
(d) Are there any risks involved with being too tough in negotiating delayed payment terms with suppliers?

## INTERPRETING FINANCIAL STATEMENTS

**BYP8-4**   The information below is from the 2008 financial statements and accompanying notes of The Scotts Company, a major manufacturer of lawn-care products.

| (in millions) | 2008 | 2007 |
|---|---|---|
| Accounts receivable | $ 270.4 | $ 259.7 |
| Allowance for uncollectible accounts | 10.6 | 11.4 |
| Sales | 2,981.8 | 2,871.8 |
| Total current assets | 1,044.9 | 999.3 |

**THE SCOTTS COMPANY**
Notes to the Financial Statements

### Note 19. Concentrations of Credit Risk

Financial instruments which potentially subject the Company to concentration of credit risk consist principally of trade accounts receivable. The Company sells its consumer products to a wide variety of retailers, including mass merchandisers, home centers, independent hardware stores, nurseries, garden outlets, warehouse clubs, food and drug stores and local and regional chains. Professional products are sold to commercial nurseries, greenhouses, landscape services and growers of specialty agriculture crops. Concentrations of accounts receivable at September 30, net of accounts receivable pledged under the terms of the New MARP Agreement whereby the purchaser has assumed the risk associated with the debtor's financial inability to pay ($146.6 million and $149.5 million for 2008 and 2007, respectively), were as follows:

|  | 2008 | 2007 |
|---|---|---|
| Due from customers geographically located in North America | 53% | 52% |
| Applicable to the consumer business | 61% | 54% |
| Applicable to Scotts LawnService®, the professional businesses (primarily distributors), Smith & Hawken® and Morning Song® | 39% | 46% |
| Top 3 customers within consumer business as a percent of total consumer accounts receivable | 0% | 0% |

The remainder of the Company's accounts receivable at September 30, 2008 and 2007, were generated from customers located outside of North America, primary retailers, distributors, nurseries and growers in Europe. No concentrations of customers of individual customers within this group account for more than 10% of the Company's accounts receivable at either balance sheet date.

The Company's three largest customers are reported within the Global Consumer segment, and are the only customers that individually represent more than 10% of reported consolidated net sales for each of the last three fiscal years. These three customers accounted for the following percentages of consolidated net sales for the fiscal years ended September 30:

|  | Largest Customer | 2nd Largest Customer | 3rd Largest Customer |
|---|---|---|---|
| 2008 | 21.0% | 13.5% | 13.4% |
| 2007 | 20.2% | 10.9% | 10.2% |
| 2006 | 21.5% | 11.2% | 10.5% |

### Instructions

Answer each of the following questions.

(a)  Calculate the receivables turnover ratio and average collection period for 2008 for the company.

(b)  Is accounts receivable a material component of the company's total 2008 current assets?

(c)  Scotts sells seasonal products. How might this affect the accuracy of your answer to part (a)?

(d)  Evaluate the credit risk of Scotts' 2008 concentrated receivables.

(e)  Comment on the informational value of Scotts' Note 19 on concentrations of credit risk.

## FINANCIAL ANALYSIS ON THE WEB

**BYP8-5** *Purpose:* To learn more about factoring from websites that provide factoring services.

*Address:* **www.ccapital.net**, or go to **www.wiley.com/college/kimmel**

*Instructions*
Go to the website, click on **Invoice Factoring**, and answer the following questions.
(a) What are some of the benefits of factoring?
(b) What is the range of the percentages of the typical discount rate?
(c) If a company factors its receivables, what percentage of the value of the receivables can it expect to receive from the factor in the form of cash, and how quickly will it receive the cash?

# Critical Thinking

## DECISION MAKING ACROSS THE ORGANIZATION

**BYP8-6** Sue and Sam Ristic own Club Fab. From its inception, Club Fab has sold merchandise on either a cash or credit basis, but no credit cards have been accepted. During the past several months, the Ristics have begun to question their credit-sales policies. First, they have lost some sales because of their refusal to accept credit cards. Second, representatives of two metropolitan banks have convinced them to accept their national credit cards. One bank, City National Bank, has stated that (1) its credit card fee is 4% and (2) it pays the retailer 96 cents on each $1 of sales within 3 days of receiving the credit card billings.

The Ristics decide that they should determine the cost of carrying their own credit sales. From the accounting records of the past 3 years, they accumulate these data:

|  | 2012 | 2011 | 2010 |
|---|---|---|---|
| Net credit sales | $500,000 | $600,000 | $400,000 |
| Collection agency fees for slow-paying customers | 2,900 | 2,600 | 1,600 |
| Salary of part-time accounts receivable clerk | 4,400 | 4,400 | 4,400 |

Credit and collection expenses as a percentage of net credit sales are as follows: uncollectible accounts 1.6%, billing and mailing costs .5%, and credit investigation fee on new customers .2%.

Sue and Sam also determine that the average accounts receivable balance outstanding during the year is 5% of net credit sales. The Ristics estimate that they could earn an average of 10% annually on cash invested in other business opportunities.

*Instructions*
With the class divided into groups, answer the following.
(a) Prepare a tabulation for each year showing total credit and collection expenses in dollars and as a percentage of net credit sales.
(b) Determine the net credit and collection expenses in dollars and as a percentage of sales after considering the revenue not earned from other investment opportunities. (*Note:* The income lost on the cash held by the bank for 3 days is considered to be immaterial.)
(c) Discuss both the financial and nonfinancial factors that are relevant to the decision.

## COMMUNICATION ACTIVITY

**BYP8-7** Stropes Corporation is a recently formed business selling the "World's Best Doormat." The corporation is selling doormats faster than Stropes can make them. It has been selling the product on a credit basis, telling customers to "pay when they can." Oddly, even though sales are tremendous, the company is having trouble paying its bills.

*Instructions*
Write a memo to the president of Stropes Corporation discussing these questions:
(a) What steps should be taken to improve the company's ability to pay its bills?
(b) What accounting steps should be taken to measure its success in improving collections and in recording its collection success?
(c) If the corporation is still unable to pay its bills, what additional steps can be taken with its receivables to ease its liquidity problems?

## ETHICS CASE

**BYP8-8** As its year-end approaches, it appears that Lopez Corporation's net income will increase 10% this year. The president of Lopez Corporation, nervous that the stockholders might expect the company to sustain this 10% growth rate in net income in future years, suggests that the controller increase the allowance for doubtful accounts to 4% of receivables in order to lower this year's net income. The president thinks that the lower net income, which reflects a 6% growth rate, will be a more sustainable rate of growth for Lopez Corporation in future years. The controller of Lopez Corporation believes that the company's yearly allowance for doubtful accounts should be 2% of receivables.

*Instructions*
(a) Who are the stakeholders in this case?
(b) Does the president's request pose an ethical dilemma for the controller?
(c) Should the controller be concerned with Lopez Corporation's growth rate in estimating the allowance? Explain your answer.

## "ALL ABOUT YOU" ACTIVITY

**BYP8-9** Credit card usage in the United States is substantial. Many startup companies use credit cards as a way to help meet short-term financial needs. The most common forms of debt for startups are use of credit cards and loans from relatives.

Suppose that you start up Brothers Sandwich Shop. You invested your savings of $20,000 and borrowed $70,000 from your relatives. Although sales in the first few months are good, you see that you may not have sufficient cash to pay expenses and maintain your inventory at acceptable levels, at least in the short term. You decide you may need to use one or more credit cards to fund the possible cash shortfall.

*Instructions*
(a) Go to the Internet and find two sources that provide insight into how to compare credit card terms.
(b) Develop a list, in descending order of importance, as to what features are most important to you in selecting a credit card for your business.
(c) Examine the features of your present credit card. (If you do not have a credit card, select a likely one online for this exercise.) Given your analysis above, what are the three major disadvantages of your present credit card?

## FASB CODIFICATION ACTIVITY

**BYP8-10** If your school has a subscription to the FASB Codification, go to **http://aaahq.org/ascLogin.cfm** to log in and prepare responses to the following.
(a) How are receivables defined in the Codification?
(b) What are the conditions under which losses from uncollectible receivables (Bad Debts Expense) should be reported?

### Answers to Insight and Accounting Across the Organization Questions

**p. 406 When Investors Ignore Warning Signs Q:** When would it be appropriate for a company to lower its allowance for doubtful accounts as a percentage of its receivables? **A:** It would be appropriate for a company to lower its allowance for doubtful accounts as a percentage of receivables if the company's collection experience had improved, or was expected to improve, and therefore the company expected lower defaults as a percentage of receivables.

**p. 409 Can Fair Value Be Unfair? Q:** What are the arguments in favor of and against fair value accounting for loans and receivables? **A:** Arguments in favor of fair value accounting for loans and receivables are that fair value would provide a more accurate view of a company's financial position. This might provide a useful early warning of when a bank or other financial institution was in trouble because its loans were of poor quality. But, banks argue that estimating fair values is very difficult to do accurately. They are also concerned that volatile fair values could cause large swings in a bank's reported net income.

**p. 413 Bad Information Can Lead to Bad Loans Q:** What steps should the banks have taken to ensure the accuracy of financial information provided on loan applications? **A:** At a minimum, the bank should have requested copies of recent income tax forms and contacted the supposed employer to verify income. To verify ownership and value of assets, it should have examined bank statements, investment statements, and title documents and should have employed appraisers.

**p. 419 eBay for Receivables Q:** What issues should management consider in deciding whether to factor its receivables? **A:** Management must prepare a cash budget and evaluate its projected cash needs. If it projects a cash deficiency, it should first pursue traditional bank financing, since it tends to be less expensive than factoring. If traditional financing is not available, management could pursue factoring. If carefully structured, a factoring arrangement can be cost-effective since it can enable the company to outsource many billing and collection activities.

## Answers to Self-Test Questions

**1.** c  **2.** c ($1,000 − $300) × (100% − 2%)  **3.** a  **4.** a ($160,000 × .075)  **5.** c ($200,000 ×.10) + ($30,000 − $18,000)  **6.** d ($800,000 − $65,000)  **7.** c  **8.** b  **9.** d  **10.** d  **11.** a $800,000 ÷ (($100,000 + $150,000) ÷ 2)  **12.** c (365 days ÷ 7)  **13.** c  **14.** a  **15.** d

# IFRS A Look at IFRS

The basic accounting and reporting issues related to recognition and measurement of receivables, such as the use of allowance accounts, how to record discounts, use of the allowance method to account for bad debts, and factoring, are essentially the same between IFRS and GAAP.

## KEY POINTS

- IFRS requires that loans and receivables be accounted for at amortized cost, adjusted for allowances for doubtful accounts. IFRS sometimes refers to these allowances as *provisions*. The entry to record the allowance would be:

| | | |
|---|---|---|
| Bad Debts Expense | xxxxxx | |
| Allowance for Doubtful Accounts | | xxxxxx |

- Although IFRS implies that receivables with different characteristics should be reported separately, there is no standard that mandates this segregation.

- The FASB and IASB have worked to implement fair value measurement (the amount they currently could be sold for) for financial instruments. Both Boards have faced bitter opposition from various factions. As a consequence, the Boards have adopted a piecemeal approach; the first step is disclosure of fair value information in the notes. The second step is the fair value option, which permits, but does not require, companies to record some types of financial instruments at fair values in the financial statements.

- IFRS requires a two-tiered approach to test whether the value of loans and receivables are impaired. First, a company should look at specific loans and receivables to determine whether they are impaired. Then, the loans and receivables as a group should be evaluated for impairment. GAAP does not prescribe a similar two-tiered approach.

- IFRS and GAAP differ in the criteria used to determine how to record a factoring transaction. IFRS is a combination of an approach focused on risks and rewards and loss of control. GAAP uses loss of control as the primary criterion. In addition, IFRS permits partial derecognition of receivables; GAAP does not.

## LOOKING TO THE FUTURE

It appears likely that the question of recording fair values for financial instruments will continue to be an important issue to resolve as the Boards work toward convergence. Both the IASB and the FASB have indicated that they believe that financial statements would be more transparent and understandable if companies recorded and reported all financial instruments at fair value. That said, in *IFRS 9*, which was issued in 2009, the IASB created a split model, where some financial instruments are recorded at fair value, but other financial assets, such as loans and receivables, can be accounted for at amortized cost if certain criteria are met. Critics say that this can result in two companies with identical securities accounting for those securities in different ways. A proposal by the FASB would require that nearly all financial instruments, including loans and receivables, be accounted for at fair value. It has been suggested that *IFRS 9* will likely be changed or replaced as the FASB and IASB continue to deliberate the best treatment for financial instruments.

In fact, one past member of the IASB said that companies should ignore *IFRS 9* and continue to report under the old standard, because in his opinion, it was extremely likely that it would be changed before the mandatory adoption date of the standard arrived in 2013.

## IFRS Self-Test Questions

1. Under IFRS, loans and receivables are to be reported on the balance sheet at:
   (a) amortized cost.
   (b) amortized cost adjusted for estimated loss provisions.
   (c) historical cost.
   (d) replacement cost.
2. Which of the following statements is *false*?
   (a) Loans and receivables include equity securities purchased by the company.
   (b) Loans and receivables include credit card receivables.
   (c) Loans and receivables include amounts owed by employees as a result of company loans to employees.
   (d) Loans and receivables include amounts resulting from transactions with customers.
3. In recording a factoring transaction:
   (a) IFRS focuses on loss of control.
   (b) GAAP focuses on loss of control and risks and rewards.
   (c) IFRS and GAAP allow partial derecognition.
   (d) IFRS allows partial derecognition
4. Under IFRS:
   (a) the entry to record estimated uncollected accounts is the same as GAAP.
   (b) loans and receivables should only be tested for impairment as a group.
   (c) it is always acceptable to use the direct write-off method.
   (d) all financial instruments are recorded at fair value.
5. Which of the following statements is *true*?
   (a) The fair value option requires that some types of financial instruments be recorded at fair value.
   (b) The fair value option allows, but does not require, that some types of financial instruments be recorded at amortized cost.
   (c) The fair value option requires that all types of financial instruments be recorded at fair value.
   (d) The FASB and IASB would like to reduce the reliance on fair value accounting for financial instruments in the future.

## IFRS Concepts and Application

**IFRS8–1**  What are some steps taken by both the FASB and IASB to move to fair value measurement for financial instruments? In what ways have some of the approaches differed?

## INTERNATIONAL FINANCIAL REPORTING PROBLEM: *Zetar plc*

**IFRS8–2**  The financial statements of Zetar plc are presented in Appendix C. The company's complete annual report, including the notes to its financial statements, is available at **www.zetarplc.com.**

*Instructions*
Use the company's annual report to answer the following questions.
   (a) According to the Operational Review of Financial Performance, what was one reason why the balance in receivables increased relative to the previous year?
   (b) According to the notes to the financial statements, how are loans and receivables defined?
   (c) In the notes to the financial statements, the company reports a "one off item" related to receivables. Explain what this item was.
   (d) Using information in the notes to the financial statements, determine what percentage the provision for impairment of receivables was as a percentage of total trade receivables for 2009 and 2008. How did the ratio change from 2008 to 2009, and what does this suggest about the company's receivables?

## Answers to IFRS Self-Test Questions
**1.** b  **2.** a  **3.** d  **4.** a  **5.** c

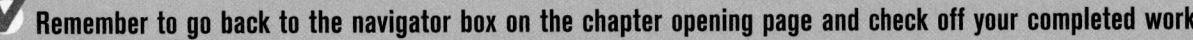
Remember to go back to the navigator box on the chapter opening page and check off your completed work.

chapter **9**

# REPORTING AND ANALYZING LONG-LIVED ASSETS

## ✔ the navigator

| | |
|---|---|
| ● Scan **Study Objectives** | ○ |
| ● Read **Feature Story** | ○ |
| ● Scan **Preview** | ○ |
| ● Read **Text and Answer** **Do it!** | |
|   p. 453 ○   p. 457 ○   p. 460 ○ | |
|   p. 464 ○   p. 472 ○ | |
| ● Work Using the **Decision Toolkit** | ○ |
| ● Review **Summary of Study Objectives** | ○ |
| ● Work **Comprehensive** **Do it!**  p. 480 | ○ |
| ● Answer **Self-Test Questions** | ○ |
| ● Complete **Assignments** | ○ |
| ● Go to **WileyPLUS** for practice and tutorials | ○ |
| ● 🌐 Read **A Look at IFRS** p. 500 | ○ |

## study objectives

**After studying this chapter, you should be able to:**

1 Describe how the cost principle applies to plant assets.

2 Explain the concept of depreciation.

3 Compute periodic depreciation using the straight-line method, and contrast its expense pattern with those of other methods.

4 Describe the procedure for revising periodic depreciation.

5 Explain how to account for the disposal of plant assets.

6 Describe methods for evaluating the use of plant assets.

7 Identify the basic issues related to reporting intangible assets.

8 Indicate how long-lived assets are reported in the financial statements.

✔ the navigator

So, you're interested in starting a new business. Have you thought about the airline industry? Your only experience with airlines is as a passenger? Don't let that stop you. Today, the most profitable airlines in the industry are not well-known majors like American Airlines and United. In fact, most giant, old airlines are either bankrupt or on the verge of bankruptcy. In a recent year, five major airlines representing 24% of total U.S. capacity were operating under bankruptcy protection.

Not all airlines are hurting. The growth and profitability in the airline industry today is found at relative newcomers like Southwest Airlines and JetBlue. These and other new airlines compete primarily on ticket prices. During a recent five-year period, the low-fare airline market share increased by 47%; the low-fare airlines now have over 22% of U.S. airline capacity.

Southwest was the first upstart to make it big. It did so by taking a different approach. It bought small, new, fuel-efficient planes. Also, instead of the "hub-and-spoke" approach used by the majors, it opted for direct, short hop, no frills flights. It was all about controlling costs—getting the most out of its efficient new planes.

Other upstarts, such as Valujet, chose a different approach. They bought planes that were 20 to 30 years old (known in the industry as zombies). By buying used planes, Valujet was able to add one or two planes a month to its fleet—an unheard of expansion. Valujet started with a $3.4 million investment and grew to be worth $630 million in its first three years.

But, a terrible crash of a Valujet aircraft focused the spotlight on its strategy of using old planes. Although the cause of the crash appears to have been unrelated to the age of its planes, in the aftermath of the crash Valujet struggled to survive under the weight of government scrutiny and lack of customer confidence. In the face of continuing financial problems and customer skepticism, Valujet merged with AirWays Corp. and took the name of its airline, AirTran Airways. AirTran is currently one of the most profitable airlines in the industry.

But with fuel costs at record high levels, AirTran is no longer in the market for old planes. Nobody is. In fact, the old Boeing 727, which until very recently was a mainstay of nearly every airline, is no longer used for passenger flights because it couldn't be operated efficiently. Today, success in the airline business comes from owning the newest and most efficient equipment, and knowing how to get the most out of it.

# A TALE OF TWO AIRLINES

**the navigator**

Was Valujet's strategy of buying used equipment really the "right formula," or was it a recipe for disaster? For airlines and many other companies, making the right decisions regarding long-lived assets is critical because these assets represent huge investments. Management must make many ongoing decisions about long-lived assets—what assets to acquire and when, how to finance them, how to account for them, and when to dispose of them.

In this chapter, we address these and other issues surrounding long-lived assets. The discussion is in two parts: plant assets and intangible assets. *Plant assets* are the property, plant, and equipment (physical assets) that commonly come to mind when we think of what a company owns. Companies also have many important *intangible assets*. These assets, such as copyrights and patents, lack physical substance but can be extremely valuable and vital to a company's success.

The content and organization of this chapter are as follows.

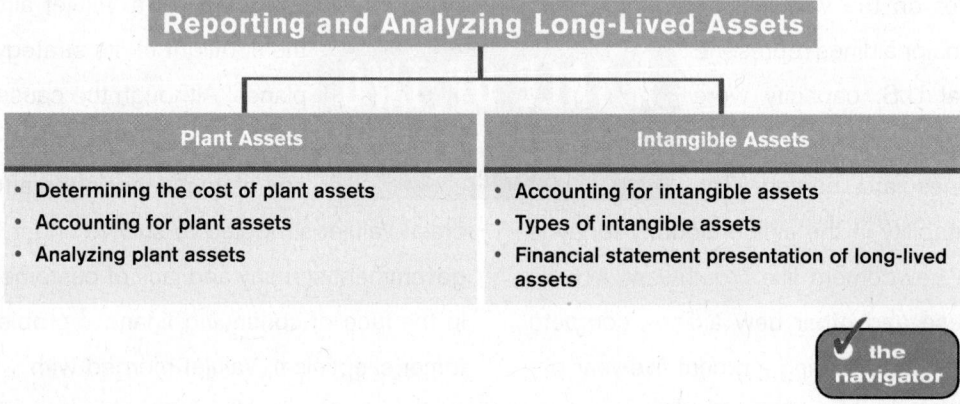

**Reporting and Analyzing Long-Lived Assets**

| **Plant Assets** | **Intangible Assets** |
|---|---|
| • Determining the cost of plant assets<br>• Accounting for plant assets<br>• Analyzing plant assets | • Accounting for intangible assets<br>• Types of intangible assets<br>• Financial statement presentation of long-lived assets |

✔ the navigator

# Plant Assets

**Plant assets** are resources that have physical substance (a definite size and shape), are used in the operations of a business, and are not intended for sale to customers. They are called various names—*property, plant, and equipment; plant and equipment;* and *fixed assets.* By whatever name, these assets are expected to provide service to the company for a number of years. Except for land, plant assets decline in service potential (value) over their useful lives.

Plant assets are critical to a company's success because they determine the company's capacity and therefore its ability to satisfy customers. With too few planes, for example, AirTran and Southwest Airlines would lose customers to their competitors. But with too many planes, they would be flying with empty seats. Management must constantly monitor its needs and acquire assets accordingly. Failure to do so results in lost business opportunities or inefficient use of existing assets and is likely to show up eventually in poor financial results.

It is important for a company to (1) keep assets in good operating condition, (2) replace worn-out or outdated assets, and (3) expand its productive assets as needed. The decline of rail travel in the United States can be traced in part to the failure of railroad companies to maintain and update their assets. Conversely, the growth of air travel in this country can be attributed in part to the general willingness of airline companies to follow these essential guidelines.

For many companies, investments in plant assets are substantial. Illustration 9-1 shows the percentages of plant assets in relation to total assets in various companies in a recent year.

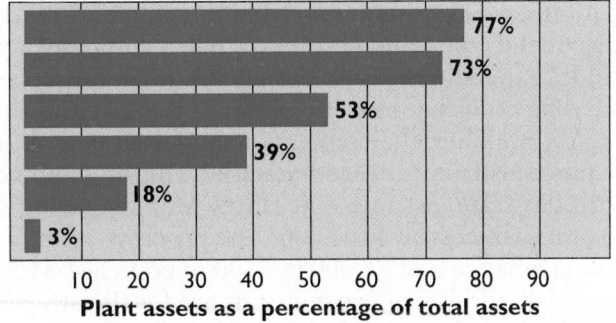

**Illustration 9-1**
Percentages of plant assets in relation to total assets

# Determining the Cost of Plant Assets

The **cost principle** requires that companies record plant assets at cost. Thus, AirTran and Southwest Airlines record their planes at cost. **Cost consists of all expenditures necessary to acquire an asset and make it ready for its intended use.** For example, the purchase price, freight costs paid by the purchaser, and installation costs are all part of the cost of factory machinery.

Determining which costs to include in a plant asset account and which costs not to include is very important. If a cost is not included in a plant asset account, then it must be expensed immediately. Such costs are referred to as **revenue expenditures**. On the other hand, costs that are not expensed immediately but are instead included in a plant asset account are referred to as **capital expenditures**.

This distinction is important; it has immediate, and often material, implications for the income statement. Some companies, in order to boost current income, have **improperly capitalized expenditures** that they should have expensed. For example, suppose that a company improperly capitalizes to a building account $1,000 of maintenance costs incurred at the end of the year. (That is, the costs are included in the asset account Buildings rather than being expensed immediately as Maintenance and Repairs Expense.) If the company is allocating the cost of the building as an expense (depreciating it) over a 40-year life, then the maintenance cost of $1,000 will be incorrectly spread across 40 years instead of being expensed in the current year. As a result, the company will understate current-year expenses by $1,000, and will overstate current-year income by $1,000. Thus, determining which costs to capitalize and which to expense is very important.

Cost is measured by the cash paid in a cash transaction or by the **cash equivalent price** paid when companies use noncash assets in payment. **The cash equivalent price is equal to the fair value of the asset given up or the fair value of the asset received, whichever is more clearly determinable.** Once cost is established, it becomes the basis of accounting for the plant asset over its useful life. Current fair value is not used to increase the recorded cost after acquisition. We explain the application of the cost principle to each of the major classes of plant assets in the following sections.

**study objective** **1**

Describe how the cost principle applies to plant assets.

**International Note** IFRS is flexible regarding asset valuation. Companies revalue to fair value when they believe this information is more relevant.

## LAND

Companies often use land as a building site for a manufacturing plant or office site. The cost of land includes (1) the cash purchase price, (2) closing costs such as title and attorney's fees, (3) real estate brokers' commissions, and (4) accrued property taxes and other liens on the land assumed by the purchaser. For example, if the cash price is $50,000 and the purchaser agrees to pay accrued taxes of $5,000, the cost of the land is $55,000.

All necessary costs incurred in making land **ready for its intended use** increase (debit) the Land account. When a company acquires vacant land, its cost includes expenditures for clearing, draining, filling, and grading. If the land has a building on it that must be removed to make the site suitable for construction of a new building, the company includes all demolition and removal costs, less any proceeds from salvaged materials, in the Land account.

To illustrate, assume that Hayes Manufacturing Company acquires real estate at a cash cost of $100,000. The property contains an old warehouse that is razed at a net cost of $6,000 ($7,500 in costs less $1,500 proceeds from salvaged materials). Additional expenditures are for the attorney's fee $1,000 and the real estate broker's commission $8,000. Given these factors, the cost of the land is $115,000, computed as shown in Illustration 9-2.

**Illustration 9-2**
Computation of cost of land

| Land | |
|---|---:|
| Cash price of property | $ 100,000 |
| Net removal cost of warehouse | 6,000 |
| Attorney's fee | 1,000 |
| Real estate broker's commission | 8,000 |
| Cost of land | **$115,000** |

When Hayes records the acquisition, it debits Land and credits Cash for $115,000.

### LAND IMPROVEMENTS

**Land improvements** are structural additions made to land, such as driveways, parking lots, fences, landscaping, and underground sprinklers. The cost of land improvements includes all expenditures necessary to make the improvements ready for their intended use. For example, the cost of a new company parking lot includes the amount paid for paving, fencing, and lighting. Thus, the company would debit the total of all of these costs to Land Improvements.

Land improvements have limited useful lives, and their maintenance and replacement are the responsibility of the company. Because of their limited useful life, companies expense (depreciate) the cost of land improvements over their useful lives.

### BUILDINGS

Buildings are facilities used in operations, such as stores, offices, factories, warehouses, and airplane hangars. Companies charge to the Buildings account all necessary expenditures relating to the purchase or construction of a building. When a building is **purchased**, such costs include the purchase price, closing costs (attorney's fees, title insurance, etc.), and real estate broker's commission. Costs to make the building ready for its intended use consist of expenditures for remodeling rooms and offices and replacing or repairing the roof, floors, electrical wiring, and plumbing. When a new building is **constructed**, its cost consists of the contract price plus payments made by the owner for architects' fees, building permits, and excavation costs.

In addition, companies add certain interest costs to the cost of a building: Interest costs incurred to finance a construction project are included in the cost of the asset when a significant period of time is required to get the asset ready for use. In these circumstances, interest costs are considered as necessary as materials and labor. However, the inclusion of interest costs in the cost of a constructed building is **limited to interest costs incurred during the construction period**. When construction has been completed, subsequent interest payments on funds borrowed to finance the construction are recorded as increases (debits) to Interest Expense.

## EQUIPMENT

**Equipment** includes assets used in operations, such as store check-out counters, office furniture, factory machinery, delivery trucks, and airplanes. The cost of equipment consists of the cash purchase price, sales taxes, freight charges, and insurance during transit paid by the purchaser. It also includes expenditures required in assembling, installing, and testing the unit. However, companies treat as expenses the costs of motor vehicle licenses and accident insurance on company trucks and cars. Such items are **annual recurring expenditures and do not benefit future periods**. Two criteria apply in determining the cost of equipment: (1) the frequency of the cost—one time or recurring, and (2) the benefit period—the life of the asset or one year.

To illustrate, assume that Lenard Company purchases a delivery truck at a cash price of $22,000. Related expenditures are sales taxes $1,320, painting and lettering $500, motor vehicle license $80, and a three-year accident insurance policy $1,600. The cost of the delivery truck is $23,820, computed as shown in Illustration 9-3.

**Illustration 9-3**
Computation of cost of delivery truck

| Delivery Truck | |
|---|---|
| Cash price | $ 22,000 |
| Sales taxes | 1,320 |
| Painting and lettering | 500 |
| **Cost of delivery truck** | **$23,820** |

Lenard treats the cost of a motor vehicle license as an expense and the cost of an insurance policy as a prepaid asset. Thus, the company records the purchase of the truck and related expenditures as follows.

| | | |
|---|---|---|
| Equipment | 23,820 | |
| License Expense | 80 | |
| Prepaid Insurance | 1,600 | |
|     Cash | | 25,500 |
|     (To record purchase of delivery truck and related expenditures) | | |

| A | = | L | + | SE |
|---|---|---|---|---|
| +23,820 | | | | |
| | | | | −80 Exp |
| +1,600 | | | | |
| −25,500 | | | | |

**Cash Flows**
−25,500

For another example, assume Merten Company purchases factory machinery at a cash price of $50,000. Related expenditures are sales taxes $3,000, insurance during shipping $500, and installation and testing $1,000. The cost of the factory machinery is $54,500, computed as in Illustration 9-4.

**Illustration 9-4**
Computation of cost of factory machinery

| Factory Machinery | |
|---|---|
| Cash price | $ 50,000 |
| Sales taxes | 3,000 |
| Insurance during shipping | 500 |
| Installation and testing | 1,000 |
| **Cost of factory machinery** | **$54,500** |

Thus, Merten records the purchase and related expenditures as follows.

| | | |
|---|---|---|
| Equipment | 54,500 | |
|     Cash | | 54,500 |
|     (To record purchase of factory machinery and related expenditures) | | |

| A | = | L | + | SE |
|---|---|---|---|---|
| +54,500 | | | | |
| −54,500 | | | | |

**Cash Flows**
−54,500

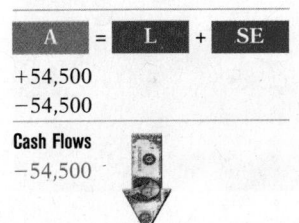

## TO BUY OR LEASE?

In this chapter, we focus on purchased assets, but we want to expose you briefly to an alternative—leasing. A lease is a contractual agreement in which the owner of an asset (the **lessor**) allows another party (the **lessee**) to use the asset for a period of time at an agreed price. In many industries, leasing is quite common. For example, one-third of heavy-duty commercial trucks are leased.

Some advantages of leasing an asset versus purchasing it are:

1. **Reduced risk of obsolescence.** Frequently, lease terms allow the party using the asset (the lessee) to exchange the asset for a more modern one if it becomes outdated. This is much easier than trying to sell an obsolete asset.

2. **Little or no down payment.** To purchase an asset, most companies must borrow money, which usually requires a down payment of at least 20%. Leasing an asset requires little or no down payment.

3. **Shared tax advantages.** Startup companies typically earn little or no profit in their early years, and so they have little need for the tax deductions available from owning an asset. In a lease, the lessor gets the tax advantage because it owns the asset. It often will pass these tax savings on to the lessee in the form of lower lease payments.

4. **Assets and liabilities not reported.** Many companies prefer to keep assets and especially liabilities off their books. Reporting lower assets improves the return on assets ratio (discussed later in this chapter). Reporting fewer liabilities makes the company look less risky. Certain types of leases, called **operating leases**, allow the lessee to account for the transaction as a rental, with neither an asset nor a liability recorded.

Airlines often choose to lease many of their airplanes in long-term lease agreements. In recent financial statements, Southwest Airlines stated that it leased 88 of its 417 planes under operating leases. Because operating leases are accounted for as rentals, these 88 planes did not show up on its balance sheet.

Under another type of lease, a **capital lease**, lessees show both the asset and the liability on the balance sheet. The lessee accounts for capital lease agreements in a way that is very similar to purchases: The lessee shows the leased item as an asset on its balance sheet, and the obligation owed to the lessor as a liability. The lessee depreciates the leased asset in a manner similar to purchased assets. Capital leases represent only about 0.5% of Southwest Airlines' property, plant, and equipment. We discuss leasing further in Chapter 10.

 ## Accounting Across the Organization

### Many U.S. Firms Use Leases

Leasing is big business for U.S. companies. For example, in a recent year leasing accounted for about 31% of all business investment ($218 billion).

Who does the most leasing? Interestingly, major banks such as Continental Bank, J.P. Morgan Leasing, and US Bancorp Equipment Finance are the major lessors. Also, many companies have established separate leasing companies, such as Boeing Capital Corporation, Dell Financial Services, and John Deere Capital Corporation. And, as an excellent example of the magnitude of leasing, leased planes account for nearly 40% of the U.S. fleet of commercial airlines. Lease Finance Corporation in Los Angeles owns more planes than any airline in the world.

In addition, leasing is becoming increasingly common in the hotel industry. Marriott, Hilton, and InterContinental are increasingly choosing to lease hotels that are owned by someone else.

 Why might airline managers choose to lease rather than purchase their planes? (See page 499.)

**Do it!** Assume that Drummond Corp. purchases a delivery truck for $15,000 cash plus sales taxes of $900 and delivery costs of $500. The buyer also pays $200 for painting and lettering, $600 for an annual insurance policy, and $80 for a motor vehicle license. Explain how the company should account for each of these costs.

**Solution**

The first four payments ($15,000 purchase price, $900 sales taxes, $500 delivery, and $200 painting and lettering) are expenditures necessary to make the truck ready for its intended use. Thus, the cost of the truck is $16,600. The payments for insurance and the license are operating expenses incurred during the useful life of the asset.

Related exercise material: **BE9-1, BE9-2, Do it!** 9-1, **E9-1, E9-2,** and **E9-3.**

**COST OF PLANT ASSETS**

**Action Plan**

- Identify expenditures made in order to get delivery equipment ready for its intended use.
- Expense operating costs incurred during the useful life of the equipment.

# Accounting for Plant Assets

## DEPRECIATION

As explained in Chapter 4, depreciation **is the process of allocating to expense the cost of a plant asset over its useful (service) life in a rational and systematic manner.** Such cost allocation is designed to properly match expenses with revenues. (See Illustration 9-5.)

**study objective 2**

Explain the concept of depreciation.

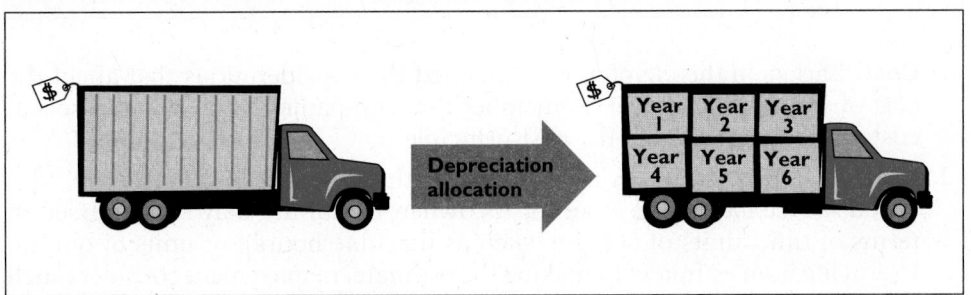

**Illustration 9-5**
Depreciation as a cost allocation concept

Depreciation Tutorial

Depreciation affects the balance sheet through accumulated depreciation, which companies report as a deduction from plant assets. It affects the income statement through depreciation expense.

It is important to understand that **depreciation is a cost allocation process, not an asset valuation process.** No attempt is made to measure the change in an asset's fair value during ownership. Thus, the **book value**—cost less accumulated depreciation—of a plant asset may differ significantly from its **fair value.** In fact, if an asset is fully depreciated, it can have zero book value but still have a significant fair value.

Depreciation applies to **three classes of plant assets**: land improvements, buildings, and equipment. Each of these classes is considered to be a **depreciable asset** because the usefulness to the company and the revenue-producing ability of each class decline over the asset's useful life. Depreciation **does not apply to land** because its usefulness and revenue-producing ability generally remain intact as long as the land is owned. In fact, in many cases, the usefulness of land increases over time because of the scarcity of good sites. Thus, **land is not a depreciable asset.**

During a depreciable asset's useful life, its revenue-producing ability declines because of wear and tear. A delivery truck that has been driven 100,000 miles will be less useful to a company than one driven only 800 miles.

A decline in revenue-producing ability may also occur because of obsolescence. **Obsolescence** is the process by which an asset becomes out of date before it physically wears out. The rerouting of major airlines from Chicago's

**Helpful Hint** Remember that depreciation is the process of *allocating cost* over the useful life of an asset. It is not a measure of value.

**Helpful Hint** Land does not depreciate because it does not wear out.

**Ethics Note** When a business is acquired, proper allocation of the purchase price to various asset classes is important, since different depreciation treatment can materially affect income. For example, buildings are depreciated, but land is not.

Midway Airport to Chicago-O'Hare International Airport because Midway's runways were too short for giant jets is an example. Similarly, many companies replace their computers long before they originally planned to do so because improvements in new computers make their old computers obsolete.

**Recognizing depreciation for an asset does not result in the accumulation of cash for replacement of the asset.** The balance in Accumulated Depreciation represents the total amount of the asset's cost that the company has charged to expense to date; **it is not a cash fund.**

## FACTORS IN COMPUTING DEPRECIATION

Three factors affect the computation of depreciation, as shown in Illustration 9-6.

**Illustration 9-6** Three factors in computing depreciation

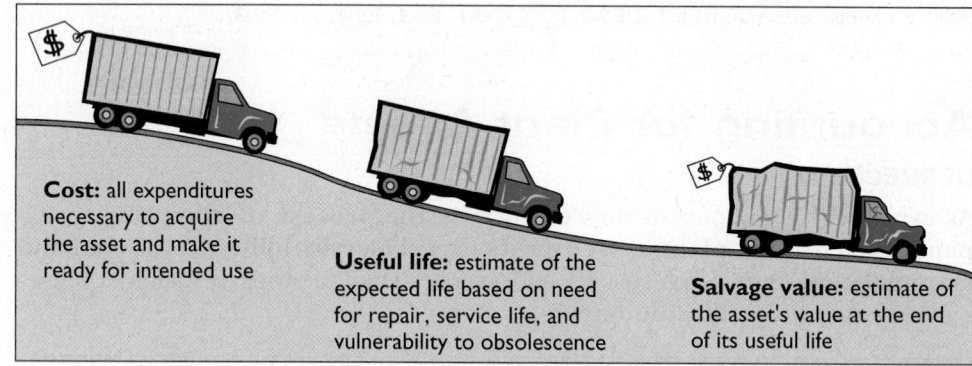

**Helpful Hint** Depreciation expense is reported on the income statement. Accumulated depreciation is reported on the balance sheet as a deduction from plant assets.

**Cost:** all expenditures necessary to acquire the asset and make it ready for intended use

**Useful life:** estimate of the expected life based on need for repair, service life, and vulnerability to obsolescence

**Salvage value:** estimate of the asset's value at the end of its useful life

1. **Cost.** Earlier in the chapter, we explained the considerations that affect the cost of a depreciable asset. Remember that companies record plant assets at cost, in accordance with the cost principle.

2. **Useful life.** Useful life is an estimate of the expected productive life, also called *service life,* of the asset for its owner. Useful life may be expressed in terms of time, units of activity (such as machine hours), or units of output. Useful life is an estimate. In making the estimate, management considers such factors as the intended use of the asset, repair and maintenance policies, and vulnerability of the asset to obsolescence. The company's past experience with similar assets is often helpful in deciding on expected useful life.

3. **Salvage value.** Salvage value is an estimate of the asset's value at the end of its useful life for its owner. Companies may base the value on the asset's worth as scrap or on its expected trade-in value. Like useful life, salvage value is an estimate. In making the estimate, management considers how it plans to dispose of the asset and its experience with similar assets.

## DEPRECIATION METHODS

**study objective  3**

Compute periodic depreciation using the straight-line method, and contrast its expense pattern with those of other methods.

Although a number of methods exist, depreciation is generally computed using one of three methods:

1. Straight-line
2. Declining-balance
3. Units-of-activity

Like the alternative inventory methods discussed in Chapter 6, each of these depreciation methods is acceptable under generally accepted accounting principles. Management selects the method it believes best measures an asset's contribution to revenue over its useful life. Once a company chooses a method, it should apply that method consistently over the useful life of the asset. Consistency enhances the ability to analyze financial statements over multiple years.

Illustration 9-7 shows the distribution of the *primary* depreciation methods in 600 of the largest U.S. companies. Clearly, straight-line depreciation is the most widely used approach. In fact, because some companies use more than one method, **straight-line depreciation is used for some or all of the depreciation taken by more than 95% of U.S. companies**. For this reason, we illustrate procedures for straight-line depreciation and discuss the alternative depreciation approaches only at a conceptual level. This coverage introduces you to the basic idea of depreciation as an allocation concept without entangling you in too much procedural detail. (Also, note that many hand-held calculators are preprogrammed to perform the basic depreciation methods.) Details on the alternative approaches are presented in Appendix 9A (pages 476–478).

Our illustration of depreciation methods, both here and in the appendix, is based on the following data relating to a small delivery truck purchased by Bill's Pizzas on January 1, 2012.

| | |
|---|---|
| Cost | $13,000 |
| Expected salvage value | $1,000 |
| Estimated useful life (in years) | 5 |
| Estimated useful life (in miles) | 100,000 |

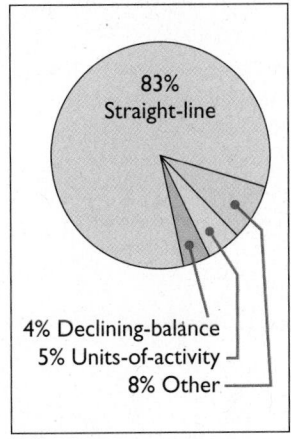

**Illustration 9-7** Use of depreciation methods in major U.S. companies

## Straight-Line

Under the **straight-line method**, companies expense an equal amount of depreciation each year of the asset's useful life. Management must choose the useful life of an asset based on its own expectations and experience.

To compute the annual depreciation expense, we divide depreciable cost by the estimated useful life. **Depreciable cost** represents the total amount subject to depreciation; it is calculated as the cost of the plant asset less its salvage value. Illustration 9-8 shows the computation of depreciation expense in the first year for Bill's Pizzas' delivery truck.

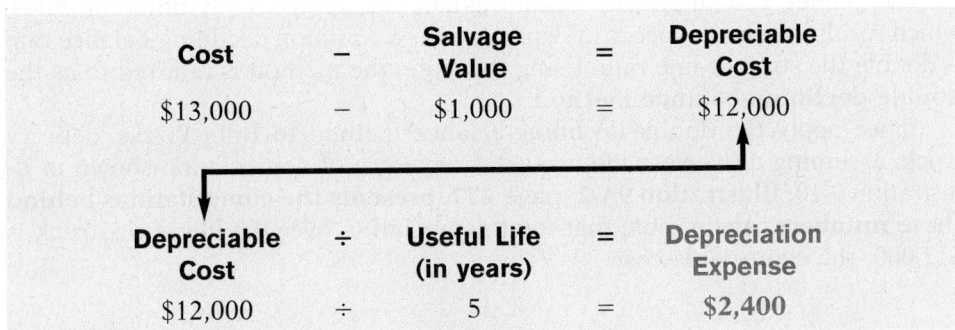

**Illustration 9-8** Formula for straight-line method

Alternatively, we can compute an annual *rate* at which the company depreciates the delivery truck. In this case, the rate is 20% (100% ÷ 5 years). When an annual rate is used under the straight-line method, the company applies the percentage rate to the depreciable cost of the asset, as shown in the **depreciation schedule** in Illustration 9-9.

**Illustration 9-9** Straight-line depreciation schedule

### BILL'S PIZZAS

| | Computation | | | Annual | End of Year | |
|---|---|---|---|---|---|---|
| Year | Depreciable Cost | × Depreciation Rate | = | Depreciation Expense | Accumulated Depreciation | Book Value |
| 2012 | $12,000 | 20% | | $ 2,400 | $ 2,400 | $10,600* |
| 2013 | 12,000 | 20 | | 2,400 | 4,800 | 8,200 |
| 2014 | 12,000 | 20 | | 2,400 | 7,200 | 5,800 |
| 2015 | 12,000 | 20 | | 2,400 | 9,600 | 3,400 |
| 2016 | 12,000 | 20 | | 2,400 | 12,000 | 1,000 |
| | | | Total | $12,000 | | |

*$13,000 − $2,400

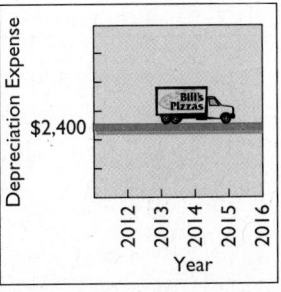

Note that the depreciation expense of $2,400 is the same each year. The book value at the end of the useful life is equal to the estimated $1,000 salvage value.

What happens when an asset is purchased **during** the year, rather than on January 1 as in our example? In that case, it is necessary to **prorate the annual depreciation** for the portion of a year used. If Bill's Pizzas had purchased the delivery truck on April 1, 2012, the company would use the truck for 9 months in 2012. The depreciation for 2012 would be $1,800 ($12,000 × 20% × $\frac{9}{12}$ of a year).

As indicated earlier, the straight-line method predominates in practice. For example, such large companies as Campbell Soup, Marriott, and General Mills use the straight-line method. It is simple to apply, and it matches expenses with revenues appropriately when the use of the asset is reasonably uniform throughout the service life. The types of assets that give equal benefits over useful life generally are those for which daily use does not affect productivity. Examples are office furniture and fixtures, buildings, warehouses, and garages for motor vehicles.

### Declining-Balance

The **declining-balance method** computes periodic depreciation using a declining book value. This method is called an **accelerated-depreciation method** because it results in higher depreciation in the early years of an asset's life than does the straight-line approach. However, because the total amount of depreciation (the depreciable cost) taken over an asset's life is the same **no matter what approach** is used, the declining-balance method produces a decreasing annual depreciation expense over the asset's useful life. In early years, declining-balance depreciation expense will exceed straight-line, but in later years, it will be less than straight-line. Managers might choose an accelerated approach if they think that an asset's utility will decline quickly.

Companies can apply the declining-balance approach at different rates, which result in varying speeds of depreciation. A common declining-balance rate is double the straight-line rate. Using that rate, the method is referred to as the **double-declining-balance method**.

If we apply the double-declining-balance method to Bill's Pizzas' delivery truck, assuming a five-year life, we get the pattern of depreciation shown in Illustration 9-10. **Illustration 9A-2, page 477, presents the computations behind these numbers.** Again, note that total depreciation over the life of the truck is $12,000, the depreciable cost.

**Illustration 9-10**
Declining-balance depreciation schedule

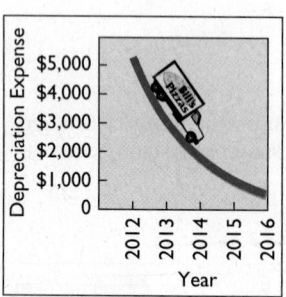

| | | Annual Depreciation Expense | End of Year | |
| | | | Accumulated Depreciation | Book Value |
| | Year | | | |
|---|---|---|---|---|
| | 2012 | $ 5,200 | $ 5,200 | $7,800 |
| | 2013 | 3,120 | 8,320 | 4,680 |
| | 2014 | 1,872 | 10,192 | 2,808 |
| | 2015 | 1,123 | 11,315 | 1,685 |
| | 2016 | 685 | 12,000 | 1,000 |
| | Total | $12,000 | | |

**BILL'S PIZZAS**

### Units-of-Activity

As indicated earlier, useful life can be expressed in ways other than a time period. Under the **units-of-activity method**, useful life is expressed in terms of the total units of production or the use expected from the asset. The units-of-activity method is ideally suited to factory machinery: Companies can measure production in terms of units of output or in terms of machine hours used in operating the machinery. It is also possible to use the method for such items as delivery equipment (miles driven) and airplanes (hours in use). The units-of-activity method is generally not suitable for such assets as buildings or furniture because activity levels are difficult to measure for these assets.

Applying the units-of-activity method to the delivery truck owned by Bill's Pizzas, we first must know some basic information. Bill's expects to be able to drive the truck a total of 100,000 miles. Illustration 9-11 shows depreciation over the five-year life based on an assumed mileage pattern. **Illustration 9A-4, pages 476–478, presents the computations used to arrive at these results.**

| | | | End of Year | |
|---|---|---|---|---|
| **BILL'S PIZZAS** | | | | |
| **Year** | **Units of Activity (miles)** | **Annual Depreciation Expense** | **Accumulated Depreciation** | **Book Value** |
| 2012 | 15,000 | $ 1,800 | $ 1,800 | $11,200 |
| 2013 | 30,000 | 3,600 | 5,400 | 7,600 |
| 2014 | 20,000 | 2,400 | 7,800 | 5,200 |
| 2015 | 25,000 | 3,000 | 10,800 | 2,200 |
| 2016 | 10,000 | 1,200 | 12,000 | 1,000 |
| Total | 100,000 | $12,000 | | |

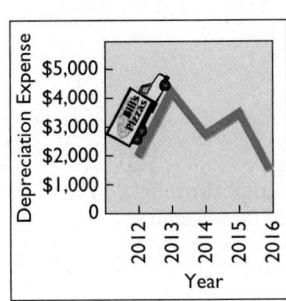

**Illustration 9-11** Units-of-activity depreciation schedule

As the name implies, under units-of-activity depreciation, the amount of depreciation is proportional to the activity that took place during that period. For example, the delivery truck was driven twice as many miles in 2013 as in 2012, and depreciation was exactly twice as much in 2013 as it was in 2012.

*before you go on...*

**Do it!** On January 1, 2012, Iron Mountain Ski Corporation purchased a new snow grooming machine for $50,000. The machine is estimated to have a 10-year life with a $2,000 salvage value. What journal entry would Iron Mountain Ski Corporation make at December 31, 2012, if it uses the straight-line method of depreciation?

**Solution**

$$\text{Depreciation expense} = \frac{\text{Cost} - \text{Salvage value}}{\text{Useful life}} = \frac{\$50,000 - \$2,000}{10} = \$4,800$$

Iron Mountain would record the first year's depreciation as follows.

| | | | |
|---|---|---|---|
| Dec. 31 | Depreciation Expense | 4,800 | |
| | Accumulated Depreciation—Equipment | | 4,800 |
| | (To record annual depreciation on snow grooming machine) | | |

Related exercise material: **BE9-3, BE9-4,** *Do it!* **9-2,** and **E9-5.**

**STRAIGHT-LINE DEPRECIATION**

**Action Plan**

• Calculate depreciable cost (Cost − Salvage value).

• Divide the depreciable cost by the asset's estimated useful life.

the navigator

### Management's Choice: Comparison of Methods

Illustration 9-12 compares annual and total depreciation expense for Bill's Pizzas under the three methods.

**Illustration 9-12**
Comparison of
depreciation methods

| Year | Straight-Line | Declining-Balance | Units-of-Activity |
|------|--------------|-------------------|-------------------|
| 2012 | $ 2,400 | $ 5,200 | $ 1,800 |
| 2013 | 2,400 | 3,120 | 3,600 |
| 2014 | 2,400 | 1,872 | 2,400 |
| 2015 | 2,400 | 1,123 | 3,000 |
| 2016 | 2,400 | 685 | 1,200 |
| | $12,000 | $12,000 | $12,000 |

Periodic depreciation varies considerably among the methods, but **total depreciation is the same for the five-year period**. Each method is acceptable in accounting because each recognizes the decline in service potential of the asset in a rational and systematic manner. Illustration 9-13 graphs the depreciation expense pattern under each method.

**Illustration 9-13** Patterns
of depreciation

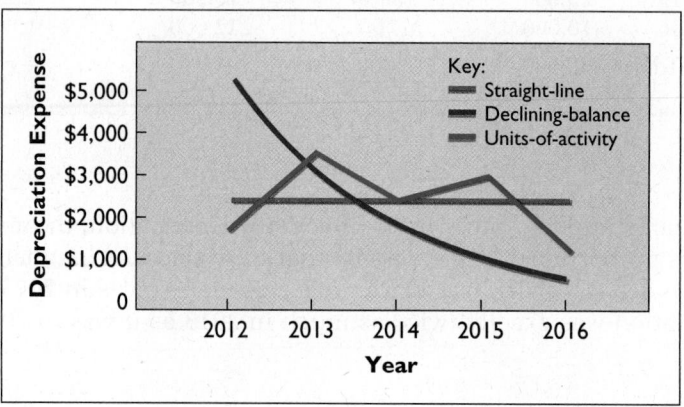

### Depreciation and Income Taxes

The Internal Revenue Service (IRS) allows corporate taxpayers to deduct depreciation expense when computing taxable income. However, the tax regulations of the IRS do not require the taxpayer to use the same depreciation method on the tax return that it uses in preparing financial statements.

Consequently, many large corporations use straight-line depreciation in their financial statements in order to maximize net income; at the same time, they use a special accelerated-depreciation method on their tax returns in order to minimize their income taxes. For tax purposes, taxpayers must use on their tax returns either the straight-line method or a special accelerated-depreciation method called the **Modified Accelerated Cost Recovery System** (MACRS).

### Depreciation Disclosure in the Notes

Companies must disclose the choice of depreciation method in their financial statements or in related notes that accompany the statements. Illustration 9-14 shows excerpts from the "Property and equipment" notes from the financial statements of Southwest Airlines.

**SOUTHWEST AIRLINES**
Notes to the Financial Statements

Illustration 9-14
Disclosure of depreciation
policies

**Property and equipment**   Depreciation is provided by the straight-line method to estimated residual values over periods ranging from 20 to 25 years for flight equipment and 5 to 30 years for ground property and equipment once the asset is placed in service. Amortization of property under capital leases is on a straight-line basis over the lease term and is included in depreciation expense.

From this note, we learn that Southwest Airlines uses the straight-line method to depreciate its planes over periods of 20 to 25 years.

## REVISING PERIODIC DEPRECIATION

Management should periodically review annual depreciation expense. If wear and tear or obsolescence indicates that annual depreciation is either inadequate or excessive, the company should change the depreciation expense amount.

When a change in an estimate is required, the company makes the change in **current and future years but not to prior periods**. Thus, when making the change, the company (1) does not correct previously recorded depreciation expense, but (2) revises depreciation expense for current and future years. The rationale for this treatment is that continual restatement of prior periods would adversely affect users' confidence in financial statements.

To determine the new annual depreciation expense, the company first computes the asset's depreciable cost at the time of the revision. It then allocates the revised depreciable cost to the remaining useful life.

To illustrate, assume that Bill's Pizzas decides at the end of 2014 (prior to the year-end adjusting entries) to extend the estimated useful life of the truck one year (a total life of six years) and increase its salvage value to $2,200. The company has used the straight-line method to depreciate the asset to date. Depreciation per year was $2,400 (($13,000 − $1,000) ÷ 5). Accumulated depreciation after three years (2011–2013) is $7,200 ($2,400 × 3), and book value is $5,800 ($13,000 − $7,200). The new annual depreciation is $1,200, computed on December 31, 2014, as follows.

study objective **4**

Describe the procedure
for revising periodic
depreciation.

**Helpful Hint** Use a step-by-step
approach: (1) determine new
depreciable cost; (2) divide by
remaining useful life.

**Illustration 9-15**   Revised
depreciation computation

| | | |
|---|---|---|
| Book value, 1/1/14 | $ 5,800 | |
| Less: New salvage value | 2,200 | |
| Depreciable cost | $ 3,600 | |
| Remaining useful life | 3 years | (2014–2016) |
| **Revised annual depreciation ($3,600 ÷ 3)** | **$1,200** | |

Bill's Pizzas does not make a special entry for the change in estimate. On December 31, 2014, during the preparation of adjusting entries, it records depreciation expense of $1,200.

Companies must disclose in the financial statements significant changes in estimates. Although a company may have a legitimate reason for changing an estimated life, financial statement users should be aware that some companies might change an estimate simply to achieve financial statement goals. For example, extending an asset's estimated life reduces depreciation expense and increases current period income.

In a recent year, AirTran Airways increased the estimated useful lives of some of its planes from 25 to 30 years and increased the estimated lives of related aircraft parts from 5 years to 30 years. It disclosed that the change in estimate decreased its net loss for the year by approximately $0.6 million, or about $0.01 per share. Whether these changes were appropriate depends on how reasonable it is to assume that planes will continue to be used for a long time. Our Feature Story suggests that although in the past many planes lasted a long time, it is also clear that because of high fuel costs, airlines are now scrapping many of their old, inefficient planes.

## before you go on...

**REVISED DEPRECIATION**

**Action Plan**

- Calculate remaining depreciable cost.
- Divide remaining depreciable cost by new remaining life.

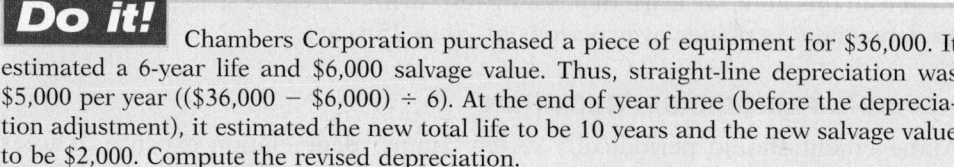 Chambers Corporation purchased a piece of equipment for $36,000. It estimated a 6-year life and $6,000 salvage value. Thus, straight-line depreciation was $5,000 per year (($36,000 − $6,000) ÷ 6). At the end of year three (before the depreciation adjustment), it estimated the new total life to be 10 years and the new salvage value to be $2,000. Compute the revised depreciation.

**Solution**

Original depreciation expense = ($36,000 − $6,000 ÷ 6) = $5,000
Accumulated depreciation after 2 years = 2 × $5,000 = $10,000
Book value = $36,000 − $10,000 = $26,000

| | |
|---|---:|
| Book value after 2 years of depreciation | $26,000 |
| Less: New salvage value | 2,000 |
| Depreciable cost | 24,000 |
| Remaining useful life | 8 years |
| Revised annual depreciation ($24,000 ÷ 8) | $3,000 |

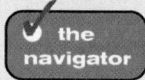

Related exercise material: **BE9-5, Do it! 9-3,** and **E9-6.**

## EXPENDITURES DURING USEFUL LIFE

During the useful life of a plant asset, a company may incur costs for ordinary repairs, additions, and improvements. **Ordinary repairs** are expenditures to maintain the operating efficiency and expected productive life of the unit. They usually are fairly small amounts that occur frequently throughout the service life. Examples are motor tune-ups and oil changes, the painting of buildings, and the replacing of worn-out gears on factory machinery. Ordinary repairs are debited to Maintenance and Repairs Expense as incurred.

In contrast, **additions and improvements** are costs incurred to **increase** the operating efficiency, productive capacity, or expected useful life of the plant asset. These expenditures are usually material in amount and occur infrequently during the period of ownership. Expenditures for additions and improvements increase the company's investment in productive facilities and are generally debited to the plant asset affected. Thus, they are **capital expenditures**. The accounting for capital expenditures varies depending on the nature of the expenditure.

Northwest Airlines at one time spent $120 million to spruce up 40 jets. The improvements were designed to extend the lives of the planes, meet stricter government noise limits, and save money. The capital expenditure was expected to extend the life of the jets by 10 to 15 years and save about $560 million compared to the cost of buying new planes. The jets were, on average, 24 years old.

## ANATOMY OF A FRAUD

Bernie Ebbers was the founder and CEO of the phone company WorldCom. The company engaged in a series of increasingly large, debt-financed acquisitions of other companies. These acquisitions made the company grow quickly, which made the stock price increase dramatically. However, because the acquired companies all had different accounting systems, WorldCom's financial records were a mess. When WorldCom's performance started to flatten out, Bernie coerced WorldCom's accountants to engage in a number of fraudulent activities to make net income look better than it really was and thus prop up the stock price. One of these frauds involved treating $7 billion of line costs as capital expenditures. The line costs, which were rental fees paid to other phone companies to use their phone lines, had always been properly expensed in previous years. Capitalization delayed expense recognition to future periods and thus boosted current-period profits.

**Total take: $7 billion**

### THE MISSING CONTROLS

*Documentation procedures.* The company's accounting system was a disorganized collection of non-integrated systems, which resulted from a series of corporate acquisitions. Top management took advantage of this disorganization to conceal its fraudulent activities.

*Independent internal verification.* A fraud of this size should have been detected by a routine comparison of the actual physical assets with the list of physical assets shown in the accounting records.

### IMPAIRMENTS

As noted earlier, the book value of plant assets is rarely the same as the fair value. In instances where the value of a plant asset declines substantially, its market value might fall materially below book value. This may happen because a machine has become obsolete, or the market for the product made by the machine has dried up or has become very competitive. A **permanent decline** in the market value of an asset is referred to as an impairment. So as not to overstate the asset on the books, the company writes the asset down to its new fair value during the year in which the decline in value occurs. For example, at one time AirTran announced a $28 million impairment loss on its DC9 jets and a $10.8 million impairment loss on its B737 jets. AirTran used appraisals and considered recent transactions and market trends involving similar aircraft in determining the fair values.

In the past, some companies **improperly** delayed recording losses on impairments until a year when it was "convenient" to do so—when the impact on the company's reported results was minimized. For example, in a year when a company has record profits, it can afford to write down some of its bad assets without hurting its reported results too much. As discussed in Chapter 4, the practice of timing the recognition of gains and losses to achieve certain income results is known as **earnings management**. Earnings management reduces earnings quality. To minimize earnings management, accounting standards now require immediate recognition of impaired assets.

Write-downs can create problems for users of financial statements. Critics of write-downs note that after a company writes down assets, its depreciation expense will be lower in all subsequent periods. Some companies improperly inflate asset write-downs in bad years, when they are going to report poor results anyway. (This practice is referred to as "taking a big bath.") Then in subsequent years, when the company recovers, its results will look even better because of lower depreciation expense.

## PLANT ASSET DISPOSALS

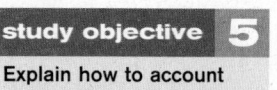

**study objective 5**

Explain how to account for the disposal of plant assets.

Companies dispose of plant assets that are no longer useful to them. Illustration 9-16 shows the three ways in which companies make plant asset disposals.

Whatever the disposal method, the company must determine the book value of the plant asset at the time of disposal in order to determine the gain or loss. Recall that the book value is the difference between the cost of the plant asset and the accumulated depreciation to date. If the disposal occurs at any time during the year, the company must record depreciation for the fraction of the year to the date of disposal. The company then eliminates the book value by reducing (debiting) Accumulated Depreciation for the total depreciation associated with that asset to the date of disposal and reducing (crediting) the asset account for the cost of the asset.

**Illustration 9-16**
Methods of plant asset disposal

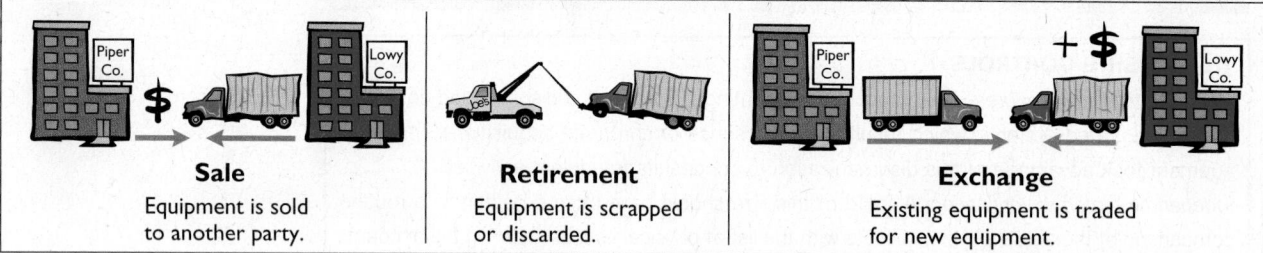

**Sale**
Equipment is sold to another party.

**Retirement**
Equipment is scrapped or discarded.

**Exchange**
Existing equipment is traded for new equipment.

### Sale of Plant Assets

In a disposal by sale, the company compares the book value of the asset with the proceeds received from the sale. If the proceeds from the sale **exceed** the book value of the plant asset, a **gain on disposal** occurs. If the proceeds from the sale **are less than** the book value of the plant asset sold, a **loss on disposal** occurs.

Only by coincidence will the book value and the fair value of the asset be the same at the time the asset is sold. Gains and losses on sales of plant assets are therefore quite common. As an example, Delta Air Lines reported a $94,343,000 gain on the sale of five Boeing B-727-200 aircraft and five Lockheed L-1011-1 aircraft.

**GAIN ON SALE.** To illustrate a gain on sale of plant assets, assume that on July 1, 2012, Wright Company sells office furniture for $16,000 cash. The office furniture originally cost $60,000 and as of January 1, 2012, had accumulated depreciation of $41,000. Depreciation for the first six months of 2012 is $8,000. Wright records depreciation expense and updates accumulated depreciation to July 1 as follows.

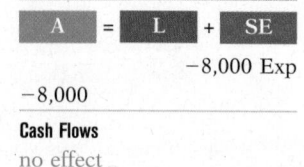

A = L + SE
                    −8,000 Exp
−8,000

**Cash Flows**
no effect

| | | | | |
|---|---|---|---|---|
| July | 1 | Depreciation Expense | 8,000 | |
| | | Accumulated Depreciation—Equipment | | 8,000 |
| | | (To record depreciation expense for the first 6 months of 2012) | | |

After the accumulated depreciation balance is updated, the company computes the gain or loss as the difference between the proceeds from sale and the book value at the date of disposal. Wright Company has a gain on disposal of $5,000, as computed in Illustration 9-17.

| Cost of office furniture | $60,000 |
| Less: Accumulated depreciation ($41,000 + $8,000) | 49,000 |
| Book value at date of disposal | 11,000 |
| Proceeds from sale | 16,000 |
| **Gain on disposal of plant asset** | **$ 5,000** |

**Illustration 9-17**
Computation of gain on disposal

Wright records the sale and the gain on sale of the plant asset as follows.

| July 1 | Cash | 16,000 | |
| | Accumulated Depreciation—Equipment | 49,000 | |
| |    Equipment | | 60,000 |
| |    Gain on Disposal of Plant Assets | | 5,000 |
| |    (To record sale of office furniture | | |
| |    at a gain) | | |

A = L + SE
+16,000
+49,000
−60,000
         +5,000 Rev

Cash Flows
+16,000

Companies report a gain on disposal of plant assets in the "Other revenues and gains" section of the income statement.

**LOSS ON SALE.** Assume that instead of selling the office furniture for $16,000, Wright sells it for $9,000. In this case, Wright experiences a loss of $2,000, as computed in Illustration 9-18.

| Cost of office furniture | $60,000 |
| Less: Accumulated depreciation | 49,000 |
| Book value at date of disposal | 11,000 |
| Proceeds from sale | 9,000 |
| **Loss on disposal of plant asset** | **$ 2,000** |

**Illustration 9-18**
Computation of loss on disposal

Wright records the sale and the loss on sale of the plant asset as follows.

| July 1 | Cash | 9,000 | |
| | Accumulated Depreciation—Equipment | 49,000 | |
| | Loss on Disposal of Plant Assets | 2,000 | |
| |    Equipment | | 60,000 |
| |    (To record sale of office furniture at a | | |
| |    loss) | | |

A = L + SE
+9,000
+49,000
         −2,000 Exp
−60,000

Cash Flows
+9,000

Companies report a loss on disposal of the plant asset in the "Other expenses and losses" section of the income statement.

## Retirement of Plant Assets

Companies simply retire, rather than sell, some assets at the end of their useful life. For example, some productive assets used in manufacturing may have very specific uses, and they consequently have no ready market when the company no longer needs them. In such a case, the asset is simply retired.

Companies record retirement of an asset as a special case of a disposal where no cash is received. They decrease (debit) Accumulated Depreciation for the full amount of depreciation taken over the life of the asset and decrease (credit) the asset account for the original cost of the asset. The loss (a gain is not possible on a retirement) is equal to the asset's book value on the date of retirement.[1]

## before you go on...

**PLANT ASSET DISPOSALS**

### Do it!

Overland Trucking has an old truck that cost $30,000 and has accumulated depreciation of $16,000. Assume two different situations:

1. The company sells the old truck for $17,000 cash.
2. The truck is worthless, so the company simply retires it.

What entry should Overland use to record each scenario?

**Action Plan**

- Compare the asset's book value and its fair value to determine whether a gain or loss has occurred.
- Make sure that both the Equipment account and Accumulated Depreciation–Equipment are reduced upon disposal.

### Solution

1. Sale of truck for cash:

| | | |
|---|---|---|
| Cash | 17,000 | |
| Accumulated Depreciation—Equipment | 16,000 | |
|     Equipment | | 30,000 |
|     Gain on Disposal of Plant Assets | | |
|       [$17,000 − ($30,000 − $16,000)] | | 3,000 |
|       (To record sale of truck at a gain) | | |

2. Retirement of truck:

| | | |
|---|---|---|
| Accumulated Depreciation—Equipment | 16,000 | |
| Loss on Disposal of Plant Assets | 14,000 | |
|     Equipment | | 30,000 |
|     (To record retirement of truck at a loss) | | |

Related exercise material: **BE9-7, BE9-8, Do it! 9-4, E9-7,** and **E9-8.**

# Analyzing Plant Assets

**study objective 6**

Describe methods for evaluating the use of plant assets.

The presentation of financial statement information about plant assets enables decision makers to analyze the company's use of its plant assets. We will use two measures to analyze plant assets: return on assets ratio, and asset turnover ratio.

### RETURN ON ASSETS RATIO

An overall measure of profitability is the **return on assets ratio**. This ratio is computed by dividing net income by average assets. (Average assets are commonly calculated by adding the beginning and ending values of assets and dividing by 2.) The return on assets ratio indicates the amount of net income generated by each dollar of assets. Thus, the higher the return on assets, the more profitable the company.

Information is provided below related to AirTran.

| | AirTran (in millions) |
|---|---|
| Net income, 2009 | $ 135 |
| Total assets, 12/31/09 | 2,284 |
| Total assets, 12/31/08 | 2,085 |
| Net sales, 2009 | 2,341 |

---

[1]More advanced courses discuss the accounting for exchanges, the third method of plant asset disposal.

Illustration 9-19 presents the 2009 and 2008 return on assets of AirTran, Southwest Airlines, and industry averages.

**Illustration 9-19**   Return on assets ratio

| Return on Assets Ratio = Net Income / Average Total Assets | | | |
| --- | --- | --- | --- |
| **AirTran** ($ in millions) | | **Southwest Airlines** | **Industry Average** |
| 2009 | 2008 | 2009 | 2009 |
| $135 / ($2,085 + $2,284)/2 = 6.2% | −12.9% | 0.7% | 3.8% |

AirTran's return on assets was better than that of Southwest's and the airline industry. The airline industry has experienced financial difficulties in recent years as it attempted to cover high labor, fuel, and security costs while offering fares low enough to attract customers. Such difficulties are reflected in the very low industry average for return on assets and in the volatility of this ratio between years for AirTran.

## Accounting Across the Organization

### Marketing ROI as Profit Indicator

Marketing executives use the basic finance concept underlying return on assets to determine "marketing return on investment (ROI)." They calculate *marketing ROI* as the profit generated by a marketing initiative divided by the investment in that initiative.

It can be tricky to determine what to include in the "investment" amount and how to attribute profit to a particular marketing initiative. However, many firms feel that measuring marketing ROI is worth the effort because it allows managers to evaluate the relative effectiveness of various programs. In addition, it helps quantify the benefits that marketing provides to the organization. In periods of tight budgets, the marketing ROI number can provide particularly valuable evidence to help a marketing manager avoid budget cuts.

*Source:* James O. Mitchel, "Marketing ROI," *LIMRA's MarketFacts Quarterly* (Summer 2004), p. 15.

? How does measuring marketing ROI support the overall efforts of the organization? (See page 499.)

## DECISION TOOLKIT

| DECISION CHECKPOINTS | INFO NEEDED FOR DECISION | TOOL TO USE FOR DECISION | HOW TO EVALUATE RESULTS |
| --- | --- | --- | --- |
| Is the company using its assets effectively? | Net income and average assets | Return on assets ratio = Net income / Average total assets | Higher value suggests favorable efficiency (use of assets). |

## ASSET TURNOVER RATIO

The **asset turnover ratio** indicates how efficiently a company uses its assets to generate sales—that is, how many dollars of sales a company generates for each dollar invested in assets. It is calculated by dividing net sales by average total assets. When we compare two companies in the same industry, the one with the higher asset turnover ratio is operating more *efficiently:* It is generating more sales per dollar invested in assets. Illustration 9-20 presents the asset turnover ratios for AirTran and Southwest Airlines.

**Illustration 9-20** Asset turnover ratios for AirTran and Southwest Airlines

| Asset Turnover Ratio = $\dfrac{\text{Net Sales}}{\text{Average Total Assets}}$ | | | |
|---|---|---|---|
| **AirTran** ($ in millions) | | **Southwest Airlines** | **Industry Average** |
| 2009 | 2008 | 2009 | 2009 |
| $\dfrac{\$2,341}{(\$2,085 + \$2,284)/2} = 1.07$ times | 1.23 times | 0.73 times | 0.60 times |

These asset turnover ratios tell us that for each dollar of assets, AirTran generates sales of $1.07 and Southwest $0.73. AirTran is more successful in generating sales per dollar invested in assets. The average asset turnover ratio for the airline industry is 0.60 times, more in line with Southwest's asset turnover.

Asset turnover ratios vary considerably across industries. The average asset turnover for electric utility companies is 0.34; the grocery industry has an average asset turnover of 2.89. Asset turnover ratios, therefore, are only comparable within—not between—industries.

## PROFIT MARGIN RATIO REVISITED

In Chapter 5, you learned about the profit margin ratio. That ratio is calculated by dividing net income by net sales. It tells how effective a company is in turning its sales into income—that is, how much income each dollar of sales provides. Illustration 9-21 shows that the return on assets ratio can be computed as the product of the profit margin ratio and the asset turnover ratio.

**Illustration 9-21** Composition of return on assets ratio

| Profit Margin | × | Asset Turnover | = | Return on Assets |
|---|---|---|---|---|
| $\dfrac{\text{Net Income}}{\text{Net Sales}}$ | × | $\dfrac{\text{Net Sales}}{\text{Average Total Assets}}$ | = | $\dfrac{\text{Net Income}}{\text{Average Total Assets}}$ |

This relationship has very important strategic implications for management. From Illustration 9-21, we can see that if a company wants to increase its return on assets, it can do so in two ways: (1) by increasing the margin it generates from each dollar of goods that it sells (the profit margin ratio), or (2) by increasing the volume of goods that it sells (the asset turnover). For example, most grocery stores have very low profit margins, often in the range of 1 or 2 cents for every dollar of goods sold. Grocery stores, therefore, focus on asset turnover: They rely on high turnover to increase their return on assets. Alternatively, a store selling luxury goods, such as expensive jewelry, doesn't generally have a high turnover. Consequently, a seller of luxury goods focuses on having a high profit margin. Recently, Apple decided to offer a less expensive version of its popular iPod. This new product would provide a lower margin, but higher volume, than Apple's more expensive version.

Let's evaluate the return on assets ratio of AirTran for 2009 by evaluating its components—the profit margin ratio and the asset turnover ratio. See Illustration 9-22.

| | Profit Margin | × | Asset Turnover | = | Return on Assets |
|---|---|---|---|---|---|
| **AirTran** | 5.8% | × | 1.07 | = | 6.2% |
| **Southwest Airlines** | 0.95% | × | 0.73 | = | 0.7% |

**Illustration 9-22**
Components of rate of return for AirTran and Southwest Airlines

AirTran's return on asset ratio of 6.2% versus Southwest's 0.7% means that Air-Tran generates approximately 6 cents per each dollar invested in assets, while Southwest generates less than 1 cent. Illustration 9-22 reveals that this superior performance occurs for two reasons. First, AirTran's profit margin ratio of 5.8% versus Southwest's of 0.95% means that for every dollar of sales, AirTran generates approximately 6 cents of net income, while Southwest generates approximately 1 cent. In addition, AirTran's asset turnover ratio of 1.07 means that it generates $1.07 of sales per each dollar invested in assets, while Southwest only generates 73 cents. Therefore, in 2009 AirTran was more effective at generating sales from its assets, and it was better at deriving profit from those sales.

## DECISION TOOLKIT

| DECISION CHECKPOINTS | INFO NEEDED FOR DECISION | TOOL TO USE FOR DECISION | HOW TO EVALUATE RESULTS |
|---|---|---|---|
| How effective is the company at generating sales from its assets? | Net sales and average total assets | Asset turnover ratio $= \dfrac{\text{Net sales}}{\text{Average total assets}}$ | Indicates the sales dollars generated per dollar of assets. A high value suggests the company is effective in using its resources to generate sales. |

## section two

# Intangible Assets

**Intangible assets** are rights, privileges, and competitive advantages that result from ownership of long-lived assets that do not possess physical substance. Many companies' most valuable assets are intangible. Some widely known intangibles are Microsoft's patents, McDonalds's franchises, the trade name iPod, and Nike's trademark "swoosh."

Analysts estimated that in the early 1980s, the fair value of intangible assets to total assets was close to 40%. By 2000, the percentage was over 80%— quite a difference. What has happened is that research and development (e.g., hi-tech and bio-tech) has grown substantially. At the same time, many companies (e.g., Nike and Gatorade) have developed brand power which enables them to maintain their market position.

As you will learn in this section, financial statements do report numerous intangibles. Yet, many other financially significant intangibles are not reported. To give an example, according to its financial statements in a recent year, Google had total stockholders' equity of $22.7 billion. But its *market* value— the total market price of all its shares on that same date—was roughly $178.5 billion. Thus, its actual market value was about $155.8 billion greater than the amount reported for stockholders' equity on the balance sheet. It is not uncommon for a company's reported book value to differ from its market value, because balance sheets are reported at historical cost. But such an extreme difference seriously diminishes the usefulness of the balance sheet to decision makers. In the case of Google, the difference is due to unrecorded intangibles. For many high-tech or so-called intellectual-property companies, most of their value is from intangibles, many of which are not reported under current accounting rules.

Intangibles may be evidenced by contracts, licenses, and other documents. Intangibles may arise from the following sources:

1. Government grants, such as patents, copyrights, licenses, trademarks, and trade names.

2. Acquisition of another business in which the purchase price includes a payment for goodwill.

3. Private monopolistic arrangements arising from contractual agreements, such as franchises and leases.

## Accounting for Intangible Assets

**study objective 7**

Identify the basic issues related to reporting intangible assets.

Companies record intangible assets at cost. Intangibles are categorized as having either a limited life or an indefinite life. If an intangible has a **limited life**, the company allocates its cost over the asset's useful life using a process similar to depreciation. The process of allocating to expense the cost of intangibles is referred to as **amortization**. The cost of intangible assets with **indefinite lives should not be amortized**.

To record amortization of an intangible asset, a company increases (debits) Amortization Expense, and decreases (credits) the specific intangible asset. (Unlike depreciation, no contra account, such as Accumulated Amortization, is usually used.)

Intangible assets are typically amortized on a straight-line basis. For example, the legal life of a patent is 20 years. Companies **amortize the cost of a patent over its 20-year life or its useful life, whichever is shorter.** To illustrate the computation of patent amortization, assume that National Labs purchases a patent at a cost of $60,000 on June 30. If National estimates the useful life of the patent to be eight years, the annual amortization expense is $7,500 ($60,000 ÷ 8) per year. National records $3,750 ($7,500 × $\frac{6}{12}$) of amortization for the six-month period ended December 31 as follows.

| A | = | L | + | SE |
|---|---|---|---|---|
| | | | | −3,750 Exp |
| −3,750 | | | | |

**Cash Flows**
no effect

| Dec. 31 | Amortization Expense | 3,750 | |
| | Patent | | 3,750 |
| | (To record patent amortization) | | |

When a company has significant intangibles, analysts should evaluate the reasonableness of the useful life estimates that the company discloses in the notes to its financial statements. In determining useful life, the company should consider obsolescence, inadequacy, and other factors. These may cause a patent or other intangible to become economically ineffective before the end of its legal life.

For example, suppose Intel obtained a patent on a new computer chip it had developed. The legal life of the patent is 20 years. From experience, however, we know that the useful life of a computer chip patent is rarely more than five years. Because new superior chips are developed so rapidly, existing chips become obsolete. Consequently, we would question the amortization expense of Intel if it amortized its patent on a computer chip for a life significantly longer than a five-year period. Amortizing an intangible over a period that is too long will understate amortization expense, overstate Intel's net income, and overstate its assets.

## DECISION TOOLKIT

| DECISION CHECKPOINTS | INFO NEEDED FOR DECISION | TOOL TO USE FOR DECISION | HOW TO EVALUATE RESULTS |
|---|---|---|---|
| Is the company's amortization of intangibles reasonable? | Estimated useful life of intangibles from notes to financial statements of this company and its competitors | If the company's estimated useful life significantly exceeds that of competitors or does not seem reasonable in light of the circumstances, the reason for the difference should be investigated. | Too high an estimated useful life will result in understating amortization expense and overstating net income. |

## Types of Intangible Assets

### PATENTS

A **patent** is an exclusive right issued by the U.S. Patent Office that enables the recipient to manufacture, sell, or otherwise control an invention for a period of 20 years from the date of the grant. **The initial cost of a patent is the cash or cash equivalent price paid to acquire the patent.**

The saying "A patent is only as good as the money you're prepared to spend defending it" is very true. Most patents are subject to some type of litigation by competitors. A well-known example is the patent infringement suit brought by Amazon.com against Barnes & Noble.com regarding its online shopping software. If the owner incurs legal costs in successfully defending the patent in an infringement suit, such costs are considered necessary to establish the validity of the patent. Thus, **the owner adds those costs to the Patent account and amortizes them over the remaining life of the patent**.

### RESEARCH AND DEVELOPMENT COSTS

**Research and development costs** are expenditures that may lead to patents, copyrights, new processes, and new products. Many companies spend considerable sums of money on research and development (R&D) in an ongoing effort to develop new products or processes. For example, in a recent year IBM spent over $5.1 billion on research and development. There are uncertainties in identifying the extent and timing of the future benefits of these expenditures. As a result, companies usually record research and development costs **as an expense when incurred**, whether the R&D is successful or not.

**Helpful Hint** Research and development costs are not intangible costs, but because these expenditures may lead to patents and copyrights, we discuss them in this section.

**International Note** IFRS allows capitalization of some development costs. This may contribute to differences in R&D expenditures across nations.

To illustrate, assume that Laser Scanner Company spent $3 million on research and development that resulted in two highly successful patents. It spent $20,000 on legal fees for the patents. It can include the legal fees in the cost of the patents but cannot include the R&D costs in the cost of the patents. Instead, Laser Scanner records the R&D costs as an expense when incurred.

Many disagree with this accounting approach. They argue that to expense these costs leads to understated assets and net income. Others argue that capitalizing these costs would lead to highly speculative assets on the balance sheet. Who is right is difficult to determine.

## COPYRIGHTS

The federal government grants **copyrights**, which give the owner the exclusive right to reproduce and sell an artistic or published work. Copyrights last for the life of the creator plus 70 years. The cost of the copyright consists of the **cost of acquiring and defending it**. The cost may be only the small fee paid to the U.S. Copyright Office, or it may amount to a great deal more if a copyright is acquired from another party. The useful life of a copyright generally is significantly shorter than its legal life.

## TRADEMARKS AND TRADE NAMES

A **trademark** or **trade name** is a word, phrase, jingle, or symbol that distinguishes or identifies a particular enterprise or product. Trade names like Wheaties, Monopoly, Sunkist, Kleenex, Coca-Cola, Big Mac, and Jeep create immediate product identification and generally enhance the sale of the product. The creator or original user may obtain the exclusive legal right to the trademark or trade name by registering it with the U.S. Patent Office. Such registration provides 20 years' protection and may be renewed indefinitely as long as the trademark or trade name is in use.

If a company purchases the trademark or trade name, the cost is the purchase price. If the company develops the trademark or trade name itself, the cost includes attorney's fees, registration fees, design costs, successful legal defense costs, and other expenditures directly related to securing it. Because trademarks and trade names have indefinite lives, they are not amortized.

## FRANCHISES AND LICENSES

When you drive down the street in your RAV4 purchased from a Toyota dealer, fill up your tank at the corner Shell station, eat lunch at Subway, or make plans to vacation at a Marriott resort, you are dealing with franchises. A **franchise** is a contractual arrangement under which the franchisor grants the franchisee the right to sell certain products, to provide specific services, or to use certain trademarks or trade names, usually within a designated geographic area.

Another type of franchise, granted by a governmental body, permits the business to use public property in performing its services. Examples are the use of city streets for a bus line or taxi service; the use of public land for telephone, electric, and cable television lines; and the use of airwaves for radio or TV broadcasting. Such operating rights are referred to as **licenses**.

Franchises and licenses may be granted for a definite period of time, an indefinite period, or perpetual. **When a company can identify costs with the acquisition of the franchise or license, it should recognize an intangible asset.** Companies record as **operating expenses** annual payments made under a franchise agreement in the period in which they are incurred. In the case of a limited life, a company amortizes the cost of a franchise (or license) as operating expense over the useful life. If the life is indefinite or perpetual, the cost is not amortized.

## GOODWILL

Usually, the largest intangible asset that appears on a company's balance sheet is goodwill. **Goodwill** represents the value of all favorable attributes that relate to a company that are not attributable to any other specific asset. These include exceptional management, desirable location, good customer relations, skilled employees, high-quality products, fair pricing policies, and harmonious relations with labor unions. Goodwill is unique because unlike other assets such as investments, plant assets, and even other intangibles, which can be sold *individually* in the marketplace, goodwill can be identified only with the business *as a whole.*

If goodwill can be identified only with the business as a whole, how can it be determined? Certainly, many business enterprises have many of the factors cited above (exceptional management, desirable location, and so on). However, to determine the amount of goodwill in these situations would be difficult and very subjective. In other words, to recognize goodwill without an exchange transaction that puts a value on the goodwill would lead to subjective valuations that do not contribute to the reliability of financial statements. **Therefore, companies record goodwill only when there is an exchange transaction that involves the purchase of an entire business. When an entire business is purchased, goodwill is the excess of cost over the fair value of the net assets (assets less liabilities) acquired.**

In recording the purchase of a business, a company debits the identifiable acquired assets and credits liabilities at their fair values, credits cash for the purchase price, and records the difference as the cost of goodwill. Goodwill is not amortized because it is considered to have an indefinite life. However, it must be written down if a company determines the value of goodwill has been permanently impaired.

## International Insight

### Should Companies Write Up Goodwill?

Softbank Corp. is Japan's biggest Internet company. At one time, it boosted the profit margin of its mobile-phone unit from 3.2% to 11.2% through what appeared to some as accounting tricks. What did it do? It wrote down the value of its mobile-phone-unit assets by half. This would normally result in a huge loss. But rather than take a loss, the company wrote up goodwill by the same amount. How did this move increase earnings? The assets were being depreciated over 10 years, but the company amortizes goodwill over 20 years. (Amortization of goodwill was allowed under the accounting standards it followed at that time.) While the new treatment did not break any rules, the company was criticized by investors for not providing sufficient justification or a detailed explanation for the sudden shift in policy.

*Source:* Andrew Morse and Yukari Iwatani Kane, "Softbank's Accounting Shift Raises Eyebrows," *Wall Street Journal* (August 28, 2007), p. C1.

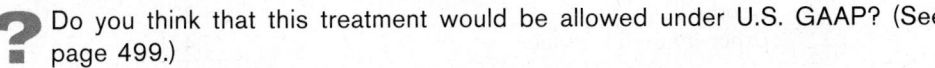

**?** Do you think that this treatment would be allowed under U.S. GAAP? (See page 499.)

## before you go on...

**CLASSIFICATION CONCEPTS**

### Do it!

Match the statement with the term most directly associated with it.

Copyright                      Amortization
Intangible assets          Franchise
Research and development costs

1. _____ The allocation to expense of the cost of an intangible asset over the asset's useful life.

2. _____ Rights, privileges, and competitive advantages that result from the ownership of long-lived assets that do not possess physical substance.

3. _____ An exclusive right granted by the federal government to reproduce and sell an artistic or published work.

4. _____ A right to sell certain products or services or to use certain trademarks or trade names within a designated geographic area.

5. _____ Costs incurred by a company that often lead to patents or new products. These costs must be expensed as incurred.

### Action Plan

- Know that the accounting for intangibles often depends on whether the item has a finite or indefinite life.
- Recognize the many similarities and differences between the accounting for plant assets and intangible assets.

  ✔ the navigator

### Solution

| | |
|---|---|
| 1. Amortization | 4. Franchise |
| 2. Intangible assets | 5. Research and development costs |
| 3. Copyright | |

Related exercise material: **BE9-10**, **Do it!** **9-5**, **E9-13**, **E9-14**, and **E9-15**.

# Financial Statement Presentation of Long-Lived Assets

**study objective 8**

Indicate how long-lived assets are reported in the financial statements.

Usually, companies show plant assets in the financial statements under "Property, plant, and equipment," and they show intangibles separately under "Intangible assets." Illustration 9-23 shows a typical balance sheet presentation of long-lived assets, adapted from The Coca-Cola Company's 2009 balance sheet.

**Illustration 9-23**
Presentation of property, plant, and equipment and intangible assets

*The Coca-Cola Company*

**THE COCA-COLA COMPANY**
Balance Sheet (partial)
(in millions)

| | |
|---|---:|
| **Property, plant, and equipment** | |
| Land | $ 699 |
| Buildings and improvements | 3,816 |
| Machinery and equipment | 10,355 |
| Containers and other | 1,597 |
| | 16,467 |
| Less: Accumulated depreciation | 6,906 |
| | 9,561 |
| | |
| **Intangible assets** | |
| Trademarks with indefinite lives | 6,183 |
| Goodwill | 4,224 |
| Other intangible assets | 2,421 |
| | $12,828 |

Intangibles do not usually use a contra asset account like the contra asset account Accumulated Depreciation used for plant assets. Instead, companies record amortization of intangibles as a direct decrease (credit) to the asset account.

Either within the balance sheet or in the notes, companies should disclose the balances of the major classes of assets, such as land, buildings, and equipment, and of accumulated depreciation by major classes or in total. In addition, they should describe the depreciation and amortization methods used and disclose the amount of depreciation and amortization expense for the period.

**KEEPING AN EYE ON CASH**

Depreciation and amortization expense are among the biggest causes of differences between accrual-accounting net income and net cash provided by operating activities. Depreciation and amortization reduce net income, but they do not use up any cash. Therefore, to determine net cash provided by operating activities, companies add depreciation and amortization back to net income. For example, if a company reported net income of $175,000 during the year and had depreciation expense of $40,000, net cash provided by operating activities would be $215,000 (assuming no other accrual-accounting differences). The operating activities section of Coca-Cola's statement of cash flows reports the following adjustment for depreciation and amortization.

**THE COCA-COLA COMPANY**
Statement of Cash Flows (partial)
(in millions)

| Cash flow from operating activities | |
|---|---|
| Net income | $6,906 |
| Plus: Depreciation and amortization | 1,236 |

The adjustment for depreciation and amortization was more than twice as big as any other adjustment required to convert net income to net cash provided by operating activities.

It is also interesting to examine the statement of cash flows to determine the amount of property, plant, and equipment a company purchased and the cash it received from property, plant, and equipment sold in a given year. For example, the investing activities section of Coca-Cola reports the following.

**THE COCA-COLA COMPANY**
Statement of Cash Flows (partial)
(in millions)

| Cash flow from investing activities | |
|---|---|
| Acquisitions and investments | $(2,452) |
| Purchases of property, plant, and equipment | (1,993) |
| Proceeds from disposals of property, plant, and equipment | 104 |
| Other | 192 |

As indicated, Coca-Cola made significant purchases and sales of property, plant, and equipment. The level of purchases suggests that Coca-Cola believes that it can earn a reasonable rate of return on these assets.

# USING THE DECISION TOOLKIT

JetBlue Airways Corporation is a low-cost airline operating primarily out of New York. It operates hundreds of flights to 51 destinations daily. Although it has operated for only eight years, it is now the tenth largest U.S. airline based on total passenger miles. It currently operates 104 planes.

## Instructions

Review the excerpts from the company's 2009 annual report that follow and then answer the following questions.

1. What method does the company use to depreciate its aircraft? Over what period is the company depreciating these aircraft?

2. What type of intangible assets does the company have, and how are they being accounted for?

3. Compute the company's return on assets ratio, asset turnover ratio, and profit margin ratio for 2009 and 2008. Comment on your results.

| (in millions) | 2009 | 2008 |
|---|---|---|
| Net income (loss) | $ 58 | $ (85) |
| Net sales | 3,286 | 3,388 |
| Beginning total assets | 6,020 | 5,598 |
| Ending total assets | 6,554 | 6,020 |

## JETBLUE AIRWAYS CORPORATION
### Notes to the Financial Statements

**Property and Equipment:** We record our property and equipment at cost and depreciate these assets on a straight-line basis to their estimated residual values over their estimated useful lives. Additions, modifications that enhance the operating performance of our assets, and interest related to predelivery deposits to acquire new aircraft and for the construction of facilities are capitalized.

Estimated useful lives and residual values for our property and equipment are as follows.

| | Estimated Useful Life | Residual Value |
|---|---|---|
| Aircraft | 25 years | 20% |
| In-flight entertainment systems | 12 years | 0% |
| Aircraft parts | Fleet life | 10% |
| Flight equipment leasehold improvements | Lease term | 0% |
| Ground property and equipment | 3–10 years | 0% |
| Leasehold improvements | 15 years or lease term | 0% |

We record impairment losses on long-lived assets used in operations when events and circumstances indicate that the assets may be impaired and the undiscounted future cash flows estimated to be generated by these assets are less than the assets' net book value. If impairment occurs, the loss is measured by comparing the fair value of the asset to its carrying amount.

**Note 8—LiveTV** Purchased technology, which is an intangible asset related to our September 2002 acquisition of the membership interests of LiveTV, was being amortized over seven years based on the average number of aircraft expected to be in service as of the date of acquisition.

**Solution**

1.  The company depreciates property and equipment using the straight-line approach. It depreciates aircraft over a 25-year life.

2.  The company has an intangible asset called "purchased technology" related to its purchase of membership interests in "LiveTV." It amortizes this intangible asset based on the company's estimate of the average number of aircraft expected to be in service over a seven-year period.

3.

|  | **2009** | **2008** |
|---|---|---|
| Return on assets | $\dfrac{\$58}{(\$6,020+\$6,554)/2} = 0.9\%$ | $\dfrac{\$(85)}{(\$5,598+\$6,020)/2} = -1.5\%$ |
| Asset turnover | $\dfrac{\$3,286}{(\$6,020+\$6,554)/2} = 0.52$ times | $\dfrac{\$3,388}{(\$5,598+\$6,020)/2} = .58$ times |
| Profit margin | $\dfrac{\$58}{\$3,286} = 1.8\%$ | $\dfrac{\$(85)}{\$3,388} = -2.5\%$ |

JetBlue's return on assets ratio increased slightly from 2008 to 2009. While its profit margin was very low in both years, JetBlue was not able to increase its asset turnover. This suggests that its ability to generate sales from its planes remained constant, while its ability to generate profits from sales remained very low.

# Summary of Study Objectives

**1** **Describe how the cost principle applies to plant assets.** The cost of plant assets includes all expenditures necessary to acquire the asset and make it ready for its intended use. Cost is measured by the cash or cash equivalent price paid.

**2** **Explain the concept of depreciation.** Depreciation is the process of allocating to expense the cost of a plant asset over its useful (service) life in a rational and systematic manner. Depreciation is not a process of valuation, and it is not a process that results in an accumulation of cash. Depreciation reflects an asset's decreasing usefulness and revenue-producing ability, resulting from wear and tear and from obsolescence.

**3** **Compute periodic depreciation using the straight-line method, and contrast its expense pattern with those of other methods.** The formula for straight-line depreciation is:

$$\frac{\text{Cost} - \text{Salvage value}}{\text{Useful life (in years)}}$$

The expense patterns of the three depreciation methods are as follows.

| Method | Annual Depreciation Pattern |
|---|---|
| Straight-line | Constant amount |
| Declining-balance | Decreasing amount |
| Units-of-activity | Varying amount |

**4** **Describe the procedure for revising periodic depreciation.** Companies make revisions of periodic depreciation in present and future periods, not retroactively.

**5** **Explain how to account for the disposal of plant assets.** The procedure for accounting for the disposal of a plant asset through sale or retirement is: (a) Eliminate the book value of the plant asset at the date of disposal. (b) Record cash proceeds, if any. (c) Account for the difference between the book value and the cash proceeds as a gain or a loss on disposal.

**6** **Describe methods for evaluating the use of plant assets.** Plant assets may be analyzed using the return on assets ratio and the asset turnover ratio. The return on assets ratio consists of two components: the asset turnover ratio and the profit margin ratio.

**7** **Identify the basic issues related to reporting intangible assets.** Companies report intangible assets at their cost less any amounts amortized. If an intangible asset has a limited life, its cost should be allocated (amortized) over its useful life. Intangible assets with indefinite lives should not be amortized.

**8** **Indicate how long-lived assets are reported in the financial statements.** Companies usually show plant assets under "Property, plant, and equipment"; they show intangibles separately under "Intangible assets." Either within the balance sheet or in the notes, companies disclose the balances of the major classes of assets, such as land, buildings, and equipment, and accumulated depreciation by major classes or in total. They describe the depreciation and amortization methods used, and disclose the amount of depreciation and amortization expense for the period. In the statement of cash flows, depreciation and amortization expense are added back to net income to determine net cash provided by operating activities. The investing section reports cash paid or received to purchase or sell property, plant, and equipment.

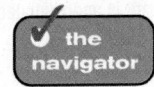

## DECISION TOOLKIT  A SUMMARY

| DECISION CHECKPOINTS | INFO NEEDED FOR DECISION | TOOL TO USE FOR DECISION | HOW TO EVALUATE RESULTS |
|---|---|---|---|
| Is the company using its assets effectively? | Net income and average assets | $$\text{Return on assets ratio} = \frac{\text{Net income}}{\text{Average total assets}}$$ | Higher value suggests favorable efficiency (use of assets). |
| How effective is the company at generating sales from its assets? | Net sales and average total assets | $$\text{Asset turnover ratio} = \frac{\text{Net sales}}{\text{Average total assets}}$$ | Indicates the sales dollars generated per dollar of assets. A high value suggests the company is effective in using its resources to generate sales. |
| Is the company's amortization of intangibles reasonable? | Estimated useful life of intangibles from notes to financial statements of this company and its competitors | If the company's estimated useful life significantly exceeds that of competitors or does not seem reasonable in light of the circumstances, the reason for the difference should be investigated. | Too high an estimated useful life will result in understating amortization expense and overstating net income. |

---

### appendix 9A

# Calculation of Depreciation Using Other Methods

**study objective 9**

Compute periodic depreciation using the declining-balance method and the units-of-activity method.

In this appendix, we show the calculations of the depreciation expense amounts that we used in the chapter for the declining-balance and units-of-activity methods.

### DECLINING-BALANCE

The **declining-balance method** produces a decreasing annual depreciation expense over the useful life of the asset. The method is so named because the computation of periodic depreciation is based on a **declining book value** (cost less accumulated depreciation) of the asset. Annual depreciation expense is computed by multiplying the book value at the beginning of the year by the declining-balance depreciation rate. **The depreciation rate remains constant from year to year, but the book value to which the rate is applied declines each year.**

Book value for the first year is the cost of the asset because the balance in accumulated depreciation at the beginning of the asset's useful life is zero. In subsequent years, book value is the difference between cost and accumulated depreciation at the beginning of the year. **Unlike other depreciation methods, the declining-balance method ignores salvage value in determining the amount to which the declining-balance rate is applied.** Salvage value, however, does limit the total depreciation that can be taken. Depreciation stops when the asset's book value equals its expected salvage value.

As noted in the chapter, a common declining-balance rate is double the straight-line rate—the **double-declining-balance method**. If Bill's Pizzas uses the double-declining-balance method, the depreciation rate is 40% (2 × the straight-line rate of 20%). Illustration 9A-1 presents the formula and computation of depreciation for the first year on the delivery truck.

**Helpful Hint** The straight-line rate is approximated as 1 ÷ Estimated life. In this case, it is 1 ÷ 5 = 20%.

**Illustration 9A-1**
Formula for declining-balance method

| Book Value at Beginning of Year | × | Declining-Balance Rate | = | Depreciation Expense |
|---|---|---|---|---|
| $13,000 | × | 40% | = | $5,200 |

Illustration 9A-2 presents the depreciation schedule under this method.

**Illustration 9A-2**
Double-declining-balance depreciation schedule

**BILL'S PIZZAS**

| | Computation | | | Annual | End of Year | |
|---|---|---|---|---|---|---|
| Year | Book Value Beginning of Year | × Depreciation Rate | = | Depreciation Expense | Accumulated Depreciation | Book Value |
| 2012 | $13,000 | 40% | | $5,200 | $ 5,200 | $ 7,800* |
| 2013 | 7,800 | 40 | | 3,120 | 8,320 | 4,680 |
| 2014 | 4,680 | 40 | | 1,872 | 10,192 | 2,808 |
| 2015 | 2,808 | 40 | | 1,123 | 11,315 | 1,685 |
| 2016 | 1,685 | 40 | | 685** | 12,000 | 1,000 |

*$13,000 − $5,200
**Computation of $674 ($1,685 × 40%) is adjusted to $685 in order for book value to equal salvage value.

**Helpful Hint** Depreciation stops when the asset's book value equals its expected salvage value.

The delivery equipment is 69% depreciated ($8,320 ÷ $12,000) at the end of the second year. Under the straight-line method, it would be depreciated 40% ($4,800 ÷ $12,000) at that time. Because the declining-balance method produces higher depreciation expense in the early years than in the later years, it is considered an **accelerated-depreciation method**.

The declining-balance method is compatible with the expense recognition principle. It matches the higher depreciation expense in early years with the higher benefits received in these years. Conversely, it recognizes lower depreciation expense in later years when the asset's contribution to revenue is less. Also, some assets lose their usefulness rapidly because of obsolescence. In these cases, the declining-balance method provides a more appropriate depreciation amount.

When an asset is purchased during the year, it is necessary to prorate the declining-balance depreciation in the first year on a time basis. For example, if Bill's Pizzas had purchased the delivery equipment on April 1, 2012, depreciation for 2012 would be $3,900 ($13,000 × 40% × $\frac{9}{12}$). The book value for computing depreciation in 2013 then becomes $9,100 ($13,000 − $3,900), and the 2013 depreciation is $3,640 ($9,100 × 40%).

## UNITS-OF-ACTIVITY

Under the **units-of-activity method**, useful life is expressed in terms of the total units of production or use expected from the asset. The units-of-activity method is ideally suited to equipment whose activity can be measured in units of output, miles driven, or hours in use. The units-of-activity method is generally not suitable for assets for which depreciation is a function more of time than of use.

**Alternative Terminology** Another term often used is the *units-of-production method.*

To use this method, a company estimates the total units of activity for the entire useful life and divides that amount into the depreciable cost to determine the depreciation cost per unit. It then multiplies the depreciation cost per unit by the units of activity during the year to find the annual depreciation for that year.

To illustrate, assume that Bill's Pizzas estimates it will drive its new delivery truck 15,000 miles in the first year. Illustration 9A-3 presents the formula and computation of depreciation expense in the first year.

**Illustration 9A-3**
Formula for units-of-activity method

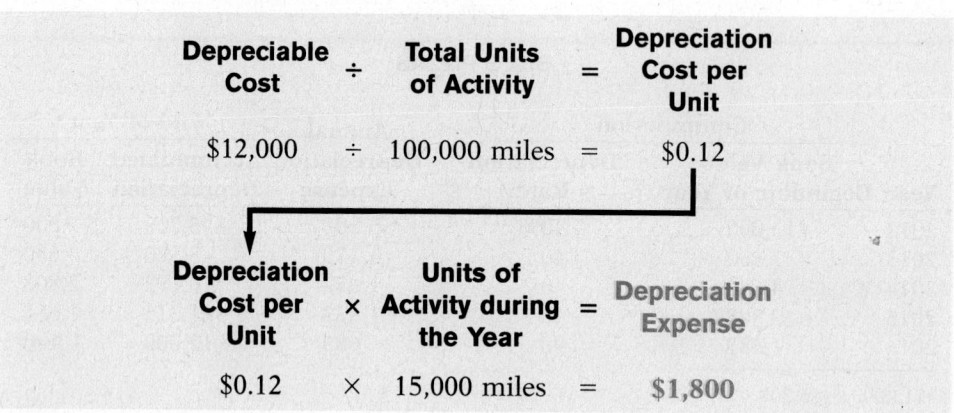

Illustration 9A-4 shows the depreciation schedule, using assumed mileage data.

**Illustration 9A-4** Units-of-activity depreciation schedule

**Helpful Hint** Depreciation stops when the asset's book value equals its expected salvage value.

**BILL'S PIZZAS**

| | Computation | | | Annual | End of Year | |
| | Units of | | Depreciation | Depreciation | Accumulated | Book |
| Year | Activity | × | Cost/Unit | = Expense | Depreciation | Value |
|---|---|---|---|---|---|---|
| 2012 | 15,000 | | $0.12 | $1,800 | $ 1,800 | $11,200* |
| 2013 | 30,000 | | 0.12 | 3,600 | 5,400 | 7,600 |
| 2014 | 20,000 | | 0.12 | 2,400 | 7,800 | 5,200 |
| 2015 | 25,000 | | 0.12 | 3,000 | 10,800 | 2,200 |
| 2016 | 10,000 | | 0.12 | 1,200 | 12,000 | 1,000 |

*$13,000 − $1,800

The units-of-activity method is not nearly as popular as the straight-line method, primarily because it is often difficult to make a reasonable estimate of total activity. However, this method is used by some very large companies, such as Standard Oil Company of California and Boise Cascade Corporation. When the productivity of the asset varies significantly from one period to another, the units-of-activity method results in the best matching of expenses with revenues.

This method is easy to apply when assets are purchased during the year. In such a case, companies use the productivity of the asset for the partial year in computing the depreciation.

# Summary of Study Objective for Appendix 9A

**9** Compute periodic depreciation using the declining-balance method and the units-of-activity method. The depreciation expense calculation for each of these methods is:

### Declining-balance:

$$\frac{\text{Book value at}}{\text{beginning of year}} \times \frac{\text{Declining-balance}}{\text{rate}} = \frac{\text{Depreciation}}{\text{expense}}$$

### Units-of-activity:

$$\frac{\text{Depreciable}}{\text{cost}} \div \frac{\text{Total units}}{\text{of activity}} = \frac{\text{Depreciation}}{\text{cost per unit}}$$

$$\frac{\text{Depreciation cost}}{\text{per unit}} \times \frac{\text{Units of activity}}{\text{during year}} = \frac{\text{Depreciation}}{\text{expense}}$$

# Glossary

**Accelerated-depreciation method** *(p. 456)*   A depreciation method that produces higher depreciation expense in the early years than the straight-line approach.

**Additions and improvements** *(p. 460)*   Costs incurred to increase the operating efficiency, productive capacity, or expected useful life of a plant asset.

**Amortization** *(p. 468)*   The process of allocating to expense the cost of an intangible asset.

**Asset turnover ratio** *(p. 466)*   Indicates how efficiently a company uses its assets to generate sales; calculated as net sales divided by average total assets.

**Capital expenditures** *(p. 449)*   Expenditures that increase the company's investment in plant assets.

**Capital lease** *(p. 452)*   A contractual agreement allowing one party (the lessee) to use another party's asset (the lessor); accounted for like a debt-financed purchase by the lessee.

**Cash equivalent price** *(p. 449)*   An amount equal to the fair value of the asset given up or the fair value of the asset received, whichever is more clearly determinable.

**Copyright** *(p. 470)* An exclusive right granted by the federal government allowing the owner to reproduce and sell an artistic or published work.

**Declining-balance method** *(pp. 456, 476)*   A depreciation method that applies a constant rate to the declining book value of the asset and produces a decreasing annual depreciation expense over the asset's useful life.

**Depreciable cost** *(p. 455)*   The cost of a plant asset less its salvage value.

**Depreciation** *(p. 453)*   The process of allocating to expense the cost of a plant asset over its useful life in a rational and systematic manner.

**Franchise** *(p. 470)*   A contractual arrangement under which the franchisor grants the franchisee the right to sell certain products, to provide specific services, or to use certain trademarks or trade names, usually within a designated geographic area.

**Goodwill** *(p. 471)*   The value of all favorable attributes that relate to a company that are not attributable to any other specific asset.

**Impairment** *(p. 461)*   A permanent decline in the fair value of an asset.

**Intangible assets** *(p. 467)*   Rights, privileges, and competitive advantages that result from the ownership of long-lived assets that do not possess physical substance.

**Lessee** *(p. 452)*   A party that has made contractual arrangements to use another party's asset for a period at an agreed price.

**Lessor** *(p. 452)*   A party that has agreed contractually to let another party use its asset for a period at an agreed price.

**Licenses** *(p. 470)*   Operating rights to use public property, granted by a governmental agency to a business.

**Operating lease** *(p. 452)*   A contractual agreement allowing one party (the lessee) to use the asset of another party (the lessor); accounted for as a rental by the lessee.

**Ordinary repairs** *(p. 460)*   Expenditures to maintain the operating efficiency and expected productive life of the asset.

**Patent** *(p. 469)*   An exclusive right issued by the U.S. Patent Office that enables the recipient to manufacture, sell, or otherwise control an invention for a period of 20 years from the date of the grant.

**Plant assets** *(p. 448)*   Tangible resources that have physical substance, are used in the operations of the business, and are not intended for sale to customers.

**Research and development costs** *(p. 469)*   Expenditures that may lead to patents, copyrights, new processes, and new products; must be expensed as incurred.

**Return on assets ratio** *(p. 464)*   A profitability measure that indicates the amount of net income generated by each dollar of assets; computed as net income divided by average assets.

**Revenue expenditures** *(p. 449)*   Expenditures that are immediately charged against revenues as an expense.

**Straight-line method** *(p. 455)*   A method in which companies expense an equal amount of depreciation for each year of the asset's useful life.

**Trademark (trade name)** *(p. 470)*   A word, phrase, jingle, or symbol that distinguishes or identifies a particular enterprise or product.

**Units-of-activity method** *(pp. 456, 477)*   A depreciation method in which useful life is expressed in terms of the total units of production or use expected from the asset.

# Comprehensive *Do it!* 1

DuPage Company purchased a factory machine at a cost of $18,000 on January 1, 2012. DuPage expected the machine to have a salvage value of $2,000 at the end of its 4-year useful life.

**Instructions**

Prepare a depreciation schedule using the straight-line method.

**Action Plan**

- Under the straight-line method, apply the depreciation rate to depreciable cost.

## Solution to Comprehensive *Do it!* 1

### DUPAGE COMPANY
### Depreciation Schedule—Straight-Line Method

| | Computation | | | Annual | End of Year | |
|---|---|---|---|---|---|---|
| Year | Depreciable Cost (a) | × Depreciation Rate (b) = | | Depreciation Expense | Accumulated Depreciation | Book Value (c) |
| 2012 | $16,000 | 25% | | $4,000 | $ 4,000 | $14,000 |
| 2013 | 16,000 | 25 | | 4,000 | 8,000 | 10,000 |
| 2014 | 16,000 | 25 | | 4,000 | 12,000 | 6,000 |
| 2015 | 16,000 | 25 | | 4,000 | 16,000 | 2,000 |

(a) $18,000 − $2,000    (b) $\frac{1}{4}$ = 25%    (c) Cost less accumulated depreciation.

# Comprehensive *Do it!* 2

On January 1, 2009, Skyline Limousine Co. purchased a limousine at an acquisition cost of $28,000. Skyline depreciated the vehicle by the straight-line method using a 4-year service life and a $4,000 salvage value. The company's fiscal year ends on December 31.

**Instructions**

Prepare the journal entry or entries to record the disposal of the limousine, assuming that it was:

(a) Retired and scrapped with no salvage value on January 1, 2013.
(b) Sold for $5,000 on July 1, 2012.

**Action Plan**

- Calculate accumulated depreciation (Depreciation expense per year × Years in use).
- At the time of disposal, determine the book value of the asset.
- Recognize any gain or loss from disposal of the asset.

## Solution to Comprehensive *Do it!* 2

| | | | |
|---|---|---|---|
| (a) Jan. 1, 2013 | Accumulated Depreciation—Equipment | 24,000* | |
| | Loss on Disposal of Plant Assets | 4,000 | |
| |     Equipment | | 28,000 |
| |       (To record retirement of limousine) | | |

*(($28,000 − $4,000) ÷ 4) × 4

| | | | |
|---|---|---|---|
| (b) July 1, 2012 | Depreciation Expense | 3,000* | |
| |     Accumulated Depreciation—Equipment | | 3,000 |
| |       (To record depreciation to date of disposal) | | |

*(($28,000 − $4,000) ÷ 4) × $\frac{1}{2}$

| | | | |
|---|---|---|---|
| | Cash | 5,000 | |
| | Accumulated Depreciation—Equipment | 21,000** | |
| | Loss on Disposal of Plant Assets | 2,000 | |
| |     Equipment | | 28,000 |
| |       (To record sale of limousine) | | |

**(($28,000 − $4,000) ÷ 4) × 3.5

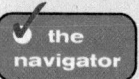

 Self-Test, Brief Exercises, Exercises, Problem Set A, and many more resources are available for practice in WileyPLUS

*Note:* All Questions, Exercises, and Problems marked with an asterisk relate to material in the appendix to the chapter.

## Self-Test Questions

Answers are on page 499.

(SO 1) **1.** Corrieten Company purchased equipment and incurred these costs:

| | |
|---|---|
| Cash price | $24,000 |
| Sales taxes | 1,200 |
| Insurance during transit | 200 |
| Installation and testing | 400 |
| Total costs | $25,800 |

What amount should be recorded as the cost of the equipment?
(a) $24,000.
(b) $25,200.
(c) $25,400.
(d) $25,800.

(SO 1) **2.** ⚒ Harrington Corporation recently leased a number of trucks from Andre Corporation. In inspecting the books of Harrington Corporation, you notice that the trucks have not been recorded as assets on its balance sheet. From this, you can conclude that Harrington is accounting for this transaction as a/an:
(a) operating lease.
(b) capital lease.
(c) purchase.
(d) None of the above.

(SO 2) **3.** Depreciation is a process of:
(a) valuation.
(b) cost allocation.
(c) cash accumulation.
(d) appraisal.

(SO 3) **4.** Cuso Company purchased equipment on January 1, 2011, at a total invoice cost of $400,000. The equipment has an estimated salvage value of $10,000 and an estimated useful life of 5 years. What is the amount of accumulated depreciation at December 31, 2012, if the straight-line method of depreciation is used?
(a) $80,000.
(b) $160,000.
(c) $78,000.
(d) $156,000.

(SO 3) **5.** ⚒ A company would minimize its depreciation expense in the first year of owning an asset if it used:
(a) a high estimated life, a high salvage value, and declining-balance depreciation.
(b) a low estimated life, a high salvage value, and straight-line depreciation.
(c) a high estimated life, a high salvage value, and straight-line depreciation.
(d) a low estimated life, a low salvage value, and declining-balance depreciation.

(SO 4) **6.** When there is a change in estimated depreciation:
(a) previous depreciation should be corrected.
(b) current and future years' depreciation should be revised.
(c) only future years' depreciation should be revised.
(d) None of the above.

(SO 4) **7.** Able Towing Company purchased a tow truck for $60,000 on January 1, 2012. It was originally depreciated on a straight-line basis over 10 years with an assumed salvage value of $12,000. On December 31, 2014, before adjusting entries had been made, the company decided to change the remaining estimated life to 4 years (including 2014) and the salvage value to $2,000. What was the depreciation expense for 2014?
(a) $6,000.
(b) $4,800.
(c) $15,000.
(d) $12,100.

(SO 4) **8.** Additions to plant assets:
(a) decrease liabilities.
(b) increase a repair expense account.
(c) increase a purchases account.
(d) are capital expenditures.

(SO 5) **9.** Bennie Razor Company has decided to sell one of its old manufacturing machines on June 30, 2012. The machine was purchased for $80,000 on January 1, 2008, and was depreciated on a straight-line basis for 10 years assuming no salvage value. If the machine was sold for $26,000, what was the amount of the gain or loss recorded at the time of the sale?
(a) $18,000 loss.
(b) $54,000 loss.
(c) $22,000 gain.
(d) $46,000 gain.

(SO 6) **10.** Which of the following measures provides an indication of how efficient a company is in employing its assets?
(a) Current ratio.
(b) Profit margin ratio.
(c) Debt to total assets ratio.
(d) Asset turnover ratio.

(SO 6) **11.** Lake Coffee Company reported net sales of $180,000, net income of $54,000, beginning total assets of $200,000, and ending total assets of $300,000. What was the company's asset turnover ratio?
(a) 0.90
(b) 0.20
(c) 0.72
(d) 1.39

(SO 7) **12.** Pierce Company incurred $150,000 of research and development costs in its laboratory to develop a new product. It spent $20,000 in legal fees for a patent granted on January 2, 2012. On July 31, 2012, Pierce paid $15,000 for legal fees in a successful defense of the patent. What is the total amount that should be debited to Patents through July 31, 2012?
(a) $150,000.
(b) $35,000.
(c) $185,000.
(d) Some other amount.

(SO 7) **13.** Indicate which one of these statements is *true.*
(a) Since intangible assets lack physical substance, they need to be disclosed only in the notes to the financial statements.

(b) Goodwill should be reported as a contra account in the stockholders' equity section.

(c) Totals of major classes of assets can be shown in the balance sheet, with asset details disclosed in the notes to the financial statements.

(d) Intangible assets are typically combined with plant assets and inventory and then shown in the property, plant, and equipment section.

(SO 7) 14. If a company reports goodwill as an intangible asset on its books, what is the one thing you know with certainty?

(a) The company is a valuable company worth investing in.

(b) The company has a well-established brand name.

(c) The company purchased another company.

(d) The goodwill will generate a lot of positive business for the company for many years to come.

(SO 7) 15. Which of the following statements is *false*?

(a) If an intangible asset has a finite life, it should be amortized.

(b) The amortization period of an intangible asset can exceed 20 years.

(c) Goodwill is recorded only when a business is purchased.

(d) Research and development costs are expensed when incurred, except when the research and development expenditures result in a successful patent.

*16. Kant Enterprises purchased a truck for $11,000 on (SO 9) January 1, 2011. The truck will have an estimated salvage value of $1,000 at the end of 5 years. If you use the units-of-activity method, the balance in accumulated depreciation at December 31, 2012, can be computed by the following formula:

(a) ($11,000 ÷ Total estimated activity) × Units of activity for 2012.

(b) ($10,000 ÷ Total estimated activity) × Units of activity for 2012.

(c) ($11,000 ÷ Total estimated activity) × Units of activity for 2011 and 2012.

(d) ($10,000 ÷ Total estimated activity) × Units of activity for 2011 and 2012.

Go to the book's companion website, **www.wiley.com/college/kimmel**, to access additional Self-Test Questions.

# Questions

1. Mrs. Villarreal is uncertain about how the cost principle applies to plant assets. Explain the principle to Mrs. Villarreal.

2. How is the cost for a plant asset measured in a cash transaction? In a noncash transaction?

3. Johnstone Company acquires the land and building owned by Briggs Company. What types of costs may be incurred to make the asset ready for its intended use if Johnstone Company wants to use only the land? If it wants to use both the land and the building?

4. Pryor Inc. needs to upgrade its diagnostic equipment. At the time of purchase, Pryor had expected the equipment to last 8 years. Unfortunately, it was obsolete after only 4 years. Justin Meyer, CFO of Pryor Inc., is considering leasing new equipment rather than buying it. What are the potential benefits of leasing?

5. In a recent newspaper release, the president of Franklin Company asserted that something has to be done about depreciation. The president said, "Depreciation does not come close to accumulating the cash needed to replace the asset at the end of its useful life." What is your response to the president?

6. Carmelita is studying for the next accounting examination. She asks your help on two questions: (a) What is salvage value? (b) How is salvage value used in determining depreciable cost under the straight-line method? Answer Carmelita's questions.

7. Contrast the straight-line method and the units-of-activity method in relation to (a) useful life and (b) the pattern of periodic depreciation over useful life.

8. Contrast the effects of the three depreciation methods on annual depreciation expense.

9. In the fourth year of an asset's 5-year useful life, the company decides that the asset will have a 6-year service life. How should the revision of depreciation be recorded? Why?

10. Distinguish between ordinary repairs and capital expenditures during an asset's useful life.

11. How is a gain or a loss on the sale of a plant asset computed?

12. Folstein Corporation owns a machine that is fully depreciated but is still being used. How should Folstein account for this asset and report it in the financial statements?

13.  What does Tootsie Roll use as the estimated useful life on its buildings? On its machinery and equipment?

14. What are the similarities and differences between depreciation and amortization?

15. During a recent management meeting, Steve Micke, director of marketing, proposed that the company begin capitalizing its marketing expenditures as goodwill. In his words, "Marketing expenditures create goodwill for the company which benefits the company for multiple periods. Therefore it doesn't make

good sense to have to expense it as it is incurred. Besides, if we capitalize it as goodwill, we won't have to amortize it, and this will boost reported income." Discuss the merits of Steve's proposal.

16. Alford Company hires an accounting intern who says that intangible assets should always be amortized over their legal lives. Is the intern correct? Explain.

17. Goodwill has been defined as the value of all favorable attributes that relate to a business enterprise. What types of attributes could result in goodwill?

18. Janis Ford, a business major, is working on a case problem for one of her classes. In this case problem, the company needs to raise cash to market a new product it developed. Mark Gordon, an engineering major, takes one look at the company's balance sheet and says, "This company has an awful lot of goodwill. Why don't you recommend that they sell some of it to raise cash?" How should Janis respond to Mark?

19. Under what conditions is goodwill recorded? What is the proper accounting treatment for amortizing goodwill?

20. Often research and development costs provide companies with benefits that last a number of years. (For example, these costs can lead to the development of a patent that will increase the company's income for many years.) However, generally accepted accounting principles require that such costs be recorded as an expense when incurred. Why?

21. In 2009, Campbell Soup Company reported average total assets of $6,265 million, net sales of $7,586 million, and net income of $736 million. What was Campbell Soup's return on assets ratio?

22. Lauren Rado, a marketing executive for Fresh Views Inc., has proposed expanding its product line of framed graphic art by producing a line of lower-quality products. These would require less processing by the company and would provide a lower profit margin. Tom Hogle, the company's CFO, is concerned that this new product line would reduce the company's return on assets. Discuss the potential effect on return on assets that this product might have.

23. Give an example of an industry that would be characterized by (a) a high asset turnover ratio and a low profit margin ratio, and (b) a low asset turnover ratio and a high profit margin ratio.

24. Allman Corporation and Bryant Corporation operate in the same industry. Allman uses the straight-line method to account for depreciation, whereas Bryant uses an accelerated method. Explain what complications might arise in trying to compare the results of these two companies.

25. Guzman Corporation uses straight-line depreciation for financial reporting purposes but an accelerated method for tax purposes. Is it acceptable to use different methods for the two purposes? What is Guzman Corporation's motivation for doing this?

26. You are comparing two companies in the same industry. You have determined that Morris Corp. depreciates its plant assets over a 40-year life, whereas Kiram Corp. depreciates its plant assets over a 20-year life. Discuss the implications this has for comparing the results of the two companies.

27. Explain how transactions related to plant assets and intangibles are reported in the statement of cash flows.

# Brief Exercises

**BE9-1** These expenditures were incurred by Patnode Company in purchasing land: cash price $60,000; accrued taxes $5,000; attorney's fees $2,100; real estate broker's commission $3,300; and clearing and grading $3,500. What is the cost of the land?

*Determine the cost of land.* (SO 1), AP

**BE9-2** Deutsch Company incurs these expenditures in purchasing a truck: cash price $24,000; accident insurance (during use) $2,000; sales taxes $1,080; motor vehicle license $300; and painting and lettering $1,700. What is the cost of the truck?

*Determine the cost of a truck.* (SO 1), AP

**BE9-3** Alan Chemicals Company acquires a delivery truck at a cost of $31,000 on January 1, 2012. The truck is expected to have a salvage value of $4,000 at the end of its 4-year useful life. Compute annual depreciation for the first and second years using the straight-line method.

*Compute straight-line depreciation.* (SO 3), AP

**BE9-4** Erin Company purchased land and a building on January 1, 2012. Management's best estimate of the value of the land was $100,000 and of the building $250,000. However, management told the accounting department to record the land at $230,000 and the building at $120,000. The building is being depreciated on a straight-line basis over 20 years with no salvage value. Why do you suppose management requested this accounting treatment? Is it ethical?

*Compute depreciation and evaluate treatment.* (SO 3), AN

**BE9-5** On January 1, 2012, the Eugene Company ledger shows Equipment $36,000 and Accumulated Depreciation $13,600. The depreciation resulted from using the straight-line method with a useful life of 10 years and a salvage value of $2,000. On this date, the

*Compute revised depreciation.* (SO 4), AP

company concludes that the equipment has a remaining useful life of only 2 years with the same salvage value. Compute the revised annual depreciation.

*Prepare entries for delivery truck costs.*

(SO 4), **AP**

**BE9-6** Sabina Company had the following two transactions related to its delivery truck.
1. Paid $38 for an oil change.
2. Paid $400 to install special shelving units, which increase the operating efficiency of the truck.

Prepare Sabina's journal entries to record these two transactions.

*Journalize entries for disposal of plant assets.*

(SO 5), **AP**

**BE9-7** Prepare journal entries to record these transactions: (a) Benton Company retires its delivery equipment, which cost $41,000. Accumulated depreciation is also $41,000 on this delivery equipment. No salvage value is received. (b) Assume the same information as in part (a), except that accumulated depreciation for the equipment is $37,200 instead of $41,000.

*Journalize entries for sale of plant assets.*

(SO 5), **AP**

**BE9-8** Clark Company sells office equipment on July 31, 2012, for $21,000 cash. The office equipment originally cost $72,000 and as of January 1, 2012, had accumulated depreciation of $42,000. Depreciation for the first 7 months of 2012 is $4,600. Prepare the journal entries to (a) update depreciation to July 31, 2012, and (b) record the sale of the equipment.

*Compute return on assets ratio and asset turnover ratio.*

(SO 6), **AP**

**BE9-9** In its 2009 annual report, McDonald's Corporation reports beginning total assets of $28.46 billion; ending total assets of $30.22 billion; net sales of $22.74 billion; and net income of $4.55 billion.
(a) Compute McDonald's return on assets ratio.
(b) Compute McDonald's asset turnover ratio.

*Account for intangibles—patents.*

(SO 7), **AP**

**BE9-10** Tanya Company purchases a patent for $156,000 on January 2, 2012. Its estimated useful life is 6 years.
(a) Prepare the journal entry to record amortization expense for the first year.
(b) Show how this patent is reported on the balance sheet at the end of the first year.

*Classification of long-lived assets on balance sheet.*

(SO 8), **AP**

**BE9-11** Nike, Inc. reported the following plant assets and intangible assets for the year ended May 31, 2009 (in millions): other plant assets $965.8; land $221.6; patents and trademarks (at cost) $515.1; machinery and equipment $2,094.3; buildings $974.0; goodwill (at cost) $193.5; accumulated amortization $47.7; and accumulated depreciation $2,298.0. Prepare a partial balance sheet for Nike for these items.

*Determine net cash provided by operating activities.*

(SO 8), **AP**

**BE9-12** Ndon Company reported net income of $157,000. It reported depreciation expense of $12,000 and accumulated depreciation of $47,000. Amortization expense was $8,000. Ndon purchased new equipment during the year for $50,000. Show how this information would be used to determine net cash provided by operating activities.

*Compute declining-balance depreciation.*

(SO 9), **AP**

*****BE9-13** Depreciation information for Alan Chemicals Company is given in BE9-3. Assuming the declining-balance depreciation rate is double the straight-line rate, compute annual depreciation for the first and second years under the declining-balance method.

*Compute depreciation using units-of-activity method.*

(SO 9), **AP**

*****BE9-14** DriveUp Taxi Service uses the units-of-activity method in computing depreciation on its taxicabs. Each cab is expected to be driven 150,000 miles. Taxi 10 cost $27,500 and is expected to have a salvage value of $500. Taxi 10 was driven 32,000 miles in 2011 and 33,000 miles in 2012. Compute the depreciation for each year.

## Do it! Review

*Explain accounting for cost of plant assets*

(SO 1), **C**

**Do it!** 9-1 Hidden Lakes Company purchased a delivery truck. The total cash payment was $30,020, including the following items.

| | |
|---|---|
| Negotiated purchase price | $24,000 |
| Installation of special shelving | 1,100 |
| Painting and lettering | 900 |
| Motor vehicle license | 180 |
| Annual insurance policy | 2,400 |
| Sales tax | 1,440 |
| Total paid | $30,020 |

Explain how each of these costs would be accounted for.

**Do it!** 9-2  On January 1, 2012, Willow Way Country Club purchased a new riding mower for $15,000. The mower is expected to have a 10-year life with a $1,000 salvage value. What journal entry would Willow Way make on December 31, 2012, if it uses straight-line depreciation?

*Calculate depreciation expense and make journal entry.*
*(SO 2), AP*

**Do it!** 9-3  Whistler Corporation purchased a piece of equipment for $50,000. It estimated an 8-year life and $2,000 salvage value. At the end of year four (before the depreciation adjustment), it estimated the new total life to be 10 years and the new salvage value to be $4,000. Compute the revised depreciation.

*Calculated revised depreciation*
*(SO 4), AP*

**Do it!** 9-4  Reinbold Manufacturing has an old factory machine that cost $50,000. The machine has accumulated depreciation of $28,000. Reinbold has decided to sell the machine.
(a)  What entry would Reinbold make to record the sale of the machine for $25,000 cash?
(b)  What entry would Reinbold make to record the sale of the machine for $15,000 cash?

*Make journal entries to record plant asset disposal.*
*(SO 5), AP*

**Do it!** 9-5  Match the statement with the term most directly associated with it.

*Match intangible assets with concepts.*
*(SO 7), C*

    Goodwill                       Amortization
    Intangible assets            Franchise
    Research and development costs

1. _____ Rights, privileges, and competitive advantages that result from the ownership of long-lived assets that do not possess physical substance.
2. _____ The allocation of the cost of an intangible asset to expense in a rational and systematic manner.
3. _____ A right to sell certain products or services, or use certain trademarks or trade names within a designated geographic area.
4. _____ Costs incurred by a company that often lead to patents or new products. These costs must be expensed as incurred.
5. _____ The excess of the cost of a company over the fair value of the net assets required.

# Exercises

**E9-1**  The following expenditures relating to plant assets were made by Newport Company during the first 2 months of 2012.
1.  Paid $7,000 of accrued taxes at the time the plant site was acquired.
2.  Paid $200 insurance to cover a possible accident loss on new factory machinery while the machinery was in transit.
3.  Paid $850 sales taxes on a new delivery truck.
4.  Paid $21,000 for parking lots and driveways on the new plant site.
5.  Paid $250 to have the company name and slogan painted on the new delivery truck.
6.  Paid $8,000 for installation of new factory machinery.
7.  Paid $900 for a 1-year accident insurance policy on the new delivery truck.
8.  Paid $75 motor vehicle license fee on the new truck.

*Determine cost of plant acquisitions.*
*(SO 1), C*

*Instructions*
(a)  ▭▭▭▷ Explain the application of the cost principle in determining the acquisition cost of plant assets.
(b)  List the numbers of the transactions, and opposite each indicate the account title to which each expenditure should be debited.

**E9-2**  Ramona Company incurred the following costs.

*Determine property, plant, and equipment costs.*
*(SO 1), C*

| | |
|---|---:|
| 1. Sales tax on factory machinery purchased | $ 5,000 |
| 2. Painting of and lettering on truck immediately upon purchase | 700 |
| 3. Installation and testing of factory machinery | 2,000 |
| 4. Real estate broker's commission on land purchased | 3,500 |
| 5. Insurance premium paid for first year's insurance on new truck | 880 |
| 6. Cost of landscaping on property purchased | 7,200 |
| 7. Cost of paving parking lot for new building constructed | 17,900 |
| 8. Cost of clearing, draining, and filling land | 13,300 |
| 9. Architect's fees on self-constructed building | 10,000 |

*Instructions*
Indicate to which account Ramona would debit each of the costs.

*Determine acquisition costs of land.*

*(SO 1),* **AP**

**E9-3** On March 1, 2012, Enrique Company acquired real estate, on which it planned to construct a small office building, by paying $80,000 in cash. An old warehouse on the property was demolished at a cost of $8,200; the salvaged materials were sold for $1,700. Additional expenditures before construction began included $1,900 attorney's fee for work concerning the land purchase, $5,200 real estate broker's fee, $9,100 architect's fee, and $14,000 to put in driveways and a parking lot.

**Instructions**
(a) Determine the amount to be reported as the cost of the land.
(b) For each cost not used in part (a), indicate the account to be debited.

*Understand depreciation concepts.*

*(SO 2),* **C**

**E9-4** Belinda Lorenz has prepared the following list of statements about depreciation.
 1. Depreciation is a process of asset valuation, not cost allocation.
 2. Depreciation provides for the proper matching of expenses with revenues.
 3. The book value of a plant asset should approximate its fair value.
 4. Depreciation applies to three classes of plant assets: land, buildings, and equipment.
 5. Depreciation does not apply to a building because its usefulness and revenue-producing ability generally remain intact over time.
 6. The revenue-producing ability of a depreciable asset will decline due to wear and tear and to obsolescence.
 7. Recognizing depreciation on an asset results in an accumulation of cash for replacement of the asset.
 8. The balance in accumulated depreciation represents the total cost that has been charged to expense.
 9. Depreciation expense and accumulated depreciation are reported on the income statement.
 10. Four factors affect the computation of depreciation: cost, useful life, salvage value, and residual value.

**Instructions**
Identify each statement as true or false. If false, indicate how to correct the statement.

*Determine straight-line depreciation for partial period.*

*(SO 3),* **AP**

**E9-5** Deloise Company purchased a new machine on October 1, 2012, at a cost of $90,000. The company estimated that the machine has a salvage value of $8,000. The machine is expected to be used for 70,000 working hours during its 8-year life.

**Instructions**
Compute the depreciation expense under the straight-line method for 2012 and 2013, assuming a December 31 year-end.

*Compute revised annual depreciation.*

*(SO 3, 4),* **AN**

**E9-6** Brett Richard, the new controller of Maldonado Company, has reviewed the expected useful lives and salvage values of selected depreciable assets at the beginning of 2012. Here are his findings:

| Type of Asset | Date Acquired | Cost | Accumulated Depreciation, Jan. 1, 2012 | Useful Life (in years) | | Salvage Value | |
|---|---|---|---|---|---|---|---|
| | | | | Old | Proposed | Old | Proposed |
| Building | Jan. 1, 2004 | $700,000 | $130,000 | 40 | 48 | $50,000 | $35,000 |
| Warehouse | Jan. 1, 2007 | 120,000 | 23,000 | 25 | 20 | 5,000 | 3,600 |

All assets are depreciated by the straight-line method. Maldonado Company uses a calendar year in preparing annual financial statements. After discussion, management has agreed to accept Brett's proposed changes. (The "Proposed" useful life is total life, not remaining life.)

**Instructions**
(a) Compute the revised annual depreciation on each asset in 2012. (Show computations.)
(b) Prepare the entry (or entries) to record depreciation on the building in 2012.

*Journalize transactions related to disposals of plant assets.*

*(SO 5),* **AP**

**E9-7** Kemp Co. has delivery equipment that cost $50,000 and has been depreciated $24,000.

**Instructions**
Record entries for the disposal under the following assumptions.
(a) It was scrapped as having no value.
(b) It was sold for $37,000.
(c) It was sold for $20,000.

**E9-8** Here are selected 2012 transactions of Eghan Corporation.

*Record disposal of equipment.*
(SO 5), **AP**

Jan. 1 Retired a piece of machinery that was purchased on January 1, 2002. The machine cost $62,000 and had a useful life of 10 years with no salvage value.

June 30 Sold a computer that was purchased on January 1, 2010. The computer cost $36,000 and had a useful life of 3 years with no salvage value. The computer was sold for $5,000 cash.

Dec. 31 Sold a delivery truck for $9,000 cash. The truck cost $25,000 when it was purchased on January 1, 2009, and was depreciated based on a 5-year useful life with a $4,000 salvage value.

**Instructions**
Journalize all entries required on the above dates, including entries to update depreciation on assets disposed of, where applicable. Eghan Corporation uses straight-line depreciation.

**E9-9** The following situations are independent of one another.

*Apply accounting concepts.*
(SO 1, 2, 6, 7), **C**

1. An accounting student recently employed by a small company doesn't understand why the company is only depreciating its buildings and equipment, but not its land. The student prepared journal entries to depreciate all the company's property, plant, and equipment for the current year-end.

2. The same student also thinks the company's amortization policy on its intangible assets is wrong. The company is currently amortizing its patents but not its goodwill. The student fixed that for the current year-end by adding goodwill to her adjusting entry for amortization. She told a fellow employee that she felt she had improved the consistency of the company's accounting policies by making these changes.

3. The same company has a building still in use that has a zero book value but a substantial fair value. The student felt that this practice didn't benefit the company's users—especially the bank—and wrote the building up to its fair value. After all, she reasoned, you can write down assets if fair values are lower. Writing them up if fair value is higher is yet another example of the improved consistency that she has brought to the company's accounting practices.

**Instructions**
Explain whether or not the accounting treatment in each of the above situations is in accordance with generally accepted accounting principles. Explain what accounting principle or assumption, if any, has been violated and what the appropriate accounting treatment should be.

**E9-10** During 2009, Federal Express reported the following information (in millions): net sales of $35,497 and net income of $98. Its balance sheet also showed total assets at the beginning of the year of $25,633 and total assets at the end of the year of $24,244.

*Calculate asset turnover ratio and return on assets ratio.*
(SO 6), **AP**

**Instructions**
Calculate the (a) asset turnover ratio and (b) return on assets ratio.

**E9-11** Mangrich International is considering a significant expansion to its product line. The sales force is excited about the opportunities that the new products will bring. The new products are a significant step up in quality above the company's current offerings, but offer a complementary fit to its existing product line. Michael Powell, senior production department manager, is very excited about the high-tech new equipment that will have to be acquired to produce the new products. Linda Huang, the company's CFO, has provided the following projections based on results with and without the new products.

*Calculate and interpret ratios.*
(SO 6), **AP**

|  | Without New Products | With New Products |
|---|---|---|
| Sales | $10,000,000 | $16,000,000 |
| Net income | $500,000 | $960,000 |
| Average total assets | $5,000,000 | $12,000,000 |

**Instructions**
(a) Compute the company's return on assets ratio, profit margin ratio, and asset turnover ratio, both with and without the new product line.
(b) Discuss the implications that your findings in part (a) have for the company's decision.

*Calculate and interpret ratios.*

(SO 6), **AP**

**E9-12** Tobias Company reports the following information (in millions) during a recent year: net sales, $11,408.5; net earnings, $264.8; total assets, ending, $4,312.6; and total assets, beginning, $4,254.3.

**Instructions**

(a) Calculate the (1) return on assets, (2) asset turnover, and (3) profit margin ratios.

(b) Prove mathematically how the profit margin and asset turnover ratios work together to explain return on assets, by showing the appropriate calculation.

(c) Tobias Company owns Villas (grocery), Tobias Theaters, Kurt Drugstores, and Cepeda (heavy equipment), and manages commercial real estate, among other activities. Does this diversity of activities affect your ability to interpret the ratios you calculated in (a)? Explain.

*Prepare adjusting entries for amortization.*

(SO 7), **AN**

**E9-13** These are selected 2012 transactions for Jendusa Corporation:

| | | |
|---|---|---|
| Jan. | 1 | Purchased a copyright for $120,000. The copyright has a useful life of 6 years and a remaining legal life of 30 years. |
| Mar. | 1 | Purchased a patent with an estimated useful life of 4 years and a legal life of 20 years for $54,000. |
| Sept. | 1 | Purchased a small company and recorded goodwill of $150,000. Its useful life is indefinite. |

**Instructions**

Prepare all adjusting entries at December 31 to record amortization required by the events.

*Prepare entries to set up appropriate accounts for different intangibles; calculate amortization.*

(SO 7), **AN**

**E9-14** Kopke Company, organized in 2012, has these transactions related to intangible assets in that year:

| | | |
|---|---|---|
| Jan. | 2 | Purchased a patent (5-year life) $280,000. |
| Apr. | 1 | Goodwill acquired as a result of purchased business (indefinite life) $360,000. |
| July | 1 | Acquired a 9-year franchise; expiration date July 1, 2021, $540,000. |
| Sept. | 1 | Research and development costs $185,000. |

**Instructions**

(a) Prepare the necessary entries to record these transactions related to intangibles. All costs incurred were for cash.

(b) Make the entries as of December 31, 2012, recording any necessary amortization.

(c) Indicate what the balances should be on December 31, 2012.

*Discuss implications of amortization period.*

(SO 7), **C**

**E9-15** Alliance Atlantis Communications Inc. changed its accounting policy to amortize broadcast rights over the contracted exhibition period, which is based on the estimated useful life of the program. Previously, the company amortized broadcast rights over the lesser of 2 years or the contracted exhibition period.

**Instructions**

 Write a short memo to your client explaining the implications this has for the analysis of Alliance Atlantis's results.

*Answer questions on depreciation and intangibles.*

(SO 2, 7), **C**

**E9-16** The questions listed below are independent of one another.

**Instructions**

Provide a brief answer to each question.

(a) Why should a company depreciate its buildings?

(b) How can a company have a building that has a zero reported book value but substantial fair value?

(c) What are some examples of intangibles that you might find on your college campus?

(d) Give some examples of company or product trademarks or trade names. Are trade names and trademarks reported on a company's balance sheet?

*Determine net cash provided by operating activities.*

(SO 8), **AN**

**E9-17** Elmbrook Corporation reported net income of $58,000. Depreciation expense for the year was $132,000. The company calculates depreciation expense using the straight-line method, with a useful life of 10 years. Top management would like to switch to a 15-year useful life because depreciation expense would be reduced to $88,000. The CEO says, "Increasing the useful life would increase net income and net cash provided by operating activities."

### Instructions

Provide a comparative analysis showing net income and net cash provided by operating activities (ignoring other accrual adjustments) using a 10-year and a 15-year useful life. (Ignore income taxes.) Evaluate the CEO's suggestion.

*E9-18    Buckeye Bus Lines uses the units-of-activity method in depreciating its buses. One bus was purchased on January 1, 2012, at a cost of $100,000. Over its 4-year useful life, the bus is expected to be driven 160,000 miles. Salvage value is expected to be $8,000.

*Compute depreciation under units-of-activity method.*
(SO 9), AP

### Instructions

(a) Compute the depreciation cost per unit.
(b) Prepare a depreciation schedule assuming actual mileage was: 2012, 40,000; 2013, 52,000; 2014, 41,000; and 2015, 27,000.

*E9-19    Basic information relating to a new machine purchased by Deloise Company is presented in E9-5.

*Compute declining-balance and units-of-activity depreciation.*
(SO 9), AP

### Instructions

Using the facts presented in E9-5, compute depreciation using the following methods in the year indicated.
(a) Declining-balance using double the straight-line rate for 2012 and 2013.
(b) Units-of-activity for 2012, assuming machine usage was 3,900 hours. (Round depreciation per unit to the nearest cent.)

## Exercises: Set B and Challenge Exercises

Visit the book's companion website, at **www.wiley.com/college/kimmel**, and choose the Student Companion site to access Exercise Set B and Challenge Exercises.

## Problems: Set A

P9-1A    Irina Company was organized on January 1. During the first year of operations, the following plant asset expenditures and receipts were recorded in random order.

*Determine acquisition costs of land and building.*
(SO 1), C

#### Debits

| | |
|---|---|
| 1. Cost of real estate purchased as a plant site (land $255,000 and building $25,000) | $ 280,000 |
| 2. Installation cost of fences around property | 6,800 |
| 3. Cost of demolishing building to make land suitable for construction of new building | 31,000 |
| 4. Excavation costs for new building | 23,000 |
| 5. Accrued real estate taxes paid at time of purchase of real estate | 3,170 |
| 6. Cost of parking lots and driveways | 29,000 |
| 7. Architect's fees on building plans | 33,000 |
| 8. Real estate taxes paid for the current year on land | 6,400 |
| 9. Full payment to building contractor | 640,000 |
| | $1,052,370 |

#### Credits

| | |
|---|---|
| 10. Proceeds from salvage of demolished building | $   12,000 |

### Instructions

Analyze the transactions using the following table column headings. Enter the number of each transaction in the Item column, and enter the amounts in the appropriate columns. For amounts in the Other Accounts column, also indicate the account title.

| Item | Land | Buildings | Other Accounts |
|---|---|---|---|

*Land $302,170*

*Journalize equipment transactions related to purchase, sale, retirement, and depreciation.*

(SO 3, 5, 8), **AP**

**P9-2A** At December 31, 2012, Rivera Corporation reported the following plant assets.

| | | |
|---|---|---|
| Land | | $ 3,000,000 |
| Buildings | $26,500,000 | |
| Less: Accumulated depreciation—buildings | 11,925,000 | 14,575,000 |
| Equipment | 40,000,000 | |
| Less: Accumulated depreciation—equipment | 5,000,000 | 35,000,000 |
| Total plant assets | | $52,575,000 |

During 2013, the following selected cash transactions occurred.

Apr.  1  Purchased land for $2,200,000.
May  1  Sold equipment that cost $600,000 when purchased on January 1, 2006. The equipment was sold for $170,000.
June  1  Sold land for $1,600,000. The land cost $1,000,000.
July  1  Purchased equipment for $1,100,000.
Dec.  31  Retired equipment that cost $700,000 when purchased on December 31, 2003. No salvage value was received.

**Instructions**

(a) Journalize the transactions. (*Hint:* You may wish to set up T accounts, post beginning balances, and then post 2013 transactions.) Rivera uses straight-line depreciation for buildings and equipment. The buildings are estimated to have a 40-year useful life and no salvage value; the equipment is estimated to have a 10-year useful life and no salvage value. Update depreciation on assets disposed of at the time of sale or retirement.

(b) Record adjusting entries for depreciation for 2013.

(c) Tot. plant assets $50,037,500

(c) Prepare the plant assets section of Rivera's balance sheet at December 31, 2013.

*Journalize entries for disposal of plant assets.*

(SO 5), **AP**

**P9-3A** Presented here are selected transactions for Snow Company for 2012.

Jan.  1  Retired a piece of machinery that was purchased on January 1, 2002. The machine cost $71,000 on that date and had a useful life of 10 years with no salvage value.
June  30  Sold a computer that was purchased on January 1, 2009. The computer cost $30,000 and had a useful life of 5 years with no salvage value. The computer was sold for $12,000.
Dec.  31  Discarded a delivery truck that was purchased on January 1, 2007. The truck cost $33,400 and was depreciated based on an 8-year useful life with a $3,000 salvage value.

**Instructions**

Journalize all entries required on the above dates, including entries to update depreciation, where applicable, on assets disposed of. Snow Company uses straight-line depreciation. (Assume depreciation is up to date as of December 31, 2011.)

*Prepare entries to record transactions related to acquisition and amortization of intangibles; prepare the intangible assets section and note.*

(SO 7, 8), **AP**

**P9-4A** The intangible assets section of Cepeda Corporation's balance sheet at December 31, 2012, is presented here.

| | |
|---|---|
| Patents ($60,000 cost less $6,000 amortization) | $54,000 |
| Copyrights ($36,000 cost less $25,200 amortization) | 10,800 |
| Total | $64,800 |

The patent was acquired in January 2012 and has a useful life of 10 years. The copyright was acquired in January 2006 and also has a useful life of 10 years. The following cash transactions may have affected intangible assets during 2013.

Jan.  2  Paid $46,800 legal costs to successfully defend the patent against infringement by another company.
Jan.–June  Developed a new product, incurring $230,000 in research and development costs. A patent was granted for the product on July 1, and its useful life is equal to its legal life. Legal and other costs for the patent were $20,000.
Sept.  1  Paid $40,000 to a quarterback to appear in commercials advertising the company's products. The commercials will air in September and October.
Oct.  1  Acquired a copyright for $200,000. The copyright has a useful life and legal life of 50 years.

### Instructions

(a) Prepare journal entries to record the transactions.

(b) Prepare journal entries to record the 2013 amortization expense for intangible assets.

(c) Prepare the intangible assets section of the balance sheet at December 31, 2013.

(d) Prepare the note to the financial statements on Cepeda Corporation's intangible assets as of December 31, 2013.

*(c) Tot. intangibles   $315,300*

**P9-5A** Due to rapid employee turnover in the accounting department, the following transactions involving intangible assets were improperly recorded by Neitzke Corporation in 2012.

*Prepare entries to correct errors in recording and amortizing intangible assets.*
*(SO 7), AP*

1. Neitzke developed a new manufacturing process, incurring research and development costs of $160,000. The company also purchased a patent for $40,000. In early January, Neitzke capitalized $200,000 as the cost of the patents. Patent amortization expense of $10,000 was recorded based on a 20-year useful life.

2. On July 1, 2012, Neitzke purchased a small company and as a result acquired goodwill of $80,000. Neitzke recorded a half-year's amortization in 2012, based on a 20-year life ($2,000 amortization). The goodwill has an indefinite life.

### Instructions

Prepare all journal entries necessary to correct any errors made during 2012. Assume the books have not yet been closed for 2012.

**P9-6A** Phelan Corporation and Keevin Corporation, two companies of roughly the same size, are both involved in the manufacture of shoe-tracing devices. Each company depreciates its plant assets using the straight-line approach. An investigation of their financial statements reveals the information shown below.

*Calculate and comment on return on assets, profit margin, and asset turnover ratio.*
*(SO 6), AN*

|  | Phelan Corp. | Keevin Corp. |
|---|---|---|
| Net income | $ 240,000 | $ 300,000 |
| Sales | 1,150,000 | 1,200,000 |
| Total assets (average) | 3,200,000 | 3,000,000 |
| Plant assets (average) | 2,400,000 | 1,800,000 |
| Intangible assets (goodwill) | 300,000 | 0 |

### Instructions

(a) For each company, calculate these values:
   (1) Return on assets ratio.
   (2) Profit margin.
   (3) Asset turnover ratio.

(b) Based on your calculations in part (a), comment on the relative effectiveness of the two companies in using their assets to generate sales. What factors complicate your ability to compare the two companies?

**\*P9-7A** In recent years, Walz Company has purchased three machines. Because of frequent employee turnover in the accounting department, a different accountant was in charge of selecting the depreciation method for each machine, and various methods have been used. Information concerning the machines is summarized in the table below.

*Compute depreciation under different methods.*
*(SO 3, 9), AP*

| Machine | Acquired | Cost | Salvage Value | Useful Life (in years) | Depreciation Method |
|---|---|---|---|---|---|
| 1 | Jan. 1, 2010 | $96,000 | $12,000 | 8 | Straight-line |
| 2 | July 1, 2011 | 85,000 | 10,000 | 5 | Declining-balance |
| 3 | Nov. 1, 2011 | 66,000 | 6,000 | 6 | Units-of-activity |

For the declining-balance method, Walz Company uses the double-declining rate. For the units-of-activity method, total machine hours are expected to be 30,000. Actual hours of use in the first 3 years were: 2011, 800; 2012, 4,500; and 2013, 6,000.

### Instructions

(a) Compute the amount of accumulated depreciation on each machine at December 31, 2013.

*(a) Machine 2   $60,520*

(b) If machine 2 was purchased on April 1 instead of July 1, what would be the depreciation expense for this machine in 2011? In 2012?

*Compute depreciation under different methods.*
*(SO 3, 9),* **AP**

***P9-8A** Rogers Corporation purchased machinery on January 1, 2012, at a cost of $250,000. The estimated useful life of the machinery is 4 years, with an estimated salvage value at the end of that period of $30,000. The company is considering different depreciation methods that could be used for financial reporting purposes.

**Instructions**

(a) Double-declining-balance
expense 2014 $31,250

(a) Prepare separate depreciation schedules for the machinery using the straight-line method, and the declining-balance method using double the straight-line rate. Round to the nearest dollar.

(b) Which method would result in the higher reported 2012 income? In the highest total reported income over the 4-year period?

(c) Which method would result in the lower reported 2012 income? In the lowest total reported income over the 4-year period?

# Problems: Set B

*Determine acquisition costs of land and building.*
*(SO 1),* **C**

**P9-1B** Franz Company was organized on January 1. During the first year of operations, the following plant asset expenditures and receipts were recorded in random order.

**Debits**

| | |
|---|---:|
| 1. Cost of real estate purchased as a plant site (land $190,000 and building $80,000) | $ 270,000 |
| 2. Accrued real estate taxes paid at time of purchase of real estate | 6,000 |
| 3. Cost of demolishing building to make land suitable for construction of new building | 32,000 |
| 4. Cost of filling and grading the land | 6,700 |
| 5. Excavation costs for new building | 21,900 |
| 6. Architect's fees on building plans | 44,000 |
| 7. Full payment to building contractor | 629,500 |
| 8. Cost of parking lots and driveways | 36,000 |
| 9. Real estate taxes paid for the current year on land | 7,300 |
| | $1,053,400 |

**Credits**

| | |
|---|---:|
| 10. Proceeds for salvage of demolished building | $ 12,700 |

**Instructions**

Analyze the transactions using the table column headings provided here. Enter the number of each transaction in the Item column, and enter the amounts in the appropriate columns. For amounts in the Other Accounts column, also indicate the account titles.

Land $302,000

| **Item** | **Land** | **Buildings** | **Other Accounts** |
|---|---|---|---|

*Journalize equipment transactions related to purchase, sale, retirement, and depreciation.*
*(SO 3, 5, 8),* **AP**

**P9-2B** At December 31, 2011, Craig Corporation reported these plant assets.

| | | |
|---|---:|---:|
| Land | | $ 4,000,000 |
| Buildings | $28,800,000 | |
| Less: Accumulated depreciation—buildings | 11,520,000 | 17,280,000 |
| Equipment | 48,000,000 | |
| Less: Accumulated depreciation—equipment | 5,000,000 | 43,000,000 |
| Total plant assets | | $64,280,000 |

During 2012, the following selected cash transactions occurred.

| | | |
|---|---|---|
| Apr. | 1 | Purchased land for $2,600,000. |
| May | 1 | Sold equipment that cost $750,000 when purchased on January 1, 2007. The equipment was sold for $367,000. |
| June | 1 | Sold land purchased on June 1, 2000, for $1,800,000. The land cost $800,000. |
| Sept. | 1 | Purchased equipment for $840,000. |
| Dec. | 31 | Retired fully depreciated equipment that cost $470,000 when purchased on December 31, 2002. No salvage value was received. |

## Instructions

(a) Journalize the transactions. (*Hint:* You may wish to set up T accounts, post beginning balances, and then post 2012 transactions.) Craig uses straight-line depreciation for buildings and equipment. The buildings are estimated to have a 40-year life and no salvage value; the equipment is estimated to have a 10-year useful life and no salvage value. Update depreciation on assets disposed of at the time of sale or retirement.

(b) Record adjusting entries for depreciation for 2012. (*Note:* The only assets that are fully depreciated are those that were retired on December 31.)

(c) Prepare the plant assets section of Craig's balance sheet at December 31, 2012.

(c) Tot. plant assets  $61,072,000

**P9-3B**  Here are selected transactions for Halverson Corporation for 2012.

*Journalize entries for disposal of plant assets.*
*(SO 5),* **AP**

| | | |
|---|---|---|
| Jan. | 1 | Retired a piece of machinery that was purchased on January 1, 2002. The machine cost $47,000 and had a useful life of 10 years with no salvage value. |
| Mar. | 31 | Sold a computer that was purchased on January 1, 2009. The computer cost $43,400 and had a useful life of 7 years with no salvage value. The computer was sold for $25,000. |
| Dec. | 31 | Discarded a delivery truck that was purchased on January 1, 2009. The truck cost $30,000 and was depreciated based on a 6-year useful life with a $3,000 salvage value. |

## Instructions

Journalize all entries required on the above dates, including entries to update depreciation on assets disposed of, where applicable. Halverson Corporation uses straight-line depreciation.

**P9-4B**  The intangible assets section of the balance sheet for Vincent Company at December 31, 2012, is presented here.

*Prepare entries to record transactions related to acquisition and amortization of intangibles; prepare the intangible assets section and note.*
*(SO 7, 8),* **AP**

| | |
|---|---|
| Patents ($70,000 cost less $7,000 amortization) | $63,000 |
| Copyrights ($48,000 cost less $18,000 amortization) | 30,000 |
| Total | $93,000 |

The patent was acquired in January 2012 and has a useful life of 10 years. The copyright was acquired in January 2010 and also has a useful life of 8 years. The following cash transactions may have affected intangible assets during 2013.

| | | |
|---|---|---|
| Jan. | 2 | Paid $36,000 legal costs to successfully defend the patent against infringement by another company. |
| Jan.–June | | Developed a new product, incurring $220,000 in research and development costs. A patent was granted for the product on July 1, and its useful life is equal to its legal life. Legal and other costs for the patent were $18,000. |
| Sept. | 1 | Paid $110,000 to an extremely large defensive lineman to appear in commercials advertising the company's products. The commercials will air in September and October. |
| Oct. | 1 | Acquired a copyright for $120,000. The copyright has a useful life and legal life of 50 years. |

## Instructions

(a) Prepare journal entries to record the transactions.

(b) Prepare journal entries to record the 2013 amortization expense.

(c) Prepare the intangible assets section of the balance sheet at December 31, 2013.

(c) Tot. intangibles       $248,950

(d) Prepare the note to the financial statements on Vincent Company's intangible assets as of December 31, 2013.

**P9-5B**  Due to rapid employee turnover in the accounting department, the following transactions involving intangible assets were improperly recorded by the Demeyer Company in 2012.

*Prepare entries to correct errors in recording and amortizing intangible assets.*
*(SO 7),* **AP**

1. Demeyer developed a new manufacturing process, incurring research and development costs of $150,000. The company also purchased a patent for $96,000. In early January, Demeyer capitalized $246,000 as the cost of the patents. Patent amortization expense of $24,600 was recorded based on a 10-year useful life.

2. On July 1, 2012, Demeyer purchased a small company and as a result acquired goodwill of $40,000. Demeyer recorded a half-year's amortization in 2012, based on a 40-year life ($500 amortization). The goodwill has an indefinite life.

**Instructions**

Prepare all journal entries necessary to correct any errors made during 2012. Assume the books have not yet been closed for 2012.

*Calculate and comment on return on assets, profit margin, and asset turnover ratio.*

*(SO 6),* **AN**

**P9-6B**  Culver Corporation and Kiltie Corporation, two corporations of roughly the same size, are both involved in the manufacture of umbrellas. Each company depreciates its plant assets using the straight-line approach. An investigation of their financial statements reveals the following information.

|  | **Culver Corp.** | **Kiltie Corp.** |
|---|---|---|
| Net income | $ 780,000 | $ 900,000 |
| Sales | 2,400,000 | 2,500,000 |
| Total assets (average) | 3,000,000 | 2,700,000 |
| Plant assets (average) | 1,400,000 | 1,200,000 |
| Intangible assets (goodwill) | 480,000 | 0 |

**Instructions**

(a) For each company, calculate these values:
  (1) Return on assets ratio.
  (2) Profit margin.
  (3) Asset turnover ratio.
(b) ▭▭▭▭▷ Based on your calculations in part (a), comment on the relative effectiveness of the two companies in using their assets to generate sales. What factors complicate your ability to compare the two companies?

*Compute depreciation under different methods.*

*(SO 3, 9),* **AP**

**\*P9-7B**  In recent years, Harper Transportation purchased three used buses. Because of frequent employee turnover in the accounting department, a different accountant selected the depreciation method for each bus, and various methods have been used. Information concerning the buses is summarized in the table below.

| Bus | Acquired | Cost | Salvage Value | Useful Life (in years) | Depreciation Method |
|---|---|---|---|---|---|
| 1 | Jan. 1, 2011 | $ 96,000 | $ 6,000 | 5 | Straight-line |
| 2 | Jan. 1, 2011 | 135,000 | 10,000 | 4 | Declining-balance |
| 3 | Jan. 1, 2011 | 100,000 | 4,000 | 5 | Units-of-activity |

For the declining-balance method, Harper Transportation uses the double-declining rate. For the units-of-activity method, total miles are expected to be 160,000. Actual miles of use in the first 3 years were: 2011, 29,000; 2012, 34,000; and 2013, 35,000.

**Instructions**

(a) Bus 1 $54,000

(a) Compute the amount of accumulated depreciation on each bus at December 31, 2013.
(b) If Bus 2 was purchased on March 1 instead of January 1, what would be the depreciation expense for this bus in 2011? In 2012?

*Compute depreciation under different methods.*

*(SO 3, 9),* **AP**

**\*P9-8B**  Kiram Corporation purchased machinery on January 1, 2012, at a cost of $350,000. The estimated useful life of the machinery is 5 years, with an estimated salvage value at the end of that period of $20,000. The company is considering different depreciation methods that could be used for financial reporting purposes.

(a) Double-declining-balance exp. 2013  $84,000

**Instructions**

(a) Prepare separate depreciation schedules for the machinery using the straight-line method, and the declining-balance method using double the straight-line rate.
(b) Which method would result in the higher reported 2012 income? In the higher total reported income over the 5-year period?
(c) Which method would result in the lower reported 2012 income? In the lower total reported income over the 5-year period?

# Problems: Set C

Visit the book's companion website, at **www.wiley.com/college/kimmel**, and choose the Student Companion site to access Problem Set C.

# Comprehensive Problem

**CP9**  Paulson Corporation's unadjusted trial balance at December 1, 2012, is presented below.

|  | Debit | Credit |
|---|---|---|
| Cash | $ 22,000 | |
| Accounts Receivable | 36,800 | |
| Notes Receivable | 10,000 | |
| Interest Receivable | –0– | |
| Inventory | 36,200 | |
| Prepaid Insurance | 3,600 | |
| Land | 20,000 | |
| Buildings | 150,000 | |
| Equipment | 60,000 | |
| Patent | 9,000 | |
| Allowance for Doubtful Accounts | | $ 500 |
| Accumulated Depreciation—Buildings | | 50,000 |
| Accumulated Depreciation—Equipment | | 24,000 |
| Accounts Payable | | 27,300 |
| Salaries and Wages Payable | | –0– |
| Notes Payable (due April 30, 2013) | | 11,000 |
| Interest Payable | | –0– |
| Notes Payable (due in 2018) | | 35,000 |
| Common Stock | | 50,000 |
| Retained Earnings | | 63,600 |
| Dividends | 12,000 | |
| Sales Revenue | | 900,000 |
| Interest Revenue | | –0– |
| Gain on Disposal of Plant Assets | | –0– |
| Bad Debts Expense | –0– | |
| Cost of Goods Sold | 630,000 | |
| Depreciation Expense | –0– | |
| Insurance Expense | –0– | |
| Interest Expense | –0– | |
| Other Operating Expenses | 61,800 | |
| Amortization Expense | –0– | |
| Salaries and Wages Expense | 110,000 | |
| Total | $1,161,400 | $1,161,400 |

The following transactions occurred during December.

Dec.  2  Paulson purchased equipment for $16,000, plus sales taxes of $800 (all paid in cash).

2  Paulson sold for $3,500 equipment which originally cost $5,000. Accumulated depreciation on this equipment at January 1, 2012, was $1,800; 2012 depreciation prior to the sale of equipment was $450.

15  Paulson sold for $5,000 on account inventory that cost $3,500.

23  Salaries and wages of $6,600 were paid.

Adjustment data:

1. Paulson estimates that uncollectible accounts receivable at year-end are $4,000.
2. The note receivable is a one-year, 8% note dated April 1, 2012. No interest has been recorded.
3. The balance in prepaid insurance represents payment of a $3,600, 6-month premium on September 1, 2012.
4. The building is being depreciated using the straight-line method over 30 years. The salvage value is $30,000.
5. The equipment owned prior to this year is being depreciated using the straight-line method over 5 years. The salvage value is 10% of cost.
6. The equipment purchased on December 2, 2012, is being depreciated using the straight-line method over 5 years, with a salvage value of $1,800.

7. The patent was acquired on January 1, 2012, and has a useful life of 9 years from that date.
8. Unpaid salaries at December 31, 2012, total $2,200.
9. Both the short-term and long-term notes payable are dated January 1, 2012, and carry a 10% interest rate. All interest is payable in the next 12 months.
10. Income tax expense was $15,000. It was unpaid at December 31.

**Instructions**

(b) Totals $1,205,400

(c) Net income $51,150

(d) Total assets $247,850

(a) Prepare journal entries for the transactions listed above and adjusting entries.
(b) Prepare an adjusted trial balance at December 31, 2012.
(c) Prepare a 2012 income statement and a 2012 retained earnings statement.
(d) Prepare a December 31, 2012, balance sheet.

# Continuing Cookie Chronicle

(*Note:* This is a continuation of the Cookie Chronicle from Chapters 1 through 8.)

**CCC9**

**Part 1**    Now that she is selling mixers and her customers can use credit cards to pay for them, Natalie is thinking of upgrading her website so that she can sell mixers online, to broaden her range of customers. She will need to known how to account for the costs of upgrading the site.

**Part 2**    Natalie is also thinking of buying a van that will be used only for business. Natalie is concerned about the impact of the van's cost on her income statement and balance sheet. She has come to you for advice on calculating the van's depreciation.

> Go to the book's companion website, at **www.wiley.com/college/kimmel**, to see the completion of this problem.

# broadening your perspective

# Financial Reporting and Analysis

**FINANCIAL REPORTING PROBLEM:** *Tootsie Roll Industries, Inc.*

**BYP9-1**    Refer to the financial statements and the Notes to Consolidated Financial Statements of Tootsie Roll Industries in Appendix A.

**Instructions**

Answer the following questions.

(a) What were the total cost and book value of property, plant, and equipment at December 31, 2009?
(b) What method or methods of depreciation are used by Tootsie Roll for financial reporting purposes?
(c) What was the amount of depreciation and amortization expense for each of the 3 years 2007–2009? (*Hint:* Use the statement of cash flows.)
(d) Using the statement of cash flows, what are the amounts of property, plant, and equipment purchased (capital expenditures) in 2009 and 2008?
(e) Explain how Tootsie Roll accounted for its intangible assets in 2009.

**COMPARATIVE ANALYSIS PROBLEM:** *Tootsie Roll vs. Hershey*

**BYP9-2**    The financial statements of The Hershey Company are presented in Appendix B, following the financial statements for Tootsie Roll Industries in Appendix A.

**Instructions**

(a) Based on the information in these financial statements and the accompanying notes and schedules, compute the following values for each company in 2009.
   (1) Return on assets ratio.
   (2) Profit margin (use "Total Revenue").
   (3) Asset turnover ratio.
(b) What conclusions concerning the management of plant assets can be drawn from these data?

## RESEARCH CASE

**BYP9-3** The September 9, 2007, issue of the *New York Times* includes an article by Denise Caruso entitled "When Balance Sheets Collide with the New Economy."

*Instructions*
Read the article and answer the following questions.
(a) What are some examples of "valuable assets" that the article says currently do not have a home on the balance sheet?
(b) What examples does the company give of the value of reputation and how it can affect a stock price?
(c) What justification does the article give for having companies report on their environmental and social responsibility, and their strategy for dealing with disasters?
(d) Are any initiatives currently being used that try to account for intangible assets that do not currently show up on the balance sheet?

## INTERPRETING FINANCIAL STATEMENTS

**BYP9-4** Bob Evans Farms, Inc. operates 714 restaurants in 31 states and produces fresh and fully cooked sausage products, fresh salads, and related products distributed to grocery stores in the Midwest, Southwest, and Southeast. For a recent 3-year period, Bob Evans Farms reported the following selected income statement data (in millions of dollars).

|  | 2009 | 2008 | 2007 |
|---|---|---|---|
| Sales | $1,750.5 | $1,737.0 | $1,654.5 |
| Cost of goods sold | 537.1 | 517.4 | 482.1 |
| Net income | 62.9* | 64.9 | 60.5 |
| Total assets | 1,147.6 | 1,207.0 | 1,197.9 |

*In 2009, the company wrote off $68.0 million of goodwill and reported a net loss of $5.1 million. Since no similar write-offs occurred in 2007 or 2008, we are using income before the write-off as net income.

*Instructions*
(a) Compute the percentage change in sales and in net income from 2007 to 2009.
(b) What contribution, if any, did the company's gross profit rate make to the change in earnings from 2007 to 2009?
(c) What was Bob Evans's profit margin ratio in each of the 3 years? Comment on any trend in this percentage.
(d) The chief executive officer's letter stated that the company slowed its expansion, opening 1 new restaurant in 2009 and 2 in 2008, compared to 10 openings in 2007. What effect would you expect this change, along with the write-off of goodwill in 2009, to have on return on assets? Calculate the company's return on assets for 2008 and 2009 to support your answer.

## FINANCIAL ANALYSIS ON THE WEB

**BYP9-5** *Purpose:* Use an annual report to identify a company's plant assets and the depreciation method used.

*Address:* **www.annualreports.com**, or go to **www.wiley.com/college/kimmel**

*Steps*
1. Select a particular company.
2. Search by company name.
3. Follow instructions below.

*Instructions*
Answer the following questions.
(a) What is the name of the company?
(b) What is the Internet address of the annual report?
(c) At fiscal year-end, what is the net amount of its plant assets?
(d) What is the accumulated depreciation?
(e) Which method of depreciation does the company use?

# Critical Thinking

## DECISION MAKING ACROSS THE ORGANIZATION

**BYP9-6** Delzer Furniture Corp. is nationally recognized for making high-quality products. Management is concerned that it is not fully exploiting its brand power. Delzer's production managers are also concerned because their plants are not operating at anywhere near full capacity. Management is currently considering a proposal to offer a new line of affordable furniture.

Those in favor of the proposal (including the vice president of production) believe that, by offering these new products, the company could attract a clientele that it is not currently servicing. Also, it could operate its plants at full capacity, thus taking better advantage of its assets.

The vice president of marketing, however, believes that the lower-priced (and lower-margin) product would have a negative impact on the sales of existing products. The vice president believes that $10,000,000 of the sales of the new product will be from customers that would have purchased the more expensive product but switched to the lower-margin product because it was available. (This is often referred to as cannibalization of existing sales.) Top management feels, however, that even with cannibalization, the company's sales will increase and the company will be better off.

The following data are available.

| (in thousands) | Current Results | Proposed Results without Cannibalization | Proposed Results with Cannibalization |
|---|---|---|---|
| Sales | $45,000 | $60,000 | $50,000 |
| Net income | $12,000 | $13,500 | $12,000 |
| Average total assets | $100,000 | $100,000 | $100,000 |

***Instructions***

(a) Compute Delzer's return on assets ratio, profit margin ratio, and asset turnover ratio, both with and without the new product line.
(b) Discuss the implications that your findings in part (a) have for Delzer's decision.
(c) Are there any other options that Delzer should consider? What impact would each of these have on the above ratios?

## COMMUNICATION ACTIVITY

**BYP9-7** The chapter presented some concerns regarding the current accounting standards for research and development expenditures.

***Instructions***

Assume that you are either (a) the president of a company that is very dependent on ongoing research and development, writing a memo to the FASB complaining about the current accounting standards regarding research and development, or (b) the FASB member defending the current standards regarding research and development. Your memo should address the following questions.

1. By requiring expensing of R&D, do you think companies will spend less on R&D? Why or why not? What are the possible implications for the competitiveness of U.S. companies?
2. If a company makes a commitment to spend money for R&D, it must believe it has future benefits. Shouldn't these costs therefore be capitalized just like the purchase of any long-lived asset that you believe will have future benefits?

## ETHICS CASE

**BYP9-8** Clean Air Anti-Pollution Company is suffering declining sales of its principal product, nonbiodegradable plastic cartons. The president, Dixon Nuber, instructs his controller, Gavin Wood, to lengthen asset lives to reduce depreciation expense. A processing line of automated plastic extruding equipment, purchased for $3.5 million in January 2011, was originally estimated to have a useful life of 8 years and a salvage value of $400,000. Depreciation has been recorded for 2 years on that basis. Dixon wants the estimated life changed to 12 years total and the straight-line method continued. Gavin is hesitant to make the change, believing it is unethical to increase net income in this manner. Dixon says, "Hey, the life is only an estimate, and I've heard that our competition uses a 12-year life on their production equipment."

***Instructions***

(a) Who are the stakeholders in this situation?
(b) Is the proposed change in asset life unethical, or is it simply a good business practice by an astute president?
(c) What is the effect of Dixon's proposed change on income before taxes in the year of change?

## "ALL ABOUT YOU" ACTIVITY

**BYP9-9** A company's tradename is a very important asset to the company, as it creates immediate product identification. Companies invest substantial sums to ensure that their product is well-known to the consumer. Test your knowledge of who owns some famous brands and their impact on the financial statements.

*Instructions*
(a) Provide an answer to the five multiple-choice questions below.
  (1) Which company owns both Taco Bell and Pizza Hut?
      (a) McDonald's.          (c) Yum Brands.
      (b) CKE.                 (d) Wendy's.
  (2) Dairy Queen belongs to:
      (a) Breyer.              (c) GE.
      (b) Berkshire Hathaway.  (d) The Coca-Cola Company.
  (3) Phillip Morris, the cigarette maker, is owned by:
      (a) Altria.              (c) Boeing.
      (b) GE.                  (d) ExxonMobil.
  (4) AOL, a major Internet provider, belongs to:
      (a) Microsoft.           (c) NBC.
      (b) Cisco.               (d) Time Warner.
  (5) ESPN, the sports broadcasting network, is owned by:
      (a) Procter & Gamble.    (c) Walt Disney.
      (b) Altria.              (d) The Coca-Cola Company.
(b) How do you think the value of these brands is reported on the appropriate company's balance sheet?

## FASB CODIFICATION ACTIVITY

**BYP9-10** If your school has a subscription to the FASB Codification, go to **http://aaahq.org/ascLogin.cfm** to log in and prepare responses to the following.
(a) What does it mean to capitalize an item?
(b) What is the definition provided for an intangible asset?
(c) Your great-uncle, who is a CPA, is impressed that you are taking an accounting class. Based on his experience, he believes that depreciation is something that companies do based on past practice, not on the basis of authoritative guidance. Provide the authoritative literature to support the practice of fixed-asset depreciation.

### Answers to Insight and Accounting Across the Organization Questions

**p. 452 Many U.S. Firms Use Leases Q:** Why might airline managers choose to lease rather than purchase their planes? **A:** The reasons for leasing include favorable tax treatment, better financing options, increased flexibility, reduced risk of obsolescence, and low airline income.

**p. 465 Marketing ROI as Profit Indicator Q:** How does measuring marketing ROI support the overall efforts of the organization? **A:** Top management is ultimately concerned about maximizing the company's return on assets. Holding marketing managers accountable for the marketing ROI will contribute to the company's overall goal of maximizing return on assets.

**p. 471 Should Companies Write Up Goodwill? Q:** Do you think that this treatment would be allowed under U.S. GAAP? **A:** The write-down of assets would have been allowed if it could be shown that the assets had declined in value (an impairment). However, the creation of goodwill to offset the write-down would not have been allowed. Goodwill can be recorded only when it results from the acquisition of a business. It cannot be recorded as the result of being created internally.

### Answers to Self-Test Questions

**1.** d ($24,000 + $1,200 + $200 + $400)  **2.** a  **3.** b  **4.** d (($400,000 − $10,000) ÷ 5) × 2  **5.** c
**6.** b  **7.** d (($60,000 − $12,000) ÷ 10) × 2 = $9,600; ($60,000 − $9,600 − $2,000) ÷ 4  **8.** d
**9.** a (($80,000 − 0) ÷ 10) × 4.5 = $36,000; ($26,000 − ($80,000 − $36,000))  **10.** d  **11.** c
$180,000 ÷ (($200,000 + $300,000) ÷ 2)  **12.** b ($20,000 + $15,000)  **13.** c  **14.** c  **15.** d
*****16.** d

 **A Look at IFRS**

IFRS related to property, plant, and equipment is found in *IAS 16* ("Property, Plant and Equipment") and *IAS 23* ("Borrowing Costs"). IFRS follows most of the same principles as GAAP in the accounting for property, plant, and equipment. There are, however, some significant differences in the implementation: IFRS allows the use of revaluation of property, plant, and equipment, and it also requires the use of component depreciation. In addition, there are some significant differences in the accounting for both intangible assets and impairments. IFRS related to intangible assets is presented in *IAS 38* ("Intangible Assets"). IFRS related to impairments is found in *IAS 36* ("Impairment of Assets").

## KEY POINTS

- The definition for plant assets for both IFRS and GAAP is essentially the same.
- Both international standards and GAAP follow the cost principle when accounting for property, plant, and equipment at date of acquisition. Cost consists of all expenditures necessary to acquire the asset and make it ready for its intended use.
- Under both IFRS and GAAP, interest costs incurred during construction are capitalized. Recently, IFRS converged to GAAP requirements in this area.
- IFRS, like GAAP, capitalizes all direct costs in self-constructed assets such as raw materials and labor. IFRS does not address the capitalization of fixed overhead, although in practice these costs are generally capitalized.
- IFRS also views depreciation as an allocation of cost over an asset's useful life. IFRS permits the same depreciation methods (e.g., straight-line, accelerated, and units-of-activity) as GAAP. However, a major difference is that IFRS requires component depreciation. *Component depreciation* specifies that any significant parts of a depreciable asset that have different estimated useful lives should be separately depreciated. Component depreciation is allowed under GAAP but is seldom used.

  To illustrate, assume that Lexure Construction builds an office building for $4,000,000, not including the cost of the land. If the $4,000,000 is allocated over the 40-year useful life of the building, Lexure reports $100,000 of depreciation per year, assuming straight-line depreciation and no disposal value. However, assume that $320,000 of the cost of the building relates to personal property and $600,000 relates to land improvements. The personal property has a depreciable life of 5 years, and the land improvements have a depreciable life of 10 years. In accordance with IFRS, Lexure must use component depreciation. It must reclassify $320,000 of the cost of the building to personal property and $600,000 to the cost of land improvements. Assuming that Lexure uses straight-line depreciation, component depreciation for the first year of the office building is computed as follows.

| | |
|---|---:|
| Building cost adjusted ($4,000,000 − $320,000 − $600,000) | $3,080,000 |
| Building cost depreciation per year ($3,080,000/40) | $ 77,000 |
| Personal property depreciation ($320,000/5) | 64,000 |
| Land improvements depreciation ($600,000/10) | 60,000 |
| Total component depreciation in first year | $ 201,000 |

- IFRS uses the term *residual value*, rather than salvage value, to refer to an owner's estimate of an asset's value at the end of its useful life for that owner.
- IFRS allows companies to revalue plant assets to fair value at the reporting date. Companies that choose to use the revaluation framework must follow revaluation procedures. If revaluation is used, it must be applied to all assets in a class of assets. Assets that are experiencing rapid price changes must be revalued on an annual basis, otherwise less frequent revaluation is acceptable.

  To illustrate asset revaluation accounting, assume that Pernice Company applies revaluation to plant assets with a carrying value of $1,000,000, a useful life of 5 years, and no residual value. Pernice makes the following journal entries in year 1, assuming straight-line depreciation.

| | | |
|---|---:|---:|
| Depreciation Expense | 200,000 | |
| Accumulated Depreciation—Plant Assets | | 200,000 |
| (To record depreciation expense in year 1) | | |

After this entry, Pernice's plant assets have a carrying amount of $800,000 ($1,000,000 − $200,000). At the end of year 1, independent appraisers determine that the asset has a fair value of $850,000. To report the plant assets at fair value, or $850,000, Pernice eliminates the Accumulated Depreciation—Plant Assets account, reduces Plant Assets to its fair value of $850,000, and records Revaluation Surplus of $50,000. The entry to record the revaluation is as follows.

| | | |
|---|---|---|
| Accumulated Depreciation—Plant Assets | 200,000 | |
|     Plant Assets | | 150,000 |
|     Revaluation Surplus | | 50,000 |
|     (To record adjusting the plant assets to fair value) | | |

Thus, Pernice follows a two-step process. First, Pernice records depreciation based on the cost basis of $1,000,000. As a result, it reports depreciation expense of $200,000 on the income statement. Second, it records the revaluation. It does this by eliminating any accumulated depreciation, adjusting the recorded value of the plant assets to fair value, and debiting or crediting the Revaluation Surplus account. In this example, the revaluation surplus is $50,000, which is the difference between the fair value of $850,000 and the book value of $800,000. Revaluation surplus is an example of an item reported as other comprehensive income, as discussed in the *A Look at IFRS* section of Chapter 5: Pernice now reports the following information in its statement of financial position at the end of year 1.

| | |
|---|---|
| Plant assets ($1,000,000 − $150,000) | $850,000 |
| Accumulated depreciation—plant assets | 0 |
| | $850,000 |
| Revaluation surplus (equity) | $ 50,000 |

As indicated, $850,000 is the new basis of the asset. Pernice reports depreciation expense of $200,000 in the income statement and $50,000 in other comprehensive income. Assuming no change in the total useful life, depreciation in year 2 will be $212,500 ($850,000 ÷ 4).

- Under both GAAP and IFRS, changes in the depreciation method used and changes in useful life are handled in current and future periods. Prior periods are not affected. GAAP recently conformed to international standards in the accounting for changes in depreciation methods.
- The accounting for subsequent expenditures, such as ordinary repairs and additions, are essentially the same under IFRS and GAAP.
- The accounting for plant asset disposals is essentially the same under IFRS and GAAP.
- Initial costs to acquire natural resources are essentially the same under IFRS and GAAP.
- The definition of intangible assets is essentially the same under IFRS and GAAP.
- Intangibles generally arise when a company buys another company. In this case, specific criteria are needed to separate goodwill from other intangibles. Both GAAP and IFRS follow the same approach to make this separation, that is, companies recognize an intangible asset separately from goodwill if the intangible represents contractual or legal rights or is capable of being separated or divided and sold, transferred, licensed, rented, or exchanged. In addition, under both GAAP and IFRS, companies recognize acquired in-process research and development (IPR&D) as a separate intangible asset if it meets the definition of an intangible asset and its fair value can be measured reliably.
- As in GAAP, under IFRS the costs associated with research and development are segregated into the two components. Costs in the research phase are always expensed under both IFRS and GAAP. Under IFRS, however, costs in the development phase are capitalized as Development Costs once technological feasibility is achieved.

To illustrate, assume that Laser Scanner Company spent $1 million on research and $2 million on development of new products. Of the $2 million in development costs, $500,000 was incurred prior to technological feasibility and $1,500,000 was incurred after technological feasibility had been demonstrated. The company would record these costs as follows.

| | | |
|---|---|---|
| Research Expense | 1,000,000 | |
| Development Expense | 500,000 | |
| Development Costs | 1,500,000 | |
|     Cash | | 3,000,000 |
|     (To record research and development costs) | | |

- IFRS permits revaluation of intangible assets (except for goodwill). GAAP prohibits revaluation of intangible assets.
- IFRS requires an impairment test at each reporting date for plant assets and intangibles and records an impairment if the asset's carrying amount exceeds its recoverable amount. The recoverable amount is the higher of the asset's fair value less costs to sell or its value-in-use. Value-in-use is the future cash flows to be derived from the particular asset, discounted to present value. Under GAAP, impairment loss is measured as the excess of the carrying amount over the asset's fair value.
- IFRS allows reversal of impairment losses when there has been a change in economic conditions or in the expected use of the asset. Under GAAP, impairment losses cannot be reversed for assets to be held and used; the impairment loss results in a new cost basis for the asset. IFRS and GAAP are similar in the accounting for impairments of assets held for disposal.
- The accounting for exchanges of nonmonetary assets has recently converged between IFRS and GAAP. GAAP now requires that gains on exchanges of nonmonetary assets be recognized if the exchange has commercial substance. This is the same framework used in IFRS.

## LOOKING TO THE FUTURE

With respect to revaluations, as part of the conceptual framework project, the Boards will examine the measurement bases used in accounting. It is too early to say whether a converged conceptual framework will recommend fair value measurement (and revaluation accounting) for plant assets and intangibles. However, this is likely to be one of the more contentious issues, given the long-standing use of historical cost as a measurement basis in GAAP.

The IASB and FASB have identified a project that would consider expanded recognition of internally generated intangible assets. IFRS permits more recognition of intangibles compared to GAAP. Thus, it will be challenging to develop converged standards for intangible assets, given the long-standing prohibition on capitalizing internally generated intangible assets and research and development costs in GAAP.

### IFRS Self-Test Questions

1. Which of the following statements is *correct*?
   (a) Both IFRS and GAAP permit revaluation of property, plant, and equipment and intangible assets (except for goodwill).
   (b) IFRS permits revaluation of property, plant, and equipment and intangible assets (except for goodwill).
   (c) Both IFRS and GAAP permit revaluation of property, plant, and equipment but not intangible assets.
   (d) GAAP permits revaluation of property, plant, and equipment but not intangible assets.
2. International Company has land that cost $450,000 but now has a fair value of $600,000. International Company decides to use the revaluation method specified in IFRS to account for the land. Which of the following statements is *correct*?
   (a) International Company must continue to report the land at $450,000.
   (b) International Company would report a net income increase of $150,000 due to an increase in the value of the land.
   (c) International Company would debit Revaluation Surplus for $150,000.
   (d) International Company would credit Revaluation Surplus by $150,000.
3. Francisco Corporation is constructing a new building at a total initial cost of $10,000,000. The building is expected to have a useful live of 50 years with no residual value. The building's finished surfaces (e.g., roof cover and floor cover) are 5% of this cost and have a useful life of 20 years. Building services systems (e.g., electric, heating, and plumbing) are 20% of the cost and have a useful life of 25 years. The depreciation in the first year using component depreciation, assuming straight-line depreciation with no residual value, is:
   (a) $200,000.        (c) $255,000.
   (b) $215,000.        (d) None of the above.
4. Research and development costs are:
   (a) expensed under GAAP.
   (b) expensed under IFRS.
   (c) expensed under both GAAP and IFRS.
   (d) None of the above.

**5.** Under IFRS, value-in-use is defined as:
   (a) net realizable value.
   (b) fair value.
   (c) future cash flows discounted to present value.
   (d) total future undiscounted cash flows.

## IFRS Concepts and Application

**IFRS9–1**   What is component depreciation, and when must it be used?

**IFRS9–2**   What is revaluation of plant assets? When should revaluation be applied?

**IFRS9–3**   Some product development expenditures are recorded as development expenses and others as development costs. Explain the difference between these accounts and how a company decides which classification is appropriate.

**IFRS9–4**   Mandall Company constructed a warehouse for $280,000. Mandall estimates that the warehouse has a useful life of 20 years and no residual value. Construction records indicate that $40,000 of the cost of the warehouse relates to its heating, ventilation, and air conditioning (HVAC) system, which has an estimated useful life of only 10 years. Compute the first year of depreciation expense using straight-line component depreciation.

**IFRS9–5**   At the end of its first year of operations, Brianna Company chose to use the revaluation framework allowed under IFRS. Brianna's ledger shows Plant Assets $480,000 and Accumulated Depreciation—Plant Assets $60,000. Prepare journal entries to record the following.
   (a) Independent appraisers determine that the plant assets have a fair value of $460,000.
   (b) Independent appraisers determine that the plant assets have a fair value of $400,000.

**IFRS9–6**   Newell Industries spent $300,000 on research and $600,000 on development of a new product. Of the $600,000 in development costs, $400,000 was incurred prior to technological feasibility and $200,000 after technological feasibility had been demonstrated. Prepare the journal entry to record research and development costs.

## INTERNATIONAL FINANCIAL STATEMENT ANALYSIS: *Zetar plc*

**IFRS9–7**   The financial statements of Zetar plc are presented in Appendix C.

### Instructions
Use the company's annual report, available at **www.zetarplc.com**, to answer the following questions.
   (a) According to the notes to the financial statements, what method or methods does the company use to depreciate "plant and equipment?" What rate does it use to depreciate plant and equipment?
   (b) According to the notes to the financial statements, how often is goodwill tested for impairment?
   (c) Using the notes to the financial statements, as well as information from the statement of cash flows, prepare the journal entry to record the disposal of property, plant and equipment during 2009. (Round your amounts to the nearest thousand.)

## Answers to IFRS Self-Test Questions
**1.** b   **2.** d   **3.** c (($10,000,000 × .05)/20) + (($10,000,000 × .20)/25) + (($10,000,000 × .75)/50)
**4.** a   **5.** c

✓ Remember to go back to the navigator box on the chapter opening page and check off your completed work.

# chapter 10

# REPORTING AND ANALYZING LIABILITIES

## ✓ the navigator

- Scan **Study Objectives** ○
- Read **Feature Story** ○
- Scan **Preview** ○
- Read **Text and Answer** **Do it!**
  p. 509 ○  p. 512 ○  p. 515 ○
  p. 520 ○  p. 521 ○
- Work **Using the Decision Toolkit** ○
- Review **Summary of Study Objectives** ○
- Work **Comprehensive** **Do it!** p. 539 ○
- Answer **Self-Test Questions** ○
- Complete **Assignments** ○
- Go to **WileyPLUS** for practice and tutorials ○
- 🌐 Read **A Look at IFRS** p. 564 ○

## study objectives

**After studying this chapter, you should be able to:**

1 Explain a current liability and identify the major types of current liabilities.

2 Describe the accounting for notes payable.

3 Explain the accounting for other current liabilities.

4 Identify the types of bonds.

5 Prepare the entries for the issuance of bonds and interest expense.

6 Describe the entries when bonds are redeemed.

7 Identify the requirements for the financial statement presentation and analysis of liabilities.

✓ the navigator

Debt can help a company acquire the things it needs to grow, but it is often the very thing that kills a company. A brief history of Maxwell Car Company illustrates the role of debt in the U.S. auto industry. In 1920, Maxwell Car Company was on the brink of financial ruin. Because it was unable to pay its bills, its creditors stepped in and took over. They hired a former General Motors executive named Walter Chrysler to reorganize the company. By 1925, he had taken over the company and renamed it Chrysler. By 1933, Chrysler was booming, with sales surpassing even those of Ford.

But the next few decades saw Chrysler make a series of blunders. By 1980, with its creditors pounding at the gates, Chrysler was again on the brink of financial ruin.

At that point, Chrysler brought in a former Ford executive named Lee Iacocca to save the company. Iacocca argued that the United States could not afford to let Chrysler fail because of the loss of jobs. He convinced the federal government to grant loan guarantees—promises that if Chrysler failed to pay its creditors, the government would pay them. Iacocca then

# AND THEN THERE WERE TWO

streamlined operations and brought out some profitable products. Chrysler repaid all of its government-guaranteed loans by 1983, seven years ahead of the scheduled final payment.

To compete in today's global vehicle market, you must be big—really big. So in 1998, Chrysler merged with German automaker Daimler-Benz, to form DaimlerChrysler. For a time, this left just two U.S.-based auto manufacturers—General Motors and Ford. But in 2007, DaimlerChrysler sold 81% of Chrysler to Cerberus, an investment group, to provide much-needed cash infusions to the automaker. In 2009, Daimler turned over its remaining stake to Cerberus. Three days later, Chrysler filed for bankruptcy. But by 2010, it was beginning to show signs of a turnaround.

These companies are giants. General Motors and Ford typically rank among the top five U.S. firms in total assets. But General Motors and Ford have accumulated a truckload of debt on their way to getting this big. Although debt has made it possible to get so big, the Chrysler story makes it clear that debt can also threaten a company's survival.

the navigator

## INSIDE CHAPTER 10 . . .

The Feature Story suggests that General Motors and Ford have tremendous amounts of debt. It is unlikely that they could have grown so large without this debt, but at times the debt threatens their very existence. Given this risk, why do companies borrow money? Why do they sometimes borrow short-term and other times long-term? Besides bank borrowings, what other kinds of debts do companies incur? In this chapter, we address these issues.

The content and organization of the chapter are as follows.

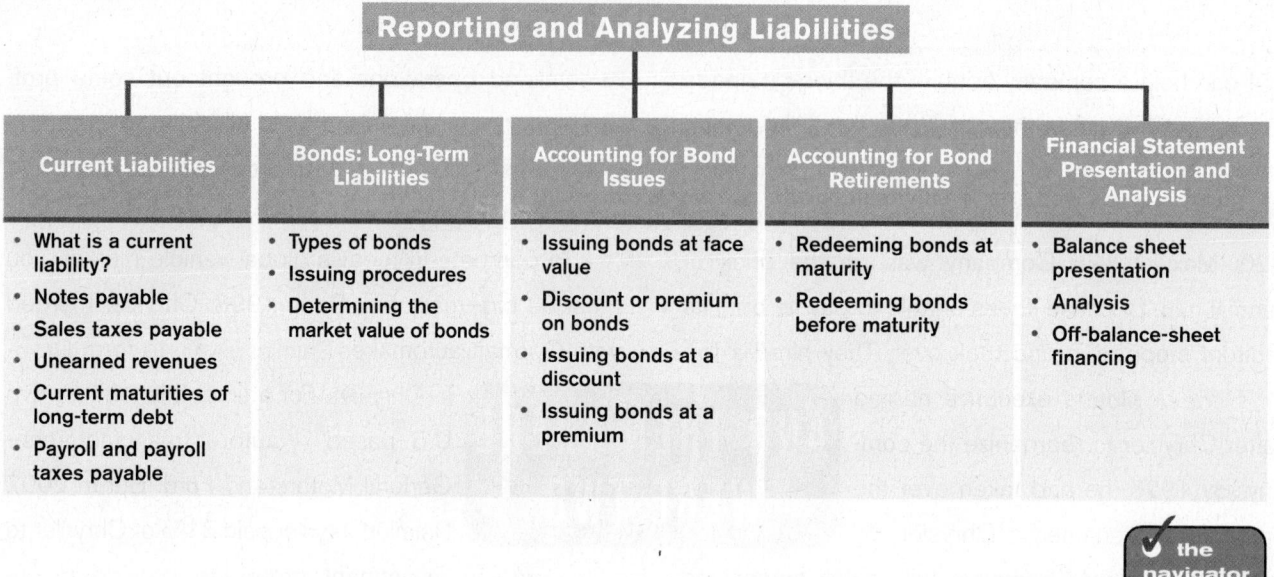

## Current Liabilities

### WHAT IS A CURRENT LIABILITY?

**study objective** 1

Explain a current liability and identify the major types of current liabilities.

You have learned that liabilities are defined as "creditors' claims on total assets" and as "existing debts and obligations." Companies must settle or pay these claims, debts, and obligations at some time in the future by transferring assets or services. The future date on which they are due or payable (the maturity date) is a significant feature of liabilities.

As explained in Chapter 2, a **current liability** is a debt that a company reasonably expects to pay (1) from existing current assets or through the creation of other current liabilities, and (2) within one year or the operating cycle, whichever is longer. Debts that do not meet both criteria are **long-term liabilities**.

Financial statement users want to know whether a company's obligations are current or long-term. A company that has more current liabilities than current assets often lacks liquidity, or short-term debt-paying ability. In addition, users want to know the types of liabilities a company has. If a company declares bankruptcy, a specific, predetermined order of payment to creditors exists. Thus, the amount and type of liabilities are of critical importance.

**Helpful Hint** In previous chapters, we explained the entries for accounts payable and the adjusting entries for some current liabilities.

The different types of current liabilities include notes payable, accounts payable, unearned revenues, and accrued liabilities such as taxes, salaries and wages, and interest. In the sections that follow, we discuss a few of the common types of current liabilities.

### NOTES PAYABLE

**study objective** 2

Describe the accounting for notes payable.

Companies record obligations in the form of written notes as **notes payable**. They often use notes payable instead of accounts payable because notes payable give the lender written documentation of the obligation in case legal remedies are needed to collect the debt. Companies frequently issue notes payable to meet short-term financing needs. Notes payable usually require the borrower to pay interest.

Notes are issued for varying periods of time. **Those due for payment within one year of the balance sheet date are usually classified as current liabilities.** Most notes are interest-bearing.

To illustrate the accounting for notes payable, assume that First National Bank agrees to lend $100,000 on September 1, 2012, if Cole Williams Co. signs a $100,000, 12%, four-month note maturing on January 1. When a company issues an interest-bearing note, the amount of assets it receives generally equals the note's face value. Cole Williams Co. therefore will receive $100,000 cash and will make the following journal entry.

| Sept. 1 | Cash | 100,000 | |
| |    Notes Payable | | 100,000 |
| |    (To record issuance of 12%, 4-month | | |
| |    note to First National Bank) | | |

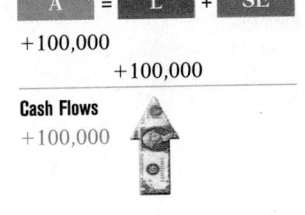

Interest accrues over the life of the note, and the issuer must periodically record that accrual. (You may find it helpful to review the discussion of interest computations that was provided in Chapter 8, page 408, with regard to notes receivable.) If Cole Williams Co. prepares financial statements annually, it makes an adjusting entry at December 31 to recognize four months of interest expense and interest payable of $4,000 ($100,000 \times 12\% \times \frac{4}{12}$):

| Dec. 31 | Interest Expense | 4,000 | |
| |    Interest Payable | | 4,000 |
| |    (To accrue interest for 4 months on First | | |
| |    National Bank note) | | |

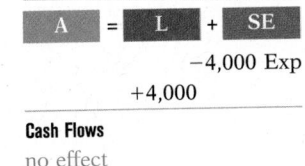

In the December 31 financial statements, the current liabilities section of the balance sheet will show notes payable $100,000 and interest payable $4,000. In addition, the company will report interest expense of $4,000 under "Other expenses and losses" in the income statement.

At maturity (January 1), Cole Williams Co. must pay the face value of the note ($100,000) plus $4,000 interest ($100,000 \times 12\% \times \frac{4}{12}$). It records payment of the note and accrued interest as follows.

| Jan. 1 | Notes Payable | 100,000 | |
| | Interest Payable | 4,000 | |
| |    Cash | | 104,000 |
| |    (To record payment of First National | | |
| |    Bank interest-bearing note and accrued | | |
| |    interest at maturity) | | |

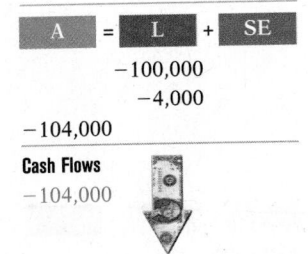

Appendix 10C at the end of this chapter discusses the accounting for long-term installment notes payable.

## SALES TAXES PAYABLE

Many of the products we purchase at retail stores are subject to sales taxes. Many states are now implementing sales taxes on purchases made on the Internet as well. Sales taxes are expressed as a percentage of the sales price. The selling company collects the tax from the customer when the sale occurs and periodically (usually monthly) remits the collections to the state's department of revenue.

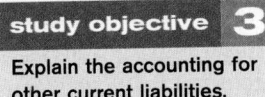

**study objective 3**

Explain the accounting for other current liabilities.

**Helpful Hint** Watch how sales are rung up at local retailers to see whether the sales tax is computed separately.

Under most state laws, the selling company must ring up separately on the cash register the amount of the sale and the amount of the sales tax collected. (Gasoline sales are a major exception.) The company then uses the cash register readings to credit Sales and Sales Taxes Payable. For example, if the March 25 cash register readings for Cooley Grocery show sales of $10,000 and sales taxes of $600 (sales tax rate of 6%), the journal entry is:

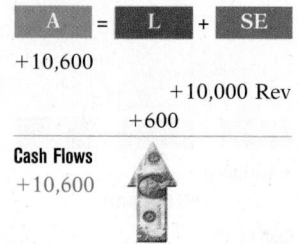

| A = L + SE |
|---|
| +10,600 |
| +10,000 Rev |
| +600 |

Cash Flows
+10,600

| | | | |
|---|---|---|---|
| Mar. 25 | Cash | 10,600 | |
| | Sales Revenue | | 10,000 |
| | Sales Taxes Payable | | 600 |
| | (To record daily sales and sales taxes) | | |

When the company remits the taxes to the taxing agency, it decreases (debits) Sales Taxes Payable and decreases (credits) Cash. The company does not report sales taxes as an expense; it simply forwards to the government the amount paid by the customer. Thus, Cooley Grocery serves only as a **collection agent** for the taxing authority.

Sometimes, companies do not ring up sales taxes separately on the cash register. To determine the amount of sales in such cases, divide total receipts by 100% plus the sales tax percentage. For example, assume that Cooley Grocery rings up total receipts of $10,600. Because the amount received from the sale is equal to the sales price 100% plus 6% of sales, or 1.06 times the sales total, we can compute sales as follows: $10,600 ÷ 1.06 = $10,000. Thus, we can find the sales tax amount of $600 by either (1) subtracting sales from total receipts ($10,600 − $10,000) or (2) multiplying sales by the sales tax rate ($10,000 × 6%).

### UNEARNED REVENUES

A magazine publisher such as Sports Illustrated may receive a customer's check when magazines are ordered. An airline company such as American Airlines often receives cash when it sells tickets for future flights. Season tickets for concerts, sporting events, and theatre programs are also paid for in advance. How do companies account for unearned revenues that are received before goods are delivered or services are provided?

1. When the company receives an advance, it increases (debits) Cash and also increases (credits) a current liability account identifying the source of the unearned revenue.

2. When the company earns the revenue, it decreases (debits) the unearned revenue account and increases (credits) an earned revenue account.

To illustrate, assume that Superior University sells 10,000 season football tickets at $50 each for its five-game home schedule. The entry is:

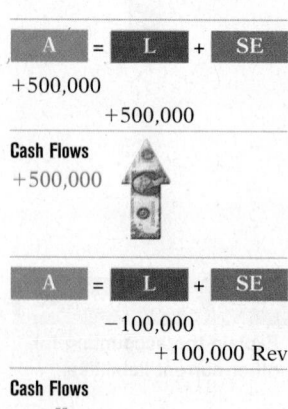

| A = L + SE |
|---|
| +500,000 |
| +500,000 |

Cash Flows
+500,000

| | | | |
|---|---|---|---|
| Aug. 6 | Cash | 500,000 | |
| | Unearned Ticket Revenue | | 500,000 |
| | (To record sale of 10,000 season tickets) | | |

As each game is completed, Superior records the earning of revenue with the following entry.

| A = L + SE |
|---|
| −100,000 |
| +100,000 Rev |

Cash Flows
no effect

| | | | |
|---|---|---|---|
| Sept. 7 | Unearned Ticket Revenue | 100,000 | |
| | Ticket Revenue | | 100,000 |
| | (To record football ticket revenues earned) | | |

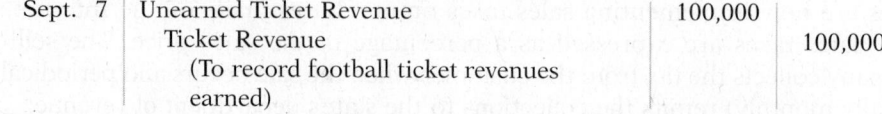

The account Unearned Ticket Revenue represents unearned revenue, and the university would report it as a current liability. As the school earns the revenue, it reclassifies the amount from unearned revenue to earned revenue. Unearned revenue is material for some companies: In the airline industry, tickets sold for future flights represent almost 50% of total current liabilities. At United Airlines, unearned ticket revenue recently was the largest current liability, amounting to more than $1 billion.

Illustration 10-1 shows specific unearned and earned revenue accounts used in selected types of businesses.

| Type of Business | Account Title | |
|---|---|---|
| | **Unearned Revenue** | **Earned Revenue** |
| Airline | Unearned Passenger Ticket Revenue | Passenger Ticket Revenue |
| Magazine publisher | Unearned Subscription Revenue | Subscription Revenue |
| Hotel | Unearned Rental Revenue | Rental Revenue |

**Illustration 10-1**
Unearned and earned revenue accounts

## CURRENT MATURITIES OF LONG-TERM DEBT

Companies often have a portion of long-term debt that comes due in the current year. As an example, assume that Wendy Construction issues a five-year, interest-bearing $25,000 note on January 1, 2011. This note specifies that each January 1, starting January 1, 2012, Wendy should pay $5,000 of the note. When the company prepares financial statements on December 31, 2011, it should report $5,000 as a current liability and $20,000 as a long-term liability. (The $5,000 amount is the portion of the note that is due to be paid within the next 12 months.) Companies often identify current maturities of long-term debt on the balance sheet as **long-term debt due within one year**. At December 31, 2009, General Motors had $724 million of such debt.

It is not necessary to prepare an adjusting entry to recognize the current maturity of long-term debt. At the balance sheet date, all obligations due within one year are classified as current, and all other obligations are long-term.

*before you go on...*

## Do it!

You and several classmates are studying for the next accounting examination. They ask you to answer the following questions.

1. If cash is borrowed on a $50,000, 6-month, 12% note on September 1, how much interest expense would be incurred by December 31?

2. How is the sales tax amount determined when the cash register total includes sales taxes?

3. If $15,000 is collected in advance on November 1 for 3-months' rent, what amount of rent revenue is earned by December 31?

### Solution

1. $50,000 × 12% × 4/12 = $2,000

2. First, divide the total cash register receipts by 100% plus the sales tax percentage to find the sales amount. Second, subtract the sales amount from the total cash register receipts to determine the sales taxes.

3. $15,000 × 2/3 = $10,000

Related exercise material: **BE10-2, BE10-3, BE10-4, Do it! 10-1, E10-1, E10-2, E10-3, E10-4, E10-6,** and **E10-7.**

**CURRENT LIABILITIES**

**Action Plan**

• Use the interest formula: Face value of note × Annual interest rate × Time in terms of one year.

• Divide total receipts by 100% plus the tax rate to determine sales; then subtract sales from the total receipts.

• Determine what fraction of the total unearned rent was earned this year.

the navigator

## PAYROLL AND PAYROLL TAXES PAYABLE

Assume that Susan Alena works 40 hours this week for Pepitone Inc., earning a wage of $10 per hour. Will Susan receive a $400 check at the end of the week? Not likely. The reason: Pepitone is required to withhold amounts from her wages to pay various governmental authorities. For example, Pepitone will withhold amounts for Social Security taxes[1] and for federal and state income taxes. If these withholdings total $100, Susan will receive a check for only $300. Illustration 10-2 summarizes the types of payroll deductions that normally occur for most companies.

**Illustration 10-2** Payroll deductions

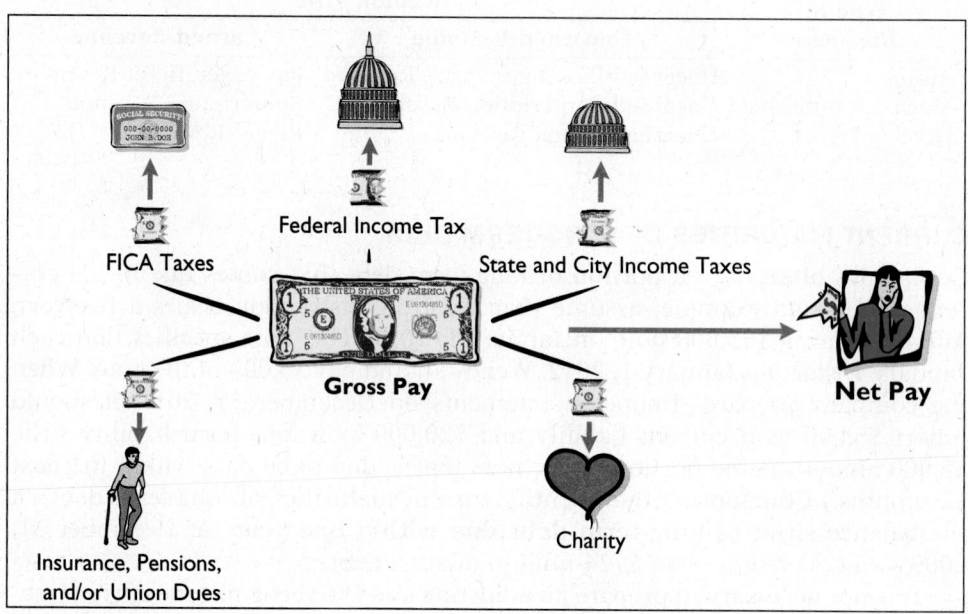

As a result of these deductions, companies withhold from employee paychecks amounts that must be paid to other parties. Pepitone therefore has incurred a liability to pay these third parties and must report this liability in its balance sheet.

As a second illustration, assume that Cargo Corporation records its payroll for the week of March 7 with the journal entry shown below.

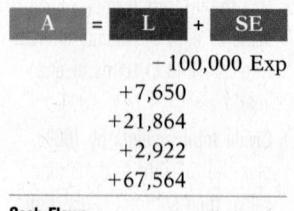

| A | = | L | + | SE |
|---|---|---|---|---|

−100,000 Exp
+7,650
+21,864
+2,922
+67,564

**Cash Flows**
no effect

| Mar. 7 | Salaries and Wages Expense | 100,000 | |
|---|---|---|---|
| | FICA Taxes Payable | | 7,650 |
| | Federal Income Taxes Payable | | 21,864 |
| | State Income Taxes Payable | | 2,922 |
| | Salaries and Wages Payable | | 67,564 |
| | (To record payroll and withholding taxes for the week ending March 7) | | |

[1]Social Security taxes are commonly called FICA taxes. In 1937, Congress enacted the Federal Insurance Contribution Act (FICA). As can be seen in the journal entry and the payroll tax journal entry on the next page, the employee and employer must make equal contributions to Social Security. The Social Security rate in 2010 was 7.65% for each.

Cargo then records payment of this payroll on March 7 as follows.

| | | | | |
|---|---|---|---:|---:|
| Mar. | 7 | Salaries and Wages Payable | 67,564 | |
| | | Cash | | 67,564 |
| | | (To record payment of the March 7 payroll) | | |

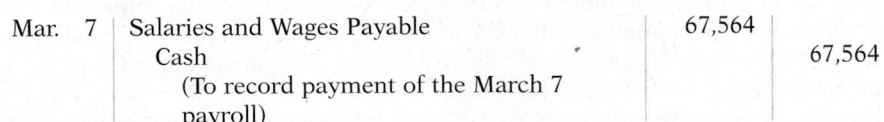

A = L + SE
$-67,564$
$-67,564$

**Cash Flows**
$-67,564$

In this case, Cargo reports $100,000 in salaries and wages expense. In addition, it reports liabilities for the salaries and wages payable as well as liabilities to governmental agencies. Rather than pay the employees $100,000, Cargo instead must withhold the taxes and make the tax payments directly. In summary, Cargo is essentially serving as a tax collector.

In addition to the liabilities incurred as a result of withholdings, employers also incur a second type of payroll-related liability. With every payroll, the employer incurs liabilities to pay various **payroll taxes** levied upon the employer. These payroll taxes include the *employer's share* of Social Security (FICA) taxes and state and federal unemployment taxes. Based on Cargo Corp.'s $100,000 payroll, the company would record the employer's expense and liability for these payroll taxes as follows.

| | | | | |
|---|---|---|---:|---:|
| Mar. | 7 | Payroll Tax Expense | 13,850 | |
| | | FICA Taxes Payable | | 7,650 |
| | | Federal Unemployment Taxes Payable | | 800 |
| | | State Unemployment Taxes Payable | | 5,400 |
| | | (To record employer's payroll taxes on March 7 payroll) | | |

A = L + SE
$-13,850$ Exp
$+7,650$
$+800$
$+5,400$

**Cash Flows**
no effect

Companies classify the payroll and payroll tax liability accounts as current liabilities because they must be paid to employees or remitted to taxing authorities periodically and in the near term. Taxing authorities impose substantial fines and penalties on employers if the withholding and payroll taxes are not computed correctly and paid on time.

## ANATOMY OF A FRAUD

Art was a custodial supervisor for a large school district. The district was supposed to employ between 35 and 40 regular custodians, as well as 3 or 4 substitute custodians to fill in when regular custodians were missing. Instead, in addition to the regular custodians, Art "hired" 77 substitutes. In fact, almost none of these people worked for the district. Instead, Art submitted time cards for these people, collected their checks at the district office, and personally distributed the checks to the "employees." If a substitute's check was for $1,200, that person would cash the check, keep $200, and pay Art $1,000.

Total take: $150,000

### THE MISSING CONTROLS

*Human Resource Controls.* Thorough background checks should be performed. No employees should begin work until they have been approved by the Board of Education and entered into the payroll system. No employees should be entered into the payroll system until they have been approved by a supervisor. All paychecks should be distributed directly to employees at the official school locations by designated employees.

*Independent internal verification.* Budgets should be reviewed monthly to identify situations where actual costs significantly exceed budgeted amounts.

*Source:* Adapted from Wells, *Fraud Casebook* (2007), pp. 164–171.

*before you go on...*

**WAGES AND PAYROLL TAXES**

### Action Plan

- Remember that wages earned are an expense to the company, but withholdings reduce the amount due to be paid to the employee.
- Payroll taxes are taxes the company incurs related to its employees.

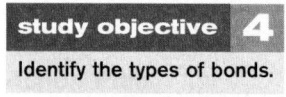

## Do it!

During the month of September, Lake Corporation's employees earned wages of $60,000. Withholdings related to these wages were $3,500 for Social Security (FICA), $6,500 for federal income tax, and $2,000 for state income tax. Costs incurred for unemployment taxes were $90 for federal and $150 for state.

Prepare the September 30 journal entries for (a) wages expense and wages payable, assuming that all September wages will be paid in October, and (b) the company's payroll tax expense.

### Solution

(a) To determine wages payable, reduce wages expense by the withholdings for FICA, federal income tax, and state income tax.

| Sept. 30 | Salaries and Wages Expense | 60,000 | |
|---|---|---|---|
| | FICA Taxes Payable | | 3,500 |
| | Federal Income Taxes Payable | | 6,500 |
| | State Income Taxes Payable | | 2,000 |
| | Salaries and Wages Payable | | 48,000 |

(b) Payroll taxes would be for the company's share of FICA, as well as for federal and state unemployment tax.

| Sept. 30 | Payroll Tax Expense | 3,740 | |
|---|---|---|---|
| | FICA Taxes Payable | | 3,500 |
| | Federal Unemployment Taxes Payable | | 90 |
| | State Unemployment Taxes Payable | | 150 |

Related exercise material: **BE10-5**, **BE10-6**, **Do it!** 10-2, and **E10-5**.

---

# Bonds: Long-Term Liabilities

**study objective** **4**

Identify the types of bonds.

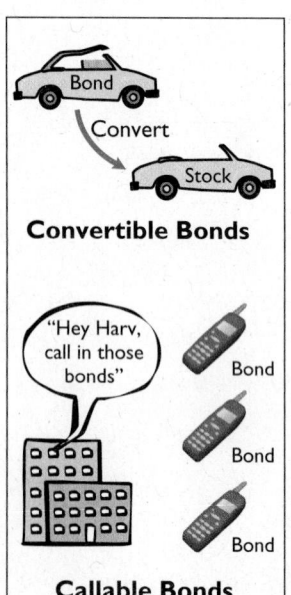

**Convertible Bonds**

"Hey Harv, call in those bonds"

Bond

Bond

Bond

**Callable Bonds**

**Long-term liabilities** are obligations that a company expects to pay more than one year in the future. In this section, we explain the accounting for the principal types of obligations reported in the long-term liabilities section of the balance sheet. These obligations often are in the form of bonds or long-term notes.

**Bonds** are a form of interest-bearing note payable issued by corporations, universities, and governmental agencies. Bonds, like common stock, are sold in small denominations (usually $1,000 or multiples of $1,000). As a result, bonds attract many investors.

### TYPES OF BONDS

Bonds may have different features. In the following sections, we describe some commonly issued types of bonds.

### Secured and Unsecured Bonds

**Secured bonds** have specific assets of the issuer pledged as collateral for the bonds. **Unsecured bonds** are issued against the general credit of the borrower. Large corporations with good credit ratings use unsecured bonds extensively. For example, at one time DuPont reported more than $2 billion of unsecured bonds outstanding.

### Convertible and Callable Bonds

Bonds that can be converted into common stock at the bondholder's option are **convertible bonds**. Bonds that the issuing company can retire at a stated dollar amount prior to maturity are **callable bonds**. Convertible bonds have features that are attractive both to bondholders and to the issuer. The conversion often gives bondholders an opportunity to benefit if the market price of the common stock increases substantially. Furthermore, until conversion, the bondholder receives interest on the bond. For the issuer, the bonds sell at a higher price and pay a lower rate of interest than comparable debt securities that do not have a conversion option. Many corporations, such as USAir, United States Steel Corp., and General Motors Corporation, have convertible bonds outstanding.

## Accounting Across the Organization

### When Convertible Bonds Don't

During the boom times of the late 1990s, many rapidly growing companies issued large quantities of convertible bonds. Investors found the convertible bonds attractive because they paid regular interest but also had the upside potential of being converted to stock if the stock price increased. At the time, stock prices were increasing rapidly, so many investors viewed convertible bonds as a cheap and safe way to buy stock.

As a consequence, companies were able to pay much lower interest rates on convertible bonds than on standard bonds. When the bonds were issued, company managers assumed that the bonds would be converted. Thus, the company would never have to repay the debt with cash. It seemed too good to be true—and it was.

When stock prices plummeted in the early 2000s, investors no longer had an incentive to convert, since the market price was below the conversion price. When many of these massive bonds came due, companies were forced either to pay them off or to issue new debt at much higher rates.

The drop in stock prices did not change the debt to total assets ratios of these companies. Discuss how the perception of a high debt to total assets ratio changed before and after the fall in stock prices. (See page 563.)

## ISSUING PROCEDURES

A **bond certificate** is issued to the investor to provide evidence of the investor's claim against the company. As Illustration 10-3 (page 514) shows, the bond certificate provides information such as the name of the company that issued the bonds, the face value of the bonds, the maturity date of the bonds, and the contractual interest rate. The **face value** is the amount of principal due at the maturity date. The **maturity date** is the date that the final payment is due to the investor from the issuing company. The **contractual interest rate** is the rate used to determine the amount of cash interest the borrower pays and the investor receives. Usually, the contractual rate is stated as an annual rate, and interest is generally paid semiannually. (We use annual payments in our examples to simplify.)

*Alternative Terminology* The contractual rate is often referred to as the *stated rate.*

## DETERMINING THE MARKET VALUE OF BONDS

If you were an investor wanting to purchase a bond, how would you determine how much to pay? To be more specific, assume that Coronet, Inc. issues a zero-interest (pays no interest) bond with a face value of $1,000,000 due in 20 years. For this bond, the only cash you receive is $1 million at the end of 20 years. Would you pay $1 million for this bond? We hope not, because $1 million received 20 years from now is not the same as $1 million received today.

The term **time value of money** is used to indicate the relationship between time and money—that a dollar received today is worth more than a dollar promised at some time in the future. If you had $1 million today, you would invest it and earn interest so that at the end of 20 years, your investment would be worth much more than $1 million. Thus, if someone is going to pay you $1 million 20 years

**Same dollars at different times are not equal.**

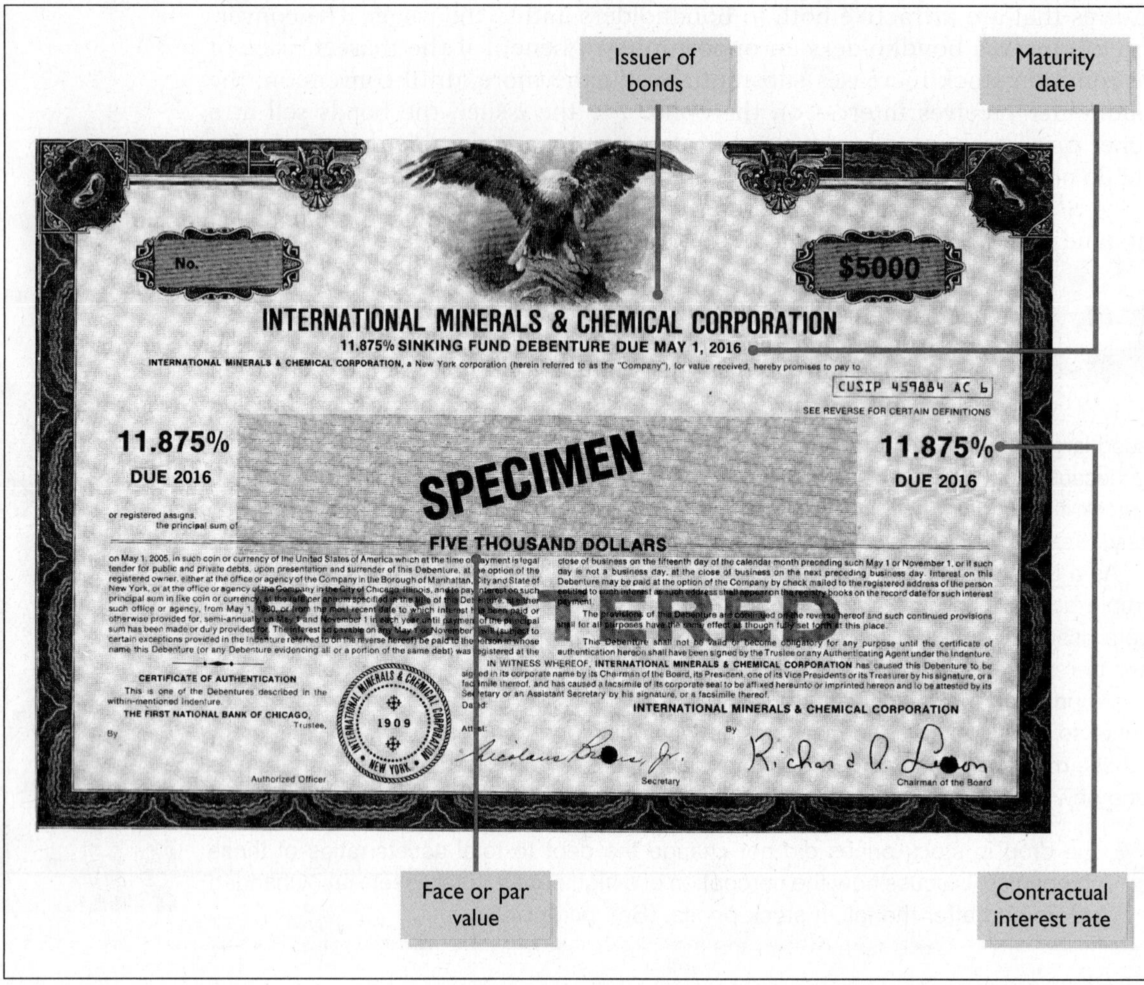

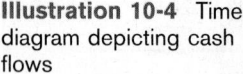

**Illustration 10-3** Bond certificate

from now, you would want to find its equivalent today, or its **present value**. In other words, you would want to determine the value today of the amount to be received in the future after taking into account current interest rates.

The current market value (present value) of a bond is therefore a function of three factors: (1) the dollar amounts to be received, (2) the length of time until the amounts are received, and (3) the market interest rate. The **market interest rate** is the rate investors demand for loaning funds. The process of finding the present value is referred to as **discounting** the future amounts.

To illustrate, assume that Acropolis Company on January 1, 2012, issues $100,000 of 9% bonds, due in five years, with interest payable annually at year-end. The purchaser of the bonds would receive the following two types of cash payments: (1) **principal** of $100,000 to be paid at maturity, and (2) five $9,000 **interest payments** ($100,000 × 9%) over the term of the bonds. Illustration 10-4 shows a time diagram depicting both cash flows.

**Illustration 10-4** Time diagram depicting cash flows

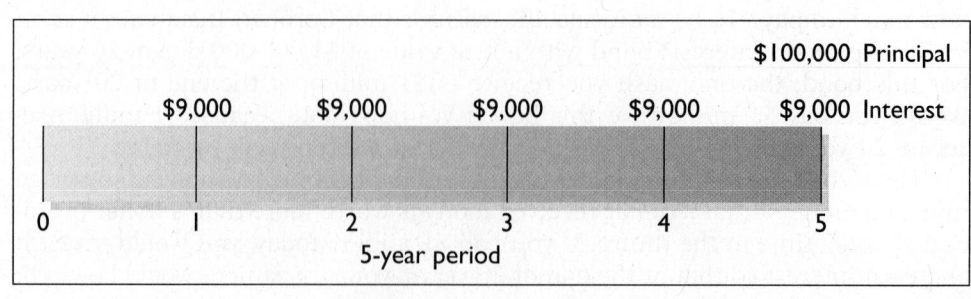

The current market value of a bond is equal to the present value of all the future cash payments promised by the bond. Illustration 10-5 lists and totals the present values of these amounts, assuming the market rate of interest is 9%.

| | |
|---|---|
| Present value of $100,000 received in 5 years | $ 64,993 |
| Present value of $9,000 received annually for 5 years | 35,007 |
| **Market price of bonds** | **$100,000** |

**Illustration 10-5**
Computing the market price of bonds

Tables are available to provide the present value numbers to be used, or these values can be determined mathematically.[2] Appendix D, near the end of the book, provides further discussion of the concepts and the mechanics of the time value of money computations.

*before you go on...*

**Do it!** State whether each of the following statements is true or false.

**BOND TERMINOLOGY**

_____ 1. Secured bonds have specific assets of the issuer pledged as collateral.

_____ 2. Callable bonds can be retired by the issuing company at a stated dollar amount prior to maturity.

_____ 3. The contractual rate is the rate investors demand for loaning funds.

_____ 4. The face value is the amount of principal the issuing company must pay at the maturity date.

_____ 5. The market value of a bond is equal to its maturity value.

**Action Plan**
• Review the types of bonds and the basic terms associated with bonds.

**Solution**

1. True.
2. True.
3. False. The contractual interest rate is used to determine the amount of cash interest the borrower pays.
4. True.
5. False. The market value of a bond is equal to the present value of all the future cash payments promised by the bond.

Related exercise material: **Do it!** 10-3.

# Accounting for Bond Issues

A corporation records bond transactions when it issues (sells) or retires (buys back) bonds and when bondholders convert bonds into common stock. If bondholders sell their bond investments to other investors, the issuing firm receives no further money on the transaction, **nor does the issuing corporation journalize the transaction** (although it does keep records of the names of bondholders in some cases).

Bonds may be issued at face value, below face value (discount), or above face value (premium). Bond prices for both new issues and existing bonds are

**study objective 5**
Prepare the entries for the issuance of bonds and interest expense.

---

[2]For those knowledgeable in the use of present value tables, the computations in this example are:
$100,000 ×.64993 = $64,993 and $9,000 × 3.88965 = $35,007 (rounded).

quoted as **a percentage of the face value of the bond. Face value is usually $1,000.** Thus, a $1,000 bond with a quoted price of 97 means that the selling price of the bond is 97% of face value, or $970.

## ISSUING BONDS AT FACE VALUE

To illustrate the accounting for bonds issued at face value, assume that Devor Corporation issues 100, five-year, 10%, $1,000 bonds dated January 1, 2012, at 100 (100% of face value). The entry to record the sale is:

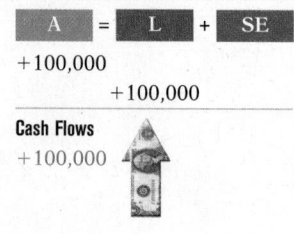

| Jan. | 1 | Cash | 100,000 | |
|---|---|---|---|---|
| | |    Bonds Payable | | 100,000 |
| | |    (To record sale of bonds at face value) | | |

Devor reports bonds payable in the long-term liabilities section of the balance sheet because the maturity date is January 1, 2017 (more than one year away).

Over the term (life) of the bonds, companies make entries to record bond interest. Interest on bonds payable is computed in the same manner as interest on notes payable, as explained earlier. If we assume that interest is payable annually on January 1 on the bonds described above, Devor accrues interest of $10,000 ($100,000 × 10% × $\frac{12}{12}$) on December 31.

At December 31 Devor recognizes the $10,000 of interest expense incurred with the following adjusting entry.

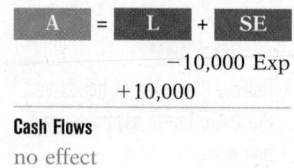

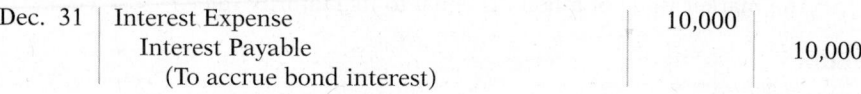

| Dec. | 31 | Interest Expense | 10,000 | |
|---|---|---|---|---|
| | |    Interest Payable | | 10,000 |
| | |    (To accrue bond interest) | | |

The company classifies **interest payable as a current liability** because it is scheduled for payment within the next year. When Devor pays the interest on January 1, 2013, it decreases (debits) Interest Payable and decreases (credits) Cash for $10,000.

Devor records the payment on January 1 as follows.

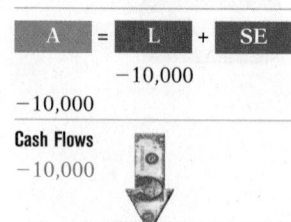

| Jan. | 1 | Interest Payable | 10,000 | |
|---|---|---|---|---|
| | |    Cash | | 10,000 |
| | |    (To record payment of bond interest) | | |

## DISCOUNT OR PREMIUM ON BONDS

The previous illustrations assumed that the contractual (stated) interest rate and the market (effective) interest rate paid on bonds were the same. Recall that the **contractual interest rate** is the rate applied to the face (par) value to arrive at the interest paid in a year. The **market interest rate** is the rate investors demand for loaning funds to the corporation. When the contractual interest rate and the market interest rate are the same, **bonds sell at face value.**

However, market interest rates change daily. The type of bond issued, the state of the economy, current industry conditions, and the company's individual performance all affect market interest rates. As a result, the contractual and market interest rates often differ. To make bonds salable when the two rates differ, bonds sell below or above face value.

To illustrate, suppose that a company issues 10% bonds at a time when other bonds of similar risk are paying 12%. Investors will not be interested in buying the 10% bonds, so their value will fall below their face value. When a bond is sold for less than its face value, the difference between the face value of a bond and its selling price is called a **discount**. As a result of the decline in the bonds' selling price, the actual interest rate incurred by the company increases to the level of the current market interest rate.

Conversely, if the market rate of interest is **lower than** the contractual interest rate, investors will have to pay more than face value for the bonds. That is, if the market rate of interest is 8% but the contractual interest rate on the bonds is 10%, the price on the bonds will be bid up. When a bond is sold for more than its face value, the difference between the face value and its selling price is called a **premium**. Illustration 10-6 shows these relationships graphically.

**Helpful Hint** Bond prices *vary inversely* with changes in the market interest rate: As market interest rates decline, bond prices will increase. When a bond is issued, if the market interest rate is below the contractual rate, the price will be higher than the face value.

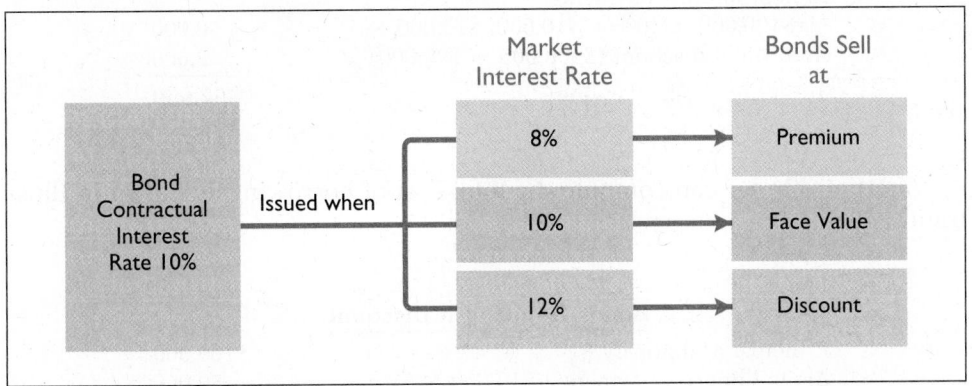

**Illustration 10-6** Interest rates and bond prices

Issuance of bonds at an amount different from face value is quite common. By the time a company prints the bond certificates and markets the bonds, it will be a coincidence if the market rate and the contractual rate are the same. Thus, the issuance of bonds at a discount does not mean that the financial strength of the issuer is suspect. Conversely, the sale of bonds at a premium does not indicate that the financial strength of the issuer is exceptional.

**Helpful Hint** Some bonds are sold at a discount by design. "Zero-coupon" bonds, which pay no interest, sell at a deep discount to face value.

## ISSUING BONDS AT A DISCOUNT

To illustrate the issuance of bonds at a discount, assume that on January 1, 2012, Candlestick Inc. sells $100,000, five-year, 10% bonds at 98 (98% of face value) with interest payable on January 1. The entry to record the issuance is:

| | | | | |
|---|---|---|---|---|
| Jan. | 1 | Cash | 98,000 | |
| | | Discount on Bonds Payable | 2,000 | |
| | | Bonds Payable | | 100,000 |
| | | (To record sale of bonds at a discount) | | |

| A | = | L | + | SE |
|---|---|---|---|---|
| +98,000 | | | | |
| | | −2,000 | | |
| | | +100,000 | | |

**Cash Flows**
+98,000

Although Discount on Bonds Payable has a debit balance, **it is not an asset**. Rather it is a **contra account**, which is **deducted from bonds payable** on the balance sheet as shown in Illustration 10-7.

**Illustration 10-7** Statement presentation of discount on bonds payable

**CANDLESTICK INC.**
Balance Sheet (partial)

Long-term liabilities
Bonds payable ............ $100,000
Less: Discount on bonds payable ....... 2,000 $98,000

**Helpful Hint** The carrying value (book value) of bonds issued at a discount is determined by subtracting the balance of the discount account from the balance of the Bonds Payable account.

The $98,000 represents the **carrying (or book) value** of the bonds. On the date of issue, this amount equals the market price of the bonds.

The issuance of bonds below face value causes the total cost of borrowing to differ from the bond interest paid. That is, the issuing corporation not only must pay the contractual interest rate over the term of the bonds but also must pay the face value (rather than the issuance price) at maturity. Therefore, the difference between the issuance price and the face value of the bonds-the discount—is an **additional cost of borrowing**. The company records this cost as **interest expense** over the life of the bonds. The total cost of borrowing $98,000 for Candlestick Inc. is $52,000, computed as shown in Illustration 10-8.

**Illustration 10-8**
Computation of total cost of borrowing–bonds issued at discount

| Bonds Issued at a Discount | |
| --- | --- |
| Annual interest payments | |
| ($100,000 × 10% = $10,000; $10,000 × 5) | $ 50,000 |
| Add: Bond discount ($100,000 − $98,000) | 2,000 |
| **Total cost of borrowing** | **$52,000** |

Alternatively, we can compute the total cost of borrowing as shown in Illustration 10-9.

**Illustration 10-9**
Alternative computation of total cost of borrowing–bonds issued at discount

| Bonds Issued at a Discount | |
| --- | --- |
| Principal at maturity | $100,000 |
| Annual interest payments ($10,000 × 5) | 50,000 |
| Cash to be paid to bondholders | 150,000 |
| Cash received from bondholders | 98,000 |
| **Total cost of borrowing** | **$ 52,000** |

To follow the expense recognition principle, companies allocate bond discount to expense in each period in which the bonds are outstanding. This is referred to as **amortizing the discount**. Amortization of the discount **increases** the amount of interest expense reported each period. That is, after the company amortizes the discount, the amount of interest expense it reports in a period will exceed the contractual amount. As shown in Illustration 10-8, for the bonds issued by Candlestick Inc., total interest expense will exceed the contractual interest by $2,000 over the life of the bonds.

As the discount is amortized, its balance declines. As a consequence, the carrying value of the bonds will increase, until at maturity the carrying value of the bonds equals their face amount. This is shown in Illustration 10-10.

**Illustration 10-10**
Amortization of bond discount

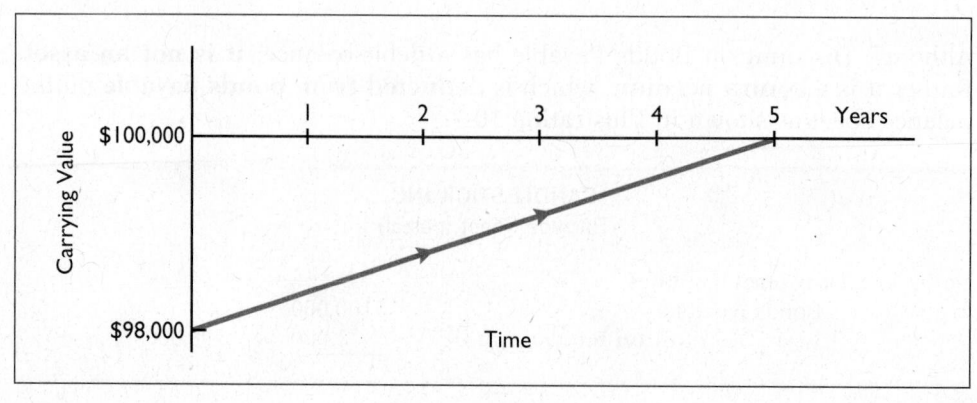

Appendix 10A and Appendix 10B at the end of this chapter discuss procedures for amortizing bond discount.

## ISSUING BONDS AT A PREMIUM

We can illustrate the issuance of bonds at a premium by now assuming the Candlestick Inc. bonds described above sell at 102 (102% of face value) rather than at 98. The entry to record the sale is:

| | | | |
|---|---|---:|---:|
| Jan. 1 | Cash | 102,000 | |
| | Bonds Payable | | 100,000 |
| | Premium on Bonds Payable | | 2,000 |
| | (To record sale of bonds at a premium) | | |

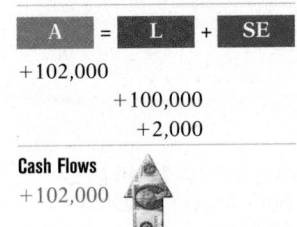

| A | = | L | + | SE |
|---|---|---|---|---|
| +102,000 | | | | |
| | | +100,000 | | |
| | | +2,000 | | |

**Cash Flows**
+102,000

Candlestick adds the premium on bonds payable **to the bonds payable** amount on the balance sheet, as shown in Illustration 10-11.

**Illustration 10-11**
Statement presentation of bond premium

### CANDLESTICK INC.
Balance Sheet (partial)

| | | |
|---|---:|---:|
| Long-term liabilities | | |
| Bonds payable | $100,000 | |
| Add: Premium on bonds payable | 2,000 | $102,000 |

The sale of bonds above face value causes the total cost of borrowing to be **less than the bond interest paid** because the borrower is not required to pay the bond premium at the maturity date of the bonds. Thus, the premium is considered to be **a reduction in the cost of borrowing** that reduces bond interest expense over the life of the bonds. The total cost of borrowing $102,000 for Candlestick Inc. is $48,000, computed as in Illustration 10-12.

**Illustration 10-12**
Computation of total cost of borrowing—bonds issued at a premium

### Bonds Issued at a Premium

| | |
|---|---:|
| Annual interest payments | |
| ($100,000 × 10% = $10,000; $10,000 × 5) | $ 50,000 |
| Less: Bond premium ($102,000 − $100,000) | 2,000 |
| **Total cost of borrowing** | **$48,000** |

Alternatively, we can compute the cost of borrowing as shown in Illustration 10-13.

**Illustration 10-13**
Alternative computation of total cost of borrowing—bonds issued at a premium

### Bonds Issued at a Premium

| | |
|---|---:|
| Principal at maturity | $100,000 |
| Annual interest payments ($10,000 × 5) | 50,000 |
| Cash to be paid to bondholders | 150,000 |
| Cash received from bondholders | 102,000 |
| **Total cost of borrowing** | **$ 48,000** |

Similar to bond discount, companies allocate bond premium to expense in each period in which the bonds are outstanding. This is referred to as **amortizing the premium**. Amortization of the premium **decreases** the amount of interest expense reported each period. That is, after the company amortizes the premium, the amount of interest expense it reports in a period will be less than the contractual amount. As shown in Illustration 10-12, for the bonds issued by Candlestick Inc., contractual interest will exceed the interest expense by $2,000 over the life of the bonds.

As the premium is amortized, its balance declines. As a consequence, the carrying value of the bonds will decrease, until at maturity the carrying value of the bonds equals their face amount. This is shown in Illustration 10-14. Appendices 10A and 10B at the end of this chapter discuss procedures for amortizing bond premium.

**Illustration 10-14**
Amortization of bond premium

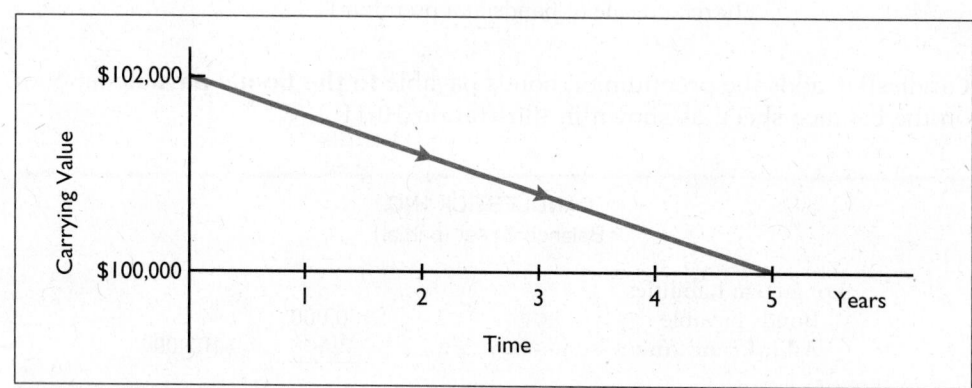

## before you go on...

**BOND ISSUANCE**

### Action Plan

- Record cash received, bonds payable at face value, and the difference as a discount or premium.
- Report discount as a deduction from bonds payable and premium as an addition to bonds payable.

**Do it!** Giant Corporation issues $200,000 of bonds for $189,000. (a) Prepare the journal entry to record the issuance of the bonds, and (b) show how the bonds would be reported on the balance sheet at the date of issuance.

### Solution

(a)

| | | |
|---|---|---|
| Cash | 189,000 | |
| Discount on Bonds Payable | 11,000 | |
| Bonds Payable | | 200,000 |
| (To record sale of bonds at a discount) | | |

(b)

| | | |
|---|---|---|
| Long-term liabilities | | |
| Bonds payable | $200,000 | |
| Less: Discount on bonds payable | (11,000) | $189,000 |

Related exercise material: **BE10-7, Do it! 10-4, E10-8, E10-9,** and **E10-10.**

## Accounting for Bond Retirements

**study objective 6**

Describe the entries when bonds are redeemed.

Bonds are retired when the issuing corporation buys back (redeems) them. The appropriate entries for these transactions are explained next.

### REDEEMING BONDS AT MATURITY

Regardless of the issue price of bonds, the book value of the bonds at maturity will equal their face value. Assuming that the company pays and records separately the interest for the last interest period, Candlestick records the redemption of its bonds at maturity as:

| | | |
|---|---|---|
| Bonds Payable | 100,000 | |
|     Cash | | 100,000 |
|       (To record redemption of bonds at maturity) | | |

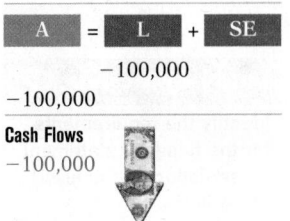

| A | = | L | + | SE |
|---|---|---|---|---|
| | | −100,000 | | |
| −100,000 | | | | |

**Cash Flows**
−100,000

## REDEEMING BONDS BEFORE MATURITY

Bonds may be redeemed before maturity. A company may decide to retire bonds before maturity in order to reduce interest cost and remove debt from its balance sheet. A company should retire debt early only if it has sufficient cash resources.

When bonds are retired before maturity, it is necessary to: (1) eliminate the carrying value of the bonds at the redemption date, (2) record the cash paid, and (3) recognize the gain or loss on redemption. The **carrying value** of the bonds is the face value of the bonds less unamortized bond discount or plus unamortized bond premium at the redemption date.

To illustrate, assume at the end of the fourth period, Candlestick Inc., having sold its bonds at a premium, retires the $100,000 face value bonds at 103 after paying the annual interest. Assume that the carrying value of the bonds at the redemption date is $100,400 (principal $100,000 and premium $400). Candlestick records the redemption at the end of the fourth interest period (January 1, 2016) as:

| | | | |
|---|---|---|---|
| Jan. 1 | Bonds Payable | 100,000 | |
| | Premium on Bonds Payable | 400 | |
| | Loss on Bond Redemption | 2,600 | |
| |     Cash | | 103,000 |
| |       (To record redemption of bonds at 103) | | |

| A | = | L | + | SE |
|---|---|---|---|---|
| | | −100,000 | | |
| | | −400 | | |
| | | | | −2,600 Exp |
| −103,000 | | | | |

**Cash Flows**
−103,000

Note that the loss of $2,600 is the difference between the $103,000 cash paid and the $100,400 carrying value of the bonds.

---

### *before you go on...*

## Do it!

R & B Inc. issued $500,000, 10-year bonds at a discount. Prior to maturity, when the carrying value of the bonds is $496,000, the company retires the bonds at 98. Prepare the entry to record the redemption of the bonds.

### Solution

There is a loss on redemption: The cash paid, $490,000 ($500,000 × 98%), is less than the carrying value of $496,000. The entry is:

| | | |
|---|---|---|
| Bonds Payable | 500,000 | |
|     Cash | | 490,000 |
|     Discount on Bonds Payable | | 4,000 |
|     Gain on Bond Redemption | | 6,000 |
|       (To record redemption of bonds at 98) | | |

**BOND REDEMPTION**

### Action Plan

- Determine and eliminate the carrying value of the bonds.
- Record the cash paid.
- Compute and record the gain or loss (the difference between the first two items).

the navigator

Related exercise material: **BE10-8,** **Do it!** **10-5, E10-11,** and **E10-12.**

# Financial Statement Presentation and Analysis

## BALANCE SHEET PRESENTATION

Current liabilities are the first category under "Liabilities" on the balance sheet. Companies list each of the principal types of current liabilities separately within the category.

Within the current liabilities section, companies usually list notes payable first, followed by accounts payable. Other items sometimes are listed in the order of their magnitude. *In your homework, you should present notes payable first, followed by accounts payable, and then other liabilities in order of magnitude.*

Companies report long-term liabilities in a separate section of the balance sheet immediately following "Current liabilities." Illustration 10-15 shows an example.

**Illustration 10-15**
Balance sheet presentation of liabilities

| MARAIS COMPANY | | |
|---|---|---|
| Balance Sheet (partial) | | |
| **Liabilities** | | |
| **Current liabilities** | | |
| Notes payable | $ 250,000 | |
| Accounts payable | 125,000 | |
| Current maturities of long-term debt | 300,000 | |
| Accrued liabilities | 75,000 | |
| Total current liabilities | | $ 750,000 |
| **Long-term liabilities** | | |
| Bonds payable | 1,000,000 | |
| Less: Discount on bonds payable | 80,000 | 920,000 |
| Notes payable, secured by plant assets | | 540,000 |
| Lease liability | | 500,000 |
| Total long-term liabilities | | 1,960,000 |
| Total liabilities | | $2,710,000 |

Disclosure of debt is very important. Failures at Enron, WorldCom, and Global Crossing have made investors very concerned about companies' debt obligations. Summary data regarding debts may be presented in the balance sheet with detailed data (such as interest rates, maturity dates, conversion privileges, and assets pledged as collateral) shown in a supporting schedule in the notes. Companies should report current maturities of long-term debt as a current liability.

**KEEPING AN EYE ON CASH**

The balance sheet presents the balances of a company's debts at a point in time. The statement of cash flows also presents information about a company's debts. Information regarding cash inflows and outflows during the year that resulted from the principal portion of debt transactions appears in the "Financing activities" section of the statement of cash flows. Interest expense is reported in the "Operating activities" section, even though it resulted from debt transactions.

The statement of cash flows shown below presents the cash flows from financing activities for Toyota Motor Corporation. From this we learn that the company issued new long-term debt of $24,481 million and repaid long-term debt of $14,628 million.

**TOYOTA MOTOR CORPORATION**
Statement of Cash Flows (partial)
2007
(in millions)

| Cash flows from financing activities | |
|---|---|
| Purchase of common stock | $ (2,505) |
| Proceeds from issuance of long-term debt | 24,481 |
| Payments of long-term debt | (14,628) |
| Increase in short-term borrowings | 2,994 |
| Dividends paid | (2,873) |
| Net cash provided by financing activities | $ 7,469 |

## ANALYSIS

Careful examination of debt obligations helps you assess a company's ability to pay its current and long-term obligations. It also helps you determine whether a company can obtain debt financing in order to grow. We will use the following information from the financial statements of Toyota Motor Corporation to illustrate the analysis of a company's liquidity and solvency.[3]

**Illustration 10-16**
Simplified balance sheets for Toyota Motor Corporation

**TOYOTA MOTOR CORPORATION**
Balance Sheets
December 31, 2007 and 2006
(in millions)

| Assets | 2007 | 2006 |
|---|---|---|
| Total current assets | $ 99,823 | $ 91,387 |
| Noncurrent assets | 176,118 | 153,200 |
| Total assets | $275,941 | $244,587 |
| **Liabilities and Stockholders' Equity** | | |
| Total current liabilities | $ 99,680 | $ 85,373 |
| Noncurrent liabilities | 75,998 | 69,315 |
| Total liabilities | 175,678 | 154,688 |
| Total stockholders' equity | 100,263 | 89,899 |
| Total liabilities and stockholders' equity | $275,941 | $244,587 |

## Liquidity

**Liquidity ratios** measure the short-term ability of a company to pay its maturing obligations and to meet unexpected needs for cash. A commonly used measure of liquidity is the current ratio (presented in Chapter 2). The current ratio

[3]We chose to use 2007 and 2006 (instead of more recent financial information) because the large losses in the auto industry during 2008 and 2009 reduce the instructional usefulness of some of the ratios in this chapter.

is calculated as current assets divided by current liabilities. Illustration 10-17 presents the current ratio for Toyota along with the industry average.

**Illustration 10-17**
Current ratio

| Ratio | Toyota ($ in millions) | | Industry Average |
|---|---|---|---|
| | 2007 | 2006 | 2007 |
| **Current Ratio** | $\dfrac{\$99{,}823}{\$99{,}680} = 1.0{:}1$ | $\dfrac{\$91{,}387}{\$85{,}373} = 1.07{:}1$ | 1.08:1 |

Toyota's current assets are approximately equal to its current liabilities. Therefore, its current ratio is about 1 in both 2006 and 2007. The industry average current ratio for manufacturers of autos and trucks is 1.08:1. Thus, Toyota's current ratio, like the industry average, is quite low.

Many companies today minimize their liquid assets (such as accounts receivable, and inventory) in order to improve profitability measures, such as return on assets. This is particularly true of large companies such as GM and Toyota. Companies that keep fewer liquid assets on hand must rely on other sources of liquidity. One such source is a **bank line of credit**. A line of credit is a prearranged agreement between a company and a lender that permits the company, should it be necessary, to borrow up to an agreed-upon amount. For example, a recent disclosure regarding debt in General Motors' financial statements states that it has $3.3 billion of unused lines of credit. This represents a substantial amount of available cash. In addition, the Management Discussion and Analysis section of GM's annual report provides an extensive discussion of the company's liquidity. In it, GM notes that even though its credit rating was downgraded during the year, its "access to the capital markets remained sufficient to meet the Corporation's capital needs." Thus, even though General Motors had a low current ratio, it believed that its available lines of credit as well as other sources of financing were adequate to meet any short-term cash deficiency it might experience.

## DECISION TOOLKIT

| DECISION CHECKPOINTS | INFO NEEDED FOR DECISION | TOOL TO USE FOR DECISION | HOW TO EVALUATE RESULTS |
|---|---|---|---|
| Can the company obtain short-term financing when necessary? | Available lines of credit, from notes to the financial statements. | Compare available lines of credit to current liabilities. Also, evaluate liquidity ratios. | If liquidity ratios are low, then lines of credit should be high to compensate. |

### Solvency

**Solvency ratios** measure the ability of a company to survive over a long period of time. The Feature Story in this chapter mentioned that although there once were many U.S. automobile manufacturers, only three U.S.-based companies remain today. Many of the others went bankrupt. This highlights the fact that when making a long-term loan or purchasing a company's stock, you must give consideration to a company's solvency.

To reduce the risks associated with having a large amount of debt during an economic downturn, some U.S. automobile manufacturers took two precautionary steps while they enjoyed strong profits. First, they built up large balances of cash and cash equivalents to avoid a cash crisis. Second, they were reluctant to build new plants or hire new workers to meet their production needs. Instead, they asked workers to put in overtime, or they "outsourced" work to other companies. In this way, when the economic downturn occurred, they hoped to avoid having to make debt payments on idle production plants and to minimize layoffs. As a result, in the middle of 2008 Ford still had cash of $29 billion, about double the amount of cash it would expect to use over a two-year period.

In Chapter 2, you learned that one measure of a company's solvency is the debt to total assets ratio. This is calculated as total liabilities divided by total assets. This ratio indicates the extent to which a company's assets are financed with debt.

Another useful solvency measure is the **times interest earned ratio**. It provides an indication of a company's ability to meet interest payments as they come due. It is computed by dividing income before interest expense and income taxes by interest expense. It uses income before interest expense and taxes because this number best represents the amount available to pay interest.

We can use the balance sheet information presented on page 523 and the additional information below to calculate solvency ratios for Toyota.

| ($ in millions) | 2007 | 2006 |
|---|---|---|
| Net income | $13,927 | $11,681 |
| Interest expense | 418 | 184 |
| Income tax expense | 7,609 | 6,769 |

The debt to total assets ratios and times interest earned ratios for Toyota and averages for the industry are shown in Illustration 10-18.

**Illustration 10-18**
Solvency ratios

$$\text{Debt to Total Assets Ratio} = \frac{\text{Total Liabilities}}{\text{Total Assets}}$$

$$\text{Times Interest Earned Ratio} = \frac{\text{Net Income} + \text{Interest Expense} + \text{Tax Expense}}{\text{Interest Expense}}$$

| Ratio | Toyota ($ in millions) 2007 | Toyota ($ in millions) 2006 | Industry Average 2007 |
|---|---|---|---|
| Debt to Total Assets Ratio | $\frac{\$175,678}{\$275,941} = 64\%$ | $\frac{\$154,688}{\$244,587} = 63\%$ | 65.0% |
| Times Interest Earned Ratio | $\frac{\$13,927 + \$418 + \$7,609}{\$418} = 52.5 \text{ times}$ | $\frac{\$11,681 + \$184 + \$6,769}{\$184} = 101.3 \text{ times}$ | 3.0 times |

Toyota's debt to total assets ratio was 64%. The industry average for manufacturers of autos and trucks is 65%. Thus, Toyota is approximately as reliant on debt financing as the average firm in the auto and truck industry.

Toyota's times interest earned ratio declined from 101.3 times in 2006 to 52.5 in 2007. This means that in 2007 Toyota had earnings before interest and taxes that were more than 50 times the amount needed to pay interest. The higher the multiple, the lower the likelihood that the company will default on interest payments. Because many of the companies in this industry had huge losses in 2007, the industry average was only 3.0. This suggests that while Toyota's ability to meet interest payments was extremely high, the average company in the industry had a much lower ability to meet interest payments.

### Investor Insight

#### Debt Masking

In the wake of the financial crisis, many financial institutions are wary of reporting too much debt on their financial statements, for fear that investors will consider them too risky. The Securities and Exchange Commission (SEC) is concerned that some companies engage in "debt masking" to make it appear that they use less debt than they actually do. These companies enter into transactions at the end of the accounting period that essentially remove debt from their books. Shortly after the end of the period, they reverse the transaction and the debt goes back on their books. The *Wall Street Journal* reported that 18 large banks "had consistently lowered one type of debt at the end of each of the past five quarters, reducing it on average by 42% from quarterly peaks."

*Source:* Tom McGinty, Kate Kelly, and Kara Scannell, "Debt 'Masking' Under Fire," *Wall Street Journal Online* (April 21, 2010).

 What implications does debt masking have for an investor that is using the debt to total assets ratio to evaluate a company's solvency? (See page 564.)

## DECISION TOOLKIT

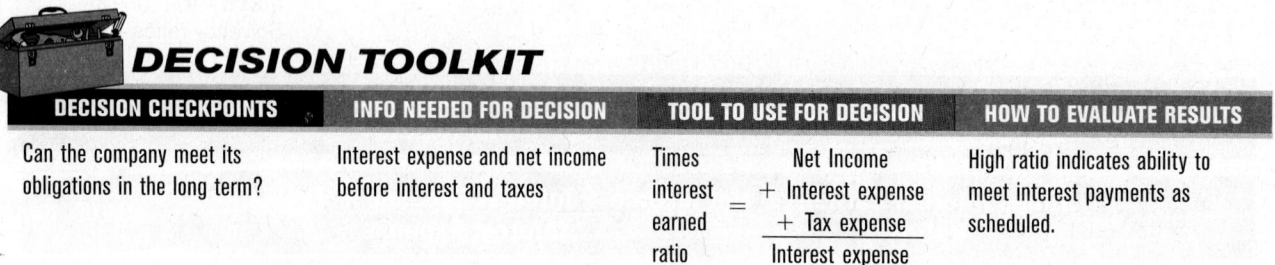

| DECISION CHECKPOINTS | INFO NEEDED FOR DECISION | TOOL TO USE FOR DECISION | HOW TO EVALUATE RESULTS |
|---|---|---|---|
| Can the company meet its obligations in the long term? | Interest expense and net income before interest and taxes | Times interest earned ratio $= \dfrac{\text{Net Income} + \text{Interest expense} + \text{Tax expense}}{\text{Interest expense}}$ | High ratio indicates ability to meet interest payments as scheduled. |

### OFF-BALANCE-SHEET FINANCING

A concern for analysts when they evaluate a company's liquidity and solvency is whether that company has properly recorded all of its obligations. The bankruptcy of Enron Corporation, one of the largest bankruptcies in U.S. history, demonstrated how much damage can result when a company does not properly record or disclose all of its debts. Many would say Enron was practicing off-balance-sheet financing. **Off-balance-sheet financing** is an intentional effort by a company to structure its financing arrangements so as to avoid showing liabilities on its balance sheet. Two common types of off-balance-sheet financing result from unreported contingencies and lease transactions.

### Contingencies

One reason a company's balance sheet might not fully reflect its potential obligations is due to contingencies. **Contingencies** are events with uncertain outcomes that may represent potential liabilities. A common type of contingency is lawsuits. Suppose, for example, that you were analyzing the financial statements of a cigarette manufacturer and did not consider the possible negative implications of existing unsettled lawsuits. Your analysis of the company's financial position would certainly be misleading. Other common types of contingencies are product warranties and environmental clean-up obligations. For example, in a recent year, Novartis AG began offering a money-back guarantee on its blood-pressure medications. This guarantee would necessitate an accrual for the estimated claims that will result from returns.

Accounting rules require that companies disclose contingencies in the notes; in some cases, they must accrue them as liabilities. For example, suppose that Waterbury Inc. is sued by a customer for $1 million due to an injury sustained by a defective product. If at the company's year-end, the lawsuit had not yet been resolved, how should Waterbury account for this event? If the company can determine **a reasonable estimate** of the expected loss and if it is **probable** it will lose the suit, then the company should accrue for the loss. It records the loss by increasing (debiting) a loss account and increasing (crediting) a liability such as Lawsuit Liability. If *both* of these conditions are not met, then the company discloses the basic facts regarding this suit in the notes to its financial statements.

## Leasing

One common type of off-balance-sheet financing results from leasing. Most lessees do not like to report leases on their balance sheets because the lease increases the company's total liabilities. Recall from Chapter 9 that **operating leases** are treated like rentals—no asset or liabilities show on the books. **Capital leases** are treated like a debt-financed purchase—increasing both assets and liabilities. **As a result, many companies structure their lease agreements to avoid meeting the criteria of a capital lease.**

Recall from Chapter 9 that many U.S. airlines lease a large portion of their planes without showing any debt related to them on their balance sheets. For example, the total increase in assets and liabilities that would result if Southwest Airlines recorded on the balance sheet its off-balance-sheet **"operating" leases** would be approximately $2.3 billion. Illustration 10-19 presents Southwest Airlines' debt to total assets ratio using the numbers presented in its balance sheet and also shows the ratio after adjusting for the off-balance-sheet leases. After those adjustments, Southwest has a ratio of 62% versus 67% before. This means that of every dollar of assets, 67 cents was funded by debt. This would be of interest to analysts evaluating Southwest's solvency.

**Ethics Note** Accounting standard-setters are attempting to rewrite rules on lease accounting because of concerns that abuse of the current standards is reducing the usefulness of financial statements.

| | **Using numbers as presented on balance sheet** | **Adjusted for off-balance-sheet leases** |
|---|---|---|
| Debt to total assets ratio | $\dfrac{\$8,803}{\$14,269} = 62\%$ | $\dfrac{\$8,803 + \$2,371}{\$14,269 + \$2,371} = 67\%$ |

**Illustration 10-19**
Debt to total assets ratio adjusted for leases

**International Note** GAAP accounting for leases is more "rules-based" than IFRS. GAAP relies on precisely defined cut-offs to determine whether an item is treated as a capital or operating lease. This rules-based approach may enable companies to structure leases "around the rules." Creating a jointly prepared leasing standard is a top priority for the IASB and FASB.

Critics of off-balance-sheet financing contend that many leases represent unavoidable obligations that meet the definition of a liability, and therefore companies should report them as liabilities on the balance sheet. To reduce these concerns, companies are required to report their operating lease obligations for subsequent years in a note. This allows analysts and other financial statement users to adjust a company's financial statements by adding leased assets and lease liabilities if they feel that this treatment is more appropriate.

# DECISION TOOLKIT

| DECISION CHECKPOINTS | INFO NEEDED FOR DECISION | TOOL TO USE FOR DECISION | HOW TO EVALUATE RESULTS |
|---|---|---|---|
| Does the company have any contingent liabilities? | Knowledge of events with uncertain negative outcomes | Notes to financial statements and financial statements | If negative outcomes are possible, determine the probability, the amount of loss, and the potential impact on financial statements. |
| Does the company have significant off-balance-sheet financing, such as unrecorded lease obligations? | Information on unrecorded obligations, such as a schedule of minimum lease payments from the notes to the financial statements | Compare liquidity and solvency ratios with and without unrecorded obligations included | If ratios differ significantly after including unrecorded obligations, these obligations should not be ignored in analysis. |

## Investor Insight

### "Covenant-Lite" Debt

In many corporate loans and bond issuances, the lending agreement specifies *debt covenants*. These covenants typically are specific financial measures, such as minimum levels of retained earnings, cash flows, times interest earned ratios, or other measures that a company must maintain during the life of the loan. If the company violates a covenant, it is considered to have violated the loan agreement; the creditors can demand immediate repayment, or they can renegotiate the loan's terms. Covenants protect lenders because they enable lenders to step in and try to get their money back before the borrower gets too deep into trouble.

During the 1990s, most traditional loans specified between three to six covenants or "triggers." In more recent years, however, when there was lots of cash available, lenders began reducing or completely eliminating covenants from loan agreements in order to be more competitive with other lenders. When the economy declined, these lenders lost big money when companies defaulted.

*Source:* Cynthia Koons, "Risky Business: Growth of 'Covenant-Lite' Debt," *Wall Street Journal* (June 18, 2007), p. C2.

 How can financial ratios such as those covered in this chapter provide protection for creditors? (See page 564.)

# USING THE DECISION TOOLKIT

Ford Motor Company has enjoyed some tremendous successes, including its popular Taurus and Explorer vehicles. Yet observers are looking for the next big hit. Development of a new vehicle costs billions. A flop is financially devastating, and the financial effect is magnified if the company has large amounts of outstanding debt.

The balance sheets on the next page provide financial information for the Automotive Division of Ford Motor Company as of December 31, 2007 and 2006. We have chosen to analyze only the Automotive Division rather than the total corporation, which includes Ford's giant financing division. In an actual analysis, you would want to analyze the major divisions individually as well as the combined corporation as a whole.

## Instructions

1. Evaluate Ford's liquidity using appropriate ratios, and compare to those of Toyota and to industry averages.

2. Evaluate Ford's solvency using appropriate ratios, and compare to those of Toyota and to industry averages.

3. Comment on Ford's available lines of credit.

## FORD MOTOR COMPANY— AUTOMOTIVE DIVISION
### Balance Sheets
### December 31, 2007 and 2006*
### (in millions)

| Assets | 2007 | 2006 |
|---|---|---|
| Current assets | $ 54,243 | $ 54,953 |
| Noncurrent assets | 64,246 | 67,681 |
| Total assets | $118,489 | $ 122,634 |
| **Liabilities and Shareholders' Equity** | | |
| Current liabilities | $ 50,218 | $ 51,690 |
| Noncurrent liabilities | 73,317 | 83,725 |
| Total liabilities | 123,535 | 135,415 |
| Total shareholders' equity | (5,046) | (12,781) |
| Total liabilities and shareholders' equity | $118,489 | $ 122,634 |
| **Other Information** | | |
| Net income (loss) | $ (4,970) | $(17,040) |
| Tax expense (refund) | (1,541) | (5,282) |
| Interest expense | 2,252 | 995 |
| Available lines of credit (Automotive Division) | 10,900 | |

*We chose to use 2007 and 2006 because the large losses in the auto industry during 2008 and 2009 reduce the instructional usefulness of some of the ratios in this discussion.

### Solution

1. Ford's liquidity can be measured using the current ratio:

| | 2007 | 2006 |
|---|---|---|
| Current ratio | $\dfrac{\$54,243}{\$50,218} = 1.08{:}1$ | $\dfrac{\$54,953}{\$51,690} = 1.06{:}1$ |

Ford's current ratio is approximately the same as the industry average of 1.08:1 and roughly the same as Toyota's. These are increasingly common levels for large companies that have reduced the amount of inventory and receivables they hold. As noted earlier, these low current ratios are not necessarily cause for concern, but they do require more careful monitoring. Ford must also make sure to have other short-term financing options available, such as lines of credit.

2. Ford's solvency can be measured with the debt to total assets ratio and the times interest earned ratio:

| | 2007 | 2006 |
|---|---|---|
| Debt to total assets ratio | $\dfrac{\$123,535}{\$118,489} = 104\%$ | $\dfrac{\$135,415}{\$122,634} = 110\%$ |
| Times interest earned ratio | $\dfrac{\$(4,970) + \$2,252 - \$1,541}{\$2,252}$ | $\dfrac{\$(17,040) + \$995 - \$5,282}{\$995}$ |
| | $= 0$ times | $= 0$ times |

The debt to total assets ratio suggests that Ford relies very heavily on debt financing. The ratio decreased from 2006 to 2007, indicating that the company's solvency improved slightly. But in both years it exceeded 100%. This is possible because we have calculated the ratio for the Automotive Division only, rather than the whole company. The debt to total assets ratio for the entire company is 94.5%. This is extremely high.

The times interest earned ratio is zero in both years. The ratio is zero because, even after adding back interest and taxes, the company's income was negative. This is well below the industry average of 3.0 times. It is likely that the company's solvency was a concern to investors and creditors and would be closely monitored. Note that because Ford reported net losses, it had tax refunds rather than tax expense. Since tax expense is added in the numerator, tax refunds are subtracted.

3. Ford has available lines of credit of $10.9 billion. These financing sources significantly improve its liquidity and help reduce the concerns of its short-term creditors.

# Summary of Study Objectives

**1** **Explain a current liability and identify the major types of current liabilities.** A current liability is a debt that a company can reasonably expect to pay (a) from existing current assets or through the creation of other current liabilities, and (b) within one year or the operating cycle, whichever is longer. The major types of current liabilities are notes payable, accounts payable, sales taxes payable, unearned revenues, and accrued liabilities such as taxes, salaries and wages, and interest payable.

**2** **Describe the accounting for notes payable.** When a promissory note is interest-bearing, the amount of assets received upon the issuance of the note is generally equal to the face value of the note, and interest expense is accrued over the life of the note. At maturity, the amount paid is equal to the face value of the note plus accrued interest.

**3** **Explain the accounting for other current liabilities.** Companies record sales taxes payable at the time the related sales occur. The company serves as a collection agent for the taxing authority. Sales taxes are not an expense to the company. Companies hold employee withholding taxes, and credit them to appropriate liability accounts, until they remit these taxes to the governmental taxing authorities. Unearned revenues are initially recorded in an unearned revenue account. As the company earns the revenue, a transfer from unearned revenue to earned revenue occurs. Companies should report the current maturities of long-term debt as a current liability in the balance sheet.

**4** **Identify the types of bonds.** The following different types of bonds may be issued: secured and unsecured bonds, and convertible and callable bonds.

**5** **Prepare the entries for the issuance of bonds and interest expense.** When companies issue bonds, they debit Cash for the cash proceeds and credit Bonds Payable for the face value of the bonds. In addition, they use the accounts Premium on Bonds Payable and Discount on Bonds Payable to show the bond premium and bond discount, respectively. Bond discount and bond premium are amortized over the life of the bond, which increases or decreases interest expense, respectively.

**6** **Describe the entries when bonds are redeemed.** When companies redeem bonds at maturity, they credit Cash and debit Bonds Payable for the face value of the bonds. When companies redeem bonds before maturity, they (a) eliminate the carrying value of the bonds at the redemption date, (b) record the cash paid, and (c) recognize the gain or loss on redemption.

**7** **Identify the requirements for the financial statement presentation and analysis of liabilities.** Current liabilities appear first on the balance sheet, followed by long-term liabilities. Companies should report the nature and amount of each liability in the balance sheet or in schedules in the notes accompanying the statements. They report inflows and outflows of cash related to the principal portion of long-term debt in the financing section of the statement of cash flows.

The liquidity of a company may be analyzed by computing the current ratio. The long-run solvency of a company may be analyzed by computing the debt to total assets ratio and the times interest earned ratio. Other factors to consider are contingent liabilities and lease obligations.

# DECISION TOOLKIT A SUMMARY

| DECISION CHECKPOINTS | INFO NEEDED FOR DECISION | TOOL TO USE FOR DECISION | HOW TO EVALUATE RESULTS |
|---|---|---|---|
| Can the company obtain short-term financing when necessary? | Available lines of credit, from notes to the financial statements | Compare available lines of credit to current liabilities. Also, evaluate liquidity ratios. | If liquidity ratios are low, then lines of credit should be high to compensate. |
| Can the company meet its obligations in the long term? | Interest expense and net income before interest and taxes | $$\text{Times interest earned ratio} = \frac{\text{Net income} + \text{Interest expense} + \text{Tax expense}}{\text{Interest expense}}$$ | High ratio indicates ability to meet interest payments as scheduled. |
| Does the company have any contingent liabilities? | Knowledge of events with uncertain negative outcomes | Notes to financial statements and financial statements | If negative outcomes are possible, determine the probability, the amount of loss, and the potential impact on financial statements. |

*(continued)*

| Does the company have significant off-balance-sheet financing, such as unrecorded lease obligations? | Information on unrecorded obligations, such as a schedule of minimum lease payments from the notes to the financial statements | Compare liquidity and solvency ratios with and without unrecorded obligations included | If ratios differ significantly after including unrecorded obligations, these obligations should not be ignored in analysis. |

## appendix 10A

# Straight-Line Amortization

### AMORTIZING BOND DISCOUNT

To follow the expense recognition principle, companies allocate bond discount to expense in each period in which the bonds are outstanding. The **straight-line method of amortization** allocates the same amount to interest expense in each interest period. The calculation is presented in Illustration 10A-1.

**study objective 8**

Apply the straight-line method of amortizing bond discount and bond premium.

| **Bond Discount** | ÷ | **Number of Interest Periods** | = | **Bond Discount Amortization** |

**Illustration 10A-1**
Formula for straight-line method of bond discount amortization

In the Candlestick Inc. example (page 517), the company sold $100,000, five-year, 10% bonds on January 1, 2012, for $98,000. This resulted in a $2,000 bond discount ($100,000 − $98,000). The bond discount amortization is $400 ($2,000 ÷ 5) for each of the five amortization periods. Candlestick records the first accrual of bond interest and the amortization of bond discount on December 31 as follows.

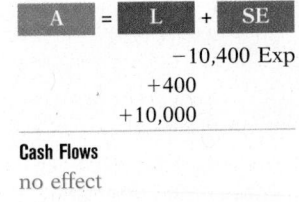

| A | = | L | + | SE |

| Dec. 31 | Interest Expense | 10,400 | |
| | Discount on Bonds Payable | | 400 |
| | Interest Payable | | 10,000 |
| | (To record accrued bond interest and amortization of bond discount) | | |

−10,400 Exp
+400
+10,000

**Cash Flows**
no effect

Over the term of the bonds, the balance in Discount on Bonds Payable will decrease annually by the same amount until it has a zero balance at the maturity date of the bonds. Thus, the carrying value of the bonds at maturity will be equal to the face value of the bonds.

Preparing a bond discount amortization schedule, as shown in Illustration 10A-2 (page 532), is useful to determine interest expense, discount amortization, and the carrying value of the bond. As indicated, the interest expense recorded each period is $10,400. Also note that the carrying value of the bond increases $400 each period until it reaches its face value of $100,000 at the end of period 5.

**Alternative Terminology** The amount in the Discount on Bonds Payable account is often referred to as *Unamortized Discount on Bonds Payable.*

**CANDLESTICK INC.**
Bond Discount Amortization Schedule
Straight-Line Method—Annual Interest Payments
$100,000 of 10%, 5-Year Bonds

| Interest Periods | (A) Interest to Be Paid (10% × $100,000) | (B) Interest Expense to Be Recorded (A) + (C) | (C) Discount Amortization ($2,000 ÷ 5) | (D) Unamortized Discount (D) − (C) | (E) Bond Carrying Value ($100,000 − D) |
|---|---|---|---|---|---|
| Issue date | | | | $2,000 | $ 98,000 |
| 1 | $10,000 | $10,400 | $ 400 | 1,600 | 98,400 |
| 2 | 10,000 | 10,400 | 400 | 1,200 | 98,800 |
| 3 | 10,000 | 10,400 | 400 | 800 | 99,200 |
| 4 | 10,000 | 10,400 | 400 | 400 | 99,600 |
| 5 | 10,000 | 10,400 | 400 | 0 | 100,000 |
| | $50,000 | $52,000 | $2,000 | | |

Column **(A)** remains constant because the face value of the bonds ($100,000) is multiplied by the annual contractual interest rate (10%) each period.
Column **(B)** is computed as the interest paid (Column A) plus the discount amortization (Column C).
Column **(C)** indicates the discount amortization each period.
Column **(D)** decreases each period by the same amount until it reaches zero at maturity.
Column **(E)** increases each period by the amount of discount amortization until it equals the face value at maturity.

**Illustration 10A-2** Bond discount amortization schedule

## AMORTIZING BOND PREMIUM

The amortization of bond premium parallels that of bond discount. Illustration 10A-3 presents the formula for determining bond premium amortization under the straight-line method.

**Illustration 10A-3**
Formula for straight-line method of bond premium amortization

| Bond Premium | ÷ | Number of Interest Periods | = | Bond Premium Amortization |
|---|---|---|---|---|

Continuing our example, assume Candlestick Inc., sells the bonds described above for $102,000, rather than $98,000. This results in a bond premium of $2,000 ($102,000 − $100,000). The premium amortization for each interest period is $400 ($2,000 ÷ 5). Candlestick records the first accrual of interest on December 31 as follows.

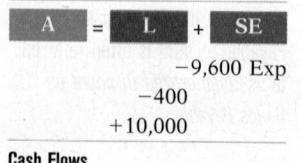

A = L + SE
−9,600 Exp
−400
+10,000

**Cash Flows**
no effect

| | | | | |
|---|---|---|---|---|
| Dec. 31 | Interest Expense | | 9,600 | |
| | Premium on Bonds Payable | | 400 | |
| | Interest Payable | | | 10,000 |
| | (To record accrued bond interest and amortization of bond premium) | | | |

Over the term of the bonds, the balance in Premium on Bonds Payable will decrease annually by the same amount until it has a zero balance at maturity.

A bond premium amortization schedule, as shown in Illustration 10A-4, is useful to determine interest expense, premium amortization, and the carrying value of the bond. As indicated, the interest expense Candlestick records each period is $9,600. Note that the carrying value of the bond decreases $400 each period until it reaches its face value of $100,000 at the end of period 5.

**Illustration 10A-4**   Bond premium amortization schedule

### CANDLESTICK INC.
### Bond Premium Amortization Schedule
### Straight-Line Method—Annual Interest Payments
### $100,000 of 10%, 5-Year Bonds

| Interest Periods | (A)<br>Interest to<br>Be Paid<br>(10% × $100,000) | (B)<br>Interest Expense<br>to Be Recorded<br>(A) − (C) | (C)<br>Premium<br>Amortization<br>($2,000 ÷ 5) | (D)<br>Unamortized<br>Premium<br>(D) − (C) | (E)<br>Bond<br>Carrying Value<br>($100,000 + D) |
|---|---|---|---|---|---|
| Issue date | | | | $2,000 | $ 102,000 |
| 1 | $10,000 | $ 9,600 | $ 400 | 1,600 | 101,600 |
| 2 | 10,000 | 9,600 | 400 | 1,200 | 101,200 |
| 3 | 10,000 | 9,600 | 400 | 800 | 100,800 |
| 4 | 10,000 | 9,600 | 400 | 400 | 100,400 |
| 5 | 10,000 | 9,600 | 400 | 0 | 100,000 |
| | $50,000 | $48,000 | $2,000 | | |

Column **(A)** remains constant because the face value of the bonds ($100,000) is multiplied by the annual contractual interest rate (10%) each period.
Column **(B)** is computed as the interest paid (Column A) less the premium amortization (Column C).
Column **(C)** indicates the premium amortization each period.
Column **(D)** decreases each period by the same amount until it reaches zero at maturity.
Column **(E)** decreases each period by the amount of premium amortization until it equals the face value at maturity.

# Summary of Study Objective for Appendix 10A

**8** **Apply the straight-line method of amortizing bond discount and bond premium.** The straight-line method of amortization results in a constant amount of amortization and interest expense per period.

appendix 10B

# Effective-Interest Amortization

To follow the expense recognition principle, companies allocate bond discount to expense in each period in which the bonds are outstanding. However, to completely comply with the expense recognition principle, interest expense as a percentage of carrying value should not change over the life of the bonds.

**study objective 9**

Apply the effective-interest method of amortizing bond discount and bond premium.

This percentage, referred to as the **effective-interest rate**, is established when the bonds are issued and remains constant in each interest period. Unlike the straight-line method, the effective-interest method of amortization accomplishes this result.

Under the **effective-interest method**, the amortization of bond discount or bond premium results in periodic interest expense equal to a constant percentage of the carrying value of the bonds. The effective-interest method results in **varying amounts** of amortization and interest expense per period but a **constant percentage rate.** In contrast, the straight-line method results in constant amounts of amortization and interest expense per period but a varying percentage rate.

Companies follow three steps under the effective-interest method:

1. Compute the **bond interest expense** by multiplying the carrying value of the bonds at the beginning of the interest period by the effective-interest rate.

2. Compute the **bond interest paid** (or accrued) by multiplying the face value of the bonds by the contractual interest rate.

3. Compute the **amortization amount** by determining the difference between the amounts computed in steps (1) and (2).

Illustration 10B-1 depicts these steps.

**Illustration 10B-1**
Computation of amortization using effective-interest method

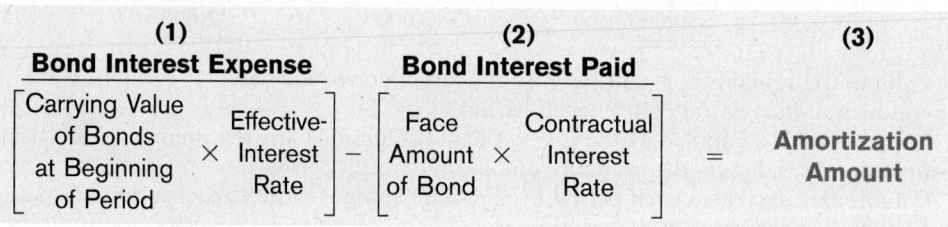

Both the straight-line and effective-interest methods of amortization result in the same total amount of interest expense over the term of the bonds. Furthermore, interest expense each interest period is generally comparable in amount. However, **when the amounts are materially different, generally accepted accounting principles (GAAP) require use of the effective-interest method.**

## AMORTIZING BOND DISCOUNT

In the Candlestick Inc. example (page 517), the company sold $100,000, five-year, 10% bonds on January 1, 2012, for $98,000. This resulted in a $2,000 bond discount ($100,000 − $98,000). This discount results in an effective-interest rate of approximately 10.53%. (The effective-interest rate can be computed using the techniques shown in Appendix D at the end of this book.)

Preparing a bond discount amortization schedule as shown in Illustration 10B-2 facilitates the recording of interest expense and the discount amortization. Note that interest expense as a percentage of carrying value remains constant at 10.53%.

**Helpful Hint** Note that the amount of periodic interest expense increases over the life of the bonds when the effective-interest method is used for bonds issued at a discount. The reason is that a constant percentage is applied to an increasing bond carrying value to compute interest expense. The carrying value is increasing because of the amortization of the discount.

### CANDLESTICK INC.
Bond Discount Amortization Schedule
Effective-Interest Method–Annual Interest Payments
10% Bonds Issued at 10.53%

| Interest Periods | (A) Interest to Be Paid (10% × $100,000) | (B) Interest Expense to Be Recorded (10.53% × Preceding Bond Carrying Value) | (C) Discount Amortization (B) − (A) | (D) Unamortized Discount (D) − (C) | (E) Bond Carrying Value ($100,000 − D) |
|---|---|---|---|---|---|
| Issue date | | | | $2,000 | $ 98,000 |
| 1 | $10,000 | $10,319 (10.53% × $98,000) | $319 | 1,681 | 98,319 |
| 2 | 10,000 | 10,353 (10.53% × $ 98,319) | 353 | 1,328 | 98,672 |
| 3 | 10,000 | 10,390 (10.53% × $ 98,672) | 390 | 938 | 99,062 |
| 4 | 10,000 | 10,431 (10.53% × $ 99,062) | 431 | 507 | 99,493 |
| 5 | 10,000 | 10,507* (10.53% × $ 99,493) | 507* | –0– | 100,000 |
| | $ 50,000 | $ 52,000 | $ 2,000 | | |

Column (A) remains constant because the face value of the bonds ($100,000) is multiplied by the annual contractual interest rate (10%) each period.
Column (B) is computed as the preceding bond carrying value times the annual effective-interest rate (10.53%).
Column (C) indicates the discount amortization each period.
Column (D) decreases each period until it reaches zero at maturity.
Column (E) increases each period until it equals face value at maturity.

*Rounded to eliminate remaining discount resulting from rounding the effective rate.

**Illustration 10B-2** Bond discount amortization schedule

For the first interest period, the computations of bond interest expense and the bond discount amortization are as follows.

| | |
|---|---|
| Bond interest expense ($98,000 × 10.53%) | $10,319 |
| Bond interest paid ($100,000 × 10%) | 10,000 |
| **Bond discount amortization** | $ 319 |

**Illustration 10B-3** Computation of bond discount amortization

As a result, Candlestick Inc. records the accrual of interest and amortization of bond discount on December 31, as follows.

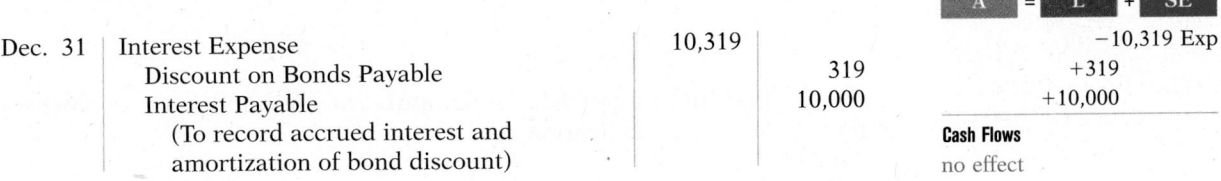

| | | | |
|---|---|---|---|
| Dec. 31 | Interest Expense | 10,319 | |
| | Discount on Bonds Payable | | 319 |
| | Interest Payable | | 10,000 |
| | (To record accrued interest and amortization of bond discount) | | |

A = L + SE

−10,319 Exp
+319
+10,000

**Cash Flows**
no effect

For the second interest period, bond interest expense will be $10,353 ($98,319 × 10.53%), and the discount amortization will be $353. At December 31, Candlestick makes the following adjusting entry.

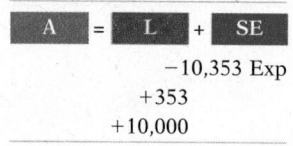

−10,353 Exp
+353
+10,000

**Cash Flows**
no effect

| | | Dec. 31 | Interest Expense | 10,353 | |
|---|---|---|---|---|---|
| | | | Discount on Bonds Payable | | 353 |
| | | | Interest Payable | | 10,000 |
| | | | (To record accrued interest and amortization of bond discount) | | |

## AMORTIZING BOND PREMIUM

Continuing our example, assume Candlestick Inc. sells the bonds described above for $102,000 rather than $98,000. This would result in a bond premium of $2,000 ($102,000 − $100,000). This premium results in an effective-interest rate of approximately 9.48%. (The effective-interest rate can be solved for using the techniques shown in Appendix D at the end of this book.) Illustration 10B-4 shows the bond premium amortization schedule.

**Illustration 10B-4** Bond premium amortization schedule

### CANDLESTICK INC.
#### Bond Premium Amortization Schedule
#### Effective-Interest Method–Annual Interest Payments
#### 10% Bonds Issued at 9.48%

| Interest Periods | (A)<br>Interest to<br>Be Paid<br>(10% × $100,000) | (B)<br>Interest Expense<br>to Be Recorded<br>(9.48% × Preceding<br>Bond Carrying Value) | (C)<br>Premium<br>Amortization<br>(A) − (B) | (D)<br>Unamortized<br>Premium<br>(D) − (C) | (E)<br>Bond<br>Carrying Value<br>($100,000 + D) |
|---|---|---|---|---|---|
| Issue date | | | | $2,000 | $102,000 |
| 1 | $10,000 | $9,670 (9.48% × $102,000) | $330 | 1,670 | 101,670 |
| 2 | 10,000 | 9,638 (9.48% × $ 101,670) | 362 | 1,308 | 101,308 |
| 3 | 10,000 | 9,604 (9.48% × $ 101,308) | 396 | 912 | 100,912 |
| 4 | 10,000 | 9,566 (9.48% × $ 100,912) | 434 | 478 | 100,478 |
| 5 | 10,000 | 9,522* (9.48% × $ 100,478) | 478* | −0− | 100,000 |
| | $ 50,000 | $ 48,000 | $ 2,000 | | |

Column (A) remains constant because the face value of the bonds ($100,000) is multiplied by the contractual interest rate (10%) each period.
Column (B) is computed as the carrying value of the bonds times the annual effective-interest rate (9.48%).
Column (C) indicates the premium amortization each period.
Column (D) decreases each period until it reaches zero at maturity.
Column (E) decreases each period until it equals face value at maturity.

*Rounded to eliminate remaining discount resulting from rounding the effective rate.

For the first interest period, the computations of bond interest expense and the bond premium amortization are:

**Illustration 10B-5**
Computation of bond premium amortization

| Bond interest paid ($100,000 × 10%) | $10,000 |
|---|---|
| Bond interest expense ($102,000 × 9.48%) | 9,670 |
| **Bond premium amortization** | $ 330 |

The entry Candlestick makes on December 31 is:

| Dec. 31 | Interest Expense | 9,670 | |
|---|---|---|---|
| | Premium on Bonds Payable | 330 | |
| | Interest Payable | | 10,000 |
| | (To record accrued interest and | | |
| | amortization of bond premium) | | |

A = L + SE

−9,670 Exp

−330

+10,000

**Cash Flows**

no effect

For the second interest period, interest expense will be $9,638, and the premium amortization will be $362. Note that the amount of periodic interest expense decreases over the life of the bond when companies apply the effective-interest method to bonds issued at a premium. The reason is that a constant percentage is applied to a decreasing bond carrying value to compute interest expense. The carrying value is decreasing because of the amortization of the premium.

## Summary of Study Objective for Appendix 10B

**9** **Apply the effective-interest method of amortizing bond discount and bond premium.** The effective-interest method results in varying amounts of amortization and interest expense per period but a constant per- centage rate of interest. When the difference between the straight-line and effective-interest method is material, GAAP requires use of the effective-interest method.

**appendix 10C**

# Accounting for Long-Term Notes Payable

The use of notes payable in long-term debt financing is quite common. Long-term notes payable are similar to short-term interest-bearing notes payable except that the terms of the notes exceed one year. In periods of unstable interest rates, lenders may tie the interest rate on long-term notes to changes in the market rate for comparable loans. Examples are the 8.03% adjustable rate notes issued by General Motors and the floating-rate notes issued by American Express Company.

A long-term note may be secured by a document called a **mortgage** that pledges title to specific assets as security for a loan. Individuals widely use **mortgage notes payable** to purchase homes, as do many small and some large companies to acquire plant assets. For example, at one time approximately 18% of McDonald's long-term debt related to mortgage notes on land, buildings, and improvements.

Like other long-term notes payable, the mortgage loan terms may stipulate either a fixed or an adjustable interest rate. Typically, the terms require the borrower to make equal installment payments over the term of the loan. Each payment consists of (1) interest on the unpaid balance of the loan and (2) a reduction of loan principal. While the total amount paid remains constant, the interest decreases each period and the portion applied to the loan principal increases.

**study objective 10**

Describe the accounting for long-term notes payable.

**Helpful Hint** Electronic spreadsheet programs can create a schedule of installment loan payments. This allows you to put in the data for your own mortgage loan and get an illustration that really hits home.

Companies initially record mortgage notes payable at face value, and subsequently make entries for each installment payment. To illustrate, assume that Porter Technology Inc. issues a $500,000, 12%, 20-year mortgage note on December 31, 2012, to obtain needed financing for the construction of a new research laboratory. The terms provide for semiannual installment payments of $33,231 (not including real estate taxes and insurance). The installment payment schedule for the first two years is as follows.

**Illustration 10C-1**
Mortgage installment payment schedule

| Semiannual Interest Period | (A) Cash Payment | (B) Interest Expense (D) × 6% | (C) Reduction of Principal (A) − (B) | (D) Principal Balance (D) − (C) |
|---|---|---|---|---|
| Issue date | | | | $500,000 |
| 1 | $33,231 | $30,000 | $3,231 | 496,769 |
| 2 | 33,231 | 29,806 | 3,425 | 493,344 |
| 3 | 33,231 | 29,601 | 3,630 | 489,714 |
| 4 | 33,231 | 29,383 | 3,848 | 485,866 |

Porter Technology records the mortgage loan and first installment payment as follows.

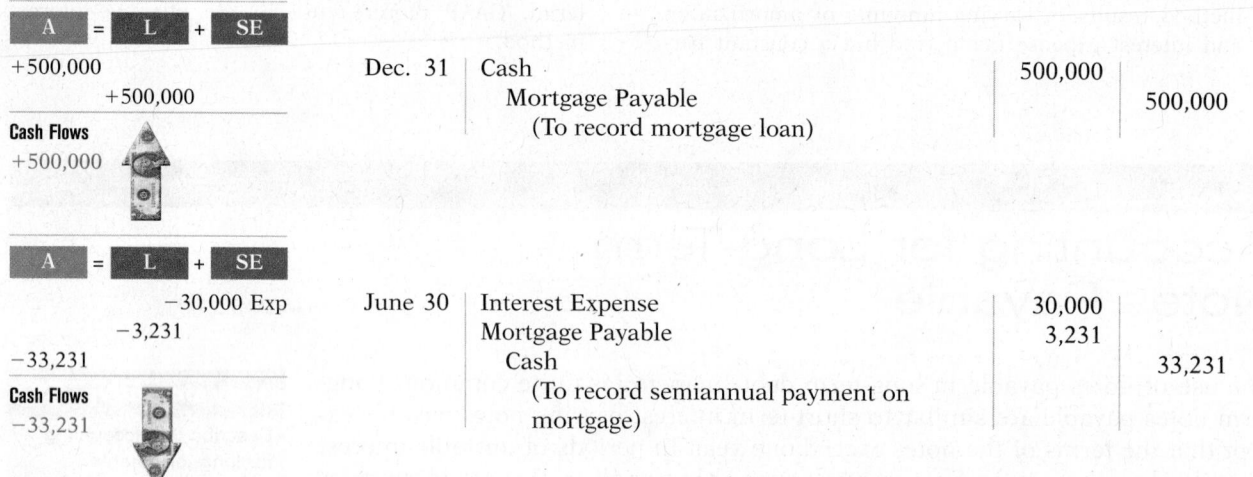

| | | | |
|---|---|---|---|
| Dec. 31 | Cash | 500,000 | |
| | Mortgage Payable | | 500,000 |
| | (To record mortgage loan) | | |

| | | | |
|---|---|---|---|
| June 30 | Interest Expense | 30,000 | |
| | Mortgage Payable | 3,231 | |
| | Cash | | 33,231 |
| | (To record semiannual payment on mortgage) | | |

A = L + SE
+500,000
+500,000
Cash Flows
+500,000

A = L + SE
−30,000 Exp
−3,231
−33,231
Cash Flows
−33,231

**In the balance sheet, the company reports the reduction in principal for the next year as a current liability, and classifies the remaining unpaid principal balance as a long-term liability.** At December 31, 2013 (the end of semiannual period 2), the total liability is $493,344, of which $7,478 ($3,630 + $3,848) is current and $485,866 ($493,344 − $7,478) is long-term.

# Summary of Study Objective for Appendix 10C

**10** **Describe the accounting for long-term notes payable.** Each payment consists of (1) interest on the unpaid balance of the loan, and (2) a reduction of loan principal. The interest decreases each period, while the portion applied to the loan principal increases each period.

# Glossary

**Bond certificate** *(p. 513)* A legal document that indicates the name of the issuer, the face value of the bonds, and such other data as the contractual interest rate and the maturity date of the bonds.

**Bonds** *(p. 512)* A form of interest-bearing notes payable issued by corporations, universities, and governmental entities.

**Callable bonds** *(p. 512)* Bonds that are the issuing company can retire at a stated dollar amount prior to maturity.

**Capital lease** *(p. 527)* A contractual agreement allowing one party (the lessee) to use the assets of another party (the lessor); accounted for like a debt-financed purchase by the lessee.

**Contingencies** *(p. 526)* Events with uncertain outcomes that may represent potential liabilities.

**Contractual (stated) interest rate** *(p. 513)* Rate used to determine the amount of interest the borrower pays and the investor receives.

**Convertible bonds** *(p. 512)* Bonds that can be converted into common stock at the bondholder's option.

**Current liability** *(p. 506)* A debt that a company reasonably expects to pay (1) from existing current assets or through the creation of other current liabilities, and (2) within one year or the operating cycle, whichever is longer.

**Discount (on a bond)** *(p. 517)* The difference between the face value of a bond and its selling price, when a bond is sold for less than its face value.

**Effective-interest method of amortization** *(p. 534)* A method of amortizing bond discount or bond premium that results in periodic interest expense equal to a constant percentage of the carrying value of the bonds.

**Effective-interest rate** *(p. 534)* Rate established when bonds are issued that remains constant in each interest period.

**Face value** *(p. 513)* Amount of principal due at the maturity date of the bond.

**Long-term liabilities** *(p. 512)* Obligations that a company expects to pay more than one year in the future.

**Market interest rate** *(p. 514)* The rate investors demand for loaning funds to the corporation.

**Maturity date** *(p. 513)* The date on which the final payment on a bond is due from the bond issuer to the investor.

**Mortgage note payable** *(p. 537)* A long-term note secured by a mortgage that pledges title to specific assets as security for the loan.

**Notes payable** *(p. 506)* An obligation in the form of a written note.

**Off-balance-sheet financing** *(p. 526)* The intentional effort by a company to structure its financing arrangements so as to avoid showing liabilities on its balance sheet.

**Operating lease** *(p. 527)* A contractual agreement allowing one party (the lessee) to use the asset of another party (the lessor); accounted for as a rental.

**Premium (on a bond)** *(p. 517)* The difference between the selling price and the face value of a bond when a bond is sold for more than its face value.

**Present value** *(p. 514)* The value today of an amount to be received at some date in the future after taking into account current interest rates.

**Secured bonds** *(p. 512)* Bonds that have specific assets of the issuer pledged as collateral.

**Straight-line method of amortization** *(p. 531)* A method of amortizing bond discount or bond premium that allocates the same amount to interest expense in each interest period.

**Time value of money** *(p. 513)* The relationship between time and money. A dollar received today is worth more than a dollar promised at some time in the future.

**Times interest earned ratio** *(p. 525)* A measure of a company's solvency, calculated by dividing income before interest expense and taxes by interest expense.

**Unsecured bonds** *(p. 512)* Bonds issued against the general credit of the borrower.

# Comprehensive Do it!

Snyder Software Inc. successfully developed a new spreadsheet program. However, to produce and market the program, the company needed additional financing. On January 1, 2011, Snyder borrowed money as follows.

1. Snyder issued $500,000, 11%, 10-year bonds. The bonds sold at face value and pay interest on January 1.

2. Snyder issued $1.0 million, 10%, 10-year bonds for $886,996. Interest is payable on January 1. Snyder uses the straight-line method of amortization.

## Instructions

(a) For the 11% bonds, prepare journal entries for the following items.
   (1) The issuance of the bonds on January 1, 2011.
   (2) Accrue interest expense on December 31, 2011.
   (3) The payment of interest on January 1, 2012.

(b) For the 10-year, 10% bonds:
   (1) Journalize the issuance of the bonds on January 1, 2011.
   (2) Prepare the entry for the redemption of the bonds at 101 on January 1, 2014, after paying the interest due on this date. The carrying value of the bonds at the redemption date was $920,897.

**Action Plan**

- Record the discount on bonds issued as a contra liability account.
- Compute the loss on bond redemption as the excess of the cash paid over the carrying value of the redeemed bonds.

**Solution to Comprehensive Do it!**

(a) (1) 2011

| Jan. 1 | Cash | 500,000 | |
|---|---|---|---|
| |     Bonds Payable | | 500,000 |
| |     (To record issue of 11%, 10-year bonds at face value) | | |

(2) 2011

| Dec. 31 | Interest Expense | 55,000 | |
|---|---|---|---|
| |     Interest Payable | | 55,000 |
| |     (To record accrual of bond interest) | | |

(3) 2012

| Jan. 1 | Interest Payable | 55,000 | |
|---|---|---|---|
| |     Cash | | 55,000 |
| |     (To record payment of accrued interest) | | |

(b) (1) 2011

| Jan. 1 | Cash | 886,996 | |
|---|---|---|---|
| | Discount on Bonds Payable | 113,004 | |
| |     Bonds Payable | | 1,000,000 |
| |     (To record issuance of bonds at a discount) | | |

(2) 2014

| Jan. 1 | Bonds Payable | 1,000,000 | |
|---|---|---|---|
| | Loss on Bond Redemption | 89,103* | |
| |     Discount on Bonds Payable | | 79,103 |
| |     Cash | | 1,010,000 |
| |     (To record redemption of bonds at 101) | | |
| | *($1,010,000 − $920,897) | | |

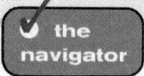

**Self-Test, Brief Exercises, Exercises, Problem Set A, and many more resources are available for practice in WileyPLUS**

*Note:* All Questions, Exercises, and Problems marked with an asterisk relate to material in the appendices to the chapter.

# Self-Test Questions

Answers are on page 564.

(SO 1)  **1.** The time period for classifying a liability as current is one year or the operating cycle, whichever is:
   (a) longer.
   (b) shorter.
   (c) probable.
   (d) possible.

**2.** To be classified as a current liability, a debt must be (SO 1) expected to be paid:
   (a) out of existing current assets.
   (b) by creating other current liabilities.
   (c) within 2 years.
   (d) Either (a) or (b).

(SO 2)  **3.** Ottman Company borrows $88,500 on September 1, 2012, from Farley State Bank by signing an $88,500, 12%, one-year note. What is the accrued interest at December 31, 2012?
(a) $2,655.  (c) $4,425.
(b) $3,540.  (d) $10,620.

(SO 2)  **4.** JD Company borrowed $70,000 on December 1 on a 6-month, 12% note. At December 31:
(a) neither the note payable nor the interest payable is a current liability.
(b) the note payable is a current liability but the interest payable is not.
(c) the interest payable is a current liability but the note payable is not.
(d) both the note payable and the interest payable are current liabilities.

(SO 3)  **5.** Alexis Company has total proceeds from sales of $4,515. If the proceeds include sales taxes of 5%, what is the amount to be credited to Sales Revenue?
(a) $4,000.
(b) $4,300.
(c) $4,289.25.
(d) The correct answer is not given.

(SO 3)  **6.** When recording payroll:
(a) gross earnings are recorded as salaries and wages payable.
(b) net pay is recorded as salaries and wages expense.
(c) payroll deductions are recorded as liabilities.
(d) More than one of the above.

(SO 3)  **7.** No Fault Insurance Company collected a premium of $18,000 for a 1-year insurance policy on April 1. What amount should No Fault report as a current liability for Unearned Insurance Premiums at December 31?
(a) $0.  (c) $13,500.
(b) $4,500.  (d) $18,000.

(SO 4)  **8.** What term is used for bonds that have specific assets pledged as collateral?
(a) Callable bonds.  (c) Secured bonds.
(b) Convertible bonds.  (d) Discount bonds.

(SO 4)  **9.** The market interest rate:
(a) is the contractual interest rate used to determine the amount of cash interest paid by the borrower.
(b) is listed in the bond indenture.
(c) is the rate investors demand for loaning funds.
(d) More than one of the above is true.

(SO 5)  **10.** Laurel Inc. issues 10-year bonds with a maturity value of $200,000. If the bonds are issued at a premium, this indicates that:
(a) the contractual interest rate exceeds the market interest rate.
(b) the market interest rate exceeds the contractual interest rate.
(c) the contractual interest rate and the market interest rate are the same.
(d) no relationship exists between the two rates.

(SO 5)  **11.** On January 1, 2012, Kelly Corp. issues $200,000, 5-year, 7% bonds at face value. The entry to record the issuance of the bonds would include a:
(a) debit to Cash for $14,000.
(b) debit to Bonds Payable for $200,000.
(c) credit to Bonds Payable for $200,000.
(d) credit to Interest Expense of $14,000.

(SO 5)  **12.** Prescher Corporation issued bonds that pay interest every July 1 and January 1. The entry to accrue bond interest at December 31 includes a:
(a) debit to Interest Payable.
(b) credit to Cash.
(c) credit to Interest Expense.
(d) credit to Interest Payable.

(SO 6)  **13.** Goethe Corporation retires its $100,000 face value bonds at 105 on January 1, following the payment of interest. The carrying value of the bonds at the redemption date is $103,745. The entry to record the redemption will include a:
(a) credit of $3,745 to Loss on Bond Redemption.
(b) debit of $3,745 to Premium on Bonds Payable.
(c) credit of $1,255 to Gain on Bond Redemption.
(d) debit of $5,000 to Premium on Bonds Payable.

(SO 7)  **14.** 🔧 In a recent year, Derek Corporation had net income of $150,000, interest expense of $30,000, and income tax expense of $20,000. What was Derek Corporation's times interest earned ratio for the year?
(a) 5.00.  (c) 6.67.
(b) 4.00.  (d) 7.50.

(SO 7)  **15.** 🔧 Which of the following is *not* a measure of liquidity?
(a) Debt to total assets ratio.
(b) Working capital.
(c) Current ratio.
(d) Current cash debt coverage.

(SO 8)  ***16.** On January 1, Xiang Corporation issues $500,000, 5-year, 12% bonds at 96 with interest payable on January 1. The entry on December 31 to record accrued bond interest and the amortization of bond discount using the straight-line method will include a:
(a) debit to Interest Expense, $57,600.
(b) debit to Interest Expense, $60,000.
(c) credit to Discount on Bonds Payable, $4,000.
(d) credit to Discount on Bonds Payable, $2,000.

(SO 8)  ***17.** For the bonds issued in question 16, what is the carrying value of the bonds at the end of the third interest period?
(a) $492,000.  (c) $472,000.
(b) $488,000.  (d) $464,000.

(SO 9)  ***18.** On January 1, Holly Ester Inc. issued $1,000,000, 10-year, 9% bonds for $938,554. The market rate of interest for these bonds is 10%. Interest is payable annually on December 31. Holly Ester uses the effective-interest method of amortizing bond discount. At the end of the first year, Holly Ester should report unamortized bond discount of:
(a) $54,900.  (c) $51,610.
(b) $57,591.  (d) $51,000.

(SO 9) *19. On January 1, Nicholas Corporation issued $1,000,000, 14%, 5-year bonds with interest payable on December 31. The bonds sold for $1,072,096. The market rate of interest for these bonds was 12%. On the first interest date, using the effective-interest method, the debit entry to Interest Expense is for:
(a) $120,000.          (c) $128,652.
(b) $125,581.          (d) $140,000.

(SO 10) *20. Sampson Corp. purchased a piece of equipment by issuing a $20,000, 6% installment note payable. Quar-

terly payments on the note are $1,165. What will be the reduction in the principal portion of the note payable that results from the first payment?
(a) $1,165.          (c) $865.
(b) $300.          (d) $1,200.

Go to the book's companion website, **www.wiley.com/college/kimmel**, to access additional Self-Test Questions.

# Questions

1. Emily Frazier believes a current liability is a debt that can be expected to be paid in one year. Is Emily correct? Explain.

2. Verona Company obtains $20,000 in cash by signing a 9%, 6-month, $20,000 note payable to First Bank on July 1. Verona's fiscal year ends on September 30. What information should be reported for the note payable in the annual financial statements?

3. (a) Your roommate says, "Sales taxes are reported as an expense in the income statement." Do you agree? Explain.
   (b) Pearl's Cafe has cash proceeds from sales of $8,550. This amount includes $550 of sales taxes. Give the entry to record the proceeds.

4. Helena University sold 9,000 season football tickets at $100 each for its five-game home schedule. What entries should be made (a) when the tickets are sold and (b) after each game?

5. Identify three taxes commonly withheld by the employer from an employee's gross pay.

6. (a) Identify three taxes commonly paid by employers on employees' salaries and wages.
   (b) Where in the financial statements does the employer report taxes withheld from employees' pay?

7. [Tootsie Roll] Identify the liabilities classified by Tootsie Roll as current.

8. (a) What are long-term liabilities? Give two examples.
   (b) What is a bond?

9. Contrast these types of bonds:
   (a) Secured and unsecured.
   (b) Convertible and callable.

10. Explain each of these important terms in issuing bonds:
    (a) Face value.
    (b) Contractual interest rate.
    (c) Bond certificate.

11. (a) ➡ What is a convertible bond?
    (b) Discuss the advantages of a convertible bond from the standpoint of the bondholders and of the issuing corporation.

12. Describe the two major obligations incurred by a company when bonds are issued.

13. Assume that Visitin Inc. sold bonds with a face value of $100,000 for $104,000. Was the market interest rate equal to, less than, or greater than the bonds' contractual interest rate? Explain.

14. Phil and Mason are discussing how the market price of a bond is determined. Phil believes that the market price of a bond is solely a function of the amount of the principal payment at the end of the term of a bond. Is he right? Discuss.

15. If a 6%, 10-year, $800,000 bond is issued at face and interest is paid annually, what is the amount of the interest payment at the end of the first period?

16. If the Bonds Payable account has a balance of $700,000 and the Discount on Bonds Payable account has a balance of $36,000, what is the carrying value of the bonds?

17. Which accounts are debited and which are credited if a bond issue originally sold at a premium is redeemed before maturity at 97 immediately following the payment of interest?

18. ➡ Barbara Monroe, the chief financial officer of Helaine Inc., is considering the options available to her for financing the company's new plant. Short-term interest rates right now are 6%, and long-term rates are 8%. The company's current ratio is 2.2:1. If she finances the new plant with short-term debt, the current ratio will fall to 1.5:1. Briefly discuss the issues that Barbara should consider.

19. 🔧
(a) In general, what are the requirements for the financial statement presentation of long-term liabilities?
(b) What ratios may be computed to evaluate a company's liquidity and solvency?

20. 🔧 Gerald Bachus says that liquidity and solvency are the same thing. Is he correct? If not, how do they differ?

21. ➡ The management of Lakeland Corporation is concerned because survey data suggest that many potential customers do not buy vehicles due to quality concerns. It is considering taking the bold step of increasing the length of its warranty from the industry standard of 3 years up to an unprecedented 10 years in an effort to increase confidence in its quality. Discuss the business as well as accounting implications of this move.

**22.** Rick Flowers needs a few new trucks for his business. He is considering buying the trucks but is concerned that the additional debt he will need to borrow will make his liquidity and solvency ratios look bad. What options does he have other than purchasing the trucks, and how will these options affect his financial statements?

**23.** Miller Corporation has a current ratio of 1.1. Ron has always been told that a corporation's current ratio should exceed 2.0. Miller argues that its ratio is low because it has a minimal amount of inventory on hand so as to reduce operating costs. Miller also points out that it has significant available lines of credit. Is Ron still correct? What do some companies do to compensate for having fewer liquid assets?

**24.** What are the implications for analysis if a company has significant operating leases?

**25.** What criteria must be met before a contingency must be recorded as a liability? How should the contingency be disclosed if the criteria are not met?

***26.** Explain the straight-line method of amortizing discount and premium on bonds payable.

***27.** Melanie Corporation issues $200,000 of 6%, 5-year bonds on January 1, 2012, at 103. Assuming that the straight-line method is used to amortize the premium, what is the total amount of interest expense for 2012?

***28.** Joslyn Topp is discussing the advantages of the effective-interest method of bond amortization with her accounting staff. What do you think Joslyn is saying?

***29.** Ziegler Corporation issues $400,000 of 9%, 5-year bonds on January 1, 2012, at 104. If Ziegler uses the effective-interest method in amortizing the premium, will the annual interest expense increase or decrease over the life of the bonds? Explain.

# Brief Exercises

**BE10-1** Jasper Company has these obligations at December 31: (a) a note payable for $100,000 due in 2 years, (b) a 10-year mortgage payable of $200,000 payable in ten $20,000 annual payments, (c) interest payable of $15,000 on the mortgage, and (d) accounts payable of $60,000. For each obligation, indicate whether it should be classified as a current liability.

*Identify whether obligations are current liabilities.*
(SO 1), **C**

**BE10-2** Canney Company borrows $90,000 on July 1 from the bank by signing a $90,000, 7%, 1-year note payable. Prepare the journal entries to record (a) the proceeds of the note and (b) accrued interest at December 31, assuming adjusting entries are made only at the end of the year.

*Prepare entries for an interest-bearing note payable.*
(SO 2), **AP**

**BE10-3** Home Town Supply does not segregate sales and sales taxes at the time of sale. The register total for March 16 is $10,388. All sales are subject to a 6% sales tax. Compute sales taxes payable and make the entry to record sales taxes payable and sales.

*Compute and record sales taxes payable.*
(SO 3), **AP**

**BE10-4** Franklin University sells 3,500 season basketball tickets at $80 each for its 10-game home schedule. Give the entry to record (a) the sale of the season tickets and (b) the revenue earned by playing the first home game.

*Prepare entries for unearned revenues.*
(SO 3), **AP**

**BE10-5** Cindy Neuer's regular hourly wage rate is $16, and she receives an hourly rate of $24 for work in excess of 40 hours. During a January pay period, Cindy works 47 hours. Cindy's federal income tax withholding is $95, and she has no voluntary deductions. Compute Cindy Neuer's gross earnings and net pay for the pay period. Assume that the FICA tax rate is 8%.

*Compute gross earnings and net pay.*
(SO 3), **AP**

**BE10-6** Data for Cindy Neuer are presented in BE10-5. Prepare the employer's journal entries to record (a) Cindy's pay for the period and (b) the payment of Cindy's wages. Use January 15 for the end of the pay period and the payment date.

*Record a payroll and the payment of wages.*
(SO 3), **AP**

**BE10-7** Palmer Corporation issued 3,000 7%, 5-year, $1,000 bonds dated January 1, 2012, at face value. Interest is paid each January 1.
(a) Prepare the journal entry to record the sale of these bonds on January 1, 2012.
(b) Prepare the adjusting journal entry on December 31, 2012, to record interest expense.
(c) Prepare the journal entry on January 1, 2013, to record interest paid.

*Prepare journal entries for bonds issued at face value.*
(SO 5), **AP**

**BE10-8** The balance sheet for Claremont Company reports the following information on July 1, 2012.

*Prepare journal entry for redemption of bonds.*
(SO 6), **AP**

**CLAREMONT COMPANY**
**Balance Sheet (partial)**

Long-term liabilities
Bonds payable                    $2,000,000
Less: Discount on bonds payable       45,000    $1,955,000

Claremont decides to redeem these bonds at 102 after paying annual interest. Prepare the journal entry to record the redemption on July 1, 2012.

*Prepare statement presentation of long-term liabilities.*
(SO 7), **AP**

**BE10-9** Presented here are long-term liability items for Borders Inc. at December 31, 2012. Prepare the long-term liabilities section of the balance sheet for Borders Inc.

| | |
|---|---|
| Bonds payable (due 2016) | $700,000 |
| Notes payable (due 2014) | 80,000 |
| Discount on bonds payable | 28,000 |

*Prepare liabilities section of balance sheet.*
(SO 7), **AP**

**BE10-10** Presented here are liability items for Azarian Inc. at December 31, 2012. Prepare the liabilities section of Azarian's balance sheet.

| | | | |
|---|---|---|---|
| Accounts payable | $157,000 | FICA taxes payable | $ 7,800 |
| Notes payable | 20,000 | | |
| (due May 1, 2013) | | Interest payable | 40,000 |
| Bonds payable (due 2016) | 900,000 | Notes payable (due 2014) | 80,000 |
| Unearned | | | |
| sales revenue | 240,000 | Income taxes payable | 3,500 |
| Discount on bonds payable | 41,000 | Sales taxes payable | 1,700 |

*Analyze solvency.*
(SO 7), **AP**

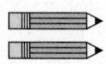

**BE10-11** The 2009 adidas financial statements contain the following selected data (in millions).

| | | | |
|---|---|---|---|
| Current assets | $4,485 | Interest expense | $169 |
| Total assets | 8,875 | Income taxes | 113 |
| Current liabilities | 2,836 | Net income | 245 |
| Total liabilities | 5,099 | | |
| Cash | 775 | | |

Compute the following values and provide a brief interpretation of each.
(a) Working capital.  (c) Debt to total assets ratio.
(b) Current ratio.  (d) Times interest earned ratio.

*Analyze solvency.*
(SO 7), **AN**

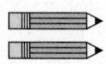

**BE10-12** The Canadian National Railway Company's (CN) total assets in a recent year were $24,004 million and its total liabilities were $14,180 million. That year, CN reported operating lease commitments for its locomotives, freight cars, and equipment totalling $740 million. If these assets had been recorded as capital leases, assume that assets and liabilities would have risen by approximately $740 million.
(a) Calculate CN's debt to total assets ratio, first using the figures reported, and then after increasing assets and liabilities for the unrecorded operating leases.
(b) Discuss the potential effect of these operating leases on your assessment of CN's solvency.

*Prepare journal entries for bonds issued at a discount.*
(SO 8), **AP**

**\*BE10-13** Strite Company issues $2 million, 10-year, 7% bonds at 99, with interest payable on December 31. The straight-line method is used to amortize bond discount.
(a) Prepare the journal entry to record the sale of these bonds on January 1, 2012.
(b) Prepare the journal entry to record interest expense and bond discount amortization on December 31, 2012, assuming no previous accrual of interest.

*Prepare journal entries for bonds issued at a premium.*
(SO 8), **AP**

**\*BE10-14** Reiden Inc. issues $4 million, 5-year, 8% bonds at 102, with interest payable on January 1. The straight-line method is used to amortize bond premium.
(a) Prepare the journal entry to record the sale of these bonds on January 1, 2012.
(b) Prepare the journal entry to record interest expense and bond premium amortization on December 31, 2012, assuming no previous accrual of interest.

*Use effective-interest method of bond amortization.*
(SO 9), **AP**

**\*BE10-15** Presented below is the partial bond discount amortization schedule for Syam Corp., which uses the effective-interest method of amortization.

| Interest Periods | Interest to Be Paid | Interest Expense to Be Recorded | Discount Amortization | Unamortized Discount | Bond Carrying Value |
|---|---|---|---|---|---|
| Issue date | | | | $38,609 | $961,391 |
| 1 | $45,000 | $48,070 | $3,070 | 35,539 | 964,461 |
| 2 | 45,000 | 48,223 | 3,223 | 32,316 | 967,684 |

**Instructions**
(a) Prepare the journal entry to record the payment of interest and the discount amortization at the end of period 1.
(b) Explain why interest expense is greater than interest paid.
(c) Explain why interest expense will increase each period.

**BE10-16** Pickeril Inc. issues a $600,000, 10%, 10-year mortgage note on December 31, 2011, to obtain financing for a new building. The terms provide for semiannual installment payments of $48,145. Prepare the entry to record the mortgage loan on December 31, 2011, and the first installment payment.

*Prepare entries for long-term notes payable.*
*(SO 10),* **AP**

# Do it! Review

**Do it! 10-1** You and several classmates are studying for the next accounting examination. They ask you to answer the following questions:
1. If cash is borrowed on a $60,000, 9-month, 10% note on August 1, how much interest expense would be incurred by December 31?
2. The cash register total including sales taxes is $42,000, and the sales tax rate is 5%. What is the sales taxes payable?
3. If $42,000 is collected in advance on November 1 for 6-month magazine subscriptions, what amount of subscription revenue is earned by December 31?

*Answer questions about current liabilities.*
*(SO 2, 3),* **C**

**Do it! 10-2** During the month of February, TriState Corporation's employees earned wages of $74,000. Withholdings related to these wages were $4,200 for Social Security (FICA), $7,100 for federal income tax, and $1,900 for state income tax. Costs incurred for unemployment taxes were $110 for federal and $160 for state.

Prepare the February 28 journal entries for (a) wages expense and wages payable assuming that all February wages will be paid in March and (b) the company's payroll tax expense.

*Prepare entries for payroll and payroll taxes.*
*(SO 3),* **AP**

**Do it! 10-3** State whether each of the following statements is true or false.

_____ 1. Convertible bonds are also known as callable bonds.

_____ 2. The market rate is the rate investors demand for loaning funds.

_____ 3. Semiannual interest on bonds is equal to the face value times the stated rate times 6/12.

_____ 4. The present value of a bond is the value at which it should sell in the market.

*Evaluate statements about bonds.*
*(SO 4),* **C**

**Do it! 10-4** Grenke Corporation issues $300,000 of bonds for $315,000. (a) Prepare the journal entry to record the issuance of the bonds, and (b) show how the bonds would be reported on the balance sheet at the date of issuance.

*Prepare journal entry for bond issuance and show balance sheet presentation.*
*(SO 5),* **AP**

**Do it! 10-5** Hanrahan Corporation issued $400,000 of 10-year bonds at a discount. Prior to maturity, when the carrying value of the bonds was $388,000, the company retired the bonds at 99. Prepare the entry to record the redemption of the bonds.

*Prepare entry for bond redemption.*
*(SO 6),* **AP**

# Exercises

**E10-1** Megan Haak and Kathy Quandt borrowed $15,000 on a 7-month, 8% note from Golden State Bank to open their business, MK's Coffee House. The money was borrowed on June 1, 2012, and the note matures January 1, 2013.

*Prepare entries for interest-bearing notes.*
*(SO 2),* **AP**

**Instructions**
(a) Prepare the entry to record the receipt of the funds from the loan.
(b) Prepare the entry to accrue the interest on June 30.
(c) Assuming adjusting entries are made at the end of each month, determine the balance in the interest payable account at December 31, 2012.
(d) Prepare the entry required on January 1, 2013, when the loan is paid back.

**E10-2** On May 15, Gruzik's Outback Clothiers borrowed some money on a 4-month note to provide cash during the slow season of the year. The interest rate on the note was 8%. At the time the note was due, the amount of interest owed was $480.

*Prepare entries for interest-bearing notes.*
*(SO 2),* **AP**

**Instructions**
(a) Determine the amount borrowed by Gruzik.
(b) Assume the amount borrowed was $18,500. What was the interest rate if the amount of interest owed was $555?
(c) Prepare the entry for the initial borrowing and the repayment for the facts in part (a).

*Prepare entries for interest-bearing notes.*
(SO 2), **AP**

**E10-3**   On June 1, Chetney Company Ltd. borrows $60,000 from First Bank on a 6-month, $60,000, 8% note. The note matures on December 1.

**Instructions**
(a) Prepare the entry on June 1.
(b) Prepare the adjusting entry on June 30.
(c) Prepare the entry at maturity (December 1), assuming monthly adjusting entries have been made through November 30.
(d) What was the total financing cost (interest expense)?

*Journalize sales and related taxes.*
(SO 3), **AP**

**E10-4**   In providing accounting services to small businesses, you encounter the following situations pertaining to cash sales.
1. Duvall Company rings up sales and sales taxes separately on its cash register. On April 10, the register totals are sales $22,000 and sales taxes $1,100.
2. Hubbard Company does not segregate sales and sales taxes. Its register total for April 15 is $13,780, which includes a 6% sales tax.

**Instructions**
Prepare the entries to record the sales transactions and related taxes for (a) Duvall Company and (b) Hubbard Company.

*Journalize payroll entries.*
(SO 3), **AP**

**E10-5**   During the month of March, Lavonis Company's employees earned wages of $64,000. Withholdings related to these wages were $4,896 for Social Security (FICA), $7,500 for federal income tax, $3,100 for state income tax, and $400 for union dues. The company incurred no cost related to these earnings for federal unemployment tax, but incurred $700 for state unemployment tax.

**Instructions**
(a) Prepare the necessary March 31 journal entry to record wages expense and wages payable. Assume that wages earned during March will be paid during April.
(b) Prepare the entry to record the company's payroll tax expense.

*Journalize unearned revenue transactions.*
(SO 3), **AP**

**E10-6**   Season tickets for the Panthers are priced at $320 and include 16 games. Revenue is recognized after each game is played. When the season began, the amount credited to Unearned Ticket Revenue was $1,728,000. By the end of October, $1,188,000 of the Unearned Ticket Revenue had been recorded as earned.

**Instructions**
(a) How many season tickets did the Panthers sell?
(b) How many home games had the Panthers played by the end of October?
(c) Prepare the entry for the initial recording of the Unearned Ticket Revenue.
(d) Prepare the entry to recognize the revenue after the first home game had been played.

*Journalize unearned subscription revenue.*
(SO 3), **AP**

**E10-7**   Sprague Company Ltd. publishes a monthly sports magazine, *Fishing Preview*. Subscriptions to the magazine cost $28 per year. During November 2012, Sprague sells 6,300 subscriptions for cash, beginning with the December issue. Sprague prepares financial statements quarterly and recognizes subscription revenue earned at the end of the quarter. The company uses the accounts Unearned Sales Revenue and Sales Revenue. The company has a December 31 year-end.

**Instructions**
(a) Prepare the entry in November for the receipt of the subscriptions.
(b) Prepare the adjusting entry at December 31, 2012, to record subscription revenue earned in December 2012.
(c) Prepare the adjusting entry at March 31, 2013, to record subscription revenue earned in the first quarter of 2013.

*Prepare journal entries for issuance of bonds and payment and accrual of interest.*
(SO 5), **AP**

**E10-8**   On August 1, 2012, Laduke Corporation issued $600,000, 7%, 10-year bonds at face value. Interest is payable annually on August 1. Laduke's year-end is December 31.

**Instructions**

Prepare journal entries to record the following events.
(a) The issuance of the bonds.
(b) The accrual of interest on December 31, 2012.
(c) The payment of interest on August 1, 2013.

**E10-9** On January 1, Krivitz Company issued $300,000, 8%, 10-year bonds at face value. Interest is payable annually on January 1.

*Prepare journal entries for issuance of bonds and payment and accrual of interest.*
*(SO 5), AP*

**Instructions**

Prepare journal entries to record the following events.
(a) The issuance of the bonds.
(b) The accrual of interest on December 31.
(c) The payment of interest on January 1.

**E10-10** Assume that the following are independent situations recently reported in the *Wall Street Journal*.
  1. General Electric (GE) 7% bonds, maturing January 28, 2013, were issued at 111.12.
  2. Boeing 7% bonds, maturing September 24, 2027, were issued at 99.08.

*Prepare entries for issue of bonds.*
*(SO 5), AN*

**Instructions**

(a) Were GE and Boeing bonds issued at a premium or a discount?
(b) Explain how bonds, both paying the same contractual interest rate, could be issued at different prices.
(c) Prepare the journal entry to record the issue of each of these two bonds, assuming each company issued $800,000 of bonds in total.

**E10-11** Olstad Company issued $350,000 of 8%, 20-year bonds on January 1, 2012, at face value. Interest is payable annually on January 1.

*Prepare journal entries to record issuance of bonds, payment of interest, and redemption at maturity.*
*(SO 5, 6), AP*

**Instructions**

Prepare the journal entries to record the following events.
(a) The issuance of the bonds.
(b) The accrual of interest on December 31, 2012.
(c) The payment of interest on January 1, 2013.
(d) The redemption of the bonds at maturity, assuming interest for the last interest period has been paid and recorded.

**E10-12** The situations presented here are independent of each other.

*Prepare journal entries for redemption of bonds.*
*(SO 6), AP*

**Instructions**

For each situation, prepare the appropriate journal entry for the redemption of the bonds.
(a) Martha Corporation retired $140,000 face value, 9% bonds on April 30, 2012, at 101. The carrying value of the bonds at the redemption date was $126,500. The bonds pay annual interest, and the interest payment due on April 30, 2012, has been made and recorded.
(b) Williams, Inc., retired $170,000 face value, 12.5% bonds on June 30, 2012, at 98. The carrying value of the bonds at the redemption date was $184,000. The bonds pay annual interest, and the interest payment due on June 30, 2012, has been made and recorded.

**E10-13** Pedrick, Inc. reports the following liabilities (in thousands) on its January 31, 2012, balance sheet and notes to the financial statements.

*Prepare liabilities section of balance sheet.*
*(SO 7), AP*

| | | | |
|---|---|---|---|
| Accounts payable | $4,263.9 | Mortgage payable | $6,746.7 |
| Accrued pension liability | 1,115.2 | Operating leases | 1,641.7 |
| Unearned sales revenue | 1,058.1 | Notes payable (due in 2015) | 335.6 |
| Bonds payable | 1,961.2 | Salaries and wages payable | 858.1 |
| Current portion of | | Notes payable (due in 2013) | 2,563.6 |
| mortgage payable | 1,992.2 | Unused operating line of credit | 3,337.6 |
| Income taxes payable | 265.2 | Warranty liability—current | 1,417.3 |

**Instructions**

(a) Identify which of the above liabilities are likely current and which are likely long-term. Say if an item fits in neither category. Explain the reasoning for your selection.
(b) Prepare the liabilities section of Pedrick's balance sheet as at January 31, 2012.

*Calculate liquidity and solvency ratios; discuss impact of unrecorded obligations on liquidity and solvency.*

(SO 7), **AP**

**E10-14** McDonald's 2009 financial statements contain the following selected data (in millions).

| | | | |
|---|---|---|---|
| Current assets | $ 3,416.3 | Interest expense | $ 473.2 |
| Total assets | 30,224.9 | Income taxes | 1,936.0 |
| Current liabilities | 2,988.7 | Net income | 4,551.0 |
| Total liabilities | 16,191.0 | | |

**Instructions**

(a) Compute the following values and provide a brief interpretation of each.
   (1) Working capital.        (3) Debt to total assets ratio.
   (2) Current ratio.         (4) Times interest earned ratio.

(b) The notes to McDonald's financial statements show that subsequent to 2009 the company will have future minimum lease payments under operating leases of $10,717.5 million. If these assets had been purchased with debt, assets and liabilities would rise by approximately $8,800 million. Recompute the debt to total assets ratio after adjusting for this. Discuss your result.

*Calculate current ratio before and after paying accounts payable.*

(SO 7), **AN**

**E10-15** 3M Company reported the following financial data for 2009 and 2008 (in millions).

**3M COMPANY**
Balance Sheet (partial)

| | **2009** | **2008** |
|---|---|---|
| Current assets | | |
| Cash and cash equivalents | $ 3,040 | $1,849 |
| Accounts receivable, net | 3,250 | 3,195 |
| Inventories | 2,639 | 3,013 |
| Other current assets | 1,866 | 1,541 |
| Total current assets | $10,795 | $9,598 |
| Current liabilities | $ 4,897 | $5,839 |

**Instructions**

(a) Calculate the current ratio for 3M for 2009 and 2008.

(b) Suppose that at the end of 2009, 3M management used $300 million cash to pay off $300 million of accounts payable. How would its current ratio change?

*Calculate current ratio before and after paying accounts payable.*

(SO 7), **AN**

**E10-16** Sportique Boutique reported the following financial data for 2012 and 2011.

**SPORTIQUE BOUTIQUE**
Balance Sheet (partial)
September 30 (in thousands)

| | **2012** | **2011** |
|---|---|---|
| Current assets | | |
| Cash and short-term deposits | $2,574 | $1,021 |
| Accounts receivable | 2,147 | 1,575 |
| Inventories | 1,201 | 1,010 |
| Other current assets | 322 | 192 |
| Total current assets | $6,244 | $3,798 |
| Current liabilities | $4,503 | $2,619 |

**Instructions**

(a) Calculate the current ratio for Sportique Boutique for 2012 and 2011.

(b) Suppose that at the end of 2012, Sportique Boutique used $1.5 million cash to pay off $1.5 million of accounts payable. How would its current ratio change?

(c) At September 30, Sportique Boutique has an undrawn operating line of credit of $12.5 million. Would this affect any assessment that you might make of Sportique Boutique's short-term liquidity? Explain.

**E10-17** A large retailer was sued nearly 5,000 times in a recent year—about once every two hours every day of the year. It has been sued for everything imaginable—ranging from falls on icy parking lots to injuries sustained in shoppers' stampedes to a murder with a rifle purchased at one of its stores. The company reported the following in the notes to its financial statements:

> The Company and its subsidiaries are involved from time to time in claims, proceedings, and litigation arising from the operation of its business. The Company does not believe that any such claim, proceeding, or litigation, either alone or in the aggregate, will have a material adverse effect on the Company's financial position or results of its operations.

*Discuss contingent liabilities.*
*(SO 7),* **C**

**Instructions**
(a) Explain why the company does not have to record these contingent liabilities.
(b) Comment on any implications for analysis of the financial statements.

*E10-18 Sanidas Company issued $500,000, 6%, 30-year bonds on January 1, 2012, at 103. Interest is payable annually on January 1. Sanidas uses straight-line amortization for bond premium or discount.

**Instructions**
Prepare the journal entries to record the following events.
(a) The issuance of the bonds.
(b) The accrual of interest and the premium amortization on December 31, 2012.
(c) The payment of interest on January 1, 2013.
(d) The redemption of the bonds at maturity, assuming interest for the last interest period has been paid and recorded.

*Prepare journal entries to record issuance of bonds, payment of interest, amortization of premium using straight-line, and redemption at maturity.*
*(SO 5, 6, 8),* **AP**

*E10-19 Gatlin Company issued $300,000, 8%, 15-year bonds on December 31, 2011, for $288,000. Interest is payable annually on December 31. Gatlin uses the straight-line method to amortize bond premium or discount.

**Instructions**
Prepare the journal entries to record the following events.
(a) The issuance of the bonds.
(b) The payment of interest and the discount amortization on December 31, 2012.
(c) The redemption of the bonds at maturity, assuming interest for the last interest period has been paid and recorded.

*Prepare journal entries to record issuance of bonds, payment of interest, amortization of discount using straight-line, and redemption at maturity.*
*(SO 5, 6, 8),* **AP**

*E10-20 Azen Corporation issued $400,000, 7%, 20-year bonds on January 1, 2012, for $360,727. This price resulted in an effective-interest rate of 8% on the bonds. Interest is payable annually on January 1. Azen uses the effective-interest method to amortize bond premium or discount.

**Instructions**
Prepare the journal entries to record (round to the nearest dollar):
(a) The issuance of the bonds.
(b) The accrual of interest and the discount amortization on December 31, 2012.
(c) The payment of interest on January 1, 2013.

*Prepare journal entries for issuance of bonds, payment of interest, and amortization of discount using effective-interest method.*
*(SO 5, 9),* **AP**

*E10-21 Perez Company issued $380,000, 7%, 10-year bonds on January 1, 2012, for $407,968. This price resulted in an effective-interest rate of 6% on the bonds. Interest is payable annually on January 1. Perez uses the effective-interest method to amortize bond premium or discount.

**Instructions**
Prepare the journal entries (rounded to the nearest dollar) to record:
(a) The issuance of the bonds.
(b) The accrual of interest and the premium amortization on December 31, 2012.
(c) The payment of interest on January 1, 2013.

*Prepare journal entries for issuance of bonds, payment of interest, and amortization of premium using effective-interest method.*
*(SO 5, 9),* **AP**

*E10-22 Kitov Co. receives $280,000 when it issues a $280,000, 6%, mortgage note payable to finance the construction of a building at December 31, 2012. The terms provide for semiannual installment payments of $14,285 on June 30 and December 31.

**Instructions**
Prepare the journal entries to record the mortgage loan and the first two installment payments.

*Prepare journal entries to record mortgage note and installment payments.*
*(SO 10),* **AP**

*Balance sheet presentation of installment note payable.*
*(SO 10),* **AP**

*\*E10-23* Berry Corporation issued a $50,000, 10%, 10-year installment note payable on January 1, 2012. Payments of $8,137 are made each January 1, beginning January 1, 2013.

***Instructions***
(a) What amounts should be reported under current liabilities related to the note on December 31, 2012?
(b) What should be reported under long-term liabilities?

# Exercises: Set B and Challenge Exercises

Visit the book's companion website, at **www.wiley.com/college/kimmel**, and choose the Student Companion site to access Exercise Set B and Challenge Exercises.

# Problems: Set A

*Prepare current liability entries, adjusting entries, and current liabilities section.*
*(SO 1, 2, 3, 7),* **AP**

**P10-1A** On January 1, 2012, the ledger of Kindt Company contained these liability accounts.

| | |
|---|---|
| Accounts Payable | $42,500 |
| Sales Taxes Payable | 6,600 |
| Unearned Service Revenue | 19,000 |

During January, the following selected transactions occurred.

Jan. 1 Borrowed $18,000 in cash from Premier Bank on a 4-month, 5%, $18,000 note.
5 Sold merchandise for cash totaling $6,254, which includes 6% sales taxes.
12 Provided services for customers who had made advance payments of $10,000. (Credit Service Revenue.)
14 Paid state treasurer's department for sales taxes collected in December 2011, $6,600.
20 Sold 500 units of a new product on credit at $48 per unit, plus 6% sales tax.

During January, the company's employees earned wages of $70,000. Withholdings related to these wages were $5,355 for Social Security (FICA), $5,000 for federal income tax, and $1,500 for state income tax. The company owed no money related to these earnings for federal or state unemployment tax. Assume that wages earned during January will be paid during February. No entry had been recorded for wages or payroll tax expense as of January 31.

***Instructions***
(a) Journalize the January transactions.
(b) Journalize the adjusting entries at January 31 for the outstanding note payable and for wages expense and payroll tax expense.
(c) Prepare the current liabilities section of the balance sheet at January 31, 2012. Assume no change in Accounts Payable.

*(c) Tot. current*
*liabilities* $146,724

*Journalize and post note transactions; show balance sheet presentation.*
*(SO 2, 7),* **AP**

**P10-2A** Connor Corporation sells rock-climbing products and also operates an indoor climbing facility for climbing enthusiasts. During the last part of 2012, Connor had the following transactions related to notes payable.

Sept. 1 Issued a $12,000 note to Patrick to purchase inventory. The 3-month note payable bears interest of 6% and is due December 1. (Connor uses a perpetual inventory system.)
Sept. 30 Recorded accrued interest for the Patrick note.
Oct. 1 Issued a $16,500, 8%, 4-month note to Canton Bank to finance the purchase of a new climbing wall for advanced climbers. The note is due February 1.
Oct. 31 Recorded accrued interest for the Patrick note and the Canton Bank note.

| Nov. | 1 | Issued a $26,000 note and paid $8,000 cash to purchase a vehicle to transport clients to nearby climbing sites as part of a new series of climbing classes. This note bears interest of 6% and matures in 12 months. |
|---|---|---|
| Nov. | 30 | Recorded accrued interest for the Patrick note, the Canton Bank note, and the vehicle note. |
| Dec. | 1 | Paid principal and interest on the Patrick note. |
| Dec. | 31 | Recorded accrued interest for the Canton Bank note and the vehicle note. |

**Instructions**
(a) Prepare journal entries for the transactions noted above.
(b) Post the above entries to the Notes Payable, Interest Payable, and Interest Expense accounts. (Use T accounts.)
(c) Show the balance sheet presentation of notes payable and interest payable at December 31.
(d) How much interest expense relating to notes payable did Connor incur during the year?

*(b) Interest Payable    $590*

**P10-3A**   The following section is taken from Paynter balance sheet at December 31, 2011.

| Current liabilities | | |
|---|---|---|
| Interest payable | | $ 40,000 |
| Long-term liabilities | | |
| Bonds payable (8%, due January 1, 2015) | | 500,000 |

Interest is payable annually on January 1. The bonds are callable on any annual interest date.

*Prepare journal entries to record interest payments and redemption of bonds.*
*(SO 5, 6),* **AP**

**Instructions**
(a) Journalize the payment of the bond interest on January 1, 2012.
(b) Assume that on January 1, 2012, after paying interest, Paynter calls bonds having a face value of $200,000. The call price is 103. Record the redemption of the bonds.
(c) Prepare the adjusting entry on December 31, 2012, to accrue the interest on the remaining bonds.

*(b) Loss    $6,000*

**P10-4A**   On October 1, 2011, Huber Corp. issued $700,000, 5%, 10-year bonds at face value. The bonds were dated October 1, 2011, and pay interest annually on October 1. Financial statements are prepared annually on December 31.

*Prepare journal entries to record issuance of bonds, interest, balance sheet presentation, and bond redemption.*
*(SO 5, 6, 7),* **AP**

**Instructions**
(a) Prepare the journal entry to record the issuance of the bonds.
(b) Prepare the adjusting entry to record the accrual of interest on December 31, 2011.
(c) Show the balance sheet presentation of bonds payable and bond interest payable on December 31, 2011.
(d) Prepare the journal entry to record the payment of interest on October 1, 2012.
(e) Prepare the adjusting entry to record the accrual of interest on December 31, 2012.
(f) Assume that on January 1, 2013, Huber pays the accrued bond interest and calls the bonds. The call price is 104. Record the payment of interest and redemption of the bonds.

*(f) Loss    $28,000*

**P10-5A**   Paprocki Company sold $6,000,000, 7%, 15-year bonds on January 1, 2012. The bonds were dated January 1, 2012, and pay interest on December 31. The bonds were sold at 98.

*Prepare journal entries to record issuance of bonds, show balance sheet presentation, and record bond redemption.*
*(SO 5, 6, 7),* **AP**

**Instructions**
(a) Prepare the journal entry to record the issuance of the bonds on January 1, 2012.
(b) At December 31, 2012, $8,000 of the bond discount had been amortized. Show the long-term liability balance sheet presentation of the bond liability at December 31, 2012.
(c) At January 1, 2014, when the carrying value of the bonds was $5,896,000, the company redeemed the bonds at 102. Record the redemption of the bonds assuming that interest for the year had already been paid.

*(c) Loss    $224,000*

*Calculate and comment on ratios.*
*(SO 7),* **AN**

**P10-6A**   You have been presented with selected information taken from the financial statements of Southwest Airlines Co., shown on the next page.

**SOUTHWEST AIRLINES CO.**
Balance Sheet (partial)
December 31
(in millions)

|  | 2008 | 2007 |
|---|---|---|
| Total current assets | $ 2,893 | $ 4,443 |
| Noncurrent assets | 11,415 | 12,329 |
| Total assets | $14,308 | $16,772 |
| | | |
| Current liabilities | $ 2,806 | $ 4,836 |
| Long-term liabilities | 6,549 | 4,995 |
| Total liabilities | 9,355 | 9,831 |
| Shareholders' equity | 4,953 | 6,941 |
| Total liabilities and shareholders' equity | $14,308 | $16,772 |

Other information:

|  | 2008 | 2007 |
|---|---|---|
| Net income (loss) | $ 178 | $ 645 |
| Income tax expense | 100 | 413 |
| Interest expense | 130 | 119 |
| Cash provided by operations | (1,521) | 2,845 |
| Capital expenditures | 923 | 1,331 |
| Cash dividends | 13 | 14 |

**Note 8. Leases**
The majority of the Company's terminal operations space, as well as 82 aircraft, were under operating leases at December 31, 2008. Future minimum lease payments under noncancelable operating leases are as follows: 2009, $376,000; 2010, $324,000; 2011, $249,000; 2012, $208,000; 2013, $152,000; after 2013, $728,000.

**Instructions**
(a) Calculate each of the following ratios for 2008 and 2007.
   (1) Current ratio.
   (2) Free cash flow.
   (3) Debt to total assets.
   (4) Times interest earned ratio.
(b) Comment on the trend in ratios.
(c) Read the company's note on leases. If the operating leases had instead been accounted for like a purchase, assets and liabilities would increase by approximately $1,600 million. Recalculate the debt to total assets ratio for 2008 in light of this information, and discuss the implictions for analysis.

*Prepare journal entries to record interest payments, straight-line discount amortization, and redemption of bonds.*
(SO 5, 6, 8), **AP**

**\*P10-7A** The following information is taken from Lima Corp.'s balance sheet at December 31, 2011.

| | | |
|---|---|---|
| Current liabilities | | |
| Interest payable | | $ 96,000 |
| Long-term liabilities | | |
| Bonds payable (4%, due January 1, 2022) | $2,400,000 | |
| Less: Discount on bonds payable | 24,000 | 2,376,000 |

Interest is payable annually on January 1. The bonds are callable on any annual interest date. Lima uses straight-line amortization for any bond premium or discount. From December 31, 2011, the bonds will be outstanding for an additional 10 years (120 months).

**Instructions**
(Round all computations to the nearest dollar.)
(a) Journalize the payment of bond interest on January 1, 2012.
(b) Prepare the entry to amortize bond discount and to accrue the interest on December 31, 2012.

(c) Assume on January 1, 2013, after paying interest, that Lima Corp. calls bonds having a face value of $400,000. The call price is 102. Record the redemption of the bonds.

(d) Prepare the adjusting entry at December 31, 2013, to amortize bond discount and to accrue interest on the remaining bonds.

(c) Loss    $11,600

**\*P10-8A**   Wong Corporation sold $2,000,000, 7%, 5-year bonds on January 1, 2012. The bonds were dated January 1, 2012, and pay interest on January 1. Wong Corporation uses the straight-line method to amortize bond premium or discount.

*Prepare journal entries to record issuance of bonds, interest, and straight-line amortization, and balance sheet presentation.*

(SO 5, 7, 8), **AP**

**Instructions**

(a) Prepare all the necessary journal entries to record the issuance of the bonds and bond interest expense for 2012, assuming that the bonds sold at 102.

(b) Prepare journal entries as in part (a) assuming that the bonds sold at 97.

(c) Show the balance sheet presentation for the bond issue at December 31, 2012, using (1) the 102 selling price, and then (2) the 97 selling price.

**\*P10-9A**   Trinh Co. sold $3,000,000, 8%, 10-year bonds on January 1, 2012. The bonds were dated January 1, 2012, and pay interest on January 1. The company uses straight-line amortization on bond premiums and discounts. Financial statements are prepared annually.

*Prepare journal entries to record issuance of bonds, interest, and straight-line amortization, and balance sheet presentation.*

(SO 5, 7, 8), **AP**

**Instructions**

(a) Prepare the journal entries to record the issuance of the bonds assuming they sold at:
  (1) 103.
  (2) 98.

(b) Prepare amortization tables for both assumed sales for the first three interest payments.

(c) Prepare the journal entries to record interest expense for 2012 under both of the bond issuances assumed in part (a).

(d) Show the long-term liabilities balance sheet presentation for both of the bond issuances assumed in part (a) at December 31, 2012.

(c) (2) 12/31/12 Interest Expense    $246,000

**\*P10-10A**   On January 1, 2012, Ross Corporation issued $1,800,000 face value, 5%, 10-year bonds at $1,667,518. This price resulted in an effective-interest rate of 6% on the bonds. Ross uses the effective-interest method to amortize bond premium or discount. The bonds pay annual interest January 1.

*Prepare journal entries to record issuance of bonds, payment of interest, and amortization of bond discount using effective-interest method.*

(SO 5, 9), **AP**

**Instructions**

(Round all computations to the nearest dollar.)

(a) Prepare the journal entry to record the issuance of the bonds on January 1, 2012.

(b) Prepare an amortization table through December 31, 2014 (three interest periods) for this bond issue.

(c) Prepare the journal entry to record the accrual of interest and the amortization of the discount on December 31, 2012.

(d) Prepare the journal entry to record the payment of interest on January 1, 2013.

(e) Prepare the journal entry to record the accrual of interest and the amortization of the discount on December 31, 2013.

(c) Interest Expense    $100,051

**\*P10-11A**   On January 1, 2012, Lehn Company issued $2,000,000 face value, 7%, 10-year bonds at $2,147,202. This price resulted in a 6% effective-interest rate on the bonds. Lehn uses the effective-interest method to amortize bond premium or discount. The bonds pay annual interest on each January 1.

*Prepare journal entries to record issuance of bonds, payment of interest, and effective-interest amortization, and balance sheet presentation.*

(SO 5, 7, 9), **AP**

**Instructions**

(a) Prepare the journal entries to record the following transactions.
  (1) The issuance of the bonds on January 1, 2012.
  (2) Accrual of interest and amortization of the premium on December 31, 2012.
  (3) The payment of interest on January 1, 2013.
  (4) Accrual of interest and amortization of the premium on December 31, 2013.

(b) Show the proper long-term liabilities balance sheet presentation for the liability for bonds payable at December 31, 2013.

(c) Provide the answers to the following questions in narrative form.
  (1) What amount of interest expense is reported for 2013?
  (2) Would the bond interest expense reported in 2013 be the same as, greater than, or less than the amount that would be reported if the straight-line method of amortization were used?

(a) (4) Interest Expense   $128,162

*Prepare installment payments schedule, journal entries, and balance sheet presentation for a mortgage note payable.*
*(SO 7, 10),* **AP**

*(c) Current portion $100,304*

**\*P10-12A** Durango purchased a new piece of equipment to be used in its new facility. The $370,000 piece of equipment was purchased with a $50,000 down payment and with cash received through the issuance of a $320,000, 8%, 3-year mortgage note payable issued on October 1, 2012. The terms provide for quarterly installment payments of $30,259 on December 31, March 31, June 30, and September 30.

### Instructions
(Round all computations to the nearest dollar.)
(a) Prepare an installment payments schedule for the first five payments of the notes payable.
(b) Prepare the journal entry related to the notes payable for December 31, 2012.
(c) Show the balance sheet presentation for this obligation for December 31, 2012. (*Hint:* Be sure to distinguish between the current and long-term portions of the note.)

*Prepare journal entries to record payments for long-term note payable, and balance sheet presentation.*
*(SO 7, 10),* **AP**

*(b) 6/30/12 Interest Expense $10,500*

**\*P10-13A** Beryl Forman has just approached a venture capitalist for financing for her new business venture, the development of a local ski hill. On July 1, 2011, Beryl was loaned $150,000 at an annual interest rate of 7%. The loan is repayable over 5 years in annual installments of $36,584, principal and interest, due each June 30. The first payment is due June 30, 2012. Beryl uses the effective-interest method for amortizing debt. Her ski hill company's year-end will be June 30.

### Instructions
(a) Prepare an amortization schedule for the 5 years, 2011–2016. Round all calculations to the nearest dollar.
(b) Prepare all journal entries for Beryl Forman for the first 2 fiscal years ended June 30, 2012, and June 30, 2013. Round all calculations to the nearest dollar.
(c) Show the balance sheet presentation of the note payable as of June 30, 2013. (*Hint:* Be sure to distinguish between the current and long-term portions of the note.)

# Problems: Set B

*Prepare current liability entries, adjusting entries, and current liabilities section.*
*(SO 1, 2, 3, 7),* **AP**

**GLS**

*(c) Tot. current liabilities $133,366*

**P10-1B** On January 1, 2012, the ledger of Fleming Company contained the following liability accounts.

| | |
|---|---|
| Accounts Payable | $52,000 |
| Sales Taxes Payable | 8,200 |
| Unearned Service Revenue | 11,000 |

During January, the following selected transactions occurred.

Jan. 1 Borrowed $18,000 from TriCounty Bank on a 3-month, 7%, $18,000 note.
 5 Sold merchandise for cash totaling $18,480, which includes 5% sales taxes.
 12 Provided services for customers who had made advance payments of $8,000. (Credit Service Revenue.)
 14 Paid state revenue department for sales taxes collected in December 2011 ($8,200).
 20 Sold 500 units of a new product on credit at $50 per unit, plus 5% sales tax.

During January, the company's employees earned wages of $54,000. Withholdings related to these wages were $4,131 for Social Security (FICA), $3,900 for federal income tax, and $1,200 for state income tax. The company owed no money related to these earnings for federal or state unemployment tax. Assume that wages earned during January will be paid during February. No entry had been recorded for wages or payroll tax expense as of January 31.

### Instructions
(a) Journalize the January transactions.
(b) Journalize the adjusting entries at January 31 for the outstanding notes payable and for wages expense and payroll tax expense.
(c) Prepare the current liabilities section of the balance sheet at January 31, 2012. Assume no change in accounts payable.

**P10-2B**  Majestic Mountain Bikes markets mountain-bike tours to clients vacationing in various locations in the mountains of Colorado. In preparation for the upcoming summer biking season, Majestic entered into the following transactions related to notes payable.

Journalize and post note transactions; show balance sheet presentation.
(SO 2, 7), AP

Mar.  1  Purchased Puma bikes for use as rentals by issuing a $9,000, 3-month, 6% note payable that is due June 1.

Mar. 31  Recorded accrued interest for the Puma note.

Apr.  1  Issued a $45,000 9-month note for the purchase of mountain property on which to build bike trails. The note bears 8% interest and is due January 1.

Apr. 30  Recorded accrued interest for the Puma note and the land note.

May  1  Issued a 4-month note to Jackson State Bank for $12,000 at 6%. The funds will be used for working capital for the beginning of the season; the note is due September 1.

May 31  Recorded accrued interest for all three notes.

June  1  Paid principal and interest on the Puma note.

June 30  Recorded accrued interest for the land note and the Jackson State Bank note.

**Instructions**

(a)  Prepare journal entries for the transactions noted above.

(b)  Post the above entries to the Notes Payable, Interest Payable, and Interest Expense accounts. (Use T accounts.)

(c)  Assuming that Majestic's year-end is June 30, show the balance sheet presentation of notes payable and interest payable at that date.

(d)  How much interest expense relating to notes payable did Majestic incur during the year?

(b) Interest Payable   $1,020

**P10-3B**  The following section is taken from Lois Corp.'s balance sheet at December 31, 2011.

Prepare journal entries to record interest payments and redemption of bonds.
(SO 5, 6), AP

Current liabilities
  Interest payable                       $    84,000
Long-term liabilities
  Bonds payable (7%, due January 1, 2016)    1,200,000

Interest is payable annually on January 1. The bonds are callable on any annual interest date.

**Instructions**

(a)  Journalize the payment of the bond interest on January 1, 2012.

(b)  Assume that on January 1, 2012, after paying interest, Lois Corp. calls bonds having a face value of $300,000. The call price is 104. Record the redemption of the bonds.

(c)  Prepare the adjusting entry on December 31, 2012, to accrue the interest on the remaining bonds.

(b) Loss     $12,000

**P10-4B**  On April 1, 2011, CMV Corp. issued $600,000, 8%, 5-year bonds at face value. The bonds were dated April 1, 2011, and pay interest annually on April 1. Financial statements are prepared annually on December 31.

Prepare journal entries to record issuance of bonds, interest, balance sheet presentation, and bond redemption.
(SO 5, 6, 7), AP

**Instructions**

(a)  Prepare the journal entry to record the issuance of the bonds.

(b)  Prepare the adjusting entry to record the accrual of interest on December 31, 2011.

(c)  Show the balance sheet presentation of bonds payable and bond interest payable on December 31, 2011.

(d)  Prepare the journal entry to record the payment of interest on April 1, 2012.

(e)  Prepare the adjusting entry to record the accrual of interest on December 31, 2012.

(f)  Assume that on January 1, 2013, CMV pays the accrued bond interest and calls the bonds. The call price is 103. Record the payment of interest and redemption of the bonds.

(f) Loss     18,000

**P10-5B**  Crescent Electric sold $5,000,000, 9%, 10-year bonds on January 1, 2012. The bonds were dated January 1 and pay interest on January 1. The bonds were sold at 103.

Prepare journal entries to record issuance of bonds, show balance sheet presentation, and record bond redemption.
(SO 5, 6, 7), AP

**Instructions**

(a)  Prepare the journal entry to record the issuance of the bonds on January 1, 2012.

(b)  At December 31, 2012, $15,000 of the bond premium had been amortized. Show the long-term liability balance sheet presentation of the bond liability at December 31, 2012.

(c) Loss $80,000

(c) At January 1, 2014, when the carrying value of the bonds was $5,120,000, the company redeemed the bonds at 104. Record the redemption of the bonds assuming that interest for the year had already been paid.

*Calculate and comment on ratios.*

(SO 7), **AN**

**P10-6B** The following selected information was taken from the financial statements of Krispy Kreme Doughnuts, Inc.

**KRISPY KREME DOUGHNUTS, INC.**
Balance Sheet (partial)
(in thousands)

|  | Jan. 31, 2010 | Feb. 1, 2009 |
|---|---|---|
| Total current assets | $ 59,223 | $ 75,806 |
| Capital assets and other long-term assets | 106,053 | 119,120 |
|  | $165,276 | $194,926 |
|  |  |  |
| Current liabilities | $ 37,673 | $ 39,616 |
| Long-term liabilities | 64,836 | 97,555 |
| Total liabilities | 102,509 | 137,171 |
| Shareholders' equity | 62,767 | 57,755 |
| Total liabilities and shareholders' equity | $165,276 | $194,926 |

Other information:

|  | 2010 | 2009 |
|---|---|---|
| Interest expense | $ 10,685 | $ 10,679 |
| Tax expense (benefit) | 575 | (503) |
| Net loss | (157) | (4,061) |
| Cash provided by operations | 19,827 | 16,593 |
| Capital expenditures | 7,967 | 4,694 |
| Cash dividends | -0- | -0- |

**Note 10. Leases**
The Company leases equipment and facilities under both capital and operating leases. The approximate future minimum lease payments under non-cancelable (operating) leases as of January 31, 2010, are set forth in the following table:

| Fiscal Year Ending in | Amount (in thousands) |
|---|---|
| 2011 | $ 8,866 |
| 2012 | 7,972 |
| 2013 | 6,769 |
| 2014 | 5,830 |
| 2015 | 5,420 |
| Thereafter | 56,667 |
|  | $91,524 |

Rent expense, net of rental income, totaled $9.6 million in fiscal 2010, $11.8 million in fiscal 2009 and $14.8 million in fiscal 2008.

**Instructions**
(a) Calculate each of the following ratios for 2010 and 2009.
   (1) Current ratio.
   (2) Free cash flow.
   (3) Debt to total assets ratio.
(b) Comment on Krispy Kreme's liquidity and solvency.

(c) Read the company's note on leases (Note 10). If the operating leases had instead been accounted for like a purchase, assets and liabilities would have increased by approximately $68,000,000. Recalculate the debt to total assets ratio for 2010 and discuss the implications for analysis.

*P10-7B   The following section is taken from Centralia Oil Company's balance sheet at December 31, 2011.

| | | |
|---|---:|---:|
| Current liabilities | | |
| Interest payable | | $ 216,000 |
| Long-term liabilities | | |
| Bonds payable (6%, due January 1, 2022) | $3,600,000 | |
| Add: Premium on bonds payable | 280,000 | 3,880,000 |

*Prepare journal entries to record interest payments, straight-line premium amortization, and redemption of bonds*
(SO 5, 6, 8), **AP**

Interest is payable annually on January 1. The bonds are callable on any annual interest date. Centralia uses straight-line amortization for any bond premium or discount. From December 31, 2011, the bonds will be outstanding for an additional 10 years (120 months).

**Instructions**
(Round all computations to the nearest dollar.)
(a) Journalize the payment of bond interest on January 1, 2012.
(b) Prepare the entry to amortize bond premium and to accrue interest due on December 31, 2012.
(c) Assume on January 1, 2013, after paying interest, that Centralia Company calls bonds having a face value of $1,800,000. The call price is 102. Record the redemption of the bonds.
(d) Prepare the adjusting entry at December 31, 2013, to amortize bond premium and to accrue interest on the remaining bonds.

(c) Gain    $90,000

*P10-8B   Champeau Company sold $2,500,000, 8%, 25-year bonds on January 1, 2012. The bonds were dated January 1, 2012, and pay interest on January 1. Champeau Company uses the straight-line method to amortize bond premium or discount.

*Prepare journal entries to record issuance of bonds, interest, and straight-line amortization, and balance sheet presentation.*
(SO 5, 7, 8), **AP**

**Instructions**
(a) Prepare all the necessary journal entries to record the issuance of the bonds and bond interest expense for 2012, assuming that the bonds sold at 102.
(b) Prepare journal entries as in part (a) assuming that the bonds sold at 96.
(c) Show the balance sheet presentation for the bond issue at December 31, 2012, using (1) the 102 selling price, and then (2) the 96 selling price.

*P10-9B   Marini Corporation sold $2,600,000, 9%, 20-year bonds on December 31, 2011. The bonds were dated December 31, 2011, and pay interest on December 31. The company uses straight-line amortization for premiums and discounts. Financial statements are prepared annually.

*Prepare journal entries to record issuance of bonds, interest, and straight-line amortization, and balance sheet presentation.*
(SO 5, 7, 8), **AP**

**Instructions**
(a) Prepare the journal entry to record the issuance of the bonds assuming they sold at:
   (1) 98.
   (2) 104.
(b) Prepare amortization tables for both of the assumed sales for the first three interest payments.
(c) Prepare the journal entries to record interest expense for the first two interest payments under both of the bond issuances assumed in part (a).
(d) Show the long-term liabilities balance sheet presentation for both of the bond issuances assumed in part (a) at December 31, 2012.

(c) (2) 12/31/12  Interest Expense    $228,800

*P10-10B   On January 1, 2012, Pedraza Corporation issued $1,000,000 face value, 6%, 10-year bonds at $1,077,217. This price resulted in an effective-interest rate of 5% on the bonds. Pedraza uses the effective-interest method to amortize bond premium or discount. The bonds pay annual interest January 1.

*Prepare journal entries to record issuance of bonds, payment of interest, and amortization of bond premium using effective-interest method.*
(SO 5, 9), **AP**

**Instructions**
(Round all computations to the nearest dollar.)
(a) Prepare the journal entry to record the issuance of the bonds on January 1, 2012.
(b) Prepare an amortization table through December 31, 2014 (three interest periods) for this bond issue.

(c) Interest
    Expense    $53,861

(c) Prepare the journal entry to record the accrual of interest and the amortization of the premium on December 31, 2012.

(d) Prepare the journal entry to record the payment of interest on January 1, 2013.

(e) Prepare the journal entry to record the accrual of interest and the amortization of the premium on December 31, 2013.

*Prepare journal entries to record issuance of bonds, payment of interest, and effective-interest amortization, and balance sheet presentation.*

*(SO 5, 7, 9), AP*

**\*P10-11B** On January 1, 2012, Witzling Company issued $4,000,000 face value, 8%, 15-year bonds at $3,391,514. This price resulted in an effective-interest rate of 10% on the bonds. Witzling uses the effective-interest method to amortize bond premium or discount. The bonds pay annual interest January 1.

**Instructions**

(a) Prepare the journal entries to record the following transactions.
    (1) The issuance of the bonds on January 1, 2012.
    (2) The accrual of interest and the amortization of the discount on December 31, 2012.
    (3) The payment of interest on January 1, 2013.
    (4) The accrual of interest and the amortization of the discount on December 31, 2013.

(b) Show the proper long-term liabilities balance sheet presentation for the liability for bonds payable at December 31, 2013.

(c) (1) $341,067

(c) Provide the answers to the following questions in narrative form.
    (1) What amount of interest expense is reported for 2013?
    (2) Would the bond interest expense reported in 2013 be the same as, greater than, or less than the amount that would be reported if the straight-line method of amortization were used?
    (3) Determine the total cost of borrowing over the life of the bond.
    (4) Would the total bond interest expense be greater than, the same as, or less than the total interest expense that would be reported if the straight-line method of amortization were used?

*Prepare installment payments schedule, journal entries, and balance sheet presentation for a mortgage note payable.*

*(SO 7, 10), AP*

**\*P10-12B** Daisy Corporation purchased a new piece of equipment to be used in its new facility. The $450,000 piece of equipment was purchased with a $50,000 down payment and with cash received through the issuance of a $400,000, 6%, 5-year mortgage note payable issued on October 1, 2012. The terms provide for quarterly installment payments of $23,298 on December 31, March 31, June 30, and September 30.

**Instructions**
(Round all computations to the nearest dollar.)

(a) Prepare an installment payments schedule for the first five payments of the notes payable.

(b) Interest Expense    $6,000

(b) Prepare the journal entry related to the notes payable for December 31, 2012.

(c) Show the balance sheet presentation for these obligations for December 31, 2012. (*Hint:* Be sure to distinguish between the current and long-term portions of the note.)

*Prepare journal entries to record payments for long-term note payable.*

*(SO 10), AP*

**\*P10-13B** Scott Robertson has just approached a venture capitalist for financing for his sailing school. The venture capitalist is willing to loan Scott $90,000 at a high-risk annual interest rate of 18%. The loan is payable over 2 years in monthly installments of $4,493. Each payment includes principal and interest, calculated using the effective-interest method for amortizing debt. Scott receives the loan on May 1, 2012, which is the first day of his fiscal year. Scott makes the first payment on May 31, 2012.

**Instructions**

(a) Prepare an amortization schedule for the period from May 1, 2012, to August 31, 2012. Round all calculations to the nearest dollar.

(b) 6/30 Interest
    Expense    $1,303

(b) Prepare all journal entries for Scott Robertson for the period beginning May 1, 2012, and ending July 31, 2012. Round all calculations to the nearest dollar.

# Problems: Set C

Visit the book's companion website, at **www.wiley.com/college/kimmel**, and choose the Student Companion site to access Problem Set C.

# Comprehensive Problem

**CP10**   Markel Corporation's balance sheet at December 31, 2011, is presented below.

**MARKEL CORPORATION**
**Balance Sheet**
**December 31, 2011**

| | | | |
|---|---|---|---|
| Cash | $ 30,000 | Accounts payable | $ 13,750 |
| Inventory | 30,750 | Interest payable | 2,500 |
| Prepaid insurance | 5,600 | Bonds payable | 50,000 |
| Equipment | 38,000 | Common stock | 25,000 |
| | $104,350 | Retained earnings | $ 13,100 |
| | | | $104,350 |

During 2012, the following transactions occurred.
1. Markel paid $2,500 interest on the bonds on January 1, 2012.
2. Markel purchased $241,100 of inventory on account.
3. Markel sold for $480,000 cash inventory which cost $265,000. Markel also collected $28,800 sales taxes.
4. Markel paid $230,000 on accounts payable.
5. Markel paid $2,500 interest on the bonds on July 1, 2012.
6. The prepaid insurance ($5,600) expired on July 31.
7. On August 1, Markel paid $10,200 for insurance coverage from August 1, 2012, through July 31, 2013.
8. Markel paid $17,000 sales taxes to the state.
9. Paid other operating expenses, $91,000.
10. Retired the bonds on December 31, 2012, by paying $48,000 plus $2,500 interest.
11. Issued $90,000 of 8% bonds on December 31, 2012, at 103. The bonds pay interest every June 30 and December 31.

**Adjustment data:**
1. Recorded the insurance expired from item 7.
2. The equipment was acquired on December 31, 2011, and will be depreciated on a straight-line basis over 5 years with a $3,000 salvage value.
3. The income tax rate is 30%. (*Hint:* Prepare the income statement up to income before taxes and multiply by 30% to compute the amount.)

**Instructions**
(You may want to set up T accounts to determine ending balances.)
(a) Prepare journal entries for the transactions listed above and adjusting entries.
(b) Prepare an adjusted trial balance at December 31, 2012.
(c) Prepare an income statement and a retained earnings statement for the year ending December 31, 2012, and a classified balance sheet as of December 31, 2012.

(b) Totals     $687,695
(c) N.I.       $72,905

# Continuing Cookie Chronicle

(*Note:* This is a continuation of the Cookie Chronicle from Chapters 1 through 9.)

**CCC10**   Recall that Cookie Creations borrowed $2,000 from Natalie's grandmother. Natalie now is thinking of repaying all amounts outstanding on that loan. She needs to know the amounts of interest payable and interest expense and needs to make the correct journal entries for repayment of the loan.

Go to the book's companion website, at **www.wiley.com/college/kimmel**, to see the completion of this problem.

# Financial Reporting and Analysis

### FINANCIAL REPORTING PROBLEM: *Tootsie Roll Industries*

**BYP10-1** Refer to the financial statements of Tootsie Roll Industries and the Notes to Consolidated Financial Statements in Appendix A.

*Instructions*

Answer the following questions.
(a) What were Tootsie Roll's total current liabilities at December 31, 2009? What was the increase/decrease in Tootsie Roll's total current liabilities from the prior year?
(b) How much were the accounts payable at December 31, 2009?
(c) What were the components of total current liabilities on December 31, 2009 (other than accounts payable already discussed above)?

### COMPARATIVE ANALYSIS PROBLEM: *Tootsie Roll vs. Hershey*

**BYP10-2** The financial statements of The Hershey Company are presented in Appendix B, following the financial statements for Tootsie Roll Industries in Appendix A.

*Instructions*

(a) Based on the information contained in these financial statements, compute the current ratio for 2009 for each company.

What conclusions concerning the companies' liquidity can be drawn from these ratios?
(b) Based on the information contained in these financial statements, compute the following 2009 ratios for each company.
   (1) Debt to total assets.
   (2) Times interest earned. (Hershey's total interest expense for 2009 was $91,336,000. See Tootsie Roll's Note 10 for its interest expense.)

What conclusions about the companies' long-run solvency can be drawn from the ratios?

### RESEARCH CASE

**BYP10-3** The September 1, 2009, edition of *CFO.com* contains an article by Marie Leone and Tim Reason entitled "Dirty Secrets." You can access this article at *www.cfo.com/article.cfm/14292477?f=singlepage*.

*Instructions*

Read the article and answer the following questions.
(a) Summarize the accounting for contingent items that is provided in this textbook.
(b) The authors of the article suggest that many companies are basically accounting for contingencies on a cash basis. Is this consistent with the approach you described in part (a)?
(c) The article suggests that many companies report one set of liability estimates to insurers and a different (lower) set of numbers in their financial statements. How is this possible, and what are the implications for investors?
(d) How do international accounting standards differ in terms of the amounts reported in these types of situations?

### INTERPRETING FINANCIAL STATEMENTS

**BYP10-4** Hechinger Co. and Home Depot are two home improvement retailers. Compared to Hechinger, founded in the early 1900s, Home Depot is a relative newcomer. But, in recent years, while Home Depot was reporting large increases in net income, Hechinger was reporting increasingly large net losses. Finally, largely due to competition from Home Depot, Hechinger was forced to file for bankruptcy. Here are financial data for both companies (in millions).

|                                   | Hechinger | Home Depot |
|-----------------------------------|-----------|------------|
| Cash                              | $   21    | $    62    |
| Receivables                       | 0         | 469        |
| Total current assets              | 1,153     | 4,933      |
| Beginning total assets            | 1,668     | 11,229     |
| Ending total assets               | 1,577     | 13,465     |
| Beginning current liabilities     | 935       | 2,456      |
| Ending current liabilities        | 938       | 2,857      |
| Beginning total liabilities       | 1,392     | 4,015      |
| Ending total liabilities          | 1,339     | 4,716      |
| Interest expense                  | 67        | 37         |
| Income tax expense                | 3         | 1,040      |
| Cash provided (used) by operations| (257)     | 1,917      |
| Net income                        | (93)      | 1,614      |
| Net sales                         | 3,444     | 30,219     |

*Instructions*
Using the data provided, perform the following analysis.
(a) Calculate working capital and the current ratio for each company. Discuss their relative liquidity.
(b) Calculate the debt to total assets ratio and times interest earned for each company. Discuss their relative solvency.
(c) Calculate the return on assets ratio and profit margin ratio for each company. Comment on their relative profitability.
(d) The notes to Home Depot's financial statements indicate that it leases many of its facilities using operating leases. If these assets had instead been purchased with debt, assets and liabilities would have increased by approximately $2,347 million. Calculate the company's debt to total assets ratio employing this adjustment. Discuss the implications.

## FINANCIAL ANALYSIS ON THE WEB

**BYP10-5** *Purpose:* Bond or debt securities pay a stated rate of interest. This rate of interest is dependent on the risk associated with the investment. Fitch Ratings provides ratings for companies that issue debt securities.

*Address:* **www.fitchratings.com**, or go to **www.wiley.com/college/kimmel**

*Instructions*
Answer the following questions.
(a) In what year did Fitch introduce its bond rating scale? (See **History** in **About Us**.)
(b) What letter values are assigned to debt investments that are considered "investment grade" and "speculative grade"? (See **Ratings Definitions**.)
(c) Search the web to identify two other major credit rating agencies.

# Critical Thinking

## DECISION MAKING ACROSS THE ORGANIZATION

**BYP10-6** On January 1, 2010, Gitzel Corporation issued $3,000,000 of 5-year, 8% bonds at 97. The bonds pay interest annually on January 1. By January 1, 2012, the market rate of interest for bonds of risk similar to those of Gitzel Corporation had risen. As a result, the market value of these bonds was $2,500,000 on January 1, 2012—below their carrying value of $2,946,000.

Jon Kanter, president of the company, suggests repurchasing all of these bonds in the open market at the $2,500,000 price. But to do so the company will have to issue $2,500,000 (face value) of new 10-year, 12% bonds at par. The president asks you, as controller, "What is the feasibility of my proposed repurchase plan?"

*Instructions*

With the class divided into groups, answer the following.

(a) Prepare the journal entry to retire the 5-year bonds on January 1, 2012. Prepare the journal entry to issue the new 10-year bonds.

(b) Prepare a short memo to the president in response to his request for advice. List the economic factors that you believe should be considered for his repurchase proposal.

## COMMUNICATION ACTIVITY

**BYP10-7** James Metallo, president of Zinda, Inc., is considering the issuance of bonds to finance an expansion of his business. He has asked you to do the following: (1) discuss the advantages of bonds over common stock financing, (2) indicate the types of bonds he might issue, and (3) explain the issuing procedures used in bond transactions.

*Instructions*

Write a memorandum to the president, answering his request.

## ETHICS CASE

**BYP10-8** The July 1998 issue of *Inc.* magazine includes an article by Jeffrey L. Seglin entitled "Would You Lie to Save Your Company?" It recounts the following true situation:

"A Chief Executive Officer (CEO) of a $20-million company that repairs aircraft engines received notice from a number of its customers that engines that it had recently repaired had failed, and that the company's parts were to blame. The CEO had not yet determined whether his company's parts were, in fact, the cause of the problem. The Federal Aviation Administration (FAA) had been notified and was investigating the matter.

What complicated the situation was that the company was in the midst of its year-end audit. As part of the audit, the CEO was required to sign a letter saying that he was not aware of any significant outstanding circumstances that could negatively impact the company—in accounting terms, of any contingent liabilities. The auditor was not aware of the customer complaints or the FAA investigation.

The company relied heavily on short-term loans from eight banks. The CEO feared that if these lenders learned of the situation, they would pull their loans. The loss of these loans would force the company into bankruptcy, leaving hundreds of people without jobs. Prior to this problem, the company had a stellar performance record."

*Instructions*

Answer the following questions.

(a) Who are the stakeholders in this situation?

(b) What are the CEO's possible courses of action? What are the potential results of each course of action? (Take into account the two alternative outcomes: the FAA determines the company (1) was not at fault, and (2) was at fault.)

(c) What would you do, and why?

(d) Suppose the CEO decides to conceal the situation, and that during the next year the company is found to be at fault and is forced into bankruptcy. What losses are incurred by the stakeholders in this situation? Do you think the CEO should suffer legal consequences if he decides to conceal the situation?

**BYP10-9** During the summer of 2002, the financial press reported that Citigroup was being investigated for allegations that it had arranged transactions for Enron so as to intentionally misrepresent the nature of the transactions and consequently achieve favorable balance sheet treatment. Essentially, the deals were structured to make it appear that money was coming into Enron from trading activities, rather than from loans.

A July 23, 2002, the *New York Times* article by Richard Oppel and Kurt Eichenwald entitled "Citigroup Said to Mold Deal to Help Enron Skirt Rules" suggested that Citigroup intentionally kept certain parts of a secret oral agreement out of the written record for fear that it would change the accounting treatment. Critics contend that this had the effect of significantly understating Enron's liabilities, thus misleading investors and creditors. Citigroup maintains that, as a lender, it has no obligation to ensure that its clients account for transactions properly. The proper accounting, Citigroup insists, is the responsibility of the client and its auditor.

*Instructions*

Answer the following questions.

(a) Who are the stakeholders in this situation?

(b) Do you think that a lender, in general, in arranging so called "structured financing" has a responsibility to ensure that its clients account for the financing in an appropriate fashion, or is this the responsibility of the client and its auditor?

(c) What effect did the fact that the written record did not disclose all characteristics of the transaction probably have on the auditor's ability to evaluate the accounting treatment of this transaction?

(d) The *New York Times* article noted that in one presentation made to sell this kind of deal to Enron and other energy companies, Citigroup stated that using such an arrangement "eliminates the need for capital markets disclosure, keeping structure mechanics private." Why might a company wish to conceal the terms of a financing arrangement from the capital markets (investors and creditors)? Is this appropriate? Do you think it is ethical for a lender to market deals in this way?

(e) Why was this deal more potentially harmful to shareholders than other off-balance-sheet transactions (for example, lease financing)?

## "ALL ABOUT YOU" ACTIVITY

**BYP10-10** For most U.S. families, medical costs are substantial and rising. But will medical costs be your most substantial expense over your lifetime? Not likely. Will it be housing or food? Again, not likely. The answer: Taxes are likely to be your biggest expense. On average, Americans work 74 days to afford their federal taxes. Companies, too, have large tax burdens. They look very hard at tax issues in deciding where to build their plants and where to locate their administrative headquarters.

*Instructions*

(a) Determine what your state income taxes are if your taxable income is $60,000 and you file as a single taxpayer in the state in which you live.

(b) Assume that you own a home worth $200,000 in your community and the tax rate is 2.1%. Compute the property taxes you would pay.

(c) Assume that the total gasoline bill for your automobile is $1,200 a year (300 gallons at $4 per gallon). What are the amounts of state and federal taxes that you pay on the $1,200?

(d) Assume that your purchases for the year total $9,000. Of this amount, $5,000 was for food and prescription drugs. What is the amount of sales tax you would pay on these purchases? (Note that many states do not have a sales tax for food or prescription drug purchases. Does yours?).

(e) Determine what your Social Security taxes are if your income is $60,000.

(f) Determine what your federal income taxes are if your taxable income is $60,000 and you file as a single taxpayer.

(g) Determine your *total* taxes paid based on the above calculations, and determine the percentage of income that you would pay in taxes based on the following formula: Total taxes paid ÷ Total income.

## FASB CODIFICATION ACTIVITY

**BYP10-11** If your school has a subscription to the FASB Codification, go to **http://aaahq.org/ asclogin.cfm** to log in and prepare responses to the following.

(a) What is the definition of current liabilities?

(b) What is the long-term obligation?

(c) What guidance does the Codification provide for the disclosure of long-term obligations?

## Answers to Insight and Accounting Across the Organization Questions

**p. 513 When Convertible Bonds Don't  Q:** The drop in stock prices did not change the debt to total assets ratios of these companies. Discuss how the perception of a high debt to total assets ratio changed before and after the fall in stock prices. **A:** When stock prices fell, the debt to total assets of these companies was unchanged: The debt was outstanding before the fall, and it was outstanding after the fall. However, before the fall, many investors did not worry if a company had a high debt to total assets ratio; they assumed that the debt would be converted to stock and so would never have to be repaid with cash. After the fall, it became clear that the debt would not be converted to stock; suddenly, a high debt to total assets ratio was a real concern.

**p. 526 Debt Masking  Q:** What implications does debt masking have for an investor that is using the debt to total assets ratio to evaluate a company's solvency? **A:** Since the debt to total assets ratio is calculated using financial statement numbers from the end of the accounting period, debt masking could result in investors making incorrect assumptions about a company's solvency. By engaging in debt masking, a company is misleading investors because what it is disclosing at the end of the period does not reflect what its normal financial position was during most of the accounting period.

**p. 528 "Covenant-Lite" Debt  Q:** How can financial ratios such as those covered in this chapter provide protection for creditors? **A:** Financial ratios such as the current ratio, debt to total assets ratio, and the times interest earned ratio provide indications of a company's liquidity and solvency. By specifying minimum levels of liquidity and solvency, as measured by these ratios, a creditor creates triggers that enable it to step in before a company's financial situation becomes too dire.

### Answers to Self-Test Questions

**1.** a  **2.** d  **3.** b ($88,500 \times .12 \times \frac{4}{12}$)  **4.** d  **5.** b ($4,515 \div 1.05$)  **6.** c  **7.** b ($18,000 \times \frac{3}{12}$)  **8.** c  **9.** c  **10.** a  **11.** c  **12.** d  **13.** b ($103,745 - $100,000$)  **14.** c ($150,000 + $30,000 + $20,000$) ÷ $30,000  **15.** a  *16. c (($500,000 \times .04) \div 5$)  *17. a ($500,000 - ($20,000 - (3 \times $4,000)$))  *18. b (($938,554 \times .10) - ($1,000,000 \times .09)$) = $3,855; ($1,000,000 - $938,554$) - $3,855  *19. c ($1,072,096 \times .12$)  *20. c ($1,165 - ($20,000 \times .015)$)

# IFRS  A Look at IFRS

IFRS and GAAP have similar definitions of liabilities. IFRSs related to reporting and recognition of liabilities are found in *IAS 1 (revised)* ("Presentation of Financial Statements") and *IAS 37* ("Provisions, Contingent Liabilities, and Contingent Assets"). The general recording procedures for payroll are similar although differences occur depending on the types of benefits that are provided in different countries.

## KEY POINTS

- The basic definition of a liability under GAAP and IFRS is very similar. In a more technical way, liabilities are defined by the IASB as a present obligation of the entity arising from past events, the settlement of which is expected to result in an outflow from the entity of resources embodying economic benefits. Liabilities may be legally enforceable via a contract or law but need not be; that is, they can arise due to normal business practices or customs.

- IFRS requires that companies classify liabilities as current or non-current on the face of the statement of financial position (balance sheet), except in industries where a *presentation* based on liquidity would be considered to provide more useful information (such as financial institutions).When current liabilities (also called short-term liabilities) are presented, they are generally presented in order of liquidity.

- Under IFRS, liabilities are classified as current if they are expected to be paid within 12 months.

- Similar to GAAP, items are normally reported in order of liquidity. Companies sometimes show liabilities before assets. Also, they will sometimes show non-current (long-term) liabilities before current liabilities.

- Under both GAAP and IFRS, preferred stock that is required to be redeemed at a specific point in time in the future must be reported as debt, rather than being presented as either equity or in a "mezzanine" area between debt and equity.

- Under IFRS, companies sometimes will net current liabilities against current assets to show working capital on the face of the statement of financial position. (This is evident in the Zetar financial statements in Appendix C.)

- IFRS requires use of the effective-interest method for amortization of bond discounts and premiums. GAAP allows use of the straight-line method where the difference is not material. Under

IFRS, companies do not use a premium or discount account but instead show the bond at its net amount. For example, if a $100,000 bond was issued at 97, under IFRS a company would record:

| | | |
|---|---|---|
| Cash | 97,000 | |
| Bonds Payable | | 97,000 |

- The accounting for convertible bonds differs across IFRS and GAAP. Unlike GAAP, IFRS splits the proceeds from the convertible bond between an equity component and a debt component. The equity conversion rights are reported in equity.

  To illustrate, assume that Harris Corp. issues convertible 7% bonds with a face value of $1,000,000 and receives $1,000,000. Comparable bonds without a conversion feature would have required a 9% rate of interest. To determine how much of the proceeds would be allocated to debt and how much to equity, the promised payments of the bond obligation would be discounted at the market rate of 9%. Suppose that this results in a present value of $850,000. The entry to record the issuance would be:

| | | |
|---|---|---|
| Cash | 1,000,000 | |
| Bonds Payable | | 850,000 |
| Equity Conversion Rights (Equity) | | 150,000 |

- The IFRS leasing standard is *IAS 17*. Both Boards share the same objective of recording leases by lessees and lessors according to their economic substance—that is, according to the definitions of assets and liabilities. However, GAAP for leases is much more "rules-based," with specific bright-line criteria (such as the "90% of fair value" test) to determine if a lease arrangement transfers the risks and rewards of ownership; IFRS is more conceptual in its provisions. Rather than a 90% cut-off, it asks whether the agreement transfers substantially all of the risks and rewards associated with ownership.
- Under GAAP, some contingent liabilities are recorded in the financial statements, others are disclosed, and in some cases no disclosure is required. Unlike GAAP, IFRS reserves the use of the term *contingent liability* to refer only to possible obligations that are *not* recognized in the financial statements but may be disclosed if certain criteria are met. Contingent liabilities are defined in *IAS 37* as being:
  - ♦ A possible obligation that arises from past events and whose existence will be confirmed only by the occurrence or non-occurrence of one or more uncertain future events not wholly within the control of the entity; or
  - ♦ A present obligation that arises from past events but is not recognized because:
    - ○ It is not probable that an outflow of resources embodying economic benefits will be required to settle the obligation; or
    - ○ The amount of the obligation cannot be measured with sufficient reliability.
- For those items that GAAP would treat as recordable contingent liabilities, IFRS instead uses the term *provisions*. **Provisions** are defined as liabilities of uncertain timing or amount. Examples of provisions would be provisions for warranties, employee vacation pay, or anticipated losses. Under IFRS, the measurement of a provision related to an uncertain obligation is based on the best estimate of the expenditure required to settle the obligation.

## LOOKING TO THE FUTURE

The FASB and IASB are currently involved in two projects, each of which has implications for the accounting for liabilities. One project is investigating approaches to differentiate between debt and equity instruments. The other project, the elements phase of the conceptual framework project, will evaluate the definitions of the fundamental building blocks of accounting. The results of these projects could change the classification of many debt and equity securities.

In addition to these projects, the FASB and IASB have also identified leasing as one of the most problematic areas of accounting. A joint project will initially focus primarily on lessee accounting. One of the first areas to be studied is, "What are the assets and liabilities to be recognized related to a lease contract?" Should the focus remain on the leased item or the right to use the leased item? This question is tied to the Boards' joint project on the conceptual framework—defining an "asset" and a "liability."

## IFRS Self-Test Questions

1. Which of the following is *false*?
   (a) Under IFRS, current liabilities must always be presented before non-current liabilities.
   (b) Under IFRS, an item is a current liability if it will be paid within the next 12 months.
   (c) Under IFRS, current liabilities are shown in order of liquidity.
   (d) Under IFRS, a liability is only recognized if it is a present obligation.
2. Under IFRS, a contingent liability is:
   (a) disclosed in the notes if certain criteria are met.
   (b) reported on the face of the financial statements if certain criteria are met.
   (c) the same as a provision.
   (d) not covered by IFRS.
3. Stevens Corporation issued 5% convertible bonds with a total face value of $3,000,000 for $3,000,000. If the bonds had not had a conversion feature, they would have sold for $2,600,000. Under IFRS, the entry to record the transaction would require a credit to:
   (a) Bonds Payable for $3,000,000.
   (b) Bonds Payable for $400,000.
   (c) Equity Conversion Rights for $400,000.
   (d) Discount on Bonds Payable for $400,000.
4. Under IFRS, if preference shares (preferred stock) have a requirement to be redeemed at a specific point in time in the future, they are treated:
   (a) as a type of asset account.
   (b) as ordinary shares (common stock).
   (c) in the same fashion as other types of preference shares.
   (d) as a liability.
5. The joint projects of the FASB and IASB could potentially:
   (a) change the definition of liabilities.
   (b) change the definition of equity.
   (c) change the definition of assets.
   (d) All of the above.

## IFRS Concepts and Application

**IFRS10–1**   Explain how IFRS defines a provision and give an example.

**IFRS10–2**   Explain how IFRS defines a contingent liability and give an example.

**IFRS10–3**   Briefly describe some of the similarities and differences between GAAP and IFRS with respect to the accounting for liabilities.

**IFRS10–4**   Ratzlaff Company issues €2 million, 10-year, 8% bonds at 97, with interest payable on July 1 and January 1.

### Instructions
   (a) Prepare the journal entry to record the sale of these bonds on January 1, 2012.
   (b) Assuming instead that the above bonds sold for 104, prepare the journal entry to record the sale of these bonds on January 1, 2012.

**IFRS10–5**   Many multinational companies find it beneficial to have their shares listed on stock exchanges in foreign countries. In order to do this, they must comply with the securities laws of those countries. Some of these laws relate to the form of financial disclosure the company must provide, including disclosures related to contingent liabilities. This exercise investigates the Tokyo Stock Exchange, the largest stock exchange in Japan.

*Address:* **www.tse.or.jp/english/,** or go to **www.wiley.com/college/kimmel**

### Steps

1. Choose **About TSE**.
2. Choose **History of TSE**. Answer questions (a) and (b).
3. Choose **Listed Company information**.
4. Choose **Disclosure**. Answer questions (c) and (d).
5. Answer the following questions.
   (a) When was the first stock exchange opened in Japan? How many exchanges does Japan have today?
   (b) What event caused trading to stop for a period of time in Japan?

    (c) What are four examples of decisions by corporations that must be disclosed at the time of their occurrence?

    (d) What are four examples of "occurrence of material fact" that must be disclosed at the time of their occurrence?

## INTERNATIONAL FINANCIAL STATEMENT ANALYSIS: *Zetar plc*

**IFRS10–6**  The financial statements of Zetar plc are presented in Appendix C. The company's complete annual report, including the notes to its financial statements, is available at **www.zetarplc.com**.

### Instructions

Use the company's annual report to answer the following questions.

    (a) According to the notes to the financial statements, what types of transactions do trade payables relate to? What was the average amount of time it took the company to pay its payables?

    (b) Note 2 (B) discusses provisions that the company records for certain types of activities. What do the provisions relate to, what are the estimates based on, and what could cause those estimates to change in subsequent periods?

    (c) What was the average interest rate paid on bank loans and overdrafts?

## Answers to IFRS Self-Test Questions

**1.** a  **2.** a  **3.** c  **4.** d  **5.** d

---

✓ **Remember to go back to the navigator box on the chapter opening page and check off your completed work.**

chapter 11

# REPORTING AND ANALYZING STOCKHOLDERS' EQUITY

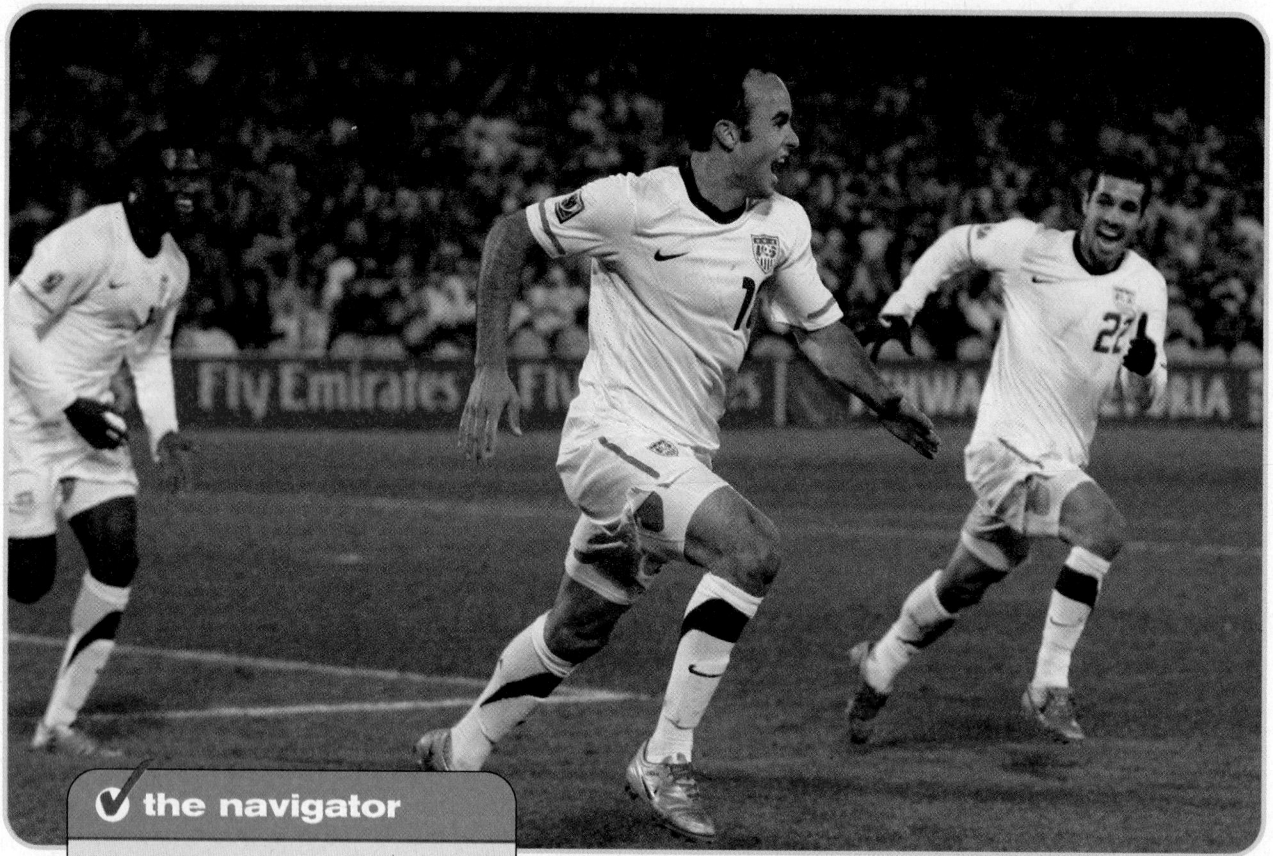


## the navigator

- Scan Study Objectives ○
- Read Feature Story ○
- Scan Preview ○
- Read Text and Answer **Do it!** p. 577 ○ p. 579 ○ p. 581 ○ p. 583 ○ p. 589 ○ p. 592 ○
- Work Using the Decision Toolkit ○
- Review Summary of Study Objectives ○
- Work Comprehensive **Do it!** p. 599 ○
- Answer Self-Test Questions ○
- Complete Assignments ○
- Go to WileyPLUS for practice and tutorials ○
- Read A Look at IFRS p. 619 ○

## study objectives

**After studying this chapter, you should be able to:**

1 Identify and discuss the major characteristics of a corporation.

2 Record the issuance of common stock.

3 Explain the accounting for the purchase of treasury stock.

4 Differentiate preferred stock from common stock.

5 Prepare the entries for cash dividends and understand the effect of stock dividends and stock splits.

6 Identify the items that affect retained earnings.

7 Prepare a comprehensive stockholders' equity section.

8 Evaluate a corporation's dividend and earnings performance from a stockholder's perspective.

the navigator

What major U.S. corporation got its start 38 years ago with a waffle iron? *Hint:* It doesn't sell food. *Another hint:* Swoosh. *Another hint:* "Just do it." That's right, Nike. In 1971 Nike co-founder Bill Bowerman put a piece of rubber into a kitchen waffle iron, and the trademark waffle sole was born. It seems fair to say that at Nike, "They don't make 'em like they used to."

Nike was co-founded by Bowerman and Phil Knight, a member of Bowerman's University of Oregon track team. Each began in the shoe business independently during the early 1960s. Bowerman got his start by making hand-crafted running shoes for his University of Oregon track team. Knight, after completing graduate school, started a small business importing low-cost, high-quality shoes from Japan. In 1964, the two joined forces, each contributing $500, and formed Blue Ribbon Sports, a partnership that marketed Japanese shoes.

It wasn't until 1971 that the company began manufacturing its own line of shoes. With the new shoes came a new corporate name—Nike—the Greek goddess of victory. It is hard to imagine that the company that now boasts a stable full of world-class athletes as

## WHAT'S COOKING?

promoters at one time had part-time employees selling shoes out of car trunks at track meets. Nike has achieved its success through relentless innovation combined with unbridled promotion.

By 1980, Nike was sufficiently established that it was able to issue its first stock to the public. In that same year, it also created a stock ownership program for its employees, allowing them to share in the company's success. Since then, Nike has enjoyed phenomenal growth, with 2009 sales reaching $19.2 billion and total dividends paid of $467 million.

Nike is not alone in its quest for the top of the sport shoe world. Reebok used to be Nike's arch rival (get it? "arch"), but then Reebok was acquired by the German company adidas. Now adidas pushes Nike every step of the way.

The shoe market is fickle, with new styles becoming popular almost daily and vast international markets still lying untapped. Whether one of these two giants does eventually take control of the pedi-planet remains to be seen. Meanwhile, the shareholders sit anxiously in the stands as this Olympic-size drama unfolds.

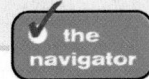

---

**INSIDE CHAPTER 11 . . .**

Corporations like Nike and adidas have substantial resources at their disposal. In fact, the corporation is the dominant form of business organization in the United States in terms of sales, earnings, and number of employees. All of the 500 largest U.S. companies are corporations. In this chapter, we look at the essential features of a corporation and explain the accounting for a corporation's capital stock transactions.

The content and organization of the chapter are as follows.

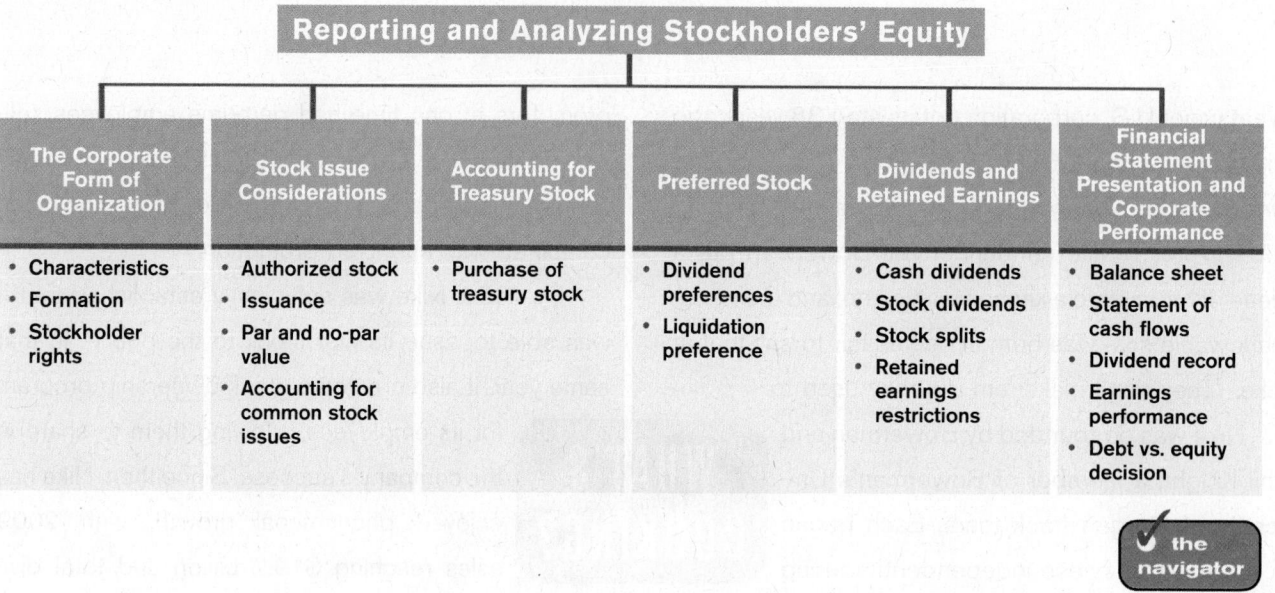

# The Corporate Form of Organization

A corporation is created by law. As a legal entity, a **corporation** has most of the rights and privileges of a person. The major exceptions relate to privileges that can be exercised only by a living person, such as the right to vote or to hold public office. Similarly, a corporation is subject to the same duties and responsibilities as a person. For example, it must abide by the law and it must pay taxes.

We can classify corporations in a variety of ways. Two common classifications are **by purpose** and **by ownership**. A corporation may be organized for the purpose of making a profit (such as Nike or General Motors), or it may be a nonprofit charitable, medical, or educational corporation (such as the Salvation Army or the American Cancer Society).

Classification by ownership differentiates publicly held and privately held corporations. A **publicly held corporation** may have thousands of stockholders, and its stock is traded on a national securities market such as the New York Stock Exchange. Examples are IBM, Caterpillar, and General Electric. In contrast, a **privately held corporation**, often referred to as a closely held corporation, usually has only a few stockholders and does not offer its stock for sale to the general public. Privately held companies are generally much smaller than publicly held companies, although some notable exceptions exist. Cargill Inc., a private corporation that trades in grain and other commodities, is one of the largest companies in the United States. This chapter deals primarily with issues related to publicly held companies.

**study objective 1**

Identify and discuss the major characteristics of a corporation.

### CHARACTERISTICS OF A CORPORATION

In 1964, when Nike's founders, Knight and Bowerman, were just getting started in the running shoe business, they formed their original organization as a partnership. In 1968, they reorganized the company as a corporation. A number of characteristics distinguish a corporation from sole proprietorships and partnerships. The most important of these characteristics are explained below.

### Separate Legal Existence

As an entity separate and distinct from its owners, the corporation acts under its own name rather than in the name of its stockholders. Nike, for example, may buy, own, and sell property, borrow money, and enter into legally binding contracts in its own name. It may also sue or be sued. It pays taxes as a separate entity.

In contrast to a partnership, in which the acts of the owners (partners) bind the partnership, the acts of corporate owners (stockholders) do not bind the corporation unless such owners are agents of the corporation. For example, if you owned shares of Nike stock, you would not have the right to purchase inventory for the company unless you were designated as an agent of the corporation.

Stockholders
**Legal existence separate from owners**

### Limited Liability of Stockholders

Since a corporation is a separate legal entity, creditors ordinarily have recourse only to corporate assets to satisfy their claims. The liability of stockholders is normally limited to their investment in the corporation. Creditors have no legal claim on the personal assets of the stockholders unless fraud has occurred. Thus, even in the event of bankruptcy of the corporation, stockholders' losses are generally limited to the amount of capital they have invested in the corporation.

Stockholders
**Limited liability of stockholders**

### Transferable Ownership Rights

Ownership of a corporation is held in shares of capital stock, which are transferable units. Stockholders may dispose of part or all of their interest in a corporation simply by selling their stock. The transfer of an ownership interest in a partnership requires the consent of each partner. In contrast, the transfer of stock is entirely at the discretion of the stockholder. It does not require the approval of either the corporation or other stockholders.

The transfer of ownership rights among stockholders normally has no effect on the operating activities of the corporation. Nor does it affect the corporation's assets, liabilities, and total stockholders' equity. The transfer of ownership rights is a transaction between individual owners. The company does not participate in the transfer of these ownership rights after the original sale of the capital stock.

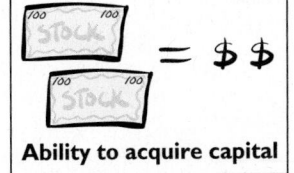

**Transferable ownership rights**

### Ability to Acquire Capital

It is relatively easy for a corporation to obtain capital through the issuance of stock. Buying stock in a corporation is often attractive to an investor because a stockholder has limited liability and shares of stock are readily transferable. Also, numerous individuals can become stockholders by investing small amounts of money.

**Ability to acquire capital**

### Continuous Life

The life of a corporation is stated in its charter. The life may be perpetual or it may be limited to a specific number of years. If it is limited, the company can extend the period of existence through renewal of the charter. Since a corporation is a separate legal entity, its continuance as a going concern is not affected by the withdrawal, death, or incapacity of a stockholder, employee, or officer. As a result, a successful corporation can have a continuous and perpetual life.

**Continuous life**

### Corporation Management

Although stockholders legally own the corporation, they manage it indirectly through a board of directors they elect. Philip Knight is the chairman of Nike's board of directors. The board, in turn, formulates the operating policies for the company. The board also selects officers, such as a president and one or more vice presidents, to execute policy and to perform daily management functions. As a result of the Sarbanes-Oxley Act, the board is now required to monitor management's actions more closely. Many feel that the failures at Enron and World-Com could have been avoided by more diligent boards.

Illustration 11-1 depicts a typical organization chart showing the delegation of responsibility.

**Illustration 11-1**
Corporation organization chart

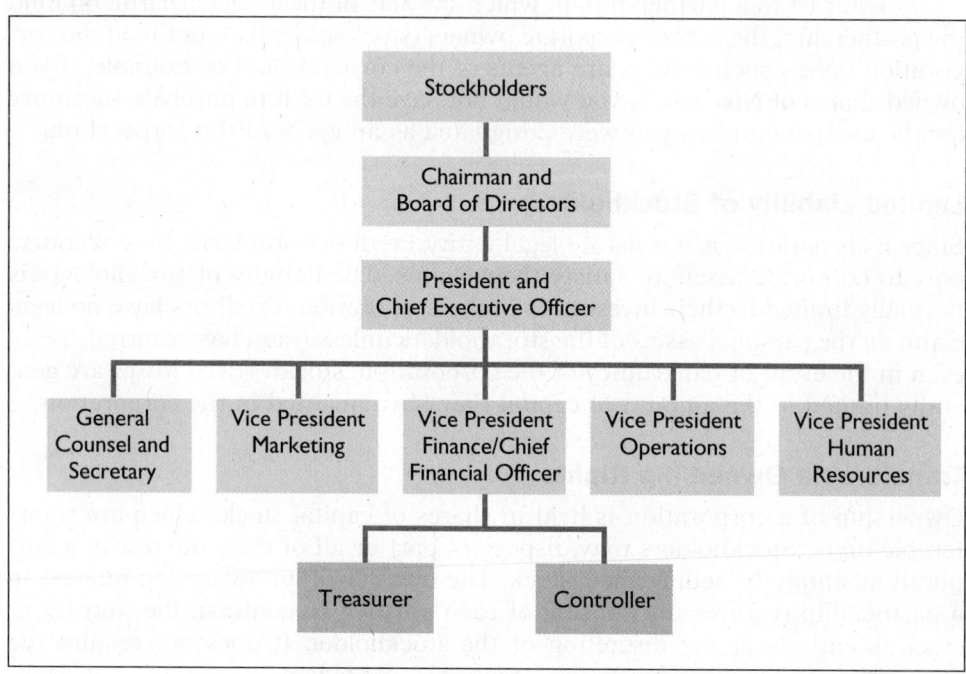

The chief executive officer (CEO) has overall responsibility for managing the business. As the organization chart shows, the CEO delegates responsibility to other officers. The chief accounting officer is the **controller**. The controller's responsibilities are to (1) maintain the accounting records, (2) maintain an adequate system of internal control, and (3) prepare financial statements, tax returns, and internal reports. The **treasurer** has custody of the corporation's funds and is responsible for maintaining the company's cash position.

The organizational structure of a corporation enables a company to hire professional managers to run the business. On the other hand, the separation of ownership and management often reduces an owner's ability to actively manage the company.

**Ethics Note** Managers who are not owners are often compensated based on the performance of the company. They thus may be tempted to exaggerate company performance by inflating income figures.

### Government Regulations

A corporation is subject to numerous state and federal regulations. For example, state laws usually prescribe the requirements for issuing stock, the distributions of earnings permitted to stockholders, and acceptable methods for retiring stock. Federal securities laws govern the sale of capital stock to the general public. Also, most publicly held corporations are required to make extensive disclosure of their financial affairs to the Securities and Exchange Commission (SEC) through quarterly and annual reports. The Sarbanes-Oxley Act increased the company's responsibility for the accuracy of these reports. In addition, when a corporate stock is listed and traded on organized securities exchanges, the corporation must comply with the reporting requirements of these exchanges.

## Additional Taxes

Owners of proprietorships and partnerships report their share of earnings on their personal income tax returns. The individual owner then pays taxes on this amount. Corporations, on the other hand, must pay federal and state income taxes as a separate legal entity. These taxes can be substantial: They can amount to as much as 40% of taxable income.

In addition, stockholders are required to pay taxes on cash dividends. Thus, many argue that corporate income is **taxed twice (double taxation)**—once at the corporate level and again at the individual level.

Illustration 11-2 shows the advantages and disadvantages of a corporation compared to a sole proprietorship and partnership.

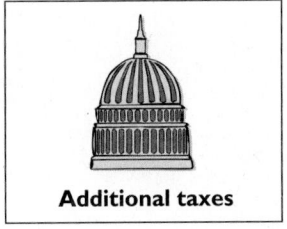

**Additional taxes**

| Advantages | Disadvantages |
| --- | --- |
| • Separate legal existence<br>• Limited liability of stockholders<br>• Transferable ownership rights<br>• Ability to acquire capital<br>• Continuous life<br>• Corporation management—professional managers | • Corporation management—separation of ownership and management<br>• Government regulations<br>• Additional taxes |

**Illustration 11-2**
Advantages and disadvantages of a corporation

## Other Forms of Business Organization

A variety of "hybrid" organizational forms—forms that combine different attributes of partnerships and corporations—now exist. For example, one type of corporate form, called an **S corporation**, allows for legal treatment as a corporation but tax treatment as a partnership—that is, no double taxation. Because of changes to the S corporation's rules, more small- and medium-sized businesses now may choose S corporation treatment. One of the primary criteria is that the company cannot have more than 75 shareholders. Other forms of organization include limited partnerships, limited liability partnerships (LLPs), and limited liability companies (LLCs).

## DECISION TOOLKIT   A SUMMARY

| DECISION CHECKPOINTS | INFO NEEDED FOR DECISION | TOOL TO USE FOR DECISION | HOW TO EVALUATE RESULTS |
|---|---|---|---|
| Should the company incorporate? | Capital needs, growth expectations, type of business, tax status | Corporations have limited liability, easier capital raising ability, and professional managers; but they suffer from additional taxes, government regulations, and separation of ownership from management. | Must carefully weigh the costs and benefits in light of the particular circumstances. |

### FORMING A CORPORATION

A corporation is formed by grant of a state **charter**. The charter is a document that describes the name and purpose of the corporation, the types and number of shares of stock that are authorized to be issued, the names of the individuals that formed the company, and the number of shares that these individuals agreed to purchase. Regardless of the number of states in which a corporation has operating divisions, it is incorporated in only one state. It is to the company's advantage to incorporate in a state whose laws are favorable to the corporate form of business organization. For example, although General Motors has its headquarters in Michigan, it is incorporated in New Jersey. In fact, more and more corporations have been incorporating in states with rules that favor existing management. For example, Gulf Oil changed its state of incorporation to Delaware to thwart possible unfriendly takeovers. There, certain defensive tactics against takeovers can be approved by the board of directors alone, without a vote by shareholders.

Upon receipt of its charter from the state of incorporation, the corporation establishes **by-laws**. The by-laws establish the internal rules and procedures for conducting the affairs of the corporation. Corporations engaged in interstate commerce must also obtain a **license** from each state in which they do business. The license subjects the corporation's operating activities to the general corporation laws of the state.

### STOCKHOLDER RIGHTS

When chartered, the corporation may begin selling shares of stock. When a corporation has only one class of stock, it is identified as **common stock**. Each share of common stock gives the stockholder the ownership rights pictured in Illustration 11-3. The articles of incorporation or the by-laws state the ownership rights of a share of stock.

Proof of stock ownership is evidenced by a printed or engraved form known as a **stock certificate**. As shown in Illustration 11-4, the face of the certificate shows the name of the corporation, the stockholder's name, the class and special features of the stock, the number of shares owned, and the signatures of authorized corporate officials. Certificates are prenumbered to ensure proper control over their use; they may be issued for any quantity of shares.

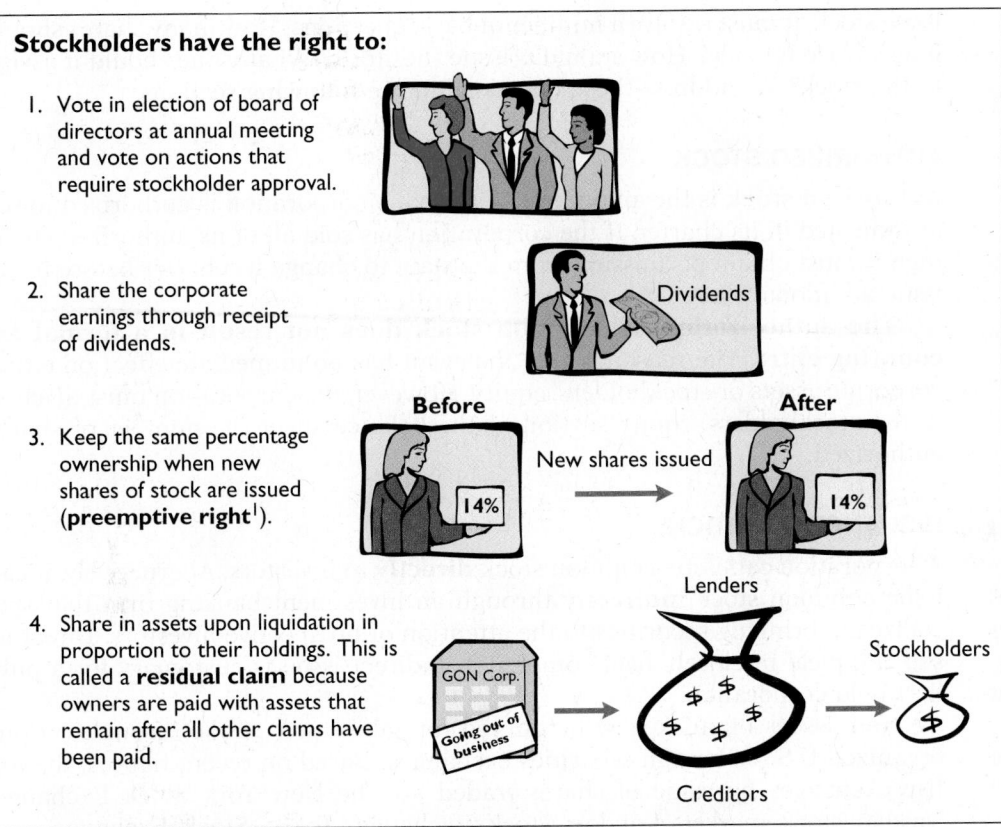

**Illustration 11-3**
Ownership rights of stockholders

**Stockholders have the right to:**

1. Vote in election of board of directors at annual meeting and vote on actions that require stockholder approval.

2. Share the corporate earnings through receipt of dividends.

3. Keep the same percentage ownership when new shares of stock are issued (**preemptive right**[1]).

4. Share in assets upon liquidation in proportion to their holdings. This is called a **residual claim** because owners are paid with assets that remain after all other claims have been paid.

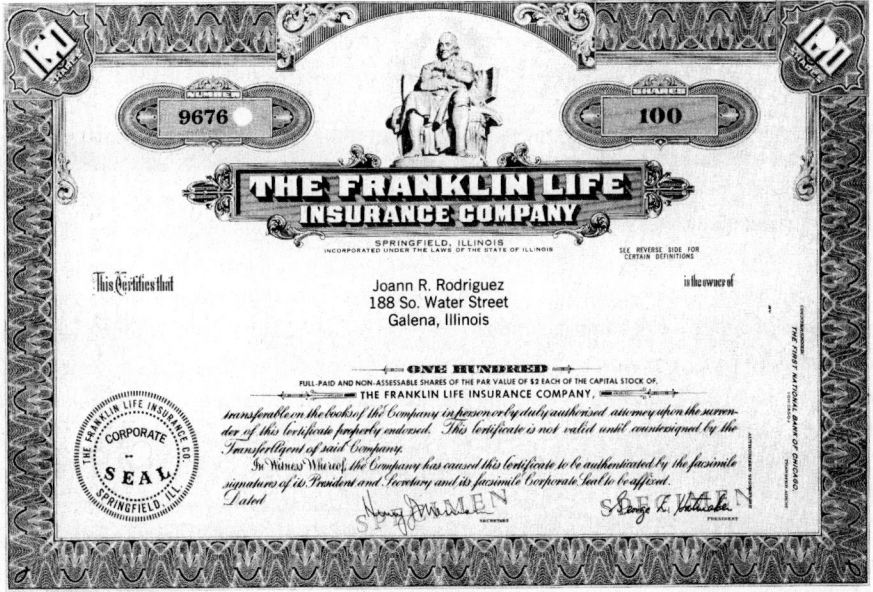

**Illustration 11-4**  A stock certificate

# Stock Issue Considerations

Although Nike incorporated in 1968, it did not sell stock to the public until 1980. At that time, Nike evidently decided it would benefit from the infusion of cash that a public sale of its shares would bring. When a corporation decides to

---

[1]A number of companies have eliminated the preemptive right because they believe it places an unnecessary and cumbersome demand on management. For example, IBM, by stockholder approval, has dropped its preemptive right for stockholders.

issue stock, it must resolve a number of basic questions: How many shares should it authorize for sale? How should it issue the stock? What value should it assign to the stock? We address these questions in the following sections.

## AUTHORIZED STOCK

**Authorized stock** is the amount of stock that a corporation is authorized to sell as indicated in its charter. If the corporation has sold all of its authorized stock, then it must obtain permission from the state to change its charter before it can issue additional shares.

**The authorization of common stock does not result in a formal accounting entry.** The reason is that the event has no immediate effect on either corporate assets or stockholders' equity. However, the corporation must disclose in the stockholders' equity section of the balance sheet the number of shares authorized.

**International Note** U.S. and U.K. corporations raise most of their capital through millions of outside shareholders and bondholders. In contrast, companies in Germany, France, and Japan acquire financing mostly from large banks or other financial institutions. Consequently, in the latter environment, shareholders are somewhat less important.

## ISSUANCE OF STOCK

A corporation can issue common stock **directly** to investors. Alternatively, it can issue common stock **indirectly** through an investment banking firm that specializes in bringing securities to the attention of prospective investors. Direct issue is typical in closely held companies. Indirect issue is customary for a publicly held corporation.

New issues of stock may be offered for sale to the public through various organized U.S. or foreign securities exchanges. Based on recent figures, the top five exchanges by value of shares traded are the New York Stock Exchange, Nasdaq stock market, London Stock Exchange, Tokyo Stock Exchange, and Euronext.

## ANATOMY OF A FRAUD

The president, chief operating officer, and chief financial officer of SafeNet, a software encryption company, were each awarded employee stock options by the company's board of directors as part of their compensation package. Stock options enable an employee to buy a company's stock sometime in the future at the price that existed when the stock option was awarded. For example, suppose that you received stock options today, when the stock price of your company was $30. Three years later, if the stock price rose to $100, you could "exercise" your options and buy the stock for $30 per share, thereby making $70 per share. After being awarded their stock options, the three employees changed the award dates in the company's records to dates in the past, when the company's stock was trading at historical lows. For example, using the previous example, they would choose a past date when the stock was selling for $10 per share, rather than the $30 price on the actual award date. In our example, this would increase the profit from exercising the options to $90 per share.

**Total take: $1.7 million**

### THE MISSING CONTROL

*Independent internal verification.* The company's board of directors should have ensured that the awards were properly administered. For example, the date on the minutes from the board meeting should be compared to the dates that were recorded for the awards. In addition, the dates should again be confirmed upon exercise.

## PAR AND NO-PAR VALUE STOCKS

**Par value stock** is capital stock that has been assigned a value per share in the corporate charter. Years ago, par value was used to determine the **legal capital** that must be retained in the business for the protection of corporate creditors. That amount is not available for withdrawal by stockholders. Thus, in the past, most states required the corporation to sell its shares at par or above.

However, the usefulness of par value as a device to protect creditors was limited because par value was often immaterial relative to the value of the company's stock in the securities markets—even at the time of issue. For example, Loews Corporation's par value is $0.01 per share, yet a new issue in 2010 would have sold at a **market value** in the $35 per share range. Thus, par has no relationship with market value and in the vast majority of cases is an immaterial amount. As a consequence, today many states do not require a par value. Instead, they use other means to protect creditors.

**No-par value stock** is capital stock that has not been assigned a value in the corporate charter. No-par value stock is fairly common today. For example, Nike and Procter & Gamble both have no-par stock. In many states, the board of directors assigns a **stated value** to the no-par shares.

*before you go on...*

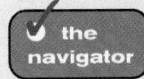 Indicate whether each of the following statements is true or false.

_____ 1. Similar to partners in a partnership, stockholders of a corporation have unlimited liability.

_____ 2. It is relatively easy for a corporation to obtain capital through the issuance of stock.

_____ 3. The separation of ownership and management is an advantage of the corporate form of business.

_____ 4. The journal entry to record the authorization of capital stock includes a credit to the appropriate capital stock account.

_____ 5. All states require a par value per share for capital stock.

### Solution

1. False. The liability of stockholders is normally limited to their investment in the corporation.
2. True.
3. False. The separation of ownership and management is a disadvantage of the corporate form of business.
4. False. The authorization of capital stock does not result in a formal accounting entry.
5. False. Many states do not require a par value.

Related exercise material: **BE11-1** and **Do it!** **11-1**.

**CORPORATE ORGANIZATION**

### Action Plan

• Review the characteristics of a corporation and understand which are advantages and which are disadvantages.

• Understand that corporations raise capital through the issuance of stock, which can be par or no-par.

 the navigator

## ACCOUNTING FOR COMMON STOCK ISSUES

The stockholders' equity section of a corporation's balance sheet includes (1) **paid-in (contributed) capital** and (2) **retained earnings (earned capital)**. The distinction between paid-in capital and retained earnings is important from both a legal and an economic point of view. **Paid-in capital** is the amount stockholders paid to the corporation in exchange for shares of ownership. **Retained earnings** is earned capital held for future use in the business. In this section,

**study objective 2**

Record the issuance of common stock.

we discuss the accounting for paid-in capital. In a later section, we discuss retained earnings.

Let's now look at how to account for new issues of common stock. The primary objectives in accounting for the issuance of common stock are (1) to identify the specific sources of paid-in capital and (2) to maintain the distinction between paid-in capital and retained earnings. As shown below, **the issuance of common stock affects only paid-in capital accounts**.

As discussed earlier, par value does not indicate a stock's market value. The cash proceeds from issuing par value stock may be equal to, greater than, or less than par value. When a company records the issuance of common stock for cash, it credits the par value of the shares to Common Stock, and records in a separate paid-in capital account the portion of the proceeds that is above or below par value.

To illustrate, assume that Hydro-Slide, Inc. issues 1,000 shares of $1 par value common stock at par for cash. The entry to record this transaction is:

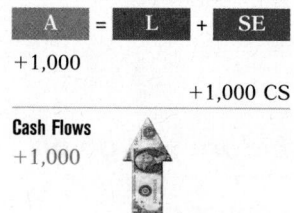

| A = L + SE |
| --- |
| +1,000 |
| +1,000 CS |

Cash Flows
+1,000

| | | |
| --- | --- | --- |
| Cash | 1,000 | |
|     Common Stock | | 1,000 |
|       (To record issuance of 1,000 shares of $1 par common stock at par) | | |

Now assume Hydro-Slide, Inc. issues an additional 1,000 shares of the $1 par value common stock for cash at $5 per share. The amount received above the par value, in this case $4 ($5 − $1), would be credited to Paid-in Capital in Excess of Par Value. The entry is:

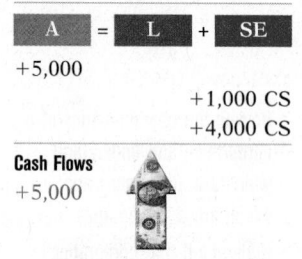

| A = L + SE |
| --- |
| +5,000 |
| +1,000 CS |
| +4,000 CS |

Cash Flows
+5,000

| | | |
| --- | --- | --- |
| Cash | 5,000 | |
|     Common Stock (1,000 × $1) | | 1,000 |
|     Paid-in Capital in Excess of Par Value | | 4,000 |
|       (To record issuance of 1,000 shares of common stock in excess of par) | | |

The total paid-in capital from these two transactions is $6,000. If Hydro-Slide, Inc. has retained earnings of $27,000, the stockholders' equity section of the balance sheet is as shown in Illustration 11-5.

**Illustration 11-5**
Stockholders' equity—paid-in capital in excess of par value

| HYDRO-SLIDE, INC. |
| --- |
| Balance Sheet (partial) |

| | |
| --- | --- |
| Stockholders' equity | |
|   Paid-in capital | |
|     Common stock | $ 2,000 |
|     **Paid-in capital in excess of par value** | 4,000 |
|     Total paid-in capital | 6,000 |
|   Retained earnings | 27,000 |
|   Total stockholders' equity | $33,000 |

Some companies issue no-par stock with a stated value. For accounting purposes, companies treat the stated value in the same way as the par value. For example, if in our Hydro-Slide example the stock was no-par stock with a stated value of $1, the entries would be the same as those presented for the par stock except the term "Par Value" would be replaced with "Stated Value." If a company issues no-par stock that does not have a stated value, then it credits to the Common Stock account the full amount received. In such a case, there is no need for the Paid-in Capital in Excess of Stated Value account.

## Investor Insight

### How to Read Stock Quotes

Organized exchanges trade the stock of publicly held companies at dollar prices per share established by the interaction between buyers and sellers. For each listed security, the financial press reports the high and low prices of the stock during the year, the total volume of stock traded on a given day, the high and low prices for the day, and the closing market price, with the net change for the day. Nike is listed on the New York Stock Exchange. Here is a recent listing for Nike:

| Stock | 52 Weeks | | Volume | High | Low | Close | Net Change |
| | High | Low | | | | | |
| --- | --- | --- | --- | --- | --- | --- | --- |
| Nike | 78.55 | 48.76 | 5,375,651 | 72.44 | 69.78 | 70.61 | −1.69 |

These numbers indicate the following: The high and low market prices for the last 52 weeks have been $78.55 and $48.76. The trading volume for the day was 5,375,651 shares. The high, low, and closing prices for that date were $72.44, $69.78, and $70.61, respectively. The net change for the day was a decrease of $1.69 per share.

**?** For stocks traded on organized exchanges, how are the dollar prices per share established? What factors might influence the price of shares in the marketplace? (See page 619.)

*before you go on...*

**Do it!** Cayman Corporation begins operations on March 1 by issuing 100,000 shares of $10 par value common stock for cash at $12 per share. Journalize the issuance of the shares.

### Solution

| | | | | |
| --- | --- | --- | --- | --- |
| Mar. 1 | Cash | | 1,200,000 | |
| | Common Stock | | | 1,000,000 |
| | Paid-in Capital in Excess of Par Value | | | 200,000 |
| | (To record issuance of 100,000 shares at $12 per share) | | | |

Related exercise material: **BE11-2, BE11-3, Do it! 11-2,** and **E11-1.**

**ISSUANCE OF STOCK**

**Action Plan**

• In issuing shares for cash, credit Common Stock for par value per share.

• Credit any additional proceeds in excess of par value to a separate paid-in capital account.

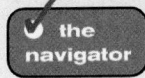
✔ the navigator

# Accounting for Treasury Stock

**Treasury stock** is a corporation's own stock that has been reacquired by the corporation and is being held for future use. A corporation may acquire treasury stock for various reasons:

1. To reissue the shares to officers and employees under bonus and stock compensation plans.

**study objective 3**

Explain the accounting for the purchase of treasury stock.

2. To increase trading of the company's stock in the securities market. Companies expect that buying their own stock will signal that management believes the stock is underpriced, which they hope will enhance its market value.

3. To have additional shares available for use in acquiring other companies.

4. To reduce the number of shares outstanding and thereby increase earnings per share.

Another infrequent reason for purchasing treasury shares is that management may want to eliminate hostile shareholders by buying them out.

Many corporations have treasury stock. For example, in the United States approximately 70% of companies have treasury stock.[2] In the first quarter of 2007, companies in the Standard & Poor's 500-stock index spent a record of about $118 billion to buy treasury stock. In a recent year, Nike purchased more than 6 million treasury shares. At one point, stock repurchases were so substantial that a study by two Federal Reserve economists suggested that a sharp reduction in corporate purchases of treasury shares might result in a sharp drop in the value of the U.S. stock market.

### PURCHASE OF TREASURY STOCK

The purchase of treasury stock is generally accounted for by the **cost method.** This method derives its name from the fact that the Treasury Stock account is maintained at the cost of shares purchased. Under the cost method, **companies increase (debit) Treasury Stock by the price paid to reacquire the shares. Treasury Stock decreases by the same amount when the company later sells the shares.**

To illustrate, assume that on January 1, 2012, the stockholders' equity section for Mead, Inc. has 100,000 shares of $5 par value common stock outstanding (all issued at par value) and Retained Earnings of $200,000. Illustration 11-6 shows the stockholders' equity section of the balance sheet before purchase of treasury stock.

**Illustration 11-6**
Stockholders' equity with no treasury stock

| MEAD, INC. | |
|---|---|
| Balance Sheet (partial) | |
| Stockholders' equity | |
| Paid-in capital | |
| Common stock, $5 par value, 400,000 shares authorized, | |
| 100,000 shares issued and outstanding | $500,000 |
| Retained earnings | 200,000 |
| Total stockholders' equity | $700,000 |

On February 1, 2012, Mead acquires 4,000 shares of its stock at $8 per share. The entry is:

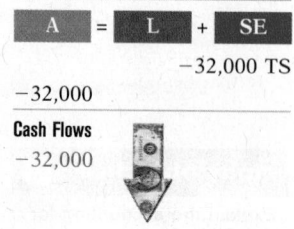

| A | = | L | + | SE |
|---|---|---|---|---|
| | | | | −32,000 TS |
| −32,000 | | | | |

**Cash Flows**
−32,000

| Feb. 1 | Treasury Stock | 32,000 | |
|---|---|---|---|
| | Cash | | 32,000 |
| | (To record purchase of 4,000 shares of treasury stock at $8 per share) | | |

[2]*Accounting Trends & Techniques—2009* (New York: American Institute of Certified Public Accountants).

The Treasury Stock account would increase by the cost of the shares purchased ($32,000). The original paid-in capital account, Common Stock, would not be affected because **the number of issued shares does not change**.

Companies show treasury stock as a deduction from total paid-in capital and retained earnings in the stockholders' equity section of the balance sheet. Illustration 11-7 shows this presentation for Mead, Inc. Thus, the acquisition of treasury stock reduces stockholders' equity.

**Ethics Note** The purchase of treasury stock reduces the cushion for creditors. To protect creditors, many states require that a portion of retained earnings equal to the cost of the treasury stock purchased be restricted from being paid as dividends.

**Illustration 11-7**
Stockholders' equity with treasury stock

| MEAD, INC. | |
|---|---|
| Balance Sheet (partial) | |
| Stockholders' equity | |
| Paid-in capital | |
| Common stock, $5 par value, 400,000 shares authorized, | |
| 100,000 shares issued and 96,000 shares outstanding | $500,000 |
| Retained earnings | 200,000 |
| Total paid-in capital and retained earnings | 700,000 |
| Less: Treasury stock (4,000 shares) | 32,000 |
| Total stockholders' equity | $668,000 |

**Helpful Hint** Treasury Stock is a contra stockholders' equity account.

Companies disclose in the balance sheet both the number of shares issued (100,000) and the number in the treasury (4,000). The difference is the number of shares of stock outstanding (96,000). The term **outstanding stock** means the number of shares of issued stock that are being held by stockholders.

In a bold (and some would say risky) move, Reebok at one time bought back nearly a *third* of its shares. This repurchase of shares dramatically reduced Reebok's available cash. In fact, the company borrowed significant funds to accomplish the repurchase. In a press release, management stated that it was repurchasing the shares because it believed that the stock was severely underpriced. The repurchase of so many shares was meant to signal management's belief in good future earnings.

Skeptics, however, suggested that Reebok's management was repurchasing shares to make it less likely that the company would be acquired by another company (in which case Reebok's top managers would likely lose their jobs). Acquiring companies like to purchase companies with large cash reserves so they can pay off debt used in the acquisition. By depleting its cash, Reebok became a less likely acquisition target.

*before you go on...*

**Do it!** Santa Anita Inc. purchases 3,000 shares of its $50 par value common stock for $180,000 cash on July 1. It expects to hold the shares in the treasury until resold. Journalize the treasury stock transaction.

**Solution**

| July | 1 | Treasury Stock | 180,000 | |
|---|---|---|---|---|
| | | Cash | | 180,000 |
| | | (To record the purchase of 3,000 shares at $60 per share) | | |

Related exercise material: **Do it!** 11-3, E11-2, and E11-5.

**TREASURY STOCK**
**Action Plan**

• Record the purchase of treasury stock at cost.

• Report treasury stock as a deduction from stockholders' equity (contra account) at the bottom of the stockholders' equity section.

the navigator

# Preferred Stock

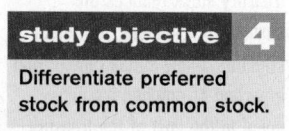

To appeal to a larger segment of potential investors, a corporation may issue an additional class of stock, called preferred stock. **Preferred stock** has contractual provisions that give it preference or priority over common stock in certain areas. Typically, preferred stockholders have a priority in relation to (1) dividends and (2) assets in the event of liquidation. However, they sometimes do not have voting rights. adidas has no outstanding preferred stock, whereas Nike has a very minor amount outstanding. Approximately 7% of U.S. companies have one or more classes of preferred stock.[3]

Like common stock, companies may issue preferred stock for cash or for noncash consideration. The entries for these transactions are similar to the entries for common stock. When a corporation has more than one class of stock, each paid-in capital account title should identify the stock to which it relates (e.g., Preferred Stock, Common Stock, Paid-in Capital in Excess of Par Value—Preferred Stock, and Paid-in Capital in Excess of Par Value—Common Stock).

Assume that Stine Corporation issues 10,000 shares of $10 par value preferred stock for $12 cash per share. The entry to record the issuance is:

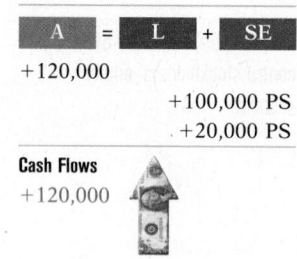

+120,000

+100,000 PS
+20,000 PS

**Cash Flows**

+120,000

| | | |
|---|---|---|
| Cash | 120,000 | |
|     Preferred Stock | | 100,000 |
|     Paid-in Capital in Excess of Par Value—Preferred Stock | | 20,000 |
|       (To record the issuance of 10,000 shares of $10 par value preferred stock) | | |

Preferred stock may have either a par value or no-par value. In the stockholders' equity section of the balance sheet, companies show preferred stock first because of its dividend and liquidation preferences over common stock.

## DIVIDEND PREFERENCES

As indicated above, **preferred stockholders have the right to share in the distribution of corporate income before common stockholders**. For example, if the dividend rate on preferred stock is $5 per share, common shareholders will not receive any dividends in the current year until preferred stockholders have received $5 per share. The first claim to dividends does not, however, **guarantee** dividends. Dividends depend on many factors, such as adequate retained earnings and availability of cash.

For preferred stock, companies state the per share dividend amount as a percentage of the par value of the stock or as a specified amount. For example, EarthLink specifies a 3% dividend, whereas Nike pays 10 cents per share on its $1 par preferred stock.

### Cumulative Dividend

Preferred stock contracts often contain a **cumulative dividend** feature. This right means that preferred stockholders must be paid both current-year dividends and any unpaid prior-year dividends before common stockholders receive dividends. When preferred stock is cumulative, preferred dividends not declared in a given period are called **dividends in arrears**.

To illustrate, assume that Scientific Leasing has 5,000 shares of 7%, $100 par value cumulative preferred stock outstanding. Each $100 share pays a $7 dividend (.07 × $100). The annual dividend is $35,000 (5,000 × $7 per share). If dividends are two years in arrears, preferred stockholders are entitled to receive in the current year the dividends as shown in Illustration 11-8.

---

[3]*Accounting Trends & Techniques—2009* (New York: American Institute of Certified Public Accountants).

| Dividends in arrears ($35,000 × 2) | $ 70,000 |
| Current-year dividends | 35,000 |
| **Total preferred dividends** | **$105,000** |

**Illustration 11-8**
Computation of total dividends to preferred stock

No distribution can be made to common stockholders until Scientific Leasing pays this entire preferred dividend. In other words, companies cannot pay dividends to common stockholders while any preferred stock dividend is in arrears.

**Dividends in arrears are not considered a liability. No obligation exists until the board of directors formally "declares" that the corporation will pay a dividend.** However, companies should disclose in the notes to the financial statements the amount of dividends in arrears. Doing so enables investors to assess the potential impact of this commitment on the corporation's financial position.

The investment community does not look favorably upon companies that are unable to meet their dividend obligations. As a financial officer noted in discussing one company's failure to pay its cumulative preferred dividend for a period of time, "Not meeting your obligations on something like that is a major black mark on your record."

### LIQUIDATION PREFERENCE

Most preferred stocks have a preference on corporate assets if the corporation fails. This feature provides security for the preferred stockholder. The preference to assets may be for the par value of the shares or for a specified liquidating value. For example, Commonwealth Edison issued preferred stock that entitled the holders to receive $31.80 per share, plus accrued and unpaid dividends, in the event of involuntary liquidation. The liquidation preference is used in litigation pertaining to bankruptcy lawsuits involving the respective claims of creditors and preferred stockholders.

*before you go on...*

**Do it!**  MasterMind Corporation has 2,000 shares of 6%, $100 par value preferred stock outstanding at December 31, 2012. At December 31, 2012, the company declared a $60,000 cash dividend. Determine the dividend paid to preferred stockholders and common stockholders under each of the following scenarios.

1. The preferred stock is noncumulative, and the company has not missed any dividends in previous years.

2. The preferred stock is noncumulative, and the company did not pay a dividend in each of the two previous years.

3. The preferred stock is cumulative, and the company did not pay a dividend in each of the two previous years.

### Solution

1. The company has not missed past dividends and the preferred stock is noncumulative; thus, the preferred stockholders are paid only this year's dividends. The dividend paid to preferred stockholders would be $12,000 (2,000 ×.06 × $100). The dividend paid to common stockholders would be $48,000 ($60,000 − $12,000).

2. The preferred stock is noncumulative; thus, past unpaid dividends do not have to be paid. The dividend paid to preferred stockholders would be $12,000 (2,000 ×.06 × $100). The dividend paid to common stockholders would be $48,000 ($60,000 − $12,000).

3. The preferred stock is cumulative; thus, dividends that have been missed (dividends in arrears) must be paid. The dividend paid to preferred stockholders would be $36,000 (3 × 2,000 ×.06 × $100). The dividend paid to common stockholders would be $24,000 ($60,000 − $36,000).

**PREFERRED STOCK DIVIDENDS**

**Action Plan**

• Determine dividends on preferred shares by multiplying the dividend rate times the par value of the stock times the number of preferred shares.

• Understand the cumulative feature: If preferred stock is cumulative, then any missed dividends (dividends in arrears) and the current year's dividend must be paid to preferred stockholders before dividends are paid to common stockholders.

Related exercise material: **Do it!** 11-4.

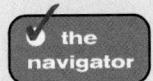
the navigator

# Dividends

**study objective 5**

Prepare the entries for cash dividends and understand the effect of stock dividends and stock splits.

As noted earlier, a **dividend is a distribution by a corporation to its stock-holders on a pro rata** (proportional to ownership) **basis**. *Pro rata* means that if you own, say, 10% of the common shares, you will receive 10% of the dividend. Dividends can take four forms: cash, property, scrip (promissory note to pay cash), or stock. Cash dividends, which predominate in practice, and stock dividends, which are declared with some frequency, are the focus of our discussion.

Investors are very interested in a company's dividend practices. In the financial press, **dividends are generally reported quarterly as a dollar amount per share**. (Sometimes they are reported on an annual basis.) For example, Nike's **quarterly** dividend rate in the fourth quarter of 2006 was 15.5 cents per share; the dividend rate for the fourth quarter of 2007 for GE was 31 cents, and for ConAgra Foods it was 18 cents.

## CASH DIVIDENDS

A **cash dividend** is a pro rata (proportional to ownership) distribution of cash to stockholders. Cash dividends are not paid on treasury shares. For a corporation to pay a cash dividend, it must have the following.

1. **Retained earnings.** Payment of dividends from retained earnings is legal in all states. In addition, loan agreements frequently constrain companies to pay dividends only from retained earnings. Many states prohibit payment of dividends from legal capital. However, payment of dividends from paid-in capital in excess of par is legal in some states.

2. **Adequate cash.** Recently, Nike had a balance in retained earnings of $5,451 million but a cash balance of only $2,291 million. If it had wanted to pay a dividend equal to its retained earnings, Nike would have had to raise $3,160 million more in cash. It would have been unlikely to do this because it would not be able to pay this much in dividends in future years. In addition, such a dividend would completely deplete Nike's balance in retained earnings, so it would not be able to pay a dividend in the next year unless it had positive net income.

3. **Declared dividends.** The board of directors has full authority to determine the amount of income to distribute in the form of dividends. Dividends are not a liability until they are declared.

The amount and timing of a dividend are important issues for management to consider. The payment of a large cash dividend could lead to liquidity problems for the company. Conversely, a small dividend or a missed dividend may cause unhappiness among stockholders who expect to receive a reasonable cash payment from the company on a periodic basis. Many companies declare and pay cash dividends quarterly. On the other hand, a number of high-growth companies pay no dividends, preferring to conserve cash to finance future capital expenditures.

Investors must keep an eye on the company's dividend policy and understand what it may mean. For most companies, for example, regular dividend boosts in the face of irregular earnings can be a warning signal. Companies with high dividends and rising debt may be borrowing money to pay shareholders. On the other hand, low dividends may not be a negative sign because it may mean the company is reinvesting in itself, which may result in high returns through increases in the stock price. Presumably, investors seeking regular dividends buy stock in companies that pay periodic dividends, and those seeking growth in the stock price (capital gains) buy stock in companies that retain their earnings rather than pay dividends.

## Entries for Cash Dividends

Three dates are important in connection with dividends: (1) the declaration date, (2) the record date, and (3) the payment date. Companies make accounting entries on the declaration date and the payment date.

On the **declaration date**, the board of directors formally authorizes the cash dividend and announces it to stockholders. The declaration of a cash dividend **commits the corporation to a binding legal obligation**. Thus, the company must make an entry to recognize the increase in Cash Dividends and the increase in the liability Dividends Payable.

To illustrate, assume that on December 1, 2012, the directors of Media General declare a $0.50 per share cash dividend on 100,000 shares of $10 par value common stock. The dividend is $50,000 (100,000 × $0.50). The entry to record the declaration is:

**Declaration Date**

| | | |
|---|---|---|
| Dec. 1 | Cash Dividends | 50,000 |
| |     Dividends Payable | 50,000 |
| |     (To record declaration of cash dividend) | |

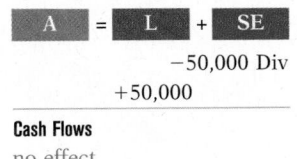

Cash Flows
no effect

In Chapter 3, we used an account called Dividends to record a cash dividend. Here, we use the more specific title Cash Dividends to differentiate from other types of dividends, such as stock dividends. Dividends Payable is a current liability: It will normally be paid within the next several months.

At the **record date**, the company determines ownership of the outstanding shares for dividend purposes. The stockholders' records maintained by the corporation supply this information.

**Helpful Hint** The record date is important in determining the dividend to be paid to each stockholder.

For Media General, the record date is December 22. No entry is required on the record date.

**Record Date**

| | |
|---|---|
| Dec. 22 | No entry necessary |

On the **payment date**, the company makes cash dividend payments to the stockholders on record as of December 22, and it also records the payment of the dividend. If January 20 is the payment date for Media General, the entry on that date is:

**Payment Date**

| | | |
|---|---|---|
| Jan. 20 | Dividends Payable | 50,000 |
| |     Cash | 50,000 |
| |     (To record payment of cash dividend) | |

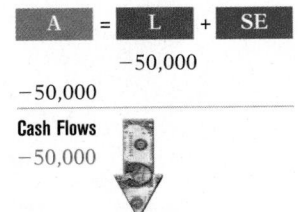

Cash Flows
−50,000

Note that payment of the dividend on the payment date reduces both current assets and current liabilities, but it has no effect on stockholders' equity. The cumulative effect of the **declaration and payment** of a cash dividend on a company's financial statements is to **decrease both stockholders' equity and total assets**.

## STOCK DIVIDENDS

A **stock dividend** is a pro rata (proportional to ownership) distribution of the corporation's own stock to stockholders. Whereas a cash dividend is paid in cash, a stock dividend is paid in stock. **A stock dividend results in a decrease in retained earnings and an increase in paid-in capital.** Unlike a cash dividend, a stock dividend does not decrease total stockholders' equity or total assets.

Because a stock dividend does not result in a distribution of assets, some view it as nothing more than a publicity gesture. Stock dividends are often issued by companies that do not have adequate cash to issue a cash dividend. These companies may not want to announce that they are not going to be issuing a cash dividend at their normal time to do so. By issuing a stock dividend, they "save face" by giving the appearance of distributing a dividend. Note that since a stock dividend neither increases nor decreases the assets in the company, investors are not receiving anything they didn't already own. In a sense, it is like asking for two pieces of pie and having your host take one piece of pie and cut it into two smaller pieces. You are not better off, but you got your two pieces of pie.

To illustrate a stock dividend, assume that you have a 2% ownership interest in Cetus Inc.; you own 20 of its 1,000 shares of common stock. If Cetus declares a 10% stock dividend, it would issue 100 shares (1,000 × 10%) of stock. You would receive two shares (2% × 100), but your ownership interest would remain at 2% (22 ÷ 1,100). **You now own more shares of stock, but your ownership interest has not changed.** Moreover, the company disburses no cash and assumes no liabilities.

What, then, are the purposes and benefits of a stock dividend? Corporations generally issue stock dividends for one of the following reasons.

1. To satisfy stockholders' dividend expectations without spending cash.
2. To increase the marketability of the stock by increasing the number of shares outstanding and thereby decreasing the market price per share. Decreasing the market price of the stock makes it easier for smaller investors to purchase the shares.
3. To emphasize that the company has permanently reinvested in the business a portion of stockholders' equity, which therefore is unavailable for cash dividends.

When the dividend is declared, the board of directors determines the size of the stock dividend and the value per share to use to record the transaction. In order to meet legal requirements, the per share amount must be at least equal to the par or stated value.

The accounting profession distinguishes between a **small stock dividend** (less than 20%–25% of the corporation's issued stock) and a **large stock dividend** (greater than 20%–25%). It recommends that the company use the **fair value per share** to record small stock dividends. The recommendation is based on the assumption that a small stock dividend will have little effect on the market price of the shares previously outstanding. Thus, many stockholders consider small stock dividends to be distributions of earnings equal to the fair value of the shares distributed. The accounting profession does not specify the value to use to record a large stock dividend. However, companies normally use **par or stated value per share**. Small stock dividends predominate in practice. In the appendix at the end of the chapter, we illustrate the journal entries for small stock dividends.

### Effects of Stock Dividends

**Helpful Hint** Because of its effects, a stock dividend is also referred to as *capitalizing retained earnings*.

How do stock dividends affect stockholders' equity? They **change the composition of stockholders' equity** because they result in a transfer of a portion of retained earnings to paid-in capital. However, **total stockholders' equity remains the same**. Stock dividends also have no effect on the par or stated value per share, but the number of shares outstanding increases.

Illustration 11-9 shows the effects that result when Medland Corp. declares a 10% stock dividend on its $10 par common stock when 50,000 shares were outstanding. The market price was $15 per share.

| | Before Dividend | Change | After Dividend |
|---|---|---|---|
| Stockholders' equity | | | |
| Paid-in capital | | | |
| Common stock, $10 par | $ 500,000 | | $ 550,000 |
| Paid-in capital in excess of par value | — | | 25,000 |
| Total paid-in capital | 500,000 | +$75,000 | 575,000 |
| Retained earnings | 300,000 | − 75,000 | 225,000 |
| Total stockholders' equity | $800,000 | $ 0 | $800,000 |
| Outstanding shares | 50,000 | + 5,000 | 55,000 |

**Illustration 11-9** Stock dividend effects

In this example, total paid-in capital increased by $75,000 (50,000 shares × 10% × $15), and retained earnings decreased by the same amount. Note also that total stockholders' equity remains unchanged at $800,000. The number of shares increases by 5,000 (50,000 × 10%).

## STOCK SPLITS

A **stock split**, like a stock dividend, involves the issuance of additional shares of stock to stockholders according to their percentage ownership. However, **a stock split results in a reduction in the par or stated value per share**. The purpose of a stock split is to increase the marketability of the stock by lowering its market value per share. This, in turn, makes it easier for the corporation to issue additional stock. After hitting a peak of 114 stock splits in 1986, the number of splits in the United States has fallen to about 30 per year. Nike was one of the few firms to split in 2007. It justified the action by noting that its stock price had increased by 70% during the previous five years.

Like a stock dividend, a stock split increases the number of shares owned by a shareholder, but it does not change the percentage of the total company that the shareholder owns. The effects of a 3-for-1 split are shown in Illustration 11-10.

**Helpful Hint** A stock split changes the par value per share but does not affect any balances in stockholders' equity.

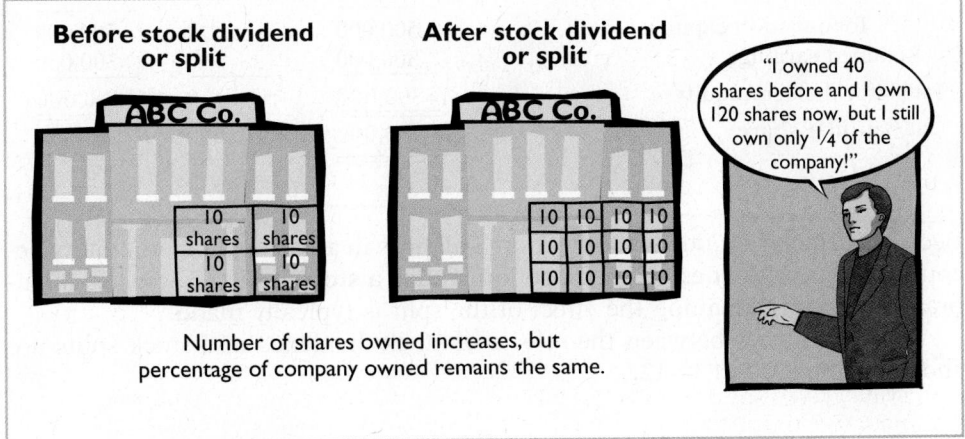

**Before stock dividend or split**

ABC Co.

10 shares | 10 shares
10 shares | 10 shares

**After stock dividend or split**

ABC Co.

10 | 10 | 10 | 10
10 | 10 | 10 | 10
10 | 10 | 10 | 10

"I owned 40 shares before and I own 120 shares now, but I still own only ¼ of the company!"

Number of shares owned increases, but percentage of company owned remains the same.

**Illustration 11-10** Effect of stock dividend or stock split for stockholders

The effect of a split on market value is generally **inversely proportional** to the size of the split. For example, after a recent 2-for-1 stock split, the market value of Nike's stock fell from $111 to approximately $55.

In a stock split, the company increases the number of shares in the same proportion that it decreases the par or stated value per share. For example, in a 2-for-1 split, the company exchanges one share of $10 par value stock for two shares of $5 par value stock. **A stock split does not have any effect on paid-in capital, retained earnings, and total stockholders' equity.** However, the number of shares outstanding increases. The effects of a 2-for-1 stock split of Medland Corporation's common stock are shown in Illustration 11-11.

**Illustration 11-11** Stock split effects

| | Before Stock Split | Change | After Stock Split |
|---|---|---|---|
| Stockholders' equity | | | |
| Paid-in capital | | | |
| Common stock | | | |
| (before: 50,000 $10 par shares; after: 100,000 $5 par shares) | $ 500,000 | | $ 500,000 |
| Paid-in capital in excess of par value | 0 | | 0 |
| Total paid-in capital | 500,000 | $ 0 | 500,000 |
| Retained earnings | 300,000 | 0 | 300,000 |
| Total stockholders' equity | $800,000 | $ 0 | $800,000 |
| **Outstanding shares** | 50,000 | + 50,000 | 100,000 |

Because a stock split does not affect the balances in any stockholders' equity accounts, a company **does not need to journalize a stock split**. However, a memorandum entry explaining the effect of the split is typically made.

The differences between the effects of stock dividends and stock splits are shown in Illustration 11-12.

**Illustration 11-12** Effects of stock splits and stock dividends differentiated

| Item | Stock Dividend | Stock Split |
|---|---|---|
| Total paid-in capital | Increase | No change |
| Total retained earnings | Decrease | No change |
| Total par value (common stock) | Increase | No change |
| Par value per share | No change | Decrease |

**Do it!** Due to five years of record earnings at Sing CD Corporation, the market price of its 500,000 shares of $2 par value common stock tripled from $15 per share to $45. During this period, paid-in capital remained the same at $2,000,000. Retained earnings increased from $1,500,000 to $10,000,000. President Joan Elbert is considering either a 10% stock dividend or a 2-for-1 stock split. She asks you to show the before and after effects of each option on retained earnings.

**STOCK DIVIDENDS; STOCK SPLITS**

**Action Plan**

- Calculate the stock dividend's effect on retained earnings by multiplying the number of new shares times the market price of the stock (or par value for a large stock dividend).
- Recall that a stock dividend increases the number of shares without affecting total equity.
- Recall that a stock split only increases the number of shares outstanding and decreases the par value per share without affecting total equity.

**Solution**

The stock dividend amount is $2,250,000 [(500,000 × 10%) × $45]. The new balance in retained earnings is $7,750,000 ($10,000,000 − $2,250,000). The retained earnings balance after the stock split is the same as it was before the split: $10,000,000. The effects on the stockholders' equity accounts are as follows.

|  | Original Balances | After Dividend | After Split |
|---|---|---|---|
| Paid-in capital | $ 2,000,000 | $ 4,250,000 | $ 2,000,000 |
| Retained earnings | 10,000,000 | 7,750,000 | 10,000,000 |
| Total stockholders' equity | $12,000,000 | $12,000,000 | $12,000,000 |
| Shares outstanding | 500,000 | 550,000 | 1,000,000 |

Related exercise material: **BE11-6, BE11-7, Do it! 11-5,** and **E11-7.**

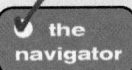

# Retained Earnings

**Retained earnings** is net income that a company retains in the business. The balance in retained earnings is part of the stockholders' claim on the total assets of the corporation. It does not, however, represent a claim on any specific asset. Nor can the amount of retained earnings be associated with the balance of any asset account. For example, a $100,000 balance in retained earnings does not mean that there should be $100,000 in cash. The reason is that the company may have used the cash resulting from the excess of revenues over expenses to purchase buildings, equipment, and other assets. Illustration 11-13 shows recent amounts of retained earnings and cash in selected companies.

**study objective 6**

Identify the items that affect retained earnings.

| Company | (in millions) | |
|---|---|---|
|  | Retained Earnings | Cash |
| Google | $20,082 | $10,198 |
| Nike, Inc. | 4,885 | 1,855 |
| Starbucks Coffee Company | 2,189 | 281 |
| Amazon.com | (1,375) | 2,539 |

**Illustration 11-13**
Retained earnings and cash balances

When expenses exceed revenues, a **net loss** results. In contrast to net income, a net loss decreases retained earnings. In closing entries, a company debits a net loss to the Retained Earnings account. **It does not debit net losses to paid-in capital accounts.** To do so would destroy the distinction between paid-in and earned capital. If cumulative losses exceed cumulative income over a company's life, a debit balance in Retained Earnings results. A debit balance in Retained Earnings, such as that of Amazon.com in a recent year, is a **deficit**. A company reports a deficit as a deduction in the stockholders' equity section of the balance sheet, as shown in Illustration 11-14 (page 590).

**Illustration 11-14**
Stockholders' equity with
deficit

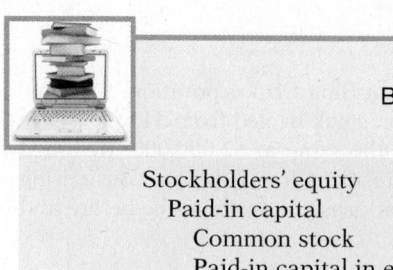

**AMAZON.COM**
Balance Sheet (partial)
(in millions)

| Stockholders' equity | | |
|---|---|---|
| Paid-in capital | | |
| Common stock | | $ 4 |
| Paid-in capital in excess of par value | | 3,068 |
| Total paid-in capital | | 3,072 |
| **Accumulated deficit** | | **(1,375)** |
| Total paid-in capital and retained earnings | | 1,697 |
| Less: Treasury stock | | 500 |
| Total stockholders' equity | | $1,197 |

## RETAINED EARNINGS RESTRICTIONS

The balance in retained earnings is generally available for dividend declarations. Some companies state this fact. In some circumstances, however, there may be **retained earnings restrictions**. These make a portion of the balance currently unavailable for dividends. Restrictions result from one or more of these causes: legal, contractual, or voluntary.

Companies generally disclose retained earnings restrictions in the notes to the financial statements. For example, Tektronix Inc., a manufacturer of electronic measurement devices, recently had total retained earnings of $774 million, but the unrestricted portion was only $223.8 million.

**Illustration 11-15**
Disclosure of unrestricted
retained earnings

**TEKTRONIX INC.**
Notes to the Financial Statements

Certain of the Company's debt agreements require compliance with debt covenants. The Company had unrestricted retained earnings of $223.8 million after meeting those requirements.

# Financial Statement Presentation of Stockholders' Equity

## BALANCE SHEET PRESENTATION

In the stockholders' equity section of the balance sheet, companies report paid-in capital and retained earnings and identify the specific sources of paid-in capital. Within paid-in capital, two classifications are recognized:

1. **Capital stock**, which consists of preferred and common stock. Companies show preferred stock before common stock because of its preferential rights. They report information about the par value, shares authorized, shares issued, and shares outstanding for each class of stock.

2. **Additional paid-in capital**, which includes the excess of amounts paid in over par or stated value.

Illustration 11-16 presents the stockholders' equity section of the balance sheet of Graber Inc. The company discloses a retained earnings restriction in the notes. The stockholders' equity section for Graber Inc. includes most of the accounts discussed in this chapter. The disclosures pertaining to Graber's common stock indicate that 400,000 shares are issued; 100,000 shares are unissued

**Illustration 11-16**
Comprehensive
stockholders' equity
section

### GRABER INC.
Balance Sheet (partial)

| | | |
|---|---:|---:|
| Stockholders' equity | | |
| Paid-in capital | | |
| Capital stock | | |
| 9% preferred stock, $100 par value, cumulative, | | |
| 10,000 shares authorized, 6,000 shares issued | | |
| and outstanding | | $ 600,000 |
| Common stock, no par, $5 stated value, | | |
| 500,000 shares authorized, 400,000 shares | | |
| issued, and 390,000 outstanding | | 2,000,000 |
| Total capital stock | | 2,600,000 |
| Additional paid-in capital | | |
| In excess of par value—preferred stock | $ 30,000 | |
| In excess of stated value—common stock | 1,050,000 | |
| Total additional paid-in capital | | 1,080,000 |
| Total paid-in capital | | 3,680,000 |
| Retained earnings (see Note R) | | 1,160,000 |
| Total paid-in capital and retained earnings | | 4,840,000 |
| Less: Treasury stock—common (10,000 shares) | | (80,000) |
| Total stockholders' equity | | $4,760,000 |

Note R: Retained earnings is restricted for the cost of treasury stock, $80,000.

**International Note** Like GAAP, under IFRS companies typically disclose separate categories of capital on the balance sheet. However, because of varying accounting treatments of certain transactions (such as treasury stock or asset revaluations), some categories used under IFRS vary from those under GAAP.

(500,000 authorized less 400,000 issued); and 390,000 shares are outstanding (400,000 issued less 10,000 shares in treasury).

In published annual reports, companies seldom present subclassifications within the stockholders' equity section. Moreover, they often combine and report as a single amount the individual sources of additional paid-in capital. Notes often provide additional detail. Illustration 11-17 is an excerpt from Procter & Gamble Company's balance sheet in a recent year.

**Illustration 11-17**
Stockholders' equity
section

### PROCTER & GAMBLE COMPANY
Balance Sheet (partial)
(in millions)

| | |
|---|---:|
| Shareholders' equity | |
| Convertible Class A preferred stock, stated value | |
| $1 per share (600 shares authorized) | $ 1,406 |
| Non-voting Class B preferred stock, stated value | |
| $1 per share (200 shares authorized) | — |
| Common stock, stated value $1 per share | |
| (10,000 shares authorized; issued: 3,989.7) | 3,990 |
| Additional paid-in capital | 59,030 |
| Total paid-in capital | 64,426 |
| Reserve for ESOP debt retirement | (1,308) |
| Retained earnings | 41,797 |
| Total paid-in capital and retained earnings | 104,915 |
| Accumulated other comprehensive income | 617 |
| Treasury stock, at cost (shares held: 857.8) | (38,772) |
| Total shareholders' equity | $ 66,760 |

The balance sheet presents the balances of a company's stockholders' equity accounts at a point in time. Companies report in the "Financing Activities" section of the statement of cash flows information regarding cash inflows and outflows during the year that resulted from equity transactions. The excerpt below presents the cash flows from financing activities from the statement of cash flows of Sara Lee Corporation in a recent year. From this information, we learn that the company's purchases of treasury stock during the period far exceeded its issuances of new common stock, and its financing activities resulted in a net reduction in its cash balance.

**SARA LEE CORPORATION**
Statement of Cash Flows (partial)
(in millions)

| | |
|---|---:|
| Cash flows from financing activities | |
| Issuances of common stock | $ 38 |
| Purchases of common stock | (686) |
| Payments of dividends | (374) |
| Borrowings of long-term debt | 2,895 |
| Repayments of long-term debt | (416) |
| Short-term (repayments) borrowings, net | (1,720) |
| Net cash used in financing activities | $ (263) |

## before you go on...

**STOCKHOLDERS'
EQUITY SECTION**

**Do it!** Jennifer Corporation has issued 300,000 shares of $3 par value common stock. It is authorized to issue 600,000 shares. The paid-in capital in excess of par value on the common stock is $380,000. The corporation has reacquired 15,000 shares at a cost of $50,000 and is currently holding those shares.

The corporation also has 4,000 shares issued and outstanding of 8%, $100 par value preferred stock. It is authorized to issue 10,000 shares. The paid-in capital in excess of par value on the preferred stock is $97,000. Retained earnings is $610,000.

Prepare the stockholders' equity section of the balance sheet.

**Action Plan**

- Present capital stock first; list preferred stock before common stock.
- Present additional paid-in capital after capital stock.
- Report retained earnings after capital stock and additional paid-in capital.
- Deduct treasury stock from total paid-in capital and retained earnings.

**Solution**

**JENNIFER CORPORATION**
Balance Sheet (partial)

| | | |
|---|---:|---:|
| Stockholders' equity | | |
| Paid-in capital | | |
| Capital stock | | |
| 8% preferred stock, $100 par value, 10,000 shares authorized, 4,000 shares issued and outstanding | $ 400,000 | |
| Common stock, $3 par value, 600,000 shares authorized, 300,000 shares issued, and 285,000 shares outstanding | 900,000 | |
| Total capital stock | 1,300,000 | |
| Additional paid-in capital | | |
| In excess of par value—preferred stock | 97,000 | |
| In excess of par value—common stock | 380,000 | |
| Total additional paid-in capital | | $ 477,000 |
| Total paid-in capital | | 1,777,000 |
| Retained earnings | | 610,000 |
| Total paid-in capital and retained earnings | | 2,387,000 |
| Less: Treasury stock—common (15,000 shares) (at cost) | | (50,000) |
| Total stockholders' equity | | $2,337,000 |

the navigator

Related exercise material: **BE11-8, Do it! 11-6, E11-8, E11-9,** and **E11-10.**

# Measuring Corporate Performance

Investors are interested in both a company's dividend record and its earnings performance. Although those two measures are often parallel, that is not always the case. Thus, investors should investigate each one separately.

## DIVIDEND RECORD

One way that companies reward stock investors for their investment is to pay them dividends. The **payout ratio** measures the percentage of earnings a company distributes in the form of cash dividends to common stockholders. It is computed by **dividing total cash dividends declared to common shareholders by net income**. Using the information shown below, the payout ratio for Nike in 2009 and 2008 is calculated in Illustration 11-18.

|                              | **2009**   | **2008**   |
|------------------------------|------------|------------|
| Dividends (in millions)      | $  475.2   | $  432.8   |
| Net income (in millions)     | 1,486.7    | 1,883.4    |

| Payout Ratio $=$ | Cash Dividends Declared on Common Stock / Net Income | |
|---|---|---|
| **($ in millions)** | **2009** | **2008** |
| **Payout Ratio** | $\dfrac{\$475.2}{\$1,486.7} = 32.0\%$ | $\dfrac{\$432.8}{\$1,883.4} = 23.0\%$ |

**Illustration 11-18**  Nike's payout ratio

The significant increase in Nike's payout ratio from 23% to 32% resulted from a combination of two factors. First, Nike increased its dividend per share from 87.5¢ to 98¢. Second, its net income declined significantly from 2008 to 2009. Nike would probably not have increased its dividend per share unless it believed it could sustain dividends at this level in future years.

Companies that have high growth rates are characterized by low payout ratios because they reinvest most of their net income in the business. Thus, a low payout ratio is not necessarily bad news. Companies that believe they have many good opportunities for growth, such as Google, will reinvest those funds in the company rather than pay high dividends. However, low dividend payments, or a cut in dividend payments, might signal that a company has liquidity or solvency problems and is trying to conserve cash by not paying dividends. Thus, investors and analysts should investigate the reason for low dividend payments.

Illustration 11-19 lists recent payout ratios of four well-known companies.

**Illustration 11-19**
Payout ratios of companies

| Company    | Payout Ratio |
|------------|--------------|
| Microsoft  | 24.5%        |
| Kellogg    | 43.3%        |
| Google     | 0%           |
| Wal-Mart   | 49.0%        |

## DECISION TOOLKIT

| DECISION CHECKPOINTS | INFO NEEDED FOR DECISION | TOOL TO USE FOR DECISION | HOW TO EVALUATE RESULTS |
|---|---|---|---|
| What portion of its earnings does the company pay out in dividends? | Net income and total cash dividends on common stock | Payout ratio $=$ Cash dividends declared on common stock / Net income | A low ratio may suggest that the company is retaining its earnings for investment in future growth. |

## EARNINGS PERFORMANCE

Another way to measure corporate performance is through profitability. A widely used ratio that measures profitability from the common stockholders' viewpoint is **return on common stockholders' equity**. This ratio shows how many dollars of net income a company earned for each dollar of common stockholders' equity. It is computed by dividing net income available to common stockholders (Net income − Preferred stock dividends) by average common stockholders' equity. Common stockholders' equity is equal to total stockholders' equity minus any equity from preferred stock.

Using the information on the previous page and the additional information presented below, Illustration 11-20 shows Nike's return on common stockholders' equity ratio.

| (in millions) | 2009 | 2008 |
|---|---|---|
| Preferred stock dividends | $ .03 | $ .03 |
| Common stockholders' equity | 8,693.1 | 7,825.3 |

| Return on Common Stockholders' Equity Ratio | = | Net Income − Preferred Stock Dividends / Average Common Stockholders' Equity |
|---|---|---|

| ($ in millions) | 2009 | 2008 |
|---|---|---|
| Return on Common Stockholders' Equity Ratio | $\dfrac{\$1{,}486.7 - \$.03}{(\$8{,}693.1 + \$7{,}825.3)/2} = 18.0\%$ | 25.4% |

**Illustration 11-20** Nike's return on common stockholders' equity

From 2008 to 2009, Nike's return on common shareholders' equity decreased. As a company grows larger, it becomes increasingly hard to sustain a high return. In Nike's case, since many believe the U.S. market for expensive sports shoes is saturated, it will need to grow either along new product lines, such as hiking shoes and golf equipment, or in new markets, such as Europe and Asia.

## DEBT VERSUS EQUITY DECISION

When obtaining long-term capital, corporate managers must decide whether to issue bonds or to sell common stock. Bonds have three primary advantages relative to common stock, as shown in Illustration 11-21.

**Illustration 11-21** Advantages of bond financing over common stock

| Bond Financing | Advantages |
|---|---|
| Ballot Box | 1. **Stockholder control is not affected.** Bondholders do not have voting rights, so current owners (stockholders) retain full control of the company. |
| Tax Bill | 2. **Tax savings result.** Bond interest is deductible for tax purposes; dividends on stock are not. |
| $/Stock | 3. **Return on common stockholders' equity may be higher.** Although bond interest expense reduces net income, return on common stockholders' equity often is higher under bond financing because no additional shares of common stock are issued. |

How does the debt versus equity decision affect the return on common stockholders' equity ratio? Illustration 11-22 shows that the return on common stockholders' equity is affected by the return on assets ratio and the amount of leverage a company uses—that is, by the company's reliance on debt (often measured by the debt to total assets ratio). **If a company wants to increase its return on common stockholders' equity, it can either increase its return on assets or increase its reliance on debt financing.**

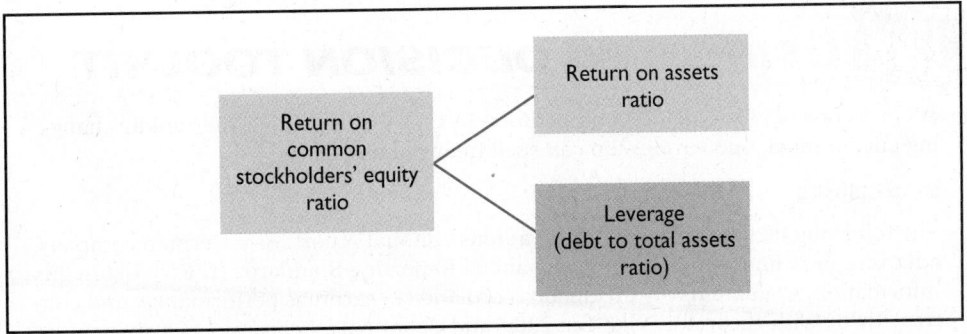

**Illustration 11-22**
Components of the return on common stockholders' equity

To illustrate the potential effect of debt financing on the return on common stockholders' equity, assume that Microsystems Inc. currently has 100,000 shares of common stock outstanding issued at $25 per share and no debt. It is considering two alternatives for raising an additional $5 million: Plan A involves issuing 200,000 shares of common stock at the current market price of $25 per share. Plan B involves issuing $5 million of 12% bonds at face value. Income before interest and taxes will be $1.5 million; income taxes are expected to be 30%. The alternative effects on the return on common stockholders' equity are shown in Illustration 11-23.

**Illustration 11-23**
Effects on return on common stockholders' equity of issuing debt

| | Plan A: Issue stock | Plan B: Issue bonds |
|---|---|---|
| Income before interest and taxes | $1,500,000 | $1,500,000 |
| Interest (12% × $5,000,000) | — | 600,000 |
| Income before income taxes | 1,500,000 | 900,000 |
| Income tax expense (30%) | 450,000 | 270,000 |
| Net income | $1,050,000 | $ 630,000 |
| Common stockholders' equity | $7,500,000 | $2,500,000 |
| Return on common stockholders' equity | 14% | 25.2% |

Note that with long-term debt financing (bonds), net income is $420,000 ($1,050,000 − $630,000) less. However, the return on common stockholders' equity increases from 14% to 25.2% with the use of debt financing because net income is spread over a smaller amount of common stockholders' equity. **In general, as long as the return on assets rate exceeds the rate paid on debt, a company will increase the return on common stockholders' equity by the use of debt.**

After seeing this illustration, one might ask, why don't companies rely almost exclusively on debt financing rather than equity? Debt has one major disadvantage: **Debt reduces solvency. The company locks in fixed payments that it must make in good times and bad. The company must pay interest on a periodic basis and must pay the principal (face value) of the bonds at maturity.** A company with fluctuating earnings and a relatively weak cash position may experience great difficulty in meeting interest requirements in periods of low earnings. In the extreme, this can result in bankruptcy. With common stock financing, on the other hand, the company can decide to pay low (or no) dividends if earnings are low.

## DECISION TOOLKIT

| DECISION CHECKPOINTS | INFO NEEDED FOR DECISION | TOOL TO USE FOR DECISION | HOW TO EVALUATE RESULTS |
|---|---|---|---|
| What is the company's return on common stockholders' investment? | Earnings available to common stockholders and average common stockholders' equity | Return on common stockholders' equity ratio $= \dfrac{\text{Net income} - \text{Preferred stock dividends}}{\text{Average common stockholders' equity}}$ | A high measure suggests strong earnings performance from common stockholders' perspective. |

# USING THE DECISION TOOLKIT

adidas is one of Nike's fiercest competitors. In such a competitive and rapidly changing environment, one wrong step can spell financial disaster.

## Instructions

The following facts are available from adidas's annual report. As a German company, adidas reports under International Financial Reporting Standards (IFRS). Using this information, evaluate its (1) dividend record and (2) earnings performance, and contrast them with those for Nike for 2009 and 2008. Nike's earnings per share were $3.07 in 2009 and $3.80 in 2008.

| (in millions)* | 2008 | 2007 | 2006 |
|---|---|---|---|
| Dividends declared | €99 | €85 | €66 |
| Net income | €642 | €551 | €496 |
| Preferred stock dividends | 0 | 0 | 0 |
| Shares outstanding at end of year | 204 | 204 | 203 |
| Common stockholders' equity | €3,400 | €3,034 | €2,836 |

*Nike has a year-end of May 31, 2009. For comparative purpose, we used adidas's December 31, 2008, data since that represents the closest year-end.

## Solution

1. *Dividend record:* A measure to evaluate dividend record is the payout ratio. For adidas, this measure in 2008 and 2007 is calculated as shown below.

| | 2008 | 2007 |
|---|---|---|
| Payout ratio | $\dfrac{€99}{€642} = 15.4\%$ | $\dfrac{€85}{€551} = 15.4\%$ |

Nike's payout ratio was 32%. adidas's payout ratio remained constant from 2007 to 2008 and was significantly less than Nike's ratio.

2. *Earnings performance:* There are many measures of earnings performance. Some of those presented thus far in the book were earnings per share (page 55) and the return on common stockholders' equity ratio (this chapter). These measures for adidas in 2008 and 2007 are calculated as shown here.

| | 2008 | 2007 |
|---|---|---|
| Earnings per share | $\dfrac{€642 - 0}{(204 + 204)/2} = €3.15$ | $\dfrac{€551 - 0}{(204 + 203)/2} = €2.71$ |
| Return on common stockholders' equity ratio | $\dfrac{€642 - 0}{(€3,400 + €3,034)/2} = 20.0\%$ | $\dfrac{€551 - 0}{(€3,034 + €2,836)/2} = 18.8\%$ |

From 2007 to 2008, adidas's net income improved 17% and its earnings per share increased 16%. Earnings per share should not be compared across companies because the number of shares varies considerably. Thus, we should not compare adidas's earnings per share with Nike's. adidas's return on common stockholders' equity increased slightly from 18.8% to 20.0%. This represents a healthy return; it is similar to Nike's.

the navigator

# Summary of Study Objectives

**1** **Identify and discuss the major characteristics of a corporation.** The major characteristics of a corporation are separate legal existence, limited liability of stockholders, transferable ownership rights, ability to acquire capital, continuous life, corporation management, government regulations, and additional taxes.

**2** **Record the issuance of common stock.** When a company records issuance of common stock for cash, it credits the par value of the shares to Common Stock; it records in a separate paid-in capital account the portion of the proceeds that is above par value. When no-par common stock has a stated value, the entries are similar to those for par value stock. When no-par common stock does not have a stated value, the entire proceeds from the issue are credited to Common Stock.

**3** **Explain the accounting for the purchase of treasury stock.** Companies generally use the cost method in accounting for treasury stock. Under this approach, a company debits Treasury Stock at the price paid to reacquire the shares.

**4** **Differentiate preferred stock from common stock.** Preferred stock has contractual provisions that give it priority over common stock in certain areas. Typically, preferred stockholders have a preference as to (1) dividends and (2) assets in the event of liquidation. However, they sometimes do not have voting rights.

**5** **Prepare the entries for cash dividends and understand the effect of stock dividends and stock splits.** Companies make entries for dividends at the declaration date and the payment date. At the declaration date the entries for a cash dividend are: debit Cash Dividends and credit Dividends Payable. The effects of stock dividends and splits: Small *stock dividends* transfer an amount equal to the fair market value of the shares issued from retained earnings to the paid-in capital accounts. *Stock splits* reduce the par value per share of the common stock while increasing the number of shares so that the balance in the Common Stock account remains the same.

**6** **Identify the items that affect retained earnings.** Additions to retained earnings consist of net income. Deductions consist of net loss and cash and stock dividends. In some instances, portions of retained earnings are restricted, making that portion unavailable for the payment of dividends.

**7** **Prepare a comprehensive stockholders' equity section.** In the stockholders' equity section of the balance sheet, companies report paid-in capital and retained earnings and identify specific sources of paid-in capital. Within paid-in capital, companies show two classifications: capital stock and additional paid-in capital. If a corporation has treasury stock, it deducts the cost of treasury stock from total paid-in capital and retained earnings to determine total stockholders' equity.

**8** **Evaluate a corporation's dividend and earnings performance from a stockholder's perspective.** A company's dividend record can be evaluated by looking at what percentage of net income it chooses to pay out in dividends, as measured by the dividend payout ratio (dividends divided by net income). Earnings performance is measured with the return on common stockholders' equity ratio (income available to common stockholders divided by average common stockholders' equity).

*the navigator*

# *DECISION TOOLKIT* A SUMMARY

| DECISION CHECKPOINTS | INFO NEEDED FOR DECISION | TOOL TO USE FOR DECISION | HOW TO EVALUATE RESULTS |
| --- | --- | --- | --- |
| Should the company incorporate? | Capital needs, growth expectations, type of business, tax status | Corporations have limited liability, easier capital raising ability, and professional managers; but they suffer from additional taxes, government regulations, and separation of ownership from management. | Must carefully weigh the costs and benefits in light of the particular circumstances. |
| What portion of its earnings does the company pay out in dividends? | Net income and total cash dividends on common stock | $\text{Payout ratio} = \dfrac{\text{Cash dividends declared on common stock}}{\text{Net income}}$ | A low ratio may suggest that the company is retaining its earnings for investment in future growth. |
| What is the company's return on common stockholders' investment? | Earnings available to common stockholders and average common stockholders' equity | $\text{Return on common stockholders' equity ratio} = \dfrac{\text{Net income} - \text{Preferred stock dividends}}{\text{Average common stockholders' equity}}$ | A high measure suggests strong earnings performance from common stockholders' perspective. |

## appendix 11A

# Entries for Stock Dividends

**study objective 9**

Prepare entries for stock dividends.

To illustrate the accounting for stock dividends, assume that Medland Corporation has a balance of $300,000 in retained earnings and declares a 10% stock dividend on its 50,000 shares of $10 par value common stock. The current fair value of its stock is $15 per share. The number of shares to be issued is 5,000 (10% × 50,000), and the total amount to be debited to Retained Earnings is $75,000 (5,000 × $15). The entry to record this transaction at the declaration date is:

| A | = | L | + | SE |
|---|---|---|---|---|
| | | | | −75,000 Div |
| | | | | +50,000 CS |
| | | | | +25,000 CS |

**Cash Flows**
no effect

| | | |
|---|---|---|
| Stock Dividends | 75,000 | |
|     Common Stock Dividends Distributable | | 50,000 |
|     Paid-in Capital in Excess of Par Value | | 25,000 |
|     (To record declaration of 10% stock dividend) | | |

At the declaration date, Medland increases (debits) Stock Dividends for the fair value of the stock issued; increases (credits) Common Stock Dividends Distributable for the par value of the dividend shares (5,000 × $10); and increases (credits) the excess over par (5,000 × $5) to an additional paid-in capital account.

Common Stock Dividends Distributable is a stockholders' equity account; it is not a liability because assets will not be used to pay the dividend. If Medland prepares a balance sheet before it issues the dividend shares, it reports the distributable account in paid-in capital as an addition to common stock issued, as shown in Illustration 11A-1.

**Illustration 11A-1**
Statement presentation of common stock dividends distributable

| MEDLAND CORPORATION | | |
|---|---|---|
| Balance Sheet (partial) | | |
| Paid-in capital | | |
|   Common stock | $500,000 | |
|   **Common stock dividends distributable** | 50,000 | $550,000 |

**Helpful Hint** Note that the dividend account title is *distributable*, not *payable*.

| A | = | L | + | SE |
|---|---|---|---|---|
| | | | | −50,000 CS |
| | | | | +50,000 CS |

**Cash Flows**
no effect

When Medland issues the dividend shares, it decreases Common Stock Dividends Distributable and increases Common Stock as follows.

| | | |
|---|---|---|
| Common Stock Dividends Distributable | 50,000 | |
|     Common Stock | | 50,000 |
|     (To record issuance of 5,000 shares in a stock dividend) | | |

# Summary of Study Objective for Appendix 11A

**9 Prepare entries for stock dividends.** To record the declaration of a small stock dividend (less than 20%), debit Stock Dividends for an amount equal to the fair value of the shares issued. Record a credit to a temporary stockholders' equity account—Common Stock Dividends Distributable—for the par value of the shares, and credit the balance to Paid-in Capital in Excess of Par Value. When the shares are issued, debit Common Stock Dividends Distributable and credit Common Stock.

# Glossary

**Authorized stock** *(p. 576)* The amount of stock that a corporation is authorized to sell as indicated in its charter.

**Cash dividend** *(p. 584)* A pro rata (proportional to ownership) distribution of cash to stockholders.

**Charter** *(p. 574)* A document that describes a corporation's name and purpose, types of stock and number of shares authorized, names of individuals involved in the formation, and number of shares each individual has agreed to purchase.

**Corporation** *(p. 570)* A company organized as a separate legal entity, with most of the rights and privileges of a person.

**Cumulative dividend** *(p. 582)* A feature of preferred stock entitling the stockholder to receive current and unpaid prior-year dividends before common stockholders receive any dividends.

**Declaration date** *(p. 585)* The date the board of directors formally authorizes the dividend and announces it to stockholders.

**Deficit** *(p. 589)* A debit balance in retained earnings.

**Dividend** *(p. 584)* A distribution by a corporation to its stockholders on a pro rata (proportional to ownership) basis.

**Dividends in arrears** *(p. 582)* Preferred dividends that were supposed to be declared but were not declared during a given period.

**Legal capital** *(p. 577)* The amount of capital that must be retained in the business for the protection of corporate creditors.

**No-par value stock** *(p. 577)* Capital stock that has not been assigned a value in the corporate charter.

**Outstanding stock** *(p. 581)* Capital stock that has been issued and is being held by stockholders.

**Paid-in capital** *(p. 577)* The amount stockholders paid in to the corporation in exchange for shares of ownership.

**Par value stock** *(p. 577)* Capital stock that has been assigned a value per share in the corporate charter.

**Payment date** *(p. 585)* The date cash dividend payments are made to stockholders.

**Payout ratio** *(p. 593)* A measure of the percentage of earnings a company distributes in the form of cash dividends to common stockholders.

**Preferred stock** *(p. 582)* Capital stock that has contractual preferences over common stock in certain areas.

**Privately held corporation** *(p. 570)* A corporation that has only a few stockholders and whose stock is not available for sale to the general public.

**Publicly held corporation** *(p. 570)* A corporation that may have thousands of stockholders and whose stock is traded on a national securities market.

**Record date** *(p. 585)* The date when the company determines ownership of outstanding shares for dividend purposes.

**Retained earnings** *(p. 589)* Net income that a company retains in the business.

**Retained earnings restrictions** *(p. 590)* Circumstances that make a portion of retained earnings currently unavailable for dividends.

**Return on common stockholders' equity ratio** *(p. 594)* A measure of profitability from the stockholders' point of view; computed by dividing net income minus preferred stock dividends by average common stockholders' equity.

**Stated value** *(p. 577)* The amount per share assigned by the board of directors to no-par stock.

**Stock dividend** *(p. 585)* A pro rata (proportional to ownership) distribution of the corporation's own stock to stockholders.

**Stock split** *(p. 587)* The issuance of additional shares of stock to stockholders accompanied by a reduction in the par or stated value per share.

**Treasury stock** *(p. 579)* A corporation's own stock that has been reacquired by the corporation and is being held for future use.

# Comprehensive **Do it!**

Rolman Corporation is authorized to issue 1,000,000 shares of $5 par value common stock. In its first year, the company has the following stock transactions.

Jan. 10  Issued 400,000 shares of stock at $8 per share.
Sept. 1  Purchased 10,000 shares of common stock for the treasury at $9 per share.
Dec. 24  Declared a cash dividend of 10 cents per share on common stock outstanding.

## Instructions

(a) Journalize the transactions.
(b) Prepare the stockholders' equity section of the balance sheet, assuming the company had retained earnings of $150,600 at December 31.

## Action Plan

- When common stock has a par value, credit Common Stock for par value and Paid-in Capital in Excess of Par Value for the amount above par value.
- Debit the Treasury Stock account at cost.

## Solution to Comprehensive Do it!

| (a) Jan. 10 | Cash | 3,200,000 | |
| | Common Stock | | 2,000,000 |
| | Paid-in Capital in Excess of Par Value | | 1,200,000 |
| | (To record issuance of 400,000 shares of $5 par value stock) | | |
| Sept. 1 | Treasury Stock | 90,000 | |
| | Cash | | 90,000 |
| | (To record purchase of 10,000 shares of treasury stock at cost) | | |
| Dec. 24 | Cash Dividends | 39,000 | |
| | Dividends Payable | | 39,000 |
| | (To record declaration of 10 cents per share cash dividend) | | |

(b)

**ROLMAN CORPORATION**
**Balance Sheet (partial)**

| Stockholders' equity | | |
| --- | --- | --- |
| Paid-in capital | | |
| Capital stock | | |
| Common stock, $5 par value, 1,000,000 shares authorized, 400,000 shares issued, 390,000 outstanding | $2,000,000 | |
| Additional paid-in capital | | |
| In excess of par value—common stock | 1,200,000 | |
| Total paid-in capital | 3,200,000 | |
| Retained earnings | 150,600 | |
| Total paid-in capital and retained earnings | 3,350,600 | |
| Less: Treasury stock (10,000 shares) | 90,000 | |
| Total stockholders' equity | $3,260,600 | |

 **Self-Test, Brief Exercises, Exercises, Problem Set A, and many more resources are available for practice in WileyPLUS**

*Note:* All Questions, Exercises, and Problems marked with an asterisk relate to material in the appendix to the chapter.

# Self-Test Questions

Answers are on page 619.

(SO 1) **1.** Which of these is *not* a major advantage of a corporation?
(a) Separate legal existence.
(b) Continuous life.
(c) Government regulations.
(d) Transferable ownership rights.

(SO 1) **2.** A major *disadvantage* of a corporation is:
(a) limited liability of stockholders.
(b) additional taxes.
(c) transferable ownership rights.
(d) None of the above.

(SO 1) **3.** Which of these statements is *false*?
(a) Ownership of common stock gives the owner a voting right.

(b) The stockholders' equity section begins with paid-in capital.
(c) The authorization of capital stock does not result in a formal accounting entry.
(d) Legal capital is intended to protect stockholders.

**4.** ABC Corp. issues 1,000 shares of $10 par value com- (SO 2) mon stock at $12 per share. When the transaction is recorded, credits are made to:
(a) Common Stock $10,000 and Paid-in Capital in Excess of Stated Value $2,000.
(b) Common Stock $12,000.
(c) Common Stock $10,000 and Paid-in Capital in Excess of Par Value $2,000.
(d) Common Stock $10,000 and Retained Earnings $2,000.

(SO 3) 5. Treasury stock may be repurchased:
   (a) to reissue the shares to officers and employees under bonus and stock compensation plans.
   (b) to signal to the stock market that management believes the stock is underpriced.
   (c) to have additional shares available for use in the acquisition of other companies.
   (d) More than one of the above.

(SO 4) 6. Preferred stock may have which of the following features?
   (a) Dividend preference.
   (b) Preference to assets in the event of liquidation.
   (c) Cumulative dividends.
   (d) All of the above.

(SO 4) 7. U-Bet Corporation has 10,000 shares of 8%, $100 par value, cumulative preferred stock outstanding at December 31, 2012. No dividends were declared in 2010 or 2011. If U-Bet wants to pay $375,000 of dividends in 2012, common stockholders will receive:
   (a) $0.          (c) $215,000.
   (b) $295,000.    (d) $135,000.

(SO 5) 8. Entries for cash dividends are required on the:
   (a) declaration date and the record date.
   (b) record date and the payment date.
   (c) declaration date, record date, and payment date.
   (d) declaration date and the payment date.

(SO 5) 9. Which of these statements about stock dividends is *true*?
   (a) Stock dividends reduce a company's cash balance.
   (b) A stock dividend has no effect on total stockholders' equity.
   (c) A stock dividend decreases total stockholders' equity.
   (d) A stock dividend ordinarily will increase total stockholders' equity.

(SO 5) 10. Zealot Inc. has retained earnings of $500,000 and total stockholders' equity of $2,000,000. It has 100,000 shares of $8 par value common stock outstanding, which is currently selling for $30 per share. If Zealot declares a 10% stock dividend on its common stock:
   (a) net income will decrease by $80,000.
   (b) retained earnings will decrease by $80,000 and total stockholders' equity will increase by $80,000.
   (c) retained earnings will decrease by $300,000 and total stockholders' equity will increase by $300,000.
   (d) retained earnings will decrease by $300,000 and total paid-in capital will increase by $300,000.

(SO 7) 11. In the stockholders' equity section of the balance sheet, common stock:
   (a) is listed before preferred stock.
   (b) is listed after retained earnings.
   (c) is part of paid-in capital.
   (d) is subtracted from treasury stock.

(SO 7) 12. In the stockholders' equity section, the cost of treasury stock is deducted from:
   (a) total paid-in capital and retained earnings.
   (b) retained earnings.
   (c) total stockholders' equity.
   (d) common stock in paid-in capital.

(SO 8) 13. The return on common stockholders' equity is usually increased by all of the following, *except*:
   (a) an increase in the return on assets ratio.
   (b) an increase in the use of debt financing.
   (c) an increase in the company's stock price.
   (d) an increase in the company's net income.

(SO 8) 14. Thomas is nearing retirement and would like to invest in a stock that will provide a good steady income. Thomas should choose a stock with a:
   (a) high current ratio.
   (b) high dividend payout.
   (c) high earnings per share.
   (d) high price-earnings ratio.

(SO 8) 15. Jackson Inc. reported net income of $186,000 during 2012 and paid dividends of $26,000 on common stock. It also paid dividends on its 10,000 shares of 6%, $100 par value, noncumulative preferred stock. Common stockholders' equity was $1,200,000 on January 1, 2012, and $1,600,000 on December 31, 2012. The company's return on common stockholders' equity for 2012 is:
   (a) 10.0%.        (c) 7.1%.
   (b) 9.0%.         (d) 13.3%.

(SO 8) 16. If everything else is held constant, earnings per share is increased by:
   (a) the payment of a cash dividend to common shareholders.
   (b) the payment of a cash dividend to preferred shareholders.
   (c) the issuance of new shares of common stock.
   (d) the purchase of treasury stock.

Go to the book's companion website, **www.wiley.com/college/kimmel**, to access additional Self-Test Questions.

# Questions

1. Max, a student, asks your help in understanding some characteristics of a corporation. Explain each of these to Max.
   (a) Separate legal existence.
   (b) Limited liability of stockholders.
   (c) Transferable ownership rights.

2. (a) Your friend B. T. Barnum cannot understand how the characteristic of corporate management is both an advantage and a disadvantage. Clarify this problem for B. T.
   (b) Identify and explain two other disadvantages of a corporation.

3. Cindy Krug believes a corporation must be incorporated in the state in which its headquarters office is located. Is Cindy correct? Explain.

4. What are the basic ownership rights of common stockholders in the absence of restrictive provisions?

5. A corporation has been defined as an entity separate and distinct from its owners. In what ways is a corporation a separate legal entity?

6. What are the two principal components of stockholders' equity?

7. The corporate charter of Elmer Corporation allows the issuance of a maximum of 100,000 shares of common stock. During its first 2 years of operation, Elmer sold 70,000 shares to shareholders and reacquired 4,000 of these shares. After these transactions, how many shares are authorized, issued, and outstanding?

8. Which is the better investment—common stock with a par value of $5 per share or common stock with a par value of $20 per share?

9. ◄ For what reasons might a company like **IBM** repurchase some of its stock (treasury stock)?

10. Rosa, Inc. purchases 1,000 shares of its own previously issued $5 par common stock for $11,000. Assuming the shares are held in the treasury, what effect does this transaction have on (a) net income, (b) total assets, (c) total paid-in capital, and (d) total stockholders' equity?

11. (a) What are the principal differences between common stock and preferred stock?
    (b) Preferred stock may be cumulative. Discuss this feature.
    (c) How are dividends in arrears presented in the financial statements?

12. Identify the events that result in credits and debits to retained earnings.

13. Indicate how each of these accounts should be classified in the stockholders' equity section of the balance sheet.
    (a) Common Stock.
    (b) Paid-in Capital in Excess of Par Value.
    (c) Retained Earnings.
    (d) Treasury Stock.
    (e) Paid-in Capital in Excess of Stated Value.
    (f) Preferred Stock.

14. What three conditions must be met before a cash dividend is paid?

15. Three dates associated with Leon Company's cash dividend are May 1, May 15, and May 31. Discuss the significance of each date and give the entry at each date.

16. Contrast the effects of a cash dividend and a stock dividend on a corporation's balance sheet.

17. Celia Ahern asks, "Since stock dividends don't change anything, why declare them?" What is your answer to Celia?

18. Burke Corporation has 10,000 shares of $15 par value common stock outstanding when it announces a 3-for-1 split. Before the split, the stock had a market price of $120 per share. After the split, how many shares of stock will be outstanding, and what will be the approximate market price per share?

19. The board of directors is considering a stock split or a stock dividend. They understand that total stockholders' equity will remain the same under either action. However, they are not sure of the different effects of the two actions on other aspects of stockholders' equity. Explain the differences to the directors.

20. [Tootsie Roll] What was the total cost of Tootsie Roll's treasury stock at December 31, 2009? What was the amount of the 2009 cash dividend? What was the total charge to Retained Earnings for the 2009 stock dividend?

21. (a) What is the purpose of a retained earnings restriction?
    (b) Identify the possible causes of retained earnings restrictions.

22. Fredo Inc.'s common stock has a par value of $1 and a current market value of $15. Explain why these amounts are different.

23. ◉━━━◉ What is the formula for the payout ratio? What does it indicate?

24. ◄ ◉━━━◉ Explain the circumstances under which debt financing will increase the return on common stockholders' equity ratio.

25. Under what circumstances will the return on assets ratio and the return on common stockholders' equity ratio be equal?

26. ◄ Haidet Corp. has a return on assets ratio of 12%. It plans to issue bonds at 8% and use the cash to repurchase stock. What effect will this have on its debt to total assets ratio and on its return on common stockholders' equity?

# Brief Exercises

*Cite advantages and disadvantages of a corporation.*
(SO 1), **K**

**BE11-1** Bonnie Decker is planning to start a business. Identify for Bonnie the advantages and disadvantages of the corporate form of business organization.

*Journalize issuance of par value common stock.*
(SO 2), **AP**

**BE11-2** On May 10, Tharp Corporation issues 2,500 shares of $5 par value common stock for cash at $13 per share. Journalize the issuance of the stock.

*Journalize issuance of no-par common stock.*
(SO 2), **AP**

**BE11-3** On June 1, Rodero Inc. issues 3,000 shares of no-par common stock at a cash price of $7 per share. Journalize the issuance of the shares.

**BE11-4** Merritt Inc. issues 8,000 shares of $100 par value preferred stock for cash at $106 per share. Journalize the issuance of the preferred stock.

*Journalize issuance of preferred stock.*
(SO 4), **AP**

**BE11-5** Wildwood Corporation has 7,000 shares of common stock outstanding. It declares a $1 per share cash dividend on November 1 to stockholders of record on December 1. The dividend is paid on December 31. Prepare the entries on the appropriate dates to record the declaration and payment of the cash dividend.

*Prepare entries for a cash dividend.*
(SO 5), **AP**

**BE11-6** The stockholders' equity section of Jumes Corporation's balance sheet consists of common stock ($8 par) $1,000,000 and retained earnings $300,000. A 10% stock dividend (12,500 shares) is declared when the market value per share is $19. Show the before and after effects of the dividend on (a) the components of stockholders' equity and (b) the shares outstanding.

*Show before and after effects of a stock dividend.*
(SO 5), **AP**

**BE11-7** Indicate whether each of the following transactions would increase (+), decrease (−), or not affect (N/A) total assets, total liabilities, and total stockholders' equity.

*Compare impact of cash dividend, stock dividend, and stock split.*
(SO 5), **K**

| Transaction | Assets | Liabilities | Stockholders' Equity |
|---|---|---|---|
| (a) Declared cash dividend. | | | |
| (b) Paid cash dividend declared in (a). | | | |
| (c) Declared stock dividend. | | | |
| (d) Distributed stock dividend declared in (c). | | | |
| (e) Split stock 3-for-1. | | | |

**BE11-8** Hewitt Corporation has these accounts at December 31: Common Stock, $10 par, 5,000 shares issued, $50,000; Paid-in Capital in Excess of Par Value $22,000; Retained Earnings $42,000; and Treasury Stock—Common, 500 shares, $11,000. Prepare the stockholders' equity section of the balance sheet.

*Prepare a stockholders' equity section.*
(SO 7), **AP**

**BE11-9** Adam Flint, president of Flint Corporation, believes that it is a good practice for a company to maintain a constant payout of dividends relative to its earnings. Last year, net income was $600,000, and the corporation paid $120,000 in dividends. This year, due to some unusual circumstances, the corporation had income of $1,600,000. Adam expects next year's net income to be about $700,000. What was Flint Corporation's payout ratio last year? If it is to maintain the same payout ratio, what amount of dividends would it pay this year? Is this necessarily a good idea—that is, what are the pros and cons of maintaining a constant payout ratio in this scenario?

*Evaluate a company's dividend record.*
(SO 8), **C**

**BE11-10** SUPERVALU, one of the largest grocery retailers in the United States, is headquartered in Minneapolis. The following financial information (in millions) was taken from the company's 2010 annual report. Net sales $44,597; net income $393; beginning stockholders' equity $2,581; and ending stockholders' equity $2,887. There were no dividends paid on preferred stock. Compute the return on common stockholders' equity ratio. Provide a brief interpretation of your findings.

*Calculate the return on stockholders' equity.*
(SO 8), **AP**

**BE11-11** Burden Inc. is considering these two alternatives to finance its construction of a new $2 million plant:
(a) Issuance of 200,000 shares of common stock at the market price of $10 per share.
(b) Issuance of $2 million, 6% bonds at face value.

*Compare bond financing to stock financing.*
(SO 8), **AP**

Complete the table and indicate which alternative is preferable.

| | Issue Stock | Issue Bond |
|---|---|---|
| Income before interest and taxes | $1,500,000 | $1,500,000 |
| Interest expense from bonds | _____ | _____ |
| Income before income taxes | | |
| Income tax expense (30%) | _____ | _____ |
| Net income | $_____ | $_____ |
| Outstanding shares | _____ | 700,000 |
| Earnings per share | $_____ | $_____ |

**\*BE11-12** Daly Corporation has 200,000 shares of $10 par value common stock outstanding. It declares a 12% stock dividend on December 1 when the market value per share is $17. The dividend shares are issued on December 31. Prepare the entries for the declaration and distribution of the stock dividend.

*Prepare entries for a stock dividend.*
(SO 9), **AP**

# Do it! Review

*Analyze statements about corporate organization.*
(SO 1), **C**

**Do it! 11-1** Indicate whether each of the following statements is true or false.

_____ 1. The corporation is an entity separate and distinct from its owners.

_____ 2. The liability of stockholders is normally limited to their investment in the corporation.

_____ 3. The relative lack of government regulation is an advantage of the corporate form of business.

_____ 4. There is no journal entry to record the authorization of capital stock.

_____ 5. No-par value stock is quite rare today.

*Journalize issuance of stock.*
(SO 2), **AP**

**Do it! 11-2** Baja Corporation began operations on April 1 by issuing 55,000 shares of $5 par value common stock for cash at $13 per share. Journalize the issuance.

*Journalize treasury stock transaction.*
(SO 3), **AP**

**Do it! 11-3** Davies Corporation purchased 2,000 shares of its $10 par value common stock for $76,000 on August 1. It will hold these in the treasury until resold. Journalize the treasury stock transaction.

*Determine dividends paid to preferred and common stockholders.*
(SO 4), **AP**

**Do it! 11-4** Aragon Corporation has 3,000 shares of 8%, $100 par value preferred stock outstanding at December 31, 2012. At December 31, 2012, the company declared a $105,000 cash dividend. Determine the dividend paid to preferred stockholders and common stockholders under each of the following scenarios.

1. The preferred stock is noncumulative, and the company has not missed any dividends in previous years.
2. The preferred stock is noncumulative, and the company did not pay a dividend in each of the two previous years.
3. The preferred stock is cumulative, and the company did not pay a dividend in each of the two previous years.

*Determine effects of stock dividend and stock split.*
(SO 5), **AP**

**Do it! 11-5** Magna CD Company has had 4 years of record earnings. Due to this success, the market price of its 400,000 shares of $2 par value common stock has increased from $12 per share to $50. During this period, paid-in capital remained the same at $2,400,000. Retained earnings increased from $1,800,000 to $12,000,000. CEO Ed Bette is considering either (1) a 15% stock dividend or (2) a 2-for-1 stock split. He asks you to show the before and after effects of each option on (a) retained earnings and (b) total stockholders' equity.

*Prepare stockholders' equity section.*
(SO 7), **AP**

**Do it! 11-6** Dwyer Corporation has issued 100,000 shares of $5 par value common stock. It was authorized 500,000 shares. The paid-in capital in excess of par value on the common stock is $263,000. The corporation has reacquired 7,000 shares at a cost of $46,000 and is currently holding those shares.

The corporation also has 2,000 shares issued and outstanding of 9%, $100 par value preferred stock. It authorized 10,000 shares. The paid-in capital in excess of par value on the preferred stock is $23,000. Retained earnings is $372,000. Prepare the stockholders' equity section of the balance sheet.

# Exercises

*Journalize issuance of common stock.*
(SO 2), **AP**

**E11-1** During its first year of operations, Pele Corporation had these transactions pertaining to its common stock.

| | | |
|---|---|---|
| Jan. | 10 | Issued 30,000 shares for cash at $5 per share. |
| July | 1 | Issued 60,000 shares for cash at $7 per share. |

**Instructions**

(a) Journalize the transactions, assuming that the common stock has a par value of $5 per share.

(b) Journalize the transactions, assuming that the common stock is no-par with a stated value of $1 per share.

*Journalize issuance of common stock and preferred stock and purchase of treasury stock.*
(SO 2, 3, 4), **AP**

**E11-2** Dukas Co. had these transactions during the current period.

| | | |
|---|---|---|
| June | 12 | Issued 80,000 shares of $1 par value common stock for cash of $300,000. |
| July | 11 | Issued 3,000 shares of $100 par value preferred stock for cash at $106 per share. |
| Nov. | 28 | Purchased 2,000 shares of treasury stock for $9,000. |

**Instructions**

Prepare the journal entries for the Dukas Co. transactions shown on page 604.

**E11-3** Vallejo Corporation is authorized to issue both preferred and common stock. The par value of the preferred is $50. During the first year of operations, the company had the following events and transactions pertaining to its preferred stock.

*Journalize preferred stock transactions and indicate statement presentation.*
*(SO 4, 7),* **AP**

Feb. 1 Issued 40,000 shares for cash at $51 per share.
July 1 Issued 60,000 shares for cash at $56 per share.

**Instructions**

(a) Journalize the transactions.
(b) Post to the stockholders' equity accounts. (Use T accounts.)
(c) Discuss the statement presentation of the accounts.

**E11-4** The stockholders' equity section of Traylor Corporation's balance sheet at December 31 is presented here.

*Answer questions about stockholders' equity section.*
*(SO 2, 3, 4, 7),* **C**

### TRAYLOR CORPORATION
### Balance Sheet (partial)

| | |
|---|---:|
| Stockholders' equity | |
| Paid-in capital | |
| Preferred stock, cumulative, 10,000 shares authorized, | |
| 6,000 shares issued and outstanding | $ 600,000 |
| Common stock, no par, 750,000 shares authorized, | |
| 580,000 shares issued | 2,900,000 |
| Total paid-in capital | 3,500,000 |
| Retained earnings | 1,158,000 |
| Total paid-in capital and retained earnings | 4,658,000 |
| Less: Treasury stock (6,000 common shares) | (32,000) |
| Total stockholders' equity | $4,626,000 |

**Instructions**

From a review of the stockholders' equity section, answer the following questions.

(a) How many shares of common stock are outstanding?
(b) Assuming there is a stated value, what is the stated value of the common stock?
(c) What is the par value of the preferred stock?
(d) If the annual dividend on preferred stock is $36,000, what is the dividend rate on preferred stock?
(e) If dividends of $72,000 were in arrears on preferred stock, what would be the balance reported for retained earnings?

**E11-5** Tofias Corporation recently hired a new accountant with extensive experience in accounting for partnerships. Because of the pressure of the new job, the accountant was unable to review what he had learned earlier about corporation accounting. During the first month, he made the following entries for the corporation's capital stock.

*Prepare correct entries for capital stock transactions.*
*(SO 2, 3, 4),* **AN**

| | | | | |
|---|---|---|---:|---:|
| May | 2 | Cash | 104,000 | |
| | | Capital Stock | | 104,000 |
| | | (Issued 8,000 shares of $10 par value | | |
| | | common stock at $13 per share) | | |
| | 10 | Cash | 530,000 | |
| | | Capital Stock | | 530,000 |
| | | (Issued 10,000 shares of $20 par value | | |
| | | preferred stock at $53 per share) | | |
| | 15 | Capital Stock | 7,200 | |
| | | Cash | | 7,200 |
| | | (Purchased 600 shares of common stock | | |
| | | for the treasury at $12 per share) | | |

**Instructions**

On the basis of the explanation for each entry, prepare the entries that should have been made for the capital stock transactions.

*Journalize cash dividends
and indicate statement
presentation.*
(SO 5), **AP**

**E11-6** On January 1, Tellier Corporation had 60,000 shares of no-par common stock issued and outstanding. The stock has a stated value of $4 per share. During the year, the following transactions occurred.

Apr. 1 Issued 9,000 additional shares of common stock for $11 per share.
June 15 Declared a cash dividend of $1.50 per share to stockholders of record on June 30.
July 10 Paid the $1.50 cash dividend.
Dec. 1 Issued 4,000 additional shares of common stock for $12 per share.
 15 Declared a cash dividend on outstanding shares of $1.60 per share to stockholders of record on December 31.

**Instructions**
(a) Prepare the entries, if any, on each of the three dates that involved dividends.
(b) How are dividends and dividends payable reported in the financial statements prepared at December 31?

*Compare effects of a stock
dividend and a stock split.*
(SO 5), **AP**

**E11-7** On October 31, the stockholders' equity section of Opio Company's balance sheet consists of common stock $648,000 and retained earnings $400,000. Opio is considering the following two courses of action: (1) declaring a 5% stock dividend on the 81,000 $8 par value shares outstanding or (2) effecting a 2-for-1 stock split that will reduce par value to $4 per share. The current market price is $17 per share.

**Instructions**
Prepare a tabular summary of the effects of the alternative actions on the company's stockholders' equity and outstanding shares. Use these column headings: **Before Action,** **After Stock Dividend**, and **After Stock Split**.

*Prepare a stockholders'
equity section.*
(SO 7), **AP**

**E11-8** Wells Fargo & Company, headquartered in San Francisco, is one of the nation's largest financial institutions. It reported the following selected accounts (in millions) as of December 31, 2009.

| | |
|---|---|
| Retained earnings | $41,563 |
| Preferred stock | 8,485 |
| Common stock—$1⅔ par value, authorized 6,000,000,000 shares; issued 5,245,971,422 shares | 8,743 |
| Treasury stock—67,346,829 shares | (2,450) |
| Additional paid-in capital—common stock | 52,878 |

**Instructions**
Prepare the stockholders' equity section of the balance sheet for Wells Fargo as of December 31, 2009.

*Prepare a stockholders'
equity section.*
(SO 7), **AP**

**E11-9** The following stockholders' equity accounts, arranged alphabetically, are in the ledger of Patel Corporation at December 31, 2012.

| | |
|---|---|
| Common Stock ($2 stated value) | $1,600,000 |
| Paid-in Capital in Excess of Par Value—Preferred Stock | 45,000 |
| Paid-in Capital in Excess of Stated Value—Common Stock | 1,050,000 |
| Preferred Stock (8%, $100 par, noncumulative) | 600,000 |
| Retained Earnings | 1,334,000 |
| Treasury Stock—Common (12,000 shares) | 72,000 |

**Instructions**
Prepare the stockholders' equity section of the balance sheet at December 31, 2012.

*Prepare a stockholders'
equity section.*
(SO 7), **AP**

**E11-10** The following accounts appear in the ledger of Sather Inc. after the books are closed at December 31, 2012.

| | |
|---|---|
| Common Stock (no-par, $1 stated value, 400,000 shares authorized, 250,000 shares issued) | $ 250,000 |
| Paid-in Capital in Excess of Stated Value—Common Stock | 1,200,000 |
| Preferred Stock ($50 par value, 8%, 40,000 shares authorized, 14,000 shares issued) | 700,000 |
| Retained Earnings | 920,000 |
| Treasury Stock (9,000 common shares) | 64,000 |
| Paid-in Capital in Excess of Par Value—Preferred Stock | 24,000 |

**Instructions**
Prepare the stockholders' equity section at December 31, assuming $100,000 of retained earnings is restricted for plant expansion. (Use Note R.)

**E11-11** The following financial information is available for Thompson Corporation.

*Calculate ratios to evaluate dividend and earnings performance.*

(SO 8), **AP**

| (in millions) | 2012 | 2011 |
|---|---|---|
| Average common stockholders' equity | $2,532 | $2,591 |
| Dividends declared for common stockholders | 298 | 611 |
| Dividends declared for preferred stockholders | 40 | 40 |
| Net income | 504 | 555 |

**Instructions**
Calculate the payout ratio and return on common stockholders' equity ratio for 2012 and 2011. Comment on your findings.

**E11-12** The following financial information is available for Walgreen Company.

*Calculate ratios to evaluate dividend and earnings performance.*

(SO 8), **AP**

| (in millions) | 2009 | 2008 |
|---|---|---|
| Average common stockholders' equity | $13,622.5 | $11,986.5 |
| Dividends declared for common stockholders | 471 | 394 |
| Dividends declared for preferred stockholders | 0 | 0 |
| Net income | 2,006 | 2,157 |

**Instructions**
Calculate the payout ratio and return on common stockholders' equity ratio for 2009 and 2008. Comment on your findings.

**E11-13** Morris Corporation decided to issue common stock and used the $300,000 proceeds to retire all of its outstanding bonds on January 1, 2012. The following information is available for the company for 2011 and 2012.

*Calculate ratios to evaluate profitability and solvency.*

(SO 8), **AN**

| | 2012 | 2011 |
|---|---|---|
| Net income | $ 182,000 | $ 150,000 |
| Dividends declared for preferred stockholders | 8,000 | 8,000 |
| Average common stockholders' equity | 1,000,000 | 700,000 |
| Total assets | 1,200,000 | 1,200,000 |
| Current liabilities | 100,000 | 100,000 |
| Total liabilities | 200,000 | 500,000 |

**Instructions**
(a) Compute the return on common stockholders' equity ratio for both years.
(b) Explain how it is possible that net income increased, but the return on common stockholders' equity decreased.
(c) Compute the debt to total assets ratio for both years, and comment on the implications of this change in the company's solvency.

**E11-14** Songbird Airlines is considering these two alternatives for financing the purchase of a fleet of airplanes:

*Compare issuance of stock financing to issuance of bond financing.*

(SO 8), **AN**

1. Issue 50,000 shares of common stock at $40 per share. (Cash dividends have not been paid nor is the payment of any contemplated.)
2. Issue 12%, 10-year bonds at face value for $2,000,000.

It is estimated that the company will earn $800,000 before interest and taxes as a result of this purchase. The company has an estimated tax rate of 30% and has 90,000 shares of common stock outstanding prior to the new financing.

**Instructions**
Determine the effect on net income and earnings per share for (a) issuing stock and (b) issuing bonds. Assume the new shares or new bonds will be outstanding for the entire year.

**E11-15** Randolph Company has $1,000,000 in assets and $1,000,000 in stockholders' equity, with 40,000 shares outstanding the entire year. It has a return on assets ratio of 10%. In the past year, it had net income of $100,000. On January 1, 2012, it issued $400,000 in debt at 4% and immediately repurchased 20,000 shares for $400,000. Management expected that, had it not issued the debt, it would have again had net income of $100,000.

*Compute ratios and interpret.*

(SO 8), **AN**

#### Instructions

(a) Determine the company's net income and earnings per share for 2011 and 2012. (Ignore taxes in your computations.)

(b) Compute the company's return on common stockholders' equity for 2011 and 2012.

(c) Compute the company's debt to total assets ratio for 2011 and 2012.

(d) Discuss the impact that the borrowing had on the company's profitability and solvency. Was it a good idea to borrow the money to buy the treasury stock?

*Journalize stock dividends.*
*(SO 5, 9),* **AP**

**\*E11-16**   On January 1, 2012, Sheperd Corporation had $1,200,000 of common stock outstanding that was issued at par and retained earnings of $750,000. The company issued 30,000 shares of common stock at par on July 1 and earned net income of $400,000 for the year.

#### Instructions

Journalize the declaration of a 15% stock dividend on December 10, 2012, for the following two independent assumptions.

(a) Par value is $10 and market value is $15.

(b) Par value is $5 and market value is $8.

# Exercises: Set B and Challenge Exercises

Visit the book's companion website, at **www.wiley.com/college/kimmel,** and choose the Student Companion site to access Exercise Set B and Challenge Exercises.

# Problems: Set A

*Journalize stock transactions, post, and prepare paid-in capital section.*
*(SO 2, 4, 7),* **AN**

**P11-1A**   Whitten Corporation was organized on January 1, 2012. It is authorized to issue 20,000 shares of 6%, $50 par value preferred stock and 500,000 shares of no-par common stock with a stated value of $1 per share. The following stock transactions were completed during the first year.

| | | |
|---|---|---|
| Jan. | 10 | Issued 70,000 shares of common stock for cash at $4 per share. |
| Mar. | 1 | Issued 12,000 shares of preferred stock for cash at $53 per share. |
| May | 1 | Issued 120,000 shares of common stock for cash at $6 per share. |
| Sept. | 1 | Issued 5,000 shares of common stock for cash at $5 per share. |
| Nov. | 1 | Issued 3,000 shares of preferred stock for cash at $56 per share. |

#### Instructions

(a) Journalize the transactions.

(b) Post to the stockholders' equity accounts. (Use T accounts.)

*(c) Tot. paid-in capital  $1,829,000*

(c) Prepare the paid-in capital portion of the stockholders' equity section at December 31, 2012.

*Journalize transactions, post, and prepare a stockholders' equity section; calculate ratios.*
*(SO 2, 3, 5, 7, 8),* **AP**

**P11-2A**   The stockholders' equity accounts of Omega Corporation on January 1, 2012, were as follows.

| | |
|---|---|
| Preferred Stock (7%, $100 par noncumulative, 5,000 shares authorized) | $ 300,000 |
| Common Stock ($4 stated value, 300,000 shares authorized) | 1,000,000 |
| Paid-in Capital in Excess of Par Value—Preferred Stock | 15,000 |
| Paid-in Capital in Excess of Stated Value—Common Stock | 480,000 |
| Retained Earnings | 688,000 |
| Treasury Stock—Common (5,000 shares) | 40,000 |

During 2012, the corporation had the following transactions and events pertaining to its stockholders' equity.

| | | |
|---|---|---|
| Feb. | 1 | Issued 5,000 shares of common stock for $30,000. |
| Mar. | 20 | Purchased 1,000 additional shares of common treasury stock at $7 per share. |
| Oct. | 1 | Declared a 7% cash dividend on preferred stock, payable November 1. |
| Nov. | 1 | Paid the dividend declared on October 1. |

Dec.   1   Declared a $0.50 per share cash dividend to common stockholders of record on December 15, payable December 31, 2012.

     31   Determined that net income for the year was $280,000. Paid the dividend declared on December 1.

**Instructions**
(a) Journalize the transactions. (Include entries to close net income and dividends to Retained Earnings.)
(b) Enter the beginning balances in the accounts and post the journal entries to the stockholders' equity accounts. (Use T accounts.)
(c) Prepare the stockholders' equity section of the balance sheet at December 31, 2012.
(d) Calculate the payout ratio, earnings per share, and return on common stockholders' equity ratio. (*Note:* Use the common shares outstanding on January 1 and December 31 to determine the average shares outstanding.)

*(c) Tot. paid-in capital $1,825,000*

**P11-3A**   On December 31, 2011, Stitch Company had 1,300,000 shares of $5 par common stock issued and outstanding. The stockholders' equity accounts at December 31, 2011, had the balances listed here.

*Prepare a stockholders' equity section.*
*(SO 7), **AP***

| | |
|---|---|
| Common Stock | $6,500,000 |
| Additional Paid-in Capital | 1,800,000 |
| Retained Earnings | 1,200,000 |

Transactions during 2012 and other information related to stockholders' equity accounts were as follows.

1. On January 10, 2012, issued at $107 per share 120,000 shares of $100 par value, 9% cumulative preferred stock.
2. On February 8, 2012, reacquired 15,000 shares of its common stock for $11 per share.
3. On June 8, 2012, declared a cash dividend of $1.20 per share on the common stock outstanding, payable on July 10, 2012, to stockholders of record on July 1, 2012.
4. On December 9, 2012, declared the yearly cash dividend on preferred stock, payable January 10, 2013, to stockholders of record on December 31, 2012.
5. Net income for the year was $3,600,000.

**Instructions**
Prepare the stockholders' equity section of Stitch's balance sheet at December 31, 2012.

*Tot. stockholders' equity $23,153,000*

**P11-4A**   The ledger of Zeta Corporation at December 31, 2012, after the books have been closed, contains the following stockholders' equity accounts.

*Reproduce retained earnings account, and prepare a stockholders' equity section.*
*(SO 5, 6, 7), **AP***

| | |
|---|---|
| Preferred Stock (10,000 shares issued) | $1,000,000 |
| Common Stock (300,000 shares issued) | 1,500,000 |
| Paid-in Capital in Excess of Par Value—Preferred Stock | 200,000 |
| Paid-in Capital in Excess of Stated Value—Common Stock | 1,600,000 |
| Retained Earnings | 2,860,000 |

A review of the accounting records reveals this information:

1. Preferred stock is 8%, $100 par value, noncumulative. Since January 1, 2011, 10,000 shares have been outstanding; 20,000 shares are authorized.
2. Common stock is no-par with a stated value of $5 per share; 600,000 shares are authorized.
3. The January 1, 2012, balance in Retained Earnings was $2,380,000.
4. On October 1, 60,000 shares of common stock were sold for cash at $9 per share.
5. A cash dividend of $400,000 was declared and properly allocated to preferred and common stock on November 1. No dividends were paid to preferred stockholders in 2011.
6. Net income for the year was $880,000.
7. On December 31, 2012, the directors authorized disclosure of a $160,000 restriction of retained earnings for plant expansion. (Use Note A.)

**Instructions**
(a) Reproduce the retained earnings account (T account) for the year.
(b) Prepare the stockholders' equity section of the balance sheet at December 31.

*(b) Tot. paid-in capital $4,300,000*
*Prepare entries for stock transactions, and prepare a stockholders' equity section.*
*(SO 2, 3, 4, 7), **AP***

**P11-5A**   Melvina Corporation has been authorized to issue 20,000 shares of $100 par value, 7%, noncumulative preferred stock and 1,000,000 shares of no-par common stock.

The corporation assigned a $5 stated value to the common stock. At December 31, 2012, the ledger contained the following balances pertaining to stockholders' equity.

| | |
|---|---:|
| Preferred Stock | $ 150,000 |
| Paid-in Capital in Excess of Par Value—Preferred Stock | 20,000 |
| Common Stock | 2,000,000 |
| Paid-in Capital in Excess of Stated Value—Common Stock | 1,520,000 |
| Treasury Stock—Common (4,000 shares) | 36,000 |
| Retained Earnings | 82,000 |

The preferred stock was issued for $170,000 cash. All common stock issued was for cash. In November 4,000 shares of common stock were purchased for the treasury at a per share cost of $9. No dividends were declared in 2012.

*Instructions*
(a) Prepare the journal entries for the following.
  (1) Issuance of preferred stock for cash.
  (2) Issuance of common stock for cash.
  (3) Purchase of common treasury stock for cash.

*(b) Tot. stockholders' equity*
*$3,736,000*

(b) Prepare the stockholders' equity section of the balance sheet at December 31, 2012.

*Prepare a stockholders'*
*equity section.*
(SO 7), **AP**

**P11-6A** On January 1, 2012, Neville Inc. had these stockholders' equity balances.

| | |
|---|---:|
| Common Stock, $1 par (2,000,000 shares authorized, 600,000 shares issued and outstanding) | $ 600,000 |
| Paid-in Capital in Excess of Par Value | 1,500,000 |
| Retained Earnings | 700,000 |

During 2012, the following transactions and events occurred.

1. Issued 50,000 shares of $1 par value common stock for $3 per share.
2. Issued 60,000 shares of common stock for cash at $4 per share.
3. Purchased 20,000 shares of common stock for the treasury at $3.80 per share.
4. Declared and paid a cash dividend of $207,000.
5. Earned net income of $410,000.

*Instructions*

*Tot. stockholders' equity $3,317,000*

Prepare the stockholders' equity section of the balance sheet at December 31, 2012.

*Evaluate a company's*
*profitability and solvency.*
(SO 8), **AP**

**P11-7A** Tejada Company manufactures backpacks. During 2012, Tejada issued bonds at 10% interest and used the cash proceeds to purchase treasury stock. The following financial information is available for Tejada Company for the years 2012 and 2011.

| | 2012 | 2011 |
|---|---:|---:|
| Sales | $ 9,000,000 | $ 9,000,000 |
| Net income | 2,240,000 | 2,500,000 |
| Interest expense | 500,000 | 140,000 |
| Tax expense | 670,000 | 750,000 |
| Dividends paid on common stock | 890,000 | 1,026,000 |
| Dividends paid on preferred stock | 300,000 | 300,000 |
| Total assets (year-end) | 14,500,000 | 16,875,000 |
| Average total assets | 15,687,500 | 17,763,000 |
| Total liabilities (year-end) | 6,000,000 | 3,000,000 |
| Avg. total common stockholders' equity | 9,400,000 | 14,100,000 |

*Instructions*
(a) Use the information above to calculate the following ratios for both years: (i) return on assets ratio, (ii) return on common stockholders' equity ratio, (iii) payout ratio, (iv) debt to total assets ratio, and (v) times interest earned ratio.
(b) Referring to your findings in part (a), discuss the changes in the company's profitability from 2011 to 2012.
(c) Referring to your findings in part (a), discuss the changes in the company's solvency from 2011 to 2012.
(d) Based on your findings in (b), was the decision to issue debt to purchase common stock a wise one?

**\*P11-8A**   On January 1, 2012, Cornell Corporation had these stockholders' equity accounts.

| | |
|---|---:|
| Common Stock ($10 par value, 70,000 shares issued and outstanding) | $700,000 |
| Paid-in Capital in Excess of Par Value | 500,000 |
| Retained Earnings | 620,000 |

During the year, the following transactions occurred.

| | | |
|---|---|---|
| Jan. | 15 | Declared a $0.50 cash dividend per share to stockholders of record on January 31, payable February 15. |
| Feb. | 15 | Paid the dividend declared in January. |
| Apr. | 15 | Declared a 10% stock dividend to stockholders of record on April 30, distributable May 15. On April 15, the market price of the stock was $14 per share. |
| May | 15 | Issued the shares for the stock dividend. |
| Dec. | 1 | Declared a $0.60 per share cash dividend to stockholders of record on December 15, payable January 10, 2013. |
| | 31 | Determined that net income for the year was $400,000. |

*Prepare dividend entries, prepare a stockholders' equity section, and calculate ratios.*
(SO 5, 7, 8, 9), **AP**

**Instructions**
(a) Journalize the transactions. (Include entries to close net income and dividends to Retained Earnings.)
(b) Enter the beginning balances and post the entries to the stockholders' equity T accounts. (*Note:* Open additional stockholders' equity accounts as needed.)
(c) Prepare the stockholders' equity section of the balance sheet at December 31.
(d) Calculate the payout ratio and return on common stockholders' equity ratio.

(c) Tot. stockholders' equity
$2,138,800

# Problems: Set B

**P11-1B**   Hennes Corporation was organized on January 1, 2012. It is authorized to issue 10,000 shares of 8%, $100 par value preferred stock and 500,000 shares of no-par common stock with a stated value of $2 per share. The following stock transactions were completed during the first year.

| | | |
|---|---|---|
| Jan. | 10 | Issued 40,000 shares of common stock for cash at $3.60 per share. |
| Mar. | 1 | Issued 5,000 shares of preferred stock for cash at $102 per share. |
| May | 1 | Issued 90,000 shares of common stock for cash at $4 per share. |
| Sept. | 1 | Issued 10,000 shares of common stock for cash at $4.40 per share. |
| Nov. | 1 | Issued 4,000 shares of preferred stock for cash at $103 per share. |

*Journalize stock transactions, post, and prepare paid-in capital section.*
(SO 2, 4, 7), **AN**

**Instructions**
(a) Journalize the transactions.
(b) Post to the stockholders' equity accounts. (Use T accounts.)
(c) Prepare the paid-in capital section of stockholders' equity at December 31, 2012.

(c) Tot. paid-in capital  $1,470,000

**P11-2B**   The stockholders' equity accounts of Nardin Corporation on January 1, 2012, were as follows.

| | |
|---|---:|
| Preferred Stock (9%, $50 par cumulative, 10,000 shares authorized) | $ 200,000 |
| Common Stock ($1 stated value, 2,000,000 shares authorized) | 1,000,000 |
| Paid-in Capital in Excess of Par Value—Preferred Stock | 16,000 |
| Paid-in Capital in Excess of Stated Value—Common Stock | 1,400,000 |
| Retained Earnings | 1,716,000 |
| Treasury Stock—Common (8,000 shares) | 20,000 |

*Journalize transactions, post, and prepare a stockholders' equity section; calculate ratios.*
(SO 2, 3, 5, 7, 8), **AP**

During 2012 the corporation had these transactions and events pertaining to its stockholders' equity.

| | | |
|---|---|---|
| Feb. | 1 | Issued 20,000 shares of common stock for $60,000. |
| Nov. | 10 | Purchased 4,000 shares of common stock for the treasury at a cost of $16,000. |
| Nov. | 15 | Declared a 9% cash dividend on preferred stock, payable December 15. |
| Dec. | 1 | Declared a $0.30 per share cash dividend to stockholders of record on December 15, payable December 31, 2012. |

Dec. 15 Paid the dividend declared on November 15.
      31 Determined that net income for the year was $408,000. The market price of the common stock on this date was $5 per share. Paid the dividend declared on December 1.

**Instructions**

(a) Journalize the transactions. (Include entries to close net income and dividends to Retained Earnings.)

(b) Enter the beginning balances in the accounts, and post the journal entries to the stockholders' equity accounts. (Use T accounts.)

(c) Prepare the stockholders' equity section of the balance sheet at December 31, 2012.

(d) Calculate the payout ratio, earnings per share, and return on common stockholders' equity ratio. (*Hint:* Use the common shares outstanding on January 1 and December 31 to determine average shares outstanding.)

*(c) Tot. paid-in capital $2,676,000*

*Prepare a stockholders' equity section.*
*(SO 7),* **AP**

**P11-3B** On December 31, 2011, Bryant Company had 600,000 shares of $1 par common stock issued and outstanding. The stockholders' equity accounts at December 31, 2011, had the balances listed here.

| | |
|---|---|
| Common Stock | $600,000 |
| Additional Paid-in Capital | 900,000 |
| Retained Earnings | 800,000 |

Transactions during 2012 and other information related to stockholders' equity accounts were as follows.

1. On January 9, 2012, issued at $52 per share 12,000 shares of $50 par value, 9% cumulative preferred stock.
2. On February 8, 2012, reacquired 15,000 shares of its common stock for $4 per share.
3. On June 10, 2012, declared a cash dividend of $1 per share on the common stock outstanding, payable on July 10, 2012, to stockholders of record on July 1, 2012.
4. On December 1, 2012, declared the yearly cash dividend on preferred stock, payable December 28, 2012, to stockholders of record on December 15, 2012.
5. Net income for the year is $2,400,000. At December 31, 2012, the market price of the common stock was $5 per share.

**Instructions**

*Tot. stockholders' equity $4,625,000*

Prepare the stockholders' equity section of Bryant Company's balance sheet at December 31, 2012.

*Reproduce retained earnings account, and prepare a stockholders' equity section.*
*(SO 5, 6, 7),* **AP**

**P11-4B** The post-closing trial balance of Flicka Corporation at December 31, 2012, contains these stockholders' equity accounts.

| | |
|---|---|
| Preferred Stock (6,000 shares issued) | $ 300,000 |
| Common Stock (350,000 shares issued) | 3,500,000 |
| Paid-in Capital in Excess of Par Value—Preferred Stock | 250,000 |
| Paid-in Capital in Excess of Par Value—Common Stock | 520,000 |
| Retained Earnings | 805,000 |

A review of the accounting records reveals this information:

1. Preferred stock is $50 par, 10%, and cumulative; 6,000 shares have been outstanding since January 1, 2011.
2. Authorized stock is 20,000 shares of preferred and 500,000 shares of common with a $10 par value.
3. The January 1, 2012, balance in Retained Earnings was $660,000.
4. On July 1, 20,000 shares of common stock were sold for cash at $16 per share.
5. A cash dividend of $380,000 was declared and properly allocated to preferred and common stock on October 1. No dividends were paid to preferred stockholders in 2011.
6. Net income for the year was $525,000.
7. On December 31, 2012, the directors authorized disclosure of a $150,000 restriction of retained earnings for plant expansion. (Use Note X.)

**Instructions**

(a) Reproduce the retained earnings account for the year.

(b) Prepare the stockholders' equity section of the balance sheet at December 31.

*(b) Tot. paid-in capital $4,570,000*

**P11-5B**  The following stockholders' equity accounts, arranged alphabetically, are in the ledger of Charlotte Corporation at December 31, 2012.

*Prepare a stockholders' equity section.*

(SO 7), **AP**

| | |
|---|---:|
| Common Stock ($2 stated value, 1,800,000 shares authorized) | $2,600,000 |
| Paid-in Capital in Excess of Par Value—Preferred Stock | 158,000 |
| Paid-in Capital in Excess of Stated Value—Common Stock | 1,950,000 |
| Preferred Stock (8%, $50 par, noncumulative, 50,000 shares authorized) | 900,000 |
| Retained Earnings | 1,958,000 |
| Treasury Stock—Common (20,000 shares) | 80,000 |

*Instructions*
Prepare the stockholders' equity section of the balance sheet at December 31, 2012.

Tot. stockholders' equity  $7,486,000

**P11-6B**  On January 1, 2012, Gabriel Inc. had these stockholder equity balances.

*Prepare a stockholders' equity section.*

(SO 7), **AP**

| | |
|---|---:|
| Common Stock, $1 par (1,000,000 shares authorized; 500,000 shares issued and outstanding) | $ 500,000 |
| Paid-in Capital in Excess of Par Value | 1,000,000 |
| Retained Earnings | 600,000 |

During 2012, the following transactions and events occurred.

1. Issued 70,000 shares of $1 par common stock for $245,000.
2. Issued 40,000 common shares for cash at $4 per share.
3. Purchased 18,000 shares of common stock for the treasury at $4 per share.
4. Declared and paid a cash dividend of $296,000.
5. Reported net income of $510,000.

*Instructions*
Prepare the stockholders' equity section of the balance sheet at December 31, 2012.

Tot. stockholders' equity  $2,647,000

**P11-7B**  Daykin Company manufactures raingear. During 2012, Daykin Company decided to issue bonds at 8% interest and then used the cash to purchase a significant amount of treasury stock. The following information is available for Daykin Company.

*Evaluate a company's profitability and solvency.*

(SO 8), **AP**

| | 2012 | 2011 |
|---|---:|---:|
| Sales | $3,000,000 | $3,000,000 |
| Net income | 780,000 | 850,000 |
| Interest expense | 120,000 | 50,000 |
| Tax expense | 166,000 | 190,000 |
| Total assets | 5,000,000 | 5,610,000 |
| Average total assets | 5,312,500 | 6,230,000 |
| Total liabilities | 2,000,000 | 1,200,000 |
| Average total stockholders' equity | 3,322,500 | 5,250,000 |
| Dividends paid on common stock | 270,000 | 300,000 |
| Dividends paid on preferred stock | 40,000 | 40,000 |

*Instructions*
(a) Use the information above to calculate the following ratios for both years: (i) return on assets ratio, (ii) return on common stockholders' equity ratio, (iii) payout ratio, (iv) debt to total assets ratio, and (v) times interest earned ratio.
(b) Referring to your findings in part (a), discuss the changes in the company's profitability from 2011 to 2012.
(c) Referring to your findings in part (a), discuss the changes in the company's solvency from 2011 to 2012.
(d) Based on your findings in (b), was the decision to issue debt to purchase common stock a wise one?

*P11-8B*  On January 1, 2012, Jason Corporation had these stockholders' equity accounts.

*Prepare dividend entries, prepare a stockholders' equity section, and calculate ratios.*

(SO 5, 7, 8, 9), **AP**

| | |
|---|---:|
| Common Stock ($20 par value, 80,000 shares issued and outstanding) | $1,600,000 |
| Paid-in Capital in Excess of Par Value | 240,000 |
| Retained Earnings | 750,000 |

During the year, the following transactions occurred.

Feb. 1  Declared a $0.50 cash dividend per share to stockholders of record on February 15, payable March 1.

Mar. 1  Paid the dividend declared in February.

July 1  Declared a 15% stock dividend to stockholders of record on July 15, distributable July 31. On July 1, the market price of the stock was $25 per share.

    31  Issued the shares for the stock dividend.

Dec. 1  Declared a $1 per share dividend to stockholders of record on December 15, payable January 5, 2013.

    31  Determined that net income for the year was $500,000. The market price of the common stock on this date was $32.

***Instructions***

(a) Journalize the transactions. (Include entries to close net income and dividends to Retained Earnings.)

(b) Enter the beginning balances and post the entries to the stockholders' equity T accounts. (*Note:* Open additional stockholders' equity accounts as needed.)

(c) Prepare the stockholders' equity section of the balance sheet at December 31.

(d) Calculate the payout ratio and return on common stockholders' equity ratio.

(c) Tot. stockholders' equity $2,958,000

## Problems: Set C

Visit the book's companion website, at **www.wiley.com/college/kimmel**, and choose the Student Companion site to access Problem Set C.

## Comprehensive Problem

**CP11**  Hampton Corporation's balance sheet at December 31, 2011, is presented below.

**HAMPTON CORPORATION**
**Balance Sheet**
**December 31, 2011**

| | | | |
|---|---|---|---|
| Cash | $ 24,600 | Accounts payable | $ 25,600 |
| Accounts receivable | 45,500 | Common stock ($10 par) | 80,000 |
| Allowance for doubtful accounts | (1,500) | Retained earnings | 127,400 |
| Supplies | 4,400 | | $233,000 |
| Land | 40,000 | | |
| Buildings | 142,000 | | |
| Accumulated depreciation—buildings | (22,000) | | |
| | $233,000 | | |

During 2012, the following transactions occurred.

1. On January 1, 2012, Hampton issued 1,200 shares of $40 par, 7% preferred stock for $49,200.
2. On January 1, 2012, Hampton also issued 900 shares of the $10 par value common stock for $21,000.
3. Hampton performed services for $320,000 on account.
4. On April 1, 2012, Hampton collected fees of $36,000 in advance for services to be performed from April 1, 2012, to March 31, 2013.
5. Hampton collected $276,000 from customers on account.
6. Hampton bought $35,100 of supplies on account.
7. Hampton paid $32,200 on accounts payable.
8. Hampton reacquired 400 shares of its common stock on June 1, 2012, for $28 per share.
9. Paid other operating expenses of $188,200.
10. On December 31, 2012, Hampton declared the annual preferred stock dividend and a $1.20 per share dividend on the outstanding common stock, all payable on January 15, 2013.
11. An account receivable of $1,700 which originated in 2011 is written off as uncollectible.

Adjustment data:

1. A count of supplies indicates that $5,900 of supplies remain unused at year-end.
2. Recorded revenue earned from item 4 above.
3. The allowance for doubtful accounts should have a balance of $3,500 at year end.
4. Depreciation is recorded on the building on a straight-line basis based on a 30-year life and a salvage value of $10,000.
5. The income tax rate is 30%. (*Hint:* Prepare the income statement up to income before taxes and multiply by 30% to compute the amount.)

*Instructions*
(You may want to set up T accounts to determine ending balances.)
(a) Prepare journal entries for the transactions listed above and adjusting entries.
(b) Prepare an adjusted trial balance at December 31, 2012.
(c) Prepare an income statement and a retained earnings statement for the year ending December 31, 2012, and a classified balance sheet as of December 31, 2012.

(b) Totals $740,690
(c) Net income $81,970
Tot. assets $421,000

# Continuing Cookie Chronicle

(*Note:* This is a continuation of the Cookie Chronicle from Chapters 1 through 10.)

**CCC11**

**Part 1**  Because Natalie has been so successful with Cookie Creations and her friend Curtis Lesperance has been just as successful with his coffee shop, they conclude that they could benefit from each other's business expertise. Curtis and Natalie next evaluate the different types of business organization. Because of the advantage of limited personal liability, they decide to form a corporation.

Natalie and Curtis are very excited about this new business venture. They come to you with information they have gathered about their companies and with a number of questions.

**Part 2**  After establishing their company's fiscal year to be October 31, Natalie and Curtis began operating Cookie & Coffee Creations Inc. on November 1, 2012. On that date, they issued both preferred and common stock. Natalie and Curtis now want to prepare financial information for the first year of operations.

> Go to the book's companion website, at **www.wiley.com/college/kimmel**, to find the completion of this problem.

## broadening your perspective

## Financial Reporting and Analysis

### FINANCIAL REPORTING PROBLEM: *Tootsie Roll Industries, Inc.*

**BYP11-1**  The stockholders' equity section of Tootsie Roll Industries' balance sheet is shown in the Consolidated Statement of Financial Position in Appendix A. You will also find data relative to this problem on other pages of Appendix A. **(Note that Tootsie Roll has two classes of common stock. To answer the following questions, add the two classes of stock together.)**

*Instructions*
Answer the following questions.
(a) What is the par or stated value per share of Tootsie Roll's common stock?
(b) What percentage of Tootsie Roll's authorized common stock was issued at December 31, 2009? (Round to the nearest full percent.)
(c) How many shares of common stock were outstanding at December 31, 2008, and at December 31, 2009?
(d) Calculate the payout ratio, earnings per share, and return on common stockholders' equity ratio for 2009.

### COMPARATIVE ANALYSIS PROBLEM: *Tootsie Roll vs. Hershey*

**BYP11-2**  The financial statements of The Hershey Company are presented in Appendix B, following the financial statements for Tootsie Roll in Appendix A.

*Instructions*

(a) Based on the information in these financial statements, compute the 2009 return on common stockholders' equity, debt to total assets ratio, and return on assets ratio for each company.

(b) What conclusions concerning the companies' profitability can be drawn from these ratios? Which company relies more on debt to boost its return to common shareholders?

(c) Compute the payout ratio for each company. Which pays out a higher percentage of its earnings?

## RESEARCH CASE

**BYP11-3** The March 15, 2010, edition of the *Wall Street Journal* includes an article by Martin Peers entitled "Media's Cash Focus is Paying Dividends."

*Instructions*

Read the article and answer the following questions.

(a) What action did Viacom take with its excess cash before it decided to consider paying dividends or stock buybacks?

(b) What percentage of free cash flow does Time Warner pay out in dividends?

(c) Why might Viacom choose to pay a lower dividend and instead use its excess cash for a stock buyback program?

(d) How might the payment of a steady, significant dividend change the nature of shareholders that invest in media companies?

(e) What message might an increased dividend or stock buybacks send to shareholders regarding what the company will do with excess cash now, as opposed to what it used to do with excess cash?

## INTERPRETING FINANCIAL STATEMENTS

**BYP11-4** Marriott Corporation split into two companies: Host Marriott Corporation and Marriott International. Host Marriott retained ownership of the corporation's vast hotel and other properties, while Marriott International, rather than owning hotels, managed them. The purpose of this split was to free Marriott International from the "baggage" associated with Host Marriott, thus allowing it to be more aggressive in its pursuit of growth. The following information (in millions) is provided for each corporation for their first full year operating as independent companies.

|  | **Host Marriott** | **Marriott International** |
|---|---|---|
| Sales | $1,501 | $8,415 |
| Net income | (25) | 200 |
| Total assets | 3,822 | 3,207 |
| Total liabilities | 3,112 | 2,440 |
| Common stockholders' equity | 710 | 767 |

*Instructions*

(a) The two companies were split by the issuance of shares of Marriott International to all shareholders of the previous combined company. Discuss the nature of this transaction.

(b) Calculate the debt to total assets ratio for each company.

(c) Calculate the return on assets and return on common stockholders' equity ratios for each company.

(d) The company's debtholders were fiercely opposed to the original plan to split the two companies because the original plan had Host Marriott absorbing the majority of the company's debt. They relented only when Marriott International agreed to absorb a larger share of the debt. Discuss the possible reasons the debtholders were opposed to the plan to split the company.

## FINANCIAL ANALYSIS ON THE WEB

**BYP11-5** *Purpose:* Use the stockholders' equity section of an annual report and identify the major components.

*Address:* www.annualreports.com, or go to www.wiley.com/college/kimmel

*Steps*

1. Select a particular company.
2. Search by company name.
3. Follow instructions below.

*Instructions*
Answer the following questions.
(a) What is the company's name?
(b) What classes of capital stock has the company issued?
(c) For each class of stock:
    (1) How many shares are authorized, issued, and/or outstanding?
    (2) What is the par value?
(d) What are the company's retained earnings?
(e) Has the company acquired treasury stock? How many shares?

# Critical Thinking

## DECISION MAKING ACROSS THE ORGANIZATION

**BYP11-6** During a recent period, the fast-food chain Wendy's International purchased many treasury shares. This caused the number of shares outstanding to fall from 124 million to 105 million. The following information was drawn from the company's financial statements (in millions).

| | Information for the Year after Purchase of Treasury Stock | Information for the Year before Purchase of Treasury Stock |
|---|---|---|
| Net income | $ 193.6 | $ 123.4 |
| Total assets | 2,076.0 | 1,837.9 |
| Average total assets | 2,016.9 | 1,889.8 |
| Total common stockholders' equity | 1,029.8 | 1,068.1 |
| Average common stockholders' equity | 1,078.0 | 1,126.2 |
| Total liabilities | 1,046.3 | 769.9 |
| Average total liabilities | 939.0 | 763.7 |
| Interest expense | 30.2 | 19.8 |
| Income taxes | 113.7 | 84.3 |
| Cash provided by operations | 305.2 | 233.8 |
| Cash dividends paid on common stock | 26.8 | 31.0 |
| Preferred stock dividends | 0 | 0 |
| Average number of common shares outstanding | 109.7 | 119.9 |

*Instructions*
Use the information provided to answer the following questions.
(a) Compute earnings per share, return on common stockholders' equity, and return on assets for both years. Discuss the change in the company's profitability over this period.
(b) Compute the dividend payout ratio. Also compute the average cash dividend paid per share of common stock (dividends paid divided by the average number of common shares outstanding). Discuss any change in these ratios during this period and the implications for the company's dividend policy.
(c) Compute the debt to total assets ratio and interest coverage ratio. Discuss the change in the company's solvency.
(d) Based on your findings in (a) and (c), discuss to what extent any change in the return on common stockholders' equity was the result of increased reliance on debt.
(e) Does it appear that the purchase of treasury stock and the shift toward more reliance on debt were wise strategic moves?

## COMMUNICATION ACTIVITY

**BYP11-7** Jim Collins, your uncle, is an inventor who has decided to incorporate. Uncle Jim knows that you are an accounting major at U.N.O. In a recent letter to you, he ends with the question, "I'm filling out a state incorporation application. Can you tell me the difference among the following terms: (1) authorized stock, (2) issued stock, (3) outstanding stock, and (4) preferred stock?"

*Instructions*
In a brief note, differentiate for Uncle Jim the four different stock terms. Write the letter to be friendly, yet professional.

## ETHICS CASES

**BYP11-8** The R&D division of Mozy Corp. has just developed a chemical for sterilizing the vicious Brazilian "killer bees" which are invading Mexico and the southern United States. The president of Mozy is anxious to get the chemical on the market because Mozy profits need a boost—and his job is in jeopardy because of decreasing sales and profits. Mozy has an opportunity to sell this chemical in Central American countries, where the laws are much more relaxed than in the United States.

The director of Mozy's R&D division strongly recommends further research in the laboratory to test the side effects of this chemical on other insects, birds, animals, plants, and even humans. He cautions the president, "We could be sued from all sides if the chemical has tragic side effects that we didn't even test for in the lab." The president answers, "We can't wait an additional year for your lab tests. We can avoid losses from such lawsuits by establishing a separate wholly owned corporation to shield Mozy Corp. from such lawsuits. We can't lose any more than our investment in the new corporation, and we'll invest just the patent covering this chemical. We'll reap the benefits if the chemical works and is safe, and avoid the losses from lawsuits if it's a disaster." The following week, Mozy creates a new wholly owned corporation called Ziegler Inc., sells the chemical patent to it for $10, and watches the spraying begin.

*Instructions*
(a) Who are the stakeholders in this situation?
(b) Are the president's motives and actions ethical?
(c) Can Mozy shield itself against losses of Ziegler Inc.?

**BYP11-9** Lesley Corporation has paid 60 consecutive quarterly cash dividends (15 years). The last 6 months have been a real cash drain on the company, however, as profit margins have been greatly narrowed by increasing competition. With a cash balance sufficient to meet only day-to-day operating needs, the president, Clint Palen, has decided that a stock dividend instead of a cash dividend should be declared. He tells Lesley's financial vice president, Becca Anderson, to issue a press release stating that the company is extending its consecutive dividend record with the issuance of a 5% stock dividend. "Write the press release convincing the stockholders that the stock dividend is just as good as a cash dividend," he orders. "Just watch our stock rise when we announce the stock dividend; it must be a good thing if that happens."

*Instructions*
(a) Who are the stakeholders in this situation?
(b) Is there anything unethical about president Palen's intentions or actions?
(c) What is the effect of a stock dividend on a corporation's stockholders' equity accounts? Which would you rather receive as a stockholder—a cash dividend or a stock dividend? Why?

## "ALL ABOUT YOU" ACTIVITY

**BYP11-10** In response to the Sarbanes-Oxley Act, many companies have implemented formal ethics codes. Many other organizations also have ethics codes.

*Instructions*
Obtain the ethics code from an organization that you belong to (e.g., student organization, business school, employer, or a volunteer organization). Evaluate the ethics code based on how clearly it identifies proper and improper behaviour. Discuss its strengths, and how it might be improved.

## FASB CODIFICATION ACTIVITY

**BYP11-11** If your school has a subscription to the FASB Codification, go to **http://aaahq.org/ascLogin.cfm** to log in and prepare responses to the following.
(a) What is the stock dividend?
(b) What is a stock split?
(c) At what percentage point does the issuance of additional shares qualify as a stock dividend, as opposed to a stock split?

### Answers to Insight and Accounting Across the Organization Questions

**p. 573 Wall Street No Friend of Facebook** Q: Why has Mark Zuckerberg, the CEO and founder of Facebook, delayed taking his company's shares public through an initial public offering (IPO)? A: Facebook doesn't need to invest in factories, distribution systems, or even marketing, so it doesn't need to raise a lot of cash. Also, by not going public, Zuckerberg has more control over the direction of the company. In addition, publicly traded companies face many more financial reporting disclosure requirements.

**p. 579 How to Read Stock Quotes** Q: For stocks traded on organized stock exchanges, how are the dollar prices per share established? What factors might influence the price of shares in the marketplace? A: The dollar prices per share are established by the interaction between buyers and sellers of the shares. The prices of shares are influenced by a company's earnings and dividends as well as by factors beyond a company's control, such as changes in interest rates, labor strikes, scarcity of supplies or resources, and politics. The number of willing buyers and sellers (demand and supply) also plays a part in the price of shares.

**p. 588 A No-Split Philosophy** Q: Why does Warren Buffett usually oppose stock splits? A: Mr. Buffett prefers to attract shareholders that make a long-term commitment to his company, as opposed to traders that only hold their investment for a short period of time. He believes that a high stock price discourages short-term investment.

### Answers to Self-Test Questions

**1.** c **2.** b **3.** d **4.** c **5.** d **6.** d **7.** d $375,000 − ($100 × 10,000 × .08 × 3) **8.** d **9.** b **10.** d (100,000 × $30 × .10) **11.** c **12.** a **13.** c **14.** b **15.** b ($186,000 − $60,000) ÷ ((1,200,000 + $1,600,000) ÷ 2) **16.** d

## IFRS A Look at IFRS

The accounting for transactions related to stockholders' equity, such as issuance of shares, purchase of treasury stock, and declaration and payment of dividends, are similar under both IFRS and GAAP. Major differences relate to terminology used, introduction of items such as revaluation surplus, and presentation of stockholders' equity information.

### KEY POINTS

• Under IFRS, the term *reserves* is used to describe all equity accounts other than those arising from contributed capital. This would include, for example, reserves related to retained earnings, asset revaluations, and fair value differences.

• Many countries have a different mix of investor groups than in the United States. For example, in Germany, financial institutions like banks are not only major creditors of corporations but often are the largest corporate stockholders as well. In the United States, Asia, and the United Kingdom, many companies rely on substantial investment from private investors.

• There are often terminology differences for equity accounts. The following summarizes some of the common differences in terminology.

| GAAP | IFRS |
|---|---|
| Common stock | Share capital—ordinary |
| Stockholders | Shareholders |
| Par value | Nominal or face value |
| Authorized stock | Authorized share capital |
| Preferred stock | Preference shares |
| Paid-in capital | Issued/allocated share capital |
| Paid-in capital in excess of par—common stock | Share premium—ordinary |
| Paid-in capital in excess of par—preferred stock | Share premium—preference |
| Retained earnings | Retained earnings or Retained profits |
| Retained earnings deficit | Accumulated losses |
| Accumulated other comprehensive income | General reserve and other reserve accounts |

As an example of how similar transactions use different terminology under IFRS, consider the accounting for the issuance of 1,000 shares of $1 par value stock for $5 per share. Under IFRS, the entry is as follows.

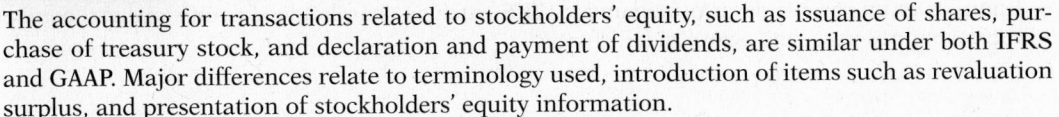

| | | |
|---|---|---|
| Cash | 5,000 | |
|   Share Capital—Ordinary | | 1,000 |
|   Share Premium—Ordinary | | 4,000 |

- The accounting for treasury stock differs somewhat between IFRS and GAAP. (However, many of the differences are beyond the scope of this course.) Like GAAP, IFRS does not allow a company to record gains or losses on purchases of its own shares. One difference worth noting is that, when a company purchases its own shares, IFRS treats it as a reduction of stockholders' equity, but it does not specify which particular stockholders' equity accounts are to be affected. Therefore, it could be shown as an increase to a contra equity account (Treasury Stock) or a decrease to retained earnings or share capital. IFRS requires that the number of treasury shares held be disclosed.

- A major difference between IFRS and GAAP relates to the account Revaluation Surplus. Revaluation surplus arises under IFRS because companies are permitted to revalue their property, plant, and equipment to fair value under certain circumstances. This account is part of general reserves under IFRS and is not considered contributed capital.

- As indicated earlier, the term *reserves* is used in IFRS to indicate all noncontributed (non–paid-in) capital. Reserves include retained earnings and other comprehensive income items, such as revaluation surplus and unrealized gains or losses on available-for-sale securities.

- IFRS often uses terms such as *retained profits* or *accumulated profit or loss* to describe retained earnings. The term *retained earnings* is also often used.

- The accounting related to prior period adjustments is essentially the same under IFRS and GAAP. IFRS addresses the accounting for errors in *IAS 8* ("Accounting Policies, Changes in Accounting Estimates, and Errors"). One area where IFRS and GAAP differ in reporting relates to error corrections in previously issued financial statements. While IFRS requires restatement with some exceptions, GAAP does not permit any exceptions.

- Equity is given various descriptions under IFRS, such as shareholders' equity, owners' equity, capital and reserves, and shareholders' funds.

## LOOKING TO THE FUTURE

As indicated in earlier discussions, the IASB and the FASB are currently working on a project related to financial statement presentation. An important part of this study is to determine whether certain line items, subtotals, and totals should be clearly defined and required to be displayed in the financial statements. For example, it is likely that the statement of stockholders' equity and its presentation will be examined closely. In addition, the options of how to present other comprehensive income under GAAP will change in any converged standard.

## IFRS Self-Test Questions

1. Under IFRS, a purchase by a company of its own shares is recorded by:
   (a) an increase in Treasury Stock.
   (b) a decrease in contributed capital.
   (c) a decrease in share capital.
   (d) All of these are acceptable treatments.
2. The term *reserves* is used under IFRS with reference to all of the following *except*:
   (a) gains and losses on revaluation of property, plant, and equipment.
   (b) capital received in excess of the par value of issued shares.
   (c) retained earnings.
   (d) fair value differences.
3. Under IFRS, the amount of capital received in excess of par value on ordinary shares would be credited to:
   (a) Retained Earnings.
   (b) Contributed Capital.
   (c) Share Premium—Ordinary.
   (d) Par value is not used under IFRS.
4. Which of the following is *false*?
   (a) Under GAAP, companies cannot record gains on transactions involving their own shares.
   (b) Under IFRS, companies cannot record gains on transactions involving their own shares.
   (c) Under IFRS, the statement of stockholders' equity is a required statement.
   (d) Under IFRS, a company records a revaluation surplus when it experiences an increase in the price of its common stock.

**5.** Which of the following does *not* represent a pair of GAAP/IFRS-comparable terms?
   (a) Additional paid-in capital/Share premium.
   (b) Treasury stock/Repurchase reserve.
   (c) Common stock/Share capital.
   (d) Preferred stock/Preference shares.

## IFRS Concepts and Application

**IFRS11-1**   On May 10, Romano Corporation issues 1,000 shares of $10 par value ordinary shares for cash at $18 per share. Journalize the issuance of the shares.

**IFRS11-2**   Ingram Corporation has the following accounts at December 31, 2012: Share Capital—Ordinary, €10 par, 5,000 shares issued, €50,000; Share Premium—Ordinary €10,000; Retained Earnings €45,000; and Treasury Shares—Ordinary, 500 shares, €11,000. Prepare the equity section of the statement of financial position.

**IFRS11-3**   Sorocaba Co. had the following transactions during the current period.

| | |
|---|---|
| June 12 | Issued 60,000 shares of $1 par value ordinary shares for cash of $375,000. |
| July 11 | Issued 1,000 shares of $100 par value preference shares for cash at $110 per share. |
| Nov. 28 | Purchased 2,000 treasury shares for $80,000. |

*Instructions*
Journalize the above transactions.

**IFRS11-4**   The January 25, 2005, edition of the *Wall Street Journal* has an article by Mary Kissel (on p. C1) entitled "Known for Growth, Asian Firms Answer Call of the Dividend."

*Instructions*
Read the article and answer the following questions.
   (a) What is the "dividend yield"? How does the dividend yield of Asian companies compare to that of companies in other regions?
   (b) What has happened to Asian company debt levels in recent years? What implications has this had for return on equity? Explain why this would be the case.
   (c) What measure is used to determine whether a company is paying out a high percentage of its earnings in the form of dividends? What percentage of their earnings are Asian firms paying out? According to the article, how have the stock prices of dividend-paying companies performed relative to non-dividend-paying companies? What explanations are given for this?

## INTERNATIONAL FINANCIAL REPORTING PROBLEM: *Zetar plc*

**IFRS11-5**   The financial statements of Zetar plc are presented in Appendix C. The company's complete annual report, including the notes to its financial statements, is available at **www.zetarplc.com**.

*Instructions*
Use the company's annual report to answer the following questions.
   (a) Using the information in the statement of changes in equity, prepare the journal entry to record the issuance of ordinary shares during the year ended April 30, 2009.
   (b) Compute the company's return on ordinary shareholders' equity for the year ended April 30, 2009.
   (c) Examine the equity section of the company's balance sheet. For each item in the equity section, provide the comparable label that would be used under GAAP.

### Answers to IFRS Self-Test Questions

**1.** d   **2.** b   **3.** c   **4.** d   **5.** b

---

✓ **Remember to go back to the navigator box on the chapter opening page and check off your completed work.**

chapter **12**

# STATEMENT OF CASH FLOWS

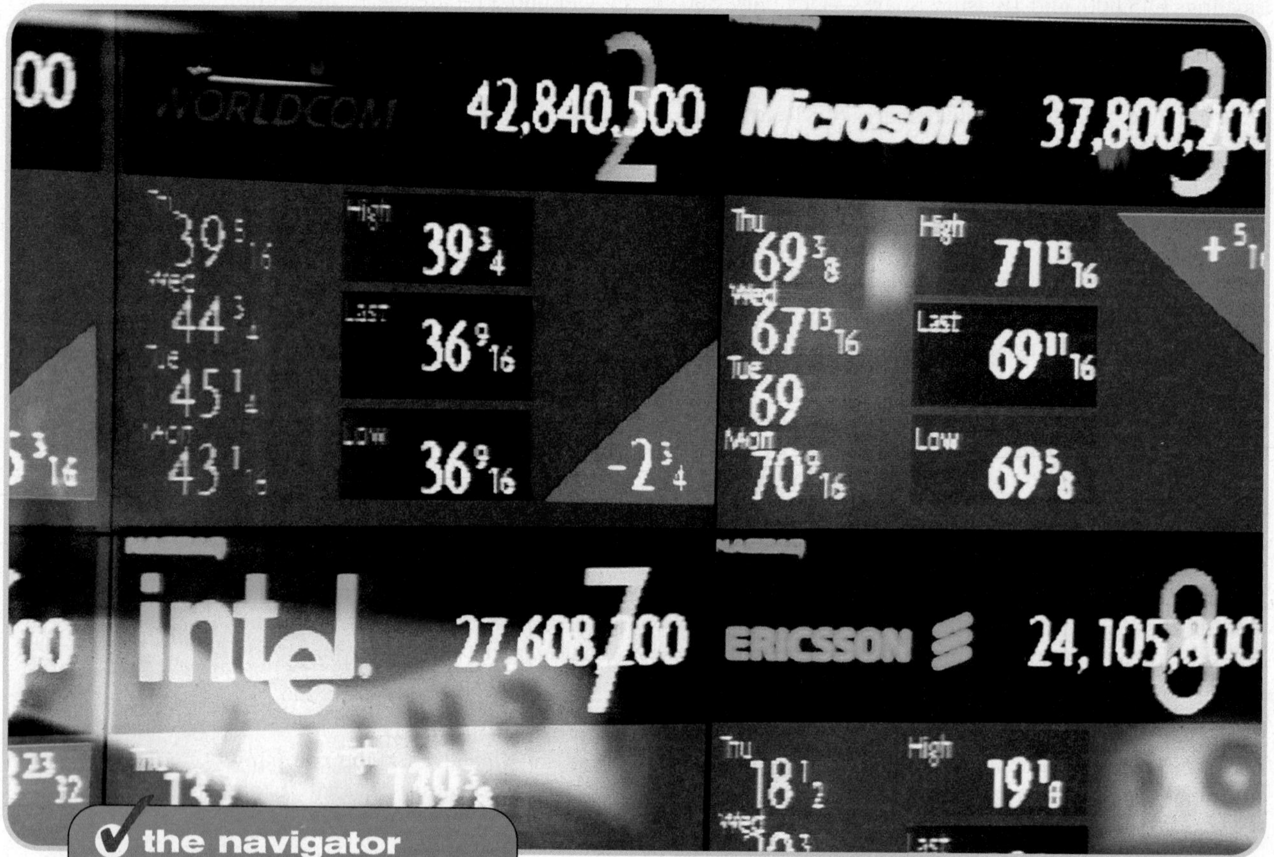


## the navigator

- Scan **Study Objectives** ○
- Read **Feature Story** ○
- Scan **Preview** ○
- Read **Text and Answer** **Do it!** p. 627 ○ p. 636 ○ p. 640 ○
- Work **Using the Decision Toolkit** ○
- Review **Summary of Study Objectives** ○
- Work **Comprehensive** **Do it!** p. 656 ○
- Answer **Self-Test Questions** ○
- Complete **Assignments** ○
- Go to **WileyPLUS** for practice and tutorials ○
- Read **A Look at IFRS** p. 680 ○

## study objectives

**After studying this chapter, you should be able to:**

1 Indicate the usefulness of the statement of cash flows.

2 Distinguish among operating, investing, and financing activities.

3 Explain the impact of the product life cycle on a company's cash flows.

4 Prepare a statement of cash flows using the indirect method.

5 Use the statement of cash flows to evaluate a company.

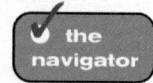

the navigator

In today's environment, companies must be ready to respond to changes quickly in order to survive and thrive. This requires that they manage their cash very carefully. One company that managed cash successfully in its early years was Microsoft. During those years, the company paid much of its payroll with stock options (rights to purchase company stock in the future at a given price) instead of cash. This strategy conserved cash and turned more than a thousand of its employees into millionaires during the company's first 20 years of business.

In recent years, Microsoft has had a different kind of cash problem. Now that it has reached a more "mature" stage in life, it generates so much cash—roughly $1 billion per month—that it cannot always figure out what to do with it. At one time, Microsoft had accumulated $60 billion.

The company said it was accumulating cash to invest in new opportunities, buy other companies, and pay off pending lawsuits. But for many years, the federal government blocked attempts by Microsoft to buy anything other than small firms because it feared that purchase of a large firm would only increase Microsoft's monopolistic position.

Microsoft's stockholders have complained for years that holding all this cash was putting a drag on the company's profitability. Why? Because Microsoft had the cash invested in very low-yielding government securities. Stockholders felt that the company either

## GOT CASH?

should find new investment projects that would bring higher returns, or return some of the cash to stockholders.

Finally, Microsoft announced a plan to return cash to stockholders, by paying a special one-time $32 billion dividend. This special dividend was so large that, according to the U.S. Commerce Department, it caused total personal income in the United States to rise by 3.7% in one month—the largest increase ever recorded by the agency. (It also made the holiday season brighter, especially for retailers in the Seattle area.) Microsoft also doubled its regular annual dividend to $3.50 per share. Further, it announced that it would spend another $30 billion buying treasury stock. In addition, Microsoft more recently offered to buy Yahoo for $44.6 billion (Yahoo declined the offer). Dividends, stock buybacks, and acquisitions will help to deplete some of its massive cash horde, but as you will see in this chapter, for a cash-generating machine like Microsoft, the company will be anything but cash-starved.

Interestingly, in 2010 Google found itself in a position similar to Microsoft's. Its cash pile of $26.5 billion was nearly 20% of the company's value. That's enough to pay a dividend of $80 per share. Unless it can find large, worthwhile projects to invest in, Google will also need to return a big chunk of its cash to shareholders.

*Source:* "Business: An End to Growth? Microsoft's Cash Bonanza," *The Economist* (July 23, 2005), p. 61.

the navigator

The balance sheet, income statement, and retained earnings statement do not always show the whole picture of the financial condition of a company or institution. In fact, looking at the financial statements of some well-known companies, a thoughtful investor might ask questions like these: How did Eastman Kodak finance cash dividends of $649 million in a year in which it earned only $17 million? How could United Airlines purchase new planes that cost $1.9 billion in a year in which it reported a net loss of over $2 billion? How did the companies that spent a combined fantastic $3.4 trillion on mergers and acquisitions in a recent year finance those deals? Answers to these and similar questions can be found in this chapter, which presents the statement of cash flows.

The content and organization of this chapter are as follows.

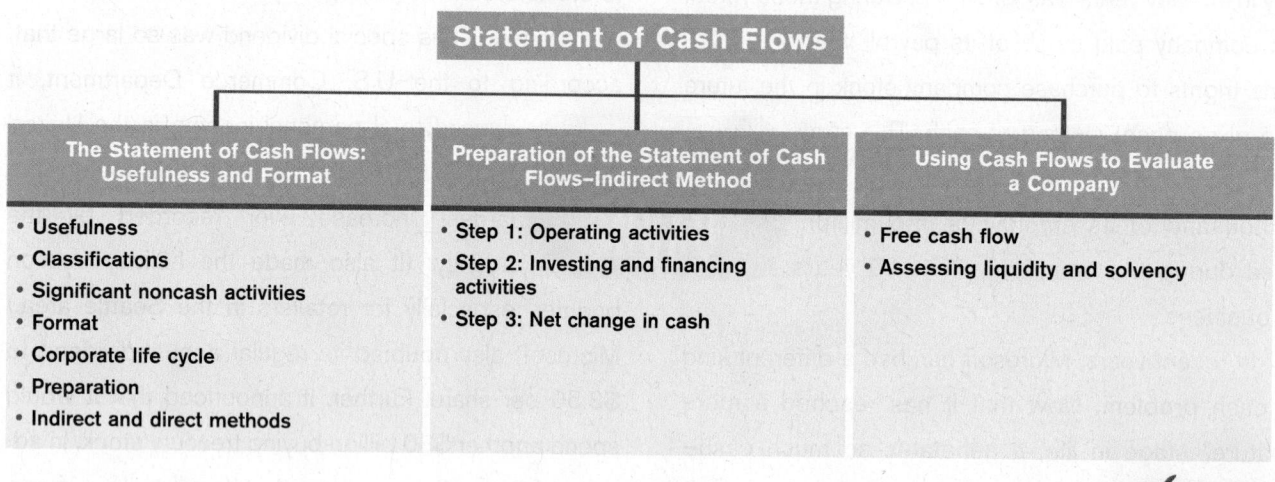

# The Statement of Cash Flows: Usefulness and Format

The balance sheet, income statement, and retained earnings statement provide only limited information about a company's cash flows (cash receipts and cash payments). For example, comparative balance sheets show the increase in property, plant, and equipment during the year. But they do not show how the additions were financed or paid for. The income statement shows net income. But it does not indicate the amount of cash generated by operating activities. The retained earnings statement shows cash dividends declared but not the cash dividends paid during the year. None of these statements presents a detailed summary of where cash came from and how it was used.

## USEFULNESS OF THE STATEMENT OF CASH FLOWS

**study objective** **1**

Indicate the usefulness of the statement of cash flows.

The statement of cash flows reports the cash receipts and cash payments from operating, investing, and financing activities during a period, in a format that reconciles the beginning and ending cash balances. The information in a statement of cash flows helps investors, creditors, and others assess:

1. **The entity's ability to generate future cash flows.** By examining relationships between items in the statement of cash flows, investors make predictions of the amounts, timing, and uncertainty of future cash flows better than they can from accrual-basis data.

2. **The entity's ability to pay dividends and meet obligations.** If a company does not have adequate cash, it cannot pay employees, settle debts, or pay dividends. Employees, creditors, and stockholders should be particularly interested in this statement because it alone shows the flows of cash in a business.

3. **The reasons for the difference between net income and net cash provided (used) by operating activities.** Net income provides information on the success or failure of a business enterprise. However, some financial statement users are critical of accrual-basis net income because it requires many estimates. As a result, users often challenge the reliability of the number. Such is not the case with cash. Many readers of the statement of cash flows want to know the reasons for the difference between net income and net cash provided by operating activities. Then they can assess for themselves the reliability of the income number.

4. **The cash investing and financing transactions during the period.** By examining a company's investing and financing transactions, a financial statement reader can better understand why assets and liabilities changed during the period.

## CLASSIFICATION OF CASH FLOWS

The statement of cash flows classifies cash receipts and cash payments as operating, investing, and financing activities. Transactions and other events characteristic of each kind of activity are as follows.

1. **Operating activities** include the cash effects of transactions that create revenues and expenses. They thus enter into the determination of net income.

2. **Investing activities** include (a) cash transactions that involve the purchase or disposal of investments and property, plant, and equipment, and (b) lending money and collecting the loans.

3. **Financing activities** include (a) obtaining cash from issuing debt and repaying the amounts borrowed, and (b) obtaining cash from stockholders, repurchasing shares, and paying dividends.

The operating activities category is the most important. It shows the cash provided by company operations. This source of cash is generally considered to be the best measure of a company's ability to generate sufficient cash to continue as a going concern.

Illustration 12-1 (page 626) lists typical cash receipts and cash payments within each of the three classifications. **Study the list carefully.** It will be very useful in solving homework exercises and problems.

Note the following general guidelines:

1. Operating activities involve income statement items.
2. Investing activities involve cash flows resulting from changes in investments and long-term asset items.
3. Financing activities involve cash flows resulting from changes in long-term liability and stockholders' equity items.

Companies classify as operating activities some cash flows related to investing or financing activities. For example, receipts of investment revenue (interest and dividends) are classified as operating activities. So are payments of interest to lenders. Why are these considered operating activities? **Because companies report these items in the income statement, where results of operations are shown.**

## SIGNIFICANT NONCASH ACTIVITIES

Not all of a company's significant activities involve cash. Examples of significant noncash activities are:

1. Direct issuance of common stock to purchase assets.
2. Conversion of bonds into common stock.
3. Direct issuance of debt to purchase assets.
4. Exchanges of plant assets.

**Ethics Note** Though we would discourage reliance on cash flows to the exclusion of accrual accounting, comparing cash from operations to net income can reveal important information about the "quality" of reported net income. Such a comparison can reveal the extent to which net income provides a good measure of actual performance.

**study objective   2**
Distinguish among operating, investing, and financing activities.

**International Note** The statement of cash flows is very similar under GAAP and IFRS. One difference is that, under IFRS, noncash investing and financing activities are not reported in the statement of cash flows but instead are reported in the notes to the financial statements.

**Illustration 12-1** Typical receipt and payment classifications

**Operating activities**

**Investing activities**

**Financing activities**

### Types of Cash Inflows and Outflows

**Operating activities—Income statement items**
 Cash inflows:
  From sale of goods or services.
  From interest received and dividends received.
 Cash outflows:
  To suppliers for inventory.
  To employees for services.
  To government for taxes.
  To lenders for interest.
  To others for expenses.

**Investing activities—Changes in investments and long-term assets**
 Cash inflows:
  From sale of property, plant, and equipment.
  From sale of investments in debt or equity securities of other entities.
  From collection of principal on loans to other entities.
 Cash outflows:
  To purchase property, plant, and equipment.
  To purchase investments in debt or equity securities of other entities.
  To make loans to other entities.

**Financing activities—Changes in long-term liabilities and stockholders' equity**
 Cash inflows:
  From sale of common stock.
  From issuance of debt (bonds and notes).
 Cash outflows:
  To stockholders as dividends.
  To redeem long-term debt or reacquire capital stock (treasury stock).

**Helpful Hint** Do not include **noncash** investing and financing activities in the body of the statement of cash flows. Report this information in a separate schedule below the statement of cash flows.

**Companies do not report in the body of the statement of cash flows significant financing and investing activities that do not affect cash.** Instead, they report these activities in either a **separate schedule** at the bottom of the statement of cash flows or in a **separate note or supplementary schedule** to the financial statements. The reporting of these noncash activities in a separate schedule satisfies the **full disclosure principle**.

*In solving homework assignments, you should present significant noncash investing and financing activities in a separate schedule at the bottom of the statement of cash flows. (See the last entry in Illustration 12-2 for an example.)*

## Accounting Across the Organization

### Net *What*?

Net income is not the same as net cash provided by operations. The differences are illustrated by the following results from recent annual reports ($ in millions). Note the wide disparity among these companies that all engaged in retail merchandising.

| Company | Net Income | Net Cash Provided by Operations |
|---|---|---|
| Kohl's Corporation | $ 1,083 | $ 1,234 |
| Wal-Mart Stores, Inc. | 11,284 | 20,169 |
| JCPenney Company, Inc. | 1,153 | 1,255 |
| Costco Wholesale Corp. | 1,082 | 2,076 |
| Target Corporation | 2,849 | 4,125 |

**?** In general, why do differences exist between net income and net cash provided by operating activities? (See page 680.)

## FORMAT OF THE STATEMENT OF CASH FLOWS

The general format of the statement of cash flows presents the results of the three activities discussed previously—operating, investing, and financing—plus the significant noncash investing and financing activities. Illustration 12–2 shows a widely used form of the statement of cash flows.

| | | |
|---|---|---|
| **COMPANY NAME** | | |
| Statement of Cash Flows | | |
| Period Covered | | |
| **Cash flows from operating activities** | | |
| (List of individual items) | XX | |
| Net cash provided (used) by operating activities | | XXX |
| **Cash flows from investing activities** | | |
| (List of individual inflows and outflows) | XX | |
| Net cash provided (used) by investing activities | | XXX |
| **Cash flows from financing activities** | | |
| (List of individual inflows and outflows) | XX | |
| Net cash provided (used) by financing activities | | XXX |
| **Net increase (decrease) in cash** | | XXX |
| **Cash at beginning of period** | | XXX |
| **Cash at end of period** | | XXX |
| **Noncash investing and financing activities** | | |
| (List of individual noncash transactions) | | XXX |

**Illustration 12-2** Format of statement of cash flows

The sum of the operating, investing, and financing sections equals the net increase or decrease in cash for the period. This amount is added to the beginning cash balance to arrive at the ending cash balance—the same amount reported on the balance sheet.

*before you go on...*

## Do it!

During its first week, Duffy & Stevenson Company had these transactions.

1. Issued 100,000 shares of $5 par value common stock for $800,000 cash.
2. Borrowed $200,000 from Castle Bank, signing a 5-year note bearing 8% interest.
3. Purchased two semi-trailer trucks for $170,000 cash.
4. Paid employees $12,000 for salaries and wages.
5. Collected $20,000 cash for services provided.

Classify each of these transactions by type of cash flow activity.

### Solution

1. Financing activity
2. Financing activity
3. Investing activity
4. Operating activity
5. Operating activity

Related exercise material: **BE12-1, BE12-2, BE12-3, Do it! 12-1, E12-1,** and **E12-2.**

**CASH FLOW ACTIVITIES**

**Action Plan**

- Identify the three types of activities used to report all cash inflows and outflows.

- Report as operating activities the cash effects of transactions that create revenues and expenses and enter into the determination of net income.

- Report as investing activities transactions that (a) acquire and dispose of investments and productive long-lived assets and (b) lend money and collect loans.

- Report as financing activities transactions that (a) obtain cash from issuing debt and repay the amounts borrowed and (b) obtain cash from stockholders and pay them dividends.

the navigator

## THE CORPORATE LIFE CYCLE

All products go through a series of phases called the **product life cycle**. The phases (in order of their occurrence) are **introductory phase**, **growth phase**, **maturity phase**, and **decline phase**. The introductory phase occurs at the beginning of a company's life, when it is purchasing fixed assets and beginning to produce and sell products. During the growth phase, the company is striving to expand its production and sales. In the maturity phase, sales and production level off. During the decline phase, sales of the product fall due to a weakening in consumer demand.

In the same way that products have life cycles, companies have life cycles as well. Companies generally have more than one product, and not all of a company's products are in the same phase of the product life cycle at the same time. This sometimes makes it difficult to classify a company's phase. Still, we can characterize a company as being in one of the four phases because the majority of its products are in a particular phase.

Illustration 12-3 shows that the phase a company is in affects its cash flows. In the **introductory phase**, we expect that the company will not be generating positive cash from operations. That is, cash used in operations will exceed cash generated by operations in the introductory phase. Also, the company will be spending considerable amounts to purchase productive assets such as buildings and equipment. To support its asset purchases, the company will have to issue stock or debt. Thus, during the introductory phase, we expect cash from operations to be negative, cash from investing to be negative, and cash from financing to be positive.

**Illustration 12-3** Impact of product life cycle on cash flows

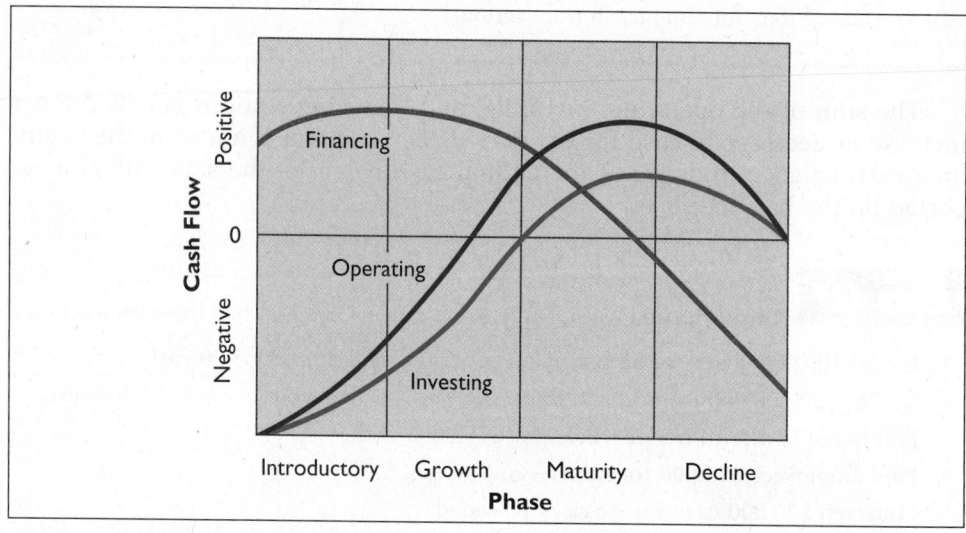

During the **growth phase**, we expect to see the company start to generate small amounts of cash from operations. During this phase, cash from operations on the statement of cash flows will be less than net income on the income statement. One reason income will exceed cash flow from operations during this period is explained by the difference between the cash paid for inventory and the amount expensed as cost of goods sold. Since the company projects increasing sales, the size of inventory purchases must increase. Thus, in the growth phase, the company will expense less inventory on an accrual basis than it purchases on a cash basis. Also, collections on accounts receivable will lag behind sales, and accrual sales during a period will exceed cash collections during that period. Cash needed for asset acquisitions will continue to exceed cash provided by operations, requiring that the company make up the deficiency by issuing new stock or debt. Thus, in the growth phase, the company continues to show negative cash from investing and positive cash from financing.

During the **maturity phase**, cash from operations and net income are approximately the same. Cash generated from operations exceeds investing needs. Thus, in the maturity phase, the company can start to pay dividends, retire debt, or buy back stock.

Finally, during the **decline phase**, cash from operations decreases. Cash from investing might actually become positive as the company sells off excess assets. Cash from financing may be negative as the company buys back stock and retires debt.

Consider Microsoft: During its early years, it had significant product development costs and little revenue. Microsoft was lucky in that its agreement with IBM to provide the operating system for IBM PCs gave it an early steady source of cash to support growth. As noted in the Feature Story, one way Microsoft conserved cash was to pay employees with stock options rather than cash. Today, Microsoft could best be characterized as being in the maturity phase. It continues to spend considerable amounts on research and development and investment in new assets. For the last three years, though, its cash from operations has exceeded its net income. Also, cash from operations over this period exceeded cash used for investing, and common stock repurchased exceeded common stock issued. For Microsoft, as for any large company, the challenge is to maintain its growth. In the software industry, where products become obsolete very quickly, the challenge is particularly great.

## Investor Insight

### Operating with Negative Cash

Listed here are recent amounts of net income and cash provided (used) by operations, investing, and financing for a variety of companies. The final column suggests their likely phase in the life cycle based on these figures.

| Company ($ in millions) | Net Income | Cash Provided (Used) by Operations | Cash Provided (Used) by Investing | Cash Provided (Used) by Financing | Likely Phase in Life Cycle |
|---|---|---|---|---|---|
| Amazon.com | $ 476 | $1,405 | $ (42) | $ (50) | Early maturity |
| LDK Solar | (144) | (81) | (329) | 462 | Introductory/ early growth |
| United States Steel | 879 | 1,745 | (4,675) | (1,891) | Maturity |
| Kellogg | 1,103 | 1,503 | (601) | (788) | Early decline |
| Southwest Airlines | 645 | 2,845 | (1,529) | 493 | Maturity |
| Starbucks | 673 | 1,331 | (1,202) | (172) | Maturity |

**?** Why do companies have negative cash from operations during the introductory phase? (See page 680.)

## PREPARING THE STATEMENT OF CASH FLOWS

Companies prepare the statement of cash flows differently from the three other basic financial statements. First, it is not prepared from an adjusted trial balance. It requires detailed information concerning the changes in account balances that occurred between two points in time. An adjusted trial balance will not provide the necessary data. Second, the statement of cash flows deals with cash receipts and payments. As a result, the company **must adjust** the effects of the use of accrual accounting **to determine cash flows**.

The information to prepare this statement usually comes from three sources:

- **Comparative balance sheets.** Information in the comparative balance sheets indicates the amount of the changes in assets, liabilities, and stockholders' equities from the beginning to the end of the period.

- **Current income statement.** Information in this statement helps determine the amount of cash provided or used by operations during the period.
- **Additional information.** Such information includes transaction data that are needed to determine how cash was provided or used during the period.

Preparing the statement of cash flows from these data sources involves three major steps, explained in Illustration 12-4 below.

**Illustration 12-4** Three major steps in preparing the statement of cash flows

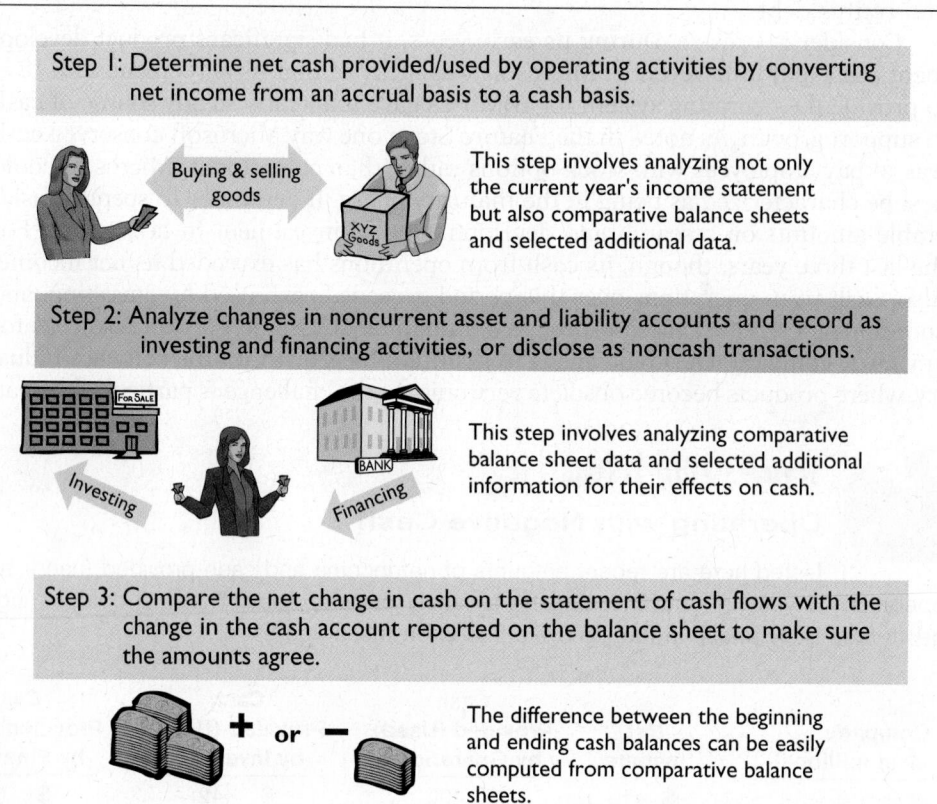

Step 1: Determine net cash provided/used by operating activities by converting net income from an accrual basis to a cash basis.

Buying & selling goods

This step involves analyzing not only the current year's income statement but also comparative balance sheets and selected additional data.

Step 2: Analyze changes in noncurrent asset and liability accounts and record as investing and financing activities, or disclose as noncash transactions.

Investing

Financing

This step involves analyzing comparative balance sheet data and selected additional information for their effects on cash.

Step 3: Compare the net change in cash on the statement of cash flows with the change in the cash account reported on the balance sheet to make sure the amounts agree.

+ or –

The difference between the beginning and ending cash balances can be easily computed from comparative balance sheets.

## INDIRECT AND DIRECT METHODS

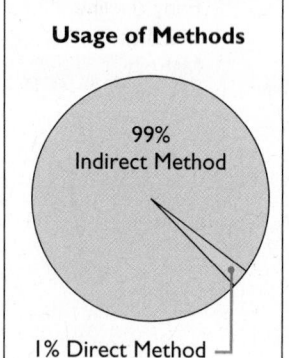

**Usage of Methods**

99% Indirect Method

1% Direct Method

In order to perform step 1, a company **must convert net income from an accrual basis to a cash basis**. This conversion may be done by either of two methods: (1) the indirect method or (2) the direct method. **Both methods arrive at the same total amount** for "Net cash provided by operating activities." They differ in **how** they arrive at the amount.

The indirect method adjusts net income for items that do not affect cash to determine net cash provided by operating activities. A great majority of companies (99%) use this method, as shown in the nearby chart.[1] Companies favor the indirect method for two reasons: (1) It is easier and less costly to prepare, and (2) it focuses on the differences between net income and net cash flow from operating activities.

The direct method shows operating cash receipts and payments. It is prepared by adjusting each item in the income statement from the accrual basis to the cash basis. The FASB has expressed a preference for the direct method, but allows the use of either method.

The next section illustrates the more popular indirect method. Appendix 12A illustrates the direct method. Appendix 12B demonstrates an approach that employs T accounts to prepare the statement of cash flows. Many students find the

---

[1]*Accounting Trends and Techniques—2009* (New York: American Institute of Certified Public Accountants, 2009).

T-account approach provides a useful structure. We encourage you to give it a try as you walk through the Computer Services example.

# Preparation of the Statement of Cash Flows—Indirect Method

To explain how to prepare a statement of cash flows using the indirect method, we use financial information from Computer Services Company. Illustration 12-5 presents Computer Services' current and previous-year balance sheets, its current-year income statement, and related financial information.

**study objective 4**

Prepare a statement of cash flows using the indirect method.

**Illustration 12-5**
Comparative balance sheets, income statement, and additional information for Computer Services Company

**COMPUTER SERVICES COMPANY**
Comparative Balance Sheets
December 31

| Assets | 2012 | 2011 | Change in Account Balance Increase/Decrease |
|---|---|---|---|
| Current assets | | | |
| Cash | $ 55,000 | $ 33,000 | $ 22,000 Increase |
| Accounts receivable | 20,000 | 30,000 | 10,000 Decrease |
| Inventory | 15,000 | 10,000 | 5,000 Increase |
| Prepaid expenses | 5,000 | 1,000 | 4,000 Increase |
| Property, plant, and equipment | | | |
| Land | 130,000 | 20,000 | 110,000 Increase |
| Buildings | 160,000 | 40,000 | 120,000 Increase |
| Accumulated depreciation—buildings | (11,000) | (5,000) | 6,000 Increase |
| Equipment | 27,000 | 10,000 | 17,000 Increase |
| Accumulated depreciation—equipment | (3,000) | (1,000) | 2,000 Increase |
| Total assets | $398,000 | $138,000 | |

| Liabilities and Stockholders' Equity | | | |
|---|---|---|---|
| Current liabilities | | | |
| Accounts payable | $ 28,000 | $ 12,000 | $ 16,000 Increase |
| Income taxes payable | 6,000 | 8,000 | 2,000 Decrease |
| Long-term liabilities | | | |
| Bonds payable | 130,000 | 20,000 | 110,000 Increase |
| Stockholders' equity | | | |
| Common stock | 70,000 | 50,000 | 20,000 Increase |
| Retained earnings | 164,000 | 48,000 | 116,000 Increase |
| Total liabilities and stockholders' equity | $398,000 | $138,000 | |

**COMPUTER SERVICES COMPANY**
Income Statement
For the Year Ended December 31, 2012

| | | |
|---|---|---|
| Revenues | | $507,000 |
| Cost of goods sold | $150,000 | |
| Operating expenses (excluding depreciation) | 111,000 | |
| Depreciation expense | 9,000 | |
| Loss on sale of equipment | 3,000 | |
| Interest expense | 42,000 | 315,000 |
| Income before income tax | | 192,000 |
| Income tax expense | | 47,000 |
| Net income | | $145,000 |

**Additional information for 2012:**
1. Depreciation expense was comprised of $6,000 for building and $3,000 for equipment.
2. The company sold equipment with a book value of $7,000 (cost $8,000, less accumulated depreciation $1,000) for $4,000 cash.
3. Issued $110,000 of long-term bonds in direct exchange for land.
4. A building costing $120,000 was purchased for cash. Equipment costing $25,000 was also purchased for cash.
5. Issued common stock for $20,000 cash.
6. The company declared and paid a $29,000 cash dividend.

We will now apply the three steps to the information provided for Computer Services Company.

### STEP 1: OPERATING ACTIVITIES

#### DETERMINE NET CASH PROVIDED/USED BY OPERATING ACTIVITIES BY CONVERTING NET INCOME FROM AN ACCRUAL BASIS TO A CASH BASIS

To determine net cash provided by operating activities under the indirect method, companies **adjust net income in numerous ways**. A useful starting point is to understand **why** net income must be converted to net cash provided by operating activities.

Under generally accepted accounting principles, most companies use the accrual basis of accounting. As you have learned, this basis requires that companies record revenue when earned and record expenses when incurred. Earned revenues may include credit sales for which the company has not yet collected cash. Expenses incurred may include some items that it has not yet paid in cash. Thus, under the accrual basis of accounting, net income is not the same as net cash provided by operating activities.

Therefore, under the **indirect method**, companies must adjust net income to convert certain items to the cash basis. The indirect method (or reconciliation method) starts with net income and converts it to net cash provided by operating activities. Illustration 12-6 lists the three types of adjustments.

| Net Income   +/− | Adjustments | = Net Cash Provided/ Used by Operating Activities |
|---|---|---|
| | • **Add back noncash expenses**, such as depreciation expense, amortization, or depletion. | |
| | • **Deduct gains and add losses** that resulted from investing and financing activities. | |
| | • **Analyze changes** to noncash current asset and current liability accounts. | |

We explain the three types of adjustments in the next three sections.

### Depreciation Expense

Computer Services' income statement reports depreciation expense of $9,000. Although depreciation expense reduces net income, it does not reduce cash. In other words, depreciation expense is a noncash charge. The company must add it back to net income to arrive at net cash provided by operating activities.

Computer Services reports depreciation expense as follows in the statement of cash flows.

**Illustration 12-7**
Adjustment for depreciation

| Cash flows from operating activities | |
|---|---|
| Net income | $145,000 |
| Adjustments to reconcile net income to net cash provided by operating activities: | |
| **Depreciation expense** | 9,000 |
| Net cash provided by operating activities | $154,000 |

As the first adjustment to net income in the statement of cash flows, companies frequently list depreciation and similar noncash charges such as amortization of intangible assets, depletion expense, and bad debt expense.

## Loss on Sale of Equipment

Illustration 12-1 states that the investing activities section should report cash received from the sale of plant assets. Because of this, **companies must eliminate from net income all gains and losses resulting from investing activities, to arrive at cash provided by operating activities**.

In our example, Computer Services' income statement reports a $3,000 loss on the sale of equipment (book value $7,000, less cash received from sale of equipment $4,000). The company's loss of $3,000 should be eliminated in the operating activities section of the statement of cash flows. Illustration 12-8 shows that the $3,000 loss is eliminated by adding $3,000 back to net income to arrive at net cash provided by operating activities.

**Illustration 12-8**
Adjustment for loss on sale of equipment

| Cash flows from operating activities | | |
|---|---|---|
| Net income | | $145,000 |
| Adjustments to reconcile net income to net cash provided by operating activities: | | |
| Depreciation expense | $9,000 | |
| **Loss on sale of equipment** | 3,000 | 12,000 |
| Net cash provided by operating activities | | $157,000 |

If a gain on sale occurs, the company deducts the gain from its net income in order to determine net cash provided by operating activities. **In the case of either a gain or a loss, companies report the actual amount of cash received from the sale as a source of cash in the investing activities section of the statement of cash flows.**

## Changes to Noncash Current Asset and Current Liability Accounts

A final adjustment in reconciling net income to net cash provided by operating activities involves examining all changes in current asset and current liability accounts. The accrual-accounting process records revenues in the period earned and expenses in the period incurred. For example, companies use Accounts Receivable to record amounts owed to the company for sales that have been made but for which cash collections have not yet been received. They use the Prepaid Insurance account to reflect insurance that has been paid for, but which has not yet expired, and therefore has not been expensed. Similarly, the Salaries and Wages Payable account reflects salaries expense that has been incurred by the company but has not been paid.

As a result, we need to adjust net income for these accruals and prepayments to determine net cash provided by operating activities. Thus, we must analyze the change in each current asset and current liability account to determine its impact on net income and cash.

**CHANGES IN NONCASH CURRENT ASSETS.** The adjustments required for changes in noncash current asset accounts are as follows: **Deduct from net income increases in current asset accounts, and add to net income decreases in current asset accounts, to arrive at net cash provided by operating activities.** We can observe these relationships by analyzing the accounts of Computer Services Company.

**DECREASE IN ACCOUNTS RECEIVABLE.** Computer Services Company's accounts receivable decreased by $10,000 (from $30,000 to $20,000) during the period. For Computer Services, this means that cash receipts were $10,000 higher than revenues. The Accounts Receivable account in Illustration 12-9 shows that Computer Services Company had $507,000 in revenues (as reported on the income statement), but it collected $517,000 in cash.

**Illustration 12-9** Analysis of accounts receivable

| Accounts Receivable | | | | |
|---|---|---|---|---|
| 1/1/12 | Balance | 30,000 | **Receipts from customers** | 517,000 |
| | Revenues | 507,000 | | |
| 12/31/12 | Balance | 20,000 | | |

As shown in Illustration 12-10, to adjust net income to net cash provided by operating activities, the company adds to net income the decrease of $10,000 in accounts receivable.

**Illustration 12-10** Adjustments for changes in current asset accounts

| Cash flows from operating activities | | |
|---|---|---|
| Net income | | $145,000 |
| Adjustments to reconcile net income to net cash provided by operating activities: | | |
| Depreciation expense | $ 9,000 | |
| Loss on sale of equipment | 3,000 | |
| Decrease in accounts receivable | 10,000 | |
| Increase in inventory | (5,000) | |
| Increase in prepaid expenses | (4,000) | 13,000 |
| Net cash provided by operating activities | | $158,000 |

When the Accounts Receivable balance increases, cash receipts are lower than revenue earned under the accrual basis. Therefore, the company deducts from net income the amount of the increase in accounts receivable, to arrive at net cash provided by operating activities.

**INCREASE IN INVENTORY.** Computer Services Company's Inventory balance increased $5,000 (from $10,000 to $15,000) during the period. The change in the Inventory account reflects the difference between the amount of inventory purchased and the amount sold. For Computer Services, this means that the cost of merchandise purchased exceeded the cost of goods sold by $5,000. As a result, cost of goods sold does not reflect $5,000 of cash payments made for merchandise. The company deducts from net income this inventory increase of $5,000 during the period, to arrive at net cash provided by operating activities (see Illustration 12-10). If inventory decreases, the company adds to net income the amount of the change, to arrive at net cash provided by operating activities.

**INCREASE IN PREPAID EXPENSES.** Computer Services' prepaid expenses increased during the period by $4,000. This means that cash paid for expenses is higher than expenses reported on an accrual basis. In other words, the company has made cash payments in the current period but will not charge expenses to income until future periods (as charges to the income statement). To adjust net income to net cash provided by operating activities, the company deducts from net income the $4,000 increase in prepaid expenses (see Illustration 12-10).

If prepaid expenses decrease, reported expenses are higher than the expenses paid. Therefore, the company adds to net income the decrease in prepaid expense, to arrive at net cash provided by operating activities.

**CHANGES IN CURRENT LIABILITIES.** The adjustments required for changes in current liability accounts are as follows: **Add to net income increases in current liability accounts, and deduct from net income decreases in current liability accounts, to arrive at net cash provided by operating activities.**

**INCREASE IN ACCOUNTS PAYABLE.** For Computer Services Company, Accounts Payable increased by $16,000 (from $12,000 to $28,000) during the period. That means the company received $16,000 more in goods than it actually paid for. As shown in Illustration 12-11 (below), to adjust net income to determine net cash provided by operating activities, the company adds to net income the $16,000 increase in Accounts Payable.

**DECREASE IN INCOME TAXES PAYABLE.** When a company incurs income tax expense but has not yet paid its taxes, it records income taxes payable. A change in the Income Taxes Payable account reflects the difference between income tax expense incurred and income tax actually paid. Computer Services' Income Taxes Payable account decreased by $2,000. That means the $47,000 of income tax expense reported on the income statement was $2,000 less than the amount of taxes paid during the period of $49,000. As shown in Illustration 12-11, to adjust net income to a cash basis, the company must reduce net income by $2,000.

**Illustration 12-11**
Adjustments for changes in current liability accounts

| Cash flows from operating activities | | |
|---|---|---|
| Net income | | $145,000 |
| Adjustments to reconcile net income to net cash | | |
| provided by operating activities: | | |
| Depreciation expense | $ 9,000 | |
| Loss on sale of equipment | 3,000 | |
| Decrease in accounts receivable | 10,000 | |
| Increase in inventory | (5,000) | |
| Increase in prepaid expenses | (4,000) | |
| Increase in accounts payable | 16,000 | |
| Decrease in income taxes payable | (2,000) | 27,000 |
| Net cash provided by operating activities | | $172,000 |

Illustration 12-11 shows that, after starting with net income of $145,000, the sum of all of the adjustments to net income was $27,000. This resulted in net cash provided by operating activities of $172,000.

## SUMMARY OF CONVERSION TO NET CASH PROVIDED BY OPERATING ACTIVITIES—INDIRECT METHOD

As shown in the previous illustrations, the statement of cash flows prepared by the indirect method starts with net income. It then adds or deducts items to arrive at net cash provided by operating activities. The required adjustments are of three types:

1. Noncash charges such as depreciation, amortization, and depletion.
2. Gains and losses from investing and financing transactions, such as the sale of plant assets.
3. Changes in noncash current asset and current liability accounts.

Illustration 12-12 provides a summary of these changes.

**Illustration 12-12**
Adjustments required to convert net income to net cash provided by operating activities

| | | Adjustment Required to Convert Net Income to Net Cash Provided by Operating Activities |
|---|---|---|
| **Noncash charges** | Depreciation expense | Add |
| | Patent amortization expense | Add |
| **Gains and losses** | Loss on sale of plant asset | Add |
| | Gain on sale of plant asset | Deduct |
| **Changes in current assets and current liabilities** | Increase in current asset account | Deduct |
| | Decrease in current asset account | Add |
| | Increase in current liability account | Add |
| | Decrease in current liability account | Deduct |

## ANATOMY OF A FRAUD

For more than a decade, the top executives at the Italian dairy products company Parmalat engaged in multiple frauds which overstated cash and other assets by more than $1 billion while understating liabilities by between $8 and $12 billion. Much of the fraud involved creating fictitious sources and uses of cash. Some of these activities incorporated sophisticated financial transactions with subsidiaries created with the help of large international financial institutions. However, much of the fraud employed very basic, even sloppy, forgery of documents. For example, when outside auditors requested confirmation of bank accounts (such as a fake $4.8 billion account in the Cayman Islands), documents were created on scanners, with signatures that were cut and pasted from other documents. These were then passed through a fax machine numerous times to make them look real (if difficult to read). Similarly, fictitious bills were created in order to divert funds to other businesses owned by the Tanzi family (who controlled Parmalat).

**Total take: Billions of dollars**

**THE MISSING CONTROL**

*Independent internal verification.* Internal auditors at the company should have independently verified bank accounts and major transfers of cash to outside companies that were controlled by the Tanzi family.

## before you go on...

**NET CASH PROVIDED BY OPERATING ACTIVITIES**

**Do it!** Josh's PhotoPlus reported net income of $73,000 for 2012. Included in the income statement were depreciation expense of $7,000 and a gain on sale of equipment of $2,500. Josh's comparative balance sheets show the following balances.

| | 12/31/12 | 12/31/11 |
|---|---|---|
| Accounts Receivable | $21,000 | $17,000 |
| Accounts Payable | 2,200 | 6,000 |

Calculate net cash provided by operating activities for Josh's PhotoPlus.

## Solution

| | | |
|---|---:|---:|
| Cash flows from operating activities | | |
| Net income | | $73,000 |
| Adjustments to reconcile net income to net cash | | |
| provided by operating activities: | | |
| Depreciation expense | $ 7,000 | |
| Gain on sale of equipment | (2,500) | |
| Increase in accounts receivable | (4,000) | |
| Decrease in accounts payable | (3,800) | (3,300) |
| Net cash provided by operating activities | | $69,700 |

Related exercise material: **BE12-5, BE12-6, BE12-7, Do it! 12-2, E12-4,** and **E12-5.**

### Action Plan

- Add noncash charges such as depreciation back to net income to compute net cash provided by operating activities.
- Deduct gains and add back losses from the sale of plant assets to compute net cash provided by operating activities.
- Use changes in noncash current asset and current liability accounts to compute net cash provided by operating activities.

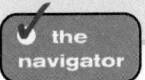

## STEP 2: INVESTING AND FINANCING ACTIVITIES

### ANALYZE CHANGES IN NONCURRENT ASSET AND LIABILITY ACCOUNTS AND RECORD AS INVESTING AND FINANCING ACTIVITIES, OR DISCLOSE AS NONCASH TRANSACTIONS

**INCREASE IN LAND.** As indicated from the change in the Land account and the additional information, the company purchased land of $110,000 by directly exchanging bonds for land. The exchange of bonds payable for land has no effect on cash. But it is a significant noncash investing and financing activity that merits disclosure in a separate schedule. (See Illustration 12–14 on page 638.)

**INCREASE IN BUILDINGS.** As the additional data indicate, Computer Services Company acquired an office building for $120,000 cash. This is a cash outflow reported in the investing section. (See Illustration 12–14 on page 638.)

**INCREASE IN EQUIPMENT.** The Equipment account increased $17,000. The additional information explains that this was a net increase that resulted from two transactions: (1) a purchase of equipment of $25,000, and (2) the sale for $4,000 of equipment costing $8,000. These transactions are both investing activities. The company should report each transaction separately. Thus, it reports the purchase of equipment as an outflow of cash for $25,000. It reports the sale as an inflow of cash for $4,000. The T account below shows the reasons for the change in this account during the year.

*Helpful Hint* The investing and financing activities are measured and reported the same under both the direct and indirect methods.

*Ethics Note* Because investors and management bonus contracts often focus on cash flow from operations, some managers have taken unethical actions to artificially increase cash flow from operations. For example, Dynegy restated its statement of cash flows because it had improperly included in operating activities $300 million that should have been reported as financing activities. This increased cash from operating activities by 37%.

**Illustration 12-13**
Analysis of equipment

| Equipment | | | |
|---|---:|---|---:|
| 1/1/12 Balance | 10,000 | Cost of equipment sold | 8,000 |
| Purchase of equipment | 25,000 | | |
| 12/31/12 Balance | 27,000 | | |

The following entry shows the details of the equipment sale transaction.

| | | |
|---|---:|---:|
| Cash | 4,000 | |
| Accumulated Depreciation | 1,000 | |
| Loss on Disposal of Plant Assets | 3,000 | |
| Equipment | | 8,000 |

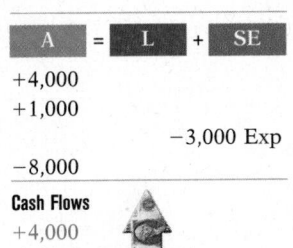

A = L + SE
+4,000
+1,000
−3,000 Exp
−8,000

Cash Flows
+4,000

**INCREASE IN BONDS PAYABLE.** The Bonds Payable account increased $110,000. As indicated in the additional information, the company acquired land by directly exchanging bonds for land. It reports this noncash transaction in a separate schedule at the bottom of the statement.

**Helpful Hint** When companies issue stocks or bonds for cash, the actual proceeds will appear in the statement of cash flows as a financing inflow (rather than the par value of the stocks or face value of bonds).

**INCREASE IN COMMON STOCK.** The balance sheet reports an increase in Common Stock of $20,000. The additional information section notes that this increase resulted from the issuance of new shares of stock. This is a cash inflow reported in the financing section.

**INCREASE IN RETAINED EARNINGS.** Retained earnings increased $116,000 during the year. This increase can be explained by two factors: (1) Net income of $145,000 increased retained earnings and (2) dividends of $29,000 decreased retained earnings. The company adjusts net income to net cash provided by operating activities in the operating activities section. Payment of the dividends (not the declaration) is a **cash outflow that the company reports as a financing activity**.

### Statement of Cash Flows–2012

Using the previous information, we can now prepare a statement of cash flows for 2012 for Computer Services Company, as shown in Illustration 12-14.

**Illustration 12-14**
Statement of cash flows, 2012–indirect method

**Helpful Hint** Note that in the investing and financing activities sections, positive numbers indicate cash inflows (receipts), and negative numbers indicate cash outflows (payments).

**COMPUTER SERVICES COMPANY**
Statement of Cash Flows–Indirect Method
For the Year Ended December 31, 2012

| | | |
|---|---:|---:|
| Cash flows from operating activities | | |
| Net income | | $ 145,000 |
| Adjustments to reconcile net income to net cash provided by operating activities: | | |
| Depreciation expense | $ 9,000 | |
| Loss on sale of equipment | 3,000 | |
| Decrease in accounts receivable | 10,000 | |
| Increase in inventory | (5,000) | |
| Increase in prepaid expenses | (4,000) | |
| Increase in accounts payable | 16,000 | |
| Decrease in income taxes payable | (2,000) | 27,000 |
| Net cash provided by operating activities | | 172,000 |
| Cash flows from investing activities | | |
| Sale of equipment | 4,000 | |
| Purchase of building | (120,000) | |
| Purchase of equipment | (25,000) | |
| Net cash used by investing activities | | (141,000) |
| Cash flows from financing activities | | |
| Issuance of common stock | 20,000 | |
| Payment of cash dividends | (29,000) | |
| Net cash used by financing activities | | (9,000) |
| Net increase in cash | | 22,000 |
| Cash at beginning of period | | 33,000 |
| Cash at end of period | | $ 55,000 |
| **Noncash investing and financing activities** | | |
| Issuance of bonds payable to purchase land | | $ 110,000 |

## STEP 3: NET CHANGE IN CASH

### COMPARE THE NET CHANGE IN CASH ON THE STATEMENT OF CASH FLOWS WITH THE CHANGE IN THE CASH ACCOUNT REPORTED ON THE BALANCE SHEET TO MAKE SURE THE AMOUNTS AGREE

Illustration 12-14 indicates that the net change in cash during the period was an increase of $22,000. This agrees with the change in Cash account reported on the balance sheet in Illustration 12-5 (page 631).

# Using Cash Flows to Evaluate a Company

Traditionally, investors and creditors have most commonly used ratios based on accrual accounting. These days, cash-based ratios are gaining increased acceptance among analysts. In this section, we review free cash flow and introduce two new measures.

**study objective 5**

Use the statement of cash flows to evaluate a company.

### FREE CASH FLOW

In the statement of cash flows, cash provided by operating activities is intended to indicate the cash-generating capability of the company. Analysts have noted, however, that **cash provided by operating activities fails to take into account that a company must invest in new fixed assets** just to maintain its current level of operations. Companies also must at least **maintain dividends at current levels** to satisfy investors. As we discussed in Chapter 2, the measurement of free cash flow provides additional insight regarding a company's cash-generating ability. **Free cash flow** describes the cash remaining from operations after adjustment for capital expenditures and dividends.

Consider the following example: Suppose that MPC produced and sold 10,000 personal computers this year. It reported $100,000 cash provided by operating activities. In order to maintain production at 10,000 computers, MPC invested $15,000 in equipment. It chose to pay $5,000 in dividends. Its free cash flow was $80,000 ($100,000 − $15,000 − $5,000). The company could use this $80,000 either to purchase new assets, pay off debt, or pay an $80,000 dividend. In practice, free cash flow is often calculated with the formula in Illustration 12-15. Alternative definitions also exist.

| Free Cash Flow | = | Cash Provided by Operations | − | Capital Expenditures | − | Cash Dividends |
|---|---|---|---|---|---|---|

**Illustration 12-15** Free cash flow

Illustration 12-16 provides basic information excerpted from the 2009 statement of cash flows of Microsoft Corporation.

**MICROSOFT CORPORATION**
Statement of Cash Flows Information (partial)
2009

| | | |
|---|---:|---:|
| Cash provided by operations | | $19,037 |
| Cash flows from investing activities | | |
| Additions to property and equipment | $ (3,119) | |
| Purchases of investments | (36,850) | |
| Sales of investments | 19,806 | |
| Acquisitions of companies | (868) | |
| Maturities of investments | 6,191 | |
| Securities lending payable | (930) | |
| Cash used by investing activities | | (15,770) |
| Cash paid for dividends | | (4,468) |

**Illustration 12-16**
Microsoft cash flow information ($ in millions)

Microsoft's free cash flow is calculated as shown in Illustration 12-17.

**Illustration 12-17**
Calculation of Microsoft's free cash flow ($ in millions)

| | |
|---|---|
| Cash provided by operating activities | $19,037 |
| Less: Expenditures on property, plant, and equipment | 3,119 |
| Dividends paid | 4,468 |
| Free cash flow | $11,450 |

Microsoft generated approximately $11.4 billion of free cash flow. This is a tremendous amount of cash generated in a single year. It is available for the acquisition of new assets, the retirement of stock or debt, or the payment of dividends.

Also note that Microsoft's cash from operations of $19 billion exceeds its 2009 net income of $14.6 billion. This lends additional credibility to Microsoft's income number as an indicator of potential future performance. If anything, Microsoft's net income might understate its actual performance.

Oracle Corporation is one of the world's largest sellers of database software and information management services. Like Microsoft, its success depends on continuing to improve its existing products while developing new products to keep pace with rapid changes in technology. Oracle's free cash flow for 2009 was $7.5 billion. This is impressive but significantly less than Microsoft's amazing ability to generate cash.

*before you go on...*

**FREE CASH FLOW**

 Chicago Corporation issued the following statement of cash flows for 2012.

**CHICAGO CORPORATION**
Statement of Cash Flows–Indirect Method
For the Year Ended December 31, 2012

| | | |
|---|---|---|
| Cash flows from operating activities | | |
| Net income | | $19,000 |
| Adjustments to reconcile net income to net cash provided by operating activities: | | |
| Depreciation expense | $ 8,100 | |
| Loss on sale of equipment | 1,300 | |
| Decrease in accounts receivable | 6,900 | |
| Increase in inventory | (4,000) | |
| Decrease in accounts payable | (2,000) | 10,300 |
| Net cash provided by operating activities | | 29,300 |
| Cash flows from investing activities | | |
| Sale of investments | 1,100 | |
| Purchase of equipment | (19,000) | |
| Net cash used by investing activities | | (17,900) |
| Cash flows from financing activities | | |
| Issuance of stock | 10,000 | |
| Payment on long-term note payable | (5,000) | |
| Payment for dividends | (9,000) | |
| Net cash used by financing activities | | (4,000) |
| Net increase in cash | | 7,400 |
| Cash at beginning of year | | 10,000 |
| Cash at end of year | | $17,400 |

(a) Compute free cash flow for Chicago Corporation. (b) Explain why free cash flow often provides better information than "Net cash provided by operating activities."

**Solution**

(a) Free cash flow = $29,300 − $19,000 − $9,000 = $1,300
(b) Cash provided by operating activities fails to take into account that a company must invest in new plant assets just to maintain the current level of operation. Companies must also maintain dividends at current levels to satisfy investors. The measurement of free cash flow provides additional insight regarding a company's cash-generating ability.

Related exercise material: **BE12-9, BE12-10, BE12-11, BE12-12, Do it! 12-3, E12-9,** and **E12-10.**

**Action Plan**

• Compute free cash flow as: Cash provided by operating activities − Capital expenditures − Cash dividends.

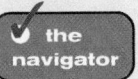 the navigator

# DECISION TOOLKIT

| DECISION CHECKPOINTS | INFO NEEDED FOR DECISION | TOOL TO USE FOR DECISION | HOW TO EVALUATE RESULTS |
|---|---|---|---|
| How much cash did the company generate to either expand operations or pay dividends? | Cash provided by operating activities, cash spent on fixed assets, and cash dividends | $\text{Free cash flow} = \text{Cash provided by operations} - \text{Capital expenditures} - \text{Cash dividends}$ | Significant free cash flow indicates greater potential to finance new investment and pay additional dividends. |

**KEEPING AN EYE ON CASH**

Cash flow is closely monitored by analysts and investors for many reasons and in a variety of ways. One measure that is gaining increased attention is "price to cash flow." This is a variant of the price to earnings (P-E) ratio, which has been a staple of analysts for a long time. The difference is that rather than divide the company's stock price by its earnings per share (an accrual-accounting–based number), the price to cash flow ratio divides the company's stock price by its cash flow per share. A high measure suggests that the stock price is high relative to the company's ability to generate cash. A low measure indicates that the company's stock might be a bargain.

The average price to cash flow ratio for companies in the Standard and Poor's 500-stock index was recently 13.6, when the average price-earnings ratio was 21.9. The following table provides values for some well-known companies. While you should not use this measure as the sole factor in choosing a stock, it can serve as a useful screen by which to identify companies that merit further investigation.

| Company | Price/Cash Flow | Price/EPS |
|---|---|---|
| Microsoft | 11.9 | 14.0 |
| Kellogg | 12.1 | 15.8 |
| Nike | 16.5 | 20.0 |
| Wal-Mart | 8.5 | 13.4 |
| Ford | 2.8 | 7.1 |
| AirTran | 4.4 | 7.7 |

## ASSESSING LIQUIDITY AND SOLVENCY USING CASH FLOWS

Previous chapters have presented ratios used to analyze a company's liquidity and solvency. Many of those ratios used accrual-based numbers from the income statement and balance sheet. In this section, we focus on ratios that are *cash-based* rather than accrual-based. That is, instead of using numbers from the income statement, these ratios use numbers from the statement of cash flows.

As discussed earlier, many analysts are critical of accrual-based numbers because they feel that the adjustment process allows too much management discretion. These analysts like to supplement accrual-based analysis with measures that use the cash flow statement. One disadvantage of these cash-based measures is that, unlike the more commonly employed accrual-based measures, there are no readily available industry averages for comparison. In the following discussion, we use cash flow-based ratios to analyze Microsoft. In addition to the cash flow information provided in Illustration 12-16 (page 639), we need the following information related to Microsoft.

| ($ in millions) | 2009 | 2008 |
|---|---|---|
| Current liabilities | $27,034 | $29,886 |
| Total liabilities | 38,330 | 36,507 |

## Liquidity

*Liquidity* is the ability to pay obligations expected to become due within the next year. In Chapter 2, you learned that one measure of liquidity is the *current ratio*: current assets divided by current liabilities. A disadvantage of the current ratio is that it uses year-end balances of current asset and current liability accounts. These year-end balances may not be representative of the company's position during most of the year.

A ratio that partially corrects this problem is the **current cash debt coverage ratio**. It is computed as cash provided by operating activities divided by average current liabilities. Because cash provided by operating activities involves the entire year rather than a balance at one point in time, this ratio is often considered a better representation of liquidity on the average day. In general, a value below .40 times is cause for additional investigation of a company's liquidity. Illustration 12-18 shows the current cash debt coverage ratio for Microsoft, with comparative numbers for Oracle. For comparative purposes, we have also provided each company's current ratio.

**Illustration 12-18**
Current cash debt coverage ratio

$$\text{Current Cash Debt Coverage Ratio} = \frac{\text{Cash Provided by Operations}}{\text{Average Current Liabilities}}$$

| | Current cash debt coverage ratio | Current ratio |
|---|---|---|
| **Microsoft** ($ in millions) | $\dfrac{\$19,037}{(\$27,034 + \$29,886)/2} = $ .67 times | 1.82:1 |
| **Oracle** | .86 times | 2.03:1 |

Microsoft's net cash provided by operating activities is .67 times its average current liabilities. Oracle's ratio of .86 times is even stronger than that of Microsoft. Both companies far exceed the threshold of .40 times. Keep in mind that Microsoft's cash position is extraordinary. For example, many large companies now have current ratios in the range of 1.0. By this standard, Oracle's current ratio of 2.03:1 and Microsoft's current ratio of 1.82:1 are both strong.

## DECISION TOOLKIT

| DECISION CHECKPOINTS | INFO NEEDED FOR DECISION | TOOL TO USE FOR DECISION | HOW TO EVALUATE RESULTS |
|---|---|---|---|
| Is the company generating sufficient cash provided by operating activities to meet its current obligations? | Cash provided by operating activities and average current liabilities | Current cash debt coverage ratio $= \dfrac{\text{Cash provided by operations}}{\text{Average current liabilities}}$ | A high value suggests good liquidity. Since the numerator contains a "flow" measure, it provides a good supplement to the current ratio. |

### Solvency

*Solvency* is the ability of a company to survive over the long term. A measure of solvency that uses cash figures is the **cash debt coverage ratio**. It is computed as the ratio of cash provided by operating activities to total debt as represented by average total liabilities. This ratio indicates a company's ability to repay its liabilities from cash generated from operations—that is, without having to liquidate productive assets such as property, plant, and equipment. A general rule of thumb is that a cash debt coverage ratio below .20 times is cause for additional investigation.

Illustration 12-19 shows the cash debt coverage ratios for Microsoft and Oracle for 2009. For comparative purposes, we have also provided the debt to total assets ratios for each company.

**Illustration 12-19**   Cash debt coverage ratio

| Cash Debt Coverage Ratio | $=\dfrac{\text{Cash Provided by Operations}}{\text{Average Total Liabilities}}$ | |
|---|---|---|
| | **Cash debt coverage ratio** | **Debt to total assets ratio** |
| **Microsoft** ($ in millions) | $\dfrac{\$19,037}{(\$38,330 + \$36,507)/2} = .51$ times | 50% |
| **Oracle** | .30 times | 47% |

Because Microsoft has long-term obligations, its cash debt coverage ratio is lower than its current cash debt coverage ratio. Obviously, Microsoft is very solvent. Oracle's cash debt coverage ratio of .30 times is not as strong as Microsoft's but still exceeds the .20 threshold. Neither the cash nor accrual measures suggest any cause for concern regarding the solvency of either company.

## DECISION TOOLKIT

| DECISION CHECKPOINTS | INFO NEEDED FOR DECISION | TOOL TO USE FOR DECISION | HOW TO EVALUATE RESULTS |
|---|---|---|---|
| Is the company generating sufficient cash provided by operating activities to meet its long-term obligations? | Cash provided by operating activities and average total liabilities | Cash debt coverage ratio $= \dfrac{\text{Cash provided by operations}}{\text{Average total liabilities}}$ | A high value suggests the company is solvent; that is, it will meet its obligations in the long term. |

# USING THE DECISION TOOLKIT

Intel Corporation is the leading producer of computer chips for personal computers. Its primary competitor is AMD. The two are vicious competitors, with frequent lawsuits filed between them. Financial statement data for Intel are provided below.

### Instructions

Calculate the following cash-based measures for Intel and compare them with the comparative data for AMD provided on page 645.

1. Free cash flow.
2. Current cash debt coverage ratio.
3. Cash debt coverage ratio.

### INTEL CORPORATION
Balance Sheets
December 31, 2009 and 2008
(in millions)

| Assets | 2009 | 2008 |
|---|---|---|
| Current assets | $21,157 | $19,871 |
| Noncurrent assets | 31,938 | 30,601 |
| Total assets | $53,095 | $50,472 |
| | | |
| **Liabilities and Stockholders' Equity** | | |
| Current liabilities | $ 7,591 | $ 7,818 |
| Long-term liabilities | 3,800 | 3,108 |
| Total liabilities | 11,391 | 10,926 |
| Stockholders' equity | 41,704 | 39,546 |
| Total liabilities and stockholders' equity | $53,095 | $50,472 |

### INTEL CORPORATION
Income Statements
For the Years Ended December 31, 2009 and 2008
(in millions)

| | 2009 | 2008 |
|---|---|---|
| Net revenues | $35,127 | $37,586 |
| Expenses | 30,758 | 32,294 |
| Net income | $ 4,369 | $ 5,292 |

**INTEL CORPORATION**
Statements of Cash Flows
For the Years Ended December 31, 2009 and 2008
(in millions)

|  | 2009 | 2008 |
|---|---|---|
| Net cash provided by operating activities | $11,170 | $10,926 |
| Net cash used for investing activities | (7,965) | (5,865) |
| Net cash used for financing activities | (2,568) | (9,018) |
| Net increase (decrease) in cash and cash equivalents | $  637 | $(3,957) |

> **Note.** Cash spent on property, plant, and equipment in 2009 was $4,515. Cash paid for dividends was $3,108.

Comparative data for AMD:

1. Free cash flow                                $7 million
2. Current cash debt coverage ratio              .21 times
3. Cash debt coverage ratio                      .06 times

### Solution

1. Intel's free cash flow is $3,547 million ($11,170 − $4,515 − $3,108). AMD's is only $7 million. This gives Intel a huge advantage in the ability to move quickly to invest in new projects.

2. The current cash debt coverage ratio for Intel is calculated as follows.

$$\frac{\$11,170}{(\$7,591 + \$7,818)/2} = 1.45 \text{ times}$$

Compared to AMD's value of .21 times, Intel is significantly more liquid.

3. The cash debt coverage ratio for Intel is calculated as follows.

$$\frac{\$11,170}{(\$11,391 + \$10,926)/2} = 1.00 \text{ times}$$

Compared to AMD's value of .06 times, Intel appears to be significantly more solvent.

# Summary of Study Objectives

**1** **Indicate the usefulness of the statement of cash flows.** The statement of cash flows provides information about the cash receipts, cash payments, and net change in cash resulting from the operating, investing, and financing activities of a company during the period.

**2** **Distinguish among operating, investing, and financing activities.** Operating activities include the cash effects of transactions that enter into the determination of net income. Investing activities involve cash flows resulting from changes in investments and long-term asset items. Financing activities involve cash flows resulting from changes in long-term liability and stockholders' equity items.

**3** **Explain the impact of the product life cycle on a company's cash flows.** During the introductory stage, cash provided by operating activities and cash from investing are negative, and cash from financing is positive.

During the growth stage, cash provided by operating activities becomes positive but is still not sufficient to meet investing needs. During the maturity stage, cash provided by operating activities exceeds investing needs, so the company begins to retire debt. During the decline stage, cash provided by operating activities is reduced, cash from investing becomes positive (from selling off assets), and cash from financing becomes more negative.

**4** **Prepare a statement of cash flows using the indirect method.** The preparation of a statement of cash flows involves three major steps: (1) Determine net cash provided/used by operating activities by converting net income from an accrual basis to a cash basis. (2) Analyze changes in noncurrent asset and liability accounts and record as investing and financing activities, or disclose as noncash transactions. (3) Compare the net change in cash on the statement of cash flows

with the change in the cash account reported on the balance sheet to make sure the amounts agree.

**5** **Use the statement of cash flows to evaluate a company.** A number of measures can be derived by using information from the statement of cash flows as well as the other required financial statements. Free cash flow indicates the amount of cash a company generated during the current year that is available for the payment of dividends or for expansion. Liquidity can be measured with the current cash debt coverage-ratio (cash provided by operating activities divided by average current liabilities). Solvency can be measured by the cash debt coverage ratio (cash provided by operating activities divided by average total liabilities).

## DECISION TOOLKIT A SUMMARY

| DECISION CHECKPOINTS | INFO NEEDED FOR DECISION | TOOL TO USE FOR DECISION | HOW TO EVALUATE RESULTS |
|---|---|---|---|
| How much cash did the company generate to either expand operations or pay dividends? | Cash provided by operating activities, cash spent on fixed assets, and cash dividends | $\text{Free cash flow} = \text{Cash provided by operations} - \text{Capital expenditures} - \text{Cash dividends}$ | Significant free cash flow indicates greater potential to finance new investment and pay additional dividends. |
| Is the company generating sufficient cash provided by operating activities to meet its current obligations? | Cash provided by operating activities and average current liabilities | $\text{Current cash debt coverage ratio} = \dfrac{\text{Cash provided by operations}}{\text{Average current liabilities}}$ | A high value suggests good liquidity. Since the numerator contains a "flow" measure, it provides a good supplement to the current ratio. |
| Is the company generating sufficient cash provided by operating activities to meet its long-term obligations? | Cash provided by operating activities and average total liabilities | $\text{Cash debt coverage ratio} = \dfrac{\text{Cash provided by operations}}{\text{Average total liabilities}}$ | A high value suggests the company is solvent; that is, it will meet its obligations in the long term. |

## appendix 12A

# Statement of Cash Flows—Direct Method

**study objective 6**

Prepare a statement of cash flows using the direct method.

To explain and illustrate the direct method, we will use the transactions of Computer Services Company for 2012, to prepare a statement of cash flows. Illustration 12A-1 presents information related to 2012 for Computer Services Company.

**Illustration 12A-1**
Comparative balance
sheets, income statement,
and additional information
for Computer Services
Company

**COMPUTER SERVICES COMPANY**
Comparative Balance Sheets
December 31

| Assets | 2012 | 2011 | Change in Account Balance Increase/Decrease |
|---|---|---|---|
| Current assets | | | |
| Cash | $ 55,000 | $ 33,000 | $ 22,000 Increase |
| Accounts receivable | 20,000 | 30,000 | 10,000 Decrease |
| Inventory | 15,000 | 10,000 | 5,000 Increase |
| Prepaid expenses | 5,000 | 1,000 | 4,000 Increase |
| Property, plant, and equipment | | | |
| Land | 130,000 | 20,000 | 110,000 Increase |
| Buildings | 160,000 | 40,000 | 120,000 Increase |
| Accumulated depreciation—buildings | (11,000) | (5,000) | 6,000 Increase |
| Equipment | 27,000 | 10,000 | 17,000 Increase |
| Accumulated depreciation—equipment | (3,000) | (1,000) | 2,000 Increase |
| Total assets | $398,000 | $138,000 | |

| Liabilities and Stockholders' Equity | | | |
|---|---|---|---|
| Current liabilities | | | |
| Accounts payable | $ 28,000 | $ 12,000 | $ 16,000 Increase |
| Income taxes payable | 6,000 | 8,000 | 2,000 Decrease |
| Long-term liabilities | | | |
| Bonds payable | 130,000 | 20,000 | 110,000 Increase |
| Stockholders' equity | | | |
| Common stock | 70,000 | 50,000 | 20,000 Increase |
| Retained earnings | 164,000 | 48,000 | 116,000 Increase |
| Total liabilities and stockholders' equity | $398,000 | $138,000 | |

**COMPUTER SERVICES COMPANY**
Income Statement
For the Year Ended December 31, 2012

| | | |
|---|---|---|
| Revenues | | $507,000 |
| Cost of goods sold | $150,000 | |
| Operating expenses (excluding depreciation) | 111,000 | |
| Depreciation expense | 9,000 | |
| Loss on sale of equipment | 3,000 | |
| Interest expense | 42,000 | 315,000 |
| Income before income tax | | 192,000 |
| Income tax expense | | 47,000 |
| Net income | | $145,000 |

**Additional information for 2012:**
1. Depreciation expense was comprised of $6,000 for building and $3,000 for equipment.
2. The company sold equipment with a book value of $7,000 (cost $8,000, less accumulated depreciation $1,000) for $4,000 cash.
3. Issued $110,000 of long-term bonds in direct exchange for land.
4. A building costing $120,000 was purchased for cash. Equipment costing $25,000 was also purchased for cash.
5. Issued common stock for $20,000 cash.
6. The company declared and paid a $29,000 cash dividend.

To prepare a statement of cash flows under the direct approach, we will apply the three steps outlined in Illustration 12-4 (page 630).

### STEP 1: OPERATING ACTIVITIES

### DETERMINE NET CASH PROVIDED/USED BY OPERATING ACTIVITIES BY CONVERTING NET INCOME FROM AN ACCRUAL BASIS TO A CASH BASIS

Under the **direct method**, companies compute net cash provided by operating activities by **adjusting each item in the income statement** from the accrual basis to the cash basis. To simplify and condense the operating activities section, companies **report only major classes of operating cash receipts and cash payments**. For these major classes, the difference between cash receipts and cash payments is the net cash provided by operating activities. These relationships are as shown in Illustration 12A-2.

**Illustration 12A-2** Major classes of cash receipts and payments

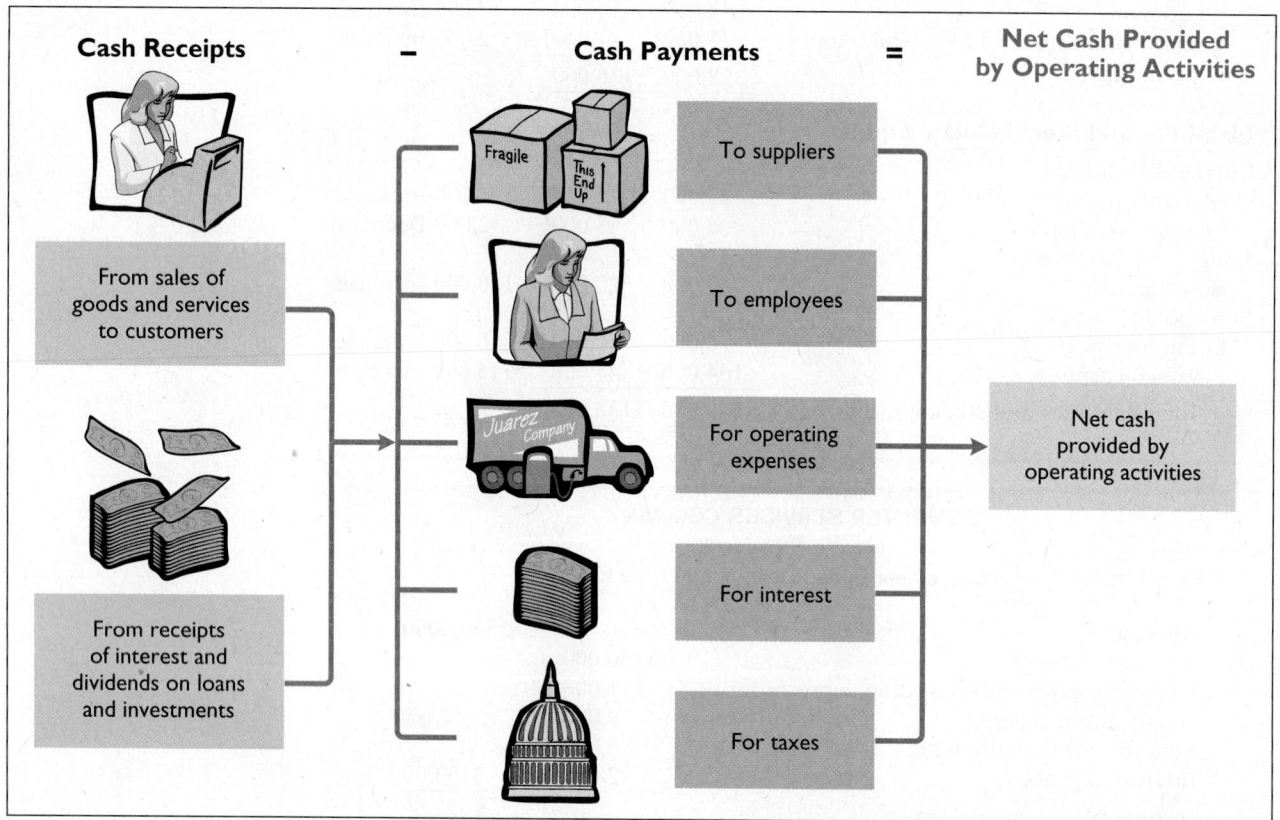

An efficient way to apply the direct method is to analyze the items reported in the income statement in the order in which they are listed. We then determine cash receipts and cash payments related to these revenues and expenses. The following pages present the adjustments required to prepare a statement of cash flows for Computer Services Company using the direct approach.

**CASH RECEIPTS FROM CUSTOMERS.** The income statement for Computer Services Company reported revenues from customers of $507,000. How much of that was cash receipts? To answer that, companies need to consider the change in accounts receivable during the year. When accounts receivable increase during the year, revenues on an accrual basis are higher than cash receipts from customers. Operations led to revenues, but not all of these revenues resulted in cash receipts.

To determine the amount of cash receipts, the company deducts from sales revenues the increase in accounts receivable. On the other hand, there may be a decrease in accounts receivable. That would occur if cash receipts from customers exceeded sales revenues. In that case, the company adds to sales revenues the decrease in accounts receivable. For Computer Services Company, accounts receivable decreased $10,000. Thus, cash receipts from customers were $517,000, computed as shown in Illustration 12A-3.

| | |
|---|---|
| Revenues from sales | $ 507,000 |
| Add: Decrease in accounts receivable | 10,000 |
| **Cash receipts from customers** | **$517,000** |

**Illustration 12A-3**
Computation of cash receipts from customers

Computer Services can also determine cash receipts from customers from an analysis of the Accounts Receivable account, as shown in Illustration 12A-4.

**Accounts Receivable**

| | | | | | |
|---|---|---|---|---|---|
| 1/1/12 | Balance | 30,000 | **Receipts from customers** | **517,000** | |
| | Revenues from sales | 507,000 | | | |
| 12/31/12 | Balance | 20,000 | | | |

**Illustration 12A-4**
Analysis of accounts receivable

**Helpful Hint** The T account shows that revenue plus decrease in receivables equals cash receipts.

Illustration 12A-5 shows the relationships among cash receipts from customers, revenues from sales, and changes in accounts receivable.

| Cash Receipts from Customers | = | Revenues from Sales | { + Decrease in Accounts Receivable<br>or<br>− Increase in Accounts Receivable |
|---|---|---|---|

**Illustration 12A-5**
Formula to compute cash receipts from customers–direct method

**CASH PAYMENTS TO SUPPLIERS.** Computer Services Company reported cost of goods sold of $150,000 on its income statement. How much of that was cash payments to suppliers? To answer that, it is first necessary to find purchases for the year. To find purchases, companies adjust cost of goods sold for the change in inventory. When inventory increases during the year, purchases for the year have exceeded cost of goods sold. As a result, to determine the amount of purchases, the company adds to cost of goods sold the increase in inventory.

In 2012, Computer Services Company's inventory increased $5,000. It computes purchases as follows.

| | |
|---|---|
| Cost of goods sold | $ 150,000 |
| Add: Increase in inventory | 5,000 |
| **Purchases** | **$155,000** |

**Illustration 12A-6**
Computation of purchases

After computing purchases, a company can determine cash payments to suppliers. This is done by adjusting purchases for the change in accounts payable. When accounts payable increase during the year, purchases on an accrual basis are higher than they are on a cash basis. As a result, to determine cash payments to suppliers, a company deducts from purchases the increase in accounts payable. On the other hand, if cash payments to suppliers exceed purchases, there may be a decrease in accounts payable. In that case, a company adds to purchases the decrease in accounts payable. For Computer Services Company, cash payments to suppliers were $139,000, computed as follows.

**Illustration 12A-7**
Computation of cash payments to suppliers

| | |
|---|---|
| Purchases | $ 155,000 |
| Deduct: Increase in accounts payable | 16,000 |
| **Cash payments to suppliers** | **$139,000** |

Computer Services also can determine cash payments to suppliers from an analysis of the Accounts Payable account, as shown in Illustration 12A-8.

**Illustration 12A-8**
Analysis of accounts payable

| Accounts Payable | | | | |
|---|---|---|---|---|
| **Payments to suppliers** | 139,000 | 1/1/12 | Balance | 12,000 |
| | | | Purchases | 155,000 |
| | | 12/31/12 | Balance | 28,000 |

**Helpful Hint** The T account shows that purchases less increase in accounts payable equals payments to suppliers.

Illustration 12A-9 shows the relationships among cash payments to suppliers, cost of goods sold, changes in inventory, and changes in accounts payable.

**Illustration 12A-9**
Formula to compute cash payments to suppliers– direct method

**CASH PAYMENTS FOR OPERATING EXPENSES.** Computer Services reported on its income statement operating expenses of $111,000. How much of that amount was cash paid for operating expenses? To answer that, we need to adjust this amount for any changes in prepaid expenses and accrued expenses payable. For example, if prepaid expenses increased during the year, cash paid for operating expenses is higher than operating expenses reported on the income statement. To convert operating expenses to cash payments for operating expenses, a company adds the increase in prepaid expenses to operating expenses. On the other hand, if prepaid expenses decrease during the year, it deducts the decrease from operating expenses.

Companies must also adjust operating expenses for changes in accrued expenses payable. When accrued expenses payable increase during the year, operating expenses on an accrual basis are higher than they are in a cash basis. As a result, to determine cash payments for operating expenses, a company deducts from operating expenses an increase in accrued expenses payable. On the other hand, a company adds to operating expenses a decrease in accrued expenses payable because cash payments exceed operating expenses.

Computer Services Company's cash payments for operating expenses were $115,000, computed as follows.

**Illustration 12A-10**
Computation of cash payments for operating expenses

| | |
|---|---|
| Operating expenses | $ 111,000 |
| Add: Increase in prepaid expenses | 4,000 |
| **Cash payments for operating expenses** | **$115,000** |

Illustration 12A-11 shows the relationships among cash payments for operating expenses, changes in prepaid expenses, and changes in accrued expenses payable.

| Cash Payments for Operating Expenses | = | Operating Expenses | + Increase in Prepaid Expense or − Decrease in Prepaid Expense | + Decrease in Accrued Expenses Payable or − Increase in Accrued Expenses Payable |
|---|---|---|---|---|

**Illustration 12A-11**
Formula to compute cash payments for operating expenses—direct method

**DEPRECIATION EXPENSE AND LOSS ON SALE OF EQUIPMENT.** Computer Services' depreciation expense in 2012 was $9,000. Depreciation expense is not shown on a statement of cash flows under the direct method because it is a noncash charge. If the amount for operating expenses includes depreciation expense, operating expenses must be reduced by the amount of depreciation to determine cash payments for operating expenses.

The loss on sale of equipment of $3,000 is also a noncash charge. The loss on sale of equipment reduces net income, but it does not reduce cash. Thus, the loss on sale of equipment is not shown on the statement of cash flows under the direct method.

Other charges to expense that do not require the use of cash, such as the amortization of intangible assets, depletion expense, and bad debts expense, are treated in the same manner as depreciation.

**CASH PAYMENTS FOR INTEREST.** Computer Services reported on the income statement interest expense of $42,000. Since the balance sheet did not include an accrual for interest payable for 2011 or 2012, the amount reported as expense is the same as the amount of interest paid.

**CASH PAYMENTS FOR INCOME TAXES.** Computer Services reported income tax expense of $47,000 on the income statement. Income taxes payable, however, decreased $2,000. This decrease means that income taxes paid were more than income taxes reported in the income statement. Cash payments for income taxes were, therefore, $49,000 as shown below.

| | |
|---|---|
| Income tax expense | $ 47,000 |
| Add: Decrease in income taxes payable | 2,000 |
| Cash payments for income taxes | $49,000 |

**Illustration 12A-12**
Computation of cash payments for income taxes

Illustration 12A-13 shows the relationships among cash payments for income taxes, income tax expense, and changes in income taxes payable.

| Cash Payments for Income Taxes | = | Income Tax Expense | + Decrease in Income Taxes Payable or − Increase in Income Taxes Payable |
|---|---|---|---|

**Illustration 12A-13**
Formula to compute cash payments for income taxes—direct method

The operating activities section of the statement of cash flows of Computer Services Company is shown in Illustration 12A-14.

**Illustration 12A-14**
Operating activities section of the statement of cash flows

| | | |
|---|---|---|
| Cash flows from operating activities | | |
| Cash receipts from customers | | $517,000 |
| Less: Cash payments: | | |
| To suppliers | $139,000 | |
| For operating expenses | 115,000 | |
| For interest expense | 42,000 | |
| For income taxes | 49,000 | 345,000 |
| Net cash provided by operating activities | | $172,000 |

When a company uses the direct method, it must also provide in a **separate schedule** (not shown here) the net cash flows from operating activities as computed under the indirect method.

## STEP 2: INVESTING AND FINANCING ACTIVITIES

### ANALYZE CHANGES IN NONCURRENT ASSET AND LIABILITY ACCOUNTS AND RECORD AS INVESTING AND FINANCING ACTIVITIES, OR DISCLOSE AS NONCASH TRANSACTIONS

**Helpful Hint** The investing and financing activities are measured and reported the same under both the direct and indirect methods.

**INCREASE IN LAND.** As indicated from the change in the Land account and the additional information, the company purchased land of $110,000 by directly exchanging bonds for land. The exchange of bonds payable for land has no effect on cash. But it is a significant noncash investing and financing activity that merits disclosure in a separate schedule. (See Illustration 12A-16.)

**INCREASE IN BUILDINGS.** As the additional data indicate, Computer Services Company acquired an office building for $120,000 cash. This is a cash outflow reported in the investing section. (See Illustration 12A-16.)

**INCREASE IN EQUIPMENT.** The Equipment account increased $17,000. The additional information explains that this was a net increase that resulted from two transactions: (1) a purchase of equipment of $25,000, and (2) the sale for $4,000 of equipment costing $8,000. These transactions are investing activities. The company should report each transaction separately. The statement in Illustration 12A-16 reports the purchase of equipment as an outflow of cash for $25,000. It reports the sale as an inflow of cash for $4,000. The T account below shows the reasons for the change in this account during the year.

**Illustration 12A-15**
Analysis of equipment

| Equipment | | | |
|---|---|---|---|
| 1/1/12 Balance | 10,000 | Cost of equipment sold | 8,000 |
| Purchase of equipment | 25,000 | | |
| 12/31/12 Balance | 27,000 | | |

The following entry shows the details of the equipment sale transaction.

| | A | = | L | + | SE |
|---|---|---|---|---|---|
| +4,000 | | | | | |
| +1,000 | | | | | |
| | | | | | −3,000 Exp |
| −8,000 | | | | | |

**Cash Flows**
+4,000

| | | |
|---|---|---|
| Cash | 4,000 | |
| Accumulated Depreciation | 1,000 | |
| Loss on Disposal of Plant Assets | 3,000 | |
| Equipment | | 8,000 |

**INCREASE IN BONDS PAYABLE.** The Bonds Payable account increased $110,000. As indicated in the additional information, the company acquired land by directly exchanging bonds for land. Illustration 12A-16 reports this noncash transaction in a separate schedule at the bottom of the statement.

**Helpful Hint** When companies issue stocks or bonds for cash, the actual proceeds will appear in the statement of cash flows as a financing inflow (rather than the par value of the stocks or face value of bonds).

**INCREASE IN COMMON STOCK.** The balance sheet reports an increase in Common Stock of $20,000. The additional information section notes that this increase resulted from the issuance of new shares of stock. This is a cash inflow reported in the financing section in Illustration 12A-16.

**INCREASE IN RETAINED EARNINGS.** Retained earnings increased $116,000 during the year. This increase can be explained by two factors: (1) Net income of $145,000 increased retained earnings and (2) dividends of $29,000 decreased retained earnings. The company adjusts net income to net cash provided by operating activities in the operating activities section. **Payment** of the dividends (not the declaration) is a **cash outflow that the company reports as a financing activity in Illustration 12A-16**.

## Statement of Cash Flows—2012

Illustration 12A-16 shows the statement of cash flows for Computer Services Company.

**Illustration 12A-16**
Statement of cash flows, 2012—direct method

| COMPUTER SERVICES COMPANY | | |
|---|---|---|
| Statement of Cash Flows—Direct Method | | |
| For the Year Ended December 31, 2012 | | |
| Cash flows from operating activities | | |
| Cash receipts from customers | | $ 517,000 |
| Less: Cash payments: | | |
| To suppliers | $ 139,000 | |
| For operating expenses | 115,000 | |
| For income taxes | 49,000 | |
| For interest expense | 42,000 | 345,000 |
| Net cash provided by operating activities | | 172,000 |
| Cash flows from investing activities | | |
| Sale of equipment | 4,000 | |
| Purchase of building | (120,000) | |
| Purchase of equipment | (25,000) | |
| Net cash used by investing activities | | (141,000) |
| Cash flows from financing activities | | |
| Issuance of common stock | 20,000 | |
| Payment of cash dividends | (29,000) | |
| Net cash used by financing activities | | (9,000) |
| Net increase in cash | | 22,000 |
| Cash at beginning of period | | 33,000 |
| Cash at end of period | | $  55,000 |
| **Noncash investing and financing activities** | | |
| Issuance of bonds payable to purchase land | | $ 110,000 |

## STEP 3: NET CHANGE IN CASH

### COMPARE THE NET CHANGE IN CASH ON THE STATEMENT OF CASH FLOWS WITH THE CHANGE IN THE CASH ACCOUNT REPORTED ON THE BALANCE SHEET TO MAKE SURE THE AMOUNTS AGREE

Illustration 12A-16 indicates that the net change in cash during the period was an increase of $22,000. This agrees with the change in balances in the cash account reported on the balance sheets in Illustration 12A-1 (page 647).

# Summary of Study Objective for Appendix 12A

**6** **Prepare a statement of cash flows using the direct method.** The preparation of the statement of cash flows involves three major steps: (1) Determine net cash provided/used by operating activities by converting net income from an accrual basis to a cash basis. (2) Analyze changes in noncurrent asset and liability accounts and record as investing and financing activities, or disclose as noncash transactions. (3) Compare the net change in cash on the statement of cash flows with the change in the cash account reported on the balance sheet to make sure the amounts agree. The direct method reports cash receipts less cash payments to arrive at net cash provided by operating activities.

# Statement of Cash Flows—T-Account Approach

Many people like to use T accounts to provide structure to the preparation of a statement of cash flows. The use of T accounts is based on the accounting equation that you learned in Chapter 1. The basic equation is:

**Assets = Liabilities + Equity**

Now, let's rewrite the left-hand side as:

**Cash + Noncash Assets = Liabilities + Equity**

Next, rewrite the equation by subtracting Noncash Assets from each side to isolate Cash on the left-hand side:

**Cash = Liabilities + Equity − Noncash Assets**

Finally, if we insert the Δ symbol (which means "change in"), we have:

**Δ Cash = Δ Liabilities + Δ Equity − Δ Noncash Assets**

What this means is that the change in cash is equal to the change in all of the other balance sheet accounts. Another way to think about this is that if we analyze the changes in all of the noncash balance sheet accounts, we will explain the change in the cash account. This, of course, is exactly what we are trying to do with the statement of cash flows.

To implement this approach, first prepare a large Cash T account, with sections for operating, investing, and financing activities. Then, prepare smaller T accounts for all of the other noncash balance sheet accounts. Insert the beginning and ending balances for each of these accounts. Once you have done this, then walk through the steps outlined on page 630. As you walk through the steps, enter debit and credit amounts into the affected accounts. When all of the changes in the T accounts have been explained, you are done. To demonstrate, we will apply this approach to the example of Computer Services Company that is presented in the chapter. Each of the adjustments in Illustration 12B-1 is numbered so you can follow them through the T accounts.

1. Post net income as a debit to the operating section of the Cash T account and a credit to Retained Earnings. Make sure to label all adjustments to the Cash T account. It also helps to number each adjustment so you can trace all of them if you make an error.
2. Post depreciation expense as a debit to the operating section of Cash and a credit to each of the appropriate accumulated depreciation accounts.
3. Post any gains or losses on the sale of property, plant, and equipment. To do this, it is best to first prepare the journal entry that was recorded at the time of the sale and then post each element of the journal entry. For example, for Computer Services the entry was:

| | | |
|---|---|---|
| Cash | 4,000 | |
| Accumulated Depreciation—Equipment | 1,000 | |
| Loss on Disposal of Plant Assets | 3,000 | |
|     Equipment | | 8,000 |

The $4,000 cash entry is a source of cash in the investing section of the Cash account. Accumulated Depreciation—Equipment is debited for $1,000. The Loss on Disposal of Plant Assets is a debit to the operating section of the Cash T account. Finally, Equipment is credited for $8,000.

4–8. Next, post each of the changes to the noncash current asset and current liability accounts. For example, to explain the $10,000 decline in Computer Services' Accounts Receivable, credit Accounts Receivable for $10,000 and debit the operating section of the Cash T account for $10,000.

9. Analyze the changes in the noncurrent accounts. Land was purchased by issuing Bonds Payable. This requires a debit to Land for $110,000 and a credit to Bonds Payable for $110,000. Note that this is a significant noncash event that requires disclosure at the bottom of the statement of cash flows.

10. Buildings is debited for $120,000, and the investing section of the Cash T account is credited for $120,000 as a use of cash from investing.

11. Equipment is debited for $25,000 and the investing section of the Cash T account is credited for $25,000 as a use of cash from investing.

12. Common Stock is credited for $20,000 for the issuance of shares of stock, and the financing section of the Cash T account is debited for $20,000.

13. Retained Earnings is debited to reflect the payment of the $29,000 dividend, and the financing section of the Cash T account is credited to reflect the use of Cash.

**Illustration 12B-1**
T-account approach

### Cash

| Operating | | | |
|---|---|---|---|
| (1) Net income | 145,000 | 5,000 | Inventory (5) |
| (2) Depreciation expense | 9,000 | 4,000 | Prepaid expenses (6) |
| (3) Loss on equipment | 3,000 | 2,000 | Income taxes payable (8) |
| (4) Accounts receivable | 10,000 | | |
| (7) Accounts payable | 16,000 | | |
| Net cash provided by operating activities | 172,000 | | |
| **Investing** | | | |
| (3) Sold equipment | 4,000 | 120,000 | Purchased building (10) |
| | | 25,000 | Purchased equipment (11) |
| | | 141,000 | Net cash used by investing activities |
| **Financing** | | | |
| (12) Issued common stock | 20,000 | 29,000 | Dividend paid (13) |
| | | 9,000 | Net cash used by financing activities |
| | 22,000 | | |

| Accounts Receivable | | Inventory | | Prepaid Expenses | | Land | |
|---|---|---|---|---|---|---|---|
| 30,000 | | 10,000 | | 1,000 | | 20,000 | |
| | 10,000 (4) | (5) 5,000 | | (6) 4,000 | | (9) 110,000 | |
| 20,000 | | 15,000 | | 5,000 | | 130,000 | |

| Buildings | | Accumulated Depreciation—Buildings | | Equipment | | Accumulated Depreciation—Equipment | |
|---|---|---|---|---|---|---|---|
| 40,000 | | | 5,000 | 10,000 | | | 1,000 |
| (10) 120,000 | | | 6,000 (2) | (11) 25,000 | 8,000 (3) | (3) 1,000 | 3,000 (2) |
| 160,000 | | | 11,000 | 27,000 | | | 3,000 |

| Accounts Payable | | Income Taxes Payable | | Bonds Payable | | Common Stock | | Retained Earnings | |
|---|---|---|---|---|---|---|---|---|---|
| | 12,000 | | 8,000 | | 20,000 | | 50,000 | | 48,000 |
| | 16,000 (7) | (8) 2,000 | | | 110,000 (9) | | 20,000 (12) | | 145,000 (1) |
| | 28,000 | | 6,000 | | 130,000 | | 70,000 | (13) 29,000 | |
| | | | | | | | | | 164,000 |

At this point, all of the changes in the noncash accounts have been explained. All that remains is to subtotal each section of the Cash T account and agree the total change in cash with the change shown on the balance sheet. Once this is done, the information in the Cash T account can be used to prepare a statement of cash flows.

# Glossary

**Cash debt coverage ratio** (p. 643) A cash-based ratio used to evaluate solvency, calculated as cash provided by operating activities divided by average total liabilities.

**Current cash debt coverage ratio** (p. 642) A cash-based ratio used to evaluate liquidity, calculated as cash provided by operating activities divided by average current liabilities.

**Direct method** (p. 630) A method of determining net cash provided by operating activities by adjusting each item in the income statement from the accrual basis to the cash basis. The direct method shows operating cash receipts and payments.

**Financing activities** (p. 625) Cash flow activities that include (a) obtaining cash from issuing debt and repaying the amounts borrowed and (b) obtaining cash from stockholders, repurchasing shares, and paying dividends.

**Free cash flow** (p. 639) Cash remaining from operating activities after adjusting for capital expenditures and dividends paid.

**Indirect method** (p. 630) A method of preparing a statement of cash flows in which net income is adjusted for items that do not affect cash, to determine net cash provided by operating activities.

**Investing activities** (p. 625) Cash flow activities that include (a) cash transactions that involve the purchase or disposal of investments and property, plant, and equipment using cash and (b) lending money and collecting the loans.

**Operating activities** (p. 625) Cash flow activities that include the cash effects of transactions that create revenues and expenses and thus enter into the determination of net income.

**Product life cycle** (p. 628) A series of phases in a product's sales and cash flows over time; these phases, in order of occurrence, are introductory, growth, maturity, and decline.

**Statement of cash flows** (p. 624) A basic financial statement that provides information about the cash receipts and cash payments of an entity during a period, classified as operating, investing, and financing activities, in a format that reconciles the beginning and ending cash balances.

## Comprehensive

The income statement for Kosinski Manufacturing Company contains the following condensed information.

### KOSINSKI MANUFACTURING COMPANY
### Income Statement
### For the Year Ended December 31, 2012

| | | |
|---|---:|---:|
| Revenues | | $6,583,000 |
| Operating expenses, excluding depreciation | $4,920,000 | |
| Depreciation expense | 880,000 | 5,800,000 |
| Income before income taxes | | 783,000 |
| Income tax expense | | 353,000 |
| Net income | | $ 430,000 |

Included in operating expenses is a $24,000 loss resulting from the sale of machinery for $270,000 cash. Machinery was purchased at a cost of $750,000. The following balances are reported on Kosinski's comparative balance sheet at December 31.

| | 2012 | 2011 |
|---|---:|---:|
| Cash | $672,000 | $130,000 |
| Accounts receivable | 775,000 | 610,000 |
| Inventory | 834,000 | 867,000 |
| Accounts payable | 521,000 | 501,000 |

Income tax expense of $353,000 represents the amount paid in 2012. Dividends declared and paid in 2012 totaled $200,000.

**Instructions**

(a) Prepare the statement of cash flows using the indirect method.

*(b) Prepare the statement of cash flows using the direct method.

**Solution to Comprehensive Do it!**

**Action Plan**

- Apply the same data to the preparation of a statement of cash flows under both the indirect and direct methods.
- Note the similarities of the two methods: Both methods report the same information in the investing and financing sections.
- Note the differences between the two methods: The cash flows from operating activities sections report different information, but the amount of net cash provided by operating activities is the same for both methods.

(a)

### KOSINSKI MANUFACTURING COMPANY
### Statement of Cash Flows—Indirect Method
### For the Year Ended December 31, 2012

| | | |
|---|---:|---:|
| Cash flows from operating activities | | |
| Net income | | $ 430,000 |
| Adjustments to reconcile net income to net cash provided by operating activities: | | |
| Depreciation expense | $ 880,000 | |
| Loss on sale of machinery | 24,000 | |
| Increase in accounts receivable | (165,000) | |
| Decrease in inventory | 33,000 | |
| Increase in accounts payable | 20,000 | 792,000 |
| Net cash provided by operating activities | | 1,222,000 |
| Cash flows from investing activities | | |
| Sale of machinery | 270,000 | |
| Purchase of machinery | (750,000) | |
| Net cash used by investing activities | | (480,000) |
| Cash flows from financing activities | | |
| Payment of cash dividends | (200,000) | |
| Net cash used by financing activities | | (200,000) |
| Net increase in cash | | 542,000 |
| Cash at beginning of period | | 130,000 |
| Cash at end of period | | $ 672,000 |

*(b)

### KOSINSKI MANUFACTURING COMPANY
### Statement of Cash Flows—Direct Method
### For the Year Ended December 31, 2012

| | | |
|---|---:|---:|
| Cash flows from operating activities | | |
| Cash collections from customers | | $6,418,000* |
| Cash payments: | | |
| For operating expenses | $(4,843,000)** | |
| For income taxes | (353,000) | (5,196,000) |
| Net cash provided by operating activities | | 1,222,000 |
| Cash flows from investing activities | | |
| Sale of machinery | 270,000 | |
| Purchase of machinery | (750,000) | |
| Net cash used by investing activities | | (480,000) |
| Cash flows from financing activities | | |
| Payment of cash dividends | (200,000) | |
| Net cash used by financing activities | | (200,000) |
| Net increase in cash | | 542,000 |
| Cash at beginning of period | | 130,000 |
| Cash at end of period | | $ 672,000 |

Direct-Method Computations:

| | |
|---|---:|
| *Computation of cash collections from customers: | |
| Revenues per the income statement | $6,583,000 |
| Deduct: Increase in accounts receivable | (165,000) |
| Cash collections from customers | $6,418,000 |
| **Computation of cash payments for operating expenses: | |
| Operating expenses per the income statement | $4,920,000 |
| Deduct: Loss from sale of machinery | (24,000) |
| Deduct: Decrease in inventories | (33,000) |
| Deduct: Increase in accounts payable | (20,000) |
| Cash payments for operating expenses | $4,843,000 |

the navigator

*Note:* All Questions, Exercises, and Problems marked with an asterisk relate to material in the appendices to the chapter.

**Self-Test, Brief Exercises, Exercises, Problem Set A, and many more resources are available for practice in WileyPLUS**

# Self-Test Questions

Answers are on page 680.

(SO 1)  1. Which of the following is *incorrect* about the statement of cash flows?
   (a) It is a fourth basic financial statement.
   (b) It provides information about cash receipts and cash payments of an entity during a period.
   (c) It reconciles the ending cash account balance to the balance per the bank statement.
   (d) It provides information about the operating, investing, and financing activities of the business.

(SO 1, 2)  2. Which of the following will *not* be reported in the statement of cash flows?
   (a) The net change in plant assets during the year.
   (b) Cash payments for plant assets during the year.
   (c) Cash receipts from sales of plant assets during the year.
   (d) Sources of financing during the period.

(SO 2)  3. The statement of cash flows classifies cash receipts and cash payments by these activities:
   (a) operating and nonoperating.
   (b) operating, investing, and financing.
   (c) financing, operating, and nonoperating.
   (d) investing, financing, and nonoperating.

(SO 2)  4. Which is an example of a cash flow from an operating activity?
   (a) Payment of cash to lenders for interest.
   (b) Receipt of cash from the sale of capital stock.
   (c) Payment of cash dividends to the company's stockholders.
   (d) None of the above.

(SO 2)  5. Which is an example of a cash flow from an investing activity?
   (a) Receipt of cash from the issuance of bonds payable.
   (b) Payment of cash to repurchase outstanding capital stock.
   (c) Receipt of cash from the sale of equipment.
   (d) Payment of cash to suppliers for inventory.

(SO 2)  6. Cash dividends paid to stockholders are classified on the statement of cash flows as:
   (a) operating activities.
   (b) investing activities.
   (c) a combination of (a) and (b).
   (d) financing activities.

(SO 2)  7. Which is an example of a cash flow from a financing activity?
   (a) Receipt of cash from sale of land.
   (b) Issuance of debt for cash.
   (c) Purchase of equipment for cash.
   (d) None of the above

(SO 2)  8. Which of the following is *incorrect* about the statement of cash flows?
   (a) The direct method may be used to report cash provided by operating activities.
   (b) The statement shows the cash provided (used) for three categories of activity.
   (c) The operating section is the last section of the statement.
   (d) The indirect method may be used to report cash provided by operating activities.

(SO 3)  9. During the introductory phase of a company's life cycle, one would normally expect to see:
   (a) negative cash from operations, negative cash from investing, and positive cash from financing.
   (b) negative cash from operations, positive cash from investing, and positive cash from financing.
   (c) positive cash from operations, negative cash from investing, and negative cash from financing.
   (d) positive cash from operations, negative cash from investing, and positive cash from financing.

**Questions 10 through 12 apply only to the indirect method.**

(SO 4)  10. Net income is $132,000, accounts payable increased $10,000 during the year, inventory decreased $6,000 during the year, and accounts receivable increased $12,000 during the year. Under the indirect method, what is net cash provided by operations?
   (a) $102,000.    (c) $124,000.
   (b) $112,000.    (d) $136,000.

(SO 4)  11. Items that are added back to net income in determining cash provided by operating activities under the indirect method do *not* include:
   (a) depreciation expense.
   (b) an increase in inventory.
   (c) amortization expense.
   (d) loss on sale of equipment.

(SO 4)  12. The following data are available for Bill Mack Corporation.

| | |
|---|---:|
| Net income | $200,000 |
| Depreciation expense | 40,000 |
| Dividends paid | 60,000 |
| Gain on sale of land | 10,000 |
| Decrease in accounts receivable | 20,000 |
| Decrease in accounts payable | 30,000 |

Net cash provided by operating activities is:
   (a) $160,000.    (c) $240,000.
   (b) $220,000.    (d) $280,000.

(SO 4, 6) **13.** The following are data concerning cash received or paid from various transactions for Orange Peels Corporation.

| | |
|---|---|
| Sale of land | $100,000 |
| Sale of equipment | 50,000 |
| Issuance of common stock | 70,000 |
| Purchase of equipment | 30,000 |
| Payment of cash dividends | 60,000 |

Net cash provided by investing activities is:
(a) $120,000.
(b) $130,000.
(c) $150,000.
(d) $190,000.

(SO 4, 6) **14.** The following data are available for Retique!

| | |
|---|---|
| Increase in bonds payable | $100,000 |
| Sale of investment | 50,000 |
| Issuance of common stock | 60,000 |
| Payment of cash dividends | 30,000 |

Net cash provided by financing activities is:
(a) $90,000.
(b) $130,000.
(c) $160,000.
(d) $170,000.

(SO 5) **15.** The cash debt coverage ratio is:
(a) a measure of liquidity.
(b) a measure of profitability.
(c) net income divided by average total liabilities.
(d) a measure of solvency.

**16.** Free cash flow provides an indication of (SO 5) a company's ability to:
(a) generate net income.
(b) generate cash to pay dividends.
(c) generate cash to invest in new capital expenditures.
(d) Both (b) and (c).

**Questions 17 and 18 apply only to the direct method.**

*17. The beginning balance in accounts receivable is (SO 6) $44,000, the ending balance is $42,000, and sales during the period are $129,000. What are cash receipts from customers?
(a) $127,000.
(b) $129,000.
(c) $131,000.
(d) $141,000.

*18. Which of the following items is reported on a cash (SO 6) flow statement prepared by the direct method?
(a) Loss on sale of building.
(b) Increase in accounts receivable.
(c) Depreciation expense.
(d) Cash payments to suppliers.

Go to the book's companion website, **www.wiley.com/college/kimmel**, to access additional Self-Test Questions.

# Questions

**1.** (a) What is a statement of cash flows?
   (b) Brad Strath maintains that the statement of cash flows is an optional financial statement. Do you agree? Explain.

**2.** What questions about cash are answered by the statement of cash flows?

**3.** Distinguish among the three activities reported in the statement of cash flows.

**4.** (a) What are the sources (inflows) of cash in a statement of cash flows?
   (b) What are the uses (outflows) of cash?

**5.** Why is it important to disclose certain noncash transactions? How should they be disclosed?

**6.** Wilma Flintstone and Barny Rubblestone were discussing the format of the statement of cash flows of Primo Pebble Co. At the bottom of Primo Pebble's statement of cash flows was a separate section entitled "Noncash investing and financing activities." Give three examples of significant noncash transactions that would be reported in this section.

**7.** Why is it necessary to use comparative balance sheets, a current income statement, and certain transaction data in preparing a statement of cash flows?

**8.** (a) What are the phases of the corporate life cycle?
   (b) What effect does each phase have on the numbers reported in a statement of cash flows?

**9.** Based on its statement of cash flows, in what stage of the product life cycle is Tootsie Roll Industries?

**10.** Contrast the advantages and disadvantages of the direct and indirect methods of preparing the statement of cash flows. Are both methods acceptable? Which method is preferred by the FASB? Which method is more popular?

**11.** When the total cash inflows exceed the total cash outflows in the statement of cash flows, how and where is this excess identified?

**12.** Describe the indirect method for determining net cash provided (used) by operating activities.

**13.** Why is it necessary to convert accrual basis net income to cash basis income when preparing a statement of cash flows?

**14.** The president of Pratt Company is puzzled. During the last year, the company experienced a net loss of $800,000, yet its cash increased $300,000 during the same period of time. Explain to the president how this could occur.

**15.** Identify five items that are adjustments to convert net income to net cash provided by operating activities under the indirect method.

**16.** Why and how is depreciation expense reported in a statement prepared using the indirect method?

**17.** Why is the statement of cash flows useful?

**18.** During 2012, Rusmussen Company exchanged $1,700,000 of its common stock for land. Indicate how the transaction would be reported on a statement of cash flows, if at all.

19.  Give examples of accrual-based and cash-based ratios to measure each of these characteristics of a company:
   (a) Liquidity.    (b) Solvency.

*20. Describe the direct method for determining net cash provided by operating activities.

*21. Give the formulas under the direct method for computing (a) cash receipts from customers and (b) cash payments to suppliers.

*22. Ambrosia Inc. reported sales of $2 million for 2012. Accounts receivable decreased $150,000 and accounts payable increased $300,000. Compute cash receipts from customers, assuming that the receivable and payable transactions are related to operations.

*23. In the direct method, why is depreciation expense not reported in the cash flows from operating activities section?

# Brief Exercises

*Indicate statement presentation of selected transactions.*
(SO 2), **K**

**BE12-1** Each of these items must be considered in preparing a statement of cash flows for Nemke Co. for the year ended December 31, 2012. For each item, state how it should be shown in the statement of cash flows for 2012.
(a) Issued bonds for $200,000 cash.
(b) Purchased equipment for $180,000 cash.
(c) Sold land costing $20,000 for $20,000 cash.
(d) Declared and paid a $50,000 cash dividend.

*Classify items by activities.*
(SO 2), **C**

**BE12-2** Classify each item as an operating, investing, or financing activity. Assume all items involve cash unless there is information to the contrary.
(a) Purchase of equipment.          (d) Depreciation.
(b) Sale of building.               (e) Payment of dividends.
(c) Redemption of bonds.            (f) Issuance of capital stock.

*Identify financing activity transactions.*
(SO 2), **AP**

**BE12-3** The following T account is a summary of the cash account of Holmes Company.

**Cash (Summary Form)**

| | | | |
|---|---|---|---|
| Balance, Jan. 1 | 8,000 | | |
| Receipts from customers | 364,000 | Payments for goods | 200,000 |
| Dividends on stock investments | 6,000 | Payments for operating expenses | 140,000 |
| Proceeds from sale of equipment | 36,000 | Interest paid | 10,000 |
| Proceeds from issuance of | | Taxes paid | 8,000 |
| bonds payable | 300,000 | Dividends paid | 40,000 |
| Balance, Dec. 31 | 316,000 | | |

What amount of net cash provided (used) by financing activities should be reported in the statement of cash flows?

*Answer questions related to the phases of product life cycle.*
(SO 3), **C**

**BE12-4**
(a) Why is cash from operations likely to be lower than reported net income during the growth phase?
(b) Why is cash from investing often positive during the late maturity phase and during the decline phase?

*Compute cash provided by operating activities—indirect method.*
(SO 4), **AP**

**BE12-5** Jeremy, Inc. reported net income of $2.5 million in 2012. Depreciation for the year was $160,000, accounts receivable decreased $350,000, and accounts payable decreased $280,000. Compute net cash provided by operating activities using the indirect approach.

*Compute cash provided by operating activities—indirect method.*
(SO 4), **AP**

**BE12-6** The net income for Bohnert Co. for 2012 was $280,000. For 2012, depreciation on plant assets was $70,000, and the company incurred a loss on sale of plant assets of $28,000. Compute net cash provided by operating activities under the indirect method.

*Compute net cash provided by operating activities—indirect method.*
(SO 4), **AP**

**BE12-7** The comparative balance sheets for Howell Company show these changes in noncash current asset accounts: accounts receivable decrease $80,000, prepaid expenses increase $28,000, and inventories increase $40,000. Compute net cash provided by operating activities using the indirect method, assuming that net income is $186,000.

**BE12-8** The T accounts for Equipment and the related Accumulated Depreciation for Anastacia Company at the end of 2012 are shown here.

*Determine cash received from sale of equipment.*
*(SO 4),* **AN**

| Equipment | | | | Accumulated Depreciation | | | |
|---|---|---|---|---|---|---|---|
| Beg. bal. | 80,000 | Disposals | 22,000 | Disposals | 5,100 | Beg. bal. | 44,500 |
| Acquisitions | 41,600 | | | | | Depr. exp. | 12,000 |
| End. bal. | 99,600 | | | | | End. bal. | 51,400 |

In addition, Anastacia Company's income statement reported a loss on the sale of equipment of $3,500. What amount was reported on the statement of cash flows as "cash flow from sale of equipment"?

**BE12-9** During 2009, Cypress Semiconductor Corporation reported cash provided by operations of $89,303,000, cash used in investing of $43,126,000, and cash used in financing of $7,368,000. In addition, cash spent for fixed assets during the period was $25,823,000. Average current liabilities were $251,522,000, and average total liabilities were $286,214,500. No dividends were paid. Calculate these values:
(a) Free cash flow.
(b) Current cash debt coverage ratio.
(c) Cash debt coverage ratio.

*Calculate cash-based ratios.*
*(SO 5),* **AP**

**BE12-10** Colburn Corporation reported cash provided by operating activities of $412,000, cash used by investing activities of $250,000, and cash provided by financing activities of $70,000. In addition, cash spent for capital assets during the period was $200,000. Average current liabilities were $150,000, and average total liabilities were $225,000. No dividends were paid. Calculate these values:
(a) Free cash flow.
(b) Current cash debt coverage ratio.
(c) Cash debt coverage ratio.

*Calculate cash-based ratios.*
*(SO 5),* **AP**

**BE12-11** Canwest Global Communications Corp. reported cash used by operating activities of $104,539,000 and revenues of $2,867,459,000 during 2009. Cash spent on plant asset additions during the year was $79,330,000. Calculate free cash flow.

*Calculate cash-based ratios.*
*(SO 5),* **AP**

**BE12-12** The management of Riggs Inc. is trying to decide whether it can increase its dividend. During the current year, it reported net income of $875,000. It had cash provided by operating activities of $734,000, paid cash dividends of $92,000, and had capital expenditures of $310,000. Compute the company's free cash flow, and discuss whether an increase in the dividend appears warranted. What other factors should be considered?

*Calculate and analyze free cash flow.*
*(SO 5),* **AN**

*BE12-13** Columbia Sportswear Company had accounts receivable of $299,585,000 at January 1, 2009, and $226,548,000 at December 31, 2009. Sales revenues were $1,244,023,000 for the year 2009. What is the amount of cash receipts from customers in 2009?

*Compute receipts from customers—direct method.*
*(SO 6),* **AP**

*BE12-14** Garvey Corporation reported income taxes of $370,000,000 on its 2012 income statement and income taxes payable of $277,000,000 at December 31, 2011, and $528,000,000 at December 31, 2012. What amount of cash payments were made for income taxes during 2012?

*Compute cash payments for income taxes—direct method.*
*(SO 6),* **AP**

*BE12-15** Yandell Corporation reports operating expenses of $90,000, excluding depreciation expense of $15,000 for 2012. During the year, prepaid expenses decreased $7,200 and accrued expenses payable increased $4,400. Compute the cash payments for operating expenses in 2012.

*Compute cash payments for operating expenses—direct method.*
*(SO 6),* **AP**

## Do it! Review

**Do it! 12-1** Kirby Corporation had the following transactions.
1. Issued $160,000 of bonds payable.
2. Paid utilities expense.
3. Issued 500 shares of preferred stock for $45,000.
4. Sold land and a building for $250,000.
5. Lent $30,000 to Dead End Corporation, receiving Dead End's 1-year, 12% note.

Classify each of these transactions by type of cash flow activity (operating, investing, or financing).

*Classify transactions by type of cash flow activity.*
*(SO 2),* **C**

*Calculate net cash from operating activities.*
(SO 4), **AP**

**Do it!** 12-2    GW Photography reported net income of $100,000 for 2012. Included in the income statement were depreciation expense of $6,300, patent amortization expense of $4,000, and a gain on sale of equipment of $3,600. GW's comparative balance sheets show the following balances.

|  | **12/31/12** | **12/31/11** |
|---|---|---|
| Accounts receivable | $21,000 | $27,000 |
| Accounts payable | 9,200 | 6,000 |

Calculate net cash provided by operating activities for GW Photography.

*Compute and discuss free cash flow.*
(SO 5), **AP**

**Do it!** 12-3    Barnish Corporation issued the following statement of cash flows for 2012.

### BARNISH CORPORATION
### Statement of Cash Flows—Indirect Method
### For the Year Ended December 31, 2012

| | | |
|---|---:|---:|
| Cash flows from operating activities | | |
| Net income | | $59,000 |
| Adjustments to reconcile net income to net cash provided by operating activities: | | |
| Depreciation expense | $ 9,100 | |
| Decrease in accounts receivable | 9,500 | |
| Increase in inventory | (5,000) | |
| Decrease in accounts payable | (2,200) | |
| Loss on sale of equipment | 3,300 | 14,700 |
| Net cash provided by operating activities | | 73,700 |
| Cash flows from investing activities | | |
| Sale of investments | 3,100 | |
| Purchase of equipment | (24,200) | |
| Net cash used by investing activities | | (21,100) |
| Cash flows from financing activities | | |
| Issuance of stock | 20,000 | |
| Payment on long-term note payable | (10,000) | |
| Payment for dividends | (13,000) | |
| Net cash used by financing activities | | (3,000) |
| Net increase in cash | | 49,600 |
| Cash at beginning of year | | 13,000 |
| Cash at end of year | | $62,600 |

(a) Compute free cash flow for Barnish Corporation.
(b) Explain why free cash flow often provides better information than "Net cash provided by operating activities."

# Exercises

*Classify transactions by type of activity.*
(SO 2), **C**

**E12-1**    Strawn Corporation had these transactions during 2012.
(a) Purchased a machine for $30,000, giving a long-term note in exchange.
(b) Issued $50,000 par value common stock for cash.
(c) Issued $200,000 par value common stock upon conversion of bonds having a face value of $200,000.
(d) Declared and paid a cash dividend of $13,000.
(e) Sold a long-term investment with a cost of $15,000 for $15,000 cash.
(f) Collected $16,000 of accounts receivable.
(g) Paid $18,000 on accounts payable.

### Instructions

Analyze the transactions and indicate whether each transaction resulted in a cash flow from operating activities, investing activities, financing activities, or noncash investing and financing activities.

**E12-2** An analysis of comparative balance sheets, the current year's income statement, and the general ledger accounts of Gygi Corp. uncovered the following items. Assume all items involve cash unless there is information to the contrary.

*Classify transactions by type of activity.*
(SO 2), **C**

(a) Payment of interest on notes payable.
(b) Exchange of land for patent.
(c) Sale of building at book value.
(d) Payment of dividends.
(e) Depreciation.
(f) Conversion of bonds into common stock.
(g) Receipt of interest on notes receivable.
(h) Issuance of capital stock.
(i) Amortization of patent.
(j) Issuance of bonds for land.
(k) Purchase of land.
(l) Receipt of dividends on investment in stock.
(m) Loss on sale of land.
(n) Retirement of bonds.

**Instructions**
Indicate how each item should be classified in the statement of cash flows using these four major classifications: operating activity (indirect method), investing activity, financing activity, and significant noncash investing and financing activity.

**E12-3** The information in the table is from the statement of cash flows for a company at four different points in time (A, B, C, and D). Negative values are presented in parentheses.

*Identify phases of product life cycle.*
(SO 3), **C**

|  | **Point in Time** | | | |
|---|---|---|---|---|
|  | **A** | **B** | **C** | **D** |
| Cash provided by operations | $ (60,000) | $ 30,000 | $120,000 | $(10,000) |
| Cash provided by investing | (100,000) | 25,000 | 30,000 | (40,000) |
| Cash provided by financing | 70,000 | (90,000) | (50,000) | 120,000 |
| Net income | (38,000) | 10,000 | 100,000 | (5,000) |

**Instructions**
For each point in time, state whether the company is most likely in the introductory phase, growth phase, maturity phase, or decline phase. In each case, explain your choice.

**E12-4** Azen Company reported net income of $190,000 for 2012. Azen also reported depreciation expense of $35,000 and a loss of $5,000 on the sale of equipment. The comparative balance sheet shows an increase in accounts receivable of $15,000 for the year, a $17,000 increase in accounts payable, and a $4,000 increase in prepaid expenses.

*Prepare the operating activities section—indirect method.*
(SO 4), **AP**

**Instructions**
Prepare the operating activities section of the statement of cash flows for 2012. Use the indirect method.

**E12-5** The current sections of Putzier Inc.'s balance sheets at December 31, 2011 and 2012, are presented here. Putzier's net income for 2012 was $153,000. Depreciation expense was $27,000.

*Prepare the operating activities section—indirect method.*
(SO 4), **AP**

|  | **2012** | **2011** |
|---|---|---|
| Current assets |  |  |
| Cash | $105,000 | $ 99,000 |
| Accounts receivable | 80,000 | 89,000 |
| Inventory | 168,000 | 172,000 |
| Prepaid expenses | 27,000 | 22,000 |
| Total current assets | $380,000 | $382,000 |
| Current liabilities |  |  |
| Accrued expenses payable | $ 15,000 | $ 5,000 |
| Accounts payable | 85,000 | 92,000 |
| Total current liabilities | $100,000 | $ 97,000 |

**Instructions**
Prepare the net cash provided by operating activities section of the company's statement of cash flows for the year ended December 31, 2012, using the indirect method.

Prepare statement of cash
flows—indirect method.
(SO 4), **AP**

**E12-6** The following information is available for Oscar Corporation for the year ended December 31, 2012.

| | |
|---|---:|
| Beginning cash balance | $ 45,000 |
| Accounts payable decrease | 3,700 |
| Depreciation expense | 162,000 |
| Accounts receivable increase | 8,200 |
| Inventory increase | 11,000 |
| Net income | 284,100 |
| Cash received for sale of land at book value | 35,000 |
| Cash dividends paid | 12,000 |
| Income taxes payable increase | 4,700 |
| Cash used to purchase building | 289,000 |
| Cash used to purchase treasury stock | 26,000 |
| Cash received from issuing bonds | 200,000 |

**Instructions**
Prepare a statement of cash flows using the indirect method.

Prepare partial statement of
cash flows—indirect method.
(SO 4), **AN**

**E12-7** The three accounts shown below appear in the general ledger of Jurena Corp. during 2012.

**Equipment**

| Date | | Debit | Credit | Balance |
|---|---|---|---|---|
| Jan. 1 | Balance | | | 160,000 |
| July 31 | Purchase of equipment | 70,000 | | 230,000 |
| Sept. 2 | Cost of equipment constructed | 53,000 | | 283,000 |
| Nov. 10 | Cost of equipment sold | | 49,000 | 234,000 |

**Accumulated Depreciation—Equipment**

| Date | | Debit | Credit | Balance |
|---|---|---|---|---|
| Jan. 1 | Balance | | | 71,000 |
| Nov. 10 | Accumulated depreciation on equipment sold | 16,000 | | 55,000 |
| Dec. 31 | Depreciation for year | | 28,000 | 83,000 |

**Retained Earnings**

| Date | | Debit | Credit | Balance |
|---|---|---|---|---|
| Jan. 1 | Balance | | | 105,000 |
| Aug. 23 | Dividends (cash) | 14,000 | | 91,000 |
| Dec. 31 | Net income | | 72,000 | 163,000 |

**Instructions**
From the postings in the accounts, indicate how the information is reported on a statement of cash flows using the indirect method. The loss on sale of equipment was $8,000. (*Hint:* Cost of equipment constructed is reported in the investing activities section as a decrease in cash of $53,000.)

Prepare a statement of cash
flows—indirect method, and
compute cash-based ratios.
(SO 4, 5), **AP**

**E12-8** Shown below and on the next page are comparative balance sheets for Padgett Company.

**PADGETT COMPANY**
**Comparative Balance Sheets**
**December 31**

| Assets | 2012 | 2011 |
|---|---:|---:|
| Cash | $ 68,000 | $ 22,000 |
| Accounts receivable | 88,000 | 76,000 |
| Inventory | 167,000 | 189,000 |
| Land | 80,000 | 100,000 |
| Equipment | 260,000 | 200,000 |
| Accumulated depreciation—equipment | (66,000) | (32,000) |
| Total | $597,000 | $555,000 |

| Liabilities and Stockholders' Equity | 2012 | 2011 |
|---|---|---|
| Accounts payable | $ 39,000 | $ 43,000 |
| Bonds payable | 150,000 | 200,000 |
| Common stock ($1 par) | 216,000 | 174,000 |
| Retained earnings | 192,000 | 138,000 |
| Total | $597,000 | $555,000 |

Additional information:

1. Net income for 2012 was $93,000.
2. Depreciation expense was $34,000.
3. Cash dividends of $39,000 were declared and paid.
4. Bonds payable amounting to $50,000 were redeemed for cash $50,000.
5. Common stock was issued for $42,000 cash.
6. No equipment was sold during 2012.
7. Land was sold for its book value.

**Instructions**
(a) Prepare a statement of cash flows for 2012 using the indirect method.
(b) Compute these cash-based ratios:
   (1) Current cash debt coverage.
   (2) Cash debt coverage.

**E12-9** Presented below is 2009 information for PepsiCo, Inc. and The Coca-Cola Company.

*Compare two companies by using cash-based ratios.*
*(SO 5),* **AN**

| ($ in millions) | PepsiCo | Coca-Cola |
|---|---|---|
| Cash provided by operations | $ 6,796 | $ 8,186 |
| Average current liabilities | 8,772 | 13,355 |
| Average total liabilities | 22,909 | 21,491 |
| Net income | 5,979 | 6,906 |
| Sales | 43,232 | 30,990 |
| Capital expenditures | 2,128 | 1,993 |
| Dividends paid | 2,732 | 3,800 |

**Instructions**
Using the cash-based measures presented in this chapter, compare the (a) liquidity and (b) solvency of the two companies.

**E12-10** Information for two companies in the same industry, Meadow Corporation and Plain Corporation, is presented here.

*Compare two companies by using cash-based ratios.*
*(SO 5),* **AN**

| | Meadow Corporation | Plain Corporation |
|---|---|---|
| Cash provided by operating activities | $ 80,000 | $100,000 |
| Average current liabilities | 50,000 | 100,000 |
| Average total liabilities | 180,000 | 250,000 |
| Net income | 200,000 | 200,000 |
| Capital expenditures | 40,000 | 70,000 |
| Dividends paid | 5,000 | 10,000 |

**Instructions**
Using the cash-based measures presented in this chapter, compare the (a) liquidity and (b) solvency of the two companies.

***E12-11** Orchard Company completed its first year of operations on December 31, 2012. Its initial income statement showed that Orchard had revenues of $198,000 and operating expenses of $83,000. Accounts receivable and accounts payable at year-end were $60,000 and $23,000, respectively. Assume that accounts payable related to operating expenses. Ignore income taxes.

*Compute cash provided by operating activities—direct method.*
*(SO 6),* **AP**

*Instructions*

Compute net cash provided by operating activities using the direct method.

*****E12-12** The 2009 income statement for McDonald's Corporation shows cost of goods sold $5,178.0 million and operating expenses (including depreciation expense of $1,216.2 million) $10,725.7 million. The comparative balance sheet for the year shows that inventory decreased $5.3 million, prepaid expenses increased $42.2 million, accounts payable (merchandise suppliers) increased $15.6 million, and accrued expenses payable increased $199.8 million.

*Instructions*

Using the direct method, compute (a) cash payments to suppliers and (b) cash payments for operating expenses.

*Compute cash flow from*
*operating activities—direct*
*method.*
(SO 6), **AP**

*****E12-13** The 2012 accounting records of Pape Transport reveal these transactions and events.

| | | | |
|---|---|---|---|
| Payment of interest | $ 10,000 | Payment of salaries and wages | $ 53,000 |
| Cash sales | 48,000 | Depreciation expense | 16,000 |
| Receipt of dividend revenue | 18,000 | Proceeds from sale of vehicles | 812,000 |
| Payment of income taxes | 12,000 | Purchase of equipment for cash | 22,000 |
| Net income | 38,000 | Loss on sale of vehicles | 3,000 |
| Payment for merchandise | 97,000 | Payment of dividends | 14,000 |
| Payment for land | 74,000 | Payment of operating expenses | 28,000 |
| Collection of accounts receivable | 195,000 | | |

*Instructions*

Prepare the cash flows from operating activities section using the direct method.

*Prepare statement of cash*
*flows—direct method.*
(SO 6), **AP**

*****E12-14** The following information is available for Washington Mills Corp. for 2012.

| | |
|---|---|
| Cash used to purchase treasury stock | $ 48,100 |
| Cash dividends paid | 21,800 |
| Cash paid for interest | 22,400 |
| Net income | 464,300 |
| Sales | 802,000 |
| Cash paid for taxes | 99,000 |
| Cash received from customers | 566,100 |
| Cash received from sale of building (at book value) | 197,600 |
| Cash paid for operating expenses | 77,000 |
| Beginning cash balance | 11,000 |
| Cash paid for goods and services | 279,100 |
| Cash received from issuing common stock | 355,000 |
| Cash paid to redeem bonds at maturity | 200,000 |
| Cash paid to purchase equipment | 113,200 |

*Instructions*

Prepare a statement of cash flows using the direct method.

*****E12-15** The following information is taken from the 2012 general ledger of Mathias Company.

| | | |
|---|---|---|
| Rent | Rent expense | $ 30,000 |
| | Prepaid rent, January 1 | 5,900 |
| | Prepaid rent, December 31 | 7,400 |
| Salaries | Salaries expense | $ 54,000 |
| | Salaries payable, January 1 | 2,000 |
| | Salaries payable, December 31 | 8,000 |
| Sales | Revenue from sales | $160,000 |
| | Accounts receivable, January 1 | 16,000 |
| | Accounts receivable, December 31 | 7,000 |

### Instructions

In each case, compute the amount that should be reported in the operating activities section of the statement of cash flows under the direct method.

# Exercises: Set B and Challenge Exercises

Visit the book's companion website, at **www.wiley.com/college/kimmel,** and choose the Student Companion site to access Exercise Set B and Challenge Exercises.

# Problems: Set A

**P12-1A** You are provided with the following transactions that took place during a recent fiscal year.

*Distinguish among operating, investing, and financing activities.*

(SO 2), C

| Transaction | Where Reported on Statement | Cash Inflow, Outflow, or No Effect? |
|---|---|---|
| (a) Recorded depreciation expense on the plant assets. | | |
| (b) Recorded and paid interest expense. | | |
| (c) Recorded cash proceeds from a sale of plant assets. | | |
| (d) Acquired land by issuing common stock. | | |
| (e) Paid a cash dividend to preferred stockholders. | | |
| (f) Distributed a stock dividend to common stockholders. | | |
| (g) Recorded cash sales. | | |
| (h) Recorded sales on account. | | |
| (i) Purchased inventory for cash. | | |
| (j) Purchased inventory on account. | | |

### Instructions

Complete the table, indicating whether each item (1) should be reported as an operating (O) activity, investing (I) activity, financing (F) activity, or as a noncash (NC) transaction reported in a separate schedule, and (2) represents a cash inflow or cash outflow or has no cash flow effect. Assume use of the indirect approach.

**P12-2A** The following account balances relate to the stockholders' equity accounts of Patil Corp. at year-end.

*Determine cash flow effects of changes in equity accounts.*

(SO 4), AN

| | 2012 | 2011 |
|---|---|---|
| Common stock, 10,500 and 10,000 shares, respectively, for 2012 and 2011 | $160,800 | $140,000 |
| Preferred stock, 5,000 shares | 125,000 | 125,000 |
| Retained earnings | 300,000 | 270,000 |

A small stock dividend was declared and issued in 2012. The market value of the shares was $8,800. Cash dividends were $20,000 in both 2012 and 2011. The common stock has no par or stated value.

### Instructions

(a) What was the amount of net income reported by Patil Corp. in 2012?

(b) Determine the amounts of any cash inflows or outflows related to the common stock and dividend accounts in 2012.

(c) Indicate where each of the cash inflows or outflows identified in (b) would be classified on the statement of cash flows.

(a) Net income          $58,800

*Prepare the operating activities section—indirect method.*
(SO 4), **AP**

**P12-3A** The income statement of Mazor Company is presented here.

### MAZOR COMPANY
### Income Statement
### For the Year Ended November 30, 2012

| | | |
|---|---:|---:|
| Sales | | $7,600,000 |
| Cost of goods sold | | |
| Beginning inventory | $1,900,000 | |
| Purchases | 4,400,000 | |
| Goods available for sale | 6,300,000 | |
| Ending inventory | 1,600,000 | |
| Total cost of goods sold | | 4,700,000 |
| Gross profit | | 2,900,000 |
| Operating expenses | | |
| Selling expenses | 450,000 | |
| Administrative expenses | 700,000 | 1,150,000 |
| Net income | | $1,750,000 |

Additional information:

1. Accounts receivable decreased $380,000 during the year, and inventory decreased $300,000.
2. Prepaid expenses increased $150,000 during the year.
3. Accounts payable to suppliers of merchandise decreased $350,000 during the year.
4. Accrued expenses payable decreased $100,000 during the year.
5. Administrative expenses include depreciation expense of $110,000.

**Instructions**

*Cash from operations*
*$1,940,000*

Prepare the operating activities section of the statement of cash flows for the year ended November 30, 2012, for Mazor Company, using the indirect method.

*Prepare the operating activities section—direct method.*
(SO 6), **AP**

*P12-4A** Data for Mazor Company are presented in P12-3A.

**Instructions**

*Cash from operations*
*$1,940,000*

Prepare the operating activities section of the statement of cash flows using the direct method.

*Prepare the operating activities section—indirect method.*
(SO 4), **AP**

**P12-5A** Retzlaff Company's income statement contained the condensed information below.

### RETZLAFF COMPANY
### Income Statement
### For the Year Ended December 31, 2012

| | | |
|---|---:|---:|
| Revenues | | $970,000 |
| Operating expenses, excluding depreciation | $614,000 | |
| Depreciation expense | 55,000 | |
| Loss on sale of equipment | 16,000 | 685,000 |
| Income before income taxes | | 285,000 |
| Income tax expense | | 56,000 |
| Net income | | $229,000 |

Retzlaff's balance sheet contained the comparative data at December 31.

| | 2012 | 2011 |
|---|---:|---:|
| Accounts receivable | $70,000 | $60,000 |
| Accounts payable | 41,000 | 32,000 |
| Income taxes payable | 13,000 | 7,000 |

Accounts payable pertain to operating expenses.

**Instructions**

*Cash from operations*
*$305,000*

Prepare the operating activities section of the statement of cash flows using the indirect method.

*P12-6A    Data for Retzlaff Company are presented in P12-5A.

**Instructions**
Prepare the operating activities section of the statement of cash flows using the direct method.

P12-7A    Presented below are the financial statements of Helwany Company.

*Prepare the operating activities section—direct method.*
(SO 6), **AP**                    Cash from
                                  operations
                                  $305,000

### HELWANY COMPANY
### Comparative Balance Sheets
### December 31

*Prepare a statement of cash flows—indirect method, and compute cash-based ratios.*
(SO 4, 5), **AP**

| Assets | 2012 | 2011 |
|---|---|---|
| Cash | $ 35,000 | $ 20,000 |
| Accounts receivable | 20,000 | 14,000 |
| Inventory | 28,000 | 20,000 |
| Property, plant, and equipment | 60,000 | 78,000 |
| Accumulated depreciation | (32,000) | (24,000) |
| Total | $111,000 | $108,000 |

| Liabilities and Stockholders' Equity | | |
|---|---|---|
| Accounts payable | $ 19,000 | $ 15,000 |
| Income taxes payable | 7,000 | 8,000 |
| Bonds payable | 17,000 | 33,000 |
| Common stock | 18,000 | 14,000 |
| Retained earnings | 50,000 | 38,000 |
| Total | $111,000 | $108,000 |

### HELWANY COMPANY
### Income Statement
### For the Year Ended December 31, 2012

| | | |
|---|---|---|
| Sales | | $242,000 |
| Cost of goods sold | | 175,000 |
| Gross profit | | 67,000 |
| Selling expenses | $18,000 | |
| Administrative expenses | 6,000 | 24,000 |
| Income from operations | | 43,000 |
| Interest expense | | 3,000 |
| Income before income taxes | | 40,000 |
| Income tax expense | | 8,000 |
| Net income | | $ 32,000 |

Additional data:

1. Depreciation expense was $17,500.
2. Dividends declared and paid were $20,000.
3. During the year equipment was sold for $8,500 cash. This equipment cost $18,000 originally and had accumulated depreciation of $9,500 at the time of sale.

**Instructions**
(a) Prepare a statement of cash flows using the indirect method.
(b) Compute these cash-based measures:
   (1) Current cash debt coverage ratio.
   (2) Cash debt coverage ratio.
   (3) Free cash flow.

(a) Cash from operations
$38,500

*P12-8A    Data for Helwany Company are presented in P12-7A. Further analysis reveals the following.

1. Accounts payable pertain to merchandise suppliers.
2. All operating expenses except for depreciation were paid in cash.
3. All depreciation expense is in the selling expense category.
4. All sales and purchases are on account.

*Prepare a statement of cash flows—direct method, and compute cash-based ratios.*
(SO 5, 6), **AP**

(a) Cash from operations
$38,500

**Instructions**
(a) Prepare a statement of cash flows for Helwany Company using the direct method.
(b) Compute these cash-based measures:
 (1) Current cash debt coverage ratio.
 (2) Cash debt coverage ratio.
 (3) Free cash flow.

*Prepare a statement of cash flows—indirect method.*
(SO 4), **AP**

**P12-9A** Condensed financial data of Lemere Inc. follow.

### LEMERE INC.
### Comparative Balance Sheets
### December 31

| Assets | 2012 | 2011 |
|---|---|---|
| Cash | $ 80,800 | $ 48,400 |
| Accounts receivable | 87,800 | 38,000 |
| Inventory | 112,500 | 102,850 |
| Prepaid expenses | 28,400 | 26,000 |
| Long-term investments | 138,000 | 109,000 |
| Plant assets | 285,000 | 242,500 |
| Accumulated depreciation | (50,000) | (52,000) |
| Total | $682,500 | $514,750 |

| Liabilities and Stockholders' Equity | | |
|---|---|---|
| Accounts payable | $102,000 | $ 67,300 |
| Accrued expenses payable | 16,500 | 21,000 |
| Bonds payable | 110,000 | 146,000 |
| Common stock | 220,000 | 175,000 |
| Retained earnings | 234,000 | 105,450 |
| Total | $682,500 | $514,750 |

### LEMERE INC.
### Income Statement Data
### For the Year Ended December 31, 2012

| | | |
|---|---|---|
| Sales | | $388,460 |
| Less: | | |
| Cost of goods sold | $135,460 | |
| Operating expenses, excluding depreciation | 12,410 | |
| Depreciation expense | 46,500 | |
| Income taxes | 27,280 | |
| Interest expense | 4,730 | |
| Loss on sale of plant assets | 7,500 | 233,880 |
| Net income | | $154,580 |

Additional information:

1. New plant assets costing $100,000 were purchased for cash during the year.
2. Old plant assets having an original cost of $57,500 and accumulated depreciation of $48,500 were sold for $1,500 cash.
3. Bonds payable matured and were paid off at face value for cash.
4. A cash dividend of $26,030 was declared and paid during the year.

Cash from operations
$176,930

**Instructions**
Prepare a statement of cash flows using the indirect method.

*Prepare a statement of cash flows—direct method.*
(SO 6), **AP**
Cash from operations
$176,930

**\*P12-10A** Data for Lemere Inc. are presented in P12-9A. Further analysis reveals that accounts payable pertain to merchandise creditors.

**Instructions**
Prepare a statement of cash flows for Lemere Inc. using the direct method.

**P12-11A**  The comparative balance sheets for Vanco Company as of December 31 are presented below.

*Prepare a statement of cash flows—indirect method.*
(SO 4), **AP**

### VANCO COMPANY
### Comparative Balance Sheets
### December 31

| Assets | 2012 | 2011 |
|---|---|---|
| Cash | $ 68,000 | $ 45,000 |
| Accounts receivable | 50,000 | 58,000 |
| Inventory | 151,450 | 142,000 |
| Prepaid expenses | 15,280 | 21,000 |
| Land | 145,000 | 130,000 |
| Equipment | 225,000 | 155,000 |
| Accumulated depreciation—equipment | (45,000) | (35,000) |
| Buildings | 200,000 | 200,000 |
| Accumulated depreciation—buildings | (60,000) | (40,000) |
| Total | $749,730 | $676,000 |
| **Liabilities and Stockholders' Equity** | | |
| Accounts payable | $ 44,730 | $ 36,000 |
| Bonds payable | 300,000 | 300,000 |
| Common stock, $1 par | 200,000 | 160,000 |
| Retained earnings | 205,000 | 180,000 |
| Total | $749,730 | $676,000 |

Additional information:

1. Operating expenses include depreciation expense of $42,000.
2. Land was sold for cash at book value.
3. Cash dividends of $12,000 were paid.
4. Net income for 2012 was $37,000.
5. Equipment was purchased for $92,000 cash. In addition, equipment costing $22,000 with a book value of $10,000 was sold for $8,000 cash.
6. 40,000 shares of $1 par value common stock were issued in exchange for land with a fair value of $40,000.

**Instructions**
Prepare a statement of cash flows for the year ended December 31, 2012, using the indirect method.

Cash from operations
$94,000

**P12-12A**  You are provided with the following transactions that took place during the year.

*Identify the impact of transactions on ratios.*
(SO 5), **C**

| Transactions | Free Cash Flow ($125,000) | Current Cash Debt Coverage Ratio (0.5 times) | Cash Debt Coverage Ratio (0.3 times) |
|---|---|---|---|
| (a) Recorded credit sales $2,500. | | | |
| (b) Collected $1,900 owed by customers. | | | |
| (c) Paid amount owed to suppliers $2,750. | | | |
| (d) Recorded sales returns of $500 and credited the customer's account. | | | |
| (e) Purchased new equipment $5,000; signed a long-term note payable for the cost of the equipment. | | | |
| (f) Purchased a patent and paid $65,000 cash for the asset. | | | |

**Instructions**
For each transaction listed above, indicate whether it will increase (I), decrease (D), or have no effect (NE) on the ratios.

# Problems: Set B

*Distinguish among operating, investing, and financing activities.*

*(SO 2),* **C**

**P12-1B** You are provided with the following transactions that took place during a recent fiscal year.

| Transaction | Where Reported on Statement | Cash Inflow, Outflow, or No Effect? |
|---|---|---|
| (a) Recorded depreciation expense on the plant assets. | | |
| (b) Incurred a loss on disposal of plant assets. | | |
| (c) Acquired a building by paying cash. | | |
| (d) Made principal repayments on a mortgage. | | |
| (e) Issued common stock. | | |
| (f) Purchased shares of another company to be held as a long-term equity investment. | | |
| (g) Paid dividends to common stockholders. | | |
| (h) Sold inventory on credit. The company uses a perpetual inventory system. | | |
| (i) Purchased inventory on credit. | | |
| (j) Paid wages to employees. | | |

**Instructions**

Complete the table indicating whether each item (1) should be reported as an operating (O) activity, investing (I) activity, financing (F) activity, or as a noncash (NC) transaction reported in a separate schedule, and (2) represents a cash inflow or cash outflow or has no cash flow effect. Assume use of the indirect approach.

*Determine cash flow effects of changes in plant asset accounts.*

*(SO 4),* **AN**

**P12-2B** The following selected account balances relate to the plant asset accounts of Karas Inc. at year-end.

| | 2012 | 2011 |
|---|---|---|
| Accumulated depreciation—buildings | $337,500 | $300,000 |
| Accumulated depreciation—equipment | 144,000 | 96,000 |
| Buildings | 750,000 | 750,000 |
| Depreciation expense | 99,500 | 85,500 |
| Equipment | 300,000 | 240,000 |
| Land | 100,000 | 70,000 |
| Loss on sale of plant assets | 6,000 | 0 |

Additional information:

1. Karas purchased $85,000 of equipment and $30,000 of land for cash in 2012.
2. Karas also sold equipment in 2012.
3. Depreciation expense in 2012 was $37,500 on building and $62,000 on equipment.

**Instructions**

*(a) Cash proceeds $5,000*

(a) Determine the amounts of any cash inflows or outflows related to the plant asset accounts in 2012.
(b) Indicate where each of the cash inflows or outflows identified in (a) would be classified on the statement of cash flows.

*Prepare the operating activities section—indirect method.*

*(SO 4),* **AP**

**P12-3B** The income statement of Hauser Company is presented on the next page.

Additional information:

1. Accounts receivable decreased $290,000 during the year, and inventory increased $140,000.
2. Prepaid expenses increased $175,000 during the year.
3. Accounts payable to merchandise suppliers increased $63,000 during the year.
4. Accrued expenses payable increased $145,000 during the year.

### HAUSER COMPANY
### Income Statement
### For the Year Ended December 31, 2012

| | | |
|---|---:|---:|
| Sales | | $5,200,000 |
| Cost of goods sold | | |
| Beginning inventory | $1,780,000 | |
| Purchases | 3,430,000 | |
| Goods available for sale | 5,210,000 | |
| Ending inventory | 1,920,000 | |
| Total cost of goods sold | | 3,290,000 |
| Gross profit | | 1,910,000 |
| Operating expenses | | |
| Selling expenses | 420,000 | |
| Administrative expense | 525,000 | |
| Depreciation expense | 105,000 | |
| Amortization expense | 15,000 | 1,065,000 |
| Net income | | $ 845,000 |

**Instructions**

Prepare the operating activities section of the statement of cash flows for the year ended December 31, 2012, for Hauser Company, using the indirect method.

*Cash from operations
$1,148,000*

**\*P12-4B**  Data for Hauser Company are presented in P12-3B.

**Instructions**

Prepare the operating activities section of the statement of cash flows using the direct method.

*Prepare the operating activities section—direct method.*
(SO 6), **AP**
*Cash from operations
$1,148,000*

**P12-5B**  The income statement of Zamora Inc. reported the following condensed information.

*Prepare the operating activities section—indirect method.*
(SO 4), **AP**

### ZAMORA INC.
### Income Statement
### For the Year Ended December 31, 2012

| | |
|---|---:|
| Revenues | $560,000 |
| Operating expenses | 400,000 |
| Income from operations | 160,000 |
| Income tax expense | 47,000 |
| Net income | $113,000 |

Zamora's balance sheet contained these comparative data at December 31.

| | 2012 | 2011 |
|---|---:|---:|
| Accounts receivable | $60,000 | $75,000 |
| Accounts payable | 35,000 | 48,000 |
| Income taxes payable | 14,000 | 6,000 |

Zamora has no depreciable assets. Accounts payable pertain to operating expenses.

**Instructions**

Prepare the operating activities section of the statement of cash flows using the indirect method.

*Cash from operations
$123,000*

**\*P12-6B**  Data for Zamora Inc. are presented in P12-5B.

**Instructions**

Prepare the operating activities section of the statement of cash flows using the direct method.

*Prepare the operating activities section—direct method.*
(SO 6), **AP**   *Cash from operations
$123,000*

**P12-7B**  Shown on the next page are the financial statements of Klemmer Company.

*Prepare a statement of cash flows—indirect method, and compute cash-based ratios.*

(SO 4, 5), **AP**

### KLEMMER COMPANY
### Comparative Balance Sheets
### December 31

| Assets | | 2012 | | 2011 |
|---|---|---|---|---|
| Cash | | $ 25,000 | | $ 33,000 |
| Accounts receivable | | 23,000 | | 14,000 |
| Inventory | | 41,000 | | 25,000 |
| Property, plant, and equipment | $ 73,000 | | $ 78,000 | |
| Less: Accumulated depreciation | (27,000) | 46,000 | (24,000) | 54,000 |
| Total | | $135,000 | | $126,000 |

| Liabilities and Stockholders' Equity | | 2012 | | 2011 |
|---|---|---|---|---|
| Accounts payable | | $ 23,000 | | $ 46,000 |
| Income taxes payable | | 26,000 | | 23,000 |
| Bonds payable | | 20,000 | | 10,000 |
| Common stock | | 25,000 | | 25,000 |
| Retained earnings | | 41,000 | | 22,000 |
| Total | | $135,000 | | $126,000 |

### KLEMMER COMPANY
### Income Statement
### For the Year Ended December 31, 2012

| | | |
|---|---|---|
| Sales | | $295,000 |
| Cost of goods sold | | 194,000 |
| Gross profit | | 101,000 |
| Selling expenses | $28,000 | |
| Administrative expenses | 9,000 | 37,000 |
| Income from operations | | 64,000 |
| Interest expense | | 7,000 |
| Income before income taxes | | 57,000 |
| Income tax expense | | 13,000 |
| Net income | | $ 44,000 |

Additional data:

1. Depreciation expense was $6,000.
2. Dividends of $25,000 were declared and paid.
3. During the year, equipment was sold for $10,000 cash. This equipment cost $13,000 originally and had accumulated depreciation of $3,000 at the time of sale.
4. Additional equipment was purchased for $8,000 cash.

**Instructions**

(a) Cash from operations
$5,000

(a) Prepare a statement of cash flows using the indirect method.
(b) Compute these cash-based measures:
   (1) Current cash debt coverage ratio.
   (2) Cash debt coverage ratio.
   (3) Free cash flow.

*Prepare a statement of cash flows—direct method, and compute cash-based ratios.*

(SO 5, 6), **AP**

(a) Cash from operations
$5,000

*P12-8B** Data for Klemmer Company are presented in P12-7B. Further analysis reveals the following.

1. Accounts payable pertains to merchandise creditors.
2. All operating expenses except for depreciation are paid in cash.
3. All depreciation expense is in the selling expense category.
4. All sales and purchases are on account.

**Instructions**

(a) Prepare a statement of cash flows using the direct method.
(b) Compute these cash-based measures:
   (1) Current cash debt coverage ratio.
   (2) Cash debt coverage ratio.
   (3) Free cash flow.

**P12-9B**   Condensed financial data of Cadet Company are shown below.

*Prepare a statement of cash flows—indirect method.*
(SO 4), **AP**

## CADET COMPANY
### Comparative Balance Sheets
### December 31

| Assets | 2012 | 2011 |
|---|---|---|
| Cash | $ 78,700 | $ 33,400 |
| Accounts receivable | 72,970 | 37,000 |
| Inventory | 121,900 | 102,650 |
| Long-term investments | 89,500 | 107,000 |
| Plant assets | 320,000 | 205,000 |
| Accumulated depreciation | (49,500) | (40,000) |
| Total | $633,570 | $445,050 |

| Liabilities and Stockholders' Equity | 2012 | 2011 |
|---|---|---|
| Accounts payable | $ 57,700 | $ 48,280 |
| Accrued expenses payable | 15,100 | 18,830 |
| Bonds payable | 140,000 | 70,000 |
| Common stock | 250,000 | 200,000 |
| Retained earnings | 170,770 | 107,940 |
| Total | $633,570 | $445,050 |

## CADET COMPANY
### Income Statement Data
### For the Year Ended December 31, 2012

| | | |
|---|---|---|
| Sales | | $294,500 |
| Gain on sale of plant assets | | 3,000 |
| | | 297,500 |
| Less: | | |
| Cost of goods sold | $104,460 | |
| Operating expenses, excluding depreciation expense | 14,670 | |
| Depreciation expense | 35,500 | |
| Income taxes | 32,100 | |
| Interest expense | 2,940 | 189,670 |
| Net income | | $107,830 |

Additional information:
1. New plant assets costing $151,000 were purchased for cash during the year.
2. Investments were sold at cost.
3. Plant assets costing $36,000 and accumulated depreciation of $26,000 were sold for $13,000.
4. A cash dividend of $45,000 was declared and paid during the year.

**Instructions**
Prepare a statement of cash flows using the indirect method.

*Cash from operations*
*$90,800*

*****P12-10B**   Data for Cadet Company are presented in P12-9B. Further analysis reveals that accounts payable pertain to merchandise creditors.

*Prepare a statement of cash flows—direct method.*
(SO 6), **AP**

**Instructions**
Prepare a statement of cash flows for Cadet Company using the direct method.

*Cash from operations*
*$90,800*

**P12-11B**   Presented on the next page are the comparative balance sheets for Lybeck Company at December 31.

*Prepare a statement of cash flows—indirect method.*
(SO 4), **AP**

**LYBECK COMPANY**
**Comparative Balance Sheets**
**December 31**

| Assets | 2012 | 2011 |
|---|---|---|
| Cash | $ 41,000 | $ 47,000 |
| Accounts receivable | 67,000 | 70,000 |
| Inventory | 182,000 | 124,000 |
| Prepaid expenses | 12,140 | 16,540 |
| Land | 130,000 | 150,000 |
| Equipment | 205,000 | 175,000 |
| Accumulated depreciation—equipment | (70,000) | (42,000) |
| Buildings | 270,000 | 270,000 |
| Accumulated depreciation—buildings | (70,000) | (50,000) |
| Total | $767,140 | $760,540 |

| Liabilities and Stockholders' Equity | | |
|---|---|---|
| Accounts payable | $ 48,000 | $ 45,000 |
| Bonds payable | 265,000 | 265,000 |
| Common stock, $1 par | 280,000 | 250,000 |
| Retained earnings | 174,140 | 200,540 |
| Total | $767,140 | $760,540 |

Additional information:

1. Operating expenses include depreciation expense $65,000 and charges from prepaid expenses of $4,400.
2. Land was sold for cash at cost.
3. Cash dividends of $57,000 were paid.
4. Net income for 2012 was $30,600.
5. Equipment was purchased for $70,000 cash. In addition, equipment costing $40,000 with a book value of $23,000 was sold for $25,000 cash.
6. 30,000 shares of $1 par value common stock were issued in exchange for land with a fair value of $30,000.

***Instructions***
Prepare a statement of cash flows for 2012 using the indirect method.

*Cash from operations*
*$46,000*

# Problems: Set C

Visit the book's companion website, at **www.wiley.com/college/kimmel**, and choose the Student Companion site to access Problem Set C.

 # Continuing Cookie Chronicle

(*Note:* This is a continuation of the Cookie Chronicle from Chapters 1 through 11.)

Natalie has prepared the balance sheet and income statement of Cookie & Coffee Creations Inc. and would like you to prepare the cash flow statement.

Go to the book's companion website, at **www.wiley.com/college/kimmel**, to find the completion of this problem.

# broadening your perspective

## Financial Reporting and Analysis

### FINANCIAL REPORTING PROBLEM: *Tootsie Roll Industries, Inc.*

**BYP12-1**   The financial statements of Tootsie Roll Industries are presented in Appendix A.

*Instructions*
Answer the following questions.
(a)  What was the amount of net cash provided by operating activities for 2009? For 2008?
(b)  What was the amount of increase or decrease in cash and cash equivalents for the year ended December 31, 2009?
(c)  Which method of computing net cash provided by operating activities does Tootsie Roll use?
(d)  From your analysis of the 2009 statement of cash flows, was the change in accounts receivable a decrease or an increase? Was the change in inventories a decrease or an increase? Was the change in accounts payable a decrease or an increase?
(e)  What was the net cash used by investing activities for 2009?
(f)  What was the amount of interest paid in 2009? What was the amount of income taxes paid in 2009?

### COMPARATIVE ANALYSIS PROBLEM: *Tootsie Roll vs. Hershey*

**BYP12-2**   The financial statements of The Hershey Company are presented in Appendix B, following the financial statements for Tootsie Roll Industries in Appendix A.

*Instructions*
(a)  Based on the information in these financial statements, compute these 2009 ratios for each company:
   (1)  Current cash debt coverage.
   (2)  Cash debt coverage.
(b)  What conclusions about the management of cash can you draw from these data?

### RESEARCH CASE

**BYP12-3**   The March 4, 2010, edition of the *Wall Street Journal Online* contains an article by Jeffrey McCracken and Tom McGinty entitled "With Fistfuls of Cash, Firms on Hunt."

*Instructions*
Read the article and answer the following questions.
(a)  How much cash did the nonfinancial (that is, nonbank-like) firms in the Standard and Poor's 500 have at the end of 2009? How big an increase in cash did this represent over the prior year?
(b)  What reasons are given in the article for why companies might not want to keep hoarding cash?
(c)  What steps did Alcoa take to try to increase the company's cash? Were these efforts successful?
(d)  Often, companies issue shares of stock to acquire other companies. This represents a significant noncash transaction. At the time the article was written, why were many companies using cash rather than stock to acquire other companies?
(e)  In addition to acquisitions, what other steps can companies take to reduce their cash balances?

### INTERPRETING FINANCIAL STATEMENTS

**BYP12-4**   The incredible growth of Amazon.com has put fear into the hearts of traditional retailers. Its stock price has soared to amazing levels. However, in 2001 many investors were very concerned about whether Amazon would survive since it had never earned a profit, and it was burning through cash. Some investors sold, but others decided to hold on to their investment in the company's stock. The following information is taken from the 2001 and 2004 financial statements of Amazon.com.

| ($ in millions) | 2001 | 2004 |
|---|---|---|
| Current assets | $1,207.9 | $2,539.4 |
| Total assets | 1,637.5 | 3,248.5 |
| Current liabilities | 921.4 | 1,620.4 |
| Total liabilities | 3,077.5 | 5,096.1 |
| Cash provided by operations | (119.8) | 566.6 |
| Capital expenditures | 50.3 | 89.1 |
| Dividends paid | 0 | 0 |
| Net income (loss) | (567.3) | 588.5 |
| Average current liabilities | 948.2 | 1,436.6 |
| Average total liabilities | 3,090.0 | 4,773.4 |

*Instructions*
(a) Calculate the current ratio and current cash debt coverage ratio for Amazon.com for 2001 and 2004, and discuss its comparative liquidity.
(b) Calculate the cash debt coverage ratio and the debt to total assets ratio for Amazon.com for 2001 and 2004, and discuss its comparative solvency.
(c) Amazon.com has avoided purchasing large warehouses. Instead, it has used those of others. In order to increase customer satisfaction Amazon may have to build its own warehouses. Calculate free cash flow for Amazon.com for 2001 and 2004, and discuss its ability to purchase warehouses and to finance expansion from internally generated cash.
(d) Based on your findings in parts (a) through (c), can you conclude whether or not Amazon.com's amazing stock price is justified?

## FINANCIAL ANALYSIS ON THE WEB

**BYP12-5** *Purpose:* Use the Internet to view SEC filings.

*Address:* **biz.yahoo.com/i**, or go to **www.wiley.com/college/kimmel**

*Steps*
1. Enter a company's name.
2. Choose **Quote**. Answer questions (a) and (b).
3. Choose **Profile**; then choose **SEC**. Answer questions (c) and (d).

*Instructions*
Answer the following questions.
(a) What company did you select?
(b) What is its stock symbol? What is its selling price?
(c) What recent SEC filings are available for your viewing?
(d) Which filing is the most recent? What is the date?

# Critical Thinking

## DECISION MAKING ACROSS THE ORGANIZATION

**BYP12-6** Bob Soakup and Clare Karr are examining the following statement of cash flows for Baldwin Company for the year ended January 31, 2012.

**BALDWIN COMPANY**
**Statement of Cash Flows**
**For the Year Ended January 31, 2012**

| | |
|---|---|
| Sources of cash | |
| From sales of merchandise | $385,000 |
| From sale of capital stock | 405,000 |
| From sale of investment (purchased below) | 80,000 |
| From depreciation | 55,000 |
| From issuance of note for truck | 20,000 |
| From interest on investments | 6,000 |
| Total sources of cash | 951,000 |

(continues on next page)

| Uses of cash | |
|---|---:|
| For purchase of fixtures and equipment | 320,000 |
| For merchandise purchased for resale | 258,000 |
| For operating expenses (including depreciation) | 170,000 |
| For purchase of investment | 75,000 |
| For purchase of truck by issuance of note | 20,000 |
| For purchase of treasury stock | 10,000 |
| For interest on note payable | 3,000 |
| Total uses of cash | 856,000 |
| Net increase in cash | $ 95,000 |

Bob claims that Baldwin's statement of cash flows is an excellent portrayal of a superb first year with cash increasing $95,000. Clare replies that it was not a superb first year. Rather, she says, the year was an operating failure, that the statement is presented incorrectly, and that $95,000 is not the actual increase in cash. The cash balance at the beginning of the year was $140,000.

*Instructions*
With the class divided into groups, answer the following.
(a) Using the data provided, prepare a statement of cash flows in proper form using the indirect method. The only noncash items in the income statement are depreciation and the gain from the sale of the investment.
(b) With whom do you agree, Bob or Clare? Explain your position.


## COMMUNICATION ACTIVITY

**BYP12-7** Alex Mabry, the owner-president of Computer Services Company, is unfamiliar with the statement of cash flows that you, as his accountant, prepared. He asks for further explanation.

*Instructions*
Write him a brief memo explaining the form and content of the statement of cash flows as shown in Illustration 12-14 (page 638).


## ETHICS CASE

**BYP12-8** Riverside Automotive Corp. is a medium-sized wholesaler of automotive parts. It has 10 stockholders who have been paid a total of $1 million in cash dividends for 8 consecutive years. The board's policy requires that, for this dividend to be declared, net cash provided by operating activities as reported in Riverside Automotive's current year's statement of cash flows must exceed $1 million. President and CEO Carl Stewart's job is secure so long as he produces annual operating cash flows to support the usual dividend.

At the end of the current year, controller Mark Heger presents president Carl Stewart with some disappointing news: The net cash provided by operating activities is calculated by the indirect method to be only $970,000. The president says to Mark, "We must get that amount above $1 million. Isn't there some way to increase operating cash flow by another $30,000?" Mark answers, "These figures were prepared by my assistant. I'll go back to my office and see what I can do." The president replies, "I know you won't let me down, Mark."

Upon close scrutiny of the statement of cash flows, Mark concludes that he can get the operating cash flows above $1 million by reclassifying a $60,000, 2-year note payable listed in the financing activities section as "Proceeds from bank loan—$60,000." He will report the note instead as "Increase in payables—$60,000" and treat it as an adjustment of net income in the operating activities section. He returns to the president, saying, "You can tell the board to declare their usual dividend. Our net cash flow provided by operating activities is $1,030,000." "Good man, Mark! I knew I could count on you," exults the president.

*Instructions*
(a) Who are the stakeholders in this situation?
(b) Was there anything unethical about the president's actions? Was there anything unethical about the controller's actions?
(c) Are the board members or anyone else likely to discover the misclassification?

### "ALL ABOUT YOU" ACTIVITY

**BYP12-9** In this chapter, you learned that companies prepare a statement of cash flows in order to keep track of their sources and uses of cash and to help them plan for their future cash needs. Planning for your own short- and long-term cash needs is every bit as important as it is for a company.

***Instructions***

Read the article "Financial 'Uh-oh'? No Problem," at **www.fool.com/savings/shortterm/02.htm**, and answer the following questions.
(a) Describe the three factors that determine how much money you should set aside for short-term needs.
(b) How many months of living expenses does the article suggest to set aside?
(c) Estimate how much you should set aside based upon your current situation. Are you closer to Cliff's scenario or to Prudence's?

### FASB CODIFICATION ACTIVITY

**BYP12-10** If your school has a subscription to the FASB Codification, go to **http://aaahq.org/ ascLogin.cfm** to log in and prepare responses to the following. Use the Master Glossary to determine the proper definitions.
(a) What are cash equivalents?
(b) What are financing activities?
(c) What are investing activities?
(d) What are operating activities?
(e) What is the primary objective for the statement of cash flow? Is working capital the basis for meeting this objective?
(f) Do companies need to disclose information about investing and financing activities that do not affect cash receipts or cash payments? If so, how should such information be disclosed?

### Answers to Insight and Accounting Across the Organization Questions

**p. 626 Net *What*? Q:** In general, why do differences exist between net income and net cash provided by operating activities? **A:** The differences are explained by differences in the timing of the reporting of revenues and expenses under accrual accounting versus cash. Under accrual accounting, companies report revenues when earned, even if cash hasn't been received, and they report expenses when incurred, even if cash hasn't been paid.

**p. 629 Operating with Negative Cash Q:** Why do companies have negative cash from operations during the introductory phase? **A:** During the introductory phase, companies usually spend more on inventory than the amount expensed for cost of goods sold because they are building up inventory and their cash collections frequently lag the amount reported for sales. Therefore, even if companies are reporting positive net income, they frequently report negative cash from operations.

### Answers to Self-Test Questions

**1.** c **2.** a **3.** b **4.** a **5.** c **6.** d **7.** b **8.** c **9.** a **10.** d ($132,000 + $10,000 + $6,000 − $12,000) **11.** b **12.** b ($200,000 + $40,000 − $10,000 + $20,000 − $30,000) **13.** a ($100,000 + $50,000 − $30,000) **14.** b ($100,000 + $60,000 − $30,000) **15.** d **16.** d *17. c ($129,000 + ($44,000 − $42,000)) *18. d

## IFRS A Look at IFRS

As in GAAP, the statement of cash flows is a required statement for IFRS. In addition, the content and presentation of an IFRS statement of cash flows is similar to the one used for GAAP. However, the disclosure requirements related to the statement of cash flows are more extensive under GAAP. *IAS 7* ("Cash Flow Statements") provides the overall IFRS requirements for cash flow information.

### KEY POINTS

- Companies preparing financial statements under IFRS must prepare a statement of cash flows as an integral part of the financial statements.
- Both IFRS and GAAP require that the statement of cash flows should have three major sections—operating, investing, and financing—along with changes in cash and cash equivalents.

- Similar to GAAP, the cash flow statement can be prepared using either the indirect or direct method under IFRS. In both U.S. and international settings, companies choose for the most part to use the indirect method for reporting net cash flows from operating activities.
- The definition of cash equivalents used in IFRS is similar to that used in GAAP. A major difference is that in certain situations, bank overdrafts are considered part of cash and cash equivalents under IFRS (which is not the case in GAAP). Under GAAP, bank overdrafts are classified as financing activities in the statement of cash flows and are reported as liabilities on the balance sheet.
- IFRS requires that noncash investing and financing activities be excluded from the statement of cash flows. Instead, these noncash activities should be reported elsewhere. This requirement is interpreted to mean that noncash investing and financing activities should be disclosed in the notes to the financial statements instead of in the financial statements. Under GAAP, companies may present this information on the face of the cash flow statement.
- One area where there can be substantial differences between IFRS and GAAP relates to the classification of interest, dividends, and taxes. The following table indicates the differences between the two approaches.

| Item | IFRS | GAAP |
|---|---|---|
| Interest paid | Operating or financing | Operating |
| Interest received | Operating or investing | Operating |
| Dividends paid | Operating or financing | Financing |
| Dividends received | Operating or investing | Operating |
| Taxes paid | Operating—unless specific identification with financing or investing activity | Operating |

- Under IFRS, some companies present the operating section in a single line item, with a full reconciliation provided in the notes to the financial statements. This presentation is not seen under GAAP.
- Similar to GAAP, under IFRS companies must disclose the amount of taxes and interest paid. Under GAAP, companies disclose this in the notes to the financial statements. Under IFRS, some companies disclose this information in the notes, but others provide individual line items on the face of the statement. In order to provide this information on the face of the statement, companies first add back the amount of interest expense and tax expense (similar to adding back depreciation expense) and then further down the statement they subtract the cash amount paid for interest and taxes. This treatment can be seen in the statement of cash flows provided for Zetar in Appendix C.

## LOOKING TO THE FUTURE

Presently, the FASB and the IASB are involved in a joint project on the presentation and organization of information in the financial statements. One interesting approach, revealed in a published proposal from that project, is that in the future the income statement and balance sheet would adopt headings similar to those of the statement of cash flows. That is, the income statement and balance sheet would be broken into operating, investing, and financing sections.

With respect to the cash flow statement specifically, the notion of *cash equivalents* will probably not be retained. That is, cash equivalents will not be combined with cash but instead will be reported as a form of highly liquid, low-risk investment. The definition of cash in the existing literature would be retained, and the statement of cash flows would present information on changes in cash only. In addition, the FASB favors presentation of operating cash flows using the direct method only. However, the majority of IASB members express a preference for not requiring use of the direct method of reporting operating cash flows. The two Boards will have to resolve their differences in this area in order to issue a converged standard for the statement of cash flows.

## IFRS Self-Test Questions

1. Under IFRS, interest paid can be reported as:
   (a) only a financing element.
   (b) a financing element or an investing element.
   (c) a financing element or an operating element.
   (d) only an operating element.

2. IFRS requires that noncash items:
   (a) be reported in the section to which they relate, that is, a noncash investing activity would be reported in the investing section.
   (b) be disclosed in the notes to the financial statements.
   (c) do not need to be reported.
   (d) be treated in a fashion similar to cash equivalents.
3. In the future, it appears likely that:
   (a) the income statement and balance sheet will have headings of operating, investing, and financing, much like the statement of cash flows.
   (b) cash and cash equivalents will be combined in a single line item.
   (c) the IASB will not allow companies to use the direct approach to the statement of cash flows.
   (d) None of the above.
4. Under IFRS:
   (a) taxes are always treated as an operating item.
   (b) the income statement uses the headings operating, investing, and financing.
   (c) dividends received can be either an operating or investing item.
   (d) dividends paid can be either an operating or investing item.
5. Which of the following is *correct*?
   (a) Under IFRS, the statement of cash flows is optional.
   (b) IFRS requires use of the direct approach in preparing the statement of cash flows.
   (c) The majority of companies following GAAP and the majority following IFRS employ the indirect approach to the statement of cash flows.
   (d) Cash and cash equivalents are reported as separate line items under IFRS.

## IFRS Concepts and Application

**IFRS 12-1** Discuss the differences that exist in the treatment of bank overdrafts under GAAP and IFRS.

**IFRS12-2** Describe the treatment of each of the following items under IFRS versus GAAP.
   (a) Interest paid.
   (b) Interest received.
   (c) Dividends paid.
   (d) Dividends received.

**IFRS 12-3** Explain how the treatment of cash equivalents will probably change in the future.

## INTERNATIONAL FINANCIAL REPORTING PROBLEM: *Zetar plc*

**IFRS12-4** The financial statements of Zetar plc are presented in Appendix C. The company's complete annual report, including the notes to its financial statements, is available at **www.zetarplc.com**.

*Instructions*
Use the company's annual report to answer the following questions.
   (a) In which section (operating, investing, or financing) does Zetar report interest paid?
   (b) Explain why the amount that Zetar reports for cash and cash equivalents in its statement of cash flows is negative.
   (c) If Zetar reported under GAAP rather than IFRS, how would its treatment of bank overdrafts differ?
   (d) Zetar's statement of cash flows reports negative "net movement in working capital" in 2009 of £2,469 (in thousands). According to the statement of cash flows, what were the components of this "net movement"?

## Answers to IFRS Self-Test Questions
**1.** c  **2.** b  **3.** a  **4.** c  **5.** c

Remember to go back to the navigator box on the chapter opening page and check off your completed work.

# chapter 13

# FINANCIAL ANALYSIS: THE BIG PICTURE

## the navigator

- Scan **Study Objectives** ○
- Read **Feature Story** ○
- Scan **Preview** ○
- Read **Text and Answer** **Do it!**
  p. 692 ○   p. 696 ○   p. 704 ○
- Work **Using the Decision Toolkit** ○
- Review **Summary of Study Objectives** ○
- Work **Comprehensive** **Do it!** p. 721 ○
- Answer **Self-Test Questions** ○
- Complete **Assignments** ○
- Go to **WileyPLUS** for practice and tutorials ○
- 🌐 Read **A Look at IFRS** p. 743 ○

## study objectives

**After studying this chapter, you should be able to:**

1 Understand the concept of sustainable income.

2 Indicate how irregular items are presented.

3 Explain the concept of comprehensive income.

4 Describe and apply horizontal analysis.

5 Describe and apply vertical analysis.

6 Identify and compute ratios used in analyzing a company's liquidity, solvency, and profitability.

7 Understand the concept of quality of earnings.

✓ the navigator

A recent issue of *Forbes* magazine listed Warren Buffett as the richest person in the world. His estimated wealth was $62 billion, give or take a few million. How much is $62 billion? If you invested $62 billion in an investment earning just 4%, you could spend $6.8 million per day—every day—forever. How did Mr. Buffett amass this wealth? Through careful investing.

However, if you think you might want to follow Mr. Buffett's example and transform your humble nest egg into a mountain of cash, be warned: His techniques have been widely circulated and emulated, but never practiced with the same degree of success.

Mr. Buffett epitomizes a "value investor." To this day, he applies the same basic techniques he learned in the 1950s from the great value investor Benjamin Graham. That means he spends his time looking for companies that have good long-term potential but are currently underpriced. He invests in companies that have low exposure to debt and that reinvest their earnings for future growth. He does not get caught up in fads or the latest trends. Instead, he looks for companies in industries with sound economics and ones that have high returns on stockholders' equity. He looks for steady earnings trends and high margins.

## IT PAYS TO BE PATIENT

Mr. Buffett sat out on the dot-com mania in the 1990s. When other investors put lots of money into fledgling high-tech firms, Mr. Buffett didn't bite because he did not find dot-com companies that met his criteria. He didn't get to enjoy the stock price boom on the way up, but on the other hand, he didn't have to ride the price back down to Earth. Instead, when the dot-com bubble burst and nearly everyone else was suffering from investment shock, Mr. Buffett swooped in and scooped up deals on companies that he had been following for years.

So, how does Mr. Buffett spend his money? Basically, he doesn't! He still lives in the same house that he purchased in Omaha, Nebraska, in 1958 for $31,500. He still drives his own car (a Cadillac DTS). And, in case you were thinking that his kids are riding the road to Easy Street, think again. Mr. Buffett has committed to giving virtually all of his money to charity before he dies.

Given that neither you nor anyone else will be inheriting Mr. Buffett's riches, you should probably start honing your financial analysis skills. A good way for you to begin your career as a successful investor is to master the fundamentals of financial analysis discussed in this chapter.

*the navigator*

**INSIDE CHAPTER 13 . . .**

We can all learn an important lesson from Warren Buffett: Study companies carefully if you wish to invest. Do not get caught up in fads but instead find companies that are financially healthy. Using some of the basic decision tools presented in this book, you can perform a rudimentary analysis on any U.S. company and draw basic conclusions about its financial health. Although it would not be wise for you to bet your life savings on a company's stock, relying solely on your current level of knowledge, we strongly encourage you to practice your new skills wherever possible. Only with practice will you improve your ability to interpret financial numbers.

Before unleashing you on the world of high finance, we will present a few more important concepts and techniques, as well as provide you with one more comprehensive review of corporate financial statements. We use all of the decision tools presented in this textbook to analyze a single company, with comparisons to a competitor and industry averages.

The content and organization of Chapter 13 are as follows.

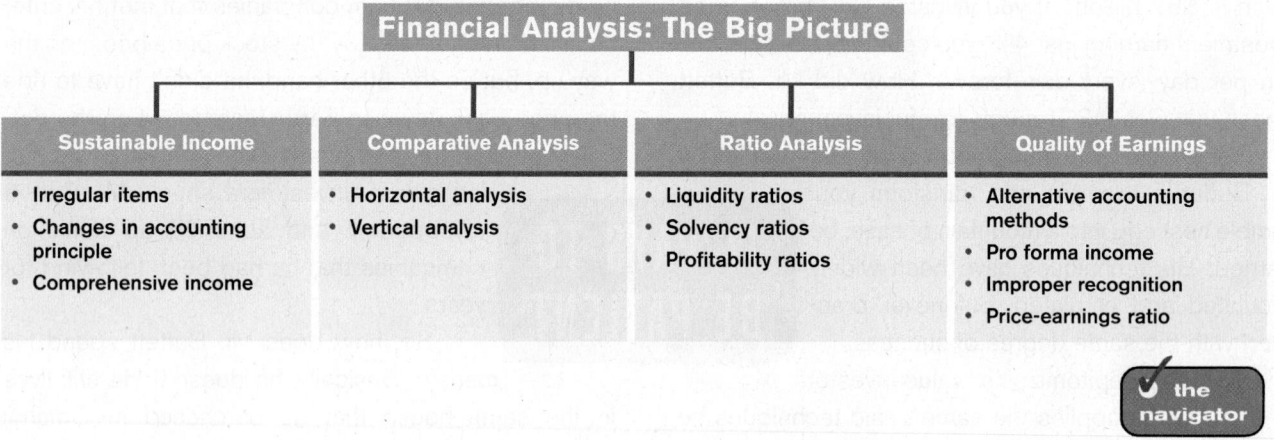

## Sustainable Income

**study objective** **1**

Understand the concept of sustainable income.

Ultimately, the value of a company is a function of its future cash flows. When analysts use this year's net income to estimate future cash flows, they must make sure that this year's net income does not include irregular (i.e., out of the ordinary) revenues, expenses, gains, or losses. Net income adjusted for irregular items is referred to as **sustainable income**. **Sustainable income is the most likely level of income to be obtained in the future.** Sustainable income differs from actual net income by the amount of irregular revenues, expenses, gains, and losses included in this year's net income.

Users are interested in sustainable income because it helps them derive an estimate of future earnings without the "noise" of irregular items. For example, suppose Rye Corporation reports that this year's net income is $500,000 but included in that amount is a once-in-a-lifetime gain of $400,000. In estimating next year's net income for Rye Corporation, we would likely ignore this $400,000 gain and estimate that next year's net income will be in the neighborhood of $100,000. That is, based on this year's results, the company's sustainable income is roughly $100,000. Therefore, identifying irregular items is important if you are going to use reported earnings to estimate a company's value.

In earlier chapters, you learned how to prepare and use a basic multiple-step income statement. In this chapter, we will explain additional components of the income statement as well as a broader measure of performance called *comprehensive income*. Illustration 13-1 presents the components of the income statement and comprehensive income; new items are presented in red. When estimating future cash flows, analysts must consider the implications that each of these components has for future cash flows.

**Income Statement**

| | |
|---|---|
| Sales | $XX |
| Cost of goods sold | XX |
| Gross profit | XX |
| Operating expenses | XX |
| Income from operations | XX |
| Other revenues (expenses) and gains (losses) | XX |
| Income before income taxes | XX |
| Income tax expense | XX |
| Income before irregular items | XX |
| Discontinued operations (net of tax) | XX |
| Extraordinary items (net of tax) | XX |
| Net income | XX |
| Other comprehensive income items (net of tax) | XX |
| Comprehensive income | $XX |

**Illustration 13-1**
Components of the income statement

## IRREGULAR ITEMS

As an aid in determining sustainable income, we identify irregular items by type on the income statement. There, companies report two types of irregular items:

1. Discontinued operations
2. Extraordinary items

**study objective  2**
Indicate how irregular items are presented.

Irregular items are reported net of income taxes. That is, a company first calculates income tax expense for the income before irregular items. Then, it calculates income tax expense for each individual irregular item. The general concept is, "Let the tax follow the income or loss."

### Discontinued Operations

To downsize its operations, General Dynamics Corp. sold its missile business to Hughes Aircraft Co. for $450 million. In its income statement, General Dynamics reported the sale in a separate section entitled "Discontinued operations." **Discontinued operations** refers to the disposal of a significant component of a business, such as the elimination of a major class of customers or an entire activity. When the disposal of a significant component occurs, the income statement should report the gain (or loss) from discontinued operations, net of tax.

To illustrate, assume that Rozek Inc. has revenues of $2.5 million and expenses of $1.7 million from continuing operations in 2012. The company therefore has income before income taxes of $800,000. During 2012, the company discontinued and sold its unprofitable chemical division. The loss on disposal of the chemical division (net of $90,000 tax savings) was $210,000. Illustration 13-2 shows the income statement presentation, assuming a 30% tax rate on income before income taxes.

**Illustration 13-2**
Statement presentation of discontinued operations

**ROZEK INC.**
Income Statement (partial)
For the Year Ended December 31, 2012

| | |
|---|---|
| Income before income taxes | $ 800,000 |
| Income tax expense | 240,000 |
| Income before irregular items | 560,000 |
| Discontinued operations | |
| Loss from disposal of chemical division, net of $90,000 income tax savings | (210,000) |
| Net income | $ 350,000 |

This presentation clearly indicates the separate effects of continuing operations and discontinued operations on net income.

## DECISION TOOLKIT

| DECISION CHECKPOINTS | INFO NEEDED FOR DECISION | TOOL TO USE FOR DECISION | HOW TO EVALUATE RESULTS |
|---|---|---|---|
| Has the company sold any major components of its business? | Discontinued operations section of income statement | Anything reported in this section indicates that the company has discontinued a major component of its business. | If a major component has been discontinued, its results during the current period should not be included in estimates of future net income. |

## Extraordinary Items

**Extraordinary items** are events and transactions that meet two conditions: They are **unusual in nature** and **infrequent in occurrence**. To be considered *unusual*, the item should be abnormal and only incidentally related to the customary activities of the entity. To be regarded as *infrequent*, the event or transaction should not be reasonably expected to recur in the foreseeable future.

A company must evaluate both criteria in terms of the environment in which it operates. Thus, Weyerhaeuser Co. reported the $36 million in damages to its timberland caused by the eruption of Mount St. Helens as an extraordinary item because the event was both unusual and infrequent. In contrast, Florida Citrus Company does not report frost damage to its citrus crop as an extraordinary item because frost damage is not viewed as infrequent.

> **Helpful Hint** Ordinary gains and losses are reported at pretax amounts in arriving at income before income taxes.

**Companies report extraordinary items net of taxes in a separate section of the income statement, immediately below discontinued operations.** To illustrate, assume that in 2012 a revolutionary foreign government expropriated property held as an investment by Rozek Inc. If the loss is $70,000 before applicable income tax savings of $21,000, the income statement presentation will show a deduction of $49,000, as in Illustration 13-3.

**Illustration 13-3**
Statement presentation of extraordinary items

**ROZEK INC.**
Income Statement (partial)
For the Year Ended December 31, 2012

| | |
|---|---:|
| Income before income taxes | $ 800,000 |
| Income tax expense | 240,000 |
| Income before irregular items | 560,000 |
| Discontinued operations: Loss from disposal of chemical division, net of $90,000 income tax savings | (210,000) |
| Extraordinary item: Expropriation of investment, net of $21,000 income tax savings | (49,000) |
| Net income | $ 301,000 |

If a transaction or event meets one but not both of the criteria for an extraordinary item, a company should report it as a separate line item in the upper portion of the income statement, rather than in the bottom portion as an extraordinary item. Usually, companies report these items under either "Other revenues and gains" or "Other expenses and losses" at their gross amount (not net of tax). This is true, for example, of gains (losses) resulting from the sale of property, plant, and equipment, as explained in Chapter 9. Illustration 13-4 shows the appropriate classification of extraordinary and ordinary items.

**Illustration 13-4**
Classification of extraordinary and ordinary items

| Extraordinary items | Ordinary items |
|---|---|

1. Effects of major natural casualties, if rare in the area.

1. Effects of major natural casualties, not uncommon in the area.

2. Expropriation (takeover) of property by a foreign government.

2. Write-down of inventories or write-off of receivables.

3. Effects of a newly enacted law or regulation, such as a condemnation action.

3. Losses attributable to labor strikes.

4. Gains or losses from sales of property, plant, or equipment.

In summary, in evaluating a company, it generally makes sense to eliminate all irregular items in estimating future sustainable income.

## Investor Insight

### What Does "Non-Recurring" Really Mean?

Many companies incur restructuring charges as they attempt to reduce costs. They often label these items in the income statement as "non-recurring" charges, to suggest that they are isolated events, unlikely to occur in future periods. The question for analysts is, are these costs really one-time, "non-recurring events," or do they reflect problems that the company will be facing for many periods in the future? If they are one-time events, then they can be largely ignored when trying to predict future earnings.

But, some companies report "one-time" restructuring charges over and over again. For example, Procter and Gamble Co. reported a restructuring charge in 12 consecutive quarters, and Motorola had "special" charges in 14 consecutive quarters. On the other hand, other companies have a restructuring charge only once in a 5- or 10-year period. There appears to be no substitute for careful analysis of the numbers that comprise net income.

 If a company takes a large restructuring charge, what is the effect on the company's current income statement versus future ones? (See page 742.)

# DECISION TOOLKIT

| DECISION CHECKPOINTS | INFO NEEDED FOR DECISION | TOOL TO USE FOR DECISION | HOW TO EVALUATE RESULTS |
|---|---|---|---|
| Has the company experienced any extraordinary events or transactions? | Extraordinary item section of income statement | Anything reported in this section indicates that the company experienced an event that was both unusual and infrequent. | These items should usually be ignored in estimating future net income. |

**Ethics Note** Changes in accounting principle should result in financial statements that are more informative for statement users. They should not be used to artificially improve the reported performance or financial position of the corporation.

## CHANGES IN ACCOUNTING PRINCIPLE

For ease of comparison, users of financial statements expect companies to prepare their statements on a basis **consistent** with the preceding period. A change in accounting principle occurs when the principle used in the current year is different from the one used in the preceding year. An example is a change in inventory costing methods (such as FIFO to average-cost). Accounting rules permit a change when management can show that the new principle is preferable to the old principle.

Companies report most changes in accounting principle retroactively.[1] That is, they report both the current period and previous periods using the new principle. As a result, the same principle applies in all periods. This treatment improves the ability to compare results across years.

# DECISION TOOLKIT

| DECISION CHECKPOINTS | INFO NEEDED FOR DECISION | TOOL TO USE FOR DECISION | HOW TO EVALUATE RESULTS |
|---|---|---|---|
| Has the company changed any of its accounting principles? | Effect of change in accounting principle on current and prior periods. | Management indicates that the new principle is preferable to the old principle. | Examine current and prior years' reported income, using new-principle basis to assess trends for estimating future income. |

## COMPREHENSIVE INCOME

**study objective 3**
Explain the concept of comprehensive income.

Most revenues, expenses, gains, and losses are included in net income. However, certain gains and losses bypass net income. Instead, companies record these items as direct adjustments to stockholders' equity. Many analysts have expressed concern about this practice because they believe it reduces the usefulness of the income statement. To address this concern, the FASB requires companies to report not only net income but also comprehensive income. Comprehensive income includes all changes in stockholders' equity during a period except those changes resulting from investments by stockholders and distributions to stockholders.

### Illustration of Comprehensive Income

Accounting standards require that companies adjust most investments in stocks and bonds up or down to their market value at the end of each accounting period. For example, assume that during 2012 Stassi Company purchased IBM stock for $10,000 as an investment. At the end of 2012, Stassi was still holding the investment, but the stock's market value was now $8,000. In this case, Stassi is required to reduce the recorded value of its IBM investment by $2,000. The $2,000 difference is an unrealized loss.

---

[1]An exception to the general rule is a change in depreciation methods. The effects of this change are reported in current and future periods. Discussion of this approach is left for more advanced courses.

Should Stassi include this $2,000 unrealized loss in net income? It depends on whether Stassi classifies the IBM stock as a trading security or an available-for-sale security. A **trading security** is bought and held primarily for sale in the near term to generate income on short-term price differences. Companies report unrealized losses on trading securities in the "Other expenses and losses" section of the income statement. The rationale: It is likely that the company will realize the unrealized loss (or an unrealized gain), so the company should report the loss (gain) as part of net income.

If Stassi did not purchase the investment for trading purposes, it is classified as available-for-sale. **Available-for-sale securities** are held with the intent of selling them sometime in the future. Companies do not include unrealized gains or losses on available-for-sale securities in net income. Instead, they report them as part of "Other comprehensive income." Other comprehensive income is not included in net income. It bypasses net income and is recorded as a direct adjustment to stockholders' equity.

## Format

One format for reporting comprehensive income is to report a combined statement of income and comprehensive income.[2] For example, assuming that Stassi Company has a net income of $300,000, the unrealized loss would be reported below net income as follows.

**STASSI CORPORATION**
Combined Statement of Income and
Comprehensive Income (partial)

| | |
|---|---|
| Net income | $300,000 |
| Unrealized loss on available-for-sale securities | 2,000 |
| Comprehensive income | $298,000 |

**Illustration 13-5** Lower portion of combined statement of income and comprehensive income

Companies also report the unrealized loss on available-for-sale securities as a separate component of stockholders' equity. To illustrate, assume Stassi Corporation has common stock of $3,000,000, retained earnings of $1,500,000, and an unrealized loss on available-for-sale securities of $2,000. Illustration 13-6 shows the balance sheet presentation of the unrealized loss.

**STASSI CORPORATION**
Balance Sheet (partial)

| | |
|---|---|
| Stockholders' equity | |
| Common stock | $3,000,000 |
| Retained earnings | 1,500,000 |
| Total paid-in capital and retained earnings | 4,500,000 |
| **Less: Unrealized loss on available-for-sale securities** | **(2,000)** |
| Total stockholders' equity | $4,498,000 |

**Illustration 13-6** Unrealized loss in stockholders' equity section

[2]Computation of comprehensive income shown in a separate statement of comprehensive income.

Note that the presentation of the loss is similar to the presentation of the cost of treasury stock in the stockholders' equity section. (An unrealized gain would be added in this section of the balance sheet.) Reporting the unrealized gain or loss in the stockholders' equity section serves two important purposes: (1) It reduces the volatility of net income due to fluctuations in fair value, and (2) it informs the financial statement user of the gain or loss that would occur if the company sold the securities at fair value.

## Complete Income Statement

The income statement for Pace Corporation in Illustration 13-7 presents the types of items found on this statement, such as net sales, cost of goods sold, operating expenses, and income taxes. In addition, it shows how companies report irregular items and comprehensive income (highlighted in red).

**Illustration 13-7**
Complete income statement

| PACE CORPORATION<br>Income Statement and<br>Statement of Comprehensive Income<br>For the Year Ended December 31, 2012 | | |
|---|---|---|
| Net sales | | $440,000 |
| Cost of goods sold | | 260,000 |
| Gross profit | | 180,000 |
| Operating expenses | | 110,000 |
| Income from operations | | 70,000 |
| Other revenues and gains | $ 5,600 | |
| Other expenses and losses | (9,600) | (4,000) |
| Income before income taxes | | 66,000 |
| Income tax expense ($66,000 × 30%) | | 19,800 |
| Income before irregular items | | 46,200 |
| **Discontinued operations: Gain on disposal of Plastics Division, net of $15,000 income taxes ($50,000 × 30%)** | | 35,000 |
| **Extraordinary item: Tornado loss, net of income tax savings $18,000 ($60,000 × 30%)** | | (42,000) |
| **Net income** | | 39,200 |
| **Add: Unrealized gain on available-for-sale securities** | | 10,000 |
| **Comprehensive income** | | $ 49,200 |

## CONCLUDING REMARKS

We have shown that the computation of the correct net income number can be elusive. In assessing the future prospects of a company, some investors focus on income from operations and therefore ignore all irregular and other items. Others use measures such as net income, comprehensive income, or some modified version of one of these amounts.

## *before you go on...*

**IRREGULAR ITEMS**

**Do it!** In its draft 2012 income statement, AIR Corporation reports income before income taxes $400,000, extraordinary loss due to earthquake $100,000, income taxes $120,000 (not including irregular items), and loss on disposal of discontinued flower division $140,000. The income tax rate is 30%. Prepare a correct income statement, beginning with income before income taxes.

**Solution**

| AIR CORPORATION<br>Income Statement (partial) | |
|---|---:|
| Income before income taxes | $400,000 |
| Income tax expense | 120,000 |
| Income before irregular items | 280,000 |
| Discontinued operations | |
| Loss on disposal of discontinued flower division, net of $42,000 tax savings | (98,000) |
| Extraordinary earthquake loss net of $30,000 tax savings | (70,000) |
| Net income | $112,000 |

Related exercise material: **BE13-1, BE13-2, BE13-3, Do it! 13-1,** and **E13-1.**

**Action Plan**

• Recall that a loss is extraordinary if it is both unusual and infrequent.

• Disclose the income tax effect of each component of income, beginning with income before any irregular items.

• Show discontinued operations before extraordinary items.

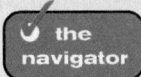

# Comparative Analysis

As indicated, in assessing the financial performance of a company, investors are interested in the core or sustainable earnings of a company. In addition, investors are interested in making comparisons from period to period. Throughout this book, we have relied on three types of comparisons to improve the decision usefulness of financial information:

1. **Intracompany basis.** Comparisons within a company are often useful to detect changes in financial relationships and significant trends. For example, a comparison of Kellogg's current year's cash amount with the prior year's cash amount shows either an increase or a decrease. Likewise, a comparison of Kellogg's year-end cash amount with the amount of its total assets at year-end shows the proportion of total assets in the form of cash.

2. **Intercompany basis.** Comparisons with other companies provide insight into a company's competitive position. For example, investors can compare Kellogg's total sales for the year with the total sales of its competitors in the breakfast cereal area, such as General Mills.

3. **Industry averages.** Comparisons with industry averages provide information about a company's relative position within the industry. For example, financial statement readers can compare Kellogg's financial data with the averages for its industry compiled by financial rating organizations such as Dun & Bradstreet, Moody's, and Standard & Poor's, or with information provided on the Internet by organizations such as Yahoo! on its financial site.

**International Note** As more countries adopt international accounting standards, the ability of analysts to compare companies from different countries should improve. However, international standards are open to widely varying interpretations. In addition, some countries adopt international standards "with modifications." As a consequence, most cross-country comparisons are still not as transparent as within-country comparisons.

We use three basic tools in financial statement analysis to highlight the significance of financial statement data:

1. Horizontal analysis
2. Vertical analysis
3. Ratio analysis

In previous chapters, we relied primarily on ratio analysis, supplemented with some basic horizontal and vertical analysis. In the remainder of this section, we introduce more formal forms of horizontal and vertical analysis. In the next section, we review ratio analysis in some detail.

## HORIZONTAL ANALYSIS

**Horizontal analysis**, also known as trend analysis, is a technique for evaluating a series of financial statement data over a period of time. Its purpose is to determine the increase or decrease that has taken place, expressed as either an amount or a percentage. For example, here are recent net sales figures (in thousands) of Chicago Cereal Company:

| 2009 | 2008 | 2007 | 2006 | 2005 |
|------|------|------|------|------|
| $11,776 | $10,907 | $10,177 | $9,614 | $8,812 |

If we assume that 2005 is the base year, we can measure all percentage increases or decreases relative to this base-period amount with the formula shown in Illustration 13-8.

**Illustration 13-8**
Horizontal analysis—
computation of changes
since base period

$$\text{Change Since Base Period} = \frac{\text{Current-Year Amount} - \text{Base-Year Amount}}{\text{Base-Year Amount}}$$

For example, we can determine that net sales for Chicago Cereal increased approximately 9.1% [($9,614 − $8,812) ÷ $8,812] from 2005 to 2006. Similarly, we can also determine that net sales increased by 33.6% [($11,776 − $8,812) ÷ $8,812] from 2005 to 2009.

Alternatively, we can express current-year sales as a percentage of the base period. To do so, we would divide the current-year amount by the base-year amount, as shown in Illustration 13-9.

**Illustration 13-9**
Horizontal analysis—
computation of current
year in relation to base
year

$$\text{Current Results in Relation to Base Period} = \frac{\text{Current-Year Amount}}{\text{Base-Year Amount}}$$

Current-period sales expressed as a percentage of the base period for each of the five years, using 2005 as the base period, are shown in Illustration 13-10.

**Illustration 13-10**
Horizontal analysis of net
sales

**CHICAGO CEREAL COMPANY**
Net Sales (in thousands)
Base Period 2005

| 2009 | 2008 | 2007 | 2006 | 2005 |
|------|------|------|------|------|
| $11,776 | $10,907 | $10,177 | $9,614 | $8,812 |
| 133.6% | 123.8% | 115.5% | 109.1% | 100% |

The large increase in net sales during 2006 would raise questions regarding possible reasons for such a significant change. Chicago Cereal's 2006 notes to the financial statements explain that the company completed an acquisition of Elf Foods Company during 2006. This major acquisition would help explain the increase in sales highlighted by horizontal analysis.

To further illustrate horizontal analysis, we use the financial statements of Chicago Cereal Company. Its two-year condensed balance sheets for 2009 and 2008, showing dollar and percentage changes, are presented in Illustration 13-11.

**Illustration 13-11**
Horizontal analysis of
balance sheets

**CHICAGO CEREAL COMPANY**
Condensed Balance Sheets
December 31 (in thousands)

| Assets | 2009 | 2008 | Increase (Decrease) during 2009 Amount | Percent |
|---|---|---|---|---|
| Current assets | $ 2,717 | $ 2,427 | $ 290 | 11.9 |
| Property assets (net) | 2,990 | 2,816 | 174 | 6.2 |
| Other assets | 5,690 | 5,471 | 219 | 4.0 |
| Total assets | $11,397 | $10,714 | $ 683 | 6.4 |
| **Liabilities and Stockholders' Equity** | | | | |
| Current liabilities | $ 4,044 | $ 4,020 | $ 24 | .6 |
| Long-term liabilities | 4,827 | 4,625 | 202 | 4.4 |
| Total liabilities | 8,871 | 8,645 | 226 | 2.6 |
| Stockholders' equity | | | | |
| Common stock | 493 | 397 | 96 | 24.2 |
| Retained earnings | 3,390 | 2,584 | 806 | 31.2 |
| Treasury stock (cost) | (1,357) | (912) | (445) | 48.8 |
| Total stockholders' equity | 2,526 | 2,069 | 457 | 22.1 |
| Total liabilities and stockholders' equity | $11,397 | $10,714 | $ 683 | 6.4 |

The comparative balance sheets show that a number of changes occurred in Chicago Cereal's financial position from 2008 to 2009. In the assets section, current assets increased $290,000, or 11.9% ($290 ÷ $2,427), and property assets (net) increased $174,000, or 6.2%. Other assets increased $219,000, or 4.0%. In the liabilities section, current liabilities increased $24,000, or 0.6%, while long-term liabilities increased $202,000, or 4.4%. In the stockholders' equity section, we find that retained earnings increased $806,000, or 31.2%.

Illustration 13-12 presents two-year comparative income statements of Chicago Cereal Company for 2009 and 2008, showing dollar and percentage changes.

**Helpful Hint** When using horizontal analysis, be sure to examine both dollar amount changes and percentage changes. It is not necessarily bad if a company's earnings are growing at a declining rate. The **amount** of increase may be the same as or more than the base year, but the **percentage** change may be less because the base is greater each year.

**Illustration 13-12**
Horizontal analysis of
income statements

**CHICAGO CEREAL COMPANY**
Condensed Income Statements
For the Years Ended December 31 (in thousands)

| | 2009 | 2008 | Increase (Decrease) during 2009 Amount | Percent |
|---|---|---|---|---|
| Net sales | $11,776 | $10,907 | $869 | 8.0 |
| Cost of goods sold | 6,597 | 6,082 | 515 | 8.5 |
| Gross profit | 5,179 | 4,825 | 354 | 7.3 |
| Selling and administrative expenses | 3,311 | 3,059 | 252 | 8.2 |
| Income from operations | 1,868 | 1,766 | 102 | 5.8 |
| Interest expense | 319 | 307 | 12 | 3.9 |
| Other income (expense), net | (2) | 13 | (15) | (115.4) |
| Income before income taxes | 1,547 | 1,472 | 75 | 5.1 |
| Income tax expense | 444 | 468 | (24) | (5.1) |
| Net income | $ 1,103 | $ 1,004 | $ 99 | 9.9 |

**Helpful Hint** Note that, in a horizontal analysis, while the amount column is additive (the total is **$99,000**), the percentage column is not additive (9.9% is **not a total**).

Horizontal analysis of the income statements shows the following changes: Net sales increased $869,000, or 8.0% ($869 ÷ $10,907). Cost of goods sold increased $515,000, or 8.5% ($515 ÷ $6,082). Selling and administrative expenses increased $252,000, or 8.2% ($252 ÷ $3,059). Overall, gross profit increased 7.3% and net income increased 9.9%. The increase in net income can be attributed to the increase in net sales and a decrease in income tax expense.

The measurement of changes from period to period in percentages is relatively straightforward and quite useful. However, complications can result in making the computations. If an item has no value in a base year or preceding year and a value in the next year, no percentage change can be computed. Likewise, no percentage change can be computed if a negative amount appears in the base or preceding period and a positive amount exists the following year.

# DECISION TOOLKIT

| DECISION CHECKPOINTS | INFO NEEDED FOR DECISION | TOOL TO USE FOR DECISION | HOW TO EVALUATE RESULTS |
|---|---|---|---|
| How do the company's financial position and operating results compare with those of the previous period? | Income statement and balance sheet | Comparative financial statements should be prepared over at least two years, with the first year reported being the base year. Changes in each line item relative to the base year should be presented both by amount and by percentage. This is called horizontal analysis. | Significant changes should be investigated to determine the reason for the change. |

## before you go on...

**HORIZONTAL ANALYSIS**

 Summary financial information for Rosepatch Company is as follows.

| | December 31, 2012 | December 31, 2011 |
|---|---|---|
| Current assets | $234,000 | $180,000 |
| Plant assets (net) | 756,000 | 420,000 |
| Total assets | $990,000 | $600,000 |

Compute the amount and percentage changes in 2012 using horizontal analysis, assuming 2011 is the base year.

**Action Plan**

• Find the percentage change by dividing the amount of the increase by the 2011 amount (base year).

**Solution**

| | Increase in 2012 | |
|---|---|---|
| | Amount | Percent |
| Current assets | $ 54,000 | 30% [($234,000 − $180,000) ÷ $180,000] |
| Plant assets (net) | 336,000 | 80% [($756,000 − $420,000) ÷ $420,000] |
| Total assets | $390,000 | 65% [($990,000 − $600,000) ÷ $600,000] |

Related exercise material: **BE13-4, BE13-6, BE13-7, BE13-9, Do it! 13-2, and E13-3.**

## VERTICAL ANALYSIS

**study objective 5**

Describe and apply vertical analysis.

**Vertical analysis,** also called common-size analysis, is a technique for evaluating financial statement data that expresses each item in a financial statement as a **percentage of a base amount.** For example, on a balance sheet we might say that current assets are 22% of total assets (total assets being the base amount). Or, on an income statement we might say that selling expenses are 16% of net sales (net sales being the base amount).

Presented in Illustration 13-13 are the comparative balance sheets of Chicago Cereal for 2009 and 2008, analyzed vertically. The base for the asset items is **total assets**, and the base for the liability and stockholders' equity items is **total liabilities and stockholders' equity**.

Illustration 13-13
Vertical analysis of balance sheets

**CHICAGO CEREAL COMPANY**
Condensed Balance Sheets
December 31 (in thousands)

| Assets | 2009 Amount | 2009 Percent* | 2008 Amount | 2008 Percent* |
|---|---|---|---|---|
| Current assets | $ 2,717 | 23.8 | $ 2,427 | 22.6 |
| Property assets (net) | 2,990 | 26.2 | 2,816 | 26.3 |
| Other assets | 5,690 | 50.0 | 5,471 | 51.1 |
| Total assets | $11,397 | 100.0 | $10,714 | 100.0 |
| **Liabilities and Stockholders' Equity** | | | | |
| Current liabilities | $ 4,044 | 35.5 | $ 4,020 | 37.5 |
| Long-term liabilities | 4,827 | 42.4 | 4,625 | 43.2 |
| Total liabilities | 8,871 | 77.9 | 8,645 | 80.7 |
| Stockholders' equity | | | | |
| Common stock | 493 | 4.3 | 397 | 3.7 |
| Retained earnings | 3,390 | 29.7 | 2,584 | 24.1 |
| Treasury stock (cost) | (1,357) | (11.9) | (912) | (8.5) |
| Total stockholders' equity | 2,526 | 22.1 | 2,069 | 19.3 |
| Total liabilities and stockholders' equity | $11,397 | 100.0 | $10,714 | 100.0 |

*Numbers have been rounded to total 100%.

In addition to showing the relative size of each category on the balance sheets, vertical analysis can show the percentage change in the individual asset, liability, and stockholders' equity items. In this case, current assets increased $290,000 from 2008 to 2009, and they increased from 22.6% to 23.8% of total assets. Property assets (net) decreased from 26.3% to 26.2% of total assets. Other assets decreased from 51.1% to 50.0% of total assets. Also, retained earnings increased by $806,000 from 2008 to 2009, and total stockholders' equity increased from 19.3% to 22.1% of total liabilities and stockholders' equity. This switch to a higher percentage of equity financing has two causes: First, while total liabilities increased by $226,000, the percentage of liabilities declined from 80.7% to 77.9% of total liabilities and stockholders' equity. Second, retained earnings increased by $806,000, going from 24.1% to 29.7% of total liabilities and stockholders' equity. Thus, the company shifted toward equity financing by relying less on debt and by increasing the amount of retained earnings.

Vertical analysis of the comparative income statements of Chicago Cereal, shown in Illustration 13-14 (page 698), reveals that cost of goods sold **as a percentage of net sales** increased from 55.8% to 56.0%, and selling and administrative expenses increased from 28.0% to 28.1%. Net income as a percentage of net sales increased from 9.1% to 9.4%. Chicago Cereal's increase in net income as a percentage of sales is due primarily to the decrease in interest expense and income tax expense as a percentage of sales.

**CHICAGO CEREAL COMPANY**
Condensed Income Statements
For the Years Ended December 31 (in thousands)

|  | 2009 | | 2008 | |
|---|---|---|---|---|
|  | **Amount** | **Percent*** | **Amount** | **Percent*** |
| Net sales | $11,776 | 100.0 | $10,907 | 100.0 |
| Cost of goods sold | 6,597 | 56.0 | 6,082 | 55.8 |
| Gross profit | 5,179 | 44.0 | 4,825 | 44.2 |
| Selling and administrative expenses | 3,311 | 28.1 | 3,059 | 28.0 |
| Income from operations | 1,868 | 15.9 | 1,766 | 16.2 |
| Interest expense | 319 | 2.7 | 307 | 2.8 |
| Other income (expense), net | (2) | .0 | 13 | .0 |
| Income before income taxes | 1,547 | 13.2 | 1,472 | 13.4 |
| Income tax expense | 444 | 3.8 | 468 | 4.3 |
| Net income | $ 1,103 | 9.4 | $ 1,004 | 9.1 |

*Numbers have been rounded to total 100%.

Vertical analysis also enables you to compare companies of different sizes. For example, one of Chicago Cereal's competitors is General Mills. General Mills has sales that are 1,000 times larger than those of Chicago Cereal. Using vertical analysis, we can more meaningfully compare the condensed income statements of Chicago Cereal and General Mills, as shown in Illustration 13-15.

**CONDENSED INCOME STATEMENTS**
For the Year Ended December 31, 2009

|  | Chicago Cereal (in thousands) | | General Mills, Inc. (in millions) | |
|---|---|---|---|---|
|  | **Amount** | **Percent*** | **Amount** | **Percent*** |
| Net sales | $11,776 | 100.0 | $14,691 | 100.0 |
| Cost of goods sold | 6,597 | 56.0 | 9,458 | 64.4 |
| Gross profit | 5,179 | 44.0 | 5,233 | 35.6 |
| Selling and administrative expenses | 3,311 | 28.1 | 2,954 | 20.1 |
| Non-recurring charges and (gains) | 0 | — | (43) | 0.3 |
| Income from operations | 1,868 | 15.9 | 2,322 | 15.8 |
| Other expenses and revenues (including income taxes) | 765 | 6.5 | 1,018 | 6.9 |
| Net income | $ 1,103 | 9.4 | $ 1,304 | 8.9 |

*Numbers have been rounded to total 100%.

Although Chicago Cereal's net sales are much less than those of General Mills, vertical analysis eliminates the impact of this size difference for our analysis. Chicago Cereal has a higher gross profit percentage 44.0%, compared to 35.6% for General Mills, but Chicago Cereal's selling and administrative expenses are 28.1% of net sales, while those of General Mills are 20.1% of net sales. Looking at net income, we see that the companies report similar percentages: Chicago Cereal's net income as a percentage of net sales is 9.4%, compared to 8.9% for General Mills.

## ANATOMY OF A FRAUD

This final *Anatomy of a Fraud* box demonstrates that sometimes relationships between numbers can be used by companies to detect fraud. The numeric relationships that can reveal fraud can be such things as financial ratios that appear abnormal, or statistical abnormalities in the numbers themselves. For example, the fact that WorldCom's line costs, as a percentage of either total expenses or revenues, differed very significantly from its competitors should have alerted people to the possibility of fraud. Or, consider the case of a bank manager, who cooperated with a group of his friends to defraud the bank's credit card department. The manager's friends would apply for credit cards and then run up balances of slightly less than $5,000. The bank had a policy of allowing bank personnel to write-off balances of less than $5,000 without seeking supervisor approval. The fraud was detected by applying statistical analysis based on Benford's Law. Benford's Law states that in a random collection of numbers, the frequency of lower digits (e.g., 1, 2, or 3) should be much higher than higher digits (e.g., 7, 8, or 9). In this case, bank auditors analyzed the first two digits of amounts written off. There was a spike at 48 and 49, which was not consistent with what would be expected if the numbers were random.

### Total take: Thousands of dollars

---

**THE MISSING CONTROL**

*Independent internal verification.* While it might be efficient to allow employees to write off accounts below a certain level, it is important that these write-offs be reviewed and verified periodically. Such a review would likely call attention to an employee with large amounts of write-offs, or in this case, write-offs that were frequently very close to the approval threshold.

---

*Source:* Mark J. Nigrini, "I've Got Your Number," *Journal of Accountancy Online* (May 1999).

 **DECISION TOOLKIT**

| DECISION CHECKPOINTS | INFO NEEDED FOR DECISION | TOOL TO USE FOR DECISION | HOW TO EVALUATE RESULTS |
|---|---|---|---|
| How do the relationships between items in this year's financial statements compare with those of last year or those of competitors? | Income statement and balance sheet | Each line item on the income statement should be presented as a percentage of net sales, and each line item on the balance sheet should be presented as a percentage of total assets or total liabilities and stockholders' equity. These percentages should be investigated for differences either across years in the same company or in the same year across different companies. This is called vertical analysis. | Any significant differences either across years or between companies should be investigated to determine the cause. |

# Ratio Analysis

In previous chapters, we presented many ratios used for evaluating the financial health and performance of a company. Here, we provide a summary listing of those ratios. (Page references to prior discussions are provided if you feel you need to review any individual ratios.) Appendix 13A provides an example of a comprehensive financial analysis employing these ratios.

 **study objective 6**

Identify and compute ratios used in analyzing a company's liquidity, solvency, and profitability.

## LIQUIDITY RATIOS

Liquidity ratios (Illustration 13-16) measure the short-term ability of the company to pay its maturing obligations and to meet unexpected needs for cash. Short-term creditors such as bankers and suppliers are particularly interested in assessing liquidity.

**Illustration 13-16**
Summary of liquidity ratios

| Liquidity Ratios | | |
|---|---|---|
| Working capital | Current assets − Current liabilities | p. 59 |
| Current ratio | $\dfrac{\text{Current assets}}{\text{Current liabilities}}$ | p. 59 |
| Current cash debt coverage ratio | $\dfrac{\text{Cash provided by operations}}{\text{Average current liabilities}}$ | p. 643 |
| Inventory turnover ratio | $\dfrac{\text{Cost of goods sold}}{\text{Average inventory}}$ | p. 297 |
| Days in inventory | $\dfrac{365 \text{ days}}{\text{Inventory turnover ratio}}$ | p. 297 |
| Receivables turnover ratio | $\dfrac{\text{Net credit sales}}{\text{Average net receivables}}$ | p. 415 |
| Average collection period | $\dfrac{365 \text{ days}}{\text{Receivables turnover ratio}}$ | p. 415 |

## Investor Insight

### How to Manage the Current Ratio

The apparent simplicity of the current ratio can have real-world limitations because adding equal amounts to both the numerator and the denominator causes the ratio to decrease.

Assume, for example, that a company has $2,000,000 of current assets and $1,000,000 of current liabilities; its current ratio is 2:1. If it purchases $1,000,000 of inventory on account, it will have $3,000,000 of current assets and $2,000,000 of current liabilities; its current ratio decreases to 1.5:1. If, instead, the company pays off $500,000 of its current liabilities, it will have $1,500,000 of current assets and $500,000 of current liabilities; its current ratio increases to 3:1. Thus, any trend analysis should be done with care because the ratio is susceptible to quick changes and is easily influenced by management.

 How might management influence a company's current ratio? (See page 743.)

## SOLVENCY RATIOS

Solvency ratios (Illustration 13-17) measure the ability of the company to survive over a long period of time. Long-term creditors and stockholders are interested in a company's long-run solvency, particularly its ability to pay interest as it comes due and to repay the balance of debt at its maturity.

**Illustration 13-17**
Summary of solvency ratios

| Solvency Ratios | | |
|---|---|---|
| Debt to total assets ratio | $\dfrac{\text{Total liabilities}}{\text{Total assets}}$ | p. 60 |
| Cash debt coverage ratio | $\dfrac{\text{Cash provided by operations}}{\text{Average total liabilities}}$ | p. 644 |
| Times interest earned ratio | $\dfrac{\text{Net income} + \text{Interest expense} + \text{Tax expense}}{\text{Interest expense}}$ | p. 529 |
| Free cash flow | $\text{Cash provided by operations} - \text{Capital expenditures} - \text{Cash dividends}$ | p. 62 |

## PROFITABILITY RATIOS

**Profitability ratios** (Illustration 13-18) measure the income or operating success of a company for a given period of time. A company's income, or lack of it, affects its ability to obtain debt and equity financing, its liquidity position, and its ability to grow. As a consequence, creditors and investors alike are interested in evaluating profitability. Profitability is frequently used as the ultimate test of management's operating effectiveness.

**Illustration 13-18**
Summary of profitability ratios

### Profitability Ratios

| | | |
|---|---|---|
| Earnings per share | $\dfrac{\text{Net income} - \text{Preferred stock dividends}}{\text{Average common shares outstanding}}$ | p. 56 |
| Price-earnings ratio | $\dfrac{\text{Stock price per share}}{\text{Earnings per share}}$ | p. 703 |
| Gross profit rate | $\dfrac{\text{Gross profit}}{\text{Net sales}}$ | p. 246 |
| Profit margin ratio | $\dfrac{\text{Net income}}{\text{Net sales}}$ | p. 247 |
| Return on assets ratio | $\dfrac{\text{Net income}}{\text{Average total assets}}$ | p. 467 |
| Asset turnover ratio | $\dfrac{\text{Net sales}}{\text{Average total assets}}$ | p. 468 |
| Payout ratio | $\dfrac{\text{Cash dividends declared on common stock}}{\text{Net income}}$ | p. 593 |
| Return on common stockholders' equity ratio | $\dfrac{\text{Net income} - \text{Preferred stock dividends}}{\text{Average common stockholders' equity}}$ | p. 594 |

### Investor Insight

#### High Ratings Can Bring Low Returns

Moody's, Standard and Poor's, and Fitch are three big firms that perform financial analysis on publicly traded companies and then publish ratings of the companies' creditworthiness. Investors and lenders rely heavily on these ratings in making investment and lending decisions. Some people feel that the collapse of the financial markets was worsened by inadequate research reports and ratings provided by the financial rating agencies. Critics contend that the rating agencies were reluctant to give large companies low ratings because they feared that by offending them they would lose out on business opportunities. For example, the rating agencies gave many so-called mortgage-backed securities ratings that suggested that they were low risk. Later, many of these very securities became completely worthless. Steps have been taken to reduce the conflicts of interest that lead to these faulty ratings.

*Source:* Aaron Lucchetti and Judith Burns, "Moody's CEO Warned Profit Push Posed a Risk to Quality of Ratings," *Wall Street Journal Online* (October 23, 2008).

**?** Why are credit rating agencies important to the financial markets? (See page 743.)

# Quality of Earnings

In evaluating the financial performance of a company, the quality of a company's earnings is of extreme importance to analysts. A company that has a high **quality of earnings** provides full and transparent information that will not confuse or mislead users of the financial statements.

 **study objective** **7**

Understand the concept of quality of earnings.

The issue of quality of earnings has taken on increasing importance because recent accounting scandals suggest that some companies are spending too much time managing their income and not enough time managing their business. Here are some of the factors affecting quality of earnings.

## ALTERNATIVE ACCOUNTING METHODS

Variations among companies in the application of generally accepted accounting principles may hamper comparability and reduce quality of earnings. For example, one company may use the FIFO method of inventory costing, while another company in the same industry may use LIFO. If inventory is a significant asset to both companies, it is unlikely that their current ratios are comparable. For example, if General Motors Corporation had used FIFO instead of LIFO for inventory valuation, its inventories in a recent year would have been 26% higher, which significantly affects the current ratio (and other ratios as well).

In addition to differences in inventory costing methods, differences also exist in reporting such items as depreciation and amortization. Although these differences in accounting methods might be detectable from reading the notes to the financial statements, adjusting the financial data to compensate for the different methods is often difficult, if not impossible.

## PRO FORMA INCOME

Companies whose stock is publicly traded are required to present their income statement following generally accepted accounting principles (GAAP). In recent years, many companies have been also reporting a second measure of income, called pro forma income. **Pro forma income** usually excludes items that the company thinks are unusual or non-recurring. For example, in a recent year, Cisco Systems (a high-tech company) reported a quarterly net loss under GAAP of $2.7 billion. Cisco reported pro forma income for the same quarter as a profit of $230 million. This large difference in profits between GAAP income numbers and pro forma income is not unusual. For example, during one 9-month period, the 100 largest companies on the Nasdaq stock exchange reported a total pro forma income of $19.1 billion but a total loss as measured by GAAP of $82.3 billion—a difference of about $100 billion!

To compute pro forma income, companies generally can exclude any items they deem inappropriate for measuring their performance. Many analysts and investors are critical of the practice of using pro forma income because these numbers often make companies look better than they really are. As the financial press noted, pro forma numbers might be called "earnings before bad stuff." Companies, on the other hand, argue that pro forma numbers more clearly indicate sustainable income because they exclude unusual and non-recurring expenses. "Cisco's technique gives readers of financial statements a clear picture of Cisco's normal business activities," the company said in a statement issued in response to questions about its pro forma income accounting.

Recently, the SEC provided some guidance on how companies should present pro forma information. Stay tuned: Everyone seems to agree that pro forma numbers can be useful if they provide insights into determining a company's sustainable income. However, many companies have abused the flexibility that pro forma numbers allow and have used the measure as a way to put their companies in a more favorable light.

## IMPROPER RECOGNITION

Because some managers have felt pressure from Wall Street to continually increase earnings, they have manipulated the earnings numbers to meet these expectations. The most common abuse is the improper recognition of revenue. One practice that some companies use is called *channel stuffing*: Offering deep discounts on their products to customers, companies encourage their customers to buy early (stuff the channel) rather than later. This lets the company report good earnings in the current period, but it often leads to a disaster in subsequent periods because customers have no need for additional goods. To illustrate, Bristol-Myers Squibb at one time indicated that it used sales incentives to encourage wholesalers to buy more drugs than needed to meet patients' demands. As a result, the company had to issue revised financial statements showing corrected revenues and income.

Another practice is the improper capitalization of operating expenses. The classic case is WorldCom. It capitalized over $7 billion of operating expenses so that it would report positive net income. In other situations, companies fail to report all their liabilities. Enron had promised to make payments on certain contracts if financial difficulty developed, but these guarantees were not reported as liabilities. In addition, disclosure was so lacking in transparency that it was impossible to understand what was happening at the company.

## PRICE-EARNINGS RATIO

Earnings per share is net income available to common stockholders divided by the average number of common shares outstanding. The market value of a company's stock changes based on investors' expectations about a company's future earnings per share. In order to make a meaningful comparison of market values and earnings across firms, investors calculate the **price-earnings (P-E) ratio**. The P-E ratio divides the market price of a share of common stock by earnings per share.

$$\text{Price-Earnings (P-E)} \atop \text{Ratio} = \frac{\text{Stock Price per Share}}{\text{Earnings per Share}}$$

**Illustration 13-19**
Formula for price-earnings (P-E) ratio

The P-E ratio reflects investors' assessment of a company's future earnings. The ratio of price to earnings will be higher if investors think that earnings will increase substantially in the future and therefore are willing to pay more per share of stock. A low price-earnings ratio often signifies that investors think the company's future earnings will not be strong. In addition, sometimes a low P-E ratio reflects the market's belief that a company has poor-quality earnings.

To illustrate, assume that two identical companies each have earnings per share of $5, but that one of the companies manipulated its accounting numbers to achieve the $5 figure. If investors perceive that one firm has lower-quality earnings, this perception will be reflected in a lower stock price and, consequently, a lower P-E.

Illustration 13-20 shows earnings per share and P-E ratios for five companies for a recent year. Note the difference in the P-E ratio of General Electric versus Google Inc.

| Company | Earnings per Share | Price-Earnings Ratio |
|---|---|---|
| Southwest Airlines | $ 0.44 | 18.6 |
| Google Inc. | 13.30 | 30.8 |
| General Electric | 2.17 | 13.2 |
| Merck | 1.49 | 14.6 |
| Nike | 3.70 | 15.9 |

**Illustration 13-20**
Earnings per share and P-E ratios of various companies

## Accounting Across the Organization

### Are Annual Reports Worth Their Weight? ⌐

Many company managers preparing their annual reports are piling on the paper in order to ease Enron-type worries on the part of investors. Natural-gas producer Williams Companies, Inc. turned out an eye-glazing annual report 1,234 pages in length. Nortel Networks Corporation added an extra two dozen pages to its annual report. Other companies have followed suit.

The trend to fuller disclosure has been a long time coming, observers say. But, they caution that more paper does not necessarily mean more information that the average investor will understand. In addition, it is important to remember that annual reports are just one piece of the puzzle as to how companies present information to decision makers.

*Source:* Elizabeth Church, "No Item Too Small as Firms Cave to Enron Disclosure Craze," *The (Toronto) Globe and Mail* (April 1, 2002), p. B1.

 Why might adding extra pages to the annual report not be beneficial to investors and analysts? What should be management's overriding objective in financial reporting? (See page 743.)

---

*before you go on...*

**QUALITY OF EARNINGS, FINANCIAL STATEMENT ANALYSIS**

 Match each of the following terms with the phrase that it best matches.

| | |
|---|---|
| Comprehensive income | Vertical analysis |
| Quality of earnings | Pro forma income |
| Solvency ratio | Extraordinary items |

1. Measures the ability of the company to survive over a long period of time.
2. Usually excludes items that a company thinks are unusual or non-recurring.
3. Includes all changes in stockholders' equity during a period except those resulting from investments by stockholders and distributions to stockholders.
4. Indicates the level of full and transparent information provided to users of the financial statements.
5. Describes events and transactions that are unusual in nature and infrequent in occurrence.
6. Expresses each item within a financial statement as a percentage of a base amount.

**Action Plan**

- Develop a sound understanding of basic methods used for financial reporting.
- Understand the use of fundamental analysis techniques.

### Solution

1. Solvency ratio: Measures the ability of the company to survive over a long period of time.
2. Pro forma income: Usually excludes items that a company thinks are unusual or non-recurring.
3. Comprehensive income: Includes all changes in stockholders' equity during a period except those resulting from investments by stockholders and distributions to stockholders.
4. Quality of earnings: Indicates the level of full and transparent information provided to users of the financial statements.
5. Extraordinary items: Describes events and transactions that are unusual in nature and infrequent in occurrence.
6. Vertical analysis: Expresses each item within a financial statement as a percentage of a base amount.

✔ the navigator

Related exercise material: **Do it!** 13-4.

# USING THE *DECISION TOOLKIT*

In analyzing a company, you should always investigate an extended period of time in order to determine whether the condition and performance of the company are changing. The condensed financial statements of Kellogg Company for 2009 and 2008 are presented here.

**KELLOGG COMPANY, INC.**
Balance Sheets
December 31 (in millions)

| Assets | 2009 | 2008 |
|---|---|---|
| Current assets | | |
| Cash | $ 334 | $ 255 |
| Accounts receivable (net) | 1,093 | 1,100 |
| Inventories | 910 | 897 |
| Other current assets | 221 | 269 |
| Total current assets | 2,558 | 2,521 |
| Property (net) | 3,010 | 2,933 |
| Other assets | 5,632 | 5,492 |
| Total assets | $11,200 | $10,946 |
| **Liabilities and Stockholders' Equity** | | |
| Current liabilities | $ 2,288 | $ 3,552 |
| Long-term liabilities | 6,637 | 5,939 |
| Stockholders' equity—common | 2,275 | 1,455 |
| Total liabilities and stockholders' equity | $11,200 | $10,946 |

**KELLOGG COMPANY, INC.**
Condensed Income Statements
For the Years Ended December 31
(in millions)

| | 2009 | 2008 |
|---|---|---|
| Net sales | $12,575 | $12,822 |
| Cost of goods sold | 7,184 | 7,455 |
| Gross profit | 5,391 | 5,367 |
| Selling and administrative expenses | 3,390 | 3,414 |
| Income from operations | 2,001 | 1,953 |
| Interest expense | 295 | 308 |
| Other (income) expense, net | 18 | 12 |
| Income before income taxes | 1,688 | 1,633 |
| Income tax expense | 476 | 485 |
| Net income | $ 1,212 | $ 1,148 |

## Instructions

Compute the following ratios for Kellogg for 2009 and discuss your findings (2008 values are provided for comparison).

1. Liquidity:
   (a) Current ratio (2008: .71:1).
   (b) Inventory turnover ratio (2008: 8.2 times).
2. Solvency:
   (a) Debt to total assets ratio (2008: 87%).
   (b) Times interest earned ratio (2008: 6.3 times).

3. Profitability:
   (a) Return on assets ratio (2008: 10.6%).
   (b) Profit margin ratio (2008: 9.0%).
   (c) Return on common stockholders' equity ratio (2008: 65%).

## Solution

1. Liquidity
   (a) Current ratio:

   $$2009: \frac{\$2,558}{\$2,288} = 1.12:1 \qquad 2008: \ .71:1$$

   (b) Inventory turnover ratio:

   $$2009: \frac{\$7,184}{(\$910 + \$897)/2} = 8.0 \text{ times} \qquad 2008: \ 8.2 \text{ times}$$

We see that between 2008 and 2009, the current ratio increased substantially. The inventory turnover ratio decreased slightly. The current ratio indicates that the company was more liquid in 2009.

2. Solvency
   (a) Debt to total assets ratio:

   $$2009: \frac{\$2,288 + \$6,637}{\$11,200} = 80\% \qquad 2008: \ 87\%$$

   (b) Times interest earned ratio:

   $$2009: \frac{\$1,212 + \$476 + \$295}{\$295} = 6.7 \text{ times} \qquad 2008: \ 6.3 \text{ times}$$

Kellogg's solvency as measured by the debt to total assets ratio improved slightly in 2009. We also can see that the times interest earned ratio improved.

3. Profitability
   (a) Return on assets ratio:

   $$2009: \frac{\$1,212}{(\$11,200 + \$10,946)/2} = 10.9\% \qquad 2008: \ 10.6\%$$

   (b) Profit margin ratio:

   $$2009: \frac{\$1,212}{\$12,575} = 9.6\% \qquad 2008: \ 9.0\%$$

   (c) Return on common stockholders' equity ratio:

   $$2009: \frac{\$1,212}{(\$2,275 + \$1,455)/2} = 65\% \qquad 2008: \ 65\%$$

Kellogg's return on assets ratio increased. Its profit margin ratio also increased, but its return on stockholders' equity held constant.

# Summary of Study Objectives

**1** **Understand the concept of sustainable income.** Sustainable income refers to a company's ability to sustain its profits from operations.

**2** **Indicate how irregular items are presented.** Irregular items—discontinued operations and extraordinary items—are presented on the income statement net of tax below "Income before irregular items" to highlight their unusual nature. Changes in accounting principle are reported retroactively.

**3** **Explain the concept of comprehensive income.** Comprehensive income includes all changes in stockholders' equity during a period except those resulting from investments by stockholders and distributions to stockholders. "Other comprehensive income" is added to or subtracted from net income to arrive at comprehensive income.

**4** **Describe and apply horizontal analysis.** Horizontal analysis is a technique for evaluating a series of data over a period of time to determine the increase or decrease that has taken place, expressed as either an amount or a percentage.

**5** **Describe and apply vertical analysis.** Vertical analysis is a technique that expresses each item in a financial statement as a percentage of a relevant total or a base amount.

**6** **Identify and compute ratios used in analyzing a company's liquidity, solvency, and profitability.** Financial ratios are provided in Illustration 13-16 (liquidity),

Illustration 13-17 (solvency), and Illustration 13-18 (profitability).

**7** **Understand the concept of quality of earnings.** A high quality of earnings provides full and transparent information that will not confuse or mislead users of the financial statements. Issues related to quality of earnings are (1) alternative accounting methods, (2) pro forma income, and (3) improper recognition. The price-earnings (P-E) ratio reflects investors' assessment of a company's future earnings potential.

*the navigator*

## DECISION TOOLKIT   A SUMMARY

| DECISION CHECKPOINTS | INFO NEEDED FOR DECISION | TOOL TO USE FOR DECISION | HOW TO EVALUATE RESULTS |
|---|---|---|---|
| Has the company sold any major components of its business? | Discontinued operations section of income statement | Anything reported in this section indicates that the company has discontinued a major component of its business. | If a major component has been discontinued, its results during the current period should not be included in estimates of future net income. |
| Has the company experienced any extraordinary events or transactions? | Extraordinary item section of income statement | Anything reported in this section indicates that the company experienced an event that was both unusual and infrequent. | These items should usually be ignored in estimating future net income. |
| Has the company changed any of its accounting principles? | Effect of change in accounting principle on current and prior periods. | Management indicates that the new principle is preferable to the old principle. | Examine current and prior years' reported income, using new-principle basis to assess trends for estimating future income. |
| How do the company's financial position and operating results compare with those of the previous period? | Income statement and balance sheet | Comparative financial statements should be prepared over at least two years, with the first year reported being the base year. Changes in each line item relative to the base year should be presented both by amount and by percentage. This is called horizontal analysis. | Significant changes should be investigated to determine the reason for the change. |
| How do the relationships between items in this year's financial statements compare with those of last year or those of competitors? | Income statement and balance sheet | Each line item on the income statement should be presented as a percentage of net sales, and each line item on the balance sheet should be presented as a percentage of total assets or total liabilities and stockholders' equity. These percentages should be investigated for differences either across years in the same company or in the same year across different companies. This is called vertical analysis. | Any significant differences either across years or between companies should be investigated to determine the cause. |

# Comprehensive Illustration of Ratio Analysis

In previous chapters, we presented many ratios used for evaluating the financial health and performance of a company. In this appendix, we provide a comprehensive review of those ratios and discuss some important relationships among them. Since earlier chapters demonstrated the calculation of each of these ratios, in this chapter we instead focus on their interpretation. Page references to prior discussions point you to any individual ratios you feel you need to review.

We used the financial information in Illustrations 13A-1 through 13A-4 to calculate Chicago Cereal Company's 2009 ratios. You can use these data to review the computations.

**Illustration 13A-1**
Chicago Cereal Company's
balance sheets

**CHICAGO CEREAL COMPANY**
Balance Sheets
December 31 (in thousands)

| Assets | 2009 | 2008 |
|---|---|---|
| Current assets | | |
| Cash and short-term investments | $   524 | $   411 |
| Accounts receivable | 1,026 | 945 |
| Inventories | 924 | 824 |
| Prepaid expenses and other current assets | 243 | 247 |
| Total current assets | 2,717 | 2,427 |
| Property assets (net) | 2,990 | 2,816 |
| Intangibles and other assets | 5,690 | 5,471 |
| Total assets | $11,397 | $10,714 |
| **Liabilities and Stockholders' Equity** | | |
| Current liabilities | $ 4,044 | $ 4,020 |
| Long-term liabilities | 4,827 | 4,625 |
| Stockholders' equity—common | 2,526 | 2,069 |
| Total liabilities and stockholders' equity | $11,397 | $10,714 |

**Illustration 13A-2**
Chicago Cereal Company's
income statements

**CHICAGO CEREAL COMPANY**
Condensed Income Statements
For the Years Ended December 31 (in thousands)

| | 2009 | 2008 |
|---|---|---|
| Net sales | $11,776 | $10,907 |
| Cost of goods sold | 6,597 | 6,082 |
| Gross profit | 5,179 | 4,825 |
| Selling and administrative expenses | 3,311 | 3,059 |
| Income from operations | 1,868 | 1,766 |
| Interest expense | 319 | 307 |
| Other income (expense), net | (2) | 13 |
| Income before income taxes | 1,547 | 1,472 |
| Income tax expense | 444 | 468 |
| Net income | $ 1,103 | $ 1,004 |

**Illustration 13A-3**
Chicago Cereal Company's
statements of cash flows

**CHICAGO CEREAL COMPANY**
Condensed Statements of Cash Flows
For the Years Ended December 31 (in thousands)

|  | 2009 | 2008 |
|---|---|---|
| Cash flows from operating activities |  |  |
| Cash receipts from operating activities | $ 11,695 | $10,841 |
| Cash payments for operating activities | 10,192 | 9,431 |
| Net cash provided by operating activities | 1,503 | 1,410 |
| Cash flows from investing activities |  |  |
| Purchases of property, plant, and equipment | (472) | (453) |
| Other investing activities | (129) | 8 |
| Net cash used in investing activities | (601) | (445) |
| Cash flows from financing activities |  |  |
| Issuance of common stock | 163 | 218 |
| Issuance of debt | 2,179 | 721 |
| Reductions of debt | (2,011) | (650) |
| Payment of dividends | (475) | (450) |
| Repurchase of common stock and other items | (645) | (612) |
| Net cash provided (used) by financing activities | (789) | (773) |
| Increase (decrease) in cash and cash equivalents | 113 | 192 |
| Cash and cash equivalents at beginning of year | 411 | 219 |
| Cash and cash equivalents at end of year | $    524 | $   411 |

**Illustration 13A-4**
Additional information for
Chicago Cereal Company

Additional information

|  | 2009 | 2008 |
|---|---|---|
| Average number of shares (thousands) | 418.7 | 418.5 |
| Stock price at year-end | $52.92 | $50.06 |

As indicated in the chapter, we can classify ratios into three types for analysis of the primary financial statements:

1. **Liquidity ratios.** Measures of the short-term ability of the company to pay its maturing obligations and to meet unexpected needs for cash.

2. **Solvency ratios.** Measures of the ability of the company to survive over a long period of time.

3. **Profitability ratios.** Measures of the income or operating success of a company for a given period of time.

As a tool of analysis, ratios can provide clues to underlying conditions that may not be apparent from an inspection of the individual components of a particular ratio. But, a single ratio by itself is not very meaningful. Accordingly, in this discussion we use the three comparisons listed below and on page 710.

1. **Intracompany comparisons** covering two years for Chicago Cereal Company (using comparative financial information from Illustrations 13A-1 through 13A-4).

2. **Intercompany comparisons** using General Mills as one of Chicago Cereal's competitors.

3. **Industry average comparisons** based on MSN.com median ratios for manufacturers of flour and other grain mill products and comparisons with other sources. For some of the ratios that we use, industry comparisons are not available. (These are denoted "na.")

### LIQUIDITY RATIOS

Liquidity ratios measure the short-term ability of the company to pay its maturing obligations and to meet unexpected needs for cash. Short-term creditors such as bankers and suppliers are particularly interested in assessing liquidity. The measures used to determine the company's short-term debt-paying ability are the current ratio, the current cash debt coverage ratio, the receivables turnover ratio, the average collection period, the inventory turnover ratio, and average days in inventory.

1. **Current ratio.** The **current ratio** expresses the relationship of current assets to current liabilities, computed by dividing current assets by current liabilities. It is widely used for evaluating a company's liquidity and short-term debt-paying ability. The 2009 and 2008 current ratios for Chicago Cereal and comparative data are shown in Illustration 13A-5.

**Illustration 13A-5**
Current ratio

| Ratio | Formula | Indicates: | Chicago Cereal 2009 | 2008 | General Mills 2009 | Industry 2009 | Page in book |
|---|---|---|---|---|---|---|---|
| Current ratio | Current assets / Current liabilities | Short-term debt-paying ability | .67 | .60 | 1.20 | 1.20 | 59 |

What do the measures tell us? Chicago Cereal's 2009 current ratio of .67 means that for every dollar of current liabilities, it has $0.67 of current assets. We sometimes state such ratios as .67:1 to reinforce this interpretation. Its current ratio—and therefore its liquidity—increased significantly in 2009. It is well below the industry average and that of General Mills.

2. **Current cash debt coverage ratio.** A disadvantage of the current ratio is that it uses year-end balances of current asset and current liability accounts. These year-end balances may not represent the company's current position during most of the year. The **current cash debt coverage ratio** partially corrects for this problem. It is the ratio of cash provided by operating activities to average current liabilities. Because it uses cash provided by operating activities rather than a balance at one point in time, it may provide a better representation of liquidity. Chicago Cereal's current cash debt coverage ratio is shown in Illustration 13A-6.

**Illustration 13A-6**
Current cash debt coverage ratio

| Ratio | Formula | Indicates: | Chicago Cereal 2009 | 2008 | General Mills 2009 | Industry 2009 | Page in book |
|---|---|---|---|---|---|---|---|
| Current cash debt coverage ratio | Cash provided by operations / Average current liabilities | Short-term debt-paying ability (cash basis) | .37 | .39 | .43 | na | 643 |

This ratio decreased slightly in 2009 for Chicago Cereal. Is the coverage adequate? Probably so. Its operating cash flow coverage of average current liabilities is similar to that of General Mills, and it approximates a commonly accepted threshold of .40. No industry comparison is available.

3. **Receivables turnover ratio.** Analysts can measure liquidity by how quickly a company converts certain assets to cash. Low values of the previous ratios can sometimes be compensated for if some of the company's current assets are highly liquid.

How liquid, for example, are the receivables? The ratio used to assess the liquidity of the receivables is the **receivables turnover ratio**, which measures the number of times, on average, a company collects receivables during the period. The receivables turnover ratio is computed by dividing net credit sales (net sales less cash sales) by average net receivables during the year. The receivables turnover ratio for Chicago Cereal is shown in Illustration 13A-7.

**Illustration 13A-7**
Receivables turnover ratio

| Ratio | Formula | Indicates: | Chicago Cereal 2009 | 2008 | General Mills 2009 | Industry 2009 | Page in book |
|---|---|---|---|---|---|---|---|
| Receivables turnover ratio | Net credit sales / Average net receivables | Liquidity of receivables | 11.9 | 12.0 | 12.8 | 14.0 | 415 |

We have assumed that all Chicago Cereal's sales are credit sales. Its receivables turnover ratio declined slightly in 2009. The turnover of 11.9 times is lower than the industry average of 14.0 times, and slightly lower than General Mills's turnover of 12.8 times.

4. **Average collection period.** A popular variant of the receivables turnover ratio converts it into an **average collection period** in days. This is done by dividing the receivables turnover ratio into 365 days. The average collection period for Chicago Cereal is shown in Illustration 13A-8.

**Illustration 13A-8**
Average collection period

| Ratio | Formula | Indicates: | Chicago Cereal 2009 | 2008 | General Mills 2009 | Industry 2009 | Page in book |
|---|---|---|---|---|---|---|---|
| Average collection period | 365 days / Receivables turnover ratio | Liquidity of receivables and collection success | 30.7 | 30.4 | 28.5 | 26.1 | 415 |

Chicago Cereal's 2009 receivables turnover of 11.9 times is divided into 365 days to obtain approximately 31 days. This means that the average collection period for receivables is about 31 days. Its average collection period is slightly longer than those of General Mills and the industry.

Analysts frequently use the average collection period to assess the effectiveness of a company's credit and collection policies. The general rule is that the collection period should not greatly exceed the credit term period (i.e., the time allowed for payment).

5. **Inventory turnover ratio.** The **inventory turnover ratio** measures the number of times average inventory was sold during the period. Its purpose is to measure the liquidity of the inventory. A high measure indicates that inventory is being sold and replenished frequently. The inventory turnover ratio is computed by dividing the cost of goods sold by the average inventory during the period. Unless seasonal factors are significant, average inventory can

be computed from the beginning and ending inventory balances. Chicago Cereal's inventory turnover ratio is shown in Illustration 13A-9.

**Illustration 13A-9**
Inventory turnover ratio

| Ratio | Formula | Indicates: | Chicago Cereal 2009 | Chicago Cereal 2008 | General Mills 2009 | Industry 2009 | Page in book |
|---|---|---|---|---|---|---|---|
| Inventory turnover ratio | Cost of goods sold / Average inventory | Liquidity of inventory | 7.5 | 7.9 | 6.2 | 6.9 | 297 |

Chicago Cereal's inventory turnover ratio decreased slightly in 2009. The turnover ratio of 7.5 times is higher than the industry average of 6.9 times and better than General Mills's 6.2 times. Generally, the faster the inventory turnover, the less cash is tied up in inventory and the less the chance of inventory becoming obsolete. Of course, a downside of high inventory turnover is that it sometimes results in lost sales because if a company keeps less inventory on hand, it is more likely to run out of inventory when it is needed.

6. **Days in inventory.** A variant of the inventory turnover ratio is the **days in inventory**, which measures the average number of days inventory is held. The days in inventory for Chicago Cereal is shown in Illustration 13A-10.

**Illustration 13A-10**
Days in inventory

| Ratio | Formula | Indicates: | Chicago Cereal 2009 | Chicago Cereal 2008 | General Mills 2009 | Industry 2009 | Page in book |
|---|---|---|---|---|---|---|---|
| Days in inventory | 365 days / Inventory turnover ratio | Liquidity of inventory and inventory management | 48.7 | 46.2 | 58.9 | 52.9 | 297 |

Chicago Cereal's 2009 inventory turnover ratio of 7.5 divided into 365 is approximately 49 days. An average selling time of 49 days is faster than the industry average and faster than that of General Mills. Some of this difference might be explained by differences in product lines across the two companies, although in many ways the types of products of these two companies are quite similar.

Inventory turnover ratios vary considerably among industries. For example, grocery store chains have a turnover of 10 times and an average selling period of 37 days. In contrast, jewelry stores have an average turnover of 1.3 times and an average selling period of 281 days. Within a company, there may even be significant differences in inventory turnover among different types of products. Thus, in a grocery store the turnover of perishable items such as produce, meats, and dairy products is faster than the turnover of soaps and detergents.

To conclude, nearly all of these liquidity measures suggest that Chicago Cereal's liquidity changed little during 2009. Its liquidity appears acceptable when compared to the industry as a whole and when compared to General Mills.

## SOLVENCY RATIOS

**Solvency ratios** measure the ability of the company to survive over a long period of time. Long-term creditors and stockholders are interested in a company's long-run solvency, particularly its ability to pay interest as it comes due and to repay the face value of debt at maturity. The debt to total assets ratio, the times interest earned ratio, and the cash debt coverage ratio provide information about debt-paying ability. In addition, free cash flow provides information about the company's solvency and its ability to pay additional dividends or invest in new projects.

7. **Debt to total assets ratio.** The debt to total assets ratio measures the percentage of total financing provided by creditors. It is computed by dividing total debt (both current and long-term) by total assets. This ratio indicates the degree of financial leveraging. It also provides some indication of the company's ability to withstand losses without impairing the interests of its creditors. The higher the percentage of debt to total assets, the greater the risk that the company may be unable to meet its maturing obligations. The lower the ratio, the more equity "buffer" is available to creditors if the company becomes insolvent. Thus, from the creditors' point of view, a low ratio of debt to total assets is desirable. Chicago Cereal's debt to total assets ratio is shown in Illustration 13A-11.

**Illustration 13A-11**
Debt to total assets ratio

| Ratio | Formula | Indicates: | Chicago Cereal 2009 | Chicago Cereal 2008 | General Mills 2009 | Industry 2009 | Page in book |
|---|---|---|---|---|---|---|---|
| Debt to total assets ratio | Total liabilities / Total assets | Percentage of total assets provided by creditors | 78% | 81% | 71% | 48% | 60 |

Chicago Cereal's 2009 ratio of 78% means that creditors have provided financing sufficient to cover 78% of the company's total assets. Alternatively, it says that it would have to liquidate 78% of its assets at their book value in order to pay off all of its debts. Its ratio is above the industry average of 48%, as well as that of General Mills. This suggests that it is less solvent than the industry average and General Mills. Chicago Cereal's solvency improved slightly during the year.

The adequacy of this ratio is often judged in light of the company's earnings. Generally, companies with relatively stable earnings, such as public utilities, have higher debt to total assets ratios than cyclical companies with widely fluctuating earnings, such as many high-tech companies.

Another ratio with a similar meaning is the **debt to equity ratio**. It shows the relative use of borrowed funds (total liabilities) compared with resources invested by the owners. Because this ratio can be computed in several ways, be careful when making comparisons with it. Debt may be defined to include only the noncurrent portion of liabilities, and intangible assets may be excluded from stockholders' equity (which would equal tangible net worth). If debt and assets are defined as above (all liabilities and all assets), then when the debt to total assets ratio equals 50%, the debt to equity ratio is 1:1.

8. **Times interest earned ratio.** The times interest earned ratio (also called interest coverage) indicates the company's ability to meet interest payments as they come due. It is computed by dividing income before interest expense and income taxes by interest expense. Note that this ratio uses income before interest expense and income taxes because this amount represents what is available to cover interest. Chicago Cereal's times interest earned ratio is shown in Illustration 13A-12.

**Illustration 13A-12**
Times interest earned ratio

| Ratio | Formula | Indicates: | Chicago Cereal 2009 | Chicago Cereal 2008 | General Mills 2009 | Industry 2009 | Page in book |
|---|---|---|---|---|---|---|---|
| Times interest earned ratio | (Net Income + Interest expense + Tax expense) / Interest expense | Ability to meet interest payments as they come due | 5.8 | 5.8 | 7.3 | 5.9 | 529 |

For Chicago Cereal, the 2009 interest coverage was 5.8, which indicates that income before interest and taxes was 5.8 times the amount needed for interest expense. This is less than the rate for General Mills, and it is slightly less than the average rate for the industry. The debt to total assets ratio decreased for Chicago Cereal during 2009, and its times interest earned ratio held constant.

9. **Cash debt coverage ratio.** The ratio of cash provided by operating activities to average total liabilities, called the **cash debt coverage ratio**, is a cash-basis measure of solvency. This ratio indicates a company's ability to repay its liabilities from cash generated from operating activities without having to liquidate the assets used in its operations. Illustration 13A-13 shows Chicago Cereal's cash debt coverage ratio.

**Illustration 13A-13**
Cash debt coverage ratio

| Ratio | Formula | Indicates: | Chicago Cereal 2009 | Chicago Cereal 2008 | General Mills 2009 | Industry 2009 | Page in book |
|---|---|---|---|---|---|---|---|
| Cash debt coverage ratio | Cash provided by operations / Average total liabilities | Long-term debt-paying ability (cash basis) | .17 | .17 | .14 | na | 644 |

An industry average for this measure is not available. Chicago Cereal's .17 is higher than General Mills's .14, and it remained unchanged from 2009. One way of interpreting this ratio is to say that net cash generated from one year of operations would be sufficient to pay off 17% of its total liabilities. If 17% of this year's liabilities were retired each year, it would take approximately 5.9 years to retire all of its debt. It would take General Mills approximately 7.1 years to do so. A general rule of thumb is that a cash debt coverage ratio above .20 is acceptable.

10. **Free cash flow.** One indication of a company's solvency, as well as of its ability to pay dividends or expand operations, is the amount of excess cash it generated after investing in capital expenditures and paying dividends. This amount is referred to as **free cash flow**. For example, if you generate $100,000 of cash from operations but you spend $30,000 on capital expenditures and pay $10,000 in dividends, you have $60,000 ($100,000 − $30,000 − $10,000) to use either to expand operations, pay additional dividends, or pay down debt. Chicago Cereal's free cash flow is shown in Illustration 13A-14.

**Illustration 13A-14**
Free cash flow

| Ratio | Formula | | | Indicates: | Chicago Cereal 2009 | Chicago Cereal 2008 | General Mills 2009 | Industry 2009 | Page in book |
|---|---|---|---|---|---|---|---|---|---|
| Free cash flow | Cash provided by operations | − Capital expenditures | − Cash dividends | Cash available for paying dividends or expanding operations | $556 (in thousands) | $507 | $686 (in millions) | na | 62 |

Chicago Cereal's free cash flow increased slightly from 2008 to 2009. During both years, the cash provided by operations was more than enough to allow it to acquire additional productive assets and maintain dividend payments. It could have used the remaining cash to reduce debt if necessary. Given that Chicago Cereal is much smaller than General Mills, we would expect its free cash flow to be substantially smaller, which it is.

## PROFITABILITY RATIOS

**Profitability ratios** measure the income or operating success of a company for a given period of time. A company's income, or the lack of it, affects its ability to obtain debt and equity financing, its liquidity position, and its ability to grow. As a consequence, creditors and investors alike are interested in evaluating profitability. Analysts frequently use profitability as the ultimate test of management's operating effectiveness.

Throughout this book, we have introduced numerous measures of profitability. The relationships among measures of profitability are very important. Understanding them can help management determine where to focus its efforts to improve profitability. Illustration 13A-15 diagrams these relationships. Our discussion of Chicago Cereal's profitability is structured around this diagram.

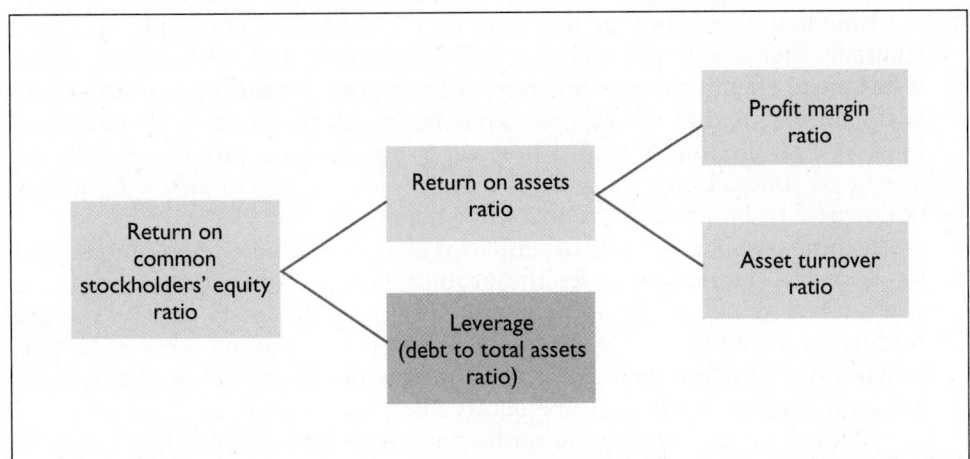

**Illustration 13A-15**
Relationships among profitability measures

11. **Return on common stockholders' equity ratio.** A widely used measure of profitability from the common stockholder's viewpoint is the return on common stockholders' equity ratio. This ratio shows how many dollars of net income the company earned for each dollar invested by the owners. It is computed by dividing net income minus any preferred stock dividends—that is, income available to common stockholders—by average common stockholders' equity. The return on common stockholders' equity for Chicago Cereal is shown in Illustration 13A-16.

**Illustration 13A-16**
Return on common stockholders' equity ratio

| Ratio | Formula | Indicates: | Chicago Cereal 2009 | Chicago Cereal 2008 | General Mills 2009 | Industry 2009 | Page in book |
|---|---|---|---|---|---|---|---|
| Return on common stockholders' equity ratio | $\dfrac{\text{Net income} - \text{Preferred stock dividends}}{\text{Average common stockholders' equity}}$ | Profitability of common stockholders' investment | 48% | 46% | 29% | 30% | 594 |

Chicago Cereal's 2009 rate of return on common stockholders' equity is unusually high at 48%, considering an industry average of 30% and General Mills's return of 29%. In the subsequent sections, we investigate the causes of this high return.

12. **Return on assets ratio.** The return on common stockholders' equity ratio is affected by two factors: the return on assets ratio and the degree of leverage. The return on assets ratio measures the overall profitability of assets in

terms of the income earned on each dollar invested in assets. It is computed by dividing net income by average total assets. Chicago Cereal's return on assets ratio is shown in Illustration 13A-17.

**Illustration 13A-17**
Return on assets ratio

| | | | Chicago Cereal | | General Mills | Industry | Page in |
| Ratio | Formula | Indicates: | 2009 | 2008 | 2009 | 2009 | book |
|---|---|---|---|---|---|---|---|
| Return on assets ratio | Net income / Average total assets | Overall profitability of assets | 10.0% | 9.4% | 8.5% | 6.7% | 467 |

Chicago Cereal had a 10.0% return on assets in 2009. This rate is significantly higher than that of General Mills and the industry average.

Note that its rate of return on common stockholders' equity (48%) is substantially higher than its rate of return on assets (10%). The reason is that it has made effective use of **leverage**. **Leveraging** or **trading on the equity** at a gain means that the company has borrowed money at a lower rate of interest than the rate of return it earns on the assets it purchased with the borrowed funds. Leverage enables management to use money supplied by nonowners to increase the return to owners.

A comparison of the rate of return on assets with the rate of interest paid for borrowed money indicates the profitability of trading on the equity. If you borrow money at 8% and your rate of return on assets is 11%, you are trading on the equity at a gain. Note, however, that trading on the equity is a two-way street: For example, if you borrow money at 11% and earn only 8% on it, you are trading on the equity at a loss.

Chicago Cereal earns more on its borrowed funds than it has to pay in interest. Thus, the return to stockholders exceeds the return on the assets because of the positive benefit of leverage. Recall from our earlier discussion that Chicago Cereal's percentage of debt financing, as measured by the ratio of debt to total assets (or debt to equity), was higher than General Mills's and the industry average. It appears that Chicago Cereal's high return on common stockholders' equity is due in part to its use of leverage.

13. **Profit margin ratio.** The return on assets ratio is affected by two factors, the first of which is the profit margin ratio. The **profit margin ratio**, or rate of return on sales, is a measure of the percentage of each dollar of sales that results in net income. It is computed by dividing net income by net sales for the period. Chicago Cereal's profit margin ratio is shown in Illustration 13A-18.

**Illustration 13A-18**
Profit margin ratio

| | | | Chicago Cereal | | General Mills | Industry | Page in |
| Ratio | Formula | Indicates: | 2009 | 2008 | 2009 | 2009 | book |
|---|---|---|---|---|---|---|---|
| Profit margin ratio | Net income / Net sales | Net income generated by each dollar of sales | 9.4% | 9.2% | 10.6% | 10.4% | 247 |

Chicago Cereal experienced a slight increase in its profit margin ratio from 2008 to 2009 of 9.2% to 9.4%. Its profit margin ratio was lower than the industry average and that of General Mills.

High-volume (high inventory turnover) businesses such as grocery stores and pharmacy chains generally have low profit margins. Low-volume businesses such as jewelry stores and airplane manufacturers have high profit margins.

14. **Asset turnover ratio.** The other factor that affects the return on assets ratio is the asset turnover ratio. The **asset turnover ratio** measures how efficiently a company uses its assets to generate sales. It is determined by dividing net sales by average total assets for the period. The resulting number shows the dollars of sales produced by each dollar invested in assets. Illustration 13A-19 shows the asset turnover ratio for Chicago Cereal.

**Illustration 13A-19**
Asset turnover ratio

| Ratio | Formula | Indicates: | Chicago Cereal 2009 | Chicago Cereal 2008 | General Mills 2009 | Industry 2009 | Page in book |
|---|---|---|---|---|---|---|---|
| Asset turnover ratio | Net sales / Average total assets | How efficiently assets are used to generate sales | 1.07 | 1.02 | .80 | 1.00 | 468 |

The asset turnover ratio shows that in 2009, Chicago Cereal generated sales of $1.07 for each dollar it had invested in assets. The ratio rose from 2008 to 2009. Its asset turnover ratio is above the industry average and that of General Mills.

Asset turnover ratios vary considerably among industries. The average asset turnover for utility companies is .45, for example, while the grocery store industry has an average asset turnover of 3.49.

In summary, Chicago Cereal's return on assets ratio increased from 9.4% in 2008 to 10.0% in 2009. Underlying this increase was an increased profitability on each dollar of sales (as measured by the profit margin ratio) and a rise in the sales-generating efficiency of its assets (as measured by the asset turnover ratio). We can analyze the combined effects of profit margin and asset turnover on return on assets for Chicago Cereal as shown in Illustration 13A-20.

**Illustration 13A-20**
Composition of return on assets ratio

| | Profit Margin | × | Asset Turnover | = | Return on Assets |
|---|---|---|---|---|---|
| Ratios: | Net Income / Net Sales | × | Net Sales / Average Total Assets | = | Net Income / Average Total Assets |
| **Chicago Cereal** | | | | | |
| 2009 | 9.4% | × | 1.07 times | = | 10.1%* |
| 2008 | 9.2% | × | 1.02 times | = | 9.4% |

*Difference from value on page 716 due to rounding.

15. **Gross profit rate.** One factor that strongly influences the profit margin ratio is the gross profit rate. The **gross profit rate** is determined by dividing gross profit (net sales less cost of goods sold) by net sales. This rate indicates a company's ability to maintain an adequate selling price above its cost of goods sold.

As an industry becomes more competitive, this ratio declines. For example, in the early years of the personal computer industry, gross profit rates were quite high. Today, because of increased competition and a belief that most brands of personal computers are similar in quality, gross profit rates have become thin. Analysts should closely monitor gross profit rates over time. Illustration 13A-21 shows Chicago Cereal's gross profit rate.

**Illustration 13A-21**
Gross profit rate

| Ratio | Formula | Indicates: | Chicago Cereal 2009 | Chicago Cereal 2008 | General Mills 2009 | Industry 2009 | Page in book |
|---|---|---|---|---|---|---|---|
| Gross profit rate | Gross profit / Net sales | Margin between selling price and cost of goods sold | 44% | 44% | 41% | 32% | 246 |

Chicago Cereal's gross profit rate remained constant from 2008 to 2009.

16. **Earnings per share (EPS).** Stockholders usually think in terms of the number of shares they own or plan to buy or sell. Expressing net income earned on a per share basis provides a useful perspective for determining profitability. **Earnings per share** is a measure of the net income earned on each share of common stock. It is computed by dividing net income by the average number of common shares outstanding during the year.

The terms "net income per share" or "earnings per share" refer to the amount of net income applicable to each share of *common stock*. Therefore, when we compute earnings per share, if there are preferred dividends declared for the period, we must deduct them from net income to arrive at income available to the common stockholders. Chicago Cereal's earnings per share is shown in Illustration 13A-22.

**Illustration 13A-22**
Earnings per share

| Ratio | Formula | Indicates: | Chicago Cereal 2009 | Chicago Cereal 2008 | General Mills 2009 | Industry 2009 | Page in book |
|---|---|---|---|---|---|---|---|
| Earnings per share (EPS) | Net income − Preferred stock dividends / Average common shares outstanding | Net income earned on each share of common stock | $2.63 | $2.40 | $3.93 | na | 56 |

Note that no industry average is presented in Illustration 13A-22. Industry data for earnings per share are not reported, and in fact the Chicago Cereal and General Mills ratios should not be compared. Such comparisons are not meaningful because of the wide variations in the number of shares of outstanding stock among companies. Chicago Cereal's earnings per share increased 23 cents per share in 2009. This represents a 9.6% increase from the 2008 EPS of $2.40.

17. **Price-earnings ratio.** The **price-earnings ratio** is an oft-quoted statistic that measures the ratio of the market price of each share of common stock to the earnings per share. The price-earnings (P-E) ratio reflects investors' assessments of a company's future earnings. It is computed by dividing the market price per share of the stock by earnings per share. Chicago Cereal's price-earnings ratio is shown in Illustration 13A-23.

**Illustration 13A-23**
Price-earnings ratio

| Ratio | Formula | Indicates: | Chicago Cereal 2009 | Chicago Cereal 2008 | General Mills 2009 | Industry 2009 | Page in book |
|---|---|---|---|---|---|---|---|
| Price-earnings ratio | Stock price per share / Earnings per share | Relationship between market price per share and earnings per share | 20.1 | 20.9 | 14.5 | 17.0 | 703 |

At the end of 2009 and 2008, the market price of Chicago Cereal's stock was $52.92 and $50.06, respectively.

In 2009, each share of Chicago Cereal's stock sold for 20.1 times the amount that was earned on each share. Chicago Cereal's price-earnings ratio is higher than General Mills's ratio of 14.5 and higher than the industry average of 17.0 times. Its higher P-E ratio suggests that the market is more optimistic about Chicago Cereal than about General Mills. However, it might also signal that Chicago Cereal's stock is overpriced. That is a matter for the analyst to determine.

18. **Payout ratio.** The payout ratio measures the percentage of earnings distributed in the form of cash dividends. It is computed by dividing cash dividends declared on common stock by net income. Companies that have high growth rates are characterized by low payout ratios because they reinvest most of their net income in the business. The payout ratio for Chicago Cereal is shown in Illustration 13A-24.

**Illustration 13A-24**
Payout ratio

| Ratio | Formula | Indicates: | Chicago Cereal 2009 | Chicago Cereal 2008 | General Mills 2009 | Industry 2009 | Page in book |
|---|---|---|---|---|---|---|---|
| Payout ratio | Cash dividends declared on common stock / Net income | Percentage of earnings distributed in the form of cash dividends | 43% | 45% | 44% | 37% | 593 |

The 2009 and 2008 payout ratios for Chicago Cereal are about the same as that of General Mills (44%) but higher than the industry average (37%).

Management has some control over the amount of dividends paid each year, and companies are generally reluctant to reduce a dividend below the amount paid in a previous year. Therefore, the payout ratio will actually increase if a company's net income declines but the company keeps its total dividend payment the same. Of course, unless the company returns to its previous level of profitability, maintaining this higher dividend payout ratio is probably not possible over the long run.

Before drawing any conclusions regarding Chicago Cereal's dividend payout ratio, we should calculate this ratio over a longer period of time to evaluate any trends and also try to find out whether management's philosophy regarding dividends has changed recently. The "Selected Financial Data" section of Chicago Cereal's Management Discussion and Analysis shows that over a 5-year period, earnings per share rose 45%, while dividends per share grew only 19%.

In terms of the types of financial information available and the ratios used by various industries, what can be practically covered in this textbook gives you only the "Titanic approach": That is, you are seeing only the tip of the iceberg compared to the vast databases and types of ratio analysis that are available on computers. The availability of information is not a problem. The real trick is to be discriminating enough to perform relevant analysis and select pertinent comparative data.

# Glossary

**Asset turnover ratio** *(p. 717)* A measure of how efficiently a company uses its assets to generate sales; computed as net sales divided by average total assets.

**Available-for-sale securities** *(p. 691)* Securities that are held with the intent of selling them sometime in the future.

**Average collection period** *(p. 711)* The average number of days that receivables are outstanding; calculated as receivables turnover divided into 365 days.

**Cash debt coverage ratio** *(p. 714)* A cash-basis measure used to evaluate solvency, computed as cash from operations divided by average total liabilities.

**Change in accounting principle** *(p. 690)* Use of an accounting principle in the current year different from the one used in the preceding year.

**Comprehensive income** *(p. 690)* A measure of income that includes all changes in stockholders' equity during a period except those resulting from investments by stockholders and distributions to stockholders.

**Current cash debt coverage ratio** *(p. 710)* A cash-basis measure of liquidity; computed as cash provided by operations divided by average current liabilities.

**Current ratio** *(p. 710)* A measure used to evaluate a company's liquidity and short-term debt-paying ability; calculated as current assets divided by current liabilities.

**Days in inventory** *(p. 712)* A measure of the average number of days inventory is held; computed as inventory turnover divided into 365 days.

**Debt to total assets ratio** *(p. 713)* A measure of the percentage of total financing provided by creditors; computed as total debt divided by total assets.

**Discontinued operations** *(p. 687)* The disposal of a significant component of a business.

**Earnings per share** *(p. 718)* The net income earned by each share of common stock; computed as net income less dividends on preferred stock divided by the average common shares outstanding.

**Extraordinary items** *(p. 688)* Events and transactions that meet two conditions: (1) unusual in nature and (2) infrequent in occurrence.

**Free cash flow** *(p. 714)* A measure of solvency. Cash remaining from operating activities after adjusting for capital expenditures and dividends paid.

**Gross profit rate** *(p. 717)* Gross profit expressed as a percentage of sales; computed as gross profit divided by net sales.

**Horizontal analysis** *(p. 694)* A technique for evaluating a series of financial statement data over a period of time to determine the increase (decrease) that has taken place, expressed as either an amount or a percentage.

**Inventory turnover ratio** *(p. 711)* A measure of the liquidity of inventory. Measures the number of times average inventory was sold during the period; computed as cost of goods sold divided by average inventory.

**Leveraging** *(p. 716)* Borrowing money at a lower rate of interest than can be earned by using the borrowed money; also referred to as trading on the equity.

**Liquidity ratios** *(p. 700)* Measures of the short-term ability of the company to pay its maturing obligations and to meet unexpected needs for cash.

**Payout ratio** *(p. 719)* A measure of the percentage of earnings distributed in the form of cash dividends; calculated as cash dividends declared on common stock divided by net income.

**Price-earnings (P-E) ratio** *(pp. 703, 718)* A comparison of the market price of each share of common stock to the earnings per share; computed as the market price of the stock divided by earnings per share.

**Pro forma income** *(p. 702)* A measure of income that usually excludes items that a company thinks are unusual or non-recurring.

**Profit margin ratio** *(p. 716)* A measure of the net income generated by each dollar of sales; computed as net income divided by net sales.

**Profitability ratios** *(p. 701)* Measures of the income or operating success of a company for a given period of time.

**Quality of earnings** *(p. 701)* Indicates the level of full and transparent information that is provided to users of the financial statements.

**Receivables turnover ratio** *(p. 711)* A measure of the liquidity of receivables; computed as net credit sales divided by average net receivables.

**Return on assets ratio** *(p. 715)* A profitability measure that indicates the amount of net income generated by each dollar of assets; calculated as net income divided by average total assets.

**Return on common stockholders' equity ratio** *(p. 715)* A measure of the dollars of net income earned for each dollar invested by the owners; computed as income available to common stockholders divided by average common stockholders' equity.

**Solvency ratios** *(p. 700)* Measures of the ability of a company to survive over a long period of time, particularly to pay interest as it comes due and to repay the balance of debt at its maturity.

**Sustainable income** *(p. 686)* The most likely level of income to be obtained in the future; calculated as net income adjusted for irregular items.

**Times interest earned ratio** *(p. 713)* A measure of a company's solvency and ability to meet interest payments as they come due; calculated as income before interest expense and income taxes divided by interest expense.

**Trading on the equity** *(p. 716)* Same as leveraging.

**Trading securities** *(p. 691)* Securities bought and held primarily for sale in the near term to generate income on short-term price differences.

**Vertical analysis** *(p. 696)* A technique for evaluating financial statement data that expresses each item in a financial statement as a percentage of a base amount.

# Comprehensive Do it!

The events and transactions of Dever Corporation for the year ending December 31, 2012, resulted in these data.

| | |
|---|---|
| Cost of goods sold | $2,600,000 |
| Net sales | 4,400,000 |
| Other expenses and losses | 9,600 |
| Other revenues and gains | 5,600 |
| Selling and administrative expenses | 1,100,000 |
| Gain from discontinued division | 570,000 |
| Loss from tornado disaster (extraordinary loss) | 600,000 |

Analysis reveals the following.

1. All items are before the applicable income tax rate of 30%.
2. The plastics division was sold on July 1.

### Instructions

Prepare an income statement for the year.

### Solution to Comprehensive Do it!

**DEVER CORPORATION**
**Income Statement**
**For the Year Ended December 31, 2012**

| | | |
|---|---|---|
| Net sales | | $ 4,400,000 |
| Cost of goods sold | | 2,600,000 |
| Gross profit | | 1,800,000 |
| Selling and administrative expenses | | 1,100,000 |
| Income from operations | | 700,000 |
| Other revenues and gains | $ 5,600 | |
| Other expenses and losses | (9,600) | (4,000) |
| Income before income taxes | | 696,000 |
| Income tax expense ($696,000 × 30%) | | 208,800 |
| Income before irregular items | | 487,200 |
| Discontinued operations: Gain from discontinued division, net of taxes of $171,000 ($570,000 × 30%) | | 399,000 |
| Extraordinary item: Tornado loss, net of income tax savings $180,000 ($600,000 × 30%) | | (420,000) |
| Net income | | $ 466,200 |

**Action Plan**

• Remember that material items not typical of operations are reported in separate sections net of taxes.

• Associate income taxes with the item that affects the taxes.

• On a corporation income statement, report income tax expense when there is income before income tax.

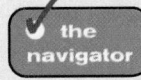

---

 Self-Test, Brief Exercises, Exercises, Problem Set A, and many more resources are available for practice in WileyPLUS

# Self-Test Questions

Answers are on page 743.

All of the Self-Test Questions in this chapter employ decision tools.

(SO 2) **1.** In reporting discontinued operations, the income statement should show in a special section:

(a) gains on the disposal of the discontinued component.
(b) losses on the disposal of the discontinued component.
(c) Neither (a) nor (b).
(d) Both (a) and (b).

(SO 2) **2.** Cool Stools Corporation has income before taxes of $400,000 and an extraordinary loss of $100,000. If the income tax rate is 25% on all items, the income statement should show income before irregular items and an extraordinary loss, respectively, of
(a) $325,000 and $100,000.
(b) $325,000 and $75,000.
(c) $300,000 and $100,000.
(d) $300,000 and $75,000.

(SO 3) **3.** Which of the following would be considered an "Other comprehensive income" item?
(a) Gain on disposal of discontinued operations.
(b) Unrealized loss on available-for-sale securities.
(c) Extraordinary loss related to flood.
(d) Net income.

(SO 4) **4.** In horizontal analysis, each item is expressed as a percentage of the:
(a) net income amount.
(b) stockholders' equity amount.
(c) total assets amount.
(d) base-year amount.

(SO 4) **5.** Adams Corporation reported net sales of $300,000, $330,000, and $360,000 in the years 2010, 2011, and 2012, respectively. If 2010 is the base year, what percentage do 2012 sales represent of the base?
(a) 77%.          (c) 120%.
(b) 108%.         (d) 130%.

(SO 5) **6.** The following schedule is a display of what type of analysis?

|                             | Amount    | Percent |
|-----------------------------|-----------|---------|
| Current assets              | $200,000  | 25%     |
| Property, plant, and equipment | 600,000 | 75%    |
| Total assets                | $800,000  |         |

(a) Horizontal analysis.      (c) Vertical analysis.
(b) Differential analysis.    (d) Ratio analysis.

(SO 5) **7.** In vertical analysis, the base amount for depreciation expense is generally:
(a) net sales.
(b) depreciation expense in a previous year.
(c) gross profit.
(d) fixed assets.

(SO 6) **8.** Which measure is an evaluation of a company's ability to pay current liabilities?
(a) Current cash debt coverage ratio.
(b) Current ratio.
(c) Both (a) and (b).
(d) None of the above.

(SO 6) **9.** Which measure is useful in evaluating the efficiency in managing inventories?
(a) Inventory turnover ratio.
(b) Days in inventory.
(c) Both (a) and (b).
(d) None of the above.

(SO 6) **10.** Which of these is *not* a liquidity ratio?
(a) Current ratio.
(b) Asset turnover ratio.
(c) Inventory turnover ratio.
(d) Receivables turnover ratio.

(SO 6) **11.** Plano Corporation reported net income $24,000; net sales $400,000; and average assets $600,000 for 2012. What is the 2012 profit margin ratio?
(a) 6%.           (c) 40%.
(b) 12%.          (d) 200%.

Use the following financial statement information as of the end of each year to answer Self-Test Questions 12–16.

|                                    | 2012    | 2011    |
|------------------------------------|---------|---------|
| Inventory                          | $ 54,000 | $ 48,000 |
| Current assets                     | 81,000  | 106,000 |
| Total assets                       | 382,000 | 326,000 |
| Current liabilities                | 27,000  | 36,000  |
| Total liabilities                  | 102,000 | 88,000  |
| Common stockholders' equity        | 240,000 | 198,000 |
| Net sales                          | 784,000 | 697,000 |
| Cost of goods sold                 | 306,000 | 277,000 |
| Net income                         | 134,000 | 90,000  |
| Tax expense                        | 22,000  | 18,000  |
| Interest expense                   | 12,000  | 12,000  |
| Dividends paid to preferred stockholders | 4,000 | 4,000 |
| Dividends paid to common stockholders | 15,000 | 10,000 |

(SO 6) **12.** Compute the days in inventory for 2012.
(a) 64.4 days.    (c) 6 days.
(b) 60.8 days.    (d) 24 days.

(SO 6) **13.** Compute the current ratio for 2012.
(a) 1.26:1.       (c) 0.80:1.
(b) 3.0:1.        (d) 3.75:1.

(SO 6) **14.** Compute the profit margin ratio for 2012.
(a) 17.1%.        (c) 37.9%.
(b) 18.1%.        (d) 5.9%.

(SO 6) **15.** Compute the return on common stockholders' equity for 2012.
(a) 54.2%.        (c) 61.2%.
(b) 52.5%.        (d) 59.4%.

(SO 6) **16.** Compute the times interest earned for 2012.
(a) 11.2 times.   (c) 14.0 times.
(b) 65.3 times.   (d) 13.0 times.

(SO 7) **17.** Which situation below might indicate a company has a low quality of earnings?
(a) The same accounting principles are used each year.
(b) Revenue is recognized when earned.
(c) Maintenance costs are capitalized and then depreciated.
(d) The company's P-E ratio is high relative to competitors.

Go to the book's companion website, **www.wiley.com/college/kimmel**, to access additional Self-Test Questions.

# Questions

All of the Questions in this chapter employ decision tools.

1. Explain sustainable income. What relationship does this concept have to the treatment of irregular items on the income statement?

2. Indicate which of the following items would be reported as an extraordinary item on Stillwell Corporation's income statement.
   (a) Loss from damages caused by a volcano eruption in Iona.
   (b) Loss from the sale of short-term investments.
   (c) Loss attributable to a labor strike.
   (d) Loss of inventory from flood damage because a warehouse is located on a flood plain that floods every 5 to 10 years.
   (e) Loss on the write-down of outdated inventory.
   (f) Loss from a foreign government's expropriation of a production facility.
   (g) Loss from damage to a warehouse in southern California from a minor earthquake.

3. Duncan Inc. reported 2011 earnings per share of $3.26 and had no extraordinary items. In 2012, earnings per share on income before extraordinary items was $2.99, and earnings per share on net income was $3.49. Do you consider this trend to be favorable? Why or why not?

4. Sandran Inc. has been in operation for 3 years and uses the FIFO method of pricing inventory. During the fourth year, Sandran changes to the average-cost method for all its inventory. How will Sandran report this change?

5. What amount did Tootsie Roll Industries report as "Other comprehensive earnings" in 2009? By what percentage did Tootsie Roll's "Comprehensive earnings" differ from its "Net earnings"?

6. (a) Kristina Desmet believes that the analysis of financial statements is directed at two characteristics of a company: liquidity and profitability. Is Kristina correct? Explain.
   (b) Are short-term creditors, long-term creditors, and stockholders interested in primarily the same characteristics of a company? Explain.

7. (a) Distinguish among the following bases of comparison: intracompany, intercompany and industry averages.
   (b) Give the principal value of using each of the three bases of comparison.

8. Two popular methods of financial statement analysis are horizontal analysis and vertical analysis. Explain the difference between these two methods.

9. (a) If Lind Company had net income of $300,000 in 2011 and it experienced a 24.5% increase in net income for 2012, what is its net income for 2012?
   (b) If 6 cents of every dollar of Lind's revenue is net income in 2011, what is the dollar amount of 2011 revenue?

10. Name the major ratios useful in assessing (a) liquidity and (b) solvency.

11. Ron Singer is puzzled. His company had a profit margin of 10% in 2012. He feels that this is an indication that the company is doing well. Teresa Ridley, his accountant, says that more information is needed to determine the company's financial well-being. Who is correct? Why?

12. What does each type of ratio measure?
    (a) Liquidity ratios.
    (b) Solvency ratios.
    (c) Profitability ratios.

13. What is the difference between the current ratio and working capital?

14. Smart Mart, a retail store, has a receivables turnover ratio of 4.5 times. The industry average is 12.5 times. Does Smart Mart have a collection problem with its receivables?

15. Which ratios should be used to help answer each of these questions?
    (a) How efficient is a company in using its assets to produce sales?
    (b) How near to sale is the inventory on hand?
    (c) How many dollars of net income were earned for each dollar invested by the owners?
    (d) How able is a company to meet interest charges as they fall due?

16. At year-end, the price-earnings ratio of General Motors was 11.3, and the price-earnings ratio of Microsoft was 28.14. Which company did the stock market favor? Explain.

17. What is the formula for computing the payout ratio? Do you expect this ratio to be high or low for a growth company?

18. Holding all other factors constant, indicate whether each of the following changes generally signals good or bad news about a company.
    (a) Increase in profit margin ratio.
    (b) Decrease in inventory turnover ratio.
    (c) Increase in current ratio.
    (d) Decrease in earnings per share.
    (e) Increase in price-earnings ratio.
    (f) Increase in debt to total assets ratio.
    (g) Decrease in times interest earned ratio.

19. The return on assets for Corwin Corporation is 7.6%. During the same year, Corwin's return on common stockholders' equity is 12.8%. What is the explanation for the difference in the two rates?

20. Which two ratios do you think should be of greatest interest in each of the following cases?
    (a) A pension fund considering the purchase of 20-year bonds.
    (b) A bank contemplating a short-term loan.
    (c) A common stockholder.

21. Hawi Inc. has net income of $200,000, average shares of common stock outstanding of 40,000,

and preferred dividends for the period of $20,000. What is Hawi's earnings per share of common stock? Sid Brey, the president of Hawi, believes that the computed EPS of the company is high. Comment.

22. Identify and explain factors that affect quality of earnings.

23.  Explain how the choice of one of the following accounting methods over the other raises or lowers a company's net income during a period of continuing inflation.

(a) Use of FIFO instead of LIFO for inventory costing.
(b) Use of a 6-year life for machinery instead of a 9-year life.
(c) Use of straight-line depreciation instead of declining-balance depreciation.

# Brief Exercises

All of the Brief Exercises in this chapter employ decision tools.

*Prepare a discontinued operations section of an income statement.*
*(SO 2),* **AP**

**BE13-1** On June 30, Amano Corporation discontinued its operations in Mexico. On September 1, Amano disposed of the Mexico facility at a pretax loss of $640,000. The applicable tax rate is 25%. Show the discontinued operations section of Amano's income statement.

*Prepare a corrected income statement with an extraordinary item.*
*(SO 2),* **AP**

**BE13-2** An inexperienced accountant for Corfeld Corporation showed the following in Corfeld's 2012 income statement: Income before income taxes $300,000; Income tax expense $72,000; Extraordinary loss from flood (before taxes) $80,000; and Net income $168,000. The extraordinary loss and taxable income are both subject to a 30% tax rate. Prepare a corrected income statement beginning with "Income before income taxes."

*Indicate how a change in accounting principle is reported.*
*(SO 2),* **C**

**BE13-3** On January 1, 2012, Gustin Inc. changed from the LIFO method of inventory pricing to the FIFO method. Explain how this change in accounting principle should be treated in the company's financial statements.

*Prepare horizontal analysis.*
*(SO 4),* **AP**

**BE13-4** Using these data from the comparative balance sheet of Rosalez Company, perform horizontal analysis.

|                     | December 31, 2012 | December 31, 2011 |
|---------------------|-------------------|-------------------|
| Accounts receivable | $ 460,000         | $ 400,000         |
| Inventory           | 780,000           | 650,000           |
| Total assets        | 3,164,000         | 2,800,000         |

*Prepare vertical analysis.*
*(SO 5),* **AP**

**BE13-5** Using the data presented in BE13-4 for Rosalez Company, perform vertical analysis.

*Calculate percentage of change.*
*(SO 4),* **AP**

**BE13-6** Net income was $500,000 in 2010, $485,000 in 2011, and $518,400 in 2012. What is the percentage of change from (a) 2010 to 2011, and (b) from 2011 to 2012? Is the change an increase or a decrease?

*Calculate net income.*
*(SO 4),* **AP**

**BE13-7** If Carolina Company had net income of $382,800 in 2012 and it experienced a 16% increase in net income over 2011, what was its 2011 net income?

*Analyze change in net income.*
*(SO 5),* **AP**

**BE13-8** Vertical analysis (common-size) percentages for Vallejo Company's sales, cost of goods sold, and expenses are listed here.

| Vertical Analysis  | 2012   | 2011   | 2010   |
|--------------------|--------|--------|--------|
| Sales              | 100.0% | 100.0% | 100.0% |
| Cost of goods sold | 60.5   | 62.9   | 64.8   |
| Expenses           | 26.0   | 26.6   | 27.5   |

Did Vallejo's net income as a percent of sales increase, decrease, or remain unchanged over the 3-year period? Provide numerical support for your answer.

*Analyze change in net income.*
*(SO 4),* **AP**

**BE13-9** Horizontal analysis (trend analysis) percentages for Spartan Company's sales, cost of goods sold, and expenses are listed here.

| Horizontal Analysis | 2012  | 2011   | 2010   |
|---------------------|-------|--------|--------|
| Sales               | 96.2% | 104.8% | 100.0% |
| Cost of goods sold  | 101.0 | 98.0   | 100.0  |
| Expenses            | 105.6 | 95.4   | 100.0  |

Explain whether Spartan's net income increased, decreased, or remained unchanged over the 3-year period.

**BE13-10**  These selected condensed data are taken from recent balance sheets of Bob Evans Farms (in thousands).

*Calculate current ratio.*
*(SO 6),* **AP**

|  | **2009** | **2008** |
|---|---|---|
| Cash | $ 13,606 | $  7,669 |
| Accounts receivable | 23,045 | 19,951 |
| Inventories | 31,087 | 31,345 |
| Other current assets | 12,522 | 11,909 |
| Total current assets | $ 80,260 | $ 70,874 |
| Total current liabilities | $245,805 | $326,203 |

Compute the current ratio for each year and comment on your results.

**BE13-11**  The following data are taken from the financial statements of Caprice Company.

*Evaluate collection of accounts receivable.*
*(SO 6),* **AN**

|  | **2012** | **2011** |
|---|---|---|
| Accounts receivable (net), end of year | $ 550,000 | $ 540,000 |
| Net sales on account | 4,300,000 | 4,000,000 |
| Terms for all sales are 1/10, n/45. | | |

Compute for each year (a) the receivables turnover ratio and (b) the average collection period. What conclusions about the management of accounts receivable can be drawn from these data? At the end of 2010, accounts receivable was $520,000.

**BE13-12**  The following data were taken from the income statements of Merlot Company.

*Evaluate management of inventory.*
*(SO 6),* **AN**

|  | **2012** | **2011** |
|---|---|---|
| Sales revenue | $6,420,000 | $6,240,000 |
| Beginning inventory | 960,000 | 840,000 |
| Purchases | 4,840,000 | 4,661,000 |
| Ending inventory | 1,020,000 | 960,000 |

Compute for each year (a) the inventory turnover ratio and (b) days in inventory. What conclusions concerning the management of the inventory can be drawn from these data?

**BE13-13**  Staples, Inc. is one of the largest suppliers of office products in the United States. It had net income of $738.7 million and sales of $24,275.5 million in 2009. Its total assets were $13,073.1 million at the beginning of the year and $13,717.3 million at the end of the year. What is Staples, Inc.'s (a) asset turnover ratio and (b) profit margin ratio? (Round to two decimals.) Provide a brief interpretation of your results.

*Calculate profitability ratios.*
*(SO 6),* **AN**

**BE13-14**  Schiller Company has stockholders' equity of $400,000 and net income of $72,000. It has a payout ratio of 18% and a return on assets ratio of 20%. How much did Schiller pay in cash dividends, and what were its average total assets?

*Calculate profitability ratios.*
*(SO 6),* **AN**

**BE13-15**  Selected data taken from a recent year's financial statements of trading card company Topps Company, Inc. are as follows (in millions).

*Calculate cash-basis liquidity and solvency ratios.*
*(SO 6),* **AN**

| | |
|---|---|
| Net sales | $326.7 |
| Current liabilities, beginning of year | 41.1 |
| Current liabilities, end of year | 62.4 |
| Net cash provided by operating activities | 10.4 |
| Total liabilities, beginning of year | 65.2 |
| Total liabilities, end of year | 73.2 |
| Capital expenditures | 3.7 |
| Cash dividends | 6.2 |

Compute these ratios: (a) current cash debt coverage ratio, (b) cash debt coverage ratio, and (c) free cash flow. Provide a brief interpretation of your results.

# Do it! Review

*Prepare income statement, including irregular items.*
(SO 2), **AP**

**Do it!** 13-1   In its draft 2012 income statement, Provision Corporation reports income before income taxes $500,000, extraordinary loss due to earthquake $180,000, income taxes $200,000 (not including irregular items), and loss on disposal of discontinued music division $24,000. The income tax rate is 40%. Prepare a correct income statement, beginning with income before income taxes.

*Prepare horizontal analysis.*
(SO 3), **AP**

**Do it!** 13-2   Summary financial information for Newburg Company is as follows.

|  | Dec. 31, 2013 | Dec. 31, 2012 |
|---|---|---|
| Current assets | $ 200,000 | $ 220,000 |
| Plant assets | 1,040,000 | 780,000 |
| Total assets | $1,240,000 | $1,000,000 |

Compute the amount and percentage changes in 2013 using horizontal analysis, assuming 2012 is the base year.

*Compute ratios.*
(SO 5), **AP**

**Do it!** 13-3   The condensed financial statements of Blondell Company for the years 2011 and 2012 are presented below.

### BLONDELL COMPANY
### Balance Sheets
### December 31 (in thousands)

|  | 2012 | 2011 |
|---|---|---|
| Current assets |  |  |
| Cash and cash equivalents | $ 330 | $ 360 |
| Accounts receivable (net) | 470 | 400 |
| Inventories | 460 | 390 |
| Prepaid expenses | 130 | 160 |
| Total current assets | 1,390 | 1,310 |
| Property, plant, and equipment (net) | 410 | 380 |
| Investments | 10 | 10 |
| Intangibles and other assets | 530 | 510 |
| Total assets | $2,340 | $2,210 |
| Current liabilities | $ 820 | $ 790 |
| Long-term liabilities | 480 | 380 |
| Stockholders' equity—common | 1,040 | 1,040 |
| Total liabilities and stockholders' equity | $2,340 | $2,210 |

### BLONDELL COMPANY
### Income Statements
### For the Year Ended December 31 (in thousands)

|  | 2012 | 2011 |
|---|---|---|
| Revenues | $3,800 | $3,460 |
| Costs and expenses |  |  |
| Cost of goods sold | 970 | 890 |
| Selling & administrative expenses | 2,400 | 2,330 |
| Interest expense | 10 | 20 |
| Total costs and expenses | 3,380 | 3,240 |
| Income before income taxes | 420 | 220 |
| Income tax expense | 168 | 88 |
| Net income | $ 252 | $ 132 |

Compute the following ratios for 2012 and 2011.
(a)  Current ratio.
(b)  Inventory turnover. (Inventory on December 31, 2010, was $340.)
(c)  Profit margin ratio.
(d)  Return on assets. (Assets on December 31, 2010, were $1,900.)
(e)  Return on common stockholders' equity. (Equity on December 31, 2010, was $900.)

(f) Debt to total assets ratio.
(g) Times interest earned.

**Do it!** 13-4   Match each of the following terms with the phrase that best describes it.

*Match terms relating to quality of earnings and financial statement analysis.*
(SO 3, 4, 5, 6, 7), **K**

Quality of earnings          Pro forma income
Current ratio                Discontinued operations
Horizontal analysis          Comprehensive income

1. A measure used to evaluate a company's liquidity.
2. Usually excludes items that a company thinks are unusual or non-recurring.
3. Indicates the level of full and transparent information provided to users of the financial statements.
4. The disposal of a significant segment of a business.
5. Determines increases or decreases in a series of financial statement data.
6. Includes all changes in stockholders' equity during a period except those resulting from investments by stockholders and distributions to stockholders.

# Exercises

⚒══⚙ All of the Exercises in this chapter employ decision tools.

**E13-1**   Tulsa Company has income before irregular items of $310,000 for the year ended December 31, 2012. It also has the following items (before considering income taxes): (1) an extraordinary fire loss of $60,000 and (2) a gain of $30,000 from the disposal of a division. Assume all items are subject to income taxes at a 30% tax rate.

*Prepare irregular items portion of an income statement.*
(SO 2), **AP**

**Instructions**
Prepare Tulsa Company's income statement for 2012, beginning with "Income before irregular items."

**E13-2**   The *Wall Street Journal* routinely publishes summaries of corporate quarterly and annual earnings reports in a feature called the "Earnings Digest." A typical "digest" report takes the following form.

*Evaluate the effects of unusual or irregular items.*
(SO 1, 2, 6), **C**

**ENERGY ENTERPRISES (A)**

|  | Quarter ending July 31 | |
| --- | --- | --- |
|  | **2012** | **2011** |
| Revenues | $2,049,000,000 | $1,754,000,000 |
| Net income | 97,000,000 | (a) 68,750,000 |
| EPS: Net income | 1.28 | 0.93 |

|  | 12 months ending July 31 | |
| --- | --- | --- |
|  | **2012** | **2011** |
| Revenues | $5,578,500,000 | $5,065,300,000 |
| Extraordinary item | (b) 1,900,000 | |
| Net income | 102,700,000 | (a) 33,250,000 |
| EPS: Net income | 1.36 | 0.48 |

(a) Includes a net charge of $26,000,000 from loss on the sale of electrical equipment
(b) Extraordinary gain on Middle East property expropriation

*The letter in parentheses following the company name indicates the exchange on which Energy Enterprises' stock is traded—in this case, the American Stock Exchange.*

**Instructions**
Answer the following questions.
(a) How was the loss on the electrical equipment reported on the income statement? Was it reported in the fourth quarter of 2011? How can you tell?
(b) Why did the *Wall Street Journal* list the extraordinary item separately?
(c) What is the extraordinary item? Was it included in income for the fourth quarter? How can you tell?
(d) Did Energy Enterprises have an operating loss in any quarter of 2011? Of 2012? How do you know?
(e) Approximately how many shares of stock were outstanding in 2012? Did the number of outstanding shares change from July 31, 2011 to July 31, 2012?

(f) As an investor, what numbers should you use to determine Energy Enterprises' profit margin ratio? Calculate the profit margin ratio for 2011 and 2012 that you consider most useful. Explain your decision.

*Prepare horizontal analysis.*
(SO 4), **AP**

**E13-3** Here is financial information for Pauletti Inc.

|  | December 31, 2012 | December 31, 2011 |
|---|---|---|
| Current assets | $106,000 | $ 90,000 |
| Plant assets (net) | 400,000 | 350,000 |
| Current liabilities | 99,000 | 65,000 |
| Long-term liabilities | 122,000 | 90,000 |
| Common stock, $1 par | 130,000 | 115,000 |
| Retained earnings | 155,000 | 170,000 |

**Instructions**
Prepare a schedule showing a horizontal analysis for 2012, using 2011 as the base year.

*Prepare vertical analysis.*
(SO 5), **AP**

**E13-4** Operating data for Gladow Corporation are presented below.

|  | 2012 | 2011 |
|---|---|---|
| Sales | $800,000 | $600,000 |
| Cost of goods sold | 520,000 | 408,000 |
| Selling expenses | 120,000 | 72,000 |
| Administrative expenses | 60,000 | 48,000 |
| Income tax expense | 30,000 | 24,000 |
| Net income | 70,000 | 48,000 |

**Instructions**
Prepare a schedule showing a vertical analysis for 2012 and 2011.

*Prepare horizontal and vertical analyses.*
(SO 4, 5), **AP**

**E13-5** The comparative balance sheets of Nike, Inc. are presented here.

**NIKE, INC.**
**Comparative Balance Sheets**
**May 31**
**($ in millions)**

| Assets | 2009 | 2008 |
|---|---|---|
| Current assets | $ 9,734 | $ 8,839 |
| Property, plant, and equipment (net) | 1,958 | 1,891 |
| Other assets | 1,558 | 1,713 |
| Total assets | $13,250 | $12,443 |
| **Liabilities and Stockholders' Equity** |  |  |
| Current liabilities | $ 3,277 | $ 3,322 |
| Long-term liabilities | 1,280 | 1,296 |
| Stockholders' equity | 8,693 | 7,825 |
| Total liabilities and stockholders' equity | $13,250 | $12,443 |

**Instructions**
(a) Prepare a horizontal analysis of the balance sheet data for Nike, using 2008 as a base. (Show the amount of increase or decrease as well.)
(b) Prepare a vertical analysis of the balance sheet data for Nike for 2009.

*Prepare horizontal and vertical analyses.*
(SO 4, 5), **AP**

**E13-6** Here are the comparative income statements of Blevins Corporation.

**BLEVINS CORPORATION**
**Comparative Income Statements**
**For the Years Ended December 31**

|  | 2012 | 2011 |
|---|---|---|
| Net sales | $598,000 | $500,000 |
| Cost of goods sold | 477,000 | 420,000 |
| Gross profit | $121,000 | $ 80,000 |
| Operating expenses | 80,000 | 44,000 |
| Net income | $ 41,000 | $ 36,000 |

## Instructions
(a) Prepare a horizontal analysis of the income statement data for Blevins Corporation, using 2011 as a base. (Show the amounts of increase or decrease.)
(b) Prepare a vertical analysis of the income statement data for Blevins Corporation for both years.

**E13-7** Nordstrom, Inc. operates department stores in numerous states. Selected financial statement data (in millions) for 2009 are presented below.

*Compute liquidity ratios.*
*(SO 6), AP*

| | End of Year | Beginning of Year |
|---|---|---|
| Cash and cash equivalents | $ 795 | $ 72 |
| Receivables (net) | 2,035 | 1,942 |
| Merchandise inventory | 898 | 900 |
| Other current assets | 326 | 303 |
| Total current assets | $4,054 | $3,217 |
| Total current liabilities | $2,014 | $1,601 |

For the year, net credit sales were $8,258 million, cost of goods sold was $5,328 million, and cash from operations was $1,251 million.

## Instructions
Compute the current ratio, current cash debt coverage ratio, receivables turnover ratio, average collection period, inventory turnover ratio, and days in inventory at the end of the current year.

**E13-8** Skie Incorporated had the following transactions involving current assets and current liabilities during February 2012.

*Perform current ratio analysis.*
*(SO 6), AP*

| Feb. | 3 | Collected accounts receivable of $15,000. |
|---|---|---|
| | 7 | Purchased equipment for $23,000 cash. |
| | 11 | Paid $3,000 for a 3-year insurance policy. |
| | 14 | Paid accounts payable of $12,000. |
| | 18 | Declared cash dividends, $4,000. |

Additional information:
As of February 1, 2012, current assets were $120,000 and current liabilities were $40,000.

## Instructions
Compute the current ratio as of the beginning of the month and after each transaction.

**E13-9** Hendi Company has these comparative balance sheet data:

*Compute selected ratios.*
*(SO 6), AP*

### HENDI COMPANY
### Balance Sheets
### December 31

| | 2012 | 2011 |
|---|---|---|
| Cash | $ 15,000 | $ 30,000 |
| Receivables (net) | 70,000 | 60,000 |
| Inventories | 60,000 | 50,000 |
| Plant assets (net) | 200,000 | 180,000 |
| | $345,000 | $320,000 |
| Accounts payable | $ 50,000 | $ 60,000 |
| Mortgage payable (15%) | 100,000 | 100,000 |
| Common stock, $10 par | 140,000 | 120,000 |
| Retained earnings | 55,000 | 40,000 |
| | $345,000 | $320,000 |

Additional information for 2012:
1. Net income was $25,000.
2. Sales on account were $375,000. Sales returns and allowances amounted to $25,000.
3. Cost of goods sold was $198,000.
4. Net cash provided by operating activities was $48,000.
5. Capital expenditures were $25,000, and cash dividends were $10,000.

*Instructions*
Compute the following ratios at December 31, 2012.
(a) Current.
(b) Receivables turnover.
(c) Average collection period.
(d) Inventory turnover.
(e) Days in inventory.
(f) Cash debt coverage.
(g) Current cash debt coverage.
(h) Free cash flow.

*Compute selected ratios.*
(SO 6), **AP**

**E13-10** Selected comparative statement data for the giant bookseller Barnes & Noble are presented here. All balance sheet data are as of the end of the fiscal year (in millions).

|  | 2008 | 2007 |
|---|---|---|
| Net sales | $5,121.8 | $5,286.7 |
| Cost of goods sold | 3,540.6 | 3,679.8 |
| Net income | 75.9 | 135.8 |
| Accounts receivable | 81.0 | 107.1 |
| Inventory | 1,203.5 | 1,358.2 |
| Total assets | 2,993.9 | 3,249.8 |
| Total common stockholders' equity | 921.6 | 1,074.7 |

*Instructions*
Compute the following ratios for 2008.
(a) Profit margin.
(b) Asset turnover.
(c) Return on assets.
(d) Return on common stockholders' equity.
(e) Gross profit rate.

*Compute selected ratios.*
(SO 6), **AP**

**E13-11** Here is the income statement for Bachus, Inc.

**BACHUS, INC.**
**Income Statement**
**For the Year Ended December 31, 2012**

| | |
|---|---|
| Sales | $400,000 |
| Cost of goods sold | 230,000 |
| Gross profit | 170,000 |
| Expenses (including $16,000 interest and $24,000 income taxes) | 98,000 |
| Net income | $ 72,000 |

Additional information:

1. Common stock outstanding January 1, 2012, was 32,000 shares, and 40,000 shares were outstanding at December 31, 2012.
2. The market price of Bachus, Inc., stock was $14 in 2012.
3. Cash dividends of $21,000 were paid, $5,000 of which were to preferred stockholders.

*Instructions*
Compute the following measures for 2012.
(a) Earnings per share.
(b) Price-earnings ratio.
(c) Payout ratio.
(d) Times interest earned ratio.

*Compute amounts from ratios.*
(SO 6), **AP**

**E13-12** Lacey Corporation experienced a fire on December 31, 2012 in which its financial records were partially destroyed. It has been able to salvage some of the records and has ascertained the following balances.

|  | December 31, 2012 | December 31, 2011 |
|---|---|---|
| Cash | $ 30,000 | $ 10,000 |
| Receivables (net) | 72,500 | 126,000 |
| Inventory | 200,000 | 180,000 |
| Accounts payable | 50,000 | 90,000 |
| Notes payable | 30,000 | 60,000 |
| Common stock, $100 par | 400,000 | 400,000 |
| Retained earnings | 113,500 | 101,000 |

Additional information:

1. The inventory turnover is 3.8 times.
2. The return on common stockholders' equity is 22%. The company had no additional paid-in capital.

3. The receivables turnover is 11.2 times.
4. The return on assets is 18%.
5. Total assets at December 31, 2011, were $605,000.

**Instructions**
Compute the following for Lacey Corporation.
(a) Cost of goods sold for 2012.
(b) Net credit sales for 2012.
(c) Net income for 2012.
(d) Total assets at December 31, 2012.

# Exercises: Set B and Challenge Exercises

Visit the book's companion website, at **www.wiley.com/college/kimmel**, and choose the Student Companion site to access Exercise Set B and Challenge Exercises.

# Problems: Set A

All of the Problems in this chapter employ decision tools.

**P13-1A** Here are comparative statement data for Silver Company and Gold Company, two competitors. All balance sheet data are as of December 31, 2012, and December 31, 2011.

*Prepare vertical analysis and comment on profitability.*
*(SO 5, 6), AN*

|  | Silver Company | | Gold Company | |
|---|---|---|---|---|
|  | **2012** | **2011** | **2012** | **2011** |
| Net sales | $1,849,000 |  | $546,000 |  |
| Cost of goods sold | 1,063,200 |  | 289,000 |  |
| Operating expenses | 240,000 |  | 82,000 |  |
| Interest expense | 6,800 |  | 3,600 |  |
| Income tax expense | 62,000 |  | 28,000 |  |
| Current assets | 325,975 | $312,410 | 83,336 | $79,467 |
| Plant assets (net) | 526,800 | 500,000 | 139,728 | 125,812 |
| Current liabilities | 66,325 | 75,815 | 35,348 | 30,281 |
| Long-term liabilities | 113,990 | 90,000 | 29,620 | 25,000 |
| Common stock, $10 par | 500,000 | 500,000 | 120,000 | 120,000 |
| Retained earnings | 172,460 | 146,595 | 38,096 | 29,998 |

**Instructions**
(a) Prepare a vertical analysis of the 2012 income statement data for Silver Company and Gold Company.
(b) Comment on the relative profitability of the companies by computing the 2012 return on assets and the return on common stockholders' equity ratios for both companies.

**P13-2A** The comparative statements of Lucille Company are presented here.

*Compute ratios from balance sheets and income statements.*
*(SO 6), AP*

**LUCILLE COMPANY**
**Income Statements**
**For the Years Ended December 31**

|  | 2012 | 2011 |
|---|---|---|
| Net sales | $1,890,540 | $1,750,500 |
| Cost of goods sold | 1,058,540 | 1,006,000 |
| Gross profit | 832,000 | 744,500 |
| Selling and administrative expenses | 500,000 | 479,000 |
| Income from operations | 332,000 | 265,500 |
| Other expenses and losses |  |  |
| Interest expense | 22,000 | 20,000 |
| Income before income taxes | 310,000 | 245,500 |
| Income tax expense | 92,000 | 73,000 |
| Net income | $ 218,000 | $ 172,500 |

## LUCILLE COMPANY
### Balance Sheets
### December 31

| Assets | 2012 | 2011 |
|---|---|---|
| Current assets | | |
| Cash | $ 60,100 | $ 64,200 |
| Short-term investments | 74,000 | 50,000 |
| Accounts receivable | 117,800 | 102,800 |
| Inventory | 126,000 | 115,500 |
| Total current assets | 377,900 | 332,500 |
| Plant assets (net) | 649,000 | 520,300 |
| Total assets | $1,026,900 | $852,800 |

| Liabilities and Stockholders' Equity | | |
|---|---|---|
| Current liabilities | | |
| Accounts payable | $ 160,000 | $145,400 |
| Income taxes payable | 43,500 | 42,000 |
| Total current liabilities | 203,500 | 187,400 |
| Bonds payable | 220,000 | 200,000 |
| Total liabilities | 423,500 | 387,400 |
| Stockholders' equity | | |
| Common stock ($5 par) | 290,000 | 300,000 |
| Retained earnings | 313,400 | 165,400 |
| Total stockholders' equity | 603,400 | 465,400 |
| Total liabilities and stockholders' equity | $1,026,900 | $852,800 |

All sales were on account. Net cash provided by operating activities for 2012 was $220,000. Capital expenditures were $136,000, and cash dividends were $70,000.

**Instructions**
Compute the following ratios for 2012.
(a) Earnings per share.
(b) Return on common stockholders' equity.
(c) Return on assets.
(d) Current ratio.
(e) Receivables turnover.
(f) Average collection period.
(g) Inventory turnover.
(h) Days in inventory.
(i) Times interest earned.
(j) Asset turnover.
(k) Debt to total assets.
(l) Current cash debt coverage.
(m) Cash debt coverage.
(n) Free cash flow.

*Perform ratio analysis, and discuss change in financial position and operating results.*
(SO 6), **AN**

**P13-3A** Condensed balance sheet and income statement data for Glassgow Corporation are presented here.

## GLASSGOW CORPORATION
### Balance Sheets
### December 31

| | 2012 | 2011 | 2010 |
|---|---|---|---|
| Cash | $ 30,000 | $ 20,000 | $ 18,000 |
| Receivables (net) | 50,000 | 45,000 | 48,000 |
| Other current assets | 90,000 | 95,000 | 64,000 |
| Investments | 55,000 | 70,000 | 45,000 |
| Plant and equipment (net) | 500,000 | 370,000 | 358,000 |
| | $725,000 | $600,000 | $533,000 |
| Current liabilities | $ 85,000 | $ 80,000 | $ 70,000 |
| Long-term debt | 145,000 | 85,000 | 50,000 |
| Common stock, $10 par | 320,000 | 310,000 | 300,000 |
| Retained earnings | 175,000 | 125,000 | 113,000 |
| | $725,000 | $600,000 | $533,000 |

### GLASSGOW CORPORATION
### Income Statements
### For the Years Ended December 31

| | 2012 | 2011 |
|---|---|---|
| Sales | $740,000 | $600,000 |
| Less: Sales returns and allowances | 40,000 | 30,000 |
| Net sales | 700,000 | 570,000 |
| Cost of goods sold | 425,000 | 350,000 |
| Gross profit | 275,000 | 220,000 |
| Operating expenses (including income taxes) | 180,000 | 150,000 |
| Net income | $ 95,000 | $ 70,000 |

Additional information:

1. The market price of Glassgow's common stock was $7.00, $7.50, and $8.50 for 2010, 2011, and 2012, respectively.
2. You must compute dividends paid. All dividends were paid in cash.

**Instructions**

(a) Compute the following ratios for 2011 and 2012.

    (1) Profit margin.               (5) Price-earnings.

    (2) Gross profit rate.           (6) Payout.

    (3) Asset turnover.             (7) Debt to total assets.

    (4) Earnings per share.

(b) Based on the ratios calculated, discuss briefly the improvement or lack thereof in the financial position and operating results from 2011 to 2012 of Glassgow Corporation.

**P13-4A**  The following financial information is for Cheaney Company.

*Compute ratios; comment on overall liquidity and profitability.*

(SO 6), **AN**

### CHEANEY COMPANY
### Balance Sheets
### December 31

| Assets | 2012 | 2011 |
|---|---|---|
| Cash | $ 70,000 | $ 65,000 |
| Short-term investments | 55,000 | 40,000 |
| Receivables | 104,000 | 90,000 |
| Inventories | 230,000 | 165,000 |
| Prepaid expenses | 25,000 | 23,000 |
| Land | 130,000 | 130,000 |
| Building and equipment (net) | 260,000 | 185,000 |
| Total assets | $874,000 | $698,000 |

| Liabilities and Stockholders' Equity | 2012 | 2011 |
|---|---|---|
| Notes payable | $170,000 | $120,000 |
| Accounts payable | 65,000 | 52,000 |
| Accrued liabilities | 40,000 | 40,000 |
| Bonds payable, due 2015 | 250,000 | 170,000 |
| Common stock, $10 par | 200,000 | 200,000 |
| Retained earnings | 149,000 | 116,000 |
| Total liabilities and stockholders' equity | $874,000 | $698,000 |

### CHEANEY COMPANY
### Income Statements
### For the Years Ended December 31

| | 2012 | 2011 |
|---|---|---|
| Sales | $882,000 | $790,000 |
| Cost of goods sold | 640,000 | 575,000 |
| Gross profit | 242,000 | 215,000 |
| Operating expenses | 190,000 | 167,000 |
| Net income | $ 52,000 | $ 48,000 |

Additional information:

1. Inventory at the beginning of 2011 was $115,000.
2. Receivables (net) at the beginning of 2011 were $86,000.
3. Total assets at the beginning of 2011 were $660,000.
4. No common stock transactions occurred during 2011 or 2012.
5. All sales were on account.

*Instructions*

(a) Indicate, by using ratios, the change in liquidity and profitability of Cheaney Company from 2011 to 2012. (*Note:* Not all profitability ratios can be computed nor can cash-basis ratios be computed.)

(b) Given below are three independent situations and a ratio that may be affected. For each situation, compute the affected ratio (1) as of December 31, 2012, and (2) as of December 31, 2013, after giving effect to the situation. Net income for 2013 was $54,000. Total assets on December 31, 2013, were $900,000.

| Situation | Ratio |
| --- | --- |
| 1. 18,000 shares of common stock were sold at par on July 1, 2013. | Return on common stockholders' equity |
| 2. All of the notes payable were paid in 2013. | Debt to total assets |
| 3. The market price of common stock was $9 and $12 on December 31, 2012 and 2013, respectively. | Price-earnings |

*Compute selected ratios, and compare liquidity, profitability, and solvency for two companies.*

*(SO 6), E*

**P13-5A** Selected financial data of Target and Wal-Mart for 2009 are presented here (in millions).

| | Target Corporation | Wal-Mart Stores, Inc. |
| --- | --- | --- |
| **Income Statement Data for Year** | | |
| Net sales | $65,357 | $408,214 |
| Cost of goods sold | 45,583 | 304,657 |
| Selling and administrative expenses | 15,101 | 79,607 |
| Interest expense | 707 | 2,065 |
| Other income (expense) | (94) | (411) |
| Income tax expense | 1,384 | 7,139 |
| Net income | $ 2,488 | $ 14,335 |
| **Balance Sheet Data (End of Year)** | | |
| Current assets | $18,424 | $ 48,331 |
| Noncurrent assets | 26,109 | 122,375 |
| Total assets | $44,533 | $170,706 |
| Current liabilities | $11,327 | $ 55,561 |
| Long-term debt | 17,859 | 44,089 |
| Total stockholders' equity | 15,347 | 71,056 |
| Total liabilities and stockholders' equity | $44,533 | $170,706 |
| **Beginning-of-Year Balances** | | |
| Total assets | $44,106 | $163,429 |
| Total stockholders' equity | 13,712 | 65,682 |
| Current liabilities | 10,512 | 55,390 |
| Total liabilities | 30,394 | 97,747 |
| **Other Data** | | |
| Average net receivables | $7,525 | $ 4,025 |
| Average inventory | 6,942 | 33,836 |
| Net cash provided by operating activities | 5,881 | 26,249 |
| Capital expenditures | 1,729 | 12,184 |
| Dividends | 496 | 4,217 |

*Instructions*

(a) For each company, compute the following ratios.

| | |
|---|---|
| (1) Current. | (8) Return on assets. |
| (2) Receivables turnover. | (9) Return on common stockholders' equity. |
| (3) Average collection period. | (10) Debt to total assets. |
| (4) Inventory turnover. | (11) Times interest earned. |
| (5) Days in inventory. | (12) Current cash debt coverage. |
| (6) Profit margin. | (13) Cash debt coverage. |
| (7) Asset turnover. | (14) Free cash flow. |

(b) Compare the liquidity, solvency, and profitability of the two companies.

# Problems: Set B

All of the Problems in this chapter employ decision tools.

**P13-1B**  Here are comparative statement data for Martin Company and Lewis Company, two competitors. All balance sheet data are as of December 31, 2012, and December 31, 2011.

*Prepare vertical analysis and comment on profitability.*
*(SO 5, 6),* **AN**

| | Martin Company | | Lewis Company | |
|---|---|---|---|---|
| | **2012** | **2011** | **2012** | **2011** |
| Net sales | $350,000 | | $1,200,000 | |
| Cost of goods sold | 180,000 | | 648,000 | |
| Operating expenses | 72,000 | | 266,000 | |
| Interest expense | 5,000 | | 10,000 | |
| Income tax expense | 17,000 | | 54,000 | |
| Current assets | 130,000 | $100,000 | 700,000 | $650,000 |
| Plant assets (net) | 400,000 | 270,000 | 1,000,000 | 750,000 |
| Current liabilities | 60,000 | 58,000 | 250,000 | 275,000 |
| Long-term liabilities | 50,000 | 72,000 | 200,000 | 150,000 |
| Common stock | 340,000 | 200,000 | 950,000 | 700,000 |
| Retained earnings | 80,000 | 40,000 | 300,000 | 275,000 |

*Instructions*

(a) Prepare a vertical analysis of the 2012 income statement data for Martin Company and Lewis Company.

(b) Comment on the relative profitability of the companies by computing the return on assets and the return on common stockholders' equity ratios for both companies.

**P13-2B**  The comparative statements of Jetson Company are shown below.

*Compute ratios from balance sheets and income statements.*
*(SO 6),* **AP**

**JETSON COMPANY**
**Income Statements**
**For the Years Ended December 31**

| | 2012 | 2011 |
|---|---|---|
| Net sales | $780,000 | $624,000 |
| Cost of goods sold | 440,000 | 405,600 |
| Gross profit | 340,000 | 218,400 |
| Selling and administrative expense | 176,880 | 149,760 |
| Income from operations | 163,120 | 68,640 |
| Other expenses and losses | | |
| Interest expense | 9,920 | 7,200 |
| Income before income taxes | 153,200 | 61,440 |
| Income tax expense | 38,000 | 14,000 |
| Net income | $115,200 | $ 47,440 |

**JETSON COMPANY**
**Balance Sheets**
**December 31**

| Assets | 2012 | 2011 |
|---|---|---|
| Current assets | | |
| Cash | $ 23,100 | $ 21,600 |
| Short-term investments | 44,800 | 33,000 |
| Accounts receivable | 106,200 | 83,800 |
| Inventory | 116,400 | 74,000 |
| Total current assets | 290,500 | 212,400 |
| Plant assets (net) | 485,300 | 439,600 |
| Total assets | $775,800 | $652,000 |

| Liabilities and Stockholders' Equity | | |
|---|---|---|
| Current liabilities | | |
| Accounts payable | $138,200 | $132,000 |
| Income taxes payable | 25,300 | 24,000 |
| Total current liabilities | 163,500 | 156,000 |
| Bonds payable | 132,000 | 120,000 |
| Total liabilities | 295,500 | 276,000 |
| Stockholders' equity | | |
| Common stock ($10 par) | 150,000 | 130,000 |
| Retained earnings | 330,300 | 246,000 |
| Total stockholders' equity | 480,300 | 376,000 |
| Total liabilities and stockholders' equity | $775,800 | $652,000 |

All sales were on account. Net cash provided by operating activities was $108,000. Capital expenditures were $47,000, and cash dividends were $30,900.

**Instructions**
Compute the following ratios for 2012.
(a) Earnings per share.
(b) Return on common stockholders' equity.
(c) Return on assets.
(d) Current.
(e) Receivables turnover.
(f) Average collection period.
(g) Inventory turnover.
(h) Days in inventory.
(i) Times interest earned.
(j) Asset turnover.
(k) Debt to total assets.
(l) Current cash debt coverage.
(m) Cash debt coverage.
(n) Free cash flow.

*Perform ratio analysis, and discuss change in financial position and operating results.*
(SO 6), **AN**

**P13-3B** The condensed balance sheet and income statement data for Finch Corporation are presented below.

**FINCH CORPORATION**
**Balance Sheets**
**December 31**

| | 2012 | 2011 | 2010 |
|---|---|---|---|
| Cash | $ 30,000 | $ 24,000 | $ 20,000 |
| Receivables (net) | 110,000 | 48,000 | 48,000 |
| Other current assets | 80,000 | 78,000 | 62,000 |
| Investments | 90,000 | 70,000 | 50,000 |
| Plant and equipment (net) | 503,000 | 400,000 | 360,000 |
| | $813,000 | $620,000 | $540,000 |
| Current liabilities | $ 98,000 | $ 75,000 | $ 70,000 |
| Long-term debt | 130,000 | 75,000 | 65,000 |
| Common stock, $10 par | 400,000 | 340,000 | 300,000 |
| Retained earnings | 185,000 | 130,000 | 105,000 |
| | $813,000 | $620,000 | $540,000 |

### FINCH CORPORATION
### Income Statements
### For the Years Ended December 31

|  | 2012 | 2011 |
|---|---|---|
| Sales | $800,000 | $750,000 |
| Less: Sales returns and allowances | 40,000 | 50,000 |
| Net sales | 760,000 | 700,000 |
| Cost of goods sold | 420,000 | 406,000 |
| Gross profit | 340,000 | 294,000 |
| Operating expenses (including income taxes) | 220,000 | 204,000 |
| Net income | $120,000 | $ 90,000 |

Additional information:

1. The market price of Finch common stock was $5.00, $3.50, and $2.80 for 2010, 2011, and 2012, respectively.
2. You must compute dividends paid. All dividends were paid in cash.

***Instructions***
(a) Compute the following ratios for 2011 and 2012.
    (1) Profit margin.           (5) Price-earnings.
    (2) Gross profit rate.      (6) Payout.
    (3) Asset turnover.        (7) Debt to total assets.
    (4) Earnings per share.

(b) Based on the ratios calculated, discuss briefly the improvement or lack thereof in the financial position and operating results from 2011 to 2012 of Finch Corporation.

**P13-4B**   Financial information for Chimera Company is presented here.

*Compute ratios; comment on overall liquidity and profitability.*
*(SO 6),* **AN**

### CHIMERA COMPANY
### Balance Sheets
### December 31

| **Assets** | 2012 | 2011 |
|---|---|---|
| Cash | $ 50,000 | $ 42,000 |
| Short-term investments | 80,000 | 50,000 |
| Receivables | 100,000 | 77,000 |
| Inventories | 410,000 | 320,000 |
| Prepaid expenses | 30,000 | 31,000 |
| Land | 75,000 | 75,000 |
| Building and equipment (net) | 570,000 | 400,000 |
| Total assets | $1,315,000 | $995,000 |

| **Liabilities and Stockholders' Equity** | 2012 | 2011 |
|---|---|---|
| Notes payable | $ 120,000 | $ 25,000 |
| Accounts payable | 160,000 | 90,000 |
| Accrued liabilities | 50,000 | 50,000 |
| Bonds payable, due 2014 | 180,000 | 100,000 |
| Common stock, $5 par | 500,000 | 500,000 |
| Retained earnings | 305,000 | 230,000 |
| Total liabilities and stockholders' equity | $1,315,000 | $995,000 |

### CHIMERA COMPANY
### Income Statements
### For the Years Ended December 31

|  | 2012 | 2011 |
|---|---|---|
| Sales | $1,050,000 | $940,000 |
| Cost of goods sold | 680,000 | 635,000 |
| Gross profit | 370,000 | 305,000 |
| Operating expenses | 240,000 | 215,000 |
| Net income | $ 130,000 | $ 90,000 |

Additional information:

1. Inventory at the beginning of 2011 was $330,000.
2. Receivables at the beginning of 2011 were $80,000.
3. Total assets at the beginning of 2011 were $1,175,000.
4. No common stock transactions occurred during 2011 or 2012.
5. All sales were on account.

***Instructions***

(a) Indicate, by using ratios, the change in liquidity and profitability of the company from 2011 to 2012. (*Note:* Not all profitability ratios can be computed nor can cash-basis ratios be computed.)

(b) Given below are three independent situations and a ratio that may be affected. For each situation, compute the affected ratio (1) as of December 31, 2012, and (2) as of December 31, 2013, after giving effect to the situation. Net income for 2013 was $125,000. Total assets on December 31, 2013, were $1,450,000.

| Situation | Ratio |
| --- | --- |
| 1. 50,000 shares of common stock were sold at par on July 1, 2013. | Return on common stockholders' equity |
| 2. All of the notes payable were paid in 2013. | Debt to total assets |
| 3. The market price of common stock on December 31, 2013, was $6.25. The market price on December 31, 2012 was $5. | Price-earnings |

*Compute selected ratios, and compare liquidity, profitability, and solvency for two companies.*

*(SO 6),* **E**

**P13-5B** Selected financial data for Stanley Black & Decker, Inc. and Snap-On Tools for 2009 are presented here (in millions).

| | Stanley Black & Decker | Snap-On Tools |
| --- | --- | --- |
| **Income Statement Data for Year** | | |
| Net sales | $3,737.1 | $2,420.8 |
| Cost of goods sold | 2,228.8 | 1,345.7 |
| Selling and administrative expenses | 1,208.2 | 824.4 |
| Interest expense | 63.7 | 47.7 |
| Other income (loss) | 42.4 | (6.1) |
| Income tax expense | 54.5 | 62.7 |
| Net income | $ 224.3 | $ 134.2 |
| **Balance Sheet Data (End of Year)** | | |
| Current assets | $1,411.9 | $1,676.1 |
| Property, plant, and equipment (net) | 575.9 | 347.8 |
| Other assets | 2,781.3 | 1,423.5 |
| Total assets | $4,769.1 | $3,447.4 |
| Current liabilities | $1,192.0 | $ 739.9 |
| Long-term debt | 1,591.0 | 1,417.5 |
| Total stockholders' equity | 1,986.1 | 1,290.0 |
| Total liabilities and stockholders' equity | $4,769.1 | $3,447.4 |
| **Beginning-of-Year Balances** | | |
| Total assets | $4,866.6 | $2,710.3 |
| Total stockholders' equity | 1,706.3 | 1,186.5 |
| Current liabilities | 1,193.2 | 547.5 |
| Total liabilities | 3,160.3 | 1,523.8 |
| **Other Data** | | |
| Average receivables (net) | $ 604.9 | $ 612.7 |
| Average inventory | 440.5 | 316.9 |
| Net cash provided by operating activities | 539.4 | 347.1 |
| Capital expenditures | 72.9 | 64.4 |
| Cash dividends | 103.6 | 69.0 |

*Instructions*

(a) For each company, compute the following ratios.

(1) Current ratio.
(2) Receivables turnover.
(3) Average collection period.
(4) Inventory turnover.
(5) Days in inventory.
(6) Profit margin.
(7) Asset turnover.

(8) Return on assets.
(9) Return on common stockholders' equity.
(10) Debt to total assets.
(11) Times interest earned.
(12) Current cash debt coverage.
(13) Cash debt coverage.
(14) Free cash flow.

(b) Compare the liquidity, solvency, and profitability of the two companies.

# Problems: Set C

Visit the book's companion website, at **www.wiley.com/college/kimmel**, and choose the Student Companion site to access Problem Set C.

# Continuing Cookie Chronicle

(*Note:* This is a continuation of the Cookie Chronicle from Chapters 1 through 12.)

**CCC13** Natalie and Curtis have comparative balance sheets and income statements for Cookie & Coffee Creations Inc. They have been told that they can use these financial statements to prepare horizontal and vertical analyses, and to calculate financial ratios, to analyze how their business is doing and to make some decisions they have been considering.

> Go to the book's companion website, at **www.wiley.com/college/kimmel**, to find the completion of this problem.

# broadening your perspective

## Financial Reporting and Analysis

**FINANCIAL REPORTING PROBLEM:** *Tootsie Roll Industries, Inc.*

**BYP13-1** Your parents are considering investing in Tootsie Roll Industries common stock. They ask you, as an accounting expert, to make an analysis of the company for them. Fortunately, excerpts from a recent annual report of Tootsie Roll are presented in Appendix A of this textbook.

*Instructions*

(a) Make a 5-year trend analysis, using 2005 as the base year, of (1) net sales and (2) net earnings. Comment on the significance of the trend results.

(b) Compute for 2009 and 2008 the (1) debt to total assets ratio and (2) times interest earned ratio. (See Note 6 for interest expense.) How would you evaluate Tootsie Roll's long-term solvency?

(c) Compute for 2009 and 2008 the (1) profit margin ratio, (2) asset turnover ratio, (3) return on assets ratio, and (4) return on common stockholders' equity ratio. How would you evaluate Tootsie Roll's profitability? Total assets at December 31, 2007, were $812,725,000, and total stockholders' equity at December 31, 2007, was $638,230,000.

(d) What information outside the annual report may also be useful to your parents in making a decision about Tootsie Roll?

**COMPARATIVE ANALYSIS PROBLEM:** *Tootsie Roll vs. Hershey*

**BYP13-2** The financial statements of The Hershey Company are presented in Appendix B, following the financial statements for Tootsie Roll Industries in Appendix A.

*Instructions*
(a) Based on the information in the financial statements, determine each of the following for each company:
   (1) The percentage increase (i) in net sales and (ii) in net income from 2008 to 2009.
   (2) The percentage increase (i) in total assets and (ii) in total stockholders' equity from 2008 to 2009.
   (3) The earnings per share for 2009.
(b) What conclusions concerning the two companies can be drawn from these data?

## RESEARCH CASE

**BYP13-3** The April 21, 2008, issue of the *Wall Street Journal Online* included an article by David Reilly entitled "A Way Charges Stay off Bottom Line."

*Instructions*
Read the article and answer the following questions.
(a) According to the article, how do companies avoid reporting losses on certain types of investment securities in net income?
(b) At what point would these losses be reported in net income?
(c) At the time of the article, what was the total estimated amount of unrealized losses that companies in the Standard and Poor's 500 Stock Index were reporting in equity?
(d) Does the article suggest that these companies are violating accounting standards?
(e) What are the implications of this accounting practice for investors?

## INTERPRETING FINANCIAL STATEMENTS

**BYP13-4** The Coca-Cola Company and PepsiCo, Inc. provide refreshments to every corner of the world. Selected data from the 2009 consolidated financial statements for The Coca-Cola Company and for PepsiCo, Inc. are presented here (in millions).

| | Coca-Cola | PepsiCo |
|---|---|---|
| Total current assets | $17,551 | $12,571 |
| Total current liabilities | 13,721 | 8,756 |
| Net sales | 30,990 | 43,232 |
| Cost of goods sold | 11,088 | 20,099 |
| Net income | 6,824 | 5,946 |
| Average (net) receivables for the year | 3,424 | 4,654 |
| Average inventories for the year | 2,271 | 2,570 |
| Average total assets | 44,595 | 37,921 |
| Average common stockholders' equity | 22,636 | 14,556 |
| Average current liabilities | 13,355 | 8,772 |
| Average total liabilities | 21,960 | 23,466 |
| Total assets | 48,671 | 39,848 |
| Total liabilities | 23,872 | 23,044 |
| Income taxes | 2,040 | 2,100 |
| Interest expense | 355 | 397 |
| Cash provided by operating activities | 8,186 | 6,796 |
| Capital expenditures | 1,993 | 2,128 |
| Cash dividends | 3,800 | 2,732 |

*Instructions*
(a) Compute the following liquidity ratios for 2009 for Coca-Cola and for PepsiCo and comment on the relative liquidity of the two competitors.
   (1) Current ratio.                    (4) Inventory turnover.
   (2) Receivables turnover.             (5) Days in inventory.
   (3) Average collection period.        (6) Current cash debt coverage.
(b) Compute the following solvency ratios for the two companies and comment on the relative solvency of the two competitors.
   (1) Debt to total assets ratio.
   (2) Times interest earned.
   (3) Cash debt coverage ratio.
   (4) Free cash flow.

(c) Compute the following profitability ratios for the two companies and comment on the relative profitability of the two competitors.
  (1) Profit margin.
  (2) Asset turnover.
  (3) Return on assets.
  (4) Return on common stockholders' equity.

## FINANCIAL ANALYSIS ON THE WEB

**BYP13-5** *Purpose:* To employ comparative data and industry data to evaluate a company's performance and financial position.

*Address:* **http://www.moneycentral.msn.com/investor/invsub/results/compare.asp**, or go to **www.wiley.com/college/kimmel**

*Steps*
(1) Identify two competing companies.
(2) Go to the above address.
(3) Type in the first company's stock symbol. (Use "symbol look-up.").
(4) Choose **Ratios**.
(5) Print out the results.
(6) Repeat steps 3–5 for the competitor.

*Instructions*
(a) Evaluate the company's liquidity relative to the industry averages and to the competitor that you chose.
(b) Evaluate the company's solvency relative to the industry averages and to the competitor that you chose.
(c) Evaluate the company's profitability relative to the industry averages and to the competitor that you chose.

# Critical Thinking

## DECISION MAKING ACROSS THE ORGANIZATION

**BYP13-6** You are a loan officer for Great Plains Bank of Davenport. David Miller, president of D. Miller Corporation, has just left your office. He is interested in an 8-year loan to expand the company's operations. The borrowed funds would be used to purchase new equipment. As evidence of the company's debt-worthiness, Miller provided you with the following facts.

|  | **2012** | **2011** |
|---|---|---|
| Current ratio | 3.1 | 2.1 |
| Asset turnover ratio | 2.8 | 2.2 |
| Cash debt coverage ratio | .1 | .2 |
| Net income | Up 32% | Down 8% |
| Earnings per share | $3.30 | $2.50 |

Miller is a very insistent (some would say pushy) man. When you told him that you would need additional information before making your decision, he acted offended and said, "What more could you possibly want to know?" You responded that, at a minimum, you would need complete, audited financial statements.

*Instructions*
With the class divided into groups, answer the following.
(a) Explain why you would want the financial statements to be audited.
(b) Discuss the implications of the ratios provided for the lending decision you are to make. That is, does the information paint a favorable picture? Are these ratios relevant to the decision?
(c) List three other ratios that you would want to calculate for this company, and explain why you would use each.

## COMMUNICATION ACTIVITY

**BYP13-7** Kevin Halen is the chief executive officer of Brenna Electronics. Halen is an expert engineer but a novice in accounting. Halen asks you, as an accounting student, to explain (a) the bases for comparison in analyzing Brenna's financial statements and (b) the limitations, if any, in financial statement analysis.

*Instructions*

Write a memo to Kevin Halen that explains the basis for comparison and the factors affecting quality of earnings.

## ETHICS CASE

**BYP13-8** Ellen Toth, president of RF Industries, wishes to issue a press release to bolster her company's image and maybe even its stock price, which has been gradually falling. As controller, you have been asked to provide a list of 20 financial ratios and other operating statistics for RF Industries' first-quarter financials and operations.

Two days after you provide the data requested, Marian Lyons, the public relations director of RF, asks you to prove the accuracy of the financial and operating data contained in the press release written by the president and edited by Marian. In the news release, the president highlights the sales increase of 25% over last year's first quarter and the positive change in the current ratio from 1.5:1 last year to 3:1 this year. She also emphasizes that production was up 50% over the prior year's first quarter.

You note that the release contains only positive or improved ratios and none of the negative or deteriorated ratios. For instance, no mention is made that the debt to total assets ratio has increased from 35% to 55%, that inventories are up 89%, and that although the current ratio improved, the current cash debt coverage ratio fell from .15 to .05. Nor is there any mention that the reported profit for the quarter would have been a loss had not the estimated lives of RF plant and machinery been increased by 30%. Marian emphasized, "The Pres wants this release by early this afternoon."

*Instructions*

(a) Who are the stakeholders in this situation?
(b) Is there anything unethical in the president's actions?
(c) Should you as controller remain silent? Does Marian have any responsibility?

## "ALL ABOUT YOU" ACTIVITY

**BYP13-9** In this chapter, you learned how to use many tools for performing a financial analysis of a company. When making personal investments, however, it is most likely that you won't be buying stocks and bonds in individual companies. Instead, when most people want to invest in stock, they buy mutual funds. By investing in a mutual fund, you reduce your risk because the fund diversifies by buying the stock of a variety of different companies, bonds, and other investments, depending on the stated goals of the fund.

Before you invest in a fund, you will need to decide what type of fund you want. For example, do you want a fund that has the potential of high growth (but also high risk), or are you looking for lower risk and a steady steam of income? Do you want a fund that invests only in U.S. companies, or do you want one that invests globally? Many resources are available to help you with these types of decisions.

*Instructions*

Go to **http://web.archive.org/web/20050210200843/http://www.cnb1.com/invallocmdl.htm** and complete the investment allocation questionnaire. Add up your total points to determine the type of investment fund that would be appropriate for you.

## FASB CODIFICATION ACTIVITY

**BYP13-10** If your school has a subscription to the FASB Codification, go to **http://aaahq.org/ascLogin.cfm** to log in and prepare responses to the following. Use the Master Glossary for determining the proper definitions.
(a) Discontinued operations.
(b) Extraordinary items.
(c) Comprehensive income.

### Answers to Insight and Accounting Across the Organization Questions

**p. 689 What Does "Non-Recurring" Really Mean? Q:** If a company takes a large restructuring charge, what is the effect on the company's current income statement versus future ones? **A:** The current period's net income can be greatly diminished by a large restructuring charge. The net incomes in future periods can be enhanced because they are relieved of costs (i.e., depreciation and labor expenses) that would have been charged to them.

**p. 700 How to Manage the Current Ratio**  Q: How might management influence a company's current ratio?  A: Management can affect the current ratio by speeding up or withholding payments on accounts payable just before the balance sheet date. Management can alter the cash balance by increasing or decreasing long-term assets or long-term debt, or by issuing or purchasing common stock.

**p. 701 High Ratings Can Bring Low Returns**  Q: Why are credit rating agencies important to the financial markets?  A: Credit rating agencies perform financial analysis on publicly traded companies and then publish research reports and credit ratings. Investors and creditors rely on the information provided by credit rating agencies in making investment and lending decisions.

**p. 704 Are Annual Reports Worth Their Weight?**  Q: Why might adding extra pages to the annual report not be beneficial to investors and analysts? What should be management's overriding objective in financial reporting?  A: When given too much information, investors may suffer from "information overload"—they may have a hard time sorting out what is important from what is not. Management's overriding financial reporting objective should be to provide an accurate depiction of the company's financial position and operating results in a clear and concise fashion. It should provide as much detail as is necessary to accomplish that.

**Answers to Self-Test Questions**

**1.** d    **2.** d ($400,000 × .75); ($100,000 × .75)    **3.** b    **4.** d    **5.** c ($360,000 ÷ $300,000)    **6.** c    **7.** a
**8.** c    **9.** c    **10.** b    **11.** a ($24,000 ÷ $400,000)    **12.** b ($306,000 ÷ (($54,000 + $48,000)/2)) = 6;
365 ÷ 6    **13.** b ($81,000 ÷ $27,000)    **14.** a ($134,000 ÷ $784,000)    **15.** d ($134,000 − $4,000) ÷
(($240,000 + $198,000)/2))    **16.** c ($134,000 + $22,000 + $12,000) ÷ $12,000    **17.** c

## IFRS | A Look at IFRS

The first sections of this chapter, dealing with the tools of financial analysis, are the same throughout the world. Techniques such as vertical and horizontal analysis, for example, are tools used by analysts regardless of whether GAAP- or IFRS-related financial statements are being evaluated. In addition, the ratios provided in the textbook are the same ones that are used internationally.

The latter part of this chapter relates to the income statement and irregular items. As in GAAP, the income statement is a required statement under IFRS. In addition, the content and presentation of an IFRS income statement is similar to the one used for GAAP. *IAS 1* (revised), "Presentation of Financial Statements," provides general guidelines for the reporting of income statement information. In general, the differences in the presentation of financial statement information are relatively minor.

## IFRS ADDITIONS TO THE TEXTBOOK

- The tools of financial statement analysis covered in this chapter are universal and therefore no significant differences exist in the analysis methods used.
- The basic objectives of the income statement are the same under both GAAP and IFRS. As indicated in the textbook, a very important objective is to ensure that users of the income statement can evaluate the earning power of the company. Earning power is the normal level of income to be obtained in the future. Thus, both the IASB and the FASB are interested in distinguishing normal levels of income from irregular items in order to better predict a company's future profitability.
- The basic accounting for discontinued operations is the same under IFRS and GAAP.
- Under IFRS, there is no classification for extraordinary items. In other words, extraordinary item treatment is prohibited under IFRS. All revenue and expense items are considered ordinary in nature. Disclosure, however, is extensive for items that are considered material to the financial results. Examples are write-downs of inventory or plant assets, or gains and losses on the sale of plant assets.
- The accounting for changes in accounting principles and changes in accounting estimates are the same for both GAAP and IFRS.
- The income statement under IFRS is referred to as a *statement of comprehensive income*. The statement of comprehensive income can be prepared under the one-statement approach or the two-statement approach.

Under the one-statement approach, all components of revenue and expense are reported in the income statement. This combined statement of comprehensive income first computes net income or loss, which is then followed by components of other comprehensive income or loss items to arrive at comprehensive income. An example appears below.

### WALTER COMPANY
### Statement of Comprehensive Income
### For the Year Ended December 31, 2012

| | |
|---|---:|
| Sales revenue | $5,100,000 |
| Cost of goods sold | 3,800,000 |
| Gross profit | 1,300,000 |
| Operating expenses | 700,000 |
| Net income | 600,000 |
| Other comprehensive income | |
|     Unrealized gain on available-for-sale securities | 75,000 |
| Comprehensive income | $ 675,000 |

Under the two-statement approach, all the components of revenues and expenses are reported in a traditional income statement *except* for other comprehensive income or loss. In addition, a second statement (the statement of comprehensive income) is then prepared, starting with net income and followed by other comprehensive income or loss items to arrive at comprehensive income. An example of the two-statement approach, using the same data as that used above for Walter Company, appears below.

### WALTER COMPANY
### Income Statement
### For the Year Ended December 31, 2012

| | |
|---|---:|
| Sales revenue | $5,100,000 |
| Cost of goods sold | 3,800,000 |
| Gross profit | 1,300,000 |
| Operating expenses | 700,000 |
| Net income | $ 600,000 |

### WALTER COMPANY
### Statement of Comprehensive Income
### For the Year Ended December 31, 2012

| | |
|---|---:|
| Net income | $600,000 |
| Other comprehensive income | |
|     Unrealized gain on available-for-sale securities | 75,000 |
| Comprehensive income | $675,000 |

- GAAP also permits the one-statement or two-statement approach. In addition, GAAP permits a third alternative, which is to show the computation of comprehensive income in the statement of stockholders' equity.

- The issues related to quality of earnings are the same under both GAAP and IFRS. It is hoped that by adopting a more principles-based approach, as found in IFRS, many of the earnings' quality issues will disappear.

## LOOKING TO THE FUTURE

The FASB and the IASB are working on a project that would rework the structure of financial statements. Recently, the IASB decided to require a statement of comprehensive income, similar to what was required under GAAP. In addition, another part of this project addresses the issue of how to classify various items in the income statement. A main goal of this new approach is to provide information that better represents how businesses are run. In addition, the approach draws attention away from one number—net income.

## IFRS Self-Test Questions

1. The basic tools of financial analysis are the same under both GAAP and IFRS *except* that:
   (a) horizontal analysis cannot be done because the format of the statements is sometimes different.
   (b) analysis is different because vertical analysis cannot be done under IFRS.
   (c) the current ratio cannot be computed because current liabilities are often reported before current assets in IFRS statements of position.
   (d) None of the above.

2. Under IFRS:
   (a) the reporting of discontinued items is different than GAAP.
   (b) the reporting of extraordinary items is prohibited.
   (c) the reporting of changes in accounting principles is different than under GAAP.
   (d) None of the above.

3. Presentation of comprehensive income must be reported under IFRS in:
   (a) the statement of stockholders' equity.
   (b) the income statement ending with net income.
   (c) the notes to the financial statements.
   (d) a statement of comprehensive income.

4. Parmalane reports the following information:

   | | |
   |---|---|
   | Sales | $500,000 |
   | Cost of goods sold | 200,000 |
   | Operating expense | 40,000 |
   | Unrealized loss on available-for-sale securities | 10,000 |

   Parmalane should report the following under the two-statement approach using IFRS:
   (a) net income of $260,000 and comprehensive income of $270,000.
   (b) net income of $270,000 and comprehensive income of $260,000.
   (c) other comprehensive income of $10,000 and comprehensive income of $270,000.
   (d) other comprehensive loss of $10,000 and comprehensive income of 250,000.

5. Assuming the same information as in question 4, Parmalane should report the following using a one-statement approach under IFRS:
   (a) net income of $260,000 and comprehensive income of $270,000.
   (b) net income of $270,000 and comprehensive income of $260,000.
   (c) other comprehensive income of $10,000 and comprehensive income of $270,000.
   (d) other comprehensive loss of $10,000 and comprehensive income of $250,000.

## IFRS Concepts and Application

**IFRS13–1**   Chen Company reports the following information for the year ended December 31, 2012: sales revenue $1,000,000, cost of goods sold $700,000, operating expenses $200,000, and an unrealized gain on available-for-sale securities of $75,000. Prepare a statement of comprehensive income using the one-statement approach.

**IFRS13–2**   Assume the same information for Chen Company as in IFRS13-1. Prepare the income statement using the two-statement approach.

## INTERNATIONAL FINANCIAL REPORTING PROBLEM: *Zetar plc*

**IFRS13–3**   The financial statements of Zetar plc are presented in Appendix C. The company's complete annual report, including the notes to its financial statements, is available at **www.zetarplc.com**.

### Instructions
Use the company's annual report to answer the following questions.
   (a) The company's income statement reports a loss on discontinued operations. What business did the company discontinue, and why did it choose to discontinue the business?
   (b) For the year ended April 30, 2009, what amount did the company lose on the operation of the discontinued business, and what amount did it lose on disposal?
   (c) What was the total recorded value of the net assets at the date of disposal, and what was the amount of costs incurred to dispose of the business?

## Answers to Self-Test Questions
1. d   2. b   3. d   4. d   5. d

✔ **Remember to go back to the navigator box on the chapter opening page and check off your completed work.**

# SPECIMEN FINANCIAL STATEMENTS: TOOTSIE ROLL INDUSTRIES, INC.

## The Annual Report

Once each year, a corporation communicates to its stockholders and other interested parties by issuing a complete set of audited financial statements. The **annual report**, as this communication is called, summarizes the financial results of the company's operations for the year and its plans for the future. Many annual reports are attractive, multicolored, glossy public relations pieces, containing pictures of corporate officers and directors as well as photos and descriptions of new products and new buildings. Yet the basic function of every annual report is to report financial information, almost all of which is produced by the corporation's accounting system.

Tootsie Roll Annual Report Walkthrough

The content and organization of corporate annual reports have become fairly standardized. Excluding the public relations part of the report (pictures, products, and propaganda), the following items are the traditional financial portions of the annual report:

Financial Highlights
Letter to the Stockholders
Management's Discussion and Analysis
Financial Statements
Notes to the Financial Statements
Management's Report on Internal Control
Management Certification of Financial Statements
Auditor's Report
Supplementary Financial Information

In this appendix, we illustrate current financial reporting with a comprehensive set of corporate financial statements that are prepared in accordance with generally accepted accounting principles and audited by an international independent certified public accounting firm. We are grateful for permission to use the actual financial statements and other accompanying financial information from the annual report of a large, publicly held company, Tootsie Roll Industries, Inc.

## Financial Highlights

Companies usually present the financial highlights section inside the front cover of the annual report or on its first two pages. This section generally reports the total or per share amounts for five to ten financial items for the current year and one or more previous years.

---

The financial information herein is reprinted with permission from the Tootsie Roll Industries, Inc. 2009 Annual Report. The complete financial statements for Tootsie Roll Industries are also available on the book's companion website.

# Corporate Profile

Tootsie Roll Industries, Inc. has been engaged in the manufacture and sale of confectionery products for 113 years. Our products are primarily sold under the familiar brand names: Tootsie Roll, Tootsie Roll Pops, Caramel Apple Pops, Child's Play, Charms, Blow Pop, Blue Razz, Cella's chocolate covered cherries, Tootsie Dots, Tootsie Crows, Junior Mints, Junior Caramels, Charleston Chew, Sugar Daddy, Sugar Babies, Andes, Fluffy Stuff cotton candy, Dubble Bubble, Razzles, Cry Baby, Nik-L-Nip and El Bubble.

*Ellen R.Gordon, President and Chief Operating Officer and Melvin J.Gordon, Chairman and Chief Executive Officer.*

# Corporate Principles

We believe that the differences among companies are attributable to the caliber of their people, and therefore we strive to attract and retain superior people for each job.

We believe that an open family atmosphere at work combined with professional management fosters cooperation and enables each individual to maximize his or her contribution to the Company and realize the corresponding rewards.

We do not jeopardize long-term growth for immediate, short-term results.

We maintain a conservative financial posture in the deployment and management of our assets.

We run a trim operation and continually strive to eliminate waste, minimize cost and implement performance improvements.

We invest in the latest and most productive equipment to deliver the best quality product to our customers at the lowest cost.

We seek to outsource functions where appropriate and to vertically integrate operations where it is financially advantageous to do so.

We view our well known brands as prized assets to be aggressively advertised and promoted to each new generation of consumers.

We conduct business with the highest ethical standards and integrity which are codified in the Company's "Code of Business Conduct and Ethics."

Financial items from the income statement and the balance sheet that typically are presented are sales, income from continuing operations, net income, earnings per share, dividends per common share, and the amount of capital expenditures. The financial highlights section from **Tootsie Roll Industries' Annual Report** is shown on page A-3. Above, we have also included Tootsie Roll's discussion of its corporate principles and corporate profile.

## Letter to the Stockholders

Nearly every annual report contains a letter to the stockholders from the chairman of the board or the president, or both. This letter typically discusses the company's accomplishments during the past year and highlights significant events such as mergers and acquisitions, new products, operating achievements, business philosophy, changes in officers or directors, financing commitments, expansion plans, and future prospects. The letter to the stockholders signed by Melvin J. Gordon, Chairman of the Board and Chief Executive Officer, and Ellen R. Gordon, President and Chief Operating Officer, of Tootsie Roll Industries is shown on the next pages.

# *To Our Shareholders*

Net product sales in 2009 were $496 million as compared with 2008 net product sales of $492 million. Most of our core brands posted solid results and Halloween was once again our largest selling season of the year.

Net earnings grew to $53 million from $39 million in 2008. The increase in earnings was attributable to margin improvements stemming from selected price increases and product weight adjustments as well as from lower energy and fuel costs and from foreign income tax benefits.

Commodity and packaging costs have risen significantly in recent years. While some of these costs abated during 2009, as a whole they remain at historically high levels. We are challenged to look for every feasible way to keep our operations lean and costs in check so that we can continue to deliver maximum value to our consumers.

We take a long-term view of our business and strive to implement measures that improve our operating results without jeopardizing the long-term strength of the Company and its

well known brands. As a value oriented confectioner, we deem it essential to be a low cost producer and actively pursue investments in the latest technology to keep us so.

To that end, capital expenditures in 2009 were $21 million. In addition to new state of the art equipment installations at a number of our plants, a portion of this figure was directed toward the latest phase of implementing our enterprise resource planning system, a comprehensive system of leading edge business software.

During 2009 we paid cash dividends of 32 cents per share and again distributed a 3% stock dividend. This was the sixty-seventh consecutive year the Company has paid cash dividends and the forty-fifth consecutive year that a stock dividend was distributed. We also repurchased 937,956 shares of common stock on the open market for an aggregate cost of $21 million.

We ended 2009 with $158 million in cash and investments and we remain poised to continue investing in our business, improving manufacturing

productivity and quality, supporting our brands, paying dividends and repurchasing common stock. We also continue to seek appropriate complementary business acquisitions.

## Sales and Marketing

During 2009 we again used carefully executed promotions to drive sales. Targeted initiatives, directed to the trade and to consumers, help to move our products into distribution and subsequently to move them off the retail shelf.

Retailers are highly selective as to the products they carry and consumers have many choices in the candy isle. We find that emphasizing high sell-through and attractive profit margins to the trade and high quality at an attractive value to the consumer is a winning strategy.

Our diverse and highly recognizable brand portfolio remains popular across all trade channels. We have a range of offerings suitable for virtually every major consumer group. Our product line undergoes continual refinement in order to retain its appeal to ever-evolving preferences and life styles. The candy marketplace is highly competitive and we are vigilant in keeping our products contemporary even as they remain iconic.

Halloween has long been our largest selling period with third quarter sales nearly double those of any other quarter in the year. We posted strong results in all major trade classes including grocery, mass merchandisers, warehouse clubs, dollar stores and drug chains. Especially popular at Halloween are our large bags of Child's Play and other mixed candy assortments,

## *Financial Highlights*

| | December 31, | |
| --- | --- | --- |
| | 2009 | 2008 |
| | (in thousands except per share data) | |
| Net Product Sales | $495,592 | $492,051 |
| Net Earnings | 53,475 | 38,777 |
| Working Capital | 155,812 | 129,967 |
| Net Property, Plant and Equipment | 220,721 | 217,628 |
| Shareholders' Equity | 652,485 | 634,770 |
| Average Shares Outstanding* | 56,072 | 56,799 |
| Per Share Items* | | |
|    Net Earnings | $0.95 | $0.68 |
|    Cash Dividends Paid | .32 | .32 |

*Adjusted for stock dividends.

which are offered in a variety of merchandising presentations.

Our bagged goods have traditionally been limited to "lay down" format that is commonly found on retailer's shelves. In addition to "lay down" bags, in 2009 we introduced a number of packs in a "vertical" format. These gusseted bags really do "stand up" on the shelf and offer a more visible, billboard-like front panel with room for expanded graphic content while creating an enhanced consumer value perception.

Other traditional merchandising presentations such as pallet packs, off shelf displays and display ready cases also continue to generate high sales volume in our Halloween packaged goods line. We continue to have some of the top selling theater box and home video items. This line was expanded in 2009 with two new Dots items that made trick-or-treating tastier. Candy Corn Dots are the classic Halloween flavor in a new gumdrop format and Bat Dots are black gumdrops with a new, mouth-watering "blood orange" flavor.

*Candy Corn and Bat Dots*

In addition to full size theater boxes, these two new frightfully good confections were packed in

mini-boxes and, together with Ghost Dots, formed the new Dots Halloween Mix. Each bag of this mix features "spook-tacular" Halloween designs, and is metallized to ensure fresh gumdrops for every trick-or-treater.

*Halloween Dots Mini Mix*

Other additions to our Halloween offerings promoted the apple theme which is so readily associated with the fall season. Apple Orchard is a mix of three mouth watering caramel apple pop flavor profiles: sour green apple, tart red Macintosh and sweet Golden Delicious. All three apple flavored hard candies are blended with luscious caramel.

Another Halloween item, Caramel Apple Sugar Babies in snack size pouches, have a caramel center encased in a tart green apple shell. The caramel apple combination is a delicious hit.

*Apple Orchard Pops*

Our unique line of wax candy products was expanded with the addition of Nik-L-Nip fruit flavored mini drinks individually wrapped and packed in a 60 count bag for sharing. For fun, we introduced Mr. Stache, a chewable wax candy moustache. These items designed for sharing are perfect

for kids parties, trick or treating or anytime.

*Mr. Stache Wax Candy*

Blow Pop sales were boosted by the introduction of an innovative new Super Blow Pop counter display. This gravity fed dispenser has a small foot print so it can be used as a counter display or it can be attached to a power wing if counter space is not available. Vivid graphics on the prominent display panel increase exposure and promote trial of this classic confection.

*Blow Pop Counter Display*

Our Andes Crème de Menthe thins have a strong selling history during the Thanksgiving and Christmas holiday seasons. Andes has also had great success selling outside the candy aisle with Andes Crème de

Menthe Baking Chips, which have grown every year since their introduction.

Building on this success, in 2009 we introduced Andes Crème de Menthe Cookies. Rich chocolate mint Andes cookies feature a crunchy cocoa cookie center, covered in a melt-in-your-mouth minty green layer, and enveloped in a rich layer of delicious chocolate. This decadent chocolate mint cookie parallels the iconic Andes Crème de Menthe thins candy, with its rectangular shape, three layers and a green center, for instant consumer recognition. Andes cookies were a sensational seasonal success for Halloween and Christmas.

*Andes Crème de Menthe Cookies*

### Advertising and Public Relations

We again promoted our long-standing "How Many Licks" Tootsie Pop message through campaigns on several children's channels on cable television in 2009. This renowned theme was further reinforced by a How Many Licks Sweepstakes that encouraged entrants to guess the correct number of licks it would take to get to the chewy Tootsie Roll center. Having evaluated thousands of estimates, we can only conclude that the answer to this riddle remains "the world may never know!"

On a whimsical note, in 2009 Tootsie Roll was featured as its own category on the long running game show *Jeopardy*. Also, Tootsie Pops were profiled on the Travel Channel's special interest

program *Extreme Mega Factories*. Repeated showing of segments such as these generate extensive exposure and awareness among viewing consumers.

Tootsie Rolls became kosher certified during 2009, making our flagship product available to a whole new group of consumers. This announcement received wide press coverage and we heard positive feedback from many enthusiastic consumers. Also, our Chairman Melvin Gordon was honored with the Kettle Award, the candy industry's highest tribute, in recognition of his lifetime achievements and dedication to the industry.

### Purchasing

Although energy costs decreased during 2009 from the record levels of 2008, other commodity prices generally remained at historically high levels. Cost decreases in edible oils, dairy products and corn based sweeteners were largely offset by surging sugar prices. In packaging, decreases in the cost of films and folding cartons were more than offset by increases in corrugated and specialty papers.

Competitive bidding, selective hedging and leveraging our high volume of purchases are some of the means we use to mitigate rising costs to the greatest extent feasible. We also embarked on an extensive internal review of cost drivers during 2009 which is a key element in our ongoing efforts to eliminate waste. A number of cost-saving ideas were identified during this review and have been implemented across all of our plants.

### Supply Chain

We continue to invest capital and resources in projects that keep our production and distribution facilities as efficient as possible, support evolving distribution patterns, improve quality and

promote growing product lines. Much of this is driven by technology, which offers continuing advancements in automation that we can incorporate on the shop floor.

2009 was also the third year of a multi-year, company-wide enterprise resource planning system upgrade. The scope of this project is comprehensive, affecting nearly every facet of the Company. We are carefully phasing in this implementation to achieve maximum results.

### International

Sales and profits in Mexico were lower in 2009 due to the devaluation of the peso. Although we promote our products in many countries throughout the world, our export business continued to be adversely affected by the relative strength of the U.S. dollar, which increases the relative cost of our products in foreign markets. Canadian sales were ahead of 2009 but profits declined due to product mix, higher commodity costs and foreign exchange rates.

### In Appreciation

We wish to express our appreciation to our many loyal employees, customers, suppliers, sales brokers and distributors throughout the world for their support in 2009. We also thank our fellow shareholders as we remain committed to the pursuit of excellence in every aspect of our operations and face the increasing challenges of today's business environment.

*Melvin J. Gordon*

Melvin J. Gordon
Chairman of the Board and
Chief Executive Officer

*Ellen R. Gordon*

Ellen R. Gordon
President and
Chief Operating Officer

# Management Discussion and Analysis

The management discussion and analysis (MD&A) section covers three financial aspects of a company: its results of operations, its ability to pay near-term obligations, and its ability to fund operations and expansion. Management must highlight favorable or unfavorable trends and identify significant events and uncertainties that affect these three factors. This discussion obviously involves a number of subjective estimates and opinions. The MD&A section of Tootsie Roll's annual report is presented below.

# Management's Discussion and Analysis of Financial Condition and Results of Operations

(in thousands except per share, percentage and ratio figures)

## FINANCIAL REVIEW

This financial review discusses the Company's financial condition, results of operations, liquidity and capital resources, significant accounting policies and estimates, new accounting pronouncements, market risks and other matters. It should be read in conjunction with the Consolidated Financial Statements and related footnotes that follow this discussion.

## FINANCIAL CONDITION

The Company's overall financial position remains very strong as a result of its 2009 net earnings and related cash flows provided by operating activities.

During 2009, the Company's cash flows from operating activities aggregated $75,281 compared to $57,042 in 2008. The Company used its cash flows to pay cash dividends of $17,825, repurchase and retire $20,723 of its outstanding shares, and make capital expenditures of $20,831. In addition, the Company's net working capital increased from $129,967 at December 31, 2008 to $155,812 at December 31, 2009.

As of December 31, 2009, the Company's aggregate cash, cash equivalents and investments, including all long-term investments in marketable securities, was $157,789 compared to $136,680 at December 31, 2008, an increase of $21,109. The 2009 amount reflects a $4,524 appreciation in market value of trading securities. The Company invests in trading securities to provide an economic hedge for its deferred compensation liabilities, as further discussed herein and in Note 7 to the Consolidated Financial Statements.

Shareholders' equity increased from $634,770 at December 31, 2008 to $652,485 as of December 31, 2009, principally reflecting 2009 net earnings of $53,475 less cash dividends and share repurchases of $17,825 and $20,723, respectively.

The Company has a relatively straight-forward financial structure and has historically maintained a conservative financial position. Except for an immaterial amount of operating leases, the Company has no special financing arrangements or "off-balance

sheet" special purpose entities. Cash flows from operations plus maturities of short-term investments are expected to be adequate to meet the Company's overall financing needs, including capital expenditures, in 2010. Occasionally, the Company considers possible acquisitions, and if the Company were to pursue and complete such an acquisition, that could result in bank borrowings.

## Results of Operations

2009 vs. 2008

Net product sales were $495,592 in 2009 compared to $492,051 in 2008, an increase of $3,541 or 1%. Although the increase in 2009 consolidated sales benefited from higher U.S. domestic sales, they were adversely affected by declines in export sales and sales of the Company's Mexican subsidiary when translated into U.S. dollar sales from a devalued foreign currency.

Product cost of goods sold were $318,645 in 2009 compared to $333,314 in 2008, a decrease of $14,669 or 4.4%. Product cost of goods sold reflects a $2,876 increase in deferred compensation expense in 2009 compared to 2008. This increase principally results from changes in the market value of investments in trading securities relating to compensation deferred in previous years and is not reflective of current operating results. Adjusting for the aforementioned, product cost of goods sold as a percentage of net product sales favorably decreased from 68.1% in 2008 to 64.1% in 2009, a decrease of 4.0% as a percent of sales. This improvement principally reflects the benefits of selective price increases, product weight declines (indirect price increases) and the favorable effects of foreign currency exchange rates on products manufactured in Canada and principally sold in the United States. Ingredient unit costs favorably decreased by approximately $700 in 2009. However, the Company was adversely affected by approximately $400 of packaging material unit cost increases in 2009 compared to 2008. The Company generally experienced significant cost increases in sugar and cocoa. However, the Company experienced favorable declines in dairy products, corn syrup and edible oils.

Due to the seasonal nature of the Company's business and corresponding variations in product mix, gross margins have historically been lower in the second half of the year, and second half of 2009 and 2008 were consistent with this trend.

Selling, marketing and administrative expenses were $103,755 in 2009 compared to $95,254 in 2008, an increase of $8,501 or 8.9%. Selling, marketing and administrative expenses reflect an $8,982 increase in deferred

compensation expense in 2009 compared to 2008. This increase principally results from changes in the market value of investments in trading securities relating to compensation deferred in previous years and is not reflective of current operating results. Adjusting for the aforementioned, selling, marketing and administrative expenses favorably decreased from $100,711 in 2008 to $100,230 in 2009, a decrease of $481 or 0.5%. As a percent of net product sales, these expenses decreased from 20.5% of net product sales in 2008 to 20.2% of product sales in 2009. The favorable decrease in such expenses principally resulted from lower freight, delivery and warehousing and distribution expenses partially offset by higher incentive compensation awards. Such higher incentive awards are due to the substantial improvement in 2009 results compared to 2008.

Selling, marketing and administrative expenses include $38,628 and $45,570 of freight, delivery and warehousing and distribution expenses in 2009 and 2008, respectively. Freight, delivery and warehousing and distribution expenses decreased from 9.3% of net product sales in 2008 to 7.8% of net product sales in 2009, primarily due to lower energy costs including lower freight fuel surcharges.

The Company believes that the carrying values of its trademarks and goodwill have indefinite lives as they are expected to generate cash flows indefinitely. In accordance with current accounting guidance, goodwill and indefinite-lived intangible assets are assessed at least annually for impairment as of December 31 or whenever events or circumstances indicate that the carrying values may not be recoverable from future cash

flows. As of December 31, 2009, management ascertained that certain trademarks were impaired, and recorded a pre-tax charge of $14,000. This 2009 impairment charge was principally driven by an increase in the discount rate required by market participants. No impairments of intangibles were recorded in 2008.

The fair values of indefinite lived intangible assets are primarily assessed using the present value of estimated future cash flows. Management believes that all assumptions used for the impairment tests are consistent with those utilized by market participants performing similar valuations. The Company's fair value estimates based on these assumptions were used to prepare projected financial information which it believes to be reasonable. Actual future results may differ from those projections and the differences may be material. Holding all other assumptions constant at the test date, a 100 basis point increase in the discount rate or a 100 basis point decrease in the royalty rate would reduce the fair value of certain trademarks by approximately 14% and 10%, respectively, indicating potential additional impairment of approximately $14,000 and $10,000, respectively, as of December 31, 2009.

Earnings from operations were $62,079 in 2009 compared to $66,527 in 2008, a decrease of $4,448. Earnings from operations includes changes in deferred compensation liabilities relating to corresponding changes in the market value of trading securities that hedge these liabilities as discussed above. Adjusting for the aforementioned deferred compensation charges of $11,858 and excluding the nonrecurring $14,000 non-cash impairment charge in 2009 relating to trademarks as discussed above, operating earnings were $80,603 and $59,193 in 2009 and 2008, respectively, an increase of $21,410 or 36.2%. Management believes this comparison is more reflective of the underlying operations of the Company. This increase principally reflects the favorable improvement in product cost of goods sold and gross profit margins, and more favorable freight, distribution and warehousing expenses as discussed above.

Other income (expense), net, was $2,100 in 2009 compared to $(10,618) in 2008, an increase of $12,718. This increase principally reflects the $11,858 favorable net change in the fair value of trading securities investments used to hedge deferred compensation liabilities, offset by a pre-tax impairment charge of $4,400 in 2009 to write down to market value the Company's 50% investment in a Spanish joint venture, and a pre-tax charge of $5,140 in prior year 2008 to write down to market value an auction rate security as discussed below.

The Company has a 50% interest in a Spanish joint venture which is accounted for under the equity method. As of December 31, 2009, management determined, based on operating losses and expectations of future results, that the carrying value of this asset was impaired. As a result, the Company recorded a pre-tax impairment charge of $4,400 in the fourth quarter 2009, resulting in an adjusted carrying value of $4,961 as of December 31, 2009. The fair value was primarily assessed using the present value of estimated future cash flows. Other income (expense), net also includes the operating results of the Company's joint venture which was a loss of $233 and $477 in 2009 and 2008, respectively.

As of December 31, 2009 and 2008, the Company's long-term investments include $7,710 and $8,410 ($13,550 original cost), respectively, of Jefferson County Alabama Sewer Revenue Refunding Warrants, originally purchased with an insurance-backed AAA rating. This is an auction rate security (ARS) that is classified as an available for sale security. Due to adverse events related to Jefferson County and its bond insurance carrier, Financial Guaranty Insurance Company (FGIC), as well as events in the credit markets, the auctions for this ARS failed throughout 2008 and 2009 (and subsequent to December 31, 2009). As such, the Company estimated the fair value of this ARS as of December 31, 2009 and 2008 utilizing a valuation model with Level 3 inputs. This valuation model considered, among others items, the credit risk of the collateral underlying the ARS, the credit risk of the bond insurer, interest rates, and the amount and timing of expected future cash flows including assumptions about the market expectation of the next successful auction.

During the prior year fourth quarter of 2008, the Company determined that the market decline in fair value of its Jefferson County ARS became other-than-temporarily impaired, as defined, and recorded a pre-tax impairment of $5,140. During the fourth quarter of 2009, the Company further evaluated this investment and concluded that an additional decline in the market value was temporary because it was not related to further credit impairment and recorded this $700 of additional decline in the market value as a charge to accumulated other comprehensive loss. Notwithstanding, the Company continues to receive all

contractual interest payments on its ARS on a timely basis, there has been no default, it is insured by FGIC and the Company has the intent and ability to hold this ARS until recovery of its amortized cost basis.

The Company has classified this ARS as non-current and has included it in long-term investments at December 31, 2009 and 2008 because the Company believes that the current financial conditions of Jefferson County and FGIC, as well as the conditions in the auction rate securities market, may take more than twelve months to resolve. Future evaluations of the fair value of this ARS could also result in additional other-than-temporary classification of declines in market value, and therefore result in additional charges to earnings.

Other income (expenses), net also includes the results of the Company's trading securities which provide an economic hedge to the Company's deferred compensation liabilities. The income (expense), on such trading securities was $4,524 and $(7,334) in 2009 and 2008, respectively. Such income or (expense) was substantially offset by a like amount of (expense) or income in aggregate product cost of goods sold and selling, marketing, and administrative expenses in the respective years as discussed above. The 2009 income principally reflects market appreciation in the equity markets in 2009, and the 2008 (expense) principally reflects the market decline in the equity markets in 2008.

The consolidated effective tax rate was 16.7% and 30.6% in 2009 and 2008, respectively. This favorable decrease in the effective tax rate principally reflects the release of Canadian income tax valuation allowances in 2009. Prior to fourth quarter 2009, Canadian income tax valuation allowances were recorded against Canadian deferred tax assets as a result of losses generated in 2009 and prior years. These Canadian income tax losses were principally the result of interest expense deductions for income tax purposes relating to an intercompany financing transaction which was eliminated in the Company's consolidated financial statements. Because the realization of such prior net operating loss (NOL) carry-forward benefits were not more-likely-than-not, a full valuation allowance was recorded as of December 31, 2008, and through third quarter 2009. In response to the Fifth Protocol to the Canada-U.S. Income Tax Convention (Treaty), during fourth quarter 2009 the Company decided to restructure its Canadian operations effective January 1, 2010. This restructuring eliminated the inter-company financing structure and related interest deduction for Canadian income taxes effective January 1, 2010. Going forward, management now expects its Canadian operation to report taxable income rather than losses for the foreseeable future. Accordingly, management determined that the Canadian NOL carry-forward benefits were more-likely-than-not realizable as of December 31, 2009. As such, the Company reversed approximately $10,700 of valuation allowances as a credit to income tax expense as of December 31, 2009. Management believes that its assessment is based on reasonable assumptions and is in accordance with accounting guidance regarding the release of valuation allowances on deferred tax assets. See also Note 4 to the Consolidated Financial Statements for further discussion.

The Treaty also provided for the phase-out of Canadian withholding tax rates for interest and allowed the Company to qualify for the 0% withholding rate effective January 1, 2010, resulting in a current tax benefit of $1,500 in 2009.

Net earnings were $53,475 in 2009 compared to $38,777 in 2008, and earnings per share were $.95 and $.68 in 2009 and 2008, respectively, an increase of $.27 or 40%. Earnings per share did benefit from the reduction in average shares outstanding resulting from common stock purchases in the open market by the Company. Average shares outstanding decreased from 56,799 in 2008 to 56,072 in 2009.

## 2008 vs. 2007

Net product sales were $492,051 in 2008 compared to $492,742 in 2007, a decrease of $691 or 0.1%. Although 2008 domestic sales increased by 0.5%, the reported consolidated net sales reflect declines in sales outside of the U.S., including the effects of a stronger dollar, which offset these domestic sales increases.

Product cost of goods sold were $333,314 in 2008 compared to $327,695 in 2007, an increase of $5,619 or 1.7%. This increase reflects a $1,877 decrease in deferred compensation expense principally resulting from the decline in the market value of investments in trading securities relating to compensation deferred in previous years. Adjusting for the aforementioned, product cost of goods sold as a percentage of net sales increased from 64.5% in 2007 to 68.1% in 2008, an increase of 3.6% as a percent of sales. This increase principally reflects significant cost increases in major ingredients, as well as higher labor and fringe benefits, including health insurance benefits, the adverse effects of

foreign currency exchange rates on products manufactured in Canada and principally sold in the United States, and generally higher plant energy costs. In 2008, increases in ingredient costs approximated $9,300, however, the Company benefited from an approximate $1,200 decrease in overall packaging material costs. The Company generally experienced significant cost increases in substantially all of its major ingredients, including sugar, corn syrup, vegetable oils, dextrose, cocoa, chocolate and gum base inputs. The adverse impact of changes in Canadian exchange rates as discussed above approximated $900 in 2008.

Due to the seasonal nature of the Company's business and corresponding variations in product mix, gross margins have historically been lower in the second half of the year, and second half of 2008 and 2007 were consistent with this trend.

Selling, marketing and administrative expenses were $95,254 in 2008 compared to $97,821 in 2007, a decrease of $2,567 or 2.6%. This decrease reflects a $5,457 decrease in deferred compensation expense principally resulting from the decline in the market value of investments in trading securities relating to compensation deferred in previous years. Adjusting for the aforementioned, selling, marketing and administrative expenses increased by $2,890 or 3.0%, and as a percent of net product sales increased from 19.9% of net product sales in 2007 to 20.5% of net product sales in 2008. These expenses include $45,570 and $41,775 of freight, delivery and warehousing and distribution expenses in 2008 and 2007 respectively. Freight, delivery and warehousing and distribution expenses increased from 8.5% of net product sales in 2007 to 9.3% of net product sales in 2008, primarily due to higher energy costs including higher freight fuel surcharges.

Earnings from operations were $66,527 in 2008 compared to $70,852 in 2007, a decrease of $4,325 or 6.1%. Earnings from operations includes changes in deferred compensation liabilities relating to corresponding changes in the market value of trading securities that hedge these liabilities as discussed above. Adjusting for the aforementioned, operating earnings were $59,193 and $72,850 in 2008 and 2007, respectively, a decrease of $13,657 or 18.7%. This decrease principally reflects the decrease in gross profit resulting from higher input costs, principally ingredients and freight and delivery, as discussed above.

Goodwill and indefinite-lived intangible assets are assessed at least annually for impairment as of December 31 or whenever events or circumstances indicate that the carrying values may not be recoverable from future cash flows. No impairments were recorded in either 2008 or 2007

Other income (expense), net, was $(10,618) in 2008 compared to $6,315 in 2007, a decrease of $16,933. This decrease principally reflects a $5,140 write-down to market value of an investment security and $9,332 relating to changes in the fair value of trading securities investments during 2008 used to hedge deferred compensation liabilities, both of which are discussed below.

As of December 31, 2008, the Company's long-term investments include $8,410 ($13,550 original cost) of Jefferson County Alabama Sewer Revenue Refunding Warrants originally purchased with an AAA rating. As discussed above, the Company estimated the fair value of this

ARS utilizing a valuation model with Level 3 inputs. During the fourth quarter 2008, the Company determined that the market decline in fair value of its Jefferson County ARS became other than temporary, as defined, and recorded an after-tax impairment of $3,328 ($5,140 pre-tax charge). Previous to fourth quarter 2008, the Company concluded that the decline in market value was temporary, as defined, and recorded declines in the market value to accumulated other comprehensive income.

Other income (expenses), net includes the results of the Company's trading securities which hedge the Company's deferred compensation liabilities. The income (expense) on such trading securities was $(7,334) and $1,998 in 2008 and 2007, respectively; such income or (expense) was substantially offset by a like amount of (expense) or income in aggregate product cost of goods sold and selling, marketing, and administrative expenses in the respective years. The 2008 (expense) of $(7,334) principally reflects the market declines in the equity markets in 2008.

Other income (expense), net also includes the results of the Company's 50% interest in a Spanish joint venture, accounted for under the equity method, which was a loss of $(477) in 2008 compared to income of $182 in 2007.

The consolidated effective tax rate was 30.6% and 33.1% in 2008 and 2007, respectively. The decrease in the effective tax rate principally reflects approximately $1,400 of reduction in tax positions resulting from the effective settlement of a state income tax audit, and approximately $700 relating to changes in foreign income tax expense due to the favorable effects of certain tax treaty

provisions between the U.S. and Canada. In addition, the 2007 effective tax rate was adversely impacted by $1,040 relating to the adoption of an interpretation of accounting guidance relating to uncertain income tax positions. During 2008 and 2007, the Company recorded $3,218 and $3,145 of valuation allowances, respectively, relating to its Canadian subsidiary tax loss carry-forwards to reduce the future income tax benefits to amounts expected to be realized.

Net earnings were $38,777 in 2008 compared to $51,625 in 2007, and earnings per share were $.68 and $.89 in 2008 and 2007, respectively, a decrease of $.21 or 24%. 2008 results were adversely affected by higher input costs, primarily relating to ingredients and freight and delivery, as well as the items discussed above in other income (expense), net. Earnings per share did benefit from the reduction in average shares outstanding resulting from common stock purchases in the open market by the Company. Average shares outstanding decreased from 58,227 in 2007 to 56,799 in 2008.

The Company has taken actions and implemented programs, including selected price increases as well as cost reduction programs, with the objective of recovering some of these higher input costs. However, these actions have not allowed the Company to recover all of these increases in ingredient and other input costs in 2008.

## LIQUIDITY AND CAPITAL RESOURCES

Cash flows from operating activities were $75,281, $57,042 and $90,064 in 2009, 2008 and 2007, respectively. The $18,239 increase in cash flows from operating activities from 2008 to 2009 principally reflects an increase of $14,698 in net income in 2009 compared to 2008, an increase of $13,260 of non-cash pre-tax impairment charges in 2009, changes in deferred income taxes, including the release of $10,700 of Canadian deferred income tax asset valuation allowances, the Company's 2008 investment in a voluntary employee association trust (VEBA) of $16,050 which is controlled solely by the Company as discussed herein, and changes in other current assets and liabilities, principally inventories and accounts receivable.

As discussed above, during 2009 the Company recorded pre-tax non-cash impairment charges of $14,000 and $4,400 relating to certain trademarks and its 50% owned Spanish joint venture, respectively; and during prior year 2008, the Company recorded a pre-tax non-cash impairment charge of $5,140 relating to its Jefferson County ARS investment.

During 2008, the Company contributed $16,050 to a VEBA trust to fund the estimated future costs of certain employee health, welfare and other benefits. The Company used the funds, as well as investment income in this VEBA trust, to pay the actual cost of such benefits during 2009 and will continue to do so through 2011. At December 31, 2009, the VEBA trust holds $12,678 of aggregate cash, cash equivalents and investments; this asset value is included in prepaid expenses in the Company's current and other assets.

Cash flows from investing activities reflect capital expenditures of $20,831, $34,355, and $14,767 in 2009, 2008 and 2007, respectively. Capital expenditures in prior year 2008

reflect $12,400 relating to the purchase of real estate that the Company placed into service as a distribution center in 2009. The 2009 and 2008 capital additions include $2,326 and $4,755, respectively, relating to computer systems and related implementation.

The Company had no bank borrowing or repayments in 2007, 2008, or 2009, and had no outstanding bank borrowings as of December 31, 2008 or 2009.

Financing activities include common stock purchases and retirements of $20,723, $21,109, and $27,300 in 2009, 2008 and 2007, respectively. Cash dividends of $17,825, $17,557, and $17,542 were paid in 2009, 2008 and 2007, respectively. The increase in cash dividends each year reflects the annual 3% stock dividend issued in each of these years less the effects of Company Common Stock purchases and retirements.

## SIGNIFICANT ACCOUNTING POLICIES AND ESTIMATES

Preparation of the Company's financial statements involves judgments and estimates due to uncertainties affecting the application of accounting policies, and the likelihood that different amounts would be reported under different conditions or using different assumptions. The Company bases its estimates on historical experience and other assumptions, as discussed herein, that it believes are reasonable. If actual amounts are ultimately different from previous estimates, the revisions are included in the Company's results of operations for the period in which the actual amounts become known. The Company's significant accounting policies are discussed in Note 1 to the Consolidated Financial Statements.

Following is a summary and discussion of the more significant accounting policies which management believes to have a significant impact on the Company's operating results, financial position, cash flows and footnote disclosure.

### Revenue recognition

Revenue, net of applicable provisions for discounts, returns, allowances and certain advertising and promotional costs, is recognized when products are delivered to customers based on a customer purchase order, and collectability is reasonably assured. The accounting for promotional costs is discussed under "Customer incentive programs, advertising and marketing" below.

Provisions for bad debts are recorded as selling, marketing and administrative expenses. Write-offs of bad debts did not exceed 0.05% of net product sales in each of 2009, 2008 and 2007, and accordingly, have not been significant to the Company's financial position or results of operations.

### Intangible assets

The Company's intangible assets consist primarily of acquired trademarks and related goodwill. In accordance with accounting guidance, goodwill and other indefinite-lived assets are not amortized, but are instead subjected to annual testing for impairment unless certain triggering events or circumstances are noted. The Company performs its annual testing impairment testing as of December 31. The Company may utilize third-party professional valuation firms to assist in the determination of certain intangibles.

The impairment test is performed by comparing the carrying value of the asset with its estimated fair value, which is calculated using estimates, including discounted projected future cash flows. These projected future cash flows are dependent on a number of factors including the execution of business plans, achievement of projected sales, including but not limited to future price increases, projected operating margins, and projected capital expenditures. Such operating results are also dependent upon future ingredient and packaging material costs, exchange rates for products manufactured or sold in foreign countries, operational efficiencies, cost savings initiatives, and competitive factors. Although the majority of the Company's trademarks relate to well established brands with a long history of consumer acceptance, projected cash flows are inherently uncertain. A change in the assumptions underlying the impairment analysis, including but not limited to a reduction in projected cash flows, the use of a different discount rate to discount future cash flows or a different royalty rate applied to the Company's trademarks, could cause impairment in the future. See above discussion and Note 12 to the Consolidated Financial Statements regarding the impairment of certain trademarks in 2009.

### Customer incentive programs, advertising and marketing

Advertising and marketing costs are recorded in the period to which such costs relate. The Company does not defer the recognition of any amounts on its consolidated balance sheet with respect to such costs. Customer incentives and other promotional costs are recorded at the time of sale based upon incentive program terms and historical utilization statistics, which are generally consistent from year to year.

The liabilities associated with these programs are reviewed quarterly and adjusted if utilization rates differ from management's original estimates. Such adjustments have not historically been material to the Company's operating results.

### Split dollar officer life insurance

The Company provides split dollar life insurance benefits to certain executive officers and records an asset equal to the cumulative premiums paid. The Company will fully recover these premiums in future years under the terms of the plan. The Company retains a collateral assignment of the cash surrender values and policy death benefits payable to insure recovery of these premiums.

### Valuation of long-lived assets

Long-lived assets, primarily property, plant and equipment, and investment in joint ventures accounted for under the equity method are reviewed for impairment as events or changes in business circumstances occur indicating that the carrying value of the asset may not be recoverable. The Company may utilize third-party professional valuation firms as necessary to assist in the determination of the fair value of long-lived assets or investments accounted for under the equity method. The estimated cash flows produced by assets, asset groups, or investments accounted for under the equity method result in an estimated fair value and are compared to the asset carrying value to determine whether impairment exists. Such estimates involve considerable management judgment and are based upon assumptions about expected future operating performance, and cash flows in the case of investments accounted for under the equity method. As a result, actual cash

flows could differ from management's estimates due to changes in business conditions, operating performance, and economic and competitive conditions. See above discussion and Note 6 regarding the impairment of the Company's Spanish joint venture recorded in 2009.

### Income taxes

Deferred income taxes are recognized for future tax effects of temporary differences between financial and income tax reporting using tax rates in effect for the years in which the differences are expected to reverse. The Company records valuation allowances in situations where the realization of deferred tax assets, including those relating to net operating tax losses, is not more-likely-than-not; and the Company adjusts and releases such valuation allowances when realization becomes more-likely-than-not as defined by accounting guidance. The Company periodically reviews assumptions and estimates of the Company's probable tax obligations using informed judgment, projections of income and losses, and historical experience.

### Valuation of investments

Investments, primarily municipal bonds and mutual funds, are reviewed for impairment at each reporting period by comparing the carrying value or amortized cost to the fair market value. The Company may utilize third-party professional valuation firms as necessary to assist in the determination of the value of investments using a valuation model with Level 3 inputs as defined. In the event that an investment security's fair value is below carrying value or amortized cost, the Company will record an other-than-temporary impairment or a temporary impairment based on accounting guidance. See above discussion and Note 10 regarding Jefferson County ARS.

***Other matters***
In the opinion of management, other than contracts for foreign currency forwards and raw materials, including currency and commodity hedges and outstanding purchase orders for packaging, ingredients, supplies, and operational services, all entered into in the ordinary course of business, the Company does not have any significant contractual obligations or future commitments. The Company's outstanding contractual commitments as of December 31, 2009, all of which are generally normal and generally recurring in nature, are summarized in the chart on page 13.

## RECENT ACCOUNTING PRONOUNCEMENTS

In February 2008, the FASB delayed the effective date of guidance for non-financial assets and non-financial liabilities, except for items that are recognized or disclosed at fair value in the financial statements on a recurring basis until fiscal and interim periods beginning after November 15, 2008. The non-financial assets and non-financial liabilities for which the Company has applied the fair value provisions of this guidance include long-lived assets, goodwill and other intangible assets. See Note 10 to the Consolidated Financial Statements.

During the first quarter of 2009, the Company adopted the authoritative guidance for disclosures about derivative instruments and hedging activities. It requires qualitative disclosures about objectives and strategies for using derivatives,

quantitative disclosures about fair value amounts of derivative instruments and related gains and losses, and disclosures about credit-risk-related contingent features in derivative agreements. The adoption did not impact the Company's financial condition, results of operations or cash flow.

In April 2009, the FASB issued guidance on (1) estimating the fair value of an asset or liability when the volume and level of activity for the asset or liability have significantly decreased and (2) identifying transactions that are not orderly. It is effective for interim and annual periods ending after June 15, 2009. The Company's adoption of the guidance during second quarter 2009 did not have a material impact on the Company's consolidated financial statements.

In April 2009, the FASB amended the other-than-temporary impairment guidance for debt securities to make the guidance more operational and to improve the presentation and disclosure of other-than-temporary impairments on debt and equity securities. It is effective for interim and annual periods ending after June 15, 2009. The Company's adoption of the guidance during second quarter 2009 did not have a material impact on the Company's consolidated financial statements.

In April 2009, the FASB issued guidance which required disclosures about the fair value of financial instruments in interim reporting periods of publicly traded companies as well as in annual financial statements. It is effective for interim periods ending after June 15, 2009. The Company's adoption of the guidance during second quarter 2009 did not have a material impact on the Company's consolidated financial statements. See Note 10 to the Consolidated Financial Statements.

In May 2009, the FASB issued guidance which established general standards of accounting for, and disclosure of, events that occur after the balance sheet date but before financial statements are issued. It includes a requirement to disclose the date through which subsequent events were evaluated. See Note 1 to the Consolidated Financial Statements.

In June 2009, the FASB issued guidance which establishes the FASB Accounting Standards Codification to become the source of authoritative U.S. generally accepted accounting principles to be applied by non-governmental entities. It is effective for interim or annual financial periods ending after September 15, 2009. The Company adopted this guidance during the third quarter of fiscal year 2009.

## MARKET RISKS

The Company is exposed to market risks related to commodity prices, interest rates, investments in marketable securities, equity price and foreign exchange.

The Company's ability to forecast the direction and scope of changes to its major input costs is impacted by significant volatility in crude oil, sugar, corn, soybean and edible oils, cocoa and dairy products markets. The prices of these commodities are influenced by changes in global demand, changes in weather and crop yields, changes in governments' farm policies, including mandates for bio-fuels and environmental matters, including global warming, and fluctuations in the U.S. dollar relative to dollar-denominated commodities in world markets. The Company believes that its competitors face the same or similar challenges.

In order to address the impact of rising input and other costs, the Company periodically reviews each item in its product portfolio to ascertain if price increases, weight declines (indirect price increases) or other actions may be taken. These reviews include an evaluation of the risk factors relating to market place acceptance of such changes and their potential effect on future sales volumes. In addition, the estimated cost of packaging modifications associated with weight changes is evaluated.

The Company also maintains ongoing cost reduction and productivity improvement programs under which cost savings initiatives are encouraged and progress monitored. The Company is not able to accurately predict the outcome of these cost savings initiatives and their effects on its future results.

### Commodity future and foreign currency forward contracts

Commodity price risks relate to ingredients, primarily sugar, cocoa, chocolate, corn syrup, dextrose, soybean and edible oils, milk, whey and gum base ingredients. The Company believes its competitors face similar risks, and the industry has historically adjusted prices to compensate for adverse fluctuations in commodity costs. The Company, as well as competitors in the confectionery industry, have taken actions, including price increases and selective product weight declines (indirect price increases) to mitigate rising input costs for ingredients, energy, freight and delivery. Although management seeks to substantially recover cost increases over the long-term, there is risk that price increases and weight declines cannot be

fully passed on to customers and, to the extent they are passed on, they could adversely affect customer and consumer acceptance and resulting sales volume.

The Company utilizes commodity futures contracts and options programs as well as annual supply agreements to hedge and plan for anticipated purchases of certain ingredients, including sugar, in order to mitigate commodity cost fluctuation. The Company also purchases forward foreign exchange contracts to hedge its costs of manufacturing certain products in Canada for sale and distribution in the United States, and periodically does so for purchases of equipment or raw materials from foreign suppliers. Such commodity futures and currency forward contracts are cash flow hedges and are effective as hedges as defined by accounting guidance. The unrealized gains and losses on such contracts are deferred as a component of accumulated other comprehensive loss and are recognized as a component of product cost of goods sold when the related inventory is sold. The Company has elected not to apply hedge accounting to commodity options contracts.

The potential change in fair value of commodity and foreign currency derivative instruments held by the Company at December 31, 2009, assuming a 10% change in the underlying contract price, was $3,018. The analysis only includes commodity and foreign currency derivative instruments and, therefore, does not consider the offsetting effect of changes in the price of the underlying commodity or foreign currency. This amount is not significant compared with the net earnings and shareholders' equity of the Company.

### Interest rates

Interest rate risks primarily relate to the Company's investments in tax exempt marketable securities, including ARS, with maturities or auction dates of generally up to three years.

The majority of the Company's investments, which are classified as available for sale, have historically been held until they mature, which limits the Company's exposure to interest rate fluctuations. The accompanying chart summarizes the maturities of the Company's investments in debt securities at December 31, 2009.

| | |
|---|---|
| Less than 1 year | $ 8,607 |
| 1–2 years | 7,858 |
| 2–3 years | 10,328 |
| Over 3 years | 7,710 |
| Total | $34,503 |

The Company had no outstanding debt at December 31, 2009 or 2008 other than $7,500 in an industrial revenue bond in which interest rates reset each week based on the current market rate. Therefore, the Company does not believe that it has significant interest rate risk with respect to its interest bearing debt.

### Investment in marketable securities

As stated above, the Company invests primarily in tax exempt marketable securities, including ARS, with maturities or auction dates generally up to three years. The Company utilizes professional money managers and maintains investment policy guidelines which emphasize quality and liquidity in order to minimize the potential loss exposures that could result in the event of a default or other adverse event, including failed auctions.

However, given events in the municipal bond and ARS markets, including failed auctions, the

Company continues to monitor these investments and markets, as well as its investment policies. Nonetheless, the financial markets have been experiencing unprecedented events, and future outcomes are less predictable than in the past.

### Equity price

Equity price risk relates to the Company's investments in mutual funds which are principally used to fund and hedge the Company's deferred compensation liabilities. At December 31, 2009, the Company has investments in mutual funds, classified as trading securities, of $32,238. Any change in the fair value of these trading securities is completely offset by a corresponding change in the respective hedged deferred compensation liability.

### Foreign currency exchange

Foreign currency exchange risk principally relates to the Company's foreign operations in Canada and Mexico, as well as periodic purchase commitments of machinery and equipment from foreign sources.

Certain of the Company's Canadian manufacturing costs, including local payroll and plant operations, and a portion of its packaging and ingredients are sourced in Canadian dollars. The Company purchases Canadian forward contracts to receive Canadian dollars at a specified date in the future and uses its Canadian dollar collections on Canadian sales as a partial hedge of its overall Canadian manufacturing obligations sourced in Canadian dollars. The Company also periodically purchases and holds Canadian dollars to facilitate the risk management of these currency changes.

From time to time the Company may use forward foreign exchange contracts and derivative instruments to mitigate its exposure to foreign exchange risks, as well as those related to firm commitments to purchase equipment from foreign vendors. As of December 31, 2009 the Company held foreign exchange forward contracts with a fair value of $3,674.

## RISK FACTORS

The Company's operations and financial results are subject to a number of risks and uncertainties that could adversely affect the Company's operating results and financial condition. Significant risk factors, without limitations that could impact the Company are the following: (i) significant competitive activity, including advertising, promotional and price competition, and changes in consumer demand for the Company's products; (ii) fluctuations in the cost and availability of various ingredients and packaging materials; (iii) inherent risks in the marketplace, including uncertainties about trade and consumer acceptance and seasonal events such as Halloween; (iv) the effect of acquisitions on the Company's results of operations and financial condition; (v) the effect of changes in foreign currencies on the Company's foreign subsidiaries operating results, and the effect of the fluctuation of the Canadian dollar on products manufactured in Canada and marketed and sold in the United States in U.S. dollars; (vi) the Company's reliance on third party vendors for various goods and services; (vii) the Company's ability to successfully implement new production processes and lines; (viii) the effect of changes in assumptions, including discount rates, sales growth and profit margins and the capability to pass along higher ingredient and other input costs through price increases, relating to the Company's impairment testing and analysis of its goodwill and trademarks; (ix) changes in the confectionery marketplace

### Open Contractual Commitments as of December 31, 2009

| Payable in | Total | Less than 1 year | 1 to 3 Years | 3 to 5 Years | More than 5 Years |
|---|---|---|---|---|---|
| Commodity options | $12,405 | $12,405 | $ — | $ — | $ — |
| Foreign currency hedges | 17,772 | 14,200 | 3,572 | — | — |
| Purchase obligations | 18,340 | 18,340 | — | — | — |
| Interest bearing debt | 7,500 | — | — | — | 7,500 |
| Operating leases | 3,281 | 1,058 | 1,139 | 723 | 361 |
| Total | $59,298 | $46,003 | $4,711 | $723 | $7,861 |

Note: Commodity options and foreign currency hedges reflect the notional amounts. The above amounts exclude deferred income tax liabilities of $44,582, liabilities for uncertain tax positions of $21,101, postretirement health care and life insurance benefits of $16,674 and deferred compensation and other liabilities of $39,839 because the timing of payments relating to these items cannot be reasonably determined.

including actions taken by major retailers and customers; (x) customer, consumer and competitor response to marketing programs and price and product weight adjustments, and new products; (xi) dependence on significant customers, including the volume and timing of their purchases, and availability of shelf space; (xii) increases in energy costs, including freight and delivery, that cannot be passed along to customers through increased prices due to competitive reasons; (xiii) any significant labor stoppages, strikes or production interruptions; (xiv) changes in governmental laws and regulations including taxes and tariffs; (xv) the risk that the market value of Company's investments could decline including being classified as "other-than-temporary" as defined; and (xvi) the potential effects of current and future macroeconomic conditions.

### Forward-looking statements

This discussion and certain other sections contain forward-looking statements that are based largely on the Company's current expectations and are made pursuant to the safe harbor provision of the Private Securities Litigation Reform Act of 1995. Forward-looking statements can be identified by the use of the words such as "anticipated," "believe," "expect," "intend," "estimate," "project," and other words of similar meaning in connection with a discussion of future operating or financial performance and are subject to certain factors, risks, trends and uncertainties that could cause actual results and achievements to differ materially from those expressed in the forward-looking statements. Such factors, risks, trends and uncertainties which in some instances are beyond the Company's control, including the overall competitive environment in the Company's industry, changes in assumptions and judgments discussed above under the heading "Significant Accounting Policies and Estimates", and factors identified and referred to above under the heading "Risk Factors."

The risk factors identified and referred to above are believed to be significant factors, but not necessarily all of the significant factors that could cause actual results to differ from those expressed in any forward-looking statement. Readers are cautioned not to place undue reliance on such forward-looking statements, which are made only as of the date of this report. The Company undertakes no obligation to update such forward-looking statements.

# Management's Report on Internal Control and Management Certifications of Financial Statements

The Sarbanes-Oxley Act of 2002 requires managers of publicly traded companies to establish and maintain systems of internal control on the company's financial reporting processes. In addition, the act requires the company's top management to provide certifications regarding the accuracy of the financial statements. The reports of Tootsie Roll are shown on page A-17.

# Management's Report on Internal Control Over Financial Reporting

The management of Tootsie Roll Industries, Inc. is responsible for establishing and maintaining adequate internal control over financial reporting, as such term is defined in the Securities Exchange Act of 1934 (SEC) Rule 13a-15(f). Our management conducted an evaluation of the effectiveness of the Company's internal control over financial reporting as of December 31, 2009 as required by SEC Rule 13a-15(c). In making this assessment, we used the criteria established in *Internal Control—Integrated Framework* issued by the Committee of Sponsoring Organizations of the Treadway Commission (the COSO criteria). Based on our evaluation under the COSO criteria, our management concluded that our internal control over financial reporting was effective as of December 31, 2009.

The effectiveness of the Company's internal control over financial reporting as of December 31, 2009 has been audited by PricewaterhouseCoopers LLP, an independent registered public accounting firm, as stated in their report which appears on page 27.

Tootsie Roll Industries, Inc.

Chicago, Illinois
March 1, 2010

## Financial Statements and Accompanying Notes

The standard set of financial statements consists of: (1) a comparative income statement for three years, (2) a comparative balance sheet for two years, (3) a comparative statement of cash flows for three years, (4) a statement of retained earnings (or stockholders' equity) for three years, and (5) a set of accompanying notes that are considered an integral part of the financial statements. The auditor's report, unless stated otherwise, covers the financial statements and the accompanying notes. The financial statements and accompanying notes plus some supplementary data and analyses for Tootsie Roll Industries follow.

CONSOLIDATED STATEMENTS OF

# *Financial Position*

TOOTSIE ROLL INDUSTRIES, INC. AND SUBSIDIARIES                    (in thousands)

# *Assets*

December 31,

| | 2009 | 2008 |
|---|---|---|
| CURRENT ASSETS: | | |
| Cash and cash equivalents | $ 90,990 | $ 68,908 |
| Investments | 8,663 | 17,963 |
| Accounts receivable trade, less allowances of $2,356 and $1,923 | 37,512 | 31,213 |
| Other receivables | 8,397 | 2,983 |
| Inventories: | | |
| Finished goods and work-in-process | 35,570 | 34,862 |
| Raw materials and supplies | 20,817 | 20,722 |
| Prepaid expenses | 8,562 | 11,328 |
| Deferred income taxes | 1,367 | 609 |
| Total current assets | 211,878 | 188,588 |
| PROPERTY, PLANT AND EQUIPMENT, at cost: | | |
| Land | 21,559 | 19,307 |
| Buildings | 102,374 | 89,077 |
| Machinery and equipment | 296,787 | 279,100 |
| Construction in progress | 6,877 | 20,701 |
| | 427,597 | 408,185 |
| Less—Accumulated depreciation | 206,876 | 190,557 |
| Net property, plant and equipment | 220,721 | 217,628 |
| OTHER ASSETS: | | |
| Goodwill | 73,237 | 73,237 |
| Trademarks | 175,024 | 189,024 |
| Investments | 58,136 | 49,809 |
| Split dollar officer life insurance | 74,642 | 74,808 |
| Prepaid expenses | 8,068 | 10,333 |
| Investment in joint venture | 4,961 | 9,274 |
| Deferred income taxes | 11,580 | 824 |
| Total other assets | 405,648 | 407,309 |
| Total assets | $838,247 | $813,525 |

(The accompanying notes are an integral part of these statements.)

(in thousands except per share data)

# *Liabilities and Shareholders' Equity*   December 31,

| | 2009 | 2008 |
|---|---|---|
| CURRENT LIABILITIES: | | |
| Accounts payable | $ 9,140 | $ 13,885 |
| Dividends payable | 4,458 | 4,401 |
| Accrued liabilities | 42,468 | 40,335 |
| Total current liabilities | 56,066 | 58,621 |
| NONCURRENT LIABILITES: | | |
| Deferred income taxes | 44,582 | 45,410 |
| Postretirement health care and life insurance benefits | 16,674 | 15,468 |
| Industrial development bonds | 7,500 | 7,500 |
| Liability for uncertain tax positions | 21,101 | 19,412 |
| Deferred compensation and other liabilities | 39,839 | 32,344 |
| Total noncurrent liabilities | 129,696 | 120,134 |
| SHAREHOLDERS' EQUITY: | | |
| Common stock, $.69-4/9 par value— | | |
| 120,000 shares authorized— | | |
| 35,802 and 35,658, respectively, issued | 24,862 | 24,762 |
| Class B common stock, $.69-4/9 par value— | | |
| 40,000 shares authorized— | | |
| 19,919 and 19,357, respectively, issued | 13,833 | 13,442 |
| Capital in excess of par value | 482,250 | 470,927 |
| Retained earnings, per accompanying statement | 145,928 | 142,872 |
| Accumulated other comprehensive loss | (12,396) | (15,241) |
| Treasury stock (at cost)— | | |
| 67 shares and 65 shares, respectively | (1,992) | (1,992) |
| Total shareholders' equity | 652,485 | 634,770 |
| Total liabilities and shareholders' equity | $838,247 | $813,525 |

CONSOLIDATED STATEMENTS OF

# Earnings, Comprehensive Earnings and Retained Earnings

TOOTSIE ROLL INDUSTRIES, INC. AND SUBSIDIARIES  (in thousands except per share data)

| | For the year ended December 31, | | |
| --- | --- | --- | --- |
| | 2009 | 2008 | 2007 |
| Net product sales | $495,592 | $492,051 | $492,742 |
| Rental and royalty revenue | 3,739 | 3,965 | 4,975 |
| Total revenue | 499,331 | 496,016 | 497,717 |
| Product cost of goods sold | 318,645 | 333,314 | 327,695 |
| Rental and royalty cost | 852 | 921 | 1,349 |
| Total costs | 319,497 | 334,235 | 329,044 |
| Product gross margin | 176,947 | 158,737 | 165,047 |
| Rental and royalty gross margin | 2,887 | 3,044 | 3,626 |
| Total gross margin | 179,834 | 161,781 | 168,673 |
| Selling, marketing and administrative expenses | 103,755 | 95,254 | 97,821 |
| Impairment charges | 14,000 | — | — |
| Earnings from operations | 62,079 | 66,527 | 70,852 |
| Other income (expense), net | 2,100 | (10,618) | 6,315 |
| Earnings before income taxes | 64,179 | 55,909 | 77,167 |
| Provision for income taxes | 10,704 | 17,132 | 25,542 |
| Net earnings | $ 53,475 | $ 38,777 | $ 51,625 |
| | | | |
| Net earnings | $ 53,475 | $ 38,777 | $ 51,625 |
| Other comprehensive earnings (loss) | 2,845 | (3,514) | 810 |
| Comprehensive earnings | $ 56,320 | $ 35,263 | $ 52,435 |
| | | | |
| Retained earnings at beginning of year | $142,872 | $156,752 | $169,233 |
| Net earnings | 53,475 | 38,777 | 51,625 |
| Cash dividends | (17,790) | (17,492) | (17,421) |
| Stock dividends | (32,629) | (35,165) | (46,685) |
| Retained earnings at end of year | $145,928 | $142,872 | $156,752 |
| Earnings per share | $ 0.95 | $ 0.68 | $ 0.89 |
| Average Common and Class B Common shares outstanding | 56,072 | 56,799 | 58,227 |

(The accompanying notes are an integral part of these statements.)

CONSOLIDATED STATEMENTS OF

# *Cash Flows*

TOOTSIE ROLL INDUSTRIES, INC. AND SUBSIDIARIES                           (in thousands)

| | For the year ended December 31, | | |
| --- | --- | --- | --- |
| | 2009 | 2008 | 2007 |
| CASH FLOWS FROM OPERATING ACTIVITIES: | | | |
| Net earnings | $ 53,475 | $ 38,777 | $ 51,625 |
| Adjustments to reconcile net earnings to net cash provided by operating activities: | | | |
| Depreciation | 17,862 | 17,036 | 15,859 |
| Impairment charges | 14,000 | — | — |
| Impairment of equity investment in joint venture | 4,400 | — | — |
| Loss from joint venture | 233 | 477 | — |
| Return on investment in joint venture | — | — | 1,419 |
| Other than temporary impairment | — | 5,140 | — |
| Amortization of marketable securities | 320 | 396 | 521 |
| Purchase of trading securities | (1,713) | (491) | (84) |
| Changes in operating assets and liabilities: | | | |
| Accounts receivable | (5,899) | (261) | 2,591 |
| Other receivables | (2,088) | (33) | 7 |
| Inventories | (675) | 1,352 | 6,506 |
| Prepaid expenses and other assets | 5,203 | (15,139) | 283 |
| Accounts payable and accrued liabilities | (2,755) | 967 | (3,234) |
| Income taxes payable and deferred | (11,731) | 8,642 | 13,481 |
| Postretirement health care and life insurance benefits | 1,028 | 3,394 | 1,272 |
| Deferred compensation and other liabilities | 3,316 | (2,385) | (12) |
| Other | 305 | (830) | (170) |
| Net cash provided by operating activities | 75,281 | 57,042 | 90,064 |
| CASH FLOWS FROM INVESTING ACTIVITIES: | | | |
| Proceeds from sale of real estate and other assets | — | — | 434 |
| Return of investment in joint venture | — | — | 1,206 |
| Capital expenditures | (20,831) | (34,355) | (14,767) |
| Purchase of available for sale securities | (11,331) | (33,977) | (59,132) |
| Sale and maturity of available for sale securities | 17,511 | 61,258 | 28,914 |
| Net cash used in investing activities | (14,651) | (7,074) | (43,345) |
| CASH FLOWS FROM FINANCING ACTIVITIES: | | | |
| Shares repurchased and retired | (20,723) | (21,109) | (27,300) |
| Dividends paid in cash | (17,825) | (17,557) | (17,542) |
| Net cash used in financing activities | (38,548) | (38,666) | (44,842) |
| Increase in cash and cash equivalents | 22,082 | 11,302 | 1,877 |
| Cash and cash equivalents at beginning of year | 68,908 | 57,606 | 55,729 |
| Cash and cash equivalents at end of year | $ 90,990 | $ 68,908 | $ 57,606 |
| Supplemental cash flow information: | | | |
| Income taxes paid | $ 22,364 | $ 12,728 | $ 11,343 |
| Interest paid | $    182 | $    252 | $    537 |
| Stock dividend issued | $ 32,538 | $ 35,042 | $ 46,520 |

(The accompanying notes are an integral part of these statements.)

# Notes to Consolidated Financial Statements

TOOTSIE ROLL INDUSTRIES, INC. AND SUBSIDIARIES

($ in thousands except per share data)

### NOTE 1—SIGNIFICANT ACCOUNTING POLICIES:

#### Basis of consolidation:

The consolidated financial statements include the accounts of Tootsie Roll Industries, Inc. and its wholly-owned subsidiaries (the Company), which are primarily engaged in the manufacture and sales of candy products. All significant intercompany transactions have been eliminated.

The preparation of financial statements in conformity with generally accepted accounting principles in the United States of America requires management to make estimates and assumptions that affect the reported amounts of assets and liabilities and disclosure of contingent assets and liabilities at the date of the financial statements and the reported amounts of revenues and expenses during the reporting period. Actual results could differ from those estimates.

Certain reclassifications have been made to the prior year financial statements to conform to the current year presentation.

#### Revenue recognition:

Products are sold to customers based on accepted purchase orders which include quantity, sales price and other relevant terms of sale. Revenue, net of applicable provisions for discounts, returns, allowances and certain advertising and promotional costs, is recognized when products are delivered to customers and collectability is reasonably assured. Shipping and handling costs of $38,628, $45,570, and $41,775 in 2009, 2008 and 2007, respectively, are included in selling, marketing and administrative expenses. Accounts receivable are unsecured. Revenues from a major customer aggregated approximately 22.9%, 23.5% and 22.4% of net product sales during the years ended December 31, 2009, 2008 and 2007, respectively.

#### Cash and cash equivalents:

The Company considers temporary cash investments with an original maturity of three months or less to be cash equivalents.

#### Investments:

Investments consist of various marketable securities with maturities of generally up to three years. The Company classifies debt and equity securities as either available for sale or trading. Available for sale are not actively traded and are carried at fair value. The Company follows current fair value

measurement guidance and unrealized gains and losses on these securities are excluded from earnings and are reported as a separate component of shareholders' equity, net of applicable taxes, until realized. Trading securities relate to deferred compensation arrangements and are carried at fair value. The Company invests in trading securities to economically hedge changes in its deferred compensation liabilities.

The Company regularly reviews its investments to determine whether a decline in fair value below the cost basis is other than temporary. If the decline in fair value is judged to be other than temporary, the cost basis of the security is written down to fair value and the amount of the write-down is included in other income (expense), net. Further information regarding the fair value of the Company's investments is included in Note 10 to the Consolidated Financial Statements.

#### Derivative instruments and hedging activities:

During the first quarter of 2009, the Company adopted the new authoritative guidance for disclosures about derivative instruments and hedging activities. This guidance requires qualitative disclosures about objectives and strategies for using derivatives, quantitative disclosures about fair value amounts of derivative instruments and related gains and losses, and disclosures about credit-risk-related contingent features in derivative agreements. The adoption of this standard did not impact the Company's consolidated financial statements.

From time to time, the Company enters into futures contracts. Commodity futures are intended and are effective as hedges of market price risks associated with the anticipated purchase of certain raw materials (primarily sugar). Foreign currency forward contracts are intended and are effective as hedges of the Company's exposure to the variability of cash flows, primarily related to the foreign exchange rate changes of products manufactured in Canada and sold in the United States, and periodic equipment purchases from foreign suppliers denominated in a foreign currency. The Company does not engage in trading or other speculative use of derivative instruments.

The Company's foreign currency forward contracts are accounted for as cash flow hedges and are recorded on the balance sheet at fair value. Changes therein are recorded in accumulated other comprehensive loss, net of tax, and are reclassified to earnings in the periods in which earnings are affected by the hedged item. Realized gains/losses are recorded as foreign exchange gains/losses in other income (expense), net.

As of December 31, 2009, the Company had foreign currency forward contracts outstanding with a notional amount of $17,772 that hedged its exposure to changes in foreign currency exchange rates for its costs of manufacturing certain products in Canada for the U.S. market. The fair value of foreign currency forward contracts, using Level 1 inputs, as discussed in Note 10, resulted in an asset of $3,674 as of December 31, 2009 which is included in other receivables. In entering into these contracts, the Company has assumed the risk that might arise from the possible inability of counterparties to meet the terms of their contracts and does not expect any significant losses from counterparty defaults.

During 2009, the Company recorded $3,365 of net derivative gains in accumulated other comprehensive loss which is a component of shareholders' equity in the statement of financial position. The Company also recognized a gain of $989, related to foreign currency contracts settled during 2009. At December 31, 2009, the Company expects to reclassify existing net gains of approximately $1,871 from accumulated other comprehensive loss to net earnings during the next twelve months.

As of December 31, 2009, the Company had commodity options contracts with a notional value of $12,405. These options have not been designated as hedges. The fair value of $1,686 is included in other receivables. In 2009 the Company recorded a gain of $1,562 in cost of goods sold.

### Inventories:

Inventories are stated at cost, not to exceed market. The cost of substantially all of the Company's inventories ($53,724 and $53,557 at December 31, 2009 and 2008, respectively) has been determined by the last-in, first-out (LIFO) method. The excess of current cost over LIFO cost of inventories approximates $13,107 and $12,432 at December 31, 2009 and 2008, respectively. The cost of certain foreign inventories ($2,663 and $2,027 at December 31, 2009 and 2008, respectively) has been determined by the first-in, first-out (FIFO) method. Rebates, discounts and other cash consideration received from vendors related to inventory purchases is reflected as a reduction in the cost of the related inventory item, and is therefore reflected in cost of sales when the related inventory item is sold.

### Property, plant and equipment:

Depreciation is computed for financial reporting purposes by use of the straight-line method based on useful lives of 20 to 35 years for buildings and 5 to 20 years for machinery and equipment. Depreciation expense was $17,862, $17,036 and $15,859 in 2009, 2008 and 2007, respectively.

### Carrying value of long-lived assets:

The Company reviews long-lived assets to determine if there are events or circumstances indicating that the amount of the asset reflected in the Company's balance sheet may not be recoverable. When such indicators are present, the Company compares the carrying value of the long-lived asset, or asset group, to the future undiscounted cash flows of the underlying assets to determine if an impairment exists. If applicable, an impairment charge would be recorded to write down the carrying value to its fair value. The determination of fair value involves the use of estimates of future cash flows that involve considerable management judgment and are based upon assumptions about expected future operating performance. The actual cash flows could differ from management's estimates due to changes in business conditions, operating performance, and economic conditions. No impairment charges of long-lived assets were recorded by the Company during 2009, 2008 and 2007.

### Postretirement health care and life insurance benefits:

The Company provides certain postretirement health care and life insurance benefits. The cost of these postretirement benefits is accrued during employees' working careers. The Company also provides split dollar life benefits to certain executive officers. The Company records an asset equal to the cumulative insurance premiums paid that will be recovered upon the death of a covered employee(s) or earlier under the terms of the plan. Split dollar premiums paid were $1,586 in 2007. No premiums were paid in 2009 and 2008.

### Goodwill and intangible assets:

In accordance with authoritative guidance, goodwill and intangible assets with indefinite lives are not amortized, but rather tested for impairment at least annually unless certain interim triggering events or circumstances require more frequent testing. All trademarks have been assessed by management to have indefinite lives because they are expected to generate cash flows indefinitely. The Company has completed its annual impairment testing of its goodwill and trademarks at December 31 of each of the years presented. As of December 31, 2009, management ascertained that certain trademarks were impaired, and recorded a pre-tax charge of $14,000. No impairments of intangibles were recorded in 2008 and 2007.

This determination is made by comparing the carrying value of the asset with its estimated fair value, which is calculated using estimates including discounted projected future cash flows. Management believes that all assumptions used for the impairment tests are consistent with those utilized by market participants performing similar valuations.

### Income taxes:

Deferred income taxes are recorded and recognized for future tax effects of temporary differences between financial and income tax reporting. The Company records valuation allowances in situations where the realization of deferred tax assets is not more–likely-than-not. Federal income taxes are provided on the portion of income of foreign subsidiaries that is expected to be remitted to the U.S. and become taxable, but not on the portion that is considered to be permanently invested in the foreign subsidiary.

### Foreign currency translation:

The U.S. dollar is used as the functional currency where a substantial portion of the subsidiary's business is indexed to the U.S. dollar or where its manufactured products are principally sold in the U.S. All other foreign subsidiaries use the local currency as their functional currency. Where the U.S. dollar is used as the functional currency, foreign currency remeasurements are recorded as a charge or credit to other income (expense), net in the statement of earnings. Where the foreign local currency is used as the functional currency, translation adjustments are recorded as a separate component of accumulated other comprehensive (loss).

### Joint venture:

The Company's 50% interest in two companies is accounted for using the equity method. The Company records an increase in its investment in the joint venture to the extent of its share of the joint venture's earnings, and reduces its investment to the extent of losses and dividends received. A dividend of $861 was paid in 2007 by the joint venture. No dividends were paid in 2009 and 2008.

As of December 31, 2009, management determined that the fair value of the asset was less than the carrying value. As a result, the Company recorded a pre-tax impairment charge $4,400 in the fourth quarter 2009, resulting in an adjusted carrying value of $4,961 as of December 31, 2009. The fair value was primarily assessed using the present value of estimated future cash flows.

### Comprehensive earnings:

Comprehensive earnings includes net earnings, foreign currency translation adjustments and unrealized gains/losses on commodity and/or foreign currency hedging contracts, available for sale securities and certain postretirement benefit obligations.

### Earnings per share:

A dual presentation of basic and diluted earnings per share is not required due to the lack of potentially dilutive securities under the Company's simple capital structure. Therefore, all earnings per share amounts represent basic earnings per share.

The Class B Common Stock has essentially the same rights as Common Stock, except that each share of Class B Common Stock has ten votes per share (compared to one vote per share of Common Stock), is not traded on any exchange, is restricted as to transfer and is convertible on a share-for-share basis, at any time and at no cost to the holders, into shares of Common Stock which are traded on the New Stock Exchange.

### Use of estimates:

The preparation of consolidated financial statements in conformity with accounting principles generally accepted in the U.S. requires management to make estimates and assumptions that affect the amounts reported. Estimates are used when accounting for sales discounts, allowances and incentives, product liabilities, assets recorded at fair value, income taxes, depreciation, amortization, employee benefits, contingencies and intangible asset and liability valuations. For instance, in determining the annual post-employment benefit costs, the Company estimates the cost of future health care benefits. Actual results may or may not differ from those estimates.

### Recent accounting pronouncements:

In February 2008, the FASB delayed the effective date of guidance for non-financial assets and non-financial liabilities, except for items that are recognized or disclosed at fair value in the financial statements on a recurring basis until fiscal and interim periods beginning after November 15, 2008. The non-financial assets and non-financial liabilities for which the Company has applied the fair value provisions of this guidance include long lived assets, goodwill and other intangible assets. See Note 10 to the Consolidated Financial Statements.

During the first quarter of 2009 the Company adopted the authoritative guidance for disclosures about derivative instruments and hedging activities. It requires qualitative disclosures about objectives and strategies for using derivatives, quantitative disclosures about fair value amounts of derivative instruments and related gains and losses, and disclosures about credit-risk-related contingent features in derivative agreements. The adoption did not impact the Company's financial condition, results of operations or cash flow.

In April 2009, the FASB issued guidance on (1) estimating the fair value of an asset or liability when the volume and level of activity for the asset or liability have significantly decreased and (2) identifying transactions that are not orderly. It is effective for interim and annual periods ending after June 15, 2009. The Company's adoption of the guidance during second quarter 2009 did not have a material impact on the Company's consolidated financial statements.

In April 2009, the FASB amended the other-than-temporary impairment guidance for debt securities to make the guidance more operational and to improve the presentation and disclosure of other-than-temporary impairments on debt and equity securities. It is effective for interim and annual periods ending after June 15, 2009. The Company's adoption of the guidance during second quarter 2009 did not have a material impact on the Company's consolidated financial statements.

In April 2009, the FASB issued guidance which required disclosures about the fair value of financial instruments in interim reporting periods of publicly traded companies as well as in annual financial statements. It is effective for interim periods ending after June 15, 2009. The Company's adoption of the guidance during second quarter 2009 did not have a material impact on the Company's consolidated financial statements. See Note 10 to the Consolidated Financial Statements.

In May 2009, the FASB issued guidance which established general standards of accounting for, and disclosure of, events that occur after the balance sheet date but before financial statements are issued. It includes a requirement to disclose the date through which subsequent events were evaluated. See Note 1 to the Consolidated Financial Statements.

In June 2009, the FASB issued guidance which establishes the FASB Accounting Standards Codification to become the source of authoritative U.S. generally accepted accounting principles to be applied by non-governmental entities. It is effective for interim or annual financial periods ending after September 15, 2009. The Company adopted this guidance during the third quarter of fiscal year 2009.

## NOTE 2—ACCRUED LIABILITIES:

Accrued liabilities are comprised of the following:

|  | December 31, | |
|---|---|---|
|  | 2009 | 2008 |
| Compensation | $ 9,254 | $11,028 |
| Other employee benefits | 2,309 | 2,552 |
| Taxes, other than income | 1,899 | 1,755 |
| Advertising and promotions | 19,350 | 17,345 |
| Other | 9,656 | 7,655 |
|  | $42,468 | $40,335 |

## NOTE 3—INDUSTRIAL DEVELOPMENT BONDS:

Industrial development bonds are due in 2027. The average floating interest rate was 0.5% and 2.6% in 2009 and 2008, respectively. See Note 10 to the Consolidated Financial Statements for fair value disclosures.

## NOTE 4—INCOME TAXES:

The domestic and foreign components of pretax income are as follows:

|  | 2009 | 2008 | 2007 |
|---|---|---|---|
| Domestic | $69,779 | $50,313 | $69,250 |
| Foreign | (5,600) | 5,596 | 7,917 |
|  | $64,179 | $55,909 | $77,167 |

The provision for income taxes is comprised of the following:

|  | 2009 | 2008 | 2007 |
|---|---|---|---|
| Current: |  |  |  |
| Federal | $22,239 | $ 6,856 | $21,785 |
| Foreign | 500 | 502 | (702) |
| State | 1,665 | 355 | 737 |
|  | 24,404 | 7,713 | 21,820 |
| Deferred: |  |  |  |
| Federal | (23) | 8,733 | 2,671 |
| Foreign | (12,987) | 264 | 918 |
| State | (690) | 422 | 133 |
|  | (13,700) | 9,419 | 3,722 |
|  | $10,704 | $17,132 | $25,542 |

Significant components of the Company's net deferred tax liability at year end were as follows:

|  | December 31, | |
|---|---|---|
|  | 2009 | 2008 |
| Deferred tax assets: |  |  |
| Accrued customer promotions | $ 4,475 | $4,299 |
| Deferred compensation | 10,667 | 9,788 |
| Postretirement benefits | 5,983 | 5,447 |
| Other accrued expenses | 5,705 | 4,785 |
| Foreign subsidiary tax loss carry forward | 14,001 | 6,068 |
| Tax credit carry forward | 1,286 | 2,540 |
| Unrealized capital loss | 6,393 | 1,799 |
|  | 48,510 | 34,726 |
| Valuation reserve | (912) | (8,506) |
| Total deferred tax assets | $47,598 | $26,220 |
| Deferred tax liabilities: |  |  |
| Depreciation | $29,657 | $23,696 |
| Deductible goodwill and trademarks | 30,585 | 25,292 |
| Accrued export company commissions | 4,179 | 4,313 |
| Employee benefit plans | 4,437 | 5,614 |
| Inventory reserves | 2,311 | 2,463 |
| Prepaid insurance | 363 | 392 |
| Accounts receivable | 57 | 455 |
| Deferred gain on sale of real estate | 7,644 | 7,972 |
| Total deferred tax liabilities | $79,233 | $70,197 |
| Net deferred tax liability | $31,635 | $43,977 |

At December 31, 2009, the tax benefits of foreign subsidiary tax loss carry forwards expiring by year are as follows: $1,083 in 2014, $2,586 in 2015, $354 in 2026, $619 in 2027, $6,365 in 2028, and $2,994 in 2029.

Also at December 31, 2009, the amounts of the foreign subsidiary tax credit carry forwards expiring by year are as follows: $152 in 2010, $152 in 2011, $152 in 2012, $152 in 2013, $152 in 2014, $152 in 2015, $222 in 2016 and $152 in 2017. A valuation allowance has been established for these carry forward credits to reduce the future income tax benefits to amounts expected to be realized.

The effective income tax rate differs from the statutory rate as follows:

| | 2009 | 2008 | 2007 |
|---|---|---|---|
| U.S. statutory rate . . . . . . . . . . . . | 35.0% | 35.0% | 35.0% |
| State income taxes, net . . . . . . . . | 1.7 | 1.0 | 0.9 |
| Exempt municipal bond interest . | (0.6) | (1.9) | (1.4) |
| Foreign tax rates . . . . . . . . . . . . . | (4.8) | (0.7) | (1.6) |
| Release of prior period valuation allowances . . . . . . . . | (13.1) | — | — |
| Qualified domestic production activities deduction . . . . . . . . . . | (2.0) | (1.4) | (1.9) |
| Tax credits receivable . . . . . . . . . | (0.4) | (1.3) | — |
| Reserve for uncertain tax benefits | 1.9 | 0.6 | 1.3 |
| Other, net . . . . . . . . . . . . . . . . . . . | (1.0) | (0.7) | 0.8 |
| Effective income tax rate . . . . . . . | 16.7% | 30.6% | 33.1% |

In connection with the acquisition in 2004 of Concord Confections, a Canadian subsidiary, the Company established an inter-company financing structure which included a loan from the U.S. parent to the Canadian subsidiary. By December of 2006, significant operating losses had accumulated in Canada and management determined that the realization of the net operating loss carry forward benefits was not more-likely-than-not, and provided a full tax valuation allowance. Consistent with relevant accounting guidance, these benefits continued to be reserved through 2008 and through the third quarter of 2009.

In December of 2008, a new U.S./Canada income tax treaty (Treaty) was ratified which effectively denies certain inter-company interest benefits to the U.S. shareholder of a Canadian company. Accordingly, in December of 2009, the Company decided to recapitalize its Canadian operations effective January 1, 2010. During the fourth quarter of 2009, the Company considered of all the evidence and relevant accounting guidance related to this recapitalization and based on reasonable assumptions, the Company concluded that it was more-likely-than-not that it would realize substantially all of the deferred tax assets related to the Canadian net operating loss carry forward benefits because it is expected that sufficient levels of income will be generated in the foreseeable future. As a result, the Company released $8.4 million of prior period valuation allowances and $2.3 million of allowances that were provided through the first nine months of 2009.

The Treaty also introduced a phase out of the withholding tax on payments from Canada to the U.S. allowing the Company to qualify for a zero percent withholding rate in 2010 if certain requirements of the Treaty were met. On January 4, 2010, the Canadian subsidiary repaid accrued interest to its U.S. parent in a manner consistent with these requirements. As a result, $1.5 million of withholding taxes accrued for 2007 and 2008 and through the third quarter of 2009 were released in the fourth quarter of 2009.

The Company has not provided for U.S. federal or foreign withholding taxes on $5,294 and $3,445 of foreign subsidiaries' undistributed earnings as of December 31, 2009 and December 31, 2008, respectively, because such earnings are considered to be permanently reinvested. It is not practicable to determine the amount of income taxes that would be payable upon remittance of the undistributed earnings.

The Company adopted the provisions of the authoritative guidance relating to unrecognized tax benefits effective January 1, 2007. The Company recognizes interest and penalties related to unrecognized tax benefits in the provision for income taxes on the Consolidated Statements of Earnings.

At December 31, 2009 and 2008, the Company had unrecognized tax benefits of $16,816 and $15,138, respectively. Included in this balance is $8,819 and $7,727, respectively, of unrecognized tax benefits that, if recognized, would favorably affect the annual effective income tax rate. As of December 31, 2009 and 2008, $4,285 and $4,274, respectively, of interest and penalties were included in the Liability for Uncertain Tax Positions.

A reconciliation of the beginning and ending balances of the total amounts of unrecognized tax benefits is as follows:

| | 2009 | 2008 | 2007 |
|---|---|---|---|
| Unrecognized tax benefits at January 1 . . . . . . . . . . . . . . . | $15,138 | $15,867 | $14,987 |
| Increases in tax positions for the current year . . . . . . . . . . . | 3,414 | 1,404 | 1,895 |
| Reductions in tax positions for lapse of statute of limitations . . . . . . . . . . . . . . . . | (890) | (1,225) | (1,015) |
| Reductions in tax positions for effective settlements . . . . . . . . | (846) | (908) | — |
| Unrecognized tax benefits at December 31 . . . . . . . . . . . . . . | $16,816 | $15,138 | $15,867 |

The Company is subject to taxation in the U.S. and various state and foreign jurisdictions. The Company remains subject to examination by U.S. federal and state and foreign tax authorities for the years 2006 through 2008. With few exceptions, the Company is no longer subject to examinations by tax authorities for the year 2005 and prior.

The Company is not currently subject to a U.S. federal examination. The Company's Canadian subsidiary is currently subject to examination by the Canada Revenue Agency for tax years 2005 and 2006. The Company is unable to determine the outcome of the examination at this time. In addition, the Company is currently subject to various state tax examinations. One of those state examinations has been effectively settled and the corresponding liability for unrecognized tax benefits has been reduced. Although the Company is unable to determine the ultimate outcome of the ongoing examinations, the Company believes that its liability for uncertain tax positions relating to these jurisdictions for such years is adequate.

Beginning in 2008, statutory income tax rates in Canada will be reduced five percentage points with the final rate reduction coming in 2014. Accordingly, the Company's Canadian subsidiary has revalued its deferred tax assets and liabilities based on the rate in effect for the year the differences are expected to reverse. Additional deferred tax expense of $1.5 million was recognized during the current period.

## NOTE 5—SHARE CAPITAL AND CAPITAL IN EXCESS OF PAR VALUE:

| | Common Stock | | Class B Common Stock | | Treasury Stock | | Capital in Excess of Par Value |
|---|---|---|---|---|---|---|---|
| | Shares | Amount | Shares | Amount | Shares | Amount | |
| | (000's) | | (000's) | | (000's) | | |
| Balance at January 1, 2007 ............... | 35,364 | $24,558 | 18,390 | $12,771 | (62) | $(1,992) | $438,648 |
| Issuance of 3% stock dividend .............. | 1,056 | 733 | 550 | 383 | (1) | — | 45,404 |
| Conversion of Class B common shares to common shares ........................ | 48 | 34 | (48) | (34) | — | — | — |
| Purchase and retirement of common shares ......... | (1,064) | (739) | — | — | — | — | (26,561) |
| Balance at December 31, 2007 ............... | 35,404 | 24,586 | 18,892 | 13,120 | (63) | (1,992) | 457,491 |
| Issuance of 3% stock dividend .............. | 1,043 | 724 | 565 | 391 | (2) | — | 33,927 |
| Conversion of Class B common shares to common shares ........................ | 100 | 69 | (100) | (69) | — | — | — |
| Purchase and retirement of common shares ......... | (889) | (617) | — | — | — | — | (20,491) |
| Balance at December 31, 2008 ............... | 35,658 | 24,762 | 19,357 | 13,442 | (65) | (1,992) | 470,927 |
| Issuance of 3% stock dividend .............. | 1,064 | 739 | 580 | 403 | (2) | — | 31,396 |
| Conversion of Class B common shares to common shares ........................ | 18 | 12 | (18) | (12) | — | — | — |
| Purchase and retirement of common shares ......... | (938) | (651) | — | — | — | — | (20,073) |
| Balance at December 31, 2009 ............... | 35,802 | $24,862 | 19,919 | $13,833 | (67) | $(1,992) | $482,250 |

Average shares outstanding and all per share amounts included in the financial statements and notes thereto have been adjusted retroactively to reflect annual three percent stock dividends.

While the company does not have a formal or publicly announced stock repurchase program, the Company's board of directors periodically authorizes a dollar amount for share repurchases.

Based upon this policy, shares were purchased and retired as follows:

| Year | Total Number of Shares Purchased | Average Price Paid Per Share |
|---|---|---|
| 2009 ..... | 938 | $22.05 |
| 2008 ..... | 889 | $23.71 |
| 2007 ..... | 1,064 | $25.61 |

## NOTE 6—OTHER INCOME (EXPENSE), NET:

Other income (expense), net is comprised of the following:

| | 2009 | 2008 | 2007 |
|---|---|---|---|
| Interest and dividend income .. | $1,439 | $ 3,451 | $3,497 |
| Gains (losses) on trading securities relating to deferred compensation plans ................... | 4,524 | (7,334) | 1,998 |
| Interest expense ........... | (243) | (378) | (535) |
| Impairment of equity investment in joint venture ........... | (4,400) | — | — |
| Joint venture income (loss) ... | (233) | (477) | 182 |
| Foreign exchange gains (losses) ................ | 951 | (963) | 656 |
| Other than temporary impairment ............. | — | (5,140) | — |
| Capital gains (losses) ........ | (38) | 88 | 228 |
| Insurance recovery .......... | — | — | 128 |
| Miscellaneous, net .......... | 100 | 135 | 161 |
| | $2,100 | $(10,618) | $6,315 |

As of December 31, 2009, management determined that the carrying value of an equity investment in a joint venture was impaired as a result of accumulated losses from operations and review of future expectations. The Company recorded a pre-tax impairment charge of $4,400 resulting in an adjusted carrying value of $4,961 as of December 31, 2009. The fair value was primarily assessed using the present value of estimated future cash flows.

## NOTE 7—EMPLOYEE BENEFIT PLANS:

### Pension plans:

The Company sponsors defined contribution pension plans covering certain non-union employees with over one year of credited service. The Company's policy is to fund pension costs accrued based on compensation levels. Total pension expense for 2009, 2008 and 2007 approximated $4,178, $3,944 and $3,589, respectively. The Company also maintains certain profit sharing and retirement savings-investment plans. Company contributions in 2009, 2008 and 2007 to these plans were $1,011, $1,003 and $873, respectively.

The Company also contributes to multi-employer defined benefit pension plans for its union employees. Such contributions aggregated $1,633, $1,392 and $1,257 in 2009, 2008 and 2007, respectively. Although the Company has been advised that the plan is currently in an underfunded status, the relative position of each employer associated with the multi-employer plan with respect to the actuarial present value of benefits and net plan assets is not determinable by the Company.

### Deferred compensation:

The Company sponsors three deferred compensation plans for selected executives and other employees: (i) the Excess Benefit Plan, which restores retirement benefits lost due to IRS limitations on contributions to tax-qualified plans, (ii) the Supplemental Plan, which allows eligible employees to defer the receipt of eligible compensation until designated future dates and (iii) the Career Achievement Plan, which provides a deferred annual incentive award to selected executives. Participants in these plans earn a return on amounts due them based on several investment options, which mirror returns on underlying investments (primarily mutual funds). The Company economically hedges its obligations under the plans by investing in the actual underlying investments. These investments are classified as trading securities and are carried at fair value. At December 31, 2009 and 2008, these investments totaled $32,238 and $26,001, respectively. All gains and losses in these investments, which are recorded in other income (expense), net, are equally offset by corresponding increases and decreases in the Company's deferred compensation liabilities. The Company recorded a gain of $4,524 in 2009 and a loss of $7,334 in 2008 on these investments.

### Postretirement health care and life insurance benefit plans:

The Company provides certain postretirement health care and life insurance benefits for corporate office and management employees. Employees become eligible for these benefits based upon their age, service and date of hire and if they agree to contribute a portion of the cost. The Company has the right to modify or terminate these benefits. The Company does not fund postretirement health care and life insurance benefits in advance of payments for benefit claims.

Amounts recognized in accumulated other comprehensive loss (pre-tax) at December 31, 2009 are as follows:

| | |
|---|---|
| Prior service credit | $ (877) |
| Net actuarial loss | 2,523 |
| Net amount recognized in accumulated other comprehensive loss | $1,646 |

The estimated actuarial loss and prior service credit to be amortized from accumulated other comprehensive income into net periodic benefit cost during 2010 are $253 and $(125), respectively.

The changes in the accumulated postretirement benefit obligation at December 31, 2009 and 2008 consist of the following:

| | December 31, | |
|---|---|---|
| | 2009 | 2008 |
| Benefit obligation, beginning of year | $15,468 | $13,214 |
| Service cost | 704 | 646 |
| Interest cost | 853 | 740 |
| Actuarial (gain)/loss | (38) | 1,172 |
| Benefits paid | (313) | (304) |
| Benefit obligation, end of year | $16,674 | $15,468 |

Net periodic postretirement benefit cost included the following components:

| | 2009 | 2008 | 2007 |
|---|---|---|---|
| Service cost—benefits attributed to service during the period | $ 704 | $ 646 | $ 667 |
| Interest cost on the accumulated postretirement benefit obligation | 853 | 740 | 694 |
| Net amortization | 140 | 33 | 90 |
| Net periodic postretirement benefit cost | $1,697 | $1,419 | $1,451 |

For measurement purposes, the 2010 annual rate of increase in the per capita cost of covered health care benefits was assumed to be 6.0% for pre-age 65 retirees, 7.5% for post 65 retirees and 9.0% for prescription drugs; these rates were assumed to decrease gradually to 5.0% for 2014 and remain at that level thereafter. The health care cost trend rate assumption has a significant effect on the amounts reported. The weighted-average discount rate used in determining the accumulated postretirement benefit obligation was 5.84% and 5.6% at December 31, 2009 and 2008, respectively.

Increasing or decreasing the health care trend rates by one percentage point in each year would have the following effect:

| | 1% Increase | 1% Decrease |
|---|---|---|
| Postretirement benefit obligation | $2,337 | $(1,930) |
| Total of service and interest cost components | $ 258 | $ (209) |

The company estimates future benefit payments will be $539, $584, $693, $782 and $911 in 2010 through 2014, respectively, and a total of $5,976 in 2015 through 2019. The future benefit payments are net of the annual Medicare Part D subsidy of approximately $1,062 beginning in 2010.

### NOTE 8—COMMITMENTS:

Rental expense aggregated $1,180, $1,311 and $1,090 in 2009, 2008 and 2007, respectively.

Future operating lease commitments are not significant.

### NOTE 9—SEGMENT AND GEOGRAPHIC INFORMATION:

The Company operates as a single reportable segment encompassing the manufacture and sale of confectionery products. Its principal manufacturing operations are located in the United States and Canada, and its principal market is the United States. The company also manufactures and sells confectionery products in Mexico, and exports products to Canada and other countries worldwide.

The following geographic data include net product sales summarized on the basis of the customer location and long-lived assets based on their physical location.

| | 2009 | 2008 | 2007 |
|---|---|---|---|
| Net product sales: | | | |
| United States | $455,517 | $448,268 | $445,820 |
| Foreign | 40,075 | 43,783 | 46,922 |
| | $495,592 | $492,051 | $492,742 |
| Long-lived assets: | | | |
| United States | $176,044 | $172,299 | $155,340 |
| Foreign | 44,677 | 45,329 | 46,061 |
| | $220,721 | $217,628 | $201,401 |

## NOTE 10—FAIR VALUE MEASUREMENTS:

Current accounting guidance defines fair value as the price that would be received in the sale of an asset or paid to transfer a liability in an orderly transaction between market participants at the measurement date. Guidance requires disclosure of the extent to which fair value is used to measure financial assets and liabilities, the inputs utilized in calculating valuation measurements, and the effect of the measurement of significant unobservable inputs on earnings, or changes in net assets, as of the measurement date. Guidance establishes a three-level valuation hierarchy based upon the transparency of inputs utilized in the measurement and valuation of financial assets or liabilities as of the measurement date. Level 1 inputs include quoted prices for identical instruments and are the most observable. Level 2 inputs include quoted prices for similar assets and observable inputs such as interest rates, foreign currency exchange rates, commodity rates and yield curves. Level 3 inputs are not observable in the market and include management's own judgments about the assumptions market participants would use in pricing the asset or liability. The use of observable and unobservable inputs is reflected in the hierarchy assessment disclosed in the table below.

As of December 31, 2009 and 2008, the Company held certain financial assets that are required to be measured at fair value on a recurring basis. These included derivative hedging instruments related to the foreign currency forward contracts and purchase of certain raw materials, investments in trading securities and available for sale securities, including an auction rate security (ARS). The Company's available for sale and trading securities principally consist of municipal bonds and mutual funds that are publicly traded.

The following tables present information about the Company's financial assets measured at fair value as of December 31, 2009 and 2008, and indicate the fair value hierarchy and the valuation techniques utilized by the Company to determine such fair value:

| | Estimated Fair Value December 31, 2009 | | | |
|---|---|---|---|---|
| | Total Fair Value | Input Levels Used | | |
| | | Level 1 | Level 2 | Level 3 |
| Cash and equivalents | $ 90,990 | $ 90,990 | $ — | $ — |
| Auction rate security (ARS) | 7,710 | — | — | 7,710 |
| Available-for-sale securities, excluding ARS | 26,851 | — | 26,851 | — |
| Foreign currency forward contracts | 3,674 | 3,674 | — | — |
| Commodity option contracts | 1,686 | 1,686 | — | — |
| Trading securities | 32,238 | 32,238 | — | — |
| Total assets measured at fair value | $163,149 | $128,588 | $26,851 | $7,710 |

| | Estimated Fair Value December 31, 2008 | | | |
|---|---|---|---|---|
| | Total Fair Value | Input Levels Used | | |
| | | Level 1 | Level 2 | Level 3 |
| Cash and equivalents | $ 68,908 | $68,908 | $ — | $ — |
| Auction rate security (ARS) | 8,410 | — | — | 8,410 |
| Available-for-sale securities excluding ARS | 33,361 | — | 33,361 | — |
| Foreign currency forward contracts | 349 | 349 | — | — |
| Trading securities | 26,001 | 26,001 | — | — |
| Total assets measured at fair value | $137,029 | $95,258 | $33,361 | $8,410 |

Available for sale securities which utilize Level 2 inputs consist primarily of municipal bonds, which are valued based on quoted market prices or alternative pricing sources with reasonable levels of price transparency.

A summary of the aggregate fair value, gross unrealized gains, gross unrealized losses, realized losses and amortized cost basis of the Company's investment portfolio by major security type is as follows:

| | December 31, 2009 | | | | |
| | Amortized Cost | Fair Value | Unrealized Gains | Unrealized Losses | Realized Losses |
|---|---|---|---|---|---|
| Available for sale: | | | | | |
| Auction rate security (ARS) | $ 8,410 | $ 7,710 | $ — | $(700) | $ — |
| Municipal bonds | 26,502 | 26,793 | 291 | — | — |
| Mutual funds | 56 | 58 | 2 | — | — |
| | $34,968 | $34,561 | $293 | $(700) | $ — |

| | December 31, 2008 | | | | |
| | Amortized Cost | Fair Value | Unrealized Gains | Unrealized Losses | Realized Losses |
|---|---|---|---|---|---|
| Available for sale: | | | | | |
| Auction rate security (ARS) | $13,550 | $ 8,410 | $ — | $ — | $(5,140) |
| Municipal bonds | 33,003 | 33,303 | 300 | — | — |
| Mutual funds | 56 | 58 | 2 | — | — |
| | $46,609 | $41,771 | $302 | $ — | $(5,140) |

As of December 31, 2008, the Company's long-term investments included an auction rate security (ARS), Jefferson County Alabama Sewer Revenue Refunding Warrants, reported at a fair value of $8,410, after reflecting a $5,140 other-than-temporary impairment against its $13,550 par value. This other-than-temporary impairment was recorded in other income (expense), net in 2008. As of December 31, 2008, this ARS was determined to be other-than-temporarily impaired due to the duration and severity of the decline in fair value. An other-than-temporary impairment must be recorded when a credit loss exists; that is when the present value of the expected cash flows from a debt security is less than the amortized cost basis of the security. The Company determined the 2008 loss to be 100% related to credit loss. The Company estimated the fair value of this ARS utilizing a valuation model with Level 3 inputs as of December 31, 2008. This valuation model considered, among other items, the credit risk of the collateral underlying the ARS, the credit risk of the bond insurer, interest rates, and the amount and timing of expected future cash flows including the Company's assumption about the market expectation of the next successful auction. During the fourth quarter of 2009, the Company further evaluated this investment and concluded that an additional decline in the fair market value was temporary, as defined, and recorded $700 of such additional decline in the fair market value as a charge to accumulated other comprehensive loss. The impairment recorded in 2009 is considered temporary as it relates to liquidity and timing of cash flows and does not represent further credit loss.

The Company classified this ARS as non-current and has included it in long-term investments on the Consolidated Statements of Financial Position at December 31, 2009 and 2008, because the Company believes that the current condition of the ARS market may take more than twelve months to improve and the Company has the ability and intent to hold the security for the foreseeable future.

Based on market conditions, the Company changed its valuation methodology for the ARS to a discounted cash flow analysis during the first quarter of 2008. Accordingly, these securities changed from Level 2 to Level 3 within the accounting guidance hierarchy.

The following tables present additional information about the Company's financial instruments (all ARS) measured at fair value on a recurring basis using Level 3 inputs at December 31, 2009 and 2008:

| | 2009 | 2008 |
|---|---|---|
| Balance at January 1 | $8,410 | $ — |
| Transfers to Level 3 | — | 27,250 |
| Other-than-temporary impairment loss recognized in earnings | — | (5,140) |
| Unrealized loss recognized in other comprehensive loss | (700) | — |
| Sales, net | — | (13,700) |
| Balance at December 31 | $7,710 | $ 8,410 |

The $7,500 carrying amount of the Company's industrial revenue development bonds at December 31, 2009 and 2008 approximates its estimated fair value as the bonds have a floating interest rate.

In addition to assets and liabilities that are recorded at fair value on a recurring basis, guidance requires the Company to record assets and liabilities at fair value on a nonrecurring basis generally as a result of impairment charges. Assets measured at fair value on a nonrecurring basis during 2009 are summarized below:

| | Twelve Months Ended December 31, 2009 | | | | | |
| | Pre-Impairment Cost Basis | 2009 Impairment Charge | New Cost Basis | Level Used to Determine New Cost Basis | | |
| | | | | Level 1 | Level 2 | Level 3 |
|---|---|---|---|---|---|---|
| Investment in joint venture | $ 9,361 | $ 4,400 | $ 4,961 | $— | $— | $ 4,961 |
| Trademarks | 189,024 | 14,000 | 175,024 | — | — | 175,024 |
| Total | $198,385 | $18,400 | $179,985 | $— | $— | $179,985 |

As discussed in Note 6, during the fourth quarter of 2009 the Company recognized an impairment of $4,400 in an equity method investment based on Level 3 inputs.

As discussed in Note 12, during the fourth quarter of 2009 the Company recognized a trademark impairment of $14,000 based on Level 3 inputs.

## NOTE 11—COMPREHENSIVE EARNINGS (LOSS):

The following table sets forth information with respect to accumulated other comprehensive earnings (loss):

| | Foreign Currency Translation Adjustment | Unrealized Gain (Loss) on | | | Accumulated Other Comprehensive Earnings (Loss) |
| | | Investments | Derivatives | Postretirement and Pension Benefits | |
|---|---|---|---|---|---|
| Balance at January 1, 2007 | $(11,224) | $ (149) | $ (271) | $ (893) | $(12,537) |
| Unrealized gains (losses) | (272) | 469 | (462) | 588 | 323 |
| (Gains) losses reclassified to net earnings | — | (61) | 1,202 | — | 1,141 |
| Tax effect | — | (151) | (273) | (230) | (654) |
| Net of tax amount | (272) | 257 | 467 | 358 | 810 |
| Balance at December 31, 2007 | (11,496) | 108 | 196 | (535) | (11,727) |
| Unrealized gains (losses) | (2,296) | (4,923) | 504 | (1,484) | (8,199) |
| (Gains) losses reclassified to net earnings | — | 5,055 | (467) | — | 4,588 |
| Tax effect | (500) | (49) | (13) | 659 | 97 |
| Net of tax amount | (2,796) | 83 | 24 | (825) | (3,514) |
| Balance at December 31,2008 | (14,292) | 191 | 220 | (1,360) | (15,241) |
| Unrealized gains (losses) | 1,183 | (709) | 4,341 | 109 | 4,924 |
| (Gains) losses reclassified to net earnings | — | — | (1,015) | — | (1,015) |
| Tax effect | (118) | 263 | (1,232) | 23 | (1,064) |
| Net of tax amount | 1,065 | (446) | 2,094 | 132 | 2,845 |
| Balance at December 31, 2009 | $(13,227) | $ (255) | $ 2,314 | $(1,228) | $(12,396) |

## NOTE 12—GOODWILL AND INTANGIBLE ASSETS:

All of the Company's intangible indefinite-lived assets are trademarks.

As of December 31, 2009, management ascertained certain trademarks were impaired, and recorded a pre-tax charge of $14,000. The principal driver of this impairment charge was an increase in the discount rate required by market participants. The fair value of indefinite-lived intangible assets was primarily assessed using the present value of estimated future cash flows. No impairments of intangibles were recorded in 2008.

The changes in the carrying amount of trademarks for 2009 and 2008 were as follows:

| | 2009 | 2008 |
|---|---|---|
| Original cost . . . . . . . . . . . . . . . . . . . . . | $193,767 | $193,767 |
| Accumulated impairment losses as of January 1 . . . . . . . . . . . . . . . . | (4,743) | (4,743) |
| Balance at January 1 . . . . . . . . . . . . . | $189,024 | $189,024 |
| Current year impairment losses . . . . . . | (14,000) | — |
| Balance at December 31 . . . . . . . . . . . | $175,024 | $189,024 |
| Accumulated impairment losses as of December 31 . . . . . . . . . . . . . | $(18,743) | $ (4,743) |

The Company has no accumulated impairment losses of goodwill.

## Auditor's Report

All publicly held corporations, as well as many other businesses and organizations (both profit and not-for-profit, large and small), engage the services of independent certified public accountants (CPAs) for the purpose of obtaining an objective, expert report on their financial statements. Based on a comprehensive examination of the company's accounting system, accounting records, and the financial statements, the outside CPA issues the auditor's report.

The standard auditor's report should identify who and what was audited and indicate the responsibilities of management and the auditor relative to the financial statements. The report should clearly state that the audit was conducted in accordance with generally accepted auditing standards and discusses the nature and limitations of the audit. Finally, the report should express an informed opinion as to (1) the fairness of the financial statements and (2) their conformity with generally accepted accounting principales. The report of PricewaterhouseCoopers LLP appearing in Tootsie Roll's annual report is shown below.

# *Report of Independent Registered Public Accounting Firm*

To the Board of Directors and Shareholders of Tootsie Roll Industries, Inc.:

In our opinion, the accompanying consolidated statements of financial position and the related consolidated statements of earnings, comprehensive earnings and retained earnings, and of cash flows present fairly, in all material respects, the financial position of Tootsie Roll Industries, Inc. and its subsidiaries at December 31, 2009 and December 31, 2008, and the results of their operations and their cash flows for each of the three years in the period ended December 31, 2009 in conformity with accounting principles generally accepted in the United States of America. Also in our opinion, the Company maintained, in all material respects, effective internal control over financial reporting as of December 31, 2009, based on criteria established in *Internal Control—Integrated Framework* issued by the Committee of Sponsoring Organizations of the Treadway Commission (COSO). The Company's management is responsible for these financial statements and financial statement schedules, for maintaining effective internal control over financial reporting and for its assessment of the effectiveness of internal control over financial reporting, included in Management's Report on Internal Control over Financial Reporting on page 14 of the 2009 Annual Report to Shareholders. Our responsibility is to express opinions on these financial statements and on the Company's internal control over financial reporting based on our integrated audits. We conducted our audits in accordance with the standards of the Public Company Accounting Oversight Board (United States). Those standards require that we plan and perform the audits to obtain reasonable assurance about whether the financial statements are free of material misstatement and whether effective internal control over financial reporting was maintained in all material respects. Our audits of the financial statements included examining, on a test basis, evidence supporting the amounts and disclosures in the financial statements, assessing the accounting principles used and significant estimates made by management, and evaluating the overall financial statement presentation. Our audit of internal control over financial reporting included obtaining an understanding of internal control over financial reporting, assessing the risk that a material weakness exists, and testing and evaluating the design and operating effectiveness of internal control based on the assessed risk. Our audits also included performing such other procedures as we considered necessary in the circumstances. We believe that our audits provide a reasonable basis for our opinions.

A company's internal control over financial reporting is a process designed to provide reasonable assurance regarding the reliability of financial reporting and the preparation of financial statements for external purposes in accordance with generally accepted accounting principles. A company's internal control over financial reporting includes those policies and procedures that (i) pertain to the maintenance of records that, in reasonable detail, accurately and fairly reflect the transactions and dispositions of the assets of the company; (ii) provide reasonable assurance that transactions are recorded as necessary to permit preparation of financial statements in accordance with generally accepted accounting principles, and that receipts and expenditures of the company are being made only in accordance with authorizations of management and directors of the company; and (iii) provide reasonable assurance regarding prevention or timely detection of unauthorized acquisition, use, or disposition of the company's assets that could have a material effect on the financial statements.

Because of its inherent limitations, internal control over financial reporting may not prevent or detect misstatements. Also, projections of any evaluation of effectiveness to future periods are subject to the risk that controls may become inadequate because of changes in conditions, or that the degree of compliance with the policies or procedures may deteriorate.

*PricewaterhouseCoopers LLP*

Chicago, IL
March 1, 2010

# Supplementary Financial Information

In addition to the financial statements and the accompanying notes, companies often present supplementary financial information. Tootsie Roll has provided stock performance information, quarterly financial data, and a five-year summary of earnings and financial highlights, which are presented on the following pages.

# *Performance Graph*

The following performance graph compares the Company's cumulative total shareholder return on the Company's Common Stock for a five-year period (December 31, 2004 to December 31, 2009) with the cumulative total return of Standard & Poor's 500 Stock Index ("S&P 500") and the Dow Jones Industry Food Index ("Peer Group," which includes the Company), assuming (i) $100 invested on December 31 of the first year of the chart in each of the Company's Common Stock, S&P 500 and the Dow Jones Industry Food Index and (ii) the reinvestment of dividends.

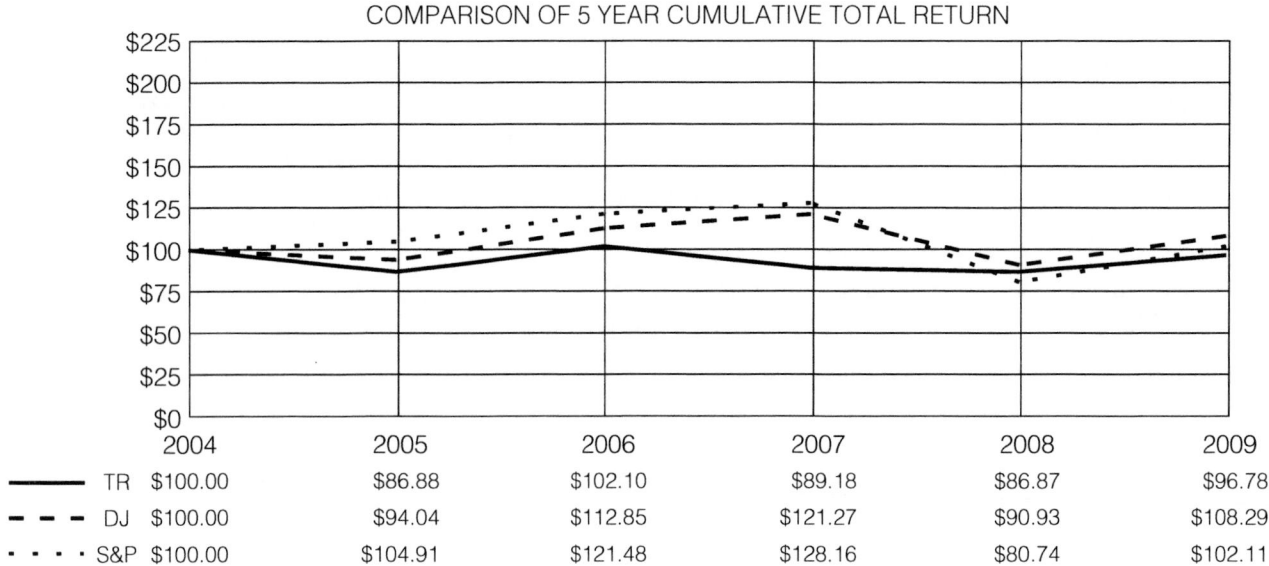

COMPARISON OF 5 YEAR CUMULATIVE TOTAL RETURN

| | 2004 | 2005 | 2006 | 2007 | 2008 | 2009 |
|---|---|---|---|---|---|---|
| TR | $100.00 | $86.88 | $102.10 | $89.18 | $86.87 | $96.78 |
| DJ | $100.00 | $94.04 | $112.85 | $121.27 | $90.93 | $108.29 |
| S&P | $100.00 | $104.91 | $121.48 | $128.16 | $80.74 | $102.11 |

# *Quarterly Financial Data (Unaudited)*

TOOTSIE ROLL INDUSTRIES, INC. AND SUBSIDIARIES

|  | (Thousands of dollars except per share data) | | | | |
| --- | --- | --- | --- | --- | --- |
| 2009 | First | Second | Third | Fourth | Total |
| Net product sales . . . . . . . . . . . . . . . . . . . | $94,054 | $107,812 | $183,408 | $110,318 | $495,592 |
| Product gross margin . . . . . . . . . . . . . . . . | 33,335 | 39,005 | 65,701 | 38,906 | 176,947 |
| Net earnings . . . . . . . . . . . . . . . . . . . . . . | 8,320 | 10,338 | 27,247 | 7,570 | 53,475 |
| Net earnings per share . . . . . . . . . . . . . . . | 0.15 | 0.18 | 0.49 | 0.14 | 0.95 |
| 2008 | | | | | |
| Net product sales . . . . . . . . . . . . . . . . . . . | $90,341 | $101,591 | $184,687 | $115,432 | $492,051 |
| Product gross margin . . . . . . . . . . . . . . . . | 29,712 | 32,850 | 59,293 | 36,882 | 158,737 |
| Net earnings . . . . . . . . . . . . . . . . . . . . . . | 6,453 | 7,246 | 19,715 | 5,363 | 38,777 |
| Net earnings per share . . . . . . . . . . . . . . . | 0.11 | 0.13 | 0.35 | 0.09 | 0.68 |

The 2009 fourth quarter net earnings included the release of tax valuation allowances, charges related to the impairment of an equity investment in joint venture and impairment charges related to certain trademarks as discussed in Notes 4, 6 and 12 to the Consolidated Financial Statements, respectively.

The 2008 fourth quarter net earnings included a charge for the other-than-temporary impairment of an auction rate security as discussed in Note 10 to the Consolidated Financial Statements.

Net earnings per share is based upon average outstanding shares as adjusted for 3% stock dividends issued during the second quarter of each year. The sum of the per share amounts may not equal annual amounts due to rounding.

2009-2008 QUARTERLY SUMMARY OF TOOTSIE ROLL INDUSTRIES, INC. STOCK PRICES AND DIVIDENDS PER SHARE

STOCK PRICES*

|  | 2009 | | 2008 | |
| --- | --- | --- | --- | --- |
|  | High | Low | High | Low |
| 1st Qtr . . . . . | $25.77 | $19.46 | $26.33 | $21.80 |
| 2nd Qtr . . . . | $24.42 | $21.82 | $27.26 | $23.27 |
| 3rd Qtr . . . . . | $24.64 | $22.67 | $31.35 | $23.67 |
| 4th Qtr . . . . . | $28.06 | $23.60 | $28.88 | $21.45 |

*NYSE—Closing Price

Estimated Number of shareholders at February 2010:

| | |
| --- | --- |
| Common Stock. . . . . . . . . . . . . . . . . . . . . . | 18,000 |
| Class B Common Stock . . . . . . . . . . . . . . . | 5,000 |

DIVIDENDS

|  | 2009 | 2008 |
| --- | --- | --- |
| 1st Qtr . . . . . | $.08 | $.08 |
| 2nd Qtr . . . . | $.08 | $.08 |
| 3rd Qtr . . . . . | $.08 | $.08 |
| 4th Qtr . . . . . | $.08 | $.08 |

NOTE: In addition to the above cash dividends, a 3% stock dividend was issued on April 9, 2009 and April 10, 2008. Cash dividends are not restated to reflect 3% stock dividends.

# *Five Year Summary of Earnings and Financial Highlights*

TOOTSIE ROLL INDUSTRIES, INC. AND SUBSIDIARIES

(Thousands of dollars except per share, percentage and ratio figures)

(See management's comments starting on page 5)

| | 2009 | 2008 | 2007 | 2006 | 2005 |
|---|---|---|---|---|---|
| **Sales and Earnings Data (2)(3)(4)** | | | | | |
| Net product sales . . . . . . . . . . . . . . | $ 495,592 | $492,051 | $492,742 | $495,990 | $487,739 |
| Product gross margin . . . . . . . . . . . . | 176,947 | 158,737 | 165,047 | 184,723 | 188,056 |
| Interest expense . . . . . . . . . . . . . . | 243 | 378 | 535 | 726 | 2,537 |
| Provision for income taxes . . . . . . . . | 10,704 | 17,132 | 25,542 | 28,796 | 36,425 |
| Net earnings . . . . . . . . . . . . . . . . . . | 53,475 | 38,777 | 51,625 | 65,919 | 77,227 |
| % of net product sales . . . . . . . . | 10.8% | 7.9% | 10.5% | 13.3% | 15.8% |
| % of shareholders' equity . . . . . . | 8.2% | 6.1% | 8.1% | 10.5% | 12.5% |
| **Per Common Share Data (1)(3)(4)** | | | | | |
| Net earnings . . . . . . . . . . . . . . . . . . | $   0.95 | $   0.68 | $   0.89 | $   1.12 | $   1.29 |
| Cash dividends declared . . . . . . . . . | 0.32 | 0.32 | 0.32 | 0.32 | 0.29 |
| Stock dividends . . . . . . . . . . . . . . . . | 3% | 3% | 3% | 3% | 3% |
| **Additional Financial Data (2)(3)(4)** | | | | | |
| Working capital . . . . . . . . . . . . . . . . | $ 155,812 | $129,967 | $141,754 | $128,706 | $132,940 |
| Net cash provided by operating activities . . . . . . . . . . . . . . . . . . . . | 75,281 | 57,042 | 90,064 | 55,656 | 82,524 |
| Net cash provided by (used in) investing activities . . . . . . . . . . . . . | (14,651) | (7,074) | (43,345) | 11,026 | 21,872 |
| Net cash provided by (used in) financing activities . . . . . . . . . . . . . | (38,548) | (38,666) | (44,842) | (79,959) | (92,379) |
| Property, plant & equipment additions . . . . . . . . . . . . . . . . . . . . | 20,831 | 34,355 | 14,767 | 39,207 | 14,690 |
| Net property, plant & equipment . . . . . | 220,721 | 217,628 | 201,401 | 202,898 | 178,760 |
| Total assets . . . . . . . . . . . . . . . . . . . | 838,247 | 813,525 | 812,725 | 791,639 | 813,696 |
| Long term debt . . . . . . . . . . . . . . . . . | 7,500 | 7,500 | 7,500 | 7,500 | 7,500 |
| Shareholders' equity . . . . . . . . . . . . . | 652,485 | 634,770 | 638,230 | 630,681 | 617,405 |
| Average shares outstanding (1) . . . . . | 56,072 | 56,799 | 58,227 | 59,048 | 59,980 |

(1) Adjusted for annual 3% stock dividends.

(2) Certain reclassifications have been made to prior year numbers to conform to current year presentation.

(3) The 2009 data included the release of tax valuation allowances, charges related to the impairment of an equity investment in joint venture and impairment charges related to certain trademarks as discussed in Notes 4, 6 and 12 to the Consolidated Financial Statements, respectively.

(4) The 2008 data included a charge for the other-than-temporary impairment of an auction rate security. Further information is included in Note 10 to the Consolidated Financial Statements.

# SPECIMEN FINANCIAL STATEMENTS: THE HERSHEY COMPANY

**THE HERSHEY COMPANY**

**CONSOLIDATED STATEMENTS OF INCOME**

| For the years ended December 31,<br>In thousands of dollars except per share amounts | 2009 | 2008 | 2007 |
|---|---|---|---|
| **Net Sales** | **$5,298,668** | $5,132,768 | $4,946,716 |
| **Costs and Expenses:** | | | |
| Cost of sales | **3,245,531** | 3,375,050 | 3,315,147 |
| Selling, marketing and administrative | **1,208,672** | 1,073,019 | 895,874 |
| Business realignment and impairment charges, net | **82,875** | 94,801 | 276,868 |
| Total costs and expenses | **4,537,078** | 4,542,870 | 4,487,889 |
| **Income before Interest and Income Taxes** | **761,590** | 589,898 | 458,827 |
| Interest expense, net | **90,459** | 97,876 | 118,585 |
| **Income before Income Taxes** | **671,131** | 492,022 | 340,242 |
| Provision for income taxes | **235,137** | 180,617 | 126,088 |
| **Net Income** | **$ 435,994** | $ 311,405 | $ 214,154 |
| **Net Income Per Share—Basic—Class B Common Stock** | **$ 1.77** | $ 1.27 | $ .87 |
| **Net Income Per Share—Diluted—Class B Common Stock** | **$ 1.77** | $ 1.27 | $ .87 |
| **Net Income Per Share—Basic—Common Stock** | **$ 1.97** | $ 1.41 | $ .96 |
| **Net Income Per Share—Diluted—Common Stock** | **$ 1.90** | $ 1.36 | $ .93 |
| **Cash Dividends Paid Per Share:** | | | |
| Common Stock | **$ 1.1900** | $ 1.1900 | $ 1.1350 |
| Class B Common Stock | **1.0712** | 1.0712 | 1.0206 |

**The notes to consolidated financial statements are an integral part of these statements.**

## THE HERSHEY COMPANY

### CONSOLIDATED BALANCE SHEETS

| December 31,<br>In thousands of dollars | 2009 | 2008 |
|---|---|---|
| **ASSETS** | | |
| **Current Assets:** | | |
| Cash and cash equivalents | $ 253,605 | $ 37,103 |
| Accounts receivable—trade | 410,390 | 455,153 |
| Inventories | 519,712 | 592,530 |
| Deferred income taxes | 39,868 | 70,903 |
| Prepaid expenses and other | 161,859 | 189,256 |
| Total current assets | 1,385,434 | 1,344,945 |
| **Property, Plant and Equipment, Net** | 1,404,767 | 1,458,949 |
| **Goodwill** | 571,580 | 554,677 |
| **Other Intangibles** | 125,520 | 110,772 |
| **Deferred Income Taxes** | 4,353 | 13,815 |
| **Other Assets** | 183,377 | 151,561 |
| Total assets | $ 3,675,031 | $ 3,634,719 |
| **LIABILITIES AND STOCKHOLDERS' EQUITY** | | |
| **Current Liabilities:** | | |
| Accounts payable | $ 287,935 | $ 249,454 |
| Accrued liabilities | 546,462 | 504,065 |
| Accrued income taxes | 36,918 | 15,189 |
| Short-term debt | 24,066 | 483,120 |
| Current portion of long-term debt | 15,247 | 18,384 |
| Total current liabilities | 910,628 | 1,270,212 |
| **Long-term Debt** | 1,502,730 | 1,505,954 |
| **Other Long-term Liabilities** | 501,334 | 504,963 |
| **Deferred Income Taxes** | — | 3,646 |
| Total liabilities | 2,914,692 | 3,284,775 |
| **Commitments and Contingencies** | — | — |
| **Stockholders' Equity:** | | |
| The Hershey Company Stockholders' Equity | | |
| Preferred Stock, shares issued: none in 2009 and 2008 | — | — |
| Common Stock, shares issued: 299,192,836 in 2009 and 299,190,836 in 2008 | 299,192 | 299,190 |
| Class B Common Stock, shares issued: 60,708,908 in 2009 and 60,710,908 in 2008 | 60,709 | 60,711 |
| Additional paid-in capital | 394,678 | 352,375 |
| Retained earnings | 4,148,353 | 3,975,762 |
| Treasury—Common Stock shares, at cost: 131,903,468 in 2009 and 132,866,673 in 2008 | (3,979,629) | (4,009,931) |
| Accumulated other comprehensive loss | (202,844) | (359,908) |
| The Hershey Company stockholders' equity | 720,459 | 318,199 |
| Noncontrolling interests in subsidiaries | 39,880 | 31,745 |
| Total stockholders' equity | 760,339 | 349,944 |
| Total liabilities and stockholders'equity | $ 3,675,031 | $ 3,634,719 |

**The notes to consolidated financial statements are an integral part of these balance sheets.**

## THE HERSHEY COMPANY

## CONSOLIDATED STATEMENTS OF CASH FLOWS

| For the years ended December 31,<br>In thousands of dollars | 2009 | 2008 | 2007 |
|---|---|---|---|
| **Cash Flows Provided from (Used by) Operating Activities** | | | |
| Net income | $ 435,994 | $ 311,405 | $ 214,154 |
| Adjustments to reconcile net income to net cash provided from operations: | | | |
| Depreciation and amortization | 182,411 | 249,491 | 310,925 |
| Stock-based compensation expense, net of tax of $19,223, $13,265 and $10,634, respectively | 34,927 | 23,583 | 18,987 |
| Excess tax benefits from exercise of stock options | (4,455) | (1,387) | (9,461) |
| Deferred income taxes | (40,578) | (17,125) | (124,276) |
| Business realignment and impairment charges, net of tax of $38,308, $61,553 and $144,928, respectively | 60,823 | 119,117 | 267,653 |
| Contributions to pension plans | (54,457) | (32,759) | (15,836) |
| Changes in assets and liabilities, net of effects from business acquisitions and divestitures: | | | |
| Accounts receivable—trade | 46,584 | 31,675 | 40,467 |
| Inventories | 74,000 | 7,681 | 45,348 |
| Accounts payable | 37,228 | 26,435 | 62,204 |
| Other assets and liabilities | 293,272 | (198,555) | (31,329) |
| Net Cash Provided from Operating Activities | 1,065,749 | 519,561 | 778,836 |
| **Cash Flows Provided from (Used by) Investing Activities** | | | |
| Capital additions | (126,324) | (262,643) | (189,698) |
| Capitalized software additions | (19,146) | (20,336) | (14,194) |
| Proceeds from sales of property, plant and equipment | 10,364 | 82,815 | — |
| Business acquisitions | (15,220) | — | (100,461) |
| Proceeds from divestitures | — | 1,960 | — |
| Net Cash (Used by) Investing Activities | (150,326) | (198,204) | (304,353) |
| **Cash Flows Provided from (Used by) Financing Activities** | | | |
| Net change in short-term borrowings | (458,047) | (371,393) | 195,055 |
| Long-term borrowings | — | 247,845 | — |
| Repayment of long-term debt | (8,252) | (4,977) | (188,891) |
| Cash dividends paid | (263,403) | (262,949) | (252,263) |
| Exercise of stock options | 28,318 | 36,996 | 50,497 |
| Excess tax benefits from exercise of stock options | 4,455 | 1,387 | 9,461 |
| Contributions from noncontrolling interests in subsidiaries | 7,322 | — | — |
| Repurchase of Common Stock | (9,314) | (60,361) | (256,285) |
| Net Cash (Used by) Financing Activities | (698,921) | (413,452) | (442,426) |
| Increase (Decrease) in Cash and Cash Equivalents | 216,502 | (92,095) | 32,057 |
| Cash and Cash Equivalents as of January 1 | 37,103 | 129,198 | 97,141 |
| Cash and Cash Equivalents as of December 31 | $ 253,605 | $ 37,103 | $ 129,198 |
| Interest Paid | $ 91,623 | $ 97,364 | $ 126,450 |
| Income Taxes Paid | 252,230 | 197,661 | 253,977 |

**The notes to consolidated financial statements are an integral part of these statements.**

## THE HERSHEY COMPANY
## CONSOLIDATED STATEMENTS OF STOCKHOLDERS' EQUITY

In thousands of dollars

| | Preferred Stock | Common Stock | Class B Common Stock | Additional Paid-in Capital | Retained Earnings | Treasury Common Stock | Accumulated Other Comprehensive Income (Loss) | Noncontrolling Interests in Subsidiaries | Total Stockholders' Equity |
|---|---|---|---|---|---|---|---|---|---|
| **Balance as of January 1, 2007** | $— | $299,085 | $60,816 | $298,243 | $3,965,415 | $(3,801,947) | $(138,189) | $ — | $683,423 |
| Net income | | | | | 214,154 | | | | 214,154 |
| Other comprehensive income | | | | | | | 110,210 | | 110,210 |
| Comprehensive income | | | | | | | | | 324,364 |
| Dividends: | | | | | | | | | |
| Common Stock, $1.135 per share | | | | | (190,199) | | | | (190,199) |
| Class B Common Stock, $1.0206 per share | | | | | (62,064) | | | | (62,064) |
| Conversion of Class B Common Stock into Common Stock | | 10 | (10) | | | | | | — |
| Incentive plan transactions | | | | 1,426 | | 2,082 | | | 3,508 |
| Stock-based compensation | | | | 29,790 | | | | | 29,790 |
| Exercise of stock options | | | | 5,797 | | 54,588 | | | 60,385 |
| Repurchase of Common Stock | | | | | | (256,285) | | | (256,285) |
| Noncontrolling interests in subsidiaries | | | | | | | | 30,598 | 30,598 |
| **Balance as of December 31, 2007** | | 299,095 | 60,806 | 335,256 | 3,927,306 | (4,001,562) | (27,979) | 30,598 | 623,520 |
| Net income | | | | | 311,405 | | | | 311,405 |
| Other comprehensive loss | | | | | | | (331,929) | | (331,929) |
| Comprehensive loss | | | | | | | | | (20,524) |
| Dividends: | | | | | | | | | |
| Common Stock, $1.19 per share | | | | | (197,839) | | | | (197,839) |
| Class B Common Stock, $1.0712 per share | | | | | (65,110) | | | | (65,110) |
| Conversion of Class B Common Stock into Common Stock | | 95 | (95) | | | | | | — |
| Incentive plan transactions | | | | (422) | | 12,989 | | | 12,567 |
| Stock-based compensation | | | | 18,161 | | | | | 18,161 |
| Exercise of stock options | | | | (620) | | 39,003 | | | 38,383 |
| Repurchase of Common Stock | | | | | | (60,361) | | | (60,361) |
| Noncontrolling interests in subsidiaries | | | | | | | | 1,147 | 1,147 |
| **Balance as of December 31, 2008** | | 299,190 | 60,711 | 352,375 | 3,975,762 | (4,009,931) | (359,908) | 31,745 | 349,944 |
| Net income | | | | | 435,994 | | | | 435,994 |
| Other comprehensive income | | | | | | | 157,064 | | 157,064 |
| Comprehensive income | | | | | | | | | 593,058 |
| Dividends: | | | | | | | | | |
| Common Stock, $1.19 per share | | | | | (198,371) | | | | (198,371) |
| Class B Common Stock, $1.0712 per share | | | | | (65,032) | | | | (65,032) |
| Conversion of Class B Common Stock into Common Stock | | 2 | (2) | | | | | | — |
| Incentive plan transactions | | | | (355) | | 4,762 | | | 4,407 |
| Stock-based compensation | | | | 44,704 | | | | | 44,704 |
| Exercise of stock options | | | | (2,046) | | 34,854 | | | 32,808 |
| Repurchase of Common Stock | | | | | | (9,314) | | | (9,314) |
| Noncontrolling interests in subsidiaries | | | | | | | | 8,135 | 8,135 |
| **Balance as of December 31, 2009** | $— | $299,192 | $60,709 | $394,678 | $4,148,353 | $(3,979,629) | $(202,844) | $39,880 | $760,339 |

**The notes to consolidated financial statements are an integral part of these statements.**

# SPECIMEN FINANCIAL STATEMENTS: ZETAR PLC

## CONSOLIDATED INCOME STATEMENT
**FOR THE YEAR ENDED 30 APRIL 2009**

| | Note | 2009 Adjusted results £'000 | 2009 Adjusting items £'000 | 2009 Total £'000 | 2008 Adjusted results £'000 | 2008 Adjusting items £'000 | 2008 Total £'000 |
|---|---|---|---|---|---|---|---|
| **Continuing operations** | | | | | | | |
| Revenue | 3 | 118,602 | — | 118,602 | 109,216 | — | 109,216 |
| Cost of sales | | (93,857) | — | (93,857) | (83,938) | — | (83,938) |
| Gross profit | | 24,745 | — | 24,745 | 25,278 | — | 25,278 |
| Distribution costs | | (4,777) | — | (4,777) | (5,013) | — | (5,013) |
| Administrative expenses | | | | | | | |
| – Other administrative expenses | | (13,917) | — | (13,917) | (11,541) | — | (11,541) |
| – One-off items | 4 | — | (1,508) | (1,508) | — | — | — |
| – Amortisation of intangible assets | 14 | — | (456) | (456) | — | (675) | (675) |
| – Share-based payments | 9 | — | 116 | 116 | — | (377) | (377) |
| Operating profit | | 6,051 | (1,848) | 4,203 | 8,724 | (1,052) | 7,672 |
| Interest income | 8 | 47 | — | 47 | 116 | — | 116 |
| Finance costs | 8 | (1,556) | (680) | (2,236) | (1,733) | (144) | (1,877) |
| Profit from continuing operations before taxation | | 4,542 | (2,528) | 2,014 | 7,107 | (1,196) | 5,911 |
| Tax on profit from continuing activities | 10 | (1,241) | — | (1,241) | (2,034) | 179 | (1,855) |
| Net result from continuing operations | | 3,301 | (2,528) | 773 | 5,073 | (1,017) | 4,056 |
| Net result from discontinued operations | 11 | — | (5,836) | (5,836) | — | (811) | (811) |
| Net result for the period | | 3,301 | (8,364) | (5,063) | 5,073 | (1,828) | 3,245 |
| Basic (losses)/earnings per share (p) | 12 | | | (42.9) | | | 29.5 |
| Diluted (losses)/earnings per share (p) | 12 | | | (42.6) | | | 25.9 |
| Adjusted basic earnings per share (p) | 12 | 28.0 | | | 46.2 | | |
| Adjusted diluted earnings per share (p) | 12 | 27.8 | | | 40.5 | | |

# CONSOLIDATED BALANCE SHEET
## AT 30 APRIL 2009

|  | Note | 2009 £'000 | 2008 £'000 |
|---|---|---|---|
| **Non-current assets** | | | |
| Goodwill | 13 | 30,821 | 32,363 |
| Other intangible assets | 14 | 623 | 1,002 |
| Property, plant and equipment | 15 | 15,283 | 18,545 |
| Deferred tax asset | 21 | 198 | 167 |
| | | 46,925 | 52,077 |
| **Current assets** | | | |
| Inventories | 16 | 14,319 | 13,364 |
| Trade and other receivables | 17 | 19,190 | 15,253 |
| Derivative financial asset | 30 | — | 72 |
| Cash at bank | 26 | 5,405 | 3,175 |
| | | 38,914 | 31,864 |
| **Total assets** | | 85,839 | 83,941 |
| **Current liabilities** | | | |
| Trade and other payables | 18 | (23,763) | (20,337) |
| Performance related contingent consideration | | (220) | (876) |
| Current tax liabilities | | (252) | (687) |
| Obligations under finance leases | 19 | (214) | (470) |
| Derivative financial instruments | 30 | (607) | — |
| Borrowings and overdrafts | 20 | (15,712) | (9,289) |
| | | (40,768) | (31,659) |
| **Net current (liabilities)/assets** | | (1,854) | 205 |
| **Non-current liabilities** | | | |
| Performance related contingent consideration | | (300) | (2,555) |
| Deferred tax liabilities | 21 | (1,575) | (1,448) |
| Obligations under finance leases | 19 | (167) | (369) |
| Borrowings and overdrafts | 20 | (4,676) | (7,609) |
| | | (6,718) | (11,981) |
| **Total liabilities** | | (47,486) | (43,640) |
| **Net assets** | | 38,353 | 40,301 |
| **Equity** | | | |
| Share capital | 22 | 1,324 | 1,151 |
| Share premium account | 23 | 28,252 | 26,449 |
| Merger reserve | | 3,411 | 3,411 |
| Equity reserve | 24 | 2,719 | 1,431 |
| Retained earnings | 24 | 2,647 | 7,859 |
| **Total equity attributable to equity holders of the parent** | | 38,353 | 40,301 |

# CONSOLIDATED STATEMENT OF CHANGES IN EQUITY
**FOR THE YEAR ENDED 30 APRIL 2009**

| | Share capital £'000 | Share premium account £'000 | Merger reserve £'000 | Equity reserve £'000 | Retained earnings £'000 | Total £'000 |
|---|---|---|---|---|---|---|
| Balance at 1 May 2007 | 1,073 | 22,673 | 3,229 | 621 | 4,914 | 32,510 |
| Profit for the year | — | — | — | — | 3,245 | 3,245 |
| Exchange gain on translation of foreign operation | — | — | — | 557 | — | 557 |
| Issue of new ordinary shares | 78 | 3,776 | 182 | — | — | 4,036 |
| Purchase of own shares | — | — | — | — | (300) | (300) |
| Share-based payment charge | — | — | — | 377 | — | 377 |
| Deferred tax on share-based payments | — | — | — | (124) | — | (124) |
| Balance at 30 April 2008 | 1,151 | 26,449 | 3,411 | 1,431 | 7,859 | 40,301 |
| Loss for the year | — | — | — | — | (5,063) | (5,063) |
| Exchange gain on translation of foreign operations | — | — | — | 1,404 | — | 1,404 |
| Issue of new ordinary shares | 173 | 1,803 | — | — | — | 1,976 |
| Purchase of own shares | — | — | — | — | (149) | (149) |
| Prior year share-based payment reversal | — | — | — | (116) | — | (116) |
| Balance at 30 April 2009 | 1,324 | 28,252 | 3,411 | 2,719 | 2,647 | 38,353 |

Attributable to equity holders of the parent

# CONSOLIDATED CASH FLOW STATEMENT
## FOR THE YEAR ENDED 30 APRIL 2009

| | Note | 2009 £'000 | 2008 £'000 |
|---|---|---|---|
| **Cash flow from operating activities** | | | |
| Profit on ordinary activities before taxation | | 2,014 | 5,911 |
| Finance costs | | 2,236 | 1,877 |
| Interest income | | (47) | (116) |
| Share-based payments | | (116) | 377 |
| Depreciation (including trademark amortisation) | 15 | 2,346 | 1,989 |
| Loss on sale of plant and equipment | | 22 | 6 |
| Amortisation of intangible assets | | 457 | 675 |
| One-off items | | 1,388 | — |
| Net movement in working capital | | (2,469) | (1,011) |
| Increase in inventories | | (1,299) | (2,646) |
| (Increase)/decrease in receivables | | (4,504) | 4,075 |
| Decrease/(increase) in payables | | 3,334 | (2,440) |
| **Cash flow from continuing operations** | | 5,831 | 9,708 |
| **Cash flow from discontinued operations** | | (1,002) | (1,260) |
| **Total cash flow from operations** | | 4,829 | 8,448 |
| Net interest paid | 8 | (1,510) | (1,646) |
| Tax paid | | (782) | (1,682) |
| **Cash generated from activities in continuing operations** | | 3,539 | 6,380 |
| **Cash flow generated from operating activities in discontinued operations** | | (1,002) | (1,260) |
| **Total cash flow from operating activities** | | 2,537 | 5,120 |
| **Cash flow from investing activities** | | | |
| Purchase of property, plant and equipment | | (3,847) | (3,722) |
| Proceeds from sale of plant and equipment | | 42 | 26 |
| Disposal of subsidiary | 11 | (220) | — |
| Total cash impact of acquisitions | | (879) | (3,733) |
| Acquisitions of businesses (including contingent consideration) | | (879) | (2,814) |
| Net borrowings assumed on acquisition | | — | (919) |
| **Net cash outflow from continuing investing activities** | | (4,904) | (7,429) |
| **Net cash outflow from discontinued investing activities** | | — | (5,244) |
| **Net cash flow from investing activities** | | (4,904) | (12,673) |
| **Cash flow from financing activities** | | | |
| Net proceeds from issue of ordinary share capital | | 1,976 | 3,851 |
| Purchase of own shares | | (149) | (300) |
| Proceeds from new borrowings | | — | 5,000 |
| Repayment of borrowings | | (3,536) | (4,819) |
| Finance lease repayments | | (457) | (472) |
| Minority interest dividends paid | | — | — |
| **Net cash flow from financing activities** | | (2,166) | 3,260 |
| **Net decrease in cash and cash equivalents** | | (4,533) | (4,293) |
| Cash and cash equivalents at beginning of the year | | (3,331) | 917 |
| Effect of foreign exchange rate movements | | (263) | 45 |
| **Cash and cash equivalents at end of the year** | | (8,127) | (3,331) |
| **Cash and cash equivalents comprise:** | | | |
| Cash at bank | 26 | 5,405 | 3,175 |
| Bank overdraft | 26 | (13,532) | (6,506) |
| | | (8,127) | (3,331) |

# TIME VALUE OF MONEY

## study objectives

**After studying this appendix, you should be able to:**

**1** Distinguish between simple and compound interest.

**2** Solve for future value of a single amount.

**3** Solve for future value of an annuity.

**4** Identify the variables fundamental to solving present value problems.

**5** Solve for present value of a single amount.

**6** Solve for present value of an annuity.

**7** Compute the present value of notes and bonds.

**8** Compute the present values in capital budgeting situations.

**9** Use a financial calculator to solve time value of money problems.

Would you rather receive $1,000 today or a year from now? You should prefer to receive the $1,000 today because you can invest the $1,000 and earn interest on it. As a result, you will have more than $1,000 a year from now. What this example illustrates is the concept of the **time value of money**. Everyone prefers to receive money today rather than in the future because of the interest factor.

## Nature of Interest

Interest is payment for the use of another person's money. It is the difference between the amount borrowed or invested (called the principal) and the amount repaid or collected. The amount of interest to be paid or collected is usually stated as a rate over a specific period of time. The rate of interest is generally stated as an annual rate.

The amount of interest involved in any financing transaction is based on three elements:

1. **Principal ($p$):** The original amount borrowed or invested.
2. **Interest Rate ($i$):** An annual percentage of the principal.
3. **Time ($n$):** The number of years that the principal is borrowed or invested.

### SIMPLE INTEREST

Simple interest is computed on the principal amount only. It is the return on the principal for one period. Simple interest is usually expressed as shown in Illustration D-1.

**study objective** **1**

Distinguish between simple and compound interest.

**Illustration D-1** Interest computation

| Interest | = | **Principal** $p$ | × | **Rate** $i$ | × | **Time** $n$ |
|---|---|---|---|---|---|---|

For example, if you borrowed $5,000 for 2 years at a simple interest rate of 12% annually, you would pay $1,200 in total interest, computed as follows.

$$
\begin{aligned}
\text{Interest} &= p \times i \times n \\
&= \$5{,}000 \times .12 \times 2 \\
&= \$1{,}200
\end{aligned}
$$

## COMPOUND INTEREST

Compound interest is computed on principal **and** on any interest earned that has not been paid or withdrawn. It is the return on (or growth of) the principal for two or more time periods. Compounding computes interest not only on the principal but also on the interest earned to date on that principal, assuming the interest is left on deposit.

To illustrate the difference between simple and compound interest, assume that you deposit $1,000 in Bank Two, where it will earn simple interest of 9% per year, and you deposit another $1,000 in Citizens Bank, where it will earn compound interest of 9% per year compounded annually. Also assume that in both cases you will not withdraw any cash until three years from the date of deposit. Illustration D-2 shows the computation of interest to be received and the accumulated year-end balances.

**Illustration D-2** Simple versus compound interest

| Bank Two | | | | Citizens Bank | | |
|---|---|---|---|---|---|---|
| Simple Interest Calculation | Simple Interest | Accumulated Year-End Balance | | Compound Interest Calculation | Compound Interest | Accumulated Year-End Balance |
| Year 1 $1,000.00 × 9% | $ 90.00 | $1,090.00 | | Year 1 $1,000.00 × 9% | $ 90.00 | $1,090.00 |
| Year 2 $1,000.00 × 9% | 90.00 | $1,180.00 | | Year 2 $1,090.00 × 9% | 98.10 | $1,188.10 |
| Year 3 $1,000.00 × 9% | 90.00 | $1,270.00 | | Year 3 $1,188.10 × 9% | 106.93 | $1,295.03 |
| | $ 270.00 | | | | $ 295.03 | |

$25.03 Difference

Note in Illustration D-2 that simple interest uses the initial principal of $1,000 to compute the interest in all three years. Compound interest uses the accumulated balance (principal plus interest to date) at each year-end to compute interest in the succeeding year—which explains why your compound interest account is larger.

Obviously, if you had a choice between investing your money at simple interest or at compound interest, you would choose compound interest, all other things—especially risk—being equal. In the example, compounding provides $25.03 of additional interest income. For practical purposes, compounding assumes that unpaid interest earned becomes a part of the principal, and the accumulated balance at the end of each year becomes the new principal on which interest is earned during the next year.

Illustration D-2 indicates that you should invest your money at a bank that compounds interest. Most business situations use compound interest. Simple interest is generally applicable only to short-term situations of one year or less.

# Future Value Concepts

## Future Value of a Single Amount

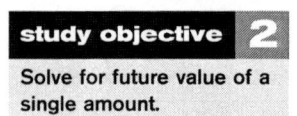

Solve for future value of a single amount.

The future value of a single amount is the value at a future date of a given amount invested, assuming compound interest. For example, in Illustration D-2, $1,295.03 is the future value of the $1,000 investment earning 9% for three years. The $1,295.03 could be determined more easily by using the following formula.

$$FV = p \times (1 + i)^n$$

where:

$$FV = \text{future value of a single amount}$$
$$p = \text{principal (or present value; the value today)}$$
$$i = \text{interest rate for one period}$$
$$n = \text{number of periods}$$

The $1,295.03 is computed as follows.

$$
\begin{aligned}
FV &= p \times (1 + i)^n \\
&= \$1,000 \times (1 + .09)^3 \\
&= \$1,000 \times 1.29503 \\
&= \$1,295.03
\end{aligned}
$$

The 1.29503 is computed by multiplying $(1.09 \times 1.09 \times 1.09)$. The amounts in this example can be depicted in the time diagram shown in Illustration D-4.

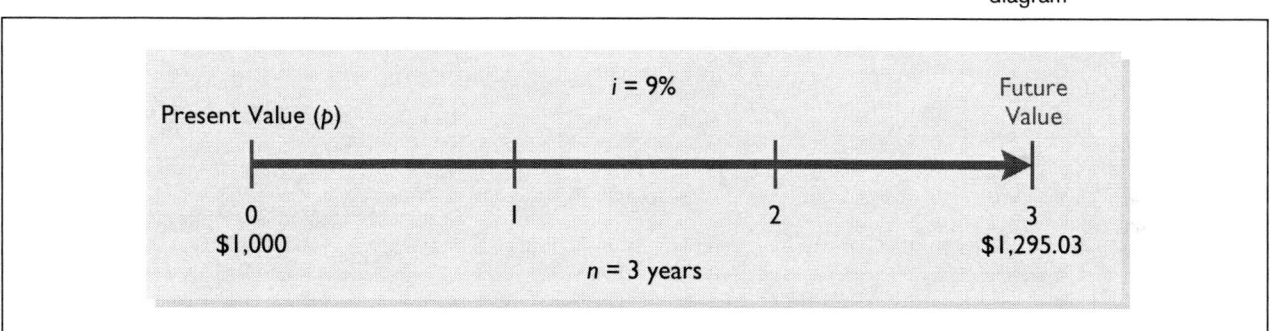

Another method used to compute the future value of a single amount involves a compound interest table. This table shows the future value of 1 for $n$ periods. Table 1 on the next page is such a table.

In Table 1, $n$ is the number of compounding periods, the percentages are the periodic interest rates, and the 5-digit decimal numbers in the respective columns are the future value of 1 factors. In using Table 1, you would multiply the principal amount by the future value factor for the specified number of periods and interest rate. For example, the future value factor for two periods at 9% is 1.18810. Multiplying this factor by $1,000 equals $1,188.10—which is the accumulated balance at the end of year 2 in the Citizens Bank example in Illustration D-2. The $1,295.03 accumulated balance at the end of the third year can be calculated from Table 1 by multiplying the future value factor for three periods (1.29503) by the $1,000.

The demonstration problem in Illustration D-5 (page D-4) shows how to use Table 1.

**TABLE 1    Future Value of 1**

| (n) Periods | 4% | 5% | 6% | 8% | 9% | 10% | 11% | 12% | 15% |
|---|---|---|---|---|---|---|---|---|---|
| 0 | 1.00000 | 1.00000 | 1.00000 | 1.00000 | 1.00000 | 1.00000 | 1.00000 | 1.00000 | 1.00000 |
| 1 | 1.04000 | 1.05000 | 1.06000 | 1.08000 | 1.09000 | 1.10000 | 1.11000 | 1.12000 | 1.15000 |
| 2 | 1.08160 | 1.10250 | 1.12360 | 1.16640 | 1.18810 | 1.21000 | 1.23210 | 1.25440 | 1.32250 |
| 3 | 1.12486 | 1.15763 | 1.19102 | 1.25971 | 1.29503 | 1.33100 | 1.36763 | 1.40493 | 1.52088 |
| 4 | 1.16986 | 1.21551 | 1.26248 | 1.36049 | 1.41158 | 1.46410 | 1.51807 | 1.57352 | 1.74901 |
| 5 | 1.21665 | 1.27628 | 1.33823 | 1.46933 | 1.53862 | 1.61051 | 1.68506 | 1.76234 | 2.01136 |
| 6 | 1.26532 | 1.34010 | 1.41852 | 1.58687 | 1.67710 | 1.77156 | 1.87041 | 1.97382 | 2.31306 |
| 7 | 1.31593 | 1.40710 | 1.50363 | 1.71382 | 1.82804 | 1.94872 | 2.07616 | 2.21068 | 2.66002 |
| 8 | 1.36857 | 1.47746 | 1.59385 | 1.85093 | 1.99256 | 2.14359 | 2.30454 | 2.47596 | 3.05902 |
| 9 | 1.42331 | 1.55133 | 1.68948 | 1.99900 | 2.17189 | 2.35795 | 2.55803 | 2.77308 | 3.51788 |
| 10 | 1.48024 | 1.62889 | 1.79085 | 2.15892 | 2.36736 | 2.59374 | 2.83942 | 3.10585 | 4.04556 |
| 11 | 1.53945 | 1.71034 | 1.89830 | 2.33164 | 2.58043 | 2.85312 | 3.15176 | 3.47855 | 4.65239 |
| 12 | 1.60103 | 1.79586 | 2.01220 | 2.51817 | 2.81267 | 3.13843 | 3.49845 | 3.89598 | 5.35025 |
| 13 | 1.66507 | 1.88565 | 2.13293 | 2.71962 | 3.06581 | 3.45227 | 3.88328 | 4.36349 | 6.15279 |
| 14 | 1.73168 | 1.97993 | 2.26090 | 2.93719 | 3.34173 | 3.79750 | 4.31044 | 4.88711 | 7.07571 |
| 15 | 1.80094 | 2.07893 | 2.39656 | 3.17217 | 3.64248 | 4.17725 | 4.78459 | 5.47357 | 8.13706 |
| 16 | 1.87298 | 2.18287 | 2.54035 | 3.42594 | 3.97031 | 4.59497 | 5.31089 | 6.13039 | 9.35762 |
| 17 | 1.94790 | 2.29202 | 2.69277 | 3.70002 | 4.32763 | 5.05447 | 5.89509 | 6.86604 | 10.76126 |
| 18 | 2.02582 | 2.40662 | 2.85434 | 3.99602 | 4.71712 | 5.55992 | 6.54355 | 7.68997 | 12.37545 |
| 19 | 2.10685 | 2.52695 | 3.02560 | 4.31570 | 5.14166 | 6.11591 | 7.26334 | 8.61276 | 14.23177 |
| 20 | 2.19112 | 2.65330 | 3.20714 | 4.66096 | 5.60441 | 6.72750 | 8.06231 | 9.64629 | 16.36654 |

John and Mary Rich invested $20,000 in a savings account paying 6% interest at the time their son, Mike, was born. The money is to be used by Mike for his college education. On his 18th birthday, Mike withdraws the money from his savings account. How much did Mike withdraw from his account?

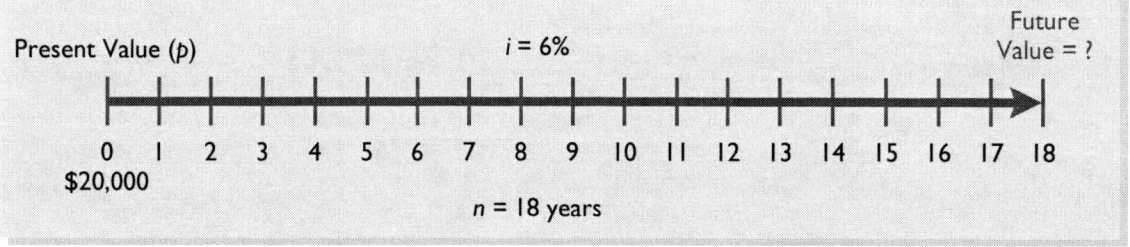

Answer: The future value factor from Table 1 is 2.85434 (18 periods at 6%). The future value of $20,000 earning 6% per year for 18 years is $57,086.80 ($20,000 × 2.85434).

**Illustration D-5**
Demonstration problem—
Using Table 1 for *FV* of 1

# Future Value of an Annuity

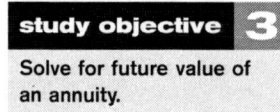

**study objective** 3

Solve for future value of an annuity.

The preceding discussion involved the accumulation of only a single principal sum. Individuals and businesses frequently encounter situations in which a **series** of equal dollar amounts are to be paid or received at evenly spaced time intervals (periodically), such as loans or lease (rental) contracts. Such payments or receipts of equal dollar amounts are referred to as annuities.

The future value of an annuity is the sum of all the payments (receipts) plus the accumulated compound interest on them. In computing the future value of an annuity, it is necessary to know (1) the interest rate, (2) the number of compounding periods, and (3) the amount of the periodic payments or receipts.

To illustrate the computation of the future value of an annuity, assume that you invest $2,000 at the end of each year for three years at 5% interest compounded annually. This situation is depicted in the time diagram in Illustration D-6.

**Illustration D-6**    Time diagram for a three-year annuity

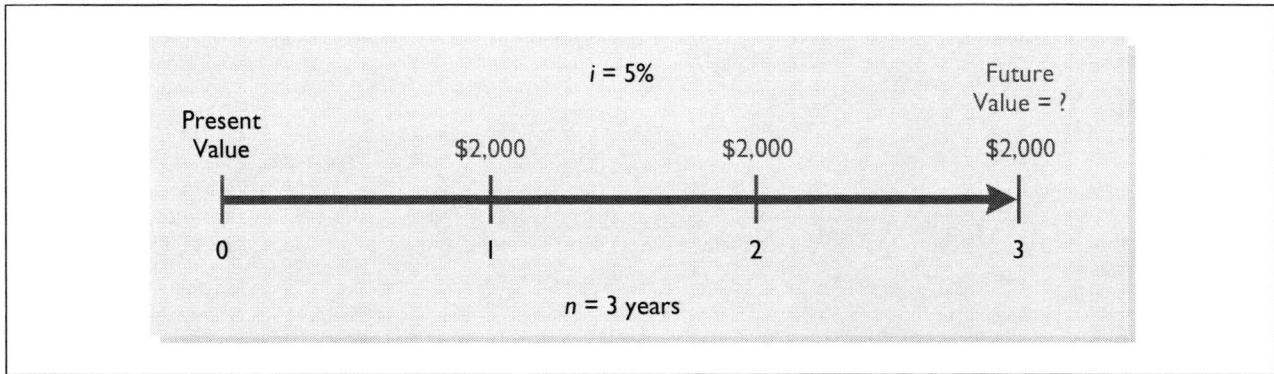

The $2,000 invested at the end of year 1 will earn interest for two years (years 2 and 3), and the $2,000 invested at the end of year 2 will earn interest for one year (year 3). However, the last $2,000 investment (made at the end of year 3) will not earn any interest. The future value of these periodic payments could be computed using the future value factors from Table 1, as shown in Illustration D-7.

**Illustration D-7**    Future value of periodic payment computation

| Invested at End of Year | Number of Compounding Periods | Amount Invested | × | Future Value of 1 Factor at 5% | = | Future Value |
|---|---|---|---|---|---|---|
| 1 | 2 | $2,000 | × | 1.10250 | | $2,205 |
| 2 | 1 | $2,000 | × | 1.05000 | | 2,100 |
| 3 | 0 | $2,000 | × | 1.00000 | | 2,000 |
| | | | | 3.15250 | | $6,305 |

The first $2,000 investment is multiplied by the future value factor for two periods (1.1025) because two years' interest will accumulate on it (in years 2 and 3). The second $2,000 investment will earn only one year's interest (in year 3) and therefore is multiplied by the future value factor for one year (1.0500). The final $2,000 investment is made at the end of the third year and will not earn any interest. Thus $n = 0$ and the future value factor is 1.00000. Consequently, the future value of the last $2,000 invested is only $2,000 since it does not accumulate any interest.

Calculating the future value of each individual cash flow is required when the periodic payments or receipts are not equal in each period. However, when the periodic payments (receipts) are **the same in each period**, the future value can be computed by using a future value of an annuity of 1 table. Table 2 (page D-6) is such a table.

**TABLE 2** Future Value of an Annuity of 1

| (n) Periods | 4% | 5% | 6% | 8% | 9% | 10% | 11% | 12% | 15% |
|---|---|---|---|---|---|---|---|---|---|
| 1 | 1.00000 | 1.00000 | 1.00000 | 1.00000 | 1.00000 | 1.00000 | 1.00000 | 1.00000 | 1.00000 |
| 2 | 2.04000 | 2.05000 | 2.06000 | 2.08000 | 2.09000 | 2.10000 | 2.11000 | 2.12000 | 2.15000 |
| 3 | 3.12160 | 3.15250 | 3.18360 | 3.24640 | 3.27810 | 3.31000 | 3.34210 | 3.37440 | 3.47250 |
| 4 | 4.24646 | 4.31013 | 4.37462 | 4.50611 | 4.57313 | 4.64100 | 4.70973 | 4.77933 | 4.99338 |
| 5 | 5.41632 | 5.52563 | 5.63709 | 5.86660 | 5.98471 | 6.10510 | 6.22780 | 6.35285 | 6.74238 |
| 6 | 6.63298 | 6.80191 | 6.97532 | 7.33592 | 7.52334 | 7.71561 | 7.91286 | 8.11519 | 8.75374 |
| 7 | 7.89829 | 8.14201 | 8.39384 | 8.92280 | 9.20044 | 9.48717 | 9.78327 | 10.08901 | 11.06680 |
| 8 | 9.21423 | 9.54911 | 9.89747 | 10.63663 | 11.02847 | 11.43589 | 11.85943 | 12.29969 | 13.72682 |
| 9 | 10.58280 | 11.02656 | 11.49132 | 12.48756 | 13.02104 | 13.57948 | 14.16397 | 14.77566 | 16.78584 |
| 10 | 12.00611 | 12.57789 | 13.18079 | 14.48656 | 15.19293 | 15.93743 | 16.72201 | 17.54874 | 20.30372 |
| 11 | 13.48635 | 14.20679 | 14.97164 | 16.64549 | 17.56029 | 18.53117 | 19.56143 | 20.65458 | 24.34928 |
| 12 | 15.02581 | 15.91713 | 16.86994 | 18.97713 | 20.14072 | 21.38428 | 22.71319 | 24.13313 | 29.00167 |
| 13 | 16.62684 | 17.71298 | 18.88214 | 21.49530 | 22.95339 | 24.52271 | 26.21164 | 28.02911 | 34.35192 |
| 14 | 18.29191 | 19.59863 | 21.01507 | 24.21492 | 26.01919 | 27.97498 | 30.09492 | 32.39260 | 40.50471 |
| 15 | 20.02359 | 21.57856 | 23.27597 | 27.15211 | 29.36092 | 31.77248 | 34.40536 | 37.27972 | 47.58041 |
| 16 | 21.82453 | 23.65749 | 25.67253 | 30.32428 | 33.00340 | 35.94973 | 39.18995 | 42.75328 | 55.71747 |
| 17 | 23.69751 | 25.84037 | 28.21288 | 33.75023 | 36.97351 | 40.54470 | 44.50084 | 48.88367 | 65.07509 |
| 18 | 25.64541 | 28.13238 | 30.90565 | 37.45024 | 41.30134 | 45.59917 | 50.39593 | 55.74972 | 75.83636 |
| 19 | 27.67123 | 30.53900 | 33.75999 | 41.44626 | 46.01846 | 51.15909 | 56.93949 | 63.43968 | 88.21181 |
| 20 | 29.77808 | 33.06595 | 36.78559 | 45.76196 | 51.16012 | 57.27500 | 64.20283 | 72.05244 | 102.44358 |

**Illustration D-8**
Demonstration problem—
Using Table 2 for *FV* of an
annuity of 1

Table 2 shows the future value of 1 to be received periodically for a given number of periods. It assumes that each payment is made at the **end** of each period. We can see from Table 2 that the future value of an annuity of 1 factor for three periods at 5% is 3.15250. The future value factor is the total of the three individual future value factors was shown in Illustration D-7. Multiplying this amount by the annual investment of $2,000 produces a future value of $6,305.

The demonstration problem in Illustration D-8 shows how to use Table 2.

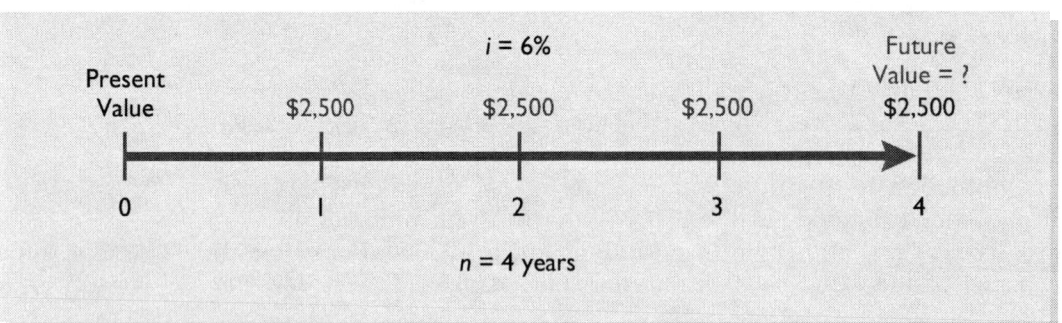

John and Char Lewis' daughter, Debra, has just started high school. They decide to start a college fund for her and will invest $2,500 in a savings account at the end of each year she is in high school (4 payments total). The account will earn 6% interest compounded annually. How much will be in the college fund at the time Debra graduates from high school?

**Answer:** The future value factor from Table 2 is 4.37462 (4 periods at 6%). The future value of $2,500 invested each year for 4 years at 6% interest is **$10,936.55** ($2,500 × 4.37462).

# Present Value Concepts

## Present Value Variables

The present value is the value now of a given amount to be paid or received in the future, assuming compound interest. The present value, like the future value, is based on three variables: (1) the dollar amount to be received (future amount), (2) the length of time until the amount is received (number of periods), and (3) the interest rate (the discount rate). The process of determining the present value is referred to as discounting the future amount.

**study objective 4**
Identify the variables fundamental to solving present value problems.

   In this textbook, we use present value computations in measuring several items. For example, Chapter 10 computed the present value of the principal and interest payments to determine the market price of a bond. In addition, determining the amount to be reported for notes payable and lease liabilities involves present value computations.

## Present Value of a Single Amount

To illustrate present value, assume that you want to invest a sum of money today that will provide $1,000 at the end of one year. What amount would you need to invest today to have $1,000 one year from now? If you want a 10% rate of return, the investment or present value is $909.09 ($1,000 ÷ 1.10). The formula for calculating present value is shown in Illustration D-9.

**study objective 5**
Solve for present value of a single amount.

$$\text{Present Value} = \text{Future Value} \div (1 + i)^n$$

**Illustration D-9**   Formula for present value

The computation of $1,000 discounted at 10% for one year is as follows.

$$
\begin{aligned}
PV &= \quad FV \quad \div (1 + i)^n \\
&= \$1,000 \div (1 + .10)^1 \\
&= \$1,000 \div 1.10 \\
&= \$909.09
\end{aligned}
$$

   The future amount ($1,000), the discount rate (10%), and the number of periods (1) are known. The variables in this situation can be depicted in the time diagram in Illustration D-10.

**Illustration D-10**
Finding present value if discounted for one period

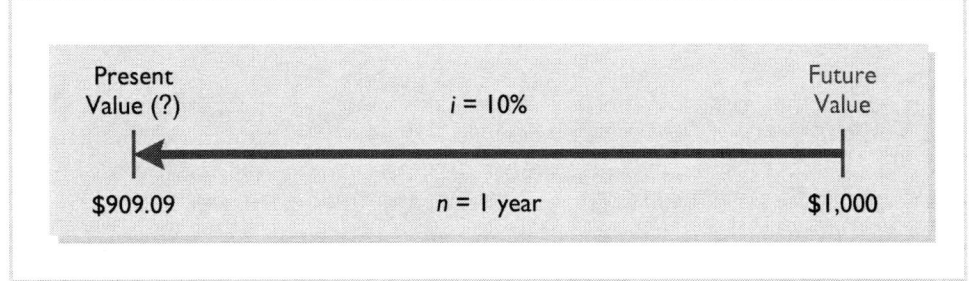

   If the single amount of $1,000 is to be received **in two years** and discounted at 10% [$PV = \$1,000 \div (1 + .10)^2$], its present value is $826.45 [($1,000 ÷ 1.21), depicted as shown in Illustration D-11 on the next page.

**Illustration D-11**
Finding present value if
discounted for two periods

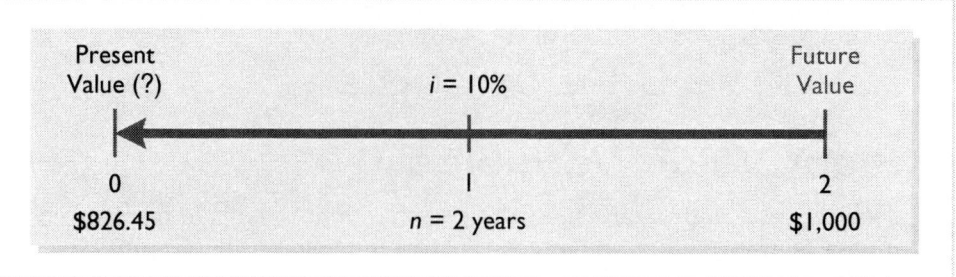

The present value of 1 may also be determined through tables that show the present value of 1 for $n$ periods. In Table 3 below, $n$ is the number of discounting periods involved. The percentages are the periodic interest rates or discount rates, and the 5-digit decimal numbers in the respective columns are the present value of 1 factors.

When using Table 3, the future value is multiplied by the present value factor specified at the intersection of the number of periods and the discount rate.

**TABLE 3    Present Value of 1**

| (n) Periods | 4% | 5% | 6% | 8% | 9% | 10% | 11% | 12% | 15% |
|---|---|---|---|---|---|---|---|---|---|
| 1 | .96154 | .95238 | .94340 | .92593 | .91743 | .90909 | .90090 | .89286 | .86957 |
| 2 | .92456 | .90703 | .89000 | .85734 | .84168 | .82645 | .81162 | .79719 | .75614 |
| 3 | .88900 | .86384 | .83962 | .79383 | .77218 | .75132 | .73119 | .71178 | .65752 |
| 4 | .85480 | .82270 | .79209 | .73503 | .70843 | .68301 | .65873 | .63552 | .57175 |
| 5 | .82193 | .78353 | .74726 | .68058 | .64993 | .62092 | .59345 | .56743 | .49718 |
| 6 | .79031 | .74622 | .70496 | .63017 | .59627 | .56447 | .53464 | .50663 | .43233 |
| 7 | .75992 | .71068 | .66506 | .58349 | .54703 | .51316 | .48166 | .45235 | .37594 |
| 8 | .73069 | .67684 | .62741 | .54027 | .50187 | .46651 | .43393 | .40388 | .32690 |
| 9 | .70259 | .64461 | .59190 | .50025 | .46043 | .42410 | .39092 | .36061 | .28426 |
| 10 | .67556 | .61391 | .55839 | .46319 | .42241 | .38554 | .35218 | .32197 | .24719 |
| 11 | .64958 | .58468 | .52679 | .42888 | .38753 | .35049 | .31728 | .28748 | .21494 |
| 12 | .62460 | .55684 | .49697 | .39711 | .35554 | .31863 | .28584 | .25668 | .18691 |
| 13 | .60057 | .53032 | .46884 | .36770 | .32618 | .28966 | .25751 | .22917 | .16253 |
| 14 | .57748 | .50507 | .44230 | .34046 | .29925 | .26333 | .23199 | .20462 | .14133 |
| 15 | .55526 | .48102 | .41727 | .31524 | .27454 | .23939 | .20900 | .18270 | .12289 |
| 16 | .53391 | .45811 | .39365 | .29189 | .25187 | .21763 | .18829 | .16312 | .10687 |
| 17 | .51337 | .43630 | .37136 | .27027 | .23107 | .19785 | .16963 | .14564 | .09293 |
| 18 | .49363 | .41552 | .35034 | .25025 | .21199 | .17986 | .15282 | .13004 | .08081 |
| 19 | .47464 | .39573 | .33051 | .23171 | .19449 | .16351 | .13768 | .11611 | .07027 |
| 20 | .45639 | .37689 | .31180 | .21455 | .17843 | .14864 | .12403 | .10367 | .06110 |

For example, the present value factor for one period at a discount rate of 10% is .90909, which equals the $909.09 ($1,000 × .90909) computed in Illustration D-10. For two periods at a discount rate of 10%, the present value factor is .82645, which equals the $826.45 ($1,000 × .82645) computed previously.

Note that a higher discount rate produces a smaller present value. For example, using a 15% discount rate, the present value of $1,000 due one year from now is $869.57 versus $909.09 at 10%. Also note that the further removed from the present the future value is, the smaller the present value. For example, using the same discount rate of 10%, the present value of $1,000 due in **five years** is $620.92. The present value of $1,000 due in **one year** is $909.09, a difference of $288.17.

The following two demonstration problems (Illustrations D-12 and D-13) illustrate how to use Table 3.

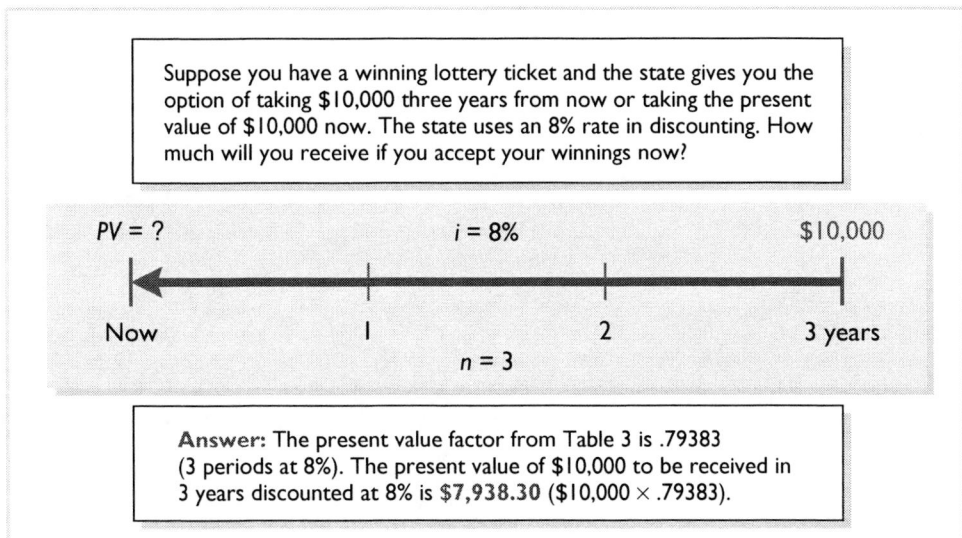

**Illustration D-12**
Demonstration problem–
Using Table 3 for *PV* of 1

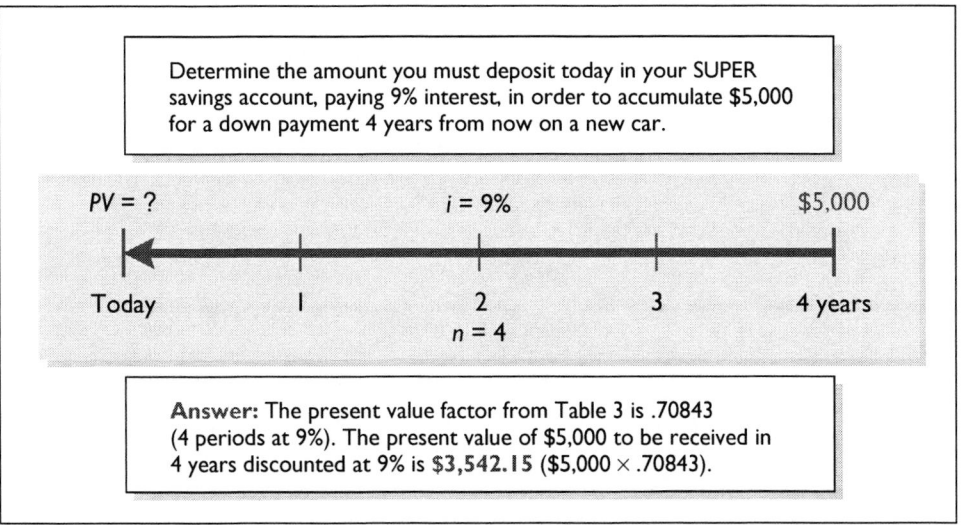

**Illustration D-13**
Demonstration problem–
Using Table 3 for *PV* of 1

# Present Value of an Annuity

The preceding discussion involved the discounting of only a single future amount. Businesses and individuals frequently engage in transactions in which a series of equal dollar amounts are to be received or paid at evenly spaced time intervals (periodically). Examples of a series of periodic receipts or payments are loan agreements, installment sales, mortgage notes, lease (rental) contracts, and pension obligations. As discussed earlier, these periodic receipts or payments are **annuities**.

The present value of an annuity is the value now of a series of future receipts or payments, discounted assuming compound interest. In computing the present value of an annuity, it is necessary to know (1) the discount rate, (2) the number of discount periods, and (3) the amount of the periodic receipts or payments. To illustrate the computation of the present value of an annuity, assume

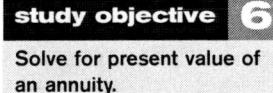

**study objective** 6

Solve for present value of an annuity.

that you will receive $1,000 cash annually for three years at a time when the discount rate is 10%. This situation is depicted in the time diagram in Illustration D-14. Illustration D-15 shows computation of the present value in this situation.

**Illustration D-14** Time diagram for a three-year annuity

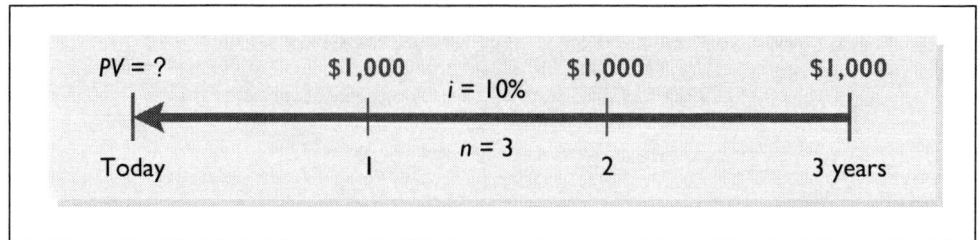

**Illustration D-15**
Present value of a series of future amounts computation

| Future Amount | × | Present Value of 1 Factor at 10% | = | Present Value |
|---|---|---|---|---|
| $1,000 (one year away) | | .90909 | | $ 909.09 |
| 1,000 (two years away) | | .82645 | | 826.45 |
| 1,000 (three years away) | | .75132 | | 751.32 |
| | | 2.48686 | | $2,486.86 |

This method of calculation is required when the periodic cash flows are not uniform in each period. However, when the future receipts are the same in each period, an annuity table can be used. As illustrated in Table 4 below, an annuity table shows the present value of 1 to be received periodically for a given number of periods.

**TABLE 4 Present Value of an Annuity of 1**

| (n) Periods | 4% | 5% | 6% | 8% | 9% | 10% | 11% | 12% | 15% |
|---|---|---|---|---|---|---|---|---|---|
| 1 | .96154 | .95238 | .94340 | .92593 | .91743 | .90909 | .90090 | .89286 | .86957 |
| 2 | 1.88609 | 1.85941 | 1.83339 | 1.78326 | 1.75911 | 1.73554 | 1.71252 | 1.69005 | 1.62571 |
| 3 | 2.77509 | 2.72325 | 2.67301 | 2.57710 | 2.53130 | 2.48685 | 2.44371 | 2.40183 | 2.28323 |
| 4 | 3.62990 | 3.54595 | 3.46511 | 3.31213 | 3.23972 | 3.16986 | 3.10245 | 3.03735 | 2.85498 |
| 5 | 4.45182 | 4.32948 | 4.21236 | 3.99271 | 3.88965 | 3.79079 | 3.69590 | 3.60478 | 3.35216 |
| 6 | 5.24214 | 5.07569 | 4.91732 | 4.62288 | 4.48592 | 4.35526 | 4.23054 | 4.11141 | 3.78448 |
| 7 | 6.00205 | 5.78637 | 5.58238 | 5.20637 | 5.03295 | 4.86842 | 4.71220 | 4.56376 | 4.16042 |
| 8 | 6.73274 | 6.46321 | 6.20979 | 5.74664 | 5.53482 | 5.33493 | 5.14612 | 4.96764 | 4.48732 |
| 9 | 7.43533 | 7.10782 | 6.80169 | 6.24689 | 5.99525 | 5.75902 | 5.53705 | 5.32825 | 4.77158 |
| 10 | 8.11090 | 7.72173 | 7.36009 | 6.71008 | 6.41766 | 6.14457 | 5.88923 | 5.65022 | 5.01877 |
| 11 | 8.76048 | 8.30641 | 7.88687 | 7.13896 | 6.80519 | 6.49506 | 6.20652 | 5.93770 | 5.23371 |
| 12 | 9.38507 | 8.86325 | 8.38384 | 7.53608 | 7.16073 | 6.81369 | 6.49236 | 6.19437 | 5.42062 |
| 13 | 9.98565 | 9.39357 | 8.85268 | 7.90378 | 7.48690 | 7.10336 | 6.74987 | 6.42355 | 5.58315 |
| 14 | 10.56312 | 9.89864 | 9.29498 | 8.24424 | 7.78615 | 7.36669 | 6.98187 | 6.62817 | 5.72448 |
| 15 | 11.11839 | 10.37966 | 9.71225 | 8.55948 | 8.06069 | 7.60608 | 7.19087 | 6.81086 | 5.84737 |
| 16 | 11.65230 | 10.83777 | 10.10590 | 8.85137 | 8.31256 | 7.82371 | 7.37916 | 6.97399 | 5.95424 |
| 17 | 12.16567 | 11.27407 | 10.47726 | 9.12164 | 8.54363 | 8.02155 | 7.54879 | 7.11963 | 6.04716 |
| 18 | 12.65930 | 11.68959 | 10.82760 | 9.37189 | 8.75563 | 8.20141 | 7.70162 | 7.24967 | 6.12797 |
| 19 | 13.13394 | 12.08532 | 11.15812 | 9.60360 | 8.95012 | 8.36492 | 7.83929 | 7.36578 | 6.19823 |
| 20 | 13.59033 | 12.46221 | 11.46992 | 9.81815 | 9.12855 | 8.51356 | 7.96333 | 7.46944 | 6.25933 |

Table 4 shows that the present value of an annuity of 1 factor for three periods at 10% is 2.48685.[1] This present value factor is the total of the three individual present value factors, as shown in Illustration D-15. Applying this amount to the annual cash flow of $1,000 produces a present value of $2,486.85.

The following demonstration problem (Illustration D-16) illustrates how to use Table 4.

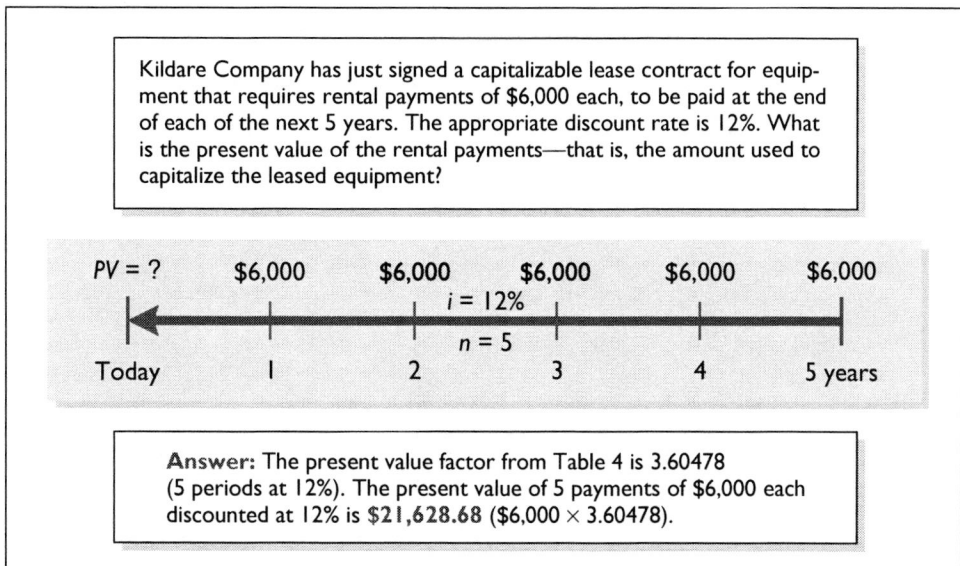

Kildare Company has just signed a capitalizable lease contract for equipment that requires rental payments of $6,000 each, to be paid at the end of each of the next 5 years. The appropriate discount rate is 12%. What is the present value of the rental payments—that is, the amount used to capitalize the leased equipment?

$PV = ?$    $6,000    $6,000    $6,000    $6,000    $6,000

$i = 12\%$

$n = 5$

Today   1   2   3   4   5 years

**Answer:** The present value factor from Table 4 is 3.60478 (5 periods at 12%). The present value of 5 payments of $6,000 each discounted at 12% is **$21,628.68** ($6,000 × 3.60478).

**Illustration D-16**
Demonstration problem—Using Table 4 for *PV* of an annuity of 1

## Time Periods and Discounting

In the preceding calculations, the discounting was done on an annual basis using an annual interest rate. Discounting may also be done over shorter periods of time such as monthly, quarterly, or semiannually.

When the time frame is less than one year, it is necessary to convert the annual interest rate to the applicable time frame. Assume, for example, that the investor in Illustration D-14 received $500 **semiannually** for three years instead of $1,000 annually. In this case, the number of periods becomes six (3 × 2), the discount rate is 5% (10% ÷ 2), the present value factor from Table 4 is 5.07569 (6 periods at 5%), and the present value of the future cash flows is $2,537.85 (5.07569 × $500). This amount is slightly higher than the $2,486.86 computed in Illustration D-15 because interest is computed twice during the same year. That is, during the second half of the year, interest is earned on the first half-year's interest.

## Computing the Present Value of a Long-Term Note or Bond

The present value (or market price) of a long-term note or bond is a function of three variables: (1) the payment amounts, (2) the length of time until the amounts are paid, and (3) the discount rate. Our illustration (on the next page) uses a five-year bond issue.

**study objective 7**

Compute the present value of notes and bonds.

---

[1]The difference of .00001 between 2.48686 and 2.48685 is due to rounding.

The first variable (dollars to be paid) is made up of two elements: (1) a series of interest payments (an annuity) and (2) the principal amount (a single sum). To compute the present value of the bond, both the interest payments and the principal amount must be discounted—two different computations. The time diagrams for a bond due in five years are shown in Illustration D-17.

**Illustration D-17**
Present value of a bond time diagram

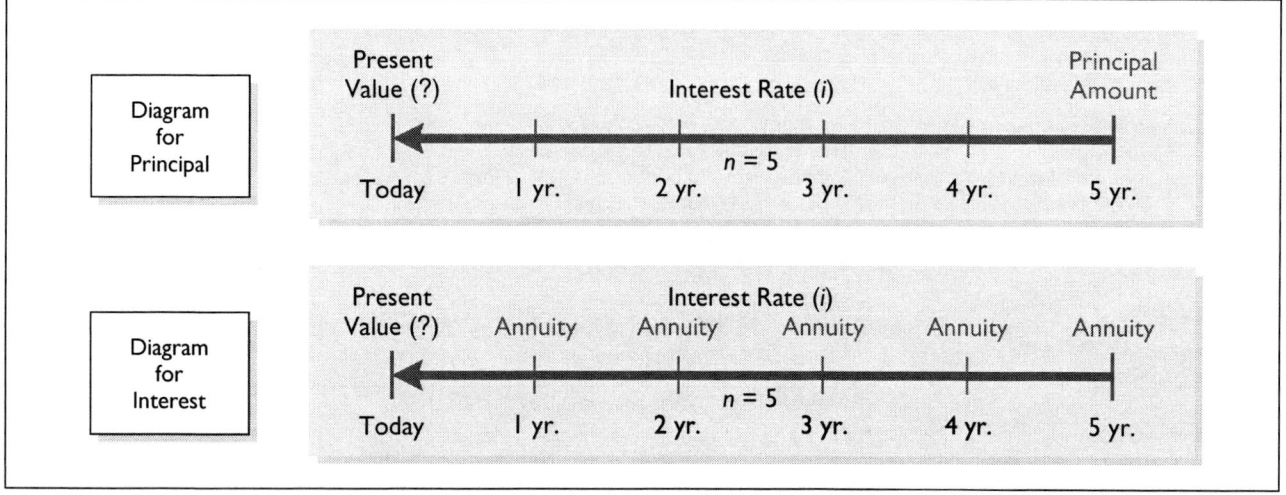

When the investor's market interest rate is equal to the bond's contractual interest rate, the present value of the bonds will equal the face value of the bonds. To illustrate, assume a bond issue of 10%, five-year bonds with a face value of $100,000 with interest payable **semiannually** on January 1 and July 1. If the discount rate is the same as the contractual rate, the bonds will sell at face value. In this case, the investor will receive (1) $100,000 at maturity and (2) a series of ten $5,000 interest payments [($100,000 × 10%) ÷ 2] over the term of the bonds. The length of time is expressed in terms of interest periods—in this case—10, and the discount rate per interest period, 5%. The following time diagram (Illustration D-18) depicts the variables involved in this discounting situation.

**Illustration D-18**
Time diagram for present value of a 10%, five-year bond paying interest semiannually

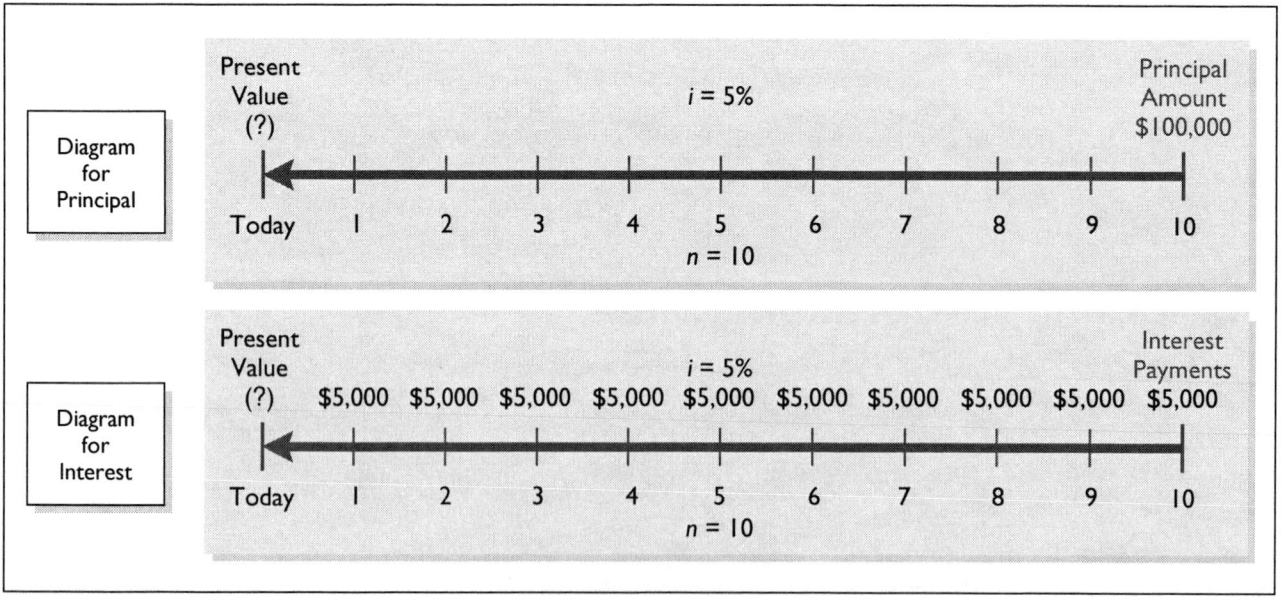

Illustration D-19 shows the computation of the present value of these bonds.

**Illustration D-19**
Present value of principal
and interest–face value

| 10% Contractual Rate—10% Discount Rate | |
|---|---|
| **Present value of principal to be received at maturity** | |
| $100,000 × *PV* of 1 due in 10 periods at 5% | |
| $100,000 × .61391 (Table 3) | $ 61,391 |
| **Present value of interest to be received periodically** | |
| **over the term of the bonds** | |
| $5,000 × *PV* of 1 due periodically for 10 periods at 5% | |
| $5,000 × 7.72173 (Table 4) | 38,609* |
| **Present value of bonds** | $100,000 |

*Rounded

Now assume that the investor's required rate of return is 12%, not 10%. The future amounts are again $100,000 and $5,000, respectively, but now a discount rate of 6% (12% ÷ 2) must be used. The present value of the bonds is $92,639, as computed in Illustration D-20.

**Illustration D-20**
Present value of principal
and interest–discount

| 10% Contractual Rate—12% Discount Rate | |
|---|---|
| **Present value of principal to be received at maturity** | |
| $100,000 × .55839 (Table 3) | $ 55,839 |
| **Present value of interest to be received periodically** | |
| **over the term of the bonds** | |
| $5,000 × 7.36009 (Table 4) | 36,800 |
| **Present value of bonds** | $92,639 |

Conversely, if the discount rate is 8% and the contractual rate is 10%, the present value of the bonds is $108,111, computed as shown in Illustration D-21.

**Illustration D-21**
Present value of principal
and interest–premium

| 10% Contractual Rate—8% Discount Rate | |
|---|---|
| **Present value of principal to be received at maturity** | |
| $100,000 × .67556 (Table 3) | $ 67,556 |
| **Present value of interest to be received periodically** | |
| **over the term of the bonds** | |
| $5,000 × 8.11090 (Table 4) | 40,555 |
| **Present value of bonds** | $108,111 |

The above discussion relied on present value tables in solving present value problems. Calculators may also be used to compute present values without the use of these tables. Many calculators, especially financial calculators, have present value (*PV*) functions that allow you to calculate present values by merely inputting the proper amount, discount rate, periods, and pressing the PV key. We discuss the use of financial calculators in the next section.

# Computing the Present Values in a Capital Budgeting Decision

The decision to make long-term capital investments is best evaluated using discounting techniques that recognize the time value of money. To do this, many companies calculate the present value of the cash flows involved in a capital investment.

To illustrate, Nagel-Siebert Trucking Company, a cross-country freight carrier in Montgomery, Illinois, is considering adding another truck to its fleet because of a purchasing opportunity. Navistar Inc., Nagel-Siebert's primary supplier of overland rigs, is overstocked and offers to sell its biggest rig for $154,000 cash payable upon delivery. Nagel-Siebert knows that the rig will produce a net cash flow per year of $40,000 for five years (received at the end of each year), at which time it will be sold for an estimated salvage value of $35,000. Nagel-Siebert's discount rate in evaluating capital expenditures is 10%. Should Nagel-Siebert commit to the purchase of this rig?

The cash flows that must be discounted to present value by Nagel-Siebert are as follows.

Cash payable on delivery (today): $154,000.

Net cash flow from operating the rig: $40,000 for 5 years (at the end of each year).

Cash received from sale of rig at the end of 5 years: $35,000.

The time diagrams for the latter two cash flows are shown in Illustration D-22.

**Illustration D-22**
Time diagrams for Nagel-Siebert Trucking Company

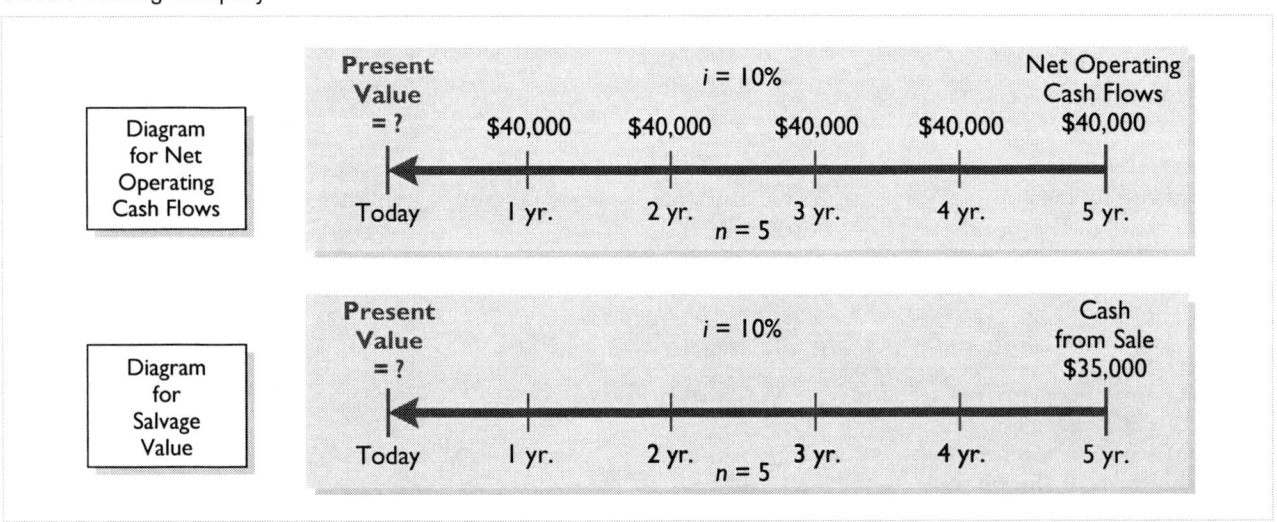

Notice from the diagrams that computing the present value of the net operating cash flows ($40,000 at the end of each year) is **discounting an annuity** (Table 4), while computing the present value of the $35,000 salvage value is **discounting a single sum** (Table 3). The computation of these present values is shown in Illustration D-23.

**Illustration D-23**
Present value computations
at 10%

### Present Values Using a 10 Percent Discount Rate

Present value of net operating cash flows received annually
over 5 years:

$40,000 × PV of 1 received annually for 5 years at 10%

$40,000 × 3.79079 =                                        $151,631.60

Present value of salvage value (cash) to be received in 5 years

$35,000 × PV of 1 received in 5 years at 10%

$35,000 × .62092 =                                          21,732.20

Present value of cash **inflows**                          173,363.80

Present value cash **outflows** (purchase price due today at 10%):

$154,000 × PV of 1 due today

$154,000 × 1.00000 =                                       154,000.00

Net present value                                         $ **19,363.80**

Because the present value of the cash receipts (inflows) of $173,363.80 ($151,631.60 + $21,732.20) exceeds the present value of the cash payments (outflows) of $154,000.00, the net present value of $19,363.80 is positive, and **the decision to invest should be accepted**.

Now assume that Nagel-Siebert uses a discount rate of 15%, not 10%, because it wants a greater return on its investments in capital assets. The cash receipts and cash payments by Nagel-Siebert are the same. The present values of these receipts and cash payments discounted at 15% are shown in Illustration D-24.

**Illustration D-24**
Present value computations
at 15 percent

### Present Values Using a 15 Percent Discount Rate

Present value of net operating cash flows received annually
over 5 years at 15%:

$40,000 × 3.35216                                          $134,086.40

Present value of salvage value (cash) to be received in 5 years
at 15%

$35,000 × .49718                                            17,401.30

Present value of cash **inflows**                         $151,487.70

Present value of cash **outflows** (purchase price due today at 15%):

$154,000 × 1.00000                                         154,000.00

Net present value                                         $ **(2,512.30)**

Because the present value of the cash payments (outflows) of $154,000 exceeds the present value of the cash receipts (inflows) of $151,487.70 ($134,086.40 + $17,401.30), the net present value of $2,512.30 is negative, and **the investment should be rejected**.

The above discussion relied on present value tables in solving present value problems. As we show in the next section, calculators may also be used to compute present values without the use of these tables. Some calculators, especially the "business" or financial calculators, have present value (PV) functions that allow you to calculate present values by merely identifying the proper amount, discount rate, periods, and pressing the PV key.

# Using Financial Calculators

**study objective** 9

Use a financial calculator to solve time value of money problems.

Business professionals, once they have mastered the underlying concepts in sections 1 and 2, often use a financial calculator to solve time value of money problems. In many cases, they must use calculators if interest rates or time periods do not correspond with the information provided in the compound interest tables.

To use financial calculators, you enter the time value of money variables into the calculator. Illustration D-25 shows the five most common keys used to solve time value of money problems.[2]

**Illustration D-25**
Financial calculator keys

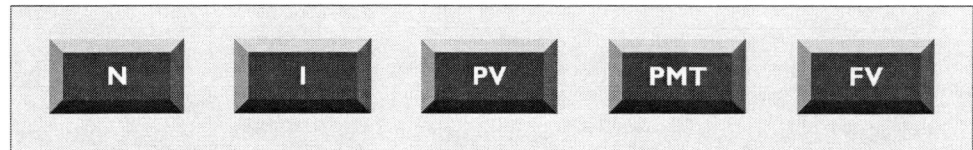

where:

    N   = number of periods
    I    = interest rate per period (some calculators use I/YR or i)
    PV  = present value (occurs at the beginning of the first period)
    PMT = payment (all payments are equal, and none are skipped)
    FV  = future value (occurs at the end of the last period)

In solving time value of money problems in this appendix, you will generally be given three of four variables and will have to solve for the remaining variable. The fifth key (the key not used) is given a value of zero to ensure that this variable is not used in the computation.

## Present Value of a Single Sum

To illustrate how to solve a present value problem using a financial calculator, assume that you want to know the present value of $84,253 to be received in five years, discounted at 11% compounded annually. Illustration D-26 depicts this problem.

**Illustration D-26**
Calculator solution for present value of a single sum

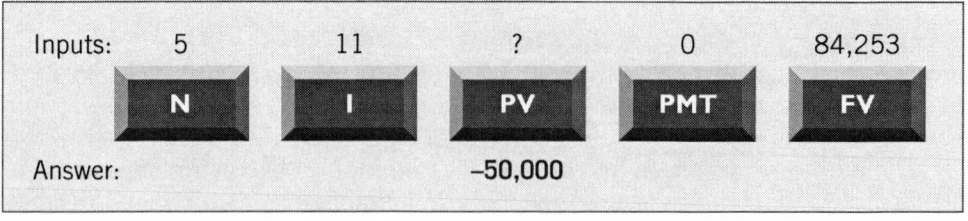

| Inputs: | 5 | 11 | ? | 0 | 84,253 |
|---|---|---|---|---|---|
| | N | I | PV | PMT | FV |
| Answer: | | | −50,000 | | |

---

[2]On many calculators, these keys are actual buttons on the face of the calculator; on others, they appear on the display after the user accesses a present value menu.

Illustration D-26 shows you the information (inputs) to enter into the calculator: N = 5, I = 11, PMT = 0, and FV = 84,253. You then press PV for the answer: −$50,000. As indicated, the PMT key was given a value of zero because a series of payments did not occur in this problem.

## PLUS AND MINUS

The use of plus and minus signs in time value of money problems with a financial calculator can be confusing. Most financial calculators are programmed so that the positive and negative cash flows in any problem offset each other. In the present value problem above, we identified the $84,253 future value initial investment as a positive (inflow); the answer −$50,000 was shown as a negative amount, reflecting a cash outflow. If the 84,253 were entered as a negative, then the final answer would have been reported as a positive 50,000.

Hopefully, the sign convention will not cause confusion. If you understand what is required in a problem, you should be able to interpret a positive or negative amount in determining the solution to a problem.

## COMPOUNDING PERIODS

In the problem above, we assumed that compounding occurs once a year. Some financial calculators have a default setting, which assumes that compounding occurs 12 times a year. You must determine what default period has been programmed into your calculator and change it as necessary to arrive at the proper compounding period.

## ROUNDING

Most financial calculators store and calculate using 12 decimal places. As a result, because compound interest tables generally have factors only up to five decimal places, a slight difference in the final answer can result. In most time value of money problems, the final answer will not include more than two decimal places.

# Present Value of an Annuity

To illustrate how to solve a present value of an annuity problem using a financial calculator, assume that you are asked to determine the present value of rental receipts of $6,000 each to be received at the end of each of the next five years, when discounted at 12%, as pictured in Illustration D-27.

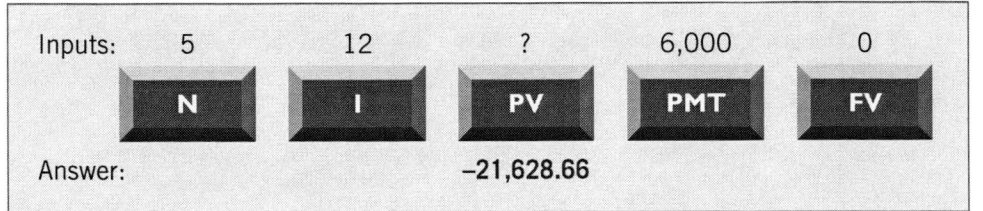

**Illustration D-27**
Calculator solution for present value of an annuity

In this case, you enter N = 5, I = 12, PMT = 6,000, FV = 0, and then press PV to arrive at the answer of −$21,628.66.

# Useful Applications of the Financial Calculator

With a financial calculator, you can solve for any interest rate or for any number of periods in a time value of money problem. Here are some examples of these applications.

### AUTO LOAN

Assume you are financing the purchase of a used car with a three-year loan. The loan has a 9.5% stated annual interest rate, compounded monthly. The price of the car is $6,000, and you want to determine the monthly payments, assuming that the payments start one month after the purchase. This problem is pictured in Illustration D-28.

**Illustration D-28**
Calculator solution for auto loan payments

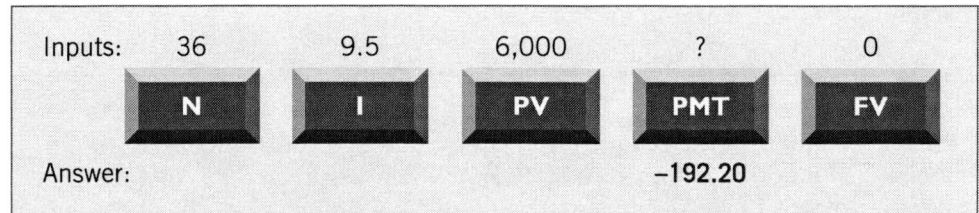

To solve this problem, you enter N = 36 (12 × 3), I = 9.5, PV = 6,000, FV = 0, and then press PMT. You will find that the monthly payments will be $192.20. Note that the payment key is usually programmed for 12 payments per year. Thus, you must change the default (compounding period) if the payments are other than monthly.

### MORTGAGE LOAN AMOUNT

Let's say you are evaluating financing options for a loan on a house. You decide that the maximum mortgage payment you can afford is $700 per month. The annual interest rate is 8.4%. If you get a mortgage that requires you to make monthly payments over a 15-year period, what is the maximum home loan you can afford? Illustration D-29 depicts this problem.

**Illustration D-29**
Calculator solution for mortgage amount

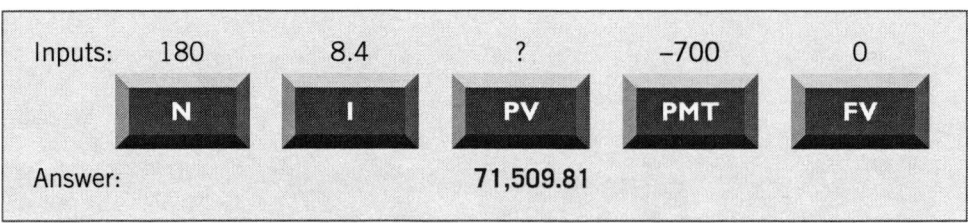

You enter N = 180 (12 × 15 years), I = 8.4, PMT = −700, FV = 0, and press PV. With the payments-per-year key set at 12, you find a present value of $71,509.81—the maximum home loan you can afford, given that you want to keep your mortgage payments at $700. Note that by changing any of the variables, you can quickly conduct "what-if" analyses for different situations.

# Summary of Study Objectives

**1** **Distinguish between simple and compound interest.** Simple interest is computed on the principal only, while compound interest is computed on the principal and any interest earned that has not been withdrawn.

**2** **Solve for future value of a single amount.** Prepare a time diagram of the problem. Identify the principal amount, the number of compounding periods, and the interest rate. Using the future value of 1 table, multiply the principal amount by the future value factor specified at the intersection of the number of periods and the interest rate.

**3** **Solve for future value of an annuity.** Prepare a time diagram of the problem. Identify the amount of the periodic payments, the number of compounding periods, and the interest rate. Using the future value of an annuity of 1 table, multiply the amount of the payments by the future value factor specified at the intersection of the number of periods and the interest rate.

**4** **Identify the variables fundamental to solving present value problems.** The following three variables are fundamental to solving present value problems: (1) the future amount, (2) the number of periods, and (3) the interest rate (the discount rate).

**5** **Solve for present value of a single amount.** Prepare a time diagram of the problem. Identify the future amount, the number of discounting periods, and the discount (interest) rate. Using the present value of a single amount table, multiply the future amount by the present value factor specified at the intersection of the number of periods and the discount rate.

**6** **Solve for present value of an annuity.** Prepare a time diagram of the problem. Identify the amount of future periodic receipts or payment (annuities), the number of discounting periods, and the discount (interest) rate.

Using the present value of an annuity of 1 table, multiply the amount of the annuity by the present value factor specified at the intersection of the number of periods and the interest rate.

**7** **Compute the present value of notes and bonds.** Determine the present value of the principal amount: Multiply the principal amount (a single future amount) by the present value factor (from the present value of 1 table) intersecting at the number of periods (number of interest payments) and the discount rate. Determine the present value of the series of interest payments: Multiply the amount of the interest payment by the present value factor (from the present value of an annuity of 1 table) intersecting at the number of periods (number of interest payments) and the discount rate. Add the present value of the principal amount to the present value of the interest payments to arrive at the present value of the note or bond.

**8** **Compute the present values in capital budgeting situations.** Compute the present values of all cash inflows and all cash outflows related to the capital budgeting proposal (an investment-type decision). If the **net** present value is positive, accept the proposal (make the investment). If the **net** present value is negative, reject the proposal (do not make the investment).

**9** **Use a financial calculator to solve time value of money problems.** Financial calculators can be used to solve the same and additional problems as those solved with time value of money tables. Enter into the financial calculator the amounts for all of the known elements of a time value of money problem (periods, interest rate, payments, future or present value), and it solves for the unknown element. Particularly useful situations involve interest rates and compounding periods not presented in the tables.

# Glossary

**Annuity** *(p. D-4)* A series of equal dollar amounts to be paid or received at evenly space time intervals (periodically).

**Compound interest** *(p. D-2)* The interest computed on the principal and any interest earned that has not been paid or withdrawn.

**Discounting the future amount(s)** *(p. D-7)* The process of determining present value.

**Future value of a single amount** *(p. D-2)* The value at a future date of a given amount invested, assuming compound interest.

**Future value of an annuity** *(p. D-5)* The sum of all the payments or receipts plus the accumulated compound interest on them.

**Interest** *(p. D-1)* Payment for the use of another person's money.

**Present value** *(p. D-7)* The value now of a given amount to be paid or received in the future assuming compound interest.

**Present value of an annuity** *(p. D-9)* The value now of a series of future receipts or payments, discounted assuming compound interest.

**Principal** *(p. D-1)* The amount borrowed or invested.

**Simple interest** *(p. D-1)* The interest computed on the principal only.

# Brief Exercises

**(Use tables to solve exercises BED-1 to BED-25.)**

*Compute the future value of a single amount.*
*(SO 2), AP*

**BED-1**   Randy Owen invested $8,000 at 5% annual interest, and left the money invested without withdrawing any of the interest for 12 years. At the end of the 12 years, Randy withdrew the accumulated amount of money. (a) What amount did Randy withdraw, assuming the investment earns simple interest? (b) What amount did Randy withdraw, assuming the investment earns interest compounded annually?

*Use future value tables.*
*(SO 2, 3), C*

**BED-2**   For each of the following cases, indicate (a) to what interest rate columns and (b) to what number of periods you would refer in looking up the future value factor.

(1)  In Table 1 (future value of 1):

|  | Annual Rate | Number of Years Invested | Compounded |
|---|---|---|---|
| Case A | 6% | 3 | Annually |
| Case B | 8% | 4 | Semiannually |

(2)  In Table 2 (future value of an annuity of 1):

|  | Annual Rate | Number of Years Invested | Compounded |
|---|---|---|---|
| Case A | 5% | 8 | Annually |
| Case B | 6% | 6 | Semiannually |

*Compute the future value of a single amount.*
*(SO 2), AP*

**BED-3**   Joyce Company signed a lease for an office building for a period of 12 years. Under the lease agreement, a security deposit of $9,200 is made. The deposit will be returned at the expiration of the lease with interest compounded at 4% per year. What amount will Joyce receive at the time the lease expires?

*Compute the future value of an annuity.*
*(SO 3), AP*

**BED-4**   Bates Company issued $1,000,000, 10-year bonds and agreed to make annual sinking fund deposits of $78,000. The deposits are made at the end of each year into an account paying 5% annual interest. What amount will be in the sinking fund at the end of 10 years?

*Compute the future value of a single amount and of an annuity.*
*(SO 2, 3), AP*

**BED-5**   Frank and Maureen Fantazzi invested $6,000 in a savings account paying 4% annual interest when their daughter, Angela, was born. They also deposited $1,000 on each of her birthdays until she was 18 (including her 18th birthday). How much was in the savings account on her 18th birthday (after the last deposit)?

*Compute the future value of a single amount.*
*(SO 2), AP*

**BED-6**   Hugh Curtin borrowed $34,000 on July 1, 2012. This amount plus accrued interest at 9% compounded annually is to be repaid on July 1, 2017. How much will Hugh have to repay on July 1, 2017?

*Use present value tables.*
*(SO 5, 6), C*

**BED-7**   For each of the following cases, indicate (a) to what interest rate columns and (b) to what number of periods you would refer in looking up the discount rate.

(1)  In Table 3 (present value of 1):

|  | Annual Rate | Number of Years Involved | Discounts per Year |
|---|---|---|---|
| Case A | 12% | 6 | Annually |
| Case B | 10% | 11 | Annually |
| Case C | 6% | 9 | Semiannually |

(2)  In Table 4 (present value of an annuity of 1):

|  | Annual Rate | Number of Years Involved | Number of Payments Involved | Frequency of Payments |
|---|---|---|---|---|
| Case A | 12% | 20 | 20 | Annually |
| Case B | 10% | 5 | 5 | Annually |
| Case C | 8% | 4 | 8 | Semiannually |

**BED-8** (a) What is the present value of $28,000 due 9 periods from now, discounted at 10%?
(b) What is the present value of $28,000 to be received at the end of each of 6 periods, discounted at 9%?

*Determine present values.*
(SO 5, 6), AP

**BED-9** Chaffee Company is considering an investment that will return a lump sum of $750,000 five years from now. What amount should Chaffee Company pay for this investment to earn a 9% return?

*Compute the present value of a single amount investment.*
(SO 5), AP

**BED-10** Lloyd Company earns 10% on an investment that will return $480,000 eight years from now. What is the amount Lloyd should invest now to earn this rate of return?

*Compute the present value of a single amount investment.*
(SO 5), AP

**BED-11** Arthur Company is considering investing in an annuity contract that will return $45,000 annually at the end of each year for 15 years. What amount should Arthur Company pay for this investment if it earns a 5% return?

*Compute the present value of an annuity investment.*
(SO 6), AP

**BED-12** Kaehler Enterprises earns 8% on an investment that pays back $90,000 at the end of each of the next 6 years. What is the amount Kaehler Enterprises invested to earn the 8% rate of return?

*Compute the present value of an annuity investment.*
(SO 6), AP

**BED-13** Hanna Railroad Co. is about to issue $300,000 of 10-year bonds paying a 9% interest rate, with interest payable semiannually. The discount rate for such securities is 8%. How much can Hanna expect to receive for the sale of these bonds?

*Compute the present value of bonds.*
(SO 5, 6, 7), AP

**BED-14** Assume the same information as BED-13 except that the discount rate was 10% instead of 8%. In this case, how much can Hanna expect to receive from the sale of these bonds?

*Compute the present value of bonds.*
(SO 5, 6, 7), AP

**BED-15** Tomas Taco Company receives a $64,000, 6-year note bearing interest of 6% (paid annually) from a customer at a time when the discount rate is 8%. What is the present value of the note received by Tomas?

*Compute the present value of a note.*
(SO 5, 6, 7), AP

**BED-16** Gleason Enterprises issued 9%, 8-year, $2,600,000 par value bonds that pay interest semiannually on October 1 and April 1. The bonds are dated April 1, 2012, and are issued on that date. The discount rate of interest for such bonds on April 1, 2012, is 10%. What cash proceeds did Gleason receive from issuance of the bonds?

*Compute the present value of bonds.*
(SO 5, 6, 7), AP

**BED-17** Mark Barton owns a garage and is contemplating purchasing a tire retreading machine for $18,000. After estimating costs and revenues, Mark projects a net cash flow from the retreading machine of $3,300 annually for 8 years. Mark hopes to earn a return of 10 percent on such investments. What is the present value of the retreading operation? Should Mark purchase the retreading machine?

*Compute the present value of a machine for purposes of making a purchase decision.*
(SO 6, 7), AP

**BED-18** Frazier Company issues an 8%, 5-year mortgage note on January 1, 2012, to obtain financing for new equipment. Land is used as collateral for the note. The terms provide for semiannual installment payments of $46,850. What were the cash proceeds received from the issuance of the note?

*Compute the present value of a note.*
(SO 6), AP

**BED-19** Leffler Company is considering purchasing equipment. The equipment will produce the following cash flows: Year 1, $38,000; Year 2, $40,000; and Year 3, $50,000. Leffler requires a minimum rate of return of 10%. What is the maximum price Leffler should pay for this equipment?

*Compute the maximum price to pay for a machine.*
(SO 6, 7), AP

**BED-20** If Colleen Mooney invests $4,172.65 now and she will receive $10,000 at the end of 15 years, what annual rate of interest will Colleen earn on her investment? (*Hint:* Use Table 3.)

*Compute the interest rate on a single amount.*
(SO 5), AN

**BED-21** Wayne Kurt has been offered the opportunity of investing $25,490 now. The investment will earn 10% per year and at the end of that time will return Wayne $80,000. How many years must Wayne wait to receive $80,000? (*Hint:* Use Table 3.)

*Compute the number of periods of a single amount.*
(SO 5), AN

**BED-22** Joanne Quick made an investment of $9,128.55. From this investment, she will receive $1,000 annually for the next 20 years starting one year from now. What rate of interest will Joanne's investment be earning for her? (*Hint:* Use Table 4.)

*Compute the interest rate on an annuity.*
(SO 6), AN

**BED-23** Patty Schleis invests $5,146.12 now for a series of $1,000 annual returns beginning one year from now. Patty will earn a return of 11% on the initial investment. How many annual payments of $1,000 will Patty receive? (*Hint:* Use Table 4.)

*Compute the number of periods of an annuity.*
(SO 6), AN

*Compute the present value of a machine for purposes of making a purchase decision.*
(SO 8), AP

**BED-24** Barney Googal owns a garage and is contemplating purchasing a tire retreading machine for $14,280. After estimating costs and revenues, Barney projects a net cash flow from the retreading machine of $2,900 annually for 8 years. Barney hopes to earn a return of 11% on such investments. What is the present value of the retreading operation? Should Barney Googal purchase the retreading machine?

*Compute the maximum price to pay for a machine.*
(SO 8), AP

**BED-25** Ramos Company is considering purchasing equipment. The equipment will produce the following cash flows: Year 1, $30,000; Year 2, $40,000; Year 3, $50,000. Ramos requires a minimum rate of return of 12%. What is the maximum price Ramos should pay for this equipment?

*Determine interest rate.*
(SO 9), AP

**BED-26** Carly Simon wishes to invest $18,000 on July 1, 2012, and have it accumulate to $50,000 by July 1, 2022.

***Instructions***
Use a financial calculator to determine at what exact annual rate of interest Carly must invest the $18,000.

*Determine interest rate.*
(SO 9), AP

**BED-27** On July 17, 2012, James Taylor borrowed $60,000 from his grandfather to open a clothing store. Starting July 17, 2018, James has to make 10 equal annual payments of $8,860 each to repay the loan.

***Instructions***
Use a financial calculator to determine what interest rate James is paying.

*Determine interest rate.*
(SO 9), AP

**BED-28** As the purchaser of a new house, Carrie Underwood has signed a mortgage note to pay the Nashville National Bank and Trust Co. $8,400 every 6 months for 20 years, at the end of which time she will own the house. At the date the mortgage is signed, the purchase price was $198,000 and Underwood made a down payment of $20,000. The first payment will be made 6 months after the date the mortgage is signed.

***Instructions***
Using a financial calculator, compute the exact rate of interest earned on the mortgage by the bank.

*Various time value of money situations.*
(SO 9), AP

**BED-29** Using a financial calculator, solve for the unknowns in each of the following situations.
(a) On June 1, 2012, Holly Golightly purchases lakefront property from her neighbor, George Peppard, and agrees to pay the purchase price in seven payments of $16,000 each, the first payment to be payable June 1, 2013. (Assume that interest compounded at an annual rate of 6.9% is implicit in the payments.) What is the purchase price of the property?
(b) On January 1, 2012, Sammis Corporation purchased 200 of the $1,000 face value, 7% coupon, 10-year bonds of Malone Inc. The bonds mature on January 1, 2020, and pay interest annually beginning January 1, 2013. Sammis purchased the bonds to yield 8.65%. How much did Sammis pay for the bonds?

*Various time value of money situations.*
(SO 9), AP

**BED-30** Using a financial calculator, provide a solution to each of the following situations.
(a) Lynn Anglin owes a debt of $42,000 from the purchase of her new sport utility vehicle. The debt bears annual interest of 7.8% compounded monthly. Lynn wishes to pay the debt and interest in equal monthly payments over 8 years, beginning one month hence. What equal monthly payments will pay off the debt and interest?
(b) On January 1, 2012, Roger Molony offers to buy Dave Feeney's used snowmobile for $8,000, payable in five equal annual installments, which are to include 7.25% interest on the unpaid balance and a portion of the principal. If the first payment is to be made on December 31, 2012, how much will each payment be?

# REPORTING AND ANALYZING INVESTMENTS

## study objectives

**After studying this appendix, you should be able to:**

**1** Identify the reasons corporations invest in stocks and debt securities.

**2** Explain the accounting for debt investments.

**3** Explain the accounting for stock investments.

**4** Describe the purpose and usefulness of consolidated financial statements.

**5** Indicate how debt and stock investments are valued and reported in the financial statements.

**6** Distinguish between short-term and long-term investments.

## Why Corporations Invest

Corporations purchase investments in debt or equity securities generally for one of three reasons. First, a corporation may **have excess cash** that it does not need for the immediate purchase of operating assets. For example, many companies experience seasonal fluctuations in sales. A Cape Cod marina has more sales in the spring and summer than in the fall and winter. The reverse is true for an Aspen ski shop. Thus, at the end of an operating cycle, many companies may have cash on hand that is temporarily idle until the start of another operating cycle. These companies may invest the excess funds to earn—through interest and dividends—a greater return than they would get by just holding the funds in the bank. The role that such temporary investments play in the operating cycle is depicted in Illustration E-1.

**study objective** 1
Identify the reasons corporations invest in stocks and debt securities.

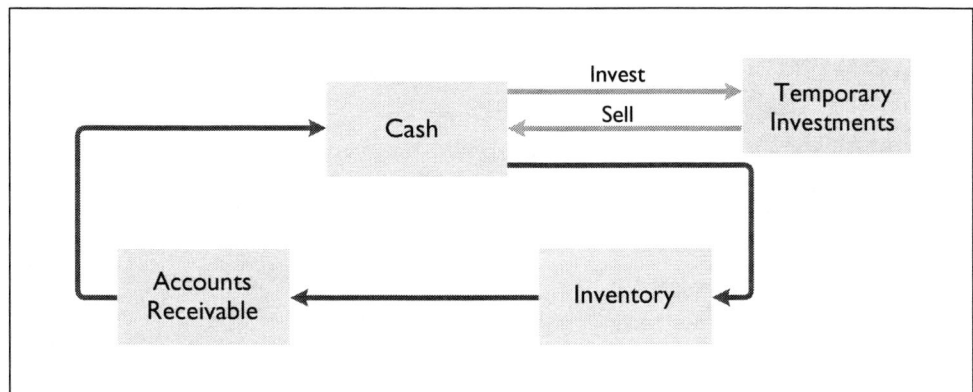

**Illustration E-1**
Temporary investments and the operating cycle

A second reason some companies such as banks purchase investments is to generate **earnings from investment income**. Although banks make most of their earnings by lending money, they also generate earnings by investing in debt and equity securities. Banks purchase investment securities because loan demand varies both seasonally and with changes in the economic climate. Thus, when loan demand is low, a bank must find other uses for its cash.

Pension funds and mutual funds are corporations that also regularly invest to generate earnings. However, they do so for *speculative reasons*. That is, they are speculating that the investment will increase in value and thus result in positive returns. Therefore, they invest primarily in the common stock of other corporations.

Third, companies also invest for **strategic reasons**. A company may purchase a noncontrolling interest in another company in a related industry in which it wishes to establish a presence. Alternatively, a company can exercise some influence over one of its customers or suppliers by purchasing a significant, but not controlling, interest in that company. Or, a corporation may choose to purchase a controlling interest in another company in order to enter a new industry without incurring the costs and risks associated with starting from scratch.

In summary, businesses invest in other companies for the reasons shown in Illustration E-2.

**Illustration E-2** Why corporations invest

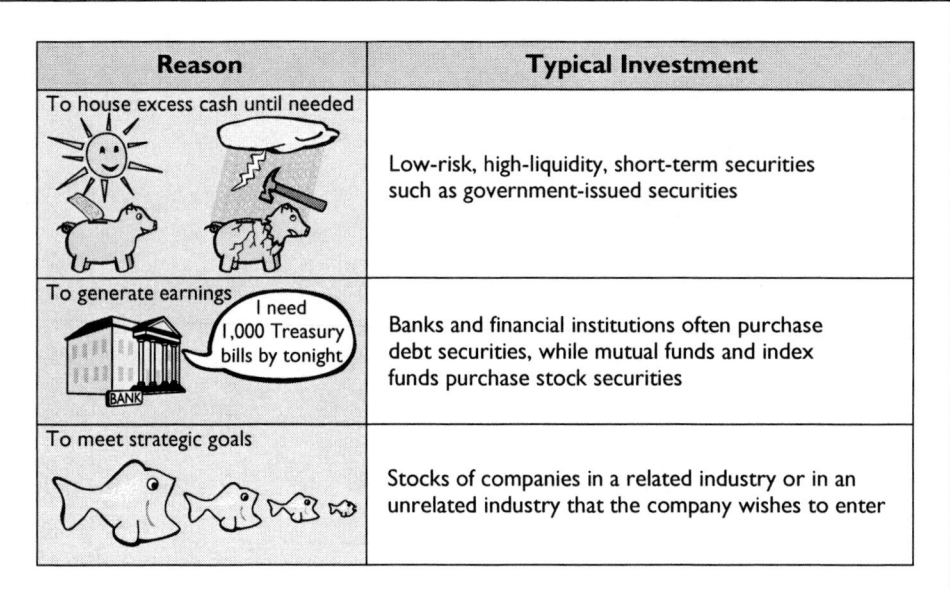

## Accounting for Debt Investments

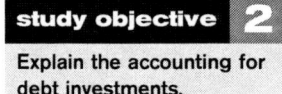

**study objective** **2**

Explain the accounting for debt investments.

Debt investments are investments in government and corporation bonds. In accounting for debt investments, companies must make entries to record (1) the acquisition, (2) the interest revenue, and (3) the sale.

### RECORDING ACQUISITION OF BONDS

**At acquisition, the cost principle applies.** Cost includes all expenditures necessary to acquire these investments, such as the price paid plus brokerage fees (commissions), if any.

For example, assume that Kuhl Corporation acquires 50 Doan Inc. 12%, 10-year, $1,000 bonds on January 1, 2012, for $54,000, including brokerage fees of $1,000. Kuhl records the investment as:

| A | = | L | + | SE |
|---|---|---|---|---|
| +54,000 | | | | |
| −54,000 | | | | |

**Cash Flows**
−$54,000

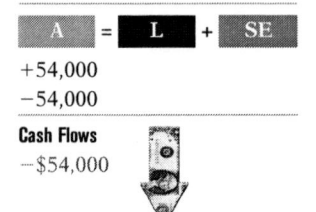

| | | | | |
|---|---|---|---|---|
| Jan. 1 | Debt Investments | | 54,000 | |
| | Cash | | | 54,000 |
| | (To record purchase of 50 Doan Inc. bonds) | | | |

## RECORDING BOND INTEREST

The Doan Inc. bonds pay interest of $3,000 semiannually on July 1 and January 1 ($50,000 \times 12\% \times \frac{1}{2}$). The entry for the receipt of interest on July 1 is:

| July 1 | Cash | 3,000 | |
| |     Interest Revenue | | 3,000 |
| |       (To record receipt of interest on Doan | | |
| |       Inc. bonds) | | |

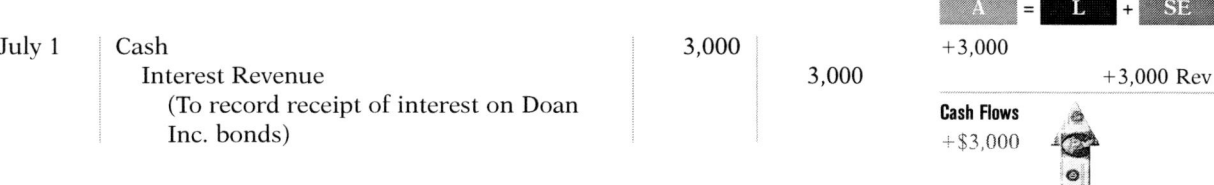

If Kuhl Corporation's fiscal year ends on December 31, it accrues the interest of $3,000 earned since July 1. The adjusting entry is:

| Dec. 31 | Interest Receivable | 3,000 | |
| |     Interest Revenue | | 3,000 |
| |       (To accrue interest on Doan Inc. | | |
| |       bonds) | | |

Kuhl reports Interest Receivable as a current asset in the balance sheet. It reports Interest Revenue under "Other revenues and gains" in the income statement.

Kuhl records receipt of the interest on January 1 as follows.

| Jan. 1 | Cash | 3,000 | |
| |     Interest Receivable | | 3,000 |
| |       (To record receipt of accrued interest) | | |

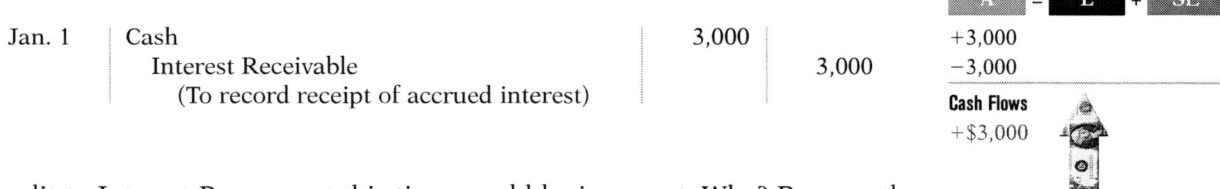

A credit to Interest Revenue at this time would be incorrect. Why? Because the company earned and accrued the interest revenue in the preceding accounting period.

## RECORDING SALE OF BONDS

When Kuhl sells the bond investments, it credits the investment account for the cost of the bonds. The company records as a gain or loss any difference between the net proceeds from the sale (sales price less brokerage fees) and the cost of the bonds.

Assume, for example, that Kuhl Corporation receives net proceeds of $58,000 on the sale of the Doan Inc. bonds on January 1, 2013, after receiving the interest due. Since the securities cost $54,000, Kuhl has realized a gain of $4,000. It records the sale as follows.

**Helpful Hint** The accounting for short-term debt investments and long-term debt investments is similar. Any exceptions are discussed in more advanced courses.

| Jan. 1 | Cash | 58,000 | |
| |     Debt Investments | | 54,000 |
| |     Gain on Sale of Debt Investments | | 4,000 |
| |       (To record sale of Doan Inc. bonds) | | |

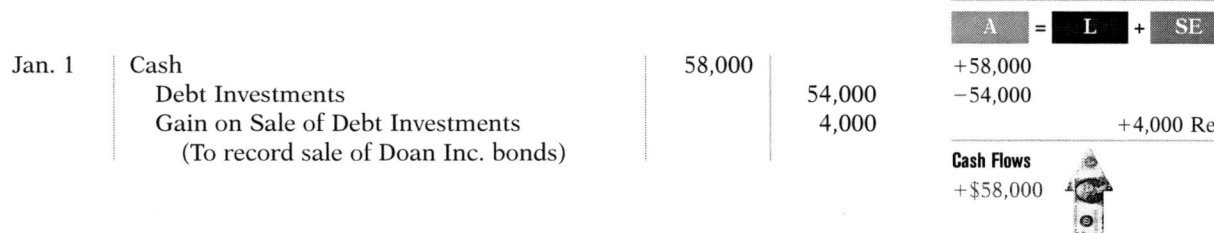

Kuhl reports the gain on the sale of debt investments under "Other revenues and gains" in the income statement and reports losses under "Other expenses and losses."

# Accounting for Stock Investments

**study objective  3**

Explain the accounting for stock investments.

Stock investments are investments in the capital stock of corporations. When a company holds stock (and/or debt) of several different corporations, the group of securities is an **investment portfolio**.

The accounting for investments in common stock depends on the extent of the investor's influence over the operating and financial affairs of the issuing corporation (the **investee**). Illustration E-3 shows the general guidelines.

**Illustration E-3**
Accounting guidelines for stock investments

| Investor's Ownership Interest in Investee's Common Stock | Presumed Influence on Investee | Accounting Guidelines |
|---|---|---|
| Less than 20% | Insignificant | Cost method |
| Between 20% and 50% | Significant | Equity method |
| More than 50% | Controlling | Consolidated financial statements |

Companies are required to use judgment instead of blindly following the guidelines.[1] We explain and illustrate the application of each guideline next.

### HOLDINGS OF LESS THAN 20%

In the accounting for stock investments of less than 20%, companies use the cost method. Under the cost method, companies record the investment at cost and recognize revenue only when cash dividends are received.

### Recording Acquisition of Stock

At acquisition, the cost principle applies. Cost includes all expenditures necessary to acquire these investments, such as the price paid plus brokerage fees (commissions), if any.

Assume, for example, that on July 1, 2012, Sanchez Corporation acquires 1,000 shares (10% ownership) of Beal Corporation common stock at $40 per share plus brokerage fees of $500. The entry for the purchase is:

A = L + SE
+40,500
−40,500

Cash Flows
−$40,500

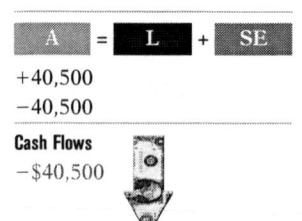

| July 1 | Stock Investments | 40,500 | |
|---|---|---|---|
| | Cash | | 40,500 |
| | (To record purchase of 1,000 shares of Beal common stock) | | |

---

[1]Among the factors that companies should consider in determining an investor's influence are whether (1) the investor has representation on the investee's board of directors, (2) the investor participates in the investee's policy-making process, (3) there are material transactions between the investor and the investee, and (4) the common stock held by other stockholders is concentrated or dispersed.

## Recording Dividends

During the time the company holds the stock, it makes entries for any cash dividends received. Thus, if Sanchez Corporation receives a $2 per share dividend on December 31, the entry is:

| | | | |
|---|---|---|---|
| Dec. 31 | Cash (1,000 × $2) | 2,000 | |
| | Dividend Revenue | | 2,000 |
| | (To record receipt of a cash dividend) | | |

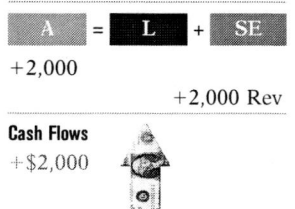

A = L + SE
+2,000
            +2,000 Rev

**Cash Flows**
+$2,000

Sanchez reports Dividend Revenue under "Other revenues and gains" in the income statement.

## Recording Sale of Stock

When a company sells a stock investment, it recognizes the difference between the net proceeds from the sale (sales price less brokerage fees) and the cost of the stock as a gain or a loss.

Assume, for instance, that Sanchez Corporation receives net proceeds of $39,500 on the sale of its Beal Corporation stock on February 10, 2013. Because the stock cost $40,500, Sanchez has incurred a loss of $1,000. It records the sale as:

| | | | |
|---|---|---|---|
| Feb. 10 | Cash | 39,500 | |
| | Loss on Sale of Stock Investments | 1,000 | |
| | Stock Investments | | 40,500 |
| | (To record sale of Beal common stock) | | |

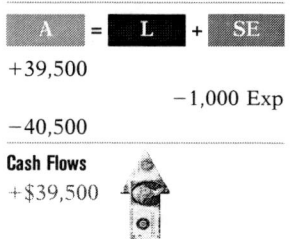

A = L + SE
+39,500
            −1,000 Exp
−40,500

**Cash Flows**
+$39,500

Sanchez reports the loss account under "Other expenses and losses" in the income statement, and would show a gain on sale under "Other revenues and gains."

### HOLDINGS BETWEEN 20% AND 50%

When an investor company owns only a small portion of the shares of stock of another company, the investor cannot exercise control over the investee. But when an investor owns between 20% and 50% of the common stock of a corporation, it is presumed that the investor has significant influence over the financial and operating activities of the investee. The investor probably has a representative on the investee's board of directors. Through that representative, the investor begins to exercise some control over the investee—and the investee company in some sense becomes part of the investor company.

For example, even prior to purchasing all of Turner Broadcasting, Time Warner owned 20% of Turner. Because it exercised significant control over major decisions made by Turner, Time Warner used an approach called the equity method. Under the **equity method, the investor records its share of the net income of the investee in the year when it is earned**. An alternative might be to delay recognizing the investor's share of net income until a cash dividend is declared. But that approach would ignore the fact that the investor and investee are, in some sense, one company, making the investor better off by the investee's earned income.

Under the equity method, the company initially records the investment in common stock at cost. After that, it adjusts the investment account **annually** to show the investor's equity in the investee. Each year, the investor does the following: (1) It increases (debits) the investment account and increases (credits) revenue for its share of the investee's net income.[2] (2) The investor also decreases (credits) the investment account for the amount of dividends received. The investment account is reduced for dividends received because payment of a dividend decreases the net assets of the investee.

### Recording Acquisition of Stock

Assume that Milar Corporation acquires 30% of the common stock of Beck Company for $120,000 on January 1, 2012. The entry to record this transaction is:

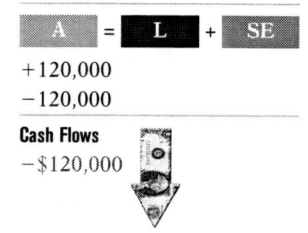

A = L + SE
+120,000
−120,000

**Cash Flows**
−$120,000

| | | | | |
|---|---|---|---|---|
| Jan. 1 | Stock Investments | | 120,000 | |
| |     Cash | | | 120,000 |
| |     (To record purchase of Beck common | | | |
| |     stock) | | | |

### Recording Revenue and Dividends

For 2012, Beck reports net income of $100,000. It declares and pays a $40,000 cash dividend. Milar must record (1) its share of Beck's income, $30,000 (30% × $100,000), and (2) the reduction in the investment account for the dividends received, $12,000 ($40,000 × 30%). The entries are:

A = L + SE
+30,000
         +30,000 Rev

**Cash Flows**
no effect

(1)

| | | | | |
|---|---|---|---|---|
| Dec. 31 | Stock Investments | | 30,000 | |
| |     Revenue from Investment in Beck Company | | | 30,000 |
| |     (To record 30% equity in Beck's 2012 | | | |
| |     net income) | | | |

A = L + SE
+12,000
−12,000

**Cash Flows**
+$12,000

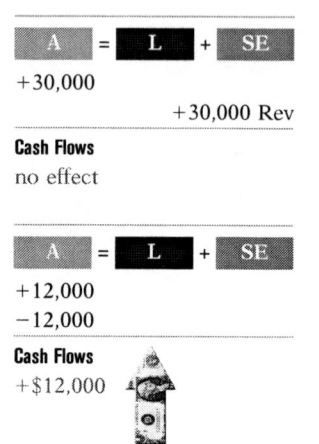

(2)

| | | | | |
|---|---|---|---|---|
| Dec. 31 | Cash | | 12,000 | |
| |     Stock Investments | | | 12,000 |
| |     (To record dividends received) | | | |

After Milar posts the transactions for the year, the investment and revenue accounts are as shown in Illustration E-4.

**Illustration E-4**
Investment and revenue accounts after posting

| Stock Investments | | | | Revenue from Investment in Beck Company | |
|---|---|---|---|---|---|
| Jan. 1 | 120,000 | Dec. 31 | 12,000 | Dec. 31 | 30,000 |
| Dec. 31 | 30,000 | | | | |
| Dec. 31 Bal. | 138,000 | | | | |

During the year, the investment account increased by $18,000. This $18,000 is Milar's 30% equity in the $60,000 increase in Beck's retained earnings ($100,000 − $40,000). In addition, Milar reports $30,000 of revenue from its investment, which is 30% of Beck's net income of $100,000.

---

[2]Conversely, the investor increases (debits) a loss account and decreases (credits) the investment account for its share of the investee's net loss.

Note that the difference between reported income under the cost method and reported revenue under the equity method can be significant. For example, Milar would report only $12,000 of dividend revenue (30% × $40,000) if it used the cost method.

### HOLDINGS OF MORE THAN 50%

A company that owns more than 50% of the common stock of another entity is known as the parent company. The entity whose stock is owned by the parent company is called the subsidiary (affiliated) company. Because of its stock ownership, the parent company has a controlling interest in the subsidiary company.

When a company owns more than 50% of the common stock of another company, it usually prepares consolidated financial statements. Consolidated financial statements present the assets and liabilities controlled by the parent company. They also present the total revenues and expenses of the subsidiary companies. Companies prepare consolidated statements **in addition to** the financial statements for the individual parent and subsidiary companies.

As noted earlier, prior to acquiring all of Turner Broadcasting, Time Warner accounted for its investment in Turner using the equity method. Time Warner's net investment in Turner was reported in a single line item—Other investments. After the merger, Time Warner instead consolidated Turner's results with its own. Under this approach, Time Warner included the individual assets and liabilities of Turner with its own assets. That is, Turner's plant and equipment were added to Time Warner's plant and equipment, its receivables were added to Time Warner's receivables, and so on. A similar sort of consolidation went on when AOL merged with Time Warner.

**Consolidated statements are useful to the stockholders, board of directors, and management of the parent company**. Consolidated statements indicate to creditors, prospective investors, and regulatory agencies the magnitude and scope of operations of the companies under common control. For example, regulators and the courts undoubtedly used the consolidated statements of AT&T to determine whether a breakup of AT&T was in the public interest. Listed here are three companies that prepare consolidated statements and some of the companies they have owned. Note that one, Disney, is Time Warner's arch rival.

**study objective 4**

Describe the purpose and usefulness of consolidated financial statements.

**Helpful Hint** If the parent (A) has three wholly owned subsidiaries (B, C, and D), there are four separate legal entities but only one economic entity from the viewpoint of the shareholders of the parent company.

| PepsiCo | Cendant | The Walt Disney Company |
|---|---|---|
| Frito-Lay | Howard Johnson | Capital Cities/ABC, Inc. |
| Tropicana | Ramada Inn | Disneyland, Disney World |
| Quaker Oats | Century 21 | Mighty Ducks |
| Pepsi-Cola | Coldwell Banker | Anaheim Angels |
| Gatorade | Avis | ESPN |

# Valuing and Reporting Investments

The value of debt and stock investments may fluctuate greatly during the time they are held. For example, in a 12-month period, the stock of Time Warner hit a high of $58\frac{1}{2}$ and a low of 9. In light of such price fluctuations, how should companies value investments at the balance sheet date? Valuation could be at cost, at fair value (market value), or at the lower-of-cost-or-market value.

Many people argue that fair value offers the best approach because it represents the expected cash realizable value of securities. Fair value is the amount for which a security could be sold in a normal market. Others counter that, unless a security is going to be sold soon, the fair value is not relevant because the price of the security will likely change again.

**study objective 5**

Indicate how debt and stock investments are valued and reported in the financial statements.

## CATEGORIES OF SECURITIES

**International Note** A recent U.S. accounting standard gives companies the "option" of applying fair value accounting, rather than historical cost, to certain types of assets and liabilities. This makes U.S. accounting closer to international standards.

For purposes of valuation and reporting at a financial statement date, debt and stock investments are classified into three categories of securities:

1. Trading securities are bought and held primarily for sale in the near term to generate income on short-term price differences.

2. Available-for-sale securities are held with the intent of selling them sometime in the future.

3. Held-to-maturity securities are debt securities that the investor has the intent and ability to hold to maturity.[3]

Illustration E-5 shows the valuation guidelines for these securities. **These guidelines apply to all debt securities and all stock investments in which the holdings are less than 20%.**

**Illustration E-5**
Valuation guidelines

**Trading**

"We'll sell within ten days."

At fair value with changes reported in net income

**Available-for-sale**

"We'll hold the stock for a while to see how it performs."

At fair value with changes reported in the stockholders' equity section

**Held-to-maturity**

"We intend to hold until maturity."

At amortized cost

### Trading Securities

Trading securities are held with the intention of selling them in a short period of time (generally less than a month). *Trading* means frequent buying and selling. As indicated in Illustration E-5, companies adjust trading securities to fair value at the end of each period (an approach referred to as mark-to-market accounting); they report changes from cost **as part of net income**. The changes are reported as **unrealized gains or losses** because the securities have not been sold. The unrealized gain or loss is the difference between the **total cost** of trading securities and their **total fair value**. Companies classify trading securities as a current asset.

As an example, Illustration E-6 shows the costs and fair values for investments classified as trading securities for Pace Corporation on December 31, 2012. Pace Corporation has an unrealized gain of $7,000 because total fair value ($147,000) is $7,000 greater than total cost ($140,000).

**Illustration E-6**
Valuation of trading securities

| Trading Securities, December 31, 2012 | | | |
|---|---|---|---|
| **Investments** | **Cost** | **Fair Value** | **Unrealized Gain (Loss)** |
| Yorkville Company bonds | $ 50,000 | $ 48,000 | $(2,000) |
| Kodak Company stock | 90,000 | 99,000 | 9,000 |
| Total | $140,000 | $147,000 | $ 7,000 |

---

[3]This category is provided for completeness. The accounting and valuation issues related to held-to-maturity securities are discussed in more advanced accounting courses.

The fact that trading securities are a short-term investment increases the likelihood that Pace will sell them at fair value for a gain. Pace records fair value and the unrealized gain through an adjusting entry at the time it prepares financial statements. In the entry, the company uses a valuation allowance account, Market Adjustment—Trading, to record the difference between the total cost and the total fair value of the securities. The adjusting entry for Pace Corporation is:

| | | | |
|---|---|---|---|
| Dec. 31 | Market Adjustment—Trading | 7,000 | |
| | Unrealized Gain—Income | | 7,000 |
| | (To record unrealized gain on trading securities) | | |

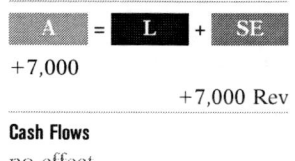

+7,000

+7,000 Rev

**Cash Flows**
no effect

The use of the Market Adjustment—Trading account enables the company to maintain a record of the investment cost. Actual cost is needed to determine the gain or loss realized when the securities are sold. The company adds the debit balance (or subtracts a credit balance) of the Market Adjustment—Trading account to the cost of the investments to arrive at a fair value for the trading securities. **The fair value of the securities is the amount companies report on the balance sheet.** They report the unrealized gain on the income statement under "Other revenues and gains." The term *income* in the account title indicates that the gain affects net income. If the total cost of the trading securities is greater than total fair value, an unrealized loss has occurred. In such a case, the adjusting entry is a debit to Unrealized Loss—Income and a credit to Market Adjustment—Trading. Companies report the unrealized loss under "Other expenses and losses" in the income statement.

The market adjustment account is carried forward into future accounting periods. No entries are made to this account during the period. At the end of each reporting period, a company adjusts the balance in the account to the difference between cost and fair value at that time. It closes the Unrealized Gain—Income account or Unrealized Loss—Income account at the end of the reporting period.

## Available-for-Sale Securities

As indicated earlier, available-for-sale securities are held with the intent of selling them sometime in the future. If the intent is to sell the securities within the next year or operating cycle, a company classifies the securities as current assets in the balance sheet. Otherwise, it classifies them as long-term assets in the investments section of the balance sheet.

Companies also report available-for-sale securities at fair value. The procedure for determining fair value and unrealized gain or loss for these securities is the same as that for trading securities. To illustrate, assume that Elbert Corporation has two securities that are classified as available-for-sale. Illustration E-7 provides information on the cost, fair value, and amount of the unrealized gain or loss on December 31, 2012. There is an unrealized loss of $9,537 because total cost ($293,537) is $9,537 more than total fair value ($284,000).

**Illustration E-7**
Valuation of available-for-sale securities

| Available-for-Sale Securities, December 31, 2012 | | | |
|---|---|---|---|
| **Investments** | **Cost** | **Fair Value** | **Unrealized Gain (Loss)** |
| Campbell Soup Corporation | | | |
| 8% bonds | $ 93,537 | $103,600 | $10,063 |
| Hershey Foods stock | 200,000 | 180,400 | (19,600) |
| Total | $293,537 | $284,000 | $(9,537) |

Both the adjusting entry and the reporting of the unrealized loss from Elbert's available-for-sale securities differ from those illustrated for trading securities. The differences result because these securities are not going to be sold in the near term. Thus, prior to actual sale it is much more likely that changes in fair value may reverse the unrealized loss. Therefore, Elbert does not report an unrealized loss in the income statement. Instead, it reports it as **a separate component of stockholders' equity**. In the adjusting entry, Elbert identifies the market adjustment account with available-for-sale securities, and identifies the unrealized gain or loss account with stockholders' equity. The adjusting entry for Elbert Corporation to record the unrealized loss of $9,537 is:

**Helpful Hint** The entry is the same regardless of whether the securities are considered short-term or long-term.

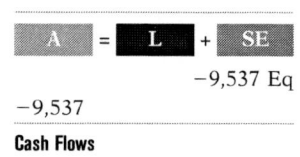

−9,537 Eq

−9,537

**Cash Flows**
no effect

| Dec. 31 | Unrealized Gain or Loss—Equity | 9,537 | |
| | Market Adjustment—Available-for-Sale | | 9,537 |
| | (To record unrealized loss on available-for-sale securities) | | |

If total fair value exceeds total cost, Elbert would record the adjusting entry as an increase (debit) to Market Adjustment—Available-for-Sale and a credit to Unrealized Gain or Loss—Equity.

For available-for-sale securities, the company carries forward the Unrealized Gain or Loss—Equity account to future periods. At each future balance sheet date, the account is adjusted with the market adjustment account to show the difference between cost and fair value at that time.

## BALANCE SHEET PRESENTATION

For balance sheet presentation, companies must classify investments as either short-term or long-term.

### Short-Term Investments

**study objective** 6

Distinguish between short-term and long-term investments.

**Helpful Hint** Trading securities are always classified as short-term. Available-for-sale securities can be either short-term or long-term.

Short-term investments (also called **marketable securities**) are securities held by a company that are (1) **readily marketable** and (2) **intended to be converted into cash** within the next year or operating cycle, whichever is longer. Investments that do not meet **both criteria** are classified as long-term investments. In a recent survey of 600 large U.S. companies, 202 reported short-term investments.

**READILY MARKETABLE. An investment is readily marketable when it can be sold easily whenever the need for cash arises.** Short-term paper[4] meets this criterion because a company can readily sell it to other investors. Stocks and bonds traded on organized securities markets, such as the New York Stock Exchange, are readily marketable because they can be bought and sold daily. In contrast, there may be only a limited market for the securities issued by small corporations and no market for the securities of a privately held company.

**INTENT TO CONVERT. Intent to convert means that management intends to sell the investment within the next year or operating cycle, whichever is longer.** Generally, this criterion is satisfied when the investment is considered a resource that the company will use whenever the need for cash arises. For example, a ski resort may invest idle cash during the summer months with the intent to sell the securities to buy supplies and equipment shortly before the next winter season. This

---

[4]Short-term paper includes (1) certificates of deposits (CDs) issued by banks, (2) money market certificates issued by banks and savings and loan associations, (3) Treasury bills issued by the U.S. government, and (4) commercial paper issued by corporations with good credit ratings.

investment is considered short-term even if lack of snow cancels the next ski season and eliminates the need to convert the securities into cash as intended.

Because of their high liquidity, companies list short-term investments immediately below Cash in the current assets section of the balance sheet. Short-term investments are reported at fair value. For example, Weber Corporation would report its trading securities as shown in Illustration E-8.

**Illustration E-8** Balance sheet presentation of short-term investments

| WEBER CORPORATION | |
|---|---|
| Balance Sheet (partial) | |
| Current assets | |
| Cash | $21,000 |
| Short-term investments, at fair value | 60,000 |

## Long-Term Investments

Companies generally report long-term investments in a separate section of the balance sheet immediately below "Current assets," as shown in Illustration E-9. Long-term investments in available-for-sale securities are reported at fair value. Investments in common stock accounted for under the equity method are reported at equity.

**Illustration E-9** Balance sheet presentation of long-term investments

| WEBER CORPORATION | | |
|---|---|---|
| Balance Sheet (partial) | | |
| Investments | | |
| Bond sinking fund | $100,000 | |
| Investments in stock of less than 20% owned companies, at fair value | 50,000 | |
| Investment in stock of 20%–50% owned company, at equity | 150,000 | |
| Total investments | | $300,000 |

## PRESENTATION OF REALIZED AND UNREALIZED GAIN OR LOSS

Companies must present in the financial statements gains and losses on investments, whether realized or unrealized. In the income statement, companies report gains and losses, as well as interest and dividend revenue, in the nonoperating activities section under the categories listed in Illustration E-10.

**Illustration E-10** Nonoperating items related to investments

| Other Revenue and Gains | Other Expenses and Losses |
|---|---|
| Interest Revenue | Loss on Sale of Investments |
| Dividend Revenue | Unrealized Loss—Income |
| Gain on Sale of Investments | |
| Unrealized Gain—Income | |

As indicated earlier, companies report an unrealized gain or loss on available-for-sale securities as a separate component of stockholders' equity. To illustrate, assume that Muzzillo Inc. has common stock of $3,000,000, retained earnings of $1,500,000, and an unrealized loss on available-for-sale securities of $100,000.

Illustration E-11 shows the financial statement presentation of the unrealized loss.

**Illustration E-11**
Unrealized loss in
stockholders' equity
section

**MUZZILLO INC.**
Balance Sheet (partial)

| | |
|---|---|
| Stockholders' equity | |
| Common stock | $3,000,000 |
| Retained earnings | 1,500,000 |
| Total paid-in capital and retained earnings | 4,500,000 |
| Less: **Unrealized loss on available-for-sale securities** | (100,000) |
| Total stockholders' equity | $4,400,000 |

Note that the presentation of the loss is similar to the presentation of the cost of treasury stock in the stockholders' equity section. (It decreases stockholders' equity.) An unrealized gain would be added in this section. Reporting the unrealized gain or loss in the stockholders' equity section serves two important purposes: (1) It reduces the volatility of net income due to fluctuations in fair value. (2) It informs the financial statement user of the gain or loss that would occur if the company sold the securities at fair value.

Companies must report, as part of a more inclusive measure called *comprehensive income,* items such as unrealized gains and losses on available-for-sale securities, which affect stockholders' equity but are not included in the calculation of net income. For example, Tootsie Roll reported other comprehensive income in 2009 of $2,845,000. Note 11 to Tootsie Roll's financial statements shows that one component of this amount was unrealized gains and losses on investment securities. Comprehensive income is discussed more fully in Chapter 13.

### STATEMENT OF CASH FLOWS PRESENTATION

As shown previously in Illustrations E-8, E-9, and E-11, the balance sheet presents a company's investment accounts at a point in time. The "Investing activities" section of the statement of cash flows reports information on the cash inflows and outflows during the period that resulted from investment transactions.

Illustration E-12 presents the cash flows from investing activities from a recent statement of cash flows of The Walt Disney Company. From this information, we learn that Disney received $1,530 million from the sale or redemption of investments during the year.

**Illustration E-12**
Statement of cash flows
presentation of investment
activities

**THE WALT DISNEY COMPANY**
Statement of Cash Flows (partial)
(in millions)

| | |
|---|---|
| Investing Activities | |
| Investments in parks, resorts and other property | $(1,566) |
| Acquisitions | (588) |
| Dispositions | — |
| **Proceeds from sale of investments** | 1,530 |
| Other | 6 |
| Cash used by investing activities | $ (618) |

# Summary of Study Objectives

**1** **Identify the reasons corporations invest in stocks and debt securities.** Corporations invest for three common reasons: (a) They have excess cash. (b) They view investment income as a significant revenue source. (c) They have strategic goals such as gaining control of a competitor or supplier or moving into a new line of business.

**2** **Explain the accounting for debt investments.** Entries for investments in debt securities are required when companies purchase bonds, receive or accrue interest, and sell bonds.

**3** **Explain the accounting for stock investments.** Entries for investments in common stock are required when companies purchase stock, receive dividends, and sell stock. When ownership is less than 20%, the cost method is used—the investment is recorded at cost. When ownership is between 20% and 50%, the equity method should be used—the investor records its share of the net income of the investee in the year it is earned. When ownership is more than 50%, consolidated financial statements should be prepared.

**4** **Describe the purpose and usefulness of consolidated financial statements.** When a company owns more than 50% of the common stock of another company, consolidated financial statements are usually prepared. These statements are especially useful to the stockholders, board of directors, and management of the parent company.

**5** **Indicate how debt and stock investments are valued and reported in the financial statements.** Investments in debt and stock securities are classified as trading, available-for-sale, or held-to-maturity for valuation and reporting purposes. Trading securities are reported as current assets at fair value, with changes from cost reported in net income. Available-for-sale securities are also reported at fair value, with the changes from cost reported in stockholders' equity. Available-for-sale securities are classified as short-term or long-term depending on their expected realization.

**6** **Distinguish between short-term and long-term investments.** Short-term investments are securities held by a company that are readily marketable and intended to be converted to cash within the next year or operating cycle, whichever is longer. Investments that do not meet both criteria are classified as long-term investments.

# Glossary

**Available-for-sale securities** *(p. E-8)* Securities that are held with the intent of selling them sometime in the future.

**Consolidated financial statements** *(p. E-7)* Financial statements that present the assets and liabilities controlled by the parent company and the total revenues and expenses of the subsidiary companies.

**Controlling interest** *(p. E-7)* Ownership of more than 50% of the common stock of another entity.

**Cost method** *(p. E-4)* An accounting method in which the investment in common stock is recorded at cost and revenue is recognized only when cash dividends are received.

**Debt investments** *(p. E-2)* Investments in government and corporation bonds.

**Equity method** *(p. E-5)* An accounting method in which the investment in common stock is initially recorded at cost, and the investment account is then adjusted annually to show the investor's equity in the investee.

**Fair value** *(p. E-7)* Amount for which a security could be sold in a normal market.

**Held-to-maturity securities** *(p. E-8)* Debt securities that the investor has the intent and ability to hold to their maturity date.

**Long-term investments** *(p. E-10)* Investments that are not readily marketable or that management does not intend to convert into cash within the next year or operating cycle, whichever is longer.

**Mark-to-market** *(p. E-8)* A method of accounting for certain investments that requires that they be adjusted to their fair value at the end of each period.

**Parent company** *(p. E-7)* A company that owns more than 50% of the common stock of another entity.

**Short-term investments (marketable securities)** *(p. E-10)* Investments that are readily marketable and intended to be converted into cash within the next year or operating cycle, whichever is longer.

**Stock investments** *(p. E-4)* Investments in the capital stock of corporations.

**Subsidiary (affiliated) company** *(p. E-7)* A company in which more than 50% of its stock is owned by another company.

**Trading securities** *(p. E-8)* Securities bought and held primarily for sale in the near term to generate income on short-term price differences.

 **Self-Test, Brief Exercises, Exercises, Problem Set A, and many more resources are available for practice in WileyPLUS**

# Self-Test Questions

Answers are at the end of the appendix.

*(SO 1)* **1.** Which of the following is *not* a primary reason why corporations invest in debt and equity securities?
  (a) They wish to gain control of a competitor.
  (b) They have excess cash.
  (c) They wish to move into a new line of business.
  (d) They are required to by law.

**2.** Debt investments are initially recorded at:    *(SO 2)*
  (a) cost.
  (b) cost plus accrued interest.

(c) book value.

(d) None of the above

(SO 2) **3.** Stan Free Company sells debt investments costing $26,000 for $28,000 plus accrued interest that has been recorded. In journalizing the sale, credits are:

(a) Debt Investments and Loss on Sale of Debt Investments.

(b) Debt Investments, Gain on Sale of Debt Investments, and Bond Interest Receivable.

(c) Stock Investments and Bond Interest Receivable.

(d) The correct answer is not given.

(SO 3) **4.** Karen Duffy Company receives net proceeds of $42,000 on the sale of stock investments that cost $39,500. This transaction will result in reporting in the income statement a:

(a) loss of $2,500 under "Other expenses and losses."

(b) loss of $2,500 under "Operating expenses."

(c) gain of $2,500 under "Other revenues and gains."

(d) gain of $2,500 under "Operating revenues."

(SO 3) **5.** The equity method of accounting for long-term investments in stock should be used when the investor has significant influence over an investee and owns:

(a) between 20% and 50% of the investee's common stock.

(b) 20% or more of the investee's bonds.

(c) more than 50% of the investee's common stock.

(d) less than 20% of the investee's common stock.

(SO 3) **6.** Assume that Horicon Corp. acquired 25% of the common stock of Sheboygan Corp. on January 1, 2012, for $300,000. During 2012, Sheboygan Corp. reported net income of $160,000 and paid total dividends of $60,000. If Horicon uses the equity method to account for its investment, the balance in the investment account on December 31, 2012, will be:

(a) $300,000.          (c) $400,000.

(b) $325,000.          (d) $340,000.

(SO 3) **7.** Using the information in the previous question, what entry would Horicon make to record the receipt of the dividend from Sheboygan?

(a) Debit Cash and credit Revenue from Investment in Sheboygan Corp.

(b) Debit Dividends and credit Revenue from Investment in Sheboygan Corp.

(c) Debit Cash and credit Stock Investment.

(d) Debit Cash and credit Dividend Revenue.

(SO 3) **8.** You have a controlling interest if:

(a) you own more than 20% of a company's stock.

(b) you are the president of the company.

(c) you use the equity method.

(d) you own more than 50% of a company's stock.

(SO 4) **9.** Which of these statements is *false*?

Consolidated financial statements are useful to:

(a) determine the profitability of specific subsidiaries.

(b) determine the aggregate profitability of enterprises under common control.

(c) determine the breadth of a parent company's operations.

(d) determine the full extent of aggregate obligations of enterprises under common control.

(SO 5) **10.** At the end of the first year of operations, the total cost of the trading securities portfolio is $120,000 and the total fair value is $115,000. What should the financial statements show?

(a) A reduction of an asset of $5,000 and a realized loss of $5,000.

(b) A reduction of an asset of $5,000 and an unrealized loss of $5,000 in the stockholders' equity section.

(c) A reduction of an asset of $5,000 in the current assets section and an unrealized loss of $5,000 under "Other expenses and losses."

(d) A reduction of an asset of $5,000 in the current assets section and a realized loss of $5,000 under "Other expenses and losses."

(SO 5) **11.** In the balance sheet, Unrealized Loss—Equity is reported as a:

(a) contra asset account.

(b) contra stockholders' equity account.

(c) loss in the income statement.

(d) loss in the retained earnings statement.

(SO 5) **12.** If a company wants to increase its reported income by manipulating its investment accounts, which should it do?

(a) Sell its "winner" trading securities and hold its "loser" trading securities.

(b) Hold its "winner" trading securities and sell its "loser" trading securities.

(c) Sell its "winner" available-for-sale securities and hold its "loser" available-for-sale securities.

(d) Hold its "winner" available-for-sale securities and sell its "loser" available-for-sale securities.

(SO 5) **13.** At December 31, 2012, the fair value of available-for-sale securities is $41,300 and the cost is $39,800. At January 1, 2012, there was a credit balance of $900 in the Market Adjustment—Available-for-Sale account. The required adjusting entry would be:

(a) Debit Market Adjustment—Available-for-Sale for $1,500, and credit Unrealized Gain or Loss—Equity for $1,500.

(b) Debit Market Adjustment—Available-for-Sale for $600, and credit Unrealized Gain or Loss—Equity for $600.

(c) Debit Market Adjustment—Available-for-Sale for $2,400, and credit Unrealized Gain or Loss—Equity for $2,400.

(d) Debit Unrealized Gain or Loss—Equity for $2,400, and credit Market Adjustment—Available-for-Sale for $2,400.

(SO 6) **14.** To be classified as short-term investments, debt investments must be readily marketable and be expected to be sold within:

(a) 3 months from the date of purchase.

(b) the next year or operating cycle, whichever is shorter.

(c) the next year or operating cycle, whichever is longer.

(d) the operating cycle.

# Questions

1. What are the reasons that companies invest in securities?

2. (a) What is the cost of an investment in bonds?
   (b) When is interest on bonds recorded?

3. Kate Denton is confused about losses and gains on the sale of debt investments. Explain these issues to Kate:
   (a) How the gain or loss is computed.
   (b) The statement presentation of gains and losses.

4. Quiddich Company sells bonds that cost $40,000 for $45,000, including $1,000 of accrued interest. In recording the sale, Quiddich books a $5,000 gain. Is this correct? Explain.

5. What is the cost of an investment in stock?

6. To acquire Bailey Corporation stock, Harris Co. pays $60,000 in cash plus $1,500 broker's fees. What entry should be made for this investment, assuming the stock is readily marketable?

7. (a) When should a long-term investment in common stock be accounted for by the equity method?
   (b) When is revenue recognized under the equity method?

8. Spock Corporation uses the equity method to account for its ownership of 30% of the common stock of English Packing. During 2012, English reported a net income of $80,000 and declares and pays cash dividends of $10,000. What recognition should Spock Corporation give to these events?

9. What constitutes "significant influence" when an investor's financial interest is less than 50%?

10. Distinguish between the cost and equity methods of accounting for investments in stocks.

11. What are consolidated financial statements?

12. What are the valuation guidelines for trading and available-for-sale investments at a balance sheet date?

13. Diana Malt is the controller of G-Products, Inc. At December 31, the company's investments in trading securities cost $74,000 and have a fair value of $70,000. Indicate how Diana would report these data in the financial statements prepared on December 31.

14. Using the data in question 13, how would Diana report the data if the investment were long-term and the securities were classified as available-for-sale?

15. Roso Company's investments in available-for-sale securities at December 31 show total cost of $202,000 and total fair value of $210,000. Prepare the adjusting entry.

16. Using the data in question 15, prepare the adjusting entry assuming the securities are classified as trading securities.

17. Where is Unrealized Gain or Loss—Equity reported on the balance sheet?

18. What purposes are served by reporting Unrealized Gains (Losses)—Equity in the stockholders' equity section?

19. Kraemer Wholesale Supply owns stock in Matlin Corporation, which it intends to hold indefinitely because of some negative tax consequences if sold. Should the investment in Matlin be classified as a short-term investment? Why?

# Brief Exercises

**BEE-1** Pegasus Corporation purchased debt investments for $40,800 on January 1, 2012. On July 1, 2012, Pegasus received cash interest of $1,660. Journalize the purchase and the receipt of interest. Assume no interest has been accrued.

*Journalize entries for debt investments.*
*(SO 2), AP*

**BEE-2** On August 1, Jewel Company buys 1,000 shares of ABC common stock for $35,000 cash plus brokerage fees of $600. On December 1, the stock investments are sold for $38,000 in cash. Journalize the purchase and sale of the common stock.

*Journalize entries for stock investments.*
*(SO 3), AP*

**BEE-3** Faye Company owns 25% of Trish Company. For the current year, Trish reports net income of $150,000 and declares and pays a $60,000 cash dividend. Record Faye's equity in Trish's net income and the receipt of dividends from Trish.

*Journalize transactions under the equity method.*
*(SO 3), AP*

**BEE-4** Cost and fair value data for the trading securities of Hayden Company at December 31, 2012, are $62,000 and $59,600, respectively. Prepare the adjusting entry to record the securities at fair value.

*Prepare adjusting entry using fair value.*
*(SO 5), AP*

**BEE-5** For the data presented in BEE-4, show the financial statement presentation of the trading securities and related accounts.

*Indicate statement presentation using fair value.*
*(SO 6), AN*

**BEE-6** In its first year of operations, Kearney Corporation purchased available-for-sale stock securities costing $72,000 as a long-term investment. At December 31, 2012, the fair value of the securities is $69,000. Prepare the adjusting entry to record the securities at fair value.

*Prepare adjusting entry using fair value.*
*(SO 5), AP*

*Indicate statement
presentation using fair value.*
(SO 6), AN

**BEE-7** For the data presented in BEE-6, show the financial statement presentation of the available-for-sale securities and related accounts. Assume the available-for-sale securities are noncurrent.

*Prepare investments section
of balance sheet.*
(SO 6), AP

**BEE-8** Sydney Corporation has these long-term investments: common stock of Russ Co. (10% ownership) held as available-for-sale securities, cost $108,000, fair value $112,000; common stock of Thomas Inc. (30% ownership), cost $210,000, equity $230,000; and a bond sinking fund of $150,000. Prepare the investments section of the balance sheet.

# Exercises

*Journalize debt investment
transactions, and accrue
interest.*
(SO 2), AP

**EE-1** Justin Corporation had these transactions pertaining to debt investments:

Jan. 1 Purchased 90 10%, $1,000 Graham Co. bonds for $90,000 cash plus brokerage fees of $1,200. Interest is payable semiannually on July 1 and January 1.
July 1 Received semiannual interest on Graham Co. bonds.
July 1 Sold 30 Graham Co. bonds for $32,000 less $400 brokerage fees.

**Instructions**
(a) Journalize the transactions.
(b) Prepare the adjusting entry for the accrual of interest at December 31.

*Journalize stock investment
transactions, and explain
income statement
presentation.*
(SO 3), AN

**EE-2** Rojas Company had these transactions pertaining to stock investments:

Feb. 1 Purchased 1,200 shares of MJ common stock (2% of outstanding shares) for $8,000 cash plus brokerage fees of $400.
July 1 Received cash dividends of $2 per share on MJ common stock.
Sept. 1 Sold 500 shares of MJ common stock for $5,500 less brokerage fees of $100.
Dec. 1 Received cash dividends of $1 per share on MJ common stock.

**Instructions**
(a) Journalize the transactions.
(b) Explain how dividend revenue and the gain (loss) on sale should be reported in the income statement.

*Journalize transactions for
investments in stock.*
(SO 3), AP

**EE-3** Glyder Inc. had these transactions pertaining to investments in common stock:

Jan. 1 Purchased 1,200 shares of Bethke Corporation common stock (5% of outstanding shares) for $58,000 cash plus $1,200 broker's commission.
July 1 Received a cash dividend of $7 per share.
Dec. 1 Sold 900 shares of Bethke Corporation common stock for $48,000 cash less $800 broker's commission.
31 Received a cash dividend of $7 per share.

**Instructions**
Journalize the transactions.

*Journalize and post
transactions under the
equity method.*
(SO 3), AP

**EE-4** On January 1, Jackson Corporation purchased a 25% equity investment in Batchelor Corporation for $150,000. At December 31, Batchelor declared and paid a $80,000 cash dividend and reported net income of $380,000.

**Instructions**
(a) Journalize the transactions.
(b) Determine the amount to be reported as an investment in Batchelor stock at December 31.

*Journalize entries under cost
and equity methods.*
(SO 3), AP

**EE-5** These are two independent situations:

1. Angel Cosmetics acquired 12% of the 300,000 shares of common stock of Chic Fashion at a total cost of $14 per share on March 18, 2012. On June 30, Chic declared and paid a $75,000 dividend. On December 31, Chic reported net income of $244,000 for the year. At December 31, the market price of Chic Fashion was $16 per share. The stock is classified as available-for-sale.

2. Randell Inc. obtained significant influence over Gatos Corporation by buying 25% of Gatos's 30,000 outstanding shares of common stock at a total cost of $11 per share on January 1, 2012. On June 15, Gatos declared and paid a cash dividend of $35,000. On December 31, Gatos reported a net income of $120,000 for the year.

**Instructions**

Prepare all the necessary journal entries for 2012 for (a) Angel Cosmetics and (b) Randell Inc.

**EE-6**   At December 31, 2012, the trading securities for Lynette, Inc., are as follows.

*Prepare adjusting entry to record fair value, and indicate statement presentation.*

*(SO 5, 6), AP*

| Security | Cost | Fair Value |
|---|---|---|
| A | $18,100 | $16,000 |
| B | 12,500 | 14,800 |
| C | 23,000 | 18,000 |
| Total | $53,600 | $48,800 |

**Instructions**

(a) Prepare the adjusting entry at December 31, 2012, to report the securities at fair value.
(b) Show the balance sheet and income statement presentation at December 31, 2012, after adjustment to fair value.

**EE-7**   Data for investments in stock classified as trading securities are presented in EE-6. Assume instead that the investments are classified as available-for-sale securities with the same cost and fair value data. The securities are considered to be a long-term investment.

*Prepare adjusting entry to record fair value, and indicate statement presentation.*

*(SO 5, 6), AN*

**Instructions**

(a) Prepare the adjusting entry at December 31, 2012, to report the securities at fair value.
(b) Show the statement presentation at December 31, 2012, after adjustment to fair value.
(c) Carla Sagen, a member of the board of directors, does not understand the reporting of the unrealized gains or losses on trading securities and available-for-sale securities. Write a letter to Ms. Sagen explaining the reporting and the purposes it serves.

**EE-8**   Redfield Company has these data at December 31, 2012:

*Prepare adjusting entries for fair value, and indicate statement presentation for two classes of securities.*

*(SO 5, 6), AN*

| Securities | Cost | Fair Value |
|---|---|---|
| Trading | $110,000 | $122,000 |
| Available-for-sale | 100,000 | 96,000 |

The available-for-sale securities are held as a long-term investment.

**Instructions**

(a) Prepare the adjusting entries to report each class of securities at fair value.
(b) Indicate the statement presentation of each class of securities and the related unrealized gain (loss) accounts.

# Problems

**PE-1**   Knuth Farms is a grower of hybrid seed corn for DeKalb Genetics Corporation. It has had two exceptionally good years and has elected to invest its excess funds in bonds. The following selected transactions relate to bonds acquired as an investment by Knuth Farms, whose fiscal year ends on December 31.

*Journalize debt investment transactions and show financial statement presentation.*

*(SO 2, 5, 6), AN*

**2012**

Jan.  1   Purchased at par $600,000 of Sullivan Corporation 10-year, 7% bonds dated January 1, 2012, directly from the issuing corporation.
July  1   Received the semiannual interest on the Sullivan bonds.
Dec. 31   Accrual of interest at year-end on the Sullivan bonds.

Assume that all intervening transactions and adjustments have been properly recorded and the number of bonds owned has not changed from December 31, 2012, to December 31, 2014.

**2015**

Jan. 1 Received the semiannual interest on the Sullivan bonds.

Jan. 1 Sold $300,000 of Sullivan bonds at 110. The broker deducted $7,000 for commissions and fees on the sale.

July 1 Received the semiannual interest on the Sullivan bonds.

Dec. 31 Accrual of interest at year-end on the Sullivan bonds.

**Instructions**

(a) Journalize the listed transactions for the years 2012 and 2015.

(b) Assume that the fair value of the bonds at December 31, 2012, was $586,000. These bonds are classified as available-for-sale securities. Prepare the adjusting entry to record these bonds at fair value.

(c) Show the balance sheet presentation of the bonds and interest receivable at December 31, 2012. Assume the investments are considered long-term. Indicate where any unrealized gain or loss is reported in the financial statements.

*Journalize investment transactions, prepare adjusting entry, and show financial statement presentation.*

(SO 2, 3, 5, 6), AN

**PE-2** In January 2012, the management of Sarah Company concludes that it has sufficient cash to purchase some short-term investments in debt and stock securities. During the year, the following transactions occurred.

Feb. 1 Purchased 1,200 shares of NJF common stock for $50,600 plus brokerage fees of $1,000.

Mar. 1 Purchased 500 shares of SEK common stock for $18,000 plus brokerage fees of $500.

Apr. 1 Purchased 70 $1,000, 8% CRT bonds for $70,000 plus $1,200 brokerage fees. Interest is payable semiannually on April 1 and October 1.

July 1 Received a cash dividend of $0.80 per share on the NJF common stock.

Aug. 1 Sold 200 shares of NJF common stock at $42 per share less brokerage fees of $350.

Sept. 1 Received $2 per share cash dividend on the SEK common stock.

Oct. 1 Received the semiannual interest on the CRT bonds.

Oct. 1 Sold the CRT bonds for $77,000 less $1,300 brokerage fees.

At December 31, the fair values of the NJF and SEK common stocks were $39 and $30 per share, respectively.

**Instructions**

(a) Journalize the transactions and post to the accounts Debt Investments and Stock Investments. (Use the T account form.)

(b) Prepare the adjusting entry at December 31, 2012, to report the investments at fair value. All securities are considered to be trading securities.

(c) Show the balance sheet presentation of investment securities at December 31, 2012.

(d) Identify the income statement accounts and give the statement classification of each account.

*Journalize transactions, prepare adjusting entry for stock investments, and show balance sheet presentation.*

(SO 3, 5, 6), AN

**PE-3** On December 31, 2011, Maxell Associates owned the following securities that are held as long-term investments.

| Common Stock | Shares | Cost |
|---|---|---|
| A Co. | 1,000 | $48,000 |
| B Co. | 5,000 | 36,000 |
| C Co. | 1,200 | 24,000 |

On this date, the total fair value of the securities was equal to its cost. The securities are not held for influence or control over the investees. In 2012, the following transactions occurred.

July 1 Received $2.00 per share semiannual cash dividend on B Co. common stock.

Aug. 1 Received $0.50 per share cash dividend on A Co. common stock.

Sept. 1 Sold 1,000 shares of B Co. common stock for cash at $9 per share less brokerage fees of $800.

Oct. 1 Sold 300 shares of A Co. common stock for cash at $54 per share less brokerage fees of $600.

Nov. 1 Received $1 per share cash dividend on C Co. common stock.

Dec. 15 Received $0.50 per share cash dividend on A Co. common stock.

31 Received $2.20 per share semiannual cash dividend on B Co. common stock.

At December 31, the fair values per share of the common stocks were: A Co. $47, B Co. $7, and C Co. $24.

**Instructions**
(a) Journalize the 2012 transactions and post to the account Stock Investments. (Use the T account form.)
(b) Prepare the adjusting entry at December 31, 2012, to show the securities at fair value. The stock should be classified as available-for-sale securities.
(c) Show the balance sheet presentation of the investments and the unrealized gain (loss) at December 31, 2012. At this date, Maxell Associates has common stock $2,000,000 and retained earnings $1,200,000.

**PE-4** Coakley Company acquired 30% of the outstanding common stock of Ginger Inc. on January 1, 2012, by paying $1,800,000 for 60,000 shares. Ginger declared and paid a $0.50 per share cash dividend on June 30 and again on December 31, 2012. Ginger reported net income of $800,000 for the year.

*Prepare entries under cost and equity methods, and prepare memorandum.*
*(SO 3), AN*

**Instructions**
(a) Prepare the journal entries for Coakley Company for 2012, assuming Coakley cannot exercise significant influence over Ginger. (Use the cost method.)
(b) Prepare the journal entries for Coakley Company for 2012, assuming Coakley can exercise significant influence over Ginger. (Use the equity method.)
(c) The board of directors of Coakley Company is confused about the differences between the cost and equity methods. Prepare a memorandum for the board that explains each method and shows in tabular form the account balances under each method at December 31, 2012.

**PE-5** Here is Maple Company's portfolio of long-term available-for-sale securities at December 31, 2011:

*Journalize stock transactions, and show balance sheet presentation.*
*(SO 3, 5, 6), AN*

| | Cost |
|---|---|
| 1,400 shares of Wickham Inc. common stock | $73,500 |
| 1,200 shares of Kerry Corporation common stock | 84,000 |
| 800 shares of H. Kelso Corporation preferred stock | 33,600 |

On December 31, the total cost of the portfolio equaled the total fair value. Maple had the following transactions related to the securities during 2012.

Jan. 20   Sold 1,400 shares of Wickham Inc. common stock at $55 per share less brokerage fees of $1,100.
     28   Purchased 400 shares of $10 par value common stock of M. McLain Corporation at $78 per share plus brokerage fees of $480.
     30   Received a cash dividend of $1.25 per share on Kerry Corporation common stock.
Feb. 8    Received cash dividends of $0.40 per share on H. Kelso Corporation preferred stock.
     18   Sold all 800 shares of H. Kelso preferred stock at $35 per share less brokerage fees of $360.
July 30   Received a cash dividend of $1.10 per share on Kerry Corporation common stock.
Sept. 6   Purchased an additional 600 shares of the $10 par value common stock of M. McLain Corporation at $82 per share plus brokerage fees of $800.
Dec. 1    Received a cash dividend of $1.50 per share on M. McLain Corporation common stock.

At December 31, 2012, the fair values of the securities were:

| | |
|---|---|
| Kerry Corporation common stock | $65 per share |
| M. McLain Corporation common stock | $77 per share |

Maple uses separate account titles for each investment, such as Investment in Kerry Corporation Common Stock.

**Instructions**
(a) Prepare journal entries to record the transactions.
(b) Post to the investment accounts. (Use separate T accounts for each investment.)

(c)  Prepare the adjusting entry at December 31, 2012, to report the portfolio at fair value.
(d)  Show the balance sheet presentation at December 31, 2012.

*Prepare a balance sheet.*
(SO 6), AP

**PE-6**  The following data, presented in alphabetical order, are taken from the records of Texton Corporation.

| | |
|---|---|
| Accounts payable | $ 150,000 |
| Accounts receivable | 90,000 |
| Accumulated depreciation—buildings | 180,000 |
| Accumulated depreciation—equipment | 52,000 |
| Allowance for doubtful accounts | 6,000 |
| Bond investments | 400,000 |
| Bonds payable (10%, due 2023) | 350,000 |
| Buildings | 900,000 |
| Cash | 63,000 |
| Common stock ($5 par value; 500,000 shares authorized, 240,000 shares issued) | 1,200,000 |
| Discount on bonds payable | 20,000 |
| Dividends payable | 50,000 |
| Equipment | 275,000 |
| Goodwill | 190,000 |
| Income taxes payable | 70,000 |
| Investment in Jansen Inc. stock (30% ownership), at equity | 240,000 |
| Land | 410,000 |
| Inventory | 170,000 |
| Notes payable (due 2013) | 70,000 |
| Paid-in capital in excess of par value | 464,000 |
| Prepaid insurance | 16,000 |
| Retained earnings | 310,000 |
| Short-term stock investment, at fair value | 128,000 |

***Instructions***
Prepare a balance sheet at December 31, 2012.

### Answers to Self-Test Questions

**1.** d  **2.** a  **3.** b  **4.** c  **5.** a  **6.** b $300,000 + (($160,000 − $60,000) × .25)  **7.** c  **8.** d
**9.** a  **10.** c  **11.** b  **12.** c  **13.** c ($41,300 − $39,800) + $900  **14.** c

# PAYROLL ACCOUNTING

## study objectives

**After studying this appendix, you should be able to:**

**1** Discuss the objectives of internal control for payroll.

**2** Compute and record the payroll for a pay period.

**3** Describe and record employer payroll taxes.

Payroll and related fringe benefits often make up a large percentage of current liabilities. Employee compensation is often the most significant expense that a company incurs. For example, General Motors recently reported total employees of 386,000 and labor costs of $21.6 billion. Add to labor costs such fringe benefits as health insurance, life insurance, disability insurance, and so on, and you can see why proper accounting and control of payroll are so important.

Payroll accounting involves more than paying employees' wages. Companies are required by law to maintain payroll records for each employee, file and pay payroll taxes, and comply with numerous state and federal tax laws related to employee compensation. Accounting for payroll has become much more complex due to these regulations.

## Payroll Defined

The term "payroll" pertains to both salaries and wages. Managerial, administrative, and sales personnel are generally paid salaries. Salaries are often expressed in terms of a specified amount per month or per year rather than an hourly rate. For example, the faculty and administrative personnel at the college or university you are attending are paid salaries. In contrast, store clerks, factory employees, and manual laborers are normally paid wages. Wages are based on a rate per hour or on a piecework basis (such as per unit of product). Frequently, the terms "salaries" and "wages" are used interchangeably.

The term "payroll" does not apply to payments made for services of professionals such as certified public accountants, attorneys, and architects. Such professionals are independent contractors rather than salaried employees. Payments to them are called **fees**, rather than salaries or wages. This distinction is important because government regulations relating to the payment and reporting of payroll taxes apply only to employees.

## Internal Control of Payroll

Internal control was introduced in Chapter 7. As applied to payrolls, the objectives of internal control are (1) to safeguard company assets against unauthorized payments of payrolls, and (2) to ensure the accuracy and reliability of the accounting records pertaining to payrolls.

**study objective** **1**

Discuss the objectives of internal control for payroll.

Irregularities often result if internal control is lax. Overstating hours, using unauthorized pay rates, adding fictitious employees to the payroll, continuing terminated employees on the payroll, and distributing duplicate payroll checks are all methods of stealing from a company. Moreover, inaccurate records will result in incorrect paychecks, financial statements, and payroll tax returns.

Payroll activities involve four functions: hiring employees, timekeeping, preparing the payroll, and paying the payroll. For effective internal control, these four functions should be assigned to different departments or individuals. To illustrate these functions, we will examine the case of Academy Company and one of its employees, Michael Jordan.

### HIRING EMPLOYEES

The human resources (personnel) department is responsible for posting job openings, screening and interviewing applicants, and hiring employees. From a control standpoint, this department provides significant documentation and authorization. When an employee is hired, the human resources department prepares an authorization form. The one used by Academy Company for Michael Jordan is shown in Illustration F-1.

**Hiring Employees**

Human Resources department documents and authorizes employment.

**Illustration F-1**
Authorization form prepared by the human resources department

ACADEMY COMPANY

Employee Name __Jordan,__ __Michael__ ___ Starting Date __9/01/10__
            LAST       FIRST     MI

Classification __Skilled-Level 10__ ___ Social Security No. __329-36-9547__

Department __Shipping__ ___ Division __Entertainment__

| | | |
|---|---|---|
| **NEW HIRE** | Classification __Clerk__ ___ Salary Grade __Level 10__ ___ Trans. from Temp. ☐ <br> Rate $ __10.00__ per __hour__ ___ Bonus __N/A__ ___ Non-exempt ☒ Exempt ☐ | |
| **RATE CHANGE** | New Rate $ __12.00__ ___ Effective Date __9/1/11__ <br> Present Rate $ __10.00__ <br> Merit ☒ Promotion ☐ Decrease ☐    Other____ <br> Previous Increase Date __None__ ___ Amount $____ per____ Type____ | |
| **SEPARATION** | Resignation ☐ Discharge ☐ Retirement ☐   Reason____ <br><br> Leave of absence ☐ From____ to____ Type____ <br> Last Day Worked____ | |
| **APPROVALS** | *BEW*     *9-1-11* <br> BRANCH OR DEPT. MANAGER    DATE | *EMW*     *9-1-11* <br> DIVISION V.P.     DATE <br> *James E. Speer* <br> PERSONNEL DEPARTMENT |

The authorization form is sent to the payroll department, where it is used to place the new employee on the payroll. A chief concern of the human resources department is ensuring the accuracy of this form. The reason is quite simple: one of the most common types of payroll frauds is adding fictitious employees to the payroll.

The human resources department is also responsible for authorizing changes in employment status. Specifically, they must authorize (1) changes in pay rates and (2) terminations of employment. Every authorization should be in writing, and a copy of the change in status should be sent to the payroll department. Notice in Illustration F-1 that Jordan received a pay increase of $2 per hour.

### TIMEKEEPING

Another area in which internal control is important is timekeeping. Hourly employees are usually required to record time worked by "punching" a time clock. Times of arrival and departure are automatically recorded by the employee by inserting a time card into the clock. Michael Jordan's time card is shown in Illustration F-2.

In large companies, time clock procedures are often monitored by a supervisor or security guard to make sure an employee punches only one card. At the end of the pay period, each employee's supervisor approves the hours shown by signing the time card. When overtime hours are involved, approval by a supervisor is usually mandatory. This guards against unauthorized overtime. The approved time cards are then sent to the payroll department. For salaried employees, a manually prepared weekly or monthly time report kept by a supervisor may be used to record time worked.

**Timekeeping**

Supervisors monitor hours worked through time cards and time reports.

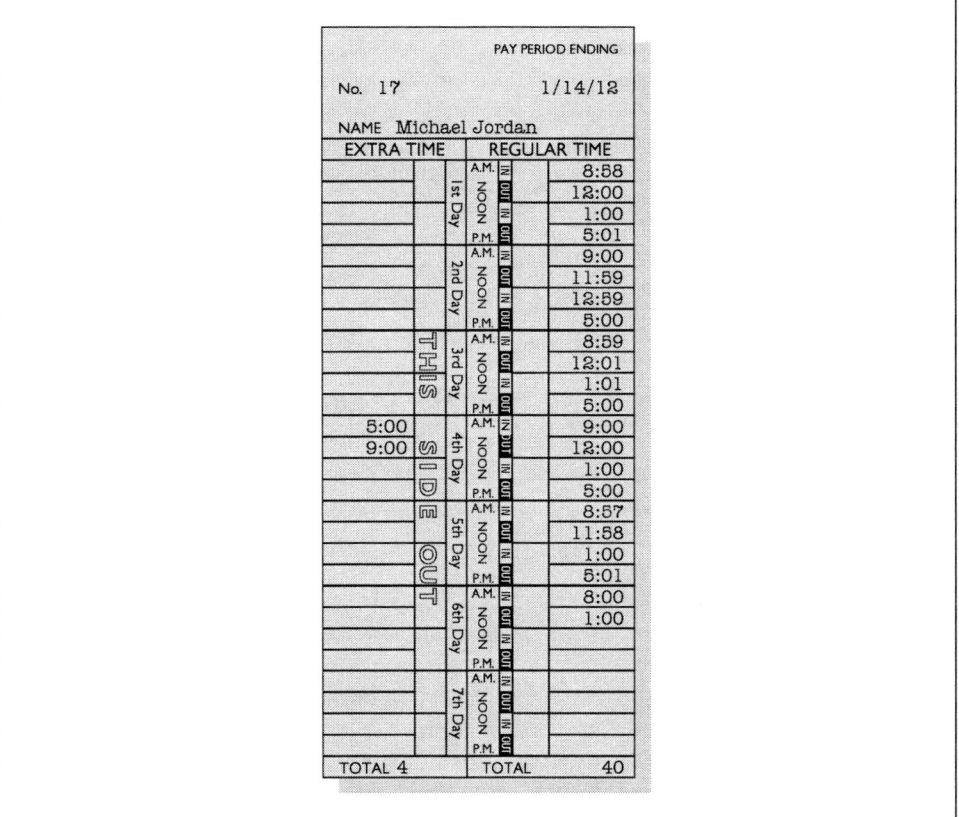

**Illustration F-2**
Time card

### PREPARING THE PAYROLL

The payroll is prepared in the payroll department on the basis of two inputs: (1) human resources department authorizations and (2) approved time cards. Numerous calculations are involved in determining gross wages and payroll deductions. Therefore, a second payroll department employee, working independently, verifies all calculated amounts, and a payroll department supervisor then approves the payroll. The payroll department is also responsible for preparing (but not signing) payroll checks, maintaining payroll records, and preparing payroll tax returns.

**Preparing the Payroll**

Two (or more) employees verify payroll amounts; supervisor approves.

**Paying the Payroll**

Treasurer signs and distributes checks.

## PAYING THE PAYROLL

The payroll is paid by the treasurer's department. **Payment by check minimizes the risk of loss from theft, and the endorsed check provides proof of payment.** For good internal control, payroll checks should be prenumbered, and all checks should be accounted for. All checks must be signed by the treasurer (or a designated agent). Distribution of the payroll checks to employees should be controlled by the treasurer's department. Many employees have their pay credited electronically to their bank account. To control such disbursements, receipts detailing gross pay, deductions, and net pay are provided to employees.

Occasionally the payroll is paid in currency. In such cases it is customary to have a second person count the cash in each pay envelope. The paymaster should obtain a signed receipt from the employee upon payment.

# Determining the Payroll

**study objective 2**

Compute and record the payroll for a pay period.

Determining the payroll involves computing three amounts: (1) gross earnings, (2) payroll deductions, and (3) net pay.

## GROSS EARNINGS

Gross earnings is the total compensation earned by an employee. It consists of wages or salaries, plus any bonuses and commissions.

Total **wages** for an employee are determined by multiplying the hours worked by the hourly rate of pay. In addition to the hourly pay rate, most companies are required by law to pay hourly workers a minimum of $1\frac{1}{2}$ times the regular hourly rate for overtime work in excess of 8 hours per day or 40 hours per week. In addition, many employers pay overtime rates for work done at night, on weekends, and on holidays.

**Helpful Hint** The law that governs pay rates is the Federal Fair Labor Standards Act. It applies to all companies involved in interstate commerce.

Michael Jordan's time card (Illustration F-2, page F-3) shows that he worked 44 hours for the weekly pay period ending January 14. The computation of his gross earnings (total wages) is shown in Illustration F-3.

**Illustration F-3**
Computation of total wages

| Type of Pay | Hours | × | Rate | = | Gross Earnings |
|---|---|---|---|---|---|
| Regular | 40 | × | $12 | = | $ 480 |
| Overtime | 4 | × | 18 | = | 72 |
| **Total wages** | | | | | **$552** |

This computation assumes that Jordan receives $1\frac{1}{2}$ times his regular hourly rate ($12 × 1.5) for his overtime hours. Union contracts often require that overtime rates be as much as twice the regular rates.

The **salary** for an employee is generally based on a monthly or yearly rate. These rates are then prorated to the payroll periods used by the company. Most executive and administrative positions are salaried. Federal law does not require overtime pay for employees in such positions.

**Ethics Note** Bonuses often reward outstanding individual performance; but successful corporations also need considerable teamwork. A challenge is to motivate individuals while preventing an unethical employee from taking another's idea for his or her own advantage.

Many companies have bonus agreements for management personnel and other employees. A recent survey found that over 94% of the largest U.S. manufacturing companies offer annual bonuses to their key executives. Bonus arrangements may be based on such factors as increased sales or net income. Bonuses may be paid in cash and/or by granting executives and employees the opportunity to acquire shares of company stock at favorable prices (called stock option plans).

## PAYROLL DEDUCTIONS

As anyone who has received a paycheck knows, gross earnings are usually very different from the amount actually received. The difference is due to payroll deductions. Such deductions do not result in payroll tax expense to the employer.

The employer is merely a collection agent, and subsequently transfers the amounts deducted to the government and designated recipients. Payroll deductions may be mandatory or voluntary. Mandatory deductions are required by law and consist of FICA taxes and income taxes. Voluntary deductions are at the option of the employee. Illustration F-4 summarizes the types of payroll deductions.

**Illustration F-4** Payroll deductions

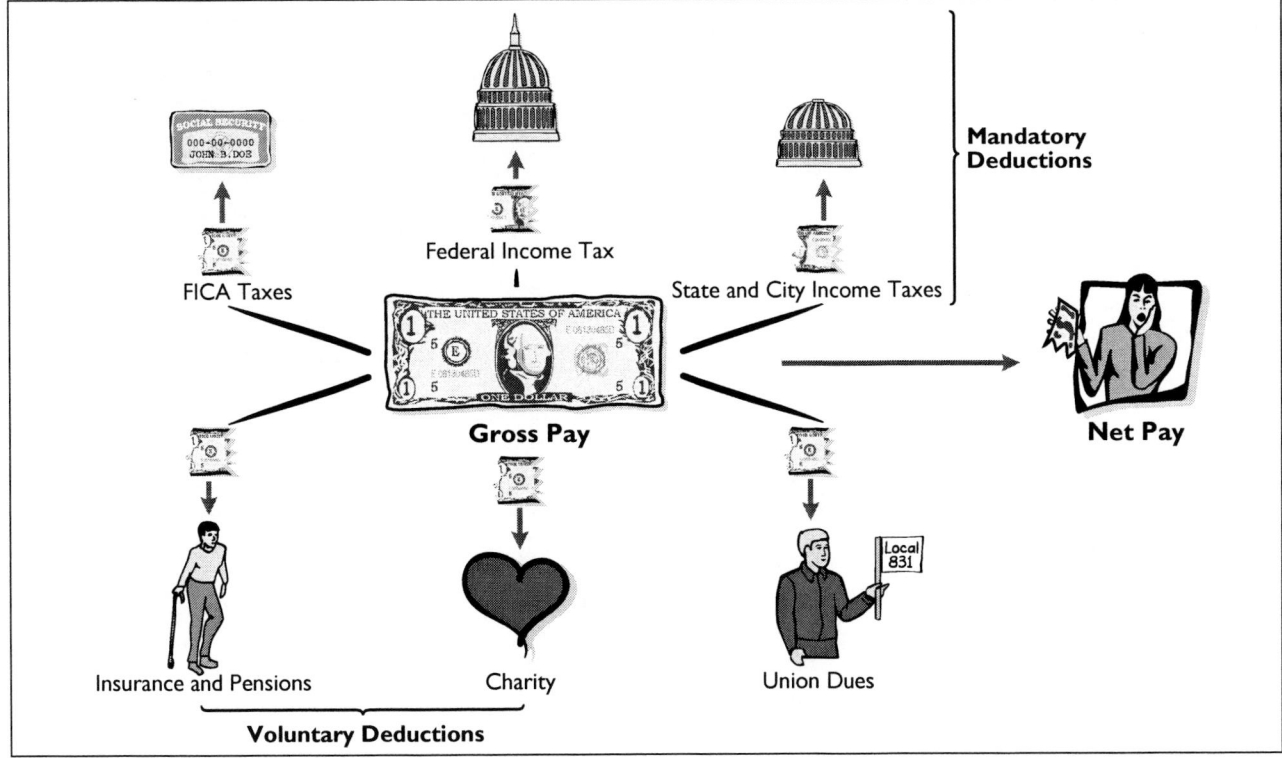

## FICA Taxes

In 1937 Congress enacted the Federal Insurance Contribution Act (FICA). FICA taxes **are designed to provide workers with supplemental retirement, employment disability, and medical benefits.** In 1965, Congress extended benefits to include Medicare for individuals over 65 years of age. The benefits are financed by a tax levied on employees' earnings. FICA taxes are commonly referred to as **Social Security taxes**.

The tax rate and the tax base for FICA taxes are set by Congress. When FICA taxes were first imposed, the rate was 1% on the first $3,000 of gross earnings, or a maximum of $30 per year. The rate and base have changed dramatically since that time! In 2010, the rate was 7.65% (6.2% Social Security plus 1.45% Medicare) on the first $102,000 of gross earnings for each employee.[1] For purpose of illustration in this appendix, we will assume a rate of 8% on the first $100,000 of gross earnings, or a maximum of $8,000. Using the 8% rate, the FICA withholding for Jordan for the weekly pay period ending January 14 is $44.16 ($552 × 8%).

## Income Taxes

Under the U.S. pay-as-you-go system of federal income taxes, employers are required to withhold income taxes from employees each pay period. The amount to be withheld is determined by three variables: (1) the employee's gross earnings;

---

[1]The Medicare provision also includes a tax of 1.45% on gross earnings in excess of $102,000. In the interest of simplification, we ignore this 1.45% charge in our end-of-chapter assignment material. We assume zero FICA withholdings on gross earnings above $100,000.

(2) the number of allowances claimed by the employee; and (3) the length of the pay period. The number of allowances claimed typically includes the employee, his or her spouse, and other dependents. **To indicate to the Internal Revenue Service the number of allowances claimed, the employee must complete an** Employee's Withholding Allowance Certificate (Form W-4). As shown in Illustration F-5, Michael Jordan claims two allowances on his W-4.

**Illustration F-5**
W-4 form

Withholding tables furnished by the Internal Revenue Service indicate the amount of income tax to be withheld. Withholding amounts are based on gross wages and the number of allowances claimed. Separate tables are provided for weekly, biweekly, semimonthly, and monthly pay periods. The withholding tax table for Michael Jordan (assuming he earns $552 per week) is shown in Illustration F-6. For a weekly salary of $552 with two allowances, the income tax to be withheld is $49.

**Illustration F-6**
Withholding tax table

**MARRIED Persons — WEEKLY Payroll Period**
**(For Wages Paid in 2012)**

| If the wages are — | | And the number of withholding allowances claimed is — | | | | | | | | | | |
|---|---|---|---|---|---|---|---|---|---|---|---|---|
| At least | But less than | 0 | 1 | 2 | 3 | 4 | 5 | 6 | 7 | 8 | 9 | 10 |
| | | The amount of income tax to be withheld is — | | | | | | | | | | |
| 490 | 500 | 56 | 48 | 40 | 32 | 24 | 17 | 9 | 1 | 0 | 0 | 0 |
| 500 | 510 | 57 | 49 | 42 | 34 | 26 | 18 | 10 | 3 | 0 | 0 | 0 |
| 510 | 520 | 59 | 51 | 43 | 35 | 27 | 20 | 12 | 4 | 0 | 0 | 0 |
| 520 | 530 | 60 | 52 | 45 | 37 | 29 | 21 | 13 | 6 | 0 | 0 | 0 |
| 530 | 540 | 62 | 54 | 46 | 38 | 30 | 23 | 15 | 7 | 0 | 0 | 0 |
| 540 | 550 | 63 | 55 | 48 | 40 | 32 | 24 | 16 | 9 | 1 | 0 | 0 |
| 550 | 560 | 65 | 57 | 49 | 41 | 33 | 26 | 18 | 10 | 2 | 0 | 0 |
| 560 | 570 | 66 | 58 | 51 | 43 | 35 | 27 | 19 | 12 | 4 | 0 | 0 |
| 570 | 580 | 68 | 60 | 52 | 44 | 36 | 29 | 21 | 13 | 5 | 0 | 0 |
| 580 | 590 | 69 | 61 | 54 | 46 | 38 | 30 | 22 | 15 | 7 | 0 | 0 |
| 590 | 600 | 71 | 63 | 55 | 47 | 39 | 32 | 24 | 16 | 8 | 1 | 0 |
| 600 | 610 | 72 | 64 | 57 | 49 | 41 | 33 | 25 | 18 | 10 | 2 | 0 |
| 610 | 620 | 74 | 66 | 58 | 50 | 42 | 35 | 27 | 19 | 11 | 4 | 0 |
| 620 | 630 | 75 | 67 | 60 | 52 | 44 | 36 | 28 | 21 | 13 | 5 | 0 |
| 630 | 640 | 77 | 69 | 61 | 53 | 45 | 38 | 30 | 22 | 14 | 7 | 0 |
| 640 | 650 | 78 | 70 | 63 | 55 | 47 | 39 | 31 | 24 | 16 | 8 | 0 |
| 650 | 660 | 80 | 72 | 64 | 56 | 48 | 41 | 33 | 25 | 17 | 10 | 2 |
| 660 | 670 | 81 | 73 | 66 | 58 | 50 | 42 | 34 | 27 | 19 | 11 | 3 |
| 670 | 680 | 83 | 75 | 67 | 59 | 51 | 44 | 36 | 28 | 20 | 13 | 5 |
| 680 | 690 | 84 | 76 | 69 | 61 | 53 | 45 | 37 | 30 | 22 | 14 | 6 |

Most states (and some cities) also require **employers** to withhold income taxes from employees' earnings. As a rule, the amounts withheld are a percentage (specified in the state revenue code) of the amount withheld for the federal income tax. Or they may be a specified percentage of the employee's earnings. For the sake of simplicity, we have assumed that Jordan's wages are subject to state income taxes of 2%, or $11.04 (2% × $552) per week.

There is no limit on the amount of gross earnings subject to income tax withholdings. In fact, the higher the earnings, the higher the amount of taxes withheld.

### Other Deductions

Employees may voluntarily authorize withholdings for charitable, retirement, and other purposes. All voluntary deductions from gross earnings should be authorized in writing by the employee. The authorization(s) may be made individually or as part of a group plan. Deductions for charitable organizations, such as the United Way, or for financial arrangements, such as U.S. savings bonds and repayment of loans from company credit unions, are made individually. Deductions for union dues, health and life insurance, and pension plans are often made on a group basis. We will assume that Jordan has weekly voluntary deductions of $10 for the United Way and $5 for union dues.

### NET PAY

Net pay is determined by subtracting payroll deductions from gross earnings. For Michael Jordan, net pay for the pay period is $432.80, computed as shown in Illustration F-7. Assuming that Michael Jordan's wages for each week during the year are $552, total wages for the year are $28,704 (52 × $552). Thus, all of Jordan's wages are subject to FICA tax during the year. Let's assume that Jordan's department head earns $2,000 per week, or $104,000 for the year. Since we are assuming that only the first $100,000 is subject to FICA taxes, the maximum FICA withholdings on the department head's earnings would be $8,000 ($100,000 × 8%).

*Alternative Terminology* Net pay is also called *take-home pay.*

| | | |
|---|---:|---:|
| Gross earnings | | $ 552.00 |
| Payroll deductions: | | |
| FICA taxes | $44.16 | |
| Federal income taxes | 49.00 | |
| State income taxes | 11.04 | |
| United Way | 10.00 | |
| Union dues | 5.00 | 119.20 |
| Net pay | | $432.80 |

**Illustration F-7**
Computation of net pay

# Recording the Payroll

Recording the payroll involves maintaining payroll department records, recognizing payroll expenses and liabilities, and recording payment of the payroll.

### MAINTAINING PAYROLL DEPARTMENT RECORDS

To comply with state and federal laws, an employer must keep a cumulative record of each employee's gross earnings, deductions, and net pay during the year. The record that provides this information is the employee earnings record. Michael Jordan's employee earnings record is shown in Illustration F-8 (next page).

**ACADEMY COMPANY**
**Employee Earnings Record**
**for the Year 2012**

| Name | Michael Jordan | Address | 2345 Mifflin Ave. |
|---|---|---|---|
| Social Security Number | 329-36-9547 | | Hampton, Michigan 48292 |
| Date of Birth | December 24, 1970 | Telephone | 555-238-9051 |
| Date Employed | September 1, 2010 | Date Employment Ended | |
| Sex | Male | Exemptions | 2 |
| Single | | Married | x |

| 2012 Period Ending | Total Hours | Regular | Overtime | Total | Cumulative | FICA | Fed. Inc. Tax | State Inc. Tax | United Fund | Union Dues | Total | Net Amount | Check No. |
|---|---|---|---|---|---|---|---|---|---|---|---|---|---|
| 1/7 | 42 | 480.00 | 36.00 | 516.00 | 516.00 | 41.28 | 43.00 | 10.32 | 10.00 | 5.00 | 109.60 | 406.40 | 974 |
| 1/14 | 44 | 480.00 | 72.00 | 552.00 | 1,068.00 | 44.16 | 49.00 | 11.04 | 10.00 | 5.00 | 119.20 | 432.80 | 1028 |
| 1/21 | 43 | 480.00 | 54.00 | 534.00 | 1,602.00 | 42.72 | 46.00 | 10.68 | 10.00 | 5.00 | 114.40 | 419.60 | 1077 |
| 1/28 | 42 | 480.00 | 36.00 | 516.00 | 2,118.00 | 41.28 | 43.00 | 10.32 | 10.00 | 5.00 | 109.60 | 406.40 | 1133 |
| Jan. Total | | 1,920.00 | 198.00 | 2,118.00 | | 169.44 | 181.00 | 42.36 | 40.00 | 20.00 | 452.80 | 1,665.20 | |

**Illustration F-8**
Employee earnings record

A separate earnings record is kept for each employee. It is updated after each pay period. The cumulative payroll data on the earnings record are used by the employer to: (1) determine when an employee has earned the maximum earnings subject to FICA taxes, (2) file state and federal payroll tax returns (as explained later in the appendix), and (3) provide each employee with a statement of gross earnings and tax withholdings for the year. Illustration F-12 (on page F-12) shows this statement.

In addition to employee earnings records, many companies find it useful to prepare a payroll register. This record accumulates the gross earnings, deductions, and net pay by employee for each pay period. It provides the documentation for preparing a paycheck for each employee. Academy Company's payroll register is presented in Illustration F-9. It shows the data for Michael Jordan in the wages section. In this example, Academy Company's total weekly payroll is $17,210, as shown in the gross earnings column.

**Illustration F-9** Payroll register

**ACADEMY COMPANY**
**Payroll Register**
**for the Week Ending January 14, 2012**

| Employee | Total Hours | Regular | Overtime | Gross | FICA | Federal Income Tax | State Income Tax | United Way | Union Dues | Total | Net Pay | Check No. | Office Salaries Expense | Wages Expense |
|---|---|---|---|---|---|---|---|---|---|---|---|---|---|---|
| Office Salaries | | | | | | | | | | | | | | |
| Arnold, Patricia | 40 | 580.00 | | 580.00 | 46.40 | 61.00 | 11.60 | 15.00 | | 134.00 | 446.00 | 998 | 580.00 | |
| Canton, Matthew | 40 | 590.00 | | 590.00 | 47.20 | 63.00 | 11.80 | 20.00 | | 142.00 | 448.00 | 999 | 590.00 | |
| Mueller, William | 40 | 530.00 | | 530.00 | 42.40 | 54.00 | 10.60 | 11.00 | | 118.00 | 412.0 | 1010 | 530.00 | |
| Subtotal | | 5,200.00 | | 5,200.00 | 416.00 | 1,090.00 | 104.00 | 120.00 | | 1,730.00 | 3,470.00 | | 5,200.00 | |
| Wages | | | | | | | | | | | | | | |
| Bennett, Robin | 42 | 480.00 | 36.00 | 516.00 | 41.28 | 43.00 | 10.32 | 18.00 | 5.00 | 117.60 | 398.40 | 1025 | | 516.00 |
| Jordan, Michael | 44 | 480.00 | 72.00 | 552.00 | 44.16 | 49.00 | 11.04 | 10.00 | 5.00 | 119.20 | 432.80 | 1028 | | 552.00 |
| Milroy, Lee | 43 | 480.00 | 54.00 | 534.00 | 42.72 | 46.00 | 10.68 | 10.00 | 5.00 | 114.40 | 419.60 | 1040 | | 534.00 |
| Subtotal | | 11,000.00 | 1,010.00 | 12,010.00 | 960.80 | 2,400.00 | 240.20 | 301.50 | 115.00 | 4,017.50 | 7,992.50 | | | 12,010.00 |
| Total | | 16,200.00 | 1,010.00 | 17,210.00 | 1,376.80 | 3,490.00 | 344.20 | 421.50 | 115.00 | 5,747.50 | 11,462.50 | | 5,200.00 | 12,010.00 |

Note that this record is a listing of each employee's payroll data for the pay period. In some companies, a payroll register is a journal or book of original entry. Postings are made from it directly to ledger accounts. In other companies, the payroll register is a memorandum record that provides the data for a general journal entry and subsequent posting to the ledger accounts. At Academy Company, the latter procedure is followed.

## RECOGNIZING PAYROLL EXPENSES AND LIABILITIES

From the payroll register in Illustration F-9, a journal entry is made to record the payroll. For the week ending January 14, the entry is:

| | | | | |
|---|---|---|---|---|
| | | | | A = L + SE |
| Jan. 14 | Office Salaries Expense | 5,200.00 | | −5,200.00 Exp |
| | Wages Expense | 12,010.00 | | −12,010.00 Exp |
| |     FICA Taxes Payable | | 1,376.80 | +1,376.80 |
| |     Federal Income Taxes Payable | | 3,490.00 | +3,490.00 |
| |     State Income Taxes Payable | | 344.20 | +344.20 |
| |     United Fund Payable | | 421.50 | +421.50 |
| |     Union Dues Payable | | 115.00 | +115.00 |
| |     Salaries and Wages Payable | | 11,462.50 | +11,462.50 |
| |       (To record payroll for the week | | | **Cash Flows** |
| |       ending January 14) | | | no effect |

Specific liability accounts are credited for the mandatory and voluntary deductions made during the pay period. In the example, debits to Office Salaries and Wages Expense are used for gross earnings because office workers are on a salary and other employees are paid on an hourly rate. In other companies, there may be debits to other accounts such as Store Salaries or Sales Salaries. The amount credited to Salaries and Wages Payable is the sum of the individual checks the employees will receive.

## RECORDING PAYMENT OF THE PAYROLL

Payment by check is made either from the employer's regular bank account or a payroll bank account. Each paycheck is usually accompanied by a detachable statement of earnings document. This shows the employee's gross earnings, payroll deductions, and net pay for the period and for the year-to-date. The Academy Company uses its regular bank account for payroll checks. The paycheck and statement of earnings for Michael Jordan are shown in Illustration F-10 (next page).

Following payment of the payroll, the check numbers are entered in the payroll register. The entry to record payment of the payroll for Academy Company is as follows.

| | | | | |
|---|---|---|---|---|
| | | | | A = L + SE |
| Jan. 14 | Salaries and Wages Payable | 11,462.50 | | −11,462.50 |
| |     Cash | | 11,462.50 |    −11,462.50 |
| |     (To record payment of payroll) | | | **Cash Flows** |
| | | | | −11,462.50 |

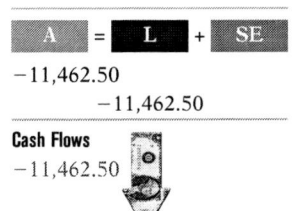

Many medium- and large-size companies use a payroll processing center that provides payroll record-keeping services. Companies send the center payroll information about employee pay rates and hours worked. The center maintains the payroll records and prepares the payroll checks. In most cases, it costs less to process the payroll through the center than if the company did so internally.

**Illustration F-10**
Paycheck and statement of earnings

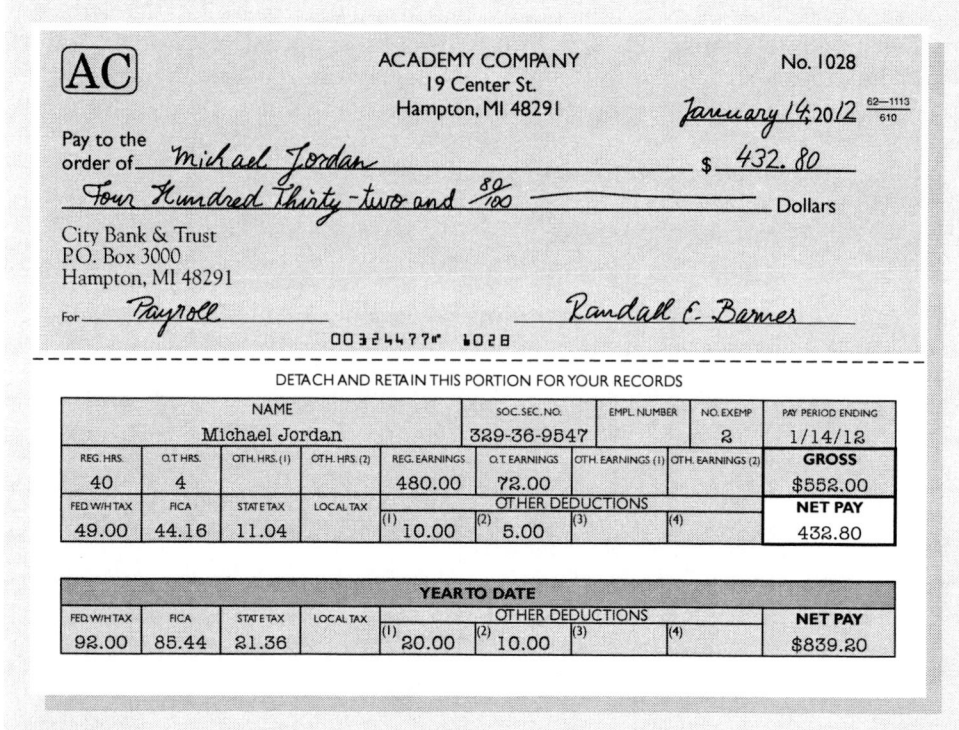

**Helpful Hint** Do any of the income tax liabilities result in payroll tax expense for the employer? *Answer:* No. The employer is acting only as a collection agent for the government.

## Employer Payroll Taxes

Payroll tax expense for businesses results from three taxes **levied on employers** by governmental agencies. These taxes are: (1) FICA, (2) federal unemployment tax, and (3) state unemployment tax. These taxes plus such items as paid vacations and pensions are collectively referred to as **fringe benefits**. As indicated earlier, the cost of fringe benefits in many companies is substantial.

### FICA TAXES

We have seen that each employee must pay FICA taxes. An employer must match each employee's FICA contribution. The matching contribution results in **payroll tax expense** to the employer. The employer's tax is subject to the same rate and maximum earnings applicable to the employee. The account, FICA Taxes Payable, is used for both the employee's and the employer's FICA contributions. For the January 14 payroll, Academy Company's FICA tax contribution is $1,376.80 ($17,210.00 × 8%).

### FEDERAL UNEMPLOYMENT TAXES

**Helpful Hint** FICA taxes are paid by both the employer and employee. Federal unemployment taxes and (in most states) the state unemployment taxes are borne entirely by the employer.

The Federal Unemployment Tax Act (FUTA) is another feature of the federal Social Security program. Federal unemployment taxes provide benefits for a limited period of time to employees who lose their jobs through no fault of their own. Under provisions of the Act, the employer is required to pay a tax of 6.2% on the first $7,000 of gross wages paid to each employee during a calendar year. The law allows the employer a maximum credit of 5.4% on the federal rate for contributions to state unemployment taxes. Because of this provision, state unemployment tax laws generally provide for a 5.4% rate. The effective federal unemployment tax rate thus becomes 0.8% (6.2% − 5.4%). This tax is borne **entirely by the employer**. There is no deduction or withholding from employees.

The account Federal Unemployment Taxes Payable is used to recognize this liability. The federal unemployment tax for Academy Company for the January 14 payroll is $137.68 ($17,210.00 × 0.8%).

## STATE UNEMPLOYMENT TAXES

All states have unemployment compensation programs under state unemployment tax acts (SUTA). Like federal unemployment taxes, state unemployment taxes provide benefits to employees who lose their jobs. These taxes are levied on employers.[2] The basic rate is usually 5.4% on the first $7,000 of wages paid to an employee during the year. The basic rate is adjusted according to the employer's experience rating: Companies with a history of unstable employment may pay more than the basic rate. Companies with a history of stable employment may pay less than 5.4%. Regardless of the rate paid, the credit on the federal unemployment tax is still 5.4%.

The account State Unemployment Taxes Payable is used for this liability. The state unemployment tax for Academy Company for the January 14 payroll is $929.34 ($17,210.00 × 5.4%).

## RECORDING EMPLOYER PAYROLL TAXES

Employer payroll taxes are usually recorded at the same time the payroll is journalized. The entire amount of gross pay ($17,210.00) shown in the payroll register in Illustration F-9 is subject to each of the three taxes mentioned above. Accordingly, the entry to record the payroll tax expense associated with the January 14 payroll is:

| | | | |
|---|---|---|---|
| Jan. 14 | Payroll Tax Expense | 2,443.82 | |
| | FICA Taxes Payable | | 1,376.80 |
| | Federal Unemployment Taxes Payable | | 137.68 |
| | State Unemployment Taxes Payable | | 929.34 |
| | (To record employer's payroll taxes on January 14 payroll) | | |

| A | = | L | + | SE |
|---|---|---|---|---|
| | | | | −2,443.82 Exp |
| | | +1,376.80 | | |
| | | +137.68 | | |
| | | +929.34 | | |

**Cash Flows**
no effect

Separate liability accounts are used instead of a single credit to Payroll Taxes Payable. Why? Because these liabilities are payable to different taxing authorities at different dates. The liability accounts are classified in the balance sheet as current liabilities since they will be paid within the next year. Payroll Tax Expense is classified on the income statement as an operating expense. Illustration F-11 summarizes the types of employer payroll taxes.

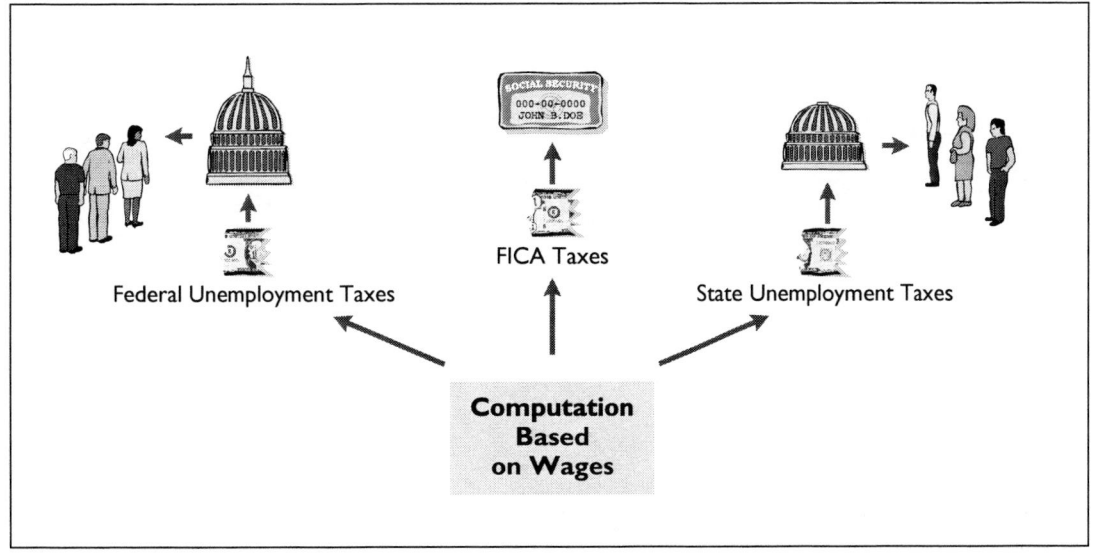

**Illustration F-11**
Employer payroll taxes

---

[2]In a few states, the employee is also required to make a contribution. In this textbook, including the homework, *we will assume that the tax is only on the employer.*

## Filing and Remitting Payroll Taxes

Preparation of payroll tax returns is the responsibility of the payroll department. Payment of the taxes is made by the treasurer's department. Much of the information for the returns is obtained from employee earnings records.

For purposes of reporting and remitting to the IRS, FICA taxes and federal income taxes that were withheld are combined. **The taxes must be reported quarterly**, no later than one month following the close of each quarter. The remitting requirements depend on the amount of taxes withheld and the length of the pay period. Remittances are made through deposits in either a Federal Reserve bank or an authorized commercial bank.

Federal unemployment taxes are generally filed and remitted **annually** on or before January 31 of the subsequent year. Earlier payments are required when the tax exceeds a specified amount. State unemployment taxes usually must be filed and paid by the **end of the month following each quarter**. When payroll taxes are paid, payroll liability accounts are debited, and Cash is credited.

The employer is also required to provide each employee with a Wage and Tax Statement (Form W-2) by January 31 following the end of a calendar year. This statement shows gross earnings, FICA taxes withheld, and income taxes withheld for the year. The required W-2 form for Michael Jordan, using assumed annual data, is shown in Illustration F-12.

The employer must send a copy of each employee's Wage and Tax Statement (Form W-2) to the Social Security Administration. This agency subsequently furnishes the Internal Revenue Service with the income data required.

**Illustration F-12**
W-2 form

| | | |
|---|---|---|
| 22222 | Void ☐ | a Employee's social security number 329-36-9547 — For Official Use Only ▶ OMB No. 1545-0008 |
| b Employer identification number (EIN) 36-2167852 | 1 Wages, tips, other compensation 26,300.00 | 2 Federal income tax withheld 2,248.00 |
| c Employer's name, address, and ZIP code<br>Academy Company<br>19 Center St.<br>Hampton, MI 48291 | 3 Social security wages 26,300.00 | 4 Social security tax withheld 2,104.00 |
| | 5 Medicare wages and tips 26,300.00 | 6 Medicare tax withheld |
| | 7 Social security tips | 8 Allocated tips |
| d Control number | 9 Advance EIC payment | 10 Dependent care benefits |
| e Employee's first name and initial: Michael — Last name: Jordan — Suff. | 11 Nonqualified plans | 12a See instructions for box 12 |
| 2345 Mifflin Ave.<br>Hampton, MI 48292 | 13 Statutory employee ☐ Retirement plan ☐ Third-party sick pay ☐ | 12b |
| | 14 Other | 12c |
| f Employee's address and ZIP code | | 12d |

| 15 State | Employer's state ID number | 16 State wages, tips, etc. | 17 State income tax | 18 Local wages, tips, etc. | 19 Local income tax | 20 Locality name |
|---|---|---|---|---|---|---|
| MI | 423-1466-3 | 26,300.00 | 526.00 | | | |
| | | | | | | |

Form **W-2** **Wage and Tax Statement** 2012

Department of the Treasury—Internal Revenue Service

**For Privacy Act and Paperwork Reduction Act Notice, see back of Copy D.**

**Copy A For Social Security Administration** — Send this entire page with Form W-3 to the Social Security Administration; photocopies are **not** acceptable.

Cat. No. 10134D

# Summary of Study Objectives

**1 Discuss the objectives of internal control for payroll.** The objectives of internal control for payroll are (1) to safeguard company assets against unauthorized payments of payrolls, and (2) to ensure the accuracy of the accounting records pertaining to payrolls.

**2 Compute and record the payroll for a pay period.** The computation of the payroll involves gross earnings, payroll deductions, and net pay. In recording the payroll, Salaries (or Wages) Expense is debited for gross earnings, individual tax and other liability accounts are credited for payroll deductions, and Salaries (Wages) Payable is credited for net pay. When the payroll is paid, Salaries and Wages Payable is debited, and Cash is credited.

**3 Describe and record employer payroll taxes.** Employer payroll taxes consist of FICA, federal unemployment taxes, and state unemployment taxes. The taxes are usually accrued at the time the payroll is recorded by debiting Payroll Tax Expense and crediting separate liability accounts for each type of tax.

# Glossary

**Bonus** *(p. F-4)* Compensation to management personnel and other employees, based on factors such as increased sales or the amount of net income.

**Employee earnings record** *(p. F-7)* A cumulative record of each employee's gross earnings, deductions, and net pay during the year.

**Employee's Withholding Allowance Certificate (Form W-4)** *(p. F-6)* An Internal Revenue Service form on which the employee indicates the number of allowances claimed for withholding federal income taxes.

**Federal unemployment taxes** *(p. F-10)* Taxes imposed on the employer that provide benefits for a limited time period to employees who lose their jobs through no fault of their own.

**FICA taxes** *(p. F-5)* Taxes designed to provide workers with supplemental retirement, employment disability, and medical benefits.

**Gross earnings** *(p. F-4)* Total compensation earned by an employee.

**Net pay** *(p. F-7)* Gross earnings less payroll deductions.

**Payroll deductions** *(p. F-4)* Deductions from gross earnings to determine the amount of a paycheck.

**Payroll register** *(p. F-8)* A payroll record that accumulates the gross earnings, deductions, and net pay by employee for each pay period.

**Salaries** *(p. F-1)* Specified amount per month or per year paid to managers and administrative personnel.

**Statement of earnings** *(p. F-9)* A document attached to a paycheck that indicates the employee's gross earnings, payroll deductions, and net pay.

**State unemployment taxes** *(p. F-11)* Taxes imposed on the employer that provide benefits to employees who lose their jobs.

**Wage and Tax Statement (Form W-2)** *(p. F-12)* A form showing gross earnings, FICA taxes withheld, and income taxes withheld which is prepared annually by an employer for each employee.

**Wages** *(p. F-1)* Amounts paid to employees based on a rate per hour or on a piece-work basis.

**Self-Test, Brief Exercises, Exercises, Problem Set A, and many more resources are available for practice in WileyPLUS**

# Questions

1. You are a newly hired accountant with Westbrook Company. On your first day, the controller asks you to identify the main internal control objectives related to payroll accounting. How would you respond?

2. What are the four functions associated with payroll activities?

3. What is the difference between gross pay and net pay? Which amount should a company record as wages or salaries expense?

4. Which payroll tax is levied on both employers and employees?

5. Are the federal and state income taxes withheld from employee paychecks a payroll tax expense for the employer? Explain your answer.

6. What do the following acronyms stand for: FICA, FUTA, and SUTA?

7. What information is shown on a W-4 statement? On a W-2 statement?

8. Distinguish between the two types of payroll deductions and give examples of each.

9. What are the primary uses of the employees earnings record?

10. (a) Identify the three types of employer payroll taxes.
    (b) How are tax liability accounts and Payroll Tax Expense classified in the financial statements?

# Brief Exercises

*Identify payroll functions.*
*(SO 1), C*

**BEF-1** Rodriguez Company has the following payroll procedures.
(a) Supervisor approves overtime work.
(b) The human resources department prepares hiring authorization forms for new hires.
(c) A second payroll department employee verifies payroll calculations.
(d) The treasurer's department pays employees.

Identify the payroll function to which each procedure pertains.

*Compute gross earnings and net pay.*
*(SO 2), AP*

**BEF-2** Erica Chambers' regular hourly wage rate is $14, and she receives an hourly rate of $21 for work in excess of 40 hours. During a January pay period, Erica works 45 hours. Erica's federal income tax withholding is $95, and she has no voluntary deductions. Compute Erica Chambers' gross earnings and net pay for the pay period.

*Record a payroll and the payment of wages.*
*(SO 2), AP*

**BEF-3** Data for Erica Chambers are presented in BEF-2. Prepare the journal entries to record (a) Erica's pay for the period and (b) the payment of Erica's wages. Use January 15 for the end of the pay period and the payment date.

*Record employer payroll taxes.*
*(SO 3), AP*

**BEF-4** In January, gross earnings in Gel Company totaled $70,000. All earnings are subject to 8% FICA taxes, 5.4% state unemployment taxes, and 0.8% federal unemployment taxes. Prepare the entry to record January payroll tax expense.

# Exercises

*Compute net pay and record pay for one employee.*
*(SO 2), AP*

**EF-1** Donna Garland's regular hourly wage rate is $16.00, and she receives a wage of 1½ times the regular hourly rate for work in excess of 40 hours. During a March weekly pay period, Donna worked 42 hours. Her gross earnings prior to the current week were $8,000. Donna is married and claims three withholding allowances. Her only voluntary deduction is for group hospitalization insurance at $15.00 per week.

*Instructions*
(a) Compute the following amounts for Donna's wages for the current week.
    (1) Gross earnings.
    (2) FICA taxes. (Assume an 8% rate on maximum of $100,000.)
    (3) Federal income taxes withheld. (Use the withholding table in the text, page F-6.)
    (4) State income taxes withheld. (Assume a 2.0% rate.)
    (5) Net pay.
(b) Record Donna's pay, assuming she is an office computer operator.

*Compute maximum FICA deductions.*
*(SO 2), AP*

**EF-2** Employee earnings records for Carnahan Company reveal the following gross earnings for four employees through the pay period of December 15.

| | | | |
|---|---|---|---|
| C. Mendez | $93,500 | D. Roberts | $99,100 |
| L. Church | $98,600 | T. Windsor | $100,000 |

For the pay period ending December 31, each employee's gross earnings is $3,000. The FICA tax rate is 8% on gross earnings of $100,000.

*Instructions*
Compute the FICA withholdings that should be made for each employee for the December 31 pay period. (Show computations.)

*Prepare payroll register and record payroll and payroll tax expense.*
*(SO 2, 3), AP*

**EF-3** Gonzalez Company has the following data for the weekly payroll ending January 31.

| | | | Hours | | | | Hourly | Federal Income Tax | Health |
|---|---|---|---|---|---|---|---|---|---|
| Employee | M | T | W | T | F | S | Rate | Withholding | Insurance |
| M. Mozart | 8 | 8 | 9 | 8 | 10 | 3 | $10 | $34 | $10 |
| E. Donnelly | 8 | 8 | 8 | 8 | 8 | 2 | 12 | 37 | 15 |
| K. Renn | 9 | 10 | 8 | 8 | 9 | 0 | 13 | 58 | 15 |

Employees are paid 1½ times the regular hourly rate for all hours worked in excess of 40 hours per week. FICA taxes are 8% on the first $100,000 of gross earnings. Gonzalez Company is subject to 5.4% state unemployment taxes and 0.8% federal unemployment taxes on the first $7,000 of gross earnings.

**Instructions**
(a)  Prepare the payroll register for the weekly payroll.
(b)  Prepare the journal entries to record the payroll and Gonzalez's payroll tax expense.

**EF-4**  Selected data from a February payroll register for Skywalker Company are presented below. Some amounts are intentionally omitted.

*Compute missing payroll amounts and record payroll.*
*(SO 2), AP*

| Gross earnings: | | State income taxes | $ (3) |
|---|---|---|---|
| Regular | $8,900 | Union dues | 100 |
| Overtime | (1) | Total deductions | (4) |
| Total | (2) | Net pay | $7,660 |
| Deductions: | | Accounts debited: | |
| FICA taxes | $ 800 | Warehouse wages | (5) |
| Federal income taxes | 1,140 | Store wages | $4,000 |

FICA taxes are 8%. State income taxes are 3% of gross earnings.

**Instructions**
(a)  Fill in the missing amounts.
(b)  Journalize the February payroll and the payment of the payroll.

**EF-5**  According to a payroll register summary of Sterrett Company, the amount of employees' gross pay in December was $800,000, of which $70,000 was not subject to FICA tax and $760,000 was not subject to state and federal unemployment taxes.

*Determine employer's payroll taxes and record payroll tax expense.*
*(SO 3), AP*

**Instructions**
(a)  Determine the employer's payroll tax expense for the month, using the following rates: FICA 8%, state unemployment 5.4%, federal unemployment 0.8%.
(b)  Prepare the journal entry to record December payroll tax expense.

# Problems

**PF-1**  Selected payroll procedures of Waegelein Company are described below.

*Identify internal control weaknesses and make recommendations for improvement.*
*(SO 1), AN*

1. Department managers interview applicants, and on the basis of the interview either hire or reject the applicants. When an applicant is hired, the applicant fills out a W-4 form (Employee's Withholding Allowance Certificate). One copy of the form is sent to the human resources department, and one copy is sent to the payroll department as notice that the individual has been hired. On the copy of the W-4 sent to payroll, the managers manually indicate the hourly pay rate for the new hire.
2. The payroll checks are manually signed by the chief accountant and given to the department managers for distribution to employees in their department. The managers are responsible for seeing that any absent employees receive their checks.
3. There are two clerks in the payroll department. The payroll is divided alphabetically; one clerk has employees A to L and the other has employees M to Z. Each clerk computes the gross earnings, deductions, and net pay for employees in the section and posts the data to the employee earning records.

**Instructions**
(a)  ▭▬▭▶ Indicate the weaknesses in internal control.
(b)  For each weakness, describe the control procedures that will provide effective internal control. Use the following format for your answer:

**(a) Weaknesses      (b) Recommended Procedures**

*Prepare payroll register and payroll entries.*

(SO 2, 3), AN

**PF-2** Stine Hardware has four employees who are paid on an hourly basis plus time-and-a half for all hours worked in excess of 40 a week. Payroll data for the week ended March 15, 2012, are presented below.

| Employee | Hours Worked | Hourly Rate | Federal Income Tax Withholdings | United Fund |
|---|---|---|---|---|
| Joe Feldon | 40 | $14.00 | $ ? | $5.00 |
| Mary Norten | 42 | 13.00 | ? | 5.00 |
| Andy Renfro | 44 | 13.00 | 60 | 8.00 |
| Kim Cheng | 46 | 13.00 | 51 | 5.00 |

Feldon and Norten are married. They claim 0 and 4 withholding allowances, respectively. The following tax rates are applicable: FICA 8%, state income taxes 3%, state unemployment taxes 5.4%, and federal unemployment 0.8%. The first three employees are sales clerks (store wages expense). The fourth employee performs administrative duties (office wages expense).

**Instructions**

(a) Net pay $1,862.06

(a) Prepare a payroll register for the weekly payroll. (Use the wage-bracket withholding table in the text for federal income tax withholdings.)

(b) Journalize the payroll on March 15, 2012, and the accrual of employer payroll taxes.

(c) Journalize the payment of the payroll on March 16, 2012.

(d) Cash paid $586.64

(d) Journalize the deposit in a Federal Reserve bank on March 31, 2012, of the FICA and federal income taxes payable to the government.

*Journalize payroll transactions and adjusting entries.*

(SO 2, 3), AN

GLS

**PF-3** The payroll liability accounts shown below are included in the ledger of Ludwick Company on January 1, 2012.

| | |
|---|---|
| FICA Taxes Payable | $ 760.00 |
| Federal Income Taxes Payable | 1,004.60 |
| State Income Taxes Payable | 108.95 |
| Federal Unemployment Taxes Payable | 288.95 |
| State Unemployment Taxes Payable | 1,954.40 |
| Union Dues Payable | 870.00 |
| U.S. Savings Bonds Payable | 360.00 |

In January, the following transactions occurred.

Jan. 10 Sent check for $870.00 to union treasurer for union dues.

12 Deposited check for $1,764.60 in Federal Reserve bank for FICA taxes and federal income taxes withheld.

15 Purchased U.S. Savings Bonds for employees by writing check for $360.00.

17 Paid state income taxes withheld from employees.

20 Paid federal and state unemployment taxes.

31 Completed monthly payroll register, which shows office salaries $14,600, store wages $28,400, FICA taxes withheld $3,440, federal income taxes payable $1,684, state income taxes payable $360, union dues payable $400, United Fund contributions payable $1,888, and net pay $35,228.

31 Prepared payroll checks for the net pay and distributed checks to employees.

At January 31, the company also makes the following accrued adjustments pertaining to employee compensation.

1. Employer payroll taxes: FICA taxes 8%, federal unemployment taxes 0.8%, and state unemployment taxes 5.4%.
2. Vacation pay: 6% of gross earnings.

**Instructions**

(b) Payroll tax expense $6,106.00; vacation benefits expense $2,580

(a) Journalize the January transactions.

(b) Journalize the adjustments pertaining to employee compensation at January 31.

**PF-4** For the year ended December 31, 2012, Bradburn Electrical Repair Company reports the following summary payroll data.

*Prepare entries for payroll and payroll taxes, and prepare W-2 data.*
*(SO 2, 3), AN*

| Gross earnings: | |
| --- | --- |
| Administrative salaries | $180,000 |
| Electricians' wages | 470,000 |
| Total | $650,000 |

| Deductions: | |
| --- | --- |
| FICA taxes | $ 45,200 |
| Federal income taxes withheld | 188,000 |
| State income taxes withheld (2.6%) | 16,900 |
| United Fund contributions payable | 32,500 |
| Hospital insurance premiums | 20,300 |
| Total | $302,900 |

Bradburn Company's payroll taxes are: FICA 8%, state unemployment 2.5% (due to a stable employment record), and 0.8% federal unemployment. Gross earnings subject to FICA taxes total $565,000, and gross earnings subject to unemployment taxes total $145,000.

**Instructions**
(a) Prepare a summary journal entry at December 31 for the full year's payroll.
(b) Journalize the adjusting entry at December 31 to record the employer's payroll taxes.
(c) The W-2 Wage and Tax Statement requires the following dollar data.

(a) Wages payable  $347,100
(b) Payroll tax
    expense  $49,985

| Wages, Tips, Other Compensation | Federal Income Tax Withheld | State Income Tax Withheld | FICA Wages | FICA Tax Withheld |
| --- | --- | --- | --- | --- |

Complete the required data for the following employees.

| Employee | Gross Earnings | Federal Income Tax Withheld |
| --- | --- | --- |
| Anna Hillman | $59,000 | $28,500 |
| Sharon Wainwright | 28,000 | 10,800 |

# PHOTO CREDITS

**Chapter 15**  Opener: Tim Mccaig/iStockphoto. Page 797: Tim Mccaig/iStockphoto. Page 800: iStockphoto. Page 811: Andrew Johnson/iStockphoto

**Chapter 16**  Opener: Lou Dematties/Reuters/©Corbis. Page 845: iStockphoto. Page 849: MTV Games/Scripps Howard Photo Service/NewsCom

**Chapter 17**  Opener: iStockphoto. Page 889: iStockphoto. Page 897: Oleksiy Maksymenko Photography/Alamy. Page 900: Jeffrey Hochstrasser/iStockphoto. Page 903: Sam Greenwood/ Getty Images, Inc. Page 908: Ramona Heim/iStockphoto

**Chapter 18**  Opener: iStockphoto. Page 939: iStockphoto. Page 942: UgurhanBetin/iStockphoto. Page 946: Pidjoe/ iStockphoto. Page 952: Digital Vision/Getty Images. Page 956: Yael/Retna

**Chapter 19**  Opener: Paul Sakuma/©AP/Wide World Photos. Page 977: Paul Sakuma/©AP/Wide World Photos. Page 982: Warchi/iStockphoto. Page 987: Dem10/iStockphoto. Page 989: Liv Friis-Larsen/iStockphoto. Page 993: Digital Vision

**Chapter 20**  Opener: Vladimir Melnikov/iStockphoto. Page 1031: Vladimir Melnikov/iStockphoto. Page 1034: Thinkstock/Comstock/Getty Images, Inc. Page 1036: Diane Bondareff/©AP/Wide World Photos. Page 1049: Wolfgang Rattya/ Reuters/Corbis. Page 1053: AP/Wide World Photos

**Chapter 21**  Opener: Marcus Clackson/iStockphoto. Page 1079: Marcus Clackson/iStockphoto. Page 1089: Eric IsselÇe/iStockphoto. Page 1093: Khuong Hoang/iStockphoto. Page 1102: Brentmelissa/iStockphoto. Page 1103: Kyodo/©AP/Wide World Photos

**Chapter 22**  Opener: Dominik Pabis/iStockphoto. Page 1137: Dominik Pabis/iStockphoto. Page 1140: SpotX/ iStockphoto. Page 1156: PhotoDisc, Inc./Getty Images. Page 1143: Hywit Dimyadi/iStockphoto

**Chapter 23**  Opener: SpxChrome/iStockphoto. Page 1185: SpxChrome/iStockphot. Page 1200: Dmitry Kutlayev/ iStockphoto

# COMPANY INDEX

# SUBJECT INDEX

**A**

ABC, *see* Activity-based costing

ABM (activity-based management), 901, 912

Absorption costing:
  defined, 1006
  variable costing vs., 996–1005

Accelerated-depreciation method, 456, 476, 477, 479

Accounts. *See also specific accounts*
  in accounting information system, 111–116
    debits and credits, 111–114
    expansion of basic equation, 104, 116
    stockholders' equity relationships, 113–116
  chart of, 120, 133
  debit and credit columns in, 111–112
  defined, 133
  permanent (real), 186–188, 197
  temporary, 186–187, 197
  uncollectible, 401–404, 423

Accounting:
  accrual-basis, *see* Accrual-basis accounting
  basic accounting equation, 3
    defined, 13, 23
    expansion, 104, 116, 654
    transaction analysis, 103–104, 109–110
  cash-basis:
    accrual basis accounting vs., 166–167
    defined, 197
    liquidity and solvency ratios, 642–643
  defined, 5, 22
  double-entry system, 112, 133
  managerial, *see* Managerial accounting
  market-to-market, E-8, E-10
  and non-accounting careers, 7
  as recruiting tool, 6

responsibility, 1078–1079, 1091–1106
  controllable vs. noncontrollable revenues/costs, 1092, 1093
  for cost centers, 1096–1097
  defined, 1110
  for investment centers, 1099–1102
  performance evaluation, 1102–1104
  for profit centers, 1097–1099
  reporting system, 1093–1096
  time periods in, 164–169

Accounting cycle:
  for manufacturing company, 770–773
  steps in, 190

Accounting information system, 100–132
  accounting transactions in, 102–110, 133
    analyzing, 103–109
    dividend payments, 108
    employee salary payments in cash, 108–109
    hiring of new employees, 108
    insurance policy purchases in cash, 107
    investment of cash by stockholders, 104–105
    note issues in exchange for cash, 105
    office equipment purchases in cash, 105
    receipt of cash in advance from customer, 105–106
    rent payments, 107
    services supplied for cash, 106–107
    supply purchases on account, 108
  accounts in, 111–116
    debits and credits, 111–114
    expansion of basic equation, 104, 116
    stockholders' equity relationships, 113–116
  accuracy in, 109
  business activities in, 9
  cash in, 130

defined, 102, 133
  for IFRS, 159
  mistakes in, 101
  recording process, 116–128
    chart of accounts, 120
    illustration, 120–128
    journalizing, 117–119, 127
    ledger entries, 119–120, 128
    posting, 120, 128
    trial balance, 129

Accounting principle, change in, 690, 720

Accounting scandals, 751, 752

Accounting standards, FASB/IASB project on, 44, 67, 159, 502, 565

Accounting transactions, 102–110, 133. *See also* Transaction analysis
  analyzing, 103–109
  dividend payments, 108
  employee salary payments in cash, 108–109
  hiring of new employees, 108
  insurance policy purchases in cash, 107
  investment of cash by stockholders, 104–105
  note issues in exchange for cash, 105
  office equipment purchases in cash, 105
  receipt of cash in advance from customer, 105–106
  rent payments, 107
  services supplied for cash, 106–107
  supply purchases on account, 108

Accounts payable, 635, G-10, G-11

Accounts payable subsidiary ledger, G-1, G-16

Accounts receivable, 399–407
  in accounting information system, 106–107
  aging the accounts receivable, 404, 423
  defined, 398–399, 423

# Chapter Content

## ACCOUNTING CONCEPTS (Chapters 2–4)

| Fundamental Qualities | Enhancing Qualities | Assumptions | Principles | Constraints |
|---|---|---|---|---|
| Relevance | Comparability | Monetary unit | Cost | Materiality |
| Faithful representation | Consistency | Economic entity | Fair value | Cost |
| | Verifiability | Periodicity | Full disclosure | |
| | Timeliness | Going concern | Revenue recognition | |
| | Understandability | Accrual basis | Expense recognition | |

## BASIC ACCOUNTING EQUATION (Chapter 3)

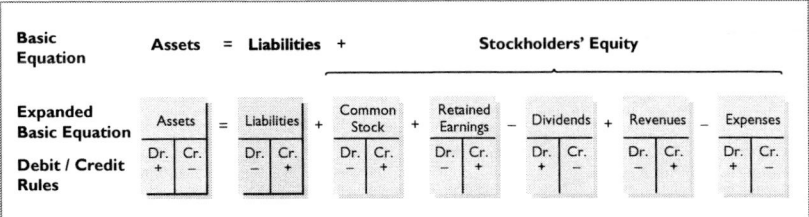

## INVENTORY (Chapters 5 and 6)

Ownership

| Freight Terms | Ownership of goods on public carrier resides with: |
|---|---|
| FOB Shipping point | Buyer |
| FOB Destination | Seller |

## ADJUSTING ENTRIES (Chapter 4)

| | Type | Adjusting Entry | |
|---|---|---|---|
| Deferrals | 1. Prepaid expenses | Dr. Expenses | Cr. Assets |
| | 2. Unearned revenues | Dr. Liabilities | Cr. Revenues |
| Accruals | 1. Accrued revenues | Dr. Assets | Cr. Revenues |
| | 2. Accrued expenses | Dr. Expenses | Cr. Liabilities |

*Note:* Each adjusting entry will affect one or more income statement accounts and one or more balance sheet accounts.

### Interest Computation

Interest = Face value of note × Annual interest rate × Time in terms of one year

## CLOSING ENTRIES (Chapter 4)

Purpose

1. Update the Retained Earnings account in the ledger by transferring net income (loss) and dividends to retained earnings.
2. Prepare the temporary accounts (revenue, expense, dividends) for the next period's postings by reducing their balances to zero.

## ACCOUNTING CYCLE (Chapter 4)

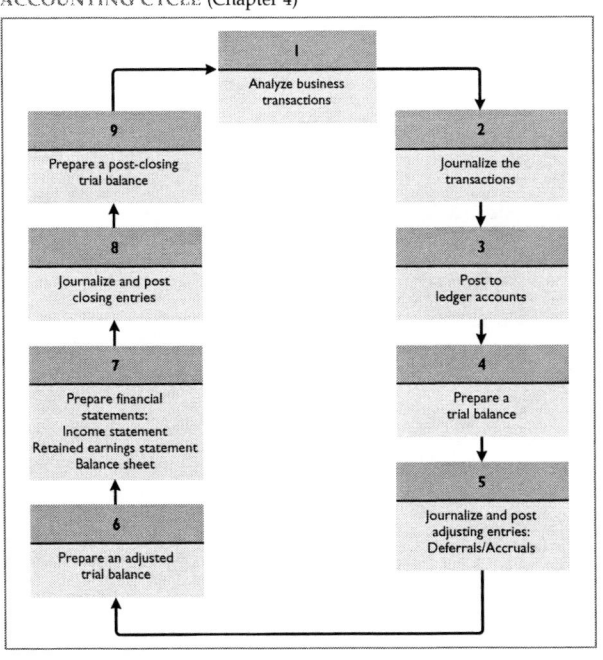

### Perpetual vs. Periodic Journal Entries

| Event | Perpetual | Periodic |
|---|---|---|
| Purchase of goods | Inventory<br>Cash (A/P) | Purchases<br>Cash (A/P) |
| Freight (shipping point) | Inventory<br>Cash | Freight-in<br>Cash |
| Return of goods | Cash (or A/P)<br>Inventory | Cash (or A/P)<br>Purchase Returns and Allowances |
| Sale of goods | Cash (or A/R)<br>Sales<br>Cost of Goods Sold<br>Inventory | Cash (or A/R)<br>Sales<br>No entry |
| End of period | No entry | Closing or adjusting entry required |

## FRAUD, INTERNAL CONTROL, AND CASH (Chapter 7)

Principles of Internal Control

Establishment of responsibility
Segregation of duties
Documentation procedures
Physical controls
Independent internal verification
Human resource controls

The Fraud Triangle

Opportunity

Financial pressure

Rationalization

### Bank Reconciliation

| Bank | Books |
|---|---|
| Balance per bank statement | Balance per books |
| Add: Deposits in transit | Add: Unrecorded credit memoranda from bank statement |
| Deduct: Outstanding checks | Deduct: Unrecorded debit memoranda from bank statement |
| Adjusted cash balance | Adjusted cash balance |

Note: 1. Errors should be offset (added or deducted) on the side that made the error.
2. Adjusting journal entries should only be made for items affecting books.

STOP AND CHECK: Does the adjusted cash balance in the Cash account equal the reconciled balance?

# Chapter Content

## RECEIVABLES (Chapter 8)

Two Methods to Account for Uncollectible Accounts

| Direct write-off method | Record bad debts expense when the company determines a particular account to be uncollectible. |
|---|---|
| Allowance method | At the end of each period, estimate the amount of uncollectible receivables. Debit Bad Debts Expense and credit Allowance for Doubtful Accounts in an amount that results in a balance in the allowance account equal to the estimate of uncollectibles. As specific accounts become uncollectible, debit Allowance for Doubtful Accounts and credit Accounts Receivable. |

Steps to Manage Accounts Receivable

1. Determine to whom to extend credit.
2. Establish a payment period.
3. Monitor collections.
4. Evaluate the receivables balance.
5. Accelerate cash receipts from receivables when necessary.

## PLANT ASSETS (Chapter 9)

Computation of Annual Depreciation Expense

| Straight-line | $\dfrac{\text{Cost} - \text{Salvage value}}{\text{Useful life (in years)}}$ |
|---|---|
| *Declining-balance | Book value at beginning of year × Declining balance rate* <br> *Declining-balance rate = 1 ÷ Useful life (in years) |
| *Units-of-activity | $\dfrac{\text{Depreciable cost}}{\text{Useful life (in units)}}$ × Units of activity during year |

Note: If depreciation is calculated for partial periods, the straight-line and declining-balance methods must be adjusted for the relevant proportion of the year. Multiply the annual depreciation expense by the number of months expired in the year divided by 12 months.

## BONDS (Chapter 10)

| Premium | Market interest rate < Contractual interest rate |
|---|---|
| Face Value | Market interest rate = Contractual interest rate |
| Discount | Market interest rate > Contractual interest rate |

Computation of Annual Bond Interest Expense

Interest expense = Interest paid (payable) + Amortization of discount
(OR − Amortization of premium)

| *Straight-line amortization | $\dfrac{\text{Bond discount (premium)}}{\text{Number of interest periods}}$ | |
|---|---|---|
| *Effective-interest amortization (preferred method) | Bond interest expense | Bond interest paid |
| | Carrying value of bonds at beginning of period × Effective-interest rate | Face amount of bonds × Contractual interest rate |

## STOCKHOLDERS' EQUITY (Chapter 11)

No-Par Value vs. Par Value Stock Journal Entries

| No-Par Value | Par Value |
|---|---|
| Cash <br>   Common Stock | Cash <br>   Common Stock (par value) <br>   Paid-in Capital in Excess of Par Value |

...rison of Dividend Effects

| | Cash | Common Stock | Retained Earnings |
|---|---|---|---|
| | ↓ | No effect | ↓ |
| | No effect | ↑ | ↓ |
| | ...o effect | No effect | No effect |

...are covered in appendix.

## STATEMENT OF CASH FLOWS (Chapter 12)

Cash flows from operating activities (indirect method)

| | | |
|---|---|---|
| Net income | | |
| Add: | Amortization and depreciation | $ X |
| | Losses on disposals of assets | X |
| | Decreases in current assets | X |
| | Increases in current liabilities | X |
| Deduct: | Increases in current assets | (X) |
| | Decreases in current liabilities | (X) |
| | Gains on disposals of assets | (X) |
| Cash provided (used) by operating activities | | $ X |

Cash flows from operating activities (direct method)

| | |
|---|---|
| Cash receipts | |
| (Examples: from sales of goods and services to customers, from receipts of interest and dividends) | $ X |
| Cash payments | |
| (Examples: to suppliers, for operating expenses, for interest, for taxes) | (X) |
| Cash provided (used) by operating activities | $ X |

## FINANCIAL STATEMENT ANALYSIS (Chapter 13)

| Discontinued operations | Income statement (presented separately after "Income from continuing operations") |
|---|---|
| Extraordinary items | Income statement (presented separately after "Discontinued operations") |
| Changes in accounting principle | In most instances, use the new method in current period and restate previous years' results using new method. For changes in depreciation and amortization methods, use the new method in the current period, but do not restate previous periods. |

Income Statement and Comprehensive Income

| | |
|---|---|
| Sales | $ XX |
| Cost of goods sold | XX |
| Gross profit | XX |
| Operating expenses | XX |
| Income from operations | XX |
| Other revenues (expenses) and gains (losses) | XX |
| Income before income taxes | XX |
| Income tax expense | XX |
| Income before irregular items | XX |
| **Irregular items (net of tax)** | **XX** |
| **Net income** | **XX** |
| **Other comprehensive income items (net of tax)** | **XX** |
| **Comprehensive income** | **$ XX** |

## MANAGERIAL ACCOUNTING (Chapter 14)

Characteristics of Managerial Accounting

| Primary Users | Internal users |
|---|---|
| Reports | Internal reports issued as needed |
| Purpose | Special purpose for a particular user |
| Content | Pertains to subunits, may be detailed, use of relevant data |
| Verification | No independent audits |

Types of Manufacturing Costs

| Direct materials | Raw materials directly associated with finished product |
|---|---|
| Direct labor | Work of employees directly associated with turning raw materials into finished product |
| Manufacturing overhead | Costs indirectly associated with manufacture of finished product |

# RAPID REVIEW
# Chapter Content

## JOB ORDER AND PROCESS COSTING (Chapters 15 and 16)

Types of Accounting Systems

| Job order | Costs are assigned to each unit or each batch of goods |
|---|---|
| Process cost | Costs are applied to similar products that are mass-produced in a continuous fashion |

Job Order and Process Cost Flow

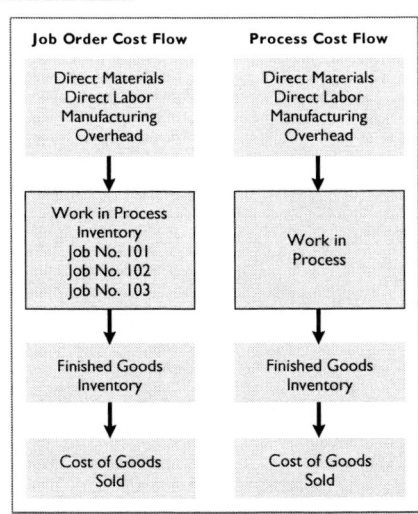

## ACTIVITY-BASED COSTING (Chapter 17)

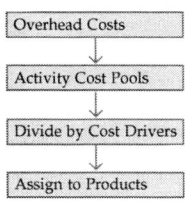

Overhead Costs

Activity Cost Pools

Divide by Cost Drivers

Assign to Products

Activity-based costing involves the following four steps:
1. Identify and classify the major activities involved in the manufacture of specific products, and allocate the manufacturing overhead costs to the appropriate cost pools.
2. Identify the cost driver that has a strong correlation to the costs accumulated in the cost pool.
3. Compute the overhead rate for each cost driver.
4. Assign manufacturing overhead costs for each cost pool to products, using the overhead rates (cost per driver).

## COST-VOLUME-PROFIT (Chapters 18 and 19)

Types of Costs

| Variable costs | Vary in total directly and proportionately with changes in activity level |
|---|---|
| Fixed costs | Remain the same in total regardless of change in activity level |
| Mixed costs | Contain both a fixed and a variable element |

CVP Income Statement Format

| | Total | Per Unit |
|---|---|---|
| Sales | $xx | $xx |
| Variable costs | xx | xx |
| Contribution margin | xx | $xx |
| Fixed costs | xx | |
| Net income | $xx | |

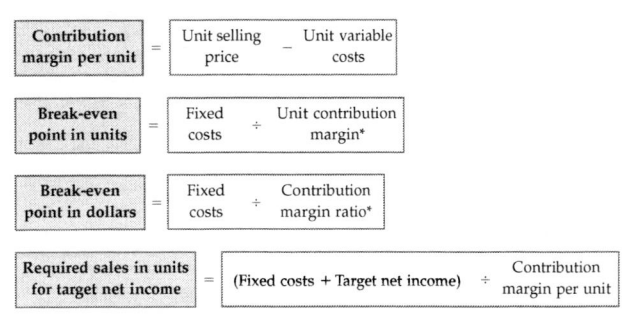

$$\text{Contribution margin per unit} = \text{Unit selling price} - \text{Unit variable costs}$$

$$\text{Break-even point in units} = \text{Fixed costs} \div \text{Unit contribution margin*}$$

$$\text{Break-even point in dollars} = \text{Fixed costs} \div \text{Contribution margin ratio*}$$

$$\text{Required sales in units for target net income} = (\text{Fixed costs} + \text{Target net income}) \div \text{Contribution margin per unit}$$

$$\text{Degree of operating leverage} = \text{Contribution margin} \div \text{Net income}$$

*For multiple products, use weighted-average.

## BUDGETS (Chapter 20)

Components of the Master Budget

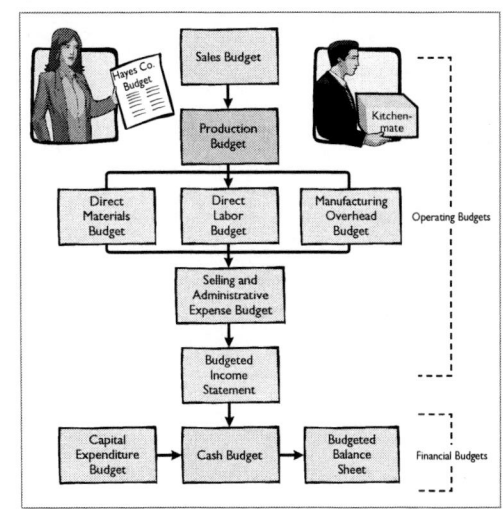

## RESPONSIBILITY ACCOUNTING (Chapter 21)

Types of Responsibility Centers

| Cost | Profit | Investment |
|---|---|---|
| Expenses only | Expenses and Revenues | Expenses and Revenues and ROI |

Return on Investment

$$\text{Return on investment (ROI)} = \text{Investment center controllable margin} \div \text{Average investment center operating assets}$$

## STANDARD COSTS (Chapter 22)

Standard Cost Variances

$$\text{Total materials variance} = \text{Materials price variance} + \text{Materials quantity variance}$$

$$\text{Total labor variance} = \text{Labor price variance} + \text{Labor quantity variance}$$

$$\text{Total overhead variance} = \text{Overhead controllable variance} + \text{Overhead volume variance}$$

Balanced Scorecard

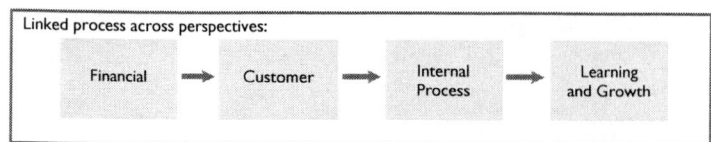

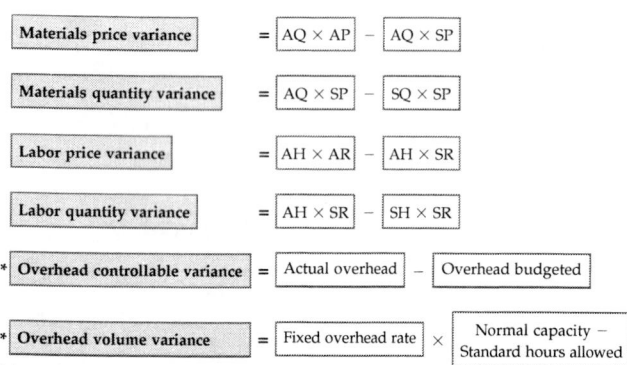

Materials price variance = |AQ × AP| − |AQ × SP|

Materials quantity variance = |AQ × SP| − |SQ × SP|

Labor price variance = |AH × AR| − |AH × SR|

Labor quantity variance = |AH × SR| − |SH × SR|

\* Overhead controllable variance = |Actual overhead| − |Overhead budgeted|

\* Overhead volume variance = |Fixed overhead rate| × |Normal capacity − Standard hours allowed|

\*Appendix coverage

## INCREMENTAL ANALYSIS AND CAPITAL BUDGETING (Chapter 23)

### Incremental Analysis

1. Identify the relevant costs associated with each alternative. Relevant costs are those costs and revenues that differ across alternatives. Choose the alternative that maximizes net income.
2. Opportunity costs are those benefits that are given up when one alternative is chosen instead of another one. Opportunity costs are relevant costs.
3. Sunk costs have already been incurred and will not be changed or avoided by any future decision. Sunk costs are not relevant costs.

### Annual Rate of Return

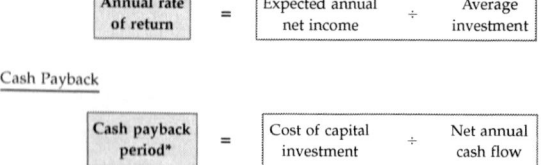

Annual rate of return = Expected annual net income ÷ Average investment

### Cash Payback

Cash payback period\* = Cost of capital investment ÷ Net annual cash flow

\*For uneven cash flows, you must calculate year-by-year

Discounted Cash Flow Approaches

| Net Present Value | Internal Rate of Return |
|---|---|
| Compute net present value (a dollar amount). If net present value is zero or positive, accept the proposal. If net present value is negative, reject the proposal. | Compute internal rate of return (a percentage). If internal rate of return is equal to or greater than the minimum required rate of return, accept the proposal. If internal rate of return is less than the minimum rate, reject the proposal. |

## INVESTMENTS (Appendix E)

Comparison of Long-Term Bond Investment and Liability Journal Entries

| Event | Investor | Investee |
|---|---|---|
| Purchase / issue of bonds | Debt Investments<br>    Cash | Cash<br>    Bonds Payable |
| Interest receipt / payment | Cash<br>    Interest Revenue | Interest Expense<br>    Cash |

Comparison of Cost and Equity Methods of Accounting for Long-Term Stock Investments

| Event | Cost | Equity |
|---|---|---|
| Acquisition | Stock Investments<br>    Cash | Stock Investments<br>    Cash |
| Investee reports earnings | No entry | Stock Investments<br>    Investment Revenue |
| Investee pays dividends | Cash<br>    Dividend Revenue | Cash<br>    Stock Investments |

RAPID REVIEW
# Financial Statements

| Order of Preparation | Date |
|---|---|
| 1. Income statement | For the period ended |
| 2. Retained earnings statement | For the period ended |
| 3. Balance sheet | As of the end of the period |
| 4. Statement of cash flows | For the period ended |

STOP AND CHECK: Net income (loss) presented on the retained earnings statement must equal the net income (loss) presented on the income statement.

Income Statement (perpetual inventory system)

**Name of Company**
**Income Statement**
**For the Period Ended**

| | | |
|---|---|---|
| Sales revenues | | |
| Sales | $ X | |
| Less: Sales returns and allowances | X | |
| Sales discounts | X | |
| Net sales | | $ X |
| Cost of goods sold | | X |
| Gross profit | | X |
| Operating expenses | | |
| (Examples: store salaries, advertising, delivery, rent, depreciation, utilities, insurance) | | X |
| Income from operations | | X |
| Other revenues and gains | | |
| (Examples: interest, gains) | X | |
| Other expenses and losses | | |
| (Examples: interest, losses) | X | X |
| Income before income taxes | | X |
| Income tax expense | | X |
| Net income | | $ X |

Income Statement (periodic inventory system)

**Name of Company**
**Income Statement**
**For the Period Ended**

| | | | |
|---|---|---|---|
| Sales revenues | | | |
| Sales | | $ X | |
| Less: Sales returns and allowances | | X | |
| Sales discounts | | X | |
| Net sales | | | $ X |
| Cost of goods sold | | | |
| Beginning inventory | | X | |
| Purchases | $ X | | |
| Less: Purchase returns and allowances | X | | |
| Net purchases | X | | |
| Add: Freight in | X | | |
| Cost of goods purchased | | X | |
| Cost of goods available for sale | | X | |
| Less: Ending inventory | | X | |
| Cost of goods sold | | | X |
| Gross profit | | | X |
| Operating expenses | | | |
| (Examples: store salaries, advertising, delivery, rent, depreciation, utilities, insurance) | | | X |
| Income from operations | | | X |
| Other revenues and gains | | | |
| (Examples: interest, gains) | | X | |
| Other expenses and losses | | | |
| (Examples: interest, losses) | | X | X |
| Income before income taxes | | | X |
| Income tax expense | | | X |
| Net income | | | $ X |

Retained Earnings Statement

**Name of Company**
**Retained Earnings Statement**
**For the Period Ended**

| | |
|---|---|
| Retained earnings, beginning of period | $ X |
| Add: Net income (or deduct net loss) | X |
| | X |
| Deduct: Dividends | X |
| Retained earnings, end of period | $ X |

Balance Sheet

**Name of Company**
**Balance Sheet**
**As of the End of the Period**

**Assets**

| | | | |
|---|---|---|---|
| Current assets | | | |
| (Examples: cash, short-term investments, accounts receivable, inventory, prepaids) | | | $ X |
| Long-term investments | | | |
| (Examples: investments in bonds, investments in stocks) | | | X |
| Property, plant, and equipment | | | |
| Land | | $ X | |
| Buildings and equipment | $ X | | |
| Less: Accumulated depreciation | X | X | X |
| Intangible assets | | | X |
| Total assets | | | $ X |

**Liabilities and Stockholders' Equity**

| | |
|---|---|
| Liabilities | |
| Current liabilities | |
| (Examples: notes payable, accounts payable, accruals, unearned revenues, current portion of notes payable) | $ X |
| Long-term liabilities | |
| (Examples: notes payable, bonds payable) | X |
| Total liabilities | X |
| Stockholders' equity | |
| Common stock | X |
| Retained earnings | X |
| Total liabilities and stockholders' equity | $ X |

STOP AND CHECK: Total assets on the balance sheet must equal total liabilities plus stockholders' equity; and, ending retained earnings on the balance sheet must equal ending retained earnings on the retained earnings statement.

Statement of Cash Flows

**Name of Company**
**Statement of Cash Flows**
**For the Period Ended**

| | |
|---|---|
| Cash flows from operating activities | |
| Note: May be prepared using the direct or indirect method | |
| Cash provided (used) by operating activities | $ X |
| Cash flows from investing activities | |
| (Examples: purchase / sale of long-term assets) | |
| Cash provided (used) by investing activities | X |
| Cash flows from financing activities | |
| (Examples: issue / repayment of long-term liabilities, issue of stock, payment of dividends) | |
| Cash provided (used) by financing activities | X |
| Net increase (decrease) in cash | X |
| Cash, beginning of the period | X |
| Cash, end of the period | $ X |

STOP AND CHECK: Cash, end of the period, on the statement of cash flows must equal cash presented on the balance sheet.

# TOOLS FOR ANALYSIS

## Liquidity

| | | |
|---|---|---|
| Working capital | Current assets − Current liabilities | p. 59 |
| Current ratio | $\dfrac{\text{Current assets}}{\text{Current liabilities}}$ | p. 59 |
| Current cash debt coverage ratio | $\dfrac{\text{Cash provided by operations}}{\text{Average current liabilities}}$ | p. 643 |
| Inventory turnover ratio | $\dfrac{\text{Cost of goods sold}}{\text{Average inventory}}$ | p. 297 |
| Days in inventory | $\dfrac{\text{365 days}}{\text{Inventory turnover ratio}}$ | p. 297 |
| Receivables turnover ratio | $\dfrac{\text{Net credit sales}}{\text{Average net receivables}}$ | p. 415 |
| Average collection period | $\dfrac{\text{365 days}}{\text{Receivables turnover ratio}}$ | p. 415 |

## Solvency

| | | |
|---|---|---|
| Debt to total assets ratio | $\dfrac{\text{Total liabilities}}{\text{Total assets}}$ | p. 60 |
| Cash debt coverage ratio | $\dfrac{\text{Cash provided by operations}}{\text{Average total liabilities}}$ | p. 644 |
| Times interest earned ratio | $\dfrac{\text{Net income + Interest expense + Tax expense}}{\text{Interest expense}}$ | p. 529 |
| Free cash flow | Cash provided by operations − Capital expenditures − Cash dividends | p. 62 |

## Profitability

| | | |
|---|---|---|
| Earnings per share | $\dfrac{\text{Net income − Preferred stock dividends}}{\text{Average common shares outstanding}}$ | p. 56 |
| Price-earnings ratio | $\dfrac{\text{Stock price per share}}{\text{Earnings per share}}$ | p. 703 |
| Gross profit rate | $\dfrac{\text{Gross profit}}{\text{Net sales}}$ | p. 246 |
| Profit margin ratio | $\dfrac{\text{Net income}}{\text{Net sales}}$ | p. 247 |
| Return on assets ratio | $\dfrac{\text{Net income}}{\text{Average total assets}}$ | p. 467 |
| Asset turnover ratio | $\dfrac{\text{Net sales}}{\text{Average total assets}}$ | p. 468 |
| ...t ratio | $\dfrac{\text{Cash dividends declared on common stock}}{\text{Net income}}$ | p. 593 |
| ...common stockholders' equity ratio | $\dfrac{\text{Net income − Preferred stock dividends}}{\text{Average common stockholders' equity}}$ | p. 594 |